COMMENTARY AND CASES
ON THE LAW OF
TRUSTS AND EQUITABLE REMEDIES

AUSTRALIA
Law Book Co.
Sydney

CANADA and USA
Carswell
Toronto

HONG KONG
Sweet & Maxwell Asia

NEW ZEALAND
Brookers
Auckland

SINGAPORE and MALAYSIA
Sweet & Maxwell Asia
Singapore and Kuala Lumpur

HAYTON AND MARSHALL

COMMENTARY AND CASES ON THE LAW OF TRUSTS AND EQUITABLE REMEDIES

TWELFTH EDITION

by

DAVID HAYTON, LL.D.

Justice of the Caribbean Court of Justice, formerly Professor of Law, King's College, London University and Fellow of Jesus College, Cambridge

and

CHARLES MITCHELL, B.A. LL.M. PH.D

Professor of Law, King's College, London University

LONDON
SWEET & MAXWELL
2005

First edition 1939 by J. A. Nathan
Second edition 1951 by O. R. Marshall
Third edition 1955 by O. R. Marshall
Fourth edition 1961 by O. R. Marshall
Second impression 1966 by O. R. Marshall
Fifth edition 1967 by O. R. Marshall
Second impression 1971 by O. R. Marshall
Sixth edition 1975 by D. J. Hayton
Seventh edition 1980 by D. J. Hayton
Eighth edition 1986 by D. J. Hayton
Second impression 1988 by D. J. Hayton

Third impression 1989 by D. J. Hayton
Ninth edition 1991 by D. J. Hayton
Second impression 1994 by D. J. Hayton
Tenth edition 1996 by D. J. Hayton
Second impression 1997 by D. J. Hayton
Third impression 1999 by D. J. Hayton
Fourth impression 2000 by D. J. Hayton
Eleventh edition 2001 by D. J. Hayton
Second impression 2001 by D.J. Hayton
Third impression 2003 by D. J. Hayton
Twelfth edition 2005 by D. J. Hayton and
C. Mitchell

Published by
Sweet & Maxwell Ltd of
100 Avenue Road,
Swiss Cottage, London NW3 3PF
(*http://www.sweetandmaxwell.co.uk*)

Phototypeset by LBJ Typesetting Ltd of Kingsclere
Printed and bound in Great Britain by TJ International Ltd, Padstow, Cornwall

No natural forests were destroyed to make this product;
only farmed timber was used and replanted.

ISBN 0 421 90190X

**A CIP catalogue record for this book is available
from the British Library**

PREFACE

If you really want a good understanding of trust law and equitable remedies this is the book for you. It is a combined textbook and case-book, designed for getting to grips with the fundamentals and so helping students appear in the top half of successful examinees. To this end, questions and problems are posed at the end of particular sections because, as someone once said, "To read without reflecting is like eating without digesting".

With the assistance of excerpts from cases, statutes, articles and Charity Commissioners' Annual Reports and Publications, the book aims to expound the law clearly and succinctly, to provide practical insight into the operation of the law and to reflect upon likely future developments (so referring occasionally to illuminating Commonwealth cases and statutes). It encourages readers to develop their analytical faculties and to think for themselves.

There is detailed investigation of those "grey" areas so favoured by examiners and often concerned with significant new developments. Of course, the syllabus for the Law Society and Bar exams is fully covered, while practitioners should find the book most useful for keeping in touch with recent developments.

Having produced the sixth edition in 1975, now that the twelfth edition has been reached and I am moving on to become a Justice of the Caribbean Court of Justice, I have a co-editor, Professor Charles Mitchell, a colleague at King's College London. He has been primarily concerned with Chapters 5, 6, 7, 10, 11, 12 and 14 and will take over as sole editor for the next edition, having done sterling work on those Chapters.

Much has happened in the four years since the last edition so that space has been found for excerpts from *Grundy v Ottey*, *Schmidt v Rosewood Trust Ltd*, *Pennington v Waine*, *Oxley v Hiscock*, *Wong v Burt*, *Abacus Trust Co v Barr*, *Twinsectra Ltd v Yardley*, *Wolff v Wolff* and *AMP(UK)Plc v Barker*. Account has also been taken of other recent cases and new developments in the Land Registration Act 2002, Civil Partnership Act 2004, Pensions Act 2004, Mental Capacity Act 2005 and the Charities Bill currently proceeding through Parliament.

To make room for the new material, excerpts from the following cases have been deleted: *Wallgrave v Tebbs*, *Re Kay ford*, *Re Baden's Deed Trusts*, *Re Barlow's W.T*, *Re Rose*, *Re Smith*, *Midland Bank v Cooke*, *Scottish Burial Reform and Cremation Society Ltd v Glasgow City*, *National Anti-Vivisection Society v IRC*, *Incorporated Council of Law Reporting v Att-Gen*, *Re South Place Ethical Society*, *Holder v Holder*, *Re Gee Seager v Copydex Ltd*, *Re Earl of Chesterfield's Trusts*, *Re Londonderry's Settlement*, *Re Rabaiotti 1989 Settlement*, *Re McGeorge*, *Tempest v Lord Camoys*, *Re Brook's Settlement*, *El Ajou v Dollar Land Holdings plc* and *Lipkin Gorman v Karpnale Ltd*.

While much has been re-written in the light of developments since the last edition, there is particularly significant new material in the following areas as one progresses through the book: the scope of proprietary estoppel principles, the extent of the beneficiary principle, and the *Re Rose* principle, sections 1 and 2 of Chapter 5 on Resulting Trusts, the re-structuring of Chapter 6 on Constructive Trusts, sections 2, 3 and 4 of Chapter 7 on Charitable Trusts, apportionments of receipts and expenses between capital and income, the rights of beneficiaries and objects of fiduciary powers to information from the trustees, the scope of the rule in *Re Hastings-Bass,* the special position of beneficiaries under pension trusts, sections 1 and 2 of Chapter 10 (dealing with falsification of trustees' accounts to provide substitutive performance of primary obligations and surcharging of trustees' accounts to provide reparation for losses arising from negligent performance of authorised activities) and the re-writing of substantial parts of Chapters 11 and 12.

The book is based upon sources available in February 2005, but at the proofs stage some up-dating has been possible so that it is hoped that the law is accurately stated as as of 1st June 2005.

For further material and new material the following websites are very useful: *www.bailii.org, www.austlii.edu.au,* www.parliament.uk, *www.charity-commission.gov.uk, www.lawcom.gov.uk* and for the work of the Trust Law Committee (of which I was Deputy Chairman from its inception in 1994 till June 2005) *www.kcl.ac.uk/depsta/law/tlc.*

David Hayton
1st June 2005

ACKNOWLEDGMENTS

The Publishers and Authors wish to thank the following for permission to reprint material from publications in which they have copyright:

Reproduced by permission of the Butterworths Division of Reed Elsevier (UK) Limited
   The All England Law Reports
   Chesterman *Charities, Trusts and Social Welfare*

Blackwell publishers
   Green: "Grey, Oughtred and Vandervell—A Contextual Reappraisal" (1984) 47 M.L.R. 385

Crown Copyright ©
   Various Acts

Her Majesty's Stationery Office:
   The Charity Commissions Annual Reports
   Charities: A Framework for the Future, White Paper Cm. 694 (1989)

Incorporated Council of Law Reporting for England & Wales:
   Appeal Cases
   Chancery Division Cases
   Weekly Law Reports

Jordan Publishing Limited
   Huntingford v Hobbs [1993] 1 F.L.R. 736

Whilst every care has been taken to establish and acknowledge copyright and contact the copyright owners, the publishers tender their apologies for any accidental infringement. They would be pleased to come to a suitable arrangement with the rightful owner in each case.

CONTENTS

Contents

TABLE OF CASES

Paragraph References in **bold** indicate that the case is discussed fully

TABLE OF STATUTES

References to Paragraphs in **bold** indicate that the text is reproduced in full

TABLE OF STATUTORY INSTRUMENTS

References to Paragraphs in **bold** indicate that the text is reproduced in full

TABLE OF EUROPEAN AND FOREIGN LEGISLATION

References to Paragraphs in **bold** indicate that the text is reproduced in full

TABLE OF TREATIES AND CONVENTIONS

References to Paragraphs in **bold** indicate that the text is reproduced in full

Chapter 1

INTRODUCTION

Section 1. What is a Trust?

A trust results from property being transferred by its owner to a trustee or **1–01** trustees to own, manage and deal with it for the benefit of beneficiaries or a charitable purpose. Trustees have two roles: first, to administer and invest the trust assets; second, to distribute the income from those assets to appropriate beneficiaries and, ultimately, to distribute the capital assets to beneficiaries.

The fundamental primary obligations of trustees are faithfully to keep **1–02** within the terms of the trust and loyally and altruistically to further the interests of the beneficiaries, rather than themselves (except to the extent the trust instrument may permit them to benefit themselves). Conduct in breach of those obligations is unauthorised and leads to strict liability for all consequences (unless they would have occurred even if there had been no such conduct). To show that they are fulfilling these obligations trustees are under a core primary obligation to produce accounts to the beneficiaries revealing precisely how the trustees have performed their duties.

Included within a trust fund are the assets from time to time held on **1–03** trust by a trustee, but these assets owned by the trustee (or a nominee or custodian to his order) never become part of the trustee's estate or patrimony so that they are not available to satisfy any claims of the trustee's private creditors, heirs or divorcing spouse. The assets must only be used to benefit the beneficiaries or to further the relevant charitable purposes— though only after satisfying any claims of the trustee for remuneration or for reimbursement of creditors with whom the trustee dealt in due performance of the trusteeship functions. It is the trustee who is sued by, or who sues, third parties duly dealt with in the trusteeship role: the trust, unlike a company incorporated under the Companies Act 1985, is not a legal person.

The priority of the beneficiaries' interests over the trustee's private **1–04** creditors is achieved by conferring on the beneficiaries equitable proprietary interests in the trust property owned by the trustee. Such proprietary interests bind anyone coming to own the trust property unless protected as a bona fide purchaser of the legal title without notice of the equitable interest or by special statutory provisions (*e.g.* the overreaching provisions simplifying the sale of land in which beneficiaries have equitable interests by conferring a good title on a purchaser free from such interests if the purchase moneys are paid to a trust corporation or to two trustees, so the beneficiaries' interests are detached from the land and attached to the proceeds of the sale).

1–05   The beneficiaries' equitable interests in the trust fund are, however, subordinated to an equitable lien (or charge) in favour of the trustee to secure payment of trustee-remuneration and creditors' duly incurred claims: creditors can take advantage of this lien by way of subrogation to the trustee's rights.

1–06   The concept of a trust fund is special, whether or not spelled out in the definition section of a trust instrument.[1] It covers the original assets (often of small value) transferred to the trustee, assets subsequently transferred to the trustee, and assets later representing such assets via successive substitutions of newly acquired assets for disposed of assets. The ring-fenced trust fund extends beyond authorised assets newly acquired by the trustee on behalf of the trust. The beneficiaries can claim unauthorised assets that the trustee wrongfully acquired on behalf of the trust and also assets that the trustee wrongfully tried to acquire for himself as part of his private estate or patrimony by using the proceeds of sale of trust assets or money obtained by abusing his office as trustee (*e.g.* by accepting a large bribe).The ring-fenced protected nature of the trust property would be illusory if it could simply be removed by the trustee lifting trust assets over the fence, selling them and buying assets put into his own house!

1–07   Equity, at the behest of the beneficiaries, will not allow the trustee to claim that he was a bad man who broke his primary obligations and so acquired an asset on his own behalf as part of his estate or patrimony. Equity insists that he was a good man and that he cannot deny that he was a good man and therefore acquired the asset on behalf of the trust so as faithfully to further the beneficiaries' interests. Thus, if the trustee sold sufficient trust assets to buy a flat for himself, then sold the flat and purchased a house with the proceeds of sale, the beneficiaries can, via the tracing process, claim that the flat and, then, the house became part of the trust fund and so held by the trustee as part of the property held on express trusts for them. The trustee cannot deny that by accepting the trusteeship he agreed to this expressly or by necessary implication. Despite his actual intention to hold the house for himself, he is compelled by Equity to hold the property on trust for the beneficiaries, such trust traditionally being regarded as a constructive trust for the beneficiaries, though there is much to be said for regarding it as directly held on an express trust for them.

1–08   Indeed, if the trustee had made a gift of the flat to his son, who had then sold it and used the proceeds of sale to buy a house, the beneficiaries can still claim that the flat and, then, the house became part of the trust fund held on trust for them. The son, as a donee with a derivatively flawed title and not a purchaser for value without notice, has throughout owned the flat and, then, the house subject to the beneficiaries' equitable proprietary interests therein. Once he becomes aware of this, he comes under a duty forthwith to transfer the flat or house to the replacement trustee of the

---

[1] See R. Nolan, "Property in a Fund" (2004) 120 L.Q.R. 108, D. Fox and D. Hayton, "Overreaching" and "Overview" respectively in P. Birks and A. Pretto (eds) *Breach of Trust* (Hart Publishing, 2002), Chapter 4 and pp.389–391 respectively, and Lord Millett on "Proprietary Restitution" in S. Degeling and J. Edelman (eds) *Equity in Commercial Law* (2005).

trust for the beneficiaries (or to the beneficiaries themselves if they have absolute interests therein and not limited or discretionary interests), meanwhile holding the property on constructive trust for them.

Normally, a trust is created by transferring property to trustees by way of **1–09** a gift from the settlor but it may be pursuant to a contract.

The law of trusts is concerned with the utilisation and preservation of wealth, whether in the form of pension funds, unit trusts, charitable funds, union funds, club funds, employee share ownership trusts, family funds or in the form of rights (whether secured or unsecured) against a borrower intended as a commercial security device to be held by trustees for the benefit of a collection of lenders. It is also about settling property on trustees so as to minimise liability to the various taxes. Much of trust law has so far developed in regard to the preservation of family wealth, tying up property so that it can be enjoyed by successive generations, protecting the family from the depredations of creditors and of particular relatives with extravagant reckless dispositions, providing secretly for mentally defective relatives, for mistresses, for illegitimate children or for institutions with which an open association is not desired.

Case law used to be much concerned with lifetime or testamentary express family trusts or trusts for employees of family companies where the funds are a small fraction of the total value of all funds held on trust. Recently, problems have arisen in respect of pension funds (leading to the Pensions Act 1995); in respect of alleged constructive trusts of family homes; in respect of assets allegedly the traceable product of property subject to a trust or other fiduciary relationship; in respect of the ambit of personal liability of recipients of trust property who no longer have it or of persons dishonestly involved in assisting in a breach of trust or other fiduciary relationship, and in respect of whether upon the liquidation of a company certain of its funds are trust funds not available for its general creditors.

The trust concept is extremely flexible and in English law can be used till **1–10** the end of a perpetuity period[2] to achieve almost any lawful end, except that problems arise where it is sought to use it to provide directly for the furtherance of abstract non-charitable purposes.[3] Some rules of trust law make it difficult to give property to unincorporated associations (which are not legal persons) on trust, though the courts now avoid this difficulty where possible by construing such gifts as out-and-out accretions to the association's funds subject to the contractual rights thereto of the members of the association under its constitution.[4] The trust concept has proved particularly useful in conveyancing so that whenever land is owned by two or more persons that land must be held on trust.[5] Maitland has quite rightly

---

[2] See paras 3–168 *et seq.*
[3] See paras 3–195 *et seq.*
[4] See paras 3–209 *et seq.*
[5] ss.34–36 of the Law of Property Act 1925, imposing a trust for sale with power to postpone sale which, under the Trusts of Land and Appointment of Trustees Act 1996 was replaced by a trust to hold land with power to sell or otherwise dispose of it as an absolute owner can. Trustees hold property as joint tenants so that on the death of one trustee the property automatically passes to the surviving trustees by virtue of the *ius accrescendi*. On the death of the last surviving trustee his personal representatives take over his function until they appoint new trustees: Trustee Act 1925, ss.18, 36.

characterised the trust concept as "the greatest and most distinctive achievement performed by Englishmen in the field of jurisprudence."[6] No lawyer can claim to provide a proper service for his private or corporate clients without a thorough grasp of trust law and its potentialities.

What then is a trust? It is impossible to define such a flexible concept. However, three quasi-definitions are now set out to provide a rough and ready introduction to trust law.

Scott, Trusts, 4th ed., para.2.3

1–11   "Even if it were possible to frame an exact definition of a legal concept, the definition would not be of great practical value. A definition cannot properly be used as though it were a major premise so that rules governing conduct can be deduced from it. Our law, at least, has not grown in that way. When the rules have been arrived at from other sources, it may be possible to attempt to frame a definition. But the definition results from the rules, and not the rules from the definition.

1–12   All that one can properly attempt to do is to give such a description of a legal concept that others will know in a general way what one is talking about. It is possible to state the principal distinguishing characteristics of the concept so that others will have a general idea of what the writer means. With this in mind, those responsible for the Restatement of Trusts proposed the following definition or description of an express trust. It is 'a fiduciary relationship with respect to property, subjecting the person by whom the title to property is held to equitable duties to deal with the property for the benefit of another person, which arises as a result of a manifestation of an intention to create it.' In this definition or description the following characteristics are to be noticed: (1) a trust is a relationship; (2) it is a relationship of a fiduciary character; (3) it is a relationship with respect to property, not one involving merely personal duties; (4) it involves the existence of equitable duties imposed upon the holder of the title to the property to deal with it for the benefit of another; and (5) it arises as a result of a manifestation of an intention to create the relationship."

Hague Convention on the Law Applicable to Trusts and on their Recognition

ARTICLE 2

1–13 "For the purposes of this Convention, the term 'trust' refers to the legal relationships created—*inter vivos* or on death—by a person, the settlor, when assets have been placed under the control of a trustee for the benefit of a beneficiary or for a specified purpose.

A trust has the following characteristics—

   a the assets constitute a separate fund and are not a part of the trustee's own estate;
   b title to the trust assets stands in the name of the trustee or in the name of another person on behalf of the trustee;

---

[6] *Selected Essays*, p.129.

c the trustee has the power and the duty, in respect of which he is accountable, to manage, employ or dispose of the assets in accordance with the terms of the trust and the special duties imposed upon him by law.

The reservation by the settlor of certain rights and powers, and the fact that the trustee may himself have rights as a beneficiary, are not necessarily inconsistent with the existence of a trust."

Principles of European Trust Law[7]

ARTICLE I

"(1) In a trust, a person called the "trustee" owns assets segregated from his private **1–14** patrimony and must deal with those assets (the "trust fund") for the benefit of another person called the "beneficiary" or for the furtherance of a purpose.
(2) There can be more than one trustee and more than one beneficiary; a trustee may himself be one of the beneficiaries.
(3) The separate existence of the trust fund entails its immunity from claims by the trustee's spouse, heirs and personal creditors.
(4) In respect of the separate trust fund a beneficiary has personal rights and may also have ["and also has" for common law countries] proprietary rights against the trustee and against third parties to whom any part of the trust fund has been wrongfully transferred."

ARTICLE II

"The general rule is that in order to create a trust a person called the "settlor" in his lifetime or on death must, with the intention of creating a segregated trust fund, transfer assets to the trustee. However, it may also be ["it is also" for common law countries] possible to create a trust by making it clear that he is to be trustee of particular assets of his."

ARTICLE III

"(1) The trust fund consists not only of the original assets and those subsequently **1–15** added, but also of those assets from time to time representing the original or added assets."

It will be seen that the last two definitions or descriptions do not refer to beneficiaries having *equitable* property interests (as opposed to the legal property interests of the trustees) since this distinction originated in English law (where a Court of Equity developed separately from the Courts of Law) and was perpetuated in its colonies (*e.g.* America, Australia, Bermuda, Bahamas, Barbados, Cayman Islands) but does not appear in the trust laws of Scotland, India, Japan, Liechtenstein or South Africa.[8]

---

[7] Published 1999 by Kluwer Law International, edited by D. Hayton, S. Kortmann and R. Verhagen.
[8] See J. Glasson (ed.) *International Trust Laws* (Jordans) and D. Hayton "The Development of the Trust Concept in Civil Law Jurisdictions" [2000] 8 Jo. Int. Trust & Corp P1 159.

The Principles of European Trust Law were prepared by an international working group so as to assist countries interested in implementing The Hague Trusts Convention. Such Principles were concerned to counter the misleading superficial impression given by Art.2 of the Trusts Convention that the term "trust" could extend to agency or mandate relationships where O, the owner, placed some of his assets under the control of another (who, could have possession of them as bailee if they were not intangible assets where ownership and possession are coterminous in common law countries but not in civil law countries).

1–16   Such impression is misconceived when the relevant part of Art.2(b) requires title to stand "in the name of another person on behalf of the trustee". If O has placed his property under the control of A, title stands in O's name not on behalf of A but on behalf of O: only control is vested in A on behalf of O.

Be that as it may the possible superficial agency construction arose from trying to deal from a layman's viewpoint with the situation where a trustee, T, does not directly own 10,000 shares (that he thought he had bought) in XYZ plc because Custodian plc owns one million XZY plc shares, 10,000 of which are recorded by it in a computer entry as held for T so that, technically, T owns a one hundredth fraction of Custodian's shareholding as equitable tenant in common. On a purposive construction, taking account of the fact that the Trusts Convention has a recital referring to the trust as a unique legal institution and has no provision as to its relationship with the earlier Hague Agency Convention and interpreting Art.2 in the light of Arts 11 and 13,[9] the Art.2 "trust" should not extend to agency or mandate or bailment. As James L.J. stated in *Smith v Anderson*,[10] "A trustee is a man who is the owner of the property and deals with it as principal as owner and as master, subject only to an equitable obligation to account to some persons to whom he stands in the relation of trustee", while in *CCSD v ISPT Pty Ltd*[11] Mason P emphasised, "It is of the essence of a trust that property is vested in the trustee."

The trustees' position

1–17   It will thus be seen that the ownership of trust property is vested in the trustees (or their nominees, though the trustees technically then own an interest in the property owned by the nominees) to be managed and dealt with wholly for the benefit of the beneficiaries.

1–18   Because the opportunities for trustees to take advantage of their position are so great Equity has imposed very strict rigorous duties upon trustees.[12] Indeed, so onerous have these duties become that properly drawn trust instruments greatly relax the standards that Equity would otherwise demand: were it not for such relaxation few individuals or companies would

---

[9] See paras 13–32 to 13–33.
[10] (1880) 15 Ch.D. 247 at 275.
[11] (1999) 2 I.T.E.L.R. 1 at 15.
[12] See Chap. 9.

be prepared to act as trustees. It should be noted that as long as illegality or public policy or uncertainty does not intervene, then draftsmen of trust instruments have a free hand to vary or negative trust principles so long as the irreducible core content of the trust concept remains. In so far as the draftsman has not made the consent of someone other than the trustees (*e.g.* an individual or a committee or a company, usually designated as a "protector") requisite before certain things are done, the trustees have an independent, unfettered discretion in their decisions though, of course, the income and capital managed by the trustees must be held according to the terms of the trust for the relevant beneficiaries.

The interests of the beneficiaries are paramount and the trustees must do **1–19** their best to hold the balance fairly between those beneficiaries (with life interests) interested in income and those beneficiaries (with absolute interests in remainder) interested in capital.[13] Indeed, the trustees have a paternalistic function of protecting each beneficiary against himself. Even if all the beneficiaries interested in a particular trust are each of full capacity and wish the trustees to do a certain thing the trustees can refuse if they consider that some of the beneficiaries are not objectively acting in their own best interests.[14] However, if all the beneficiaries are between them absolutely entitled to the trust property and are each of full capacity then under the *Saunders v Vautier*[15] principle, the beneficiaries have a fundamental proprietary power to call for the trust property to be vested in them (or their nominees) by the trustees, so terminating the trust.

Since the beneficiaries' interests are paramount the trustees cannot (in **1–20** the absence of authorisation in the trust instrument) invest trust moneys as they might invest their own: they have to play "safe" and invest only in investments authorised under the Trustee Act 2000, replacing the Trustee Investments Act 1961.[16] Even if they have a broad express power of investment they cannot speculate because (in the absence of a contrary provision in the trust instrument) they have to exercise as much care as a prudent man of business would exercise if investing for other persons for whom he felt morally obliged to provide.[17] On the other hand, whilst trustees when selling their own houses might feel bound to honour the commercial morality code and reject out of hand a higher offer when they had orally agreed, subject to contract, to sell to a purchaser who had just submitted his part of the contract to them, trustees, when selling trust property in such circumstances, must not reject the higher offer without probing it with a view to acceptance.[18] Any authority given by the trust instrument to the trustees is deemed to exclude ordinary trust law as little as possible and will be presumed not to allow the trustees to act in a way detrimental to the beneficiaries.

---

[13] See Chap. 9.
[14] *Re Brockbank* [1949] Ch. 206, subject to the beneficiaries' power to direct the trustees to retire and appoint other designated persons to become Trustees under the Trusts of Land & Appointment of Trustees Act 1996 s.19.
[15] *Saunders v Vautier* (1841) 4 Beav. 115, see at para.9–123; *Re Smith* [1928] Ch. 915.
[16] See Chap. 9.
[17] See para.9–53.
[18] *Buttle v Saunders* [1950] W.N. 255.

1–21   A trust, unlike a company,[19] has no legal personality; thus, it cannot own property or enter into contracts, sue or be sued. It is the trustees who own the trust property, enter into contracts, sue or are sued. A trustee as such has no distinct legal personality in his representative capacity separate from himself in his personal capacity.[20] Thus, he is personally liable to the extent of his whole personal fortune for debts contracted in managing the trust fund,[21] whether contracting in his own name or as trustee,[22] unless he makes it clear that he is to be liable only to the extent that the trust fund is available to him to satisfy the liability.[23] To discharge liabilities properly incurred by him as trustee he has a right of indemnity against the trust fund[24] (but only after discharging any liability for any breaches of trust[25]) and creditors may be subrogated to this right.[26]

1–22   Generally, one can say that the external aspects of a trust are governed by common law rules whilst the internal aspects are governed by rules of equity.[27] Thus, before turning the spotlight from the trustees to the beneficiaries one needs to consider the development of equity and the trust so that one can then examine the nature of the interest of a beneficiary under a trust.

Section 2. The Development of Equity and the Trust

1–23   A trust is the creature of Equity and not of the common law so what is "Equity?" In this context Equity can only be described as the body of rules which evolved from those rules applied and administered by the Court of Chancery before the Judicature Act 1873. Since that Act came into force on November 1, 1875 the rules of Equity and the rules of common law have been concurrently applied and administered in all Courts.[28]

The Court of Chancery grew out of the residuum of justice left in the King where his common law courts for some special reason brought about an unjust result, *e.g.* because they provided no remedy owing to the rigidity

---

[19] A company needs to be created formally and registered under the Companies Act 1985. A trust can be created informally: see Chap. 2.

[20] However, for some taxation purposes trustees are considered a single continuing body of persons distinct from the actual individuals who are from time to time trustees: Taxation of Chargeable Gains Act 1992, s.69; *Bond v Pickford* [1983] S.T.C. 517.

[21] *Fraser v Murdoch* (1881) 6 App. Cas. 855 at 874; *Staniar v Evans* (1886) 34 Ch.D. 470 at 477.

[22] *Watling v Lewis* [1911] 1 Ch. 414 at 423–424; *Burt, Boulton & Hayward v Bull* [1895] 1 Q.B. 276 at 285.

[23] *Lumsden v Buchanan* (1865) 4 Macq. 950 at 955; 13 L.T. 174; *Muir v City of Glasgow Bank* (1879) 4 App. Cas. 337 at 355 and 388.

[24] *Re Blundell* (1888) 40 Ch.D. 370 at 377; *Re Exhall Coal Co. Ltd* (1886) 35 Beav. 449 at 453.

[25] *Jacubs v Rylance* (1874) L.R. 17 Eq. 341; *Doering v Doering* (1889) 42 Ch.D. 203.

[26] *Re Johnson* (1880) 15 Ch.D. 548; *Re Firth* [1902] 1 Ch. 342; *Re Raybould* [1900] 1 Ch. 199; *Re Suco Gold Pty. Ltd* (1983) 7 Australian C.L.R. 873.

[27] At common law no *ultra vires* doctrine (like that applicable to companies) applied to trustees who had the full powers of individuals, but the internal equitable interest of beneficiaries came in equity to bind all donees and all purchasers with notice. The trustee having legal ownership could enforce his legal rights against third parties in the common law courts. The beneficiary having only equitable rights could enforce these against the trustee in the Court of Chancery. If the trustee wrongfully refused to exercise his legal rights the beneficiary could be authorised to take legal proceedings in the trustee's name as plaintiff. Since 1875 in such a case the beneficiary will be claimant and will merely join the trustee as a co-defendant to ensure that all necessary parties will be bound by the decision in the case: *Parker-Tweedale v Dunbar Bank plc* [1990] 2 All E.R. 577 at 583.

[28] Supreme Court of Judicature Act 1873, ss.24, 25, now Supreme Court Act 1981, s.49.

of the writ system or only an inadequate remedy or because a party could not succeed due to the power or wealth of the other party.[29] An aggrieved person would petition the King who would refer it to his Chancellor as his right-hand man. The Chancellor, who was an ecclesiastic, with some knowledge of Roman law and canon law, first advised the King and his Council, but towards the end of the fifteenth century began making decrees on his own authority. He was concerned with affording relief in hard cases and acted *in personam* against defendants who were imprisoned for contempt if they did not observe his decrees. At first, Equity varied according to the Chancellor's conscience—or the size of the Chancellor's foot as Selden remarked.[30] The work of hearing petitions led to increasing judicial activity of the Chancellor in what came to be known as the Court of Chancery. Lawyers, like Lord Nottingham at the end of the seventeenth century, instead of ecclesiastics, became Chancellors and began systematically developing a body of rules of equity. The Chancellor, Lord Eldon, observed in 1818,[31] "Nothing would inflict on me greater pain than the recollection that I had done anything to justify the reproach that the Equity of this Court varies like the Chancellor's foot." However, as Jessel M.R. commented in 1880[32]:

> "The rules of Courts of Equity are not supposed to have been established from time immemorial. It is perfectly well-known that they have been established from time to time—altered, improved and refined from time to time. The doctrines are progressive, refined and improved."

Subsequently,[33] Harman L.J. complained, that equitable principles are: **1–24**

> "rather too often bandied about in common law courts as though the Chancellor still had only the length of his own foot to measure when coming to a conclusion,"

though as Bagnall J. remarked in 1972[34]:

> "In the field of equity the length of the Chancellor's foot has been measured or is capable of measurement. This does not mean that equity is past child-bearing; simply that its progeny must be legitimate—by precedent out of principle."

---

[29] For fuller accounts see Holdsworth's *History of English Law*, Vol. 1 at p.395 *et seq.*; Potter's *Historical Introduction to English Law* (4th ed.) at p.152 *et seq.*; Milsom's *Historical Foundations of the Common Law* (2nd ed.) at p.82 *et seq.*; J. H. Baker's *Introduction to English Legal History* (4th ed.), Chaps 6, 14, 15, 16.

[30] *Table Talk of John Selden* (Pollock ed., 1927), p.43.

[31] *Gee v Pritchard* (1818) 2 Swans. 402 at 414.

[32] *Re Hallett's Estate* (1880) 13 Ch.D. 696 at 710.

[33] *Campbell Discount Co. Ltd v Bridge* [1961] 1 Q.B. 445 at 459, (similarly see *per* Lord Radcliffe in *Bridge v Campbell Discount Co. Ltd* [1962] A.C. 600 at 626).

[34] *Cowcher v Cowcher* [1972] 1 All E.R. 943 at 948.

Nowadays, Megarry V.-C. has pointed out[35] there is a:

> "tendency in equity to put less emphasis on detailed rules that have
> emerged from the cases and more weight on the underlying principles
> that engendered those rules, treating the rules less as rules requiring
> complete compliance and more as guidelines to assist the court in
> applying the principles."

1–25   It is crucial to appreciate that Equity is only a gloss on, or supplement
to,[36] the common law that is a self-sufficient system whose rigour needed
mitigating in the interests of justice and of social and economic change.
Thus, Equity's trust concept was used to enable landowners in their
lifetimes in effect to devise land (viz. pass land on by will) or married
women in effect to have separate property or merchant venturers to do
business under deeds of settlement almost as if they were limited companies, when at common law such was not possible due respectively to the
lack of testamentary power, to married men having control of their wives'
property and to the absence of limited companies. Equity developed a
modern law of mortgages (including tacking, marshalling, consolidation and
the crucial doctrine of the equity of redemption) and of restrictive
covenants when the common law had closed the category of negative
easements, while Equity also gave effect to interests in land created for
value without satisfying formal common law requirements. It developed its
remedies of injunction and specific performance and its auxiliary jurisdiction to assist proceedings at law by interrogatories, discovery nowadays
"disclosure", set-off and the taking of accounts, while being ready to relieve
against the rigidity of the law where there was proof of fraud, mistake,
undue influence or misrepresentation. The supplementary nature of Equity
is very evident here, but in respect of Equity's greatest invention, the trust,
a self-sufficient system has developed.

The relationship between equity and the common law

1–26 There are three aspects to the relationship between Equity and the
common law as emphasised by the draftsman of the Judicature Acts 1873–
75, Sir Arthur Wilson.[37] First, Equity recognises and enforces rights and
duties known to the common law but then goes further in recognising and
enforcing other rights and duties. The classic example is the trust, *e.g.*
where property is vested in trustees for A for life, remainder to B
absolutely. The common law protects the trustees' title to the property and
facilitates their dealing with third parties but if A or B wishes to enforce his
rights then it is equity that governs the position. Hence the trustees' rights
are legal rights and the beneficiaries' rights are equitable rights.

1–27   The trust derives from the mediaeval practice of a "feoffor" conveying a
legal estate in land to a "feoffee to uses" to hold it to the use of a *cestui
que use.*" This was done to enable a knight to go off to the Crusades,

---

[35] *Re Montagu's S.T.* [1987] Ch. 264 at 278, [1992] 4 All E.R. 308 at 324.
[36] F. W. Maitland, *Equity* (2nd ed.) pp.18–19; Meagher, Gummow and Lehane (4th ed.) Chap. 1.
[37] See (1875) 19 Sol. Jo. at pp.633–634.

leaving someone to safeguard his land for himself and his family,[38] or to enable some body to benefit as a *"cestui que use"* which could not directly benefit as a feoffee owing to the Mortmain Statutes[39] or vows of poverty.[40] Indeed, lifetime "uses" could be exploited to enable land to be devised in effect and as a tax avoidance device to avoid burdensome feudal incidents. The number of trustees could be kept up so that there was never a death of a sole individual to provoke the levy of feudal dues on death of the estate owner. Accordingly, the Statute of Uses 1535, "executed" the use so that the legal estate vested automatically in the *cestui que use* and not the feoffee to uses.[41] What happened if a legal estate was purportedly conveyed to A to the use of B to the use of C? At first, B held the legal estate as his own property, the first use being executed and the second use being void as repugnant to the first use. However, by the middle of the seventeenth century the second use came to be enforced as a matter of course (not just to prevent fraud or remedy a mistake) and it came to be known as a trust to distinguish it from the first use. The drafting formula became "Unto and to the use of B and his heirs in trust for C and his heirs" and C came to be known as the *cestui que trust*. After the repeal of the Statute of Uses in 1925 land was conveyed "to B in fee simple on trust for C in fee simple."

Over the years C's equitable interest came to be enforced in the Court of Chancery not just against the trustee or a donee of the legal estate from the trustee but against anyone having the legal estate, other than a bona fide purchaser for value of it without notice ("equity's darling"). Notice comprised actual knowledge and knowledge which a person should have had if he had made reasonable inquiries and inspections ("constructive notice"); such actual or constructive notice of a purchaser's agent will be imputed to the purchaser ("imputed notice") unless the agent was acting in fraud of his principal and the matter of which he had notice was relevant to the fraud.

The second aspect is that common law and equity may provide different **1–28** remedies but each leave the claimant free to enjoy whatever remedy was allowed by the other. After all, the common law affords the "bad man" the fundamental freedom to break his contract or misappropriate another person's property and pay damages, while where circumstances justify the intervention of Equity, Equity insists that the man be a "good man" and does not allow him to maintain that he is a "bad man": Equity looks on as done that which ought to be done and declares that the bad man holds particular property on trust for the good man (who can then require legal ownership of the property to be transferred to him) or decrees specific performance or grants an injunction against a legal title owner.[42] Where the

---

[38] To protect the land a "real" action to recover the land (the *"rem"*) had to be brought by an adult male "seised" of the land by virtue of feoffment with livery of seisin and present in court.

[39] The Mortmain Statutes prevented land being conveyed without a royal licence into the "dead hand" of a corporation (not liable to the feudal dues payable on marriage, death or the heir being under age).

[40] *e.g.* the Order of Franciscan Friars.

[41] This soon led to a rebellion as it prevented land being indirectly devised: hence the Statute of Wills 1540 was enacted to enable land to be directly devised, with anti-tax-avoidance provisions in the statute of Explanation of Wills 1542 treating certain lifetime dispositions as if devices by will.

[42] *Att.-Gen. for Hong Kong v Reid* [1994] 1 A.C. 324; *Bromage v Genning* (1616) 1 Roll. Rep. 368; O. W. Holmes, *The Common Law* and (1897) 10 Harv. L.R. 457; Millett L.J. in [1993] Restitution L.R. 7 and 19–21.

common law only allows damages for breach of contract or for nuisance Equity may decree specific performance or grant an injunction. A contract relating to land, before becoming void at law for lack of writing required by the Law of Property (Miscellaneous Provisions) Act 1989[43] was not enforceable in court if written evidence was lacking, though the deposit could be forfeited or recovered for failure of consideration, but in Equity specific performance could be ordered if there was an act of part performance. A voluntary, (*i.e.* gratuitous) covenant under seal enables the covenantee to obtain common law damages for breach thereof[44] but Equity will not decree specific performance since "Equity will not assist a volunteer," *i.e.* an intended donee. At common law a claimant can generally only obtain damages for his losses but if there is a breach of a trust or other fiduciary relationship a claimant can always make the defendant account for any profit he has made.[45]

1–29   Beneficiaries do not sue trustees for damages but seek to make trustees liable to account in equity so as to discover the proper amount due after finalising accounts. Thus, if a trustee acts beyond her powers in the trust deed the beneficiaries can "falsify" the trustee's accounts. If T wrongfully sells 1,000 ABC Ltd shares to purchase 2,000 XYZ Ltd shares which depreciate in value, the sale is "falsified", so that T's accounts should still reveal ownership of 1,000 ABC Ltd shares and T must sell the XYZ shares and purchase 1,000 ABC shares even if they have doubled in value. If T's negligent conduct within her powers causes £10,000 loss to the trust fund then the accounts are "surcharged" by the addition of £10,000 to the trust fund, so requiring T to make up this loss. Moreover, if T wrongfully sells trust assets to purchase a house privately for herself, Equity looks on as done that which the beneficiaries claim ought to have been done and requires the house to be treated as trust property, unless it is worth less than the replacement cost of the sold the trust assets; in this eventuality, T is personally liable for the amount of the replacement cost but the beneficiaries have an equitable charge over the house enabling them to be treated as secured creditors up to the value of the house.

1–30   The Chancellors also established that the beneficiaries have more than a personal right to seek the proper amount due to them from the trustee on a taking of accounts. The beneficiaries have an equitable proprietary interest in the trust fund in T's ownership. This has the effect of affording them priority over T's creditors, heirs or divorcing spouse. Moreover, because the beneficiaries have a property interest they can recover the property from X to whom T has wrongfully transferred the property, unless X is a bona fide purchaser of a legal interest in the property for value without notice of the trust (or a successor thereto). Indeed, if X is such a purchaser, then the beneficiaries can trace the proceeds of sale so as to recover any asset

---

[43] See at para.2–07.
[44] *Cannon v Hartley* [1949] Ch. 213, at para.4–53.
[45] *Surrey C.C. v Bredero Homes* [1993] 1 W.L.R. 1361 (plaintiff received only nominal damages, not being entitled to profit that defendant made from his breach). Exceptionally, the amount of profits may have to be paid over at common law: *Att.-Gen. v Blake* [2001] 1 A.C. 268.

purchased by T with such proceeds considered to be the beneficiaries' moneys in the eyes of Equity. The input value of the beneficiaries can be traced from asset to asset (*e.g.*, to stocks and shares, to the proceeds of sale thereof, to a painting purchased therewith, to the proceeds of sale thereof and to a flat purchased therewith) until such value is wholly dissipated, *e.g.*, by being used to pay off unsecured debts.

The third aspect of the relationship between Equity and the common law **1–31** is that there are some very rare cases where the rules of Equity and of common law actually conflict. In 1616[46] it was held that Equity prevailed because the Court of Chancery could effectively issue common injunctions restraining parties successful in common law courts from enforcing their judgments or restraining parties from continuing with a common law action. Now the Supreme Court Act 1981, s.49 (replacing the Judicature Act 1873, s.25(11) and the Judicature Act 1925, s.44) states, "Every Court exercising jurisdiction in England or Wales in any civil cause or matter shall continue to administer law and equity on the basis that, wherever there is any conflict or variance between the rules of equity and the rules of common law with reference to the same matter, the rules of equity shall prevail."

Examples of conflict are cases where in an action on a deed at law it was **1–32** no defence for a defendant to plead a written variation for value not in a deed but such a defendant could obtain a common injunction in equity.[47] Similarly, if a legal estate owner purportedly granted a lease exceeding three years in writing, instead of by deed, and the document contained a term enabling the landlord to claim a year's rent in advance then at law the landlord (only being entitled to rent in arrear at law) could not sue for such rent or levy distress for such rent, so he could be liable to the tenant for illegal distress. Since Equity would be prepared to decree specific performance so as to have a legal lease by deed executed and before then look on as done that which ought to be done, the landlord could obtain a common injunction in respect of the tenant's action for legal distress.[48] An example of variance arises where a claimant seeks contribution from sureties where one of them is insolvent. At law if A, B and C are sureties for £30,000 and A becomes insolvent then B and C are only liable for £10,000 each. In Equity B and C are liable for £15,000 each.[49] The claimant receives less at law than in Equity so no question arose before 1875 of a defendant seeking a common injunction as happened in cases of conflict.

The fusion fallacy

The Judicature Act 1873 enabled the one Court concurrently to administer **1–33** the rules of common law and the rules of Equity. It did not provide for the fusion of these two systems of principle; it only provided for the fusion of

---

[46] *Earl of Oxford's Case* (1615) 1 Rep. Ch. 1.
[47] *Berry v Berry* [1929] 2 K.B. 316.
[48] *Walsh v Lonsdale* (1882) 21 Ch.D. 9, on which see *Chan v Cresdon Pty. Ltd* (1989) 168 C.L.R. 242.
[49] *Lowe & Sons v Dixon & Sons* (1885) 16 Q.B.D. 455.

the Courts administering the two systems. As Sir George Jessel M.R. stated in *Salt v Cooper*,[50] having himself as Solicitor General piloted the Act through the Commons, the main object of the Act

> "has been sometimes inaccurately called 'the fusion of Law and Equity'; but it is not any fusion, or anything of the kind; it was the vesting in one tribunal the administration of Law and Equity in every cause, action or dispute which should come before that tribunal."

After all, section 25(11) of the 1873 Act and its statutory replacements assume the continued existence of two separate systems for otherwise there would be no need to provide for the resolution of conflicts between them. In Ashburner's vivid metaphor,[51] "the two streams of jurisdiction though they run in the same channel run side by side and do not mingle their waters."

Surprisingly, Lord Diplock in *obiter dicta* has stated[52]:

> "My Lords, by 1977 this metaphor has in my view become both mischievous and deceptive. The innate conservatism of English lawyers may have made them slow to recognise that by the Judicature Act 1873 the two systems of substantive and adjectival law formerly administered by Courts of Law and Courts of Chancery were fused. As at the confluence of the Rhone and Saone, it may be possible for a short distance to discern the source from which each part of the combined stream came, but there comes a point at which this ceases to be possible. If Professor Ashburner's fluvial metaphor is to be retained at all, the waters of the confluent streams of law and equity have surely mingled now."

But how can law and equity be fused? If a trustee does what he is not entitled to do, at the behest of the beneficiaries he is treated as if he had only done what he was entitled to do, and so must restore the value of the trust fund to what it would have been if he had been a good trustee duly performing his primary obligation in the best interests of the beneficiaries: hence questions of foreseeability and causation of losses do not arise once it is established that loss would not have occurred but for the original authorised conduct. Such questions are crucial for common law liability in

---

[50] (1880) 16 Ch.D. 544 at 549. In an extempore interlocutory judgment (where the right to specific performance was conceded) in *Walsh v Lonsdale* (1882) 21 Ch.D. 9 at 14, Jessel M.R. got carried away and erroneously said: "There are not two estates as there were formerly, one estate at common law by reason of the payment of rent from year to year and an estate in equity under the agreement. There is only one court and the equity rules prevail in it." Legal leases and equitable leases co-exist without conflict: Megarry & Wade's *Law of Real Property* (6th ed.), paras 14–039 *et seq*; Meagher Gummow and Lehane, Equity (4th ed.), paras 2–180 to 2–225; *Tinsley v Milligan* [1994] 1 A.C. 340.
[51] *Principles of Equity* (2nd ed., 1933), p.18.
[52] *United Scientific Holdings Ltd v Burnley Borough Council* [1978] A.C. 904 at 924–925. His common law colleagues all spoke in the same vein. See also Lord Denning in *Nelson v Larholt* [1948] 1 K.B. 339 at 343 and *Errington v Errington* [1952] 1 K.B. 290 at 298. Contrast the views of Lord Brandon in *Bank of Boston v European Grain* [1989] 1 All E.R. 545 at 557 and Mummery L.J. in *MCC Proceeds Inc. v Lehman Bros International* [1998] 4 All E.R. 675 at 691.

tort and contract. Moreover, in the law of trusts there is legal and equitable ownership and a beneficiary, having only an equitable title, cannot sue a third party at law for negligently damaging trust property[53]; in property law there are legal and equitable rights with different effects, especially as regards third parties who find that equitable rights are normally much less obvious than legal rights; common law claims in respect of breach of contract extend to losses caused to the plaintiff but not normally to profits made by the defendant[54]; equitable rights can only be enforced by equitable remedies and not by common law damages,[55] equitable defences like hardship and not affording assistance to volunteers or to those who come without "clean hands" cannot be defences to common law actions, *e.g.* for debt. It is a fallacy[56] to assume that law and equity have been fused into a new body of principles. It would be possible to dispense with the terms "legal" and "equitable" and have a unitary system of rules replicating the effect of the current rules, but why bother when the current taxonomy works well?

The modern trust concept

(1) The trustees own and manage segregated assets as a trust fund for   **1–34** the benefit of beneficiaries, who are not ordinary creditors of the trustees but have an interest in the fund that survives the insolvency, dissolution, death or divorce of the trustees.

(2) The beneficiaries, indeed, have an equitable proprietary interest binding not only the trustee's creditors, heirs or spouse but extending to property, whether the original trust property or property traceable[57] as representing the original trust property, either owned by the trustees or a third party transferee who is not a bona fide purchaser of a legal interest without notice of the trust nor protected by statutory provisions (*e.g.*, conferring a good title on a purchaser of land if paying the purchase moneys to two trustees or a trust corporation, irrespective of notice of the trust).

(3) In the absence of express provisions in the trust instrument there is implied a regime not just of trustees' powers but also of trusteeship obligations to ensure the trustees' impartiality, loyalty and prudence and so protect the beneficiaries[58]; but there are certain irreducible

---

[53] *Leigh & Sillavan v Aliakmon Shipping* [1986] 2 All E.R. 145 at 151; *Parker-Tweedale v Dunbar Bank plc* [1990] 2 All E.R. 577.

[54] *Surrey C.C. v Bredero Homes* [1993] 1 W.L.R. 1361; *In data v ACL* [1997] *The Times,* August 14; for exceptional circumstances see *Attorney-General v Blake* [2001] 1 A.C. 268.

[55] *Downsview Nominees v First City Corp* [1993] A.C. 295 at 315; *China & South Seas Bank Ltd v Tan* [1990] 1 A.C. 536 at 543. By the Supreme Court Act 1981, s.50 (replacing provisions originally in Chancery Amendment Act 1858) damages may be awarded in lieu of or in addition to specific performance or an injunction, which is how the unexplained award of damages in *Seager v Copydex* (1967) 2 All E.R. 414 is explained by Slade J. in *English v Dedham Vale Properties Ltd* [1978] 1 All E.R. 382 at 399, although in the view of the Canadian Supreme Court in *Cadbury Schweppes Inc. v FBI Foods* (1999) 167 D.L.R. (4th) 577 equitable compensation is available under the inherent equitable jurisdiction.

[56] As emphasised by Holdsworth (1935) 51 L.Q.R. 142; Lord Evershed (1954) 70 L.Q.R. 326; P. V. Baker (1977) 93 L.Q.R. 529; Meagher Gummow & Lehane, *Equity* (4th ed.) paras 2–100 to 2–110; J.E. Martin [1994] Conv. 13; D. Capper (1994) 14 *Legal Studies* 315.

[57] See Chap. 12.

[58] See at paras 9–08 *et seq.*

core obligations that cannot be ousted[59] *e.g.* to produce accounts to beneficiaries for falsification or surcharge.

(4) The trust instrument can create whatever flexible or inflexible structure the settlor desires, whether concerning the creation of a variety of rights for beneficiaries or concerning matters of internal management.

(5) It is the trustees who sue or are sued, the trust not being a legal person, so there is the possibility of "look-through" or "conduit" taxation of beneficiaries, avoiding entity-level taxation unless statute intervenes.

(6) The court, in addition to its usual punitive, regulatory role, has a paternalistic supporting role to advise trustees and resolve doubts or enlarge trustees' powers in the unforeseeable circumstances that can arise in the lengthy life of a trust.

(7) A trust is not a contract like a contract for the benefit of a third party or parties[60] or a contract of agency.

   (a) Once the settlor (gratuitously or pursuant to a contract) has made his unilateral transfer of his assets to the trustee to own as a segregated patrimony, he drops out of the picture and cannot tell the trustee what to do[61]: the trustee's obligations are independent obligations owed exclusively to the beneficiaries who alone have correlative rights against the trustee.[62] Indeed, in the rare case where all the beneficiaries collectively between them entitled to the whole equitable proprietory interest are all of full capacity they can unanimously act to terminate the trust against the opposition of the trustee and of the settlor.

   (b) The fact that the settlor later dies or becomes mentally incapacitated or discovers a breach of trust has been committed is totally immaterial.

   (c) The death or incapacity of the trustee does not affect the continuing existence of the trust: it only means that someone else will need to take over the office of trustee. Indeed, equitable interests under a trust can arise without the knowledge and agreement of the trustee (*e.g.* in the case of a testamentary trust or the case of property, like land or shares, that can be transferred into the name of another without the need to tell such person) but the obligations of trusteeship will not arise if the trustee refuses to act and disclaims, in which event, the settlor or his executor takes the property as trustee.[63]

   (d) A settler can be sole trustee of designated property of his own on trust for others or for charity: a person cannot contract with himself.

---

[59] See at paras 9–167, 9–250.
[60] First permitted by Contracts (Rights of Third Parties) Act 1999.
[61] *Re Astor's ST* [1952] Ch 534 at 542, *Bradshaw v University College of Wales* [1987] 3 All E.R. 200 at 203.
[62] Powers of appointment or of revocation or to direct or veto certain action may, however, be reserved to others, *e.g.* the settlor, his widow, a designated protector.
[63] Equity will not allow a trust to fail for want of a trustee: at para.8–39.

    (e) A major breach of trust confers no right to treat the trust as terminated: it merely enables the beneficiaries to falsify or surcharge the trustee's accounts and to apply to the court to replace the trustee.

    (f) A beneficiary need suffer no loss before requiring the trustee to restore to the trust fund value lost due to breaches of trust: a claimant suing in contract (or tort) has to show she suffered loss.

The past utility, versatility and vitality of the trust

The trust has been to the fore in reflecting economic and social changes **1–35** and leading to statutory reform of the law.

  (a) It enabled land indirectly to be left on death to someone other than the owner's legal heir until Parliament made this possible directly in 1540.

  (b) It enabled members of an unincorporated association to trade via trustees with the apparent benefit of limited liability until the courts after 80 years or so held the members to be personally liable, thereby compelling Parliament to enact legislation permitting limited liability corporations in the mid twentieth century.

  (c) When married women would otherwise have no property rights, the father of a married woman could transfer property to trustees to hold to her "separate use", so that she had some financial independence before legislation conferred independence on wives.

  (d) With the increase in cohabitation over the last 30 years, problems have arisen where W has moved into a house or flat owned by M and then acted in detrimental reliance on a belief encouraged by M that F is to acquire some share in the property. Here the courts have been prepared to impose a constructive or resulting trust upon M so that the property is regarded in equity as co-owned in shares decreed by the court.

Where the King or Parliament has considered that there has been an abuse **1–36** of the trust then legislation has blocked such abuse.

  (a) Thus, transfers to trustees with intent to avoid creditors were first blocked in 1376, while transfers to trustees to the use of a corporation (to whom transfers could not be made directly due to the Statute of Mortmain) were blocked in 1391.

  (b) Transfers to trustees to avoid wardship rights of feudal lords were blocked in 1490, while the general device of using "uses" to avoid feudal incidents was blocked in 1535.

  (c) More recently, transfers made within six years of death to trustees (or others) with intent to defeat claims of the transferor's dependants under the Inheritance (Provision for Family & Dependants) Act 1975 can be set aside as far as necessary, as can dispositions to trustees (or others) with intent to defeat the Matrimonial Causes Act 1973 claims of the transferor's spouse or children.

On the tax front, legislation ensures that settlors cannot make transfers to trustees so as to obtain unfair tax advantages, *e.g.* settlors are taxed on trust income if creating a trust for their infant children or a trust under which the settlor or his spouse can receive any benefit, while taxes on death in respect of property are not avoided by a settlor who is not entirely excluded from benefiting for such property under his lifetime trust.

The modern utility, versatility and vitality of the trust

A. The family context

1–37 Trusts are particularly common to provide for the management of the affairs of beneficiaries who are mentally or physically handicapped or who are spendthrift or who are young or who are old. They are also used to prevent the law of succession operating to vest the deceased's property absolutely in his adult children who could then dissipate the property. Thus a settlor's trust can preserve and generate family assets for three or four generations, successive family members benefiting from avoiding division of the assets into smaller and smaller shares each generation and from economies of scale in the management of the large pool of family assets.
Examples of family trusts are:

(a) a grandparent's fixed trust for such of the grandchildren who attain 25 years in equal shares;

(b) a testator's fixed trust for the surviving spouse for life, remainder to their children equally, but with power for the spouse by will or by deed to appoint the capital unequally between such of the children and the children's children as may be seen fit in the spouse's absolute discretion;

(c) a testator's fixed trust for the surviving spouse for life, remainder equally to each of their children for the life of each respective child, with the capital of such child's share to pass equally to such child's children, subject to an overriding power for the surviving spouse to appoint as in (b) and after the death of such spouse for the trustees to have such power of appointment;

(d) a discretionary trust for such of the descendants of the settlor/ testator as the trustees shall see fit in their absolute discretion from time to time to pay income or capital to, before expiry of an eighty year perpetuity period.

1–38 The settlor can provide a legally significant (but not legally binding) letter of wishes to guide the trustees in the exercise of their discretions, while family members can be trustees and employ professional discretionary portfolio managers to manage investments and other professionals for other tasks. Often a professional trust corporation is trustee, while family input can be preserved via the trust instrument providing for a "protector" with arrangements for the appointment of successor protectors. The protector may be the settlor or his surviving spouse or a specified child or a committee or board or, even, a company whose shares are owned by family members. The protector may have powers of vetoing trustees' proposed distributions of capital or proposed sales of particular assets and power to replace the trustees, even with foreign trustees to be subjected to a new foreign trust law replacing English law as the law governing the trust. The protector will generally be subject to similar fiduciary duties as trustees in exercising his powers unless the trust instrument or special circumstances indicate otherwise.

Lifetime trusts are more useful than testamentary trusts because the probate process on death is a public one revealing the terms of the will and the taxable size of the deceased's estate. Moreover, if a settlor has assets in many jurisdictions he does not want those assets to pass on death subject to different succession laws and a variety of forced heirship regimes, forcing different fractions of his estate to pass to his children and treating gifts made within differing periods before death as part of such estate.

To avoid such complex situations, well-advised wealthy persons with valuable assets in a variety of countries put most of their assets into a lifetime trust so as to escape the application of laws governing succession to a deceased's estate.

If a person dies intestate then his administrators hold his estate on a statutory trust with a power of sale. A similar trust arises whenever land is co-owned if an express trust is not created in the co-ownership documentation.

B. The commercial context

As seen, trusts developed in the context of preserving and developing **1–39** family wealth and of furthering charitable purposes. Private client lawyers specialise in these areas, thereby helping their clients in generating family wealth and using any surplus to advance philanthropic purposes.

In the twentieth century, the story of the trust has been the story of corporate finance lawyers utilising the trust structure, so that it is estimated that no more than 10 per cent of trust assets are comprised in family and charitable trusts. Thus, the most important dimension of the trust concept is as an instrument of commerce, particularly for money-raising, with the key attributes of protection against insolvency, the protective regime of fiduciary trust law and the flexibility of provisions that can be inserted in trust instruments. In this context the trust results from a contract rather than a gift.

The key attributes of trusts can be employed in whatever ways the ingenious mind of man can devise. Common uses of the trusts are as follows.

1. Pensions for employees

To ensure funding of pensions for retired employees, money is paid **1–40** (pursuant to the contract of employment) to trustees to manage as a segregated fund. The retired employee then receives thereout either a percentage of his final salary or a lump sum that must be used to purchase an annuity.

2. Collective investment schemes

1–41 A trust is used as an open ended collective investment vehicle (with no fixed or irreducible capital base) in which the value of units in the unit trust held for a particular unit-holder-investor is directly related to the value of the assets held by the custodian trustee to the order of the managing trustee. Investors can sell their units back to the manager whenever they wish, whereupon a charge to capital gains tax will arise (but no such charge arises against the trustees or the unit holders on the disposal and reinvestment of underlying trust assets).

"Unit trusts" (known as "mutual funds" in North America) differ from "investment trusts" (as featured in share price pages of newspapers) because the latter actually are companies so that the investor owns shares in the company, the value of which will depend not just on the value of the assets owned by the company but also upon the dividend policy of the company, so that the share price will stand at a discount to the net asset value. Open-ended investment companies (OEICs)—as open-ended as unit trusts—can now be created with share prices directly reflecting the value of underlying assets.

Unit trusts can quote one price for acquisition of units and another for redemption of units, while OEICs have a single pricing system, leading many unit trusts to move to a single pricing system. A unit trust can only issue "income" or "accumulation" units while an OEIC can issue different classes of share intended for different types of investment or investor.

3. Collective security trusts for holders of bonds or debenture stock

1–42 The trustee has the benefit of the borrower's promise to repay the loan collectively provided by a group of lenders and often also has assets of the borrower as security for repayment.

The trustee is an independent professional person (not the agent of either the lenders or the borrower) who can be relied upon confidentially to monitor matters and to decide the proper response to any default or even to modify the terms of the loan without the expense and trouble of a meeting with the lenders except in defined special circumstances.

The rights of the trustee and any fruits of such rights (*e.g.*, proceeds of sale of a security) are held as a separate fund for the lenders (of whom there are too many to be co-owners of the security interest, four being the maximum for co-ownership of interests in land), so protecting them against the insolvency of the trustee whose office as trustee will then be filled by another trustee.

4. Syndicated loan trusts

1–43 Where slices of capital will be provided at differing times and may be from lenders different from the original lenders, trustees of collective security trusts can have overriding powers to afford subsequent lenders the same priority as earlier lenders or even a higher priority but, perhaps, only if a specified proportion of the earlier lenders agree.

Indeed, to deal with the case where all the lenders are repaid but further loans are needed (*e.g.* in financing the Channel Tunnel) matters can be arranged so that the trustee continues to hold the security but for the new lenders without the need for anything further to be done (like registration of a new charge if the old charge were considered to have ceased when all the old lenders had been paid).

5. Subordination trusts

Subordination of a creditor occurs where one creditor, the "subordinated" **1–44** or "junior" creditor, agrees not to be paid by a debtor until another creditor, the "senior" creditor, of the common debtor has been paid.

To avoid the insolvency rule that requires rateable distributions to creditors from an insolvent debtor, a trust deed is executed under which the junior debt is payable by the debtor to a trustee, who is to hold any payment made in respect of the junior debt on trust first for the benefit of the senior creditor to the amount of the senior debt, and then, if any money remains, for the junior creditor. The senior creditor is thus protected against the insolvency of both the junior creditor and the debtor. Prospective lenders often will not lend unless they obtain this priority over existing debts.[64]

6. Securitisation trusts of special purpose vehicles (SPV)

For the purposes of enabling a complex portfolio of assets (*e.g.*, secured or **1–45** unsecured debts, credit card receivables) to be available as security to investors, a company, known as an SPV, purchases the portfolio, borrowing the money via a collective security bond issue (as in 3 above). The shares in the SPV and the portfolio are held on trust to repay the bondholders with any (small) surplus held on trust for the bondholders or for charitable purposes (or for non-charitable purposes where expressly permitted by foreign laws, *e.g.* of Bermuda, Cayman Islands, Isle of Man, Jersey).[65]

This avoids the original owner of the portfolio beneficially owning shares in the SPV, and so avoids the SPV's debt appearing on such owner's consolidated balance sheet. Where there is a shortage in the financial markets of AAA rated bonds or of high yielding bonds it is possible to use this securitisation trust device to put together a "ring-fenced" package of corporate bonds to help satisfy the shortage.

7. Project financing and future income streams

If L contracts to lend £50 million to B and actually pays over the money to **1–46** B on the basis that B will hold on trust for L all money B expects to acquire from a particular source once B acquires it, then as soon as B does acquire

---

[64] *e.g. Manning v AIG Europe UK Ltd* [2004] E.W.H.C. (Ch.) 1760.
[65] Further on commercial and financial uses of trusts see S. Moerman, "Non-charitable purposes trusts" (1999–2000) 6 Trusts & Trustees at 7–13; C. Duffet, "Using Trusts in International Financial and Commercial Transactions" (1992) 1 Jo Int Planning at 23–30; J.H. Langbein "The Secret Life of the Trust: The Trust as an Instrument of Commerce (1997) 107 Yale L.J. pp.165–189: and D.J. Hayton (ed.). Extending the Boundaries of Trusts and Similar Ring-Fenced Funds (Kluwer, 2002), Chapters by D. Hayton, S. Worthington, P. O'Hogan and A. Anderson.

it B holds it on trust for L.[66] Such acquired money is not available for B's creditors: after all, by paying over the £50 million to B, L made such available to B's creditors, who should not therefore benefit further by also having available to them the asset purchased by L as the price of the loan.

This enables B to acquire money now in respect of a future income stream expected from a particular project *e.g.* a tunnel, a mine, an oil well. Such income will be used to service the debt interest and to repay capital.

8. Temporary purpose trusts of money until debtor-creditor relationship arises (Quistclose[67] trusts)

1–47 C can transfer money to T or to D on trust for C until the money is used for a specified purpose benefiting D, whereupon D is merely to be a debtor of C.

This protects C against the insolvency of D if the money is not so used (unless C paid the money on trust to D, and D wrongfully dissipated it so it became untraceable).

9. Client accounts e.g. of solicitors

If X, involved in a profession or business, has an office (or private) account with a bank and a separate client account for clients' money, then the client account money is held on trust for the clients, who are thus safe if X becomes insolvent. It is a fundamental feature of the trust concept that anyone can open in his own name an account designated as a trust account for the benefit of others, who are then protected against the insolvency of the account holder. In such event they are entitled to the balance in the account and to assets wrongfully purchased by the account holder in his own name with money drawn from the account or wrongfully given away to a third party.

10. Trusts affecting personal accounts of agents or purchasers so as to protect interests of principals or vendors

1–48 P Co may sell its fleet of cars or its airline tickets through the agency of A Co which will merely be in a debtor-creditor relationship with P Co, having to pay it an amount corresponding to the proceeds of sale less A Co's commission. Purchasers from A Co will not make out one cheque in favour of A Co for its commission and a second cheque in favour of P Co for the balance, but just a cheque for the whole amount in favour of A Co, which will pay such cheque into its personal account. P Co then runs the risk of A Co's insolvency.

To avoid such risk,[68] P Co can negotiate an arrangement whereby A Co contractually agrees that it will hold a specified (fractional or percentage)

---

[66] *Re Lind* [1915] 2 Ch. 345, *Palette Shoes Pty. Ltd v Krohn* (1937) 58 C.L.R. 1 at 26–27.
[67] *Barclays Bank v Quistclose Investment Ltd* [1970] A.C. 567 as explained in *Twinsectra Ltd v Yardley* [2002] 2 A.C. 164.
[68] *Re Fleet Disposal Services Ltd* [1995] 1 B.C.L.C. 345; *Re Lewis of Leicester Ltd* [1995] 1 B.C.L.C. 428; *Re ILG Travel* [1995] 2 B.C.L.C. 128; *Air Canada v M & L Travel Ltd* (1994) 108 DLR (4th) 592; background position to *Royal Brunei Airlines v Tan* [1995] 2 A.C. 378.

part of the proceeds of sale that represents the whole proceeds less its commission on trust for P Co, it will pay an amount of money corresponding to such part to P Co within a specified period of, say, five working days (such payment to discharge the relevant indebtedness of A Co to P Co) and will not let the balance in the account within such period fall below the amount due to P Co.[69]

V Co may sell raw materials to P Co which P Co uses to produce manufactured products belonging wholly to P Co and which P Co then sells. To avoid the insolvency risk arising from P Co only being a debtor of V Co, V Co can negotiate in its contract of sale with P Co, that P Co will be trustee of such a (fractional or percentage) part of the proceeds of sale of the newly manufactured products as is equivalent to the amount owing to V Co by P Co at the time P Co received such proceeds,[70] P Co will pay to V Co such amount within a specified period of, say, 5 working days and will not let the balance in its account within such period fall below such amount due to V Co.

In both these instances of principal-agent and vendor-purchaser the principal or vendor will be able to invoke equitable tracing processes so as to have an equitable lien or charge for the amount of its money[71] over the personal bank account of the agent or purchaser and an equitable proprietary interest in any traceable product purchased with its money. Under the general law, the principal or vendor will not have such rights if the alleged trust was a sham (both parties from the outset agreeing on irregular payments under a debtor-creditor relationship to help the cash-flow of the agent or purchaser) or will lose such rights if expressly or impliedly agreeing to ouster of the trust relationship by a debtor-creditor relationship.

11. Building contracts: retention trusts

Standard form building construction contracts have a clause for the **1–49** employer of the management contractor, which employs various works contractors, to set up a retention trust fund of a percentage (*e.g.*, three or five per cent) of each amount certified by the architect as due to the management contractor for itself and the works contractors. Half of this fund is payable when the architect issues the certificate of practical completion and the final half upon issue of the certificate of completion of making good defects.

---

[69] One cannot trace beyond the lowest intermediate balance (*Roscoe v Winder* [1915] 1 Ch. 62): this clause is not vital but serves to emphasise the trust relationship.

[70] *Associated Alloys Pty Ltd v ACN 001 452 106 Pty Ltd* (in Liquidation) 2000 74 A.L.J.R. 862 where at 869 Gaudron, McHugh, Gummow and Hayne JJ. state "There being value [provided by V Co], and equity regarding as done that which ought to be done, a completely constituted trust would arise in respect of those proceeds as they were received by the Buyer [P Co]".

[71] Such charge arises by operation of law from the creation of the trust, and a trust affecting a company's property does not require registration under s.395 Companies Act 1985 unlike an expressly created charge. If the contract between V Co and P Co related not to a trust of a specific ascertainable part (say half) of the proceeds (say £100,000) received by P Co, but to a trust of an amount corresponding to the amount of the debt (say £50,000) a problem arises as to certainty of subject matter of a trust, there being no £50,000 fund segregated from the remaining £50,000, so that only a contractual charge would arise, falling within s.395.

Thus, the employer has a measure of security to ensure the building is properly completed and the management contractor and works contractors have some protection against the insolvency of the employer.

12. Sinking fund trusts

1–50 Where major expenditure will be needed after a number of years, money can be paid regularly to a trustee so that an adequate amount will certainly be available to carry out a particular purpose, for example major repairs or renewals for blocks of flats, for old heritage property, or for good environmental land reclamation after working out of a mine.

13. Employee share ownership trusts

A company can arrange for some of its shares to be held on trust for allocation to particular employees in due course (who then receive favoured tax treatment if they do not sell their shares for three years). Thus its employees are encouraged to work hard (so helping it and the English economy to develop) The trust also provides a market for shares in the employer company. "All employee" trusts of shares are particularly encouraged by provisions in the Finance Act 2000, the Inland Revenue even publishing model trust deeds.

14. Trusts of shares to separate control from ownership of the company

1–51 It may be useful to have voting rights vested in independent trustees rather than in those owning the economic value. Thus, where A and B are 60:40 shareholders in a joint venture company they can transfer their shares to T on the basis T must vote 75 per cent as B directs, which provides B with greater protection than if A merely contracted with B to vote 35 of his 60 as B directs, in which case A could break his contract and harm B's interests.

Independent trustees may be controlling directors of a company so that those owning the economic value do not have control which would contravene public interest laws, *e.g.* for the conduct of banking business or for regulating fair competition (where the regulatory authority may require the shares to be sold but afford the trustees a reasonable time for this, so avoiding a forced sale at a depressed price that would have had to occur if the beneficiary controlled the company).

15. Custodian trusts in the financial or securities markets

1–52 To facilitate speedy inexpensive dealings in stocks and shares, many of such securities are held by a corporate custodian, often for a sub-custodian, which holds for a broker who holds for a client. Because there can be no bailment or custody of intangibles, intangibles must be owned by the custodian as trustee, with sub-custodians, brokers and their clients having only a proportionate equitable co-ownership interest in the fungible pool of securities legally owned by the custodian as trustee.

This trust of a pool of assets for persons entitled to proportionate shares therein as equitable co-owners provides purchasers of securities with a proprietary interest and avoids technical certainty problems concerning which specific securities belong to whom. Thus, if Nominee plc is registered shareholder of ten million shares in Bigg plc and Subcustodian plc is interested in two million shares out of which it sold 100,000 to P, P does not actually own a specific 100,000 shareholding. P owns a one twentieth share of Subcustodian's one fifth share of Nominee's shareholding.

16. Pledges of bills of lading

Pledging the bill of lading with the other shipping documents requires **1–53** delivery to the lender, but the buyer-borrower needs these documents to obtain the goods from the shipping company. If the lender parts with the documents unconditionally the pledge will be extinguished.

Thus, the buyer provides the lender with a trust letter or receipt in which, in return for the release of the documents, the buyer undertakes he will hold the documents and then the goods and any proceeds of sale on trust for the lender, who is thereby deemed to continue in constructive possession of the documents, so that the pledge remains valid.

The nature of a beneficiary's interest

There has been much controversy over the nature of a beneficiary's interest **1–54** under a trust based upon the differences between *in personam* rights against trustees and *in rem* rights against property.[72] However, much depends on the meaning in context of *in personam* and *in rem* and whether one is dealing with a *bare* trust (A holds on trust for X absolutely) or a *fixed* trust (A holds on trust for X for life, remainder to Y for life, remainder to Z absolutely) or a *discretionary* trust (A holds on trust to distribute the income and capital between such of X Y or Z or their spouses and issue as he sees fit).

In all cases X has an equitable chose in action, a right *in personam* **1–55** against the trustee to verify or falsify the trusteeship accounts and to compel due administration of the trust: the *situs* of that chose is in the jurisdiction where the trustees reside and administer the trust. As beneficiary under a bare trust he may demand transfer of the legal title from the trustee and so obtain the trust property *in rem* for himself as legal and beneficial owner[73]; he may, instead, assign or declare a sub-trust of his equitable interest in the trust property; he may trace the trust property into the hands of third-party recipients from the trustee unless the third party is a bona fide purchaser of the legal title for value without notice of his equitable interest[74] or a purchaser who complies with the overreaching requirements of the Law of Property Act or the Settled Land Act[75] or a person who validly acquired title under a foreign *lex situs*.[76] Thus he has

---

[72] Hart (1899) 15 L.Q.R. 294; Scott (1917) 17 Col.L.R. 269; Stone (1917) 17 Col.L.R. 467; Hanbury (1929) 45 L.Q.R. 198; Latham (1954) 32 Can.B.R. 520; Waters (1967) 45 Can.B.R. 219; *Baker v Archer-Shee* [1927] A.C. 844.
[73] *Saunders v Vautier* (1841) 4 Beav. 115; see at para.9–123.
[74] *Re Diplock* [1948] Ch. 465.
[75] LPA 1925, s.27; SLA 1925, s.18.
[76] Art.11, para, 2(d) of The Hague Trust Convention, implemented by Recognition of Trusts Act 1987.

proprietary *in rem* rights in the relevant assets. However, in this last eventuality if the trustee has dissipated the proceeds of sale then X has lost his equitable proprietary interest and is left merely with his equitable chose in action against the trustee personally, which will be worthless if the trustee is bankrupt or disappears with all his assets. For tax purposes X is properly regarded as *in rem* owner of the relevant assets. However, X is properly regarded as enforcing an *in personam* right against A where A holds a French immovable on express or resulting trust for X,[77] but refuses to transfer title to X, so that X's English proceedings against A resident in England are not "proceedings which have as their object rights *in rem* in, or tenancies of, immovable property" when the court of the *lex situs* has exclusive jurisdiction.[78] As the European Court stated[79]:

> "The aim of the proceedings before the national court is to obtain a declaration that the son holds the flat for the exclusive benefit of the father and that he is under a duty to execute the documents necessary to convey ownership of the flat to the father. The father . . . seeks only to assert rights as against the son. Consequently his action is an action *in personam* . . . the immovable nature of the property held in trust and its location are irrelevant to the issues which have to be determined in the main proceedings, which would have been the same if the dispute had concerned a flat situated in the U.K. or a yacht."

1–56 If X be a beneficiary with a limited interest under a fixed trust, he has a disposable equitable proprietary interest but he cannot claim the trust capital unless the other beneficiaries, Y and Z, are each of full capacity and join in demanding it from the trustees so that they can then divide it between themselves as they agree. He has a right to the income produced by the trust assets and is regarded as having part of the equitable ownership of the assets themselves[80] so that if they are situate in New York State he is treated for tax purposes as interested in foreign assets, namely New York assets[81]; it being immaterial that the trustees reside in and administer the trust in England so that his equitable chose in action is English.

1–57 If he is a beneficiary under a discretionary trust, X merely has a hope of receiving something. He cannot compel the trustees to pay him anything (so that the source of any entitlement is the exercise of the trustees' discretion) and cannot substitute another person for himself as a potential recipient of discretionary sums but he can release his rights[82] and he has *in*

---

[77] *Webb v Webb* [1994] Q.B. 696 (Ct. of Justice of EU). See also *Ashurst v Polland* [2001] 2 All E.R. 75.
[78] Art.16(1) of Convention on Jurisdiction and the Enforcement of Judgments in Civil and Commercial Matters implemented by Civil Jurisdiction and Judgments Act 1982, replaced by Council Regulation No.44 of 2001.
[79] [1994] Q.B. 696 at 716.
[80] *New Zealand Insurance Co. Ltd v C.P.D. (Victoria)* [1973] V.R. 659.
[81] *Baker v Archer-Shee* [1927] A.C. 844; *Hamilton-Russell's Executors v I.R.C.* (1943) 25 T.C. 200 at 207–208; *I.R.C. v Berrill* [1982] 1 All E.R. 867 at 880. Where the trust is not an English trust but a New York trust then, by the New York proper law, a life tenant only has an equitable chose in action and not a proprietary interest in the trust assets: *Archer-Shee v Garland* [1931] A.C. 212. Further see *Memec v I.R.C.* [1996] S.T.C. 1336 at 1351 and, on appeal, [1998] S.T.C. 754 at 764.
[82] *Re Gulbenkian's Settlement (No.2)* [1970] Ch. 408.

rem standing to trace for the benefit of all those interested under the trust.[83] However, it seems that just as personal representatives of an unadministered estate[84] and a company subject to a winding-up order[85] have ownership subject to onerous duties in circumstances where the devisees, legatees or creditors have no equitable proprietary interest but only choses in action, so trustees of a discretionary trust with a large fluctuating class of beneficiaries have ownership subject to onerous fiduciary duties in circumstances where the beneficiaries under the discretionary trust only have an equitable chose in action.[86] Indeed, Viscount Radcliffe[87] has rejected the view that "for all purposes and at every moment of time the law requires the separate existence of two different kinds of estate or interest in property, the legal and the equitable . . . Equity in fact calls into existence and protects equitable rights and interests in property only where their recognition has been found to be required in order to give effect to its doctrines."[88]

To conclude, in order to understand the working operation of a trust it is **1–58** better to regard the interest of a beneficiary as an *in personam* right to compel the trustees to perform the trust, *i.e.* as an equitable chose in action situated where the trustees reside and administer the trust. However, where the trustee has become insolvent or things have gone wrong and trust property finds its way wrongly into the hands of a third party (other than equity's darling) then it is appropriate to regard the interest of a beneficiary, as a result of his having throughout had[89] an interest in a fund, as an equitable *in rem* right.[90]

Where the state is seeking to recover tax which hinges upon the *situs* of the taxable asset the better approach (in the absence of express statutory guidance) is to say that if X is a bare beneficiary or a life tenant he should in substance be regarded as having an *in rem* interest in the trust assets wherever they may be situated. But if X is a discretionary beneficiary then in substance he should be regarded as having an *in personam* equitable chose in action[91] situate where the trustees reside and administer the trust.

From a tax point of view a beneficiary's interest (leaving aside bare **1–59** trusts) will be one of two basic types. He will either have a current fixed entitlement to such net income as remains after a proper exercise of the trustees' administrative powers (an interest in possession,[92] *e.g.* a life

---

[83] After all, a residuary beneficiary under an unadministered estate can assert "the estate's right of property": *Commissioner for Stamp Duties v Livingston* [1965] A.C. 694 at 714.

[84] *Commissioner for Stamp Duties v Livingston* [1965] A.C. 694.

[85] *Ayerst v C. & K. Constructions Ltd* [1976] A.C. 168.

[86] If the class is a fixed class of, say, seven persons of full capacity then the seven have *Saunders v Vautier* (1841) 4 Beav 115 proprietary interests: *Schmidt v Rosewood Trust Ltd* [2003] 2 A.C. 709, para.40.

[87] Trustees of a charitable purpose trust would seem to be in a similar position, having ownership subject to onerous duties enforceable by the Attorney-General: see *Att.-Gen. v Cocke* [1988] Ch. 414 and *Von Ernst & Cie SA v IRC* [1980] 1 All E.R. 677.

[88] [1965] A.C. 694 at 712.

[89] See R. C. Nolan, "Property in a Fund" (2004) 120 L.Q.R. 108.

[90] Unless the *lex situs* governing transfer of the relevant property was a foreign one having no concept of equitable proprietary right in its code of property principles.

[91] *cf. Sainsbury v I.R.C.* [1970] 1 Ch. 712.

[92] *Pearson v I.R.C.* [1981] A.C. 753. The distinction between trusts with an interest in possession and trusts where no such interest exists, is crucial for inheritance tax purposes: Inheritance Tax Act 1984, ss.49–57, 58–85.

interest) or he will have no fixed entitlement to anything, merely hoping that the trustees will from time to time give him some of the trust income (*i.e.* he will merely be beneficiary of a discretionary trust)[93] or will not use their dispositive powers to divert to others the income he would otherwise have received (*e.g.* to A for life subject to the trustees' power within six months of income arising to pay such income instead to B or C).

Section 3. A Discretionary Trust Precedent (Modern and Traditional)

1–60 As seeing something for yourself is so much better than any description there now follows a discretionary trust precedent. Read it now, read it after reading Chapter 3, section 1, and read it at later stages when the significance of its administrative clauses will be more apparent. The trust in question where no interest in possession exists usefully reveals the flexibility of a trust and common administrative clauses. It is worthwhile considering how you would explain to a lay person the effect of clauses 3 and 4 and how accountable (or free from accountability) are the trustees. Trust instruments are normally drafted so as drastically to lighten the otherwise onerous duties of trustees.

TRADITIONAL TRUST PRECEDENT

1–61 THIS SETTLEMENT is made the _____day of _____19 _____
BETWEEN _____of _____(hereinafter called "the Settlor") of the one part and _____ of _____and _____of _____ (hereinafter called "the Original Trustees")[94] of the other part

WHEREAS:

(A) The Settlor is desirous of making irrevocable provision for the Specified Class as herein defined [and for charity[95]] in manner hereinafter appearing
(B) With the intention of making such provision the Settlor has prior to the execution hereof transferred to the Original Trustees the assets specified in the Second Schedule hereto and is desirous of declaring such trusts thereof as hereinafter appear
(C) The Settlor may hereafter pay or transfer further assets to or into the control of the Trustees hereof to be held by them on the trusts of this Settlement

NOW THIS DEED WITNESSETH as follows:
   1.—(1) THE perpetuity period applicable to this Settlement under the rule against perpetuities shall be the period of eighty years from the execution of this deed
   (2) IN this Settlement and the Schedules hereto the following expressions shall have the following meanings that is to say:

---

[93] See Chap. 4, section 2 and at para.3–59.
[94] As to the identity of the Trustees see clause 8(a).
[95] Delete reference to charity if settlor does not wish to benefit charity.

(a) "the Trustees" means the Original Trustees or other the trustees or trustee for the time being of this Settlement and "Trustee" has a corresponding meaning;

(b) subject to any and every exercise of the powers conferred by Clause 5 hereof "the Specified Class" has the meaning attributed to it in the First Schedule hereto;

(c) "the Appointed Day" means the day on which shall expire the period of eighty years less three days from the execution of this Deed;

(d) "The Trust Fund" means and includes:

(i) the said assets specified in the Second Schedule hereto;

(ii) all assets paid or transferred to or into the control of and accepted by the Trustees as additions to the Trust Fund; and

(iii) the assets from time to time representing the said assets specified in the Second Schedule hereto and the said additions to the Trust Fund or any part or parts thereof respectively

(e) "Spouse" means a party to a marriage which is for the time being subsisting and does not include a party to a former marriage which has terminated by death or divorce or otherwise

[(f)[96] "charity" means any institution whether corporate or not (including a trust) which is established for exclusively charitable purposes and "charities" bears a corresponding meaning]

(g) "the Nominating Beneficiaries" means such of the persons referred to in the First Schedule hereto as are for the time being members of the Specified Class and *sui juris*

2. THE Trustees shall stand possessed of the Trust Fund UPON TRUST at their **1–62** discretion to retain the same (so far as not consisting of cash) in its existing form of investment or to sell the same or any part or parts thereof and to invest or apply the net proceeds of any sale and any other capital moneys in or upon any kind of investment or for any of the purposes hereinafter authorised with power at any time and from time to time to vary such investments or applications for others of any nature hereby authorised.

3.—(1)[97] THE Trustees shall stand possessed of the Trust Fund and the income **1–63** thereof UPON TRUST for all or such one or more exclusively of the others or other of the members of the Specified Class if more than one in such shares and either absolutely or at such age or time or respective ages or times upon and with such limitations conditions and restrictions and such trusts and powers (including discretionary trusts and powers over income and capital exercisable by any person or persons other than the Settlor or any Spouse of the Settlor whether similar to the discretionary trusts and powers herein contained or otherwise) and with such provisions (including provisions for maintenance and advancement and the accumulation of income for any period or periods authorised by law and provisions for investment and management of any nature whatsoever and provisions for the appointment of separate trustees of any appointed fund) and generally in such manner as the Trustees (being not less than two in number or being a corporate trustee) shall in their absolute discretion from time to time by any deed or deeds revocable or irrevocable appoint PROVIDED THAT:

(i) no such appointment shall invalidate any payment or application of capital or income previously made under the trusts or powers herein elsewhere contained; and

---

[96] Delete sub-clause (f) if charities are not intended to benefit.
[97] Delete numeral (1) if sub-clause (2) deleted.

(ii) every appointment shall be made and every interest limited thereunder shall vest in interest (if at all) not later than the Appointed Day and no appointment shall be revoked later than the Appointed Day

[(2)[98] Subject to any appointment previously made by the Trustees under the powers hereinbefore contained the Trustees may in their absolute discretion and without prejudice to the generality of the said powers at any time and from time to time before the Appointed Day:

(a) pay or transfer the whole or any part or parts of the income or capital of the Trust Fund to any charity or charities or apply the same for any exclusively charitable purpose or purposes;

(b) revocably or irrevocably in writing appoint that the whole or any part or share of the income of the Trust Fund or any annual or other periodic sum out of the same income shall during any period or periods ending before the Appointed Day be paid to any charity or charities;

(c) enter into any covenant or other arrangement with any charity or charities to enable or facilitate the recovery of any tax by such charity or charities in respect of any such payment transfer or appointment (as aforesaid)

PROVIDED ALWAYS that the receipt of the person purporting or appearing to be the treasurer or other proper officer of any charity or (in the case of a charitable trust) of the persons purporting or appearing to be the trustees thereof shall be a good discharge to the Trustees for any capital or income paid or transferred to such charity without the necessity for the Trustees to see further to the application thereof]

1–64   **4.**—(1) IN default of and subject to and until any or every exercise of the powers conferred on the Trustees by the preceding clause hereof the Trustees shall until the Appointed Day hold the income of the Trust Fund upon the trusts and with and subject to the powers and provisions following namely:

(a) During the period of twenty-one years from the execution of this Deed the Trustees shall have power to pay or apply the whole or any part or parts of such income as it arises to or for the maintenance and support or otherwise for the benefit of all or such one or more exclusively of the others or other of the persons who shall for the time being be living and members of the Specified Class if more than one in such shares and in such manner as the Trustees shall in their absolute discretion without being liable to account for the exercise of such discretion think fit.

(b) Subject to any and every exercise of the last-mentioned power the Trustees shall during the said period of twenty-one years accumulate the whole or the balance (as the case may be) of the said income by investing the same in any manner hereby authorised and shall hold the accumulations so made as an accretion to the capital of the Trust Fund for all purposes.

(c) After the expiration of the same period of twenty-one years the Trustees shall until the Appointed Day pay or apply the whole of the annual income of the Trust Fund as it arises to or for the maintenance and support or otherwise for the benefit of all or such one or more exclusively of the others or other of the persons who shall for the time being be living and members

---

[98] Delete sub-clause (2) if charities are not intended to benefit.

of the Specified Class if more than one in such shares and in such manner as the Trustees shall in their absolute discretion without being liable to account for the exercise of such discretion think fit

(2) In default of and subject to any or every exercise of the said powers conferred on the Trustees by the preceding clause hereof the Trustees shall stand possessed of the Trust Fund on the Appointed Day UPON TRUST for such persons as shall be then living and members of the Specified Class if more than one in equal shares per capita absolutely

(3) Any income or capital of the Trust Fund which but for this present sub-clause would be undisposed of by this Deed shall be held by the Trustees Upon Trust for [[99] _____ and his/her executors administrators and assigns absolutely][1] [_____and _____ and their respective executors administrators and assigns in equal shares absolutely][2] _____ (as a registered charity) absolutely and in the event of the failure of this present trust then for charitable purposes generally][3]

5. THE Trustees (being not less than two in number or being a corporate trustee) may from time to time and at any time before the Appointed Day by any deed or deeds: **1–65**

(a) declare that any person or class or description of person shall cease to be a member or members of the Specified Class and thereupon such person or class or description of person shall cease to be a member or members of the Specified Class in the same manner as if he she or they had originally been expressly excluded therefrom but without prejudice to any previous payment of capital or income to such person or any member of such class or description of person or application thereof for his her or their benefit PROVIDED that the removal of any such person or class or description of person as aforesaid shall not prejudice modify or affect any appointment of capital or income then already made [AND PROVIDED ALSO[4] that the removal of any such person or class or description of person as aforesaid shall not prejudice modify or affect the trust in favour of [_____ and his/her executors administrators and assigns][5] [_____ and _____ and their executors administrators and assigns][6] contained in sub-clause (3) of the last preceding clause hereof]

(b) declare that any person or persons (not being the Settlor or a Spouse of the Settlor or one of the Trustees) previously nominated in writing in that behalf by any one or more of the Nominating Beneficiaries shall thenceforth be included in the Specified Class and thereupon such person or persons shall become a member or members of the Specified Class for all the purposes hereof PROVIDED that (subject to obtaining any necessary Exchange Control consents) the Trustees shall have an absolute discretion whether or not to make any such declaration in relation to any person or persons nominated as aforesaid and PROVIDED FURTHER that any addition of any such person or persons to the Specified Class shall not prejudice modify or affect any appointment of capital or income then already made

---

[99] The beneficiaries under this ultimate trust should not be the settlor or his spouse or anyone whom he might marry or detrimental tax consequences follow.
[1] These are alternatives, so delete as appropriate.
[2] *ibid.*
[3] *ibid.*
[4] This proviso is not required if the ultimate trust in clause 4(3) is in favour of charity.
[5] Delete as appropriate, for these are alternatives.
[6] *ibid.*

(c) wholly or partially release or restrict all or any of the powers and discretions conferred upon them (including this present power) whether in relation to the whole Trust Fund or any part or parts thereof or the income thereof respectively

6. WHENEVER the Trustees shall determine to apply any income for the benefit of an infant the Trustees may either themselves so apply that income or for that purpose may pay the same to any parent guardian or other person for the time being having the care or custody of such infant (other than the Settlor or any Spouse of the Settlor) without being responsible for seeing to the further application thereof

7.—(1) MONEYS to be invested under this Settlement may be invested or otherwise applied on the security of or in the purchase or acquisition of real or personal property (including the purchase or acquisition of chattels and the effecting or maintaining of policies of insurance or assurance) rights or interests of whatsoever kind and wheresoever situate including any stocks funds shares securities or other investments of whatsoever nature and wheresoever (but including derivatives for the purpose only of controlling or limiting risk) whether producing income or not and whether involving liability or not or on personal loan with or without interest and with or without security to any person (other than the Settlor or any Spouse of the Settlor) anywhere in the world including loans to any member of the Specified Class and the Trustees may grant indulgence to or release any debtor (other than as aforesaid) with or without consideration and may enter into profit sharing agreements and give and take options with or without consideration and accept substitution of any security for other security or of one debtor for another debtor to the intent that the Trustees (subject as herein provided) shall have the same unrestricted powers of investing and using moneys and transposing invest-ments and altering the user of moneys arising under these presents as if they were absolutely entitled thereto beneficially

1–66 (2) IT IS HEREBY EXPRESSLY DECLARED that without prejudice to the generality of the foregoing sub-clause and without prejudice to any powers conferred by law the Trustees shall (subject to the terms of any appointment made under the powers hereinbefore contained) have the following additional powers-exercisable until the Appointed Day namely:

(a) The Trustees may:
   (i) at any time or times lay out any part or parts of the Trust Fund in the purchase or acquisition of and paying the expenses of purchasing or acquiring and making improvements in or repairs to or on any land and buildings of freehold leasehold or of any other tenure or interest of whatsoever description situate in any part of the world whether or not in the occupation of or intended for occupation by any member or members of the Specified Class;
   (ii) at any time or times lay out any part or parts of the Trust Fund in the purchase of household furniture plate linen china cutlery and articles of household use ornament or equipment or any other chattels whatsoever for the use or enjoyment of any member or members of the Specified Class whether occupying a building purchased as aforesaid or otherwise
(b) (i) any land purchased by the Trustees shall if situate in England or Wales be assured to the Trustees upon trust for sale with power to postpone sale and if situate elsewhere be assured to the Trustees either with or

without any trust for sale as the Trustees shall think fit but nevertheless with power to sell the same;

(ii) in relation to any land situate outside England and Wales the powers and indemnities given to the Trustees in relation to land in England by English law shall apply as if expressed in this Deed and the net rents and profits thereof shall be applicable in like manner as if they arose from land in England;

(iii) the Trustees shall stand possessed of any land so purchased and the net proceeds of sale thereof and other capital moneys arising under this Settlement upon the trusts and with and subject to the powers and provisions (including power to purchase land) upon with and subject to which the money laid out in the purchase of such land would have been held if the same had not been so laid out;

(iv) until the sale of any land purchased as aforesaid the Trustees may permit any member or members of the Specified Class to occupy the same upon such terms (if any) as to payment or non-payment of rent rates taxes and other expenses and outgoings and as to repair and decoration and for such period or periods before the Appointed Day as the Trustees may think fit;

(v) the Trustees shall be indemnified out of the Trust Fund against all costs rents covenants obligations and outgoings relating to any land purchased as aforesaid or for which the Trustees may be liable in respect of the said premises or the said purchase

(c) Any household furniture or other chattels purchased by the Trustees as aforesaid may be handed over to any member or members of the Specified Class for his or her or their use or enjoyment for any period before the Appointed Day upon and subject to such terms and conditions (if any) as to maintaining such inventory or inventories (if any) and as to insurance and preservation as the Trustees shall think fit **1–67**

(d) (i) The Trustees shall be at liberty to borrow money (otherwise than from the Settlor or any Spouse of the Settlor) for any of the purposes of this Settlement (including the provision of money to give effect to any appointment authorised hereunder or for the purpose of effecting or maintaining any policies or purchasing or subscribing for any shares or stocks securities properties options rights or interests or other property of whatsoever description) and they may pledge or mortgage the whole or any part of the Trust Fund or the future income thereof by way of security for any such loan and no lender shall be obliged to inquire as to the purpose for which any loan is required or whether the money borrowed exceeds any such requirement

(ii) The Trustees may pledge or mortgage the whole or any part of the Trust Fund by way of principal collateral or other security or by way of guarantee to secure any bank overdraft or other moneys borrowed by any member or members of the Specified Class *Provided* that neither the Settlor nor any Spouse of the Settlor is the lender or one of the lenders in respect of or has any interest in such overdraft or other moneys and *Provided* further that no person other than a member or members of the Specified Class is liable for the repayment thereof

(e) The Trustees may at any time or times enter into any compromise or arrangement with respect to or may release all or any of their rights as shareholders stockholders or debenture stockholders or creditors of any company and whether in connection with a scheme of reconstruction or amalgamation or otherwise and may accept in or towards satisfaction of all or any of such rights such consideration as they shall in their discretion think fit whether in the form of shares stock debenture stock cash obligations or securities of the same or of any other company or companies or in any other form whatsoever

1–68   (f)   (i)   The Trustees may effect purchase or acquire any policy or policies assuring payment to the Trustees in the event of the death of any person of such sum as the Trustees in their absolute discretion (having regard to any prospective liability for tax that may arise in respect of the Trust Fund or any part thereof on the death of such person) may think fit or any endowment or sinking fund policy or policies of whatsoever nature and may pay any premium or premiums thereon out of income or capital

(ii)   Without prejudice to the last-mentioned powers or to any powers vested in them under the general law the Trustees may from time to time apply any part or parts of the income or capital of the Trust Fund in or towards payment of the premium or premiums on any policy or policies in which any one or more of the members of the Specified Class shall (whether under this Settlement or any other deed or otherwise) have any beneficial interest whether vested or contingent and whether indefeasible or defeasible PROVIDED ALWAYS that no person except one or more of the members of the Specified Class shall have any beneficial interest whatsoever in the said policy or policies and so that (subject to the said proviso) the Trustees shall have power if they think fit to effect any such policy or policies on any life or lives in which any one or more of the members of the Specified Class shall have an insurable interest

(iii)   PROVIDED ALWAYS that no income shall be paid or applied under the foregoing powers after the expiration of twenty-one years from the execution hereof if such payment or application would involve an accumulation of the said income

(iv)   In relation to any policy held by them hereunder the Trustees shall have all the powers of a beneficial owner including (without prejudice to the generality of such powers) power to surrender any such policy or to convert the same into a paid up policy or into any other form of assurance or otherwise or to exercise any option thereunder or to sell mortgage charge or otherwise realise or dispose of the same

1–69   (g)   The Trustees may exercise all voting rights appertaining to any investments comprised in the Trust Fund in as full free and absolute a manner as if they were absolute owners of such investments and in particular but without prejudice to the generality of the foregoing provisions shall be at liberty to exercise such voting rights either by voting or by abstaining from voting so as to ensure or further the appointment or reappointment of any one or more of their number to be directors secretaries or employees of any company in which any part of the Trust Fund may for the time being be invested or of any subsidiary of any such company and any Trustee receiving from any such company or subsidiary any fees salary bonuses or commissions for services rendered to such company or subsidiary shall be entitled to retain the same for his own benefit and shall not be required to account therefor to any person interested hereunder

(h)   The Trustees shall not be bound or required to interfere in the management or conduct of the affairs or business of any company in which the Trust

Fund may be invested (whether or not the Trustees have the control of such company) and so long as no Trustee has actual knowledge of any fraud dishonesty recklessness or negligence on the part of the directors having the management of such company they may leave the same (including the payment or non-payment of dividends) wholly to such directors without being liable for any loss thereby arising

(i) The Trustees shall have the powers of appropriation and other incidental **1–70** powers conferred on a personal representative by Section 41 of the Administration of Estates Act 1925 but without the necessity of obtaining the consent of any person to the exercise thereof

(j) The Trustees may apportion as they think fit any funds subject to different trusts which may have become blended and (without prejudice to the jurisdiction of the Court) may determine as they shall consider just whether any money is to be considered as capital or income and whether any expense ought to be paid out of capital or income and all other questions and matters of doubt of whatsoever description arising in the execution of the trusts of these presents and none of the Trustees and no person having formerly been one of the Trustees and no estate of any deceased Trustee shall be liable for or for the consequences of any act done or omitted to be done or for any payment made or omitted to be made in pursuance of any such determination notwithstanding that such determination shall subsequently be held to have been wrongly made

(k) The Trustees may in addition and without prejudice to any powers to employ agents or attorneys conferred by law employ and remunerate on such terms and conditions as they shall think fit any Solicitors Brokers or other agents or advisers (being in each case a person firm or corporation other than and excluding the Settlor and any Spouse of the Settlor) for the purpose of transacting all or any business of whatever nature or doing any act or giving any advice requiring to be transacted done or given in relation to the trusts hereof including any business act or advice which a trustee not being in any profession or business could have transacted done or given personally and any such Solicitor Broker or other agent or adviser shall be entitled to retain any such remuneration or his share thereof notwithstanding that he or any partner of his is a trustee or the sole trustee hereof or is a member officer or employee of or is otherwise interested in any body corporate which is a trustee or the sole trustee hereof and notwithstanding that such agent or adviser is a body corporate of which one or more of the trustees is a member officer or employee or in which one or more of the Trustees is otherwise interested. And the Trustees shall not be responsible for the default of any such Solicitor Broker or other agent or adviser or for any loss occasioned by the employment thereof in good faith

(l) The Trustees may employ and remunerate as they see fit an investment **1–71** manager (who may be one of themselves or any person associated with any of themselves) so as to delegate to him full discretion to manage the Trust Fund or any part thereof within the limits and for the period stipulated by the Trustees providing his investment activities are subject to review by the Trustees no less than every six months and providing he is reasonably believed by the Trustees to be someone qualified and authorised to engage in the business of managing investments for others and the Trustees shall have authority to enter into an agreement with such investment manager on the same terms (including, for example, terms as to self-dealing and sub-delegation) as a prudent man of business can agree for the management of his own funds and the Trustees shall not be liable for any loss resulting from the exercise of the powers herein conferred so long as they act in good faith nor for any profit made by the investment manager if a Trustee or associated with a Trustee so long as management fees and commissions do not exceed those paid by an unassociated client with a portfolio of investments of similar value to that of the Trust Fund

1–72   (m) The Trustees may deposit any moneys deed securities or investments (including shares and securities to bearer) held by them as trustees with any banker or any person firm or corporation (other than and excluding the Settlor and any Spouse of the Settlor) whether in the United Kingdom or abroad for safe custody or receipt of dividends and may pay out of the income or capital of such part of the Trust Fund as they shall think proper any sum payable for such deposit and custody

(n) Assets of the Trust may be held in the names of any two or more of the Trustees and the Trustees may vest such assets in a stakeholder or in a nominee or nominees anywhere in the world (other than the Settlor or any Spouse of the Settlor) on behalf of the Trustees and entrust or concur in entrusting the realisation and reinvestment of such assets to such stakeholder nominee or nominees upon such terms as the Trustees may deem reasonable

(o) The Trustees may (at the expense of the Trust Fund) incorporate or register or procure the incorporation or registration of any company (with limited or unlimited liability) in any part of the world for any purpose including the acquisition of the Trust Fund or any part thereof and so that (if thought fit) the consideration on the sale of the Trust Fund to any such company may consist wholly or partly of fully paid shares debentures debenture stock or other securities of the company credited as fully paid which shall be allotted to or otherwise vested in the Trustees and be capital moneys in the Trustees' hands

1–73   (p) The trustees may embark upon or carry on whether alone or in partnership or as a joint venture with any other person or persons (except the Settlor or any Spouse of the Settlor) or corporation or corporations at the expense of the Trust Fund and the income thereof any trade or business whatsoever including (without prejudice to the generality of the foregoing) any forestry timber farming development insurance banking or other agricultural com-mercial industrial financial or professional trade or business whatsoever and may assist or finance to any extent the commencement or carrying on of any trade or business by any other or others (except as aforesaid)

(q) The trustees may effect any transaction relating to the management administration or disposition of property within the Trust Fund which falls within the jurisdiction of a court to authorise under section 57 of the Trustee Act 1925 without the necessity of obtaining an order of the court authorising such transactions

8.   THE following provisions shall apply to the trusts and trusteeship hereof:

(a) The statutory powers of appointing trustees shall apply hereto and shall be exercisable by [the Settlor][7] during [his/her][8] life PROVIDED that neither the

---

[7] Amend as appropriate.
[8] *ibid.*

Settlor nor any Spouse of the Settlor shall be appointed a trustee of these presents

(b) Any person whether an individual or a body corporate may be appointed as **1–74** a trustee of this settlement whether or not he or it shall be resident domiciled or incorporated in the United Kingdom and the appointment as sole trustee of a body corporate ranking as a trust corporation under the law governing its incorporation shall validly discharge the trustees from all the trusts of this settlement except those if any relating to English or Welsh land then comprised in this settlement

(c) The Trustees shall have power to carry on the administration of the trusts of this settlement in any part of the world whether inside or outside the United Kingdom and power to that end to appoint and pay agents and investment managers with general discretion as to investment and disinvestment of the whole or a specified part of the trust fund upon such terms (including, for example, terms as to self-dealing and sub-delegation) as a prudent man of business can agree for the management of his own funds

(d) No Trustee shall be capable of being removed or replaced on the grounds that he has remained out of the United Kingdom for more than 12 months

(e) Subject to subclause (b) hereof the law according to which the trusts powers and provisions of this settlement shall for the time being be governed and administered shall be the law of England and Wales

(f) The Trustees shall have power exercisable at any time or time by deed or **1–75** deeds executed before the Perpetuity Day in their absolute discretion (but during the lifetime of the Settlor not without his prior consent in writing) to declare that the law governing the validity of this settlement or the law governing the administration of this settlement shall from the date of such deed or from some later date specified therein and subject to any further exercise of this power be the law of some other State specified therein provided that such State has its own internal law of trusts and recognises the effectiveness of the exercise of this power and providing always that this power shall not be exercisable so as to render this settlement revocable or unenforceable in whole or in part or otherwise to affect the beneficial trusts and powers thereof other than the powers incorporated by Trustee Act 1925 sections 31 and 32 and analogous powers in other States and "administration" matters shall include all matters other than those governing the validity of the beneficial interests created or capable of being created under this settlement

(g) Any Trustee engaged in any profession or business shall be entitled to charge and be paid all professional or other charges made by him or his firm for business done by him or his firm in relation to the execution of the trusts hereof whether or not in the ordinary course of his profession or business and whether or not of a nature requiring the employment of a professional or business person

(h) Any corporation appointed to be a trustee hereof shall have the powers rights and benefits as to remuneration or otherwise as at or prior to its appointment may be agreed in writing between such corporation and the person or persons (or corporation or corporations) making such appointment

9. THE following provisions shall apply to the powers and discretions of the **1–76** Trustees hereunder:

(1) Any Trustee may concur in exercising any such power or discretion notwithstanding that he may have a direct or other personal interest in the

mode or result of exercising the same Provided that at least one of the Trustees has no such direct or other personal interest

(2) The Trustees shall not be concerned to see to the insurance preservation repair or renewal of any freehold leasehold or other property household furniture or other chattels occupied used or enjoyed by any member of the Specified Class and in the professed execution of the trusts and powers hereof no Trustee shall be liable for any loss to the trust premises arising by reason of any improper investment or application of the Trust Fund or any part thereof made in good faith

(3) Every discretion hereby conferred upon the Trustees shall be an absolute and unfettered discretion and the Trustees shall not be required to furnish to any beneficiary hereunder any reason or justification for the manner in which any such discretion may be exercised

(4) No power or discretion hereunder to which the rule against perpetuities applies shall be exercisable after the Appointed Day

1–77   **10.** NOTWITHSTANDING anything hereinbefore or in the schedules hereto contained:

(a) the Trust Fund and the income thereof shall be possessed and enjoyed to the entire exclusion of the Settlor and of any benefit to the Settlor by contract or otherwise;

(b) no part of the Trust Fund or the income thereof shall be paid lent or applied for the benefit of the Settlor or any Spouse of the Settlor nor shall any power or discretion hereunder be exercised so as to confer any benefit on the Settlor or any Spouse of the Settlor in any circumstances whatsoever

1–78   **11.** THIS Settlement and the dispositions hereby made are intended to be and are irrevocable

IN WITNESS whereof the parties hereto have hereunto set their respective hands or seals the day and year first before written

THE FIRST SCHEDULE[9] hereinbefore referred to

The Specified Class consists (subject to any exercise of the powers contained in Clause 5 of the foregoing Deed) of the following persons namely:

[(1) the children and remoter issue of the Settlor whether living at the date hereof or born hereafter;

(2) any person (other than a Trustee) who shall (whether before or after the date hereof) have married any of such children or remoter issue of the Settlor as aforesaid (whether or not such marriage shall for the time being be subsisting);

(3) A.B. (the brother of the Settlor);

(4) the children and remoter issue of the said A.B. whether living at the date hereof or born hereafter;

(5) any person (other than a Trustee) who shall (whether before or after the date hereof) have married any of such children or remoter issue of the said A.B. as aforesaid (whether or not such marriage shall for the time being be subsisting);

---

[9] This schedule has been completed by way of example.

(6) any adopted child of the Settlor or of any of such children or remoter issue of the Settlor as aforesaid and the children and remoter issue of any such adopted child;

(7) any person (other than a Trustee) who shall (whether before or after the date hereof) have married any such adopted child or any child or remoter issue of any such adopted child as aforesaid (whether or not such marriage shall for the time being be subsisting)

Provided that for the purposes of this present definition a person shall be deemed to be the adopted child of another person only if he or she shall be recognised as the adopted child of such other person by the Law of England for the time being in force.]

THE SECOND SCHEDULE hereinbefore referred to

MODERN TRUST SETTLEMENT

(From J. Kessler, *Drafting Trusts and Will Trusts*, 7th ed. (2004)

This settlement is made [date] between: **1–79**

1 [Name of settlor] of [address] ("the Settlor") of the one part and
2   2.1 [Name of first trustee] of [address] and
     2.2 [Name of second trustee] of [address]
     ("the Original Trustees") of the other part.

Whereas:

1 The Settlor has [two] children:
   1.1 [Adam Smith] ("[Adam]") who was born on [date] and
   1.2 [Mary Smith] ("[Mary]") who was born on [date].
2 This Settlement shall be known as the [Name-of-settlor Settlement 2000].

Now this deed witnesses as follows:

1. Definitions

In this settlement: **1–80**

1.1 **"The Trustees"** means the Original Trustees or the trustees of the settlement for the time being.
1.2 **"The Trust Fund"** means:
   1.2.1 property transferred to the Trustees to hold on the terms of this Settlement; and
   1.2.2 all property from time to time representing the above.
1.3 **"Trust Property"** means any property comprised in the Trust Fund.
1.4 **"The Trust Period"** means the period of 80 years beginning with the date of this Settlement. That is the perpetuity period applicable to this Settlement under the rule against perpetuities.
1.5 **"The Accumulation Period"** means the period of 21 years beginning with the date of this Settlement.

1.6 **"The Beneficiaries"** means:
    1.6.1 The children and descendants of the Settlor.
    1.6.2 The spouses, widows and widowers (whether or not remarried) of paragraph .1 of this sub-clause:
    1.6.3 The [widow] (whether or not remarried) of the Settlor.
    1.6.4 Any Person or class of Persons nominated to the Trustees by:
        1.6.4.1 the Settlor or
        1.6.4.2 two Beneficiaries (after the death of the Settlor)

    and whose nomination is accepted in writing by the Trustees.
    1.6.5 At any time during which there are no Beneficiaries within paragraph .1 of this sub-clause.
        1.6.5.1 [specify "fall back" beneficiaries if desired, *e.g.* nieces and nephews and their families].
        1.6.5.2 [any company, body or trust established for charitable purposes only].
1.7 **"Person"** includes a person anywhere in the world and includes a Trustee.

2. Trust Income

1–81 Subject to the Overriding Powers below:

2.1 The Trustees may accumulate the whole or part of the income of the Trust Fund during the Accumulation Period. That income shall be added to the Trust Fund.
2.2 The Trustees shall pay or apply the remainder of the income to or for the benefit of any Beneficiaries, as the Trustees think fit, during the Trust Period.

3. Overriding Powers

1–82 The Trustees shall have the following powers ("Overriding Powers"):

3.1 Power of appointment
    3.1.1 The Trustees may appoint that they shall hold the Trust Fund for the benefit of any Beneficiaries, on such terms as the Trustees think fit.
    3.1.2 An appointment may create any provisions and in particular:
        3.1.2.1 discretionary trusts;
        3.1.2.2 dispositive or administrative powers;
        exercisable by any Person.
    3.1.3 An appointment shall be made by deed and may be revocable or irrevocable.
3.2 *Transfer of Trust Property to new settlement*
    The Trustees may by deed declare that they hold any Trust Property on trust to transfer it to trustees of a Qualifying Settlement, to hold on the terms of that Qualifying Settlement, freed and released from the terms of this Settlement.
    "A Qualifying Settlement" here means any settlement, wherever established, under which every Person who may benefit is (or would if living be) a Beneficiary of this Settlement.
3.3 *Power of advancement*
    The Trustees may pay or apply any Trust Property for the advancement or benefit of any Beneficiary.

3.4 The Overriding Powers shall be exercisable only:

    3.4.1 during the Trust Period; and

    3.4.2 at a time when there are at least two Trustees, or the Trustee is a company carrying on a business which consists of or includes the management of trusts.

4. Default Clause

Subject to that, the Trust Fund shall be held on trust for [Adam and Mary in equal **1–83** shares—or specify default trusts as appropriate] absolutely.

5. Appointment of Trustees

The power of appointing trustees is exercisable by the Settlor during [his] life and by will.

6. Further Provisions

The provisions set out in the schedule below shall have effect [For a shorter form, say instead of the above:

> "The standard provisions of the Society of Trust and Estate Practitioners (1st Edition) shall apply with the deletion of paragraph 5. Section 11 Trusts of Land & Appointment of Trustees Act 1996 (consultation with beneficiaries) shall not apply."

And omit the schedule.]

7. Exclusion of Settlor and Spouse

Notwithstanding anything else in this Settlement, no power conferred by this **1–84** settlement shall be exercisable, and no provision shall operate so as to allow Trust Property or its income to become payable to or applicable for the benefit of the Settlor or the spouse of the Settlor in any circumstances whatsoever.

In witness, [etc.]

THE SCHEDULE: FURTHER PROVISIONS

1. Additional Powers

The Trustees have the following additional powers: **1–85**

1.1 Investment

    1.1.1 The Trustees may make any kind of investment that they could make if they were absolutely entitled to the Trust Fund. In particular the Trustees may invest in land in any part of the world and unsecured loans.

    1.1.2 The Trustees are under no obligation to diversify the Trust Fund.

    1.1.3 The Trustees may invest in speculative or hazardous investments but this power may only be exercised at the time when there are at least two Trustees, or the Trustee is a company carrying on a business which consists of or includes the management of trusts.

1.2 Joint property

The Trustees may acquire property jointly with any Person and may blend Trust Property with other property.

1.3 General power of management and disposition
   The Trustees may effect any transaction relating to the management or disposition of Trust Property as if they were absolutely entitled to it.

1.4 Improvement

The Trustees may develop or improve Trust Property in any way. Capital expenses need not be repaid out of income under section 84(2) of the Settled Land Act 1925, if the Trustees think fit.

1.5 Income and capital

     1.5.1 The Trustees may acquire:
          1.5.1.1 wasting assets and
          1.5.1.1 assets which yield little or no income
          for investment or any other purpose.
     1.5.2 The Trustees are under no duty to procure distributions from a company in which they are interested.
     1.5.3 The Trustees may pay taxes and other expenses out of income although they would otherwise be paid out of capital
     1.5.4 Generally, the Trustees are under no duty to hold a balance between conflicting interests of Beneficiaries.
     1.5.5 The Trustees may (subject to the jurisdiction of the Court) determine whether receipts and liabilities are to be considered as capital or income, and whether expenses ought to be paid out of capital or income. The Trustees shall not be liable for any act done in pursuance of such determination (in the absence of fraud or negligence) even though it shall subsequently be held to have been wrongly made.
     1.5.6 Income may be set aside and invested to answer any liabilities which in the opinion of the Trustees ought to be borne out of income or to meet depreciation of the capital value of any Trust Property. In particular, income may be applied for a leasehold sinking fund policy.

1.6 Application of trust capital as income

1–86 The Trustees may apply Trust Property as if it were income arising in the current year. In particular, the Trustees may pay such income to a Beneficiary as his income, for the purpose of augmenting his income.

1.7 Use of trust property

     1.7.1 The Trustees may acquire any interest in property anywhere in the world for occupation or use by a Beneficiary.
     1.7.2 The Trustees may permit a Beneficiary to occupy or enjoy the use of Trust Property on such terms as they think fit.
     1.7.3 The Trustees may lend trust money to a Beneficiary. The loan may be interest free and unsecured, or on such terms as the Trustees think fit. The Trustees may charge Trust Property as security for any debts or obligations of a Beneficiary.

1.8 Trade

The Trustees may carry on a trade, in any part of the world, alone or in partnership. **1–87**

1.9 Borrowing

The Trustees may borrow money for investment or any other purpose. Money borrowed shall be treated as Trust Property.

1.10 Delegation

A Trustee or the Trustees jointly (or other Person in a fiduciary position) may authorise any person to exercise all or any functions on such terms as to remuneration and other matters as they think fit. A Trustee shall not be responsible for the default of that Person (even if the delegation was not strictly necessary or convenient) provided he took reasonable care in his selection and supervision.

1.11 Nominees and custodians

    1.11.1 The Trustees may appoint a person to act as their nominee in relation to such of the assets of the trust as they may determine. They may take such steps as are necessary to secure that those assets are vested in the nominee.

    1.11.2 The Trustees may appoint a person to act as custodian in relation to such of the assets of the trust as they may determine. The Trustees may give the custodian custody of the assets and any documents or records concerning the assets. The Trustees are not obliged to appoint a custodian of securities payable to bearer.

    1.11.3 The Trustees may appoint a person to act as nominee or custodian on such terms as to remuneration and other matters as they may think fit.

1.12 Offshore administration

The Trustees may carry on the administration of this Settlement anywhere they think fit.

1.13 Indemnities

The Trustees may indemnify any Person for any liability relating to the Settlement. **1–88**

1.14 Security

The Trustees may mortgage or charge Trust Property as security for any liability incurred by them as Trustees (and may grant a floating charge so far as the law allows).

1.15 Supervision of company

The Trustees are under no duty to enquire into the conduct of a company in which they are interested, unless they have knowledge of circumstances which call for inquiry.

1.16 Appropriation

The Trustees may appropriate Trust Property to any Person or class of Persons in or towards the satisfaction of their interest in the Trust Fund.

1.17 Receipt by charities

Where Trust Property is to be paid or transferred to a charity, the receipt of the treasurer or appropriate officer of the charity shall be a complete discharge to the Trustees.

1.18 Release of powers

1–89   The Trustees (or other persons in a fiduciary position) may by deed release wholly or in part any of their rights or functions and (if applicable) so as to bind their successors.

1.19 Ancillary powers

The Trustees may do anything which is incidental or conducive to the exercise of their functions.

1.20 Insurance policies

The trustees may pay premiums of any insurance policy out of income.

2. Minors

1–90   2.1 Where the Trustees may apply income for the benefit of a minor, they may do so by paying the income to the minor's parent or guardian on behalf of the minor, or to the minor if he has attained the age of 16. The Trustees are under no duty to inquire into the use of the income unless they have knowledge of circumstances which call for inquiry.

2.2 Where the Trustees may apply income for the benefit of a minor, they may do so by resolving that they hold that income on trust for the minor absolutely and:

2.2.1 The Trustees may apply that income for the benefit of the minor during his minority.

2.2.2 The Trustees shall transfer the residue of that income to the minor on attaining the age of 18.

2.2.3 For investment and other administrative purposes that income shall be treated as Trust Property.

3. Mentally handicapped beneficiary

1–91   Where income or capital is payable to a Beneficiary who does not have the mental capacity to appoint an attorney with an enduring general power, the Trustees may (subject to the directions of the Court or his Receiver) apply that income or capital for his benefit.

4. Disclaimer

A Person may disclaim his interest in this Settlement wholly or in part.

5. Apportionment

Income and expenditure shall be treated as arising when payable, and not from day to day, so that no apportionment shall take place.

6. Conflicts of interest

6.1 In this paragraph: **1–92**
    6.1.1 **"A Fiduciary"** means a Person subject to fiduciary duties under the Settlement.
    6.1.2 **"An Independent Trustee"**, in relation to a Person, means a Trustee who is not:
        6.1.2.1 a brother, sister, ancestor, descendant or dependent of the Person;
        6.1.2.2 a spouse of paragraph .1.2.1 above, or a spouse of the Person;
        6.1.2.3 a company controlled by one or more of any of the above.
    6.1.3 Subject to the next sub-clause a Fiduciary may:
        6.1.3.1 enter into a transaction with the Trustees, or
        6.1.3.2 be interested in an arrangement in which the Trustees are or might have been interested, or
        6.1.3.3 act (or not act) in any other circumstances;
        even though his fiduciary duty under the Settlement conflicts with other duties or with his personal interest;
    6.1.4 The above sub-clause only has effect if:
        6.1.4.1 the Fiduciary first discloses to the Trustees the nature and extent of any material interest conflicting with his fiduciary duties, and
        6.1.4.2 there is an Independent Trustee in respect of whom there is no conflict of interest, and he considers that the transaction arrangement or action is not contrary to the general interest of the Settlement.
    6.1.5 The powers of the Trustees may be used to benefit a Trustee (to the same extent as if he were not a Trustee) provided that there is an Independent Trustee in respect of whom there is no conflict of interest.

7. Absolute discretion clause

7.1 The Powers of the Trustees may be exercised: **1–93**
    7.1.1 at their absolute discretion; and
    7.1.2 from time to time as occasion requires.
7.2 The Trustees are not under any duty to consult with any Beneficiaries or to give effect to the wishes of any Beneficiaries.

8. Trustee remuneration

8.1 A Trustee acting in a professional capacity is entitled to receive reasonable remuneration out of the Trust Fund for any services that he provides on behalf of the Trust
8.2 For this purpose, a trustee acts in a professional capacity if he acts in the course of a profession or business which consists of or includes the provision of services in connection with:
    8.2.1 the management or administration of trusts generally or a particular kind of trust, or
    8.2.2 any particular aspect of the management or administration of trusts generally or a particular kind of trust.
8.3 The Trustees may make arrangements to remunerate themselves for work done for a company connected with the Trust Fund.

9. Commissions and bank charges

1–94 9.1 A Person may retain any reasonable commission or profit in respect of any transaction relating to this Settlement even though that commission or profit was procured by an exercise of fiduciary powers (by that Person or some other Person) provided that:

9.1.1 The Person would in the normal course of business receive and retain the commission or profit on such transaction.

9.1.2 The receipt of the commission or profit shall be disclosed to the Trustees.

9.2 A bank may make loans to the Trustees and generally provide banking services upon its usual terms and shall not be liable to account for any profit so made even though the receipt of such profit was procured by an exercise of fiduciary powers (by the bank or some other Person).

10. Liability of trustees

1–95 10.1 The duty of reasonable care (set out in s. 1, Trustee Act 2000) applies to all the functions of the Trustees.

10.2 A Trustee shall not be liable for a loss to the Trust Fund unless that loss was caused by his own fraud or negligence.

10.3 A Trustee shall not be liable for acting in accordance with the advice of Counsel, of at least five years' standing, with respect to the settlement. A Trustee may recover from the Trust Fund any expenses where he has acted in accordance with such advice. The Trustees may in particular conduct legal proceedings in accordance with such advice without obtaining a court order.

10.4 The above paragraph does not apply if:

10.4.1 the Trustee knows or has reasonable cause to suspect that the advice was given in ignorance of material facts; or

10.4.2 proceedings are pending to obtain the decision of the court on the matter.

10.5 The Trustees may distribute Trust Property or income in accordance with this Settlement but without having ascertained that there is no Person who is or may be entitled to any interest therein by virtue of any illegitimate relationship. The Trustees shall not be liable to such a Person unless they have notice of his claim at the time of the distribution.

10.6 This paragraph does not prejudice any right of any Person to follow property or income into the hands of any Person, other than a purchaser, who may have received it.

11. Appointment and retirement of trustees

1–96 11.1 A Person may be appointed Trustee of the Settlement even though he has no connection with the United Kingdom.

11.2 A Trustee who has reached the age of 65 shall retire if:

11.2.1 he is requested to do so by his co-trustees, or by a Person interested in Trust Property; and

11.2.2 he is effectually indemnified against liabilities properly incurred as Trustee.

On that retirement a new Trustee shall be appointed if necessary to ensure that there will be at least two Trustees. This sub-paragraph does not apply to a Trustee who is the Settlor or the spouse or widow of the Settlor.

11.3 A Trustee may be discharged even though there is neither a trust corporation nor two Persons to act as trustees provided that there remains at least one trustee.

Section 4. Taxation Aspects of Trusts

Just as a swimmer's environment is water so a trust's environment is a fiscal **1–97** system. Necessarily, space allows of only a superficial treatment here, especially as regards those anti-avoidance provisions designed to prevent the versatile flexibility of the trust from being manipulated to obtain tax advantages. After all, in trust law a settlor may himself be a trustee and a beneficiary, may have power to add or subtract beneficiaries, may have powers of appointing income and capital amongst the beneficiaries or on new trusts, and may have power to revoke his trust, whilst the trustees may have power to accumulate income within the trust and to invest in non-income-producing assets. A trust is like a sponge capable of soaking up liquid funds and retaining them without undue leakage, yet capable of being squeezed lightly or harshly or of being totally squashed so as to yield its contents into the required hands; it can even be split up into smaller pieces having the same qualities as the whole.

Income tax

(1) *The settlor's position.* An individual's taxable income is taxed progres- **1–98** sively at rates laid down annually in the Finance Act. There is a Starting Rate of 10 per cent (up to £2,090), then a 22 per cent Basic Rate (up to £32,400) and a 40 per cent Higher Rate (over £32,400), though, previously, progressively higher slices of taxable income were taxed at progressively higher rates (up to a top rate as high as 83 per cent). For dividend income the rate is 10 per cent for those below the Higher Rate limit, and 32.5 per cent for those above it. For other savings income there is a starting rate of 10 per cent, a lower rate of 20 per cent and then the higher rate of 40 per cent. The progressive nature of the tax is such that, in circumstances not covered by anti-avoidance provisions, a tax saving can be achieved by a wealthy person hiving off some of his income to trustees or an individual or a charity not taxable at the higher rates or at all. He can do this either by covenanting to pay income to them or by transferring the income-producing capital itself. If capital taxes have lower rates than income tax (as was the case until 1988) or have the advantage that the first £8,500 of gains each year are exempt from capital gains tax, further tax savings can be achieved by using trustees' powers of accumulation of income to convert income into capital and eventually pass it over to beneficiaries as capital, although there is less scope for this now that from 6 April 2004 the maximum rate of tax on accumulated trust income has been raised to 40 per cent from 34 per cent.[10] Tax-efficient benefits in kind (*e.g.* free loans of cash, chattels, houses) may also be conferred on beneficiaries.

---

[10] Income and Corporation Taxes Act 1988 (ICTA), ss.686, 687 as amended by Finance Act 2004, s.29.

Anti-avoidance provisions, however, reduce the opportunities for settlements to be used to avoid income tax. In considering whether such provisions apply one must ask three questions:

1–99   (i) Do the settlor and his spouse retain any possibility of benefiting from the settled property other than in very limited contingencies.[11] If so then the trust income is treated as wholly his.[12] If a settlor receives a capital sum by way of loan from the trust or repayment of his loan to the trust, he is treated as receiving taxed net income (to the extent of available undistributed income for that year and the next 10 years) equal to such sum.[13]

(ii) If the settlor is not caught by (i) but income is actually paid by the trustees to or for the benefit of the settlor's minor unmarried children (or allocated on a bare trust to pay the income therefrom to such children[14]) such income ranks as the settlor's.[15] If income is accumulated, then any capital payment to or for the benefit of the unmarried minor is deemed to be a payment of income, ranking as the settlor's income, to the extent that there is accumulated income available to cover the payment.[16]

(iii) Was a covenanted payment of income either a maintenance payment for an ex-spouse or a separated spouse or an annual payment made for bona fide commercial reasons in connection with his trade profession or vocation or a covenant for charity capable of lasting for more than three years so that it is then deductible from the settlor's income.[17]

1–100   (2) *The trustees' position.* The trustees are liable to basic rate tax, or 20 per cent lower rate tax on savings (except for dividends taxed at 10 per cent) under the appropriate income tax schedules on all the income produced by the trust fund. Such income is quite separate from their own personal income. Trust income can have no deduction against it for personal allowances or for expenses incurred in administering the trust.[18] It cannot be liable to higher rate tax. Much income will be received by the trustees after deduction of tax (*e.g.* dividends or building society interest) but in other cases (*e.g.* profits of carrying on a trade[19]) the trustees will need to pay the basic rate tax.

In an exceptional case where trust income without passing through the hands of a trustee is paid directly to an interest in possession beneficiary who has no liability to income tax because of non-residence or charitable status the trustees will not be assessed to tax.[20]

---

[11] ICTA, s.660A, substituted by Finance Act 1995, Sch.17.
[12] *ibid.* and s.660E and F, enabling tax paid by the settlor to be recovered from the recipient of the income. Further see Simon's *Tiley and Collison UK Tax Guide 2004–05*, Chap.14.
[13] ICTA, s.677. These anti-avoidance provisions are now consolidated in the Income Tax (Trading and Other Income) Act 2005 Ch.5. Note also that civil partners of settlors are to be treated as if spouses: Finance Act 2005 s.103."
[14] ICTA, s.660B as amended by Finance Act 1999 s.64.
[15] ICTA, s.660B, substituted by F.A. 1995 Sched. 17.
[16] ICTA, s.660B(2), (3).
[17] ICTA, s.347A and s.660A as added by Finance Act 1995, Sch,17.
[18] *Aikin v Macdonald's Trustees* (1894) 3 T.C. 306.
[19] Of course, expenses incurred in earning the profits may be deducted and loss relief may be claimed.
[20] *Williams v Singer* [1921] A.C. 65.

Where no one such as a life tenant has an interest in possession[21] in the **1–101** trust entitling him as of right to the income then the trustees have to pay tax at the section 686 rate applicable to trusts which is 40 per cent except for dividend income taxed at the 32.5 per cent schedule F trust rate.[22] This is because in such cases there would otherwise be too much scope for minimising liability to tax by exercising powers of accumulation or by delaying exercising discretionary powers over income until a tax-efficient beneficiary materialised. However, in the case of these accumulation trusts and discretionary trusts the expenses incurred in administering the trust which are properly chargeable to income (under the general law if ignoring express authority in the trust instrument) can be deducted from the income liable to the additional rate charge.[23]

(3) *The beneficiary's position.* A beneficiary who is currently entitled to **1–102** trust income as it arises (*i.e.* who has an interest in possession like a life tenant) is liable to income tax for the year of assessment in which that income arises, even if none of the income was actually paid to him that year[24] One should note that the effect of Trustee Act 1925, s.31[25] (which may be excluded by the trust instrument) is to convert a minor's apparent entitlement to income under a trust for him for life into a contingent interest, since it imposes a duty upon the trustees to accumulate income (so far as not needed for his maintenance, education or benefit) until his majority, and if he dies before attaining his majority the accumulated income passes with the capital, to which it has accrued, to the person entitled to capital after his death.[26] The beneficiary will be entitled to the balance after the trustees have paid basic rate tax or lower rate or the 10 per cent dividend tax and their administration expenses. This net sum (*e.g.* £7,000 where gross income of £10,000 has borne £2,200 basic rate tax and £800 expenses) is then grossed up by the relevant rate of tax.

$$(£7,000 \times \frac{100}{100 - 22} = £8,974)$$

to find the taxable sum to rank as part of the beneficiary's total taxable income. He is given a tax credit for the difference (£8,974 − £7,000 = £1,974) (except for the 10 per cent dividend tax) so if his total income is such that he bears basic rate tax only then this credit satisfies his liability.[27]

---

[21] For the meaning of interest in possession see *Pearson v IRC* [1981] A.C. 753 and at para.1–109.

[22] ICTA, ss.686, 687 as amended by FA 2002, s.29(2). These provisions do not apply if the income is treated as the settlor's under the anti-avoidance provisions above.

[23] ICTA, s.686(2A); *Carver v Duncan* [1985] A.C. 1082.

[24] *Baker v Archer-Shee* [1927] A.C. 844; *Hamilton-Russell's Executors v I.R.C.* (1943) 25 T.C. 200; [1943] 1 All E.R. 474.

[25] At para.9–181. One should also note that a person with a contingent right, *e.g.* upon attaining 30 years of age obtains a vested right to income on attaining majority: Trustee Act 1925, s.31(1)(ii) at para.9–179.

[26] *Stanley v I.R.C.* [1944] 1 All E.R. 230.

[27] Where the trustees deduct their administration expenses the beneficiary is only entitled to gross up his net receipt *after* tax and these expenses, so his grossed-up income will be less than the trustees' gross income: *Macfariane v I.R.C.*, 1929 S.C. 453; 14 T.C. 532. If the trustees had paid him the gross £10,000 less £2,200 tax then if he were below the tax threshold he would reclaim the £2,200 and then pay the trustees their £800 expenses, so leaving him with £9,200 instead of £8,974 where the trustees first paid their expenses before paying him.

If he is not liable to tax then he can reclaim the amount of the tax credit from the Revenue (£1,974, and not the £2200 actually paid by the trustees); if he is liable to higher rate tax then he only has to pay the difference between the amount of such liability and the amount of the tax credit.

1–103   A beneficiary not entitled to trust income as it arises (*i.e.* who does not have an interest in possession but depends upon the discretion of the trustees) is charged[28] on what he receives. He will receive the income net of the s.686 trust rate tax of 40 per cent deducted by the trustees[29]: he obtains a tax credit for this deduction and will be able to reclaim some of this sum if his total income is such that he is assessable at some lower rate than 40 per cent. The imposition of tax at 40 per cent on the trustees is thus not a worrying factor where the trustees distribute the income to beneficiaries liable to basic rate tax or no tax at all. However, if the income is accumulated it will now also suffer tax at 40 per cent except in one case. If trust capital is so applied that it becomes *income* in the beneficiary's hands, then to the extent that the amount of capital distributed is less than the net amount of accumulated income after tax, the beneficiary will be treated as having received such gross amount of income as after deduction of tax at 40 per cent[30] leaves the amount of the capital distributed and he will be able to claim repayment of tax if liable to tax at a lower rate than 40 per cent.

The increase in the rate of tax applicable to trusts to 40 per cent was announced by the Chancellor on December 10, 2003 as part of his plans to modernise and simplify the income and capital gains tax systems for trusts and settlements with effect on and after April 6, 2005. A further consultative document was issued by the Inland Revenue on August 13, 2004. Other possible changes include: the introduction of an income tax basic rate tax band of £500 (after expenses) for all trusts; exemption from the tax trust rate for most trusts where income and capital gains pass quickly through the trust to the beneficiaries, who will then pay tax at their own marginal rates; treating the allowable losses of a settlor deemed to benefit from his trust as accruing to him, so that he receives the benefit of any losses as well as the burden of paying tax on capital gains; and, allowing the beneficiaries of trusts for the disabled and orphans to elect to be taxed as if they were the owners of the trust assets, so that for tax purposes they will be taxed as if they directly received income and gains. Much has been left to the 2006 Budget.

Schedule F dividend income taxed at 32.5 per cent raises major problems for trustees who invest in shares. If the trustees receive a gross dividend of £1000 they actually receive a net £900 and need to pay a further £225 tax (£325 tax at 32.5 per cent, less £100 credit) so they can actually distribute £675 to a discretionary beneficiary. Such distribution must be grossed up to £1125 so that £675 is received after payment of 40 per cent tax on £1125. Other trust income must be found to pay the £125 on top of the £225.

---

[28] Under Sch.D, Case III.
[29] ICTA, ss.686, 687.
[30] ICTA, s.687. This tax will actually have been paid earlier when the income was accumulated.

Once income has been accumulated it loses its character as income and **1–104** accrues to the capital fund becoming part thereof (*i.e.* it becomes capitalised), so payments of accumulated income will be payments of capital and will normally be receipts of capital in the beneficiary's hands and so not liable to income tax. However, if a beneficiary is given £x p.a. and the trustees have a duty or a power to make up that sum out of capital if trust income is less than £x, such "topping up" payments of capital will be taxed as income in the beneficiary's hands.[31] Moreover, regular payments out of capital may be characterised as income receipts of the beneficiary if paid to enable him to keep up his standard of living.[32] However, a disposition of capital in exercise of a power over capital will normally not rank as income in the beneficiary's hands even if used for what might be termed as an income purpose.[33]

Capital payments may involve liabilities to inheritance tax and capital gains tax.

Inheritance tax

(1) *The settlor's position.* When a settlor transfers assets to trustees or **1–105** declares himself trustee of specific assets this amounts to a transfer of value (*i.e.* a disposition diminishing the value of the disposer's estate[34]).

A transfer of value may be chargeable, exempt or potentially exempt,[35] and on death the deceased is treated as making a transfer of value of the whole of his estate immediately before his death.[36] If a donor makes a gift on trusts (or outright) but reserves any benefit[37] then the gifted property is treated as still belonging to him so as to be taxable on his death with the rest of his estate at 40 per cent, *e.g.* if he is one of the beneficiaries of his discretionary trust or a remunerated trustee or, not being a beneficiary, retains the *de facto* use of the gifted property, so creating a major problem for parents who give away their house to their children but continue to live there.

Transferring property into a discretionary trust (other than a favoured **1–106** accumulation and maintenance trust) is a chargeable transfer[38] whilst transferring property into an interest in possession trust or accumulation and maintenance trust is a potentially exempt transfer[39] (so no I.H.T. is payable) ripening into an exempt transfer if the settlor survives for seven years. Inheritance tax ("I.H.T.") is charged at 40 per cent for death transfers and those within three years of death and half that for lifetime

---

[31] *Brodies's Will Trustees v I.R.C.* (1933) 17 T.C. 432; *Lindus & Horton v I.R.C.* (1933) 17 T.C. 442.
[32] *Cunard's Trustees v I.R.C.* [1962] 1 All E.R. 159.
[33] *Stevenson v Wishart* [1987] 1 W.L.R. 1204.
[34] Inheritance Tax Act 1984 (IHTA), s.3(1). A transfer will be exempt from being a chargeable transfer if within the exemption for small annual amounts (£3,000), or for normal expenditure out of income or for a transfer between spouses, or gifts in consideration of marriage, or to charities, or to political parties or for certain national purposes: IHTA, ss.18–29.
[35] IHTA, s.3A.
[36] IHTA, s.4.
[37] Finance Act 1986, s.102.
[38] IHTA, s.2.
[39] IHTA, s.3A(2).

transfers unless the transferor dies within seven years, a sliding scale operating between three and seven years of the transfer.[40] No tax is payable if the transfer falls within the nil rate band, currently £275,000, taking account of the transferor's cumulative total in the seven years immediately preceding the relevant transfer. Thus, everyone who is wealthy enough can give away £275,000 every seven years without any I.H.T. liability.

1–107   If the settlor pays the I.H.T. *inter vivos* in respect of his discretionary settlement, so diminishing his estate further, he is treated as having made a transfer of value of such amount as after payment of I.H.T. thereon leaves the value of the settled property, *i.e.* his gift is grossed up.[41] This does not happen if the trustees pay the I.H.T. out of the trust fund.[42]

1–108   (2) *Interest in possession trusts.* The person beneficially entitled to the interest in possession (*e.g.* a life interest) is deemed to own the whole settled capital so when he disposes of his interest (*e.g.* gives it away or sells it) or his interest comes to an end[43] (other than upon his becoming absolutely entitled to the capital[44]) there is deemed to be a transfer of value equal to that of the whole settled capital. Where he sells his interest the amount of the transfer of value is reduced by the proceeds of sale.[45] His lifetime transfer of value will be potentially exempt but if he dies within seven years or died owning the interest the amount of I.H.T. payable will depend upon his cumulative total in the preceding seven years.[46] It is, however, the trustees who are primarily liable to pay the I.H.T. out of the trust property.[47]

According to an Inland Revenue Press Notice[48]:

1–109   "An interest in possession in settled property exists where the person having the interest has the immediate entitlement (subject to any prior claim by the trustees for expenses or other outgoings properly payable out of income) to any income produced by that property as the income arises; but that a discretion or power, in whatever form, which can be exercised after income arises so as to withhold it from that person negatives the existence of an interest in possession. For this purpose a power to accumulate income is regarded as a power to withhold it, unless any accumulations must be held solely for the person having the interest or his personal representatives.

On the other hand the existence of a mere power of revocation or appointment, the exercise of which would determine the interest wholly or in part (but which so long as it remains unexercised, does not

---

[40] IHTA, s.7.
[41] IHTA, ss.3(1), 162(3), 164.
[42] *ibid.* and s.199(1)(c).
[43] IHTA, s.52(1). If the interest terminates on his death then the settled capital is aggregated with his estate: ss.4(1), 49(1).
[44] IHTA, s.53(2) or if the capital reverts to the settlor or passes to the beneficiary's spouse: s.53(3), (4).
[45] IHTA, s.52(2).
[46] IHTA, ss.51(1), 52(2), 7.
[47] IHTA, ss.201(1)(a), 212(1). A new beneficiary with an interest in possession may also be liable though he has power to recoup the tax: ss.201(1)(b), 212(1), (2).
[48] [1976] B.T.R. 418.

affect the beneficiary's immediate entitlement to income) does not in the Board's view prevent the interest from being an interest in possession."

This Notice was issued since the legislation does not define the crucial **1–110** concept "interest in possession." Since then the Notice has been withdrawn because its contents were supported by the House of Lords in *Pearson v I.R.C.*,[49] which 3:2 rejected the traditional Chancery view that the mere existence of a power to accumulate or otherwise divert *income* from life tenant, L, did not prevent L having an interest in possession, L being entitled to income unless the trustees positively diverted it. Thus, a beneficiary does not have an interest in possession if the trustees have power to divert the income away from him (*e.g.* by accumulating it, so that it accrues to capital to which he has no certainty of succeeding, or by paying it or applying it for the benefit of another beneficiary). A power to terminate an interest in possession (*e.g.* a power to appoint or advance some or all the *capital* to X) does not prevent the interest being an interest in possession so long as the power is not exercised.

There is a distinction between *dispositive* powers, by which income can be **1–111** diverted away from a beneficiary, and *administrative* powers by which income can also be so diverted. Dispositive powers enabling net income after expenses to be diverted to another beneficiary prevent an interest in possession arising. Administrative powers enabling gross income to be used for payment of expenses and other outgoings properly payable out of income[50] do not prevent an interest in possession arising in the net income. Indeed, Viscount Dilhorne in *Pearson*[51] said *obiter* that a power [perhaps ancillary and not independent] to use income to pay taxes otherwise payable out of capital was an administrative power.[52]

Interests in remainder or reversion after an interest in possession are normally excluded property so that a transfer of them occasions no charge to I.H.T.[53]: after all, the beneficiary with the interest in possession is already treated as owning the whole settled capital.[54]

(3) *Trusts with no interest in possession.* Unless these are privileged trusts **1–112** (*infra*) they are liable to a periodic charge to I.H.T. every tenth anniversary[55] and it is up to the trustees to pay this out of the trust fund.[56] If during

---

[49] [1981] A.C. 753; [1980] 2 All E.R. 479, developed in *Re Trafford* [1985] Ch. 32.
[50] For such expenses see *Carver v Duncan* [1985] A.C. 1082.
[51] [1981] A.C. 753 at 775; [1980] 2 All E.R. 479, 486, followed in *Miller v I.R.C.* [1987] S.T.C. 108.
[52] Powers to allow a beneficiary to have rent-free use of a house or interest-free use of cash raise thorny problems: the Revenue treat the exercise of such powers as creating interests in possession and so occasioning an I.H.T. charge if previously no interest in possession subsisted or if causing the partial termination of an existing interest in possession: *I.R.C. v Lloyds Private Banking Ltd* [1998] S.T.C. 559. While the house remains trust property for the user to have an interest in possession in trust property, loaned cash becomes the property of the borrower absolutely and his debt is the trust property. The trust property is thus transposed from cash into a debt due to the trust and it can hardly be said that the borrower has an interest in possession in that debt that is trust property.
[53] IHTA, ss.47, 48. Certain exceptions exist to prevent use of such interests to avoid I.H.T.
[54] IHTA, s.49(1).
[55] IHTA, ss.61, 64.
[56] IHTA, ss.201(1)(a), 212.

a 10-year period capital ceases to be subject to such trusts (*e.g.* because distributed to a beneficiary or because resettled or subsettled on interest in possession trusts or privileged trusts) there is an exit charge in respect of such capital.[57] Basically, the exit charge represents a proportion of the periodic charge payable on the next 10-year anniversary of the trust and depends on the time elapsed since the last such anniversary. Calculation of the tax actually payable is complex involving a hypothetical transfer of value by a hypothetical transferor with a cumulative total including that of the settlor in the seven years before creating the trust.[58] The rate of I.H.T. is calculated at 30 per cent of the lifetime rates applicable to the hypothetical transfer,[59] so the maximum rate is 6 per cent (30 per cent of 20 per cent). Thus discretionary trusts can still be useful propositions, especially if they are kept just below the £263,000 threshold and are made by settlors with small cumulative totals of chargeable transfers. Additions of property by the original settlor to his trust should be avoided since they will often cause more I.H.T. to be charged (at the next 10-year anniversary) than would be the case if he created a new separate settlement.[60]

If the trustees pay I.H.T. in respect of the exit charge out of property remaining in the discretionary settlement then the chargeable amount has to be grossed up[61]: This does not happen if the recipient of the capital ceasing to be subject to the discretionary trust pays the I.H.T.[62]

1–113 (4) *Privileged trusts.* For policy reasons some trusts which would other- wise fall to be taxed as trusts with no interest in possession receive privileged treatment. Accumulation and maintenance trusts for minors are the most significant privileged trusts for private tax planning. Such trusts are privileged so as not to discriminate between gifts to minors or to adults contingent upon attaining 25 years of age (which must take effect behind trusts) and outright gifts to adults of 25 years or more. No periodic or exit charges are payable and no charge arises when a beneficiary becomes entitled to the settled property.[63]

1–114 Such privileged treatment is accorded to settled property if[64]:

(1) One or more persons ("beneficiaries") *will*,[65] on or before attaining a specified age not exceeding 25,[66] become beneficially entitled to it or to an interest in possession in it; and

(2) No interest in possession subsists in it, and the income from it is to be accumulated so far as not applied for the maintenance education or benefit of a beneficiary; and

---

[57] IHTA, s.65.
[58] IHTA, ss.66, 68, 69. The exit charge rate necessarily has to be calculated as a proportion of the effective rate of the last periodic charge.
[59] IHTA, s.66(1).
[60] IHTA, s.67.
[61] IHTA, s.65(2)(b).
[62] IHTA, s.65(2)(a).
[63] IHTA, ss.58(1)(b), 71(4).
[64] IHTA, s.71(1), (2).
[65] "Will" means "must under the terms of the settlement become entitled" ignoring possibilities of the beneficiary dying, becoming bankrupt, assigning his interest or losing his interest under the Variation of Trusts Act 1958: *Inglewood v I.R.C* [1983] 1 W.L.R. 366.
[66] No age need be specified in the settlement or an age greater than 25 can be specified for entitlement to *capital* so long as Trustee Act 1925, s.31(1)(ii) applies to confer a vested right to *income* on a beneficiary attaining majority.

(3) Either (a) all the persons who are or have been beneficiaries are or were either (i) grandchildren of a common grandparent, or (ii) children, widows or widowers of such grandchildren who were themselves beneficiaries but died before the time when, had they survived, they would have become entitled as in (1) above, or (b) not more than 25 years have elapsed since the commencement of the settlement or, if it was later, since the time when the conditions in (1) and (2) became satisfied with respect to the property.

There are other privileged trusts which receive special treatment, *e.g.* charitable trusts and protective trusts.[67]

Capital gains tax

(1) *The settlor's position.* On settling capital assets (other than cash or his **1–115** principal private residence[68]) *inter vivos* a settlor will be chargeable to C.G.T. on this disposal even if he (or his spouse) is a trustee or sole trustee or life tenant or if the settlement is revocable.[69] The chargeable gain will be the excess of the property's then market value over its March 31, 1982 value or its subsequent original acquisition (or "base") cost to the settlor.[70] However, on a transfer into a discretionary trust (a chargeable I.H.T. transfer taxable only if the nil band is exceeded) the settlor can elect that the gain be held over, the trustees taking the property over at the settlor's original base value.[71] However, after December 9, 2003 no such election can be made if the settlor retains an interest in the settlement.[72] The settlor should not settle assets on which he has made a loss since such loss can only be set off against gains on subsequent disposals to the trustees.[73] The rate of C.G.T. payable by the settlor will be the same as his income tax basic or higher rate, *i.e.* 22 per cent or 40 per cent.[74] An indexation allowance (to deal with inflation) calculated to 5 April 1998 is available to reduce the chargeable gain. Thereafter tapering relief[75] is available to reduce the gain by 5 per cent (for non-business assets) for each whole year of ownership of the disposed of asset up to a maximum of 10 years, but the reductions do not start till the third year of ownership, so the maximum reduction is 40 per cent for non-business assets thereby reducing the tax rate to the equivalent of 24 per cent. For business assets the maximum reduction is 75

---

[67] IHTA, ss.72–77, 86–89.
[68] Taxation of Chargeable Gains Act 1992 (TCGA), s.21(1)(b) and ss.222–226 as amended by F.A. 2004, s.117.
[69] TCGA, s.70: no charge to C.G.T. arises where a testator's will creates a trust since his estate is already liable to I.H.T.: the trustees (and then the legatees) take over the value of the property at the testator's death as their base value: TCGA, s.62. However, if the settlor or his spouse retains any interest in the settled property subsequent capital gains of the trustees are charged to the settlor: *Billingham v Cooper* [2001] S.T.C. 1177.
[70] TCGA, s.17: the first £8,200 of gains are exempt and there is an indexation allowance to cope with inflation until 5 April 1998, and tapering relief thereafter.
[71] TCGA, s.260 as amended by F.A. 2004, s.116.
[72] This closes the loophole exposed in *Melville v I.R.C.* [2001] S.T.C. 1271.
[73] TCGA, s.18.
[74] TCGA, s.4.
[75] Finance Act 1998, s.122.

per cent after four years (reducing the tax rate to 10 per cent) with reductions respectively of 12.5 per cent, 25 per cent, and 50 per cent after one, two and three years.

1–116   (2) *Actual disposals by trustees*. Normal principles apply to calculating the gain or loss on sales of chargeable assets by trustees which are chargeable at the trusts' rate of 40 per cent on their gains but only have an annual exemption of half that of individuals.[76] Losses must be set off against gains of the same year or of future years.[77] Any unrelieved losses when the trust ends and a beneficiary becomes absolutely entitled to the settled property will enure for the benefit of the beneficiary.[78] Incidentally, settled property is trust property other than nominee property where the trustees are bare trustees or nominees for a beneficiary (or beneficiaries between them) absolutely entitled to the trust property, subject to the trustees' lien for costs and expenses.[79] Bare trusts are ignored, the acts of the bare trustees being treated as the acts of the beneficiaries.[80]

1–117   (3) *Actual disposals of beneficiaries' equitable interests*. To prevent double taxation there is no C.G.T. charge when a beneficiary disposes of his underlying equitable interest in settled property so long as that interest had not at any time been acquired for money or money's worth (other than another interest under the settlement).[81]

(4) *Life interest in possession trusts*. On the death of a life tenant in possession where the settlement continues the trustees are deemed to dispose of and re-acquire the settled property at its then market value, but C.G.T. will not be charged.[82] After all, I.H.T. will be charged on the settled property.[83] Thus the property's base value gets a C.G.T.-free uplift. However, any held-over gain on the creation of the settlement will be chargeable, and payable by the trustees.[84]

1–118   If the life interest terminates other than on the life tenant's death but the settlement continues (*e.g.* to A for life or until remarriage, then B for life, then C absolutely and A remarries or releases her interest) there is no charge to C.G.T.[85] The original base value of the property in the trustees' hands remains unaltered.

If the life tenant dies and the settlement ends because a person becomes absolutely entitled to the settled property, the trustees are deemed to dispose of and re-acquire the settled property at its then market value, but C.G.T. will not be charged.[86] After all, I.H.T. will be charged on the

---

[76] Finance Act 1998, s.118 TCGA, Sch.1: the fraction dwindles to one-tenth if the settlor creates 10 or more settlements. Gains of £8,500 are exempt in 2005–2006 for individuals.
[77] TCGA, s.2.
[78] TCGA, s.71.
[79] TCGA, ss.68, 60.
[80] TCGA, s.60.
[81] TCGA, s.76. If the trust is non-resident there will be a charge: TCGA, s.85(1).
[82] TCGA, s.72.
[83] IHTA, ss.4, 49(1).
[84] TCGA, ss.74, 65: hold-over relief was available for transfers to trustees of interest in possession trusts until March 14, 1989: Finance Act 1989, s.124.
[85] The event falls outside the charging provisions, TCGA, ss.71, 72. However, I.H.T. will be payable: IHTA, ss.51, 52.
[86] TCGA, ss.71, 73.

property that has now become nominee property.[87] The absolutely entitled beneficiary will take over the property with its base value as at the life tenant's death. However, any held-over gain on the creation of the settlement will be chargeable at the beneficiary's expense.

If the life interest terminates other than on the life tenant's death and the settlement ends in respect of particular property because a person becomes absolutely entitled to the settled property, such property is deemed to have been disposed of by the trustees and C.G.T. is chargeable at the trusts' rate of 40 per cent.[88] The position is as set out in the next paragraph, except that no hold-over relief is available because the disposition will be a potentially exempt transfer for I.H.T. purposes.[89] If the trustees do not pay the tax within six months then the absolutely entitled person becomes liable.[90]

(5) *Trusts with no life interest in possession.* When a person becomes **1–119** absolutely entitled to any settled property as against the trustees, the assets comprised in the part to which he has become entitled are deemed to have been disposed of by the trustees for market value and C.G.T. is chargeable.[91] The rate of C.G.T. is the trusts' rate of 40 per cent.[92] However, because the absolute entitlement occasions an exit charge to IHT an election can be made to hold over the gain and this can extend to any held-over gain on the creation of the settlement.[93]

The charge to C.G.T. arises whether the person becoming absolutely **1–120** entitled does so in his personal capacity as beneficiary or in a fiduciary capacity as trustee of another trust.[94] If trust assets wholly cease to be subject to the trusts, powers and provisions of one settlement and become subject to the trusts, powers and provisions of another settlement, there is a deemed disposal of the assets even if the trustees of the two settlements happen to be the same persons.[95] The trustees of a settlement are treated as a single continuing body of persons distinct from the actual persons who may from time to time be the trustees[96] (so that a change of trustees occasions no charge to C.G.T. or I.H.T.).

Difficult questions arise where trustees of a settlement containing a **1–121** power of appointment or of allocation or of appropriation or of advancement exercise such power so that part of the settled property falls to be held by them on trusts other than those to which it was subject immediately beforehand. Does the exercise of the power create a new trust, whose trustees are absolutely entitled against the old trustees, so that there has been a deemed disposal, or does it merely create a sub-trust under the

---

[87] IHTA, ss.4, 49(1).
[88] TCGA, s.71, Finance Act 1998, s.120.
[89] Except where discretionary trustees become absolutely entitled against interest in possession trustees (not a potentially exempt transfer) when hold-over relief will be available; TCGA, s.260.
[90] TCGA, s.69(4).
[91] TCGA, s.7.
[92] Finance Act 1998, s.120, F.A. 2004, s.29.
[93] TCGA, s.260. However, if the gain on an asset is held over then on a subsequent sale taper relief is only available for the seller's period of ownership.
[94] *Hoare Trustees v Gardner* [1979] Ch. 10 at 13–14.
[95] *Hart v Briscoe* [1979] Ch. 1 at 5; *Bond v Pickford* [1983] S.T.C. 517; *cf. Swires v Renton* [1991] S.T.C. 490.
[96] *Roome v Edwards* [1982] A.C. 279 (English trustees liable for gain on non-resident trustee's part of the trust property: see [1981] C.L.J. 240; *Bond v Pickford,* above; TCGA, s.69(1).

umbrella of the old original trust so that there has been no deemed disposal? If the power is in a wide form authorising an application of the trust fund freed and released from the original trusts of the settlement, so that the original trusts are replaced by other exhaustive trusts, then such an application of the trust fund will be a deemed disposal.[97] If the power is in a narrow form, *e.g.* a special power to appoint the trust fund on trusts for a class of beneficiaries, their spouses and children (but with no unusual provision allowing the trustees to delegate their duties to other persons or otherwise contemplating the creation of an entirely new trust) then any appointed property will be regarded as a sub-trust within the original trust, even if the sub-trusts are exhaustive, so there will be no deemed disposal.[98]

Section 5. Significance of Matters of Construction

1–122   Before a court can apply a legal rule to validate or invalidate a provision in a document or something purportedly done thereunder it is vital to construe the provision to determine exactly what it means in the context of the document as a whole and in the light of such extrinsic evidence as is admissible, *e.g.* allowing the judge to put himself in the testator's armchair and take advantage of section 21 of the Administration of Justice Act 1982.[99]

1–123   Every provision requires minute scrutiny to see how many meanings it may have—nothing must be taken for granted. Words like "relatives" or "customers" may seem straightforward enough. But does "relatives of X" mean just those persons who would be his statutory next-of-kin taking under the intestacy rules if X were dead or does it cover the huge number who are descended like X from some common ancestor thousands of years ago?[1] Does "customer of the Y Co.," cover a purchaser who has not ordered any goods from the Y Co. for six months, one year, six years or more?[2] Can "small" have a meaning where a testator leaves his residuary estate on trust for "those who have only received small legacies?"[3] Can "gay guys" extend to lesbians and bi-sexuals? Can "Madonna fans" be restricted to members of her official fan club?

1–124   It is often crucial whether words have any obligatory sense ("must") or merely a permissive sense ("may"), though complex clauses can make the distinction difficult to discern.[4] If a trustee is protected when lending on mortgage if acting upon a report as to the value of property "made by a

---

[97] Hold-over relief will be available in respect of business or agricultural assets or if an I.H.T. charge arises because interest in possession trusts are the new trusts.

[98] See *Bond v Pickford*, above. Trusts are exhaustive if the beneficial interest is fully disposed of so that there is no need to refer elsewhere to discover what happens after someone dies or fails to obtain a vested interest. See also *Swires v Renton* [1991] S.T.C. 490 and *Revenue* SP 7/84. The taxation of non-resident trusts is ignored as a very complex topic containing many tax avoidance provisions; see R. Venables Q.C., *Non-Resident Trusts* (Key Haven plc).

[99] See at para.3–65; *Re Williams* [1985] 1 W.L.R. 905; *Re Benham's W.T.* [1995] S.T.C. 210.

[1] *Re Baden's Deed Trusts (No.2)* [1972] Ch. 607.

[2] *Sparfax (1965) Ltd v Dommett, The Times*, July 14, 1972.

[3] *Re Steel* [1978] 2 All E.R. 1026; *cf. O'Rourke v Binks* [1992] S.T.C. 703.

[4] See Chap. 3, sections 1 and 3 and *McPhail v Doulton* [1971] A.C. 424.

person whom he reasonably believed to be an able practical surveyor or valuer instructed and employed independently of any owner of the property," must the valuer *in fact* be independently instructed or is the trustee's reasonable belief sufficient?[5] Does "charitable or benevolent" mean that a purpose can be charitable or instead it can be benevolent, so that the trust is void, or can it be treated as meaning that the purpose must be both charitable and benevolent so that the trust is valid?[6] If property is left to D "on condition she provides a home for her infirm sister, I," does this mean that if D takes the property she will be subject to this condition or can the apparent condition really be treated as only expressing the testator's motive.[7] Indeed, what does the condition mean? Is it certain enough to be enforceable and valid? If not, can the clause be treated as expressing motive only so that D can inherit the property?

If a testator leaves his residuary estate "for the Hull Judeans Association **1–125** in memory of my late wife to be used solely in the work of constructing the new buildings for the Association and/or improvements to the said buildings" can this be construed not as a purpose trust to endow the Association, (and so void) but as an out-and-out gift accruing to the Association's funds, subject to the contractual rights thereto of the Association members under its constitution?[8]

From the outset one has to be alert to the possibilities of construction. **1–126** Judges are only human and once they have seen the merits of a case they may be prepared to construe a document—or even interpret circumstances[9]—in a way that one would not normally construe it—or interpret them—coming "cold" to the situation. Some judges, however, do prefer to adopt a strict approach. The rest of this book contains plenty of examples of both sorts, though the modern judicial trend is to be facilitative and uphold trustlike arrangements so far as possible.

Section 6. Aspects of Wills and Intestacy Law

In a study of trust law there are many occasions when points relating to **1–127** wills or intestacies crop up. A general outline knowledge of the laws applicable thereto is thus useful before embarking on a detailed study of trust law.[10]

First, one needs to distinguish the position of personal representatives (P.R.s) winding up a deceased person's estate from the position of trustees holding the trust property. The P.R.s' function is to collect in the deceased's assets, pay off all debts, taxes and expenses and, then, to distribute the

---

[5] Contrast *Re Walker* (1890) 62 L.T. 449 at 452 and *Re Somerset* [1894] 1 Ch. 231 at 253 with *Re Stuart* [1897] 2 Ch. 583 at 592, *Shaw v Cates* [1909] 1 Ch. 389 at 403 and *Re Solomon* [1912] 1 Ch. 261 at 281.
[6] *Chichester Diocesan Fund v Simpson* [1944] A.C. 341 at para.7–138; *cf.* a trust for purposes connected with the education and welfare of children: *Att.-Gen. of Bahamas v Royal Trust Co.* [1986] 1 W.L.R. 1001.
[7] *Re Brace* [1954] 1 W.L.R. 955; *cf. Re Frame* [1939] Ch. 700.
[8] *Re Lipinski's W.T.* [1976] Ch. 235 at para.3–242.
[9] *Re Vandervell's Trusts (No.2)* [1974] Ch. 269 at para.2–67; *Hammond v Mitchell* [1991] 1 W.L.R. 1127; *Wayling v Jones* (1993) 69 P. & C.R. 170.
[10] For further reference see *Theobald on Wills*; Parry & Clark's *Law of Succession*.

Conclusion?

assets to those entitled under the will or intestacy. Their duty is owed to the estate as a whole so that they are under no duty to consider the effect of the exercise of their administrative powers so as to keep an even hand between those interested in income and those interested in capital.[11] Until they assent to the assets passing to the legatees or devisees the legal and beneficial title to the assets is vested in the P.R.s.[12] The legatees or devisees have no equitable interest in such assets: they merely have an equitable right to compel due administration of the estate though this chose in action (unlike the right of a beneficiary under a discretionary trust) can be assigned or bequeathed.[13] To assist them in their functions P.R.s have a statutory power to appropriate assets to legatees or devisees[14] and if only a sole P.R. has been appointed then, acting as such, he can give a valid receipt for capital moneys arising on a sale of a trust of land.[15] P.R.s can only be appointed by will or by the court.[16] Finally, one of two or more P.R.s has full power to deal with the deceased's pure personalty[17] However, in respect of freehold or leasehold land the concurrence of all the P.R.s is required to enter into any contract and then to convey the land.[18]

1–128   When P.R.s have completed administration of the deceased's estate they become trustees of the residuary estate[19] and their conduct will be sufficient to imply an assent of personalty to themselves as trustees.[20] As trustees they can exercise the statutory power that trustees have to appoint new or additional trustees.[21] Such appointment makes the new or additional trustees trustees of the trusts of the residuary estate but it does not obtain the benefit of Trustee Act 1925, s.40 (at para.8–23): thus, to the extent that the residuary estate consists of land, the legal estate therein remains outstanding in the P.R.s until a written assent is executed by them (or their successors in title) in favour of such trustees,[22] no earlier implied assent from conduct being possible for legal[23] estates in land. Thus, personal

---

[11] *Re Hayes's W.T.* [1971] 1 W.L.R. 758, Trustees have such a duty.

[12] "Whatever property comes to the executor *virtute officii* comes to him in full ownership without distinction between legal and equitable interests: the whole property in his": *Commissioner for Stamp Duties v Livingston* [1965] A.C. 694, 701. Thus "no legatee, devisee or next of kin has any beneficial interest in the assets being administered"; *Re Hayes's W.T.* [1971] 1 W.L.R. 758 at 764.

[13] *Re Leigh's W.T.* [1970] Ch. 277; *P. V. Baker* (1970) 86 Q.L.R. 20; *Crowden v Aldridge* [1993] 1 W.L.R. 433; *Marshall v Kerr* [1994] 3 All E.R. 106 at 112, 119; *Wu v Wu* [1996] 3 W.L.R. 778.

[14] Administration of Estates Act 1925, s.41. Trustees only have such power if expressly conferred upon them.

[15] Law of Property Act 1925, s.27(2). *cf.* Settled Land Act 1925, s.30(3).

[16] Trustees can be appointed under Trustee Act 1925, s.36 at para.8–01.

[17] *Attenborough v Solomon* [1913] A.C. 76 where a P.R., three years after he had become a trustee of the deceased's silver, pledged it and this was invalid since trustees must act jointly.

[18] Law of Property (Miscellaneous Provisions) Act 1994, s.16.

[19] *Eaton v Daines* [1894] W.N. 32; *Re Ponder* [1921] 2 Ch. 59; *Re Cockburn's W.T.* [1957] 1 Ch. 438.

[20] *Attenborough v Solomon* [1913] A.C. 76; C. Stebbings [1984] Conv. 423.

[21] *Re Cockburn's W.T.* [1957] 1 Ch. 438.

[22] *Re King's W.T.* [1964] Ch. 542, criticised by Professor E. C. Ryder [1976] *Current Legal Problems* 60. The Limitation Act 1980 may remedy defects in title. Take E and F who completely administer T's estate and are to hold the residue (including Blackacre) upon trust for sale for A for life, remainder to B absolutely. Five years later E dies. Then F as surviving trustee purports to appoint G and H additional trustees with himself. Four years later F dies. G and H as trustees then sell and convey Blackacre to P. Later P contracts to sell to Q who objects to P's title. The objection is valid (unless P can prove 12 years' adverse possession). The legal estate is in F's personal representatives and not P since E and F never executed a written assent of Blackacre in favour of themselves in their new capacity as trustees. Thus they could not take advantage of Trustee Act 1925, s.40, para.8–23.

[23] An implied informal assent is possible for equitable interests if the P.R. is also beneficially entitled: *Re Edwards's W.T.* [1982] Ch. 30.

representatives need to execute a written assent in favour of themselves as trustees so that subsequent appointments by them are effective under s.40.

If a testator leaves his residuary estate on trust for A absolutely or for A **1–129** for life, remainder to B absolutely, it has already been seen that no trust arises until the P.R.s have completed winding up the estate and ascertained the residue. Before then where the P.R.s dispose of assets other than to legatees C.G.T. will be payable by the P.R.s.[24] However, for I.H.T. purposes a legatee with an interest in possession in a deceased's residuary estate is treated as having such interest from the deceased's death.[25] For income tax purposes sums paid to the legatees to the extent that residuary estate income is available are taxed on the grossed up equivalent of such sums[26]:

Basically, a will (unless made by a privileged military testator) must be in **1–130** writing signed at the end by the testator (or by some other person in his presence and by his direction).[27] The testator's signature has to be made or acknowledged by him in the presence of two witnesses both with the testator at the same time. The witnesses must then sign their names in the testator's presence. The document must be intended to take effect only on the testator's death.[28] Thus, if S by deed settles £50,000 upon trust for himself for life and then for R absolutely, the formalities for a will are not applicable since S's settlement takes effect immediately, giving R a present vested interest in remainder and entitling S only to the income from the £50,000 for the rest of his life. If S, instead had made a will bequeathing £50,000 to R absolutely, S could use in his lifetime not only the income from the £50,000 but also the whole £50,000: he could also revoke his will and bequeath the £50,000 to X instead. Incidentally, personal property is said to be bequeathed to legatees and real property to be devised to devisees by will.

Gifts by will may fail to take effect by reason *inter alia* of ademption, **1–131** abatement, lapse, the beneficiary being an attesting witness or the spouse or civil partner thereof[29] or the beneficiary disclaiming the gift or the beneficiary's marriage to the testator having been disolved or annulled unless a contrary intention appears in the will.[30] Ademption occurs if T specifically leaves some property such as "my Ming dynasty vase" or "my house Blackacre" but no longer has the property when he dies: the legacy or devise is adeemed and the legatee or devisee receives nothing. Abatement is a little less drastic: if T's debts are such that the Ming vase and Blackacre forming part of T's estate at T's death have to be sold but that a surplus remains after using the proceeds to pay off the debts then a rateable

---

[24] *Cochrane v I.R.C.* [1974] S.T.C. 335; *Prest v Bettinson* [1980] S.T.C. 607; TCGA, s.62. P.R.s have the annual exemption (£8,200) for the year in which the deceased died and for the next two years of assessment. Where P.R.s' gains do not exceed their losses any surplus losses cannot be passed on to the legatees unlike the position for trustees and beneficiaries under TCGA, s.71(2). Assets received by legatees are taken over at their base value at the deceased's death: TCGA, s.62(4).

[25] IHTA, s.91.

[26] ICTA 1988, ss.695 and 696 as amended by Finance Act 1995 Sch.18.

[27] Wills Act 1837, s.9 at para.2–109.

[28] *Att.-Gen. v Jones* (1817) 3 Price 368, *Governors of Foundling Hospital v Crane* [1911] 2 K.B. 367.

[29] Wills Act 1837, s.15 as restricted by Wills Act 1968 (at para.2–132 below) and extended by Civil Partnership Act 2004 Sch.4 para.3.

[30] Law Reform (Succession) Act 1995, s.3, substituting Wills Act 1837, s.18A.

proportion will pass to the legatee and devisee. General legacies such as "I bequeath £5,000 to A, £3,000 to B and £1,000 to C" must first abate to their entire extent before resort can be had to specific gifts.[31]

1–132   Lapse occurs if a legatee or devisee predeceases the testator unless the legatee or devisee was a child (or other issue) of the testator and left issue alive at the testator's death: in such an exceptional case the gift is effective in favour of the surviving issue *per stirpes*.[32] Where lapse occurs the gift fails and will fall into any residuary gift of the testator (*e.g.* "I leave all the residue of my property not otherwise hereinbefore disposed of to R"). Necessarily, if it is the residuary legatee, R, who has predeceased the testator and occasioned the lapse, then the gifted property must be undisposed of and so pass to the next-of-kin under the intestacy rules applicable on the partial intestacy of the testator. Similarly, if a trust in a will fails, the property purportedly subject to the trust will pass under the residuary gift unless the trust was of the residuary property when the property will pass to the next-of-kin under the intestacy rules.

1–133   If it is uncertain whether or not a beneficiary predeceased the testator (*e.g.* where they are both killed by a bomb or in a car or plane crash) the younger is presumed to have survived the elder under the *commorientes* rule in s.184 of the Law of Property Act 1925.

1–134   A beneficiary under a will or intestacy may disclaim the gift to him.[33] The gift then falls back into the deceased's estate and passes to whomsoever would have been entitled if the disclaiming beneficiary had predeceased the deceased.[34] Once a beneficiary has accepted the gift he cannot disclaim it[35] but he can assign it on to whomsoever he wants. This will occasion another charge to C.G.T. or I.H.T. unless this occurs within two years of the deceased's death and takes the form of a written instrument varying the will or the intestacy rules and executed by the bountiful beneficiary, who then elects for such variation to take effect as if made by the deceased in his will.[36] Unfortunately, for income tax purposes the variation is not so treated so that the bountiful beneficiary will be treated[37] as a settlor of the benefit conferred by him.[38]

1–135   This leaves us with the intestacy rules but first it should be noted that, whilst a testator in his will can appoint "executors" to administer the testator's estate and who will obtain "probate" of the will, where a person dies intestate his closest relatives normally have to take out "letters of

---

[31] The order in which property has to be resorted to to pay debts, etc., is laid down in Pt II, 1st Sch. to the Administration of Estates Act 1925.

[32] Wills Act 1837, s.33, as substituted by Administration of Justice Act 1982, s.19. Illegitimate issue count: Family Law Reform Act 1969, s.16. *Per stirpes* means through their stocks of descent so that children of a deceased child take the share their parent would have taken had he survived.

[33] *Townson v Tickell* (1819) 3 B. & Ald. 31; *Re Scott* [1975] 1 W.L.R. 1260. A gift of a single whole (*e.g.* residue) must be wholly accepted or wholly disclaimed, partial acceptance amounting to whole acceptance: *Re Joel* [1943] Ch. 311; *Guthrie v Walrond* (1882) 22 Ch.D. 573.

[34] *Re Backhouse* [1931] W.N. 168.

[35] *Re Hodge* [1940] Ch. 260.

[36] IHTA 1984, s.142; TCGA 1992, s.62(6).

[37] See *Schnieder v Mills* [1993] S.T.C. 430 at 435.

[38] If a variation is made by a beneficiary in favour of his minor unmarried child then the income arising (unless accumulated in a capital settlement) will be assessed as that of the beneficiary: ICTA 1988, s.660B, above at para.1–94.

administration" and act as "administrators": the phrase "personal representatives" covers both executors and administrators. A testator's will, if
professionally drafted, will, after specific gifts, usually give everything to the
executors on a trust for sale, and, on an intestacy, statute[39] directs the
administrators to hold the intestate's property on a trust with a power of
sale.

Where an intestate is survived by a spouse and issue[40] the spouse takes
the intestate's personal chattels absolutely and the net sum of £125,000 free
of death duties and costs[41]: the residue is held on "the statutory trusts" for
the issue subject to the spouse having a life interest[42] in half the residue. If
the intestate is survived by a spouse and one or more of the following, that
is to say, a parent, a brother or sister of the whole blood, or issue of such a
brother or sister, but leaves no issue, then, the spouse takes the personal
chattels absolutely and the net sum of £200,000 free of death duties and
costs: half of any residue is held for the surviving spouse absolutely and the
other half is held for the surviving parents or parent or, if there is no
surviving parent, it is held on "the statutory trusts" for the brothers and
sisters of the whole blood. If the intestate leaves a spouse and no issue and
no parent or brother or sister of the whole blood and no issue of such
brother or sister then the surviving spouse takes everything.

If the intestate leaves issue, but no surviving spouse, everything is held on **1–136**
"the statutory trusts" for the issue. If the intestate leaves no spouse and no
issue any surviving parent or parents of the intestate take the assets
absolutely. If, in such circumstances, there is no such surviving parent the
intestate's relatives are entitled in the following order so that if any member
of one class takes a vested interest he excludes all members of subsequent
classes:

  (i) the brothers and sisters of the whole blood on "the statutory trusts,"
 (ii) brothers and sisters of the half blood on "the statutory trusts,"
(iii) grandparents,
 (iv) uncles and aunts of the whole blood on "the statutory trusts,"
  (v) uncles and aunts of the half blood on "the statutory trusts." In
      default the Crown (or the Duchy of Lancaster or of Cornwall) takes
      everything as *bona vacantia*.

---

[39] Administration of Estates Act 1925, s.33 as amended by Trusts of Land and Appointment of Trustees Act 1996, Sch.2.
[40] "Issue" includes illegitimate issue: Family Law Reform Act 1987, s.1. Indeed, unless s.1 of that Act is excluded any disposition (by will or deed) referring to various relatives (*e.g.* child, nephew) covers both legitimate and illegitimate relatives. Civil partners now have the same rights as spouses: Civil Partnership Act 2004 Sch.4 paras 7 *et seq.*
[41] The rules are in AEA 1925, s.46 and the current amount of the statutory legacies in Family Provision (Intestate Succession) Order 1993 (SI 1993/2906). Interest of 4 per cent is payable on unpaid statutory legacies. The spouse must survive the intestate by 28 days to take the legacy: Law Reform (Succession) Act 1995, s.1.
[42] The surviving spouse has a right to require the personal representatives purchase or redeem the life interest by paying over its capital value: Administration of Estates Act 1925, s.47A. For calculation see Intestate Succession (Interest and Capitalisation) Order 1977 (SI 1977/1491), as amended by SI 1983/1374. She also has a right to compel the personal representatives to appropriate the matrimonial home at a proper valuation towards satisfaction of her interest under the intestacy: Intestates' Estate Act 1952, s.5; *Re Phelps* [1980] Ch. 275.

1–137   If property is held on the statutory trusts, *e.g.* for issue, this means that the property is held upon trust equally for all the intestate's children living at his death who have attained or subsequently attain 18 years of age or who marry under that age: if a child predeceased the intestate, but left issue living or conceived at the death of the intestate, then such issue stand in the parent's shoes and take his share if they go on to attain 18 years of age or marry thereunder.[43] Thus, if an intestate widower dies leaving a 40-year-old son (with two daughters of his own) and two grandchildren aged 20 and 15, being the children of a deceased son of the intestate, then the 40-year-old son takes one-half of the intestate's property, and the two grandchildren acquire interests in the other half. The elder grandchild takes one-quarter of the property absolutely whilst the other quarter is held for the younger grandchild contingent upon his attaining 18 or marrying thereunder: if he should die before then his elder brother would then obtain the whole half share that would have passed to his father had he not predeceased the intestate.

1–138   Finally, mention may be made of the fact that if a testator's will or the intestacy rules fail to make reasonable financial provision for the testator's or intestate's dependants then an application under the Inheritance (Provision for Family and Dependants) Act 1975 can be made to the court for the court to order reasonable provision to be made. Sections 10 and 11 have special provisions to deal with dispositions within six years of death intended to defeat applications for financial provision and with contracts to leave property by will.

Section 7. Classification of Trusts

1–139   Traditionally trusts have been classified as express, implied, resulting or constructive. Classification is significant in the following respects. No formalities are required for the creation of implied, resulting or constructive trusts.[44] A person who is incapable of being an express trustee may become a resulting or constructive trustee.[45] A constructive trust imposed on A, the owner of Blackacre, in favour of B as to a half interest therein may be void against A's trustee in bankruptcy under s.339 of the Insolvency Act 1986 as not being a settlement upon B for valuable consideration.[46] A resulting trust imposed on A, the owner of Blackacre, in favour of B due to B contributing half the purchase moneys will not be void against A's trustees in bankruptcy under s.339.

There is no authoritative classification of trusts but for our purposes the following classification is adopted.

1–140   *Express trust*: a trust where the settlor has positively expressed his intention to create a trust of specific property and subsequent substituted property from time to time comprised within the trust fund, whether using the word "trust" or other informal words expressing the same idea.

---

[43] Administration of Estates Act 1925, s.47(1).
[44] LPA 1925, s.53(2) at para.2–06 and Law of Property (Miscellaneous Provisions) Act 1989, s.2(5).
[45] *Re Vinogradoff* [1935] W.N. 68.
[46] *Re Densham* [1975] 3 All E.R. 726.

Implied trust: a resulting or constructive trust.[47]

Resulting trust[48]: a resulting trust arises, where A transfers property or causes property to be transferred without intending to dispose of his beneficial interest, so that if he transfers property to B gratuitously, then B is rebuttably presumed to hold such property on trust for A, or if A and B equally put up the purchase price but have Blackacre put into B's name alone, then B will hold on resulting trust for A and B equally, or if A transfers property to B on trusts which, for some reason, leave some or all of the beneficial interest undisposed of, B automatically holds such property on a resulting trust for A to the extent of the undisposed of beneficial interest.

Constructive trust[49]: a trust of specific property declared by Equity on proof of special circumstances (which require the owner's conscience to be affected by knowledge of the special circumstances) where Equity considers it unconscionable for the owner of specific property to hold it for his own benefit to the exclusion of the claimant. Thus, a proprietary interest subsists in that specific property which makes it necessary to prove facts which fit the accepted special circumstances directly or by analogy, because the court cannot impose a constructive trust over an owner's property whenever justice and good conscience require it and thereby indulge idiosyncratic notions of fairness and justice,[50] especially if the owner has become insolvent. The special circumstances normally involve the defendant having agreed expressly or impliedly to hold property wholly or partly for the claimant in cases where it would be unconscionable for the agreed trust to be unenforceable, *e.g.* due to lack of certainty or of requisite formalities or due to an impermissible change of mind.

Exceptionally, a person, though not constructive trustee of specific **1–141** property (so that this exception may more accurately be thought of as constructive *trusteeship*) may, through his dishonest involvement with a breach of trust or other fiduciary duty, be treated constructively as if he were a trustee so that he may be made personally liable to account like an express trustee, *i.e.* be personally liable to make good the loss of trust property.[51] Historically, the terminology of personal liability to account in equity as a constructive trustee has been utilised: logically, this equitable remedy of *personal* liability to account should be kept distinct from *proprietary* constructive trusts of property, so it is excluded from Chapter 6 and discussed in Chapter 11.

The classic proprietary constructive trust arises in support of pre-existing **1–142** rights in respect of property: it is a substantive proprietary right that is a natural incident of the trust institution or another fiduciary obligation in respect of property. As such, it arises automatically on the occurrence of certain factual situations involving property subject to a trust or other fiduciary obligation, so that any court decree will be retrospective.

---

[47] *Cowcher v Cowcher* [1972] 1 All E.R. 943 at 949, though Trustee Act 1925, s.68(17) in speaking of "implied and constructive trusts" means "resulting and constructive trusts."
[48] See Chap. 5.
[49] See Chap. 6.
[50] See at paras 6–93 to 6–123.
[51] See Chap. 11.

1–143   Different from the English constructive trust (sometimes referred to as an "institutional" or "substantive" constructive trust) is the remedial constructive trust found in the USA, Canada and Australia[52] which does not arise automatically in accordance with settled principles but which is imposed by the court as a remedy in its discretion when it discovers it just, the court's decree being prospective except to the rare extent it considers it should be retrospective against a specified person.[53] Once the defendant property owner is insolvent it is clear that no remedial constructive trust should be imposed by the courts because this would undermine the statutory regime covering assets of insolvent persons.[54] However, there is scope[55] for the courts to develop a doctrine enabling them to impose a remedial constructive trust against the property of a solvent defendant.

1–144   It should be noted that in some judgments "constructive trust" is sometimes used to cover automatic resulting trusts which may be said to arise as a matter of construction. "Implied trust" is sometimes used to mean informally created express trusts not using the word "trust", sometimes to mean resulting trusts, sometimes to mean only presumed resulting trusts,[56] and sometimes to mean presumed resulting trusts and constructive trusts arising out of informally expressed common intentions.[57] This has created problems for parliamentary counsel.[58] Ideally, since the concept of "implied trust" has no useful function it should cease to be used, but the compendious expression "implied resulting or constructive trusts" has its attractions to judges and parliamentary counsel who act with abundant caution.

---

[52] *Giumelli v Giumelli* [1999] 73 A.L.J.R. 547 (Australia), *Peter v Beblow* (1993) 101 D.L.R. (4th) 621 (Canada).
[53] *Westdeutsche Landesbank v Islington B.C.* [1996] A.C. 669 at 714.
[54] *Re Polly Peck (No.2)* [1998] 3 All E.R. 812, 824, 830.
[55] *Westdeutsche Landesbank v Islington B.C.* [1996] A.C. 669 at 716, *Re Goldcorp* [1994] 2 All E.R. 806 at 826–827.
[56] See, *e.g. Soar v Ashwell* [1893] 2 Q.B. 390; *Cook v Fountain* (1676) 3 Swan. 585; *Re Llanover Estates* [1926] Ch. 626; *Lloyd v Spillil* (1740) Barn. Ch. 384 at 388; *Allen v Snyder* [1977] 2 New South Wales L.R. 685.
[57] Sir Christopher Slade, *The Informal Creation of Interests in Land* (The Childe & Co. Oxford Lecture, 1984), p.4.
[58] *e.g.* LPA 1925, s.53(2); Trustee Act 1925, s.68(17).

Chapter 2

FORMAL REQUIREMENTS

Section 1. Lifetime and testamentary dispositions distinguished

A testamentary disposition is one that requires to be made in the form of a **2–01** will complying with the Wills Act 1837, as amended. A will has been defined[1] as "an instrument by which a person makes a disposition of his property to take effect after his decease and which is in its own nature ambulatory and revocable during his life": such person is a testator or testatrix. As Lord Oliver remarked,[2] "It is, of course, axiomatic that an essential characteristic of a will is that, during the lifetime of the testator, it is a mere declaration of his present intention and may be freely revoked or altered. It does not follow that every document intended to operate on death and containing a power of revocation is necessarily testamentary in character."

He also stated[3] "the most obvious example of such a revocable but non-testamentary instrument is the exercise of a revocable power of appointment under a settlement *inter vivos*." A testator has to make a disposition of his own property. Thus if trustees hold property for T for life, and then to distribute the capital between such of T's descendants as the trustees shall select in their absolute discretion, but subject to T's power, revocably or irrevocably, to appoint shares of capital to pass after his death to such of his descendants as he may see fit, T is not disposing of his own property if he revocably appoints all the capital to pass on his death to his son, S.

What if T has disposed of his property in his lifetime to trustees on trusts **2–02** for himself for life, remainder to B and C equally, where he has expressly reserved to himself the power to revoke the trust wholly or partly at any time during his life or to appoint capital to such of XYZ as he might choose? In default of any exercise of the power, capital will pass equally to B and C on the death of the life tenant, T, but as a result of T's earlier *lifetime disposition* to the trustees which took effect immediately, conferring an equitable interest in capital on B and C, although subsequently defeasible if the power of revocation or appointment were exercised. Thus, a settlor's revocable trusts taking effect in his lifetime are not testamentary dispositions.[4]

---

[1] Lord Oliver in *Baird v Baird* [1990] 2 A.C. 548 at 556 adopting *Jarman on Wills* (8th ed., 1951), p.26.
[2] *Baird v Baird* [1990] 2 A.C. 548 at 557.
[3] *ibid.* at 556.
[4] *Kauter v Hilton* (1953) 90 C.L.R. 86 at 98–99 and 100–101, *Young v Sealey* [1949] Ch. 279 at 284 and 294, *Choithram International SA v Pagarani* [2001] 2 All E.R. 492 at 500, *Anderson v Patton* [1948] 2 D.L.R. 202. The creation of a joint bank account is not a testamentary disposition: see para.5–116.

2–03   What if T went further and disposed of his property in his lifetime to trustees to hold the income *and the capital* on trust for himself or such other persons as he might direct and, then, on his death to distribute whatever remained to B and C equally? Here T has the full equitable interest in all the trust property to do whatever he wants with it: B and C have no interest whatsoever in the trust property, only a hope that something will remain at T's death and that it will then pass to them. At the outset T made a lifetime disposition of his legal (but not his beneficial) interest in the trust property: he retained the whole beneficial interest as his to do with as he wished in the rest of his lifetime. Thus, T's intentions to benefit B and C are testamentary intentions concerned with disposing of his beneficial interest in the trust property, so that such intentions will be ineffective unless complying with the Wills Act 1837 requiring two witnesses.[5] All the trust property is held from the outset to T's order in his lifetime until he orders how the remaining capital is to be dealt with on his death, such orders being testamentary in nature.

2–04   One needs to distinguish the situation where trustees hold to the order of the settlor from the outset and the situation where the trustees hold to the order of the settlor only after he exercises a power so to order, as where they hold on trusts for various persons subject to the settlor's power (via a power of revocation or a power of appointment in his own favour) to defeat the existing equitable interests of the beneficiaries by directing the trustees for the future to hold to his order. In the former situation from the outset the full equitable interest is owned by the settlor, while in the latter situation such equitable interest from the outset is held by all the beneficiaries and it is only at some subsequent date that the settlor can acquire an equitable interest by exercising his reserved overriding powers. In the former case there is no lifetime disposition of the settlor's equitable interest, while in the latter case there is, the settlor only acquiring an equitable interest if he exercises his overriding powers.

Section 2. Lifetime or Inter Vivos Trusts

THE STATUTORY PROVISIONS

Law of Property Act 1925

2–05   *Section 52(1)*: "All conveyances of land or of any interest therein are void for the purpose of conveying or creating a legal estate unless made by deed."

---

[5] *Anderson v Patton* (above) and *Kauter v Hilton* (above) at 100 endorsing Dixon and Evatt JJ. in *Russell v Scott* (1936) 55 C.L.R. 440 at 454 "What can be accomplished only by will is the voluntary transmission on death of an interest which up to the moment of death belongs absolutely and indefeasibly to the deceased." See also *Governors of Foundling Hospital v Crane* [1911] 2 K.B. 367 at 379–380. An agreement between T and L, intended to be a legatee under T's formally valid will, that L will hold the legacy on secret trust for B amounts to a testamentary disposition, but will be effective under a constructive trust: see section 3 below.

Section 53(1): "Subject to the provisions hereinafter contained with respect to the creation of interests in land by parol:

(*a*) No interest in land can be created or disposed of except by writing signed by the person creating or conveying the same, or by his agent thereunto lawfully authorised in writing, or by will, or by operation of law;

(*b*) A declaration of trust respecting any land or any interest therein must be manifested and proved by some writing signed by some person who is able to declare such trust or by his will;

(*c*) A disposition of an equitable interest or trust subsisting at the time of the disposition, must be in writing signed by the person disposing of the same, or by his agent thereunto lawfully authorised in writing or by will.

(2) This section does not affect the creation or operation of resulting, implied or **2–06** constructive trusts."

Section 54(1): "All interests in land created by parol and not put in writing and signed by the persons so creating the same, or by their agents thereunto lawfully authorised in writing, have, notwithstanding any consideration having been given for the same, the force and effect of interests at will only.

(2) Nothing in the foregoing provisions . . . shall affect the creation by parol of leases taking effect in possession for a term not exceeding three years at the best rent which can reasonably be obtained without taking a fine."

Section 55: "Nothing in the last two foregoing sections shall—

(*a*) Invalidate dispositions by will . . .

(*d*) Affect the operation of the law relating to part performance."

Section 205(1): "In this Act unless the context otherwise requires, the following expressions have the meanings hereby assigned to them— . . .

(ii) "Conveyance" includes a mortgage, charge, lease, assent, vesting declaration, vesting instrument, disclaimer, release and every other assurance of property or of an interest therein by any instrument, except a will; "convey" has a corresponding meaning; and "disposition" includes a conveyance and also a devise, bequest, or an appointment of property contained in a will; and "dispose of" has a corresponding meaning . . .

(ix) "Land" includes land of any tenure, and mines and minerals, whether or not held apart from the surface, buildings or parts of buildings . . . and other corporeal hereditaments; also a manor, an advowson, and a rent and other incorporeal hereditaments, and an easement, right, privilege, or benefit in, over, or derived from land; but not an undivided share in land . . .

(x) "Legal estates" mean the estates, interests and charges, in or over land (subsisting or created at law) which are by this Act authorised to subsist or be created as legal estates; "equitable interests" mean all the other interests and charges in or over land or in the proceeds of sale thereof."

LAW OF PROPERTY (MISCELLANEOUS PROVISIONS) ACT 1989

Section 2.—(1) A contract for the sale or other disposition of an interest in land **2–07** can only be made in writing and only by incorporating all the terms which the parties have expressly agreed in one document or, where contracts are exchanged, in each.

(2) The terms may be incorporated in a document either by being set out in it or by reference to some other document.

(3) The document incorporating the terms or, where contracts are exchanged, one of the documents incorporating them (but not necessarily the same one) must be signed by or on behalf of each party to the contract.

(4) Where a contract for the sale or other disposition of an interest in land satisfies the conditions of this section by reason only of the rectification of one or more documents in pursuance of an order of a court, the contract shall come into being, or be deemed to have come into being, at such time as may be specified in the order.

(5) This section does not apply in relation to—

2–08   (*a*) a contract to grant such a lease as is mentioned in section 54(2) of the Law of Property Act 1925 (short leases);
(*b*) a contract made in the course of a public auction; or
(*c*) a contract regulated under the Financial Services Act 1986;

and nothing in this section affects the creation or operation of resulting, implied or constructive trusts.

(6) In this section—
"disposition" has the same meaning as in the Law of Property Act 1925;
"interest in land" means any estate, interest or charge in or over land or in or over the proceeds of sale of land.

(7) Nothing in this section shall apply in relation to contracts made before this section comes into force.

(8) Section 40 of the Law of Property Act 1925 (which is superseded by this section) shall cease to have effect.

CONTRACTS TO CREATE TRUSTS OR DISPOSE OF EQUITABLE INTERESTS

2–09   Section 2 of the 1989 Act applies to a contract to create a trust of any interest in land and to a contract to dispose of an equitable interest in land, *e.g.* a life interest or a co-owner's equitable interest under a trust of land. Unlike the previous position under Law of Property Act 1925, s.40,[6] the contract is void if all the terms are not in one document signed[7] by both parties or in exchanged documents signed by each exchanger (or on his

---

[6] "(1) No action may be brought upon any contract for the sale or other disposition of land or any interest in land, unless the agreement upon which such action is brought, or some memorandum or note thereof, is in writing, and signed by the party to be charged or by some other person thereunto by him lawfully authorised.
(2) This section does not affect the law relating to part performance."
[7] Old, liberal authorities on what constituted a sufficient signature for Statute of Frauds 1677 and Law of Property Act 1925 are no longer relevant: the 1989 Act has a different philosophy, so a signature must be a handwritten signature: *Firstpost Homes Ltd v Johnson* [1995] 4 All E.R. 355. The 1989 Act does not apply to the exercise of an option to purchase an interest in land (*Spiro v Glencrown Properties Ltd* [1991] Ch. 537) nor to a lock-out agreement not to consider any further offers if the purchaser exchanges contracts within two weeks (*Pitt v PHH Asset Management Ltd* [1994] 1 W.L.R. 327) nor to a collateral contract (*Record v Bell* [1991] 1 W.L.R. 853) nor to an agreement supplemental to a completed contract (*Tootal Clothing Ltd v Guinea Properties Management Ltd* (1992) 64 P. & C.R. 452): it applies to variations, *McCausland v Duncan Lawrie* [1996] 4 All E.R. 995. If an agreed term is omitted then rectification can be obtained so that the rectified document complies with the 1989 Act: *Wright v Robert Leonard (Developments) Ltd* [1994] E.G.C.S. 69.

behalf), though it is possible to incorporate terms set out in another document by referring to that document. Under s.40 the contract had not been required to be created by signed writing, but only to be evidenced by writing signed by or on behalf of the defendant by the time a court action was brought, and the contract was unenforceable by action,[8] but not void, until the requisite signed written evidence materialised or part performance of the contract occurred.

For a claimant to rely on the equitable doctrine of part performance to **2–10** obtain specific performance or damages in lieu (under the equitable jurisdiction originally enshrined in Lord Cairns' Act 1858) he needed to show that he had acted to his detriment in reliance upon the inadequately evidenced contract and that his acts were such as to indicate, on a balance of probabilities, that they had been performed in reliance upon a contract with the defendant concerning land and consistent with the contract alleged.[9] The doctrine of part performance is not available in support of a void obligation but a claimant may, instead, rely on the imposition of a constructive trust[10] to prevent a defendant unconscionably relying upon lack of the necessary signed writing. Thus, if a defendant contracted to sell a building plot to the claimant for £30,000, so that the claimant then spent £200,000 on erecting a house on the plot, the defendant would not be able to take unconscionable advantage of the omission of some minor term from the terms of the written agreement. He would be compelled to hold the plot on constructive trust for the claimant, subject to payment of the £30,000 (if not already paid), so that the claimant would be entitled to a conveyance of the plot.[11]

A contract to create a trust of pure personalty need satisfy no special **2–11** formalities as also seems to be the case for a contract to dispose of an equitable interest in pure personalty.[12]

THE CREATION OF TRUSTS AND SECTION 53(1)(b)[13]

Transactions within s.53(1)(b), unlike those within s.53(1)(a) or within **2–12** s.53(1)(c), need only be evidenced at some time by signed writing and do not actually have to be carried out by signed writing if they are to be effective. It would seem that s.53(1)(a) needs to be construed as covering the creation of equitable interests in land (*e.g.* equitable charges, restrictive covenants) other than equitable interests under a trust, leaving s.53(1)(b) to

---

[8] A deposit could be forfeited or recovered: *Monnickendam v Leanse* (1923) 39 T.L.R. 445; *Pulbrook v Lawes* (1876) 1 Q.B.D. 284.

[9] *Steadman v Steadman* [1976] A.C. 536 as narrowly interpreted in *Re Gonin* [1979] Ch. 16 and commented upon in *Actionstrength Ltd v International Glass Engineering SpA* [2003] 2 A.C. 541 paras 23 and 47.

[10] *Yaxley v Gotts* [2000] 1 All E.R. 74. See s.2(5) of the 1989 Act and para.2–30 (equitable proprietary estoppel interests) and Chap.6, s.3.

[11] If D holds on trust for P who is of full capacity then P can demand that D transfer the property to P. See *Saunders v Vautier* principle, para.9–123. As a short-cut the court would here direct the defendant to execute a conveyance in the plaintiff's favour: *cf. Pascoe v Turner* [1979] 1 W.L.R. 431.

[12] See *Chinn v Collins* [1981] A.C. 533 at 548 and the discussion of *Oughtred v I.R.C.* [1960] A.C. 206, paras 2–47 to 2–49.

[13] Replacing Statute of Frauds 1677, s.7 with fresh wording: see *Grey v I.R.C.* [1960] A.C. 1.

cover creation of equitable interests in land under a trust.[14] This protects a landowner and his heirs from the perils of oral evidence and enables purchasers to know whether or not to pay the purchase money to at least two trustees.

2–13   A settlor may create a trust of Blackacre either by declaring that he himself is henceforth to hold Blackacre on specified trusts or by conveying Blackacre to trustees and declaring specified trusts on which the trustees are to hold Blackacre. In both cases the declaration of the trusts must be in writing specifying the beneficiaries, the trust property and the nature of the trusts.[15] As was the case with Law of Property Act 1925, s.40 the writing may be comprised in linked documents[16] and also the trust is unenforceable, but not void, until the requisite written evidence is present,[17] or part performance of the trusts occurs.[18]

The signing must be "by some person who is able to declare such trust," *e.g.* by A where A conveys Blackacre to B and contemporaneously declares signed written trusts for C or by T1 and T2 where they hold property on trust for A for life, remainder to B but with power for the trustees to declare new trusts in favour of C or his issue. It has been assumed that the absence from s.53(1)(b), unlike s.53(1)(a) or (c), of an express reference to an agent precludes the settlor's agent authorised in writing from being "some person who is able to declare" a trust on the settlor's behalf, but such assumption may yet prove to be unfounded because the duly authorised agent may be regarded as "some person who is able to declare such trust." The signatory should be the person who, at the time of the signature, would seem to be the beneficial owner (or, perhaps, the agent thereof) if the declaration of trust were ignored.[19] Such person will be A where A declares himself trustee of Blackacre for B, and such person will be B if, subsequently, B declares that he holds his equitable interest on trust for C for life, remainder to D.[20] However, if A conveys Blackacre to B and contemporaneously declares *oral* trusts for C, then subsequent written evidence of the trust signed by B satisfies s.53(1)(b)[21] though it may well be that until B signs such writing (or an act of part performance occurs) A

---

[14] In view of LPA 1925, s.52(1), s.53(1)(a) cannot be restricted to legal interests and so that s.53(1)(a) does not make s.53(1)(b) otiose para.(b) should be construed applying the maxim "*generalia specialibus non derogant*," general clauses cannot derogate from special clauses, so that declarations of trust of land are outside s.53(1)(a): *Hagen v Waterhouse* (1991) 34 N.S.W.L.R. 308 at 385–386.

[15] *Smith v Matthews* (1861) 3 De G.F. & J. 139; *Morton v Tewart* (1842) 2 Y. & C.Ch. Case 67.

[16] *Forster v Hale* (1798) 3 Ves. 696.

[17] *Rochefoucauld v Boustead* [1897] 1 Ch. 1962, 206; *Gardner v Rowe* (1828) 5 Russ. 258. (A granted a lease to B on oral trusts for C, and after B became bankrupt B executed a deed stating the trusts. *Held* valid declaration of trust prior to B's bankruptcy so his creditors had no claim to the lease. Note under the *Rochefoucauld* doctrine, at para.2–21, B was bound from the time he took the lease so if, instead, A orally declared *himself* trustee of land for C and provided written evidence only after his own bankruptcy he would not be bound by the trust until the written evidence, so his creditors would have a claim to the land, assuming C had not earlier acted to his detriment, *e.g.* by building a house on the land, in reliance on A's declaration of trust.)

[18] LPA s.55(d).

[19] See T. G. Youdan [1984] C.L.J. 306 at 316–320.

[20] *Tierney v Wood* (1854) 19 Beav. 330; *Kronheim v Johnson* (1877) 7 Ch.D. 60.

[21] *Gardner v Rowe*, above; *Smith v Matthews*, above; *Mountain v Styak* [1922] N.Z.L.R. 131. If the oral trusts had been for A himself then he would have an equitable interest under a constructive trust which he could then sub-settle; *Tierney v Wood*, above.

retains the equitable interest[22] which he can dispose of as he wishes (unless C has earlier acted to his detriment, *e.g.* by building on Blackacre, such performance giving rise to an equitable estoppel).

If A had conveyed land or transferred other property to B to hold to A's **2–14** order and on some subsequent date told B to hold on trust for C, this would amount to A disposing of his subsisting equitable interest in C's favour: such disposition would be void under s.53(1)(c) unless in writing signed by A or his agent.[23]

Declarations of trust of property other than land or interests in land can be made orally[24] since no special evidential or other requirements exist, but care must be taken where A purports to declare himself trustee of an equitable interest in any property for X absolutely where X is of full capacity. In substance it seems that the apparent sub-trust is a disposition of A's subsisting equitable interest within s.53(1)(c) because the head trustee, whom X can directly sue, is now holding on trust for X and not for A, who has no active duties to perform and so drops out of the picture.[25]

DISPOSITIONS OF EQUITABLE INTERESTS AND SECTION 53(1)(c)

In context the meaning of "equitable interest" must comprise interests in **2–15** land or in personalty and "disposition" must comprise a disposition in writing or otherwise.[26]

The signed writing is essential to the validity of the disposition: failure to satisfy s.53(1)(c) makes the disposition void. Subsequent written evidence will be of no avail unless it can be construed as a "belt and braces" device capable of making a disposition as of its date insofar as necessary if the earlier disposition were void.[27] The signed writing may comprise linked documents.[28] Where the assignee is to hold the assigned equitable interest as trustee the writing need not contain the particulars of the trust which may thus be communicated orally,[29] though if the interest is in land some subsequent written evidence will be necessary to satisfy s.53(1)(b). If no communication of the particulars of the trust is made to the assignee, T, taking as trustee, then the assigned interest will be held on resulting trust for the assignor, A, and any subsequent disposition in favour of B by the assignor will fall within section 53(1)(c). It is vital to appreciate that A's direction to T to hold the property for B, instead of A, amounts to A disposing of his subsisting equitable interest to B within s.53(1)(c): *Grey v I.R.C.*, paras 2–50 *et seq.*

---

[22] See at para.2–23.
[23] *Grey v I.R.C.* [1960] A.C. 1, above.
[24] *Rowe v Prance* [2000] W.T.L.R. 249 (boat), *Paul v Constance* [1977] 1 W.L.R. 527 (a bank account, a chose in action).
[25] See at para.2–42.
[26] Assumed in *Grey v I.R.C.*, above; *Oughtred v I.R.C.* [1960] A.C. 206, *Vandervell v I.R.C.* [1967] 2 A.C. 291, and treated as well established in *Re Tyler's Fund Trusts* [1967] 3 All E.R. 389 at 392. The context must oust L.P.A. 1925, s.205(1)(ii), (x).
[27] See *Grey v I.R.C.* [1958] Ch. 690 at 706–707 and B. Green (1984) 47 M.L.R. 385 at 391–92.
[28] *Re Danish Bacon Co. Ltd Staff Pension Fund* [1971] 1 W.L.R. 248.
[29] *Re Tyler's Fund Trusts* [1967] 2 All E.R. 389.

2–16   There is no disposition of a subsisting equitable interest when a legal owner with full beneficial ownership makes a declaration of trust. He is not regarded as having two estates one legal and the other equitable,[30] the equitable or beneficial interest is merged or subsumed in the legal estate and will pass automatically when the legal estate is transferred.[31] If he declares a trust this creates a new equitable interest so no evidential or other writing will be necessary except in the case of land within s.53(1)(b). Similarly, if T holds property on trust for A for life, remainder to B, but has an overriding power to appoint the trust fund on trust for X and X's family which he exercises, this creates a new equitable interest in favour of X and X's family.

However, where trustees hold property on trust for B absolutely and, pursuant to B's direction they transfer the property to X absolutely then B's interest is extinguished and X obtains full legal and beneficial ownership so there is no separate disposition by B of his equitable interest that requires compliance with s.53(1)(c): *Vandervell v I.R.C.*, paras 2–63, 2–67. If this last example were extended one step further because X had previously agreed to hold the property on trust for Y one might think that this should make no difference. Nevertheless, in substance B is responsible for disposing of his subsisting equitable interest now in the hands of Y so that s.53(1)(c) should be applicable,[32] there being a need for a paper trail where the equitable interest has been separated from the legal interest so that Y can prove his interest against X's executors after X's death. This need for a paper trail could justify a need for writing where a legal beneficial owner, A, declares he holds specific personalty on trust for Y, or a trustee, T, who holds on trust for X, exercises an overreaching power of appointment to declare that T now holds for Y instead of X, but in neither case is writing required.[33] The key in each case is that neither A nor T owns a separate subsisting equitable interest which he disposes of to Y.

2–17   It would seem that there is a disposition where there is a release or a surrender of a subsisting equitable interest[34] but not where there is a disclaimer.[35] Variations of trusts under the Variation of Trusts Act 1958 escape s.53(1)(c) either by implication under the 1958 Act or by virtue of a constructive trust within s.53(2).[36] Also escaping s.53(1)(c) (and the Wills Act 1837) is the exercise of an employee's contractual right to nominate revocably a person to receive moneys payable under a pension trust fund in the event of the employee's death in service: there is no subsisting interest

---

[30] *Westdeutsche Landesbank v Islington B.C.* [1996] A.C. 669 at 706; *D.K.L.R. Holding Co. v C.S.D.(N.S.W.)* (1982) 40 Austr.L.R. 1; a person cannot hold on trust for himself: *Re Cook* [1948] Ch. 212.
[31] *Vandervell v I.R.C.* [1967] 2 A.C. 291.
[32] *cf. Grey v I.R.C.* [1960] A.C. 1 where trustees held shares on trust for Mr. Hunter and he told them to hold the shares not (so to speak) in their left hands for him but in their right hands as trustees of existing trusts for his grandchildren: this ranks as a CGT disposal by one trustee to another even if the same individual is concerned: *Hoare Trustees v Gardner* [1978] 1 All E.R. 791.
[33] See note 24 above and *Re Vandervell's Trusts (No 2)* [1974] Ch. 269
[34] LPA 1925, s.205(1)(ii), G. Battersby [1979] Conv. 17 at 20–21.
[35] *Re Paradise Motor Co. Ltd* [1968] 1 W.L.R. 1125; disclaimer "operates by way of avoidance and not by way of disposition." See also *Allied Dunbar Assurance plc v Fowler* [1994] 25 Est. Gaz. 149 and LPA 1925, s.52(2)(b).
[36] *Re Holt's S.T.* [1969] 1 Ch. 100.

in property to dispose of[37] Similarly, if L takes out a policy on his life where rights to a money payment only crystallise on his death, there is no disposition of a subsisting equitable interest if he orally nominates X to receive the money and hold it on trust for Y and Z.[38]

It is important to realise that in the case of shares in public companies most are dematerialised securities that are transferred through CREST.[39] This is an electronic system owned and operated by CRESTCo Limited (which is owned by Euroclear Bank) in accordance with the Uncertificated Securities Regulations 2001, SI 2001/3755. While a plc company may have a register of shareholders with certificates relating to their paper shares, the CREST records constitute a register of title. Thus a transfer from one CREST member account to another operates to transfer legal title, *e.g.* from Cazenove & Co. to Barclays Bank Trust Co. whose clients' interests are pooled in a single account maintained by the CREST member, although in its discretion it may note with CREST designated different accounts for different clients (who only have equitable interests) but without giving any identification of the particular clients.[40]

To avoid formalities problems for dispositions of equitable interests or for assignments of legal chooses in action, reg.38(5) provides "Sections 53(1)(c) and 136 of the Law of Property Act 1925 shall not apply (if they would otherwise do so) to (a) any transfer of title to uncertificated units of a security by means of a relevant system and (b) any disposition or assignment of a security title to which is held by a relevant nominee", which, by reg.38(6), is a subsidiary undertaking of an Operator (of the system) designated by the Operator as a relevant nominee.

2–18

However, without the need for reg.38, it seems likely that the replacement of V by P on the computer record of a financial intermediary, like Cazenove & Co., is in itself effective to transfer V's interest. After all, a change in the membership list of a deed of settlement "company", which was an unincorporated society with trustees holding property on trust for members of the "company", has been accepted as valid without the need for any writing signed by the transferor, V[41]

Because a security is defined by reg.3 as including an interest in a security, it seems that if a relevant nominee holds title to a security on trust for X, then X, whether for value or gratuitously, can assign his interest in the security to Y or declare a trust thereof for Z without the need for signed writing.

---

[37] *Re Danish Bacon Co. Ltd Staff Pension Fund* [1971] 1 W.L.R. 248; *Baird v Baird* [1990] 2 A.C. 548.
[38] *Gold v Hill* (1998–99) 1 I.T.E.L.R. 27.
[39] See CREST Reference Manual and J. Benjamin and M. Yates, *The Law of Global Custody* Butterworths (2nd ed., 2002), Ch.9.
[40] "A designation may be alphanumeric but should not give any indication of the identity of any beneficial owner"—CREST Reference Manual Chap. 2, section 5.
[41] *Ashby v Blackwell and Mullion Bank* (1765) Amb 503, K. F. Sin, *The Legal Nature of the Unit Trust* (Oxford 1997, p.17). It has been taken for granted that resigning members (or executors of deceased members) of a club do not need to provide signed writing to part with their equitable interests, while new members do not need to show any signed assignments to them: members can be regarded as contractually bound to recognise the running of their membership list.

STATUTE MAY NOT BE USED AS AN INSTRUMENT OF FRAUD,
CONSTRUCTIVE TRUSTS AND RESULTING TRUSTS

2–19 If A either transfers land to B or buys land in B's name on an oral understanding with B that B is to hold the land on trust for A, case law[42] assumes that A cannot prove the express trust owing to s.53(1)(b), so that it will be necessary for signed writing of B to satisfy s.53(1)(b).[43]

It would, however, be monstrous if B could plead the statute (passed to prevent fraud) so as fraudulently to keep the land for himself. Accordingly, A can have his claim to the land recognised on one of three grounds.

2–20 He can accept that s.53(1)(b) prevents proof of the express trust, but then he can rely on s.53(2) on the basis of either a resulting trust[44] (arising from the gratuitous circumstances in which there was no intention to transfer any beneficial interest) or a constructive trust[45] (imposed upon B because it would be fraudulent and unconscionable for him to keep the land for himself and so unjustly enrich himself).

Alternatively, since there is a valid trust, though unenforceable by virtue of s.53(1)(b), A can rely on equity estopping B from raising the issue of unenforceability under s.53(1)(b)[46] since otherwise B would be using statute as an instrument of fraud, so that the court thus enforces the express trust.

2–21 As Lindley L.J. stated in *Rochefoucauld v Boustead*.[47]

> "It is a fraud on the part of a person to whom land is conveyed as a trustee and who knows it is so conveyed to deny the trust and to claim the land for himself. Consequently, notwithstanding the statute, it is competent for a person claiming land conveyed to another to prove by parol evidence that it was so conveyed upon trust for the claimant, and that the grantee, knowing the facts, is denying the trust and relying upon the form of conveyance and the statute in order to keep the land himself. . . . The trust which the plaintiff has established is clearly an express trust . . . one which the plaintiff and the defendant intended to create. The case is not one in which an equitable obligation [*i.e.* a constructive trust] arises although there may have been no intention to create a trust."[48]

2–22 This equitable maxim "Equity will not allow a statute to be used as an instrument of fraud" is not confined to cases in which the conveyance was itself fraudulently obtained. "The fraud which brings the principle into play

---

[42] *Hutchins v Lee* (1737) 1 Atk. 447; *Young v Peachy* (1741) 2 Atk 255; *Re Duke of Marlborough* [1894] 2 Ch. 133.

[43] *Ambrose v Ambrose* (1716) 1 P. Wms. 321; *Smith v Matthews* (1861) 3 De G.F. & J. 139; *Gardner v Rowe* (1828) 5 Russ. 258; *Mountain v Styak* [1922] N.Z.L.R. 131.

[44] See paras 5–29, 5–113; *Hodgson v Marks* [1971] Ch. 892; *Davies v. Otty (No.2)* (1865) 35 Beav. 208; *Haigh v Kaye* (1872) L.R. 7 Ch. 469. The circumstances oust the impact of LPA 1925, s.60(3); see para.5–113.

[45] *Scheuerman v Scheuerman* (1916) 28 D.L.R. 223; *Bannister v Bannister* [1948] 2 All E.R. 133; *Binions v Evans* [1972] Ch. 359; *British Railways Board v Pickin* [1974] A.C. 765, 795–796.

[46] This could also be the case where T holds personalty on oral or written trusts but sells it and wrongfully uses the proceeds to buy land in his private capacity for himself.

[47] [1897] 1 Ch. 196 at 206, 208.

[48] The trust was held to be an express trust for the purpose of the Statute of Limitations. For classification of trusts see above, para. 1–39.

arises as soon as the absolute character of the conveyance is set up for the purpose of defeating the beneficial interest."[49] So if A sells her two adjoining cottages to B for below market value, B orally agreeing to let her live in one cottage for the rest of her days, B will be compelled to hold that cottage on trust for A for life if he subsequently changes his mind and tries to defeat her interest by relying on s.53(1)(b).[50]

Where A's oral understanding with B is that B will hold the land on trust **2–23** for C, B clearly cannot keep the land for himself. Can A claim beneficial entitlement if he has repented of his intention to benefit C? After all, he can argue that his failure to satisfy s.53(1)(b) means that there is no completely constituted trust for C and equity will not perfect imperfect gifts, assuming C can make no special proprietary estoppel claim by virtue of detrimental reliance.[51] Thus B holds the land on resulting trust for A since A has failed effectively to dispose of his beneficial interest,[52] if indeed, he does not hold on constructive trust for A to prevent B's fraudulent conduct from unjustly enriching B.[53] Whilst B would be estopped from pleading s.53(1)(b) against A or C, A can argue that nothing should stop A from pleading s.53(1)(b) against C. It is true that A intended to make a gift of the beneficial interest to C but A had failed to comply with the requisite formalities, and intended donees cannot complain if the donor's original purported gift was ineffective and the donor then repents of his intentions and so refuses to perfect the gift.[54]

C can invoke the analogous case where X by will devises land to Y on the **2–24** oral understanding with Y that Y is to hold the land on trust for Z. After all, the wills formalities provisions and s.53 of the Law of Property Act were originally all contained in the Statute of Frauds. It is clear that X's secret trust in favour of Z will be enforced against Y.[55] However, Y is clearly intercepting property definitively intended by X for Z, X dying happy with the secret trust, while A is alive and the last thing he wants is for C to benefit.

C might then emphasise that the oral trust of land is valid, though **2–25** unenforceable due to s.53(1)(b),[56] so that if B wished B could carry out the trust and sign the necessary writing himself.[57] A will reply that B's authority to sign the required writing can be revoked by A's notification to him or by A's death.[58] Once A has so notified B then it would fly in the face of the statute to allow C to adduce oral evidence to establish his interest. Thus, C cannot prove any unjust deprivation to justify the imposition of a constructive trust.

---

[49] *Bannister v Bannister* [1948] 2 All E.R. 133 at 136; *Ungurian v Lesnoff* [1990] Ch. 206.
[50] *ibid.*
[51] See paras 2–30 *et seq.*
[52] *Hodgson v Marks* [1971] Ch. 892.
[53] *Bannister v Bannister*, above; *Last v Rosenfeld* [1972] 2 N.S.W.L.R. 923 at 937.
[54] See *Re Brooks' S.T.*, paras 4–45 and 4–80.
[55] *Ottaway v Norman* [1972] Ch. 698, *infra*, para.2–110.
[56] *Gardner v Rowe* (1828) 5 Russ. 258; *Rochefoucauld v Boustead* [1897] 1 Ch. 196 at 206.
[57] *Ambrose v Ambrose* (1716) 1 P. Wms. 321; *Smith v Matthews* (1861) 3 De G.F. & J. 139; *Mountain v Styak* [1922] N.Z.L.R. 131.
[58] *Rudkin v Dolman* (1876) 35 L.T. 791; *Scheurman v Scheurman* (1916) 52 S.C.R. 625 at 636.

After all, if A had orally declared himself trustee of Blackacre for C, C could adduce no oral evidence to establish the interest (unless taking advantage of detrimental reliance to establish an equitable proprietary claim).[59] It should make no difference that A transferred the land to B and declared oral trusts for C: if it did there would hardly be any scope for the application of s.53(1)(b) with its cautionary and evidentiary functions.[60]

2–26 It may be argued[61] that there should be no difference between (1) A simply conveying Blackacre to B with intent manifested by oral evidence to make an outright gift to B (effective in B's favour) and (2) A conveying Blackacre to B with intent manifested by oral evidence for B to hold on trust for C as intended donee of an equitable gift. However, s.53(1)(b) deliberately creates a difference in expressly requiring written evidence of trusts of land where legal title is in one person (B) and equitable title is in another (C) so that A's claim should prevail over C's claim. This evidence provides a paper trail to enable C to enforce his interest against B's executors after B's death, as is the case.

So far, we have been concerned with a gratuitous conveyance by A to B for C. However, if A sells and conveys land to B at an undervalue (so losing all interest therein) on the express understanding that B will hold the land on trust to give effect to an equitable interest of C or to a licence conferred by A on C, then C has enforceable rights against B.[62] B is not allowed to claim that C's rights are unenforceable against him because this would be fraudulent.

AMBIT AND NATURE OF EQUITABLE MAXIM

2–27 The equitable maxim, "Equity will not allow a statute to be used as an instrument of fraud", is available not just against the transferee-trustee but to volunteers claiming under him[63] and to purchasers with notice.

Indeed, Ungoed-Thomas J. has held[64] that it is available against a bona fide purchaser for value without notice of the trusts affecting his vendor's title, taking the view that such a purchaser is acting fraudulently if he seeks to rely on s.53(1)(b) once he discovers the trusts. It is difficult to see why such purchaser is acting fraudulently. Even if the trusts had originally satisfied s.53(1)(b) a purchaser without notice would take free from the trusts, so that even if the trusts flouting s.53(1)(b) are allowed to be proved under *Rochefoucauld* a purchaser without notice should still take free from the trusts.

---

[59] *Wratten v Hunter* [1978] 2 N.S.W.L.R. 367; *Midland Bank v Dobson* [1986] 1 F.L.R. 171; *Gissing v Gissing* [1971] A.C. 886 at 905.

[60] J. D. Feltham [1987] Conv. 246.

[61] T. G. Youdan [1988] Conv. 267.

[62] *Ashburn Anstalt v Arnold* [1989] Ch. 1; *Lyus v Prowsa Developments Ltd* [1982] 1 W.L.R. 1044. Since the Contracts (Rights of Third Parties) Act 1999 C can also rely on it.

[63] *Lincoln v Wright* (1859) 4 De G. & J. 16; *Re Duke of Marlborough* [1894] 2 Ch. 133.

[64] *Hodgson v Marks* [1971] Ch. 892 at 909; see inconsistency with *Dodds v Hill* (1865) 2 H. & M. 424 endorsed in *Macmillan v Bishopsgate (No.3)* [1995] 3 All E.R. 747 at 773.

In cases[65] where A has transferred an interest in land to B but orally for **2–28** the benefit of A, the effect of the equitable maxim is to create a resulting trust,[66] even though in *Bannister v Bannister* Scott L.J.[67] described the doctrine as "the equitable principle on which a constructive trust is raised against a person who insists on the absolute character of a conveyance to himself for the purpose of defeating a beneficial interest." Subsequent purchasers are bound by resulting or constructive trusts if they have notice,[68] so it matters not whether the trusts be resulting or constructive trusts, each being within s.53(2) of the Law of Property Act. However, in cases where A has transferred an interest in land to B but orally for the benefit of C, and the court does not hold there to be a resulting trust in A's favour but, exceptionally, compels B to hold the land for C's benefit there is a constructive trust. These exceptional cases arise in testamentary situations where A leaves property by will to B on fully or half-secret trusts[69] or in *inter vivos* situations where the detrimental reliance of C creates an estoppel interest.[70] The key to the enforcement of C's interest against B is not just the intention of A (which is the key to express trusts[71]) but B's agreement to hold property for C, whether leading A to die happy in the belief that C's interests were secure so that he need not take other steps to secure C's interests (*viz.* secret trusts) or leading C to carry out detrimental acts of reliance in relation to the property (*viz.* proprietary estoppel interests).

As a final point on the equitable maxim it is important to realise that **2–29** where certain interests are required to be registered or protected under the Land Charges Act 1972[72] or the Land Registration Act 1925 or 2002[73] or the Companies Act 1985[74] on pain of a purchaser taking free from such interests, it is not fraud for the purchaser merely to take advantage of his strict statutory rights by relying on the absence of the registration or protection stipulated for in the statute. It is fraud, however, if he positively misleads the interest owner to leave the interest unprotected.

EQUITABLE PROPRIETARY ESTOPPEL
(BY ACQUIESCENCE OR ENCOURAGEMENT)

If O encourages or acquiesces in X acting to his detriment in reliance on **2–30** the belief that O's property is X's property or that O has given or will give X the property or an interest therein, then, to prevent unconscionable

---

[65] *Rochefoucauld v Boustead* [1897] 1 Ch. 196; *Bannister v Banister* [1948] 2 All E.R. 133.
[66] *Hodgson v Marks* [1971] 1 Ch. 892.
[67] [1948] 2 All E.R. 133 at 136.
[68] In the case of unregistered land or if the beneficiary is in actual occupation with an overriding interest in registered land.
[69] See paras 2–103 *et seq.*
[70] See paras 2–30 *et seq.*
[71] See Ford & Lee, *Principles of Law of Trusts*, para.6350.
[72] *Hollington Bros Ltd v Rhodes* [1951] 2 T.L.R. 691; *Miles v Bull (No.2)* [1969] 3 All E.R. 1585; *Midland Bank Trust Co. v Green* [1981] A.C. 513; *Lloyds Bank plc v Carrick* [1996] 4 All E.R. 630.
[73] *De Lusignan v Johnson* (1973) 230 Est.Gaz. 499; *Freer v Unwins Ltd* [1976] Ch. 288; *Williams & Glyn's Bank v Boland* [1981] A.C. 487.
[74] *Re Monolithic Building Co.* [1915] 2 Ch. 643.

behaviour, equity will estop O from asserting his full legal and beneficial ownership and from claiming that non-compliance with statutory requirements bars X's claim. Such estoppel gives rise to an equity in X's favour which may entitle him to an injunction against O[75] or an equitable lien[76] on O's property for X's expenditure[77] or for the value of X's improvements,[78] or for a sum of an appropriate proportionate amount to satisfy his equity,[79] or to a decree perfecting O's imperfect gift and ordering O to convey[80] or lease[81] land to X unconditionally or on payment of some money by X,[82] or grant X an easement[83] or a licence as long as X uses the premises as his private residence[84] or as long as X's loan is not repaid by O.[85]

2–31   Court of Appeal cases[86] indicate a cautious approach to ensure that X should receive the minimum equity to do justice to him, having regard to the way in which he changed his position for the worse[87] by reason of the acquiescence and encouragement of O. As Walker L.J. stated in *Gillett v Holt*,[88]

> "Detriment is required. But the authorities show that it is not a narrow or technical concept. The detriment need not consist of the expenditure of money or other quantifiable financial detriment, so long as it is something substantial. The requirement must be approached as part of a broad inquiry as to whether repudiation of an assurance is or is not unconscionable in all the circumstances . . . There must be sufficient causal link between the assurance relied on and the detriment asserted. The issue of detriment must be judged at the moment when the person who has given the assurance seeks to go back on it. Whether the detriment is sufficiently substantial is to be tested by whether it would

[75] *Jackson v Cator* (1800) 5 Ves. 688 or damages in lieu of an injunction: *Shaw v Applegate* [1978] 1 All E.R. 123.
[76] Instead of a lien the Court may make the order for possession in favour of O conditional upon repayment to X of X's expenditure: *Dodsworth v Dodsworth* (1973) 228 Est. Gaz. 1115.
[77] *Unity Joint Stock Mutual Banking Assoc. v King* (1858) 25 Beav. 72; *Hussey v Palmer* [1972] 1 W.L.R. 1286; *Morris v Morris* [1982] 1 N.S.W.L.R. 61; *Lee-Parker v Izzet (No.2)* [1972] 2 All E.R. 800 at 804–805.
[78] *Raffaele v Raffaele* [1962] W.R. 238; (1963) 79 L.Q.R. 228 (D. E. Allan).
[79] *Baker v Baker* (1993) 25 H.L.R. 408; *Burrows v Sharp* (1989) 23 H.L.R. 82; *Gillett v Holt* [2001] Ch. 210, *Jennings v Rice* [2002] W.T.L.R. 367, *Campbell v Griffin* [2001] W.T.L.R. 981.
[80] *Pascoe v Turner* [1979] 1 W.L.R. 431; *Gillett v Holt* [2001] Ch. 210. X may even obtain O's residuary estate: *Re Basham* [1986] 1 W.L.R. 1498. If the land has been sold X will be entitled to its proceeds of sale: *Wayling v Jones* (1993) 69 P. & C.R. 170.
[81] *Siew Soon Wah v Yong Tong Hong* [1973] A.C. 836; *Griffiths v Williams* (1977) 248 E.G. 947; *Taylor Fashions Ltd v Liverpool Victoria Trustees Co.* [1982] Q.B. 133; *Yaxley v Gotts* [2000] Ch. 162.
[82] *Lim Teng Huan v Ang Swee Chin* [1992] 1 W.L.R. 113 (O ordered to convey his half share to X upon X paying him its value as bare land, X having built upon it.).
[83] *Ward v Kirkland* [1967] Ch. 194; *Ives Investments Ltd v High* [1967] 2 Q.B. 379; *Crabb v Arun D.C.* [1976] Ch. 179.
[84] *Inwards v Baker* [1965] 2 Q.B. 29; *Greasley v Cooke* [1980] 1 W.L.R. 1306.
[85] *Re Sharpe* [1980] 1 W.L.R. 219.
[86] *Crabb v Arun D.C.* [1976] Ch. 179; *Pascoe v Turner* [1979] 1 W.L.R. 431; *Sledmore v Dalby* 1996 72 P & CR 1961; *Baker v Baker* (1993) 25 H.L.R. 408; *Gillett v Holt* [2001] Ch. 210, *Jennings v Rice* [2002] W.T.L.R. 367; *Grundy v Ottey* [2003] W.T.L.R. 1253, para.2–90.
[87] *Pascoe v Turner* [1979] 2 All E.R. 945 at 950. "The person claiming must have incurred expenditure or otherwise have prejudiced himself or acted to his detriment," *per* Dunn L.J. in *Greasley v Cooke* [1980] 1 W.L.R. 1306 at 1313–14.
[88] [2001] Ch. 210 at 232, on which see R. Wells [2000] Conv. 13. The Court of Appeal rejected the judge's view that a promise to leave property by will had to be irrevocable and required some mutual understanding as to the quid pro quo for the promise.

be unjust or inequitable to allow the assurance to be disregarded—that is, again, the essential test of unconscionability. The detriment alleged must be pleaded and proved."

Once it is proved that the assurance was made and that there has been **2–32** conduct by the claimant of such a nature that inducement may be inferred, then the burden of proof switches to the defendant to establish that the claimant did not rely on the assurance[89]

Originally, the courts regarded matters from O's viewpoint so that it was **2–33** considered that O had to be at fault in some way before X could claim an equity. So, if O did not know the true position and so did not know of his right to object when he either acquiesced in or encouraged X's belief then O was not estopped from subsequently asserting his rights against X.[90] This may still be the position in cases of acquiescence where O has stood by without protest while his rights were being infringed at a time when he did not realise he had such rights.[91]

In cases of encouragement the courts now regard matters from X's **2–34** viewpoint. Fault on O's part is no longer crucial: attention is focused on X's position and how unconscionable it would be if he were to suffer from O enforcing his strict legal rights once O had discovered his rights.[92] Indeed, a broad approach is suggested "directed at ascertaining whether, in particular circumstances it would be unconscionable for a party to be permitted to deny that which, knowingly or unknowingly, he has allowed or encouraged another to assume to his detriment."[93] Lord Browne-Wilkinson thus stated.[94]

> "In order to found a proprietary estoppel it is not essential that the representor should have been guilty of unconscionable conduct in permitting the representee to assume that he could act as he did: it is enough if, in all the circumstances, it is unconscionable for the representor to go back on the assumption that he permitted the representee to make."

O's ignorance of the true position and of his strict rights is merely one of **2–35** the relevant factors in the overall inquiry. The court considers whether it would be unconscionable for O to insist on his strict legal rights, and if it would, then the court, taking into account *all circumstances to the date of the trial*,[95] qualifies, suspends or extinguishes those rights (perhaps on

---

[89] *Wayling v Jones* (1999) 69 P & CR 170 at 173 endorsed in *Gillett v Holt* [2001] Ch. 210 at 226 and *Gunndy v Ottey* [2003] W.T.L.R. 1253 paras 56 and 60 para.2–90.

[90] *Wilmot v Barber* (1880) 15 Ch.D. 96; *Falcke v Scottish Imperial Insurance Co.* (1886) 34 Ch.D. 234 at 243, 253; *Re Vandervell's Trusts (No.2)* [1974] Ch. 269 at 300–301.

[91] *Taylor Fashions Ltd v Liverpool Victoria Trustees Co.* [1982] Q.B. 133 at 147; *Amalgamated Investment & Property Co. v Texas Commerce International Bank* [1982] Q.B. 84 at 104.

[92] *ibid.* See also *McMahon v Kerry C.C.* [1981] ILRM 419.

[93] *Taylor Fashions Ltd v Liverpool Victoria Trustees Co.* [1982] Q.B. 133 at 151; approved in *Habib Bank Ltd v Habib Bank A.G. Zurich* [1981] 2 All E.R. 650 at 666. Compare the approach to consents to breach of trust, para.10–79.

[94] *Lim Teng Huan v Ang Swee Chin* [1992] 1 W.L.R. 113 at 117 overlooked in *Matharu v Matharu* (1994) 68 P. & C.R. 93.

[95] *Willis v Willis* (1986) 277 E.G. 1133; *Williams v Staite* [1979] Ch. 291.

monetary terms) so far as necessary for X to receive the minimum equity to do justice to him. As the Court of Appeal[96] stated in 2004, "The scope of the court's inquiry is not limited to what it would be unconscionable for the Testator to have done in 1976 but should take account of subsequent events affecting the conscience of the Testator" which, in the circumstances, ousted a claim to inherit a farm as promised in 1976.

2–36   In family property cases the courts are very ready to find that once X acted detrimentally this was in reliance upon O's representation: once detriment is shown the burden falls on O to prove that X did not act in reliance on the representation.[97] In *Wayling v Jones*[98] O and X lived together as homosexuals for 16 years before O died, X being a chef who, for less than full wages, helped O run his hotel business. After 10 years O promised to leave X the hotel in his will, and did so. Unfortunately that hotel was sold and a new one purchased but without O changing his will: hence the gift of the old hotel was adeemed when O died. The new hotel was sold and X claimed the proceeds of sale successfully, despite having answered "Yes" in cross-examination to the question, "If he had not made the promise to you, would you still have stayed?" thereby indicating that he stayed with O for low wages because he loved him and had not relied on any promise that the hotel would be his on O's death.

2–37   The Court of Appeal held that since O did make the promise and since X in his evidence in chief had said that if O had then reneged on his promise he, X, would have left, this was sufficient to prevent O's executors from showing that X had not relied upon the promise. Thus, exceptionally, the court acted not on evidence of what the promisee actually did in reliance on the promise but on speculation as to what the promisee might have done.

2–38   The key question to be asked of a claimant cohabitant is, therefore, "What would you have done if the defendant had revoked his promise?" If the answer is on the lines "Nothing. I would have stayed with him because I loved him", then the claim fails. If the answer is on the lines, "I would have left and gone elsewhere", then the claimant's case is established unless somehow the defendant promisor can show that the claimant had not, in fact, relied on his promise. The second answer is not treated merely as indicating the claimant left simply because the defendant's new attitude revealed that their close loving relationship had ended so there was little point in staying, such having no significance as to whether or not the claimant had detrimentally relied upon the defendant's promise.

As made clear in *Grundy v Ottey*[99] (see para.2–90) "the purpose of proprietary estoppel is not to enforce an obligation that does not amount to

---

[96] *Uglow v Uglow* [2004] W.T.L.R. 1183 (the 1975 assurance implicitly assumed that the farming partnership between the claimant and his uncle, the testator, would work out, but it collapsed and the testator in 1984 conscionably granted the claimant a secure agricultural tenancy of 175 of the 235 acres but did not enforce the rental provisions). Coming to Equity with "unclean hands" may bar a claim as in *Gonthier v Orange Contract Scaffolding Ltd* [2003] EWCA Civ 873.

[97] *Greasley v Cooke* [1980] 1 W.L.R. 1306; *Coombes v Smith* [1986] 1 W.L.R. 808; *Grant v Edwards* [1986] Ch. 638; *Maharaj v Chand* [1986] A.C. 898.

[98] (1993) 69 P. & C.R. 170 discussed by E. Cooke (1995) 111 L.Q.R. 389.

[99] [2003] W.T.L.R. 1253, para.61.

a contract nor yet to reverse the detriment which the claimant has suffered but to grant an appropriate remedy in respect of the unconscionable conduct".

Because the court tailors the remedy to fit the unconscionable conduct **2–39** and can take account of factors up to the court hearing, one might have thought that a proprietary estoppel claim was too uncertain and too unstable to rank as a proprietary interest unless and until the court decreed that the claimant was to have a specific type of proprietary interest and not a mere licence or a sum of money.[1] However, in the family homes context proprietary estoppel claims to a promised specific share or a fair share have become indistinguishable[2] from claims to a common intention constructive trust of a specific or fair share, which give rise to a proprietary interest once detrimental reliance has been incurred by the claimant.

Thus s.116 of the Land Registration Act 2002 states, "It is hereby declared for the avoidance of doubt that, in relation to registered land . . . (a) an equity by estoppel . . . has effect from the time the equity arises as an interest capable of binding successors in title". This means that a proprietary estoppel takes effect as an interest capable of binding successors in title from the time the equity arises upon detrimental reliance being incurred, and not from the date of the court order establishing that the equity created a proprietary interest as opposed to a personal obligation to pay a sum of money.[3]

In the case of unregistered land the Court of Appeal has taken the same **2–40** attitude.[4] Purchasers of land thus need to check if any occupier not having legal title has some proprietary estoppel claim. However, if the claim is to an equitable co-ownership interest it will be overreached if the purchase moneys are paid to two trustees or a trust corporation.[5]

IMPORTANCE OF FORMAL REQUIREMENTS

Formal requirements are designed to ensure that an owner of property **2–41** seriously considers what he or she is doing and to provide documentary evidence making fraud more difficult and avoiding problems as to who is entitled to what, especially when many years have elapsed and persons may have died. The validity and consequences of a transaction may depend on compliance with a particular form. Thus a testator's legatees and devisees will receive nothing under his will if it is void for non-compliance with the Wills Act 1837 formalities. Through not having used the requisite formalities a man, like Mr. Vandervell, may find that he has not divested himself of all interest in property settled by him with the result that he is

---

[1] See D. Hayton [1990] Conv. 370, Lord Browne-Wilkinson (1996) 10 Trust L.I. 98, P. Ferguson (1993) 109 L.Q.R. 114, D. Hayton (1993) 109 L.Q.R. 485.
[2] *Yaxley v Gotts* [2000] Ch. 162, *Gillet v Holt* [2001] Ch. 210.
[3] See B. Macfarlane "Proprietary Estoppel and Third Parties after the Land Registration Act 2002" (2003) 62 Camb. L.J. 661.
[4] *Campbell v Griffin* [2001] 1 W.T.L.R. 981 at 994, *Lloyds Bank v Carrick* [1996] 4 All E.R. 630 at 642, *Voyce v Voyce* (1991) 62 P. & C.R. 290 (but contrast *United Bank of Kuwait plc v Sahib* [1997] Ch. 107 at 142).
[5] *Birmingham Midshires Mortgage Services Ltd v Sabherwal* (1999) 80 P. & C.R. 256.

liable to a large amount of tax he had intended to avoid.[6] If a disposition can be effected orally then no stamp duty will be payable: stamp duty is payable on *instruments* (physically capable of being impressed with a stamp) transferring property or interests in property and so will be escaped if the transfer is effected orally and a subsequent written instrument merely records this for the benefit of the trustees. However, section 82 of the Finance Act 1985 has made conveyances or transfers by way of gift no longer subject to *ad valorem* duty.

EXAMPLES OF APPLICATION OF FORMALITIES

2–42 T1 and T2 hold property on trust for A absolutely in the following five examples:

(1) *A declares that he is to hold his equitable interest on trust for such of L to Z as may appoint*. Here A remains in the picture with active trust duties so this is a declaration of trust where the declaration may be oral if the property is pure personalty but must be evidenced in writing within section 53(1)(b) if the property is land.[7]

(2) *A declares himself trustee of his interest for D absolutely*. Whilst superficially a declaration of trust requiring only compliance with s.53(1)(b) if the property is land, this probably amounts to a disposition of A's entire equitable interest which must itself be in writing within s.53(1)(c) whether the property is land or pure personalty.[8] After all, A is a simple bare trustee with no active duties to perform, (having, essentially, made himself an agent for D), so that he should drop out of the picture, T1 and T2 now holding for D instead of A: by A's action A's equitable interest has passed to D who can directly enforce his rights against T1 and T2 merely joining A as a co-defendant to the action.[9] It seems that if A declared himself trustee for D for life, remainder to E, then if A's duty is as bare trustee to transfer actual income to D and then the actual capital assets to E, A will be regarded as a passive trustee.[10]

2–43 (3) *A directs T1 and T2 to transfer the property to E absolutely for E's own benefit*. Here, it has been held that the transfer of the legal title to E automatically carries with it the equitable interest so that there is no separate disposition by A of his equitable interest that requires compliance with s.53(1)(c): *Vandervell v I.R.C.* set out at para.2–63. However, the reasoning is not very satisfactory because in the case of a transfer by the

---

[6] *Vandervell v I.R.C.* [1967] 2 A.C. 291.

[7] *Onslow v Wallis* (1849) 1 Mac. & G. 506 approved in *Re Lashmar* [1891] 1 Ch. 253.

[8] *Grainge v Wilberforce* (1889) 5 T.L.R. 436, 437; *Re Lashmar* [1891] 1 Ch. 253; *Grey v I.R.C.* [1958] Ch. 375 at 382, *per* Upjohn J. [1958] Ch. 690 at 715, *per* Evershed M.R. *Corin v Patton* (1990) 169 C.L.R. 540 at 579 *per* Deane J.

[9] Brian Green in (1984) 47 M.L.R. 385 at 396–399 prefers the declaration to be treated as a sub-trust carving out a subsidiary equitable entitlement in B's favour out of A's original equitable interest but he goes on to submit that it should fall within s.53(1)(c) as a part disposal of A's equitable interest, a disposal of the beneficial part of A's bundle of hitherto subsisting equitable rights.

[10] *Re Lashmar* [1891] 1 Ch. 258 at 269. He would be an active trustee if he declared he held his interest on trust to sell it and invest the proceeds for D for life, remainder to E, when he would need to invest so as to keep a fair balance between D and E.

legal and beneficial[11] owner the beneficial interest is merged or subsumed in the legal interest, whereas when T holds the legal title on trust for A the legal and equitable interests are obviously separated and the issue is whether they can be joined without a separate assignment or surrender by A, so that the beneficial interest is then at home with the legal interest in T and so capable of transfer by T to E.

Looking at matters from A's viewpoint, A is not seeking to replace **2–44** himself as beneficiary owning an equitable interest with someone else as owner of his subsisting equitable interest.[12] He is authorising T to transfer legal beneficial ownership of the trust property to E freed and discharged from A's rights. In the case of an authorised sale to E, it is clear that A's equitable interest is overreached, being detached from the sold assets and attached to the proceeds of sale and then any assets purchased therewith.[13] If, under the original terms of S's trust for W for life, remainder to A absolutely, T had express power after W's death to transfer to E such assets as T chose in T's discretion and T chose to transfer particular assets to E, this exercise of T's power would overreach A's equitable interest. Where, instead, T holds property on trust for A or as A directs as absolute beneficial owner, then a transfer by T to E of particular assets as directed by A should similarly overreach A's equitable interest in those assets.[14]

In any event, it is the transfer to E as legal beneficial owner[15] that is **2–45** crucial. Thus, if before legal title was transferred A revoked his direction to T, then A would remain entitled to the equitable interest and E could not in law complain about the promised gift not materialising. In the case of shares (or registered land) the legal title is not actually transferred till the transferee becomes registered as owner (or the relevant documents are delivered to the appropriate District Land Registry) but equity treats the transfer as complete when the transferor has done everything necessary to be done by him,[16] *e.g.* delivery of the share or land certificate and the transfer form to the transferee. Thus once T has posted off such documents to the registry or the transferee or has agreed to hold the documents as agent of the transferee[17] A will not be allowed to revoke his gift and claim that E on becoming registered owner holds the property on trust for A.[18]

(4) *A directs T1 and T2 to hold the property on trust for F absolutely.* This is a disposition of A's equitable interest and so must be in writing within s.53(1)(*c*): *Grey v I.R.C.* set out in para.2–50. After all, as a result of A's

---

[11] No separate equitable interest subsists where A is sole legal beneficial owner: *Westdeutsche Landesbank v Islington B.C.* [1996] A.C. 669 at 706.

[12] As in *Grey v I.R.C.* [1960] AC I; see para 2–16.

[13] C. Harpum, "Overreaching, Trustees' Powers and the Reform of the 1925 Legislation" [1990] Camb. L.J. 277, C. Harpum (ed.) Megarry & Wade, *Law of Real Property* (6th ed.), paras 4–079 to 4–080, *State Bank of India v Sood* [1997] Ch. 276.

[14] R. Nolan, "*Vandervell v I.R.C.*: A Case of Overreaching" [2002] Camb. L.J. 169.

[15] It is immaterial that as in *Vandervell v I.R.C.* [1967] 2 A.C. 291 T has the option to reacquire the assets and holds such option on trust for A or someone else.

[16] *Re Rose* [1952] Ch. 499.

[17] *Pennington v Waine* [2002] 1 W.L.R. 2075.

[18] B. Green (1984) 47 M.L.R. 385 at 410, and see, n.36, para.2–660.

direction T1 and T2 hold on trust for F instead of A, so A has been responsible for his equitable interest passing from himself to F.[19]

2–46   If T1 and T2 held the property on trust for A until A *or the trustees* appoint the property to be held on trust for such of C to Z as might be seen fit, then such appointment by the trustees on trust for F absolutely would not be "a disposition of an equitable interest subsisting at the time of the disposition" within s.53(1)(c), but the creation of a new interest automatically extinguishing A's formerly subsisting equitable interest.[20] If, however, A, and not the trustees, appointed property on trust for F absolutely this would seem a disposition of A's subsisting equitable interest since by virtue of A's act it passes from him to F. As Viscount Simonds stated in *Grey v I.R.C.*,[21] "If the word 'disposition' is given its natural meaning it cannot be denied that a direction given by Mr. Hunter [the settlor-beneficiary] whereby the beneficial interest theretofore vested to him became vested in another is a disposition." However, in *obiter dicta* Lord Denning[22] suggests that if T1 and T2 held property on a resulting trust for A until A or the trustees appointed new trusts then an appointment *by A* or the trustees should be treated as the creation of a new interest, A's equitable interest (under the resulting trust arising to plug the gap in the beneficial ownership) automatically ceasing "as soon as the gap is filled by the creation or declaration of a valid trust."[23] These dicta seem unsound where the appointment is by A: in *Re Vandervell's Trusts (No.2)* it was surely only because *the trustees* made the appointment that there was created a valid trust to displace the resulting trust as emphasised by Stephenson L.J.

2–47   (5) *A contracts with G to transfer his equitable interest to G.* If A's equitable interest is in land, whether or not held on trust for sale, then all the terms of the contract must be in writing as required by s.2 of Law of Property (Miscellaneous Provisions) Act 1989. Otherwise, it seems writing is not required. Certainly, a contract to make a disposition of an equitable

---

[19] An exception from the *Grey v I.R.C.* principle is implicit in *Re Bowden* [1936] Ch. 31 and *Re Adlard* [1954] Ch. 29 on which see para.4–47. No writing seems required where S has executed a voluntary "S" settlement and therein covenanted to transfer to his trustee (*e.g.* Lloyds Bank) after-acquired property appointed to him under the "T" trust or bequeathed to him under T's will, and Lloyds Bank becomes trustee of the "T" trust or of T's will when property is appointed or bequeathed to S (giving S an equitable interest) and S authorises Lloyds Bank *qua* trustee of the "T" trust or of T's will to hold the property *qua* trustee of the "S" trust. Where CREST enables title to securities to be evidenced and transferred electronically without a written instrument (pursuant to Companies Act 1989, s.207) Regulation 38(5) of the Uncertificated Securities Regulations 2001 provides "sections 53(1)(c) and 136 of the Law of the Property Act 1925 shall not apply (if they otherwise would do so) to (a) any transfer of title to uncertificated units of a security by means of a relevant system and (b) any disposition or assignment of a security, title to which is held by a relevant nominee."

[20] *Commissioners of State Revenue v Lam & Kym Pty Ltd* [2004] Victoria S.C.A. 204, para.45; *Re Vandervell's Trusts (No.2)* [1974] Ch. 269, see at para.2–67, criticised on its estoppel grounds by Brian Green, at para.2–86.

[21] [1960] A.C. 1 at 12.

[22] *Re Vandervell's Trusts (No.2)* [1974] Ch. 269 at 320.

[23] One cannot restrict Lord Denning's views to equitable interests under *resulting* trusts, falling outside s.53(1)(c): equitable interests under *express* trusts are similarly displaced by the creation of new valid trusts. In *Re Tyler's Fund Trusts* [1967] 3 All E.R. 389 at 391–392, Pennycuick J. applied s.53(1)(c) to an equitable interest under a resulting trust. In *Oughtred v I.R.C.* [1960] A.C. 206 at 253, Lord Denning considered s.53(1)(c) to apply to an equitable interest under a constructive trust which falls under s.53(2) like a resulting trust.

interest does not seem itself to be a disposition. However, it can be said that the constructive trusteeship imposed upon A when he enters into a specifically enforceable contract[24] to sell his equitable interest to G means that T1 and T2 hold on trust for A who holds on constructive trust for G, so that if A is or becomes (after receipt of the purchase price) a simple bare trustee with no active duties to perform he disappears from the picture, leaving T1 and T2 holding on trust for G. Thus A has disposed of his equitable interest and this requires writing within s.53(1)(c).[25]

Against such a conclusion is s.53(2) which states that s.53(1) is not to affect the creation or operation of constructive trusts so that without the need for any s.53(1)(c) writing G becomes owner of the equitable interest due to the constructive trust in his favour: this view has been taken by Upjohn J.,[26] Lord Radcliffe,[27] Megarry J.[28] and by Goff and Shaw L.JJ.,[29] and has been held correct by the Court of Appeal in *Neville v Wilson*,[30] at para.2–53. In any event as Lord Cohen has indicated[31] once G had paid the purchase price to A, A would not be able to put forward successfully any claim to the equitable interest. Furthermore, A's self-interested trusteeship in ensuring the contract is observed and the purchase price paid to him means that when the contract is first made he is not a simple bare trustee with no active duties so that the constructive trust in G's favour is a true sub-trust outside s.53(1)(c). The position is analogous to the case where A declares a sub-trust of his equitable interest for S for one month, remainder to T absolutely (outside s.53(1)(c)) and after a month S's interest automatically ceases and by operation of law T becomes full beneficial owner (outside s.53(1)(c)).

2–48

In *Chinn v Collins* the House of Lords regarded the availability of specific performance and the creation of a constructive trust immaterial in a case concerned with non-specifically enforceable contractual dealings relating to an equitable interest in shares (in an English public company held by an English private company as nominee for a Guernsey trustee). Lord Wilberforce asserted,[32] "Dealings related to the equitable interest in these [shares] required no formality. As soon as there was an agreement for their sale accompanied or followed by payment of the price, the equitable title passed at once to the purchaser and all that was needed to perfect his title was notice to the trustee or the nominee."[33]

2–49

---

[24] See at para.6–82.
[25] See Lord Denning in *Oughtred v I.R.C.* [1960] A.C. 206 at 233. Stamp duty may then be payable under Stamp Act 1891, s.59(1).
[26] *Oughtred v I.R.C.* [1958] Ch. 383.
[27] *Oughtred v I.R.C.* [1960] A.C. 206 at 227–228.
[28] *Re Holt's Settlement* [1969] 1 Ch. 100.
[29] *DHN Food Distributors Ltd v Tower Hamlets London Borough Council* [1976] 1 W.L.R. 852 at 865,867.
[30] [1997] Ch. 144.
[31] *Oughtred v I.R.C.* [1960] A.C. 206 at 230.
[32] [1981] A.C. 533 at 548 without giving reasons, though the emphasis on payment of the price indicates support for Lord Cohen's view in *Oughtred*, above. The other Law Lords agreed with him.
[33] Under the rule in *Dearle v Hall* (1828) 3 Russ. 1 the first assignee to give notice of the dealing with the equitable interest to the trustee takes priority over other assignees.

GREY v INLAND REVENUE COMMISSIONERS

2–50   House of Lords [1960] A.C. 1; [1959] 3 W.L.R. 759; 103 S.J 896; [1959] 3 All E.R.
603; [1959] T.R. 311 (Viscount Simonds, Lords Radcliffe, Cohen, Keith of
Avonholm and Reid)

On February 1, Mr. Hunter, as settlor, transferred 18,000 shares of £1 each to the
appellants as nominees for himself. The appellants were the trustees of six
settlements, which Mr. Hunter had previously created. On February 18, 1955, Mr.
Hunter orally directed the trustees to divide the 18,000 shares into six parcels of
3,000 shares each and to appropriate the parcels to the trusts of the six settlements,
one parcel to each settlement.

  On March 25, 1955, the trustees executed six deeds of declaration of trust (which
Mr. Hunter also executed in order to testify to the oral direction previously given by
him) declaring that since February 18, 1955, they held each of the parcels of 3,000
shares on the trusts of the relevant settlement. The Commissioners of Inland
Revenue assessed the deeds of declaration of trust to *ad valorem* stamp duty on the
basis that the oral declaration did not effectively create trusts of the shares so that it
was the subsequent deeds that created trusts of the shares and were stampable as
instruments transferring an interest in property: they were not exempt as merely
confirming an earlier effective transfer. The trustees appealed against this view
upheld by a majority in the Court of Appeal.

2–51   LORD RADCLIFFE: "My Lords, if there is nothing more in this appeal than the short
question whether the oral direction that Mr. Hunter gave to his trustees on
February 18, 1955, amounted in any ordinary sense of the words to a 'disposition of
an equitable interest or trust subsisting at the time of the disposition,' I do not feel
any doubt as to my answer. I think that it did. Whether we describe what happened
in technical or in more general terms, the full equitable interest in the eighteen
thousand shares concerned, which at that time was his, was (subject to any statutory
invalidity) diverted by his direction from his ownership into the beneficial ownership
of the various equitable owners, present and future, entitled under his six existing
settlements . . .

2–52   "In my opinion, it is a very nice question whether a parol declaration of trust of
this kind was or was not within the mischief of section 9 of the Statute of Frauds.
The point has never, I believe, been decided and perhaps it never will be. Certainly
it was long established as law that while a declaration of trust respecting land or any
interest therein required writing to be effective a declaration of trust respecting
personalty did not. Moreover, there is warrant for saying that a direction to his
trustee by the equitable owner of trust property prescribing new trusts of that
property was a declaration of trust. But it does not necessarily follow from that that
such a direction, if the effect of it was to determine completely or *pro tanto* the
subsisting equitable interest of the maker of the direction, was not also a grant or
assignment for the purposes of section 9 and therefore required writing for its
validity. Something had to happen to that equitable interest in order to displace it in
favour of the new interests created by the direction: and it would be at any rate
logical to treat the direction as being an assignment of the subsisting interest to the
new beneficiary or beneficiaries or, in other cases, a release or surrender of it to the
trustee.

  "I do not think, however, that that question has to be answered for the purposes
of this appeal. It can only be relevant if section 53(1) of the Law of Property Act
1925 is treated as a true consolidation of the three sections of the Statute of Frauds

concerned and as governed, therefore, by the general principle, with which I am entirely in agreement, that a consolidating Act is not to be read as effecting changes in the existing law unless the words it employs are too clear in their effect to admit of any other construction. But, in my opinion, it is impossible to regard section 53 of the Law of Property Act 1925 as a consolidating enactment in this sense."[34] *Appeal dismissed.*

NEVILLE v WILSON

Court of Appeal [1997] Ch. 144, [1996] 3 W.L.R. 460, [1996] 3 All ER 171 (Nourse, **2–53** Rose and Aldous L.JJ.)

NOURSE L.J.: "We are therefore of the opinion that in about April 1969 the shareholders of JEN entered into an agreement with one another for the informal liquidation of JEN as contended for by Mr Jacob and thus, as part of it, for the division of JEN's equitable interest in the 120 ordinary shares in UEC registered in the names of the widow and Mr Wilson amongst themselves, as Mr Hyde put it, 'on a shareholding basis'; in other words, in proportions corresponding to their existing shareholdings. . . . In consequence, JEN's equitable interest in the shares would, as the plaintiffs now claim, be divided amongst the shareholders in the proportions: 104 for the trustees of the will of the testator, and 4 each for the widow, Mr Neville, Mrs Hill and Mrs Wilson.

The effect of the agreement, more closely analysed, was that each shareholder **2–54** agreed to assign his interest in the other shares of JEN's equitable interest in exchange for the assignment by the other shareholders of their interests in his own aliquot share. Each individual agreement having been a disposition of a subsisting equitable interest not made in writing, there then arises the question whether it was rendered ineffectual by s.53 of the Law of Property Act 1925 . . .

The simple view of the present case is that the effect of each individual agreement **2–55** was to constitute the shareholder an implied or constructive trustee for the other shareholders, so that the requirement for writing contained in sub-s.(1)(c) of s.53 was dispensed with by sub-s.(2). That was the view taken by Upjohn J at first instance and by Lord Radcliffe in the House of Lords in *Oughtred v IRC*. In order to see whether it is open to us to adopt it in this court, we must give careful consideration to those views and to the other speeches in the House of Lords.

In *Oughtred v IRC* [1960] A.C. 206 a mother and son were the tenant for life and **2–56** absolute reversioner respectively under a settlement of shares in a private company. By an oral agreement made on 18 June 1956 they agreed that on 26 June the son would exchange his reversionary interest under the settlement for shares in the same company owned by the mother absolutely, to the intent that her life interest in the settled shares should be enlarged into an absolute interest. On 26 June the mother and the son released the trustees by a deed which recited, amongst other things, that the settled shares were "accordingly now held in trust for [the mother] absolutely", and that it was intended to transfer them to her. On the same day the trustees transferred the settled shares to the mother by deed, the consideration being

---

[34] Would *ad valorem* stamp duty have been avoided if (1) H had orally declared himself trustee of the shares on trust for his grandchildren; (2) H had retired as trustee in favour of the trustees of the six settlements, legal title to the shares being transferred to such trustees by instrument bearing fixed 50p duty; (3) the trustees later signed an instrument recording they hold the shares on specified trusts declared earlier by H?

expressed to be ten shillings. It was held by Lord Keith of Avonholm, Lord Denning and Lord Jenkins, (Lord Radcliffe and Lord Cohen dissenting), that the transfer was assessable to ad valorem stamp duty. The basis of decision adopted by the majority was that, even if the oral agreement was effective to pass the equitable interest in the settled shares to the mother, the transfer, as the instrument by which the transaction was completed, was none the less a conveyance on sale within s.54 of the Stamp Act 1891.

2–57   Upjohn J, having said that s.53(2) of the 1925 Act was a complete answer to the argument that s.53(1)(c) applied, continued ([1958] Ch. 383 at 390):

> "This was an oral agreement for value, and, accordingly, on the making thereof Peter the vendor became a constructive trustee of his equitable reversionary interest in the trust funds for the appellant. No writing to achieve that result was necessary, for an agreement of sale and purchase of an equitable interest in personalty (other than chattels real) may be made orally, and s.53 has no application to a trust arising by construction of law."

Lord Radcliffe, having expressed the view that the judgment of Upjohn J was correct and agreeing with his reasons, said ([1960] A.C. 206 at 227):

> "The reasoning of the whole matter, as I see it, is as follows: On June 18, 1956, the son owned an equitable reversionary interest in the settled shares; by his oral agreement of that date he created in his mother an equitable interest in his reversion, since the subject-matter of the agreement was property of which specific performance would normally be decreed by the court. He thus became a trustee for her of that interest sub modo; having regard to sub-s.(2) of s.53 of the Law of Property Act, 1925, sub-s.(1) of that section did not operate to prevent that trusteeship arising by operation of law."

2–58   Lord Cohen, the other member of the minority, said ([1960] A.C. 206 at 230):

> "Before your Lordships, counsel for the Crown was prepared to agree that, on the making of the oral agreement, Peter became a constructive trustee of his equitable reversionary interest in the settled funds for the appellant, but he submitted that, none the less, s.53(1)(c) applied and, accordingly, Peter could not assign that equitable interest to the appellant except by a disposition in writing. My Lords, with that I agree, but it does not follow that the transfer was a conveyance of that equitable interest on which ad valorem stamp duty was payable under the Stamp Act, 1891."

Having held that the transfer was not such a conveyance, he dissented on that ground.

2–59   Lord Denning said [1960] A.C. 206 at 233):

> "I do not think it necessary to embark on a disquisition on constructive trusts; because I take the view that, even if the oral agreement of June 18, 1956, was effective to transfer Peter's reversionary interest to his mother, nevertheless, when that oral agreement was subsequently implemented by the transfer, then the transfer became liable to stamp duty. But I may say that I do not think the oral agreement was effective to transfer Peter's reversionary interest to his mother. I should have thought that the wording of s.53(1)(c) of the Law of Property Act, 1925, clearly made a writing necessary to effect a transfer, and s. 53(2) does not do away with that necessity."

The views of their Lordships as to the effect of s.53 can be summarised as follows. **2–60** Lord Radcliffe, agreeing with Upjohn J, thought that sub-s.(2) applied. He gave reasons for that view. Lord Cohen and Lord Denning thought that it did not. Although neither of them gave reasons, they may be taken to have accepted the submissions of Mr Wilberforce Q.C. (see [1960] A.C. 206 at 220–222). Lord Keith and Lord Jenkins expressed no view either way. We should add that when the case was in this court, Lord Evershed MR, in delivering the judgment of himself, Morris and Ormerod LJJ, said [1958] Ch. 678 at 687):

> "In this court the case for the Crown has, we think, been somewhat differently presented, and in the end of all, the question under s.53 of the Law of Property Act [1925] does not, in our judgment, strictly call for a decision. We are not, however, with all respect to the learned judge, prepared to accept, as we understand it, his conclusion on the effect of s.53 of the Law of Property Act."

The basis of this court's decision was the same as that adopted by the majority of the House of Lords.

We do not think that there is anything in the speeches in the House of Lords **2–61** which prevents us from holding that the effect of each individual agreement was to constitute the shareholder an implied or constructive trustee for the other share-holders. In this respect we are of the opinion that the analysis of Lord Radcliffe, based on the proposition that a specifically enforceable agreement to assign an interest in property creates an equitable interest in the assignee, was unquestionably correct (*cf. London and South Western Rly Co. v Gomm* (1882) 20 Ch.D. 562 at 581 *per* Jessel M.R.). A greater difficulty is caused by Lord Denning's outright rejection of the application of s.53(2), with which Lord Cohen appears to have agreed.

So far as it is material to the present case, what sub-s.(2) says is that sub-s.(1)(c) does not affect the creation or operation of implied or constructive trusts. Just as in *Oughtred v IRC* the son's oral agreement created a constructive trust in favour of the mother, so here each shareholder's oral or implied agreement created an implied or constructive trust in favour of the other shareholders. Why then should sub-s.(2) not apply? No convincing reason was suggested in argument and none has occurred to us since. Moreover, to deny its application in this case would be to restrict the effect of general words when no restriction is called for, and to lay the ground for fine distinctions in the future. With all the respect which is due to those who have thought to the contrary, we hold that sub-s.(2) applies to an agreement such as we have in this case.

For these reasons, we have come to the conclusion that the agreement entered **2–62** into by the shareholders of JEN in about April 1969 was not rendered ineffectual by s.53 of the 1925 Act."

VANDERVELL v INLAND REVENUE COMMISSIONERS

House of Lords [1967] 2 A.C. 291 [1967] 2 W.L.R. 97 [1967] 1 All ER 1 (Lords **2–63** Pearce, Upjohn and Wilberforce; Lords Reid and Donovan dissenting)

The detailed facts appear in the judgment of Lord Denning M.R. in *Re Vandervell's Trusts (No.2)* set out at para.2–67.

The following extracts from the speeches in the House of Lords concern the point whether the transfer by the bare trustee of the legal title to shares carried with it the equitable interest of the taxpayer beneficiary without any separate written disposition by him.

LORD UPJOHN: ". . . the object of the section, as was the object of the old Statute of Frauds, is to prevent hidden oral transactions in equitable interests in fraud of those truly entitled, and making it difficult, if not impossible, for the trustees to ascertain who are in truth the beneficiaries. When the beneficial owner, however, owns the whole beneficial estate and is in a position to give directions to his bare trustee with regard to the legal as well as the equitable estate there can be no possible ground for invoking the section where the beneficial owner wants to deal with the legal estate as well as the equitable estate.

2–64   "I cannot agree with Diplock L.J. that prima facie a transfer of the legal estate carries with it the absolute beneficial interest in the property transferred; this plainly is not so, *e.g.* the transfer may be on a change of trustee; it is a matter of intention in each case. If, however, the intention of the beneficial owner in directing the trustee to transfer the legal estate to X is that X should be the beneficial owner, I can see no reason for any further document or further words in the document assigning the legal estate also expressly transferring the beneficial interest; the greater includes the less. X may be wise to secure some evidence that the beneficial owner intended him to take the beneficial interest in case his beneficial title is challenged at a later date but it certainly cannot, in my opinion, be a statutory requirement that to effect its passing there must be some writing under section 53(1)(c).

2–65   "Counsel for the Crown admitted that where the legal and beneficial estate was vested in the legal owner and he desired to transfer the whole legal and beneficial estate to another he did not have to do more than transfer the legal estate and he did not have to comply with section 53(1)(c); and I can see no difference between that case and this.

"As I have said, that section is, in my opinion, directed to cases where dealings with the equitable estate are divorced from the legal estate and I do not think any of their Lordships in *Grey v I.R.C.*[35] and *Oughtred v I.R.C.*[36] had in mind the case before your Lordships. To hold the contrary would make assignments unnecessarily complicated; if there had to be assignments in express terms of both legal and equitable interests that would make the section more productive of injustice than the supposed evils it was intended to prevent . . ."

2–66   LORD WILBERFORCE: ". . . On November 14, 1958, the taxpayer's solicitor received from the bank a blank transfer of the shares, executed by the bank, and the share certificate. So at this stage the taxpayer was the absolute master of the shares and only needed to insert his name as transferee in the transfer and to register it to become the full legal owner. He was also the owner in equity. On November 19, 1958, the solicitor . . . on behalf of the taxpayer, who intended to make a gift, handed the transfer to the College, which in due course, sealed it and obtained registration of the shares in the College's name. The case should then be regarded as one in which the taxpayer himself has, with the intention to make a gift, put the College in a position to become the legal owner of the shares, which the College in fact became. If the taxpayer had died before the College had obtained registration, it is clear on the principle of *Re Rose*[37] that the gift would have been complete, on the basis that he had done everything in his power to transfer the legal interest, with

---

[35] [1960] A.C. 1.
[36] [1960] A.C. 206.
[37] [1949] Ch. 78. However, in *Re Rose* the taxpayer was entitled legally and equitably to the shares and did all he could to transfer them by executing a share transfer and delivering the transfer and the share certificate to the donee. Vandervell was only equitably entitled and to say that he had done all he could to vest the shares in the College is to beg the s.53(1)(c) question of what was required of an owner of a subsisting equitable interest to achieve a disposition of that interest in the first place.

an intention to give, to the College. No separate transfer, therefore, of the equitable interest ever came to or needed to be made and there is no room for the operation of the subsection. What the position would have been had there simply been an oral direction to the legal owner (*viz.* the bank) to transfer the shares to the College, followed by such a transfer, but without any document in writing signed by the taxpayer as equitable owner, is not a matter which calls for consideration here . . ."[38]

RE VANDERVELL'S TRUSTS (NO.2)

Court of Appeal [1974] Ch. 269; [1974] 3 All E.R. 205 [1973] 3 W.L.R. 744 (Lord Denning M.R., Stephenson and Lawton L.JJ.)

LORD DENNING M.R.: "During his lifetime Mr. Vandervell was a very successful **2–67** engineer. He had his own private company—Vandervell Products Ltd—'the products company,' as I will call it—in which he owned virtually all the shares. It was in his power to declare dividends as and when he pleased. In 1949 he set up a trust for his children. He did it by forming Vandervell Trustees Ltd—'the trustee company,' as I will call it. He put three of his friends and advisers in control of it. They were the sole shareholders and directors of the trustee company. Two were chartered accountants. The other was his solicitor. He transferred money and shares to the trustee company to be held in trust for the children. Such was the position at the opening of the first period.

The first period: 1958–61

"The first period covers the three years from October 1958 to October 1961. Mr. **2–68** Vandervell decided to found a chair of pharmacology at the Royal College of Surgeons. He was to endow it by providing £150,000. But he did not do it by a direct gift. In November 1958 he transferred to the Royal College of Surgeons 100,000 'A' shares in his products company. His intention was that his products company should declare dividends in favour of the Royal College of Surgeons which would amount in all to £150,000 or more. But, when that sum had been provided, he wanted to be able to regain the shares—so as to use the dividends for other good purposes. So, about the time of the transfer, on December 1, 1958, he got the Royal College of Surgeons to grant an option to the trustee company. By this option the Royal College of Surgeons agreed to transfer the 100,000 'A' shares to the trustee company for the sum of £5,000 at any time on request within the next five years. (This £5,000 was far less than the real value of the shares.) At the time when the option was granted, Mr. Vandervell did not state definitely the trusts on which the trustee company was to hold the option. He meant the trustee company to hold the option on trust—not beneficially for itself—but on trust for someone or other. He did not specify the trusts with any kind of precision. But at a meeting with the chairman of the trustee company it was proposed—and Mr. Vandervell approved— that the option should be held *either* on trust for his children (as an addition to the children's settlement) *or* alternatively on trust for the employees of his products company. He had not made up his mind which of those should benefit. But one thing he was clear about. He thought that he himself had parted with all interest in the shares and in the option. Afterwards, during the years from 1958 to 1961, he saw

[38] See N. Strauss (1967) 30 M.L.R. 461; Gareth Jones [1966] C.L.J. 19–25; S. M. Spencer (1967) 31 Conv.(N.S.) 175–181; B. Green (1984) 47 M.L.R. 385, 410.

to it that his products company declared dividends on these 100,000 shares which were paid to the Royal College of Surgeons. They amounted to £266,000 gross (before tax), or £157,000 net (after tax). So the Royal College of Surgeons received ample funds to found the Chair of Pharmacology.

2–69 "But there were other advantages hoped for. The Royal College of Surgeons thought that, being a charity, they could claim back the tax from the Revenue. And Mr. Vandervell thought that, having parted with all interest in the shares, he was not subject to pay surtax on these dividends. The Revenue authorities, however, did not take that view. They claimed that Mr. Vandervell had not divested himself of all interest in the shares. They argued that he was the beneficial owner of the option and liable for surtax on the dividends. Faced with this demand, in October 1961, the trustee company, on the advice of counsel, and with the full approval of Mr. Vandervell, decided to exercise the option. It did it so as to avoid any question of surtax thereafter being payable by Mr. Vandervell. This ended the first period (when the option was in being) and started the second period (after the option was exercised).

The second period: 1961–65

2–70 "In October 1961 the trustee company exercised the option. It did it by using the money of the children's settlement. It paid £5,000 of the children's money to the Royal College of Surgeons. In return the Royal College of Surgeons, on October 27, 1961 transferred the 100,000 'A' shares to the trustee company. The intention of Mr. Vandervell and of the trustee company was that the trustee company should hold the shares (which had replaced the option) on trust for the children as an addition to the children's settlement. The trustee company made this clear to the Revenue authorities in an important letter written by its solicitors on November 2, 1961, which I will read:

"G.A. Vandervell, Esq.—Surtax

'Further to our letter of the 7th September last, we write to inform you that in accordance with the advice tendered by Counsel to Vandervell Trustees Ltd, the latter have exercised the option granted to them by the Royal College of Surgeons of the 1st December 1958, and procured a transfer to them of the shares referred to in the option, with funds held by them upon the trusts of the Settlement created by Mr. G. A. Vandervell and dated the 3rd December 1959, and consequently such shares will henceforth be held by them upon the trusts of that Settlement.'

2–71 "Mr. Vandervell believed that thenceforward the trustee company held the 100,000 'A' shares on trust for the children. He acted on that footing. He got his products company to declare dividends on them for the years 1962 to 1964 amounting to the large sum of £1,256,458 gross (before tax) and £769,580 10s. 9d. (after tax). These dividends were received by the trustee company and added to the funds of the children's settlement. They were invested by the trustee company for the benefit of the children exclusively. But even now Mr. Vandervell had not shaken off the demands of the Revenue authorities. They claimed that, even after the exercise of the option, Mr. Vandervell had not divested himself of his interest in the 100,000 'A' shares and that he was liable for surtax on the dividends paid to the children's settlement. Faced with this demand Mr. Vandervell, on the advice of counsel, took the final step. He executed a deed transferring everything to the trustee company on trust for the children. This ended the second period, and started the third.

The third period: 1965–67

"On January 19, 1965, Mr. Vandervell executed a deed by which he transferred to **2–72** the trustee company all right, title or interest which he had on the option or the shares or in the dividends—expressly declaring that the trustee company was to hold them on the trusts of the children's settlement. At last the Revenue authorities accepted the position. They recognised that from January 19, 1965, Mr. Vandervell had no interest whatever in the shares or the dividends. They made no demands for surtax thenceforward.

On January 27, 1967, Mr. Vandervell made his will. It was in contemplation of a **2–73** new marriage. In it he made no provision for his children. He said expressly that this was because he had already provided for them by the children's settlement. Six weeks later, on March 10, 1967, he died.

Summary of the claims

"The root cause of all the litigation is the claim of the Revenue authorities.
"*The first period—1958–61.* The Revenue authorities claimed that Mr. Vandervell was the beneficial owner of the *option* and was liable for surtax on the dividends declared from 1958 to 1961. This came to £250,000. The claim of the Revenue was upheld by the House of Lords: see *Vandervell v Inland Revenue Coms.*[39]
"*The second period—1961–65.* The Revenue authorities claimed that Mr. Vander- **2–74** vell was the beneficial owner of the shares. They assessed him for surtax in respect of the dividends from October 11, 1961, to January 19, 1965, amounting to £628,229. The executors dispute the claim of the Revenue. They appealed against the assessments. But the appeal was, by agreement, stood over pending the case now before us. The executors have brought this action against the trustee company. They seek a declaration that, during the second period, the dividends belonged to Mr. Vandervell himself, and they ask for an account of them. The Revenue asked to be joined as parties to the action. This court did join them: see *Vandervell Trustees Ltd v White*;[40] but the House of Lords reversed the decision.[41] So this action has continued—without the presence of the Revenue—whose claim to £628,229 has caused all the trouble.
"*The third period—1965–67.* The Revenue agreed that they have no claim against the estate for this period.

The law for the first period

"The first period was considered by the House of Lords in *Vandervell v Inland* **2–75** *Revenue Comrs.*[42] They held, by a majority of three to two, that during this period the trustee company held the option as a trustee. The terms of the trust were stated in two ways. Lord Upjohn (with the agreement of Lord Pearce) said[43] that the proper inference was that—

'the trustee company should hold as trustee on such trusts as [Mr. Vandervell] or the trustee company should from time to time declare.'

---

[39] [1967] 2 A.C. 291; [1967] 1 All E.R. 1.
[40] [1970] Ch. 44; [1969] 3 All E.R. 496.
[41] [1971] A.C. 912; [1970] 3 All E.R. 16.
[42] [1967] 2 A.C. 291; [1967] 1 All E.R. 1.
[43] [1967] 2 A.C. 315 at 317; [1967] 1 All E.R. 10 at 11.

Lord Wilberforce said[44] that 'the option was held [by the trustee company] on trusts not at the time determined, but to be decided on a later date.'

"The trouble about the trust so stated was that it was too uncertain. The trusts were not declared or defined with sufficient precision for the trustees to ascertain who the beneficiaries were. It is clear law that a trust (other than a charitable trust) must be for ascertainable beneficiaries: see *Re Gulbenkian's Settlement Trusts*[45] *per* Lord Upjohn. Seeing that there were no ascertainable beneficiaries, there was a resulting trust for Mr. Vandervell. But if and when Mr. Vandervell should declare any defined trusts, the resulting trust would come to an end. As Lord Upjohn said[44] 'until these trusts should be declared there was a resulting trust for [Mr. Vandervell].'

2–76   "During the first period, however, Mr. Vandervell did not declare any defined trusts. The option was, therefore, held on a resulting trust for him. He had not divested himself absolutely of the shares. He was, therefore, liable to pay surtax on the dividends.

The law for the second period

2–77   "In October and November 1961 the trustee company exercised the option. It paid £5,000 out of the children's settlement. The Royal College of Surgeons transferred the legal estate in the 100,000 'A' shares to the trustee company. Thereupon the trustee company became the legal owner of the shares. This was a different kind of property altogether. Whereas previously the trustee company had only a chose in action of one kind—an option—it now had a chose in action of a different kind—the actual shares. This trust property was not held by the trustee company beneficially. It was held by the company on trust. On this occasion a valid trust was created at the time of the transfer. It was manifested in clear and unmistakable fashion. It was precisely defined. The shares were to be held on the trusts of the children's settlement. The evidence of intention is indisputable: (i) the trustee company used the children's money—£5,000—with which to acquire the shares; this would be a breach of trust unless they intended the shares to be an addition to the children's settlement; (ii) the trustee company wrote to the Revenue authorities the letter of November 2, 1961, declaring expressly that the shares 'will henceforth be held by them upon the trusts of the children's settlement'; (iii) thenceforward all the dividends received by the trustee company were paid by it to the children's settlement and treated as part of the funds of the settlement. This was all done with the full assent of Mr. Vandervell. Such being the intention, clear and manifest, at the time when the shares were conveyed to the trustee company, it is sufficient to create a trust.

2–78   "Counsel for the executors admitted that the intention of Mr. Vandervell and the trustee company was that the shares should be held on trust for the children's settlement. But he said that this intention was of no avail. He said that during the first period Mr. Vandervell had an equitable interest in the property, namely, a resulting trust; that he never disposed of this equitable interest (because he never knew he had it); and that in any case it was the disposition of an equitable interest which, under section 53 of the Law of Property Act 1925, had to be in writing, signed by him or his agent, lawfully authorised by him in writing (and there was no such writing produced). He cited *Grey v Inland Revenue Comrs.*[46] & *Oughtred v Inland Revenue Comrs.*[47]

---

[44] [1967] 2 A.C. 325 at 328; [1967] 1 All E.R. 16 at 17.
[45] [1970] A.C. 508 at 523, 524; [1968] 3 All E.R. 785 at 792, 793.
[46] [1960] A.C. 1.
[47] [1960] A.C. 206; [1959] 3 All E.R. 623.

"There is a complete fallacy in that argument. A resulting trust for the settlor is born and dies without any writing at all. It comes into existence wherever there is a gap in the beneficial ownership. It ceases to exist whenever that gap is filled by someone becoming beneficially entitled. As soon as the gap is filled by the creation or declaration of a valid trust, the resulting trust comes to an end. In this case, before the option was exercised, there was a gap in the beneficial ownership. So there was a resulting trust for Mr. Vandervell. But, as the option was exercised and the shares registered in the trustees' name there was created a valid trust of the shares in favour of the children's settlement. Not being a trust of land, it could be created without any writing. A trust of personalty can be created without writing. Both Mr. Vandervell and the trustee company had done everything which needed to be done to make the settlement of these shares binding on them. So there was a valid trust: see *Milroy v Lord*[48] *per* Turner L.J.

The law as to third period

"The executors admit that from January 19, 1965, Mr. Vandervell had no interest **2–79** whatsoever in the shares. The deed of that date operated so as to transfer all his interest thenceforward to the trustee company to be held by them on trust for the children. I asked counsel for the executors: what is the difference between the events of October and November 1961 and the event of January 19, 1965? He said that it lay in the writing. In 1965 Mr. Vandervell disposed of his equitable interest in writing, whereas in 1961 there was no writing. There was only conduct or word of mouth. That was insufficient. And, therefore, his executors were not bound by it.

"The answer to this argument is what I have said. Mr. Vandervell did not dispose **2–80** in 1961 of any equitable interest. All that happened was that his resulting trust came to an end—because there was created a new valid trust of the shares for the children's settlement.

Estoppel

"Even if counsel for the executors were right in saying that Mr. Vandervell **2–81** retained an equitable interest in the shares, after the exercise of the option, the question arises whether Mr. Vandervell can in the circumstances be heard to assert the claim against his children. Just see what happened. He himself arranged for the option to be exercised. He himself agreed to the shares being transferred to the trustee company. He himself procured his products company to declare dividends on the shares and to pay them to the trustee company for the benefit of the children. Thenceforward the trustee company invested the money and treated it as part of the children's settlement. If he himself had lived, and not died, he could not have claimed it back. He could not be heard to say that he did not intend the children's trust to have it. Even a court of equity would not allow him to do anything so inequitable and unjust. Now that he has died, his executors are in no better position. If authority were needed, it is to be found in *Milroy v Lord*[49] In that case Thomas Medley assigned to Samuel Lord 50 shares in the Bank of Louisiana on trust for his niece; but the shares were not formally transferred into the name of Samuel Lord. The bank, however, paid the dividends to Samuel Lord.[50] He paid them to the niece, and then, at Thomas Medley's suggestion, the niece used those

---

[48] (1862) 4 De G.F. & J. 264 at 274; [1861–73] All E.R. Rep.783 at 789.
[49] 4 De G.F. & J. 264; [1861–73] All E.R. Rep.783, para.4–03.
[50] Since he had a power of attorney from Medley authorising him to the dividends.

dividends to buy shares in a fire insurance company—taking them in the name of Thomas Medley. After Thomas Medley's death, his executors claimed that the bank shares belonged to them as representing him, and also the fire insurance shares. Knight-Bruce and Turner L.JJ. held that the executors were entitled to the bank shares, because 'there is no equity in this Court to perfect an imperfect gift.' But the executors were not entitled to the fire insurance shares. Turner L.J. said:[51]

> '. . . the settlor made a perfect gift to [the niece] of the dividends upon these shares, so far as they were handed over or treated by him as belonging to her, and these insurance shares were purchased with dividends which were so handed over or treated.'

2–82 "So here Mr. Vandervell made a perfect gift to the trustee company of the dividends on the shares, so far as they were handed over or treated by him as belonging to the trustee company for the benefit of the children. Alternatively, there was an equitable estoppel. His conduct was such that it would be quite inequitable for him to be allowed to enforce his strict rights (under a resulting trust) having regard to the dealings which had taken place between the parties: see *Hughes v Metropolitan Railway Co.*[52]

"I would allow the appeal and dismiss the claim of the executors."

2–83 STEPHENSON L.J.: "I have had more doubt than my brethren whether we can overturn the judgment of Megarry J.[53] in what I have not found an easy case.

"To expound my doubts would serve no useful purpose; to state them shortly may do no harm. The cause of all the trouble is what the judge called 'the illfated option' and its incorporation in a deed which was 'too short and simple' to rid Mr. Vandervell of the beneficial interest in the disputed shares, as a bare majority of the House of Lords held, not without fluctuation of mind on the part of one of them (Lord Upjohn), in *Vandervell v Inland Revenue Comrs.*[54] The operation of law or equity kept for Mr. Vandervell or gave him back an equitable interest which he did not want and would have thought he had disposed of if he had ever known it existed. It is therefore difficult to infer that he intended to dispose or ever did dispose of something he did not know he had until the judgment of Plowman J. in *Vandervell v Inland Revenue Comrs.*, which led to the deed of 1965, enlightened him, or to find a disposition of it in the exercise by the trustee company in 1961 of its option to purchase the shares. And even if he had disposed of his interest, he did not dispose of it by any writing sufficient to comply with section 53(1)(c) of the Law of Property Act 1925 . . .

2–84 "*But Lord Denning M.R. and Lawton L.J. are able to hold that no disposition is needed because (1) the option was held on such trusts as might thereafter be declared by the trustee company or Mr. Vandervell himself, and (2) the trustee company has declared that it holds the shares in the children's settlement,*[55] I doubt the first, because it was apparently the view of the majority of the House of Lords in *Vandervell v Inland Revenue Comrs.* I should be more confident of the second if it had been pleaded or argued either here or below and we had had the benefit of the learned judge's views on it. I see, as perhaps did counsel, difficulties in the way of a limited

---

[51] 4 De G.F. & J. at 277; [1861–73] All E.R.Rep. at 790.
[52] (1877) 2 App.Cas. 439 at 448.
[53] [1973] 3 W.L.R. 744; [1974] 1 All E.R. 47.
[54] [1967] 2 A.C. 291; [1967] 1 All E.R. 1.
[55] Editor's italics.

company declaring a trust by parol or conduct and without a resolution of the board of directors, and difficulties also in the way of finding any declaration of trust by Mr. Vandervell himself in October or November 1961, or any conduct then or later which would in law or equity estop him from denying that he made one.

"However, Lord Denning M.R. and Lawton L.J. are of the opinion that these **2–85** difficulties, if not imaginary, are not insuperable and that these shares went into the children's settlement in 1961 in accordance with the intention of Mr. Vandervell and the trustee company—a result with which I am happy to agree as it seems to me to be in accordance with the justice and the reality of the case."

B. GREEN (1984) 47 M.L.R. 418 (COMMENTING ON *RE VANDERVELL'S TRUST* (NO.2))

"Lord Denning isolated estoppel as a basis for his decision quite separate to the **2–86** declaration of new trusts ground upon which he primarily founded himself: but then complicated the picture by (i) intertwining his 'estoppel' reasoning with the 'perfect gift' approach of Turner L.J. in relation to the Louisiana Bank shares' dividends in *Milroy v Lord*[56] and (ii) citing as his 'estoppel' authority *Hughes v Metropolitan Railway*[57] Lawton L.J., on the other hand, concertinaed the declaration of new trusts and estoppel arguments; and it is not clear whether in his judgment it was V's procurement of the payment of the second phase dividends or his wilful agreement to V.T.'s exercise of the option using children's settlement monies, or both factors, which achieved the estoppel result. Both judgments ignored the question of whether V (and hence his executors) were merely estopped in respect of recovery of the second phase dividends or whether estoppel extended to recovery of the shares on which the dividends had been declared as well, no doubt since that question had become otiose since V's execution of his stage (10) assignment and release upon which the second phase had terminated.

"The estoppel raised by the majority was, despite the misleading citation of **2–87** *Hughes*, 'estoppel by encouragement':[58] a genus of what is today increasingly referred to, along with the related doctrine of 'estoppel by acquiescence,' by the blanket term 'proprietary estoppel.' The difficulty here is not so much seeing how an 'estoppel by encouragement' might be made out on the facts of *Vandervell (No. 2)*, but rather as to how it could be said that the 'minimum equity' necessary to satisfy the objects of the children's settlement involved the retention of the £770,000 dividends appropriated on their behalf by V.T. It is clear that proprietary estoppels can be raised in respect of personalty just as in respect of realty.[59] Furthermore, even though it may not have been generally perceived in 1974,[60] it has now been

---

[56] (1862) 2 De G.F. & J. 264. The shares could only be transferred by complying with all due forms, but there was no such obstacle to a gift of the money dividends arising on the shares where the donor was *not* merely entitled to those dividends in equity. Had Thomas Medley only been entitled to the dividends in equity, s.9 of the Statute of Frauds 1677 would have been just as great a problem to him as was s.53(1)(*c*) to V. Lord Denning's use of *Milroy v Lord* in the present connection begs precisely the same question as does Lord Wilberforce in *Vandervell v I.R.C.* where he adopts the view of Jenkins J. in *Re Rose*: see above, at para.2–66, n.38.

[57] (1877) 2 App.Cas. 439. The root authority on the waiver of contractual rights doctrine of promissory estoppel: generally seen as unconnected with the present subject-matter. (Although see the widest treatment of this area by Robert Goff J. in *Amalgamated Investment & Property Co. Ltd v Texas Commerce International Bank Ltd* [1981] 1 All E.R. 923, which was too much even for Lord Denning's wholesale adoption when that case reached the Court of Appeal: [1981] 3 All E.R. 577).

[58] The majority cast V in an active role: he is not alleged to have simply acquiesced but positively to have encouraged: see [1974] Ch. 269 at 321A–B and 325G; *per* Denning and Lawton L.JJ. respectively.

[59] See, *e.g. Falcke v Scottish Imperial Insurance Co.* (1886) 34 Ch.D. 234.

[60] See Megarry J. in *Vandervell (No.2)* at first instance [1974] Ch. 269, 301B espousing the conventional assumption in this regard.

convincingly established[61] that (whatever may be the position in regard to 'acquiescence'[62]) neither principle nor previous authority requires the person estopped in an 'encouragement' case to have known of his legal right inconsistent to that on the faith of which the person seeking to raise an equity against him acted to his detriment. And the children's settlement had incurred a certain detriment in reliance on V's encouragement, since on such facts as were emergent V.T. had considered itself honour bound to follow V's wishes and it was V's wish (on the advice of his legal advisers) that the children's settlement should exercise the option with its own monies. But even if V's encouragement of V.T.'s actions for and on behalf of the children's settlement was theoretically capable of grounding an estoppel despite V's lack of knowledge of his true rights at all material times, it is impossible to see how the comparatively trivial estoppel thereby entailed could conceivably justify the children's settlement's retention of over £3/4 million. Under normal conditions it would require deeply unconscientious behaviour by a representor, which had induced an extremely substantial (if not wholly proportionate) irreversible act of detriment on the part of a representee to raise an equity of that extent.

2–88   "Yet when one searches for the villain in V, one finds an innocent. As for substantial detriment, there was no evidence whatsoever that the children's settlement had changed its position at all in the face of V's encouragement, beyond expending £5,000 in exercise of the option in the first place. The £770,000 dividends had simply been credited to the children's settlement's account, none of it had been distributed, let alone dissipated, on an assumption that V.T. was entitled to deal with it as part of the children's fund[63] Nor does it even appear that the mechanism of estoppel was, on the facts, necessary to do justice to the objects of the children's settlement at all. The £5,000 could easily have been ordered to be repaid (with interest) by V's executors as a condition of the payment over of the dividends (with interest) to them.[64]

2–89   "The only party to the second phase transactions who had actually acted to his detriment in reliance on the property and future legal defensibility of V.T. holding the £770,000 as an accretion to the children's settlement trust fund, was V himself. He had assumed that he had adequately provided for his children *inter vivos*, and hence cut them out of his will: an act of detrimental reliance rendered irreversible by his death. One is left with the impression that it was V's reliance on his own mistaken belief that he had successfully vested beneficial entitlement to the dividends in the children's settlement which was the real and substantial basis for raising an equity against his executors: which makes V the only person in English law ever to have stood in the shoes of both 'estopped' and 'estopper' at one and the same time."

---

[61] By Oliver J. in *Taylor Fashions Ltd v Liverpool Victoria Trustees Co. Ltd* [1981] 1 All E.R. 897 pointing up the divergences between Cranworth L.C. and Lord Westbury in *Ramsden v Dyson* (1866) L.R. 1 H.L. 129: a distinction obscured by the accessible "five probanda" of Fry J. in *Wilmot v Barber* (1880) 15 Ch.D. 96 at 105–106, too easily cited as a substitute for analysis for too long.

[62] Where arguably *Wilmot v Barber* (1880) 15 Ch.D. 96 stands. Had V merely "acquiesced," probandum number 4 would have prevented an estoppel being raised against him as one mistaken as to his legal rights. A mistake of secondary fact, not law: *cf. Cooper v Phibbs* (1867) L.R. 2 H.L. 149.

[63] *per* Megarry J. in *Vandervell (No.2)* at first instance: [1974] Ch. 269 at 301F–G.

[64] Which is to cast *Vandervell (No.2)* as the "trust unravelling" case it essentially should have been; with the children's settlement obtaining restitution of its £5,000 as money paid under a mistake of fact as to what it would be getting for it: *cf. Cooper v Phibbs* (1867) L.R. 2 H.L. 149.

GRUNDY v OTTEY

Court of Appeal [2003] EWCA Civ 1176, [2003] WTLR 1253 (Pill, Laws and Arden L.JJ.)

ARDEN L.J.: [52] . . . "It is common ground that proprietary estoppel can arise **2–90** where an owner of property encourages another to act to his detriment in the belief that he will obtain an interest in that other property. The underlying rationale is that it would be unconscionable for the maker of the assurance not to give effect to his promise. The matter must be looked at in the round. As Robert Walker LJ (with whom Beldam and Waller LJJ agreed) said in *Gillett v Holt* [2001] Ch 210 at 225:

> '. . . it is important to note at the outset that the doctrine of proprietary estoppel cannot be treated as subdivided into three or four watertight compartments. Both sides are agreed on that, and in the course of the oral argument in this court it repeatedly became apparent that the quality of the relevant assurance may influence the issue of reliance, that reliance and detriment are often intertwined, and that whether there is a distinct need for a "mutual understanding" may depend on how the other elements are formulated and understood. Moreover the fundamental principle that equity is concerned to prevent unconscionable conduct permeates all the elements of the doctrine. In the end of the court must look at the matter in the round.'

[53] Later in his judgment, Robert Walker LJ set out the relevant principles as to **2–91** the reliance and detriment required in proprietary estoppel, citing the judgment of Balcombe LJ in *Wayling v Jones* (1993) 69 P&CR 170 as follows:

> '(1) There must be a sufficient link between the promises relied upon and the conduct that constitutes the detriment—see *Eves v Eves* [1975] 1 WLR 1338, 1345E-F, in particular per Brightman J, *Grant v Edwards* [1986] Ch 638, 648–649, 655–657, 656G–H, per Nourse LJ and per Browne-Wilkinson V-C and in particular the passage where he equates the principles applicable in cases of constructive trust to those of proprietary estoppel.
> (2) The promises relied upon do not have to be the sole inducement for the conduct: it is sufficient if they are an inducement—*Amalgamated Property Co v Texas Bank* [1982] QB 84, 104–105.
> (3) Once it has been established that promises were made, and that there has been conduct by the plaintiff of such a nature that inducement may be inferred, then the burden of proof shifts to the defendants to establish that he did not rely on the promises—*Greasley v Cooke* [1980] 1 WLR 1306; *Grant v Edwards* [1980] Ch 638, 657.'

[54] In the course of his judgment, Robert Walker LJ by implication accepted the **2–92** argument that what makes an assurance binding is the detrimental reliance on the promise by the person to whom the assurance is given (see [2001] Ch 210 at 227). After that time, it is too late for the maker of the assurance to change his mind.

[55] Robert Walker LJ also discussed the requirement for detriment. The **2–93** detriment must be sufficiently substantial to make it unjust or inequitable or unconscionable for the maker of the assurance to withdraw it ([2001] Ch 210 at 232F). Once the claim to equitable relief is satisfied, the court has to decide the appropriate form of relief: 'The court approaches this task in a cautious way, in

order to achieve . . . the minimum equity to do justice to the plaintiff.' (Per Robert Walker LJ in *Gillett v Holt* [2001] Ch 210 at 235.)

2–94   [56] In order to show that the person to whom the assurance was made was induced to act to his detriment, it is not necessary to show that he would have left the maker of the assurance if the promise had not been made, but only that he would have left the maker of the assurance if the promise had been withdrawn— *Wayling v Jones* (1993) 69 P&CR 170. Once the claimant shows that the promise was made, and that his conduct was such that inducement could be inferred, the burden of proof shifts to the maker of the promise to show that the claimant did not, in fact, rely on the promise—*Wayling v Jones*.

2–95   [57] As to the remedy that the court should grant when proprietary estoppel has been established, this should be no more than is necessary to protect against unconscionable conduct: see *Jennings v Rice* [2002] WTLR 367, 378. The remedy must be proportionate to the detriment suffered (*ibid*, 378, 381, 386). The following passage from the judgment of Robert Walker LJ suggests that the requirement of proportionality is more easily satisfied where it is proposed to implement an assurance to transfer specific property:

> 'Sometimes the assurances, and the claimant's reliance on them, have a consensual character falling not far short of an enforceable contract (if the only bar to the formation of a contract is non-compliance with *s2* of the *Law of Property (Miscellaneous Provisions) Act 1989*, the proprietary estoppel may become indistinguishable from a constructive trust—*Yaxley v Gotts* [2000] Ch 162). In a case of that sort both the claimant's expectations and the element of detriment to the claimant will have been defined with reasonable clarity. A typical case would be an elderly benefactor who reaches a clear understanding with the claimant (who may be a relative, a friend, or a remunerated companion or carer) that if the claimant resides with and cares for the benefactor, the claimant will inherit the benefactor's house (or will have a home for life). In a case like that the consensual element of what has happened suggests that the claimant and the benefactor probably regarded the expected benefit and the accepted detriment as being (in a general, imprecise way) equivalent, or at any rate not obviously disproportionate. Cases of that sort, if free from other complications, fit fairly comfortably into Dr Gardner's first or second hypothesis (both of which aim to vindicate the claimant's expectations as far as possible, and if possible by providing the claimant with the specific property which the benefactor has promised).
>
> However, the claimant's expectations may not be focused on any specific property. In *Re Basham* [1986] 1 WLR 1498 the deputy judge (Mr Edward Nugee QC) rejected the submission that there must be some clearly identified piece of property, and that decision has been approved more than once in this court. Moreover (as the judge's findings in this case vividly illustrate) the claimant's expectations may have been formed on the basis of vague and inconsistent assurance. The judge said of Mrs Royle that she: ". . . was prone to saying different things at different times and, perhaps deliberately, couched her promises. . . in non-specific terms." He made that observation in relation to the failure of the contract claim, but it is relevant to the estoppel claim also.
>
> If the claimant's expectations are uncertain (as will be the case with many honest claimants) then their specific vindication cannot be the appropriate test. A similar problem arises if the court, although satisfied that the claimant has a genuine claim, is not satisfied that the high level of the claimant's expectations is fairly derived from his deceased patron's assurances, which may have justified

only a lower level of expectation. In such cases the court may still take the claimant's expectations (or the upper end of any range of expectations) as a starting point, but unless constrained by authority I would regard it as no more than a starting point.'

[58] For my part I do not read this passage from the judgement of Robert **2–96** Walker LJ as detracting from the general proposition that the relationship between the promise and the remedy must be proportionate, and that the promise, even if of a specific property, is only a starting point: 'if the claimant's expectations are. . . out of all proportion to the detriment which the claimant has suffered, the court can and should recognise that the claimant's equity should be satisfied in another (and generally more limited) way' (per Robert Walker LJ at 384). 'The essence of the doctrine of proprietary estoppel is to do what is necessary to avoid an unconscionable result, and a disproportionate remedy cannot be the right way of doing that' (per Robert Walker LJ at 386).

. . .

[60] Miss Rich also submits the judge placed too much emphasis on the answer **2–97** to the *Wayling v Jones* question. In my judgment, Miss Ottey was asked the question which that case establishes is the relevant one and the judge was entitled to act on her answer. Once there was reliance, then on the authorities, the promise became irrevocable in equity. The onus shifted to Mr Grundy to disprove any causal connection with the promise, and the judge found, as he was entitled to do, that this burden had not been discharged.

[61] As respects the cross-appeal, Mr Garnett submits that the judge did not **2–98** properly analyse *Jennings v Rice* and should have started with specific assurances. In my judgment, this submission does not accord with the judgment. The judge's starting point in paragraph 43 is the value in money terms of the expectation which Mr Andreae raised. Moreover, the purpose of proprietary estoppel is not to enforce an obligation that does not amount to a contract nor yet to reverse the detriment which the claimant has suffered but to grant an appropriate remedy in respect of the unconscionable conduct. In my judgment, this was the exercise which the judge performed and he did so in a way in which he was entitled so to do."

QUESTIONS

1. T1 and T2 hold property on trust for X. What formalities are required if: **2–99**

   (i) X assigns his equitable interest to Y or to A and B on trust for Y;

 (ii) X directs T1 and T2 to hold the property on trust for Y;

(iii) X contracts with Y to transfer his equitable interest to him;

 (iv) X declares himself a trustee of his interest for Y;

  (v) X declares himself trustee of his interest for himself for life, remainder for Y absolutely;

 (vi) X directs T1 and T2 to transfer the property to P and Q on trust for Y; what should T1 and T2 do if X died or revoked his direction before T1 and T2 had transferred the legal title?

(vii) X directs T1 and T2 that they henceforth have power to appoint the property to such of Y, his spouse and issue as they may see fit, and a month later T1 and T2 declare they therefore hold the property on trust for Y for life, remainder to his children equally.

Does it matter if the property is land or personalty? Does it matter if the property were held on resulting trust for X?

2–100   2. All Heels' College, Durham, to which Archibald Alumnus who has just died has left all his property by will, seeks your advice on the property to which it is entitled (taking account of Law of Property Act 1925, s.60(3)).

On February 1, last year, Archibald did three things:

(i)   he transferred £25,000 from his bank account into the bank account of Roger Randall as his nominee;

(ii) he executed a share transfer of his 15,000 shares in Up and Down Ltd in favour of Simon Sharp (not intending him to become beneficial owner) and Simon in due course became registered owner of the shares;

(iii) for no consideration he conveyed his holiday cottage, Tree-Tops, to Theodore Thin for an estate in fee simple in possession.

2–101   On March 1, Archibald orally stated, "I declare that I hold my interest in the £25,000, which I recently transferred into Roger Randall's name, upon trust for my two adult children in equal shares."

On April 1, by unsigned writing Archibald directed Simon to hold half the Up and Down Ltd shares upon trust for Gay Gibson and to transfer the other half into the name of Maud Molesworth legally and beneficially, which Simon duly did.

As far as Tree-Tops is concerned there is cogent evidence that prior to the execution of the conveyance Theodore had orally agreed with Archibald to hold it upon trust for Wendy Williams.

2–102   3. Two years ago Brian transferred his cottage to Tom, orally telling Tom to hold it for Brian for life and then for Clarissa absolutely. He also transferred 10,000 ICI plc shares, 8,000 Hanson plc shares and 6,000 British Gas shares to his sister, Susan, orally telling her to hold them for himself or for such of their relatives as she might select. He soon told her to hold the ICI shares for Clarissa absolutely. Susan complied but said that she was now going to hold the Hanson shares for her cousin, Joy. Brian then told her to transfer the British Gas shares to Tom, who had already orally agreed to hold them on the same trusts as he held the cottage. Susan did so transfer the shares.

A year ago Brian had a row with Clarissa and so told Tom, "Hold the cottage and the shares for me absolutely until I decide what to do about them." Last month he wrote a letter to Tom, "When I die I want you to transfer the cottage and the shares to Joy."

A fortnight ago Brian died, having, by will, left everything to Eric.

Advise Eric.

Section 3. Post Mortem Trusts: Secret Trusts

I. General

2–103   The doctrine of secret trusts developed as a product of equity not allowing statutes to be used as an instrument of fraud.[65] It will already have been

---

[65] *McCormick v Grogan* (1869) L.R. 4 H.L. 82 at 88–89; *Blackwell v Blackwell* [1929] A.C. 318, p.94; *Jones v Badley* (1868) 3 Ch. App.362 at 364.

seen that statutes prescribe certain formalities for declarations of trust respecting land and for dispositions of equitable interests.[66] In addition, s.9 of the Wills Act 1837 set out at para.2–109, prescribes special formalities for the validity of testamentary dispositions whilst the Administration of Estates Act 1925 lays down rules of intestate succession. All too often a person might be induced to die intestate leaving X as his intestate successor[67] or to leave property by will to X on the secret oral understanding that X was to hold the property he received on trust for B. If X were allowed to retain the property beneficially, instead of taking merely as trustee, then this would be allowing statutes to be used as an instrument of fraud by X. Accordingly, equity treats X as a trustee despite the absence of the requisite formalities.

Secret trusts most commonly concern trusts engrafted on wills and in this **2–104** context it is most important to distinguish between (1) fully secret trusts, (2) half-secret trusts, and (3) cases where the probate doctrine of incorporation by reference arises. Respective examples (where X has agreed to hold on trust for B) are (1) I devise Blackacre to X absolutely (2) I devise Blackacre to X upon trusts which I have communicated to him and (3) I devise Blackacre to X upon trusts which I have communicated to him by letter dated November 11, 2004. In this last example since the will refers to a written instrument, already existing at the date of the will, in such terms that the written instrument can be ascertained, the requirements of the doctrine of incorporation are satisfied[68] so that the incorporated document is admitted to public probate as part of the testator's will, the will's compliance with the requirements of s.9 of the Wills Act being sufficient to cover the unattested written instrument referred to in the will. It will be seen that the application of the doctrine of incorporation renders the imposition of a secret trust unnecessary as the requisite formalities for an express trust are present, preventing any possibility of fraud upon X's part.

Testators, today, who do not want their testamentary wishes to become **2–105** public by admission to probate as part of their will can take advantage of the doctrine of secret trusts to make provision for mistresses, illegitimate children, relatives whom they do not wish to appear to be helping or organisations which they do not wish to appear to be helping. Indecisive, aged testators can also leave everything by will absolutely to their solicitors, from time to time calling upon or phoning their solicitors with their latest wishes.

Proving secret trusts can be a problem, though the standard of proof is **2–106** the ordinary civil standard on a balance of probabilities unless fraud is involved when a higher standard is required.[69] A good practical precaution is for the testator to have a document signed by the intended trustee put into the possession of the secret beneficiaries.

---

[66] Law of Property Act 1925, s.53, above, at para.2–05.
[67] *Sellack v Harris* (1708) 2 Eq.Ca.Ab. 46.
[68] *In the goods of Smart* [1902] P. 238; *Re Jones* [1942] Ch. 328, restricted by *Re Edwards W.T.* [1948] Ch. 440.
[69] *Re Snowden* [1979] 2 All E.R. 172 at 179 (disagreeing with *Ottaway v Norman* [1971] 3 All E.R. 1325 at 1333), but if P has proved intent to create a trust on a balance of probabilities is it not illogical to require a higher standard of proof if the legatee is alleged to be fraudulent—see [1979] C.L.J. 260 (C. Rickett).

2–107   The obligation on the secret trustee, T, may be a simple obligation to transfer the bequeathed property to X, or to hold the property on trusts (whether of a fixed interest or discretionary nature) for specified beneficiaries, or to pass the property by will on to Z after T has had the income therefrom or the use thereof in T's lifetime,[70] or to pass by will to Z whatever remains of the property after bona fide resort to it by T in his lifetime.[71]

II. FULLY SECRET TRUSTS

2–108   A fully secret trust is one where neither the existence of the trust nor its terms are disclosed by the will.[72]

If a testator makes a valid will bequeathing or devising property to X, apparently beneficially, and communicates to X his intention that X is to hold the property on certain trusts or subject to certain conditions or charges, which X accepts either expressly by promise or impliedly by silence, oral evidence is admissible to prove both the existence and the terms of the trust or conditions or charges which, if clearly proved, X will be compelled to carry out: *Ottaway v Norman*, below. Nothing short of an express or implied acceptance by X will raise a trust (or condition or charge): *Wallgrave v Tebbs*, below. Communication and acceptance must be of a definite legally binding obligation of X, not of a mere hope or confidence expressed by the testator.[73] Communication and acceptance[74] may be effected at any time during the life of the testator, whether before or after the execution of the will and communication may be made through an agent.[75] It may also be made by handing to X a sealed envelope containing the terms of the trust, and requiring X not to open it until after the testator's death: *Re Keen*, below. If X is told in the testator's lifetime that he is to hold the property on trust, but is not informed of the terms of the trust, he holds the property on a resulting trust for the testator's residuary legatee or devisee, or if there is no such person, or the property is residuary property, then for the testator's intestate successors:[76] *Re Boyes*.[77]

---

[70] *Howell v Hyde* [2003] N.S.W.S.C. 732, so if T does not retain shares in a company as required but sells them and buys new shares the beneficiaries can claim the new shares.

[71] *Ottaway v Norman* [1972] Ch. 698.

[72] It can also arise in cases of intestacy: *Sellack v Harris* (1708) 2 Eq.Ca.Ab. 46.

[73] See *Kasperbauer v Griffith* [2000] W.T.L.R. 333 at 343 *Att.-Gen. v Chamberlain* (1904) 90 L.T. 581; *Re Snowden* [1979] Ch. 528 at 534. Whether the obligation is technically a trust or a condition or a charge (see para.3–23) it seems that equity will intervene.

[74] The full extent of the property to be covered by the obligation must be communicated and accepted so that where a secret trust for a £5,000 legacy has been communicated to and accepted by the trustee and the legacy is increased by £5,000 in a further codicill but nothing said to the trustee the further £5,000 is not caught by the secret trust: *Re Colin Cooper* [1939] Ch. 580 at 811. The further £5,000 is taken beneficially by the fully secret "trustee."

[75] *Moss v Cooper* (1861) 1 J. & H. 352. If the agent were unauthorised but the legatee did not approach the testator to clarify the matter would this amount to acquiescence?

[76] If X himself is the residuary beneficiary or next-of-kin it seems the court should not impose an arbitrary salutary rule removing all temptation to make self-serving statements by prohibiting X from taking *qua* residuary beneficiary or next-of-kin. Only if X appeared to be lying and it was impossible to ascertain the trust terms should public policy prevent X from obtaining any advantage from his own wrong and pass the property to the person who would have taken under the intestacy rules if X had not survived the testator; *cf. Re Sigsworth* [1935] Ch. 89.

[77] (1884) 26 Ch.D. 531.

If X is not so told he takes the property beneficially as is also the case if X is told that he is to take the property subject to a condition or charge but is not informed of the terms of the condition or charge.

Wills Act 1837

Section 9.[78] "No will shall be valid unless—

2–109

(*a*) it is in writing, and signed by the testator, or by some other person in his presence and by his direction; and

(*b*) it appears that the testator intended by his signature to give effect to the will; and

(*c*) the signature is made or acknowledged by the testator in the presence of two or more witnesses present at the same time; and

(*d*) each witness either—

(i) attests and signs the will; or

(ii) acknowledges his signature, in the presence of the testator (but not necessarily in the presence of any other witness), but no form of attestation shall be necessary."

OTTAWAY v NORMAN

Chancery Division [1972] Ch. 698; [1972] 2 W.L.R. 50; [1971] 3 All E.R. 1325

A testator, Harry Ottaway, by will devised his bungalow (with fixtures, fittings and furniture) to his housekeeper Miss Hodges in fee simple and gave her a legacy of £1,500 and half the residue of his estate. It was alleged that Miss Hodges had orally agreed with the testator to leave the bungalow, etc., by her will to the plaintiffs, who were the testator's son and daughter-in-law, Mr. and Mrs. William Ottaway, and that she had also orally agreed to leave to them whatever money was left at her death. By her will Miss Hodges left all her property away from the plaintiffs, who thus brought an action against Miss Hodges' executor, Mr. Norman, for a declaration that the appropriate parts of Miss Hodges' estate were held by him on trust for the plaintiffs.

2–110

Brightman J. upheld the plaintiffs' claim except in respect of the moneys.

BRIGHTMAN J.: ". . . It will be convenient to call the person on whom such a trust is imposed the 'primary donee' and the beneficiary under that trust the 'secondary donee.' The essential elements which must be proved are: (i) the intention of the testator to subject the primary donee to an obligation in favour of the secondary donee; (ii) communication of that intention to the primary donee; and (iii) the acceptance of that obligation by the primary donee either expressly or by acquiescence. It is immaterial whether these elements precede or succeed the will of the donor. I am informed that there is no recent reported case where the obligation imposed on the primary donee is an obligation to make a will in favour of the secondary donee as distinct from some form of *inter vivos* transfer. But it does not

2–111

---

[78] Superseding the Statute of Frauds 1677, s.5 and itself substituted by Administration of Justice Act 1982, s.17.

seem to me that that can really be a distinction which can validly be drawn on behalf
of the defendant in the present case. The basis of the doctrine of a secret trust is the
obligation imposed on the conscience of the primary donee and it does not seem to
me that there is any materiality in the machinery by which the donor intends that
that obligation shall be carried out . . .

2–112   "I find as a fact that Harry Ottaway intended that Miss Hodges should be obliged
to dispose of the bungalow in favour of the plaintiffs at her death, that he
communicated that intention to Miss Hodges and that Miss Hodges accepted the
obligation. I find the same facts in relation to the furniture, fixtures and fittings
which passed to Miss Hodges under clause 4 of Harry Ottaway's will. I am not
satisfied that any similar obligation was imposed and accepted as regards any
contents of the bungalow which had not devolved on Miss Hodges under clause 4 of
Harry Ottaway's will.

"I turn to the question of money. In cross-examination William Ottaway said the
trust extended to the house, furniture and money:

> 'Everything my father left to Miss Hodges was to be in the trust. The trust
> comprised the lot. She could use the money as she liked. She had to leave my
> wife and me whatever money was left.'

2–113   In cross-examination Mrs. Ottaway said that her understanding was that Miss
Hodges was bound to make a will giving her and her husband the bungalow,
contents and any money she had left. "She could please herself about the money.
She did not have to save it for us. She was free to spend it." It seems to me that two
questions arise. First as a matter of fact what did the parties intend should be
comprised in Miss Hodges's obligation? All money which Miss Hodges had at her
death, including money which she had acquired before Harry's death and money she
acquired after his death from all sources? Or, only money acquired under Harry's
will? Secondly, if such an obligation existed would it as a matter of law create a valid
trust? On the second question I am content to assume for present purposes but
without so deciding that if property is given to the primary donee on the
understanding that the primary donee will dispose by his will of such assets, if any,
as he may have at his command at his death in favour of the secondary donee, a
valid trust is created in favour of the secondary donee which is in suspense during
the lifetime of the primary donee, but attaches to the estate of the primary donee at
the moment of the latter's death. There would seem to be at least some support for
this proposition in an Australian case to which I was referred: *Birmingham v
Renfrew*.[79] I do not, however, find sufficient evidence that it was Harry Ottaway's
intention that Miss Hodges should be compelled to leave all her money, from
whatever source derived, to the plaintiffs. This would seem to preclude her giving
even a small pecuniary legacy to any friend or relative. I do no think it is clear that
Harry Ottaway intended to extract any such far-reaching undertaking from Miss
Hodges or that she intended to accept such a wide obligation herself. Therefore the
obligation, if any, is in my view to be confined to money derived under Harry
Ottaway's will. If the obligation is confined to money derived under Harry Ottaway's
will, the obligation is meaningless and unworkable unless it includes the requirement that she shall keep such money separate and distinct from her own money. I
am certain that no such requirement was ever discussed or intended. If she had the
right to mingle her own money with that derived from Harry, there would be no
ascertainable property on which the trust could bite at her death.[80]

---

[79] (1937) 57 C.L.R. 666, para.2–152.
[80] On this principle see *Henry v Hammond* [1913] 2 K.B. 515 at 521; endorsed in *R. v Clowes* [1994] 2 All
E.R. 316 at 325.

"There is another difficulty. Does money in this context include only cash or cash **2–114** and investments, or all moveable property of any description? The evidence is quite inconclusive. In my judgment the plaintiff's claim succeeds in relation to the bungalow and in relation to the furniture, fixtures and fittings which devolved under clause 4 of Harry Ottaway's will subject, of course, to normal wastage and fair wear and tear, but not to any other assets."

III. HALF-SECRET TRUSTS

A half-secret trust is one where the existence of the trust is disclosed by the **2–115** will but the terms are not.

If a testator makes a valid will bequeathing or devising property to X on trust, without specifying in the will the objects of the trust, but communicates the objects to X *before or at the time of* the execution of the will, which states that the objects have been so communicated, and X accepts the trust then X will be compelled to carry out the trust for the specified objects:[81] *Blackwell v Blackwell*, below. If, however, the testator communicates the objects to X *after* the execution of the will, X will hold the property on trust, because the will has created a trust; but since the objects have not been effectively specified, the beneficial interest will belong to the testator's residuary legatee or devisee, or if there is no such person, or if the property is residuary property, to the testator's intestate successors[82]: *Re Keen*, below.

The supposed justification of this is that a testator cannot, through the **2–116** medium of a valid will which imposes a trust but does not create the beneficial interests of that trust, reserve to himself a power to create the beneficial interests in an informal non-testamentary manner, so giving the go-by to the requirements of the Wills Act 1837. After all, as we have seen, in the case of the probate doctrine of incorporation of documents by reference the documents must exist prior to or contemporaneously with the execution of the will, for to allow otherwise would be to give the go-by to the Wills Act. However, the doctrine of incorporation by reference operates within the ambit of the statutory formalities, whilst the whole justification for secret trusts is to impose them just where the statutory formalities have not been satisfied: they operate outside the will and independently of the Wills Act.[83] Fully secret trusts, allowing communication of the trusts

---

[81] The full extent of the property to be covered by the obligation must be communicated so that if £5,000 is bequeathed on a half-secret trust accepted by the trustee and then a codicil increases that sum to £15,000 but the trustee is not informed of this increase, the surplus £10,000 will not be held on the half-secret trust but on trust for the residuary legatee or next-of-kin: *cf. Re Colin. Cooper* [1939] Ch. 580 and 811. If the trustee had undertaken to hold the original legacy and anything extra that the testator might subsequently bequeath, then the trustee would be bound to hold everything bequeathed on the half-secret trust.

[82] If a testator, having created a valid half-secret trust, subsequently tells the trustee not to hold for the old beneficiaries but to hold for new beneficiaries the trust for the new beneficiaries will fail by *Re Keen*, and it is possible that the revocation of the old trusts will fall on the basis that it was conditional on the creation of valid new trusts: it will succeed if construed as unconditional (*cf.* conditional revocation of wills, *e.g. Re Finnemore* [1992] 1 All E.R. 800) so the property will pass to the residuary legatee (or the statutory next-of-kin).

[83] *Re Young* [1951] Ch. 344; *Re Gardner (No.2)* [1923] 2 Ch. 230; *Cullen v Att.-Gen. for N. Ireland* (1866) L.R. 1 H.L. 190 at 198 (in the tax context); *Blackwell v Blackwell* [1929] A.C. 318 at 340, 342; *Re Snowden* [1979] 2 All E.R. 172 at 177. However, as P. Critchley in (1999) 115 LQR 631 at 641 correctly states, "the mistake is to confuse 'outside the will' with 'outside the Wills Act' ": a disposition by way of secret trust is a testamentary disposition, being revocable and ambulatory, as made clear in section 1 of this Chapter, so as to fall within the Wills Act. It is the harmful effect of the secret trustee's wrongful conduct that justifies Equity's intervention.

between execution of the will and the testator's death, allow the go-by to be given to the Wills Act, and since a will is ambulatory, being of no effect till death, there is logically no difference between declarations of trusts before and after the will. After all, in the case of both fully and half-secret trusts communicated after the will it is fraudulent for X to deprive B of his beneficial interest which but for the testator relying on X's promise would have been secured to B by the testator altering his will, so choosing a compliant legatee as trustee. Logically, half-secret trusts in this respect should be assimilated to fully secret trusts, as in Ireland,[84] Australia's New South Wales[85] and most American jurisdictions,[86] rather than have a different rule based upon a misplaced analogy with the doctrine of incorporation by reference. At present, there are the following differences between half-secret trusts and the probate doctrine of incorporation;

2–117   (i) In half-secret trusts the will need not specify the type of communication with any precision; in incorporation by reference the will must refer to the document to be incorporated with sufficient precision to enable it to be identified.[87]

(ii) In half-secret trusts the communication may be oral; in incorporation by reference the document to be incorporated must be in writing.

(iii) In half-secret trusts the testator must take the intended trustee into his confidence; in incorporation by reference the intended trustee need not be told of the document to be incorporated. Indeed, incorporation by reference may be effected in cases of absolute gift as well as in cases of trust.

2–118   (iv) In half-secret trusts the names of the beneficiaries are not made public; in incorporation by reference the incorporated document is admitted to probate and so made public.

(v) A beneficiary under a half-secret trust who witnesses the will does not forfeit his beneficial interest, whereas a beneficiary named in an incorporated document who witnesses the will does.[88]

(vi) The interest of a beneficiary under a half-secret trust who predeceases the testator does not lapse (*sed quaere*, para.2–139): in like circumstances that of a beneficiary named in an incorporated document does.[89]

2–119   One special requirement for half-secret trusts which is inapposite for fully secret trusts and is probably derived from the false analogy with the probate doctrine of incorporation, is that the communication of the trusts and the terms of the trust must not conflict with the wording of the will, for to allow otherwise would be to allow oral evidence to contradict the express words of the will: *Re Keen*, below. Thus, leaving property to four persons

---

[84] *Re Browne* [1944] Ir. R. 90; 67 L.Q.R. 413 (L. A. Sheridan; *Re Prendiville* (unreported) noted [1992] Conv. 202 by J. Mee). If a testator expressly specifies that Irish law shall govern the validity of any half-secret trust he creates should English law nullify such choice on public policy grounds? See: Arts 6 and 18 Hague Trusts Convention at paras 13–30, 13–35.
[85] Ledgerwood v Petpetual Trustee Co. Ltd (1997) 41 N.S.W.L.R. 532.
[86] *Restatement of Trusts*, para.55(*c*)(*h*).
[87] *Re Edwards' W.T.* [1948] Ch. 440.
[88] *Re Young* [1951] Ch. 344.
[89] *Re Gardner (No. 2)* [1923] 2 Ch. 230; *Bizzey v Flight* (1876) 3 Ch.D. 269.

"to be dealt with in accordance with my wishes which I have made known *to them*" is ineffective to create a half-secret trust unless the wishes were communicated to all four:[90] communication to less than four would only be effective if the words "or any one or more of them" had been added.[91] Furthermore, if property is left by will to X as trustee, evidence is not admissible to show that X was meant to have some part of that property beneficially.[92]

By way of contrast if the wording of the will gives property "to X **2–120** absolutely" or "to X relying on him, but not by way of trust, to carry out my wishes . . ." then oral evidence is admissible to prove a fully-secret trust, contradicting the express words of the will, for to allow otherwise would be to allow the possibility of the perpetration of fraud: *Re Spencer's Will*.[93]

Should there really be such distinctions between fully- and half-secret trusts if their basis[94] is that whilst the will must first operate to vest the property in the secret trustee, thereafter the secret trusts themselves arise outside the will for equity "makes him do what the will in itself has nothing to do with; it lets him take what the will gives him and then makes him apply it as the court of conscience directs, and it does so in order to give effect to the wishes of the testator which would not otherwise be effectual"? Is it not illogical in the case of half-secret trusts for the court to concern itself so strictly with the wording of the will and to require communication of the trust in accordance therewith before or at the time of the will?

BLACKWELL v BLACKWELL

House of Lords [1929] A.C. 318; 98 L.J. Ch. 251; 140 L.T. 444 (Lord Hailsham L.C., **2–121** Viscount Sumner, Lords Buckmaster, Carson and Warrington)

A testator by a codicil bequeathed £12,000 to five persons upon trust to invest according to their discretion and "to apply the income . . . for the purposes indicated by me to them." Before the execution of the codicil the objects of the trust were communicated in outline to four of the legatees and in detail to the fifth, and the trust was accepted by all of them. The fifth legatee also made a memorandum, on the same day as (though a few hours after) the execution of the codicil, of the testator's instructions. The plaintiffs (the residuary legatees) now claimed a declaration that no valid trust in favour of the objects so communicated had been created, on the ground principally that parol evidence was inadmissible to establish the purposes indicated by the testator.

Eve J. and the Court of Appeal held that the evidence was admissible, and here **2–122** proved a valid secret trust for the persons named by the testator in his instructions to the legatees. The appellants appealed unsuccessfully.

---

[90] *Re Spence* [1949] W.N. 237 following *Re Keen*.
[91] "to them or either of them" was used in *Re Keen*.
[92] *Re Rees* [1950] Ch. 204; *Re Tyler* [1967] 1 W.L.R. 1269; *Re Pugh's W.T.* [1967] 1 W.L.R. 1262; *Re Baillie* (1886) 2 T.L.R. 660; *Re Marsten* [1953] N.Z.L.R. 456. *Aliter* if property given under a fully secret trust when the possibilities of trust, conditional gift and equitable charge have to be examined: *Irvine v Sullivan* (1869) L.R. 8 Eq. 673; *Re Foord* [1922] 2 Ch. 519.
[93] (1887) 57 L.T. 519; *Re Williams* [1933] 1 Ch. 244; *Irvine v Sullivan*, above; cf. *Re Falkiner* [1924] 1 Ch. 88; *Re Stirling* [1954] 1 W.L.R. 763.
[94] *Blackwell v Blackwell* [1929] A.C. 318 at 335; *Re Young* [1951] Ch. 344; *Re Snowden* [1979] 2 All E.R. 172 at 177.

VISCOUNT SUMNER: ". . . In itself the doctrine of equity, by which parol evidence is admissible to prove what is called 'fraud' in connection with secret trusts, and effect is given to such trusts when established, would not seem to conflict with any of the Acts under which from time to time the legislature has regulated the right of testamentary disposition. A court of conscience finds a man in the position of an absolute legal owner of a sum of money, which has been bequeathed to him under a valid will, and it declares that, on proof of certain facts relating to the motives and actions of the testator, it will not allow the legal owner to exercise his legal right to do what he will with his own. This seems to be a perfectly normal exercise of general equitable jurisdiction. The facts commonly, but not necessarily, involve some immoral and selfish conduct on the part of the legal owner. The necessary elements, on which the question turns, are intention, communication and acquiescence. The testator intends his absolute gift to be employed as he and not as the donee desires; he tells the proposed donee of this intention and, either by express promise or by the tacit promise, which is satisfied by acquiescence, the proposed donee encourages him to bequeath the money in the faith that his intentions will be carried out. For the prevention of fraud equity fastens on the conscience of the legatee a trust, a trust, that is, which otherwise would be inoperative; in other words it makes him do what the will in itself has nothing to do with; it lets him take what the will gives him and then makes him apply it as the court of conscience directs, and it does so in order to give effect to wishes of the testator which would not otherwise be effectual.

2–123   "To this, two circumstances must be added to bring the present case to the test of the general doctrine, first, that the will states on its face that the legacy is given on trust but does not state what the trusts are, and further contains a residuary bequest, and, second, that the legatees are acting with perfect honesty, seek no advantage to themselves, and only desire, if the court will permit them, to do what in other circumstances the court would have fastened it on their conscience to perform.

2–124   "Since the current of decisions down to *Re Fleetwood*[95] and *Re Huxtable*[96] has established that the principles of equity apply equally when these circumstances are present as in cases where they are not, the material question is whether and how the Wills Act affects this case. It seems to me that, apart from legislation, the application of the principle of equity which was made in *Fleetwood's* case and *Huxtable's* case was logical, and was justified by the same considerations as in the cases of fraud and absolute gifts. Why should equity forbid an honest trustee to give effect to his promise, made to a deceased testator, and compel him to pay another legatee, about whom it is quite certain that the testator did not mean to make him the object of his bounty? In both cases the testator's wishes are incompletely expressed in his will. Why should equity, over a mere matter of words, give effect to them in one case and frustrate them in the other? No doubt the words 'in trust' prevent the legatee from taking beneficially, whether they have simply been declared in conversation or written in the will, but the fraud, when the trustee, so called in the will, is also the residuary legatee, is the same as when he is only declared a trustee by word of mouth accepted by him. I recoil from interfering with decisions of long standing, which reject this anomaly, unless constrained by statute . . .

---

[95] (1880) 15 Ch.D. 594, where a testatrix by a codicil bequeathed to X all her personalty "to be applied as I have requested him to do." Before the execution of the codicil she had stated to X the trusts on which she intended the property to be held, and X made a memorandum of the details in her presence. Hall V.-C. held that external evidence was admissible to prove the terms of the understanding between X and the testatrix.
[96] [1902] 2 Ch. 793.

"The limits, beyond which the rules as to unspecified trusts must not be carried, **2–125** have often been discussed. A testator cannot reserve to himself a power of making future unwitnessed dispositions by merely naming a trustee and leaving the purposes of the trust to be supplied afterwards, nor can a legatee give testamentary validity to an unexecuted codicil by accepting an indefinite trust, never communicated to him in the testator's lifetime: *Johnson v Ball*,[97] *Re Boyes*[98] *Riordan v Banon*,[99] *Re Hetley*[1] To hold otherwise would indeed be to enable the testator to 'give the go-by' to the requirements of the Wills Act, because he did not choose to comply with them. It is communication of the purpose to the legatee, coupled with acquiescence or promise on his part, that removes the matter from the provision of the Wills Act and brings it within the law of trusts, as applied in this instance to trustees, who happen also to be legatees. . . ." *Appeal dismissed.*

RE KEEN, EVERSHED v GRIFFITHS

Court of Appeal [1937] Ch. 236; 106 L.J. Ch. 177; 156 L.T. 207; 53 T.L.R. 320; 81 S.J. 97; [1937] 1 All E.R. 452 (Wright M.R., Greene and Romer L.JJ.)

The testator by clause 5 of his will, dated August 11, 1932, gave to his executors **2–126** and trustees, Captain Hazelhurst and Mr. Evershed, the sum of £10,000 free of duty "to be held upon trust and disposed of by them among such person, persons or charities as may be notified by me to them or either of them during my lifetime, and in default of such notification and so far as such notification shall not extend I declare that the said sum of £10,000 or such part thereof as shall not be disposed of in manner aforesaid shall fall into and form part of my residuary estate." Earlier, on March 31, 1932, the testator had made a will containing an identical gift. He had on that date handed to Mr. Evershed a sealed envelope containing the name of the intended beneficiary, but he had not disclosed its contents to Mr. Evershed, having directed that it was not to be opened until after his death. Mr. Evershed regarded himself as having undertaken to hold the £10,000 in accordance with the directions contained in the sealed envelope. A new will was executed on August 11, 1932, but no fresh directions were given. Mr. Evershed still regarded himself as being bound by the previous communication. On the testator's death the question arose whether the £10,000 was held by Captain Hazelhurst and Mr. Evershed on trust for the intended beneficiary or whether it fell into residue. It was held by Farwell J. and the Court of Appeal that it fell into residue.

LORD WRIGHT M.R.: "Farwell J. . . . decided adversely to the claims of the lady **2–127** [the intended beneficiary] on the short ground that she could not prove that she was a person notified to the trustees by the testator during his lifetime within the words of clause 5 [of the will]. His opinion seems to be that the clause required the name and identity of the lady to be expressly disclosed to the trustees during the testator's lifetime, so that it was not sufficient to place these particulars in the physical possession of the trustees, or one of them, in the form of a memorandum which they were not to read till the testator's death.

"I am unable to accept this conclusion, which appears to me to put too narrow a construction on the word 'notified' as used in clause 5 in all the circumstances of the

---

[97] (1851) 5 De G. & Son 85.
[98] (1884) 26 Ch.D. 531.
[99] (1876) 10 I.R.Eq. 469.
[1] [1902] 2 Ch. 866.

case. To take a parallel, a ship which sails under sealed orders is sailing under orders though the exact terms are not ascertained by the captain till later. I note that the case of a trust, put into writing, which is placed in the trustees' hands in a sealed envelope, was hypothetically treated by Kay J. as possibly constituting a communication in a case of this nature[2] This, so far as it goes seems to support my conclusion. The trustees had the means of knowledge available whenever it became necessary and proper to open the envelope. I think Mr. Evershed was right in understanding that the giving of the sealed envelope was a notification within clause 5.

2–128   "This makes it necessary to examine the matter on a wider basis . . .

". . . The principles of law or equity relevant in a question of this nature have now been authoritatively settled or discussed by the House of Lords in *Blackwell v Blackwell*[3] [in the case of half-secret trusts and *McCormick v Grogan*[4] in the case of fully secret trusts. The Master of the Rolls then analysed the facts and decisions in those cases, and continued:] As, in my judgment, clause 5 should be considered as contemplating future dispositions, and as reserving to the testator the power of making such dispositions without a duly attested codicil, simply by notifying them during his lifetime, the principles laid down by Lord Sumner [in *Blackwell v Blackwell*] must be fatal to the appellant's claim. Indeed, they would be equally fatal even on the construction for which Mr. Roxburgh contended, that the clause covered both anterior or contemporaneous notifications and future notifications. The clause would be equally invalid, but as already explained I cannot accept that construction. In *Blackwell v Blackwell*[5] *Re Fleetwood*[6] and *Re Huxtable*[7] the trusts had been specifically declared to some or all of the trustees, at or before the execution of the will, and the language of the will was consistent with that fact. There was, in these cases, no reservation of a future power to change the trusts, in whole or in part. Such a power would involve a power to change a testamentary disposition by an unexecuted codicil, and would violate section 9 of the Wills Act. This was so held in *Re Hetley*.[8] *Johnson v Balt*[9] is, again, a somewhat different example of the rule against dispositions made subsequently to the date of the will in cases where the will in terms leaves the property on trust, and shows that the position may be different from the position where the will in terms leaves the gift absolutely. The trusts referred to, but undefined in the will, must be described in the will as established prior to, or at least contemporaneously with, its execution.

2–129   "But there is a still further objection which, in the present case, renders the appellant's claim unenforceable: the trusts which it is sought to establish by parol evidence would be inconsistent with the express terms of the will. That such an objection is fatal appears from the cases already cited, such as *Re Huxtable*. In that case, an undefined trust of money for charitable purposes was declared in the will, as in respect of the whole corpus and, accordingly, evidence was held inadmissible that the charitable trust was limited to the legatee's life, so that he was free to dispose of the corpus after his death. Similarly in *Johnson v Ball* the testator by the will left the property to trustees, upon the uses contained in a letter signed 'by them and myself': it was held that that evidence was not admissible to show that, though

---

[2] *Re Boyes* (1884) 26 Ch.D. 531 at 536.
[3] [1929] A.C. 318; see above, para.2–121.
[4] (1869) L.R. 4 H.L. 82.
[5] [1929] A.C. 318.
[6] (1880) 15 Ch.D. 594.
[7] [1902] 2 Ch. 793.
[8] [1902] 2 Ch. 866.
[9] (1851) 5 De G. & Sm. 85.

no such letter was in existence at the date of the will, the testator had made a subsequent declaration of trust; the court held that these trusts could not be enforced. Lord Buckmaster in *Blackwell's* case[10] described *Johnson v Ball* as an authority pointing 'to a case where the actual trusts were left over after the date of the will to be subsequently determined by the testator.' That, in his opinion, would be a contravention of the Wills Act. I know of no authority which would justify such a contravention. Lord Buckmaster also quotes[11] the grounds on which Parker V.-C. based his decision as being both 'that the letter referred to in the will had no existence at the time when the will was made and that, supposing it referred to a letter afterwards signed, it is impossible to give effect to it as a declaration of the trusts since it would admit the document as part of the will and it was unattested.'

"In the present case, while clause 5 refers solely to a future definition, or to future **2–130** definitions, of the trust, subsequent to the date of the will, the sealed letter relied on as notifying the trust was communicated (as I find the facts) before the date of the will. That it was communicated to one trustee only, and not to both, would not, I think, be an objection (see Lord Warrington's observation in the *Blackwell* case).[12] But the objection remains that the notification sought to be put in evidence was anterior to the will, and hence not within the language of clause 5, and inadmissible simply on that ground, as being inconsistent with what the will prescribes. . . ." *Appeal dismissed.*[13]

IV. THE BASIS OF SECRET TRUSTS

Before dealing with the basis of secret trusts it is as well to examine certain **2–131** unusual secret trust situations since they will shed light thereon.

(i) *Attestation of will by secret beneficiary*

Section 15 of the Wills Act 1837: "If any person shall attest the execution of any will to whom or to whose wife or husband any beneficial devise, legacy, estate, interest, gift, or appointment, of or affecting any real or personal estate (other than and except charges and directions for the payment of any debt or debts), shall be thereby given or made, such devise, legacy, estate, interest, gift, or appointment shall, so far only as concerns such person attesting the execution of such will, or the wife or husband of such person, or any person claiming under such person or wife or husband, be utterly null and void, and such person so attesting shall be admitted as a witness to prove the execution of such will, or to prove the validity or invalidity thereof, notwithstanding such devise, legacy, estate, interest, gift, or appointment mentioned in such will."

Section 1 of the Wills Act 1968: "For the purposes of section 15 of the **2–132** Wills Act 1837 the attestation of a will by a person to whom or to whose spouse there is given or made any such disposition as is described in that

---

[10] [1929] A.C. 318, 331.
[11] *ibid.* at 330.
[12] *ibid.* at 341.
[13] In *Re Bateman's W.T.* [1970] 1 W.L.R. 1463; [1970] 3 All E.R. 817, *Re Keen* was followed without argument where a testator had directed his trustees to set aside £24,000 and pay the income thereof "to such persons and in such proportions *as shall* be stated by me in a sealed letter to my trustees": "[The direction] clearly imports that the testator may, in the future after the date of the will, give a sealed letter to his trustees. It is impossible to confine the words to a sealed letter already so given. If that be the true construction of the wording it is not in dispute that the direction is invalid": *per* Pennycuick V.-C. at 1468 and 820, respectively.

section shall be disregarded if the will is duly executed without his attestation and without that of any other such person."

In Re Young[14] there was a bequest by a testator to his wife with a direction that on her death she should leave the property for the purposes which he had communicated to her. Before execution of his will, a direction was given by him and accepted by wife that she would leave a legacy of £2,000 to testator's chauffeur. The chauffeur had witnessed the testator's will. Danckwerts J. held that the chauffeur had not forfeited his legacy under s.15 of the Wills Act 1837 for "the whole theory of the formulation of a secret trust is that the Wills Act has nothing to do with the matter because the forms required by the Wills Act are entirely disregarded, since the persons do not take by virtue of the gift in the will, but by virtue of the secret trusts imposed upon the beneficiary who does in fact take under the will."

2–133   But why is it that the secret beneficiary does not obtain an interest in the testator's property (or rights against the secret trustee) at the date of the testator's death by virtue of a testamentary disposition within the Wills Act when, until the testator dies the relevant property is his absolutely to deal with as he pleases? Why should the attesting secret beneficiary be allowed to benefit if the function of s.15 is to ensure there is an impartial witness with nothing to gain or lose by his testimony? He may know he is a beneficiary at the time of attestation. He could be lying if he said he did not know: for this reason a beneficiary taking on the face of a will is subject to s.15 even if, in fact, he just witnessed the signature at the end of the will and so did not know of its contents.

2–134   It seems likely that persons taking under a fully secret trust would receive nothing if the trustee taking absolutely beneficially on the face of the will had witnessed the will so he should receive nothing on which the trusts could bite,[15] though some might argue[16] that the admission of oral evidence to establish the trusteeship should carry the day: half-secret trustees taking as trustees on the face of the will clearly cannot infringe s.15 of the Wills Act 1837.

(ii) *Trustee predeceasing testator*

2–135   Generally, a gift by will to X is said to lapse if X predeceases the testator and the gift fails.[17] If, however, the gift is to X on trust for B and B survives the testator then despite X's predecease the gift will not lapse for equity will not allow a trust to fail for want of a trustee: the testator's personal representative will take over as trustee.[18]

---

[14] [1951] Ch. 344. Civil partners are now treated like husbands and wives: Civil Partnership Act 2004 Sch.4 para.3.

[15] Compare "trustee predeceasing testator" in following paragraph.

[16] See *Inchiquin v French* (1745) 1 Cox Eq. Cas. 1.

[17] Exceptionally, if issue predecease a testator leaving issue of their own surviving the testator, the gift takes effect in favour of the surviving issue: Wills Act 1837, s.33. The persons benefiting from this exception will not be able to disregard the deceased legatee-trustee's undertaking: *cf. Huguenin v Baseley* (1807) 14 Ves. 273.

[18] *Sonley v Clock Makers' Company* (1780) 1 Bro.C.C. 81; *Mallott v Wilson* [1903] 2 Ch. 494; *Re Smirthwaite's Trusts* (1871) L.R. 11 Eq. 251; *Re Armitage* [1972] Ch. 438. See para.8–39.

According to dicta of Cozens-Hardy L.J. in *Re Maddock*,[19] a case concerning a fully secret trust, "if the legatee renounces and disclaims, or dies in the lifetime of the testator, the persons claiming under the memorandum [*i.e.* the secret trusts] can take nothing." This is based upon the view that the secret trusts only arise when the property intended to be the subject-matter of the trust vests in someone under the terms of the will.[20] It follows that if by reason of the fully secret trustee's death the property does not so vest then no trust can arise.

(iii) *Trustee disclaiming after testator's death*

A beneficiary under a will after the testator's death can always disclaim a legacy or devise before acceptance and a person can always disclaim the office of trustee before acceptance.[21] If a person named as a half-secret trustee disclaimed the office then it would seem clear that the testator's personal representative would hold on the trusts for the secret beneficiaries. Where disclaimer by fully secret trustees is concerned although Cozens-Hardy L.J. opined in *Re Maddock*, above that no trusts would arise in such a case there are contrary dicta of Lord Buckmaster and Lord Warrington in *Blackwell v Blackwell*:[22] "In the case where no trusts are mentioned the legatee might defeat the whole purpose by renouncing the legacy and the breach of trust would not in that case inure to his own benefit, but I entertain no doubt that the court having once admitted the evidence of the trust, would interfere to prevent its defeat." Lord Buckmaster's dicta presuppose the existence of a trust whereof the legatee is in breach and apply the maxim that equity will not allow a trust to fail for want of a trustee. Whether the trusts arose on the testator's death or at an earlier time is not stated by Lord Buckmaster. By analogy with mutual wills the testator's death should be the appropriate time, it being immaterial whether or not gifts are disclaimed.[23] Disclaimer would, however, be material if the testator's orally communicated intentions to the legatee were construed not as imposing trusts but as conferring a gift subject to a personal condition.[24]

2–136

(iv) *Trustee revoking acceptance before the testator's death*

Compare the three following examples:

2–137

---

[19] [1902] 2 Ch. 220 at 231.

[20] "The obligation can be enforced if the donee becomes entitled": *per* Romer J. in *Re Gardner* [1923] 2 Ch. 230, 232. "The doctrine must, in principle, rest on the assumption that the will has first operated according to its terms": *per* Viscount Sumner [1929] A.C. 318, 334. "The whole basis of secret trusts is that they operate outside the will, changing nothing that is written in it and allowing it to operate according to its tenor, but then fastening a trust on to the property in the hands of the recipient": *per* Megarry V.-C. *Re Snowden* [1979] 2 All E.R. 172 at 177.

[21] *Smith v Smith* [2001] 1 W.L.R. 1937; *Re Sharman's W.T.* [1942] Ch. 311.

[22] [1929] A.C. 318 at 328, 341.

[23] *Re Dale* [1993] 4 All E.R. 129; see also *Blackwell v Blackwell* [1929] A.C. 318 at 341, *per* Lord Warrington: "It has long been settled that if a gift be made to a person in terms absolutely but in fact upon a trust communicated to the legatee and accepted by him, the legatee, would be bound to give effect to the trust, on the principle that the gift may be presumed to have been made on the faith of his acceptance of the trust, and a refusal after the death of the testator to give effect to it would be a fraud on the part of the legatee." See also (1972) 36 Conv. (N.S.) 113 (R. Burgess).

[24] See at para.3–25.

(a) Testator, T, bequeaths £10,000 to X absolutely, having told X that
     he wants X to hold the money on trust for Y. A year later X tells T
     that he is no longer prepared to hold the money on trust for anyone.
     Five years later T dies without having changed his will;

(b) The bequest as before but X tells T that he is no longer prepared to
     hold the money on trust for anyone only three days before T dies of
     a week-long illness;

(c) The bequest as before but T is incurably insane when informed by X
     as before and T remains so till his death five years later.

2–138 Does X take the £10,000 beneficially only in case (a)? Is X under any
obligations before T's death? What if the trust had been half secret?

(v) *Secret beneficiary predeceasing testator*

2–139   If T by will left property to X on trust expressly for B, and B predeceased
T, the gift to B would lapse just as an *inter vivos* trust for B fails if B is not
alive when the trust is created.[25] One would have imagined that the result
would be the same if T, having asked X to hold on trust for B, left property
"to X absolutely" or "to X upon trusts that I have communicated to him."
However, in *Re Gardner (No.2)*[26] Romer J. held that B's interest did not
lapse as B obtained an interest as soon as T communicated the terms of the
trust to X and X accepted the trust. B's interest derived not from T's will
(to which the rules regarding lapse would have applied) but under the
agreement between T and X. "The rights of the parties appear to me to be
exactly the same as though the husband (X), after the memorandum had
been communicated to him by the testatrix (T) in the year 1909 had
executed a declaration of trust binding himself to hold any property that
should come to him upon his wife's (T's) partial intestacy upon trust as
specified in the memorandum."[27]

     Such a declaration, however, does not create a properly constituted trust
since the subject-matter is future property.[28] It may be that Romer J.
considered that the vesting of the property in X on T's death in 1919
completely constituted the trust[29] but on the terms of the memorandum.
However, the interests of those taking under the memorandum only
became vested proprietory interests after T's death: until then the so-
called interests only amounted to mere hope that T would not change her
mind and make a different testamentary disposition or die insolvent and

---

[25] *Re Corbishley's Trusts* (1880) 14 Ch.D. 846; *Re Tilt* (1896) 74 L.T. 163, both concerned with personalty
where a gift to B gave B an absolute interest: for realty a gift by will after 1837 to B gave an absolute
interest whilst till 1925 a gift by deed to B gave B only a life interest in the absence of proper words of
limitation.

[26] [1923] 2 Ch. 230.

[27] *ibid.* at 233. Here Romer J. may have been thinking that if B had an absolute vested interest in a 1909
settlement then funds accruing under a will taking effect in 1919 would be treated as an accretion to the
1909 settlement rather than as comprised in a separate 1919 referential settlement: see *Re Playfair* [1951]
Ch. 4.

[28] *Re Ellenborough* [1903] 1 Ch. 697; *Re Northcliffe* [1925] Ch. 651; *Williams v C.I.R.* [1965] N.Z.L.R. 395, see
at para.4–92.

[29] *cf. Re Ralli's W.T.* [1964] Ch. 288; *Re Adlard* [1954] Ch. 29.

that X would not revoke his acceptance, so that ultimately X would receive property to hold on trust for them. Just as an *inter vivos* trust constituted by X in 1919 declaring himself trustee of certain property for the benefit of A, B and C equally would give B no interest, if at that date B were dead and so no longer an existing legal entity, so the trust arising in *Re Gardner* after T's death in 1919 could give B no interest, B being dead by that date. It makes no difference that whilst B was alive he might have had some sort of hope that if he lived long enough a trust might come into existence for his benefit at a later date. The authority of *Re Gardener* is thus very weak indeed.

(vi) *Bequest to two on a promise by one*

The orthodox position is laid down in *Re Stead*[30] by Farwell J.:   **2–140**

"If A induced B either to make, or to leave unrevoked, a will leaving property to A and C as tenants in common, by expressly promising or tacitly consenting, that he and C will carry out the testator's wishes and C knows nothing of the matter until after the testator's death, A is bound, but C is not bound: *Tee v Ferris*;[31] the reason stated being, that to hold otherwise would be to enable one beneficiary to deprive the rest of their benefits by setting up a secret trust. If, however, the gift were to A and C as joint tenants, the authorities have established a distinction between those cases in which the will is made on the faith of an antecedent promise by A and those in which the will is left unrevoked on the faith of a subsequent promise. In the former case the trust binds both A and C: *Russell v Jackson*;[32] *Jones v Bradley*,[33] the reason stated being that no person can claim an interest under a fraud committed by another; in the latter case A and not C is bound: *Burney v Macdonald*[34] and *Moss v Cooper*,[35] the reason stated being that the gift is not tainted with any fraud in procuring the execution of the will. Personally, I am unable to see any difference between a gift made on the faith of an antecedent promise and a gift left unrevoked on the faith of a subsequent promise to carry out the testator's wishes; but apparently a distinction has been made by the various judges who have had to consider the question. I am bound, therefore, to decide in accordance with these authorities . . ."

However, Bryn Perrins in (1972) 88 L.Q.R. 225 examines these author-   **2–141** ities to different effect, persuasively concluding that the only question to be asked is: was the gift to C induced by A's promise? If yes, C is bound; if no, he is not:

---

[30] [1900] 1 Ch. 231, 247, The principles here discussed apply only to fully secret trusts. In the case of half-secret trusts, if the will permits communication to be made to one only of several trustees, a communication made before or at the time of the execution of the will to one only of the trustees binds all of them, the trust being a joint office: *Blackwell v Blackwell* [1929] A.C. 318; *Re Spence* [1949] W.N. 237; *Ward v Duncombe* [1893] A.C. 369; *Re Gardom* [1914] 1 Ch. 662 at 673.
[31] (1856) 2 K. & J. 357.
[32] (1852) 10 Hare 204.
[33] (1868) L.R. 3 Ch. 362.
[34] (1845) 15 Sim. 6.
[35] (1861) 1 J. & H. 352.

BRYN PERRINS (1972) 88 L.Q.R. 225

2–142 "The reasons stated by Farwell J. in *Re Stead* are at first sight contradictory. One consideration is that a person must not be allowed, by falsely setting up a secret trust, to deprive another of his benefits under the will. Apparently this is decisive if the parties are tenants in common but not if they are joint tenants. On the other hand one person must not profit by the fraud of another. Apparently this is decisive only if the parties are joint tenants and not if they are tenants in common. Yet again it is apparently only fraud in procuring the execution of a will that is relevant, and not fraud in inducing a testator not to revoke a will already made. All very confusing, but add *Huguenin v Baseley*[36] and the whole picture springs into focus and the confusion disappears. Returning to A and C, whether they are tenants in common or joint tenants, C is not bound *if his gift was not induced by the promise of A* because to hold otherwise would be to enable A to deprive C of his benefit by setting up a secret trust; but C is bound *if his gift was induced by the promise of A* because he cannot profit by the fraud of another; and if the trust was communicated to A after the will was made, then C takes free *if this gift was not* induced by the promise of A because if there is no inducement there is no fraud affecting C.

2–143 This, it is submitted, is what was decided by the cases cited in Farwell J.'s judgment."

CONCLUSIONS

In the light of the foregoing discussion of unusual secret trust situations it will be seen that the title of a beneficiary under a fully secret and a half-secret trust arises outside the will and is regarded by many judges[37] as arising outside the Wills Act and so not by virtue of a testamentary disposition. Even then, it seems that, except in the case of disclaimer by a fully secret trustee after the testator's death, such a trust is conditional and dependent upon the gift by will taking effect according to its terms. Section 9 of the Wills Act 1837 should however, be relevant because the intended secret trust property belongs absolutely and indefeasibly to the testator who is free to deal with it howsoever he pleases before he dies,[38] so that the disposition thereof by the conduct outside his will[39] is a testamentary disposition.[40] How then does there arise an equitable obligation binding the trustee's conscience?

2–144 The equitable principle that equity will not allow a statute to be used as an instrument of fraud was the basis for not allowing the Statute of Frauds 1677 to be invoked by persons intended to be secret trustees of testamentary gifts or to be trustees of inter vivos trusts of land.[41] The provisions of

---

[36] (1807) 14 Ves. 273. This is authority for the principle, "No man may profit by the fraud of another." A widow was persuaded by Rev. Baseley, who managed her property, to settle some of it on him and his family. Later, she married Mr. Huguenin and sought to set aside the conveyance for undue influence. She succeeded, for Lord Eldon held that the Rev. Baseley's wife and children, though innocent, were not purchasers but volunteers who could not profit from Baseley's fraud and retain their vested interests.

[37] *Re Snowden* [1979] 2 All E.R. 172 at 177, *Re Young* [1951] Ch. 344, *Re Gardner (No.2)* [1923] 2 Ch. 230, *Blackwell v Blackwell* [1929] 2 A.C. 318 at 340, 342.

[38] *Kasperbauer v Griffith* [2000] W.T.L.R. 333 at 343.

[39] Since secret trusts operate outside the will it is illogical in the case of a half-secret trust not to allow communication after the date of the will but before the testator's death and claim that otherwise the Wills Act would be avoided: see above, para.2–116.

[40] See P. Critchley (1999) 115 L.Q.R. 631 at 639–641.

[41] *McCormick v Grogan* (1868) L.R. 4 H.L. 82 at 88–89; *Jones v Badley* (1868) 3 Ch. App. 362 at 364; *Wattgrave v Tebbs* (1855) 2 K. & J. 313 at 321–322; *Rochefoucauld v Boustead* [1897] 1 Ch. 196.

the 1677 Statute are now to be found in the Wills Act 1837 and the Law of Property Act 1925. The equitable principle should apply since there would be fraud if the secret trustee attempted to rely on the statute, whether dishonestly to try to retain a beneficial interest or to defeat a beneficial interest which he had led the testator to believe would belong to another. There would be not just a fraud on the testator in betraying the testator's confidence[42] but there would be harmful fraud on the secret beneficiary who would be deprived of the benefit which, but for the trustee agreeing to carry out the testator's wishes, would surely have been secured for him by other means.[43] Thus, in a fully secret trust and also in a half-secret trust the trustee holds the testator's property not on resulting or constructive trust for the testator's residuary legatee (or next of kin as the case may be) but on the express trust for the beneficiary: it would be unconscionable for the trustee to hold the property otherwise by invoking the Wills Act for that would enable statute to be used as an instrument of fraud. Thus, C can enforce his interest where A devises land by will to B on an oral trust for C.[44]

2–145 The same result can better be achieved in accordance with statute if one treats such trusts as constructive trusts—exempted from LPA, s. 53(1) by s.53(2)—on the ground that such trusts, unlike ordinary express trusts which can be created unilaterally, depend crucially upon the trustee's express or tacit promise to honour the trust in favour of the secret beneficiary.[45] As Robert Walker LJ states,[46] "There must be an agreement between A and B conferring a benefit on C because it is the agreement which would make it unconscionable for B to resile from his agreement." This was his view of secret trusts as well as mutual wills: "both doctrines show equity intervening to prevent unconscionable conduct".[47]

Section 4. Post Mortem Trusts: Mutual Wills[48]

2–146 The term "mutual wills" is used to describe documents of a testamentary character made as the result of a contract between husband and wife, or other persons, to create irrevocable interests in favour of ascertainable beneficiaries. The revocable nature of the wills under which the interests are created is fully recognised by the court of probate,[49] but, in certain circumstances, the court of equity will protect and enforce the interests

---

[42] As stated in *Re Dale* [1993] 4 All E.R. 129 at 142 in relation to mutual wills made by two testators, T1 and T2, where T1 dies and T2 makes a will departing from what was agreed, "I am unable to see why it should be any the less a fraud on T1 if the agreement was that each testator should leave his or her property to particular beneficiaries, *e.g.* their children, rather than to each other."

[43] D.R. Hodge [1980] Conv. 341. This point seems overlooked by B. Perrins in [1985], Conv. 248.

[44] *Ottaway v Norman* [1972] Ch. 698 and see above, para.2–24. In *Re Baillie* (1886) 2 T.L.R. 660, 661 a half-secret trust of land failing for one reason also failed for not complying with written formalities: this seems erroneous.

[45] In *Re Cleaver* [1981] 2 All E.R. 1018 at 1024 Nourse J. categorised secret trusts as constructive trusts and Peter Gibson LJ endorsed this in *Kasperbauer v Griffith* [2000] W.T.L.R. 333 at 342.

[46] *Gillett v Holt* [2000] 2 All E.R. 289 at 305.

[47] *ibid.* at 304.

[48] See Oakley's *Constructive Trusts* (3rd ed.), Chap. 5; (1989) 105 L.Q.R. 534 (C.E.F. Rickett).

[49] *Re Heys* [1914] P. 192.

created by the agreement despite the revocation of the will by one party
after the death of the other without having revoked his will.

2–147   A typical case of mutual wills arises in the following circumstances:
H(usband) and W(ife) agree to execute mutual wills (or a joint will) leaving
their respective properties to the survivor of them for life, with remainder
to the same ultimate beneficiary (B). H dies, W makes a fresh will leaving
her property away from B to her second husband (S).

2–148   In these circumstances, H's will (or the joint will) is admitted to probate
on his death and, under it, W gets a life interest and B an interest in
remainder. On W's death, her second will is admitted to probate. Under it
her property vests in her personal representatives upon trust, not for S, but
to give effect to the terms of the agreement upon which the mutual wills
were made, *i.e.* upon trust for B.

B's interest in W's property arises as soon as H dies. It prevails over the
interest of S therein by virtue of the maxim that "where the equities are
equal the first in time prevails." Indeed, if B survives H but predeceases W
his interest in W's property does not lapse but is payable to his personal
representatives, and forms part of his estate.[50] B's interest arises irrespective of whether W disclaims her benefit under H's will[51] and even if H and
W left no property to each other, leaving everything to B.[52] It is the death[53]
of H, no longer having the opportunity to revoke his own will, which
concludes performance of the contract and renders the will of W irrevocable in equity, though, it is always revocable at law.

2–149   The courts will not infer a trust merely because mutual wills are made in
almost identical terms. There must be evidence of an agreement to create
interests under the mutual wills which are intended to be irrevocable after
the death of the first to die. As Leggatt L.J. stated a *Re Goodchild*.[54] "A key
feature of mutual wills is the irrevocability of the mutual intentions. Not
only must they be [contractually] binding when made, but the testators must
have undertaken, and so must be bound, not to change their intentions
after the death of the first testator." Where there is no such evidence the
fact that the survivor takes an absolute interest is a factor against the
implication of an agreement.[55] Where, however, the evidence is clear, as,
for example, where it is contained in recitals in the wills themselves, the fact
that each testator gave the other an absolute interest with a substitutional
gift in the event of the other's prior death does not prevent a trust from
arising.[56]

2–150   The requirement for mutual wills sometimes expressed as the need for
"an agreement not to revoke" the wills is more aptly expressed as the need
for "acceptance of an obligation imposed by the other party" as the

---

[50] *Re Hagger* [1930] 2 Ch. 190.
[51] *Dufour v Pereira* (1769) 1 Dick. 419 at 421; *Stone v Hoskins* [1905] P. 194 at 197; *Re Hagger* [1930] 2 Ch.
190; J. D. B. Mitchell (1951) 14 M.L.R. 136 at 138.
[52] *Re Dale* [1994] Ch. 31.
[53] *Quaere*: would incurable insanity on the part of H have the same effect? Consider Mental Health Act
1983, ss.95, 96.
[54] [1997] 3 All E.R. 63 at 71.
[55] *Re Oldham* [1925] Ch. 75.
[56] *Re Green* [1951] Ch. 148.

obligation may well allow the will of the survivor to be revoked so long as a new will is made giving effect to the agreed arrangements.[57] The acceptance of an obligation may be difficult to prove in husband and wife situations where there is less likely to be an intention to impose legal relationships, neither party making the gifts by will on the faith of a promise by the other to accept legal obligations, but instead, making the gifts without any strings attached, confidently assuming the other party will do as asked.[58]

The principle is that the survivor becomes a trustee for the performance **2–151** of the mutual agreement after the death of the first to die. Accordingly, if the agreement is too vague to be enforced, there will be no trust. Subject to this, however, the agreement can define the property, which is to be subject to the trust, in any way it pleases. The trust may give the survivor nothing[59] or just give the survivor a life interest in all or a specific part of the deceased's property or it may also provide for the survivor to have a life interest in all or a specific part of his own property at the date of death of the deceased.[60] The life interest may even extend to capital acquired after the deceased's death though practical problems arise if there is no power of appointment of capital in favour of the life tenant.[61] Sometimes, it may appear that the survivor is to be absolute owner of the deceased's property passing to him under the will and of his own existing and subsequently acquired property, but that he is supposed to be under some binding obligation to bequeath whatever he has left at his death to the agreed beneficiaries.[62]

A purported trust of such uncertain property would normally be void,[63] **2–152** but it seems that the express contract between the parties that led the party first dying to leave his property in the agreed manner may give the ultimate beneficiaries a remedy by way of a "floating" trust, suspended during the survivor's lifetime and crystallising into a proper trust on his death: *Re Cleaver*, below. The survivor will be under a fiduciary duty not to make *inter vivos* gifts deliberately intended to defeat the contract and, presumably, the proceeds of sale of any property within the fiduciary obligation and any property purchased with such proceeds will be subject to such obligation.[64] Perhaps the "floating" trust may develop doctrinally by analogy with the floating charge over company assets and crystallise not only on the death of the survivor but also when the survivor attempts to make a mala fide gift or sale at an undervalue designed to defeat his contract,[65] especially if such intent is expressed in the contract.

---

[57] *Lewis v Cotton* [2001] W.T.L.R. 1117 at 1129, NZCA.
[58] *Gray v Perpetual Trustee Ltd* [1928] A.C. 391; *Re Oldham* [1925] Ch 75, *Re Goodchild* [1997] 3 All E.R. 63.
[59] *Re Dale* [1994] Ch. 31.
[60] *Re Hagger* [1930] 2 Ch. 190.
[61] J. D. B. Mitchell (1953) 14 M.L.R. 136; R. Burgess (1972) 36 Conv. 113.
[62] Such beneficiaries may well not have vested interests liable to be divested: the parties probably intend them to benefit only if alive on the survivor's death so that if they all predecease the survivor his fiduciary obligation will cease.
[63] *Re Jones* [1898] 1 Ch. 438 *Re Goodchild* [1997] 3 All E.R. 63 at 76 and see at para.3–80.
[64] The fiduciary relationship should give rise to a right to trace. The survivor might be compared to an executor who has full title to the testator's estate in which the beneficiaries have no proprietary interest (see *Commissioner for Stamp Duties v Livingston* [1965] A.C. 694 at 701; *Re Diplock* [1948] Ch. 465). Because the obligation is rather nebulous a well-advised testator should leave the property to S for life, remainder to B but give S and the trustees a joint power to appoint capital to S.
[65] *Healey v Brown* [2002] W.T.L.R. 849, para.13.

2–153   Before the death of the first to die the agreement is a contractual one made in consideration of the mutual promises of H and W for the benefit of B, who neither is a party to the contract nor supplies consideration.[66] Whether H would be in breach of the contract if he told W that he no longer intended to give effect to their arrangement, or if his will was automatically revoked by remarriage to someone else after divorcing W, or if he revoked his will without informing W but predeceased W, depends on the construction of the contract. Prime facie it seems that the contract will be presumed revocable upon notice to the other party or upon the will automatically being revoked by marriage so as not to be broken if such circumstances occur.[67] However, if H makes a new will containing new arrangements without informing W, but predeceases W, it seems that W can sue H's executors for damages for losses flowing from the breach of contract (though W will be released from her obligations under contract) or for specific performance if willing to fulfil her obligations.[68]

2–154   If H died first, by his will carrying into effect the mutual arrangement, then, in order to protect B and to prevent W repudiating her obligations, a constructive trust is imposed since B is unable to bring an action for specific performance[69] of the express terms of the contract or was unable until advantage could be taken of the Contracts (Rights of Third Parties) Act 1999. If the contract relates not just to whatever assets might be owned at death but to interests in land then equity will not allow LPA 1925, s.40 or now Law of Property (Miscellaneous Provisions) Act 1989, s.2 to be pleaded since this would be to use the statute as an instrument of fraud.[70]

2–155   It seems that the principles underlying mutual wills extend to an agreement subsequent to the making of the wills[71] and to an agreement between joint tenants not to sever their interest on terms that the survivor will dispose of the asset in an agreed manner.[72]

RE CLEAVER (DECEASED)

Chancery Division [1981] 1 W.L.R. 939; [1981] 2 All E.R. 1018

The testator and testatrix married in their seventies and in 1974 made wills on the same date and in similar terms, leaving their property to each other absolutely and in default of survival to the plaintiffs. The testator died in 1975. The testatrix made a new will in 1977 and cut out the plaintiffs and died in 1978. The plaintiffs successfully claimed her executors held her estate on the terms of the 1974 will.

---

[66] *Dufour v Pereira* (1769) 1 Dick. 419 at 421; *Lord Walpole v Lord Oxford* (1797) 3 Ves. 402; *Gray v Perpetual Trustee Co.* [1928] A.C. 391; *Birmingham v Renfrew* (1937) 57 C.L.R. 666.
[67] *Dufour v Pereira*, above at 420; *Stone v Hoskins* [1905] P. 194 at 197; *Re Marsland* [1939] Ch. 820; *Lewis v Cotton* [2001] W.T.L.R. 1117 at 1129.
[68] See C. E. F. Rickett (1991) 54 M.L.R. 581 and M. Cope, *Constructive Trusts*, pp.534–537.
[69] *Birmingham v Renfrew* (1937) 57 C.L.R. 666; *Re Dale* [1994] Ch. 31.
[70] *Birmingham v Renfrew* (1937) 57 C.L.R. 666 at 690; *Lewis v Cotton* [2001] W.T.L.R. 1117 at 1131. *Healey v Brown* [2002] W.T.L.R. 849, a decision of a commercial law Q.C. sitting as a deputy judge, is clearly wrong in applying the 1989 Act to enable a widower to dispose of a flat, formerly owned with his wife as joint tenants at law and in equity, so as to defeat his agreement with his wife: see Underhill and Hayton, *Law of Trusts and Trustees* (16th ed., 2003), pp.429–430.
[71] *Re Fox* [1951] Ontario R. 378.
[72] *Re Newey* [1994] 2 N.Z.L.R. 590, *Manitoba University v Sandeman* (1998) 155 D.L.R. (4th) 40, *Healey v Brown* [2002] W.T.L.R. 849.

NOURSE J.: "I have derived great assistance from the decision of the High Court **2–156** of Australia in *Birmingham v Renfrew* (1936) 57 C.L.R. 666. That was a case where the available extrinsic evidence was held to be sufficient to establish the necessary agreement between two spouses. . . . I would like to read three passages from the judgment of Dixon J., which state, with all the clarity and learning for which the judgments of that most eminent judge are renowned, what I believe to be a correct analysis of the principles on which a case of enforceable mutual wills depends. First (at 682–683):

'I think the legal result was a contract between husband and wife. The contract **2–157** bound him, I think, during her lifetime not to revoke his will without notice to her. If she died without altering her will, then he was bound after her death not to revoke his will at all. She on her part afforded the consideration for his promise by making her will. His obligation not to revoke his will during her life without notice to her is to be implied. For I think the express promise should be understood as meaning that if she died leaving her will unrevoked then he would not revoke his. But the agreement really assumes that neither party will alter his or her will without the knowledge of the other. It has long been established that a contract between persons to make corresponding wills gives rise to equitable obligations when one acts on the faith of such an agreement and dies leaving his will unrevoked so that the other takes property under its dispositions. It operates to impose upon the survivor an obligation regarded as specifically enforceable. It is true that he cannot be compelled to make and leave unrevoked a testamentary document and if he dies leaving a last will containing provisions inconsistent with his agreement it is nevertheless valid as a testamentary act. But the doctrines of equity attach the obligation to the property. The effect is, I think, that the survivor becomes a constructive trustee and the terms of the trust are those of the will which he undertook would be his last will.'

"Next (at 689):

'There is a third element which appears to me to be inherent in the nature of **2–158** such a contract or agreement, although I do not think it has been expressly considered. The purpose of an arrangement for corresponding wills must often be, as in this case, to enable the survivor during his life to deal as absolute owner with the property passing under the will of the party first dying. That is to say, the object of the transaction is to put the survivor in a position to enjoy for his own benefit the full ownership so that, for instance, he may convert it and expend the proceeds if he choose. But when he dies he is to bequeath what is left in the manner agreed upon. It is only by the special doctrines of equity that such a floating obligation, suspended, so to speak, during the life-time of the survivor can descend upon the assets at his death and crystallise into a trust. No doubt gifts and settlements, *inter vivos*, if calculated to defeat the intention of the compact, could not be made by the survivor and his right of disposition, *inter vivos*, is, therefore, not unqualified. But, substantially, the purpose of the arrangement will often be to allow full enjoyment for the survivor's own benefit and advantage upon condition that at his death the residue shall pass as arranged.'

"Finally (at 690):

'In *Re Oldham* Astbury J. pointed out, in dealing with the question whether an **2–159** agreement should be inferred, that in *Dufour v Pereira* the compact was that the survivor should take a life estate only in the combined property. It was, therefore, easy to fix the corpus with a trust as from the death of the survivor. But I do not see any difficulty in modern equity in attaching to the assets a constructive trust which allowed the survivor to enjoy the property subject to a fiduciary duty which, so to speak, crystallised on his death and disabled him only from voluntary disposition *inter vivos*.'

"I interject to say that Dixon J. was there clearly referring only to voluntary dispositions *inter vivos* which are calculated to defeat the intention of the compact. No objection could normally be taken to ordinary gifts of small value. He went on:

2–160   'On the contrary, as I have said, it seems rather to provide a reason for the intervention of equity. The objection that the intended beneficiaries could not enforce a contract is met by the fact that a constructive trust arises from the contract and the fact that testamentary dispositions made upon the faith of it have taken effect. It is the constructive trust and not the contract that they are entitled to enforce.'

"It is also clear from *Birmingham v Renfrew* that these cases of mutual wills are only one example of a wider category of cases, for example secret trusts, in which a court of equity will intervene to impose a constructive trust. A helpful and interesting summary of that wider category of cases will be found in the argument of counsel for the plaintiffs in *Ottaway v Norman* [1972] Ch. 698 at 701–702. The principle of all these cases is that a court of equity will not permit a person to whom property is transferred by way of gift, but on the faith of an agreement or clear understanding that it is to be dealt with in a particular way for the benefit of a third person, to deal with that property inconsistently with that agreement or understanding. If he attempts to do so after having received the benefit of the gift equity will intervene by imposing a constructive trust on the property which is the subject-matter of the agreement or understanding.

2–161   "I would emphasise that the agreement or understanding must be such as to impose on the donee a legally binding obligation to deal with the property in the particular way and that the other two certainties, namely those as to the subject-matter of the trust and the persons intended to benefit under it, are as essential to this species of trust as they are to any other. In spite of an argument by counsel for Mr. and Mrs. Noble to the contrary, I find it hard to see how there could be any difficulty about the second or third certainties in a case of mutual wills unless it was in the terms of the wills themselves. There, as in this case, the principal difficulty is always whether there was a legally binding obligation or merely an honourable engagement.

"Before turning in detail to the evidence which relates to the question whether there was a legally binding obligation on the testatrix in the present case or not I must return once more to *Birmingham v Renfrew*. It is clear from that case, if from nowhere else, that an enforceable agreement to dispose of property in pursuance of mutual wills can be established only by clear and satisfactory evidence. That seems to me to be no more than a particular application of the general rule that all claims relating to the property of deceased persons must be scrutinised with very great care. However, that does not mean that there has to be a departure from the ordinary standard of proof required in civil proceedings. I have to be satisfied on the balance of probabilities that the alleged agreement was made, but before I can be satisfied of that I must find clear and satisfactory evidence to that effect."

QUESTIONS

1. Is a sound approach to gifts by will where secret trusts or mutual wills may be **2–162** involved as follows:

(1) Is there appearance of (a) incorporation by reference (b) half-secret trust (c) fully secret trust (d) mutual wills?

(2) If (a) does the will refer to an ascertainable already existing document or does it attempt to incorporate a future document or an assortment of present and future documents?

(3) If (b) so that on the face of the will there really was an intent to create a binding obligation were the terms of the obligation (i) communicated before or after the will and, if before, were they (ii) communicated in accordance with the will (iii) to a person who accepted them and (iv) who does not take beneficially under the trust if the obligation was a trust and not a gift upon condition?

(4) If (c) so that there was an intention outside of the will to create a binding obligation were the terms of the obligation (i) communicated in the testator's lifetime (ii) to a person who accepted the obligation?

(5) If (d) so that the arrangements were agreed by each testator, resulting in the alike wills, was there an acceptance that the survivor would be legally obliged to carry out the arrangements?

2. In 2000 Alan made his will as follows: "Whatever I die possessed of I give to **2–163** my wife Brenda." The will was witnessed by two of Alan's daughters, Diana and Edwina. Shortly afterwards, Alan asked Brenda if she would hold half the property she received under his will for their three daughters, Diana, Edwina and Freda equally. Brenda assented to this. In 2003 Freda ran away with a merchant seaman, Wayne. As a result Alan told Brenda to keep Freda's share for herself. A year ago Diana died, childless, and a week later Alan died after a long illness. How should his £150,000 estate be distributed? Would it make any difference if Brenda disclaimed all benefits due to pass to her under the will and relied, instead, upon her rights under the intestacy rules?

3. H and W make wills in identical terms *mutatis mutandis* in pursuance of an **2–164** agreement that they were each to leave their estates upon trust for sale for the survivor absolutely, the survivor being obliged to leave half of the property he owned at his death to their nephews. A and B equally. Each agreed not to withdraw from the arrangement without giving notice to the other. W died childless having left all her estate upon trust for sale for H absolutely.

H later married S and made a second will leaving half his property to A and B equally, one quarter to S absolutely and one quarter to S "upon trusts which have been communicated to her." In a sealed envelope given to S shortly before H made his second will there were directions that S was to hold the quarter share given to her as trustee on trust for X for life remainder to Y absolutely, whilst one month before his death H asked S to hold her absolute quarter share upon trust for Z and she agreed. H and S were involved in a bad car crash resulting in S predeceasing H by one day.

How should H's estate be distributed if the property received by H under W's will **2–165** was worth £150,000 whilst the property passing under H's will was worth £100,000? Would it make any difference if two years after W's death and seven years before his own death H had created a settlement of £40,000 on trust for X for life, remainder to Y absolutely? Would the position be any different if W's estate had been worth £500,000 and she had died intestate owing to her will failing to comply with the formalities required by the Wills Act 1837?

4. A month before he died Tim conveyed his freehold estate, Longways, to Brian Bluff, having obtained Brian's oral agreement to hold it on trust for Lucy Lovejoy. Lucy first learned of this after Tim's death, she and Tim having had a major row two weeks before Tim's death so Tim then told Brian to hold Longways for Tim.

In 2003 Tim made his will in which he appointed Roger Robinson to be his executor, he gave Braeside to Bluff "to deal with as I have directed him" and he gave his residuary estate to his widow.

2–166   Tim's signature to his will was properly witnessed by Robinson and by Bluff. Tim contemporaneously handed Bluff a diskette from an Amstrad word processor saying, "This tells you what to do with Braeside after my death but you will not find the code word to its special contents until after my death, when the code word will be in my deed box at my Bank in Buty High Street." Bluff took the diskette saying, "That's fine by me."

Tim died last week in a car crash. Bluff discovered that in the deed box there were two undated slips of paper headed "Codeword," one containing the word "Scylla," the other containing the word "Charybdis." The former makes the diskette state: "Memo to B. Bluff. Please sell Braeside, invest the proceeds and pay the income to Sue Grabbitt till her death when you can have the capital." The latter makes the diskette state: "Memo to B. Bluff. Please transfer Braeside to Sue Grabbitt." Obviously, Tim had put both messages on the diskette before making his will but the codeword device left him still able to decide which message should be the binding one.

Bluff seeks your advice about entitlement to Braeside and to Longways.

2–167   5. If trustees hold property upon trust to pay or transfer the income and or capital to the settlor or his nominee in accordance with such written directions as may from time to time be received by the trustees from the settlor in his lifetime, and on his death to transfer the property remaining to X Y and Z equally (or unequally if the settlor so directs in writing in his lifetime) then is this not a bare *Saunders v Vautier* (at para.9–123) trusteeship or agency until the settlor's death (especially, if the trustees have to invest as the settlor directs or can only invest or disinvest with the settlor's consent) so that the property remains part of the settlor's disposable estate and the settlement actually amounts to a testamentary disposition requiring compliance with the Will Act 1837? Is this also the case where trustees hold a £10 million fund on trust to accumulate the income in the settlor's lifetime, remainder to X Y and Z equally (or unequally if the settlor so directs in his lifetime in writing), where the settlor retains a power to revoke the trust wholly or partly and a power to appoint income or capital to anyone (including himself) at any time?

Is there a distinction between (1) trustees holding to the order of the settlor and (2) trustees holding to the settlor's order if he orders it?

Chapter 3

THE ESSENTIALS OF A TRUST

To create a trust any requisite formalities for vesting property in the **3–01** trustees (known as completely constituting the trust) must be complied with and the "three certainties" must be present: certainty of intention to create a trust, certainty of subject matter of the trust and certainty of beneficiaries. These are mechanisms for trying to ensure that there are obligations that are administratively workable and capable of being "policed" by the court. To underpin the binding obligation inherent in the trust concept the trust must be directly or indirectly for the benefit of persons (individual or corporate) so that some person has *locus standi* to apply to the court to enforce the trust and make the trustees liable to account,[1] unless the trust is either for a limited anomalous number of testamentary non-charitable purposes relating to the maintenance of animals, tombs, etc.,[2] or for charitable purposes when the Attorney-General or the Charity Commissioners enforce the charitable purposes. Charitable trusts, where there is a general charitable intention, are also favoured in that they do not have to satisfy the requirement of certainty of objects (so long as the objects are sufficiently certain to be classified as exclusively charitable) and they can endure for ever, whilst private trusts are limited by the perpetuity rules to a perpetuity period. As charitable trusts are a special category they are dealt with in Chapter 7.

In the vast majority of cases the trustees know that they are trustees, **3–02** having agreed with the settlor to be trustees, and the beneficiaries know that they are beneficiaries, but a trust can be created unilaterally by a settlor in circumstances where the trustees do not know that they are trustees[3] and the beneficiaries do not know that they are beneficiaries.[4]

Take the case of a trust created by will where the testator before he dies does not tell the trustees or the beneficiaries about his testamentary trust, which arises as soon as he dies. Equity does not allow a trust to fail for want of a trustee,[5] so if the trustees refuse to act and disclaim the intended trust property, such property falls to be held on trust by the person in whom the deceased's estate is vested, the executor or the administrator with the will annexed to the grant of letters of administration. Such person holds the

---

[1] See section 5, at paras 3–195 *et seq.*
[2] See at paras 3–206 *et seq.*
[3] *Fletcher v Fletcher* (1844) 4 Hare 67; *Childers v Childers* (1857) 1 De G.&J. 482.
[4] *Fletcher v Fletcher* (above); *Re Lewis* [1904] 2 Ch. 656, *Rose v Rose* (1986) 7 N.S.W.L.R. 679 at 686, *Re Kayford* [1975] 1 W.L.R. 279. Indeed, there may be no beneficiaries for a period while income is being accumulated and the ultimate contingent beneficiary may not be born or otherwise ascertained for some time, especially for jurisdictions other than England where the accumulation period can be as long as the perpetuity period.
[5] *Mallott v Wilson* [1903] 2 Ch. 494, *Harris v Sharp*, (1989) [2003] W.T.L.R. 1541.

trust property (to the extent not properly used for the payment of the deceased's debts and expenses) on trust for the beneficiaries until such person exercises his power[6] to appoint new trustees.

3–03   Similarly, a settlor in his lifetime might transfer legal title to his registered land or his shares in a company[7] by making the transferee(s) registered proprietor(s) of the land or shares without telling them, and by signing a document showing he intends them to become trustees thereof for specified beneficiaries. If the trustees disclaim on learning the true situation, then, after rectification of the register, the legal title remains with the settlor to hold it as trustee on trust for the beneficiaries. In the case of chattels the settlor can execute a deed of gift to a person as trustee on declared trusts.[8]

Thus, the key event that gives rise to a trust is the unilateral act of the settlor. The intended trustee's decision to accept the trust property and act as trustee then makes that trustee the trustee of the trust, but if he decided against it, the trust still subsists so the beneficiaries still have equitable interests, albeit with the settlor or the settlor's personal representative as trustee until new trustees are appointed. The trustee is then entitled to remuneration under the trust instrument or statute[9] as an incident of the office of trustee and not by virtue of any agreement or contract with the settlor.[10] The trustee cannot sue the settlor for trusteeship fees, while the settlor cannot sue the trustee if the trustee in breach of trust carries out the trusteeship negligently or improperly. The trustee reimburses itself out of the trust fund for properly incurred expenses and pays its fees thereout, while it is the beneficiaries (and not the settlor) who can sue the trustee if it acts negligently or improperly so that the trustee tops up the trust fund to its proper level. A breach of contract can lead to termination of the contract, but a breach of trust does not terminate the trust, although enabling termination of the wrongdoing trustee's term of office and replacement by a new person as trustee.

3–04   A person cannot be burdened with the duties of trusteeship until that person's conscience is affected by the trust,[11] *e.g.* by actual knowledge of the trust or by turning a "Nelsonian" blind eye to the trust or by being suspicious that a trust affects property but then deliberately or recklessly failing to make the further inquiries that an honest reasonable person would take.[12] However, property in the hands of a person whose conscience

---

[6] Trustee Act 1925, s.36.
[7] S could also covenant on behalf of himself and his personal representatives with T that one year after his death his personal representatives will pay £100,000 to T to the intent that T will hold the benefit of this covenant on trust for S's illegitimate children who attain 25 years.There is an immediate trust of this chose in action (even if T subsequently disclaims on learning of the covenant): *Fletcher v Fletcher* (1844) 4 Hare 67. There is a danger that if the intended trustee is kept in the dark, then the trust could be a sham, with the property remaining beneficially owned by the settlor, *e.g. Midland Bank plc v Wyatt* [1995] 1 F.L.R. 696.
[8] Title passes on due execution of the deed: *Naas v Westminster Bank* [1940] A.C. 366.
[9] Trustee Act 2000, s.29, para.9–42.
[10] *Re Duke of Norfolk's S.T* [1982] Ch. 61. *Galmerrow Securities Ltd v National Westminster Bank* [2002] W.T.L.R. 125.
[11] *Westdeutsche Landesbank v Islington B.C.* [1996] A.C. 669 at 705, 707.
[12] Further on such actual, "Nelsonian" or "naughty" knowledge see at para.11–22.

is not affected by any equitable interest is subject from the time of receipt by such person to equitable interests then burdening the property under the priority rules governing proprietary interests,[13] whether such equitable interests are interests under trusts or charges (or equitable easements or restrictive covenants).

Section 1. Certainty of Intention to Create a Trust

RELATIONSHIPS OTHER THAN TRUSTS

A person may deal with his property in a variety of ways, His expressed **3–05** wishes have to be examined in the context of the surrounding circumstances for indications as to the consequences he expects to flow from his actions, so that these indicia may then be seen as appropriate to the creation of a trust relationship or some other relationship. A person can create a trust without knowing it[14]; while, no matter how clear the intention to create a trust, if the essence of the obligation created is that of a charge[15] or of a debt[16] then a charge or a debt will arise and not a trust.

Bailment

If an owner delivers possession (as opposed to ownership) of her goods to **3–06** another on condition that they will be redelivercd to the owner or according to the owner's directions when the purpose of delivering the goods (*e.g.* for cleaning or for use for a year or for safe custody or as security for a loan) has been carried out, this will be a bailment.[17] This is a common law relationship where the bailee receives a special property in the goods, the general property in which remains in the bailor.

Bailment of intangibles cannot exist because intangibles (*e.g.* copyrights, shares in companies, debts) cannot be possessed without being owned.

Agency

If an owner transfers ownership or possession of property to another to **3–07** enable him to do things on his behalf an agency relationship will arise. The principal can direct the agent and can terminate the agency (except in certain limited circumstances[18]). The agent (unlike a trustee *vis-à-vis* the

---

[13] *Westdeutsche Landesbank v Islington B.C.* [1996] A.C. 669 at 707.
[14] *e.g. Paul v Constance* [1977] 1 W.L.R. 54; *Re Vandervell's Trusts (No.2)* [1974] Ch. 269; *Re Chelsea Cloisters Ltd* (1980) 41 P. & C.R. 98.
[15] *Clough v Martin* [1985] 1 W.L.R. 111; *Re Bond Worth Ltd* [1980] Ch. 228.
[16] *Commissioners of Customs & Excise v Richmond Theatre Management Ltd* [1995] S.T.C. 257.
[17] See N. E. Palmer, *Bailment* (2nd ed.) and A. P. Bell, *Modern Law of Personal Property*, Chap. 5. There can be sufficient fiduciary relationship between bailor and bailee to give the bailor the equitable right to trace the bailed goods and their product: *Aluminium Industries Vaasen v Romalpa* [1976] 1 W.L.R. 676 but this has been much restricted as a special case: *Clough Mill Ltd v Martin* [1985] 1 W.L.R. 111
[18] Neither the settlor nor beneficiaries of a trust (unless between them absolutely entitled and *sui juris* when they can terminate the trust) have such rights.A person can be a trustee but not an agent for unborn or unascertained persons: *Swain v Law Society* [1981] 3 All E.R. 797 at 822. Further see Markesinis & Munday's *Outline of Agency*, Chap. 6.

settlor or beneficiaries) has power to subject his principal to liability in contract and in tort. The agency normally arises as a result of a contract between principal and agent. Thus, an agency normally creates a debtor-creditor relationship. However, if a principal sells his cars via an agent obliged to pay the proceeds of each sale into a designated account and to remit to the principal by separate cheques the proceeds of such sales less commission and costs within five days then a trust arises.[19] This is crucial where the agent goes into liquidation.

Equitable charges and reservation of title

3–08 To protect his financial interests as much as possible against creditors' insolvencies, S, a supplier of materials to a manufacturer, M Ltd, may seek to obtain[20] an equitable interest in (a) the materials; (b) any products produced using his materials and (c) any proceeds of sale of the materials or the products either until the price of the particular materials is paid or even until the price of all materials supplied by S to M Ltd is paid. If M Ltd did hold (a), (b) and (c) on trust for S then S would be entitled to such on the insolvency of M Ltd in priority to M Ltd's creditors. However, if S only had a charge then such would be void against M Ltd's liquidator unless registered under the Companies Act when (impractically) no dealings with the assets could take place without S's consent.

3–09 In *Re Bond Worth Ltd*[21] it was held that if S transfers legal title in fibre to M Ltd, purporting to reserve equitable ownership of the fibre until resale and to become equitable owner of the proceeds of sale and of any products produced using the fibre and of the proceeds of sale thereof until full payment be made for the relevant fibre, this amounts to the creation of an equitable charge by M Ltd by way of security. Such a charge needed to be registered under the Companies Act (now section 395 of the 1985 Act) and was not, and so was void against creditors and the liquidator.

3–10 The alternative effective approach for S to adopt is to retain full legal beneficial ownership in the materials supplied until full payment to S of money due from M Ltd[22] when there can be no question of M Ltd granting a registrable charge because M Ltd owns nothing out of which a grant can be made.[23] Thus S can recover such raw materials in the event of the insolvency of M Ltd However, if S goes further and claims to obtain legal ownership of products produced using his materials with others supplied by M Ltd or a third party until paid the money due from M Ltd, this will

---

[19] *Re Fleet Disposal Services Ltd* [1995] 1 B.C.L.C. 345 above at para.1–48 and for sales of airline tickets: *Royal Brunei Airlines v Tan* [1995] 3 All E.R. 97; *Re Air Canada and M & L Travel Ltd* (1994) 108 D.L.R. (4th) 592.

[20] S is legal and beneficial owner: he cannot obtain a separate equitable interest until full ownership is vested in another: *Westdentsche Landesbank v Islington BC* [1996] A.C. 669 at 706, 714; *DKLR Holding Co (No.2) Pty Ltd v Commissioner of Stamp Duties* (1982) 149 C.L.R. 431.

[21] [1980] Ch. 228. See also *Specialist Plant Ltd v Braithwaite* [1987] BCLC, where the Court of Appeal held that the suppliers' attempt to become part owner of the products made with his suppliers till payment actually created an equitable charge: also is *ICI New Zealand Ltd v Agnew* [1998] 2 N.Z.L.R. 129.

[22] *Armour v Thyssen Edelstahlwerke A.G.* [1991] 2 A.C. 339.

[23] *Clough Mill Ltd v Martin* [1985] 1 W.L.R. 111, para.3–25; *Re Highway Foods International Ltd* [1995] 1 B.C.L.C. 209.

normally be construed as giving rise to a charge on the products in S's favour.[24] Similarly, any clause purporting to make S owner of the proceeds of sale of such products until paid the money due from M Ltd will be construed as creating a charge.[25]

The substance of the matter is that M Ltd is intended to be entitled to **3–11** the new products or the proceeds of sale thereof once it has paid the debt due to S, so that, really, S has a charge over property subject to M Ltd's equity of redemption. What, however, if M Ltd expressly contracted that it will be trustee of re-sale proceeds received by it, holding one fifth for S and four fifths for itself (so as to cover S's input and profit), or, better still, holding on trust for S such fractional part of such proceeds then received as is equivalent to the amount then owing by M Ltd to S and the rest on trust for itself? No charge within section 395 arises here.[26] On receipt of the proceeds "Equity looks on that as done which ought to be done", and because of this, "even if the proceeds were paid into a general bank account there could be a tracing remedy where the recipient was obliged to hold a particular portion of the proceeds on trust."[27] To reinforce S's position, M Ltd should be expressly placed under an obligation to transfer the relevant amount of money into M Ltd's account within a short period (between five to 10 working days) and under an obligation in that period not to permit the amount credited in the general account to fall below the relevant amount held on trust for S.

Where M Ltd is simply selling goods supplied by S then the contract can **3–12** contain a provision that M Ltd is to hold proceeds of sale of the goods forthwith as trustee thereof for S to the extent of the fraction thereof representing the amounts then due to S by M Ltd in respect of such goods, providing that moneys subject to such trust may be paid into M Ltds' general bank account subject to being transferred into S's own account within ten working days (but without liability to pay interest thereon for such ten days) and providing that the money to the credit of M Ltd in its general bank account shall never fall below the amount held on trust for S. S should then have equitable entitlement to such money[28] supported by equitable tracing rights,[29] though they will be valueless if such money is used to pay off creditors without notice of S's rights.

Because effective reservation of title clauses are a form of security that potential creditors of a company ought to be able to discover, the Law

---

[24] *Clough v Martin* [1985] 1 W.L.R. 111; *Modelboard Ltd v Outer Box Ltd* [1993] B.C.L.C. 623.

[25] *Pfeiffer v Arbuthnot Factors* [1988] 1 W.L.R. 150; *Company Computer Ltd v Abercorn Group* [1993] B.C.L.C. 603; *Re Highway Foods International Ltd* [1995] 1 B.C.L.C. 209.

[26] *Associated Alloys Pty Ltd v ACN 001 452 106 Pty Ltd* (2000) 202 C.L.R. 588. If the contract related not to a trust of a specific fraction or percentage but only to a trust of an amount of money then owed by M Ltd to S a problem arises as to certainty of subject matter because such amount is not segregated from the remaining amount of M Ltd's money, so that no more than a contractual charge can arise, requiring registration under s.395 Companies Act 1985.

[27] *ibid.* at 870.

[28] *Associated Alloys Pty Ltd v ACN 001 452 106 Pty Ltd* (2000) 202 C.L.R. 588. *Re Fleet Disposal Services Ltd* [1995] 1 B.C.L.C. 345; *Re Lewis's of Leicester Ltd* [1995] 1 B.C.L.C. 428, *Royal Trust Bank v National Westminster Bank* [1996] 2 B.C.L.C. 128

[29] For the extensiveness of tracing via an equitable charge see *El Ajou v Dollar Land Holdings* [1993] 3 All E.R. 717, 736–737, reversed on another point [1994] 2 All E.R. 685.

Commission in its Consultation Paper No.164, "Registration of Security Interests", recommends that they should be registrable like charges on a company's property.

Loans

3–13   If A transfers to B £50,000 not by way of gift but as part of the purchase price of Blackacre for £150,000 in B's name, then A will have one-third of the equitable interest in Blackacre (under a resulting trust) which will obviously appreciate or depreciate with the value of Blackacre. If A had merely lent B the £50,000 to help B acquire the whole beneficial interest in Blackacare, then A would merely have a personal claim against B for the debt. If the £50,000 loan had been secured by a charge on Blackacre then A would have the right to sell Blackacre to repay himself the debt out of the proceeds of sale. It is also possible that A could also forgive the debt in consideration for purchasing a specified share of Blackacre.

3–14   The one arrangement cannot be both a loan and a trust since the concepts are mutually exclusive.[30] However, a loan arrangement may commence with the borrower receiving the lender's money to be used only for a particular purpose, resulting if the purpose is performed in a pure loan relationship excluding any trust relationship, but with the money being held on trust (whether express or resulting) for the lender in the event of non-performance of the purpose.[31] Thus where Quistclose loaned Rolls Razor Ltd £209,000 only for the purpose of paying a dividend on July 24, and Rolls Razor went into liquidation on July 17, so preventing any dividend being paid, the House of Lords held the money to be held on trust for Quistclose. This approach was applied in *Re EVTR*, at para.3–50.

Prepayments

3–15   When a company goes into liquidation (or an individual becomes bankrupt) it will be crucial whether a claimant has merely a personal claim, whether contractual or quasi-contractual, or has a proprietary claim under a trust or a charge. If a customer sent money to a company for goods and the company went into liquidation before supplying the goods the customer with his personal claim will be a mere unsecured creditor. If the customer in his letter had stipulated that his money was to be held in trust for him till he received title to the goods, then he will have an equitable interest giving him priority over the company's creditors in so far as it is possible to trace such money. If the company, fearful of liquidation, had expressly opened a trust bank account in which it had deposited customers' payments then, again, such a customer will have an equitable interest.[32]

---

[30] *Re Sharpe* [1980] 1 W.L.R. 219; *Spence v Browne* (1988) 18 Fam. Law 291. In an exceptional case, a female not seeking repayment of her loan to a male houseowner, with whom she cohabits, nor any interest on the loan may thereby act to her detriment on the basis of a common intention that she should acquire a share of the house so that she acquires such a share: *Risch v McFee* [1991] 1 F.L.R. 105.

[31] *Barclays Bank Ltd v Quistclose Investments Ltd* [1970] A.C. 567; *Carreras Rothmans Ltd v Freeman Mathews Treasure Ltd* [1985] 1 All E.R. 155; *Re EVTR Ltd* [1987] B.C.L.C. 646; *Twinsectra Ltd v Yardley* [2002] 2 A.C. 164. Further on purpose trusts and the beneficiary principle see at paras 3–205 *et seq.*

[32] *Re Kayford Ltd* [1975] 1 W.L.R. 279. Also *see Re Chelsea Cloisters Ltd* (1980) 41 P. & C.R. 98 (tenants' damage deposit account moneys held on trust by company landlord in liquidation).

One could take the view[33] that the company's unilateral declaration of **3–16** trust is a voidable preference of the customers as creditors. The customer would expect to be a mere creditor, having done nothing to prevent his payment going into the ordinary bank account of the company to be available to creditors generally. The company's voluntary act preferred the customers' interests above those of ordinary creditors, and this is a voidable preference resulting in the customers being relegated to the position of ordinary creditors. However, the courts[34] have taken the view that the company's unilateral declaration of trust prevents the customers from becoming creditors by making them beneficiaries under a trust, just as if the customers themselves had created the trust, or does not result from the requisite subjective desire to prefer the customers. Indeed, even where there is no clear declaration of trust by the company the courts have become quite ready to infer the requisite intent to create a trust where a separate bank account has been opened when the company was in a parlous financial situation.[35]

The most extreme case is *Neste Oy v Lloyd's Bank plc*[36] where the plaintiff **3–17** shipowners made a series of payments to PSL, their agents, to discharge present and future liabilities relating to their vessels. Such were paid into PSL's general account with the Bank, without being subjected to any trusts.

> "[The last] payment was credited to PSL at a time when Peckston Group Ltd had already resolved that it and its group companies should cease trading immediately (one of the directors supporting the resolution being a director of PSL) at a time when PSL had not paid for the services for which the funds had been remitted and at a time when, in all the circumstances, there was no chance that PSL could pay for the services".[37]

The directors of PSL would have been liable for wrongful trading if PSL had continued in business. Bingham J. held,[38]

> "Given the situation of PSL when the last payment was received, any honest and reasonable directors (or the actual directors had they known of it) would, I feel sure, have arranged for the repayment of that sum to the plaintiffs without hesitation or delay . . . and, accordingly, a constructive trust is to be inferred."

He thus refused to allow the Bank to set off the payment against money **3–18** due to it when he held that the Bank had constructive notice of the trust.

---

[33] Goodhart and Jones (1980) 43 M.L.R. 489 at 496–498 querying whether Kayford's unilateral voluntary declaration of trust contravened the Companies Act 1948, ss.302, 320, now Insolvency Act 1986, ss.238, 239, but because Kayford could have declined the order and returned the prepayment could it not also accept the order only on the basis the prepayment was trust money as indicated by RM Goode, *Payment Obligations in Commercial & Financial Transactions* (2nd ed., 1989), p.18 n.64?

[34] *Re Kayford Ltd* [1975] 1 W.L.R. 279; *Re Chelsea Cloisters Ltd* (1980) 41 P. & C.R. 989; *Re Lewis's of Leicester Ltd* [1995] 1 B.C.L.C. 428 applying *Re M.C. Bacon* [1991] 1 Ch. 127.

[35] *Re Chelsea Cloisters Ltd, above; Re Lewis's of Leicester Ltd, above;* M. Bridge (1992) 12 O.J.L.S. 333, 335–357.

[36] [1983] 2 Lloyds Rep. 658.

[37] *ibid.* at 666.

[38] *ibid.* at 665.

Subsequently in *Re Japan Leasing (Europe) Plc*[39] the judge applied the views of Bingham J. to the case where a purchaser paid the instalment of the purchase price of an aeroplane to company A, the head vendor, to divide the instalment between itself and three companies B, C and D, A's co-vendors. The intended beneficial payment to A discharged the purchaser of its liability to A B C and D under contractual arrangements which also expressly excluded any trust relationship arising between A on the one hand and B, C and D on the other hand in respect of instalments received by A: A was only to be under a personal contractual obligation as agent to account to B, C and D in respect thereof. However, the judge held that when A received the instalment after its financial problems had led to it going into administration the exclusion clause did not extend to the constructive trust that the judge held to arise by operation of law against A because[40] "it would be unconscionable for the Company [A], as agent, to receive money as agent knowing that it could not account for it to its principal [B, C, and D]".

3–19   Thus, a contractual arrangement became a trust arrangement by operation of law. It is equally possible, of course, for a contractual relationship to become a trust relationship upon events specified in the contract. Thus, it may be expressly stipulated that unit holders under a unit trust only have personal rights to a sum of money calculated by reference to the number of units owned and the underlying value of the assets subject to the unit trust (rather than a proprietary interest in the underlying assets), such rights to be remediable only by monetary compensation, until the unit trust comes to the end of its life whereupon the then unit holders are to have a proprietary interest in the assets then owned by the trustees.[41] Similarly, a life policy may consist of an investment element linked with a unit trust, premiums being applied in the acquisition of units. However, unit-linked policies normally provide that the policy-holder has no proprietary interest in the units allocated to the policy which are merely to be units of account establishing the extent of the insurance company's personal liability.[42]

Privity of contract

3–20   The well-established common law rule is that only a party to a contract can sue on it, so that if A contracts with B for the benefit of C, C cannot enforce the contract or prevent A and B from varying its terms.[43] B alone can enforce the contract: normally he can only claim nominal damages for his own loss,[44] though sometimes the equitable remedy of specific performance may be available.[45] Statutory rules in the Contracts (Rights of Third Parties) Act 1999 now permit A and B if they wish, to enable C to enforce A's contract with B.

---

[39] [2000] W.T.L.R. 301.
[40] *ibid.* at 316.
[41] See K.F. Sin, *The Legal Nature of the Unit Trust*, Oxford, (1997), Chap. 5.
[42] *Foskett v McKeown* 2001 1 A.C. 102 at 143.
[43] *Dunlop v Selfridge* [1915] A.C. 847; *Scruttons v Midland Silicones* [1962] A.C. 440.
[44] *Panatown Ltd v Alfred McAlpine Construction Ltd* [2000] 4 All E.R. 97, HL.
[45] *Beswick v Beswick* [1968] A.C. 58, para.11–310.

In contrast, if A transfers property to B on trust for C, then Equity has always held that only C can enforce the trust and compel restitution to the trust fund of any losses or profits because A drops out of the picture as a donor who has made an irrevocable gift.[46]

Exceptionally, where A contracted with B if it is positively provided[47] that **3–21** they both[48] intended B to be the trustee of the benefit of A's promise (a chose in action capable of being the subject matter of a trust) for C, then C will be able to enforce the trust, subject to joining B as a necessary party to be bound by any judgment in the action.[49] In such circumstances A and B will not be able to vary their contract without C's consent, unless such a power was expressly or by necessary implication reserved at the creation of the contract in circumstances where the power is a personal one for the benefit of A or B and not a fiduciary power for the benefit of C.

In the absence of clear trust language it is difficult to forecast exactly **3–22** what are the circumstances when a court will find that a trust has been affirmatively established.[50] The courts are reluctant[51] to find an intent to create a trust, suspecting that such a claim is normally a transparent device to avoid the privity of contract doctrine.

Where there is a contract between A and B for the benefit of C, B cannot unilaterally[52] improve's C's position (and worsen A's position) by declaring himself trustee for C or assigning his rights to C where B's rights are inherently for nominal damages only. However, if both A and B contracted on the footing that B would be able to enforce contractual rights for the benefit of those who suffered from defective performance but who could not acquire any rights to hold A liable for breach, then B may assign such rights[53] and be regarded as trustee of such rights.[54] Such an exception to the general rule that refuses to recognise a *ius quaesitum tertio* may be regarded as "a judicial subterfuge"[55] providing "a remedy where no other would be available to a person sustaining loss which under a national legal system ought to be compensated by the person who has caused it."[56] "The legal position in cases such as these is now fundamentally affected by the Contracts (Rights of Third Parties) Act 1999"[57] which enables rights to be expressly enforceable by a third party like C if the contracting parties so wish.

---

[46] *Paul v Paul* (1882) 20 Ch.D. 742; *Re Astor's S.T.* [1952] Ch. 534 at 542; *Bradshaw v University College of Wales* [1987] 3 All E.R. 200, 203; *Goulding v James* [1997] 2 All E.R. 239 at 247.

[47] *West v Houghton* 1879 L.R. 4 C.P.D. 197 at 203.

[48] *Re Schebsman* [1994] Ch. 83 at 89, 104: B cannot unilaterally increase the measure of A's liability.

[49] *Vandepitte v Preferred Accident Insurance Co* [1933] A.C. 70 at 79; *Parker-Tweedale v Dunbar Bank plc* [1991] Ch. 26.

[50] See *Trident General Insurance Co. v McNeice Bros* (1988) 165 C.L.R. 107, pointing out how *Re Foster* [1938] 4 All E.R. 357 and *Re Sinclair's Life Policy* [1938] Ch. 799 cannot logically be distinguished from *Royal Exchange Assurance v Hope* [1928] Ch. 179 and *Re Webb* [1941] Ch. 225.

[51] *Re Schebsman* [1944] Ch. 538; *Green v Russell* [1959] 2 Q.B. 220; *Beswick v Beswick* [1966] Ch. 538; *Swain v Law Society* [1983] 1 A.C. 598.

[52] *Re Schebsman*, above, n.48; *Darlington B.C. v Wiltshier Northern Ltd* [1995] 1 W.L.R. 68.

[53] *Dunlop v Lambert* (1839) 6 Cl. & F. 600; *The Albazero* [1977] A.C. 774; *St Martin's Property Corporation Ltd v Sir Robert McAlpine Ltd* [1994] 1 A.C. 85; *Darlington B.C. v Wiltshier Northern Ltd,* above.

[54] *Darlington B.C. v Wiltshier Northern Ltd,* above; *Panatown Ltd v Alfred McAlpine Construction Ltd* [2001] 1 A.C. 518.

[55] *Swain v Law Society* [1983] 1 A.C. 598 at 611.

[56] *St Martin's Property Corporation Ltd v Sir Robert McAlpine Ltd* [1994] A.C. 85 at 115.

[57] *Panatown Ltd v Alfred McAlpine Construction Ltd* [2001] 1 A.C. 518 at 575.

Possibilities of construction for testamentary gifts

3–23   If a testator by will leaves property to B and requires B to make some payment to C or perform some obligation in favour of C, there are five possible constructions open to a court. The testator's words may be treated as:

    (i) Merely indicating his motive, so that B takes an absolute beneficial interest, *e.g.* "to my wife, B, so that she may support herself and the children according to their needs" or "to my daughter B, on condition she provides a home for my handicapped daughter, C."[58]

    (ii) Creating a charge on the property given to B, so that B takes the property beneficially subject to the charge for securing payment of money to C,[59] *e.g.* "my office block, Demeter House, to my son, B, subject to paying thereout £10,000 p.a. to my widow, C."

3–24   (iii) Creating a trust in favour of C,[60] *e.g.* "my office block, Demeter House, to B absolutely but so that he must pay an amount equal to the income therefrom to my widow C for the rest of her life."

    (iv) Creating a personal obligation binding B to C so that if B accepts the property he must perform the obligation in C's favour[61] (even if it costs him more than the value of the property[62]) *e.g.* "my leasehold cottage currently subleased to X I hereby devise to B absolutely on condition that he agrees to pay my widow C £15,000 p.a. for the rest of her life."

    (v) Creating a condition subsequent that affects the property in B's hands making B liable to forfeit the property if the condition is broken;[63] *e.g.* "my 500,000 £1 shares ICI plc to B Charity Co. on condition that it pays my widow, C, an annuity of £10,000 for her life and properly maintains my family burial vault, and upon any failure to observe this condition then the R.S.P.C.A. shall become entitled to the shares."

CLOUGH MILL LTD v MARTIN

Court of Appeal [1984] 3 All E.R. 982; [1985] 1 W.L.R. 111.

3–25   ROBERT GOFF L.J.: "This appeal is concerned with what is sometimes called 'a retention of title clause', but more frequently nowadays a 'Romalpa clause.' The appellants, Clough Mills Ltd, carry on business as spinners of yarn. Under four

---

[58] *Re Brace* [1954] 1 W.L.R. 955; *cf. Re Frame* [1939] Ch. 700 and *Re Lipinski* [1976] Ch. 235. Further see Administration of Justice Act 1982 s.22, at para.3–66.

[59] *Re Oliver* (1890) 62 L.T. 533. B is under no personal obligation to make up any deficiency caused by insufficiency of the property charged.

[60] *e.g. Irvine v Sullivan* (1869) L.R. 8 Eq. 673.

[61] *Re Lester* [1942] Ch. 324.

[62] *Re Hodge* [1940] Ch. 260.

[63] *Att.-Gen. v Cordwainers' Company* (1833) 3 My. & K.; 40 E.R. 203; *Re Oliver* (1890) 62 L.T. 533; *Re Tyler* [1891] 3 Ch. 252, *Ellis v Chief Adjudication Officer* [1998] 1 F.L.R. 184 (E who gifted flat to D on condition D repaid E's mortgage and allowed E to reside therein under D's care could invoke valid conditions when evicted by D and D sold the flat).

contracts entered into between December 1979 and March 1980 they contracted to supply yarn to a company called Heatherdale Fabrics Ltd (which I shall refer to as 'the buyers'), which carried on business as manufacturers of fabric. When the appellants entered into these contracts, they knew that the yarn to be supplied under them was to be used by the buyers for such manufacture. Each of the contracts incorporated the appellants' standard conditions. These included a condition (condition 12) entitled 'Passing of title'; this is the Romalpa clause, with the construction and effect of which this case is concerned . . . It reads as follows:

> 'However the ownership of the material shall remain with the Seller, which **3–26** reserves the right to dispose of the material until payment in full for all the material has been received by it in accordance with the terms of this contract or until such time as the Buyer sells the material to its customers by way of bona-fide sale at full market value.
>
> If such payment is overdue in whole or in part the Seller may (without prejudice to any of its other rights) recover or re-sell the material or any of it and may enter upon the Buyer's premises by its servants or agents for that purpose.
>
> Such payments shall become due immediately upon the commencement of any act or proceeding in which the Buyer's solvency is involved.
>
> If any of the material is incorporated in or used as material for other goods before such payment the property in the whole of such goods shall be and remain with the Seller until such payment has been made, or the other goods have been sold as aforesaid, and all the Seller's rights hereunder in the material shall extend to those other goods.'

On March 11, 1980 the respondent, Geoffrey Martin, was appointed receiver of **3–27** the buyers. On that date the buyers still retained at their premises 375 kg of unused yarn supplied under contracts and still unpaid for. So on March 11, 1980 the appellants wrote to the receiver expressing their intention to repossess the unused yarn . . . the solicitors acting for the receiver replied that the appellants' retention of title clause was invalid for, *inter alia*, non-registration under section 95 of the Companies Act 1948 and that the receiver would therefore continue to allow the yarn to be used and would refuse the appellants admission to collect it. The appellants therefore commenced proceedings, claiming damages from the receiver for conversion of the yarn. His Honour Judge O'Donoghue, sitting as a judge of the High Court, dismissed the claim, holding that, on its true construction, condition 12 created a charge on the yarn and that such charge was void for non-registration under section 95. It is against that decision that the appellants now appeal to this court . . .

"The submission of counsel for the appellants as to the nature of the appellants' **3–28** retention of title under the first sentence of the condition was extremely simple. Under the Sale of Goods Act 1979 a seller of goods is fully entitled, after delivery of the goods to the buyer, to retain title in the goods until he has been paid: see section 19(1) of that Act. That is precisely what the appellants have done by condition 12. The appellants' title did not derive from the contract; on the contrary, it was simply retained by them, though under the contract power was conferred on the buyers both to sell the goods and to use them in manufacturing other goods. As the buyers never acquired any title to the unused yarn in question, they could not charge the yarn to the appellants. So the appellants were, quite simply, the owners of the yarn; and there was no question of there being any charge on the yarn in their favour, which was void if unregistered.

3–29   "This attractively simple approach was challenged by counsel for the receiver. He submitted, first of all, that, if the first sentence of condition 12 is read literally, as counsel for the appellants suggested it should be read, the buyers can only have had possession of the yarn in a fiduciary capacity, whether as bailees or as fiduciary agents. But, he said, the power conferred on the buyers under the contract, not merely to sell the material but also to mix it with other materials in the manufacture of goods, was inconsistent with the existence of any fiduciary capacity in the buyers, or indeed with the appellants' unqualified ownership of the yarn.

3–30   "Now this is a submission which I am unable to accept. In every case, we have to look at the relevant documents and other communications which have passed between the parties, and to consider them in the light of the relevant surrounding circumstances, in order to ascertain the rights and duties of the parties *inter se*, always paying particular regard to the practical effect of any conclusion concerning the nature of those rights and duties. In performing this task, concepts such as bailment and fiduciary duty must not be allowed to be our masters, but must rather be regarded as the tools of our trade. I for my part can see nothing objectionable in an agreement between parties under which A, the owner of goods, gives possession of those goods to B, at the same time conferring on B a power of sale and a power to consume the goods in manufacture, though A will remain the owner of the goods until they are either sold or consumed. I do not see why the relationship between A and B, pending sale or consumption, should not be the relationship of bailor and bailee, even though A has no right to trace the property in his goods into the proceeds of sale. If that is what the parties have agreed should happen, I can see no reason why the law should not give effect to that intention. I am happy to find that both Staughton and Peter Gibson J.J. have adopted a similar approach in *Hendy Lennox (Industrial Engines) Ltd v Grahame Puttick Ltd* [1984] 1 W.L.R. 485 and *Re Andrabell Ltd* [1984] 3 All E.R. 407.

3–31   "Even so, it is necessary to examine counsel for the appellants' construction in a little more detail. If, under this condition, retention of title applied only to goods not yet paid for, I can see that his construction could be given effect to without any problem. But the difficulty with the present condition is that the retention of title applies to material, delivered and retained by the buyer, until payment in full for *all* the material delivered under the contract has been received by the seller. The effect is therefore that the seller may retain his title in material still held by the buyer, even if part of that material has been paid for. Furthermore, if in such circumstances the seller decides to exercise his rights and resell the material, questions can arise concerning (1) whether account must be taken of the part payment already received in deciding how much the seller should be entitled to sell and (2) whether, if he does resell, he is accountable to the buyer either in respect of the part payment already received, or in respect of any profit made on the resale by reason of a rise in the market value of the material . . .

3–32   "To me, the answer to these questions lies in giving effect to the condition in accordance with its terms, and on that approach I can discern no intention to create a trust. The condition provides that the seller retains his ownership in the material. He therefore remains owner; but, during the subsistence of the contract, he can only exercise his powers as owner consistently with the terms, express and implied, of the contract. On that basis, in my judgment, he can during the subsistence of the contract only resell such amount of the material as is needed to discharge the balance of the outstanding purchase price; and, if he sells more, he is accountable to the buyer for the surplus. However, once the contract has been determined, as it will be if the buyer repudiates the contract and the seller accepts the repudiation, the seller will have his rights as owner (including, of course, his right to sell the goods) uninhibited by any contractual restrictions; though any part of the purchase price received by him and attributable to the material so resold will be recoverable by the buyer on the ground of failure of consideration, subject to any set-off arising from a crossclaim by the seller for damages for the buyer's repudiation.

". . . If this approach is right, I can see no reason why the retention of title in the **3–33** first sentence of condition 12 should be construed as giving rise to a charge on the unused material in favour of the seller. In the course of his argument counsel for the receiver prayed in aid another proposition culled from the judgment of Slade J. in *Re Bond Worth Ltd* [1980] Ch. 228 at 248; [1979] 3 All E.R. 919 at 939 when he said:

> 'In my judgment, any contract which, by way of security for payment of a debt, confers an interest in property defeasible or destructible on payment of such debt, or appropriates such property for the discharge of the debt, must necessarily be regarded as creating a mortgage or charge, as the case may be. The existence of the equity of redemption is quite inconsistent with the existence of a bare trustee-beneficiary relationship.'

"However, so far as the retention of title in unused materials is concerned, I see no **3–34** difficulty in distinguishing the present case from that envisaged by Slade J. Under the first sentence of the condition, the buyer does not, by way of security, *confer* on the seller an interest in property defeasible on the payment of the debt so secured. On the contrary, the seller *retains* the legal property in the material.

"There is however one further point which I must consider. Counsel for the receiver relied, in support of his argument, on the fourth sentence of the condition. It will be remembered that this reads as follows:

> 'If any of the material is incorporated in or used as material for other goods before such payment the property in the whole of such goods shall be and remain with the Seller until such payment has been made, or the other goods have been sold as aforesaid, and all the Seller's rights hereunder in the material shall extend to those other goods.'

"The submission of counsel for the receiver was that the effect of this provision is **3–35** to confer on the seller an interest in the buyer's property and so must have been to create a charge; and he further submitted that, having regard to the evident intention that the seller's rights in goods in which the material provided by him has been incorporated shall be the same as his rights in unused material, the seller's rights in unused material should likewise be construed as creating a charge.

"Now it is no doubt true that, where A's material is lawfully used by B to create **3–36** new goods, whether or not B incorporates other material of his own, the property in the new goods will generally vest in B, at least where the goods are not reducible to the original materials (see Bl. Com. (14th ed. pp.404–405). But it is difficult to see why, if the parties agree that the property in the goods shall vest in A, that agreement should not be given effect to. On this analysis, under the fourth sentence of the condition as under the first, the buyer does not *confer* on the seller an interest in property defeasible on the payment of the debt; on the contrary, when the new goods come into existence the property in them *ipso facto* vests in the seller, and he thereafter retains his ownership in them, in the same way and on the same terms as he retains his ownership in the unused material. However, in considering the fourth sentence, we have to take into account not only the possibility that the buyer may have paid part of the price for the material, but also that he will have borne the cost of manufacture of the new goods, and may also have provided other materials for incorporation into those goods; and the condition is silent, not only about repaying such part of the price for the material as has already been paid by the buyer, but also about any allowance to be made by the seller to the buyer for the cost of manufacture of the new goods, or for any other material incorporated by the buyer into the new goods. Now, no injustice need arise from the exercise of the seller's power to resell such goods provided that, having applied the price received from the resale in satisfaction of the outstanding balance of the price owed to him by the buyer, he is bound to account for the remainder to the buyer. But the difficulty of construing the fourth sentence as simply giving rise to a retention by the seller of title to the new goods is that it would lead to the result that, on the determination of the contract under which the original material was sold to the buyer, the ownership of the seller in the new goods would be retained by the seller uninhibited by any terms of the contract, which had then ceased to apply; and I find it impossible to believe that it was the intention of the parties that the seller would thereby gain the windfall of the full value of the new product, deriving as it may well do not merely from the labour of the buyer but also from materials that were his, without any duty to account to him for any surplus of the proceeds of sale above the outstanding balance of the price due by him to the seller. It follows that the fourth sentence must be read as creating either a trust or a charge. In my judgment, however, it cannot have been intended to create a trust. Those who insert Romalpa clauses in their contracts of sale must be aware that other suppliers might do the same; and the prospect of two lots of material, supplied by different sellers, each subject to a Romalpa clause which vests in the seller the legal title in a product manufactured from both lots of material, is not at all sensible. Accordingly, consistent with the approach to a similar provision in *Re Peachdart Ltd* [1984] Ch. 131, I have come to the conclusion that, although it does indeed do violence to the language of the fourth sentence of the condition, that sentence must be read as giving rise to a charge on the new goods in favour of the seller.

3–37   "Even so, I do not see why the presence of the last sentence in the condition should prevent us from giving effect to the first sentence in accordance with its terms . . .

3–38   "I recognise that, on the view which I have formed of the retention of title in the first sentence of condition 12 in this case, its effect is very similar to that of a charge on goods created by the buyer in favour of the seller. But the simple fact is that under the first sentence of the condition the buyer does not in fact confer a charge on his goods in favour of the seller: on the contrary, the seller retains his title in his goods, for the purpose of providing himself with security. I can see no reason in law why a seller of goods should not adopt this course, and, if the relevant contractual term is effective to achieve that result, I can see no reason why the law should not give effect to it in accordance with its terms."

ASSOCIATED ALLOYS PTY LIMITED v ACN 001 452 106 PTY LIMITED
(IN LIQUIDATION)

High Court of Australia (2000) H.C.A. 25, 74 A.L.J.R. 862; (2000) 202 C.L.R. 588

GAUDRON, McHUGH, GUMMOW & HAYNE JJ

3–39   "The appellant, Associated Alloys Pty Ltd ('the Seller'), sold steel to the first respondent, ACN 001 452 106 Pty Limited (In Liquidation) (formerly Metropolitan Engineering and Fabrications Pty Ltd) ('the Buyer'), between 1981 and 1996. In about 1987 or 1988, the Seller began to issue invoices to the Buyer with the registration of title clause, the subject-matter of this appeal, printed on the reverse side.

"Invoices were issued by the Seller to the Buyer on August 31, September 26 and October 26, 1995. Each individually numbered invoice recorded the details of the supply and shipment of steel by the Seller, in accordance with an individually numbered order of the Buyer. Each invoice also recorded a particular United States dollar sum owed by the Buyer to the Seller in respect of the particular shipment of steel supplied thereunder. On the front of the Invoices was recorded, under the heading 'PAYMENT TERMS', 'PAYMENT DUE APPROX MID/END NOVEMBER '95'. The bottom of the front of the Invoices was marked 'Romalpa Clause set forth on the reverse side hereof applies' . . .

"The clause provided:

"Reservation of Title

'[1] It is expressly agreed and declared that the title of the subject goods/ **3–40** product shall not pass to the [Buyer] until payment in full of the purchase price. The [Buyer] shall in the meantime take custody of the goods/product and retain them as the fiduciary agent and bailee of the [Seller].

[2] The [Buyer] may resell but only as a fiduciary agent of the [Seller]. Any right to bind the [Seller] to any liability to any third party by contract or otherwise is however expressly negatived. Any such resale is to be at arms length and on market terms and pending resale or utilisation in any manufacturing or construction process, is to be kept separate from its own, properly stored, protected and insured.

[3] The [Buyer] will receive all proceeds whether tangible or intangible, direct or indirect of any dealing with such goods/product in trust for the [Seller] and will keep such proceeds in a separate account until the liability to the [Seller] shall have been discharged.

[4] The [Seller] is to have power to appropriate payments to such goods and accounts as it thinks fit notwithstanding any appropriation by the [Buyer] to the contrary.

[5] *In the event that the [Buyer] uses the goods/product in some manufacturing* **3–41** *or construction process of its own or some third party, then the [Buyer] shall hold such part of the proceeds of such manufacturing or construction process as relates to the goods/product in trust for the [Seller]. Such part shall be deemed to equal in dollar terms the amount owing by the [Buyer] to the [Seller] at the time of the receipt of such proceeds'."* (paragraph numbers and emphasis added)

It is the operation of the fifth paragraph of the clause ("the Proceeds Subclause") which is of prime importance for this appeal . . .

The Proceeds Subclause operates, conditionally, "[i]n the event that the [Buyer] **3–42** uses the goods/product in some manufacturing or construction process of its own or some third party". This event occurred on each occasion the Buyer used the steel supplied by the Seller to manufacture the Steel Products. No question arises as to the Seller retaining any proprietary interest in the steel it supplied under the Invoices to the Buyer. This is because the steel supplied by the Seller was no longer capable of being ascertained in the Steel Products manufactured by the Buyer. This loss of ascertainability may be contrasted with the circumstances in which the first paragraph of the reservation of title clause applies. This paragraph has an operation where the steel supplied by the Seller remains intact in the hands of the Buyer or is otherwise dealt with by the Buyer in such a way that the steel supplied does not lose its ascertainability. In such a case, the goods would remain the property of the Seller and an action in trover or detinue would lie against the Buyer[64] and, in support of such an action, injunctive relief might be available in an appropriate case.[65]

3–43   The remainder of the Proceeds Subclause is divisible into two parts. The first part describes a subject-matter of commercial value. The second part operates to confer an interest in equity in that subject-matter . . .

The proper construction of the phrase "the proceeds" is revealed by a consideration of the Proceeds Subclause as a whole. The phrase has the meaning employed by Sir George Jessel MR in his ex tempore judgment in *In re Hallett's Estate*,[66] where the Master of the Rolls eloquently states the principles of tracing in equity. The phrase "the proceeds" is to be construed as referring to moneys received by the Buyer and not debts which may be set out in the Buyer's books (or computer records) from time to time.[67] The concluding sentence of the Proceeds Subclause would be strained if the phrase "the proceeds" were to include book debts. In the event that a debt were subject to conditions, it may prove to be difficult to determine when the Buyer is in "receipt" of that intangible obligation. Moreover, to attempt to equate a chose in action, "in dollar terms", to a sum of money, namely "the amount owing by the [Buyer] to the [Seller] at the time of the receipt of such proceeds", is, at the very least, conceptually problematic. In contrast, limiting the phrase "the proceeds" to refer to payments made to the Buyer results in this equation operating with certainty.

3–44   It is necessary to determine the equitable rights, liabilities and remedies which arise from the purported operation of the Proceeds Subclause. A pendent question also arises as to the manner in which the Buyer's contractual rights and obligations are affected by equitable considerations . . .

The contracts, in respect of each of the Invoices, spoke for the future and provided the attachment of a trust for "the proceeds" received from time to time. There being value, and equity regarding as done that which ought to be done, a completely constituted trust would arise in respect of those "proceeds" (giving that word the meaning considered above) as they were received by the Buyer.[68]

In their joint judgment in *Kauter v Hilton*, Dixon CJ, Williams and Fullagar JJ identified[69]:

> "the established rule that in order to constitute a trust the intention to do so must be clear and that it must also be clear what property is subject to the trust and reasonably certain who are the beneficiaries".

3–45   In the present case, it is no objection to the effective creation of a trust that the property to be subjected to it is identified to be a proportion of the proceeds received by the Buyer; a proportion referable to moneys from time to time due and owing but unpaid by the Buyer to the Seller.

---

[64] *Penfolds Wines Pty Ltd v Elliott* (1946) 74 C.L.R. 204 at 229; *Gollan v Nugent* (1988) 166 C.L.R. 18 at 25.
[65] As was sought in *Penfolds Wines Pty Ltd v Elliott* (1946) 74 CLR 204, and see *Puma Australia Pty Ltd v Sportsman's Australia Limited (No.2)* [1994] 2 Qd R 159 at 166–169, 171–173.
[66] (1880) 13 Ch.D. 696 at 708–709.
[67] Questions as to the application of moneys received, which it is unnecessary now to answer, may arise where a running account exists between a supplier (*e.g.* the Seller) and purchaser (*e.g.* the Buyer).
[68] *Palette Shoes Pty Ltd v Krohn* (1937) 58 C.L.R. 1 at 26–27; *Federal Commissioner of Taxation v Everett* (1980) 143 C.L.R. 440 at 450. See also the United States authorities considered under the heading "Debtor Declaring Himself Trustee for Creditor" in Bogert, *The Law of Trusts and Trustees*, 2nd ed. rev (1984), §19.
[69] (1953) 90 C.L.R. 86 at 97.

In respect of those proceeds from time to time bound by the trust, there is **3–46** nothing in the terms of the trust to negative the ordinary consequence that the trustee (the Buyer) is bound to apply that sum by accounting to or at the direction of a beneficiary (the Seller). It is convenient to identify the condition which limits the beneficiary's entitlement to call upon the trust property later in this judgment. As Professor Hayton points out,[70] with reference to authority,[71] because equity treats as done that which ought to be done, even if the proceeds were paid into a general bank account of the Buyer there could be a tracing remedy where the recipient was obliged to hold a particular portion of the proceeds on trust.

In the situation just considered, where the trust is performed and discharged by appropriation of the proceeds by the Seller, the relevant trust relationship between the Buyer and the Seller is brought to an end. A question may then arise whether, despite the Seller having been funded in this way, it might retain a good claim for that amount by an action in debt against the Buyer. The answer to that will be found not in trust law but in the terms, express or implied, of the contract between the Buyer and the Seller. In the formulation of those terms, particularly any implied terms, there is, to adapt the words of Lord Wilberforce, "surely no difficulty in recognising the co-existence in one transaction of legal and equitable rights and remedies"[72] and the giving of effect to "practical arrangements" by "the flexible interplay of law and equity" . . .[73]

The contractual agreements of the Buyer and Seller, in respect of each of the **3–47** Invoices, included the amount to be paid by the Buyer for the steel supplied under each Invoice and stated "PAYMENT DUE APPROX MID/END NOVEMBER '95". This latter term operated as a period of credit, commercially benefiting the Buyer. The question that arises is whether this term is inconsistent with the intention to constitute a trust in the manner described above. That is, whether the purported liberty of the Buyer not to pay the Seller is consistent with the obligation to create a trust of "proceeds" which might be received by the Buyer during the period of credit. This question is resolved by reference to the contract as a whole, including the implied terms that arise.

The rules governing the implication of an implied term as a matter of fact were **3–48** stated by the Privy Council in *BP Refinery (Westernport) Pty Ltd v Shire of Hastings* . . .[74]

The implication of an implied term operates to align, or give congruence to, the rights and obligations of the Buyer and Seller in contract and the intention of these parties to create a trust in the manner described above. An implied contractual term arises, as a matter of business efficacy, that upon the receipt by the Buyer of the relevant "proceeds" (and thus the constitution of a trust of part of those proceeds), the obligation in debt is discharged. The express term in the agreement (referred to above) which provides for a period of credit within which the debt need not be paid by the Buyer is, in turn, incorporated as an express term of the trust. This term thereby prescribes the period within which the Seller, as beneficiary, cannot call

---

[70] Underhill and Hayton, *Law Relating to Trusts and Trustees*, 15th ed. (1995) at 12(n); *cf.* Hayton, "The Uses of Trusts in the Commercial Context", in Hayton (ed.), *Modern International Developments in Trust Law*, (1999), p.145 at p.168.
[71] Including that of the Supreme Court of Canada in *Air Canada v M & L Travel Ltd* [1993] 3 S.C.R. 787 at 804–805 in which reliance was placed upon the judgment of Hope J.A. in *Stephens Travel Service International Pty Ltd (Receivers and Managers Appointed) v Qantas Airways Ltd* (1988) 13 N.S.W.L.R. 331 at 348–349, with which Kirby P. and Priestley J.A. agreed.
[72] *Quistclose Investments Ltd v Rolls Razor Ltd* [1970] A.C. 567 at 581.
[73] *Quistclose Investments Ltd v Rolls Razor Ltd* [1970] A.C. 567 at 582.
[74] (1977) 180 C.L.R. 266 at 283.

upon the trust property (if the trust is constituted during the credit period). The implied term thus provides one means of discharging the debt by performance. No relevant inconsistency arises between this implied term and the express term in the agreement providing for a period of credit for the Buyer . . .

3–49   Further, no inconsistency arises between the contractual agreement and the creation of a trust of property "equal in dollar terms [to] the amount owing by the [Buyer] to the [Seller] at the time of the receipt" of the proceeds.[75] Manifestly, this term did not operate to constitute a trust in respect of the whole of the proceeds received by the Buyer except, perhaps, coincidentally.

The Proceeds Subclause is an agreement to constitute a trust of future-acquired property. It is therefore not a "charge" within the meaning of s. 9 of the Law and the detailed provisions of the Law governing charges thus do not apply to it. The Proceeds Subclause is not a "registrable charge" within s. 262 and the Seller had no obligation to lodge a notice under s. 263 within the prescribed period (s 266(1)(c)). In turn, the Proceeds Subclause is not void as against the administrators or liquidator of the Buyer (see s. 266(1))."

RE EVTR

Court of Appeal [1987] B.C.LC 646

3–50   The appellant, who had won £240,000 on premium bonds, wanted to help the penurious company, which had employed him, to purchase new equipment. He deposited £60,000 with the company's solicitors to be released to the company "for the sole purpose of buying new equipment." The money was paid into the company's general funds and paid out in pursuit of the purpose. Receivers were appointed and the company ceased trading before delivery of the equipment, so that £48,536 of the £60,000 was returned to the company. The trial judge rejected the appellants claim to the money but the Court of Appeal upheld it.

3–51   DILLON L.J.: "In the forefront of the appellant's case counsel for the appellant (Mr Jackson) refers to the decision of the House of Lords in *Barclays Bank Ltd v Quistclose Investments Ltd* [1970] A.C. 567. There, Quistclose had lent money to a company (Rolls Razor Ltd) on an agreed condition that the money be used only for the purpose of paying a particular dividend which the company had declared. In the event the company went into liquidation, after receiving Quistclose's money, but without having paid the dividend. It was held that Quistclose could claim the whole of the money back, as on a resulting trust, the specific purpose having failed, and Quistclose was not limited to proving as an unsecured creditor in the liquidation of the company.

3–52   In the present case the £60,000 was released by Knapp-Fishers to the company on the appellant's instructions for a specific purpose only, namely the sole purpose of buying new equipment. Accordingly, I have no doubt, in the light of *Quistclose*, that, if the company had gone into liquidation, or the receivers had been appointed, and the scheme had become abortive before the £60,000 had been disbursed by the company, the appellant would have been entitled to recover his full £60,000, as between himself and the company, on the footing that it was impliedly held by the company as a resulting trust for him as the particular purpose of the loan had failed.

"At the other end of the spectrum, if after the £60,000 had been expended by the company as it was, the Encore System had been duly delivered to, and accepted by,

---

[75] See Underhill and Hayton, *Law Relating to Trusts and Trustees*, 15th ed. (1995), pp.11–12.

the company, there could be no doubt that the appellant's only right would have been as an unsecured creditor of the company for the £60,000. There would have been no question of the Encore System, or any interest in it, being held on any sort of trust for the appellant, and if, after it had been delivered and installed, the company had sold the system, the appellant could have had no claim whatsoever to the proceeds of sale as trust moneys held in trust for him.

"The present case lies on its facts between those two extremes of the spectrum . . .

"On *Quistclose* principles, a resulting trust in favour of the provider of the money **3–53** arises when money is provided for a particular purpose only, and that purpose fails. In the present case, the purpose for which the £60,000 was provided by the appellant to the company was, as appears from the authority to Knapp-Fishers, the purpose of (the company) buying new equipment. But in any realistic sense of the words that purpose has failed in that the company has never acquired any new equipment, whether the Encore System which was then in mind or anything else. True it is that the £60,000 was paid out by the company with a view to the acquisition of new equipment, but that was only at half-time, and I do not see why the final whistle should be blown at half-time. The proposed acquisition proved abortive and a large part of the £60,000 has therefore been repaid by the payees. The repayments were made because of, or on account of, the payments which made up the £60,000 and those were payments of trust moneys. It is a long-established principle of Equity that, if a person who is a trustee receives money or property because of, or in respect of, trust property, he will hold what he receives as a constructive trustee on the trusts of the original trust property. It follows, in my judgment, that the repayments made to the receivers are subject to the same trusts as the original £60,000 in the hands of the company. There is now, of course, no question of the £48,536 [*i.e.* the repayments] being applied in the purchase of new equipment for the company, and accordingly, in my judgment, it is now held on a resulting trust for the appellant."

TRUSTS AND POWERS

Special attention has to be given to the distinction between trusts and **3–54** powers which is complicated by the fact that the trustees will in many cases not just have trusts which they *must* carry out (*e.g.* "on trust to distribute the income between such of my descendants as they see fit from time to time") but also distributive (as opposed to administrative) powers concerning distributing income or capital (*e.g.* "but so that my trustees may instead distribute the income between such charities as they may see fit from time to time") which they *may or may not* exercise. Furthermore, in construing a clause in a trust deed there may be a fine (and perhaps artificial) distinction between (a) a power of distribution of income coupled with a trust to dispose of the undistributed surplus and (b) a trust for distribution coupled with a power to withhold a portion and accumulate it or otherwise dispose of it, (*e.g.* (a) on trust to pay or apply the income to or for the benefit of such of my family company's employees, ex-employees and their relatives and dependants as my trustees may see fit but so that my trustees shall pay or apply any income not so paid or applied within three months of receipt by my trustees to or for the benefit of such of my issue as my trustees shall see fit and (b) on trust to pay or apply the income to or for the benefit of such of my family company's employees, ex-employees and their relatives and dependants as my trustees shall see fit but so that my trustees may pay or apply any income within three months of receiving it to or for the benefit of such of my issue as my trustees may see fit).

3–55   A trustee *must*[76] act in accordance with the terms of the trust and whilst such terms may leave him no discretion (*e.g.* if holding on trust for A for life, remainder to B, when he must pay the income to A and then, on A's death, pay the capital to B) sometimes such terms may afford him some discretion, as in the case of a discretionary trust (*e.g.* on trust to distribute the income and capital as he sees fit between such of A, B, C, D and E and their spouses and issue as he may choose). Lack of someone to enforce a trust is fatal to its validity.[77]

3–56   A power, which is the authority to deal with property which one does not own, may be legal where it is a statutory power of attorney[78] or a mortgagee's statutory power of sale,[79] but it is usually a power to choose who are to be the beneficial recipients of property and such power of appointment is equitable[80] and will arise under a trust. Such a power will be a special power unless the donee can on his own appoint to himself when it will be a general power.[81] Where a special power is exercisable in favour of everyone but a small excepted class (*e.g.* the settlor and his spouse and past and present trustees) it is often referred to as a hybrid or intermediate power.[82] The validity of a trust depends upon the existence of a person with *locus standi* positively to enforce it but this does not appear necessary for the validity of a power.[83]

3–57   The donee of a special power will usually be a trustee but, as far as the power is concerned, the donee *may or may not* exercise it as he chooses, *e.g.* where he holds on trust with power to distribute income amongst such of V, W, X, Y, Z as he sees fit but in default of appointment upon trust for A for life, remainder to B absolutely. Here, he can choose whether or not to pay income to V, W, X, Y, Z but, if he does not so choose or does not exercise his discretion in respect of particular income within a reasonable time so that his discretion is extinguished,[84] then the income in question must be paid to A. A trustee with a special power must ask two interrelated questions: (1) "Shall I exercise the power?" (2) "If so, how shall I exercise it?" A trustee of a discretionary trust just asks "How shall I exercise my duty to distribute income amongst the beneficiaries?"

---

[76] If he does not then the court will intervene to ensure that the trusts are carried out: *McPhail v Doulton* [1971] A.C. 424 at 457, see at para.3–135.
[77] Except in limited anomalous cases where the "trusts" are in substance "powers," see at para.3–206.
[78] Powers of Attorney Act 1971; Trustee Delegation Act 1999.
[79] Law of Property Act 1925, ss.88, 101, 104.
[80] *ibid.* s.1(7).
[81] *Re Penrose* [1933] Ch. 793, Perpetuities Act 1964, s.7.
[82] *Re Hay's Settlement* [1982] 1 W.L.R. 202.
[83] *Re Shaw*, [1957] 1 All E.R. 745 at 759 endorsed by *Re Wooton's W.T.* [1968] 2 All E.R. 618 at 624; Morris Leach, *Rule Against Perpetuities* (2nd ed.), p.320.
[84] *Re Allen-Meyrick's W.T.* [1966] 1 W.L.R. 499; *Re Gulbenkian's S.T. (No.2)* [1970] Ch. 408.

Powers are fiduciary or personal

Whilst the donee of a power of appointment need not exercise it he will, if **3–58**
a trustee, be under an obligation bona fide to consider exercising the power
and to this end to take reasonable steps to discover the identities and needs
of objects of the power, before considering the appropriateness of individual appointments.[85] Someone who is donee of a special power in a personal,
as opposed to a fiduciary, capacity is not under the obligation to consider
exercising the power (*e.g.* where a testator's will trusts have E and F as
trustees but the widow life tenant is given power to appoint capital between
grandchildren). The personal donee of a special power can release it unlike
a fiduciary donee who can only do so if authorised by the trust instrument.[86]
Powers vested in trustees as such are fiduciary (*i.e.* the power is conferred
upon a trustee the better to enable him to fulfil his trusteeship role and not
for his personal use unconstrained by any obligations relating to its use[87])
unless there is express contrary intent in the trust instrument.

Position of beneficiaries and of objects of powers

Beneficiaries under a discretionary trust and objects of a fiduciary power **3–59**
held by trustees have some common rights.[88] Both have a right to retain any
sums properly paid by the trustees in exercise of their discretion; both have
a right to be considered by the trustees with a view to a distribution in their
favour, though the trustees' duty of inquiry of possible recipients is higher
where they have to carry out discretionary trusts than where they merely
have to consider whether or not to exercise a power.[89] However, where
under discretionary trusts income has to be distributed year by year (an
exhaustive discretionary trust)[90] amongst a discretionary class then if all
members of such class are ascertained and of full capacity they can, if
unanimous, call for the income and so have a collectively enforceable right:
they can have a similar right if also similarly interested in capital.[91] The
collective objects of a special power can have no such right. Furthermore,
discretionary trusts over income remain exercisable despite the passing of
time, though only in favour of such persons as would have been possible
beneficiaries if the discretion had been exercised within a reasonable time,
whilst if powers over income are not exercised within a reasonable time the
discretion is extinguished and the default beneficiaries are entitled.[92]

---

[85] *McPhail v Doulton* [1971] A.C. 424; *Re Manisty* [1974] Ch. 17; *Re Hay's S.T.* [1982] 1 W.L.R. 202, see
para.3–137.
[86] *Re Wills's Trust Deeds* [1964] Ch. 219. See further, para.3–103.
[87] *Re Bacon* [1907] 1 Ch. 475 at 487; *Re Wills' Trust Deed* [1964] Ch. 219 at 231; *Re Gulbenkian's Settlements*
[1970] A.C. 508 at 518.
[88] *Vestey v I.R.C.* [1979] 2 All E.R. 225 at 235–236.
[89] *McPhail v Doulton* [1971] A.C. 424.
[90] A discretionary trust is "exhaustive" where the trustees must distribute the income amongst class "A" and
"non-exhaustive" where the trustees must distribute the income amongst class "A" *only* if they fail to
exercise a power to withhold the income for some purpose such as accumulating it or using it for class
"B." There is a fine line between the latter situation and a trust for accumulation or for benefiting
discretionary class "B" with a power to benefit discretionary class "A." See *Sainsbury v I.R.C.* [1970] 1 Ch.
712; *McPhail v Doulton* [1971] A.C. 424 at 448.
[91] *Re Smith* [1928] Ch. 915; *Saunders v Vautier* (1841) Cr. & Ph. 240. Rights to capital are often contingent
upon being alive at the "closing date" of the trust, so preventing a *Saunders v Vautier* right arising.
[92] *Re Locker's S.T.* [1977] 1 W.L.R. 1323; *Re Allen-Meyrick's W.T.* [1966] 1 W.L.R. 499.

Finally, trustees are under a core duty, so far as practicable, to inform beneficiaries of full capacity and objects of fiduciary powers of full capacity who are primary objects of the settlor's bounty that they are beneficiaries or objects, so as to give substance to their core right to make the trustees account for the stewardship of the trust fund.[93] Indeed, the settlor can be forced to tell them the name and address of the trustees.[94] However, it is open to a settlor by expressly creating only a personal power to exclude any rights of objects of powers other than the first right mentioned at the beginning of the paragraph.[95]

Problems as to trust or power intentions

3–60   Problems can arise in ascertaining the intentions of a testator. He may intend to leave property to his executors and trustees on trust for W for life with:

(1) a mere power for her to appoint the capital amongst such of their children as she may see fit, so that if the power is not exercised the capital is held on a resulting trust for the testator's estate[96];

(2) a mere power for her to appoint the capital amongst such of their children as she may see fit, but in default of appointment remainder for their children equally[97] (a fixed trust);

(3) a mere power for her to appoint the capital amongst such of their children as she may see fit, but in default of appointment for such of their children and in such shares as his executors and trustees shall select in their absolute discretion[98] (a discretionary trust);

(4) a "trust" power whereby she *must* exercise her power to appoint the capital (vested in the executors and trustees) amongst such of their children as she sees fit.[99] If this discretionary trust is unexercised at her death then the court will order equal division on the basis that

---

[93] *Schmidt v Rosewood Trust Ltd* [2003] 2 A.C. 709.

[94] *Re Murphy's Settlements* [1999] 1 W.L.R. 282.

[95] See *Re Manisty's S.T.* [1974] Ch. 17 at, 25, 27–28, *Steele v Paz Ltd* [1993–95] Manx L.R. 426.

[96] *Re Weekes's Settlement* [1897] 1 Ch. 289, see at para.3–63; *Re Combe* [1925] 1 Ch. 210 (after life interest, "in trust for such persons as my said son shall by will appoint but such appointment must be confined to relations of mine of the whole blood": held resulting trust when no appointment made); *Re Poulton's W.T.* [1987] 1 All E.R. 1068.

[97] *Wilson v Duguid* (1883) 24 Ch.D. 244 (trust for A for life, remainder to such of his children as he should by any writing appoint: held children had vested interests, liable to be divested by exercise of power, since there was an *implied* gift to the children equally in default of appointment). If A's power had only been exercisable by will then the implied gift in default of appointment would have been only to those children alive at A's death, since any appointment could only have been in favour of those children: *Walsh v Wallinger* (1830) 2 Russ.& M. 78 at 81. One should note that "to W for life, remainder to our children equally, but so that W may instead appoint the capital between our children in such shares as she may see fit" is equivalent to "to W for life, with power for her to appoint the capital amongst our children as she sees fit, but in default of appointment for our children equally": the children in both cases have immediate vested interests liable to be divested. See *Re Llewellyn's Settlement* [1921] 2 Ch. 281; *Re Arnold* [1947] Ch. 131.

[98] This gift on discretionary trust in default of appointment will need to be express, whereas a gift to beneficiaries equally in default of appointment may well be implied. If the trustees do not select beneficiaries then new trustees can be appointed or the court may order equal distribution in the absence of a more appropriate basis for distribution: *McPhail v Doulton* [1971] A.C. 424 at 457.

[99] *Brown v Higgs* (1803) 8 Ves.561; M. C. Cullity (1976) 54 Can.B.R. 229.

equality is equity[1] unless some other basis for distribution appears more appropriate[2] (which may well be the case if the class of objects is broader, *e.g.*, my children and my nephews and nieces and the children of such persons).

Where the class of objects is so large that they cannot all be listed then, **3–61** obviously, there can be no question of equal division under an implied gift in default of appointment. Thus, in welfare trusts for employees, ex-employees and their relations and dependants where the trustees are empowered to make grants to such persons, the question that arises is whether the relevant clause in the trust deed is a mere power or a "trust" power.[3] Where the person with the "trust" power has the trust property vested in him it has become the modern usage simply to say that he holds the property on discretionary trust.[4]

The similarities between discretionary trusts and powers have led to the certainty test being the same for both: both are valid if it can be said with certainty of any given beneficiary or object that he is or is not a member of the class of beneficiaries or objects.[5] For a fixed trust for equal division, however, since it is necessary to know the exact number of beneficiaries to arrange for equal arithmetical division, the trust will only be valid if a comprehensive list of all the beneficiaries can be drawn up.

In reading cases and textbooks it is necessary to be aware of the fact that **3–62** discretionary trusts are sometimes referred to as trust powers or powers in the nature of a trust, and that the situation where, after a power, there is implied a trust in default for persons equally, is sometimes referred to as a trust power or a power in the nature of a trust or a power coupled with a trust.

In ascertaining whether or not only a mere power and no more is intended the following propositions[6] can be stated:

(1) If there is a gift over in default of appointment, the power is a mere power,[7] even where the gift over is void for some reason.[8]

---

[1] In *Wilson v Duguid* (1883) 24 Ch.D. 244 at 249 Chitty J. adverts to the distinction between a trust power and a trust in default of appointment under a mere power. Where the class is small like "children," then the class members take equally on either view (*e.g. Burrough v Philcox* (1840) 5 My. & Cr. 72) so why create the paradoxical concept of a trust power as inquired by M. G. Unwin (1962) 26 Conv 92? See also [1984] Conv 227 (Bartlett and Stebbings). However, unequal division is possible in the case of a trust power and this may be appropriate where the class is larger, *e.g.* my children and my nephews and nieces and their issue. Moreover, even where the class is as small as children it may be that the class includes children who predeceased W and the court may prefer to divide the capital only between those alive at W's death. If the class is children or grandchildren it is likely the gift to grandchildren will be treated as a substitutionary gift in the event of predeceasing children, so the children will take *per stirpes* like the statutory trusts on intestacy: *above*, para.1–137.
[2] *McPhail v Doulton* [1971] A.C. 424, at para.3–124.
[3] *ibid.*
[4] *e.g. Re Baden's Deed Trusts (No.2)* [1973] Ch. 9; *Re Hay's S.T.* [1982] 1 W.L.R. 202, at para.3–137.
[5] *McPhail v Doulton* [1971] A.C. 424, at para.3–124.
[6] It should be noted that general powers of appointment are never considered to be in the nature of trusts, since there is no class of persons in whose favour the trust could operate. The question, therefore, arises only in connection with special powers of appointment.
[7] *e.g. Re Mills* [1930] 1 Ch. 654.
[8] *Re Sprague* (1880) 43 L.T. 236; *Re Sayer* [1957] Ch. 423.

(2) A residuary gift in favour of the donee of the power is not a gift over for this purpose.[9]

(3) To cause a power to be treated as a mere power only, the gift over must be in default of appointment, and not for any other event. Thus in the absence of a gift in default of appointment, a gift over on the failure of the appointees or any of them to reach a specified age will not necessarily prevent the power from being treated as a discretionary trust or prevent the implication of a trust for the objects equalty in default of appointment.[10]

(4) Where there is no gift over in default of appointment, the power may be only a mere power, or a power coupled with an implied trust in default of appointment, or a trust power or discretionary trust, according to the true intention of the settlor.[11]

RE WEEKES' SETTLEMENT

Chancery Division [1897] 1 Ch. 289; 66 L.J.Ch. 179; 76 L.T. 112.

3–63 A testatrix gave a life interest in property to her husband with a "power to dispose of all such property by will amongst our children in accordance with the power granted to him as regards the other property which I have under my marriage settlements."[12] There was in her will no gift over in default of appointment, and the husband died intestate without having exercised the power. The surviving children of the marriage claimed the property in equal shares, on the ground that there was an implied gift to them in default of appointment.

ROMER J.: ". . . The husband did not exercise the power of appointment, and the question is whether the children take in default of appointment.

"Now, apart from the authorities, I should gather from the terms of the will that it was a mere power that was conferred on the husband, and not one coupled with a trust that he was bound to exercise. I see no words in the will to justify me in holding that the testatrix intended that the children should take if her husband did not execute the power.

3–64 "This is not a case of a gift to the children with power to the husband to select, or to such of the children as the husband should select by exercising the power.

"If in this case the testatrix really intended to give a life interest to her husband and a mere power to appoint if he chose, and intended if he did not think fit to appoint that the property should go as in default of appointment according to the settlement, why should she be bound to say more than she has said in this will?

"I come to the conclusion on the words of this will that the testatrix only intended to give a life interest and a power to her husband—certainly she has not said more than that.

"Am I then bound by the authorities to hold otherwise? I think I am not. The authorities do not show, in my opinion, that there is a hard-and-fast rule that a gift

---

[9] *Re Brierley* [1894] 43 W.R. 36.
[10] *Re Llewellyn's Settlement* [1921] 2 Ch. 281.
[11] *Burrough v Philcax* (1840) 5 My. & Cr. 72; *Re Weekes's Settlement*, below; *Re Combe* [1925] Ch. 210; *Re Perowne* [1951] Ch. 785; *Re Scarisbrick* [1951] Ch. 622; *Re Arnold's Trusts* [1947] Ch. 131; *McPhail v Doulton* [1971] A.C. 424.
[12] There were gifts over in default of appointment in those settlements.

to A for life with a power to A to appoint among a class and nothing more must, if there is no gift over in the will, be held a gift by implication to the class in default of the power being exercised. In my opinion the cases show (though there may be found here and there certain remarks of a few learned judges which, if not interpreted by the facts of the particular case before them, might seem to have a more extended operation) that you must find in the will an indication that the testatrix did intend the class or some of the class to take—intended in fact that the power should be regarded in the nature of a trust, only a power of selection being given, as, for example, a gift to A for life with a gift over to such of a class as A shall appoint . . ."

Held, the power was a mere power only so the children were therefore not entitled in default of appointment.

THE NECESSARY LANGUAGE TO REVEAL INTENT TO CREATE A TRUST

No technical expressions are necessary to create a trust so long as some **3–65** imperative formula is used to indicate that the person owning the property in question is to be subject to a legally binding obligation to hold and manage the property for others (or himself and others). Wills often create problems where a testator expresses his confidence, wish, hope or request that a particular legatee should use the legacy in a certain way. Originally, the courts[13] were only too ready to treat such precatory words as creating a trust and as James L.J. said in *Lamb v Eames*[14] "the officious kindness of the Court of Chancery in interposing trusts where in many cases the father of the family never meant to create trusts, must have been a very cruel kindness indeed." Since the 1870s the courts have not allowed precatory words to create a trust unless on the consideration of the will as a whole it was clearly the intention of the testator to create a trust.[15] By Administration of Justice Act 1982, section 21 extrinsic evidence, including evidence of the testator's intention, may be admitted to assist in its interpretation (a) in so far as any part of the will is meaningless (b) in so far as the language used in any part of it is ambiguous on the face of it and (c) in so far as evidence, *other than evidence of the testator's intention*, shows that the language used in any part of it is ambiguous in the light of the surrounding circumstances.

The following clauses have been held, in context, not to create a trust: **3–66** "feeling confident that she will act justly to our children in dividing the same when no longer required by her,"[16] "it is my desire that she allows A.G. an annuity of £25 during her life,"[17] "I wish them to bequeath the same equally between the families of O and P,"[18] "in the fullest trust and

---

[13] *Eade v Eade* (1820) 5 Madd. 118 at 121; *Palmer v Simmonds* (1854) 2 Drew 221; *Gutty v Cregoe* (1857) 24 Beav 185.

[14] (1871) 6 Ch.App. 597.

[15] *Lamb v Eames* (1871) 6 Ch.App. 597; *Re Adams and Kensington Vestry* (1884) 27 Ch.D. 394. In *Re Steele's W.T.* [1948] Ch. 603 an unusual precatory formula for disposing of jewellery which Page-Wood V.-C. in *Shelley v Shelley* (1868) L.R. 6 Eq. 540, had held created a trust was also apt to create a trust since it was likely the professional draftsman had the earlier formula in mind: (1968) 32 Conv 361 (P. St. J. Langan).

[16] *Mussoorie Bank Ltd v Raynor* (1882) 7 App.Cas.221.

[17] *Re Diggles* (1888) 39 Ch.D. 253.

[18] *Re Hamilton* (1895) 2 Ch. 370.

confidence that she will carry out my wishes in the following particulars,"[19]
"I request that C on her death leave her property to my four sisters."[20]
Nowadays, Administration of Justice Act 1982, section 22 states, "Except
where a contrary intent is shown, it shall be presumed that if a testator
devises or bequeaths property to his spouse in terms which in themselves
would give an absolute interest to the spouse but by the same instrument
purports to give his issue an interest in the same property, the gift to the
spouse is absolute notwithstanding the purported gift to the issue", *e.g.* "all
my property to my wife and after her death to our children."

3–67   In *Comiskey v Bowring-Hanbury*[21] a testator left to his wife "the whole of
my real and personal estate in full confidence that she will make such use of
it as I should have made myself and that at her death she will devise *it* to
such one or more of my nieces as she may think fit and in default of any
disposition by her thereof by her will I hereby *direct* that all my estate and
property acquired by her under this my will *shall* at her death be equally
divided among the surviving said nieces." The House of Lords (Lord
Lindley dissenting) held a trust had been created: the widow could have the
use of the property (*e.g.* income, occupation of the house) and could
manage it (she was Settled Land Act tenant for life) but the capital had to
pass on her death to the nieces equally if not passed to them in other shares
by her will.

3–68   Recently the Court of Appeal[22] has not been as strict as formerly in
requiring clear evidence of an intent to create a trust, but it does recognise
that a settlor does not actually need to know that it is technically a trust
that he is creating: he is taken to intend the legal consequences that would
be apparent to a lawyer.[23]

An intention to create a trust of property normally requires indications
that the alleged trustee is to be obliged to keep the specific trust property
separate from his own.[24] After all if a recipient of money:

> "is not bound to keep the money separate, but is entitled to mix it with
> his own money and deal with it as he pleases, and when called upon to
> hand over an equivalent sum of money, then he is not a trustee of the
> money but merely a debtor."[25]

---

[19] *Re Williams* [1897] 2 Ch. 12.
[20] *Re Johnson* [1939] 2 All E.R. 458.
[21] [1905] A.C. 84.
[22] *Paul v Constance*, below, para.3–73; *Re Vandervell's Trusts (No.2)* [1974] Ch. 269, *above*, at para.2–67; *Re Chelsea Cloisters Ltd* (1980) 41 P. & C.R. 98.
[23] See also Buckley L.J. on the creation of an equitable charge in *Swiss Bank Corporation v Lloyds Bank* [1980] 2 All E.R. 419 at 426: "notwithstanding that the matter depends on the intention of the parties, if on the true construction of the relevant documents in the light of any admissible evidence as to surrounding circumstances the parties have entered into a transaction the legal effect of which is to give rise to an equitable charge, the fact that they may not have realised this consequence will not mean that there is no charge. They must be presumed to intend the consequences of their acts." Also *Clough Mill Ltd v Martin,* above, paras 3–25 *et seq.*
[24] *Paragon Finance plc v Thakerar & Co* [1999] 1 All E.R. 400 at 416; *Re Goldcorp Exchange Ltd* [1995] 1 A.C. 74; *Re English & American Insurance Co. Ltd* [1994] 1 B.C.L.C. 345.
[25] *Henry v Hammond* [1913] 2 K.B. 515 at 521; *R. v Clowes (No.2)* [1994] 2 All E.R. 316 at 325; *Commissioners of Customs & Excise v Richmond Theatre Management Ltd* [1995] S.T.C. 257.

However, mingling of funds will not be fatal to the funding of a trust **3–69**
where T receives funds from A, B and C for such funds or investments
purchased therewith to be held separately from T's own assets, on a trust
for A, B and C in their proportionate shares[26] or where T adds funds of A,
B and C to funds of his in a separate account so that such funds or ·
investments purchased therewith are held separately from T's own assets on
trust for A, B and C and T in proportionate shares.[27] T can also contract
with X that if he receives proceeds of sale materialising from some
specified future property, he will hold all or a specified part on trust for X,
such trust then affecting the certain whole or part of the ascertained
proceeds when received by T. Thus, even if they are mingled with T's funds
in T's general bank account X has a right to trace such amount until
properly placed in a separate account for X.[28]

Shams

Even if language is used that would clearly suffice to create a trust for **3–70**
beneficiaries subsequent language in the trust instrument may indicate that
there is no true trust for those beneficiaries, only a sham trust, the true trust
being to hold the trust fund (as to capital and income) for the settlor
absolutely, albeit with power to benefit beneficiaries, so the settlor remains
full beneficial owner of the trust fund. An example would be where a later
clause stipulates that during the life of the settlor no beneficiary is to be
informed of the trust and any beneficiary who discovers the trust cannot sue
the trustees in respect of anything occurring or not occurring in the lifetime
of the settlor, so beneficiaries have no rights in the settlor's lifetime.[29]

Instead of a trust being a sham on the face of the trust instrument, a trust **3–71**
can be a sham in substance[30] because the *common understanding*[31] at the
outset between the settlor and the trustee is that the trustee is to do
whatever the settlor wants with the trust property.

If for some reason (*e.g.* a settlor's poor understanding of English) a trust **3–72**
company put a simple discretionary trust for the settlor's descendants in
front of the settlor and unknowingly allowed the settlor to believe the trust
fund was held to his order like a bank account, although the trust company
intended to run a proper trust for the settlor's descendants, the settlor
could recover the property as his own if the trust company refused his
request to pay him monies after two years or so of giving effect to his
requests because they were in favour of his children and the trust company

---

[26] *R. v Clowes (No.2)*, above; *Re Goldcorp Exchange Ltd*, above.
[27] *Re Lewis's of Leicester Ltd* [1995] 1 B.C.L.C. 428.
[28] *Re Fleet Disposal Services Ltd* [1995] 1 B.C.L.C. 345: *Associated Alloys Pty Ltd ACN 001 452 106 Pty Ltd (in liquidation)* (2000) 74 A.L.J.R 862, above, at para.3–39; *cf. Re ILG Travel* [1995] 2 B.C.L.C. 128; *Pullan v Koe* [1913] 1 Ch. 9; *Palette Shoes Pty Ltd. v Krohn* (1937) 58 C.L.R. 1 at 27 and para.6–86.
[29] The disposition in their favour is a testamentary disposition requiring compliance with the formalities for wills."If the beneficiaries have no rights enforceable against the trustees there are no trusts" for the beneficiaries: *Armitage v Nurse* [1998] Ch. 241, 253 *per* Millett L.J.
[30] *R v Dimsey, R v Allen* [1999] S.T.C. 846, 870–871, *Rahman v Chase Bank (C.I) Trust Co Ltd* [1991] Jersey L.R., *Midland Bank v Wyatt* [1995] 1 F.L.R. 697, *Chase Manhattan Equities Ltd v Goodman* [1991] B.C.L.C. 897.
[31] *Shalon v Russo* [2003] W.T.L.R. 1165, *Re Esteem Settlement* [2004] W.T.L.R. 1.

itself considered it sensible to benefit the children as requested. Strictly, it would seem that the trust property from the outset has been held to his order in accordance with his intention so he can order the return of the property, although if regarded as creating a true trust by mistake he can anyhow set it aside for mistake.[32]

PAUL v CONSTANCE

Court of Appeal [1977] 1 W.L.R. 527; [1977] 1 All E.R. 195 (Scarman, Bridge and Cairns L.JJ.)

3–73   SCARMAN L.J.: "Mr. Dennis Albert Constance was a wage earner living in Cheltenham until he died on March 9, 1974. He was married to Bridget Frances Constance, the defendant in this action. But they parted in June 1965. In 1967 Mr. Constance met Mrs. Doreen Grace Paul, who is the plaintiff in this action. The two of them set up house together in December of that year, and they lived to all appearances as man and wife up to the date of Mr. Constance's death. The house in which they lived was the property of the plaintiff.

3–74   "In August 1969 Mr. Constance was injured at his work. He claimed damages against his employers . . . his claim was disposed of by the payment to him of a sum of £950. This money he received by cheque early in 1973. He discussed with the plaintiff what to do with the money, and the evidence is clear that they decided it was to go into a bank account. The two of them went to see the manager of the St. George's Square branch of Lloyds Bank in Cheltenham, and there they had a discussion about opening a bank account. According to the notes of evidence which the trial judge made, the two of them had a discussion with the bank manager. He explained to them the different sorts of accounts which they could open, and the decision was taken to open a deposit account. At that stage Mr. Constance revealed that they were not married. It is perhaps of some significance in understanding this interview if one recalls the evidence that was given by a Mr. Thomas, a fellow employee of Mr. Constance's, who said that he knew that they were not married but most people did not. After Mr. Constance had told the manager that they were not married the manager said: 'Well, it will be in your name only then?' Mr. Constance said; 'Yes.' Then Mr. Constance asked the manager what was to happen if the plaintiff wanted to draw on the account, or if he wanted the plaintiff to draw on it, and the manager said that that could be done if she used a note with Mr. Constance's signature on it authorising her to draw on the account.

3–75   "The account that was opened on that day in February 1973 is at the very heart of this case. The account was maintained in Mr. Constance's name from that date until the date of his death. Over the period between 1973 and his death, some 13 months later in 1974, further sums were paid into the account including, in particular, some sums which represented 'bingo' winnings. It is clear from the evidence that Mr. Constance and the plaintiff did play 'bingo,' and they played it really as a joint venture. They did have winnings from time to time, and at any rate three of such winnings—none of them very great—were paid into the account. It is clear from the plaintiff's evidence that they thought of those winnings as 'their winnings': neither hers nor his alone, but theirs. Nevertheless, when the account was closed on the death of Mr. Constance the ultimate balance, after the addition of interest,

---

[32] *Gibbon v Mitchell* [1990] 3 All E.R. 338, *Dent v Dent* [1996] I W.L.R. 683.

consisted largely of the initial sum of £950 representing Mr. Constance's damages as a result of his injury at work. There was one withdrawal during this period, a sum of £150, and the evidence was that that money was divided between the two of them after part of it had been used for buying Christmas presents and some food.

"The plaintiff began her action after the death of Mr. Constance against his lawful wife, the defendant, who took out letters of administration for his estate since he died intestate. The plaintiff claims that the bank account in his name, to which I have referred, was held by him on trust for the benefit of himself and the plaintiff jointly. She claims that it was an express trust declared orally by him on numerous occasions. The defendant maintains that the whole fund contained in the account was the beneficial property of the deceased at the time of his death, and, as such, became part of his estate after death.

"The matter came on for trial and on August 12 the Judge found in favour of the plaintiff. He found the existence of an express trust, a trust for the benefit of the plaintiff and the deceased jointly, and he ordered that the sum of £499.21 be paid to the plaintiff as representing one half share of the fund to which she was beneficially entitled.

"The only point taken by the defendant on her appeal to this court goes to the question whether or not there was, in the circumstances of this case, an express declaration of trust. **3–76**

"Counsel for the defendant drew the attention of the court to the so- called three certainties that have to be established before the court can infer the creation of a trust. We are concerned only with one of the three certainties, and it is this (Snell's Equity 27th ed at 111):

> 'The words [that is the words of the declaration relied on] must be so used that on the whole they ought to be construed as imperative. [A little later on the learned author says:] No particular form of expression is necessary for the creation of a trust, if on the whole it can be gathered that a trust was intended. A trust may well be created, although there may be an absence of any expression in terms imposing confidence. A trust may thus be created without using the word "trust," for what the court regards is the substance and effect of the words used.'

"Counsel for the defendant has taken the court through the detailed evidence and submits that one cannot find anywhere in the history of events a declaration of trust in the sense of finding the deceased man, Mr. Constance, saying: 'I am now disposing of my interest in this fund so that you, Mrs. Paul, now have a beneficial interest in it.' Of course, the words which I have just used are stilted lawyers' language, and counsel for the plaintiff was right to remind the court that we are dealing with simple people, unaware of the subtleties of equity, but understanding very well indeed their own domestic situation. It is right that one should consider the various things that were said and done by the plaintiff and Mr. Constance during their time together against their own background and in their own circumstances. **3–77**

"Counsel for the defendant drew our attention to two cases [*Jones v Lock*[33] and *Richards v Delbridge*],[34] and he relies on them as showing that, though a man may say in clear and unmistakable terms that he intends to make a gift to some other person, for instance his child or some other member of his family, yet that does not

---

[33] (1865) 1 Ch.App. 25.
[34] (1874) L.R. 18 Eq. 11.

necessarily disclose a declaration of trust; and, indeed, in the two cases to which we have been referred the court held that, though there was a plain intention to make a gift, it was not right to infer any intention to create a trust . . .

3–78   "There is no suggestion of a gift by transfer in this case. The facts of those cases do not, therefore, very much help the submission of counsel for the defendant, but he was able to extract from them this principle: that there must be a clear declaration of trust, and that means there must be clear evidence from what is said or done of an intention to create a trust, or as counsel for the defendant put it, 'an intention to dispose of a property or a fund so that somebody else to the exclusion of the disponent acquires the beneficial interest in it.' He submitted that there was no such evidence.

"When one looks to the detailed evidence to see whether it goes as far as that— and I think that the evidence does have to go as far as that—one finds that from the time that Mr. Constance received his damages right up to his death he was saying, on occasions, that the money was as much the plaintiff's as his. When they discussed the damages, how to invest them or what to do with them, when they discussed the bank account, he would say to her: 'The money is as much yours as mine.' The judge, rightly treating the basic problem in the case as a question of fact, reached this conclusion. He said:

'I have read through my notes, and I am quite satisfied that it was the intention of [the plaintiff] and Mr. Constance to create a trust in which both of them were interested.'

3–79   "In this court the issue becomes: was there sufficient evidence to justify the judge reaching that conclusion of fact? In submitting that there was, counsel for the plaintiff draws attention first and foremost to the words used. When one bears in mind the unsophisticated character of Mr. Constance and his relationship with the plaintiff during the last few years of his life, counsel for the plaintiff submits that the words that he did use on more than one occasion namely: 'This money is as much yours as mine,' convey clearly a present declaration that the existing fund was as much the plaintiff's as his own. The judge accepted that conclusion. I think he was well justified in doing so and, indeed, I think he was right to do so. There are, as counsel for the plaintiff reminded us, other features in the history of the relation- ship between the plaintiff and Mr. Constance which support the interpretation of those words as an express declaration of trust. I have already described the interview with the bank manager when the account was opened. I have mentioned also the putting of the 'bingo' winnings into the account, and the one withdrawal for the benefit of both of them.

The question, therefore, is whether in all the circumstances the use of those words on numerous occasions as between Mr. Constance and the plaintiff constituted an express declaration of trust. The judge found that they did. For myself, I think he was right so to find. I therefore would dismiss the appeal."[35]

Section 2. Certainty of Subject-matter

3–80   Certainty of subject-matter requires that the property to be held on trust must be certain for otherwise there will be nothing specific to which the

---

[35] Why was Mrs.Paul not entitled to the whole £998.42 as surviving joint tenant? *cf. Re Osoba* [1979] 2 All E.R. 393. Ought it not to be possible to identify a declaration of trust at a particular time, *e.g.* to know when Mrs.Paul's right commenced for limitation purposes, or for entitlement to interest?

trust can attach.[36] It is also necessary that the beneficial interests to be taken by the beneficiaries must be certain,[37] However, where a court is imposing a constructive trust to prevent fraudulent or unconscionable behaviour of a defendant trying to take advantage of uncertainty it will circumvent problems of uncertainty.[38] This justifies the imposition of the common intention constructive trust of a fair share in a family home and even the "floating trust" discussed in *Birmingham v Renfrew*[39] (and accepted in *Ottaway v Norman*[40] and *Re Cleaver*[41]) against a defendant who agreed (under a mutual will or a secret trust) with a deceased testator to accept such a trust.

Where property is transferred to a trustee to hold separately from the **3–81** rest of his assets such property is necessarily identified by virtue of the transfer. Identifiability problems, however, arise if T purports to declare himself trustee of some of his property. "It makes no difference what the parties intended, if what they intend is impossible: as is the case with an immediate transfer of [legal or equitable] title to goods whose identity is not yet known"[42] Thus, if T gratuitously purports to declare himself trustee for B of 20 cases of Chateau Latour 1983 when he has 80 cases thereof, or 20 of his 80 gold bars, B acquires no equitable interest until 20 cases or 20 bars have been segregated and appropriated for B.[43] It similarly follows from the very nature of things (*viz.* that it is impossible to have title to specific assets when nobody knows to what assets the title relates) that if T gratuitously declares himself trustee of 50 of his Wonder Ltd shares when he has 950 of them or £50 in his building society account (then containing £950) on trust for B, B acquires no equitable interest until such shares or moneys have been segregated from T's so as to be separately held for B.[44]

Most surprisingly, in *Hunter v Moss*[45] the Court of Appeal upheld a **3–82** gratuitous trust of 50 of T's shares in MEL when T had 950 of them on the basis that:[46]

---

[36] *Palmer v Simmonds* (1854) 2 Drew. 221, 227 ("the bulk of my residuary estate" cannot satisfy the certainty requirement though "my residuary estate" can; *Re London Wine Co. (Shippers) Ltd* [1986] Palmer's Company Cases 121 (settlor cannot declare itself trustee of unascertained 20 out of 80 bottles of Lafite 1970 in its cellar though it could declare it held its holding of 80 bottles on trust as for three-quarters for itself and one-quarter for X).

[37] *Boyce v Boyce* (1849) 16 Sim. 476 where T devised four houses on trust to convey whichever one she chose to Maria and to convey the others to Charlotte; and upon Maria predeceasing T so that she could not choose any house it was held the trust in favour of Charlotte was void for uncertainty. However in *Re Golay's W.T.* [1965] 1 W.L.R. a trust for B to receive an objectively reasonable income was upheld.

[38] *Pallant v Morgan* [1953] Ch. 43; *Banner Homes Group plc v Luff Developments Ltd* [2000] 2 All E.R. 117; *Gissing v Gissing* [1971] A.C. 886 at 909 ("fair" share of family home); *Eves v Eves* [1975] 3 All E.R. 768 at 772; *Passee v Passee* [1988] 1 F.L.R. 263 at 271.

[39] (1936) 57 C.L.R. 666 at 689, above at para.2–156.

[40] [1972] Ch. 698, also *Healey v Brown* [2002] W.T.L.R. 849

[41] [1981] 1 W.L.R. 939.

[42] *Re Goldcorp Exchange* [1994] 2 All E.R. 806 at 814 *per* Lord Mustill.

[43] *ibid. Re London Wine Co. Shippers Ltd* [1986] P.C.C. 121; *Re Stapylton Fletcher Ltd* [1995] 1 All E.R. 192. These problems in the sale of goods context have now been remedied by Sale of Goods Amendment Act 1995.

[44] *cf. Re Innes* [1910] 1 Ch. 188 at 193; *MacJordan Construction Ltd v Brookmount Erostin* [1992] B.C.L.C. 350.

[45] [1994] 1 W.L.R. 452 criticised (1994) 110 L.Q.R. 335; it seems inconsistent with the later *Re Goldcorp Exchange* [1994] 2 All E.R. 806 at 814. It has been followed in an undefended case as applicable to intangibles but not tangibles (*Re Harvard Securities* [1997] 2 B.C.L.C. 369) and applied in Hong Kong: *Re CA Pacific Finance Ltd* [2000] 1 B.C.L.C. 494 at 509.

[46] *ibid.* at 459.

"just as a person can give by will a specified number of his shares in a
certain company, so equally he can declare himself a trustee of 50 of
his shares in MEL and that is effective to give a beneficial proprietary
interest to the beneficiary under the trust".

This overlooks a crucial difference between inter vivos and testamentary
dispositions. By his death a testator does everything necessary to divest
himself of all his legal and beneficial title in all his assets in favour of his
executor,[47] who is then obliged to implement his wishes subject to payment
of debts, expenses and taxes. In his lifetime a donor-settlor only divests
himself of his beneficial entitlement to his assets when he has done
everything necessary to identify those assets to which he has relinquished
entitlement, *i.e.* when he has separated 50 shares from the remaining 900
shares which he retains. Until then, how can one tell whether 100 shares
sold by him are all his or only half his? Having made an imperfect gift, he is
entitled to sell all as his own shares.

3–83   The problem facing B can be overcome easily enough[48] by T declaring
himself trustee of specified assets in proportionate undivided shares for
himself and B. Thus, T himself could have declared that he held the chose
in action representing his 950 shares on trust as to eighteen nineteenths for
himself and one nineteenth for B: it is then clear that T and B have
eighteen nineteenths and one nineteenth undivided shares in the *chose*
thereby enabling B to take advantage of the tracing rules in respect of such
one nineteenth, which cannot be done for an imperfect equitable gift of 50
unsegregated shares because one cannot tell which 50 of the 950 shares
were supposed to be beneficially B's.

3–84   An intention to create a trust of one nineteenth of a shareholding is a
different intention from an intention to create a trust of 50 shares, which is
a feasible intention where T is registered shareholder of 950 shares. To give
effect to such intention he can send the share certificate for 950 shares to
the company registrar with a signed transfer form requesting a share
certificate for 900 shares and one for 50 shares. He can then declare a trust
of the 50 shares covered by the latter certificate, and tracing principles are
available if such shares are sold or given away.[49]

3–85   However, what of the much more common situation where T owns
shares in a public company, all of whose 5 million shares are registered in
the name of Custodian plc, whose computer records it as holding 1 million
shares for Cazenove & Co, whose computer records it as holding 20,000
shares for T? Here, T does not actually own 20,000 shares and so cannot

---

[47] See above, at para.1–127. If T in his lifetime declared himself trustee of 50 shares for A and 900 for B so
as to have divested himself in equity of all interest in the 950 shares he owned, then A and B, between
them absolutely entitled to the 950 shares, could demand transfer of legal title to themselves and treat
themselves as entitled to one nineteenth and eighteen nineteenths of T's chose in action.

[48] Hence the approach in Sale of Goods Amendment Act 1995, s.1(3) deeming a vendor of a number of
assets in a larger whole owned by him to be tenant in common as to the proportionate share reflecting the
proportion that the number of goods contracted to be sold bears to the total owned by him. Thus, if he
received the purchase price for 10 out of 40 cases of Ch. Lafite 1983 still in his cellar (without the 10
having been allocated by markings or otherwise to the purchaser) he is treated as holding a quarter of
such stock of wine on trust for the purchaser, which is crucial if he has become insolvent.

declare a trust of 20,000 shares nor of 5,000 shares, for that matter. Actually, T owns a fiftieth equitable interest in Cazenove's one fifth equitable interest in the pool of 5 million shares legally owned by Custodian plc. Thus, the court has to construe T's declaration of trust of his notional 20,000 shares for B not as impossible and nonsensical but as reflecting an intention to make a declaration of trust of his one fiftieth interest in Cazenove's interest in the shares owned by Custodian plc. It seems to follow that if T happened to declare himself trustee of a notional 5,000 of his 20,000 shares, then, because he does not own any shares, he should be treated as intending to declare himself trustee of a quarter of the one fiftieth interest he does own in Cazenove's interest in the shares owned by Custodian plc. Thus certainty of subject matter of the trust is present.[49]

One problem that remains concerns the application of section 53(1) (c) **3–86** of the Law of Property Act 1925 which requires a disposition of a subsisting equitable interest to be in signed writing or be void. Prima facie, where T declares himself trustee of his equitable interest for B (where B is of full capacity) this is a disposition of his subsisting equitable interest to B because B replaces T as owner of the equitable interest,[50] just as where T sells his equitable interest to B.

However, subsidiary legislation ousts the application of s.53 (1) (c) for dealings in shares held in the CREST system for paperless dealings in shares in United Kingdom public companies.[51]

Section 3. Certainty of Beneficiaries and Administrative Workability

The comprehensive list test

Prior to the radical decision in *McPhail v Doulton*, below, a distinction had **3–87** to be drawn between trusts and powers for certainty purposes. Since trusts, even if discretionary, *have* to be carried out by trustees it must be possible in default for the courts positively to enforce and control the trust: for this reason there must be no linguistic or semantic uncertainty, otherwise known as conceptual uncertainty, in the description of the beneficiaries nor can the class of beneficiaries be so described that the trust is administratively unworkable. It used to be considered that if trustees failed to carry out a discretionary trust then, since it would be individious and injudicial for the courts to distinguish between the possible discretionary beneficiaries, the court would have to intervene positively by acting on the

---

[49] Sir Roy Goode in "Are Intangible Assets Fungibles?" [2003] L.M.C.L.Q. 309 argues that this should be the case even for shares in a private company on the basis that shares in a company are merely notional units of co-ownership of a single legally indivisible asset, though this is disputed by Guy Morton in S. Worthington (ed.) *Commercial Law and Commercial Practice* (Hart Publishing, 2003), pp.296–302. However, a shareholder, S, in a private company may have legal title to a shareholding of 200 shares and a shareholding of 750 shares where the gratuitous transfer to him of the 200 shares was a forgery. If he then declares himself trustee of 50 shares for X he can perfect this equitable gift by sending one of his two share certificates to the company for it to be split into two share certificates, one representing the 50 shares held for X. The position is then clear for the victim of the forgery and also for X if S subsequently sells shares in the company.
[50] See at para.2–42 *above*.
[51] Regulation 38(5) of the Uncertified Securities Regulations 2001 (SI 2001/3755); see para.2–18 above.

maxim "Equality is equity" and so distribute the trust assets equally. It followed that for an equal division it must be possible to draw up a comprehensive list of the beneficiaries. Accordingly, discretionary trusts used to fail for uncertainty if such a list could not be drawn up.[52] This must still be the position for "fixed" trusts which require equal division amongst the beneficiaries. Thus a trust for "my relations in equal shares," has to be construed as for "my statutory next-of-kin in equal shares" to save it from being void for uncertainty.[53]

The conceptually clear "is or is not" test

3–88 On the other hand, where powers of appointment for objects are concerned, the court does not positively intervene to compel exercise of the power (except in extremely exceptional circumstances[54]). So long as the trustees consider whether or not to exercise the powers and do not go beyond the scope of the powers the courts cannot intervene in negative fashion unless the trustees can be shown to have acted mala fide or capriciously, *i.e.* for reasons which are irrational, perverse or irrelevant to any sensible expectation of the settlor. It is purely up to the trustees whether or not they exercise the powers, so all that is required is that they are in an adequately informed position to consider the exercise of the powers,[55] *i.e.* if they can say with certainty of any given person that he is or is not within the scope of the power: see *Re Gulbenkian's S.T.*, below, rejecting the view expressed in the Court of Appeal that it suffices if the trustees can say of any *one or a few* persons with certainty that he or they are within the scope of the power though uncertainty may exist in respect of many other persons. Accordingly, a power fails for uncertainty only if the court cannot with certainty determine whether any given individual is or is not within the scope of the power.

3–89 In *McPhail v Doulton*, below, the House of Lords were faced with a quasi-charitable trust that was a type of private pension trust where it would have been regarded as unsatisfactory on social policy grounds for such a discretionary trust to be void when it would have been valid if a discretionary power. They thus held by a 3:2 majority that the *Gulbenkian* test for powers is also the appropriate test for discretionary trusts as it was possible for the court to carry out a discretionary trust by distributing the trust assets not equally amongst all possible beneficiaries (surely the last thing the settlor ever intended) but in such proportions as appropriate in the circumstances "so as to give effect to the settlor's or testator's intentions. It may do so by appointing new trustees or authorising or directing representative persons of the classes of beneficiaries to prepare a scheme of distribution, or even, should the proper basis for distribution appear, by itself directing the trustees so to distribute."[56] The case was then remitted

[52] *I.R.C. v Broadway Cottages Trust* [1955] Ch. 20.
[53] *Re Gansloser's W.T.* [1952] Ch. 30; *Re Poulton's W.T.* [1987] 1 All E.R. 1068 since it is impossible to establish all persons related by blood, however remotely.
[54] *Schmidt v Rosewood Trust Ltd* [2003] 2 A.C. 709, paras 42 and 51.
[55] *R. v Charity Commissioner Ex p. Baldwin* [2001] W.T.L.R. 137 at 148–149.
[56] [1971] A.C. 424 at 457, such methods seemingly also being available for powers of appointment to be exercised: *Schmidt v Rosewood Trust Ltd* [2003] 2 A.C. 709.

to the High Court for determination whether on the new test the trust was valid or void for uncertainty.

Application of the "is or is not" test

In *Re Baden's Deed Trusts (No.2)*, below, on appeal from the High Court **3–90** the Court of Appeal unanimously held the trust valid. Stamp L.J. considered the court must be able to say of any given postulant that he definitely is a member of the beneficiary class or he definitely is *not* such a member, *i.e.* the name of a postulant must be capable of being put either in a "Yes" box or a "No" box. Thus a discretionary trust would be void if some postulants' names had to go into a "Don't know" box: if "relatives" meant descendants of a common ancestor there would be a very large number of persons (in those pre-DNA testing days), neither known to be relatives nor to be non-relatives, needing to be placed within the "Don't know" box, so invalidating a discretionary trust for relatives. However, Stamp L.J. was prepared to treat relatives as meaning "next-of-kin" in which case any postulant would fall within the "Yes" box or the "No" box, so validating the trust.

Sachs and Megaw L.JJ., however, held the trust valid with "relatives" **3–91** bearing its broadest meaning as descendants of a common ancestor. Sachs L.J. took the robust practical view that if a postulant could not prove that his name should go into the "Yes" box then it went into the "No" box. Megaw L.J. treated Stamp L.J.'s view that a discretionary trust will fail if it cannot be shown of any individual that he definitely is or *definitely is not* a member of the class is to contend "in substance and reality that it does fail simply because it is impossible to ascertain every member of the class"[57] and draw up a comprehensive list thereof, a contention rejected by *McPhail v Doulton*. However, in ascertaining whether *any* (as opposed to every) individual is or is not a class member it is surely not necessary to ascertain *every* class member and draw up a comprehensive list. Be that as it may, Megaw L.J. considered the "is or is not" test satisfied if "as regards a substantial number of objects it can be said with certainty that they fall within the trust, even though as regards a substantial number of other persons the answer would have to be not 'they are outside the trust' but 'it is not proven whether they are in or out.' What is a substantial number may well be a question of common sense and of some degree in relation to the particular trust."[58]

However, initially one wonders whether it is so wrong for Stamp L.J. to **3–92** emphasise the need to ascertain those who are *not* class members when a person alleging a breach of trust will need to prove that the trustees distributed to an individual who was *not* a class member. There is also obvious uncertainty in the word "substantial". What, indeed, if a class like that in *McPhail v Doulton* was enlarged by there being added a conceptually uncertain clause such as "or any of my company's customers or any of my

---

[57] [1973] Ch. 9 at 23.
[58] *ibid.* at 24.

old friends." Surely the whole trust would be void just as a discretionary trust for "my desandants and my friends" would be void, though the concept of "descendant is clear enough.[59] Moreover, the "substantial" view is only a question of degree removed from the view rejected by the Lords in *Re Gulbenkian* in relation to powers, and so in relation to trusts by *McPhail v Doulton*, namely the view[60] that a power or discretionary trust is valid if it can be said with certainty of any one or a few persons[61] that he or they are within the scope of the power or discretionary trust though uncertainty exists as to whether other persons are within or without the power or discretionary trust.

3–93   The crux of the matter is how the court will deal with B's allegation that the trustees committed a breach of trust by paying income to X, who is alleged to be not a relative of A. There is no evidence capable of proving that X is or is not such a relative. Does this mean that, since B has not discharged the burden of proving that X is not a relative of A, B's action fails? If so, then the trustees are free to pay income to X and, indeed, to any Tom, Dick or Harriet and so do whatever they like without the risk of any sanctions for breach of any obligation: if it is in practice impossible to prove that anyone is not a relative of A, for anyone might well be if we could go back far enough, *e.g.* to 4,000 B.C. However, if, although the *legal* burden of proving such a breach of trust lies on B, the *evidential* burden of proving payment to a beneficiary lies on the trustees once B has provided prima facie evidence that the payee is not a beneficiary, then B's action will succeed. If so, then the trustees will be under an enforceable duty to pay only those who can produce the relevant birth and marriage certificates or other sufficient evidence to prove relationship. Sachs[62] and Megaw L.JJ. expressly agreed with the judge of first instance, Brightman J., for the reasons he gave and these justify the pragmatic majority view in the Court of Appeal. He said[63]:

3–94   "In practice, the use of the expression 'relatives' cannot cause the slightest difficulty. A supposed relative to whom a grant is contemplated would, in strictness, be bound to produce the relevant birth and marriage certificates or other sufficient evidence to prove his or her relationship. If the relationship is sufficiently proved the trustees will be entitled to make the grant. If no sufficient evidence can be produced the trustees would have no option but to decline to make a grant."

---

[59] Is there scope for the court to develop a power to strike out an offending concept and sever it from the valid concepts within the class or classes of beneficiaries?: *Re Leek* [1969] 1 Ch. 563, 586; *Re Gulbenkian's Settlement* [1968] Ch. 126 at 138. It seems not: see *Re Gulbenkian's Settlement* [1970] A.C. 508 at 524; *McPhail v Doulton* [1971] A.C. 424 at 456; *Tatham v Huxtable* (1950) 81 C.L.R. 639, 652. The trust for a large group is wholly valid or wholly void.

[60] *Re Gulbenkian's Settlement* [1968] Ch. 126, CA.

[61] Megaw L.J. in *Re Baden (No.2)* [1973] Ch. 9 at 24, treats the rejected view as concerning one person but Lord Upjohn in *Re Gulbenkian's Settlement* [1970] A.C. 508 at 524, in his example of two or three individuals being clearly "old friends" treats the rejected view as concerning one or a few persons.

[62] Sachs L.J. considered that if a postulant is not proved to be within the beneficial class then he is outside it, so placing the evidential burden on the trustees to prove the payee is a relative. See *Cross on Evidence*, Chap. 4 on legal and evidential burdens of proof.

[63] [1971] 3 All E.R. 985 at 995.

Thus the trustees are liable if they do not discharge the evidential burden of proving payment to a relative. Nowadays, DNA testing makes this straightforward but creates administrative unworkability problems if the class size and the purposes of the trust do not make the trust charitable.

Conceptual certainty, evidential certainty, ascertainability and administrative workability

As Carl Emery has emphasised,[64] questions concerning "certainty" of **3–95** beneficiaries of trusts or objects of powers may relate to one or more of the following:

> "(a) 'Conceptual uncertainty': this refers to the precision of language used by the settlor to define the classes of persons whom he intends to benefit.
>
> (b) 'Evidential uncertainty': this refers to the extent to which the evidence available in a particular case enables specific persons to be identified as members of those classes—and so as beneficiaries or potential beneficiaries.
>
> (c) 'Ascertainability': this refers to the extent to which 'the whereabouts or continued existence' of persons identified as beneficiaries or potential beneficiaries can be ascertained.
>
> (d) 'Administrative workability': this refers to the extent to which it is practicable for trustees to discharge the duties laid upon them by the settlor towards beneficiaries or potential beneficiaries."

Evidential uncertainty does not invalidate a discretionary trust or a **3–96** power since if a person is not proved to be within the beneficial class then he is outside it.[65] Ascertainability problems (*e.g.* over the where-abouts or continued existence of a relative, A, or an ex-employee, B) do not invalidate a discretionary trust or a power because such problems are valid reasons for trustees deciding not to exercise their discretions or powers, and because, in the case of a trust, the court may give leave to distribute the trust fund on the basis that X is dead[66] or may direct a scheme for distribution amongst ascertained beneficiaries.[67]

If a discretionary trust is not conceptually certain or not administratively **3–97** workable then the express trust fails and the property will be held on resulting trust for the settlor. If a trust is not conceptually certain then it cannot be administratively workable, *e.g.* a discretionary trust "for such persons as have moral claims upon me."[68] "for my old friends[69] and

---

[64] (1982) 98 L.Q.R. 551 at 552.

[65] *Re Baden's Deed Trust (No.2)* [1973] Ch. 9 at 20, *per* Sachs L.J. [1972] Ch. 607, *per* Brightman J. The minority view of Stamp L.J. was to the effect that the evidential uncertainty (which he considered could not be resolved so simplistically) converted the apparent black and white certainty of concept into an uncertain grey concept.

[66] *Re Benjamin* [1902] 1 Ch. 723.

[67] *McPhail v Doulton* [1971] A.C. 424 at 457; *Re Hain* [1961] 1 W.L.R. 440 and *Muir v I.R.C.* [1966] 3 All E.R. 38 at 44 show that a trust will not be invalidated because some of the class of beneficiaries may have disappeared or become impossible to find or it has been forgotten who they were.

[68] *Re Leek* [1969] 1 Ch. 563.

[69] *Brown v Gould* [1972] 53 at 57; *Re Barlow's W.T.* [1979] 1 All E.R. 296.

business associates," "for worthy causes,"[70] "for those of my friends and relations who are good citizens," "for my customers"[71] (because uncertain when they become ex-customers), "for my fans" (unless restricted to members of a particular fan club), "for Cambridge students" (unless restricted to students from time to time studying as junior members of the University of Cambridge). As Lord Hailsham emphasised in *I.R.C. v McMullen*,[72] "Where it is claimed that there is an ambiguity, a benignant construction should be given if possible. This was the maxim of the civil law: *semper in dubiis benigniora praeferenda sunt*. There is a similar maxim in English law: *ut res magis valeat quam pereat*. It applied where a gift is capable of two constructions one of which would make it void and the other effectual."

3–98   In a very rare case a discretionary trust may be conceptually certain but, nonetheless, may be administratively unworkable, *e.g.* "for everyone in the world except the settlor, his spouse and past and present trustees"[73] or even "for the benefit of any or all or some of the inhabitants of the County of West Yorkshire."[74] Such a "trust" would not be capable of being effectively "policed" by the court when a default beneficiary complains of the trustee's exercise of a power in favour of an object. A court must act judicially according to some criteria, expressly or impliedly provided by the trust instrument or by extrinsic admissible evidence, so that it may control or execute the trusts: it cannot resort to pure guesswork for such is a non-justiciable function.[75] If you were trustee of a discretionary trust for everyone in the world but five persons, how on earth would you begin to try to decide what to do?

3–99   However, trustees' *powers* to add anyone in the world (excepting the settlor, his spouse, past and present trustees) to the class of discretionary trust beneficiaries[76] and trustees' powers to appoint capital or income to anyone in the world (excepting the above small class) have been upheld by judges of first instance as not capable of being invalidated by the test of administrative workability which has been restricted to trusts.[77] The basis for this distinction is that in the case of a discretionary trust a trustee is under more extensive obligations which the beneficiaries can positively enforce because they may lead to the court seeing to the carrying out of the trusts. In the case of powers a trustee only need consider periodically

---

[70] *Re Atkinson* [1978] 1 All E.R. 1275.
[71] *Sparfax (1965) Ltd v Dommett* [1972] *The Times,* July 14.
[72] [1981] A.C. 1 at 11, [1980] 1 All E.R. 884 at 890 at para.7–178.
[73] *Re Hay's S.T.* [1982] 1 W.L.R. 202, para.3–137 *Yeap Cheo Neo v Ong Chen Neo* (1875) L.R. 6 P.C. 381; *Blausten v I.R.C.* [1972] Ch. 256 at 266, 271, 272. The question of conceptual certainty and of administrative workability must be determined at the date of creation of the trust: *Re Baden's Deed Trust (No.2)* [1972] Ch. 607.
[74] *R. v District Auditor Ex p. West Yorkshire County Council* (1985) 26 R.V.R. 24, [2001] W.T.L.R. 795 there were about 2,500,000 potential beneficiaries.
[75] On justiciability see *Buttes Gas & Oil Co. v Hamer (No.3)* [1982] A.C. 888 at 938 *per* Lord Wilberforce.
[76] *Re Manisty's Settlement* [1974] Ch. 17. In this case, as held by Templeman J, it is more easy to discern the intention of the settlor than in the case of a power to appoint to anyone but four specified persons—unless a settlor's letter of wishes is available.
[77] *Re Hay's S.T.* [1982] 1 W.L.R. 202, para.3–137, *Re Beatty's W.T.* [1990] 3 All E.R. 844. In *Re Denley's Trust Deed* [1969] 1 Ch. 373 Goff J. with little discussion upheld the power of trustees to allow any persons other than the trust beneficiaries to use the sports ground primarily intended for the beneficiaries' use.

whether or not he should exercise the power, taking into account the range of objects of the power and the appropriateness of possible individual appointments; the only control exercisable by the court in the words of Templeman J.[78] "is the removal of the trustees and the only 'due adminstration' which can be 'directed' is an order requiring the trustees to consider the exercise of the power, and, in particular a request from a person within the ambit of the power." He contemplated[79] it being possible for objects to have no right to be informed they were objects and no right to go through the trust accounts. However, he accepted[80] that the court must be able to intervene if a wide power is exercised capriciously, *i.e.* for reasons which are irrational, perverse or irrelevant to any sensible expectation of the settlor.

But if this is the case, then for the trustees' power to be justiciable the **3–100** settlor's expectations must somehow be discerned.[81] If they cannot be discerned so that the power is not justiciable then it cannot be a fiduciary power, yet a power exercisable *virtute officii* can only be a fiduciary power unless expressly stated not to be fiduciary but only personal.[82] The object of a fiduciary power has, like a beneficiary in default of exercise of the power, a right to seek the court's removal of the trustees for exercising the power for reasons which are irrational, perverse or irrelevant to any sensible expectation of the settlor. If such expectation cannot be discerned then the court cannot adjudicate on the matter and cannot determine rights and duties. Thus, Buckley L.J. considered *obiter*[83] that a power to add anyone in the world to a class of trust beneficiaries (and, presumably, by parity of reasoning a power to appoint to anyone in the world) would be void. Templeman J.[84] and Megarry V.-C.[85] have rejected this, considering[86] that "dispositions ought, if possible, to be upheld and the court ought not to be astute to find grounds on which a power can be invalidated."

The need for justiciability underlies the requirement of administrative **3–101** workability yet the High Court has created a distinction between trusts where there is positive and negative justiciability and fiduciary powers where there is allegedly, only negative justiciability. The distinction may well be disputed in an appellate court. After all, in *McPhail v Doulton*[87] the House of Lords regarded discretionary trusts ("trust powers" in the terminology of Lord Wilberforce) and powers of appointment as so similar in substance that the same certainty test should apply to both, so why only have the test of administrative workability apply to discretionary trusts?

---

[78] [1974] Ch. 17 at 27–28. Also see *Re Gulbenkian's S.T.* [1970] A.C. 508 at 525.
[79] *ibid.* at 24–25.
[80] *ibid.* at 26.
[81] In *Re Manisty's Settlement* [1974] Ch. 17 at 24–25 Templeman J. significantly stated, "In the present case if the settlement is read as a whole the expectations of the settlor are not difficult to discern."
[82] *Re Gulbenkian's S.T.* [1970] A.C. 508 at 518, *per* Lord Reid, unless the trust instrument expressly makes clear that the powers are to be regarded as personal and not fiduciary.
[83] *Blausten v I.R.C.* [1972] Ch. 256 at 273 and Orr and Salmon L.J.J. agreed with him at 274 and 175. The moral is to couch the power as a power for the trustees to add to the class of beneficiaries anyone from a list submitted to them by any existing beneficiary: see trust precedent at para 1–65, above.
[84] *Re Manisty's S.T.* [1974] Ch. 17.
[85] *Re Hay's S.T.* [1982] 1 W.L.R. 202, applied in *I.R.C. v Schroder* [1983] S.T.C. 480.
[86] *ibid.* at 212. So long as conceptual certainty is present it does not matter that in substance the testator is effectively delegating his function of choosing legatees to another: *Re Abraham's W.T.* [1969] 1 Ch. 463; *Re Park* [1932] 1 Ch. 580; *Re Nicholls* (1987) 34 D.L.R. (4th) 321; *Re Beatty's W.T.* [1990] 3 All E.R. 844.
[87] [1971] A.C. 424.

Furthermore, despite the views of Templeman J. in *Re Manisty*, the court may positively intervene in an extreme case where there is an improper refusal to consider exercising a power so as to direct the exercise of the power in an obviously proper way (albeit a power to benefit a beneficiary as opposed to an object of a power of appointment).[88] This has recently taken on particular significance in the context of pension fund trusts in favour of beneficiaries who have earned their interests and have legitimate expectations that powers of augmenting pensions will be exercised in their favour.[89] Warner J.[90] indeed, regarded Lord Wilberforce's remarks on how the court can positively see to the carrying out of discretionary trusts as equally applicable to fiduciary powers though in the context of a power to benefit beneficiaries (not objects of a power) who had earned their pension rights and expectations. Moreover, Lord Walker has apparently accepted that Lord Wilberforce's remarks are applicable for the court to implement powers as well as discretionary trusts.[91]

3–102   On the safety-first principle a power of appointment should be restricted to a workable ascertainable class of persons and a power to add persons to a beneficial class should be restricted, for example, to persons nominated in writing by existing members of the class who shall give written reasons why such an addition would have been likely to have met with the settlor's approval. Otherwise, a memorandum of wishes expressed to be of no binding legal effect, but merely indicative of the settlor's purposes in creating the trust, will probably be held by the courts to set workable parameters for the exercise of the trustee's discretion under a power (or even a trust). The power should clearly be upheld if the trust instrument expressly states that it is to be a personal power such that its exercise is to be unchallengeable unless providing the trustee with a tangible benefit so as to be a fraud on the power.

Fiduciary powers and personal powers

3–103   There is a personal power where the holder of the power (known as the "donee" of the power) does not have to consider from time to time whether or not to exercise the power and can even release the power so it can never be exercised.[92] If he does decide to exercise the power, then he "is entitled to prefer one object to another from any motive he pleases, and however capriciously he exercises the power the Court will uphold it",[93] so long as he commits no fraud on the power by exercising it to benefit someone (like himself) outside the scope of the power[94] *e.g.* appoints to an object on the basis that the object will give him half the money appointed as a gift or to repay a debt due to him.

---

[88] *Klug v Klug* [1918] 2 Ch. 67, *White v Grane* (1854) 18 Beav 571, *Re Lofthause* (1885) 29 Ch.D. 921.
[89] *Mettoy Pension Trustees Ltd v Evans* [1991] 2 All E.R. 513, *Thrells Ltd v Lomas* [1993] 1 W.L.R. 456, below.
[90] *Mettoy*, above at 549 at para.3–152.
[91] *Schmidt v Rosewood Trust Ltd* [2003] 2 A.C. 309, paras 42 and 51, below at para.3.155.
[92] *Re Gulbenkian's S.T.* [1982] 1 W.L.R. 202, *Re Wills' Trust Deeds* [1964] Ch. 219.
[93] *Re Wright* [1920] 1 Ch. 108 at 118. The court cannot take a personal power away from its holder: *Re Park* [1932] 1 Ch. 580.
[94] *Re Somes* [1896] 1 Ch. 250, 255, *Palmer v Locke* (1880) 15 Ch.D. 294 at 302–303.

One type of a personal power can be regarded as a "beneficial" power where the holder of the power can exercise it for his own benefit[95] *e.g.* appoint money to himself or to another to satisfy a legal or moral obligation or refuse to consent to the trustee selling shares in a company of which he is a director or selling a house he occupies.

There is a fiduciary power where the settlor intends the donee to exercise **3–104** a discretion to benefit beneficiaries or objects of a power of appointment in a responsible manner for the purposes for which the discretion was conferred on the donee by the settlor.[96] This requires the donee to consider periodically—or when consent is sought by the trustees—whether or not to exercise the discretion, and the discretion cannot be released or fettered in any way unless expressly authorised in the trust instrument.[97] The exercise or non-exercise of the discretionary power must take account of the range of possibilities within the power and must be in good faith and not be irrational, perverse or irrelevant to any sensible expectation of the settlor.[98] The donee cannot benefit from the discretionary power unless authorised expressly or by necessary implication.[99]

Powers vested in an office-holder like a trustee or a protector are presumed to be fiduciary powers,[1] while powers relating to distribution of capital or income to beneficiaries or objects and which are vested in individuals *qua* individuals like the settlor or a testator's widow or eldest child are presumed to be personal.[2] Powers vested in such individuals which relate to the appointment and replacement of trustees or the investment role thereof are, however, presumed fiduciary[3] because the trustees' investment role is at the core of the trust, protecting and furthering the interests of the beneficiaries as a whole.

One has to construe the terms of the trust instrument in the light of the **3–105** surrounding background circumstances to determine the obligations affecting the donee of a power,[4] so that express assistance from the draftsman is advisable. Indeed, expressly or by necessary implication a power could be semi-fiduciary.

For example, an individual donee of a power could be under no duty to consider periodically whether or not to exercise the power, and could even refuse to bother ever thinking about it, but if she did exercise the power then it would have to be exercised subject to the obligations affecting full fiduciary powers.[5] Alternatively, a trustee could be under an obligation to consider periodically whether or not to exercise a power (*e.g.* a power to

---

[95] *Re Wills' Trust Deeds* [1964] Ch. 214 at 228, *Steele v Paz Ltd*. [1993–95] Manx LR 102 especially on appeal at 426, *Re Z Trust* [1997] Cayman I.L.R. 248.
[96] *Re Hay's S.T.* [1981] 3 All E.R. 788 at 792, *Re Beatty's W.T.* [1990] 3 All E.R. 844 at 846.
[97] *Re Hay's S.T.* (above).
[98] *ibid.* and *Re Manisty's Settlement* [1974] Ch. 17.
[99] *Re Z Trust* [1997] Cayman I.L.R. 248.
[1] *Re Wills' Trust Deeds* [1964] Ch. 219, *Re Gulbenkian's S.T.* [1970] A.C. 508 at 518.
[2] *Re Somes* [1896] 1 Ch. 250, *Palmer v Locke* (1880) 15 Ch.D. 294.
[3] *IRC v Schroder* [1983] S.T.C. 480, *Commissioner of Stamp Duties v Way* [1942] 1 All E.R. 191, *Vestey's Executors v IRC* [1949] 1 All E.R. 1108; *Re Osiris Trustees Ltd* [2003] W.T.L.R. 933.
[4] *Botnar v IRC* [1999] S.T.C. 711 (CA), applying Lord Hoffmann's approach in *Investors Compensation Scheme v West Bromwich B.S.* [1998] 1 W.L.R. 896.
[5] *Re Osiris Trustees Ltd* [2000] W.T.L.R. 933.

appoint to anyone except the settlor, the settlor's spouse and the trustee) but if he did exercise the power then he would be treated as the donee of a personal power, so that the exercise of the power could not be challenged except under the fraud on a power doctrine (*e.g.* if property were appointed to X on condition X gave half of it to the settlor, the settlor's spouse or the trustee). This latter construction by way of an allegedly necessary implication could be used by the courts to justify the validity of trustees' powers to appoint to anyone in the world except X,Y and Z, courts being reluctant to overturn old cases on the basis of which property has changed hands over many years.

3–106   Normally, all the powers of a trustee are fidiciary,[6] while in the case of protectors their powers will be fiduciary if for the benefit of the beneficiaries as a whole, but it is possible for some powers to be conferred on the protector to safeguard the interests of the protector (*e.g.* if the protector be the settlor or a beneficiary[7]) or even of the settlor (*e.g.* if the protector be the settlor's lawyer and confidant[8]). While protectors can be indemnified as to expenses properly incurred in fulfilling the duties of their office, the draftsperson needs not only to consider spelling out the nature of their powers—and the implications for the trustees' relationship with them—but to provide for protectors to charge for their services and, perhaps, have the benefit of a clause exempting them from liability for negligent breach of their fiduciary duties. The court, having inherent jurisdiction to appoint a protector (*e.g.* if no name appears in the schedule to the trust where the protector's name was accidentally never inserted[9]) must also have similar jurisdiction to replace a protector in breach of his fiduciary duties.[10]

3–107   There seems no reason why a personal power which does not have to be administratively workable[11] should have to satisfy the test for conceptual certainty of fiduciary powers. Instead of the concept being certain enough to enable the court to say of any given postulant that he definitely is or is not an object of the power, it should suffice that the court can say of one or more persons that they are within the "core" meaning of the concept (*e.g.* "friends"[12]) even if the penumbra may be so uncertain that the court cannot say of many persons whether they qualify or not.[13] Thus, a widow's personal power should be valid where her husband leaves his residuary estate to trustees upon particular discretionary trusts, but gives his widow power to appoint thereout up to 10 separate sums of £2,000 to up to 10 friends of the testator not otherwise benefited by his will, or power to appoint up to

---

[6] *Re Gulbenkian's S.T.* [1970] A.C. 508 at 518.
[7] *Rawson Trust v Perlman* 1 Butts O.C.M. 135, *Re Z Trust* [1997] Cayman I.L.R. 248. Further see D. J. Hayton (1999) 32 Vanderbilt Jo. of Transnational Law 559, 579–589.
[8] *Re Star Trust Knierem v Bermuda Trust Co.* 1 Butts O.C.M. 116.
[5] *Steele v Paz Ltd.* [1993–95] Manx LR 102 and, on appeal, 426.
[10] *Re Papadimitriou* [2004] W.T.L.R. 1141, para.71.
[11] *Re Hay's Settlement* [1982] 1 W.L.R. 202, below, para.3–137.
[12] See Browne-Wilkinson J on "friends" in *Re Barlow's W.T.* [1979] 1 W.L.R. 278.
[13] See C. T. Emery (1982) 98 L.Q.R. 551, 582 where he uses the expression "bare power" to distinguish a personal power from a fiduciary power. Exercise of the personal power would be effective so long as confined to those within the "core" meaning of the concept. Query whether it should be ineffective only when in favour of some person clearly outside the penumbra of meaning, *e.g.* where the alleged old friend had never met or corresponded with the testator: see below at para.3–119.

£20,000 thereout between business associates of the testator not otherwise benefited by his will as she might see fit. After all, this is not so different from a testator leaving his residuary estate to trustees upon discretionary trusts "for my old friends, A, B, C, and D, and for my good business associates, V, W, X and Y, with power for my widow to add as beneficiaries anyone else (apart from herself or past and present trustees) but particularly any person she considers to be other friends or business associates of mine as she may see fit." This last power would enable her to benefit the testator's "friends" and "business associates" by making them eligible to benefit from the exercise of the trustees' discretion.

Conditions subsequent and conditions precedent

Trusts may contain conditions subsequent or conditions precedent. If **3–108** property is held subject to a condition subsequent so that the beneficiary's vested interest will be liable to forfeiture on the subsequent happening of the proscribed event, the condition must be such that the court can see from the outset precisely and distinctly upon the happening of what event the interest is to be forfeited.[14] The circumstances involving forfeiture must be clearly known in advance so that the beneficiary knows precisely where he stands and the condition must not be void for public policy[15] for being repugnant to the essential alienability of the interest given.[16]

Where property is held on trust for persons subject to the fulfilment of a **3–109** condition so that it is up to them positively to show that they satisfy such condition precedent then a less strict standard of certainty is usually required, except where the trust is a fixed trust for equal division amongst all those who can satisfy a particular condition when the condition must be certain enough to enable a complete list to be drawn up of those who satisfy the condition.[17] However, if instead of a fixed trust for a class there is a discretionary trust or a fiduciary power for a class of people who can satisfy a particular condition, then the condition must contain conceptually clear criteria so that it can be said of any given postulant that he is or is not a member of the class.[18]

Where, instead of a fixed amount being is held on trust for distribution **3–110** between qualifying members of a class there is a trust to enable qualifying individuals to benefit to a specified extent (*i.e.* not "£100,000 to be distributed between such of my relatives as marry persons of the Jewish faith and of Jewish parentage as my trustees may see fit"[19] but "£5,000 to each of my relatives as marry persons of the Jewish faith and of Jewish

---

[14] *Clavering v Ellison* (1859) 7 H.L.Cas.707; *Blathwayt v Lord Cawley* [1976] A.C. 397 at 429 ("being or becoming a Catholic" valid).
[15] *Church Property Trustees of Newcastle Diocese v Ebbeck* (1960) 104 C.L.R. 394: "profess Protestant faith" certain but void for public policy as designed by testator to encourage his three sons to divorce their Catholic wives. Nowadays Art.8 Human Rights Convention also relevant.
[16] *Re Scientific Investment Pension Plan Trusts* [1999] C.L. 53 at 59.
[17] *e.g.* the case of a trust for my relatives 'within three degrees of consanguinity', to create certainty in equal shares as envisaged in *Re Barlow's W.T.* [1979] 1 W.L.R. 278.
[18] *McPhail v Doulton* [1971] A.C. 424.
[19] Void for uncertainty: *Clayton v Ramsden* [1943] A.C. 320.

parentage" or "£25,000 to my daughter Naomi if she marries a person of the Jewish faith and of Jewish parentage") Browne-Wilkinson J. has held[20] that the qualifying condition is valid if it is possible to say of one or more persons that he or they undoubtedly qualify, even though it may be impossible to say of others whether or not they qualify. This is fine where someone like Naomi is named, but otherwise not, which Brown-Wilkinson J. failed to appreciate.

3–111   In *Re Barlow* Browne-Wilkinson J. was faced with a testatrix who directed her executor "to allow any member of my family and any friends of mine who may wish to do so to purchase" particular paintings in the testatrix's estate at a low 1970 valuation. He held that the disposition was properly to be regarded as a series of individual gifts to persons answering the description friends or blood relations of the testatrix, since the effect of the disposition was to confer on such persons a series of options to purchase. It was not necessary to discover who all the friends or relations were: all that was required was for the executors to be able to say of any individual coming forward that he had proved that he was a friend or relation on which qualifications he provided guidance.[21] He justified this on the basis of *Re Allen*[22] where the Court of Appeal had upheld a devise "to the eldest of the sons of A who shall be a member of the Church of England and an adherent to the doctrine of that Church," so allowing the eldest son to seek to establish that he qualified, even if the conditions were conceptually uncertain so that it would be impossible to say of others whether or not they qualified. He considered *Re Allen* still to be good law after *McPhail v Doulton* since the Court of Appeal in *Re Tuck's S.T.*[23] had mentioned it approvingly (but only in the context of revealing a distinction between conditions precedent and conditions subsequent, which he overlooked).

3–112   He was much impressed by Lord Evershed's dictum[24] that a gift to A if he is a tall man will be valid, enabling A if he is 6ft. 6ins. to claim the gift. Where there is one ascertained individual, who is the only possible beneficiary, then one can accept his entitlement if he can prove he comes within the "core" meaning of the qualifying condition, even if the penumbra is so conceptually uncertain that it may often be impossible to judge whether the condition is satisfied.[25] This exception will cover several

---

[20] *Re Barlow's W.T.* [1979] 1 W.L.R. 278. This was the test suggested by Lord Denning in *Re Gulbenkian's S.T.* [1968] Ch. 126 at 134 for judging certainty of powers and rejected by the House of Lords on appeal. "Jewish faith and parentage" was held void for uncertainty in *Clayton v Ramsden* [1943] A.C. 320 but in *Re Tepper's W.T.* [1987] Ch. 358 Scott J. was reluctant to find "Jewish faith" uncertain and so adjourned the case to see if evidence of the Jewish faith as practised by the testator would clarify the matter. Both cases involved conditions subsequent.

[21] *Re Baden's Deed Trusts (No.2)* [1973] Ch. 9 enables relations to be ascertained on the basis that he who does not prove he is a relation is not a relation, the concept of descendant of a common ancestor being clear. The concept of friendship is not clear. If one picture was particularly good and available at a particularly low price, so that everyone wanted this best bargain, would the purchaser have to be found by putting all possible names into a hat and drawing out one name? But would not this be impossible since the uncertain penumbra of meaning of friendship would make it impossible for the executor or the court to decide whether many persons were friends or not?

[22] [1953] Ch. 810.

[23] [1978] Ch. 49.

[24] [1953] Ch. 810 at 817.

[25] L. McKay [1980] Conv 263 at 277; C. T. Emery (1982) 98 L.Q.R. 551 at 564.

ascertained beneficiaries where each is the only possible beneficiary, *e.g.* "£15,000 to each of my sons A, B, C and D if he is tall."

However, one ought not to extend the exception beyond individuals **3–113** whose identity is ascertained from the outset to individuals whose identity can only be ascertained after deciding whether or not others have satisfied a particular condition which is conceptually uncertain, *e.g.* £20,000 to my first daughter to marry (or to the eldest of my daughters who shall marry) a tall adherent to the doctrine of the Church of England. If the eldest daughter, A, marries someone within the penumbra of the conceptually uncertain condition so that it is impossible to say whether she qualifies or not then it cannot help B, the second eldest, if she is within the "core" of the condition by marrying a 6ft. 6ins. Church of England vicar. Whether B satisfies the condition depends on the *ex hypothesi* insoluble question whether or not A has satisfied the condition.[26] The condition would fail more clearly if the gift had been to "my first female friend to marry a tall adherent to Church of England doctrine" since "friend" is a highly imprecise concept.

Browne-Wilkinson J. considered that "a gift of £10,000 to each of my **3–114** friends" was valid, whilst accepting that a discretionary trust or power for "my friends" would be void[27] Such a less strict approach is anomalous and illogical. After all, a trustee or executor directed to make specific payments to qualifying beneficiaries has a duty to make such payments which may be enforced by each qualifying beneficiary, unlike the weaker position of beneficiaries or objects under discretionary trusts or powers. Furthermore, the person entitled to the fund after payment thereout of the sums to the "friends" must have a clear right to sue the trustee or executor for paying sums out to persons not ranking as "friends", so that it needs to be possible to draw up a comprehensive fixed list of friends. To protect themselves the trustees or executors (caught between the claims of the alleged friend and the residuary beneficiary) must have a right to obtain the court's directions as to the comprehensive list of persons to whom to make the payments. "Friends" gives rise not just to evidential uncertainty but to conceptual uncertainty having an uncertain penumbra making it impossible in many instances for the court to say whether a person is or is not a friend. If, pragmatically, one is to have Browne-Wilkinson J.'s exception for persons within the "core" meaning of friend why not allow discretionary trusts and powers to be validly exercised in favour of persons within the "core" meaning of friend, though House of Lords authority[28] is against this?

Resolution of uncertainty

Questions of evidential uncertainty can be resolved by the court in the last **3–115** resort, though it is possible for the trust instrument to contain a clause empowering someone like the trustees[29] or the testator's widow, or the testator's business partner to resolve any evidential uncertainty.

---

[26] C. T. Emery (1982) 98 L.Q.R. 551 at 564–565. The Court of Appeal in *Re Allen* [1953] Ch. 810 did not face up to this when dealing with a claim by the eldest son (or rather, his executor).
[27] *Re Barlow's W.T.* [1979] 1 W.L.R. 278 at 281.
[28] *Re Gulbenkian's S.T.* [1970] A.C. 508, below para.3–121; *McPhail v Doulton* [1971] A.C. 424, below para.3–124.
[29] *Dundee General Hospital Board v Walker* [1952] 1 All E.R. 896.

Apparent conceptual uncertainty may not be such if the court restrictively construes the concept, *e.g.* restricts "Cambridge students" to students from time to time studying as junior members of the University of Cambridge or restrict "fans of Elvis Presley" to members of Elvis Presley fan clubs or restricts a residuary bequest to "those beneficiaries who have only received small amounts" to those who had received legacies of £25, £50 and £100 where other legatees had received legacies of £200 and £250.[30] A proviso that in cases of doubt the decision of the Registrary of the University of Cambridge or of the secretaries of official Elvis Presley fan clubs shall be conclusive may assist the court restrict the concept so that it is actually certain.

3–116 However, actual conceptual uncertainty cannot be resolved by such provisos,[31] except, it seems, where a person acting as an expert (as opposed to acting as an arbitrator) is given power to resolve the matter *e.g.* the Chief Rabbi is to determine whether or not beneficiaries are of the Jewish faith.[32] If the concept is "my tall relations" or "my old friends" or "my good business associates," and the testator's trustees are given power to resolve any doubts as to whether any persons qualify or not then since *ex hypothesi* the court cannot resolve the uncertainty caused by the conceptual uncertainty it is difficult to see how the trustees can. There are no clear conceptual criteria to guide them or, indeed, the court if their exercise of the power is challenged. An inherently irresolvable issue is just that; it cannot be resolved, whether by a judge or anyone else.

3–117 If the concept is "persons whom my trustees consider to be my tall relatives or my old friends or my good business associates" the concept still seems uncertain. As Jenkins J. said in *Re Coxen*[33]:

> "If the testator had insufficiently defined the state of affairs on which the trustees were to form their opinion he would not have saved the condition from invalidity on the ground of uncertainty merely by making their opinion the criterion, although the declaration by the trustees of this or that opinion would be an event about which in itself there could be no uncertainty."

3–118 This view was followed in *Re Jones*[34] and then in *Re Wright's W.T.*[35] where a gift of property to trustees "to use the same at their absolute discretion for such people and institutions as they think have helped me or my late husband" failed for conceptual uncertainty. How can the trustees consider

---

[30] *Re Steel* [1978] 2 All E.R. 1026 at 1032; also see *O'Rourke v Bicks* [1992] S.T.C. 703.

[31] *Re Coxen* [1948] Ch. 747 at 761–762; *Re Jones* [1953] Ch. 125; *Re Wright's W.T.* [1981] L.S. Gaz. 841. Lord Denning's dicta to the contrary in *Re Tuck's S.T.* [1978] Ch. 49 at 60, 62 are out of line and seem based on a misinterpretation of *Dundee General Hospital Board, above* as Eveleigh L.J. indicates [1978] Ch. 49 at 66. See also P. Matthews (1983) 133 New L.J. 915.

[32] Lord Denning's approach in *Re Tuck's ST* [1978] Ch. 49 at 60, 62 can nowadays be so justified e.g. *The Glacier Bay* [1996] 14 Rep 370, *Brown v G10 Insurance Ltd* [1998] Lloyds Rep. I.R. 201 [1998] *The Times* February 18.

[33] [1948] Ch. 747 at 761–762.

[34] [1953] Ch. 125: "if at any time B shall in the uncontrolled opinion of the trustee have social or other relationship with C."

[35] [1981] L.S. Gaz. 841. Also see *Tatham v Huxtable* (1950) 81 C.L.R. 639, 653.

someone to have helped a testatrix or to be a tall relative or old friend or good business associate without knowing what exactly they are supposed to consider as criteria justifying their conclusion? If their conclusion is challenged how can the court adjudicate upon the matter?[36]

If a power to resolve conceptual uncertainty is given not as a fiduciary **3–119** power but as a personal power, for example, to the testator's widow, might this validate a prima facie uncertain trust? What if a testator left his residuary estate to his executors and trustees on discretionary trust for his old friends but stated that if any doubts or disputes arose as to membership of such class then his widow's decision was to be final unless it was unreasonable, as rejecting a person clearly within the "core" meaning of "old friends" or admitting a person clearly outside the "penumbra" of meaning of "old friend," like someone whom the testator had never met or corresponded with?[37] It would seem unreasonable for a court not to accept the validity of such a personal power with the above express or implied limitation that it may not be exercised unreasonably. But if one concedes the validity of such power of the widow why should one not concede the validity of such power if vested in trustees in such terms indicating it is to be regarded not as a fiduciary power.[38] If such power was *expressly* limited as above the court might well accept it as conferring dispositive leeway on the trustees, just as much as on the widow, but the court would be reluctant to find such validating *implied* limitation on the power vested in the trustees as such.

Absence of certainties

If there is no intention to create a trust the alleged settlor or his estate **3–120** retains the beneficial interest in relevant property. If there is uncertainty of subject-matter then the alleged trust is ineffective since there is nothing for the alleged trust to "bite" on. If certainty of intention and of subject-matter are present but there is uncertainty of beneficiaries then the trustee holds the property on a resulting trust for the settlor or the testator's estate as the case may be.

If property is given by will or other instrument to someone absolutely and subsequently in that instrument trusts are imposed on that absolute interest then if these trusts fail for uncertainty or otherwise the donee takes the property for himself absolutely.[39]

---

[36] The jurisdiction of the court cannot be ousted: *Re Raven* [1915] 1 Ch. 673: *Re Wynn's W.T.* [1952] Ch. 271. One should note that a court should construe a discretionary trust "for my old friends but so that my trustees shall have power to resolve any doubts as to whether anyone is or is not an old friend of mine" as being a discretionary trust for "persons whom my trustees consider to be my old friends" so that the position should be the same on either construction.

[37] This is narrower than taking advantage of *Re Hay's S.T.* [1982] 1 W.L.R. 202, para.3–137 to give the widow power to add to the class of beneficiaries anyone else (apart from herself or past or present trustees) but particularly anyone she considers to be an old friend of the testator. Also see *Re Coates* [1955] Ch. 495 for the court's liberal approach before establishment of the "is or is not" test.

[38] Perhaps this may have been at the back of Harman L.J.'s mind in *Re Leek* [1969] 1 Ch. 563 at 579 when, whilst accepting that a discretionary trust for such persons as have moral claims on the settlor would be void for conceptual uncertainty, he uttered unorthodox dicta to the effect that if the trustees were arbiters of the class of beneficiaries, being such persons as the trustees considered to have a moral claim on the settlor, the trust would be valid.

[39] *Hancock v Watson* [1902] A.C. 14: *Re Burton's S.T.* [1955] Ch. 348.

RE GULBENKIAN'S SETTLEMENT TRUSTS

3–121 House of Lords [1970] A.C. 508; [1968] 3 W.L.R. 1127; [1968] 3 All E.R. 785.

Settlements were made including a special power for trustees to appoint in favour of Nubar Gulbenkian "and any wife and his children or remoter issue . . . and any person . . . in whose house or apartment or in whose company or under whose care or control or by or with whom [he] may from time to time be employed or residing," and with trusts in default of appointment.

The House of Lords unanimously upheld the power and (Lord Donovan reserving his opinion though "inclined to share" Lord Upjohn's views) rejected *obiter* the broad view that a power was valid if any one person clearly fell within the scope of the power. The House construed the clause as meaning "and any person or persons by whom Nubar may from time to time be employed and any person or persons with whom N from time to time is residing whether in the house or apartments of such person or persons or whether in the company or under the care and control of such person or persons" and held that it could be said with certainty whether any given individual was or was not a member of that class so that the power was valid.

LORD UPJOHN (with whom Lords Guest and Hodson concurred): "My lords, that is sufficient to dispose of the appeal, but the reasons of two members of the Court of Appeal went further and so must be examined.

3–122 "Lord Denning M.R.,[40] propounded a test in the case of powers collateral, namely, that if you can say of one particular person meaning thereby, apparently, any one person only that he is clearly within the category the whole power is good though it may be difficult to say in other cases whether a person is or is not within the category, and he supported that view by reference to authority. Winn L.J. said[41] that where there was not a complete failure by reason of ambiguity and uncertainty the court would give effect to the power as valid rather than hold it defeated since it will not have wholly failed, which put—though more broadly—the view expressed by Lord Denning M.R. Counsel for the respondents in his second line of argument relied on these observations as a matter of principle but he candidly admitted that he could not rely on any authority. Moreover, Lord Denning M.R. expressed the view[42] that the different doctrine with regard to trust powers should be brought into line with the rule with regard to conditions precedent and powers collateral . . .

[After pointing out that a fixed trust for equal division among my old friends would be void even if two or three individuals plainly were old friends, he continued]

"Suppose the donor does not direct an equal division but gives a power of selection to his trustees among the class: exactly the same principles apply. The trustees have a duty to select the donees of the donor's bounty from among the class designated by the donor; he has not entrusted them with any power to select the donees merely from among known claimants within the class, for that is constituting a narrower class and the donor has given them no power to do this . . .

3–123 "But with respect to mere powers,[43] while the court cannot compel the trustees to exercise their powers, yet those entitled to the fund in default must clearly be entitled to restrain the trustees from exercising it save among those within the

---

[40] [1968] Ch. 126 at 133, 134.
[41] [1968] Ch. 126 at 138.
[42] *ibid.*
[43] He had just pointed out that in the case of trust powers (*viz.* discretionary trusts) "the trustees *must* exercise their power of selection and in default the court will", so he could not "see how it is possible to apply to the execution of a trust power the principles applicable to the permissible exercise by the donees, even if trustees, of mere powers."

power. So the trustees, or the court, must be able to say with certainty who is within and who is without the power. It is for this reason that I find myself unable to accept the broader position advanced by Lord Denning M.R. and Winn L.J., mentioned earlier.

"My lords, I would dismiss these appeals." *Appeals dismissed.*

MCPHAIL v DOULTON

House of Lords [1971] A.C. 424; [1970] 2 W.L.R. 1110; [1970] 2 All E.R. 228.   **3–124**

The facts and the issues appear clearly in the following speech of Lord Wilberforce with which Lord Reid and Viscount Dilhorne concurred, though dissenting speeches were delivered by Lords Hodson and Guest.

LORD WILBERFORCE: "My Lords, this appeal is concerned with the validity of a trust deed dated July 17, 1941, by which Mr. Bertram Baden established a fund for the benefit, broadly, of the staff of the respondent company Matthew Hall & Co. Ltd
The critical clauses are as follows:

'9. (a) The Trustees shall apply the net income of the Fund in making at their absolute discretion grants to or for benefit of any of the officers and employees or ex-officers or ex-employees of the Company or any relatives or dependants of any such persons in such amounts at such times and on such conditions (if any) as they think fit and any such grant may at their discretion be made by payment to the beneficiary or to any institution or person to be applied for his or her benefit and in the latter case the Trustees shall be under no obligation to see to the application of the money.
'(b) The Trustees shall not be bound to exhaust the income of any year or other period in making such grants as aforesaid and any income not so applied shall be dealt with as provided by clause 6(a) hereof enabling moneys to be placed with any Bank or to be invested.
'(c) The Trustees may realise any investments representing accumulations of income and apply the proceeds as though the same were income of the Fund and may also (but only with the consent of all the Trustees) at any time prior to the liquidation of the Fund realise any other part of the capital of the Fund which in the opinion of the Trustees it is desirable to realise in order to provide benefits for which the current income of the Fund is insufficient.
'10. All benefits being at the absolute discretion of the Trustees, no person shall have any right title or interest in the Fund otherwise than pursuant to the exercise of such discretion, and nothing herein contained shall prejudice the right of the Company to determine the employment of any officer or employee.'

"Clause 11 defines a perpetuity period within which the trusts are, in any event, to   **3–125**
come to an end and clause 12 provides for the termination of the fund. On this event the trustees are directed to apply the fund in their discretion in one or more of certain specified ways of which one is in making grants as if they were grants under clause 9(a) . . .

"In this House, the appellants contended that the provisions of clause 9(a) constitute a trust and not a power. If that is held to be the correct result both sides agree that the case must return to the Chancery Division for consideration, on this footing, whether this trust is valid. But here comes a complication. In the present state of authority, the decision as to validity would turn on the question whether a complete list (or on another view a list complete for practical purposes) can be drawn up of all possible beneficiaries. This follows from the Court of Appeal's decision in *Inland Revenue Comrs. v Broadway Cottages Trust*[44] as applied in later cases by which, unless this House decides otherwise, the Court of Chancery would be bound. The respondents invite your Lordships to review this decision and challenge its correctness. So the second issue which arises, if clause 9(a) amounts to a trust, is whether the existing test for its validity is right in law and if not, what the test ought to be.

3–126   "Before dealing with these two questions some general observations, or reflections, may be permissible. It is striking how narrow and in a sense artificial is the distinction, in cases such as the present, between trusts or as the particular type of trust is called, trust powers, and powers. It is only necessary to read the learned judgments in the Court of Appeal[45] to see that what to one mind may appear as a power of distribution coupled with a trust to dispose of the undistributed surplus, by accumulation or otherwise, may to another appear as a trust for distribution coupled with a power to withhold a portion and accumulate or otherwise dispose of it. A layman and, I suspect, also a logician, would find it hard to understand what difference there is.

3–127   "It does not seem satisfactory that the entire validity of a disposition should depend on such delicate shading. And if one considers how in practice reasonable and competent trustees would act, and ought to act, in the two cases, surely a matter very relevant to the question of validity, the distinction appears even less significant. To say that there is no obligation to exercise a mere power and that no court will intervene to compel it, whereas a trust is mandatory and its execution must be compelled, may be legally correct enough, but the proposition does not contain an exhaustive comparison of the duties of persons who are trustees in the two cases. A trustee of an employees' benefit fund, whether given a power or a trust power, is still a trustee and he would surely consider in either case that he has a fiduciary duty; he is most likely to have been selected as a suitable person to administer it from his knowledge and experience, and would consider he has a responsibility to do so according to its purpose. It would be a complete misdescription of his position to say that, if what he has is a power unaccompanied by an imperative trust to distribute, he cannot be controlled by the court if he exercised it capriciously, or outside the field permitted by the trust (*cf.* Farwell on Powers[46]). Any trustee would surely make it his duty to know what is the permissible area of selection and then consider responsibly, in individual cases, whether a contemplated beneficiary was within the power and whether, in relation to other possible claimants, a particular grant was appropriate.

3–128   "Correspondingly a trustee with a duty to distribute, particularly among a potentially very large class, would surely never require the preparation of a complete list of names, which anyhow would tell him little that he needs to know. He would examine the field, by class and category; might indeed make diligent and careful enquiries, depending on how much money he had to give away and the means at his disposal, as to the composition and needs of particular categories and of individuals within them; decide on certain priorities or proportions, and then

---

[44] [1955] Ch. 20.
[45] [1969] 2 Ch. 388.
[46] (3rd ed., 1916), p.524.

select individuals according to their needs or qualifications. If he acts in this manner, can it really be said that he is not carrying out the trust?

"Differences there certainly are between trusts (trust powers) and powers, but as   **3–129**
regards validity should they be so great as that in one case complete, or practically complete ascertainment is needed, but not in the other? Such distinction as there is would seem to lie in the extent of the survey which the trustee is required to carry out; if he has to distribute the whole of a fund's income, he must necessarily make a wider and more systematic survey than if his duty is expressed in terms of a power to make grants. But just as, in the case of a power, it is possible to underestimate the fiduciary obligation of the trustee to whom it is given, so, in the case of a trust (trust power), the danger lies in overstating what the trustee requires to know or to enquire into before he can properly execute his trust. The difference may be one of degree rather than of principle; in the well-known words of Sir George Farwell (*Farwell on Powers*[47]) trusts and powers are often blended, and the mixture may vary in its ingredients.

"I now consider whether the provisions of clause 9(a) constitute a trust or a power. Naturally read, the intention of the deed seems to me clear: clause 9(a), whose language is mandatory ('shall'), creates, together with a power of selection, a trust for distribution of the income, the strictness of which is qualified by clause 9(b) which allows the income of any one year to be held up and (under clause 6(a)) either placed, for the time, with a bank, or, if thought fit, invested. Whether there is, in any technical sense an accumulation, seems to me in the present context a jejune enquiry; what is relevant is that clause 9(c) marks the difference between 'accumulations' of income and the capital of the fund: the former can be distributed by a majority of the trustees, the latter cannot. As to clause 10, I do not find in it any decisive indication. If anything it seems to point in favour of a trust, but both this and other points of detail are insignificant in the face of the clearly expressed scheme of clause 9. I therefore declare that the provisions of clause 9(a) constitute a trust and remit the case to the Chancery Division for determination whether on this basis clause 9 is (subject to the effects of section 164 of the Law of Property Act 1925) valid or void for uncertainty.

"This makes it necessary to consider whether, in so doing, the court should   **3–130**
proceed on the basis that the relevant test is that laid down in the *Broadway Cottages* case[48] or some other test. That decision gave the authority of the Court of Appeal to the distinction between cases where trustees are given a *power* of selection and those where they are bound by a *trust* for selection. In the former case the position, as decided by this House, is that the power is valid if it can be said with certainty whether any given individual is or is not a member of the class and does not fail simply because it is impossible to ascertain every member of the class. (The *Gulbenkian* case.[49]) But in the latter case it is said to be necessary, for the trust to be valid, that the whole range of objects (I use the language of the Court of Appeal) should be ascertained or capable of ascertainment.

"The respondents invited your Lordships to assimilate the validity test for trusts   **3–131**
to that which applies to powers. Alternatively, they contended that in any event the test laid down in the *Broadway Cottages* case was too rigid, and that a trust should be upheld if there is sufficient practical certainty in its definition for it to be carried out, if necessary with the administrative assistance of the court, according to the

---

[47] *ibid.* at 10.
[48] [1955] Ch. 20.
[49] [1970] A.C. 508.

expressed intention of the settlor. I would agree with this, but this does not dispense from examination of the wider argument. The basis for the *Broadway Cottages* case principle is stated to be that a trust cannot be valid unless, if need be, it can be executed by the court, and that the court can only execute it by ordering an equal distribution in which every beneficiary shares. So it is necessary to examine the authority and reason for this supposed rule as to the execution of trusts by the court.

3–132   "Assuming, as I am prepared to do for present purposes, that the test of validity is whether the trust can be executed by the court, it does not follow that execution is impossible unless there can be equal division. As a matter of reason, to hold that a principle of equal division applies to trusts such as the present is certainly paradoxical. Equal division is surely the last thing the settlor ever intended; (equal division among all may, probably would, produce a result beneficial to none) Why suppose that the court would lend itself to a whimsical execution? And as regards authority, I do not find that the nature of the trust, and of the court's powers over trusts, calls for any such rigid rule. Equal division may be sensible and has been decreed, in cases of family trusts for a limited class, here there is life in the maxim 'equality is equity,' but the cases provide numerous examples where this has not been so, and a different type of execution has been ordered, appropriate to the circumstances. . . .

3–133   "So I come to *Inland Revenue Comrs. v Broadway Cottage Trusts.*[50] This was certainly a case of trust, and it proceeded on the basis of an admission, in the words of the judgment, 'that the class of "beneficiaries" is incapable of ascertainment.' In addition to the discretionary trust of income, there was a trust of capital for all the beneficiaries living or existing at the terminal date. This necessarily involved equal division and it seems to have been accepted that it was void for uncertainty since there cannot be equal division among a class unless all the members of the class are known. The Court of Appeal[51] applied this proposition to the discretionary trust of income, on the basis that execution by the court was only possible on the same basis of equal division. They rejected the argument that the trust could be executed by changing the trusteeship, and found the relations cases of no assistance as being in a class by themselves. The court could not create an arbitrarily restricted trust to take effect in default of distribution by the trustees. Finally they rejected the submission that the trust could take effect as a power, a valid power could not be spelt out of an invalid trust.

3–134   "So I think we are free to review the *Broadway Cottages* case. The conclusion which I would reach, implicit in the previous discussion, is that the wide distinction between the validity test for powers and that for trust powers, is unfortunate and wrong, that the rule recently fastened on the courts by the *Broadway Cottages* case ought to be discarded, and that the test for the validity of trust powers ought to be similar to that accepted by this House in *Re Gulbenkian's Settlement Trusts* for powers, namely that the trust is valid if it can be said with certainty that any given individual is or is not a member of the class.

3–135   "Assimilation of the validity test does not involve the complete assimilation of trust powers with powers. As to powers, I agree with my noble and learned friend Lord Upjohn in *Re Gulbenkian's Settlement* that although the trustees may, and normally will, be under a fiduciary duty to consider whether or in what way they should exercise their power, the court will not normally compel its exercise. It will intervene if the trustees exceed their powers, and possibly if they are proved to have

---

[50] [1955] Ch. 20.
[51] [1968] Ch. 126.

exercised it capriciously. But in the case of a trust power, if the trustees do not exercise it, the court will; I respectfully adopt as to this the statement in Lord Upjohn's opinion.[52] I would venture to amplify this by saying that the court, if called on to execute the trust power, will do so in the manner best calculated to give effect to the settlor's or testator's intentions. It may do so by appointing new trustees, or authorising or directing representative persons of the classes of beneficiaries to prepare a scheme of distribution, or even, should the proper basis for distribution appear, by itself directing the trustees so to distribute. The books give many instances where this has been done and I see no reason in principle why they should not do so in the modern field of discretionary trusts (see *Brunsden v Woolredge*,[53] *Supple v Lowson*,[54] *Liley v Hey*[55] and Lewin on Trusts[56]). Then, as to the trustees' duty of enquiry or ascertainment, in each case the trustees ought to make such a survey of the range of objects or possible beneficiaries as will enable them to carry out their fiduciary duty (*cf. Liley v Hey*). A wider and more comprehensive range of enquiry is called for in the case of trust powers than in the case of powers.

"Two final points: first, as to the question of certainty, I desire to emphasise the **3–136** distinction clearly made and explained by Lord Upjohn,[57] between linguistic or semantic uncertainty which, if unresolved by the court, renders the gift void, and the difficulty of ascertaining the existence or whereabouts of members of the class, a matter with which the court can appropriately deal on an application for directions. There may be a third case where the meaning of the words used is clear but the definition of beneficiaries is so hopelessly wide as not to form 'anything like a class' so that the trust is administratively unworkable or in Lord Eldon L.C.'s words one that cannot be executed (*Morice v Bishop of Durham*[58]). I hesitate to give examples for they may prejudice future cases, but perhaps 'all the residents of Greater London' will serve. I do not think that a discretionary trust for 'relatives' even of a living person falls within this category . . ."

Appeal allowed. Declaration that the provisions of clause 9(a) constituted a trust. Case remitted for determination whether on this basis clause 9 was (subject to the effects of section 164 of the Law of Property Act 1925) valid or void for uncertainty.

RE HAY'S SETTLEMENT TRUSTS

Chancery Division [1982] 1 W.L.R. 202; [1981] 3 All E.R. 786

By clause 4 of Lady Hay's settlement made in 1958, trustees held the trust fund **3–137** "on trust for such persons or purposes for such interests and with such gifts over and (if for persons) with such provisions for their respective maintenance or advancement at the discretion of the Trustees or of any other persons as the Trustees shall by any deed or deeds revocable or irrevocable (but if revocable not after the expiration of 21 years from the date hereof) executed within 21 years from the date hereof appoint . . . and in default of such appointment in trust for the nieces and nephews of the Settlor now living in equal shares." A proviso precluded any appointment being made to the settlor, any husband of her, and any trustee or

---

[52] [1970] A.C. 508 at 525.
[53] (1765) Amb. 507.
[54] (1773) Amb. 729.
[55] (1842) 1 Hare 580.
[56] (16th ed., 1964), p.630.
[57] [1970] A.C. 508 at 524.
[58] (1805) 10 Ves. at 527.

past trustee. For the first five years income was to be accumulated and then the income was to be held on discretionary trusts for the nieces and nephews or charities until the clause 4 power of appointment was exercised or ceased to be exercisable (by expiry of the 21 years).

3–138   In 1969 a deed of appointment was executed, clause 1 conferring a power of appointment on the trustees (exercisable till expiry of the 21-year period in the 1958 settlement) to hold "the trust fund and the income thereof on trust for such persons and such persons as shall be appointed." Clause 2 directed that the undisposed-of income (until full exercise of the clause 1 power) be held on discretionary trusts for the benefit of any persons whatsoever (the settlor, any husband of her, any existing or former trustee excepted) or for any charity.

Was the vast power of appointment in the 1958 settlement valid or not? If valid was its exercise void in creating a vast discretionary trust that could be said to infringe the rule "*delegatus non potest delegare*" or the rule that a trust must be administratively workable?

3–139   MEGARRY V.-C.: ". . . The starting point must be to consider whether the power created by the first limb of clause 4 of the settlement is valid . . . The essential point is whether a power for trustees to appoint to anyone in the world except a handful of specified persons is valid. Such a power will be perfectly valid if given to a person who is not in a fiduciary position: the difficulty arises when it is given to trustees, for they are under certain fiduciary duties in relation to the power, and to a limited degree they are subject to the control of the courts. At the centre of the dispute there are *Re Manisty's Settlement Trusts*; [1974] Ch. 17; (in which Templeman J. differed from part of what was said in the Court of Appeal in *Blausten v Inland Revenue Comrs*,; [1972] Ch. 256; *McPhail v Doulton*; [1971] A.C. 424; (which I shall call *Re Baden (No. 1)*); and *Re Baden's Deed Trusts (No. 2)*; [1973] Ch. 9, which I shall call *Re Baden (No. 2)*. Counsel for the defendants, I may say, strongly contended that *Re Manisty's Settlement* was wrongly decided.

3–140   "In *Re Manisty's Settlement* a settlement gave trustees a discretionary power to apply the trust fund for the benefit of a small class of the settlor's near relations, save that any member of a smaller 'excepted class' was to be excluded from the class of beneficiaries. The trustees were also given power at their absolute discretion to declare that any person, corporation or charity (except a member of the excepted class or a trustee) should be included in the class of beneficiaries. Templeman J. held that this power to extend the class of beneficiaries was valid. In *Blausten v Inland Revenue Comrs.* which had been decided some eighteen months earlier, the settlement created a discretionary trust of income for members of a 'specified class' and a power to pay or apply capital to or for the benefit of members of that class, or to appoint capital to be held on trust for them. The settlement also gave the trustees power 'with the previous consent in writing of the settlor' to appoint any other person or persons (except the settlor) to be included in the 'specified class.' The Court of Appeal decided the case on a point of construction; but Buckley L.J.; ([1972] Ch. 256 at 271) also considered a contention that the trustees' power to add to the 'specified class' was so wide that it was bad for uncertainty, since the power would enable anyone in the world save the settlor to be included. He rejected this contention on the ground that the settlor's prior written consent was requisite to any addition to the 'specified class'; but for this, it seems plain that he would have held the power void for uncertainty. Orr L.J. simply concurred, but Salmon L.J. expressly confined himself to the point of construction, and said nothing about the power to add to the 'specified class.' In *Re Manisty's Settlement*; [1974] Ch. 17 at 29, Templeman J. rejected the view of Buckley L.J. on this point on the ground that *Re*

Gestetner (deceased); [1953] Ch. 672, *Re Gulbenkian's Settlement Trusts*; [1970] A.C. 508 and the two *Baden* cases did not appear to have been fully explored in the *Blausten* case, and the case did not involve any final pronouncement on the point. In general, I respectfully agree with Templeman J.

"I propose to approach the matter by stages. First, it is plain that if a power of **3–141** appointment is given to a person who is not in a fiduciary position, there is nothing in the width of the power which invalidates it per se. The power may be a special power with a large class of persons as objects; the power may be what is called a 'hybrid' power, or an 'intermediate' power, authorising appointment to anyone save a specified number or class of persons; or the power may be a general power. Whichever it is, there is nothing in the number of persons to whom an appointment may be made which will invalidate it. The difficulty comes when the power is given to trustees as such, in that the number of objects may interact with the fiduciary duties of the trustees and their control by the court. The argument of counsel for the defendants carried him to the extent of asserting that no valid intermediate or general power could be vested in trustees.

"That brings me to the second point, namely, the extent of the fiduciary obligations of trustees who have a mere power vested in them, and how far the court exercises control over them in relation to that power. In the case of a trust, of course, the trustee is bound to execute it, and if he does not, the court will see to its execution. A mere power is very different. Normally the trustee is not bound to exercise it, and the court will not compel him to do so. That, however, does not mean that he can simply fold his hands and ignore it, for normally he must from time to time consider whether or not to exercise the power, and the court may direct him to do this.

"When he does exercise the power, he must, of course (as in the case of all trusts **3–142** and powers) confine himself to what is authorised, and not go beyond it. But that is not the only restriction. Whereas a person who is not in a fiduciary position is free to exercise the power in any way that he wishes, unhampered by any fiduciary duties, a trustee to whom, as such, a power is given is bound by the duties of his office in exercising that power to do so in a responsible manner according to its purpose. It is not enough for him to refrain from acting capriciously; he must do more. He must 'make such a survey of the range of objects or possible beneficiaries' as will enable him to carry out his fiduciary duty. He must find out 'the permissible area of selection and then consider responsibly, in individual cases, whether a contemplated beneficiary was within the power and whether, in relation to the possible claimants, a particular grant was appropriate': per Lord Wilberforce in *Re Baden (No. 1)*; [1971] A.C. 424 at 449, 457. . .

"That brings me to the third point. How is the duty of making a responsible **3–143** survey and selection to be carried out in the absence of any complete list of objects? This question was considered by the Court of Appeal in *Re Baden (No. 2)*. That case was concerned with what, after some divergences of judicial opinion, was held to be a discretionary trust and not a mere power; but plainly the requirements for a mere power cannot be more stringent than those for a discretionary trust. The duty, I think, may be expressed along the following lines. The trustee must not simply proceed to exercise the power in favour of such of the objects as happen to be at hand or claim his attention. He must first consider what persons or classes of persons are objects of the power within the definition in the settlement or will. In doing this, there is no need to compile a complete list of the objects, or even to make an accurate assessment of the number of them: what is needed is an appreciation of the width of the field, and thus whether a selection is to be made merely from a dozen or, instead, from thousands or millions . . . Only when the trustee has applied his mind to 'the size of the problem' should he then consider in individual cases whether, in relation to other possible claimants, a particular grant is appropriate. In doing this, no doubt he should not prefer the undeserving to the deserving; but he is not required to make an exact calculation whether, as between deserving claimants, A is more deserving than B: see *Re Gestetner (deceased)*; [1953] Ch. 672 at 688, approved in *Re Baden (No.1)* [1971] A.C. 424 at 453.

3–144   "If I am right in these views, the duties of a trustee which are specific to a mere power seem to be threefold. Apart from the obvious duty of obeying the trust instrument, and in particular of making no appointment that is not authorised by it, the trustee must, first, consider periodically whether or not he should exercise the power; second, consider the range of objects of the power; and third, consider the appropriateness of individual appointments. I do not assert that this list is exhaustive; but as the authorities stand it seems to me to include the essentials, so far as relevant to the case before me.

"On this footing, the question is thus whether there is something in the nature of an intermediate power which conflicts with these duties in such a way as to invalidate the power if it is vested in a trustee. The case that there is rests in the main on *Blausten v Inland Revenue Comrs.* which I have already summarised. The power there was plainly a mere power; and it authorised the trustees, with the settlor's previous consent in writing, to add any other person or persons (except the settlor) to the specified class.

3–145   "After referring to *Re Park* [1932] 1 Ch. 581 at 583, Buckley L.J. went on; ([1972] Ch. 256 at 273:

> ". . . this is not a power which suffers from the sort of uncertainty which results from the trustees being given a power of so wide an extent that it would be impossible for the court to say whether or not they were properly exercising it and so wide that it would be impossible for the trustees to consider in any sensible manner how they should exercise it, if at all, from time to time. The trustees would no doubt take into consideration the possible claims of anyone having any claim in the beneficence of the [settlor]. That is not a class of persons so wide or so indefinite that the trustees would not be able rationally to exercise their duty to consider from time to time whether or not they should exercise the power."

"It seems quite plain that Buckley L.J. considered that the power was saved from invalidity only by the requirement for the consent of the settlor. The reason for saying that in the absence of such a requirement the power would have been invalid seems to be twofold. First, the class of persons to whose possible claims the trustees would be duty-bound to give consideration was so wide as not to form a true class, and this would make it impossible for the trustees to perform their duty of considering from time to time whether to exercise the power.

3–146   "I feel considerable difficulty in accepting this view. First, I do not see how mere numbers can inhibit the trustees from considering whether or not to exercise the power, as distinct from deciding in whose favour to exercise it. Second, I cannot see how the requirement of the settlor's consent will result in any 'class' being narrowed from one that is too wide to one that is small enough. Such a requirement makes no difference whatever to the number of persons potentially included: the only exclusion is still the settlor. Third, in any case I cannot see how the requirement of the settlor's consent could make it possible to treat 'anyone in the world save X' as constituting any real sort of a 'class,' as that term is usually understood.

3–147   "The second ground of invalidity if there is no requirement for the settlor's consent seems to be that the power is so wide that it would be impossible for the trustees to consider in any sensible manner how to exercise it, and also impossible for the court to say whether or not they were properly exercising it. With respect, I do not see how that follows. If I have correctly stated the extent of the duties of trustees in whom a mere power is vested, I do not see what there is to prevent the trustees from performing these duties. It must be remembered that Buckley L.J., though speaking after *Re Gulbenkian's Settlement* and *Re Baden (No. 1)* had been decided, lacked the advantage of considering *Re Baden (No. 2)*, which was not decided until some five months later. He thus did not have before him the explanation in that case of how the trustees should make a survey and consider individual appointments in cases where no complete list of objects could be compiled. I also have in mind that the settlor in the present case is still alive, though I do not rest my decision on that.

"From what I have said it will be seen that I cannot see any ground on which the **3–148** power in question can be said to be void. Certainly it is not void for linguistic or semantic uncertainty; there is no room for doubt in the definition of those who are or are not objects of the power. Nor can I see that the power is administratively unworkable. The words of Lord Wilberforce in *Re Baden (No. 1)* [1971] A.C. 424 at 457 are directed to discretionary trusts, not powers. Nor do I think that the power is void as being capricious. In *Re Manisty's Settlement* [1974] Ch. 17 at 27 Templeman J. appears to be suggesting that a power to benefit 'residents in Greater London' is void as being capricious 'because the terms of the power negative any sensible intention on the part of the settlor.' In saying that, I do not think that the judge had in mind a case in which the settlor was, for instance, a former chairman of the Greater London Council, as subsequent words of his on that page indicate. In any case, as he pointed out earlier, this consideration does not apply to intermediate powers, where no class which could be regarded as capricious has been laid down. Nor do I see how the power in the present case could be invalidated as being too vague, a possible ground of invalidity considered in *Re Manisty's Settlement* [1974] Ch. 17 at 24. Of course, if there is some real vice in a power, and there are real problems of administration or execution, the court may have to hold the power invalid: but I think that the court should be slow to do this. Dispositions ought if possible to be upheld, and the court ought not to be astute to find grounds on which a power can be invalidated. Naturally, if it is shown that a power offends against some rule of law or equity, then it will be held to be void: but a power should not be held void on a peradventure. In my judgment, the power conferred by clause 4 of the settlement is valid.

"With that, I turn to the discretionary trust of income under clause 2 of the deed **3–149** of appointment. Apart from questions of the validity of the trust per se, there is the prior question whether the settlement enabled the trustees to create such a trust, or, for that matter, the power set out in clause 1 of the deed of appointment. The power conferred by clause 4 of the settlement provides that the trustees are to hold the trust fund on trust 'for such persons or purposes for such interests and with such gifts over and (if for persons) with such provision for their respective maintenance or advancement at the discretion of the Trustees or any other persons as the trustees shall appoint. Clause 2 of the deed of appointment provides that the trustees are to hold the trust fund on trust to pay the income 'to or for the benefit of any person or persons whatsoever . . . or to any charity' in such manner and shares and proportions as the trustees think fit. I need say nothing about purposes or charities as no question on them has arisen. The basic question is whether the appointment has designated the 'persons' to whom the appointment is made.

"Looked at as a matter of principle, my answer would be 'No.' There is no such **3–150** person to be found in clause 2 of the deed of appointment. That seems to me to be a plain case of delegation.

"Counsel for the defendants relied on *Re Hunter's Will Trusts* [1963] Ch. 372; [and *Re Morris' S.T.* [1951] 2 All E.R. 528] as supporting his contention that clause 2 of the deed of appointment was void.

"Now it is clear that in these authorities the rule delegatus non potest delegare was in issue. Does this rule apply to intermediate powers? This was not explored in argument, but I think that it is clear from *Re Triffitt's Settlement* [1958] Ch. 852 that the rule does not apply to an intermediate power vested in a person beneficially. Here, of course, the power is an intermediate power, but it is vested in trustees as such, and not in any person beneficially; and the rule is that 'trustees cannot delegate unless they have authority to do so': *per* Viscount Radcliffe in *Re Pilkington's Will Trusts* [1964] A.C. 612 at 639. Accordingly, I do not think that the fact that the power is an intermediate power excludes it from the rule against delegation. On the contrary, the fact that the power is vested in trustees subjects it to that rule unless there is something in the settlement to exclude it. I can see nothing in the settlement which purports to authorise any such appointment or to exclude the normal rule against delegation. In my judgment, both on principle and on authority clause 2 of the deed of appointment is void as being an excessive execution of the power.

3–151   "That, I think, suffices to dispose of the case. I have not dealt with the submission which counsel for the defendants put in the forefront of his argument. This was that even if the power had been wide enough to authorise the creation of the discretionary trust, that trust was nevertheless as bad as being a trust in favour of 'so hopelessly wide' a definition of beneficiaries 'as not to form anything like a class so that the trust is administratively unworkable': see *per* Lord Wilberforce in *Re Baden (No. 1)*; [1971] A.C. 424 at 457. I do not propose to go into the authorities on this point. I consider that the duties of trustees under a discretionary trust are more stringent than those of trustees under a power of appointment (see *Re Baden (No. 1)*; [1971] A.C. 424 at 457), and as at present advised I think that I would, if necessary, hold that an intermediate trust such as that in the present case is void as being administratively unworkable. In my view there is a difference between a power and a trust in this respect. The essence of that difference, I think, is that beneficiaries under a trust have rights of enforcement which mere objects of a power lack."

[He then held that the nieces and nephews living at the date of the settlement had become entitled to the trust fund on the expiration of 21 years from the date of the settlement by virtue of the gift over in default of any valid appointment within the 21 years.]

METTOY PENSION TRUSTEES LTD v EVANS

Chancery Division [1990] 1 W.L.R. 1587; [1991] 2 All E.R. 515.

3–152   On the liquidation of a company, which was sole trustee of its company pension fund, it became impossible for it to exercise its fiduciary power as trustee to apply surplus trust funds to benefit the beneficiaries; nor could the liquidator exercise the power because of his conflicting duties to the creditors of the company otherwise entitled to the surplus and to the beneficiary. Could the court exercise the power in the same way that the court can give effect to discretionary trusts? Yes.

3–153   WARNER J.: "The question then arises, if the discretion is a fiduciary power which cannot be exercised either by the receivers or by the liquidator, who is to exercise it? I heard submissions on that point. The discretion cannot be exercised by the directors of the company, because on the appointment of the liquidator all the powers of the directors ceased. I was referred to a number of authorities on the circumstances in which the court may interfere with or give directions as to the exercise of discretions vested in trustees, namely *Gisborne v Gisborne* (1877) 2 App.Cas. 300; *Re Hodges, Dovey v Ward* (1878) 7 Ch.D. 754; *Tabor v Brooks* (1878) 10 Ch. D 273; *Klug v Klug* [1918] 2 Ch. 67; *Re Allen-Meyrick's Will Trusts; Mangnall v Allen-Meyrick* [1966] 1 W.L.R. 499; *McPhail v Doulton* [1971] A.C. 424; *Re Manisty's Settlement* [1974] Ch. 17 at 25–26 and *Re Locker's Settlement Trusts; Meachem v Sachs* [1977] 1 W.L.R. 1323. None of those cases deals directly with a situation in which a fiduciary power is left with no one to exercise it. They point however to the conclusion that in that situation the court must step in. Mr Inglis-Jones and Mr Walker urge me to say that in this case the court should step in by giving directions to the trustees as to the distribution of the surplus in the pension fund. They relied in particular on this passage in the speech of Lord Wilberforce in *McPhail v Doulton* [1971] A.C. 424 at 456–457:

> "As to powers, I agree with my noble and learned friend Lord Upjohn in *Re Gulbenkian's Settlement* [1970] A.C. 508 that although the trustees may, and formally will, be under a fiduciary duty to consider whether or in what way they should exercise their power, the court will not normally compel its exercise. It will intervene if the trustees exceed their powers, and possibly if they are proved to have exercised it capriciously. But in the case of a trust power, if the trustees do not exercise it, the court will; I respectfully adopt as to this the statement in Lord Upjohn's opinion (see [1970] A.C. 508 at 525). I would venture to amplify this by saying that the court, if called upon to execute the trust power, will do so in the manner best calculated to give effect to the settlor's or testator's intentions. It may do so by appointing new trustees, or by authorising or directing representative persons of the classes of beneficiaries to prepare a scheme of distribution, or even, should the proper basis for distribution appear, by itself directing the trustees so to distribute. The books give many instances where this has been done and I see no reason in principle why they should not do so in the modern field of discretionary trusts . . ."

"Clearly, in the first two sentences of that passage Lord Wilberforce was referring to   **3–154** a discretion in category 2[59] and in the following part of it to a discretion in category 4. In that latter part he was indicating how the court might give effect to a discretionary trust when called upon to execute it. It seems to me however that the methods he indicated could be equally appropriate in a case where the court was called upon to intervene in the exercise of a discretion in category 2. In saying that I do not overlook that in *Re Manisty's Settlement* [1974] Ch. 17 at 25 Templeman J. expressed the view that the only right and the only remedy of an object of the power who was aggrieved by the trustees' conduct would be to apply to the court to remove the trustees and appoint others in their place. However, the earlier authorities to which I was referred, such as *Re Hodges* and *Klug v Klug*, had not been cited to

---

[59] Note that in Warner J.'s classification, category 1 comprises any power given to a person to determine the destination of trust properly without that person being under any obligation to exercise the power or to preserve it (a personal power); category 2 comprises any power conferred on the trustees of the property or on any other person as a trustee of the power itself (a fiduciary power); category 3 comprises any discretion which is really a duty to form a judgment as to the existence or otherwise of particular circumstances giving rise to particular consequences; and category 4 comprises discretionary trusts where someone, usually the trustees, is under a duty to select from among a class of beneficiaries those who are to receive amounts of income or capital of the trust fund.

Templeman J. I conclude that, in a situation such as this, it is open to the court to adopt whichever of the methods indicated by Lord Wilberforce appears most appropriate in the circumstances."

SCHMIDT v ROSEWOOD TRUST LIMITED

Privy Council [2003] UKPC 26; [2003] 2 A.C. 709; [2003] 2 W.L.R. 1442; [2003] 3 All E.R. 76 (Lords, Nicholls, Hope Hutton, Hobhouse and Walker)

3–155 LORD WALKER [after citing Lord Wilberforce in *McPhail v Doulton* [1971] A.C. 424 at 448–449, set out in paragraphs 3–126 to 3–129 above]

"[40] This passage gives a very clear and eminently realistic account of both the points of difference and the similarities between a discretionary trust and a fiduciary dispositive power. The outstanding point of difference is of course that under a discretionary trust of income distribution of income (within a reasonable time) is mandatory, the trustees' discretion being limited to the choice of the recipients and the shares in which they are to take. If there is a small, closed class of discretionary objects who are all *sui juris*, their collective entitlement gives them a limited power of disposition over the income subject to the discretionary trust, as is illustrated by *In re Smith* [1928] Ch. 915 and *In re Nelson* (1918) reported as a note to *In re Smith*. But the possibility of such a collective disposition will be rare, and on his own the object of a discretionary trust has no more of an assignable or transmissible interest than the object of a mere power.

3–156 [41] Apart from the test for certainty being the same and the fact that an individual's interest or right is non-assignable, there are other practical similarities between the positions of the two types of object. Either has the negative power to block a family arrangement or similar transaction proposed to be effected under the rule in *Saunders v Vautier* (1841) 4 Beav 115 (unless in the case of a power the trustees are specially authorised to release, that is to say extinguish, it). Both have a right to have their claims properly considered by the trustees. But if the discretion is exercisable in favour of a very wide class the trustees need not survey mankind from China to Peru (as Harman J, echoing Dr Johnson, said in *In re Gestetner Settlement* [1953] Ch. 672, 688–9) if it is clear who are the prime candidates for the exercise of the trustees' discretion.

3–157 [42] That thought was developed by Templeman J in *In re Manisty's Settlement* [1974] Ch. 17, although he was mainly concerned to contrast the exercise by trustees of an intermediate power (in the sense mentioned above) with the exercise by trustees of a wide special power. He said (at p.27) that a wide power, whether special or intermediate, does not negative or prohibit a sensible approach by trustees to the consideration and exercise of their powers. After referring to some very well-known observations by Lord Eldon LC in *Morice v Bishop of Durham* (1805) 10 Ves Jun 522, 539, Templeman J continued (at pp.27–28):

"Nor does an intermediate power break the principles laid down by Lord Eldon LC in the passage which I have read because, in relation to a power exercisable by the trustees at their absolute discretion, the only 'control' exercisable by the court is the removal of the trustees, and the only 'due administration' which can be 'directed' is an order requiring the trustees to consider the exercise of the power, and in particular a request from a person within the ambit of the power."

However in *Mettoy Pension Trustees Ltd v Evans* [1990] 1 W.L.R. 1587, 1617–8, Warner J. (after referring to Lord Wilberforce's observations in *McPhail v Doulton* at pp.456–7 and to some authorities not cited in *In re Manisty's Settlement*) took a broader view of the court's power to intervene in the case of a fiduciary dispositive power.

Disclosure to discretionary beneficiaries: a proprietary basis?

[43] Much of the debate before the Board addressed the question whether a **3–158** beneficiary's right or claim to disclosure of trust documents should be regarded as a proprietary right. Mr Brownbill argued that it should be classified in that way, and from that starting point he argued that no object of a mere power could have any right or claim to disclosure, because he had no proprietary interest in the trust property. . .

. . .

[51] Their Lordships consider that the more principled and correct approach is to regard the right to seek disclosure of trust documents as one aspect of the court's inherent jurisdiction to supervise, and if necessary to intervene in, the administration of trusts. The right to seek the court's intervention does not depend on entitlement to a fixed and transmissible beneficial interest. The object of a discretion (including a mere power) may also be entitled to protection from a court of equity, although the circumstances in which he may seek protection, and the nature of the protection he may expect to obtain, will depend on the court's discretion: see Lord Wilberforce in *Gartside v Inland Revenue Commissioners* [1968] A.C. 553, 617–8 and in *McPhail v Doulton* [1971] A.C. 424, 456–7; Templeman J. in *In re Manisty's Settlement* [1974] Ch. 17, 27–8; and Warner J in *Mettoy Pension Trustees Ltd v Evans* [1990] 1 W.L.R. 1587, 1617–8. Mr Brownbill's submission to the contrary effect tends to prove too much, since he would regard the object of a discretionary trust as having a proprietary interest even though it is not transmissible (except in the special case of collective action taken unanimously by all the members of a closed class).

[52] Their Lordships are therefore in general agreement with the approach **3–159** adopted in the judgments of Kirby P and Sheller JA in the Court of Appeal of New South Wales in *Hartigan Nominees Pty Ltd v Rydge* (1992) 29 N.S.W.L.R. 405. . .

. . .

[54] It will be observed that Kirby P said that for an applicant to have a **3–160** proprietary right might be sufficient, but was not necessary. In the Board's view it is neither sufficient nor necessary. Since *In re Cowin* well over a century ago the court has made clear that there may be circumstances (especially of confidentiality) in which even a vested and transmissible beneficial interest is not a sufficient basis for requiring disclosure of trust documents; and *In re Londonderry's Settlement* and more recent cases have begun to work out in some detail the way in which the court should exercise its discretion in such cases. There are three such areas in which the court may have to form a discretionary judgment: whether a discretionary object (or some other beneficiary with only a remote or wholly defeasible interest) should be granted relief at all; what classes of documents should be disclosed, either completely or in a redacted form; and what safeguards should be imposed (whether by undertakings to the court, arrangements for professional inspection, or otherwise) to limit the use which may be made of documents or information disclosed under the order of the court.

. . .

Conclusion

3–161   [66] Their Lordships have already indicated their view that a beneficiary's right to seek disclosure of trust documents, although sometimes not inappropriately described as a proprietary right, is best approached as one aspect of the court's inherent jurisdiction to supervise (and where appropriate intervene in) the administration of trusts. There is therefore in their Lordships' view no reason to draw any bright dividing-line either between transmissible and non-transmissible (that is, discretionary) interests, or between the rights of an object of a discretionary trust and those of the object of a mere power (of a fiduciary character). The differences in this context between trusts and powers are (as Lord Wilberforce demonstrated in *McPhail v Doulton*) a good deal less significant than the similarities. The tide of Commonwealth authority, although not entirely uniform, appears to be flowing in that direction.

3–162   [67] However the recent cases also confirm (as had been stated as long ago as *In re Cowin* in 1886) that no beneficiary (and least of all a discretionary object) has any entitlement as of right to disclosure of anything which can plausibly be described as a trust document. Especially when there are issues as to personal or commercial confidentiality, the court may have to balance the competing interests of different beneficiaries, the trustees themselves, and third parties. Disclosure may have to be limited and safeguards may have to be put in place. Evaluation of the claims of a beneficiary (and especially of a discretionary object) may be an important part of the balancing exercise which the court has to perform on the materials placed before it. In many cases the court may have no difficulty in concluding that an applicant with no more than a theoretical possibility of benefit ought not to be granted any relief."

R. v DISTRICT AUDITOR Ex p WEST YORKSHIRE METROPOLITAN COUNTY COUNCIL

Divisional Court (1985) 26 R.V.R. 24; [2001] W.T.L.R. 785.

3–163   To spend money under Local Government Act 1972, section 137 just before its abolition the Metropolitan Council resolved to create a trust (to which £400,000 would be transferred), in which the capital and income had to be spent within 11 months, "for the benefit of any or all or some of the inhabitants of the County of West Yorkshire" in any one of four specified ways: (i) to assist economic development in the county in order to relieve unemployment and poverty, (ii) to assist bodies concerned with youth and community problems, (iii) to assist and encourage ethnic and other minority groups, (iv) to inform all interested and influential persons of the consequences of the proposed abolition of the Council (and other metropolitan councils). Was the trust administratively workable?

3–164   LLOYD L.J. (with whom Taylor J. concurred): "Counsel for the county council did not seek to argue that the trust is valid as a charitable trust, though he did not concede the point in case he should have second thoughts in a higher court. His case was that the trust could take effect as an express private trust. For the creation of an express private trust three things are required. First, there must be a clear intention to create the trust. Secondly there must be certainty as to the subject matter of the trust; and thirdly there must be certainty as to the persons intended to benefit. Two of the three certainties, as they are familiarly called, were present here. Was the third? He argued that the beneficiaries of the trust were all or some of the inhabitants of the county of West Yorkshire. The class might be on the large side, containing as it does some two and a half million potential beneficiaries. But the definition, it was said, is straightforward and clear cut. There is no uncertainty as to the concept. If anyone were to come forward and claim to be a beneficiary, it could be said of him at once whether he was within the class or not.

"I cannot accept counsel for the county council's argument. I am prepared to **3–165** assume in favour of the council, without deciding, that the class is defined with sufficient clarity. I do not decide the point because it might, as it seems to me, be open to argument what is meant by 'an inhabitant' of the county of West Yorkshire. But I put that difficulty on one side. For there is to my mind a more fundamental difficulty. A trust with as many as two and a half million potential beneficiaries is, in my judgment, quite simply unworkable. The class is far too large. In *Re Gulbenkian's Settlements* [1970] A.C. 508 Lord Reid said at 518:

'It may be that there is a class of case where, although the description of a class **3–166** of beneficiaries is clear enough, any attempt to apply it to the facts would lead to such administrative difficulties that it would for that reason be held to be invalid.'

[His Lordship quoted Lord WILBERFORCE's final paragraph in *McPhail v Doulton* [1971] A.C. 424 at 457, above, para.3–136, and continued]:
"It seems to me that the present trust comes within the third case to which Lord Wilberforce refers . . .
"There can be no doubt that the declaration of trust in the present case created a trust and not a power. Following Lord Wilberforce's dictum, I would hold that the definition of the beneficiaries of the trust is 'so hopelessly wide' as to be incapable of forming 'anything like a class.' I would therefore reject counsel for the county council's argument that the declaration of trust can take effect as an express private trust.
"Since, as I have already said, it was not argued that the trust can take effect as a valid charitable trust, it follows that the declaration of trust is ineffective. What we have here, in a nutshell, is a non-charitable purpose trust. It is clear law that, subject to certain exceptions, such trusts are void: see *Lewin on Trusts* (16th ed.), at 17–19. The present case does not come within any of the established exceptions. Nor can it be brought within the scope of such recent decisions as *Re Denley's Trust Deed* [1969] 1 Ch. 373 (below at para.3–232), and *Re Lipinski's Will Trusts* [1976] Ch. 235 (below at para.3–242), since there are, for the reasons I have given, no ascertained or ascertainable beneficiaries."

Section 4. Compliance with the Rules against Perpetuity

Reference is often made to a trust offending the perpetuity rule without it **3–167** being made clear whether the trust infringes the rule against remoteness of vesting, directed at persons' interests vesting at too remote a time, or infringes the rule against inalienability, directed at immediately effective interests which can go on for too long, so tying up the use of the income of trust property for too long. The two rules are mutually exclusive, the former applying to "people" trusts and the latter to "purpose" trusts. Thus, the 1964 Perpetuities and Accumulations Act, which helps to validate people trusts, leaves the rule against inalienability well alone because it cannot invalidate people trusts.

THE RULE AGAINST REMOTENESS[60]

The common law rule

3–168   Where capital is set on one side to be kept intact ("endowment" capital) with only the income thereof being used, this cannot last indefinitely. A settlor cannot be allowed to rule the living from his grave for thousands of years nor to compel capital to be used for ever as "safe" trust capital instead of absolutely owned capital available for risky entrepreneurial ventures. Thus, where a settlor created successive interests a future interest (contingent on birth or whatever) was, under the common law rule, void unless *at the creation of the trust* it was *absolutely certain* that the contingency would be satisfied—and so the interest would become "vested in interest"—within the perpetuity period.

3–169   The perpetuity period cannot exceed 21 years from the death of some expressly or impliedly relevant life in being at the creation of the trust. A settlor can expressly stipulate that his beneficiaries are only those described by him who take a vested interest before the expiry of 21 years from the death of the last survivor of all the descendants of King George VI living at the date of the settlement (a "royal lives" clause). If T died, leaving his estate on trust for his widow, W, for life, remainder to S, his only child, for life, remainder to such of his grandchildren who attained 21 years of age, all the trusts are valid. W has a life interest "vested in possession" (a present right of present enjoyment), S has a life interest "vested in interest" (a present right to future enjoyment), while grand-children under 21 have contingent interests (a contingent right to future enjoyment), which must become vested in interest within 21 years of the deaths of S and his spouse, even though in the case of class gifts a member's interest does not vest in interest (for perpetuity purposes) until the size of the share is fixed when the last class member is ascertained.[61] The grandchildren's parents' lives are impliedly causally relevant in restricting the period within which the contingent interests inevitably must, if at all, become vested interests.

The 1964 Act "wait and see" rule

3–170   If, by any stretch of the imagination, a contingent interest might possibly not become vested in interest within the perpetuity period, it was void. To mitigate this harshness the Perpetuities and Accumulations Act 1964 radically reformed the rule against remoteness. Where a contingent future interest would have been void at common law one now "waits and sees" what actually happens in a statutory perpetuity period.[62] The interest is valid until it becomes clear that it must vest in interest (if at all) outside the period prescribed by statute, which replaces causally relevant common law

---

[60] See Morris & Leach, *The Rule against Perpetuities* (2nd ed.), Megarry & Wade *Real Property*, Chap.7 but in the light of J. Dukeminier (1986) 102 L.Q.R. 250 on relevant lives in being.

[61] The class gift to grandchildren would therefore have been void if the age to be attained exceeded 21 years; hence s.163, Law of Property Act 1925 and s.4 of the Perpetuities and Accumulations Act 1964.

[62] Perpetuities and Accumulations Act 1964, s.3(1), (2), (3), at para.3–189.

lives by a list of statutory lives in being[63] and, as an alternative, expressly allows a specified period of years not exceeding 80 to be chosen as the perpetuity period.[64] Modern practice is to use the 80-year period because one then knows in advance exactly when the trust will terminate.

The 1964 Act only affects settlements created after July 16, 1964 but in **3–171** the case of settlements made by the exercise of a special power of appointment only applies where the head-settlement containing the special power was created after July 16, 1964.[65] The reason for this exception is that the perpetuity period for special powers runs not from the date the power is exercised but from the date of the head-settlement creating the power.[66]

Discretionary trusts

The rule against remoteness originated in dealing with contingent, life or **3–172** absolute, interests in remainder. How did it deal with the validity of discretionary trusts? It dealt with them by regarding them as trust *powers* and so, like special powers of appointment, they were void unless they were absolutely bound to be completely exercised within the perpetuity period so that all the trust property became absolutely owned by some of the discretionary beneficiaries within the period.[67] Under the 1964 Act discretionary trusts and special powers of appointment that would have been void at common law are valid to the extent that the trustees actually exercise their fiduciary powers within the statutory perpetuity period.[68] Thereafter, there will be a resulting trust of the property in favour of the settlor[69] (unless, exceptionally, there is a gift over to a person with a vested interest[70]).

Class gifts

The 1964 Act deals specifically with class gifts,[71] particularly where **3–173** beneficiaries have to attain an age greater than 21 years. Thus, if a testator, T, left property to his only child, C, for life, remainder to such of his grandchildren as attained 25 years of age this remainder would have been wholly void at common law because a grandchild might theoretically attain 25 years of age more than 21 years after the death of impliedly relevant lives in being.[72] The 1964 Act reduces the age from 25 years to 24 years if

---

[63] *ibid.* s.3(5), at below para.3–191.
[64] *ibid.* s.1.
[65] *ibid.* s.15(5).
[66] *Pilkington v I.R.C.* [1964] A.C. 612.
[67] *Re Coleman* [1936] Ch. 528.
[68] 1964 Act, ss.3(3), 15(2).
[69] 1964 Act, s.4(4), like the rest of s.4, only seems applicable to fixed trusts in favour of a class and not discretionary trusts, "class" gifts traditionally being restricted to cases where the property is divisible into shares varying according to the number of persons in the class and the "class-closing" rule in *Andrews v Partington* (1791) 3 Bro. C.C. 401 applying when the first member of the class becomes entitled to claim his share.
[70] 1964 Act, s.6.
[71] See above, n.69, 1964 Act, s.4.
[72] A class gift could not be partly valid and partly void: the size of the benefit of each member of the class had to be certain before expiry of the perpetuity period so the possibility of the number of members increasing outside the period made the gift to the class wholly void.

the youngest grandchild is only three years old at the death of the last statutory life in being, so that in the next 21 years, if at all, the grandchild will obtain a vested interest, so the remainder is valid.

3–174   Where the problem relates not to attaining a specified age outside the perpetuity period but to persons by birth, or marriage or otherwise, becoming members of a class outside the period the Act provides a statutory guillotine. At the end of the period such persons will be excluded from the class of beneficiaries so the property will then be held absolutely for the then existing beneficiaries.[73] Thus, if a testator leaves £1 million to be distributed equally amongst any great-grandchildren whenever born and at the end of the period of statutory lives plus 21 years there are 20 great-grandchildren, then the class will close to the exclusion of future-born great-grandchildren. It also seems likely that if a testator leaves £100,000 to the persons who are at his death the Chairman and Treasurer of the Wheatsheaf Darts Club to hold the same on trust solely for present and future members of the club one waits and sees if the club is dissolved within the period of statutory lives plus 21 years, because the then members would divide the property (or, rather, its proceeds of sale) equally between themselves. Otherwise, because at the end of the period persons can still become members and so obtain an interest in the property, the 1964 Act may well apply[74] to exclude such future persons from the class of beneficiaries. Those happening to be members at the end of the period will become absolutely entitled to the property. Hopefully, they will agree that the property should then be vested in four club members on a bare trust to be administered for current members according to the rules of the club.

Re Denley-type locus standi purpose trusts

3–175   As will be seen in the next section, *Re Denley*[75] upheld a trust of land to be maintained and used as a recreation or sports ground for the benefit of employees from time to time of a particular company, while in *Wicks v Firth*[76] the House of Lords assumed that there can be a valid trust to award scholarships to assist in the education of children of employees of a company from time to time. Both trusts were limited expressly to a valid perpetuity period but what would have happened if such trusts were left open-ended to last indefinitely?

3–176   It seems likely that for perpetuity purposes such a trust would be regarded as analogous to a discretionary trust before the 1964 Act.[77] Thus, because the powers of the trustees to benefit the beneficiaries were not bound to have been exhaustively exercised within the common law perpetuity period the trusts would have been void. However, under the Act the

---

[73] 1964 Act, s.4(4).
[74] With members having fixed rights to property on dissolution under the Club rules the case seems more appropriately treated within s.4(4) (like a fixed trust for a class) rather than within s.3(3) as a discretionary trust followed by a resulting trust upon expiry of the perpetuity period or earlier dissolution of the club.
[75] [1969] 1 Ch. 373.
[76] [1983] A.C. 214.
[77] See *Re Grant's W.T.* [1979] 3 All E.R. 359 at 368.

trusts are valid to the extent that the trustees exercise their fiduciary powers within the statutory perpetuity period.[78] At the end of such period the property will be held on resulting trust for the settlor.

An alternative approach is to say that *Re Denley*-type purpose trusts **3–177** should be treated like other permitted non-charitable purpose trusts[79] and so be subject not to the rule against remoteness but to the rule against inalienability.[80] This will make them void unless at the outset it is certain that by the end of the perpetuity period the trust fund will be wholly alienable by some absolute owners.[81] Because of the modern, praiseworthy, judicial tendency to facilitate, rather than frustrate, the intentions of settlors and testators it seems likely that the courts will not invoke the harsh application of the rule against inalienability that applies to purpose trusts but will regard *Re Denley*-type purpose trusts as trusts for those persons with locus standi to sue.[82]

After all, under the rule in *Saunders v Vautier*[83] if S creates a trust to **3–178** spend £10,000 in planting trees on land held for A for life, remainder to B, A and B can together claim the £10,000 since they are intended to benefit absolutely between them and so can choose how to take such benefit.[84] Similarly, if a testator leaves £10,000 to provide for publishing his manuscript books so that there will be sufficient money to provide for his grandson's university education, the grandson can claim the £10,000 if publication is not a paying proposition, because the request was solely for his benefit.[85]

It should make no difference if the class of beneficiaries benefiting from **3–179** a trust's purposes is a fluctuating class so that *Saunders v Vautier* rights cannot be invoked,[86] *e.g.* present and future members of a club or present and future members of a class under a discretionary trust. The key question of construction[87] is whether the trust is primarily for the benefit of individuals, with the specified way in which they are to enjoy the benefits being secondary, or whether the specified purpose in which they will be involved to some extent is of the essence of the trust, with the indirect benefit to individuals being secondary.

The former category will include trusts to provide a maintenance fund **3–180** for historic buildings and gardens held by trustees for the benefit of individuals[88] or to provide a sinking fund for repairs to a block of flats for the benefit of lessees from time to time[89] or to provide for the education of employees' children.[90] The latter category will include trusts for furthering

---

[78] 1964 Act, s.3(3).
[79] See below at para.3–183.
[80] *Re Northern Developments (Holdings) Ltd* (October 6, 1978, unreported) at (1991) 107 L.Q.R. 608 at 611.
[81] See next sub-heading.
[82] See Vinelott J. in *Re Grant's W.T.* [1979] 3 All E.R. 359 at 368; P.J. Millett Q.C. (now Lord Millett) (1985) 101 L.Q.R. 268 at 281–282.
[83] See at para.9–123.
[84] *Re Bowes* [1896] 1 Ch. 507.
[85] *Re Skinner's Trusts* (1860) 1 John & H 102.
[86] *Re Levy* [1960] Ch. 346 at 363; *Re Westphal* [1972] N.Z.L.R. 792 at 794–795.
[87] See P. J. Millett Q.C. (now Lord Millett) (1985) 101 L.Q.R. 269, 282.
[88] *Re Aberconway's S.T.* [1953] Ch. 647; *Raikes v Lygon* [1988] 1 W.L.R. 281.
[89] Landlord and Tenant Act 1987, s.42.
[90] *Wicks v Firth* [1983] A.C. 214; see also *Re Sanderson's Trusts* (1857) 3 K & J; *Re Abbott Fund Trust* [1900] 2 Ch. 326; *Re Gillingham Bus Disaster Fund* [1958] Ch. 300.

the overriding purposes of a political party[91] or a non-charitable religious order[92] or of an unincorporated society,[93] such trusts being void for infringing the rule against inalienability (if not restricted to the perpetuity period) and the beneficiary principle.

3–181   The former category will have the benefit of the 1964 Act. Prima facie, there will be a discretionary trust for the benefit of the class until expiry of the statutory period of statutory lives plus 21 years, when a resulting trust in favour of the settlor's estate will arise.[94] Exceptionally, in the case of a class of club members with fixed rights under the club rules it may be that those members will be allowed to divide the property between themselves on dissolution of the club within the statutory perpetuity period or, if later, upon expiry of such period by virtue of section 4(4) of the Act.[95]

THE RULE AGAINST INALIENABILITY (OR PERPETUAL PURPOSE TRUSTS)

3–182   The common law rule against remoteness ensured that endowment trusts for persons were void unless one could be absolutely sure from the outset that by the end of the perpetuity period the beneficiaries would have obtained vested interests enabling them to deal with the trust fund as they wished. Under the rule in *Saunders v Vautier*[96] if trustees hold property on trust for A absolutely or for B for life, remainder to C absolutely then (assuming each is *sui juris*) A or B and C, as the case may be, can direct the trustees how to deal with the property, *e.g.* vest it in A absolutely or divide it absolutely between B and C in the shares agreed by B and C. Persons like B must obtain vested interests before the end of the perpetuity period but there is no requirement that their interests must terminate within the perpetuity period so that someone must become absolutely entitled to the relevant property in such period.[97] Thus, if at the end of the period B has a life interest the trust continues till C acquires the property on B's death.

3–183   The rule against inalienability makes the few permitted[98] non-charitable endowment purpose trusts void unless from the outset it is certain that persons will become absolutely entitled beneficiaries by the end of the perpetuity period,[99] 21 years from the death of the last survivor of any causally relevant lives in being.[1] Such a rule was necessary because purposes unlike individuals can last forever and because a rule against remoteness of vesting is inappropriate when interests cannot vest in purposes as opposed to persons. Thus, testamentary trusts to erect and then maintain a sepulchral monument, to say private masses for the testator and to maintain

---

[91] *Re Grant's W.T.* [1979] 3 All E.R. 359; *Bacon v Pianta* (1966) 114 C.L.R. 634.
[92] *Leahy v Att-Gen. for New South Wales* [1959] A.C. 457.
[93] *Came v Long* (1860) 2 De. G.F. & J. 75; *Re Macauley's Estate* [1943] Ch. 435n.
[94] 1964 Act, s.3(3).
[95] See above, at para.3–174.
[96] (1841) 4 Beav. 115, below at para.9–123.
[97] *Re Chardon* [1928] Ch. 464; *Re Gage* [1898] 1 Ch. 506; *Wainwright v Miller* [1897] 2 Ch. 255.
[98] See para.3–206.
[99] *Leahy v Att.-Gen. for New South Wales* [1959] A.C. 457; *Cocks v Manners* (1871) L.R. 12 Eq. 574.
[1] *Re Astor's S.T.* [1952] Ch. 534; *Re Khoo Cheng Teow* [1932] Straits Settlement Reports 226. The statutory period of 80 years is available only for the rule against remoteness: see next note.

the testator's horse or cat are void unless restricted to a specified perpetuity period, which will be 21 years unless, say, a royal lives clause is used.

Section 15(4) of the Perpetuities and Accumulation Act 1964 prevents the Act having any effect in relation to the rule against inalienability.[2]

Alienability of trust assets but inalienability of trust fund

Whatever happen from time to time to be the particular trust *assets*   **3–184**
comprised in the trust *fund* will be alienable under the Trustee Act 2000, the Settled Land Act 1925 or the Law of Property Act 1925. However, if trust income has to be used for a particular purpose then the trust fund producing that income must be kept intact for as long as the income is required for that purpose. The inalienability of the trust income inevitably leads to the inalienability of the trust fund. The rule against inalienability is concerned to ensure that the length of time for which trustees must retain the trust fund (in whatever assets it is from time to time invested) does not exceed the perpetuity period.

Only endowment trusts are subject to rule

If the trustees do not have to keep the capital intact and use only the   **3–185**
income thereof but can spend trust money on the trust purposes without the need to consider whether or not the money represents capital or income and whether the purpose is a "capital" or "income" type of purpose, then the rule against inalienability has no application.[3] Usually, the settlor will make it clear if the trustees are to hold his property on trust only to use the income within a specified perpetuity period for particular purposes and at the end of the period to distribute the capital to beneficiaries. Exceptionally, he may make it clear that his property is to be used without distinction between capital and income until fully consumed.

THE RULE AGAINST EXCESSIVE ACCUMULATIONS

Fearful of the implications for the English economy if megawealthy men   **3–186**
like Thellusson could by will[4] have the income of their estate accumulated for the full perpetuity period of royal lives plus 21 years—and more fearful for the finances of themselves and their children—English MPs passed the

---

[2] See para.3–194. It is oddly worded. In context "the rule of law rendering void for remoteness" is the rule against inalienability (which the draftsman considers to make purpose trusts void if they can continue till too remote a time). The draftsman in s.1 uses "the rule against perpetuities" when referring to the rule against remoteness of vesting and allowing the 80-year period expressly to be specified. One should add implicitly to the end of s.15(4) "applicable to the relevant disposition under such rule of law."

[3] *Re Lipinski's W.T.* [1976] Ch. 235 at 245, see below para.3–242; *Re Drummond* [1914] 2 Ch. 90 at 98; *Re Prevost* [1930] 2 Ch. 383 at 388; *Re Price* [1943] Ch. 422 at 428, 430; *Re Macaulay's Estate* [1943] Ch. 435 at 436 (H.L); R. H. Maudsley, *The Modern Law of Perpetuities*, p.173. In *Leahy v Att.-Gen. for New South Wales* [1959] A.C. 457 at 483, see, para.3–223. Viscount Simonds doubted whether a society's liberty to spend the capital and income of a gift as it saw fit saved a gift on trust to the society unless its members are treated as the immediate beneficiaries capable of disposing of the gifted property. This is too restrictive a view of the beneficiary principle: there can be *Re Denley-type* purpose trusts benefiting individuals within a fluctuating class who have no right to make the trust property their own but do have a right to ensure that the property is used for their benefit.

[4] *Thellusson v Woodford* (1799) 4 Ves. 227.

Accumulations Act 1800 (the "Thellusson Act") to restrict the period for which income could be accumulated. The modern position is as follows.

If a trust is concerned with a trust or power to accumulate, it is crucial to restrict the accumulation to one of the six periods allowed by section 164 of the Law of Property Act 1925 and section 13 of the 1964 Act unless section 31 of the Trustee Act 1925 allows accumulations during a beneficiary's minority:

(a) the life of the grantor or settlor;

(b) twenty-one years from the death of the grantor, settlor or testator;

(c) the duration of the minority or respective minorities of any person(s) living or *en venture sa mère* at the death of the grantor, settlor or testator;

(d) the duration of the minority or respective minorities only of any persons(s) who under the limitations of the instrument directing the accumulations would, for the time being, if of full age, be entitled to the income directed to be accumulated;

(e) twenty-one years from the date of the making of the disposition;

(f) the duration of the minority or respective minorities of any person(s) in being at that date.

3–187   If an excessive accumulation infringed the perpetuity period it was void *in toto*.[5] If within the perpetuity period it is cut down to the nearest appropriate period of the six permitted, and only the excess was void.[6] After the 1964 Act it may well be that the "wait and see" provisions will validate accumulations within the statutory perpetuity period, so that the excessive accumulation will be cut down to the nearest appropriate permitted period.

Indirectly, "excessive" accumulation may be provided for by empowering trustees to transfer trust assets to a company formed by them in return for shares in the company: the company can then retain profits and not declare dividends. Indeed, the company can settle assets on accumulation trusts without being bound by the statute which only applies to natural persons.[7] It seems likely that a settlor can expressly choose a foreign law to govern accumulations without offending English public policy.[8] The English Accumulations Act 1800 never extended to colonies or dependencies under whose laws accumulations can continue for as long as the perpetuity period. The Law Commission has strongly recommended that the accumulation period should be the same as the perpetuity period which should be extended to 125 years.[9]

POWER TO SPECIFY PERPETUITY PERIOD

3–188   **1.**—(1) Subject to section 9(2) of this Act and subsection (2) below, where the instrument by which any disposition is made so provides, the perpetuity period applicable to the disposition under the rule against perpetuities, instead of being of

---

[5] *Curtis v Lukin* (1842) 5 Beav. 147.
[6] *Re Watt's W.T.* [1936] 2 All E.R. 1555 at 1562; *Re Ransome* [1957] Ch. 348 at 361.
[7] *Re Dodwell & Co's Trust Deed* [1979] Ch. 301.
[8] Consider Arts 6 and 18 of Hague Convention on Trust and problem at paras 13–30 and 13–35.
[9] Law Commission Report No.251 (1998), accepted by the Government in March 2001.

any other duration, shall be of a duration equal to such number of years not exceeding eighty as is specified in that behalf in the instrument.

(2) Subsection (2) above shall not have effect where the disposition is made in exercise of a special power of appointment, but where a period is specified under that subsection in the instrument creating such a power the period shall apply in relation to any disposition under the power as it applies in relation to the power itself.

Uncertainty as to remoteness

3.—(1) Where, apart from the provisions of this section and sections 4 and 5 of **3–189** this Act, a disposition would be void on the ground that the interest disposed of might not become vested until too remote a time, the disposition shall be treated, until such time (if any) as it becomes established that the vesting must occur, if at all, after the end of the perpetuity period, as if the disposition were not subject to the rule against perpetuities; and its becoming so established shall not affect the validity of anything previously done in relation to the interest disposed of by way of advancement, application of intermediate income or otherwise.

(2) Where, apart from the said provisions, a disposition consisting of the conferring of a general power of appointment would be void on the ground that the power might not become exercisable until too remote a time, the disposition shall be treated, until such time (if any) as it becomes established that the power will not be exercisable within the perpetuity period, as if the disposition were not subject to the rule against perpetuities.

(3) Where, apart from the said provisions, a disposition consisting of the conferring of any power, option or other right would be void on the ground that the right might be exercised at too remote a time, the disposition shall be treated as regards any exercise of the right within the perpetuity period as if it were not subject to the rule against perpetuities and, subject to the said provisions, shall be treated as void for remoteness only if, and so far as, the right is not fully exercised within that period.

(4) Where this section applies to a disposition and the duration of the **3–190** perpetuity period is not determined by virtue of section 1 or 9(2) of this Act, it shall be determined as follows:—

(a) where any persons falling within subsection (5) below are individuals in being and ascertainable at the commencement of the perpetuity period the duration of the period shall be determined by reference to their lives and no others, but so that the lives of any description of persons falling within paragraph (b) or (c) of that subsection shall be disregarded if the number of persons of that description is such as to render it impracticable to ascertain the date of death of the survivor;

(b) where there are no lives under paragraph (a) above the period shall be twenty-one years.

(5) The said persons are as follows:— **3–191**

(a) the person by whom the disposition was made;
(b) a person to whom or in whose favour the disposition was made, that is to say—
(i) in the case of a disposition to a class of persons, any member or potential member of the class;

> (ii) in the case of an individual disposition to a person taking only on certain conditions being satisfied, any person as to whom some of the conditions are satisfied and the remainder may in time be satisfied;
>
> (iii) in the case of a special power of appointment exercisable in favour of members of a class, any member or potential member of the class;
>
> (iv) in the case of a special power of appointment exercisable in favour of one person only, that person or, where the object of the power is ascertainable only on certain conditions being satisfied, any person as to whom some of the conditions are satisfied and the remainder may in time be satisfied;
>
> (v)   in the case of any power, option or other right, the person on whom the right is conferred;
>
> (c) a person having a child or grandchild within sub-paragraphs (i) to (iv) of paragraph (b) above, or any of whose children or grandchildren, if subsequently born, would by virtue of his or her descent fall within those sub-paragraphs;
>
> (d) any person on the failure or determination of whose prior interest the disposition is limited to take effect.

Reduction of age and exclusion of class members to avoid remoteness

3–192 **4.**—(1) Where a disposition is limited by reference to the attainment by any person or persons of a specified age exceeding 21 years, and it is apparent at the time the disposition is made or becomes apparent at a subsequent time—

> (a) that the disposition would, apart from this section, be void for remoteness, but
>
> (b) that it would not be so void if the specified age had been twenty-one years,

the disposition shall be treated for all purposes as if, instead of being limited by reference to the age in fact specified, it had been limited by reference to the age nearest to that age which would, if specified instead, have prevented the disposition from being so void.

(2) Where in the case of any disposition different ages exceeding 21 years are specified in relation to different persons—

> (a) the reference in paragraph (b) of subsection (1) above to the specified age shall be construed as a reference to all the specified ages, and
>
> (b) that subsection shall operate to reduce each such age so far as is necessary to save the disposition from being void for remoteness.

3–193 (3) Where the inclusion of any persons, being potential members of a class or unborn persons who at birth would become members or potential members of the class, prevents the foregoing provisions of this section from operating to save a disposition from being void for remoteness, those persons shall thenceforth be deemed for all the purposes of the disposition to be excluded from the class, and the said provisions shall thereupon have effect accordingly.

(4) Where, in the case of a disposition to which subsection (3) above does not apply, it is apparent at the time the disposition is made or becomes apparent at a subsequent time that, apart from this subsection, the inclusion of any persons, being potential members of a class or unborn persons who at birth would become

members or potential members of the class, would cause the disposition to be treated as void for remoteness, those persons shall, unless their exclusion would exhaust the class, thenceforth be deemed for all the purposes of the disposition to be excluded from the class.

(5) Where this section has effect in relation to a disposition to which section 3 above applies, the operation of this section shall not affect the validity of anything previously done in relation to the interest disposed of by way of advancement, application of intermediate income or otherwise.

Short title, interpretation and extent

15.—(1) This Act may be cited as the Perpetuities and Accumulations Act 1964. **3–194**
(2) In this Act—

"disposition" includes the conferring of a power of appointment and any other disposition of an interest in or right over property, and references to the interest disposed of shall be construed accordingly;
"in being" means living or en ventre sa mere;
"power of appointment" includes any discretionary power to transfer a beneficial interest in property without the furnishing of valuable consideration;
"will" includes a codicil;

and for the purposes of this Act a disposition contained in a will shall be deemed to be made at the death of the testator.

(3) For the purposes of this Act a person shall be treated as a member of a class if in his case all the conditions identifying a member of the class are satisfied, and shall be treated as a potential member if in his case some only of those conditions are satisfied but there is a possibility that the remainder will in time be satisfied.

(4) Nothing in this Act shall affect the operation of the rule of law rendering void for remoteness certain dispositions under which property is limited to be applied for purposes other than the benefit of any person or class of persons in cases where the property may be so applied after the end of the perpetuity period.

(5) The foregoing sections of this Act shall apply (except as provided in section 8(2) above) only in relation to instruments taking effect after the commencement of this Act, and in the case of an instrument made in the exercise of a special power of appointment shall apply only where the instrument creating the power takes effect after that commencement:

Section 5. The Beneficiary Principle

Because enforceable obligations of the trustee are at the heart of the **3–195** trust it is a hallowed principle that Courts of Equity will not uphold any alleged trust that cannot be effectively supervised and sanctioned by the Courts at the behest of somebody in whose favour the Courts can decree performance.[10] Leaving aside charitable purpose trusts enforceable by the Crown in the public interest via the Attorney-General and the Charity

---

[10] *Morice v Bishop of Durham* (1804) 9 Ves. 399, 405, (1805) 10 Ves. 521 at 539. "A court of equity does not recognise as valid a trust which it cannot both enforce and control "per Roxburgh J in *Re Astor's S.T.* [1952] Ch. 534 at 549.

Commissioners, a trust "to be effective must have ascertained or ascertainable beneficiaries", as Lord Evershed MR emphasised in *Re Endacott*.[11] Indeed, Viscount Simonds[12] explained "a trust may be created for the benefit of persons as *cestuis que trust* but not for a purpose or object unless the purpose or object be charitable, for a purpose or object cannot sue, but if it be charitable the Attorney General can sue to enforce it". In the case of a trust for persons it is those persons who sue to enforce their rights as beneficiaries against the trustees, the settlor dropping out of the picture like a donor who has made an outright gift.[13] It is thus taken for granted that "A trust for non-charitable purposes, as distinct from a trust for individuals, is clearly void because there is no beneficiary."[14]

3–196   Thus, a trust to further the abstract impersonal purposes of a contemplative (non-charitable) Catholic Order of nuns[15] or of the Labour Party is void.[16] This sort of overriding purpose trust is in the words of Goff J in *Re Denley's Trust Deed*[17]:

> "A purpose trust, the carrying out of which would benefit an individual or individuals but where that benefit is so indirect or intangible or which is otherwise so framed as not to give those persons any *locus standi* to apply to the court to enforce the trust, in which case the beneficiary principle would apply to invalidate the trust, quite apart from any question of uncertainty or perpetuity"

3–197   He then upheld a trust of a corporate settlor's land "to be maintained and used as and for the purposes of a recreation or sports ground primarily for the benefit of the employees of the company and secondarily for the benefit of such other persons (if any) as the trustees may allow to use the same." The attainment of these trust purposes was sufficiently for the benefit of individuals taken to be intended to have *locus standi* to enforce the trust positively in their favour.[18] After all, the trust was primarily for the benefit of people, with the specified way in which they were to be benefited being secondary: the specified purpose was not of the essence of the trust with an indirect secondary benefit to people.[19] As trusts for the benefit of people and similar to discretionary trusts, such trusts should have the benefit

---

[11] *Re Endacott* [1960] Ch. 232 at 246.
[12] *Leahy v Att-Gen for New South Wales* [1959] A.C. 457 at 479.
[13] *Re Astor's S.T.* [1952] Ch. 534 at 542, *Bradshaw v University College of Wales* [1987] 3 All E.R. 200 at 203.
[14] *Re Recher's W.T.* [1972] Ch. 526 at 538, thoroughly endorsed by P. Matthews in D. Hayton (ed.), *Extending the Boundaries of Trusts and Similar Ring-Fenced Funds* (Kluwer, 2002), pp.203–242, commented upon pp.6–7. A power to carry out abstract impersonal purposes can be valid: *Re Douglas* [1887] 35 Ch.D. 472, *Goff v Nairne* (1876) 3 Ch.D. 278, *Re Shaw* [1957] 1 W.L.R. 729; *Re Wooton's W.T.* [1968] 2 All E.R. 618 at 623–624.
[15] *Leahy v Att-Gen for New South Wales* [1959] A.C. 457.
[16] *Re Grant's W.T.* [1979] 3 All E.R. 359. See also *Re Astor's S.T.* [1952] Ch. 534, *Re Shaw* [1957] 1 W.L.R. 729, *Re Endacott* [1960] Ch. 232.
[17] [1969] 1 Ch. 373 at 382–383.
[18] Also see *Wicks v Firth* [1983] A.C. 214 and *Re Saxone Shoe Co's Trust Deed* [1962] 1 W.L.R. 934 (which would now be valid under the *McPhail v Doulton* [1971] A.C. 424 test). Persons named in a trust deed and benefiting directly or indirectly (*e.g.* as employees) but not intended to have a right to enforce the trust have no *locus standi* to apply to the court: *Shaw v Lawless* (1838) 5 Cl. & Fin. 129, 153; *Gandy v Gandy* (1885) 30 Ch.D. 57 at 69–70; L. McKay (1973) 37 Conv. 420, 426–427.
[19] P. J. Millett Q.C. (now Lord Millett) (1985) 101 L.Q.R. 269, 282 and para.3–179 above.

of the liberal Perpetuities and Accumulations Act 1964 and not be subject to the strict rule against inalienability already discussed in the last section.

The orthodox view that non-charitable purpose trusts are void and that **3–198** settlors (unless beneficiaries) have no rights to enforce their trusts enforceable only by beneficiaries has led to offshore jurisdictions filling a gap in the trusts "market" by enacting legislation validating non-charitable purpose trusts so long as the trust instrument appoints an enforcer (who could be the settlor or an independent or related third party) with provision for further enforcers after his death or retirement.

What then would happen under English conflict of laws (known also as private international law) principles if the English court were faced with a non-charitable purpose trust of English assets governed by a foreign law (such as that of Jersey or the Isle of Man or Bermuda or the British Virgin Islands or the Cayman Islands) treating such a trust as valid where the terms of the trust appoint an enforcer and provide for the appointment of a successor to any enforcer? The English court can only hold the trust to be void for infringing the beneficiary principle (so that a resulting trust arises for the settlor, whose creditors, heirs or divorcing spouse can then enforce their claims against the trust assets) if such a foreign trust concept is either repugnant to the core of the trust concept or contrary to English public policy.[20]

English law is not so insular as to refuse to recognise any aspect of **3–199** foreign law that is different from English law.[21] English law can accept that just as a car needs an engine so a trust needs an enforcer, whether a beneficiary or the Attorney-General or Charity Commissioners for charitable purpose trusts or some person expressly appointed by the trust instrument to be enforcer with *locus standi*[22] positively[23] to enforce the trust? After all, as made clear in *Schmidt v Rosewood Trust Ltd*,[24] rights to disclosure of trust documents and supporting information are not based on beneficiaries' proprietary interests but on the court's inherent jurisdiction to supervise matters and make the trustees account for their trusteeship at the behest of sufficiently interested persons, *e.g.* objects of powers[25] or new trustees[26] or protectors.[27]

Take the case of a Jersey trust (limited to a perpetuity period of 80 years) to further the interests of the U.K. Conservative Party expressed to be

---

[20] See approach to wide exemption clauses in *Armitage v Nurse* [1998] Ch. 241, 253, and the right under the Recognition of Trusts Act 1987 to choose any foreign trust law to govern a trust so long as not "manifestly incompatible with public policy" (at para.13–16 below).

[21] The inalienability of an alimentary life interest under Scots law was accepted by the Court of Appeal in *Re Fitzgerald* [1904] 1 Ch. 573 though English life interests cannot be inalienable.

[22] See the emphasis on *locus standi* to enforce in *Re Denley's Trust Deed* [1969] 1 Ch. 373, 382–383, *Re Astor's S.T.* [1952] Ch. 534, 542, *Re Shaw* [1957] 1 W.L.R. 729 at 745. See D. Hayton "Developing the Obligation Characteristic of the Trust (2001) 117 L.Q.R. 96.

[23] The fact that the residuary legatees or the next-of-kin will take property in default of specific purposes being carried out does not indicate that the settlor-testator intended such "negatively" interested persons to be enforcers, so the presence of such persons will not save a trust for non-charitable purposes: *Re Shaw* [1957] 1 W.L.R. 729 at 745; *Re Davidson* [1909] 1 Ch. 567 at 571.

[24] [2003] 2 A.C. 709, above para.3–155.

[25] *ibid.*

[26] *Young v Murphy* [1996] 1 V.R. 279.

[27] *Re Hare Trust* (2001) 4 I.T.E.L.R. 288, *Von Knierem v Bermuda Trust Co. Ltd* Butts O.C.M. Vol. 1, pp.116–125; Civil Procedure Rules Pt. 64 and Practice Directions thereto which are very wide: see para.9–223.

enforceable by the Leader from time to time of such Party, or to further the purposes of a specified contemplative Order of Nuns expressed to be enforceable by the Head from time to time of such Order, or to further the professional interests of barristers entitled to practice in the English Courts expressed to be enforceable by the Chair from time to time of the Bar Council or to further the business and reputation of a named Set of Barristers' Chambers expressed to be enforceable only by the Head of Chambers from time to time. The trusts clearly supply a mechanism for the positive enforcement of the trusts so that the trustees are under an obligation to account to someone in whose favour the court can positively decree performance, unlike the cases of void non-charitable purpose trusts so far considered by the English courts[28] where there was no-one who had been given *locus standi* positively to sue to enforce the trust.

3–200   Thus, the English courts should not hold the above Jersey trusts to be void so that the settlor is entitled from the outset to the beneficial interest under a resulting trust. Where then is the beneficial interest? Should a non-charitable purpose trust be treated like a charitable purpose trust where the trustees are the legal beneficial owners[29] but are under fiduciary and equitable duties owed to the Attorney-General and the Charity Commissioners or any "interested person"[30] having the permission of the Commissioners? The trustees of a non-charitable purpose trust can similarly owe fiduciary and equitable duties to the enforcer, but what if the enforcer does not enforce the trusts or, worse still, the trustee and the enforcer appropriate the property for themselves (though an individual enforcer cannot bind his *ex officio* successors not to enforce the trustee's duties)? Under the rule in *Saunders v Vautier*[31] they are not entitled to take the trust property for themselves unless they are the persons exclusively beneficially entitled to the trust property. This cannot be the case where another person becomes beneficially entitled at the end of the trust period with the right to make the trustee account for its trusteeship.

3–201   The key issue then is whether until the end of this trust period it is correct that the beneficial interest is not vested in the settlor under a resulting trust subject to the trustee having a valid power to carry out the non-charitable purposes[32] and the enforcer having a valid power to ensure that the trustee exercises its power: such powers seem to be valid even under English domestic law because the approach of the courts is to facilitate settlor's intentions unless illegal or otherwise contrary to public policy.

3–202   Surely, by expressly using language imposing a duty to the enforcer upon the trustee to use all the trust property exclusively to carry out the non-charitable purposes (and so not to benefit the settlor), the settlor by

---

[28] *E.g. Re Nottage* [1895] 2 Ch. 649, *Re Wightwick's W.T.* [1950] Ch. 260, *Leahy v Att-Gen for New South Wales* [1959] A.C. 457 (all void for perpetuity in any event, except for a saving statute in the New South Wales Case); and *Re Astor's S.T.* [1952] Ch. 534 (void for uncertainty, unworkability and unenforceabiltiy, through within perpetuity period).
[29] Just like executors of a testator: *Commissioners of Stamp Duty v Livingston* [1965] A.C. 694.
[30] Charities Act 1993, s.33.
[31] See para.3–208.
[32] *Re Shaw* [1957] 1 All E.R. 745 at 759 endorsed in *Re Wooton's W.T.* [1968] 2 All E.R. 618 at 624.

necessary implication has abandoned any beneficial interest in the trust property so as to oust any resulting trust.[33] Thus, the trustee must have legal beneficial ownership of the trust property but subject to fiduciary and equitable duties owed to the enforcer.

This position achieved by *foreign* trust legislation does not appear to be **3–203** so out of line as to be repugnant to the core trust concept or contrary to English public policy. Indeed, if in an *English* trust deed, a settlor abandoned all beneficial interest in the trust property to the intent that the trustee must use its legal beneficial ownership of the trust property to carry out workable non-charitable purposes for a royal lives and 21 years perpetuity period and appointed an enforcer expressly required to ensure that the trustee carries out the trusts and expressly given sufficient enforcement rights against the trustee, there seems plenty of scope for the House of Lords or a bold Court of Appeal to accept the validity of such non-charitable purpose trust where, crucially, there is a designated enforcer to whom the trustee owes duties in respect of its legal beneficial ownership of all the trust property.

It matters not that the enforcer only has a power and not a duty to **3–204** enforce the trustee's obligations: a beneficiary is in exactly the same position. A beneficiary has much self-interest in enforcing the trust, but so will often be the case for the person appointed to be enforcer who may, indeed, have something to lose if not enforcing the trust eg removal by the members of his body from the office that led him to be the enforcer or censure at an extraordinary general meeting. Moreover, a reputable trustee duly performs trusteeship duties because good at them, enjoying doing them and getting paid for them, while any successor trustee is under a duty to make the old trustee remedy any breaches of duty that are discovered.[34]

Quistclose Money Purpose Trusts

These trusts, like *Re Denley* purpose trusts,[35] have been construed in **3–205** accordance with traditional doctrine to be trusts for persons and not special cases where there is a valid purpose trust. Where P (the payer) and R (the recipient) have agreed that the money is loaned by P to R for a specific purpose and no other purpose, such that the money is not freely at the disposal of R as if R's own money, then the relationship only becomes one of creditor and debtor once R has used the money for the prescribed purpose. Until then, the position will either be that P created an express trust[36] of the money for himself, subject to R's power as trustee to use the money for the prescribed purpose, or that P created a resulting trust[37] to the same effect (presumed in the absence of any intent of P to transfer the

---

[33] "If the settlor has expressly, or by necessary implication, abandoned any beneficial interest in the trust property, there is in my view no resulting trust": Lord Brown-Wilkinson in *Westdeutsche Landesbank v Islington LBC* [1966] A.C. 669 at 708.
[34] *Young v Murphy* [1996] 1 V.R. 279.
[35] See para.3–197 and *Re Grant's W.T.* [1979] 3 All E.R. 359 at 368.
[36] As held by Lord Hoffmann in *Twinsectra Ltd v Yardley* [2002] UKHL 12; [2002] 2 A.C. 164.
[37] As held by Lord Millett, *ibid.*, paras 77–102, extensively dealing with all aspects.

beneficial interest to R). So long as the power is stated with sufficient clarity for the court to be able to determine whether it is still capable of being carried out or whether the money has been misapplied, it is sufficiently certain to be valid.[38]

ANOMALOUS VALID TESTAMENTARY PURPOSE TRUSTS

3-206   The Court of Appeal[39] has accepted that there are some anomalous cases, not to be extended, where testamentary trusts infringing the beneficiary (or enforcer) principle have been held valid as concessions to human sentiment. These anomalous cases are:

(1) trusts for the maintenance of particular animals[40];
(2) trusts for the erection or maintenance of graves and sepulchral monuments[41];
(3) trusts for the saying of masses in private[42];
(4) trusts for the promotion and furtherance of fox-hunting but this has been made illegal by virtue of the Hunting Act 2004.[43]

These trusts are sometimes referred to as trusts of imperfect obligation[44] since the trustees are not obliged to carry out the trusts in the absence of anyone able to apply to the court to enforce the trust. The trusts are subject to the rule against inalienability and so must be restricted directly or indirectly[45] to the common law perpetuity period. If the trustees do not take advantage of what, in substance, amounts to a power to carry out a purpose, then the person otherwise entitled to the trust property will be

---

[38] The commercially important but intellectually complex issues surrounding the *Quistclose* purpose trust have led to W. Swadling (ed.), *The Quistclose Trust* (Hart Publishing, 2004).

[39] *Re Endacott* [1960] Ch. 232 (residuary gift to a parish council "for the purpose of providing some useful memorial to" the testator held void for uncertainty and for infringing the beneficiary principle).

[40] *Pettingall v Pettingall* (1842) 11 L.J. Ch. 176; *Re Dean* (1889) 41 Ch.D. 552. Many trusts for animals generally are charitable: *Re Wedgwood* [1915] 1 Ch. 113.

[41] *Re Hooper* [1932] Ch. 38; *Mussett v Bingle* [1876] W.N. 170; *Pirbright v Salwey* [1896] W.N. 86; *Trimmer v Danby* (1856) 25 L.J. Ch. 424. The maintenance of private graves may be possible for 99 years under the Parish Council and Burial Authorities (Miscellaneous Provisions) Act 1970, s.1. If the construction is part of the fabric of a church the trust is charitable and valid: *Hoare v Osborne* (1866) L.R. 1 Eq. 585.

[42] *Bourne v Keane* [1919] A.C. 815 at 874–875. Gifts for the saying of masses in public are charitable because of the public benefit in assisting in the endowment of priests but not for the saying of masses in private: *Re Hetherington* [1989] 2 All E.R. 129 (but the endowment ground seems applicable in both cases). In Malaysia and Singapore trusts for ancestor worship (Sin Chew or Chin Shong ceremonies) have been held valid anomalous non-charitable purpose gifts if restricted to the perpetuity period: *Tan v. Tan* (1946) 12 M.L.J. 159,; *Hong Kong Bank Trustee Co. v Farrer Tan* [1988] 1 M.L.J. 485.

[43] *Re Thompson* [1934] Ch. 342, but the default beneficiary, a charity, only objected *pro forma*. If any of these anomalous cases is to be overruled this seems the prime candidate: it certainly should not be extended to other forms of sport like angling Romer J. erroneously based his judgment on negative enforceability by the default beneficiary: positive enforceability is, however, necessary (*Re Davidson* [1909] 1 Ch. 567, 571; *Re Shaw* [1957] 1 W.L.R. 729 at 745). Snell's *Equity*, Part II, Chap.1, sect. 3.3.

[44] Snell's *Equity*, Part II, Chap.1, sect. 3.3.

[45] *Pedulla v Nasti* (1990) 20 N.S.W.L.R. 720. If a will restricts a bequest expressly "so far as the law allows" this is construed as restricting the period to 21 years so satisfying the rule against inalienability: *Re Hooper* [1932] Ch. 38. The court will not imply such a term: *Re Compton* [1946] 1 All E.R. 117. If the legacy does not have to be kept intact as endowment capital but can be spent as soon as practicable on the purpose then the rule against inalienability has no application: *Trimmer v Danby* (1856) 25 L.J.Ch. 424; *Mussett v Bingle* [1876] W.N. 170.

able to claim it. The courts here have created an exception to the principle[46] that they will not treat words creating a trust as if only creating a power.

PURPOSES CONSTRUED AS TRUSTS FOR BENEFICIARIES

Re Denley-type purpose trusts typically involve a large fluctuating class of beneficiaries never intended to have, and never capable[47] of having, absolute ownership of the trust property, and only having a positive right to the performance of the trustee's duties in the form prescribed by the settlor. What of the cases, however, where there is a small class of identified beneficiaries who could be intended to have absolute ownership of the trust property, though the settlor purportedly qualifies this by requiring the property to be used for a specified purpose? **3–207**

Take the case of a trust fund set up for the education of the seven children of a deceased clergyman. Once their formal education was over, Kekewich J.[48] held this to be an absolute gift with the reference to education expressing merely the motive of the gift. He applied the well-established, and difficult to rebut,[49] presumption of construction,[50] "If a gross sum be given, or if the whole income of property be given, and a special purpose be assigned for this gift this court regards the gift as absolute and the purpose merely as the motive of the gift, and therefore holds that the gift takes effect as to the whole sum or the whole income as the case may be."

This was applied by the Court of Appeal in *Re Osoba*[51] where a bequest to the testator's widow upon trust "for her maintenance and for the training of my daughter, Abiola, up to university grade and for the maintenance of my aged mother" was held to be a trust for the three females absolutely as joint tenants. In *Re Bowes*[52] a trust to spend £5,000 on planting trees for shelter on the Wemmergill Estate was held to be a trust for the estate owners absolutely with the motive of having trees planted, so the owners could have the £5,000 to spend as they wished. **3–208**

Thus, if S creates a trust for the maintenance of B for B's life and, subject thereto, for C absolutely, B will be absolutely entitled to the whole income for whatever purpose he wants,[53] being entitled by the *Saunders v Vautier*

---

[46] *IRC v Broadway Cottage Trust* [1955] Ch. 20 at 36, *Re Shaw* [1957] 1 W.L.R. 729 at 746.

[47] A fluctuating class can never exercise *Saunders v Vautier* rights to make the trust, property their own: *Re Levy* [1960] Ch. 346 at 363; *Re Westphal* [1972] N.Z.L.R. 792 at 764–765. Exceptionally, where the beneficial class consists of members from time to time of a club who, on dissolution of the club, are entitled to divide the assets between them, the beneficiariaries will be able to acquire absolute ownership: see above at para.3–174.

[48] *Re Andrew's Trust* [1905] 2 Ch. 48.

[49] *Re Abbott Fund Trust* [1900] 2 Ch. 326: fund subscribed for maintenance of two deaf and dumb ladies (so not of normal capacity) held after their deaths to pass to subscribers under resulting trust and not to survivor's estate. For other cases where the beneficiary was only entitled to claim what was necessary for the specified purpose see *Re Sanderson's Trusts* (1857) 3 K.&J. 497; *Re Gillingham Bus Disaster Fund* [1958] Ch. 300.

[50] *Re Sanderson's Trusts* (1857) 3 K. & J. 497 and see *Re Skinner* (1860) 1 J. & H. 102 at 105.

[51] [1979] 2 All E.R. 393.

[52] [1896] 1 Ch. 507.

[53] Unless the circumstances such as B's mental and physical incapacity indicate otherwise: *Re Sanderson's Trusts* (1859) 3 K.&J. 497.

principle[54] to obtain for himself any interest in property (whether capital or income) to which he is absolutely indefeasibly entitled *sui juris*. On the other hand, if S creates a trust for the trustees to apply so much of the income as is necessary for the maintenance of B for B's life, and subject thereto, for C absolutely B will only have *Saunders v Vautier* rights to so much of the income as is necessary for the specified purpose.[55]

GIFTS FOR PURPOSES OF UNINCORPORATED BODIES

3–209 Unincorporated bodies, whether called associations, clubs or societies, raise special problems since an unincorporated body, unlike a corporate body, is not a legal person capable of owning property or entering into contracts or floating charges or of being the subject of legal rights and duties.[56] For this reason clubs, often incorporated themselves by registration as an Industrial and Provident Society under the 1965 Act of that title, which is considerably cheaper than converting the club into a limited company under the Companies Act 1985 and which enables the structure of the club for most practical purposes to remain fundamentally the same, so that the club is run by a committee elected by the member-shareholders. Tax legislation treats an unincorporated body formed for business purposes as a partnership with tax liability attributed to the individual partners, but if not formed for business purposes then the unincorporated body is regarded as a beneficiary under a bare trust, so making the trustees liable for corporation tax or, until its abolition, development land tax.[57]

3–210 The body's property will be vested in trustees under a bare trust for the members of the body (except to the extent that statute may prevent members of certain bodies from winding up the body and dividing its property between themselves.[58]) The trustees or other organ under the body's constitution may enter into contracts, thereby putting the body's property at risk *vis-à-vis* the claims of creditors, and may even be authorised to declare trusts binding the body's property.[59] To the extent such valid trusts have not been declared the body's property belongs to the members, subject to their contract made between themselves under the body's constitution and subject to any claims that third parties may have resulting from contracts made by the trustees.[60]

---

[54] (1841) 4 Beav. 115, at para.9–123.
[55] See *Re Sanderson's Trusts, supra.* If the trustees had a discretion to decide how much income they considered to be necessary for B's maintenance then B would be bound to accept such subjectively determined amount (unless B could prove bad faith or invoke *Re Hastings-Bass* principles discussed below at para.9–235).
[56] Trade unions are unincorporated associations (if not incorporated as a special register body) but by the Trade Union and Labour Relations Act 1974, s.2 they can make contracts in their own names, may sue or be sued in their own names, judgments can be enforced against them as if they were bodies corporate, and property may be vested in trustees on trust "for the union".
[57] *Conservative Central Office v Burrell* [1982] 1 W.L.R. 522; *Frampton v I.R.C.* [1985] S.T.C. 186, Income and Corporation Tax Act 1988, s.111; Development Land Tax Act 1976, s.47, Interpretation Act 1978, s.5 and Sch.1 defining person to include a body corporate or incorporate.
[58] *e.g.* Literary and Scientific Institutions Act 1854, s.30; *Re Bristol Athenaeum* (1899) 43 Ch.D. 236.
[59] Anything they do may be ratified by the membership since unincorporated associations have no capacity to be limited and so unlike companies cannot act *ultra vires*, though most of the *ultra vires* doctrine for companies has been abolished where outsiders dealing with the company are concerned: Companies Act 1989, s.108.
[60] *Re Bucks Constabulary Fund Friendly Society (No.2)* [1979] 1 All E.R. 623, at para.5–66.

A member or his spouse (or anyone) may give property in their lifetime **3–211** by will to the officers of the body as trustees upon certain trusts that are germane to the purpose of the body. Such trusts may be to use the property as soon as convenient in payment of everyday expenses so that the property is treated as part of the body's general assets. However, such trust property may not be intended to become the body's property to be spent as part of its general assets. The trust property may be intended to be held under a separate endowment account (so that income but not capital is spent) and managed separately from the body's general assets: neither the body's constitution nor the agreement of its members can then change the trustees' obligations as trustees of the trust property.

Associations with no unifying contract

An unincorporated body has the following features: **3–212**

(1) it is composed of two or more persons bound together for a common purpose;
(2) these persons have mutual rights and duties arising from a contract between them;
(3) the body has rules to determine (a) who controls the body and its funds and (b) the terms on which such control is exercisable;
(4) the body can be joined or left at will.

For lack of the second and third features the Conservative Party was held not to be an unincorporated association liable to corporation tax.[61] The Revenue had argued that the party was an unincorporated association since members' contributions surely took effect as an accretion to the funds which were the subject-matter of a contract which such members had made between themselves. How else could there be a legal relationship between a contributor and the recipient of the contribution so as to safeguard the contributor's interest?

Vinelott J.[62] suggested that the answer is that the contributor enters into **3–213** a contract with the treasurer whereby in consideration of payment of the subscription the treasurer undertakes to apply the subscription towards the association's purposes: breach of this undertaking can be enjoined on normal contractual principles at the suit of the contributor. On appeal,[63] Brightman L.J. opined that the contributor, by way of mandate or agency, gives his contribution to the treasurer to add it to the general funds of the association. Once that has been done the mandate becomes irrevocable but the contributor will have a remedy to restrain or have made good a

---

[61] *Conservative Central Office v Burrell* [1982] 1 W.L.R. 522. The fourth feature was not in issue but it seems too restrictive since an association may well have restrictions on new membership or rules curtailing the freedom of members to leave at will.

[62] *Conservative Central Office v Burrell* [1980] 3 All E.R. 42. He appears to suggest as an alternative that the treasurer by accepting the subscription comes under a special equitable obligation similar to an executor.

[63] [1982] 1 W.L.R. 522, and see [1983] Conv. 150 (P. Creighton) and (1983) 133 New L.J. 87 (C. T. Emery). Brightman L.J. made no comment on Vinelott J.'s views.

misapplication of the mixed fund, unless it appeared on ordinary accounting principles that his own contribution had already been properly
expended.

A transfer of assets for purposes (whether of an unincorporated body or
otherwise[64]) may thus take effect by way of contract or of mandate (which
may be gratuitous) if the donor is to retain some measure of control. Effect
cannot be given to a testator's bequests in such fashion since one cannot
imply a contract or mandate between a deceased person and another,[65]
though a deceased may authorise or direct his personal representatives to
enter into a contract or mandate. A deceased may also in his lifetime
contract to leave property by will to someone for a purpose, and if he does
die, leaving such a will, then his rights and duties under the contract will
vest in his personal representatives who will be able to enforce the
contractual undertakings given to him.

3–214   There is no need for any of the above artificial reasoning in the case of
gifts for unincorporated associations as Brightman L.J. has emphasised,[66]
since lifetime or testamentary gifts can validly take effect "as an accretion
to the funds which are the subject-matter of the contract which the
members [of the unincorporated association] have made *inter se.*"[67]

Different constructions of gifts to unincorporated bodies

Before the 1964 Perpetuities and Accumulations Act there were particular
legal obstacles confronting gifts to unincorporated bodies. The gift could
not be an absolute gift to such a body because such a body has no legal
personality. It could not be a valid gift if construed as a gift to the present
and future members of the body because the intent to ensure benefiting
future members required the capital to be kept intact and held on trust for
only the income to be used, so that the capital would remain available for
the benefit of future members.[68] This rendered the gift void for infringing
the rule against remoteness, though since the 1964 Act such a gift would be
valid for the statutory perpetuity period.[69] If the gift were construed as a
gift to the body on trust for carrying out purposes, with the gift being an
endowment fund to be used for those purposes only, and not to be used
without distinction between capital and income nor to be capable (on
dissolution of the body) for sharing out between the then members, then
such a purpose trust was void for infringing the rule against inalienability,
unless it was a charitable purpose trust. The 1964 Act has not affected
this.[70]

3–215   The gift would be valid if construed as an absolute gift to the persons
happening to be current members of the body, so that any such person
could claim his proportionate share. This might not be quite what the

---

[64] *e.g.* a disaster appeal committee in a situation like that in *Re Gillingham Bus Disaster Fund* [1958] Ch. 300.
[65] As accepted by Vinelott J. and Brightman L.J. in the *Conservative Central Office* case, also *Re Wilson*
[1908] 1 Ch. 839.
[66] *Conservative Central Office v Burrell* [1982] 2 All E.R. 1 at 7.
[67] *ibid.*
[68] *Leahy v Att.-Gen. for New South Wales* [1959] A.C. 457.
[69] See above at para.3–170.
[70] See s.15(4) of 1964 Act, above para.3–194.

deceased donor wished but, at least, his gift was not void. There developed a sophisticated construction, more likely to give effect testator's intention to benefit future members, but without imposing a trust to benefit future members with the attendant void for remoteness problem before the 1964 Act.

The sophisticated construction construes the gift as an absolute gift to the current members beneficially, but as an accretion to the body's property held subject to the terms of the contract which the members are subjected to by virtue of their membership of the body. This contract determines how the body's assets are to be enjoyed and what are the rights of the members in respect of such assets, while the treasurer or other worthy members will hold the assets on a bare trust for current members to be dealt with according to the contract (the constitution of the body).

Possible constructions to consider

1. The gift is a valid absolute gift (though, if testamentary, the **3–216** testator's executors will be under a fiduciary duty to give effect to the intended absolute gift after paying debts, etc.) to the persons currently members of the unincorporated body, so that any such person can claim his proportionate share.[71] The donor-testator is not providing endowment capital, but giving his property so that each donee can deal with his share as he wishes. Exceptionally, if the contract between the donees as members of the body requires gifts to members in their capacity, or under their description, as members to be treated as an accretion to the body's fund to be dealt with according to the body's rules[72] then the donor's property will have to be so treated.[73]

2. The gift is a valid absolute gift to the current members, taking effect as an accretion to the body's funds which are to be dealt with (under a bare trust) according to the rules of the body by which the members are all contractually bound.[74] The donor/testator is not providing endowment capital but giving his property to be freely spent[75] on day-to-day expenses or something of a more lasting nature, or to be divided up and pocketed by the members if the contractual rules allow this on dissolution or otherwise. It ought not

---

[71] *Cocks v Manners* (1871) L.R. 12 Eq. 574; *Re Smith* [1916] 1 Ch. 937; *Re Ogden* [1933] Ch. 678; *Re Clarke* [1901] 2 Ch. 110 (revealing that an expression of the purpose of the gift may merely be regarded as motive).

[72] Like property caught by a donee's covenant to settle after-acquired property: *Pullan v Koe* [1913] 1 Ch. 9 and at para.4–55.

[73] P. Matthews [1995] Conv. 302; as Viscount Simonds stated in *Leahy v Att.-Gen. for New South Wales* [1959] A.C. 457 at 478, "If it is a gift to individuals, each of them is entitled to his distributive share (unless he has previously bound himself by the rules of the society that it should be devoted to some other purpose)".

[74] *Re Recher's W.T.* [1972] Ch. 526, below at para.3–237; *Re Lipinski's W.T.* [1976] Ch. 235, below at para.3–242 at 211; *Universe Tankships Inc. of Monrovia v International Transport Workers Federation* [1983] A.C. 366; *News Group Ltd v Sogat* [1986] I.C.R. 716; *Bacon v O'Dea* (1989) 88 A.L.R. 486; *Re Bucks Constabulary Fund (No. 2)* [1979] 1 All E.R. 623, below, at para.5–66.

[75] *Re Macaulay's Estate* [1943] Ch. 435; *Re Price* [1943] Ch. 422; *Re Lipinski* [1976] Ch. 235; *Re Drummond* [1914] 2 Ch. 90 at 97–98; *Re Prevost* [1930] 2 Ch. 383.

to matter that because of some statute or subordination to some outside legal entity the members are unable to wind up the body and pocket its assets.[76] The gift in augmentation of the body's general assets is freely alienable other than directly to members: it can be totally consumed in supporting the body's purposes directly or indirectly benefiting the members who all have *locus standi* to sue. The gift does not have to be kept intact as endowment capital, so no trust rules concerning remoteness or inalienability can be applicable. However, if the testator knew that it was impossible or very difficult in practice for members to wind up the body and pocket its assets, so that the body was designed to carry on indefinitely, his bequest could well be construed as intending to set up endowment capital so that the income would benefit members from time to time indefinitely as under construction 3.[77]

3–217   3. The gift is intended to ensure that present and future members are either directly benefited or indirectly benefited (sufficiently to have *locus standi* to sue under *Re Denley's Trust Deed*) by the carrying out of the purposes of the body to which they belong. Thus, the gift is of endowment capital to be held upon trust (separate from the body's general assets available to be spent like current income) so that the income will always be available for the members from time to time or for purposes benefiting such members.

3–218   One can have an obvious example like £100,000 left on trust "to The Club Treasurer to apply the income for the benefit qua members of those from time to time members of the Club" or a less obvious example like "to The Club Treasurer to apply the income for the general purposes of the Club" or for a particular purpose within its various purposes. Another example would be if a testator left £1 million to The Club Treasurer "for the benefit of members from time to time of the Club" or "for the lasting benefit of the Club". Here, by necessary implication the *capital* needs to be set aside as an endowment so that the income can be used indefinitely for the benefit of the members directly or indirectly. Such endowment gifts before the 1964 Perpetuities and Accumulation Act would have been void for infringing the rule against remoteness. Nowadays, the trend[78] is to stretch matters to hold that there is no endowment capital, so that there is an absolute gift accruing to the body's assets under the second construction above.

3–219   If the court cannot so hold then what is to happen if the members wind up the body, wanting to make its assets their own, or if the body is continuing its functions at expiry of the perpetuity period? In

---

[76] The suggestion of Vinelott J. in *Re Grant's W.T.* [1979] 3 All E.R. 359 that a "necessary characteristic" of any gift within this second construction is the members' power to alter the rules and divide the assets between them seems unsound. It surely suffices that the gifted property is not endowment capital but can be freely spent on purposes benefiting the members. The members' contractual rights to enforce spending the property for their benefit suffices even if they cannot personally "pocket" the property: their position is similar to that of beneficiaries with *locus standi* to enforce purpose trusts directly benefiting them even if they have no *Saunders v Vautier* right to "pocket" the trust property.

[77] *Carne v Long* (1860) 2 De G.F. & J. 75; *Bacon v Pianta* (1966) 114 C.L.R. 634 (to the Communist Party of Australia "for its sole use and benefit"); *Re Grant's W.T.* [1979] 3 All E.R. 359.

[78] See above, n.74.

the former case, it seems likely the courts will construe the trust as a discretionary trust for members[79] until the winding up resolution, whereupon a fixed trust arises for the members equally[80] in accordance with the body's constitution. Thus the trust property passes to the members. In the latter case, the courts could take the strict view that on expiry of the perpetuity period the discretionary trust terminates[81] and there is a resulting trust in favour of the settlor's estate. However, to avoid practical problems in tracing the devolution of such estate and to achieve a more just outcome, it seems likely that the courts will be prepared to interpret s.4(4) of the 1964 Act liberally so as to treat the settlor's gift as a class gift within the subsection. Thus, the class of members will close so as to exclude persons becoming members outside the perpetuity period. The current members at the end of that period should between them be absolutely entitled to the gifted capital. No doubt, in practice, they will be happy to transfer it to trustees as an accretion to the club's funds but a member could claim his proportionate share (at the risk of not having his membership renewed) unless the club rules expressly provided that any assets passing to a member by virtue of the membership must accrue to the club's funds.[82]

Where the members cannot make the club assets their own because statute prohibits this[83] or because on dissolution the assets must pass to another body[84] then the trust will be construed as a purpose trust under constructions 4 and 5. **3–220**

4. The gift is intended to be of endowment capital to be held on trust for the income to be applied to a charitable purpose. This is a valid charitable trust (exempt from the beneficiary principle and the rule against inalienability) whose funds will need to be kept separate from the non-charitable funds of the body and will remain subject to the charitable purpose, even after dissolution of the body.[85]

5. The gift is intended to be of endowment capital to be held on trust for the income to be applied for the club's abstract non-charitable purposes where any benefit for persons is so indirect or intangible that no person has *locus standi* to apply for enforcement of the trust. The trust will be void for infringing the beneficiary principle[86] unless it is one of the anomalous permitted testamentary purpose trusts,[87] but even these must be restricted to the common law perpetuity period if they are not to infringe the rule against inalienability.[88]

---

[79] See *Re Grant's W.T.* [1979] 3 All E.R. 359 at 368 on *Re Denley* purpose trusts.
[80] Or otherwise as provided in the body's constitution, *e.g.* country members only receiving half that of town members.
[81] Perpetuities and Accumulations Act 1964, s.3(3).
[82] See above, n.71 and 73.
[83] *e.g.* Literacy and Scientific Institutions Act 1854, s.30. *Re Bristol Athenaeum* (1889) 43 Ch.D. 236.
[84] *e.g. Re Grant's W.T.* [1979] 3 All E.R. 359.
[85] *Brooks v Richardson* [1986] 1 All E.R. 952; *Re Finger's W.T.* [1972] Ch. 300 revealing the predisposition of the court to treat a gift to an unincorporated charitable body as a trust for purposes, so as to prevent the gift lapsing if the body had been earlier dissolved and the second construction had been applied.
[86] *Leahy v Att.-Gen. for New South Wales* [1959] A.C. 457.
[87] See above, at para.3–206.
[88] *ibid.*

3–221   In *Re Grant's W.T.*[89] a testator left his estate "to the Labour Party
Property Committee for the benefit of the Chertsey Headquarters of
the Chertsey and Walton Constituency Labour Party" ("C.L.P.")
providing that if the headquarters ceased to be in the Chertsey UDC
area (1972) his estate should pass to the National Labour Party
("N.L.P.") absolutely. The C.L.P. constitution subordinated it to the
N.L.P., who could direct changes in the constitution and prevent the
C.L.P. changing its constitution without N.L.P. approval. Vinelott J.
held that the estate was meant to be kept intact as endowment
capital on trust for Labour Party purposes and so was void for
infringing the beneficiary principle and the rule against
inalienability.

3–222   6. The gift is intended to be of endowment capital (in which the settlor
has abandoned all interest) to be held on trust for the income to be
applied for the club's abstract non-charitable purposes, the chairman
from time to time of the club to be sole enforcer of the trust. The
House of Lords may be prepared to acept this,[90] but it would need
to be restricted from the outset to a common law perpetuity period
so as not to infringe the rule against inalienability, and the purposes
would need to be certain enough to enable the restrictions on the
use of the income to be identified and enforced.[91]

LEAHY v ATTORNEY-GENERAL FOR NEW SOUTH WALES

3–223 Privy Council [1959] A.C. 457; [1959] 2 All E.R. 300 (Viscount Simonds, Lords
Morton of Henryton, Cohen, Somervell of Harrow and Denning)

By his will the testator provided as follows: "As to my property known as
'Elmslea' situated at Bungendore aforesaid and the whole of the land comprising
the same and the whole of the furniture contained in the homestead thereon upon
trust for such order of nuns of the Catholic Church or the Christian Brothers as my
executors and trustees shall select."

Counsel for the trustees argued that the disposition made thereby was good as it
stood. Once the trustees selected the recipient of the gift, whether an order of nuns
or the Christian Brothers, the selected body became absolutely entitled to the gift.
No question of uncertainty or perpetuity was therefore involved and the gift was
valid. It should be observed that this argument, if successful, would enable the
trustees to select as the recipient an order of nuns which was not charitable in the
legal sense of that term. The phrase "order of nuns" included "contemplative" as
well as "active" orders, the former of which were not charitable[92] Counsel,

---

[89] [1979] 3 All E.R. 359. *Obiter dicta* overlook the impact of the 1964. Perpetuities and Accumulations Act
and the significance of *Re Lipinski's W.T.* [1976] Ch. 235. See further (1980) 39 Camb. L.J. 88 (C. E. F.
Rickett) and (1980) 44 M.L.R. 459 (B. Green). In *News Group Newspapers Ltd v Society of Graphical &
Allied Trades* [1986] I.C.R. 716 Lloyd L.J. seems to accept that the NLP's power to obtain CLP assets for
its own needs justified the conclusions of Vinelott J.

[90] See para.3–198 above.

[91] See *Twinsectra Ltd v Yardley* [2000] W.T.L.R. 527, 560 (reversed on other grounds in [2002] UKHL 12,
[2002] 2 A.C. 164) on certainty of analogous *Quistclose*-type trust restrictions: where the purposes are
spelled out in certain workable fashion one could have all the club members as enforcers.

[92] See *Gilmour v Coats* [1949] A.C. 426; at para.7–236.

accordingly, argued, in the alternative, that, if the disposition made by clause 3 was not valid as it stood, it was nevertheless saved from invalidity by section 37D of the Conveyancing Act 1919–54, which would, at least, enable active (though not contemplative) orders to be selected.

VISCOUNT SIMONDS: "The disposition made by clause 3 must now be considered. **3–224** As has already been pointed out, it will in any case be saved by the section so far as orders other than contemplative orders are concerned, but the trustees are anxious to preserve their right to select such orders. They can only do so if the gift is what is called an absolute gift to the selected order, an expression which may require examination.

"The difficulty arises out of the artificial and anomalous conception of an **3–225** unincorporated society which, though it is not a separate entity in law, is yet for many purposes regarded as a continuing entity and, however inaccurately, as something other than an aggregate of its members. In law a gift to such a society simpliciter (*i.e.*, where, to use the words of Lord Parker in *Bowman v Secular Society Ltd*,[93] neither the circumstances of the gift nor the directions given nor the objects expressed impose on the donee the character of a trustee) is nothing else than a gift to its members at the date of the gift as joint tenants or tenants in common. It is for this reason that the prudent conveyancer provides that a receipt by the treasurer or other proper officer of the recipient society for a legacy to the society shall be a sufficient discharge to executors. If it were not so, the executors could only get a valid discharge by obtaining a receipt from every member. This must be qualified by saying that by their rules the members might have authorised one of themselves to receive a gift on behalf of them all.

"It is in the light of this fundamental proposition that the statements, to which **3–226** reference has been made, must be examined. What is meant when it is said that a gift is made to the individuals comprising the community and the words are added 'it is given to them for the benefit of the community?' If it is a gift to individuals, each of them is entitled to his distributive share (unless he has previously bound himself by the rules of the society that it shall be devoted to some other purpose). It is difficult to see what is added by the words 'for the benefit of the community.' If they are intended to import a trust, who are the beneficiaries? If the present members are the beneficiaries, the words add nothing and are meaningless. If some other persons or purposes are intended, the conclusion cannot be avoided that the gift is void. For it is uncertain and beyond doubt tends to a perpetuity.

"The question then appears to be whether, even if the gift to a selected order of nuns is prima facie a gift to the individual members of that order, there are other considerations arising out of the terms of the will, or the nature of the society, its organisation and rules, or the subject-matter of the gift, which should lead the court to conclude that though prima facie the gift is an absolute one (absolute both in quality of estate and in freedom from restriction) to individual nuns, yet it is invalid because it is in the nature of an endowment and tends to a perpetuity or for any other reason.

"The prima facie validity of such a gift (by which term their Lordships intend a **3–227** bequest or devise) is a convenient starting-point for the examination of the relevant law. For, as Lord Tomlin (sitting at first instance in the Chancery Division) said in *Re Ogden*,[94] a gift to a voluntary association of persons for the general purposes of

---

[93] [1917] A.C. 406 at 437.
[94] [1933] Ch. 678 at 681.

the association is an absolute gift and prima facie a good gift. He was echoing the words of Lord Parker in *Bowman's* case[95] that a gift to an unincorporated association for the attainment of its purposes 'may . . . be upheld as an absolute gift to its members.' These words must receive careful consideration, for it is to be noted that it is because the gift can be upheld as a gift to the individual members that it is valid, even though it is given for the general purpose of the association. If the words 'for the general purposes of the association' were held to import a trust, the question would have to be asked, what is the trust and who are the beneficiaries? A gift can be made to persons (including a corporation) but it cannot be made to a purpose or to an object: so, also, a trust may be created for the benefit of persons as *cestuis que trust* but not for a purpose or object unless the purpose or object be charitable. For a purpose or object cannot sue, but, if it be charitable, the Attorney-General can sue to enforce it . . ." [He then considered *Cocks v Manners* (1871) L.R. 12 Eq. 574; *Re Smith* [1914] 1 Ch. 937; *Re Clarke* [1901] 2 Ch. 110; *Re Drummond* [1914] 2 Ch. 90; *Re Taylor* [1940] Ch. 481; *Re Price* [1943] Ch. 422; *Re Prevost* [1930] 2 Ch. 383 and *Re Ray's W.T.* [1936] Ch. 520.]

3–228   "The cases that have been referred to are all cases in which gifts have been upheld as valid either on the ground that, where a society has been named as legatee, its members could demand that the gift should be dealt with as they should together think fit; or on the ground that a trust has been established (as in *Re Drummond*) which did not create a perpetuity . . .

3–229   "Their Lordships must now turn to the recent case of *Re Macaulay's Estate*,[96] which appears to be reported only in a footnote to *Re Price*.[97] There the gift was to the Folkestone Lodge of the Theosophical Society absolutely for the maintenance and improvement of the Theosophical Lodge at Folkestone. It was assumed that the donee 'the Lodge' was a body of persons. The decision of the House of Lords in July 1933, to which both Lord Buckner and Lord Tomlin were parties, were that the gift was invalid. A portion of Lord Buckmaster's speech may well be quoted. He had previously referred to *Re Drummond* and *Carne v Long*. 'A group of people,' he said, 'defined and bound together by rules and called by a distinctive name can be the subject of gift as well as any individual or incorporated body. The real question is what is the actual purpose for which the gift is made. There is no perpetuity if the gift is for the individual members for their own benefit, but that, I think, is clearly not the meaning of this gift. Nor again is there a perpetuity if the society is at liberty in accordance with the terms of the gift to spend both capital and income as they think fit . . . If the gift is to be for the endowment of the society to be held as an endowment and the society is according to its form perpetual, the gift is bad: but, if the gift is an immediate beneficial legacy, it is good.' In the result he held the gift for the maintenance and improvement of the Theosophical Lodge at Folkestone to be invalid. Their Lordships respectfully doubt whether the passage in Lord Buckmaster's speech in which he suggests the alternative ground of validity, *viz*, that the society is at liberty in accordance with the terms of the gift to spend both capital and income as they think fit, presents a true alternative. It is only because the society, *i.e.*, the individuals constituting it, are the beneficiaries that they can dispose of the gift. Lord Tomlin came to the same conclusion. He found in the words of the will 'for the maintenance and improvement' a sufficient indication that it was the permanence of the Lodge at Folkestone that the testatrix was seeking to secure and

---

[95] [1917] A.C. 406 at 442.
[96] [1943] Ch. 435n.
[97] [1943] Ch. 422.

this, he thought, necessarily involved endowment. Therefore a perpetuity was created. A passage from the judgment of Lord Hanworth M.R. (which has been obtained from the records) may usefully be cited. He said: 'The problem may be stated in this way. If the gift is in truth to the present members of the society described by their society name so that they have the beneficial use of the property and can, if they please, alienate and put the proceeds in their own pocket, then there is a present gift to individuals which is good: but if the gift is intended for the good not only of the present but of future members so that the present members are in the position of trustees and have no right to appropriate the property or its proceeds for their personal benefit, then the gift is invalid. It may be invalid by reason of there being a trust created, or it may be by reason of the terms that the period allowed by the rule against perpetuities would be exceeded.'

"It is not very clear what is intended by the dichotomy suggested in the last **3–230** sentence of the citation, but the penultimate sentence goes to the root of the matter. At the risk of repetition their Lordships would point out that if a gift is made to individuals, whether under their own names or in the name of their society, and the conclusion is reached that they are not intended to take beneficially, then they take as trustees. If so, it must be ascertained who are the beneficiaries. If, at the death of the testator, the class of beneficiaries is fixed and ascertained or ascertainable within the limit of the rule against perpetuities, all is well. If it is not so fixed and not so ascertainable, the trust must fail.

"It must now be asked, then, whether in the present case there are sufficient indications to displace the prima facie conclusion that the gift made by clause 3 of the will is to the individual members of the selected order of nuns at the date of the testator's death so that they can together dispose of it as they think fit. It appears to their Lordships that such indications are ample.

"In the first place, it is not altogether irrelevant that the gift is in terms upon trust **3–231** for a selected order. It is true that this can in law be regarded as a trust in favour of each and every member of the order. But at least the form of the gift is not to the members, and it may be questioned whether the testator understood the niceties of the law. In the second place, the members of the selected order may be numerous, very numerous perhaps, and they may be spread over the world. If the gift is to the individuals it is to all the members who were living at the death of the testator, but only to them. It is not easy to believe that the testator intended an 'immediate beneficial legacy' (to use the words of Lord Buckmaster) to such a body of beneficiaries. In the third place, the subject-matter of the gift cannot be ignored. It appears from the evidence filed in the suit that Elmslea is a grazing property of about 730 acres, with a furnished homestead containing twenty rooms and a number of outbuildings. With the greatest respect to those judges who have taken a different view, their Lordships do not find it possible to regard all the individual members of an order as intended to become the beneficial owners of such a property. Little or no evidence has been given about the organisation and rules of the several orders, but it is at least permissible to doubt whether it is a common feature of them that all their members regard themselves or are to be regarded as having the capacity of (say) the Corps of Commissionaires (see *Re Clarke*) to put an end to their association and distribute its assets. On the contrary it seems reasonably clear that, however little the testator understood the effect in law of a gift to an unincorporated body of persons by their society name, his intention was to create a trust not merely for the benefit of the existing members of the selected order but for its benefit as a continuing society and for the furtherance of its work.

". . . Their Lordships, therefore, humbly advise Her Majesty that the appeal should be dismissed, but that the gift made by clause 3 of the will is valid by reason only of the provisions of section 37D of the Conveyancing Act 1919–54, and that the power of selection thereby given to the trustees does not extend to contemplative orders of nuns." *Appeal dismissed.*

RE DENLEY'S TRUST DEED

Chancery Division [1969] 1 Ch. 373; [1968] 3 W.L.R. 457; [1968] 3 All E.R. 65.

3–232   In 1936 land was conveyed by a company to trustees so that until the expiration of 21 years from the death of the last survivor of certain specified persons the land should under clause 2(c) of a trust deed "be maintained and used as and for the purpose of a recreation or sports ground primarily for the benefit of the employees of the company and secondarily for the benefit of such other person or persons (if any) as the trustees may allow to use the same." The main question was dealt with as follows in a reserved judgment:

GOFF J.: "It was decided in *Re Astor's Settlement Trusts*,[98] that a trust for a number of non-charitable purposes was not merely unenforceable but void on two grounds; first that they were not trusts for the benefit of individuals, which I refer to as 'the beneficiary principle,' and, secondly, for uncertainty.

"Counsel for the first defendant has argued that the trust in clause 2(c) in the present case is either a trust for the benefit of individuals, in which case he argues that they are an unascertainable class and therefore the trust is void for uncertainty, or it is a purpose trust, that is a trust for providing recreation, which he submits is void on the beneficiary principle, or alternatively it is something of a hybrid having the vices of both kinds.

3–233   *"I think that there may be a purpose or object trust, the carrying out of which would benefit an individual or individuals, where that benefit is so indirect or intangible or which is otherwise so framed as not to give those persons any locus standi to apply to the court to enforce the trust, in which case the beneficiary principle would, as it seems to me, apply to invalidate the trust, quite apart from any question of uncertainty or perpetuity. Such cases can be considered if and when they arise. The present is not, in my judgment, of that character, and it will be seen that clause 2(d) of the trust deed expressly states that, subject to any rules and regulations made by the trustees, the employees of the company shall be entitled to the use and enjoyment of the land.*

"Apart from this possible exception, in my judgment the beneficiary principle of *Re Astor*,[99] which was approved in *Re Endacott (decd.)*,[1] see particularly by Harman L.J.,[2] *is confined to purpose or object trusts which are abstract or impersonal. The objection is not that the trust is for a purpose or object per se, but that there is no beneficiary or cestui que trust. The rule is so expressed in* Lewin on Trusts *(16th ed.), p.17, and, in my judgment, with the possible exception which I have mentioned, rightly so. In* Re Wood[3] *Harman J. said:*

'There has been an interesting argument on the question of perpetuity, but it seems to me, with all respect to that argument, that there is an earlier obstacle which is fatal to the validity of this bequest, namely, that a gift on trust must

---

[98] [1952] Ch. 534.
[99] [1952] Ch. 534. Editor's italics for cross-referencing purposes.
[1] [1960] Ch. 232.
[2] [1960] Ch. 232 at 250.
[3] [1949] Ch. 498 at 501.

have a cestui que trust, and there being here no cestui que trust the gift must fail.'

"Again, in *Leahy v Att.-Gen. of New South Wales*[4] Viscount Simonds, delivering the   **3–234**
judgment of the Privy Council, said:

> 'A gift can be made to persons (including a corporation) but it cannot be made to a purpose or to an object: so, also [and these are the important words] a trust may be created for the benefit of persons as cestuis que trust but not for a purpose or object unless the purpose or object be charitable. For a purpose or object cannot sue, but, if it be charitable, the Attorney-General can sue to enforce it.'

"Where, then, the trust, though expressed as a purpose, is directly or indirectly for the benefit of an individual or individuals, it seems to me that it is in general outside the mischief of the beneficiary principle.

"I am fortified in this conclusion by the dicta of Lord Evershed M.R. and Harman L.J. in *Re Harpur's Will Trusts, Haller v Att.-Gen.*[5]

"Some further support for my conclusion is, I think, to be found in *Re Aberconway's Settlement Trusts*[6] where it was assumed that a trust for the upkeep and development of certain gardens which were part of a settled estate was valid.

"I also derive assistance from what was said by North J. in *Re Bowes*.[7] That was a   **3–235**
bequest of a sum of money on trust to expend the same in planting trees for shelter on certain settled estates. It happened that there was a father and a son of full age, tenant for life in possession and tenant in tail in remainder respectively; so that, subject to the son disentailing, they were together absolutely entitled, and the actual decision was that they could claim the money, but North J. said[8]:

> 'If it were necessary to uphold it, the trees can be planted upon the whole of it until the fund is exhausted. Therefore, there is nothing illegal in the gift itself . . .';

and[9]: 'I think there clearly is a valid trust to lay out money for the benefit of the persons entitled to the estate.'

"The trust in the present case is limited in point of time so as to avoid any infringement of the rule against perpetuities and, for the reasons which I have given, it does not offend against the beneficiary principle; and unless, therefore, it be void for uncertainty, it is a valid trust.

"There is, however, one other aspect of uncertainty which has caused me some   **3–236**
concern; that is, whether this is in its nature a trust which the court can control, for, as Lord Eldon L.C. said in *Morice v Bishop of Durham*[10]:

> 'As it is a maxim that the execution of a trust shall be under the control of the court, it must be of such a nature that it can be under that control; so that the

---

[4] [1959] A.C. 457 at 478.
[5] [1962] Ch. 78 at 91, 96.
[6] [1953] Ch. 647.
[7] [1896] 1 Ch. 507.
[8] [1896] 1 Ch. 507 at 510.
[9] [1896] 1 Ch. 507 at 511.
[10] (1805) 10 Ves. 522 at 539.

administration of it can be reviewed by the court; or, if the trustee dies, the court itself can execute the trust: a trust, therefore, which, in case of maladministration could be reformed; and a due administration directed; and then, unless the subject and the objects can be ascertained upon principles familiar in other cases, it must be decided that the court can neither reform maladministration nor direct a due administration.'

"In my judgment, however, it would not be right to hold the trust void on this ground. The court can, as it seems to me, execute the trust both negatively by restraining any improper disposition or use of the land, and positively by ordering the trustees to allow the employees and such other persons (if any) as they may admit to use the land for the purpose of a recreation or sports ground. Any difficulty there might be in practice in the beneficial enjoyment of the land by those entitled to use it is, I think, really beside the point. The same kind of problem is equally capable of arising in the case of a trust to permit a number of persons—for example, all the unmarried children of a testator or settlor—to use or occupy a house or to have the use of certain chattels; yet no one would suggest, I fancy, that such a trust would be void.

"In my judgment, therefore, the provisions of clause 2(c) are valid."

RE RECHER'S WILL TRUSTS

3–237 Chancery Division [1972] Ch. 526; [1971] 3 W.L.R. 321; [1971] 3 All E.R. 401.

By will dated May 23, 1957, T gave a share of her residue to what the judge interpreted as "The London and Provincial Anti-Vivisection Society" which had ceased to exist on January 1, 1957. T died in 1962. In a reserved judgment consideration was first given to the question whether the gift would have been valid if the unincorporated society had existed at T's death:

BRIGHTMAN J.: "Having reached the conclusion that the gift in question is not a gift to the members of the London and Provincial Society at the date of death, as joint tenants or tenants in common so as to entitle a member as of right to a distributive share, nor an attempted gift to present and future members beneficially, and is not a gift in trust for the purpose of the society, I must now consider how otherwise, if at all, it is capable of taking effect.

3–238 "As I have already mentioned, the rules of the London and Provincial Society do not purport to create any trusts except insofar as the honorary trustees are not beneficial owners of the assets of the society, but are trustees on trust to deal with such assets according to the directions of the committee.

3–239 "A trust for non-charitable purposes, as distinct from a trust for individuals, is clearly void because there is no beneficiary. It does not, however, follow that persons cannot band themselves together as an association or society, pay subscriptions and validly devote their funds in pursuit of some lawful non-charitable purpose. An obvious example is a members' social club. But it is not essential that the members should only intend to secure direct personal advantages to themselves. The association may be one in which personal advantages to the members are combined with the pursuit of some outside purpose. Or the association may be one which offers no personal benefit at all to the members, the funds of the association being applied exclusively to the pursuit of some outside purpose. Such an association of persons is bound, I would think, to have some sort of constitution; *i.e.* the rights and liabilities of the members of the association will inevitably depend on some form of contract *inter se*, usually evidenced by a set of rules. In the present case it appears to me clear that the life members, the ordinary members and the associate members of the London Provincial Society were bound together by a contract *inter se*. Any such member was entitled to the rights and subject to the liabilities defined by the rules. If the committee acted contrary to the rules, an individual member would be entitled to take proceedings in the courts to compel observance of the rules or to recover damages for any loss he had suffered as a result of the breach of contract. As and when a member paid his subscription to the association, he would be subjecting his money to the disposition and expenditure thereof laid down by the rules. That is to say, the member would be bound to permit, and entitled to require, the honorary trustees and other members of the society to deal with that subscription in accordance with the lawful directions of the committee. Those directions would include the expenditure of that subscription, as part of the general funds of the association, in furthering the objects of the association. The resultant situation, on analysis, is that the London and Provincial Society represented an organisation of individuals bound together by a contract under which their subscriptions became, as it were, mandated towards a certain type of expenditure as adumbrated in rule 1. Just as the two parties to a bipartite bargain can vary or terminate their contract by mutual assent, so it must follow that the life members, ordinary members and associate members of the London and Provincial Society could, at any moment of time, by unanimous agreement (or by majority vote if the rules so prescribe), vary or terminate their multipartite contract. There would be no limit to the type of variation or termination to which all might agree. There is no private trust or trust for charitable purposes or other trust to hinder the process. It follows that if all members agreed, they could decide to wind up the London and Provincial Society and divide the net assets among themselves beneficially. No one would have any locus standi to stop them so doing. The contract is the same as any other contract and concerns only those who are parties to it, that is to say, the members of the society.

3–240 "The funds of such an association may, of course, be derived not only from the subscriptions of the contracting parties but also from donations from non-contracting parties and legacies from persons who have died. In the case of a donation which is not accompanied by any words which purport to impose a trust, it seems to me that the gift takes effect in favour of the existing members of the association as an accretion to the funds which are the subject-matter of the contract which such members have made *inter se*, and falls to be dealt with in precisely the same way as the funds which the members themselves have subscribed. So, in the case of a legacy. In the absence of words which purport to impose a trust, the legacy is a gift to the members beneficially, not as joint tenants or as tenants in common so as to entitle each member to an immediate distributive share, but as an accretion to the funds which are the subject-matter of the contract which the members have made *inter se*.

3–241 "In my judgment the legacy in the present case to the London and Provincial Society ought to be construed as a legacy of that type, that is to say, a legacy to the members beneficially as an accretion to the funds subject to the contract which they had made *inter se*. Of course, the testatrix did not intend the members of the society to divide their bounty between themselves, and doubtless she was ignorant of that remote but theoretical possibility. Her knowledge or absence of knowledge of the true legal analysis of the gift is irrelevant. The legacy is accordingly in my view valid, subject only to the effect of the events of January 1, 1957."

RE LIPINSKI'S WILL TRUSTS

Chancery Division [1976] Ch. 235; [1977] 1 All E.R. 33; [1976] 3 W.L.R. 522.

3–242   The testator bequeathed his residuary estate to trustees on trust "as to one half thereof for the Hull Judeans (Maccabi) Association in memory of my late wife to be used solely in the work of constructing the new buildings for the association and/or improvements to the said buildings." Was this valid?

OLIVER J.: "I approach question 1 of the summons, therefore, on the footing that this is a gift to an unincorporated non-charitable association. Such a gift, if it is an absolute and beneficial one, is of course perfectly good: see, for instance, the gift to the Corps of Commissionaires in *Re Clarke*.[11] What I have to consider, however, is the effect of the specification by the testator of the purposes for which the legacy was to be applied. The principles applicable to this type of case were stated by Cross J. in *Neville Estates Ltd v Madden*[12] and they are conveniently summarised in *Tudor on Charities*, where it is said[13]:

3–243   "In *Neville Estates Ltd v Madden* Cross J. expressed the opinion (which is respectfully accepted as correct) that every such gift might, according to the actual words used, be construed in one of three quite different ways: (*a*) As a gift to the members of the association at the date of the gift as joint tenants so that any member could sever his share and claim it whether or not he continues to be a member. (*b*) As a gift to the members of the association at the date of the gift not as joint tenants, but subject to their contractual rights and liabilities towards one another as members of the association. In such a case a member cannot sever his share. It will accrue to the other members on his death or resignation, even though such members include persons who become members after the gift took effect. If this is the effect of the gift, it will not be open to objection on the score of perpetuity or uncertainty unless there is something in its terms or circumstances or in the rules of the association which precludes the members at any given time from dividing the subject of the gift between them on the footing that they are solely entitled to it in equity. (*c*) The terms or circumstances of the gift or the rules of the association may show that the property in question—*i.e.* the subject of the gift—is not to be at the disposal of the members for the time being but is to be held in trust for or applied for the purposes of the association as a quasi-corporate entity. In this case the gift will fail unless the association is a charitable body."

3–244   "That summary may require, I think, a certain amount of qualification in the light of subsequent authority, but for the present purposes I can adopt it as a working guide. Counsel for the next-of-kin argues that the gift in the present case clearly does not fall within the first category, and that the addition of the specific direction as to its employment by the association prevents it from falling into the second category. This is, therefore, he says, a purpose trust and fails both for that reason and because the purpose is perpetuitous . . .

"Counsel for the next-of-kin points out, first, that the gift is in memory of the testator's late wife (which, he says, suggests an intention to create a permanent

---

[11] [1901] 2 Ch. 110.
[12] [1962] Ch. 832.
[13] 6th ed., 1967), p.150.

memorial or endowment); secondly, that the gift is *solely* for a particular purpose (which would militate strongly against any suggestion that the donees could wind up and pocket the money themselves, even though their constitution may enable them to do so); and, thirdly, that the gift contemplates expenditure on 'improvements,' which connotes a degree of continuity or permanence. All this, he says, shows that what the testator had in mind was a permanent endowment in memory of his late wife.

"For my part, I think that very little turns on the testator's having expressed the **3–245** gift as being in memory of his late wife. I see nothing in this expression which suggests any intention to create a permanent endowment. It indicates merely, I think, a tribute which the testator wished to pay, and it is not without significance that this self-same tribute appeared in the earlier will in which he made an absolute and outright gift to the association. The evidential value of this in the context of a construction summons may be open to doubt, and I place no reliance on it. It does, however, seem to me that nothing is to be derived from these words beyond the fact that the testator wished the association to know that his bounty was a tribute to his late wife.

"I accept, however, the submission of counsel for the next-of-kin that the designation of the sole purpose of the gift makes it impossible to construe the gift as one falling into the first of Cross J.'s categories, even if that were otherwise possible. But I am not impressed by the argument that the gift shows an intention of continuity. Counsel prays in aid *Re Macaulay*[14] where the gift was for the 'maintenance and improvement of the Theosophical Lodge at Folkestone.' The House of Lords held that it failed for perpetuity, the donee being a non-charitable body. But it is clear from the speeches of both Lord Buckmaster and Lord Tomlin that their Lordships derived the intention of continuity from the reference to 'maintenance.' Here it is quite evident that the association was to be free to spend the capital of the legacy.

"*Re Price*[15] itself is authority for the proposition that a gift to an unincorporated **3–246** non-charitable association for objects on which the association is at liberty to spend both capital and income will not fail for perpetuity, although the actual conclusion in that case has been criticised, the point that the trust there (the carrying on of the teachings of Rudolf Steiner) was a 'purpose trust' and thus unenforceable on that ground was not argued. It does not seem to me, therefore, that in the present case there is a valid ground for saying that the gift fails for perpetuity.

"But that is not the end of the matter. If the gift were to the association *simpliciter*, it would, I think, clearly fall within the second category of Cross J.'s categories. At first sight, however, there appears to be a difficulty in arguing that the gift is to members of the association subject to their contractual rights *inter se* when there is a specific direction or limitation sought to be imposed on those contractual rights as to the manner in which the subject-matter of the gift is to be dealt with. This, says counsel for the next-of-kin, is a pure 'purpose trust' and is invalid on that ground, quite apart from any question of perpetuity. I am not sure, however, that it is sufficient merely to demonstrate that a trust is a 'purpose' trust . . .

"There would seem to me to be, as a matter of common sense, a clear distinction **3–247** between the case where a purpose is described which is clearly intended for the benefit of ascertained or ascertainable beneficiaries, particularly where those beneficiaries have the power to make the capital their own, and the case where no

---

[14] [1943] Ch. 435.
[15] [1943] Ch. 422.

beneficiary at all is intended (for instance, a memorial to a favourite pet) or where the beneficiaries are unascertainable (as for instance in *Re Price*[16]). If a valid gift may be made to an unincorporated body as a simple accretion to the funds which are the subject-matter of the contract which the members have made *inter se*, and *Neville Estates v Madden*[17] and *Re Recher's Will Trusts*[18] show that it may, I do not really see why such a gift, which specifies a purpose which is within the powers of the unincorporated body and of which the members of that body are the beneficiaries, should fail. Why are not the beneficiaries able to enforce the trust or, indeed, in the exercise of their contractual rights, to terminate the trust for their own benefit? Where the donee body is itself the beneficiary of the prescribed purpose, there seems to me to be the strongest argument in common sense for saying that the gift should be construed as an absolute one within the second category, the more so where, if the purpose is carried out, the members can by appropriate action vest the resulting property in themselves, for here the trustees and the beneficiaries are the same persons.

. . .

3–248   "A striking case which seems to be not far from the present is *Re Turkington*,[19] where the gift was to a masonic lodge 'as a fund to build a suitable temple in Stafford.' The members of the lodge being both the trustees and the beneficiaries of the temple, Luxmoore J. construed the gift as an absolute one to the members of the lodge for the time being. Directly in point is the more recent decision of Goff J. in *Re Denley's Trust Deed*,[20] where the question arose as to the validity of a deed under which land was held by trustees as a sports ground:

> ". . . primarily for the benefit of the employees of [a particular] company and secondarily for the benefit of such other person or persons . . . as the trustees may allow to use the same"

the latter provision was construed by Goff J. as a power and not a trust. The same deed conferred on the employees a right to use and enjoy the land subject to regulations made by the trustees. Goff J. held that the rule against enforceability of non-charitable "purpose or object" trusts was confined to those which were abstract or impersonal in nature where there was no beneficiary or *cestui que trust*. A trust which, though expressed as a purpose, was directly or indirectly for the benefit of an individual or individuals was valid provided that those individuals were ascertainable at any one time and the trust was not otherwise void for uncertainty.

"I respectfully adopt [the view of Goff J, italicised, *supra*, at para.3–233], as it seems to me to accord both with authority and with common sense.

3–249   "If this is the right principle, then on each side of the line does the present case fall? Counsel for the Attorney-General has submitted in the course of his argument in favour of charity that the testator's express purpose 'solely in the work of constructing the new buildings for the association' referred and could only refer to the youth centre project, which was the only project for the erection of buildings which was under consideration at the material time. If this is right, then the trust must, I think, fail, for it is quite clear that that project is ultimately conceived

[16] [1943] Ch. 422.
[17] [1962] Ch. 832.
[18] [1972] Ch. 526.
[19] [1937] 4 All E.R. 501.
[20] [1969] 1 Ch. 373 at 375.

embraced not only the members of the association, but the whole Jewish community in Hull, and it would be difficult to argue that there was any ascertainable beneficiary. I do not, however, so construe the testator's intention. The evidence is that the testator knew the association's position and that he took a keen interest in it. I infer that he was kept informed of its current plans. The one thing that is quite clear from the minutes is that from 1965 right up to the testator's death there was great uncertainty about what was going to be done. There was a specific project for the purchase of a house in 1965. By early 1966 the youth centre was back in favour. By October 1966 it was being suggested that the association should stay where it was in its rented premises. The meeting of March 21, is, I think, very significant because it shows that it was again thinking in terms of its own exclusive building and that the patrons (of whom the testator was one) would donate the money when it was needed. At the date of the will, the association had rejected the youth centre plans and was contemplating again the purchase of premises of its own; and thereafter interest shifted to the community centre. I am unable to conclude that the testator had any specific building in mind; and, in my judgment, the reference to 'the . . . buildings for the association' means no more than whatever buildings the association may have or may choose to erect or acquire. The reference to improvements reflects, I think, the testator's contemplation that the association might purchase or might, at his death, already have purchased an existing structure which might require improvement or conversion or even that it might, as had at one time been suggested, expend money in improving the premises which it rented from the Jewish Institute. The association was to have the legacy to spend in this way for the benefit of its members.

"I have already said that, in my judgment, no question of perpetuity arises here, **3–250** and accordingly the case appears to me to be one of the specification of a particular purpose for the benefit of ascertained beneficiaries, the members of the association for the time being. There is an additional factor. This is a case in which, under the constitution of the association, the members could, by the appropriate majority, alter their constitution so as to provide, if they wished, for the division of the association's assets among themselves. This has, I think, a significance. I have considered whether anything turns in this case on the testator's direction that the legacy shall be used 'solely' for one or other of the specified purposes. Counsel for the association has referred me to a number of cases where legacies have been bequeathed for particular purposes and in which the beneficiaries have been held entitled to override the purpose, even though expressed in mandatory terms.

"Perhaps the most striking in the present context is the case of *Re Bowes*,[21] where **3–251** money was directed to be laid out in the planting of trees on a settled estate. That was a 'purpose' trust, but there were ascertainable beneficiaries, the owners for the time being of the estate; and North J. held that the persons entitled to the settled estate were entitled to have the money whether or not it was laid out as directed by the testator. He said:[22]

"The owners of the estate now say 'It is a very disadvantageous way of spending this money; the money is to be spent for our benefit, and that of no one else; it was not intended for any purpose other than our benefit and that of the estate. That is no reason why it should be thrown away by doing what is not for our benefit, instead of being given to us, who want to have the enjoyment of it.' I

---

[21] [1896] 1 Ch. 507.
[22] [1896] 1 Ch. 507 at 511.

think their contention is right. I think the fund is devoted to improving the estate, and improving the estate for the benefit of the persons who are absolutely entitled to it."

3–252   "I can see no reason why the same reasoning should not apply in the present case simply because the beneficiary is an unincorporated non-charitable association. I do not think the fact that the testator has directed the application 'solely' for the specified purpose adds any legal force to the direction. The beneficiaries, as members of the association for the time being, are the persons who could enforce the purpose and they must, as it seems to me, be entitled not to enforce it or, indeed, to vary it.

"Thus, it seems to me that whether one treats the gift as a 'purpose' trust or as an absolute gift with a superadded direction or, on the analogy of *Re Turkington*,[23] as a gift where the trustees and the beneficiaries are the same persons, all roads lead to the same conclusion.

"In my judgment, the gift is a valid gift."

REFORM?

Section 16 of the Ontario Perpetuities Act 1966

3–253   (1) A trust for a specific non-charitable purpose that creates no enforceable equitable interest in a specific person shall be construed as a power[24] to appoint the income or the capital, as the case may be, and, unless the trust is created for an illegal purpose or a purpose contrary to public policy, the trust is valid so long as, and to the extent that it is exercised either by the original trustee or his successor, within a period of twenty-one years, notwithstanding that the limitation creating the trust manifested any intention, either expressly or by implication, that the trust should or might continue for a period in excess of that period, but, in the case of such a trust that is expressed to be of perpetual duration, the court may declare the limitation to be void if the court is of opinion that by so doing the result would more closely approximate to the intention of the creator of the trust than the period of validity provided by this section.

3–254   (2) To the extent that the income or capital of a trust for a specific non-charitable purpose is not fully expended within a period of twenty-one years, or within any annual or other recurring period within which the limitation creating the trust provided for the expenditure of all or a specified portion of the income or the capital, the person or persons, or his or their successors, who would have been entitled to the property comprised in the trust if the trust had been invalid from the time of its creation, are entitled to such unexpended income or capital.

Bermuda Trusts (Special Provisions) Amendment Act 1998

Purpose trusts

3–255   **2.** For Part II of the Trusts (Special Provisions) Act 1989 (trusts for a purpose) there shall be substituted—

---

[23] [1937] 4 All E.R. 501.
[24] The courts are not prepared to do this artificially of their own volition: see *IRC v Broadway Cottages Trust* [1955] Ch. 20 at 36.

"Part II Purpose Trusts

Purpose trusts

12A—(1) A trust may be created for a non-charitable purpose or purposes **3–256** provided that the conditions set out in subsection (2) are satisfied; and in this Part such a trust is referred to as a "purpose trust".
(2) The conditions are that the purpose or purposes are—

(a) sufficiently certain to allow the trust to be carried out,
(b) lawful, and
(c) not contrary to public policy.

(3) A purpose trust may only be created in writing.
(4) The rule of law (known as the rule against excessive duration or the rule against perpetual trusts) which limits the time during which the capital of a trust may remain unexpendable to the perpetuity period under the rule against perpetuities shall not apply to a purpose trust.
(5) The rule against perpetuities (also known as the rule against remoteness of vesting) as modified by the Perpetuities and Accumulations Act 1989 shall apply to a purpose trust.

Enforcement and variation of purpose trust by the court

12B—(1) The Supreme Court may make such order as it considers expedient **3–257** for the enforcement of a purpose trust on the application of any of the following persons—

(a) any person appointed by or under the trust for the purposes of this subsection;
(b) the settlor, unless the trust instrument provides otherwise;
(c) a trustee of the trust;
(d) any other person whom the court considers has sufficient interest in the enforcement of the trust;

and where the Attorney-General satisfies the court that there is no such person who is able and willing to make an application under this subsection, the Attorney-General may make an application for enforcement of the trust.
(2) On an application in relation to a purpose trust by any of the following persons—

(a) any person appointed by or under the trust for the purposes of this subsection;
(b) the settlor, unless the trust instrument provides otherwise;
(c) a trustee of the trust,

the court may if it thinks fit approve a scheme to vary any of the purposes of the trust, or to enlarge or otherwise vary any of the powers of the trustees of the trust.
(3) Where any costs are incurred in connection with any application under this section, the Supreme Court may make such order as it considers just as to payment of those costs (including payment out of the property of the trust).

QUESTIONS

3–258   **1.** A testator who died a month ago by his will made the following bequests:

  (i) £10,000 to Alan and at his death the remaining part of what is left that he does not want for his own use to be divided equally between Xerxes and Yorick;

 (ii) £50,000 to my trustees Tom and Tim to distribute amongst such of the inhabitants of Cambridge as they shall in their unfettered discretion think fit;

(iii) £100,000 to my said trustees to distribute amongst Brian, Charles, David, Ellen, Oswald, Peter, Quentin and Roger and such of my other business associates and old friends as they shall see fit;

 (iv) £100,000 to my said trustees to use the income for 80 years from my death as the applicable perpetuity period or such other period as the law allows if less for providing holidays for employees and ex-employees their spouses and relatives of I.C.I. plc and of companies on whose boards of directors, directors of I.C.I. plc sit, and thereafter to use the income for the education of my relatives;

  (v) residue to my son Simon trusting that he will see to it that my old friends shall have the contents of my wine cellar; and in case of any doubts he shall have power to designate who are my business associates and old friends.

Consider the validity of these bequests, the testator having lived in Cambridge all his life.

3–259   **2.** "If the practical distinctions between discretionary trusts and fiduciary powers are so slight as to justify the decisions in *McPhail v Doulton* and *Schmidt v Rosewood Trust Ltd* it cannot be right to have one but not the other subject to the test of administrative workability; nor, in light of *McPhail v Doulton*, can *Re Barlow's W.T.* be justified." Discuss.

3. Simon Small, who was only 4 feet 11 inches tall, has just died. In his home-made will, he directed his executors:

   "(a) to pay £2,000 to each of my small relatives;

   (b) to distribute £8,000 as they see fit amongst such persons as they consider to be friends of mine;

   (c) to hold my residuary estate on trust to pay the income therefrom to my four daughters equally in their respective lifetimes but if a daughter marries a supporter of Watford Football Club the share of such daughter shall accrue to the other daughters, as shall also be the case on the death of a daughter, but on the death of my last surviving daughter they shall distribute the capital within one year amongst such persons connected with me who have been benefited by me in my lifetime as they shall see fit."

Advise on the validity of the above bequests.

4. By his will Tony left:

  (a) "£1,000,000 to my executor and trustee Eric to use the income to further the purposes of the UK Socialist Party so far as the law allows, such trust to be enforceable by the Leader from time to time of such Party";

  (b) "£50,000 to the Treasurer of the Cambridge University Law Society to deal with it as the Society wishes";

   (c) "£50,000 to the Treasurer of the Manchester Literary and Philosophical Society on trust to apply the income for the benefit of its members";

   (d) "£150,000 to be used at the discretion of the chairman and executive council of the Anthroposophical Society of Great Britain to further the teachings of Rudolph Steiner";

   (e) "the proceeds of sale of my residuary estate to the Treasurer of the Manchester Mavericks Darts Club to apply half the income for the purposes of the Club and half the income for providing educational assistance to the children of Club members."

Statute prevents the members of the "Lit. and Phil." Society from winding up the Society and dividing its assets between themselves, while this is possible in the case of the Darts Club only if membership falls below five, though the rules can be changed by a 90 per cent majority vote.

Advise on the validity of the above bequests.

5. How satisfactory are the reforms enacted in sections 12A and 12B of the **3–260** Bermudan Trusts (Special Provisions) Act 1989 (as substituted by the Trusts Special Provisions Amendment Act 1998) when under the old law enforcement was possible only where there was an expressly appointed enforcer? Where is the beneficial equitable ownership if a settlor transfers £500,000 and all the shares in Wonder Co. Ltd to trustees to the intent that he be forthwith divested of all interest in the assets which are to be used exclusively for the purpose of developing Wonder Co. Ltd? How does the position differ if the trustees are under a duty to accumulate the income for the full 100 year period allowed by Bermudan law and on the expiry thereof in their discretion to distribute the trust property between such of the settlor's relatives then alive as they see fit, but with the power at any earlier time to appoint capital or income to the settlor or any of his relatives as they may see fit or to any other person nominated in writing to them by the settlor?

6. Do you have any anxieties over a structure where a £20 million portfolio of shares, land and paintings is owned by a company, all of whose shares are held by a private trust company holding the shares on trust for the purpose of developing the value of the shares, and where the shares in the trust company are held by individuals on trust for the purpose of running the business of the trust company as trustee of only one trust?

Chapter 4

EXPRESS PRIVATE TRUSTS

Section 1. Completely and Incompletely Constituted Trusts[1]

4–01 There are two ways of completely constituting an *inter vivos* trust: (1) by the settlor (or a donee of a power of appointment conferred by the settlor) transferring the property intended to be the subject-matter of the trust to persons as trustees upon certain trusts declared by him or (2) by the settlor (or a donee of a power of appointment conferred by the settlor) declaring that he himself will hold certain of his property as trustee upon certain trusts.

In the case of testamentary trusts by virtue of the death there is a perfect gift of the legal beneficial ownership to the executor(s)[2] or administrator(s)[3] who are under equitable obligations,[4] once debts, expenses and taxes have been paid, to transfer the relevant property to legatees or devisees entitled in their own right or as trustees for others. So long as the three certainties are present[5] and debts expenses and taxes do not exhaust the relevant property, a testamentary trust will be constituted though the named trustee disclaims or is unable to take the property through incapacity or predeceasing the testator.[6] Whoever succeeds to the legal title takes subject to the trust, for equity will not allow a trust to fail for want of a trustee.[7]

I. Creation of Express Trusts by an Effectual Transfer upon Trust

4–02 A purported voluntary transfer of legal title is ineffectual both at law and in equity where something remains to be done by the transferor in order to render the transfer effectual: *Milroy v Lord*, below. When, however, the transferor has done everything which it is obligatory for him alone to do to render the transfer of legal title effectual, but something remains to be done by a third party, the transfer, though invalid at law, is nevertheless valid in equity. In *Pennington v Waine* below it is made clear that the settlor must either have put it out of her power to stop the transfer proceeding, having irrevocably put the transferee or his agent in a position to complete the gift (*e.g.* by registration of the transferee as owner of shares or land) or

---

[1] For the formalities required for the creation of trusts, see Chap.2.
[2] Administration of Estates Act 1925, ss.1, 25, 32.
[3] *ibid.* and s.9 as substituted by Law of Property Miscellaneous Provisions Act 1994, s.14.
[4] *Commissioner of Stamp Duties v Livingston* [1965] A.C. 694; *Marshall v Kerr* [1995] 1 A.C. 148.
[5] See Chap.3.
[6] *Sonley v Clock Makers' Company* (1780) 1 Bro.C.C. 81; *Re Smirthwaite's Trusts* (1871) L.R. 11 Eq. 251.
[7] *Re Armitage* [1972] Ch. 438 at 445 (where it is pointed out that very exceptionally the trust can fail if the personality of the named trustee is vital to the carrying out of the trust).

circumstances akin to equitable proprietary estoppel must make it unconscionable for her (or her personal representatives) to insist on ownership of
the relevant property.

MILROY v LORD

Court of Appeal in Chancery (1862) 4 De G.F. & J. 264; 31 L.J. Ch. 798; 7 L.T. 178;
    8 Jur. 806 (Turner and Knight-Bruce L.JJ.)

Thomas Medley executed what was treated as a voluntary deed[8] purporting to
assign 50 shares in the Louisiana Bank to Samuel Lord upon trust for the benefit of
the plaintiffs. The shares were transferable only by entry in the books of the bank;
but no such transfer was ever made. Samuel Lord held at the time a general power of
attorney authorising him to transfer Thomas Medley's shares, and Thomas Medley,
after the execution of the settlement, gave him a further power of attorney
authorising him to receive the dividends on the bank shares. Thomas Medley lived
three years after the execution of the deed, during which period the dividends were
received by Samuel Lord and remitted by him to the plaintiffs, sometimes directly
and sometimes through Thomas Medley. *There was thus a perfect gift of the
dividends.*

Shortly after the execution of the deed, the settlor had delivered to Samuel Lord
the certificates for the shares; and on the death of the settlor, Samuel Lord gave up
the certificates to the settlor's executor. The shares stood in the settlor's name
before and at the time of his death.

Stuart V.-C. held that a trust had been created for the plaintiffs but was reversed
upon an appeal by the executor.

TURNER L.J.: "Under the circumstances of this case, it would be difficult not to **4–03**
feel a strong disposition to give effect to this settlement to the fullest extent, and
certainly I have spared no pains to find the means of doing so, consistently with
what I apprehend to be the law of the court; but, after full and anxious
consideration, I find myself unable to do so. *I take the law of this court to be well
settled, that, in order to render a voluntary settlement valid and effectual, the settlor
must have done everything which, according to the nature of the property comprised in
the settlement, was necessary to be done in order to transfer the property and render the
settlement binding upon him. He may, of course, do this by actually transferring the
property to the persons for whom he intends to provide, and the provision will then be
effectual, and it will be equally effectual if he transfers the property to a trustee for the
purposes of the settlement, or declares that he himself holds it in trust for those
purposes;[9] and if the property be personal, the trust may, as I apprehend, be declared
either in writing or by parol; but, in order to render the settlement binding, one or other
of these modes must, as I understand the law of this court, be resorted to, for there is no
equity in this court to perfect an imperfect gift. The cases, I think, go further to this*

---

[8] The deed (apparently executed in Louisiana) was expressed to be made in consideration of one dollar. In
Mountford v Scott [1975] Ch. 258, the Court of Appeal treated £1 as valuable consideration enabling
specific performance to be ordered. If a transfer or grant of a legal title for consideration fails (*e.g.* a
purported legal lease is not granted by deed) equity will treat this as a contract to transfer or grant the
legal title properly, and if the contract is specifically enforceable (complying with the requisite formalities
in Law of Property Miscellaneous Provisions Act 1989, s.2) equity will treat it as having been carried out,
so that the transfer or grant is effective to create an equitable interest: *Walsh v. Lonsdale* (1882) 21
Ch.D.9.
[9] See section 1(II). The italicised passage has been much quoted and applied.

extent: that if the settlement is intended to be effectuated by one of the modes to which I have referred, the court will not give effect to it by applying another of those modes. If it is intended to take effect by transfer, the court will not hold the intended transfer to operate as a declaration of trust,[10] *for then every imperfect instrument would be made effectual by being converted into a perfect trust.* These are the principles by which, as I conceive, this case must be tried.

4–04   "Applying, then, these principles to the case, there is not here any transfer either of the one class of shares or of the other[11] to the objects of the settlement, and the question therefore must be whether a valid and effectual trust in favour of those objects was created in the defendant Samuel Lord or in the settlor himself as to all or any of these shares. Now it is plain that it was not the purpose of this settlement, or the intention of the settlor, to constitute himself a trustee of the bank shares. The intention was that the trust should be vested in the defendant Samuel Lord, and I think therefore that we should not be justified in holding that by the settlement, or by any parol declaration made by the settlor, he himself became a trustee of these shares for the purposes of the settlement. By doing so we should be converting the settlement or the parol declaration to a purpose wholly different from that which was intended to be effected by it and, as I have said, creating a perfect trust out of an imperfect transaction. . . .

4–05   "The more difficult question is whether the defendant Samuel Lord did not become a trustee of these shares. Upon this question I have felt considerable doubt; but in the result, I have come to the conclusion that no perfect trust was ever created in him. The shares, it is clear, were never legally vested in him; and the only ground on which he can be held to have become a trustee of them is that he held a power of attorney under which he might have transferred them into his own name; but he held that power of attorney as the agent of the settlor; and if he had been sued by the plaintiffs as trustee of the settlement for an account under the trust, and to compel him to transfer the shares into his own name as trustee, I think he might well have said: 'These shares are not vested in me; I have no power over them except as the agent of the settlor, and without his express directions I cannot be justified in making the proposed transfer, in converting an intended into an actual settlement.' A court of equity could not, I think, decree the agent of the settlor to make the transfer, unless it could decree the settlor himself to do so, and it is plain that no such decree could have been made against the settlor. In my opinion, therefore, this decree cannot be maintained as to the fifty Louisiana Bank shares . . ."

PENNINGTON v WAINE

Court of Appeal (Schiemann, Clarke and Arden L.JJ.) [2002] EWCA Civ. 227 [2002] 1 W.L.R. 2075; [2002] 4 All E.R. 215.

4–06   Ada owned 1,500 out of 2,000 shares in C Ltd which had custody of her share certificate. She told her nephew Harold, who was company secretary, that she was giving him 400 shares and wanted him to become a director. She instructed a partner, P, in the company's auditors' firm to prepare a transfer form, which she executed and returned to P, who put it in the firm's company's file, not Ada's file, in his office. P then told Harold of Ada's gift, saying Harold need take no further

---

[10] See section 1(III).
[11] A similar question arose in the case with reference to a second set of shares.

action, and asked Harold to sign the necessary form of consent to act as director now that he had qualifying shares. Harold signed the form and Ada as director countersigned it. Ada then made a will bequeathing 620 shares to Harold so that after her death he would have 1,020 of the 2,000 shares. A month later she died.

Judge Howarth held there had been a valid gift of the 400 shares.

ARDEN L.J. (gave the following reserved judgment with which Schiemann L.J. simply concurred) **4–07**

"[50] Counsel have taken the court through the authorities in detail and it will thus be unnecessary for me to cite from the authorities at length. To reduce confusion, I will refer to the decision of Jenkins J in *Re Rose* [1949] Ch. 78 as *Re Rose, Midland Bank v Rose* and to the decision of this court in the (unconnected) case of *Re Rose* [1952] Ch 449 as *Re Rose, Rose v IRC*. **4–08**

[51] The legal title to a share may today be conveyed by the execution and registration of an instrument of transfer (section 182(1) of the Companies Act 1985). However, the equitable interest in a share may pass under a contract of sale even if the contract is not completed by registration (*Hawks v McArthur* [1951] 1 All E.R. 22). In addition, a share may also be the subject of a valid equitable assignment: see for example *Re Rose, Rose v IRC*. **4–09**

[52] This appeal raises the question of what is necessary for the purposes of a valid equitable assignment of shares by way of gift. If the transaction had been for value, a contract to assign the share would have been sufficient: neither the execution nor the delivery of an instrument of transfer would have been required. However, where the transaction was purely voluntary, the principle that equity will not assist a volunteer must be applied and respected. This principle is to be found in *Milroy v Lord* and other cases . . . Accordingly the gift must be perfected, or "completely constituted". **4–10**

[53] The principle that equity will not assist a volunteer has been lucidly explained in Maitland's *Lectures on Equity* (1932) at page 73: **4–11**

"I have a son called Thomas. I write a letter to him saying 'I give you my Blackacre estate, my leasehold house in the High Street, the sum of £1000 Consols standing in my name, the wine in my cellar.' This is ineffectual—I have given nothing—a letter will not convey freehold or leasehold land, it will not transfer Government stock, it will not pass the ownership in goods. Even if, instead of writing a letter, I had executed a deed of covenant—saying not I do convey Blackacre, I do assign the leasehold house and the wine, but I covenant to convey and assign—even this would not have been a perfect gift. It would be an imperfect gift, and being an imperfect gift the Court will not regard it as a declaration of trust. I have made quite clear that I do not intend to make myself a trustee, I meant to give. The two intentions are very different—the giver means to get rid of his rights, the man who is intending to make himself a trustee intends to retain his rights but to come under an onerous obligation. The latter intention is far rarer than the former. Men often mean to give things to their kinsfolk, they do not often mean to constitute themselves trustees. An imperfect gift is no declaration of trust. This is well illustrated by the cases of *Richards v Delbridge* (1874) L.R. 18 Eq. 11 and *Heartley v Nicholson* (1875) L.R. 19 Eq. 233."

[54] Thus explained, the principle that equity will not assist a volunteer at first sight looks like a hard-edged rule of law not permitting much argument or exception. Historically the emergence of the principle may have been due to the **4–12**

need for equity to follow the law rather than an intuitive development of equity. The principle against imperfectly constituted gifts led to harsh and seemingly paradoxical results. Before long, equity had tempered the wind to the shorn lamb (*i.e.* the donee). It did so on more than one occasion and in more than one way.

4–13   [55] Firstly it was held that an incompletely constituted gift could be upheld if the gift had been completed to such an extent that the donee could enforce his right to the shares as against third parties without forcing the donor to take any further step. Accordingly, if a share transfer has been executed by the donor and duly presented to the company for registration, the donee would be entitled, if necessary, to apply to the court for an order for rectification of the share register under section 359 of the Companies Act 1985. Such an order would not, of course, be granted if for example the directors had a discretion to refuse to register the transfer and had timeously passed a valid resolution to decline to register the transfer (see *Buckley on the Companies Acts* 15 ed (2000) paragraph [359.277]).

4–14   [56] That exception was extended in *Re Rose, Rose v IRC* and other cases by holding that for this exception to apply it was not necessary that the donor should have done all that it was necessary to be done to complete the gift, short of registration of the transfer. On the contrary it was sufficient if the donor had done all that it was necessary for him or her to do.

. . .

[Reference was then made to the exceptional circumstances in *T. Choithram International SA v Pagarani* [2001] 1 W.L.R. 1]

4–15   [60] . . . In that case the donor signed the trust deed setting up the foundation and then simply made an oral declaration of gift of all his wealth to the foundation. The Privy Council held that the gift to "the foundation" could only properly be construed as a gift to the purposes declared by the trust deed and administered by the trustees. Lord Browne-Wilkinson giving the judgment of the Privy Council referred to the arguments that the courts below had accepted, namely that

> ". . . the court will not give a benevolent construction so as to treat ineffective words of outright gift as taking effect as if the donor had declared himself a trustee for the donee (see *Milroy v Lord*). So, it is said, in this case TCP used words of gift to the foundation (not words declaring himself a trustee): unless he transferred the shares and deposits so as to vest title in all the trustees, he had not done all that he could in order to effect the gift. It therefore fails. Further it is said that it is not possible to treat TCP's words of gift as a declaration of trust because they make no reference to trusts. Therefore the case does not fall within either of the possible methods by which a complete gift can be made and the gift fails."

Lord Browne-Wilkinson disagreed with this conclusion:

> "*Although equity will not aid a volunteer, it will not strive officiously to defeat a gift.* This case falls between the two common-form situations mentioned above. Although the words used by TCP [the donor] are those normally appropriate to an outright gift—'I give to X'—in the present context there is no breach of the principle in *Milroy v Lord* if the words of TCP's gift (ie to the foundation) are given their only possible meaning in this context. The foundation has no legal existence apart from the trust declared by the foundation trust deed. Therefore the words 'I give to the foundation' can only mean 'I give to the trustees of the

foundation trust deed to be held by them on the trusts of the foundation trust deed'. Although the words are apparently words of outright gift they are essentially words of gift on trust.

But, it is said, TCP vested the properties not in *all* the trustees of the foundation but only in one, ie TCP. Since equity will not aid a volunteer, how can a court order be obtained vesting the gifted property in the whole body of trustees on the trusts of the foundation? . . . In their Lordships' view there should be no question. TCP has, in the most solemn circumstances, declared that he is giving (and later that he has given) property to a trust which he himself has established and of which he has appointed himself to be a trustee. All this occurs at one composite transaction taking place on 17 February. There can in principle be no distinction between the case where the donor declares himself to be sole trustee for a donee or a purpose and the case where he declares himself to be one of the trustees for that donee or purpose. In both cases his conscience is affected and it would be unconscionable and contrary to the principles of equity to allow such a donor to resile from his gift." (See [2001] 1 WLR at 11–12).

[61] Accordingly the principle that, where a gift is imperfectly constituted, the **4–16** court will not hold it to operate as a declaration of trust, does not prevent the court from construing it to be a trust if that interpretation is permissible as a matter of construction, which may be a benevolent construction. The same must apply to words of gift. An equity to perfect a gift would not be invoked by giving a benevolent construction to words of gift or, it follows, words which the donor used to communicate or give effect to his gift.

[62] The cases to which Counsel have referred us do not reveal any, or any **4–17** consistent single policy consideration behind the rule that the court will not perfect an imperfect gift. The objectives of the rule obviously include ensuring that donors do not by acting voluntarily act unwisely in a way that they may subsequently regret. This objective is furthered by permitting donors to change their minds at any time before it becomes completely constituted. This is a paternalistic objective, which can outweigh the respect to be given to the donor's original intention as gifts are often held by the courts to be incompletely constituted despite the clearest intention of the donor to make the gift. Another valid objective would be to safeguard the position of the donor: suppose, for instance, that (contrary to the fact) it had been discovered after Ada's death that her estate was insolvent, the court would be concerned to ensure that the gift did not defeat the rights of creditors. But, while this may well be a relevant consideration, for my own part I do not consider that this need concern the court to the exclusion of other considerations as in the event of insolvency there are other potent remedies available to creditors where insolvents have made gifts to defeat their claims. (see for example sections 339 and 423 of the Insolvency Act 1986). There must also be, in the interests of legal certainty, a clearly ascertainable point in time at which it can be said that the gift was completed, and this point in time must be arrived at on a principled basis.

[63] There are countervailing policy considerations which would militate in favour **4–18** of holding a gift to be completely constituted. These would include effectuating, rather than frustrating, the clear and continuing intention of the donor, and preventing the donor from acting in a manner which is unconscionable. As Mr McGhee points out, both these policy considerations are evident in *Choithram*. It does not seem to me that this consideration is inconsistent with what Jenkins LJ said in *Re McArdle* [1951] Ch 669. His point is that there is nothing unconscionable in simply (without more) changing your mind. That is also the point which Professor Worthington makes in the passage I have cited above.

4–19   [64] If one proceeds on the basis that a principle which animates the answer to the question whether an apparently incomplete gift is to be treated as completely constituted is that a donor will not be permitted to change his or her mind if it would be unconscionable, in the eyes of equity, vis a vis the donee to do so, what is the position here? There can be no comprehensive list of factors which makes it unconscionable for the donor to change his or her mind: it must depend on the court's evaluation of all the relevant considerations. What then are the relevant facts here? Ada made the gift of her own free will: there is no finding that she was not competent to do this. She not only told Harold about the gift and signed a form of transfer which she delivered to Mr Pennington for him to secure registration: her agent also told Harold that he need take no action. In addition Harold agreed to become a director of the Company without limit of time, which he could not do without shares being transferred to him. If Ada had changed her mind on (say) 10 November 1998, in my judgment the court could properly have concluded that it was too late for her to do this as by that date Harold signed the form 288A, the last of the events identified above, to occur.

4–20   [65] There is next the pure question of law: was it necessary for Ada deliver the form of transfer to Harold? I have referred above to the difference of view between Evershed MR and Jenkins LJ. In *Re Rose, Rose v IRC* the issue was whether the gift was perfected by 10 April 1943, by which date the donor had executed the declarations of gift and delivered the share transfers to reflect the gifts to the transferees. Argument was not therefore directed to the question whether a beneficial interest in the shares passed on the dates of the declarations of trust or on the date on which the share transfers were handed over. For my own part I do not consider that it was necessary to the conclusions of Evershed MR that the gift should have taken effect before the transfers were delivered to the transferees. Indeed for him so to hold would not in my view be consistent with the second sentence cited from the relevant part of his judgment (set out above) or with the fact that he went on to approve as a correct statement of the law the decision of Jenkins J in *Re Rose, Midland Bank v Rose* (where, the share transfers having been delivered to the donee, the gift was held to be perfect because there was nothing else the donor could do) or with the fact that Morris LJ agreed with both judgments. . . . The conclusion of Jenkins LJ was predicated on the basis that delivery of the transfer to the donee was necessary and had occurred. Likewise the decision of this court in *Mascall v Mascall* (1984) 50 P & CR 199 and of the Privy Council in *Pehrsson v von Greyerz* (16 June 1999, unreported), were predicated on the same basis. I have summarised those cases earlier in this judgment. Accordingly the ratio of *Re Rose, Rose v IRC* was as I read it that the gifts of shares in that case were completely constituted when the donor executed share transfers and delivered them to the transferees even though they were not registered in the register of members of the company until a later date.

4–21   [66] However, that conclusion as to the ratio in *Re Rose, Rose v IRC* does not mean that this appeal must be decided in the appellants' favour. Even if I am correct in my view that the Court of Appeal took the view in *Re Rose, Rose v IRC* that delivery of the share transfers was there required, it does not follow that delivery cannot in some circumstances be dispensed with. Here, there was a clear finding that Ada intended to make an immediate gift. Harold was informed of it. Moreover, I have already expressed the view that a stage was reached when it would have been unconscionable for Ada to recall the gift. It follows that it would also have been unconscionable for her personal representatives to refuse to hand over the share transfer to Harold after her death. In those circumstances, in my judgment, delivery of the share transfer before her death was unnecessary so far as perfection of the gift was concerned.

[67] It is not necessary to decide the case simply on that basis. After transfers were executed Mr Pennington wrote to Harold on Ada's ? informing him of the gift and stating that there was no action that he take. I would also decide this appeal in favour of the respondent on this basis. If I am wrong in the view that delivery of the share transfers to the company or the donee is required and is not dispensed with by reason of the fact that it would be unconscionable for Ada's personal representatives to refuse to hand the transfers over to Harold, the words used by Mr Pennington should be construed as meaning that Ada and, through her, Mr Pennington became agents for Harold for the purpose of submitting the share transfer to the Company. This is an application of the principle of benevolent construction to give effect to Ada's clear wishes. Only in that way could the result "This requires no action on your part" and an effective gift be achieved. Harold did not question this assurance and must be taken to have proceeded to act on the basis that it would be honoured.

[68] Accordingly in my judgment the judge was right in the conclusion that he reached.
. . ."

4–23

Clarke L.J. gave a separate judgment holding that mere execution of the signed share transfer form on its own amounted to a valid equitable assignment, but, if wrong on that, he agreed with Arden L.J.'s reasons.

Note

A gift of shares (not within the CREST system) is, therefore, valid in equity **4–24** if (1) the transferor has executed the form of transfer required by the company's articles[12] and (2) has done everything else (*e.g.* delivered the share certificate) which it is obligatory for *him* alone to do to make the transfer effective and binding upon him,[13] so that it is then out of his power to prevent the transferee (or the agent thereof) from proceeding to do what is necessary.[14] The gift is effective at law when registration of the transfer is made, and until this is done a transferor who complies with (1) and (2) above is a constructive trustee for the transferee.

---

[12] In *Milroy v Lord*, above the form used was a deed poll; in *Antrobus v Smith* (1805) 12 Ves. 39, unsealed writing, both of which were inappropriate forms according to the company's articles. Under Companies Act 1989, s.207 the Secretary of State for Trade and Industry has promulgated the Uncertificated Securities Regulations 2001 which have enabled securities to be evidenced and transferred without a written instrument. There is now a paperless computerised system (CREST) for public companies. Regulation 38(5) of the above Regulations disapplies Law of Property Act 1925 s.53(1)(c) for transfers of equitable interests in shares, the title to which is in another under the CREST system.

[13] *Corin v Patton* (1990) 169 C.L.R. 540. In *Re Fry* [1946] Ch. 312 although the American donor had sent the necessary forms to obtain Treasury exchange control consent no consent had been obtained before his death. If the gift was imperfect because such consent had not been obtained why was the gift in *Re Rose* not imperfect because the directors' consent to register the shares had not been obtained at the relevant time? Is it because the directors' consent is the ultimate consent and is a negative requirement in that transfers must automatically be registered within two months unless the directors' discretion to refuse is exercised within the two months: Companies Act 1985, s.183(5), *Re Swaledale Cleaners Ltd* [1968] 1 W.L.R. 1710?

[14] In very exceptional circumstances like those in *Pennington v Waine* [2002] 1 W.L.R. 2075 it will, however, be unconscionable for the settlor to claim he still has ownership of the relevant property, by analogy with equitable proprietary estoppel circumstances, the donee having taken on liabilities as director believing himself so qualified.

The identical principle applies to a gift of a debt or other legal chose in action. If, therefore, the donor makes an absolute written assignment of the debt,[15] the gift is good in equity, though it will not be valid at law until written notice is received by the debtor whether from the assignor or the assignee.[16] A voluntary oral assignment on the other hand would be ineffective both at law and in equity.[17]

4–25   In the case of a gift of an equitable interest statute[18] requires action only by the donor so that there is no scope for *Milroy v Lord*. If the donor has made a written assignment, whether of the whole or a part of the equitable interest, the gift is good. This was so in *Kekewich v Manning*,[19] where the donor made a voluntary assignment by deed of his equitable interest in a trust fund. A voluntary *promise* to assign an equitable interest is unenforceable even if in signed writing since it is not an assignment and the absence of consideration means the promisee is a volunteer whom equity will not assist.[20]

Legal estates in freehold or leasehold property must be transferred by deed or in the case of registered land by a transfer form which is subsequently registered. Delivery by the registered proprietor to the transferee of the executed transfer form and the land certificate will satisfy the *Re Rose* principle.[21] as clarified in *Pennington v Waine* above.

Personal chattels must be transferred by delivery or by deed of gift. It is noteworthy that money is not effectively given by the donor giving his cheque for the money[22] for a cheque is merely a revocable authority or mandate and can be stopped before clearance. A bill of exchange must be transferred by endorsement[23] and copyright by writing.[24]

4–26   As will be seen (at para.4–37), existing rights to have property now or in the future and whether or not such rights are conditional (*e.g.* on marrying or attaining 25 years) or defeasible (*e.g.* by exercise of a power of appointment) are capable of being gratuitously assigned: a *spes* or expectancy (*e.g.* a hope of receiving property if a power of appointment is exercised or a hope of inheriting property under T's will) is not property and so cannot be assigned,[25] although a person can enter into a contract for sale of a *spes*.

---

[15] As required by s.136 of the Law of Property Act 1925.
[16] *Holt v Heatherfield Trust* [1942] 2 K.B. 1; *Norman v F.C.T.* (1963) 109 C.L.R. 28.
[17] *Olsson v Dyson* (1969) 120 C.L.R. 365; *cf. Tibbits v George* (1836) 5 A. & E. 107.
[18] s.53(1)(c) of the Law of Property Act 1925.
[19] (1851) 1 De G.M. & G. 176; such an assignment may take the form of a written direction to the trustees to hold on trust for the third party; *Grey v I.R.C.*, above, at para.2–50.
[20] *Re McArdle* [1951] Ch. 669.
[21] *Re Ward* [1968] W.A.R. 33; *Scoones v Galvin* [1934] N.Z.L.R. 1004; *Brunker v Perpetual Trustee Co.* (1937) 57 C.L.R. 555; *Mascall v Mascall* (1984) 49 P. & C.R. 119.
[22] *Re Swinburne* [1926] Ch. 38; *Re Owen* [1949] W.N. 201; [1949] 1 All E.R. 901.
[23] Bills of Exchange Act 1882, s.31; Cheques Act 1957, ss.1, 2.
[24] Copyright Designs and Patents Act 1988, s.90(3).
[25] *Williams v Commissioners of Inland Revenue* [1965] N.Z.L.R. 395, below at para.4–92.

II. CREATION OF AN EXPRESS TRUST BY AN EFFECTUAL DECLARATION OF TRUST

In each case where a declaration of trust of the settlor as trustee is relied on **4–27** the court must be satisfied that the subject matter of the trust has been clearly identified or segregated from the settlor's other assets[26] and that a *present binding* declaration of trust has been made complying with the requisite formalities,[27] though the trust interest may be defeasible upon exercise of a power of appointment or a power of revocation.[28]

A declaration of trust, to be effectual, need not be literal. It is not necessary for an intending declarant to say: "I declare myself a trustee." What is necessary is some form of expression which in the circumstances shows that he intended to constitute himself trustee and another a beneficiary even if he did not know that the obligation he was creating amounted to a trust, see *Paul v Constance*, above, para.3–73. An illustration of this is *Choithram International S.A. v Pagarani*.[29] A month before he died of cancer, TCP organised an elaborate ceremony at his London bedside to establish a philanthropic Foundation in the form of a Jersey trust of which he was Settlor and one of the Trustees. He executed the trust deed in the presence of three (of the other six) trustees and of his accountant and the First Secretary of the Indian High Commission. They recollected him as orally making an immediate absolute gift to the Foundation of all his wealth in his shareholdings and credit balances with four British Virgin Island Companies. Indeed, the minutes of those companies' meetings later that day recorded that the directors (including TCP, who signed the minutes) acknowledged TCP's gift of such wealth to the Foundation and that the Trustees (who included TCP) of the Foundation were henceforth the holders of the shares and assets in the relevant companies. Before TCP died the gifted property was not vested in the other Trustees, so it was alleged the gift was an imperfect gift.

Lord Browne-Wilkinson for the Privy Council held in context that "the words 'I give to the Foundation' can only mean 'I give to the Trustees of the Foundation trust deed to be held by them on the trusts of the Foundation trust deed'. Although the words are apparently words of outright gift they are essentially words of gift on trust." In substance, it seems that TCP was regarded as having said: "As sole legal beneficial owner of the assets and as legal trustee of the Foundation I'm giving my beneficial interest on trust for the Foundation and so as trustee now holding such interest on the trusts of the Foundation deed".

What of the fact that he had not actually transferred the gifted assets to **4–28** all seven Trustees, including himself as one of the Trustees? As Lord Browne-Wilkinson stated, "what then is the position where the trust

---

[26] See above, paras 3–81 *et seq*. A declaration of trust of £100 (of the larger sum of money) in my bank account should be ineffective, though a trust of all (or half) the money currently in my bank account should be an effective trust of a chose in action.

[27] Neville J. in *Re Cozens* [1913] 2 Ch. 478 at 486; Romilly M.R. in *Grant v Grant* (1865) 34 Beav. 623 at 626.

[28] *Copp v Wood* [1962] 2 D.L.R. 224; *Beecher v Major* (1865) 2 Drew & Son 431 at 437; *Young v Sealey* [1949] Ch. 278 at 284, 294; *Choithram International S.A. v Pagarani* [2001] 2 All E.R. 492, 500. A transfer or declaration of trust of property is presumed irrevocable: *Newton v Askew* (1848) 11 Beav. 145, *Miller v Harrison* (1871) L.R. 5 Eq. 324.

[29] [2001] 2 All E.R. 492 at 501–502. See para.4–15 above.

property is vested in one of the body of Trustees *viz* TCP? TCP has, in the
most solemn circumstances, declared that he is giving (and later that he has
given) property to a trust which he himself has established and of which he
has appointed himself to be a Trustee. All this occurs in one composite
transaction taking place on February 17. There can in principle be no
distinction between the case where the donor declares himself to be sole
Trustee for a donee or a purpose and the case where he declares himself to
be one of the Trustees. In both cases his conscience is affected and it would
be unconscionable and contrary to the principles of equity to allow such a
donor to resile from his gift . . . in the absence of special factors,[30] where
one out of a larger body of trustees has the trust property vested in him he
is bound by the trust and must give effect to it by transferring the trust
property into the name of all the Trustees".

As it happened, the four companies had altered their share registers after
TCP's death so that legal title to the shares actually vested in the remaining
six Trustees. The Privy Council held that the administrators of TCP's
intestate estate could not claim the shares or the deposit balances with the
companies.

Neville J., in *Re Cozens*,[31] referred to a "present irrevocable[32] declaration
of trust." The distinction is apparently between these declarations: "I
declare a trust for X to be entitled on my death" and "I declare that on my
death I will declare a trust for X." The latter is a mere promise to create a
testamentary trust in the future, an example being *Bayley v Boulcott*.[33] The
former could operate as a declaration of trust in favour of the declarant for
life, remainder to X, an example being *Kelly v Walsh*.[34]

An interesting example of a declaration of trust occurred in *Re Ralli's
Will Trusts*.[35] H, the owner of a reversionary interest (after her mother's life
interest) under the will of her deceased father, covenanted with the trustees
of her marriage settlement to settle, as soon as circumstances would admit,
all her existing and after-acquired property (thinking particularly of the
future actual assets she would become entitled to on her mother's death)
upon certain trusts (which failed) and ultimately upon trusts for the benefit
of the children of H's sister who were volunteers. A declaration of trust
clause in the marriage settlement declared that all property comprised
within the terms of the covenant should be subject in equity to the trusts of
the settlement pending transfer to the trustees. H never assigned the
reversionary interest to the trustees before she died. Buckley J. held that
the reversionary interest being existing property of H at the time of her
declaration of trust there was a valid trust of the interest so that the actual
assets materialising on the death of H's mother years after H's death passed
(not under H's will or intestacy but) under her settlement to her sister's

---

[30] *e.g.* if the settlor intended no trust to arise until he had vested the intended trust property in the names of all the intended trustees.
[31] [1913] 2 Ch. 478 at 486.
[32] A valid trust may be revocable and so fully effective unless and until revoked: see cases in n.28 above.
[33] (1828) 4 Russ. 345.
[34] (1878) 1 L.R.Ir. 275; see also *Re Smith* (1890) 64 L.T. 13.
[35] [1964] Ch. 288 at 298, below at para.4–85.

children. It would appear that if her reversionary interest had only been acquired by her subsequently to her settlement so as to be after-acquired property then no trust of the interest would have arisen in favour of the volunteer nieces and nephews as declarations of trust in respect of after-acquired property are ineffective at law and in equity where volunteers are concerned.[36]

III. INEFFECTUAL TRANSFERS NOT SAVED BY BEING REGARDED AS EFFECTUAL DECLARATIONS

No matter how clearly there may have been an intention to create a **4–29** voluntary trust by transfer, if the intending transferor has used an ineffectual method of transfer, this will not be construed into a declaration of trust. *Milroy v Lord*, above, at para.4–03 and *Paul v Constance*, above, at para.3–73, show that the attempted out-and-out *transfer* to other persons as trustees is the clearest evidence that the donor did not intend to *retain* the property and himself be trustee thereof.

Exceptionally, in the case of shares within the *Re Rose* principle it seems that if the directors refuse to register the share transfer then the transferor remains indefinitely as constructive trustee of the shares for the transferee.[37] It would further seem that if the transferee lost the transfer form or it was destroyed in a fire then the equitable interest he had acquired should justify the court requiring the transferor to execute a fresh transfer.[38]

Where the transferee disclaims the intended trust as soon as he hears of it it has been held that the transfer is not void *ab initio* but is valid until disclaimer when the legal interest, now subject to the trust, revests in the settlor.[39]

IV. THE IMPORTANCE OF THE DISTINCTION BETWEEN COMPLETELY AND INCOMPLETELY CONSTITUTED TRUSTS

Position of volunteers

If a will creates trusts it is immaterial that the beneficiary is a volunteer **4–30** just as it is immaterial that a legatee is a volunteer: subject to payment of debts, expenses and liabilities the personal representatives must vest the subject-matter of the gift in the trustees or in the legatee.[40]

If an *inter vivos* trust is completely constituted, whether by a transfer to trustees upon trusts declared by the settlor or by the settlor himself

---

[36] *Williams v C.I.R.* [1965] N.Z.L.R. 395 at para.4–92.

[37] *Re Rose* [1952] Ch. 499 at 510; *Tett v Phoenix Property Investment Co.* [1984] BCLC 599 at 619, noted (1985) 48 M.L.R. 220; A. J. Oakley, *Constructive Trusts*, (3rd ed.), Chap.8.

[38] Zines, (1965) 38 Australian L.J. 344; Seddon (1974) 48 A.L.J. 13; Trustee Act 1925, s.51; *Mascall v Mascall* (1984) 49 P. & C.R. 119.

[39] *Jones v Jones* (1874) 31 L.T. 535; *Mallott v Wilson* [1903] 2 Ch. 494, *Harris v. Sharp* [2003] W.T.L.R. 1541 at 1549 *per* Fox L.J. Also see *Fletcher v Fletcher* (1844) 4 Hare 67 below at para.4–59.

[40] Until the personal representatives appropriate the assets, having decided recourse to them will not be necessary for payment of debts, etc., or having paid off all debts, etc., the legatees only have a chose in action and not a full equitable interest: see above, at para.1–127.

declaring trusts of certain of his property, then the beneficiaries under the trust can enforce it despite being volunteers.[41] "Once a trust relationship is established between trustee and beneficiary, the fact that a beneficiary has given no value is irrelevant."[42] If the trust has not been completely constituted then the "settlor" can only be treated as having promised to make a gift on trust and so if the "beneficiary" is only a volunteer, no consideration having been supplied for the promise, he cannot enforce the promise:[43] "equity will not assist a volunteer." However, if a beneficiary who is not a volunteer seeks to enforce the promise the court will enforce the promise so that the trust becomes completely constituted and then a volunteer beneficiary will be in a position to enforce the now completely constituted trust.[44]

4–31   A person is not a volunteer if he provided value or can bring himself within a marriage consideration: *Pullan v Koe*, para.4–52. A promise to create a trust made before and in consideration of marriage is regarded as having been made for value. If the trust is created after marriage and contains a true recital that it was made in pursuance of an ante-nuptial promise to create the trust it will be treated as having been made for value.[45] Within the scope of marriage consideration are the parties to the marriage, their children and remoter issue.[46] Old cases allowing children of a former marriage or a possible later remarriage or illegitimate children to be within the scope of marriage consideration and to enforce trust deed covenants to settle after-acquired property, can now only be supported on the basis that such children's interests were so closely interwoven with the interests of the children of the marriage that the latter could only benefit on terms allowing the former to benefit.[47]

4–32   Once a trust is completely constituted a settlor cannot "undo" it or revoke it on the basis that the beneficiaries are only volunteers[48]—unless he reserved a power to revoke at the time he created the trust. After all, if A makes a birthday or Christmas gift to B, A cannot recover the property if she subsequently falls out with B.

Covenants to settle or transfer property

If A covenants (*i.e.* promises in a deed) to pay £11,000 or transfer 1,000 I.C.I. ordinary shares or transfer his unique fifth dynasty Ming vase to B, a volunteer, then B has a chose in action enforceable at law against A, the deed's formalities supplying the consideration.[49] However, equity does not

---

[41] *Paul v Paul* (1882) 20 Ch.D. 742. If the trustees wrongfully refuse to sue they will be joined as co-defendants: *Parker-Tweedale v Dunbar Bank plc* [1991] Ch. 26; *Bradstock Trustee Services Ltd v Nabarro Nathanson* [1995] 1 W.L.R. 1405.

[42] Per Lord Browne-Wilkinson is *Choithram International S.A. v Pagarini* [2001] 2 All E.R. 492 at 501.

[43] *Re Plumptre's Marriage Settlement* [1910] 1 Ch. 609; *Re D'Angibau* (1880) 15 Ch.D. 228.

[44] *Davenport v Bishopp* (1843) 2 Y. & C.C.C. 451, affd. (1846) 1 Ph. 698.

[45] *Re Holland* [1902] 2 Ch. 360.

[46] *Att.-Gen. v Jacobs-Smith* [1895] 2 Q.B. 341; *Re Cook's S.T.* [1965] Ch. 902.

[47] *Mackie v Herbertson* (1884) 9 App.Cas. 303 at 337; *De Mestre v West* [1891] A.C. 264 at 270; *Rennell v. I.R.C.* [1962] Ch. 329, 341; *Re Cook's S.T.* [1965] Ch. 902 at 914.

[48] *Re Bowden* [1936] Ch. 71; *Re Adlard* [1954] Ch. 29.

[49] *Cannon v Hartley* [1949] Ch. 213, below at 4–66, seals being required for deeds until August 1990.

regard the deed's formalities as consideration and so treats B as a volunteer and "equity will not assist a volunteer." Thus B cannot obtain specific performance of the Ming vase covenant but will have to be satisfied with common law damages, as for the £11,000 covenant or the 1,000 I.C.I. shares covenant, specific performance never being available in such cases where money compensation is itself adequate.[50] Equity, however, will not frustrate a volunteer suing at law[51] and so B may recover as damages £11,000, or the money equivalent of the shares or the Ming vase.

Since B has a chose in action this is property that he himself as beneficial **4–33** owner can settle on trusts, whether declaring himself trustee of it or assigning it to trustees on trusts for C for life, remainder to D.

If A covenants with B to transfer £60,000 to B as trustee with express or implied intent that B shall hold the benefit of the covenant upon trust for C and D if they attain 21 years of age, then A has created a completely constituted trust of the benefit of the covenant held by B as trustee, so this may be enforced by C and D, though volunteers, just as trusts are ordinarily enforceable by volunteers: *Fletcher v Fletcher*,[52] para.4–59.

If A merely covenants with B to pay money or transfer property[53] to B on **4–34** trust for C and D if they attain 21 the question arises whether A intended to create a trust *of the covenant* for C and D (an immediate equitable gift of the covenant) or intended only to create a trust *of the subject-matter of the covenant* if or when transferred to B (a future equitable gift of such subject-matter). Though volunteers, C and D will be able to enforce their claims if there is a completely constituted trust of the benefit of the covenant,[54] but they will fail if A is treated as merely promising to make a gift to B of the property to which the covenant relates, for a trust will only arise when the property is effectively given to B.[55]

Originally, the courts were quite sympathetic to the claims of the likes of **4–35** C and D, just as originally they were quite ready to find an intention to create a trust in precatory words like "wish," "request," "in full confidence

---

[50] *Harnett v Yielding* (1805) 2 Sch. & Lef. 549 at 552; *Beswick v Beswick* [1968] A.C. 58.

[51] *Cannon v Hartley* [1949] Ch. 213, unless fraud, undue influence or oppressive unconscionable behaviour were involved: *Hart v O'Connor* [1985] 2 All E.R. 880 at 891–892, *per* Lord Brightman. To succeed at law the volunteer, if not a covenantee under a deed poll, will have to be a party to the *inter partes* deed as well as a covenantee, LPA 1925, s.56, covering only land: *Beswick v Beswick* (3:2 majority view) [1968] A.C. 58 at 76, 81, 87, 94, 105.

[52] (1844) 4 Hare 67 where the intention was not express but implied in rather special circumstances at a time when courts were more ready to find an intent to create a trust than they now are. Other examples are *Williamson v Codrington* (1750) 1 Ves.Sen. 511; *Cox v Barnard* (1850) 8 Hare 310; *Watson v Parker* (1843) 6 Beav. 283; *Dowling v Dowling* [1917] Victoria L.R. 208.

[53] M. W. Friend [1982] Conv. 280 distinguishes between covenants to settle (i) money; (ii) specific and presently existing property other than money and (iii) future or after-acquired property. For (i) a trust of the benefit of the covenant should be inferred simply because A has constituted himself the debtor of B in his capacity as trustee for C. For (ii) no debt is automatically created and B can only obtain nominal damages unless A intended to create a trust of the covenant. A covenant of type (iii) is incapable of being the subject-matter of a trust. His view on type (i) covenants is attractive but for other covenants full damages should always be available, and the covenant and damages relating thereto should be held on trust if A clearly intended such: see Feltham (1982) 98 L.Q.R. 17 and at paras 4–35 to 4–40.

[54] *Fletcher v Fletcher* (1844) 4 Hare 67; *Cox v Barnard* (1850) 8 Hare 310 at 312 at 313; *Milroy v Lord* (1862) 4 De G.F. & J. 264, 278, and *Re Cavendish-Browne* [1916] W.N. 341, indicate that a covenant for further assurance may assist the court to find an intent to create a trust of a covenant to transfer property or of the covenant for further assurance itself. After all, the benefit of the covenant for further assurance can hardly be held on a resulting trust for the settlor without making the covenant futile and meaningless: see further nn.58 and 84 and text thereto.

[55] *Re Plumptre's Marriage Settlement* [1910] 1 Ch. 609.

that," etc.[56] In the twentieth century the courts have become reluctant to find an intention to create a completely constituted trust of the benefit of a covenant.

This seems quite justifiable. Where in the context of a lengthy trust deed, typically a marriage settlement (wholly enforceable by the issue within the marriage consideration but not by the next-of-kin beneficiaries in default of issue so far as not completely constituted) there is a covenant by the settlor to transfer after-acquired property to the trustees, surely the settlor is only promising to make a gift of such property to the trustees, so that a completely constituted trust enforceable by next-of-kin volunteers will only arise upon the property being gifted to the trustees.[57] It would be most unusual for the settlor to intend to create a trust of the covenant forthwith enforceable by next-of-kin volunteers, so a clear express intention should be required for this, *e.g.* "to the intent that the benefit of this covenant shall be held by my trustees upon trust for."

If a deed merely contains one covenant, *e.g.* "A covenants with B to transfer £10,000 to him on C's twenty-fifth birthday to hold on trust for C if C attains twenty-five" then since A has constituted himself debtor of B in his capacity as trustee for C and the deed would otherwise be futile[58] it seems it should be treated as creating a trust of the covenant as if it read "A covenants with B to transfer £10,000 to him on C's twenty-fifth birthday to the intent that B shall hold the benefit of this covenant on trust for C if he attains twenty-five." This will be the position, anyhow, under the Contracts (Rights of Third Parties) Act 1999 if the covenant was created after May 10, 2000.

4–36   It has been suggested[59] that since four[60] of the cases where there was held to be no trust of the benefit of the covenant concerned covenants to settle after-acquired property or analogous covenants, such covenants are never capable of being the subject-matter of a trust just as a *spes* or future property cannot be the subject of a trust or of an assignment. While one can *contract* to transfer not-yet-existing property one cannot *give* or transfer or declare a trust of not-yet-existing property. This calls for a digression which will show that future property is non-existent property so there is nothing for a trust to "bite" on, whilst a covenant relating to future property is an existing chose in action[61] which a trust can "bite" on. "A

---

[56] See above, at para.3–65.

[57] *Re Plumptre's M.S.* [1910] 1 Ch. 609; *Re Pryce* [1917] 1 Ch. 234. Really the settlor intends the covenant to be for the enforceable benefit of his spouse and issue and not the next-of-kin, while any actual transfer is to be for the benefit of all the beneficiaries. On this basis the position should not be affected by the Contracts (Rights of Third Parties) Act 1999: see s.1(2) thereof preventing a third party suing "if on a proper construction of the contract it appears that the parties did not intend the term to be enforceable by the third party". It appears from s.7(3) that promises in a deed, known as specialties, are treated as contracts under s.1.

[58] *cf. Fletcher v Fletcher* (1844) 6 Hare 67, below at para.4–59. *Ex hypothesi* if B does not hold the benefit of the covenant on trust for C, he must hold it on resulting trust for A, and so cannot sue A for damages for breach of covenant.

[59] W. A. Lee (1969) 85 L.Q.R. 313.

[60] *Re Plumptre's M.S.* [1910] 1 Ch. 609; *Re Pryce* [1917] 1 Ch. 234; *Re Kay's Settlement* [1939] Ch. 329; *Re Cook's S.T.* [1965] Ch. 902, below at para.4–77.

[61] LPA 1925, s.205(1)(xx) defines property as including any thing in action.

chose in action is no less a chose in action because it is not immediately recoverable by action" as Lord Oliver has made clear.[62]

Future property must be distinguished from existing vested or contingent **4–37** rights to obtain property at some future time.[63] While a contingent equitable interest in remainder under a trust (*e.g.* to A for life, remainder to B if he attains 30 and is alive on A's death, where B has an assignable, saleable interest) is existing property, examples of future property are the hope of inheriting upon the death of some live person or of receiving property under the exercise of a power of appointment or of acquiring book-debts arising in a business or of acquiring royalties arising on a book. At law an assignment of future property is void as an assignment of nothing,[64] though, if the assignee gave valuable consideration equity will treat the assignment as a contract to assign the property when received if received,[65] the assignment being wholly inoperative if no value was given.[66] Just as an assignment of future property to trustees is void at law and inoperative in equity unless for value, a declaration of trust by S that he holds future property on trust is inoperative unless for value: *Williams v C.I.R.*, para.4–92. If S covenants to assign future property, when received if received, then equity will not enforce this in favour of volunteers but only in favour of someone who provided value or is within a marriage consideration.[67] However, at common law a covenantee can obtain full damages under a deed poll or, if also a party, where the deed is *inter partes*. Thus, if S in a deed with B covenants to assign to B, a volunteer, any property S may acquire under S's father's will or intestacy B may obtain full damages at common law if S breaks the covenant: *Cannon v Hartley*, para.4–666.

In this case since B has the beneficial ownership of a presently existing **4–38** covenant it seems B may declare himself trustee of the covenant for C. It follows that S when entering into the after-acquired property covenant with B should be able intentionally to create a trust of the covenant for C, *e.g.* "I, S, hereby covenant to assign to B any property that I may inherit under my father's will or intestacy to the intent that B shall immediately hold the benefit of this covenant as trustee on trust for C." Since there is a completely constituted trust of the covenant it is then enforceable by C though a volunteer. In *Davenport v Bishopp*[68] Knight-Bruce V.-C. indicated there could be a completely constituted trust of a covenant to settle after-acquired property *viz.* relating to an indefinite amount at an indefinite future time. Further, in *Lloyd's v Harper*[69] the Court of Appeal held there was a trust of the benefit of a contractual promise to pay an uncertain amount on an uncertain future date, which is similar to a promise to assign

---

[62] *Kwok Chi Leung Karl v Commissioner of Estate Duty* [1988] 1 W.L.R. 1035 at 1040, applied in *Re Landau* [1997] 3 All E.R. 322 at 328.
[63] See *Re Earl of Midleton's W.T.* [1969] 1 Ch. 600 at 607.
[64] *Holroyd v Marshall* (1862) 10 H.L.Cas. 191 at 220; *Re Tilt* (1896) 74 L.T. 163.
[65] *ibid.*
[66] *Re Ellenborough* [1903] 1 Ch. 697.
[67] *ibid.*; *Re Lind* [1915] 2 Ch. 345; *Palette Shoes Pty. Ltd v Krohn* (1937) CLR 1 at 27; *Re Brooks's S.T.* [1939] Ch. 993, below at para.4–80.
[68] (1843) 2 Y. & C.C.C. 451 at 460.
[69] (1880) 16 Ch.D. 290.

an expectancy, and in *Royal Exchange Assurance v Hope*[70] Tomlin J. upheld a trust of a contractual promise to pay a sum arising only on a person's death before a certain date which might or might not occur. Thus, a covenant to settle after-acquired property or an analogous covenant can itself be the subject-matter of a completely constituted trust,[71] though where the covenant relates to future property there should be a rebuttable presumption that the settlor intended not to create a trust of the covenant (an immediate equitable gift) but only a trust of the property when acquired and transferred to trustees (a future equitable gift of future property).[72]

4–39   The elliptical judgment of Buckley J. in *Re Cook's S.T.*, at para.4–77 is best interpreted as based on the fact that there was no intention to create a trust of the covenant so as to be forthwith enforceable by the children volunteers, but only an intention to create a trust of the subject-matter of the covenant if or when it materialised and was transferred to the trustees for the children; so only then would the children have enforceable equitable rights, though, meanwhile, Sir Herbert would be able to enforce the covenant, having provided consideration therefor. It is considered that *if* the settlor had ended his covenant with the clause, "to the intent that the benefit of this covenant shall forthwith be held by my trustees upon the trusts hereof" Buckley J. surely would have upheld a trust of the covenant even though it related to a sum of money that might never arise. A good draftsman should, of course, expressly state the intention of the settlor.[73] Sir Herbert or, it seems,[74] his executors could have enforced his contractual rights and the proceeds of sale thereby placed in the trustees' hands would then be held on trust for the children volunteers. The trustees could not compel Sir Herbert or his executors to take such action nor could they join him or his executors as co-defendants in an attempt to take advantage of his contractual rights.[75]

Can the covenantee sue?

4–40   If A enters into a deed with B and gratuitously covenants with B to transfer existing or after-acquired property to B, but breaks the covenant, then equity will not assist B as a volunteer but it will not frustrate B from obtaining damages at common law: *Cannon v Hartley*, at para.4–66. Similarly, if A covenants with X that he will transfer £20,000 to B on trust for C then A is liable at law only to X if he fails to transfer the money.[76]

---

[70] [1928] Ch. 179.
[71] Further, see (1976) 92 L.Q.R. 427 (Meagher and Lehane) (though not dealing with the resulting trust difficulty where the covenantee sues the settlor); (1975) 91 L.Q.R. 236 (J. L. Barton); D. Wright (1996) 70 Austr. L.J. 911 also dealing with Australian cases where the judges have become readier to infer a trust from an intent to benefit X in circumstances where a trust is the appropriate vehicle to deliver that benefit: *Trident General Insurance Co. Ltd v McNiece Bros. Pty. Ltd* (1988) 165 C.L.R. 107, 121, 147, *Re Australian Elizabethan Theatre Trust* (1991) FCR 491, 503.
[72] See *Re Plumptre's M.S.* [1910] 1 Ch. 609.
[73] Just as where the settlor intends to create a trust of the benefit of a contract: see above, at para.4–41.
[74] *Beswick v Beswick* [1968] A.C. 58.
[75] Since Sir Herbert and his executors are under no obligation to the trustees or the children to exercise Sir Herbert's contractual rights, they cannot be forced against their will to become parties to an action concerning such rights.
[76] *Colyear v Lady Mulgrave* (1836) 2 Keen 81.

If A covenants with B to transfer property to B on trust for C to the **4–41** intent that B as trustee will hold the benefit of the covenant on trust for C then there is a completely constituted trust of the benefit of the covenant.[77] As with all trusts B as trustee is under a duty to get in the trust property and so enforce the covenant so as to benefit C. If B breaks his duty then C can sue A and join B as co-defendant.[78]

If A covenants with B to transfer property to B on trust for C in circumstances where there is no intention to create a trust of the covenant then A is treated as voluntarily promising to make a gift of the property referred to in the covenant, so that C will only have enforceable rights as a volunteer if A actually carries out his promise and transfers the property to B.[79]

However, cannot B sue A for damages for breach of the covenant with **4–42** B[80] and recover full damages[81] to be held on trust for C? The difficulty is that *ex hypothesi* B does not hold the covenant on trust for C so that he must either hold the covenant for his own benefit or by way of resulting trust for A and it is clear that he is not intended to hold the covenant beneficially. If, therefore, the covenant and the right to damages for breach of covenant are held on resulting trust for the settlor, A, then surely so must any damages for breach of covenant.[82] Since A is, under the resulting trust, an absolutely entitled beneficiary of full capacity he must under the *Saunders v Vautier* principle[83] be able to terminate such trust and prevent the trustees from launching upon such a pointless exercise as a suit against himself for damages.[84] A further difficulty is that if B could choose to sue and so constitute a trust of the damages this would contravene the principle in *Re Brook's S.T.*, at para.4–80, that only a settlor (or his authorised agent) can completely constitute his trust, just as only a donor or his agent can complete a gift. Moreover, for the matter to be at the whim of B whether he sues or not, not only puts B in an invidious position, it contravenes the principle that the acts, neglects or defaults of the trustees cannot be allowed to affect the rights of their beneficiaries.[85]

---

[77] *Fletcher v Fletcher*, at para.4–59.

[78] *Vandepitte v Preferred Accident Insurance Co.* [1933] A.C. 70 at 79; *Wills v Cooke* (1979) 76 Law Soc. Gaz. 706; *Parker-Tweedale v Dunbar Bank plc (No.1)* [1991] Ch. 26.

[79] *Re Plumptre's M.S.* [1910] 1 Ch. 609; *Re Pryce* [1917] 1 Ch. 234.

[80] Old cases tend to assume that B could be left to pursue his common law remedy without considering for whom such damages should be held: *Davenport v Bishopp* (1843) 2 Y. & C.C.C. 451 at 460; *Milroy v. Lord* (1862) 4 De G.F. & J. 264 at 278; *Re Flavell* (1883) 25 Ch.D. 89 at 99; *Re Plumptre's M.S.* [1910] 1 Ch. 609 (damages claim statute-barred).

[81] *Robertson v Wait* (1853) 8 Exch. 299; *Lamb v Vice* (1840) 6 M. & W. 862 (J. L. Barton) (1975) 91 L.Q.R. 236, 238–239 though M. W. Friend has pointed out that *Lamb v Vice* concerned a bond and the bond created a debt: [1982] Conv. 280, 283; surely, at law if a covenantor did not transfer property worth £X to the covenantee then the loss was £X, the position in equity of the beneficiaries being immaterial before the Judicature Act and the position has not changed since then: see D. Goddard [1988] Conv. 19 and *Re Cavendish-Browne's S.T.* [1916] W.N. 341, though this inadequately reported case may be an example of a completely constituted trust of a covenant for further assurance.

[82] *cf.* resulting trust of £500 in *Re Tilt* (1896) 74 L.T. 163.

[83] See at para.9–123.

[84] See *I.R.C. v Ingram* [1997] 4 All E.R. 395, 424 where Millett L.J. endorses *Hirachand Punamchand v Temple* [1911] 2 K.B. 330, where plaintiff money-lenders accepted a lesser sum from the defendant's father in satisfaction of a debt and then sued the defendant for the balance. Vaughan Williams L.J. (at 337) and Fletcher-Moulton L.J. (at 342) held any moneys recovered would be held on trust for the father: "a court of equity would have regarded the plaintiffs as disentitled to sue except as trustees for the father and would have restrained them from suing" (at 342).

[85] *Fletcher v Fletcher* (1844) 4 Hare 67 at 78; *Re Richerson* [1892] 1 Ch. 379.

4–43   In practice, if a trustee like B were considering suing A to benefit C he would seek to obtain the leave of the court for, otherwise, he would be at personal risk as to costs if he sued and could not prove his costs were properly incurred.[86] It is plain that the court will direct B that he must not sue for common law damages for breach of covenant where A did not create a completely constituted trust of the benefit of the covenant.[87] Equity thus goes beyond passively not assisting volunteers by positively intervening (which can only be justified on the grounds set out in the penultimate paragraph rather than the basis mouthed by the courts that "equity will not assist a volunteer"). This negative direction is so well-established that there is no need for trustees like B to bother the court: there is a complete defence if any beneficiary like C brings a breach of trust action against B for failing to sue the covenantor for damages.[88]

4–44   If a bold trustee like B did sue (*e.g.* because married to the beneficiary or fully indemnified as to costs by the beneficiary) it is submitted such action would fail on the basis that since the settlor had not created a trust of the voluntary covenant he must *ex hypothesi* have reserved to himself the right, if he chooses, at a later date to constitute a trust of the property referred to in his covenant, having lined up the trustee as his agent to receive the property, but who meanwhile is to hold the covenant on a resulting trust for the settlor, making any action against the settlor groundless.

Only the settlor (or his authorised agent) can constitute a trust

4–45   Like the donor of a gift, the settlor must be responsible for the trust property becoming duly vested in the trustees whether he or his duly authorised agent is directly responsible.[89] This is obvious where S has created the "S" settlement and a trustee, Y, whose daughter is life tenant, steals from S a painting (that S has talked about transferring to the trust but as to which S is still undecided) so that it will grace his daughter's lounge very nicely. Equity respects the common law rule that only a donor or his agent can make an effective gift so there is no trust of the painting. The position would be the same if S mistakenly left the painting behind at Y's house, having taken it there merely to show it to Y and his daughter.

4–46   If S in his 1998 voluntary settlement has covenanted to transfer to the trustees of his settlement after-acquired property appointed to S under a special power in the 1976 "T" trust or devolving upon S under T's will or intestacy, and property is appointed to S in 2005 or bequeathed to S on T's death in 2005, what happens if, fortuitously, the "S" trustees happen to be

---

[86] *Re Beddoe* [1893] 1 Ch. 547; *Re Yorke* [1911] 1 Ch. 370. Wherever trustees have reasonable doubts they may at the cost of the trust obtain directions from the court: Civil Procedure Rules, Pt 64.

[87] *Re Pryce* [1917] 1 Ch. 234 (though Eve J.'s reasoning is fallacious in that the Judicature Act fusion did not make defences available to a defendant in Chancery also available to a defendant at law: *Cannon v. Hartley* [1949] Ch. 213; (1960) 76 L.Q.R. 100 at 109, 111 (D. W. Elliot); Meagher Gummow & Lehane's *Equity: Doctrines & Remedies*, para.2–170 of 4th ed.); *Re Kay's Settlement* [1939] Ch. 329, discussed by Romer J., at para.4–00; *Re Cook's S.T.* [1965] Ch. 902.

[88] *Re Ralli's W.T.* [1964] Ch. 288 at 301–302.

[89] *Re Brooks's S.T.* [1939] 1 Ch. 993 (there could hardly be a clearer case for allowing a trustee to constitute the trust if the law were to allow this); *Re Adlard* [1954] Ch. 29; *Milroy v Lord,* above, at para.4–05, last paragraph of quoted judgment of Turner L.J.

trustees of the "T" trust or of T's will, not so unlikely if the "S" trustees are a trust corporation like Barclays Bank Trust Co? Can the trustees of the "T" trust or of T's will claim to hold the appointed or bequeathed property as trustees of the "S" settlement, so completely constituting a trust of such property in the "S" settlement, even though S is himself demanding the appointed or bequeathed property? No, S is entitled to the property free from any trusts since his voluntary obligation is unenforceable and he is in no way responsible for vesting title to the property in the "S" trustees: *Re Brooks' S.T.*, para.4–80.

However, if S in 2005 had authorised the trustees of the "T" trust or of **4–47** T's will to hold the appointed or bequeathed property *qua* trustees of the "S" settlement, the "S" settlement of such property would be completely constituted and so S would not be able to claim the property for himself.[90] Similarly, if S in his 1998 settlement had inserted a clause authorising the "S" trustees to receive property appointed or bequeathed to him and the "S" trustees had received such property from the trustees of the "T" trust or of T's will then the "S" settlement of such property would be completely constituted,[91] so long as the authority had not been revoked before such receipt, such authority being voluntary[92] and therefore unenforceable and revocable.[93]

In *Re Ralli's W.T.*, at para.4–85, Buckley J. *obiter* took a view incon- **4–48** sistent[94] with the *Re Brooks's S.T.* principle, that case not being cited to him. S voluntarily covenanted in her 1924 settlement to assign her interest in remainder under the "T" trust of 1899 to the "S" trustees as soon as circumstances might admit, but did not do so before she died in 1956. Her interest in remainder fell into possession in 1961 by which time it so happened that X, the sole surviving trustee of S's 1924 settlement (and one of the original trustees thereof) had been appointed by a third party to be a trustee of the 1899 "T" trust and was, in fact, sole surviving trustee of the "T" trust. Buckley J. considered that since X had the title to the covenanted

---

[90] *Re Adlard* [1954] Ch. 29. If S had been deliberately misled by the trustees telling him he was bound to authorise them he might have a claim if he acted promptly after finding out.

[91] *Re Bowden* [1936] Ch. 71, discussed in *Re Ralli's W.T.*, at para.4–85. By LPA s.53(1)(c) writing is required for the assignment of S's interest under the "T" trust or T's will to the trustees of S's settlement: see *Grey v I.R.C.* [1960] A.C. 1, as discussed at para.2–15. Where the same persons are trustees of both trusts it seems implicit in *Re Bowden* and *Re Adlard* [1954] Ch. 29, that there is an exception from the *Grey v I.R.C.* [1960] A.C. 1 principle discussed at para.2–15 where the S settlement with S's consent receives S's T property pursuant to an after-acquired property clause (whether general or specifically relating to property appointed under a special power or bequeathed under a will): it is then inequitable for S to claim the interest and so the Revenue will not be able to tax S as if the interest were still his.

[92] Or not otherwise binding as an irrevocable power of attorney or to give effect to a condition contained in a will: *Re Burton's Settlements* [1955] Ch. 82.

[93] *Re Bowden* [1936] Ch. 71, though *cf.* dicta in *Re Burton's Settlements* [1955] Ch. 82 at 104.

[94] Perhaps one can reconcile the cases on the basis that *Re Brooks' S.T.* concerned a live settlor who had changed his mind while in *Re Ralli's W.T.* the settlor had died happy without having changed her mind, having a continuing intention like that in *Re James* [1935] Ch. 449 if such extension of the *Strong v Bird* principle is justifiable despite the countering view in *Re Gonin* [1979] Ch. 16, at para.4–51 and in *Re Pagarini* [1998/99] 2 O.F.L.R. 1 (B.V.I. Court of Appeal). Nevertheless, the view of Buckley J. should be rejected as making life impossibly difficult for trust companies managing thousands of trusts: see J. Penner, *Law of Trusts*, 4th ed., paras 8–60 to 8–61.

property as sole[95] trustee of the 1899 "T" trust and was also trustee of S's 1924 settlement containing the covenant, this completely constituted S's voluntary settlement of the assets in question. However, S was in no way responsible for the assets becoming vested in X so that according to *Re Brooks's S.T.*, at para.4–80, no trust of the assets within the 1924 settlement should have arisen. The position might have been different if S *herself* had appointed X to be trustee of the "T" trust or if she had appointed X to be her executor, for she would then have been responsible for X as trustee of her settlement acquiring title to the covenanted property so impliedly authorising the position. To appreciate this it is necessary to consider the rule in *Strong v Bird*.

The rule in Strong v Bird

4–49   *Strong v Bird*[96] decides that in certain circumstances equity should allow the common law position to prevail where a deceased creditor had appointed his debtor as his executor, and the executor could not sue himself. The *common law* treated the appointment[97] as extinguishing or releasing the debt on the basis[98] "that a debt was no more than the right to sue for the money owing to the creditor and that a personal action was discharged when it was suspended by the voluntary act of the person entitled to bring it . . . [the true basis of the common law rule] lay in the significance attributed to the voluntary act [of appointing the executor] on the part of the testator. Once this is recognised the true character of the rule is perceived. It reflected the presumed intention of the party having the right to bring the action and was not absolute in its operation." Since administrators are not chosen by the testator the common law did not treat the court appointment of the administrator as the release of any debt due to the deceased from the administrator.[99] In *equity* the debtor (whether the deceased creditor's executor or administrator) had to account for the debt to the estate so that such moneys were available to pay off creditors of the estate or to be distributed amongst the estate beneficiaries.[1]

In *Strong v Bird* the court of equity decided that the common law should prevail, and thus the executor did not have to account for the debt, if the

---

[95] If there had been another trustee, Y, then Y would need to seek the directions of the court. Trustees hold property jointly and must act unanimously. Since Y is not a trustee-covenantee under the 1924 settlement does not Y hold the assets on trust for S's estate so that he will be liable for breach of trust if he co-operates with X to transfer the assets to X to be held on the trusts of the 1924 settlement? If this is so then X will need to co-operate with Y to transfer the assets to S's estate and X will not be liable to the 1924 settlement beneficiaries since he was never able himself to obtain the assets for the 1924 settlement.

[96] (1874) L.R. 18 Eq. 315, Waters's *Law of Trusts in Canada*, pp.166–174; Meagher Gummow and Lehane's *Equity: Doctrines & Remedies*, paras 2901–2908.

[97] Taking out the grant of probate or becoming an executor *de son tort* by intermeddling sufficed and, it seems, the appointment itself, though the executor died before taking out probate or intermeddling; *Wankford v Wankford* (1704) 1 Salk. 299; *Re Bourne* [1906] 1 Ch. 697; *Jenkins v Jenkins* [1928] 2 K.B. 501; *Bone v Stamp Duties Commissioner* (1974) 132 C.L.R. 38; *Re Applebee* [1891] 3 Ch. 422; *Williams on Wills* (15th ed.), p.717.

[98] Per Mason J. in *Bone v Stamp Duties Commissioner* (1974) 132 C.L.R. 38 at 53.

[99] *Wankford v Wankford* (1704) 1 Salk. 299; *Seagram v Knight* (1867) 2 Ch. App.628; *Re Gonin* [1977] 2 All E.R. 720 at 734. Now see Administration of Estates Act 1925, s.21A added by Limitation Amendment Act 1980, s.10.

[1] *Berry v Usher* (1805) 11 Ves. 87; *Jenkins v Jenkins* [1928] 2 K.B. 501.

testator had manifested an intent to forgive the debt in his lifetime and this intent had continued till death.

Where a donor intends to make an immediate gift of specific property **4–50** but fails to satisfy the legal formalities for vesting legal title in the intended donee and goes on to appoint the donee his executor and then dies, the appointment itself is no perfect gift at law of the specific property although it is in the case of a release of a debt due from an imperfectly released debtor. However, Neville J. in *Re Stewart*[2] extended *Strong v Bird*, which *negatively* left the situation as it was at law, since he *positively* treated a gift as effective though the law did not, so perfecting an imperfect gift made by the testator in his lifetime to his wife who was one of his appointed executors. He said:[3]

> "Where a testator has expressed the intention of making a gift of personal estate to one who upon his death becomes his executor, the intention continuing unchanged, the executor is entitled to hold the property for his own benefit. The reasoning is first that the vesting of the property in the executor at the testator's death completes the imperfect gift made in the lifetime and secondly that the intention of the testator to give the beneficial interest to the executor is sufficient to countervail the equity of beneficiaries under the will, the testator having vested the legal estate in the executor."

Re Stewart has been followed many times at first instance[4] and treated as **4–51** good law by the Court of Appeal.[5] In *Re James*[6] Farwell J. extended *Re Stewart* to perfect an imperfect gift of real property made by a donor to his housekeeper who, on the donor's intestacy, had herself appointed by the court one of two administratrices of the deceased donor's estate, thereby obtaining legal title to the house. This extension has been doubted by Walton J. in *Re Gonin*[7] and rejected by the British Virgin Islands' Court of Appeal in *Re Pagarini*:[8] after all, it is the voluntary act of the testator in appointing his debtor as his executor that extinguishes the debt at law, so that the fortuitous appointment by the court of an administrator who was a debtor of the intestate did not extinguish the debt, and so *Strong v Bird* would have been differently decided if the defendant had been an administrator and not an executor. However, the reasoning in the above-cited dicta of Neville J. suggests that, what, perhaps, should more aptly be known as the rule in *Re Stewart* is only concerned with the acquisition of legal title like the *tabula in naufragio* "plank in the shipwreck" doctrine.[9]

---

[2] [1908] 2 Ch. 251.
[3] *ibid.* at 254.
[4] *Re Comberback* (1929) 73 Sol. J. 403; *Re James* [1935] Ch. 449; *Re Nelson* (1967) 91 Sol. J. 533: see also *Re Ralli's W.T.* [1964] Ch. 288; *Re Gonin* [1979] Ch. 16.
[5] *Re Freeland* [1952] Ch. 110, counsel unreservedly accepting *Re Stewart*.
[6] [1935] Ch. 449.
[7] [1979] Ch. 16. The extension is acceptable to P. V. Baker (1977) 93 L.Q.R. 485 and G. Kodilinye [1982] Conv. 14.
[8] [1998/99] 2 O.F.L.R. 1.
[9] This doctrine confers priority upon later equitable interests whose owners somehow manage to obtain the legal estate: it was particularly significant before 1926 and still can have some effect: Megarry and Wade, *Law of Real Property* (6th ed.) 19–244 *McCarthy & Stone Ltd v Hodge* [1971] 1 W.L.R. 1547. *MacMillan v Bishopsgate Investment Management (No.3)* [1995] 3 All E.R. 747 at 770–773.

4–52   What is traditionally known as the rule in *Strong v Bird* has now developed into the principle that an imperfect *immediate*[10] gift of specific[11] existing[12] real or personal property[13] will be perfected if the intended donee is appointed the testator's executor or administrator alone or with others so long as the intention to make the gift continues unchanged till the testator's death.[14] The gift is perfected *vis-à-vis* those beneficially entitled to the deceased's estate but probably not *vis-à-vis* creditors since a common law extinguishment of a debt by appointment of the debtor as executor did not avail against creditors.[15]

Where the imperfect gift is to trustees and one (or more) of them is appointed the donor's executor this should perfect the trust, the equity of the beneficiaries under the intended trust of the property being sufficient to countervail the equity of the testamentary residuary beneficiaries.[16]

4–53   With voluntary covenants, where there is no completely constituted trust of such covenants, difficulties arise in applying the rule in *Strong v Bird* where one of the trustee-covenantees is appointed executor of the deceased settlor. First, the rule requires separate specific identifiable property[17] so as to be incapable of applying where S has voluntarily covenanted to pay £20,000 or transfer shares to the value of £20,000. Secondly, *ex hypothesi* S has neither transferred the property nor completely constituted a trust of the covenant itself and so does not have "a present intention to make an immediate gift"[18] of the subject-matter, if indeed the covenant does not expressly refer to transferring the subject-matter at a future date. The covenant is thus "an announcement of what a man intends to do in the future and is not intended by him as a gift in the present"[19] so as not to comply with the requirement of a present intention to make an immediate gift. Query whether this requirement is logically justifiable since once the pass has been sold by equity assisting a volunteer and perfecting an imperfect immediate gift it seems inconsistent for equity to refrain from assisting a volunteer under an imperfect gift of specific property to be made at a future time (other than the donor's death when testamentary formalities must be complied with[20]) once that time has arrived.[21] Thirdly, it

---

[10] *Re Innes* [1910] 1 Ch. 188; *Re Freeland* [1952] Ch. 110; *Re Gonin* [1979] Ch. 16; *Re Pink* [1912] 2 Ch. 528 at 536–539; *Simpson v Simpson* [1992] 1 F.L.R. 423. *Re Goff* (1914) 111 L.T. 34 is out of line since the donor only intended to forgive the debt if the donor predeceased the donee.

[11] *Re Innes* [1910] 1 Ch. 188 at 193.

[12] *Morton v Brighouse* [1927] 1 D.L.R. 1009.

[13] *Re James* [1935] Ch. 449.

[14] It seems contrary expressions before death may be ignored if the intent to make the imperfect gift is confirmed in the will: *Re Stoneham* [1919] 1 Ch. 149 at 158. For cases on contrary intention see *Re Freeland* [1952] Ch. 110; *Re Eiser's W.T.* [1937] 1 All E.R. 244; *Re Wale* [1956] 1 W.L.R. 1346; *Morton v. Brighouse* [1927] 1 D.L.R. 1009 (property imperfectly given to X subsequently specifically bequeathed to Y).

[15] *Bone v Stamp Duties Comr.* (1974) 132 C.L.R. 38.

[16] *Re Ralli's W.T.* [1964] Ch. 288.

[17] *Re Innes* [1910] 1 Ch. 188.

[18] *Re Freeland* [1952] Ch. 110 at 118, the Court of Appeal assuming this to be good law since counsel did not argue that *Re Innes* was wrong on this point.

[19] *Re Innes* [1910] 1 Ch. 188 at 193.

[20] *Re Pink* [1912] 2 Ch. 528 at 536, 538–539.

[21] In *Re Ralli's W.T.* [1964] Ch. 288, Buckley J. assumed a covenant to transfer property as soon as circumstances would admit could come within the rule in *Strong v Bird*. See also *Re Goff* (1914) 111 L.T. 34.

may be difficult to show that the settlor's intention continued unchanged till death.

If S makes an imperfect gift to trustees of his settlement and dies, his **4–54** intention to make the gift continuing unchanged till his death, and his executor, mistakenly believing himself legally bound to perfect the gift, does so, Astbury J. opined[22] this would be effective against the beneficiaries entitled under S's will. Can this really be so when an executor does not have as much freedom as the deceased to release debts and perfect gifts since the executor holds the estate under fiduciary obligations owed to the will beneficiaries and not as absolute owner like the deceased?[23] Would *Strong v Bird* not have been decided differently (and the debtor remain accountable in equity if the executor could not personally satisfy all creditors' claims) if the debtor had not been appointed executor but whoever was the executor had released the debt?

PULLAN v KOE

Chancery Division [1913] 1 Ch. 9; 82 L.J. Ch. 37.

A marriage settlement of 1859 contained a covenant by the husband and wife to **4–55** settle the wife's after-acquired property of the value of £100 or upwards.

In 1879 the wife received £285 and paid it into her husband's banking account, on which she had power to draw. Part of it was shortly after invested in two bearer bonds which remained at the bank till the husband's death in 1909 and were now in his executors' possession:

Held, that the moment the wife received the £285 it was specifically bound by the covenant[24] and was consequently subject in equity to a trust enforceable in favour of all persons within the marriage consideration, and therefore, the trustees were entitled to follow and claim the bonds as trust property, though their legal remedy on the covenant was statute-barred.

SWINFEN EADY J. (in a reserved judgment): "The defence of laches and acquiescence was given up by the defendants, but they insisted that, although they still retained the bonds, they were under no liability to the plaintiffs. They put their case in this way—that the plaintiff trustees could not follow the bonds into their hands, that the only liability of the husband was upon his covenant, and the claim of the trustees was for damages only, and that as this claim accrued in 1879 it was long since barred by the Statutes of Limitation. . . .

"[The husband] received the bonds, purchased with his wife's money, with full **4–56** notice of the trusts of the settlement, and knowing that the £285 and the bonds purchased with part of it were bound by the covenant. The trustees having traced the property into his hands are entitled to claim it from his executors.

---

[22] *Carter v Hungerford* [1917] 1 Ch. 260 at 273. Astbury J.'s *ratio* was based on the false assumption that the settler held the benefit of the covenant on trust for beneficiaries: but see *Re Pryce* [1917] 1 Ch. 234; *Re Kay's S.T.* [1939] Ch. 329.

[23] *Stamp Duties Comr. v Livingstone* [1965] A.C. 694; *Re Diplock* [1948] Ch. 465.

[24] Where consideration has been provided (so that equitable remedies are not precluded by the maxim "Equity will not assist a volunteer") and specific ascertained sums of money come into the hands of X, who is bound to hold them on particular trusts, "Equity looks on as done that which ought to be done", so treating the money as forthwith subject to the relevant trusts: *Pullan v Koe* [1913] 1 Ch. 9; *Re Lind* [1915] 2 Ch. 345; *Re Gillott's Settlements* [1934] Ch. 97; *Palette Shoes Pty. Ltd v Krohn* (1937) C.L.R. 1 at 27, However, if X covenants for value or contracts that X will hold, or transfer to trustees, £10,000 of his money on trust for certain beneficiaries, the lack of an ascertained segregated £10,000 ousts any equitable remedy if common law damages are inadequate: *Stone v Stone* (1869) 5 Ch.App. 74; *MacJordan Construction Ltd v Brookmount Erostin Ltd* [1992] B.C.L.C. 350.

"It was contended that the bonds never in fact became trust property, as both the wife and husband were only liable in damages for breach of covenant, and that the case was different from cases where property which has once admittedly become subject to the trusts of an instrument has been improperly dealt with, and is sought to be recovered. In my opinion as soon as the £285 was paid to the wife it became in equity bound by and subject to the trusts of the settlement. The trustees could have claimed that particular sum, could have obtained at once the appointment of a receiver of it, if they could have shown a case of jeopardy, and, if it had been invested and the investment could be traced, could have followed the money and claimed the investment.

4–57 "This point was dealt with by Jessel M.R. in *Smith v Lucas*,[25] where he said: 'What is the effect of such a covenant in equity? It has been said that the effect in equity of the covenant of the wife, as far as she is concerned, is that it does not affect her personally, but that it binds the property: that is to say, it binds the property under the doctrine of equity that that is to be considered as done which ought to be done. That is in the nature of specific performance of the contract no doubt. If therefore, this is a covenant to settle the future-acquired property of the wife, and nothing more is done by her, the covenant will bind the property.'

"Again in *Collyer v Isaacs*[26] Jessel M.R. said: 'A man can contract to assign property which is to come into existence in the future, and when it has come into existence, equity, treating as done that which ought to be done, fastens upon that property, and the contract to assign thus becomes a complete assignment. If a person contract for value, *e.g.* in this marriage settlement, to settle all such real estate as his father shall leave him by will, or purports actually to convey by the deed all such real estate, the effect is the same. It is a contract for value which will bind the property if the father leaves any property to his son.'

4–58 "Again the trustees are entitled to come into a Court of Equity to enforce a contract to create a trust, contained in a marriage settlement, for the benefit of the wife and the issue of the marriage, all of whom are within the marriage consideration. The husband covenanted that he and his heirs, executors, and administrators should, as soon as circumstances would admit, convey, assign, and surrender to the trustees the real or personal property to which his wife should become beneficially entitled. The trustees are entitled to have that covenant specifically enforced by a Court of Equity. In *Re D'Angibau*[27] and in *Re Plumptre's Marriage Settlement*[28] it was held that the Court would not interfere in favour of volunteers, not within the marriage consideration, but here the plaintiffs are the contracting parties and the object of the proceeding is to benefit the wife and issue of the marriage."

FLETCHER v FLETCHER

Vice-Chancellor (1844) 4 Hare 67; 14 L.J.Ch. 66; 8 Jur.(O.S.) 1040.

4–59 The bill was filed by Jacob, a natural son of the testator, Ellis Fletcher, demanding payment by the defendants, who were the testator's executors of the sum of £60,000 from the assets (and interest calculated from a date 12 months after the death of the testator). The claim was founded upon a voluntary deed executed by

---

[25] 18 Ch.D. 531 at 543.
[26] 19 Ch.D. 342 at 351.
[27] (1880) 15 Ch.D. 228 at 242.
[28] [1910] 1 Ch. 609 at 616.

the testator some years before his death and discovered for the first time some years after his death. The deed had been retained by the testator in his own possession and, so far as appeared, he had not communicated its contents either to the trustees or to the beneficiaries.

The deed was made on September 1, 1829, between Ellis Fletcher and five trustees therein named; it recited that Ellis Fletcher, being desirous of making provision for his two natural sons, John and Jacob, thereby covenanted for himself, his heirs, executors and administrators, with the said trustees, their heirs, executors, administrators and assigns, that if either or both of the sons should survive the testator, the latter's heirs, etc., would pay to the trustee, their heirs, etc., the sum of £60,000 within twelve months of the death of the testator to be held upon the following trusts: if both sons were alive at the testator's death and attained the age of twenty-one the trustees were to hold the money on trust for them both in equal shares as tenants in common; if only one son fulfilled these conditions the money was to be held on trust for him alone. In the event of either or both of the sons surviving the testator but neither attaining the age of twenty-one, the money was to fall back into residue.

Both sons survived the testator but John died without attaining twenty-one. Jacob **4–60** accordingly claimed that he had become solely entitled to the £60,000 and interest under the indenture of covenant.

The executors admitted assets. The surviving trustees said that they had not accepted or acted in the trusts of the indenture; and they declined to accept or act in such trusts.

At the close of the argument, Wigram V.-C. said: "It is not denied that, if the plaintiff in this case had brought an action in the name of the trustees, he might have recovered the money; and it is not suggested that, if the trustees had simply allowed their name to be used in the action, their conduct could have been impeached. There are two classes of cases, one of which is in favour of, and the other, if applicable, against, the plaintiff's claim. The question is to which of the two classes it belongs.

"In trying the equitable question I shall assume the validity of the instrument at **4–61** law. If there was any doubt of that it would be reasonable to allow the plaintiff to try the right by suing in the name of the surviving trustee. The first proposition relied upon against the claim in equity was that equity will not interfere in favour of a volunteer. That proposition, though true in many cases, has been too largely stated. A court of equity, for example, will not, in favour of a volunteer, enforce the performance of a contract *in specie*. That it will, however, sometimes act in favour of a volunteer is proved by the common case of a volunteer on a bond who may prove his bond against the assets. Again, where the relation of trustee and *cestui que trust* is constituted, as where property is transferred from the author of the trust into the name of a trustee, so that he has lost all power of disposition over it, and the transaction is complete as regards him, the trustee, having accepted the trust, cannot say he holds it, except for the purposes of the trust; and the court will enforce the trust at the suit of a volunteer. According to the authorities I cannot, I admit, do anything to perfect the liability of the author of the trust if it is not already perfect. The covenant, however, is already perfect. The covenantor is liable at law, and the court is not called upon to do any act to perfect it. One question made in argument has been whether there can be a trust of a covenant the benefit of which shall belong to a third party; but I cannot think there is any difficulty in that. Suppose, in the case of a personal covenant to pay a certain annual sum for the benefit of a third person, the trustee were to bring an action against the covenantor; would he be afterwards allowed to say he was not a trustee? If he cannot do so after once acknowledging the trust, then there is a case in which there is a trust of a covenant for another. In the case of *Clough v Lambert*[29] the question arose; the point does not appear to have been taken during the argument, but the Vice-Chancellor was of opinion that the covenant bound the party; that the *cestui que trust* was entitled to the benefit of it; and that the mere intervention of a trustee made no difference. The proposition, therefore, that in no case can there be a trust of a covenant is clearly too large, and the real question is whether the relation of trustee and *cestui que trust* is established in the present case.

4-62   WIGRAM V.-C.: "The objections made to the relief sought by the plaintiff under the covenant were three: first, that the covenant was voluntary; secondly, that it was executory; and, thirdly, that it was testamentary, and had not been proved as a will. For the purpose of considering these objections I shall first assume that the surviving trustee of the deed of September 1829 might recover upon the covenant at law; and upon that assumption the only questions will be, first, whether I shall assist the plaintiff in this suit so far as to allow him the use of the name of the surviving trustee, upon the latter being indemnified, a course which the trustee does not object to if the court shall direct it; and, secondly, whether I shall further facilitate the plaintiff's proceeding at law by ordering the production of the deed of covenant for the purposes of the trial.

4-63   "Now, with regard to the first objection, for the reasons which I mentioned at the close of the argument, I think the proposition insisted upon, that because the covenant was voluntary therefore the plaintiff could not recover in equity, was too broadly stated. I referred to the case of a volunteer by specialty claiming payment out of assets, and to the case of one claiming under a voluntary trust, where a fund has been transferred. The rule against relief to volunteers cannot, I conceive, in a case like that before me, be stated higher than this, that a court of equity will not, in favour of a volunteer, give to a deed any effect beyond what the law will give to it. But if the author of the deed has subjected himself to a liability at law, and the legal liability comes regularly to be enforced in equity, as in the cases before referred to, the observation that the claimant is a volunteer is of no value in favour of those who represent the author of the deed. If, therefore, the plaintiff himself were the covenantee,[30] so that he could bring the action in his own name, if follows, from what I have said, that in my opinion he might enforce payment out of the assets of the covenantor in this case. Then, does the interposition of the trustee of this covenant make any difference? I think it does not. Upon this part of the case I have asked myself the question, proposed by Vice-Chancellor Knight-Bruce in *Davenport v Bishopp*,[31] whether, if the surviving trustee chose to sue, there would be any equity on the part of the estate to restrain him from doing so,[32] or, which is the same question, in principle, whether in a case in which the author of the deed has conferred no discretion on the trustees (upon which supposition the estate is liable at law) the right of the plaintiff is to depend upon the caprice of the trustee, and to be kept in suspense until the Statute of Limitations might become a bar to an action by the trustee.

4-64   Or, in the case of new trustees being appointed (perhaps by the plaintiff himself, there being a power to appoint new trustees), supposing his own nominees to be willing to sue, the other trustees might refuse to sue. I think the answer to these and

---

[29] (1839) 10 Sim. 174.
[30] A case of this type is *Cannon v Hartley* [1949] Ch. 213.
[31] (1843) 2 Y. & C.C.C. 451.
[32] See (1960) 76 L.Q.R. 100 (Elliott).

like questions must be in the negative. The testator has bound himself absolutely. There is a debt created and existing. I give no assistance against the testator. I only deal with him as he has dealt by himself, and, if in such a case the trustee will not sue without the sanction of the court, I think it is right to allow the *cestui que trust* to sue for himself, in the name of the trustee, either at law, or in this court, as the case may require. The rights of the parties cannot depend upon mere accident and caprice. Having come to this conclusion upon abstract reasoning, it was satisfactory to me to find that this view of the case is not only consistent with, but is supported by, the cases of *Clough v Lambert*[33] and *Williamson v Codrington*.[34] If the case, therefore, depended simply upon the covenant being voluntary my opinion is that the plaintiff would be entitled to use the name of the trustee at law, or to recover the money in this court, if it were unnecessary to have the right decided at law, and, where the legal right is clear, to have the use of the deed, if that use is material.

"The second question is whether, taking the covenant to be executory, the title of **4–65** the plaintiff to relief is affected by that circumstance. The question is answered by what I have already said. Its being executory makes no difference, whether the party seeks to recover at law in the name of the trustee, or against the assets in this court.

"The third question is whether the plaintiff is precluded from relief in this court, on the ground suggested that this is a testamentary paper . . . There is, therefore, no ground for the argument that the interest is testamentary.

"The only other question arises from the circumstances of the instrument having been kept in the possession of the party—does that affect its legal validity? In the case of *Dillon v Coppin*[35] I had occasion to consider that subject, and I took pains to collect the cases upon it. The case of *Doe v Knight*[36] shows that, if an instrument is sealed and delivered, the retainer of it by the party in his possession does not prevent it from taking effect. No doubt the intention of the parties is often disappointed by holding them to be bound by deeds which they have kept back, but such unquestionably is the law . . .

"Declare that the deed of September 1, 1829, constitutes a debt at law, and decree payment of the principal and interest on the same to the plaintiff."

CANNON v HARTLEY

Chancery Division [1949] Ch. 213.

By a deed of separation made on January 23, 1941, between the defendant of the **4–66** first part, his wife of the second part and the plaintiff, their daughter, of the third part, the defendant covenanted, *inter alia*, "If and whenever during the lifetime of the wife or the daughter the husband shall become entitled . . . under the will or codicil . . . of either of his parents . . . to any money or property exceeding in net amount or value £1,000, he will forthwith at his own expense . . . settle one-half of such money or property upon trust for himself for life and for the wife for life after his death and subject thereto in trust for the daughter absolutely . . ." In 1944 the defendant became entitled, subject to a prior life interest therein of his mother, to a quarter share of a fund of approximately £50,000. The defendant's wife died in 1946. The defendant refused to execute a settlement in accordance with the said covenant. On a claim by the plaintiff for damages for breach of the covenant:

---

[33] (1839) 10 Sim. 174.
[34] (1750) 1 Ves.Sen. 511.
[35] (1839) 4 Myl. & Cr. 647 at 660.
[36] (1826) 5 B. & C. 671.

Held, that the plaintiff was entitled to damages.

4–67   Romer J.: "It has been argued on behalf of the defendant that the plaintiff, not having given any consideration for this covenant by her father, is not only unable to apply to a court of equity for the enforcement of the covenant by way of specific performance, but that she is also disqualified from suing at common law for damages for breach of the covenant.

"It is, of course, well established that in such a case as this a volunteer cannot come to a court of equity and ask for relief which is peculiar to the jurisdiction of equity, *viz*. Specific performance; but for my part I thought it was reasonably clear that, the document being under seal, the covenantee's claim for damages would be entertained, and that is still my belief . . .

"But the defendant relies upon some observations made by Eve J. in *Re Pryce*,[37] and on the subsequent decision of Simonds J. in *Re Kay's Settlement*.[38] I think the point of the observations of Eve J. in *Re Pryce* appear sufficiently in *Re Kay's Settlement*. The headnote of that case is: 'A voluntary settlement executed by a spinster contained a covenant in the usual form to settle any after-acquired property, with certain exceptions. The settlor afterwards married and had three children. Having become entitled under a will to a legacy and a share of residue which fell within the covenant, and a share in an appointed fund, she was asked by the trustees of the settlement to settle this property, but refused to do so: Held, on an application by the trustees for directions, that the children, being volunteers, had no right to enforce the covenant, and therefore the trustees ought to be directed not to take any proceedings to enforce the covenant, by action for damages for breach or otherwise.'

4–68   "Simonds J., after referring to the facts of the case, said at 338:

> 'It is in these circumstances that the trustees have issued this summons, making as parties to it, first, the settlor herself and, secondly, her infant children, who are beneficiaries under the settlement. But, be it observed, though beneficiaries, her children are, for the purpose of this settlement, to be regarded as volunteers, there being no marriage consideration, which would have entitled them to sue, though they are parties to this application. The trustees asked whether, in the event which has happened of the settlor having become entitled to certain property, they should take proceedings against her to compel performance of the covenant or to recover damages on her failure to implement it.

4–69
> 'I am bound to say that that does not seem to me to be a very happy form of proceeding, though perhaps it is difficult to see how else the trustees should act. It is to be observed that one of the persons made a party is the very person as to whom the trustees ask the question whether she should be sued. She, the settlor, has appeared by Mr. Evershed and has contended, as she was entitled to contend, that the only question before the court was whether the trustees ought to be directed to take such proceedings; that is to say, she contended that the only question before the court was precisely that question which Eve J. had to deal with in *Re Pryce*. She has said that the question before me is not primarily whether, if she were sued, such an action would succeed (as to which she might have a defence, I know not what), but whether, in the circumstances

---

[37] [1917] 1 Ch. 234.
[38] [1939] Ch. 329 at 338.

as they are stated to the court, the trustees ought to be directed to take proceedings against her.

'As to that, the argument before me has been, on behalf of the children of **4–70** the marriage, beneficiaries under the settlement, that, although it is conceded that the trustees could not successfully take proceedings for specific performance of the agreements contained in the settlement, yet they could successfully, and ought to be directed to, take proceedings at law to recover damages for the non-observance of the agreements contained in the settlement, first, the covenant for further assurance of the appointed share of the first-mentioned £20,000 and, secondly, the covenant with regard to the after-acquired property. In the circumstances I must say that I felt considerable sympathy for the argument which was put before me by Mr. Winterbotham on behalf of the children, that there was, at any rate, on the evidence before the court today, no reason why the trustees should not be directed to take proceedings to recover what damages might be recoverable at law for breach of the agreements entered into by the settlor in her settlement. But on a consideration of *Re Pryce* it seemed to me that so far as this court was concerned the matter was concluded and that I ought not to give any directions to the trustees to take the suggested proceedings.

'In *Re Pryce* the circumstances appear to me to have been in no wise **4–71** different from those which obtain in the case which I have to consider. In that case there was a marriage settlement made in 1887. It contained a covenant to settle the wife's after-acquired property. In 1904 there was a deed of gift under which certain interests in reversion belonging to the husband were assured by him absolutely to his wife. The husband was also entitled to a one-third share in certain sums appointed to him by the will of his father in exercise of a special power of appointment contained in a deed of family arrangements. The share of the £9,000 fell into possession in 1891 on the death of his father, and was paid to him, unknown to the trustees of his marriage settlement, and spent. The interests given by the husband to the wife and his share of the £4,700 came into possession in 1916 on the death of the husband's mother, and were outstanding in the trustees of his parents' settlement and of the deed of family arrangement respectively. The husband died in 1907, and there was no issue of the marriage. Subject to his widow's life interest in both funds, the ultimate residue of the wife's fund was held in trust for her statutory next-of-kin, and the husband's fund was held in trust for him absolutely. The widow was also tenant for life under her husband's will. The trustees of the marriage settlement in that case took out a summons 'to have it determined whether these interests and funds were caught by the provisions of the settlement, and, if so, whether they should take proceedings to enforce them.'

In those proceedings, apparently, the plaintiffs were the trustees of the **4–72** marriage settlement, and the only defendant appears to have been the widow of the settlor; that is to say, there were no other parties to the proceedings to whose beneficial interest it was to argue in favour of the enforceability and enforcement of the covenant, but the trustees no doubt argued in favour of their interests, as it was their duty to do. Eve J., in a considered judgment, held that although the interests to which I have referred were caught by the covenant of the wife and the agreement by the husband respectively, yet the trustees ought not to take any steps to recover any of them. In the case of the wife's fund he said that her next of kin were volunteers, who could neither maintain an action to enforce the covenant nor for damages for breach of it, and that the court would not give them by indirect means what they could not obtain by direct procedure; therefore he declined to direct the trustees to take proceedings either to have the covenant specifically enforced or to recover damages at law. Many of the cases which have been cited to me, though not

4–73   all of them apparently, were cited to him, and after deciding that no steps should be taken to enforce specific performance of the covenant he used these words: "The position of the wife's fund is somewhat different, in that her next of kin would be entitled to it on her death; but they are volunteers, and although the court would probably compel fulfilment of the contract to settle at the instance of any persons within the marriage consideration—see, *per* Cotton L.J. in *Re D'Angibau*[39] and in their favour will treat the outstanding property as subjected to an enforceable trust—*Pullan v Koe*[40] "volunteers have no right whatever to obtain specific performance of a mere covenant which has remained as a covenant and has never been performed": see, *per* James L.J. in *Re D'Angibau*. Nor could damages be awarded either in this court, or, I apprehend, at law,[41] where, since the Judicature Act, 1873, the same defences would be available to the defendant as would be raised in an action brought in this court for specific performance or damages."

4–74   "That is the exact point which has been urged on me with great insistence by Mr. Winterbotham. Whatever sympathy I might feel for his argument, I am not justified in departing in any way from this decision, which is now twenty-one years old. The learned judge went on: "In these circumstances, seeing that the next-of-kin could neither maintain an action to enforce the covenant nor for damages for breach of it, and that the settlement is not a declaration of trust constituting the relationship of trustee and cestui que trust between the defendant and the next of kin, in which case effect could be given to the trusts even in favour of volunteers, but is a mere voluntary contract to create a trust, ought the court now for the sole benefit of these volunteers to direct the trustees to take proceedings to enforce the defendant's covenant? I think it ought not; to do so would be to give the next of kin by indirect means relief they cannot obtain by any direct procedure, and would in effect be enforcing the settlement as against the defendant's legal right to payment and transfer from the trustees of the parents' marriage settlement." It is true that in those last words the learned judge does not specifically refer to an action for damages, but it is clear that he has in his mind directions both with regard to an action for specific performance and an action to recover damages at law— or, now, in this court. In those circumstances it appears to me that I must follow the learned judge's decision and I must direct the trustees not to take any steps either to compel performance of the covenant or to recover damages through her failure to implement it."

4–75   "Now it appears to me [this is Romer J. after the lengthy citation of Simonds J.] that neither in *Re Pryce*[42] nor in *Re Kay's Settlement*[43] is any authority for the proposition which has been submitted to me on behalf of the defendant. In neither case were the claimants parties to the settlement in question, nor were they within the consideration of the deed. When volunteers were referred to in *Re Pryce* it seems to me that what Eve J. intended to say was that they were not within the class

---

[39] (1880) 5 Ch.D. 228 at 242, 246.
[40] [1913] 1 Ch. 9.
[41] But see above at para.4–43, n.87.
[42] [1917] 1 Ch. 234.
[43] [1939] Ch. 329.

of non-parties, if I may use that expression, to whom Cotton L.J. recognised in *Re D'Angibau*[44] that the court would afford assistance. In the present case the plaintiff, although a volunteer, is not only a party to the deed of separation but is also a direct covenantee under the very covenant upon which she is suing. She does not require the assistance of the court to enforce the covenant for she has a legal right herself to enforce it. She is not asking for equitable relief but for damages at common law for breach of covenant.

"For my part, I am quite unable to regard in *Re Pryce*, which was a different case dealing with totally different circumstances, or anything which Eve J. said therein, as amounting to an authority negativing the plaintiff's right to sue in the present case. I think that what Eve J. was pointing out in *Re Pryce* was that the next of kin who were seeking to get an indirect benefit had no right to come to a court of equity because they were not parties to the deed and were not within the consideration of the deed and, similarly, they would have no right to proceed at common law by an action for damages, as the court of common law would not entertain a suit at the instance of volunteers who were not parties to the deed which was sought to be enforced, any more than the court of equity would entertain such a suit.

"I shall accordingly direct an inquiry as to the damages sustained by the plaintiff for breach by the defendant of the covenant with the plaintiff."

4–76

RE COOK'S S.T.

Chancery Division [1965] Ch. 902; [1965] 2 W.L.R. 179; [1964] 3 All E.R. 898.

Sir Herbert as life tenant and his son, Sir Francis, as remainderman agreed that certain settled property (including a Rembrandt) should become Sir Francis's absolutely subject to Sir Francis resettling some of the property (not the Rembrandt) and covenanting with the trustees of the resettlement that in case any of certain pictures (including the Rembrandt) should be sold during Sir Francis's lifetime the net proceeds of sale should be paid over to the trustees to be held by them on the resettlement trusts in favour of Sir Francis's children. A settlement was executed pursuant to this contract.

4–77

Sir Francis gave the Rembrandt to his wife who desired to sell it. The trustees, therefore, took out a summons as to whether or not upon any sale of the Rembrandt the trustees would be obliged to take steps to enforce the covenant.

Held, (1) Since Sir Francis's children were volunteers they could not enforce the covenant so that the trustees would be directed not to enforce the covenant on the principles in *Re Pryce*[45] and *Re Kay*[46] but (2) that in any case the covenant operated only upon a sale by Sir Francis and not by his wife.

As to (1):

BUCKLEY J.: ". . . Counsel appearing for Sir Francis submitted that as a matter of law the covenant . . . is not enforceable against him by the trustees of the settlement . . . [He] submits that the covenant was a voluntary and executory contract to make a settlement in a future event and was not a settlement of a covenant to pay a sum of money to the trustees. He further submits that, as regards the covenant, all the beneficiaries under the settlement are volunteers with the consequence that not only

4–78

---

[44] (1880) 15 Ch.D. 228.
[45] [1917] 1 Ch. 234.
[46] [1939] Ch. 329.

should the court not direct the trustees to take proceedings on the covenant but also that it should positively direct them not to take proceedings. He relies on *Re Pryce* and *Re Kay's Settlement*.

4–79   "Counsel for the second and third defendants have contended that, on the true view of the facts, there was an immediate settlement of the obligation created by the covenant, and not merely a covenant to settle something in the future. It was said, as counsel for the second defendant put it, that, by the agreement, Sir Herbert bought the rights arising under the covenant for the benefit of the cestuis que trust under the settlement and that, the covenant being made in favour of the trustees, these rights became assets of the trust. He relied on *Fletcher v Fletcher*;[47] *Williamson v Codrington*[48] and *Re Cavendish Browne's Settlement Trusts*.[49] I am not able to accept this argument. The covenant with which I am concerned did not, in my opinion, create a debt enforceable at law, that is to say, a property right, which, although to bear fruit only in the future and on a contingency, was capable of being made the subject of an immediate trust, as was held to be the case in *Fletcher v Fletcher*. Nor is this covenant associated with property which was the subject of an immediate trust, as in *Williamson v Codrington*. Nor did the covenant relate to property which then belonged to the covenantor, as in *Re Cavendish Browne's Settlement Trusts*. In contrast to all these cases, this covenant on its true construction is, in my opinion, an executory contract to settle a particular fund or particular funds of money which at the date of the covenant did not exist and which might never come into existence. It is analogous to a covenant to settle an expectation or to settle after-acquired property. The case, in my judgment, involves the law of contract, not the law of trusts . . .

"Accordingly, the second and third defendants are not in my judgment entitled to require the trustees to take proceedings to enforce the covenant, even if it is capable of being construed in a manner favourable to them."

RE BROOKS' SETTLEMENT TRUSTS

Chancery Division [1939] 1 Ch. 993.

4–80   By the terms of a marriage settlement the income of the settled fund was directed to be paid to the wife during her life and the fund was to be held in trust for such of her issue as she might by deed or will appoint; in default of any appointment the fund was to be held in trust for all her children who being sons should attain the age of twenty-one years or being daughters should attain that age or marry in equal shares. In 1929 one of her children. A.T., executed a voluntary settlement whereby he assigned to Lloyds Bank as trustees "all the part or share, parts or shares and other interest whether vested or contingent to which the settlor is now or may hereafter become entitled whether in default of appointment, or under any appointment hereafter to be made or on failure of any such appointment of and in the trust property" subject to the marriage settlement. By an appointment in pursuance of the power executed in 1939, his mother appointed him a sum of £3,517 and released her life interest. Thereupon Lloyds Bank Ltd, who had by then become trustees of the marriage settlement as well as the voluntary settlement took out a summons asking whether they should pay A.T. the £3,517.

[47] (1844) 4 Hare 67.
[48] (1750) 1 Ves.Sen. 511.
[49] (1916) 61 S.J. 27.

Held, that A.T. was entitled to require payment of the sum appointed, and could **4–81** not be compelled to permit the bank to retain the £3,517.

FARWELL J.: "When one looks at the voluntary settlement, at first sight the answer would seem to be quite clearly that the trustees' duty was to retain the sum of £3,517 as part of the funds which the son had voluntarily settled, and the language of the voluntary settlement would seem to leave no doubt on that score, because the settlor assigned to the bank 'all the part or share parts or shares and other interest whether vested or contingent to which the settlor is now or may hereafter become entitled whether in default of appointment or under any appointment hereafter to be made or on failure of any such appointment of and in the trust property which is now or may at any time hereafter become subject to the trusts of the wife's settlement.' One would say, looking at the language of the settlement, that it would be difficult to find words more apt to embrace in the voluntary settlement all the interests which the son had then or might thereafter have under the marriage settlement and that accordingly the answer should be that it is the duty of the trustees to retain this as part of the voluntary settlement fund. But, when one considers the legal position in this matter, a different aspect seems to appear. If the matter could be tested simply as one of construction, the answer would appear to be in favour of the trustees of the voluntary settlement; but the question is not one of construction only, and I have to consider whether the attempt to assign that which the son has now become entitled to by virtue of the exercise of the power is enforceable against him.

"The legal position in the case of a special power of appointment is not in any **4–82** doubt at all. Referring to *Farwell on Powers*, (3rd ed.), p.310, I find this statement of principle, which will be found in exactly the same language in earlier editions of the book, and therefore is not in any way the creation of the editor: 'The exercise of a power of appointment divests (either wholly or partially according to the terms of the appointment) the estates limited in default of appointment and creates a new estate, and that, too, whether the property be real or personal.' The effect of this is that in the case of a special power the property is vested in the persons who take in default of appointment, subject, of course, to any prior life interest, but liable to be divested at any time by a valid exercise of the power, and the effect of such an exercise of the power is to defeat wholly or *pro tanto* the interests which up to then were vested in the persons entitled in default of appointment and to create new estates in those persons in whose favour the appointment had been made. That being so, it is, in my judgment, impossible to say that until an appointment has been made in favour of this son the son had any interest under his mother's settlement other than an interest as one of the people entitled in default of appointment; he had an interest in that; but that interest was liable to be divested, and, if an appointment was made in favour of the son, then to that extent the persons entitled in default were defeated and he was given an interest in the funds which he had never had before and which came into being for the first time when the power was exercised. No doubt it is quite true to say that the appointment has to be read in to the marriage settlement, but, in my judgment, that is not sufficient ground for saying that at the time when this voluntary settlement was made the son had any interest at all in the fund other than his vested interest in default of appointment; for the rest, he had nothing more than a mere expectancy, the hope that at some date his mother might think fit to exercise the power of appointment in his favour, but, until she did so choose, he had nothing other than his interest in default of appointment to which he could point and say: 'That is a fund to which I shall become entitled in future or to which I am contingently entitled.' Apart from this he was not contingently entitled at all; he had no interest whatever in the fund until the appointment had been executed.

4–83   "If that be the true view, as I believe it to be, the result must be that, whatever the language of the settlement may be, the settlor under the voluntary settlement was purporting to assign to the trustees something to which he might in certain circumstances become entitled in the future, but to which he was not then entitled in any sense at all, and if that be so, then it is plain on the authorities that the son cannot be compelled to hand over or to permit the trustees to retain this sum and that he is himself entitled to call upon them to pay it over to him.

"There are two cases to which I have been referred. One of them is a decision of Buckley J. (as he then was) in a case of *In re Ellenborough*.[50] What Buckley J. said was this: 'The question is whether a volunteer can enforce a contract made by deed to dispose of an expectancy. It cannot be and is not disputed that if the deed had been for value the trustees could have enforced it. If value be given, it is immaterial what is the form of assurance by which the disposition is made, or whether the subject of the disposition is capable of being thereby disposed of or not. An assignment for value binds the conscience of the assignor. A Court of Equity as against him will compel him to do that which ex hypothesi he has not yet effectually done. Future property, possibilities, and expectancies are all assignable in equity for value: *Tailby v Official Receiver*.[51] But when the assurance is not for value, a Court of Equity will not assist a volunteer, the reason for that being, that, since it is merely a voluntary act and not an act for consideration at all, the conscience of the assignor is not affected so as in equity to prevent him from saying: "I am not going to hand over this property to which now for the first time I have become entitled." ' If that be the true view, it must follow that this particular interest, which for the first time came into being when the appointment was made, is not caught by the settlement.

4–84   "Notwithstanding the fact that the language of this voluntary settlement as a matter of construction is wide enough to comprise this interest, the principle of law which I have stated makes it impossible to enforce the settlement to that extent and prevents the settlor from being compelled by this Court to transfer or permit the trustees to retain this money as part of the funds subject thereto.

RE RALLI'S WILL TRUSTS

Chancery Division [1964] Ch. 288; [1963] 3 All E.R. 940.

4–85   From 1899 Helen was entitled to one-half of her father's residuary estate subject to her mother's life interest. The mother died in 1961 so Helen's reversionary interest then fell into possession. In 1924 Helen in her marriage settlement had covenanted to assign to the trustees thereof as soon as circumstances would admit all her existing and after-acquired property upon certain trusts for her children which failed (Helen dying a childless widow) and ultimately upon trusts for the benefit of the children of Helen's sister, Irene, who were volunteers. A subsequent clause in the marriage settlement was held on its proper construction to declare that all property comprised within the terms of the covenant should be subject in equity to the trusts of the settlement pending assignment to the trustees. Helen never assigned the reversionary interest before dying in 1956.

The plaintiff was one of the three original trustees of the 1924 marriage settlement and was sole surviving trustee thereof. It so happened that in 1946 he

---

[50] [1903] 1 Ch. 697 at 700.
[51] (1888) 13 App.Cas. 523.

had also become a trustee of Helen's father's will and was indeed sole surviving trustee. He claimed that Helen's reversion in half the residue was held on the trusts of the marriage settlement whilst the defendants, Helen's personal representatives, claimed her estate was entitled.

BUCKLEY J. held that the vested reversionary interest, being existing property of **4–86** Helen at the time she made what he construed as an independent declaration of trust pending assignment to the trustees of her marriage settlement, was held on the trusts of the marriage settlement. He then continued:

"If this view is right, this disposes of the case, but I think I should go on to state what would be my view, if I were mistaken in the view I have expressed. The investments representing the share of residue in question stand in the name of the plaintiff. This is because he is now the sole surviving trustee of the testator's will. Therefore, say the defendants, he holds these investments primarily on the trusts of the will, that is to say, in trust for them as part of Helen's estate. The plaintiff is, however, also the sole surviving covenantee under clause 7 of the settlement, as well as the sole surviving trustee of that settlement. This, however, affords him no answer, say the defendants, to their claim under the will unless the plaintiff, having transferred the property to them in pursuance of the trusts of the will, could compel them to return it in pursuance of their obligation under the covenant, and this, they say, he could not do. In support of this last contention they rely on *Re Plumptre's Marriage Settlement*,[52] *Re Pryce*,[53] and *Re Kay's Settlement*.[54]

"The plaintiff, on the other hand, contends that, as he already holds the **4–87** investments, no question of his having to enforce the covenant arises. The fund having come without impropriety into his hands is now, he says, impressed in his hands with the trusts on which he ought to hold it under the settlement; and because of the covenant it does not lie in the mouth of the defendants to say that he should hold it in trust for Helen's estate. He relies on *Re Bowden*[55] in which case a lady by a voluntary settlement purported to assign to trustees *inter alia* such property as she should become entitled to under the will of her father, who was still alive, and authorised the trustees to receive the property and give receipts for it. In due course her father died and the property to which the lady became entitled under his will was transferred to the trustees of the settlement. Many years later the lady claimed that the property belonged to her absolutely. Bennett, J. [held] that she was not entitled to the property.

"Counsel for the defendants says that *Re Bowden* and *Re Adlard's Settlement* **4–88** *Trust*[56] are distinguishable from the present case because in each of those cases the fund had reached the hands of the trustees of the relevant settlement and was held by them in that capacity, whereas in the present case the fund is, as he maintains, in the hands of the plaintiff in the capacity of trustee of the will and not in the capacity of trustee of the settlement. He says that *Re Burton's Settlements*,[57] the complicated facts of which I forbear to set out here, should be distinguished on the ground that, when the settlement there in question was made, the trustee of that settlement and the trustee of the settlement under which the settlor had expectations was the same, so that the settlor by her settlement gave directions to the trustee of the settlement under which she had expectations, who then already held the relevant fund.

---

[52] [1910] 1 Ch. 609.
[53] [1917] 1 Ch. 234.
[54] [1939] Ch. 329.
[55] [1936] Ch. 71.
[56] [1954] Ch. 29.
[57] [1955] Ch. 82.

4–89   "Counsel for the plaintiff says that the capacity in which the trustee has become possessed of the fund is irrelevant. Thus in *Strong v Bird*,[58] an imperfect gift was held to be completed by the donee obtaining probate of the donor's will of which he was executor, notwithstanding that the donor died intestate as to her residue and that the donee was not a person entitled as on her intestacy. Similarly in *Re James*,[59] a grant of administration to two administrators was held to perfect an imperfect gift by the intestate to one of them, who had no beneficial interest in the intestate's estate.

4–90   "In my judgment the circumstance that the plaintiff holds the fund because he was appointed a trustee of the will is irrelevant. He is at law the owner of the fund and the means by which he became so have no effect on the quality of his legal ownership. The question is: for whom, if any one, does he hold the fund in equity? In other words, who can successfully assert an equity against him disentitling him to stand on his legal right? It seems to me to be indisputable that Helen, if she were alive, could not do so,[60] for she has solemnly covenanted under seal to assign the fund to the plaintiff and the defendants can stand in no better position. It is, of course, true that the object of the covenant was not that the plaintiff should retain the property for his own benefit, but that he should hold it on the trusts of the settlement. It is also true that, if it were necessary to enforce performance of the covenant, equity would not assist the beneficiaries under the settlement, because they are mere volunteers; and that for the same reason the plaintiff, as trustee of the settlement, would not be bound to enforce the covenant and would not be constrained by the court to do so, and indeed, it seems, might be constrained by the court not to do so. As matters stand, however, there is no occasion to invoke the assistance of equity to enforce the performance of the covenant. It is for the defendants to invoke the assistance of equity to make good their claim to the fund. To do so successfully they must show that the plaintiff cannot conscientiously withhold it from them. When they seek to do this, he can point to the covenant which, in my judgment, relieves him from any fiduciary obligation that he would otherwise owe to the defendants as Helen's representatives. In so doing the plaintiff is not seeking to enforce an equitable remedy against the defendants on behalf of persons who could not enforce such a remedy themselves: he is relying on the combined effect of his legal ownership of the fund and his legal right to enforce the covenant. That an action on the covenant might be statute-barred is irrelevant, for there is no occasion for such an action.

4–91   "Had someone other than the plaintiff been the trustee of the will and held the fund, the result of this part of the case would, in my judgment, have been different; and it may seem strange that the rights of the parties should depend on the appointment of the plaintiff as a trustee of the will in 1946, which for present purposes may have been a quite fortuitous event. The result, however, in my judgment, flows—and flows, I think, quite rationally—from the consideration that the rules of equity derive from the tenderness of a court of equity for the consciences of the parties. *There would have been nothing unconscientious in Helen or her personal representatives asserting her equitable interests under trusts of the will against a trustee who was not a covenantee under clause 7 of the settlement*,[61] and it would have been unconscientious for such a trustee to disregard those interests. Having obtained a transfer of the fund, it would not have been unconscientious in

---

[58] (1874) L.R. 18 Eq. 315.
[59] [1935] Ch. 449.
[60] Is this right in view of *Re Brooks's S.T.* [1939] 1 Ch. 993, above, at para.4–80.
[61] Author's italics.

Helen to refuse to honour her covenant, because the beneficiaries under her settlement were mere volunteers: nor seemingly would the court have regarded it as unconscientious in the plaintiff to have abstained from enforcing the covenant either specifically or in damages, for the reason, apparently, that he would have been under no obligation to obtain for the volunteers indirectly what they could not obtain directly. In such circumstances Helen or her personal representatives could have got and retained the fund. In the circumstances of the present case, on the other hand, it is not unconscientious in the plaintiff to withhold from Helen's estate the fund which Helen covenanted that he should receive: on the contrary, it would have been unconscientious in Helen to seek to deprive the plaintiff of that fund, and her personal representatives can be in no better position. The inadequacy of the volunteers' equity against Helen and her estate consequently is irrelevant, for that equity does not come into play; but they have a good equity as against the plaintiff, because it would be unconscientious in him to retain as against them any property which he holds in consequence of the provisions of the settlement.

"For these reasons I am of opinion that in the events which have happened the plaintiff now holds the fund in question on the trusts of the marriage settlement, and I will so declare."

WILLIAMS v COMMISSIONERS OF INLAND REVENUE

New Zealand Court of Appeal [1965] N.Z.L.R. 395.

Williams, who had a life interest under a trust, executed a voluntary deed, in which "the assignor by way of gift hereby assigns to the assignee for the religious purposes of the Parish of the Holy Trinity Gisborne for the four years commencing on June 30, 1960 the first £500 of the net income which shall accrue to the assignor personally while he lives in each of the said four years from the Trust. . . . And the assignor hereby declares that he is trustee for the sole use and benefit of the assignee for the purpose aforesaid of so much (if any) of the said income as may not be capable of assignment (or may come to his hands)." **4–92**

The question arose whether Williams had effectively divested himself of his interest in the £500 so as not to be liable for income tax on it. The New Zealand Court of Appeal held that he had not.

TURNER J. (delivering the judgment of North P. and himself) said: "Mr. Thorp, for the appellant, submitted that what was assigned by this document was a defined share in the existing life estate of the assignor in the trust property, and hence that the deed of assignment took effect, as at its date, to divest the assignor of the annual sums of £500 so that he did not thereafter derive them for taxation purposes in the years under consideration. For the respondent Commissioner it was contended that the deed was ineffective to divest the assignor of the sums, and that its effect was no more than that of an order upon the trustees still revocable by the assignor until payment.

"The life interest of the appellant in the trust was at the date of the execution of the deed an existing equitable interest. Being an existing interest, it was capable in equity of immediate effective assignment. Such an assignment could be made without consideration, if it immediately passed the equitable estate: *Kekewich v Manning*.[62] There is no doubt that if the deed before us had purported to assign, not **4–93**

---

[62] (1851) 1 De G.M. & G. 176; 42 E.R. 519.

'the first £500,' but the whole of the appellant's life interest under the trust, such an assignment would have been good in equity.

"But while equity will recognise a voluntary assignment of an existing equitable interest, it will refuse to recognise in favour of a volunteer an assignment of an interest, either legal or equitable, not existing at the date of the assignment, but to arise in the future. Not yet existing, such property cannot be owned, and what may not be owned may not be effectively assigned: *Holroyd v Marshall*.[63] If, not effectively assigned, it is made the subject of an agreement to assign it, such an agreement may be good in equity, and become effective upon the property coming into existence but if, and only if, the agreement is made for consideration (as in *Spratt v Commissioner of Inland Revenue*[64]), for equity will not assist a volunteer: In *Re Ellenborough*.[65]

4–94 "The deed on which this appeal is founded was not made for consideration. The simple question is therefore—was that which it purported to assign (*viz.* 'the first five hundred pounds of the net income which shall accrue') an existing property right, or was it a mere expectancy, a future right not yet in existence? If the former, counsel agree that the deed was effective as an immediate assignment: if the latter, it is conceded by Mr. Thorp that it could not in the circumstances of this case have effect.

"What then was it that the assignor purported to assign? What he had was the life interest of a *cestui que trust* in a property or partnership adventure vested in or carried on by trustees for his benefit. Such a life interest exists in equity as soon as the deed of trust creating it is executed and delivered. Existing, it is capable of immediate assignment. We do not doubt that where it is possible to assign a right completely it is possible to assign an undivided interest in it. The learned Solicitor-General was therefore right, in our opinion, in conceding that if here, instead of purporting to assign 'the first £500 of the income,' the assignor had purported to assign (say) an undivided one-fourth share in his life estate, then he would have assigned an existing right, and in the circumstances effectively.

4–95 "But in our view, as soon as he quantified the sum in the way here attempted, the assignment became one not of a share or a part of his right, but of moneys which should arise from it. Whether the sums mentioned were ever to come into existence in whole or in part could not at the date of assignment be certain. In any or all of the years designated the net income might conceivably be less than five hundred pounds; in some or all of them the operations of the trust might indeed result in a loss. The first £500 of the net income, then, might or might not (judging the matter on the date of execution of the deed) in fact have any existence.

"We accordingly reject Mr. Thorp's argument that what was here assigned was a part or share of the existing equitable right of the assignor. He did not assign part of his right to income; he assigned a right to a part of the income, a different thing. The £500 which was the subject of the purported assignment was five hundred pounds *out of the net income*. There could be no such income for any year until the operations of that year were complete, and it became apparent what debits were to be set off against the gross receipts. For these reasons we are of opinion that what was assigned here was money; and that was something which was not presently owned by the assignor. He had no more than an expectation of it, to arise, it is true, from an existing equitable interest—but that interest he did not purport to assign. . . .

---

[63] (1862) 10 H.L.C. 191, 210; 11 E.R. 999 at 1006, *per* Lord Westbury L.C.
[64] [1964] N.Z.L.R. 272.
[65] [1903] 1 Ch. 697.

"It was argued in the alternative by Mr. Thorp, but somewhat faintly that if the **4–96** document were not effective as an assignment it was effective as a declaration of trust, and that this result was sufficient to divest the appellant of the enjoyment of the annual sums so that he did not derive them as income. It will be recalled in this regard that the text of the deed includes an express declaration of trust. Mr. Thorp's submission was that this express declaration is effective even if the assignment fails. We agree that there may be circumstances in which a purported assignment, ineffective for insufficiency of form or perhaps through lack of notice, may yet perhaps be given effect by equity by reason of the assignor having declared himself to be a trustee; but it is useless to seek to use this device in the circumstances of the present case. Property which is not presently owned cannot presently be impressed with a trust any more than it can be effectively assigned; property which is not yet in existence may be the subject of a present agreement to impress it with a trust when it comes into the hands of the donor; but equity will not enforce such an agreement at the instance of the *cestui que trust* in the absence of consideration: *Ellison v Ellison*.[66] For the same reasons therefore as apply in this case to the argument on assignment Mr. Thorp's second alternative submission must also fail."

V. EXCEPTIONS TO THE RULE THAT EQUITY WILL NOT ASSIST A VOLUNTEER

There seem to be four exceptions. **4–97**

1. *Equitable exceptions*

(a) The rule in *Strong v Bird*.[67] This has already been considered, above, at paras 4–49 to 4–54.

(b) *Donationes mortis causa*. Cases of *donationes mortis causa* sometimes provide an exception to the rule that equity will not perfect an imperfect gift. A *donatio mortis causa* must comply with the following essential requirements:

(i) The donor must have made the gift in contemplation, though not necessarily in expectation, of death.

(ii) He must have delivered the subject-matter of the gift to the donee or transferred to him the means or part of the means of getting at that subject-matter, *e.g.* delivering a key, like car keys[68] or a key to a box containing essential indicia of title,[69] intending to part with dominion over the property to which the key relates.

(iii) The circumstances must have been such as to establish that the gift **4–98** was to be absolute and complete only on the donor's death so as to be revocable before then. A condition to this effect need not be expressed and will normally be implied from the fact that the gift was made when the donor was ill.[70]

---

[66] (1802) 6 Ves.Jun. 656 at 662, *per* Lord Eldon.
[67] (1874) L.R. 18 Eq. 315.
[68] *Woodard v Woodard* (1991) 21 Fam. Law 470 (not necessary to hand over log book).
[69] *Re Lillingston* [1952] 2 All E.R. 184, *Sen v Headley* [1991] Ch. 425.
[70] *See Re Eillingston* [1952] 2 All E.R. 184; *Re Mustapha* (1891) 8 T.L.R. 160.

Since, in the case of a chose in action, physical delivery is impossible, it follows that the title of the donee will not be completely vested at the death of the donor. The question is, therefore, whether the donee can, as a volunteer, compel the personal representatives of the donor to complete the gift. Equity will not grant its assistance to the donee in every such case; it will do so only in those cases in which the donor has delivered to the donee a document which is necessary to prove title to the chose in action, *i.e.* a document the possession or production of which is necessary in order to entitle the possessor or producer to payment of the money as property purported to be given.[71] It is not necessary that the document should contain all the terms on which the subject-matter of the chose in action is held.[72] In the case of a bank deposit book, delivery of the book is sufficient to pass the money in the deposit account if the bank insists on production of the book before paying out. Delivery of title deeds to land or of share certificates is capable of amounting to a *d.m.c.* of the land[73] or of the shares.[74] Delivery of a donor's own cheque cannot amount to a *d.m.c.* of the sum represented by the cheque,[75] although delivery of a cheque payable to the donor can amount to a *d.m.c*[76]

4–99   (c) *Equitable proprietary estoppel.* As already seen above at paras 2–30 to 2–40, In some circumstances equity will prevent an owner of land, who has made an imperfect gift of some estate or interest in it, from asserting his title against the donee. The equity of the donee exists where he has expended money on the land in the mistaken belief that he has or will acquire an interest in it and the owner, knowing of the mistake, stood by and allowed the expenditure to be incurred. This type of equity has a wider sphere of operation than an estoppel of the ordinary kind, and in some cases nothing short of a conveyance of the owner's estate or interest to the donee will be sufficient to satisfy the equity.

2. Statutory exception

4–100   The Trusts of land and Appointment of Trustees Act 1996 provides a further exception to the rule.

Conveyance to an infant. Although after 1925 an infant cannot hold a legal estate in land, an attempt to transfer a legal estate to him is not wholly ineffective. It operates as a declaration of trust by the grantor in favour of the minor.[77]

---

[71] *Moore v Darton* (1851) 4 De G. & Sm. 517; *Re Dillon* (1890) 44 Ch.D. 76; *Birch v Treasury Solicitor* [1951] Ch. 298.

[72] *Birch v Treasury Solicitor* [1951] Ch. 298; disapproving dicta in *Re Weston* [1902] 1 Ch. 680 and *Delgoffe v Fader* [1939] Ch. 922.

[73] *Sen v Headley* [1991] 2 All E.R. 636 (appeal to H.L. settled).

[74] *Dufficy v Mollica* [1968] 3 NSWLR 751 at 759. This clearly should be the position if a share transfer form is properly executed and handed over; *Staniland v Willott* (1850) 3 Mac. & G. 664; *Re Craven's Estate* [1937] Ch. 423; or if land is actually conveyed; *Cooper v Seversen* (1955) 1 D.L.R. (2d) 161.

[75] *Re Beaumont* [1902] 1 Ch. 889; *Re Leaper* [1916] 1 Ch. 579.

[76] *Re Mead* (1880) 15 Ch.D. 651.

[77] Trusts of Land and Appointment of Trustees Act 1996, Sch.1, para.1.

QUESTIONS

1. Sam is freehold owner of some unregistered land in Wales, registered shareholder of 10,000 OK Ltd shares, a depositor of £12,000 with Bigg Bank and of £14,000 with Great Bank, and is entitled to XYZ Ltd shares held for him by Eric, executor of his father's will.

Sam gives the title deed to the Welsh land to Dawn, signing a hand-written endorsement on the conveyance to himself, "Dawn, this is now yours." He orally tells Frances he is holding 4,000 of his OK shares on trust for her, tells George he is holding his Bigg account on trust for him, has Great Bank write a letter to Harriet informing her that at Sam's telephoned request it is now holding his £14,000 on trust for her, tells Ian he is holding one half of his remaining 6,000 OK shares on trust for him, and tells Eric to transfer the XYZ shares to Jennifer. Eric signs a duly completed share transfer form and encloses it with the relevant share certificate in an envelope which he gives to Jennifer, who accidentally throws it out with some old newspapers and empty envelopes.

One month later a financial disaster strikes Sam, who seeks to recover the above property if at all possible. Advise him. Would your answer be different in respect of the OK shares if he had made a further declaration of trust of 3,000 OK shares in favour of Keith?

2. Under A's father's will trusts property is settled on trust for W for life, **4–101** remainder to his sons A and B equally, but W has express power to appoint the capital between A and B as she sees fit. If A assigns *inter alia* "All my interest under my father's will trusts to Bigg Bank on trust for X for life, remainder to Y", advise the bank if W dies either (i) without having made an appointment so that A receives £450,000, or (ii) having appointed £500,000 to A a month before her death, so that A's half share on her death brings him assets worth £200,000.

Would your advice differ if, instead, A had assigned to the Bank *inter alia* "all such assets whatsoever as shall come into my possession on my mother's death under the terms of my father's will trusts"? Would it matter if these words were followed by "but pending transfer of such assets I shall hold all my interest under my father's will trusts on the trusts applicable to such assets"?

Would any of your advice to the bank differ if unknown to A the bank happened to be trustee of his father's will trusts?

3. Five years ago, 26-year-old Sheila executed a voluntary settlement of certain **4–102** property and further assigned to Barclays Bank as her trustee all property to which she might become entitled under anybody's will or intestacy and she covenanted with the bank[78] to transfer to it upon the trusts of the settlement the sum of £30,000 to which she would become entitled under another trust if she attained 30.

Last year Sheila's mother died, by her will appointing Barclays Bank her executor and leaving £20,000 to Sheila. After receiving the £30,000 on attaining 30 Sheila, who then banked with Lloyds Bank, sent off her cheque for that sum in favour of Barclays Bank but stopped the cheque before it was met and sent off a cheque for £12,000 in its place. This cheque was cashed.

Sheila now claims to be entitled to recover this £12,000 and to be under no obligation to pay the £18,000 balance. She further demands that Barclays Bank pay her the £20,000 due to her under her mother's will. Advise the bank.

---

[78] Would it have been better for the bank (and the beneficiaries under Sheila's voluntary settlement) if Sheila had, instead, expressly assigned to the bank her contingent equitable interest in £30,000 or had, additionally, declared herself trustee of such interest on the trusts of her voluntary settlement?

Would it make any difference if Sheila had died last month having appointed Barclays Bank executor of her will and having left everything to her husband, Barry, whom she had married last year and who persisted with her claims and demands?

4–103   4. "When it comes to Chancery judges directing trustees not to sue on covenants, that are not themselves the subject-matter of a trust, the judges cannot justify their directions simply on the negative basis that 'Equity will not assist a volunteer' because Equity is positively intervening to prevent trustees exercising their common law rights." Discuss.

5. On Albert's hundredth birthday he asked his three children Maud, George and Emma, to visit him.

To Maud he said, "Here is a large envelope for you but don't open it till you've left me." To George he said, "Here is my share certificate for 4,000 ordinary shares in P.Q. Ltd, together with a transfer in your favour which I've signed. You can also have my car." To Emma he said, "I feel awful. If I die I want you to have everything else including this house and all my furniture. All the necessary papers are in this deed box underneath my bed. Here is the only key."

Albert died in his sleep that very night. His will appointed George his executor and left everything equally amongst his children.

In Maud's envelope were a cheque for £2,000 and the deeds of some freehold land and on the last conveyance to Albert he had written and signed, "I hold this for Maud." In the deed box Emma found several share certificates, Albert's Trustee Savings Bank passbook showing a balance of £1,000, and a receipt acknowledging that the bank had the safe custody of the title deeds to the house. George was unable to get himself registered in respect of the 4,000 shares as the directors refused to register him and were entitled to do so under the company's articles.

Advise Albert's executor on the distribution of Albert's estate.

4–104   6. Is the following approach to completely and incompletely constituted trusts a sound one?

(1) Has a trust been completely constituted by a declaration of trust by S himself or by property having been effectively given by him to trustees, bearing in mind that the strict rules as to gifts have been attenuated by *Strong v Bird* principles and *donatio mortis causa* principles and that if the intent is clear there may be a completely constituted trust of a covenant?

(2) If a trust is incompletely constituted is the beneficiary seeking to enforce the trust
  (a) a convenanting party,
  (b) someone who gave consideration for the settlor's covenant,
  (c) someone within the marriage consideration if the settlement was made in consideration of marriage?

(3) If a beneficiary cannot enforce the trust can the trustees as convenantees sue at common law and hold the damages on trust—but for whom?[79]

---

[79] If the trustee-covenantee assigned the benefit of the covenant to the person beneficially claiming the subject-matter of the covenant should the covenant not still be held on resulting trust for the settlor? Similarly, if the trustee resigned on appointing the alleged beneficiary to be trustee.

Section 2. Discretionary and Protective Trusts[80]

Discretionary Trusts

If a settlor wishes to provide for B by creating a trust for the benefit of B **4–105** (*e.g.* conferring a life interest upon B) he ought to consider whether his intention will best be carried out by conferring a distinct fixed interest upon B. After all, if B becomes bankrupt his life interest, like his other property, will pass to his trustee in bankruptcy for the benefit of his creditors. Moreover, B himself could sell his life interest and lose the proceeds on a gambling holiday so as then to be unprovided for.

If, however, B were merely a beneficiary of a discretionary trust[81] of **4–106** income, B would have no right to any of the trust income: he would merely have a hope that the trustees' discretion would be exercised in his favour. The essence of a discretionary trust is, of course, the complete discretion of the trustees as to the amount of income, if any, to be paid to the various beneficiaries of the trust. If the trustees have no power to retain income for accumulation the whole income[82] has to be distributed though only amongst such of the beneficiaries and in such proportions as the trustees see fit.[83] Only if all the beneficiaries of the discretionary trust are each of full capacity and between themselves absolutely entitled to either the income or the income and capital of the trust and call for the trustees to transfer the income or the trust property (as the case may be) to them (or to their nominee) do the trustees' discretions determine.[84] Till then neither individually nor collectively do the beneficiaries have an interest in possession.[85]

If B is beneficiary of a discretionary trust and then sells his interest or **4–107** becomes bankrupt his assignee or trustee in bankruptcy has no more right than he to demand payment from the trustees. If the trustees do exercise their discretion in favour of B by paying money to him or delivering goods to him then B's assignee or trustee in bankruptcy is entitled to the money or goods.[86] Indeed, where the trustees have had notice of the assignment or bankruptcy but have still paid money to B they have been held liable to his assignee or trustee in bankruptcy for the money so paid.[87] It seems, however, that if the trustees spend trust money on the maintenance of B by

---

[80] See generally Sheridan, "Discretionary Trusts" (1957) 21 Conv. (N.S.) 55; "Protective Trusts," *ibid.* 110; A. J. Hawkins (1967) 31 Conv. (N.S.) 117, Hardingham and Baxt, *Discretionary Trusts*.

[81] For the nature of an interest under a discretionary trust see *Gartside v I.R.C.* [1968] A.C. 553; *Re Weir's Settlement* [1969] 1 Ch. 657 (reversed [1971] Ch. 145 on grounds not affecting these principles); *Schmidt v Rosewood Trust Ltd* [2003] 2 A.C. 709. For an example of a draft discretionary settlement see above, at para.1–60.

[82] An "exhaustive" discretionary trust: *Sainsbury v I.R.C.* [1970] 1 Ch. 712.

[83] *Re Gourju's W.T.* [1943] Ch. 24; *Re Gulbenkian's Settlements (No.2)* [1970] Ch. 408; *Re Allen Meyrick's W.T.* [1966] 1 W.L.R. 499.

[84] *Re Smith* [1928] Ch. 915, *Schmidt v Rosewood Trust Ltd* [2003] 2 A.C. 709.

[85] *Re Trafford* [1984] 1 All E.R. 1108; *Vestey v I.R.C. (No.2)* [1979] 2 All E.R. 225 at 235–236.

[86] *Re Coleman* (1888) 39 Ch.D. 443. The assignment must be for value if the assignment of what B hopes to receive from an exercise of the trustees' discretion is to be enforceable once B has actually received property from the trustees; see, at para.6–85.

[87] *Re Neil* (1890) 62 L.T. 649; *Re Bullock* (1891) 60 L.J. Ch. 341 though *Re Ashby* [1892] 1 Q.B. 872 has created some uncertainty by indicating that an assignee or a trustee in bankruptcy can only claim to the extent to which sums paid are in excess of the amount necessary for B's maintenance: see Hardingham & Baxt's *Discretionary Trusts*, p.144.

paying third parties for food, clothes or accommodation for B then the assignee or trustee in bankruptcy will have no claim.[88]

Discretionary trusts thus have the advantage of protecting beneficiaries from themselves besides the obvious advantages of flexibility. However, there is the corresponding disadvantage that such trusts create uncertainty for a beneficiary since he has no fixed entitlement as he would have, say, if he had a life interest.

Protective Trusts

4–108   To tackle this disadvantage there arose the protective trust[89] conferring upon B a life (or lesser) interest determinable upon the bankruptcy of B or upon any other event which would deprive B of the right to receive all the income of the trust, whereupon a discretionary trust springs up in favour of B and her spouse and issue. It has long been established that, whilst a condition or proviso for forfeiture of an interest on bankruptcy or attempted alienation of the interest is void, a determinable limitation of an interest to last until bankruptcy or attempted alienation is valid,[90] except that where a settlor purports to create such a protective trust for himself the determining event will be void against his trustee in bankruptcy for reasons of public policy.[91] The justification for such a distinction is that a limitation merely sets a natural limit to an interest whilst a condition or proviso cuts down an interest before it reaches its natural limit: if such a condition or proviso is void for being contrary to a course of devolution prescribed by law, in cutting down the natural length of an interest to prevent creditors obtaining the benefit of the interest, or for being repugnant to the nature of the alienable interest granted, then the whole natural interest is available for creditors and for alienation. A limitation, however, creates a determinable interest lasting until the limiting event happens and such interest itself is the whole natural interest. The conceptual difference between conditional and determinable interests may be stated as the difference between giving someone a 12-inch ruler subject to being cut down to a six-inch ruler in certain conditions and giving someone a six-inch ruler in the first place.

4–109   Protective trusts are now normally created by use of the shorthand phrase "protective trusts" which invokes the detailed trusts set out in s.33 of the Trustee Act 1925. It is also quite common in the cause of fiscal flexibility to insert some express provision enabling the protected life tenant during the currency of his determinable life interest, if he obtains the written approval of the trustees, to enter into arrangements with the other beneficiaries under the settlement for dividing up the trust funds or

---

[88] *Re Coleman* (1888) 39 Ch.D. 443 at 451; *Re Allan-Meyrick's W.T.* [1966] 1 W.L.R. 499.

[89] See the statutory form invoked by use of the phrase "protective trusts" set out in the Trustee Act 1925, s.33, at para.4–111. They have favoured treatment for inheritance tax purposes: Inheritance Tax Act 1984, s.88; *Cholmondeley v I.R.C.* [1986] S.T.C. 384.

[90] *Brandon v Robinson* (1811) 18 Ves. 429; *Re Leach* [1912] 2 Ch. 422; *Re Scientific Investment Pension Plan Trusts* [1999] Ch. 53 at 59.

[91] *Re Burroughs-Fowler* [1916] 2 Ch. 251, at para.4–133, *Official Assignee v NZI Life Assurance* [1995] 1 N.Z.L.R. 684.

otherwise rearranging the beneficial interests as if he had an absolute life interest. Indeed, the protected life tenant may be given a general power of appointment exercisable only with the written consent of the trustees (for this purpose being a trust corporation or not less than two persons other than or in addition to the protected life tenant) so as to be able to vary the beneficial or administrative provisions of the settlement or even completely to revoke the settlement.[92] For the reasons set out in an extract para.4–113 from a case note by R.E. Megarry (later Vice-Chancellor) it became not uncommon to create a series of protective trusts, *e.g.* one set until a beneficiary is 30, another from 30 to 40, a third from 40 to 50 and another for the rest of his life. Nowadays, particularly to deal with eventualities where it may or may not be clear whether forfeiture has occurred and where forfeiture may or may not be a "good" thing, a settlor seeking to provide for a profligate beneficiary may as well give the beneficiary a fixed interest but revocable at the trustees' discretion. The beneficiary then has a transferable but unsaleable interest, and whenever it would help the beneficiary to avoid claims the trustees can revoke his interest in favour of his having an interest under a discretionary trust or no interest at all for a few years till things have blown over.

As will be seen upon examining section 33 of the Trustee Act 1925 a **4–110** protective trust contains three parts: (1) a life or lesser interest determinable on certain events; (2) a forfeiture clause specifying the determining events; (3) a discretionary trust which arises after forfeiture.

The Trustee Act 1925

Section 33.—(1) Where any income, including an annuity or other periodical **4–111** income payment, is directed to be held on protective trusts for the benefit of any person[93] (in this section called "the principal beneficiary") for the period of his life or for any less period, then, during that period (in this section called the "trust period") the said income shall, without prejudice to any prior interest, be held on the following trusts, namely:

(i) Upon trust for the principal beneficiary during the trust period or until he, whether before or after the termination of any prior interest, does or attempts to do or suffers any act or thing, or until any event happens, other than an advance under any statutory or express power,[94] whereby, if the said income were payable during the trust period to the principal beneficiary absolutely during that period, he would be deprived of the right to receive the same or any part thereof, in any of which cases, as well as on the termination of the trust period, whichever first happens, this trust of the said income shall fail or determine.

---

[92] Such a general power falls to be treated as a special power for perpetuity purposes so that the perpetuity period runs not from the date of the exercise of the power of appointment but from the date of the settlement creating the power: *Re Earl of Coventry's Indentures* [1974] Ch. 77; Perpetuities and Accumulations Act 1964, s.7.

[93] Person means a human being and not a company: *I.R.C. v Brandenburg* [1982] S.T.C. 555 at 565, 569.

[94] See *Re Hodgson* [1913] 1 Ch. 34; *Re Shaw's Settlement* [1951] Ch. 833; *Re Rees* [1954] Ch. 202; *cf. Re Stimpson's Trusts* [1931] 2 Ch. 77, which should now be confined to its own facts, that is where an express advancement clause is lacking and where no use is made of s.33 of the Trustee Act. Even so, it must be regarded as of doubtful authority: see *Re Rees* [1954] Ch. 202 at 209.

(ii) If the trust aforesaid fails or determines during the subsistence of the trust period, then, during the residue of that period, the said income shall be held upon trust for the application thereof[95] for the maintenance or support, or otherwise for the benefit, of all or any one or more exclusively of the other or others of the following persons (that is to say)—

    (a) the principal beneficiary and his or her wife or husband, if any, and his or her children or more remote issue, if any; or

    (b) if there is no wife or husband or issue of the principal beneficiary in existence, the principal beneficiary and the persons who would, if he were actually dead, *be entitled to the trust property or the income thereof* or to the annuity fund, if any, or arrears of the annuity, as the case may be; as the trustees in their absolute discretion, without being liable to account for the exercise of such discretion, think fit.

4–112   (2) This section does not apply to trusts coming into operation before the commencement of this Act, and has effect subject to any variation[96] of the implied trusts aforesaid contained in the instrument creating the trust.

(3) Nothing in this section operates to validate any trust which would, if contained in the instrument creating the trust, be liable to be set aside.[97]

R. E. MEGARRY (1958) 74 L.Q.R. 184

4–113   "This sequence of events [in *Re Richardson's W.T.* [1958] Ch. 504] points a moral for draftsmen. Hitherto the normal course of drafting has been to give a life interest simply 'on protective trusts,' with or without variations. The result is that a single mistaken act by the beneficiary may deprive him of his determinable life interest and reduce him for the rest of his life to the status of merely one of the beneficiaries of a discretionary trust. *Re Richardson* suggests that there may be advantages in setting up a series of protective trusts, *e.g.* one set until the beneficiary is twenty-five, another from twenty-five to thirty-five, a third from thirty-five to forty-five, and another for the rest of his life. The result would be that a youthful indiscretion at, say, twenty-two, would not irretrievably condemn the beneficiary to the mere hopes of a beneficiary under a discretionary trust, dependent upon the exercise of the trustees' discretion, but would give him a fresh start when he was twenty-five. Again, a bankruptcy at the age of thirty would not *per se* mean that when he was twice that age he would still have not an income as of right, but a mere hope of a well-exercised discretion. Indeed, instead of relating the stages to the age of the beneficiary, they might be related to a period of time (*e.g.* five years) after the occurrence of any event which had made the initial trust pass from Stage 1 to Stage 2. England lacks the device of the spendthrift trust in the American sense, but it is far from clear that the fullest possible use is being made of the existing machinery of

---

[95] The income must be distributed: *Re Gourju's W.T.* [1934] Ch. 24.

[96] See, *e.g. Re Wittke* [1944] Ch. 166: bequest of residue upon protective trusts for testatrix's sister, no period being specified, but trustees being given a power to pay capital to the sister from time to time. *Held* by Vaisey J. that a protected life interest had been created, for, had an absolute interest been given, it would have been open to the sister to call for an immediate transfer of the capital, which would have been inconsistent with the power given to the trustees.

[97] This preserves *inter alia* the rule that although a settlor may validly create in favour of another person a life interest determinable by bankruptcy, such a limitation in favour of himself is void against his trustee in bankruptcy. See *Re Burroughs-Fowler* [1916] 2 Ch. 251; *Re Detmoid* (1889) 40 Ch.D. 585 (where a determining event, other than bankruptcy, occurred, and it was held that the life interest determined). See, below, Sect. 3.

protective and discretionary trusts." [The American spendthrift trust is a result of most American jurisdictions allowing inalienable beneficial interests to be created, though legislation sometimes intervenes to allow creditors to reach income in excess of a specified amount.]

Forfeiting Events

Whether the interest of the beneficiary is determined in the events which **4–114** have happened is a question of construction of the forfeiture clause in each particular case. It is sometimes said that forfeiture clauses should be construed in favour of the principal beneficiary, but it must be remembered that he is not the sole object of the testator's bounty, and that there are other persons upon whom the testator intended to confer a benefit.[98] It is only if, after construing the clause, a doubt remains that this should be resolved in favour of the principal beneficiary, for "the burden is upon those who allege a forfeiture to satisfy the court that a forfeiture has occurred."[99]

The forfeiture clause contained in s.33 of the Trustee Act 1925 is very **4–115** wide, for it includes not only the acts and omissions of the principal beneficiary, but also the happening of any event which deprives him of his right to receive the income or any part thereof. Such an event was the Trading with the Enemy Act 1939 and orders made thereunder, whereby the property of those resident in enemy territory vested in the Custodian of Enemy Property.[1] It was otherwise with express forfeiture clauses which were drafted in narrower terms. Thus in *Re Hall*[2] forfeiture was to occur "if the annuitant should alienate or charge her annuity or become bankrupt or do or suffer any act or thing whereby the said annuity or any part thereof would or might become vested in or payable to any other person." It was held by Uthwatt J. that the clause was directed to the forfeiture of the annuity in the event of the annuitant doing *personally* certain classes of things whereby she would be deprived of her annuity. Accordingly, the Trading with the Enemy Act 1939 did not bring about a forfeiture.

Apart from these special cases, involving the application of the Trading **4–116** with the Enemy Act to protective trusts, the following events have been held to cause a forfeiture:

Re Balfour's Settlement[3]: the impounding by the trustees of part of the income of the principal beneficiary to repair a breach of trust committed by them in paying part of the trust fund to him at his own instigation.

Re Walker[4]: the bankruptcy of the principal beneficiary, even if this had occurred before the trust first came into operation.

---

[98] *Re Sartoris's Estate* [1892] 1 Ch. 11 at 16.
[99] *Re Baring's Settlement Trusts* [1940] Ch. 737 (Morton J.).
[1] *e.g.* Trading with the Enemy (Custodian) Order 1939 (S.R. & O. 1939 No.1198). Later orders contained a proviso that vesting in the custodian should not take place if it would cause a forfeiture (*e.g.* S.R. & O. 1945 No.887).
[2] [1944] Ch. 46; so too *Re Furness, Wilson v Kenmare (No.1)* [1944] 1 All E.R. 575; *Re Harris* [1945] Ch. 316; *Re Pozot's Settlement Trusts* [1952] Ch. 427.
[3] [1938] Ch. 928.
[4] [1939] Ch. 974.

Re Baring's Settlement Trusts[5]: an order of sequestration of the income for contempt of court, even though the contempt is subsequently purged.

Re Dennis's Settlement Trusts[6]: the execution by the principal beneficiary of a deed of variation relinquishing his right to part of the income in certain events.

4–117   *Re Richardson's W.T.*[7]: an order of the Divorce court attempting to impose a charge (to secure maintenance of £50 p.a.) which though ineffectual for that purpose was sufficient to bring about a forfeiture thereby conveniently benefiting the principal beneficiaries, who had been adjudicated bankrupt a year after such order and who would still benefit under the discretionary trusts of income (whereas the trustee in bankruptcy would have acquired all the income but for the forfeiture).

On the other hand no forfeiture occurred in the following cases:

Re Tancred's Settlement[8]: the appointment by the principal beneficiary of an attorney to receive the income, even though the attorney's expenses are to be deducted from the income, and the balance paid over to the principal beneficiary.

Re Mair[9]: the making by the court of an order under s.57 of the Trustee Act 1925 authorising capital moneys to be raised to enable the principal beneficiary to pay certain pressing liabilities: s.57 is an overriding section whose provisions are read into every settlement. Contrast *Re Salting*,[10] where the scheme sanctioned by the court under s.57 involved the doing of certain acts by the principal beneficiary—and *his* omission to do them caused a forfeiture. The scheme provided for the life tenant to pay premiums on insurance policies with a proviso that the trustees were to pay the premiums out of his income if the premiums were not duly paid: his failure to pay was held to create a forfeiture.

4–118   *Re Westby's Settlement*[11]: the charge of a lunacy per centage upon the estate of a lunatic under s.148(3) of the Lunacy Act 1890 (replaced by Mental Health Act 1983, s.106(6)), since the fees payable were to be regarded as management expenses, and, even if a charge was created by the section, it was not such an incumbrance as was contemplated by the forfeiture clause.[12]

4–119   *Re Longman*[13]: a testatrix left the income of her residuary estate on certain trusts for her son under which he would forfeit his interest if he should "commit permit or suffer any act default or process whereby the

---

[5] [1940] Ch. 737.

[6] [1942] Ch. 283; see (1942) 58 L.Q.R. 312. It may be possible to set aside a deed for mistake as in *Gibbon v Michell* [1990] 1 W.L.R. 1304.

[7] See also *Edmonds v Edmonds* [1965] 1 W.L.R. 58 (attachment of earnings order to secure former wife's maintenance held to cause forfeiture of husband's protected interest in pension fund). Further see [1993] So.Jo. 919, indicating that no attachment can be made to sums paid to the pensioner under the discretionary trusts arising upon forfeiture of the pensioner's fixed entitlements.

[8] [1903] 1 Ch. 715.

[9] [1935] Ch. 562.

[10] [1932] 2 Ch. 57.

[11] [1950] Ch. 296; overruling *Re Custance's Settlements* [1946] Ch. 42; see also *Re Oppenheim's Will Trusts* [1950] Ch. 633 (appointment of receiver of person of unsound mind did not effect a forfeiture).

[12] The same result was then achieved, independently of the cases, by the Law Reform (Miscellaneous Provisions) Act 1949, s.8.

[13] [1955] 1 W.L.R. 197.

said income or any part thereof would or might but for this present proviso become vested in or payable to any other person." The son authorised the trustee to pay his creditors specified sums out of a particular future dividend due on shares forming part of the residuary estate. The son later withdrew this authority, and the company afterwards did not declare a dividend. It was held by Danckwerts J. that the withdrawal of authority would not by itself prevent forfeiture;[14] but the failure to declare a dividend did, since the income of the residuary estate never included anything to which the authority could possibly have attached.

General Accident Fire and Life Assurance Corporation Ltd v I.R.C.[15]: **4–120** order of the Divorce court diverting income from husband to wife and taking effect in priority to the protective trusts was held by the Court of Appeal not to create a forfeiture, so the husband retained a life interest liable to estate duty on death. Although the case turned on a narrow ground of construction of s.33 it is possible to treat it on the same basis as *Re Mair*, above (order under section 57 of the Trustee Act): all protective trusts must be read as subject to the court's jurisdiction to make orders under s.57 of the Trustee Act and ss.24 and 31 of the Matrimonial Causes Act 1973. If this be the case then *Re Richardson's W.T.*[16] above (not cited to the Court of Appeal) is out of line like *Re Carew*[17] which the Court of Appeal overruled.

An order of the court may sometimes do more than cause a forfeiture: it **4–121** may destroy the protected life interest and discretionary trusts altogether. This happened in *Re Allsopp's Marriage Settlement Trusts*,[18] where an express protective trust was created by a marriage settlement in 1916 with discretionary trusts after forfeiture. In 1928 on the dissolution of the marriage the court made an order varying the marriage settlement by *extinguishing* the rights of the husband as if he were already dead. Vaisey J. held that the husband's protected life interest was extinguished for all purposes and the discretionary trusts were so closely connected with the life interest that they also were destroyed.

The effect of the forfeiture is to determine the principal beneficiary's life **4–122** interest and to bring the discretionary trusts into operation. Thus in *Re Gourju's Will Trusts*,[19] the Trading with the Enemy Act 1939 and orders made thereunder having brought about a forfeiture of the principal beneficiary's interests, and the discretionary trusts having arisen, it was held by Simonds J. that income which had accrued due before the forfeiture was payable to the Custodian of Enemy Property, but income which accrued due after that event was to be held on the discretionary trusts for the benefit of the beneficiaries, and that since the Act contemplated a continuous benefit to those beneficiaries, the trustees were not to retain the

---

[14] See *Re Baker* [1904] 1 Ch. 157.
[15] [1963] 1 W.L.R. 1207; (1963) 27 Conv.(N.S.) 517 (F. R. Crane).
[16] [1958] Ch. 504 Further see Parker & Mellows, *The Modern Law of Trusts* 7th ed. A. J. Oakley, at 236.
[17] (1910) 103 L.T. 658.
[18] [1959] Ch. 81.
[19] [1943] Ch. 24.

income, but were to apply it for the beneficiaries as and when it came in, subject to such reasonable exceptions as the exigencies of the case demanded.[20] Thus the trustees could not accumulate the income so as to pay it at the end of the war to the principal beneficiary (a woman marooned in German-occupied Nice).

Section 3. Attempts by a Settlor to Deprive his Creditors

4–123 Although a settlor may validly create in favour of another person a life interest determinable upon bankruptcy such a limitation in favour of himself is void as a matter of public policy[21] against his trustee in bankruptcy though effective between himself and the other beneficiaries under the settlement; *Re Burroughs-Fowler*. Where there are several determinable events including bankruptcy then the occurrence before bankruptcy of some other determinable event is, however, valid against the trustee in bankruptcy.[22] A settlement upon discretionary trusts where the settlor is one of the discretionary beneficiaries is prima facie valid but may be impeached under s.423 of the Insolvency Act 1986 (replacing s.172 of the Law of Property Act 1925) or ss.339 and 341 of the Insolvency Act 1986 (replacing s.42 of the Bankruptcy Act 1914).

INSOLVENCY ACT 1986, SS.423–425, 339–342

4–124 These sections are broad enough to catch many dispositions by a settlor in favour of third parties. Section 423, at para.4–136, operates *independently of any bankruptcy* of the settlor and covers all voluntary settlements and settlements in consideration of marriage (whenever made) if the settlor made the settlement "*for the purpose* (a) of putting assets beyond the reach of a person who is making, or may at some time make, a claim against him, or (b) of otherwise prejudicing the interests of such a person in relation to the claim which he is making or may make." This purpose needs to be a substantial purpose (*e.g.* a co-equal purpose) but not a dominant purpose.[23]

4–125 Sections 339 and 341, paras 4–140 to 4–141, only apply *if the settlor is adjudged bankrupt* (and apply only in favour of the trustee in bankruptcy) and only if the settlement[24] was not created more than five years before the

---

[20] If the trustees fail to exercise their discretion, the discretionary trusts over income remain exercisable despite the passing of time though only in favour of such persons as would have been objects of the discretion had it been exercised within a reasonable time: *Re Locker's S.T.* [1978] 1 All E.R. 216.

[21] Some offshore trust juridictions (*e.g.* Belize and the Cook Islands) have abolished the rule that a settlor may not create a protective trust determinable on his bankruptcy so as to prevent his interest passing on bankruptcy to his trustee in bankruptcy. If property subject to such a Belize trust is found in England it is almost certain that it will be made available to the trustee in bankruptcy, taking advantage of Art.18 of The Hague Trusts Convention implemented by Recognition of Trusts Act 1987.

[22] *Re Detmold* (1889) 40 Ch.D. 585.

[23] *I.R.C. v Hashmi* [2002] EWCA Civ 981, [2002] W.T.L.R. 1027. There is no limitation period for a claim under s.423 but if an action is brought 20 or 30 years after the relevant transaction it could be attacked under the right to a fair hearing in Art.6 of the Human Rights Convention.

[24] Exercise of a special power of appointment under a settlement created more than 5 years before the settlor's bankruptcy is outside s.339 even if occurring well within the 5 years: *Clarkson v Clarkson* (unreported CA April 26, 1994, Underhill & Hayton, *Law of Trusts*, 16th ed., p.289).

bankruptcy, but no purposive intent to defraud creditors is required: merely entering into a transaction at an undervalue suffices. This includes a man trying to prevent his major creditor obtaining his farm by granting a protected agricultural tenancy to his wife at full market rent, but depreciating the value of the man's interest, where the wife thereby would safeguard the family home and the farming business and obtain a "ransom" surrender-value against the creditor.[25] Valuation of the transaction (*e.g.* assignment of a life policy) to see if there was an undervalue can take account of subsequent events (*e.g.* where the assignment was made one week after the assignor learned of the policy-holders imminent death which followed two months later).[26]

The basic period is within two years of presentation of the bankruptcy petition but is extended to five years if the settlor-transferor was insolvent, as defined in s.341(3), at the time of the transfer or became so as a result of the transfer. It is rebuttably presumed that such insolvency existed if the transfer benefited "associates", including relatives of the bankrupt or spouse, as defined in section 435.

Section 423, replacing Law of Property Act 1925, s.172 (itself replacing a **4–126** statute of 1571) probably encapsulates in modern language the effect of the old case law. The section clearly extends to "present" creditors (with existing enforceable claims) and "subsequent" creditors (identifiable persons who have claims that may reasonably be anticipated to mature into existing enforceable claims, *e.g.* holders of guarantees executed by the donor, or persons who had issued writs or informed the donor that they would be issuing a writ or would have so informed the donor if they had his knowledge, such as his knowledge of his negligence in relation to them).

In some circumstances the section is capable of extending to "potential future" creditors, *viz.* presently unidentifiable persons, who may or may not surface at any time in the future to bring presently unascertainable claims of indeterminate amounts against the donor.

In *Re Butterworth*[27] Butterworth, who had been a successful baker for many years, decided to expand and buy a grocery business, a trade in which he had no experience. He therefore settled most of his property on his family just before buying the grocery business. It was not a success but Butterworth was able to sell it six months later for the same price he had paid. He continued with his bakery until it failed three years later. The Court of Appeal held that the settlement was made "with intent to defraud" under the 1571 Statute of Elizabeth and so could be upset by the creditors of the bakery.

Jessel M.R. said,[28] "The principle of *Mackay v Douglas* is this, that a man **4–127** is not entitled to go into a hazardous business, and immediately before doing so settle all his property voluntarily, the object being this: 'If I succeed in business, I make a fortune for myself. If I fail, I leave my

---

[25] *Agricultural Mortgage Corporation v Woodward* [1995] 1 B.C.L.C. 1, [1996] 1 F.L.R. 226.
[26] *Reid v Ramlort Ltd* [2003] 1 B.C.L.C. 499.
[27] (1882) 19 Ch.D. 588.
[28] *ibid.* at 598, also see Lindley L.J. at 60 and *Cadogan v Cadogan* [1977] 1 W.L.R. 1041.

creditors unpaid. They will bear the loss.' That is the very thing which the Statute of Elizabeth was meant to prevent. The object of the settlor was to put his property out of the reach of his future creditors. He contemplated engaging in this new trade and he wanted to preserve his property from his future creditors. That cannot be done by a voluntary settlement. That is, to my mind, a clear and satisfactory principle."

4–128　　In these days when lawyers, accountants and doctors may find that they can only insure themselves against negligence up to a ceiling of £x, but that they may possibly become liable for £2x, what can they do? They can, of course, settle their property on their families, but can one distinguish their activities as professions and not hazardous trades so as to fall outside Jessel M.R.'s statement of principle? Should it matter whether a business is a trade or a profession in these days when there should be no room for class distinction? Can s.423(3) be treated as changing the law through speaking of "putting assets beyond the reach of *a* person who may at some time make a claim" rather than "*any* person," so that it could be said to contemplate only an identifiable person rather than any future potential creditors?[29] Probably not.

4–129　　This point was not raised in *Midland Bank plc v Wyatt*[30] where s.423, following *Re Butterworth* was held to cover the voluntary disposition of assets to trustees to avoid future but unknown creditors, whether or not the transferor was about to go into a "hazardous business", and whether or not the transferor was about to undertake the business as a sole trade or a partnership or via a limited liability company he controlled. Section 423 applies if a substantial[31] purpose is avoiding existing, potential or future creditors but not if such purpose is estate planning. Once there is a strong prima facie case that the purpose of a transaction was to prejudice the interests of creditors no legal privilege attaches to documents relating to such transactions.[32]

4–130　　To avoid problems one may seek to take advantage of favourable asset protection trust legislation in some off-shore trust jurisdictions (*e.g.* Belize, Cook Islands) which protects a settlor against potential future creditors and also introduces a short limitation period (there being no limitation period in England) where present and subsequent creditors are concerned, but assets could be at risk if they can be traced to England or the USA where the courts could find such legislation contrary to public policy. By ss.352 and 357 of the Insolvency Act 1986 a bankrupt is guilty of an offence if in the 5 years before his bankruptcy commenced he made or caused to be made any gift or transfer of or charge on his property unless he proves that at the time he had no intent to defraud creditors under s.423 or to conceal the state of his affairs. Assisting such a person to commit such a crime is an offence.

---

[29] A question posed by Moffat & Chesterman, *Trusts Law: Text & Materials*, 3rd ed., p.231. After all, a prospective hazardous trader can form a company with limited liability to engage in the trade (though creditors may well insist on him personally guaranteeing company debts). Professionals can now create a limited liability partnership under Limited Liability Partnerships Act 2000.
[30] [1995] 1 F.L.R. 696.
[31] *IRC v Hashmi* [2003] W.T.L.R. 1027.
[32] *Barclays Bank plc v Eustice* [1995] 1 W.L.R. 1238.

The burden of proving the settlor's purpose is on the applicant while the **4–131** burden of proving exemption under s.425(2) is on the transferee who seeks exemption.[33] Proving the settlor's purpose is a question of fact and the surrounding circumstances may be capable of establishing a rebuttable presumption that the requisite purpose was present, *e.g.* where the settlor settles virtually all his assets, or settles so much of his assets that his liabilities then exceed what he has left, or makes the settlement secretly and hastily.[34]

Dispositions to defeat spouses

Under s.37 of the Matrimonial Causes Act 1973 the Family Division has jurisdiction to set aside dispositions made with the intention of defeating a spouse's claim to financial relief,[35] such an intention being presumed for a disposition made within three years of the application to the court if it actually has the effect of defeating such claim: s.37(5).

Dispositions to defeat heirs

Under the Inheritance (Provision for Family and Dependants) Act 1975 **4–132** the court has power to make various orders in relation to dispositions effected by a deceased, other than for full valuable consideration, and made with the intention of defeating applications for financial provision.[36] Section 10 applies to dispositions made less than six years before the deceased's death but not including appointments made in exercise of a special power of appointment. Section 13 provides protection for trustee-disponees against liability beyond trust property at hand.

RE BURROUGHS-FOWLER

Chancery Division [1916] 2 Ch. 251.

By an ante-nuptial settlement dated March 24, 1905, freeholds and leaseholds **4–133** belonging to W. J. Fowler, the intended husband, were conveyed to the trustees upon trust to sell subject to certain consents and "to pay the rents profits and income thereof to the said W. J. Fowler or to permit him to receive the same during his life or until he shall be outlawed or be declared bankrupt or become an insolvent debtor within the meaning of some Act of Parliament for the relief of insolvent debtors or shall do or suffer something whereby the said rents profits and income or some part thereof respectively might if absolutely belonging to him become vested in or payable to some other person or persons. And from and immediately after the

---

[33] *Lloyds Bank Ltd v Marcan* [1974] 1 W.L.R. 370 on LPA 1925, s.172 but similar principles seem applicable to s.423.

[34] *Re Wise* (1886) 17 Q.B.D. 290; *Freeman v Pope* (1870) 5 Ch.App.538; *Re Sinclair* (1884) 26 Ch.D. 319; *Lloyds Bank Ltd v Marcan* [1974] 1 W.L.R. 370; *Agricultural Mortgage Corporation v Woodward* [1995] 1 B.C.L.C. 1.

[35] *e.g. Kemmis v Kemmis* [1988] 1 W.L.R. 1307; *Sherry v Sherry* [1991] 1 F.L.R. 307; but a notice to quit given to a landlord by a joint tenant of a periodic tenancy is not a disposition of any property, such notice merely signifying the tenant was not willing to consent to the continuation of the tenancy beyond the date when if would otherwise expire: *Newlon Housing Trust v Alsulaimen* [1999] 1 A.C. 813.

[36] *e.g. Re Dawkins* [1986] 2 F.L.R. 360.

death of the said W. J. Fowler or other the determination of the trust for his benefit
in his lifetime to pay the said rents profits and income unto the" wife if she should
survive him during her life for her separate use without power of anticipation, and
after the death of the survivor upon the usual trusts for the children of the marriage.

4–134   After the marriage the husband took the name of Burroughs-Fowler. He was
adjudicated bankrupt in 1915. The trustee in bankruptcy offered for sale the
husband's life interest under the settlement, but the intending purchaser objected
that the debtor's life interest remained defeasible if the debtor should do or suffer
any of the other specified acts of forfeiture.

4–135   PETERSON J.: "Now the limitation until the settlor is declared bankrupt is void
against the trustee in bankruptcy, and therefore, so far as the trustee in bankruptcy
is concerned, the words relating to the bankruptcy and insolvency of the settlor must
be treated as if they were omitted altogether from the clause. But on the other hand
the provision as to bankruptcy and insolvency is not void as between the husband
and the wife; for it was decided in *Re Johnson*[37] that, while the provision for the
cessation of the life interest on bankruptcy was void as against the trustee in
bankruptcy, it was effective for the purpose of producing a forfeiture as between the
person who had the protected life interest and the persons interested in remainder.
What, then, is the result? It is said that the result may be that the trustee in
bankruptcy will be in a position to dispose of more than was vested in the bankrupt
himself. That would be so in any case, because, so far as the trustee is concerned,
the provisions for terminating the protected life interest upon bankruptcy are void.
It seems to me that the true view is that, so far as the trustee in bankruptcy is
concerned, the provisions as to bankruptcy and insolvency must be treated as
excluded from the settlement, and the trustee is therefore in a position to deal with
the interest of the husband under the settlement, whatever it may be, as if those
provisions were excluded. So far, however, as the wife is concerned the forfeiture by
reason of the bankruptcy has already taken place, and, therefore, it is no longer
possible for the husband hereafter to do or suffer something which would determine
his interest. The result is that the trustee in bankruptcy is in possession of the life
interest of the bankrupt, which is now incapable of being affected by any subsequent
forfeiture."

Insolvency Act 1986

4–136   **423. Transactions defrauding creditors.**—(1) This section relates to transactions
entered into at an undervalue; and a person[38] enters into such a transaction with
another person if—

   (a) he makes a gift to the other person or he otherwise enters into a transaction
       with the other on terms that provide for him to receive no consideration;
   (b) he enters into a transaction with the other in consideration of marriage; or
   (c) he enters into a transaction with the other for a consideration the value of
       which, in money or money's worth, is significantly less than the value, in
       money or money's worth, of the consideration provided by himself.

4–137   (2) Where a person has entered into such a transaction, the court may, if satisfied
under the next subsection, make such order as it thinks fit[39] for—

---

[37] [1904] 1 K.B. 134.
[38] The section has extra-territorial effect: *Re Paramount Airways* [1993] Ch. 223. See also Enterprise Act
2002, s.254, and note that by s.262 thereof a trustee in bankruptcy cannot bring an action under ss.339, 340
or 423 without the consent of the creditors' committee or of the court.
[39] s.425(1) sets out specific orders "without prejudice to the generality of s.423."

(a) restoring the position to what it would have been if the transaction had not been entered into, and

(b) protecting the interests of persons who are victims of the transaction.

(3) In the case of a person entering into such a transaction, an order shall only be made if the court is satisfied that it was entered into by him for the purpose—

(a) of putting assets beyond the reach of a person who is making, or may at some time make, a claim against him, or

(b) of otherwise prejudicing the interests of such a person in relation to the claim which he is making or may make. . . .

(5) In relation to a transaction at an undervalue, references here and below to a victim of the transaction are to a person who is, or is capable of being, prejudiced by it; and in the following two sections the person entering into the transaction is referred to as "the debtor."

424. Those who may apply for an order under s.423.—(1) An application for an **4–138** order under section 423 shall not be made in relation to a transaction except—

(a) in a case where the debtor has been adjudged bankrupt or is a body corporate which is being wound up or in relation to which an administration order is in force, by the official receiver, by the trustee of the bankrupt's estate or the liquidator or administrator of the body corporate or (with the leave of the court) by a victim of the transaction. . . .

    (c) in any other case, by a victim of the transaction.

(2) An application made under any of the paragraphs of subsection (1) is to be treated as made on behalf of every victim of the transaction.

425. Provision which may be made by order under s.423.—(2) An order under **4–139** section 423 may affect the property of, or impose any obligation on, any person whether or not he is the person with whom the debtor entered into the transaction; but such an order—

(a) shall not prejudice any interest in property which was acquired from a person other than the debtor and was acquired in good faith, for value and without notice[40] of the relevant circumstances, or prejudice any interest deriving from such an interest, and

(b) shall not require a person who received a benefit from the transaction in good faith, for value and without notice of the relevant circumstances to pay any sum unless he was a party to the transaction.

(3) For the purposes of this section the relevant circumstances in relation to a transaction are the circumstances by virtue of which an order under section 423 may be made in respect of the transaction.

339. Transactions at an undervalue.—(1) Subject as follows in this section and **4–140** sections 341 and 342, where an individual is adjudged bankrupt and he has at a relevant time (defined in section 341) entered into a transaction with any person at

---

[40] Notice will include constructive notice: *Lloyds Bank Ltd v Marcan* [1973] 1 W.L.R. 339 at 345.

an undervalue, the trustee of the bankrupt's estate may apply to the court for an order under this section.

(2) The court shall, on such an application, make such order as it thinks fit for restoring the position to what it would have been if that individual had not entered into that transaction.

(3) For the purposes of this section and sections 341 and 342, an individual enters into a transaction with a person at an undervalue if—

(a) he makes a gift to that person or he otherwise enters into a transaction with that person on terms that provide for him to receive no consideration,

(b) he enters into a transaction with that person in consideration of marriage, or

(c) he enters into a transaction with that person for a consideration the value of which, in money or money's worth, is significantly less than the value, in money or money's worth, of the consideration provided by the individual.

4–141   **341. "Relevant time" under ss.339, 340.**—(1) Subject as follows, the time at which an individual enters into a transaction at an undervalue . . . is a relevant time if the transaction is entered into or the preference given—

(a) in the case of a transaction at an undervalue at a time in the period of 5 years ending with the day of the presentation of the bankruptcy petition on which the individual is adjudged bankrupt . . .

(2) Where an individual enters into a transaction at an undervalue . . . at a time mentioned in paragraph (a) . . . of subsection (1) (not being, in the case of a transaction at an undervalue, a time less than 2 years before the end of the period mentioned in paragraph (a)), that time is not a relevant time for the purposes of section 339 . . . unless the individual—

(a) is insolvent at that time, or

(b) becomes insolvent in consequence of the transaction . . . but the requirements of this subsection are presumed to be satisfied, unless the contrary is shown, in relation to any transaction at an undervalue which is entered into by an individual with a person who is an associate of his (otherwise than by reason only of being his employee).

(3) For the purposes of subsection (2), an individual is insolvent if—

(a) he is unable to pay his debts as they fall due, or

(b) the value of his assets is less than the amount of his liabilities, taking into account his contingent and prospective liabilities.

4–142   **342. Orders under ss.339, 340.**—(2) An order under section 339 or 340 may affect the property of, or impose any obligation on, any person whether or not he is the person with whom the individual in question entered into the transaction . . . but such an order—

(a) shall not prejudice any interest in property which was acquired from a person other than that individual and was acquired in good faith and for value or prejudice any interest deriving from such an interest, and

(b) shall not require a person who received a benefit from the transaction . . . in good faith and for value to pay a sum to the trustee of the bankrupt's estate, except where he was a party to the transaction . . .

(2A)[41]   Where a person has acquired an interest in property from a person other **4–143**
than the individual in question, or has received a benefit from the transaction . . .,
and at the time of that acquisition or receipt—

(a) he had notice of the relevant surrounding circumstances and of the relevant
    proceedings, or
(b) he was an associate of, or was connected with, either the individual in
    question or the person with whom that individual entered into that
    transaction . . .

then, unless the contrary is shown, it shall be presumed for the purposes of para. (a)
or para. (b) of subsection (2) that the interest was acquired or the benefit was
received otherwise than in good faith.

(4) For the purposes of subsection (2A)(a), the relevant surrounding circumstances are

(a) the fact that the individual in question entered into the transaction at an
    undervalue; or
(b) . . .

(5) For the purposes of subsection (2A)(a), a person has notice of the relevant
proceedings if he has notice—

(a) of the fact that the petition on which the individual in question is
    adjudicated bankrupt has been presented; or
(b) of the fact that the individual in question has been adjudged bankrupt.

QUESTIONS

1. Sharp transferred various assets to trustees to be held on trust for Sharp **4–144**
himself for life or until he should become bankrupt or his property should otherwise
become available to his creditors. On any such event occurring the trustees were
directed to pay the income to Sharp's wife for her life. Subject to those trusts the
trustees were to hold on trust for Sharp's children absolutely in equal shares.

Four years after making the settlement Sharp was adjudicated bankrupt when he
had a wife and two adult children.

Advise Sharp's trustee in bankruptcy as to the position if he wishes (1) to sell or
(2) to retain Sharp's interest under the settlement.

2. Valiant has just been asked to become a partner in the ten partner firm of **4–145**
solicitors, "Chance & Hope." He knows that the firm has not been able to obtain
sufficient insurance cover in respect of negligence claims, so the partners would then
be personally liable for any excess claims which might amount to £20 million. He
owns a £½ million house and has just inherited £1,680,000. His wife is likely to be
elected a local councillor in the next election. Her party is likely to win and impose

---

[41] These provisions came into force on July 26, 1994 by virtue of Insolvency (No.2) Act 1994, s.6 to remove
the previous difficulties for purchasers of property that had been given away in the previous five years and
who could be adversely affected merely because they had notice of such a transaction at an undervalue. A
purchaser will now be protected if his conveyancing searches do not reveal any bankruptcy proceedings
being brought against the donor.

financial policies contravening the law, so that she could be surcharged by the District Auditor and be bankrupted if unable to pay. They have twin sons, aged two years.

He seeks your advice on what they can do to safeguard their assets, and mentions the possibility that his wife's involvement with politics might lead them to divorce, ultimately.

Chapter 5

RESULTING TRUSTS

Section 1. Overview of Resulting and Constructive Trusts

Trusts are either express trusts or trusts imposed by law. Express trusts are **5–01**
created when a settlor who intends to create a trust takes appropriate steps
to bring the trust into being. All other trusts are imposed by law: by statute,
or by the rules of equity. Laying statutory trusts to one side,[1] only two types
of trust are imposed by law: resulting trusts and constructive trusts.[2] Under
English law, these trusts arise because the rules of equity stipulate that they
will be imposed on property in particular circumstances. These rules give
the courts no discretion to bring trusts into being, or to refuse to do so,
according to their assessment of the equities of a case.[3]

What are resulting and constructive trusts?

The word "resulting" derives from the Latin word *resalire*: "to jump **5–02**
back". Hence a resulting trust is literally a trust which returns beneficial
ownership of the trust property to a person who owned the property before
it reached the trustee's hands: in equity, the beneficial interest "jumps
back" to its previous owner. Using the term "resulting trust" in a literal
sense, we could therefore meaningfully say that an "express resulting trust"
would be created if I transferred £500 to you with the instruction that you
should hold the money on trust for me. However, trust lawyers rarely use
the term "resulting trust" to describe an *express* trust which carries the
beneficial interest back to its previous owner.[4] They almost always use it to
describe a trust which conforms to this pattern, *and which is imposed by
law.*[5]

The verb "to construe" means "to interpret". Hence the word "con- **5–03**
structive" is used to denote the fact that the law interprets—or, effectively,
deems—a party's actions or words to have had some effect in law, even
though they may not actually have had this effect in fact.[6] For example, a
person with "constructive notice" is deemed to know the answers to

---

[1] Statutory trusts are imposed in various situations in different Commonwealth countries; they are not
discussed at any length in this book, but for one example, see paras 1–135 to 1–137, above.
[2] There is no separate category of "implied trust": see para.1–144, above.
[3] The position is different in some other jurisdictions: see para.6–03.
[4] But see, *e.g. Latimer v C.I.R.* [2004] 1 W.L.R. 1466 at [41], *per* Lord Millett.
[5] *e.g. Lane v Dighton* (1762) Amb. 409 at 411, *per* Sir Thomas Clarke M.R.; *Barton v Muir* (1874) L.R. 6
P.C. 134 at 145, *per* Sir John Stuart; *Churcher v Martin* (1889) 42 Ch.D. 312 at 319, *per* Kekewich J.; *Re
English & American Insurance Co. Ltd* [1994] 1 B.C.L.C. 649 at 651, *per* Harman J.; *Air Jamaica Ltd v
Charlton* [1999] 1 W.L.R. 1399 at 1412, *per* Lord Millett.
[6] Sir R. Megarry, "Historical Development" in *Special Lectures of the Law Society of Upper Canada 1990—
Fiduciary Duties* (1991) 1, 5: "'Constructive' seems to mean 'It isn't, but has to be treated as if it were'."

questions that a reasonable person in his position would have asked, even if he does not actually know them because he has not actually asked the questions. In the case of a "constructive trust", the law deems a defendant to have conferred the same proprietary rights[7] on a claimant as he would have acquired, had the defendant validly declared an express trust in his favour, even though no such valid declaration has actually been made.[8] Thus a "constructive trust" is literally a trust which is not an express trust, and which is imposed by law.

Why are resulting and constructive trusts imposed?

5–04   Why are resulting and constructive trusts imposed, and what (if any) are the differences between them? Unfortunately, these questions are difficult to answer. We can list the situations in which the courts have imposed resulting and constructive trusts, but establishing a more rigorous taxonomy of these situations is a challenging task. One problem is that the classifications "resulting trust" and "constructive trust" seem to cut across one another. If a constructive trust is a trust imposed by law in circumstances where no express trust has been validly declared, and a resulting trust is a trust which returns beneficial ownership of the trust property to a previous owner, then it seems to follow that some trusts can be both resulting trusts and constructive trusts. Different judges have drawn different conclusions from this. On one view, all trusts imposed by law are constructive trusts, and resulting trusts are a sub-set of constructive trusts which conform to a particular fact-pattern,[9] so that the two are effectively interchangeable whenever these facts are encountered.[10] On another view, resulting trusts and constructive trusts are distinct categories of trust, imposed by the courts for different reasons.[11] We cannot decide which of these views is correct unless we know why constructive and resulting trusts are imposed. If they are imposed for the same reasons, then they are identical and it does not matter which label we use, although it would make life easier if we only used one label. If they are imposed for different reasons, then we can say that one type of trust is used in one set of circumstances, and the other in another set of circumstances, though we must stay alert to the possibility that these sets of circumstances may sometimes coincide.[12]

---

[7] But not the same personal rights: see paras 5–06 to 5–08.

[8] L. D. Smith, "Constructive Trusts and Constructive Trustees" [1999] C.L.J. 294, 294–298.

[9] *Re Llanover Settled Estates* [1926] Ch. 626 at 637, *per* Astbury J., approving the statement to this effect in A. Underhill, *The Law Relating to Trusts and Trustees* (8th ed., 1926), p.9.

[10] *Gissing v Gissing* [1971] A.C. 886 at 905, *per* Lord Diplock; *Cowcher v Cowcher* [1972] 1 W.L.R. 425 at 431, *per* Bagnall J.; *Hussey v Palmer* [1972] 1 W.L.R. 1286 at 1289, *per* Lord Denning M.R.; *Collings v Lee* [2001] 2 All E.R. 332 at 336, *per* Nourse L.J.

[11] *Allen v Snyder* (1977) 2 N.S.W.L.R. 685 at 698, *per* Samuels J.A.; *Drake v Whipp* [1996] 1 F.L.R. 826 at 829–30, *per* Peter Gibson L.J.; *Westdeutsche Landesbank Girozentrale v Islington LB.C.* [1996] A.C. 669 at 715, *per* Lord Browne-Wilkinson, followed in *Papamichael v National Westminster Bank plc* [2003] 1 Lloyd's Rep. 341 at [239], *per* Judge Chambers Q.C.; *Air Jamaica Ltd v Charlton* [1999] 1 W.L.R. 1399 at 1412, *per* Lord Millett.

[12] For example, if resulting trusts respond to a defendant's unjust enrichment, and constructive trusts respond to a defendant's wrongdoing, then it could be appropriate to impose either type of trust where a defendant takes a claimant's money in breach of a pre-existing duty and uses it to buy a new asset. Here, the new asset might be characterized either as an unjust enrichment or as a wrongful gain: R. Chambers "Tracing and Unjust Enrichment" in J. W. Neyers *et al.* (eds.) *Understanding Unjust Enrichment* (2004) 263, p.279.

Some legal scholars have recently sought to explain resulting and **5–05** constructive trusts by analysing them as "responses" to legally significant "causative events",[13] methodology that was first propounded by the late Professor Peter Birks.[14] On this approach, legal rights are understood to respond to various causative events, such as consent, wrongs, and unjust enrichment. In some cases these rights include not only personal rights, but also proprietary rights arising under trusts imposed by law. Hence the key to understanding trusts imposed by law is to identify the source of the rights which they afford to the beneficiaries: *i.e.* the "causative events" to which these rights respond. The writers who have taken this approach have differed in their conclusions, but their work confirms that Professor Birks' methodology is a powerful analytical tool. It enables us to understand more clearly the ways in which the law of trusts might align with the law of obligations, and the ways in which resulting and constructive trusts might differ from one another. We shall return to event-based analyses of resulting trusts in section 5 below, and to similar analyses of constructive trusts in Chapter 6.[15]

Personal and proprietary rights distinguished

The trustee of a resulting or constructive trust owes the same core duty **5–06** as an express trustee, to hold the trust property for the beneficiary and convey it to his order.[16] However, this is the limit of his obligations, and he does not also owe the fiduciary duty of loyalty which attaches to express trusteeship,[17] since this must be undertaken voluntarily.[18] Hence the beneficiary of a resulting or constructive trust does not enjoy the same personal

---

[13] Professor Robert Chambers' work in this field is particularly important: R. Chambers, *Resulting Trusts* (1997); R. Chambers, "Constructive Trusts in Canada" (1999) 37 Alberta L.R. 173, reprinted (2001) 15 Tru L.I. 214 and (2002) 16 Tru. L.I. 2; R. Chambers, "Resulting Trusts in Canada" (2000) 38 Alberta L.R. 378, reprinted (2002) 16 Tru. L.I. 104 and 138. His work on resulting trusts builds on P. Birks "Restitution and Resulting Trusts" in S. Goldstein (ed.), *Equity and Contemporary Legal Developments* (1992) 335, reprinted P. Birks and F. D. Rose (eds), *Restitution and Equity* (2000) 265. Differing analyses founded on the same methodology include: W. J. Swadling, "A New Role for Resulting Trusts?" (1996) 16 L.S. 110; C. E. F. Rickett, "The Classification of Trusts" (1999) 18 N.Z Law Rev. 305; C. E. F. Rickett and R. Grantham, "Resulting Trusts: A Rather Limited Doctrine" in P. Birks and F. D. Rose (eds), *Restitution and Equity* (2000) 39; B. Macfarlane, "Constructive Trusts Arising on Receipt of Property *Sub Conditione*" (2004) 120 L.Q.R. 667.
[14] *e.g.* P. Birks, "Equity in the Modern Law: An Exercise in Taxonomy" (1996) 26 U.W.A.L.R. 1; P. Birks, "Equity, Conscience, and Unjust Enrichment" (1999) 23 University of Melbourne L.R. 1.
[15] See paras 6–04 *et seq.* Express trusts arise in response to the settlor's intention to confer proprietary rights on the beneficiaries. These can come into existence even if the beneficiaries and the trustee are unaware of the settlor's intention until later, *e.g.* where the trust is created on death by the settlor's will. If the trustee disclaims, equity will not allow the trust to fail for want of a trustee and the settlor himself or his personal representative will become trustee for the beneficiaries: *Mallott v Wilson* [1903] 2 Ch. 49; *Harris v Sharp* [2003] W.T.L.R. 1541. In virtually all cases, however, a settlor sensibly obtains the agreement of the trustee to act as such in advance of his declaration of trust.
[16] *Allied Carpets Group plc v Nethercott* Q.B.D. January 28, 2000, Colman J.; *Re Holmes* [2005] 1 All E.R. 490 at [22], *per* Burnton J. Hence the beneficiary can obtain an order against the trustee akin to the orders for conveyance made in *Dillwyn v Llewelyn* (1862) 4 De G. F. & J. 517 at 523, *per* Lord Westbury L.C., and more recently in *Riches v Hogben* [1985] 2 Qd. R. 292 at 302, *per* McPherson J. The trustee may also be obliged to get in the trust estate where this is necessary: *Evans v European Bank Ltd* (2004) 7 I.T.E.L.R. 19 at [116], *per* Spigelman C.J.; *Bracken Partners Ltd v Gutteridge* [2004] 1 B.C.L.C. 373.
[17] *Lonrho plc v Fayed (No.2)* [1992] 1 W.L.R. 1 at 12, *per* Millett J. Nor need he undertake the administrative and managerial duties with which express trustees are commonly charged, as discussed in Chapter 9.
[18] A. Scott, "The Fiduciary Principle" (1949) 37 Cal. L.R. 539, 540; *Hospital Products Ltd v United States Surgical Corp.* (1984) 156 C.L.R. 41 at 96–97.

rights against the trustee as those which are generally enjoyed by the beneficiaries of an express trust.[19]

5–07   There is a significant difference between a beneficiary's proprietary rights under a resulting or constructive trust, and his personal rights against the trustee. In *Westdeutsche Landesbank Girozentrale v Islington L.B.C.*,[20] Lord Browne-Wilkinson thought that it would be inappropriate to fix a resulting or constructive trustee with personal liability to account to the beneficiaries for the trust property, unless his conscience were affected with knowledge of the circumstances which led to the creation of the beneficiary's equitable proprietary interest. Situations can certainly be imagined in which it would seem harsh to hold a resulting or constructive trustee liable to make good losses out of the trust funds when he does not know that the beneficiary has an equitable interest in the property: where the trustee is an infant, for example.[21] However, it need not follow from this, as Lord Browne-Wilkinson also held, that a resulting or constructive trust should not arise at all unless and until the trustee's conscience is affected by knowledge of the relevant circumstances.[22]

5–08   Less drastic strategies than denying the existence of the trust altogether are open to a court that wishes to avoid fixing a resulting or constructive trustee with personal liability for spending the trust assets in good faith: for example, placing the trustee under no greater duty than "an obligation to restore the property on demand, if still in possession of it" at the time when the trustee becomes aware of the trust's existence.[23] Various authorities contradict the view that trusts cannot be imposed by law unless and until the trustee's conscience is affected,[24] and in Professor Chambers' words:[25]

> "delaying the creation of the trust until the trustees have sufficient notice to affect their consciences may have a drastic effect on a number of important matters which depend on the timing of the creation of the resulting [or constructive] trust, such as entitlement to income, liability for taxation, risk and insurance, commencement of limitation periods, transfer and transmission of property interests, and priority of competing claims."

In principle, therefore, the best view is that a resulting or constructive trust can arise whatever the state of the trustee's conscience, and that when it

---

[19] R. H. Maudsley, "Constructive Trusts" (1977) 28 N.I.L.R. 123, 124; R. Chambers, *Resulting Trusts* (1997) 194–200; L. D. Smith, "Constructive Fiduciaries?" in P. Birks (ed.), *Privacy and Loyalty* (1997) 249, 263–267; Lord Millett, "Restitution and Constructive Trusts" (1998) 114 L.Q.R. 399, 404–5. *Quaere* whether a resulting or constructive trustee enjoys the same right of indemnity as an express trustee? On this point, see *Nolan v Collie* (2003) 7 V.R. 287 at [32]–[34]; *Re Loftus (deceased)* [2005] EWHC 406 (Ch) at [201].
[20] [1996] A.C. 669 at 705–706. See paras 5–186 to 5–190.
[21] As in *Re Vinogradoff* [1935] W.N. 68.
[22] [1996] A.C. 669 at 706–707; at paras 5–195 to 5–197; recognising that an equitable proprietary interest can burden a defendant's legal estate before his conscience is affected, but refusing to use the term "trust" to describe this interest.
[23] J. Hackney, *Understanding Equity & Trusts* (1987) 167. Other possible strategies are explored in R. Chambers, *Resulting Trusts* (1997), pp.209–212.
[24] *Birch v Blagrave* (1755) Amb. 264; *Childers v Childers* (1857) 1 De G. & J. 482; *Re Vinogradoff* [1935] W.N. 68; *Re Diplock* [1948] Ch. 465; *Re Muller* [1953] N.Z.L.R. 879.
[25] R. Chambers, *Resulting Trusts* (1997), p.206.

does so the beneficiary immediately acquires an equitable proprietary interest in the trust assets,[26] along with a concomitant right to see an account of the trustee's dealings with the property from the moment of receipt. However, this need not mean that the trustee will be personally liable for disposing of the trust assets before his conscience is affected by knowledge of the circumstances which led to the imposition of the trust.[27]

Exemption from formality rules

Neither resulting nor constructive trusts are subject to the Law of Property Act 1925, s.53(1), a fact which takes on particular significance in cases where spouses or unmarried cohabitees have both contributed towards the purchase or upkeep of a shared home without any writing being used to set out the respective size of each party's equitable interest in the property.[28]   **5–09**

Classifying resulting trusts

Lord Millett has written extra-judicially that: "Resulting trusts arise in three situations: voluntary payment or transfer; purchase in the name of another; and incomplete disposal of the beneficial interest. The first two have been described as 'apparent gifts'; the last as 'failing trusts'."[29] We shall adopt this classification for the purpose of expounding the cases in sections 3 and 4. First, though, we must explain what lawyers mean when they speak of "automatic" and "presumed resulting trusts", and we must examine the role of presumptions and intention in this area of the law.   **5–10**

Section 2. "Automatic" and "Presumed Resulting Trusts"

In *Re Vandervell's Trusts (No.2)*, Megarry J. held that there are two types of resulting trusts: "automatic resulting trusts" and "presumed resulting trusts".[30] In his Lordship's view, the former arise "automatically" when some or all of the beneficial interest in property held on an express trust has not been exhausted. On Megarry J.'s view, for example, an "automatic resulting trust" would arise if X transferred property to Y on trust for Z, for the period of Z's life, remainder to Z's children, and Z then died without issue. In this situation, X would have failed to dispose of the whole beneficial interest in the trust property, and since it cannot have been his   **5–11**

---

[26] *Cf. Hardoon v Belilios* [1901] A.C. 118 at 123, *per* Lord Lindley: a trust exists when "the legal title [is] in the plaintiff and the equitable title in the defendant."

[27] *R. v Chester and North Wales Legal Aid Area Office Ex p Floods of Queensferry Ltd* [1998] 1 W.L.R. 1496 at 1500, *per* Millett L.J.; *Allan v Rea Brothers Trustees Ltd* [2002] P.L.R. 169 at [55], *per* Robert Walker L.J.; *Waxman v Waxman* (2004) 7 I.T.E.L.R. 162 at [583], *per curiam* (Ont. CA); *Clark v Cutland* [2004] 1 W.L.R. 783 (D can hold property on constructive trust though C concedes that D not personally liable to account). See too R. Chambers, *Resulting Trusts* (1997), pp.200–209; W. J. Swadling, "Property and Conscience" (1998) 14 Tru L.I. 228; Lord Millett, "Restitution and Constructive Trusts" (1998) 114 L.Q.R. 399, 403–406.

[28] See paras 5–89 *et seq.* and 6–93 *et seq.*

[29] Lord Millett, "Pension Schemes and the Law of Trusts" (2000) 14 Tru L.I. 66, 73.

[30] [1974] Ch. 269 at 288 *et seq.*, glossing *Vandervell v I.R.C.* [1967] 2 A.C. 291 at 312 *et seq.*, *per* Lord Upjohn.

intention for the remainder interest to go to Y, or to the Crown as *bona vacantia*, a resulting trust "automatically" returns it to X.

5–12   In contrast, Megarry J. thought that a "presumed resulting trust" would arise in cases where X buys property in Y's name, or gratuitously transfers property to Y. In these situations, X may have made his intentions clear, but if he does not, then equity presumes what they must have been. It is inherently more likely in these cases than in the first case that X intended to give Y the property. Nonetheless equity views the transaction with a cynical eye and raises a presumption in X's favour, failure to rebut which by Y will lead to the imposition of a resulting trust in X's favour. In Megarry J.'s view, the relevant presumption in cases of this sort is that X intends Y to be trustee for him, a point to which we shall return below.

5–13   Megarry J.'s analysis was doubted by Lord Browne-Wilkinson in *Westdeutsche Landesbank Girozentrale v Islington L.B.C.* His Lordship observed that there is no real difference between the two classes of case which Megarry J. identified.[31] In the first case as in the second, X transfers legal title to property to Y and gets nothing in return for it. In the first case as in the second, the imposition of a resulting trust leads to the creation of a new equitable property right for X, and as a new right, as Professor Chambers has written, "it cannot be explained as the inertia of a pre-existing beneficial interest".[32] In the first case, as in the second, a resulting trust will not arise if Y can prove that X meant to benefit him. So, in the example given above, Y could keep the remainder interest for himself if he could show that X meant him to do so in the event that Z died childless.[33] This all suggests that there are not two types of resulting trust, but only one, imposed by law when property is transferred gratuitously and the transferee cannot establish that the transferor meant him to take the beneficial interest for himself.

---

[31] See too Lord Browne-Wilkinson, "Constructive Trusts and Unjust Enrichment" (1996) 10 Tru. L.I. 98, 99–100; Lord Millett, "Restitution and Constructive Trusts" (1998) 114 L.Q.R. 399, 402 n.17; Lord Millett, "Pension Schemes and the Law of Trusts" (2000) 14 Tru L.I. 66, 73.

[32] R. Chambers, "Resulting Trusts in Canada" (2000) 38 Alberta L.R. 379, 389.

[33] A resulting trust would also be precluded in this case if X intended to abandon the property, as it would then go to the Crown as *bona vacantia*. The courts are generally reluctant to find that settlors mean to abandon their property: *Davis v Richards & Wallington Ltd* [1990] 1 W.L.R. 1511 at 1540–1542, *per* Scott J., following *Jones v Williams*, Ch.D., 15 March 1988, Knox J. But for a rare case where the court so found, see *Environment Agency v Hilldridge Ltd* [2004] 2 B.C.L.C. 358, and note too that in the case of street collections, where thousands of individual donors contribute money towards a purpose which is then accomplished leaving a surplus, the courts are likely to find a general intention to part utterly with contributed money so as to exclude any resulting trust in their favour. In such cases, the money will pass to the Crown, as in *e.g. Re West Sussex Constabulary's Fund Trusts* [1971] Ch. 1, para.5–58, unless accruing to the funds of an unincorporated association for which the collections were made, as in *e.g. Re Bucks Constabulary Fund Friendly Society (No.2)* [1979] 1 W.L.R. 936, para.5–66. *Cf.* Lord Millett, "Pension Schemes and the Law of Trusts" (2000) 14 Tru L.I. 66, 74, professing the unorthodox view that if no resulting trust arises on the failure of an express trust, then the trustees should become the beneficial owners of the trust assets, so that these would become *bona vacantia* only if the trustees disclaimed their interest.

RE VANDERVELL'S TRUSTS (NO.2)

Chancery Division [1974] Ch. 269; [1974] 1 All E.R. 47; [1973] 3 W.L.R. 744

See paras 2–67 *et seq.* for the facts of the case revealing that while the Court of **5–14** Appeal disagreed with Megarry J.'s view of the facts no adverse comment was made on his propositions on resulting trusts.

MEGARRY J. (in a reserved judgment): "It seems to me that the relevant points on **5–15** resulting trusts may be put in a series of propositions . . . as follows.

"(1) If a transaction fails to make any effective disposition of any interest it does **5–16** nothing. This is so at law and in equity, and has nothing to do with resulting trusts.

"(2) Normally the mere existence of some unexpressed intention in the breast of **5–17** the owner of the property does nothing: there must at least be some expression of that intention before it can effect any result. To yearn is not to transfer.

"(3) Before any doctrine of resulting trust can come into play, there must at least **5–18** be some effective transaction which transfers or creates some interest in property.

"(4) Where A effectually transfers to B (or creates in his favour) any interest in **5–19** any property, whether legal or equitable, a resulting trust for A may arise in two distinct classes of case. For simplicity, I shall confine my statement to cases in which the transfer or creation is made without B providing any valuable consideration, and where no presumption of advancement can arise; and I shall state the position for transfers without specific mention of the creation of new interests.

"(a) The first class of case is where the transfer to B is not made on any trust. If, **5–20** of course, it appears from the transfer that B is intended to hold on certain trusts, that will be decisive, and the case is not within this category; and similarly if it appears that B is intended to take beneficially. But in other cases there is a rebuttable presumption that B holds on a resulting trust for A. The question is not one of the automatic consequences of a dispositive failure by A, but one of presumption: the property has been carried to B, and from the absence of consideration and any presumption of advancement B is presumed not only to hold the entire interest on trust, but also to hold the beneficial interest for A absolutely. The presumption thus establishes both that A is to take on trust and also what that trust is. Such resulting trusts may be called 'presumed resulting trusts'."

"(b) The second class of case is where the transfer to B is made on trusts which **5–21** leave some or all of the beneficial interest undisposed of. Here B automatically holds on a resulting trust for A to the extent that the beneficial interest has not been carried to him or others. The resulting trust here does not depend on any intentions or presumptions, but is the automatic consequence of A's failure to dispose of what is vested in him. Since *ex hypothesi* the transfer is on trust, the resulting trust does not establish the trust but merely carries back to A the beneficial interest that has not been disposed of. Such resulting trusts may be called 'automatic resulting trusts'."

"(5) Where trustees hold property in trust for A, and it is they who, at A's **5–22** direction, make the transfer to B, similar principles apply, even though on the face of the transaction the transferor appears to be the trustees and not A. If the transfer to B is on trust, B will hold any beneficial interest that has not been effectually disposed of on an automatic resulting trust for the true transferor, A. If the transfer to B is not on trust, there will be a rebuttable presumption that B holds on a resulting trust for A."

WESTDEUTSCHE LANDESBANK GIROZENTRALE v ISLINGTON L.B.C.

House of Lords, [1996] A.C. 669; [1996] 2 W.L.R. 802; [1996] 2 All E.R. 961

5–23   See para.5–173 for the facts of the case.

5–24   LORD BROWNE-WILKINSON: "Under existing law a resulting trust arises in two sets of circumstances:

5–25   "(A) Where A makes a voluntary payment to B or pays (wholly or in part) for the purchase of property which is vested either in B alone or in the joint names of A and B, there is a presumption that A did not intend to make a gift to B: the money or property is held on trust for A (if he is the sole provider of the money) or in the case of a joint purchase by A and B in shares proportionate to their contributions. It is important to stress that this is only a presumption, which presumption is easily rebutted either by the counter-presumption of advancement or by direct evidence of A's intention to make an outright transfer.[34]

5–26   "(B) Where A transfers property to B on express trusts, but the trusts declared do not exhaust the whole beneficial interest.[35]

5–27   "Both types of resulting trust are traditionally regarded as examples of trusts giving effect to the common intention of the parties. A resulting trust is not imposed by law against the intentions of the trustee (as is a constructive trust) but gives effect to his presumed intention. Megarry J. in *Re Vandervell's Trusts (No.2)* suggests that a resulting trust of type (B) does not depend on intention but operates automatically. I am not convinced that this is right. If the settlor has expressly, or by necessary implication, abandoned any beneficial interest in the trust property, there is in my view no resulting trust: the undisposed-of equitable interest vests in the Crown as *bona vacantia*.[36]"

5–28   On the traditional view of the law espoused by Megarry J. in *Re Vandervell's Trusts (No.2)*, above, and by Lord Browne-Wilkinson in the *Westdeutsche* case, above, resulting trusts arise where property is transferred gratuitously, and the transferor X's intentions are unclear, because he is presumed to intend that the transferee Y should hold the property on trust for him.[37] However, this analysis suffers from a significant drawback: it cannot account for cases where resulting trusts have been imposed, but it is clear that X had no intention that Y should be his trustee, or even that the one thing X intended was precisely that Y should not be his trustee. In such cases, Y should have been able to rebut a presumption that he was to hold the property on trust, and yet a resulting trust was still imposed. For example, in *Vandervell v IRC*,[38] as we have seen,[39] Vandervell thought that he had disposed of his property completely, and did not want the remainder of the property to result to him, as this rendered him liable to tax that he had sought to avoid; in *Re Vinogradoff*,[40] the transferor could not have

---

[34] Underhill & Hayton, pp.317 ff.; *Vandervell v I.R.C.* [1967] 2 A.C. 291 at 312ff.; *Re Vandervell's Trusts (No.2)* [1974] Ch. 269 at pp.288ff.
[35] *ibid.* and *Barclays Bank Ltd v Quistclose Investments Ltd* [1970] A.C. 567.
[36] *Re West Sussex Constabulary's Widows, Children and Benevolent (1930) Fund Trusts* [1971] Ch. 1.
[37] W. J. Swadling, "A New Role for Resulting Trusts?" (1996) 16 L.S. 110, 115.
[38] [1967] 2 A.C. 291.
[39] Above at para.2–16.
[40] [1935] W.N. 68.

intended the transferee to be trustee for her because the transferee was her seven year-old grand-daughter; and in *El Ajou v Dollar Land Holdings plc*,[41] the transferor had no such intention because it was unaware of the fact that the property had been taken from it in the first place.

This problem can be solved by recognizing that resulting trusts are not **5–29** imposed in response to X's (actual or presumed) intention to create a trust, but in response to the fact that X (actually or presumably) did not intend to make a gift to Y.[42] This analysis makes sense of all the cases, including those listed above: it is clear, for example, that although Vandervell did not wish the share option to result to him, he did not wish to make an outright gift of it to the trustee company, either, as Lord Millett pointed out in *Air Jamaica Ltd v Charlton*.[43] Hence, as Lord Phillips M.R. recently held in *Lavelle v Lavelle*, the best view of the law is that:[44]

> "where one person, A, transfers the legal title of a property he owns or purchases to another, B, without receipt of any consideration, the effect will depend on his intention. . . . Normally there will be evidence of the intention with which a transfer is made. Where there is not, the law applies presumptions. Where there is no close relationship between A and B, there will be a presumption that A does not intend to part with the beneficial interest in the property . . . [If B fails to rebut this presumption, then he will] take the legal title under a resulting trust for A."[45]

There are also cases where X transfers property to Y and he does **5–30** actually intend that Y should hold the property on trust for X. If all relevant formalities are complied with, then the arrangement will simply take effect as an express trust. If they are not, then the express trust intended by X will be unenforceable, and if X is to receive an equitable beneficial interest then it must be under a resulting trust, as in *Hodgson v Marks*. However, even cases of this sort can be explained on the basis that evidence of X's intention to create a trust for himself demonstrates that he had no intention to benefit Y.

Resulting trusts respond only to a transferor's lack of intention to benefit **5–31** a transferee. Lord Browne-Wilkinson thought that "a resulting trust arises in order to give effect to the intention of the parties":[46] *i.e.* he saw them as responding to the intentions of both the transferor and the transferee. In this, however, his Lordship confused resulting trusts with common intention

---

[41] [1993] 3 All E.R. 717.
[42] R. Chambers, *Resulting Trusts* (1997), pp.19–27; P. Birks, *Unjust Enrichment* (2003), pp.136–137.
[43] [1999] 1 W.L.R. 1399 at 1412; at para.5–48. See too *Twinsectra Ltd v Yardley* [2000] W.T.L.R. 527 at 562, *per* Potter L.J.; [2002] 2 A.C. 164 at [91], *per* Lord Millett.
[44] [2004] 2 F.C.R. 418 at [13]–[14].
[45] Where there *is* a close relationship between A and B, such as father and child, a countervailing presumption of advancement will be raised: see para.5–117.
[46] "Constructive Trusts and Unjust Enrichment" (1996) 10 Tru L.I. 98, 99, echoed in *Tinsley v Milligan* [1994] 1 A.C. 340 at 371; *Westdeutsche Landesbank Girozentrale v Islington L.B.C.* [1996] A.C. 669 at 708.

constructive trusts,[47] and his view is inconsistent with cases where resulting trusts were imposed on property held by transferees who had no intention of becoming trustees, for example because they were legally incapable of forming any intention at all.[48] Hence, the better view is that the only person whose intentions are relevant is the transferor.[49]

5–32   A presumption in the transferor's favour will only be made in cases where there is no evidence that he intended to create a trust, or to make a gift, or to make a loan of the property to the transferee.[50] In cases where the court has heard sufficient evidence to determine the transferor's intention on the facts, there is no need for any presumption to be made.[51]

HODGSON v MARKS

Court of Appeal [1971] Ch. 892, [1971] 2 All E.R. 684; [1971] 2 W.L.R. 1263 (Russell, Buckley, and Caisus L.JJ.).

5–33   Mrs. Hodgson was an elderly widow who transferred legal title to her house to her lodger, Mr. Evans, to stop her nephew from turning him out of the house. Mr. Evans sold the house to Mr. Marks, who granted a registered mortgage over the house to a building society to secure a purchase loan. Mr. Marks and Mrs. Hodgson knew nothing of one another at this time. When she found out what had happened, she sued Mr. Marks and the building society, and asked for the house to be reconveyed to her free of the mortgage. At first instance the judge held that Mrs. Hodgson had not intended to make a gift to Mr. Evans, but that she had intended that he should hold the house on an express trust for her. This trust was *prima facie* unenforceable for non-compliance with the LPA 1925, s.53(1)(b), but relying on *Rochefoucauld v Boustead*,[52] the judge held that the statute should not be used to prevent her from giving evidence of fraud, with the result that she should be permitted to prove the oral trust. However, the judge dismissed Mrs. Hodgson's claim because he considered that she had no overriding interest under the LRA 1925, s.70(1)(g) as a person "in actual occupation of the land". On appeal, the Court of Appeal held that she did have an overriding interest binding on Mr. Marks and the building society.

5–34   RUSSELL L.J. (with whom the other judges agreed) decided that Mrs. Hodgson had relevantly been in "actual occupation" of the house during the relevant period, and then proceeded: "I turn next to the question whether s.53(1) of the Law of

---

[47] For which see paras 6–93 *et seq.* It seems likely that his Lordship was misled by Lord Diplock's unfortunately expressed speech in *Gissing v Gissing* [1971] A.C. 886 at 904–5 and 922. Certainly a misreading of this speech led the Canadian courts to use unorthodox "common intention resulting trusts" to resolve shared homes cases (*e.g. Rathwell v Rathwell* [1978] 2 S.C.R. 436), an approach which has now given way to the application of statutes and constructive trust reasoning: *Oosterhoff on Trusts* 6th ed. (2004), pp.554–560.

[48] *e.g. Lench v Lench* (1805) 10 Ves. Jun. 511; *Childers v Childers* (1857) 1 De G. & J. 482; *Re Vinogradoff* [1935] W.N. 68.

[49] R. Chambers, *Resulting Trusts* (1997), 35–37; J. Mee, *The Property Rights of Cohabitees* (1999), pp.39–43. This is not to deny that a transferee's intentions can be relevant as circumstantial evidence of the transferor's intentions, as in, *e.g. Ali v Khan* (2002) 5 I.T.E.L.R. 232 at [28], *per* Morritt V.-C.

[50] *Air Jamaica Ltd v Charlton* [1999] 1 W.L.R. 1399 at 1412, *per* Lord Millett; *Twinsectra Ltd v Yardley* [2000] W.T.L.R. 527 at 562, *per* Potter L.J.; *Lavelle v Lavelle* [2004] 2 F.C.R. 418 at [13], *per* Lord Phillips M.R.

[51] *Stockholm Finance Ltd v Garden Holdings Inc.* Ch.D. October 26, 1995, *per* Robert Walker J.; *United Overseas Bank Ltd v Iwuanyanwu* Ch.D. 5 March 2001 at [33]; *Ali v Khan* (2002) 5 I.T.E.L.R. 232 at [30], *per* Morritt V.-C.; *Popely v Ayton Ltd* [2004] All E.R. (D) 149 (Apr.) at [7].

[52] [1897] 1 Ch. 196.

Property Act 1925 prevents the assertion by the plaintiff of her entitlement in equity to the house. Let me first assume that, contrary to the view expressed by the judge, the first defendant is not debarred from relying on the section, and the express oral arrangement or declaration of trust between the plaintiff and Mr. Evans found by the judge was not effective as such. Nevertheless, the evidence is clear that the transfer was not intended to operate as a gift and, in those circumstances, I do not see why there was not a resulting trust of the beneficial interest to the plaintiff, which would not, of course, be affected by s.53(1). It was argued that a resulting trust is based on implied intention, and that where there is an express trust for the transferor intended and declared—albeit ineffectively—there is no room for such an implication. I do not accept that. If an attempted express trust fails, that seems to me just the occasion for implication of a resulting trust, whether the failure be due to uncertainty, or perpetuity, or lack of form. It would be a strange outcome if the plaintiff were to lose her beneficial interest because her evidence had not been confined to negativing a gift but had additionally moved into a field forbidden by s.53(1) for lack of writing. I remark in this connection that we are not concerned with the debatable question whether on a voluntary transfer of land by A to stranger B there is a presumption of a resulting trust. The accepted evidence is that this was not intended as a gift, notwithstanding the reference to love and affection in the transfer, and s.53(1) does not exclude that evidence. . .

"On the above footing it matters not whether the first defendant was or was not **5–35** debarred from relying on s.53(1) by the principle that the section is not to be used as an instrument for fraud. The first defendant was in fact ignorant of her interest and it is forcefully argued that there is nothing fraudulent in his taking advantage of the section. I do not propose to canvass the general point further, more particularly in the light of the nature of the subject-matter with which we are dealing—an overriding interest. Quite plainly Mr. Evans could not have placed any reliance on s.53, for that would have been to use the section as an instrument of fraud. Accordingly, at the moment before registration of the first defendant as registered proprietor there was in existence an overriding interest in the plaintiff, and by force of the statute the registration could only take effect subject thereto."

QUESTIONS

Did the trust which arose in Mrs. Hodgson's favour respond to her **5–36** intention to create a trust for herself,[53] or to her lack of intention to give the house to Mr. Evans? If the former, then did it not subvert the underlying purpose of the formality rules contained in s.53 to give her enforceable rights against Mr. Marks and the building society? Would a resulting trust have arisen in Mrs. Hodgson's favour if she had transferred the house to Mr. Evans on an unenforceable oral trust for the benefit of a third party?

---

[53] As argued in W. J. Swadling, "A Hard Look at *Hodgson v Marks*", in P. Birks and F. D. Rose (eds.), *Restitution and Equity* (2000) 61.

Section 3. Failing Trusts

I. Where Resulting Trusts Arise

5–37　Resulting trusts arise in favour of the settlor where he has transferred property to trustees[54] on express trusts which fail, whether for failure of marriage consideration, uncertainty, lapse, disclaimer, perpetuity, illegality, non-compliance with requisite statutory formalities, or for any other reason.[55] They also arise if settlors fail to dispose exhaustively of the whole beneficial interest under their express trusts.[56] Where express trusts of funds subscribed by many settlors do not exhaust the funds there is a resulting trust in favour of the settlors rateably in proportion to the amounts subscribed by them.[57] In the case of charitable trusts that fail the funds will usually be applied *cy-près* as will be seen in Chapter 7.

5–38　　Whether or not the settlor has failed to dispose effectively of the entire beneficial interest is often a difficult matter. In *Re Abbott*[58] a fund had been subscribed for the maintenance and support of two deaf and dumb women and Stirling J. held, not as a matter of construction of the documents by which the subscriptions had been sought, but as an inference from all the facts, that the surplus left after both women had died was held on a resulting trust for the subscribers. In *Re Andrew's Trust*[59] a fund was subscribed solely for the education of the children of a deceased clergyman and not for the exclusive use of one child or for equal division among them but as necessary, and after the formal education of the children had been completed Kekewich J. held that the children were entitled to the balance equally. He construed "education" in the broadest sense as an ongoing process that did not come to an end with the conclusion of formal education, and he treated the reference to education as expressing merely the motive of the gift. Thus, he held that: "If a gross sum be given, or if the whole income of property be given, and a special purpose be assigned for the gift this court [rebuttably] regards the gift as absolute and the purpose merely as the motive of the gift, and therefore holds that the gift takes effect as to the whole sum or the whole income as the case may be".[60]

---

[54] If a settlor declares *himself* trustee of a trust which fails, he will become absolute beneficial owner of the property once more. A resulting trust is not needed to accomplish this, and in fact would be impossible, as a person cannot be a trustee solely for his own benefit: *Westdeutsche Landesbank Girozentrale v Islington L.B.C.* [1996] A.C. 669 at 703, *per* Lord Browne-Wilkinson.

[55] *Hodgson v Marks* [1971] Ch. 892 at 933 *per* Russell L.J.; *Re Ames's Settlement* [1946] Ch. 217 though see now ss.16 and 24 of the Matrimonial Causes Act 1973. If the settlor were a testator then the property would result to his estate: if the property were specifically devised or bequeathed it would fall into residue; if the property were comprised in the residuary gift then it would pass to the next-of-kin under the intestacy rules set out in the Administration of Estates Act 1925 as amended. On the impact of illegality, see paras 5–124 *et seq.*

[56] *Re West* [1900] 1 Ch. 84; *Re Gillingham Bus Disaster Fund* [1958] Ch. 300.

[57] See too *Re British Red Cross Balkan Fund* [1914] 2 Ch. 419 (where in the absence of the Att.-Gen. a resulting trust was erroneously admitted); *Re Welsh Hospital Fund* [1921] 1 Ch. 655 at 662; *Re Hobourn Aero Components Ltd's Air Raid Disaster Fund* [1946] Ch. 194; *Air Jamaica Ltd v Charlton* [1999] 1 W.L.R. 1399 (for which, see paras 5–45 *et seq.*).

[58] [1900] 2 Ch. 326.

[59] [1905] 2 Ch. 48.

[60] *ibid.* at 52–53, citing Page-Wood V.-C. in *Re Sanderson's Trust* (1857) 3 K. & J. 497 at 503.

This was applied by the Court of Appeal in *Re Osoba*[61] holding that a **5–39** bequest to the testator's widow upon trust "for her maintenance and for the training of my daughter Abiola up to university grade and for the maintenance of my aged mother" was a trust for the three women absolutely as joint tenants so that nothing resulted to the testator's estate after Abiola finished her university education, the widow and the mother having died by then, so that Abiola was absolutely entitled as the surviving joint tenant.

It was formerly thought that a resulting trust conforming to the pattern **5–40** described here would also arise following the failure of a purpose trust to apply money lent for a specific purpose. In *Barclays Bank Ltd v Quistclose Investments Ltd*[62] a company lent money to another company in the same corporate group for the purpose of paying a dividend to the shareholders of the second company, and the second company became insolvent before the dividend was paid. The House of Lords held that the money was held for the first company on a resulting trust which arose on the failure of a primary express trust to pay the dividend. However, this was difficult to reconcile with various trust law principles, *e.g.* the beneficiary principle which suggests that if the primary trust was a trust for a private purpose then it should have been void.[63] Building on his extra-judicial criticisms of the reasoning in *Quistclose* and subsequent cases applying the principle,[64] Lord Millett therefore reinterpreted these authorities in *Twinsectra Ltd v Yardley*.[65] In essence, he held that where X lends money to Y on the condition that Y applies the money to a specific purpose in circumstances such as those which obtained in the *Quistclose* case, a trust of the money immediately arises in X's favour, but this trust is defeasible by the exercise of a power vested in Y to apply the money to the specified purpose.[66] It seems from his extra-judicial writings that Lord Millett formerly thought that the trust for X would always be an express trust, but his speech in *Twinsectra* suggests that he was persuaded by Professor Chambers' general work on resulting trusts to modify this opinion,[67] and to hold that in cases where the transferor does not declare an express trust for himself when he lends the money to the transferee, a resulting trust can arise in his favour.[68]

---

[61] [1979] 2 All E.R. 393.
[62] [1970] A.C. 567. See too *ETVR* [1987] B.C.L.C. 646.
[63] R. Chambers, *Resulting Trusts* (1997), pp.68–89; W. J. Swadling, "Orthodoxy" in W. J. Swadling (ed.) *The Quistclose Trust: Critical Essays* (2004) 9.
[64] P. J. Millett Q.C. "The *Quistclose* Trust: Who Can Enforce It?" (1985) 101 L.Q.R. 269.
[65] [2002] A.C. 164; at para.11–87.
[66] The nature of this power is discussed in L. Smith "Understanding the Power" in Swadling, above, 67.
[67] Although not his analysis of the *Quistclose* case, which his Lordship thought vulnerable to the criticisms made in L. Ho and P. St.J. Smart "Reinterpreting the *Quistclose* Trust: A Critique of Chambers' Analysis" (2001) 21 O.J.L.S. 267. Professor Chambers answers these criticisms, and restates his position on *Quistclose*, in "Restrictions on the Use of Money" in Swadling, above, 77; see too J. Glister, "The Nature of *Quistclose* Trusts: Classification and Reconciliation" [2004] C.L.J. 632.
[68] As noted in J. Penner, "Lord Millett's Analysis" in Swadling, above, 41, pp.50–56. See also Lord Millett's own comments in the foreword to this book, at p.ix.

II. WHERE RESULTING TRUSTS DO NOT ARISE

5–41 There is no resulting trust for the settlor or his estate on the failure of an express trust if the trustee is expressly intended to take the property beneficially for himself subject to a charge for some purpose. Thus, in *Re Foord*[69] where a testator left his estate to his sister "absolutely . . . on trust" to pay his widow an annuity and the estate exceeded the annuity the sister was held beneficially entitled to the balance. Likewise, there is no resulting trust where the rule in *Hancock v Watson*[70] applies. This rule states that "if you find an absolute gift to a legatee in the first instance, and trusts are engrafted or imposed on that absolute interest which fail, either from lapse or invalidity or any other reason, then the absolute gift takes effect so far as the trusts have failed to the exclusion of the residuary legatee or next-of-kin as the case may be."[71] The rule is equally applicable to *inter vivos* settlements.[72]

5–42 There is no resulting trust if the doctrine of acceleration applies to prevent there being a temporary failure to exhaust the beneficial interest under a trust.[73] Thus, if T by will leaves property to A for life and after A's death to B absolutely, and A disclaims his interest, B's interest is accelerated so as to take effect immediately, thereby ousting any possible resulting trust of the income until A's death. For the doctrine to apply the remainderman must have a vested interest and there must be no contrary intention manifested in the trust document.[74]

5–43 There is usually no resulting trust where a party has transferred property under a contract (save for the rare cases in which a *Quistclose*-style arrangement has been agreed by the parties, as discussed above[75]). Thus, in the case of a society formed to raise funds by subscriptions from its members for the purpose of providing for their widows, which had surplus funds after the death of the last widow, there could be no resulting trust for the deceased members' estates: each member had parted absolutely with his money in return for contractual benefits for his widow.[76] Similarly, no resulting trust can arise where donors part absolutely with their money for tickets contractually entitling them to participate in raffles, sweepstakes, beetle drives, whist drives, discos, or to watch live entertainment, and the purposes for which such money has been raised fail to exhaust the profits arising after deducting expenses.[77]

5–44 *Davis v Richard & Wallington Ltd*[78] concerned a surplus within a pension scheme. The funds of the scheme were held on trust but the trust deed was silent as to the destination of any surplus, and there was no way to amend

---

[69] [1922] 2 Ch. 519. See too *Cook v Hutchinson* (1836) 1 Keen 42. But contrast the resulting trust in *Re West* [1900] 1 Ch. 84.
[70] [1902] A.C. 14. See too *Lassence v Tierney* (1849) 1 Mac. & G. 551.
[71] *ibid.* at 22 (Lord Davey).
[72] *A.-G. v Lloyd's Bank* [1935] A.C. 382; *Re Burton's S.T.* [1955] Ch. 348; *Watson v Holland* [1985] 1 All E.R. 290.
[73] *Re Flower's S.T.* [1957] 1 W.L.R. 401.
[74] *Re Scott* [1975] 2 All E.R. 1033.
[75] See para.5–40, above.
[76] *Cunnack v Edwards* [1896] 2 Ch. 679.
[77] *Re West Sussex Constabulary's Benevolent Fund Trusts* [1971] Ch. 1; at para.5–58.
[78] [1990] 1 W.L.R. 1511.

the deed to deal with the surplus.[79] Scott J. held that the surplus derived primarily from over funding arising from the contributions of the employer (which was obliged to make up any deficiencies if the employees' contributions proved inadequate), and that the portion of the surplus which derived from the employer's contributions should result to the employer. However, as regards the surplus derived from the employees' contributions he held that this should pass to the Crown as *bona vacantia* because the circumstances of the case pointed "firmly and clearly to the conclusion that a resulting trust in favour of the employees should be excluded." Why? Because equity should not impute to the employees an intention that would lead to an unworkable result, the value of benefits being different for each employee.[80] Nor should equity impose a resulting trust if this would lead to employees receiving more than the legislature intended when stipulating the statutory limits under exempt approved schemes. However, these reasons for refusing to impose a resulting trust for the employees were regarded as unconvincing by Lord Millett in *Air Jamaica Ltd v Charlton*.

AIR JAMAICA LTD v CHARLTON

Privy Council [1999] 1 W.L.R. 1399 (Lords Steyn, Hope and Millett, Sir Christopher Slade, and Sir Andrew Leggatt).

Air Jamaica Ltd was privatised and its employee pensions plan was discontinued, **5–45** leaving a surplus of $400 million. The pensions plan was established by a trust deed, one clause of which (clause 13.3) provided that "any balance of the Fund shall be applied to provide additional benefits for Members and after their death for their widows or their designated beneficiaries in such equitable and non-discriminatory manner as the Trustees may determine". The surplus would have been distributed in line with this clause if it had been valid, but the Privy Council advised that it was void for perpetuity. Clause 4 of the trust deed stated: "No moneys which at any time have been contributed by the Company under the terms hereof shall in any circumstances be repayable to the Company". The company purported to amend the trust deed, by removing clause 4 and replacing clause 13.3 with a clause providing that the surplus would be held on trust for the company. The Privy Council advised that clause 4 invalidated these amendments, but that it did not prevent a resulting trust from arising in the company's favour in respect of the surplus funds.

LORD MILLETT (speaking for the court): "*Prima facie* the surplus is held on a **5–46** resulting trust for those who provided it. This sometimes creates a problem of some perplexity. In the present case, however, it does not. Contributions were payable by the members with matching contributions by the company. In the absence of any evidence that this is not what happened in practice, the surplus must be treated as provided as to one half by the company and as to one half by the members.

"The Attorney General contended that neither the company nor the members **5–47** can take any part in the surplus, which has reverted to the Crown as *bona vacantia*. He argued that cl. 4 of the trust deed precludes any claim by the company, while the

---

[79] See now Pensions Act 1985, ss.68, 69.
[80] But if the proportionate return under a resulting trust were effectively impossible to calculate and administer, why not have a *per capita* distribution to cut the Gordian knot, in line with Goff J.'s recommendation in *Re West Sussex Constabulary's Fund Trusts* [1970] 1 All E.R. 544 at 548?

members cannot claim any part of the surplus because they have received all that they are entitled to. There is authority for both propositions. Their Lordships consider that they can be supported neither in principle nor as a matter of construction.

5–48   "In *Re A.B.C. Television Ltd Pension Scheme*[81] Foster J. held that a clause similar to cl. 4 of the present trust deed 'negatives the possibility of implying a resulting trust'. This is wrong in principle. Like a constructive trust, a resulting trust arises by operation of law, though unlike a constructive trust it gives effect to intention. But it arises whether or not the transferor intended to retain a beneficial interest—he almost always does not—since it responds to the absence of any intention on his part to pass a beneficial interest to the recipient. It may arise even where the transferor positively wished to part with the beneficial interest, as in *Vandervell v I.R.C.*[82] In that case the retention of a beneficial interest by the transferor destroyed the effectiveness of a tax avoidance scheme which the transferor was seeking to implement. The House of Lords affirmed the principle that a resulting trust is not defeated by evidence that the transferor intended to part with the beneficial interest if he has not in fact succeeded in doing so. As Plowman J. had said in the same case at first instance:[83]

> 'As I see it, a man does not cease to own property simply by saying "I don't want it". If he tries to give it away the question must always be, has he succeeded in doing so or not?'

Lord Upjohn expressly approved this.[84]

5–49   "Consequently their Lordships think that clauses of this kind in a pension scheme should generally be construed as forbidding the repayment of contributions under the terms of the scheme, and not as a pre-emptive but misguided attempt to rebut a resulting trust which would arise *dehors* the scheme. The purpose of such clauses is to preclude any amendment that would allow repayment to the company. Their Lordships thus construe cl. 4 of the trust deed as invalidating the 1994 amendments, but not as preventing the company from retaining a beneficial interest by way of a resulting trust in so much of the surplus as is attributable to its contributions.

5–50   "The members' contributions stand on a similar footing. In *Davis v Richards & Wallington Industries Ltd*[85] Scott J. held that the fact that a party has received all that he bargained for is not necessarily a decisive argument against a resulting trust, but that in the circumstances of the case before him a resulting trust in favour of the employees was excluded. The circumstances that impressed him were twofold. He considered that it was impossible to arrive at a workable scheme for apportioning the employees' surplus among the different classes of employees and he declined[85a] to 'impute to them an intention that would lead to an unworkable result'. He also considered that he was precluded by statute from 'imputing to the employees an intention' that they should receive by means of a resulting trust sums in excess of the maximum permitted by the relevant tax legislation.

5–51   "These formulations also adopt the approach to intention that their Lordships have already considered to be erroneous. Their Lordships would observe that, even in the ordinary case of an actuarial surplus, it is not obvious that, when employees

---

[81] May 22, 1973, unreported.
[82] [1967] 1 All E.R. 1.
[83] [1966] Ch. 261 at 275.
[84] [1967] 1 All E.R. 1 at 9.
[85] [1991] 2 All E.R. 563.
[85a] At 1544.

are promised certain benefits under a scheme to which they have contributed more than was necessary to fund them, they should not expect to obtain a return of their excess contributions. In the present case, however, the surplus does not arise from over-funding but from the failure of some of the trusts. It is impossible to say that the members 'have received all that they bargained for'. One of the benefits they bargained for was that the trustees should be obliged to pay them additional benefits in the event of the scheme's discontinuance. It was the invalidity of this trust that gave rise to the surplus. Their Lordships consider that it would be more accurate to say that the members claim such part of the surplus as is attributable to their contributions because they have not received all that they bargained for.

"Pension schemes in Jamaica, as in England, need the approval of the Inland **5–52** Revenue if they are to secure the fiscal advantages that are made available. The tax legislation in both countries places a limit on the amount which can be paid to the individual employee. Allowing the employees to enjoy any part of the surplus by way of resulting trust would probably exceed those limits. This fact is not, however, in their Lordships' view a proper ground on which to reject the operation of a resulting trust in favour of the employees. The Inland Revenue had an opportunity to examine the pension plan and to withhold approval on the ground that some of its provisions were void for perpetuity. They failed to do so. There is no call to distort principle in order to meet their requirements. The resulting trust arises by operation of the general law, *dehors* the pension scheme and the scope of the relevant tax legislation.

"Scott J. was impressed by the difficulty of arriving at a workable scheme for **5–53** apportioning the surplus funds among the members and the executors of deceased members. This was because he thought it necessary to value the benefits that each member had received in order to ascertain his share in the surplus. On the separate settlement with mutual insurance analysis which their Lordships have adopted in the present case, however, no such process is required. The members' share of the surplus should be divided *pro rata* among the members and the estates of deceased members in proportion to the contributions made by each member without regard to the benefits each has received and irrespective of the dates on which the contributions were made."

III. Dissolution of Unincorporated Associations

When an unincorporated association is dissolved it is necessary to ascertain **5–54** whether its property falls to be distributed on a resulting trust to persons providing such property or on a contractual basis to the members of the association or as *bona vacantia* to the Crown.

The rules of an unincorporated association usually vest the assets of the **5–55** association in trustees on trust for the members. However, this trust bears no relation to the members' claims to the surplus assets when the association is dissolved. So far as these are concerned, the old view[86] that they arise under resulting trusts has been totally discredited. It is now well established that the interests and rights of persons who are members of any

---

[86] *Re Printers and Transferrers Amalgamated Trades Protection Society* [1899] 2 Ch. 184; *Re Lead Co.'s Workmen's Fund Society* [1904] 2 Ch. 196.

type of unincorporated association are governed exclusively by contract.[87] Hence, if the rules of the association by which the members are contractually bound *inter se* provide for a particular method of distribution when the association is dissolved, this method will be used,[88] subject to the rights of third parties to share in the surplus assets.

5–56   Third party rights to share in the fund will arise either by the duly authorised procedure in the association's constitution for creating contracts or express trusts, or by declarations of trust made by a donor at the time of transferring property to the association. However, to avoid invalidating a donor's declaration of trust for infringing the beneficiary principle or perpetuity rules, the courts tend to interpret such gifts not as declarations of trust, but as out-and-out gifts to the members as an accretion to the funds which are the subject-matter of the contract by which the members are all bound *inter se*, with the result that such gifts will fall to be dealt with in just the same way as the funds which the members themselves have subscribed to the association's funds.[89] Only if the association has become moribund, as where all the members or all but one has died, will the assets be treated as *bona vacantia* and pass to the Crown.[90]

5–57   The present position is set out in *Re Bucks Constabulary Fund Friendly Society (No.2)*. This decision is to be preferred to *Re West Sussex Constabulary's Benevolent Fund*, because it pays proper attention to the primacy of the members' contracts in determining beneficial entitlements to the assets of the association, as stipulated in *Re Recher's W.T.*[91]

RE WEST SUSSEX CONSTABULARY'S WIDOWS, CHILDREN AND BENEVOLENT (1930) FUND TRUSTS

Chancery Division [1971] Ch. 1; [1970] 2 W.L.R. 848; [1970] 1 All E.R. 544

5–58   In 1930 members of the West Sussex Constabulary established a fund to provide for their widows and orphans. In 1968 the West Sussex Constabulary was amalgamated with other forces, and the question arose how the assets of the fund should be dealt with. These came from (1) contributions of past and present members; (2) entertainments, raffles, sweepstakes; (3) collecting boxes; (4) donations and legacies.

5–59   Goff J. held that (4) were held on resulting trusts for the donors whilst (1), (2), and (3) were *bona vacantia*. These holdings are now of doubtful value in view of the next case, *Re Bucks Constabulary Fund Friendly Society (No.2)*. However, the following dicta are good law.

---

[87] *Tierney v Tough* [1914] 1 I.R. 142; *Re St. Andrew's Allotment Association* [1969] 1 W.L.R. 229; *Re William Denby Ltd's Sick Fund* [1971] 1 W.L.R. 973; *Re West Sussex Constabulary's Benevolent Fund Trusts* [1971] Ch. 1; *Re Sick & Funeral Society of St. John's Sunday School* [1973] Ch. 51 (*per capita* basis but child members only to have a half share); *Re GKN Nuts and Bolts Ltd Sports and Social Club* [1982] 1 W.L.R. 774; *Re Bucks Constabulary Fund Friendly Society (No.2)* [1979] 1 All E.R. 623; *Boyle v Collins* [2004] 2 B.C.L.C. 471 at [26]–[27], *per* Lewison J., considering *Abbatt v Treasury Solicitor* [1969] 1 W.L.R. 561.
[88] Otherwise, distribution will be on the basis of equality.
[89] *Re Recher's W.T.* [1972] Ch. 526; *Re Lipinski's W.T.* [1976] Ch. 235, above at paras 3–242 *et seq.*
[90] *Re Bucks Constabulary Fund Friendly Society (No.2)* [1979] 1 All E.R. 623; *Cunnack v Edwards* [1896] 2 Ch. 679. *Re West Sussex Constabulary's Benevolent Fund* [1971] Ch. 1 holds otherwise but it is probably wrong. If under the association's rules the last member can claim the property without having to call a meeting, *e.g.* in the case of a tontine society, then he or his estate will be entitled to the property.
[91] [1972] Ch. 526 at 538–539, above, at paras 3–237 *et seq.*

GOFF J.: "I must now turn to the moneys raised from outside sources. Counsel for **5–60** the Treasury Solicitor made an overriding general submission that there cannot be a resulting trust of any of the outside moneys because in the circumstances it is impossible to identify the trust property; no doubt something could be achieved by complicated accounting, but this, he submitted, would not be identification but notional reconstruction. I cannot accept that argument. In my judgment, in a case like the present, equity will cut the Gordian knot by simply dividing the ultimate surplus in proportion to the sources from which it has arisen. . . . There may be cases of tolerable simplicity where the court will be more refined, but in general, where a fund has been raised from mixed sources, interest has been earned over the years and income—and possibly capital—expenditure has been made indiscriminately out of the fund as an entirety, and then the venture comes to an end prematurely or otherwise, the court will not find itself baffled but will cut the Gordian knot as I have said.

"Then counsel divided the outside moneys into three categories, first, the **5–61** proceeds of entertainments, raffles and sweepstakes; secondly, the proceeds of collecting-boxes; and, thirdly, donations, including legacies if any, and he took particular objections to each.

"I agree that there cannot be any resulting trust with respect to the first category. **5–62** I am not certain whether Harman J. in *Re Gillingham Bus Disaster Fund*[92] meant to decide otherwise. In stating the facts he referred to 'street collections and so forth.'[93] In the further argument[94] there is mention of whist drives and concerts but the judge himself did not speak of anything other than gifts. If, however, he did, I must respectfully decline to follow his judgment in that regard, for whatever may be the true position with regard to collecting-boxes, it appears to me to be impossible to apply the doctrine of resulting trust to the proceeds of entertainments and sweepstakes and such-like money-raising operations for two reasons: first, the relationship is one of contract and not of trust, the purchaser of a ticket may have the motive of aiding the cause or he may not; he may purchase a ticket merely because he wishes to attend the particular entertainment or to try for the prize, but whichever it be, he pays his money as the price of what is offered and what he receives; secondly, there is in such cases no direct contribution to the fund at all; it is only the profit, if any, which is ultimately received and there may even be none.

"In any event, the first category cannot be any more susceptible to the doctrine **5–63** than the second to which I now turn. Here one starts with the well-known dictum of P.O. Lawrence J. in *Re Welsh Hospital (Netley) Fund* where he said[95]:

> 'So far as regards the contributors to entertainments, street collections etc., I have no hesitation in holding that they must be taken to have parted with their money out-and-out. It is inconceivable that any person paying for a concert ticket or placing a coin in a collecting-box presented to him in the street should have intended that any part of the money so contributed should be returned to him when the immediate object for which the concert was given or the collection made had come to an end. To draw such an inference would be absurd on the face of it.'

This was adopted by Upjohn J., in *Re Hillier's Trusts*[96] where the point was actually decided.

---

[92] [1958] Ch. 300.
[93] *ibid.* at 304.
[94] *ibid.* at 309.
[95] [1921] 1 Ch. 655 at 660.
[96] [1954] 1 W.L.R. 9.

5–64   ". . . In *Re Ulverston and District New Hospital Building Trusts*[97] Jenkins L.J. threw
out a suggestion that there might be a distinction in the case of a person who could
prove that he put a specified sum in a collecting-box, and, in the *Gillingham* case[98]
Harman J. after noting this, decided that there was a resulting trust with respect to
the proceeds of collections. He said:[99]

> 'In my judgment the Crown has failed to show that this case should not follow
> the ordinary rule merely because there was a number of donors who, I will
> assume, are unascertainable. I see no reason myself to suppose that the small
> giver who is anonymous has any wider intention than the large giver who can
> be named. They all give for the one object. If they can be found by enquiry the
> resulting trust can be executed in their favour. If they cannot I do not see how
> the money could then, with all respect to Jenkins L.J., change its destination
> and become *bona vacantia*. It will be merely money held upon a trust for which
> no beneficiary can be found. Such cases are common and where it is known that
> there are beneficiaries the fact that they cannot be ascertained does not entitle
> the Crown to come in and claim. The trustees must pay the money into court
> like any other trustee who cannot find his beneficiary. I conclude, therefore,
> that there must be an enquiry for the subscribers to this fund.'

5–65   ". . . [For] for my part I cannot reconcile the decision of Upjohn J. in *Re Hillier's
Trusts* with that of Harman J. in the *Gillingham* case. As I see it, therefore, I have to
choose between them. On the one hand it may be said that Harman J. had the
advantage, which Upjohn J. had not, of considering the suggestion made by Jenkins
L.J. On the other hand that suggestion with all respect, seems to me somewhat
fanciful and unreal. I agree that all who put their money into collecting-boxes
should be taken to have the same intention, but why should they not all be regarded
as intending to part with their money out and out absolutely in all circumstances? I
observe that P. O. Lawrence J. in *Re Welsh Hospital*[1] used very strong words. He
said any other view was inconceivable and absurd on the face of it. That commends
itself to my humble judgment, and I therefore prefer and follow the judgment of
Upjohn J. in *Re Hillier's Trusts*."

RE BUCKS CONSTABULARY FUND FRIENDLY SOCIETY (NO.2)

Chancery Division [1979] 1 W.L.R. 936; [1979] 1 All E.R. 623.

5–66   The Bucks Constabulary Fund Friendly Society was established to provide for the
relief of widows and orphans of deceased members of the Bucks Constabulary. It
was an unincorporated association registered under the Friendly Societies Act 1896
but it had no rules providing for the distribution of its assets in the event of it being
wound up. When it was wound up the question arose whether the surplus assets
were *bona vacantia* passing to the Crown or whether they should be distributed
among the members equally *per capita* or on some other basis.

5–67   WALTON J.: "There are basically two claimants to the fund, the Solicitor for the
Affairs of Her Majesty's Treasury, who claims the assets as ownerless property, *bona
vacantia*, and the members of the friendly society at the date of its dissolution on
14th October 1969.

---

[97] [1956] Ch. 622 at 633.
[98] [1958] Ch. 300.
[99] *ibid.* at 314.
[1] [1921] Ch. 655 at 661.

"Before considering the relevant legislation . . . and the decided cases, it is I think **5–68** desirable to view the question of the property of unincorporated associations in the round. If a number of persons associate together, for whatever purpose, if that purpose is one which involves the acquisition of cash or property of any magnitude, then, for practical purposes, some one or more persons have to act in the capacity of treasurers or holders of the property. In any sophisticated association there will accordingly be one or more trustees in whom the property which is acquired by the association will be vested. These trustees will of course not hold such property on their own behalf. Usually there will be a committee of some description which will run the affairs of the association; though of course in a small association the committee may well comprise all the members; and the normal course of events will be that the trustee, if there is a formal trustee, will declare that he holds the property of the association in his hands on trust to deal with it as directed by the committee. If the trust deed is a shade more sophisticated it may add that the trustee holds the assets on trust for the members in accordance with the rules of the association. Now in all such cases it appears to me quite clear that, unless under the rules governing the association the property thereof has been wholly devoted to charity, or unless and to the extent to which the other trusts have validly been declared of such property, the persons, and the only persons, interested therein are the members. Save by way of a valid declaration or trust in their favour, there is no scope for any other person acquiring any rights in the property of the association, although of course it may well be that third parties may obtain contractual or proprietary rights, such as a mortgage, over those assets as the result of a valid contract with the trustees or members of the committee as representing the association.

"I can see no reason for thinking that this analysis is any different whether the **5–69** purpose for which the members of the association associate are a social club, a sporting club, to establish a widows' and orphans' fund, to obtain a separate Parliament for Cornwall, or to further the advance of alchemy. It matters not. All the assets of the association are held in trust for its members (of course subject to the contractual claims of anybody having a valid contract with the association) save and expect to the extent to which valid trusts have otherwise been declared of its property. I would adopt the analysis made by Brightman J. in *Re Recher's Will Trusts*[2] . . .

"All this doubtless seems quite elementary, but it appears to me to have been lost **5–70** sight of to some extent in some of the decisions which I shall hereafter have to consider in detail in relation to the destination on dissolution of the funds of unincorporated associations.

"Now in the present case I am dealing with a society which was registered under **5–71** the Friendly Societies Act 1896. This does not have any effect at all on the unincorporated nature of the society, or (as I have in substance already indicated) on the way in which its property is held. But the latter point is in fact made very explicit by the provisions of s.49(1) of the 1896 Act which reads as follows:

'All property belonging to a registered society, whether acquired before or after the society is registered, shall vest in the trustees for the time being of the society, for the use and benefit of the society and the members thereof, and of all persons claiming through the members according to the rules of the society.'

"There can be doubt, therefore, that in the present case the whole of the property **5–72** of the society is vested in the trustees for the use and benefit of the society and the members thereof and of all persons claiming through the members according to the

---

[2] [1972] Ch. 526 at 538–539, set out above at paras 3–237 *et seq*.

rules of the society. I do not think I need go through the rules in detail. They are precisely what one would expect in the case of an association whose main purpose in life was to enable members to make provision for widows and orphans. Members paid a contribution in exchange for which in the event of their deaths their widows and children would receive various benefits. There is a minimal benefit for which provision is made in the case of a member suffering very sever illness indeed, but, as counsel for the Treasury Solicitor was able to demonstrate from an analysis of the accounts, virtually the entire expenditure of the association was, as indeed one would expect, on the provision of widows' and orphans' benefits. But, of course, there is no trust whatsoever declared in their favour. I am not called on, I think, to decide whether they are, within the meaning of s.49(1), persons claiming through the members according to the rules of the society, or whether they are simply the beneficiaries of stipulations by the members for the benefit of third parties. All parties are agreed that accrued rights of such persons must be given full effect. There is indeed no rule which says what is to happen to surplus assets of the society on a dissolution. But in view of s.49(1) there is no need. The assets must continue to be held, the society having been dissolved, and the widows and orphans being out of the way, simply for the use and benefit of the members of the society, albeit they will all now be former members.

5–73   "This indeed appears so obvious that in a work of great authority on all matters connected with friendly societies, *Baden Fuller*, the learned author says this:[3]

> 'If the rules provide for the termination of the society they usually also provide for the distribution of the funds in that event, but if on the termination of a society no provision has been made by the rules for the distribution of its funds, such funds are divisible among the existing members at the time of the termination or dissolution in proportion to the amount contributed by each member for entrance fees and subscriptions, but irrespective of fines or payments made to members in accordance with the rules.'

5–74   "In my judgment this accurately represents the law, at any rate so far as the beneficiaries of the trust on dissolution are concerned, although not necessarily so far as the quantum of their respective interests is concerned; a matter which still remains to be argued. The effective point is that the claims of the Treasury Solicitor to the funds as *bona vacantia* are unsustainable in the present case. I say 'in the present case' because there are undoubtedly cases where the assets of an unincorporated association do become *bona vacantia*. To quote *Baden Fuller* again:[4]

> 'A society may sometimes become defunct or moribund by its members either all dying or becoming so reduced in numbers that it is impossible either to continue the society or to dissolve it by instrument; in such cases the surplus funds, after all existing claims (if any) under the rules have been satisfied or provided for, are not divisible among the surviving members. . . or the last survivor. . . or the representative of the last survivor. . . nor is there any resulting trust in favour of the personal representatives of the members of the society . . . not even in favour of honorary members in respect of donations by them . . . but a society which, though moribund, had at a testator's death one member and three annuitant beneficiaries, was held to be existing so as to

---

[3] *The Law of Friendly Societies* (4th ed., 1926), p.186.
[4] *ibid.*, pp.186–187.

prevent the lapse of a legacy bequeathed to it by the testator . . . . In these circumstances two cases seem to occur: if the purposes of the society are charitable, the surplus will be applicable cy-pres . . . but if the society is not a charity, the surplus belongs to the Crown as *bona vacantia*.'

"Before I turn to a consideration of the authorities, it is I think pertinent to **5–75** observe that all unincorporated societies rest in contract to this extent, that there is an implied contract between all of the members *inter se* governed by the rules of the society. In default of any rule to the contrary, and it will seldom if ever be that there is such a rule, when a member ceases to be a member of the association he *ipso facto* ceases to have any interest in its funds. Once again, so far as friendly societies are concerned, this is made very clear by s.49(1), that it is the members, the present members, who, alone, have any right in the assets. As membership always ceases on death, past members or the estates of deceased members therefore have no interest in the assets. Further, unless expressly so provided by the rules, unincorporated societies are not really tontine societies, intended to provide benefits for the longest liver of the members. Therefore, although it is difficult to say in any given case precisely when a society becomes moribund, it is quite clear that if a society is reduced to a single member neither he, still less his personal representatives on his behalf, can say he is or was the society and therefore entitled solely to its fund. It may be that it will be sufficient for the society's continued existence if there are two members, but if there is only one the society as such must cease to exist. There is no association, since one can hardly associate with oneself or enjoy one's own society. And so indeed the assets have become ownerless.

"I now turn to the authorities. The first case is that of *Cunnack v Edwards*.[5] . . . **5–76** The association there in question was established in 1810 to raise a fund by the subscriptions, fines and forfeitures of its members, to provide annuities for the widows of its deceased members. It was later registered under the Friendly Societies Act 1829. . . . A careful examination of that case reveals that the really crucial fact was that the rules were required to state all the uses applicable to the assets of the society and they stated none in favour of members. On dissolution s.26 governed, and following on the absence of any provision in favour of members in the rules the members were not entitled to any interest in the assets. Hence the inescapable conclusion that the surplus assets had no owner and must go to the Crown. At the risk of repetition, the combined effect of the rules and the 1829 Act made it quite impossible for any argument to the effect that on dissolution the assets vested in then members in some shares and proportions, which is the normal argument to be put forward in such a case. The case therefore did not decide that this was not the usual position in the case of an unincorporated association not then registered under the Friendly Societies Act.

[The judge referred to various cases and went on:] "Finally . . . there comes a **5–77** case which gives me great concern, *Re West Sussex Constabulary's Widows, Children and Benevolent (1930) Fund Trusts*.[6] The case is indeed easily distinguishable from the present case in that what was there under consideration was a simple unincorporated association and not a friendly society, so that the provisions of s.49(1) of the 1869 Act do not apply. Otherwise the facts in that case present remarkable parallels to the facts in the present case. Goff J. decided that the surplus funds had become *bona vacantia*. [See paras 5–58 *et seq*.] . . .

---

[5] [1895] 1 Ch. 489; on appeal [1896] 2 Ch. 679.
[6] [1971] Ch. 1.

5–78   "It will be observed that the first reason given by the judge for his decision is that he could not accept the principle of the members' clubs as applicable. This is a very interesting reason, because it is flatly contrary to the successful argument of Mr. Ingle Joyce who appeared for the Attorney-General in the case Goff J. purported to follow, *Cunnack v Edwards*. His argument was as follows:[7]

> 'This society was nothing more than a club, in which the members had no transmissible interest: *Re St. James' Club*.[8] Whatever the members, or even the surviving member, might have done while alive, when they died their interest in the assets of the club died with them';

and in the Court of Appeal[9] he used the arguments he had used below. If all that Goff J. meant was that the purposes of the fund before him were totally different from those of a members' club then of course one must agree, but if he meant to imply that there was some totally different principle of law applicable one must ask why that should be. His second reason is that in all the cases where the surviving members had taken, the organisation existed for the benefit of the members for the time being exclusively. This may be so, so far as actual decisions go, but what is the principle? Why are the members not in control, complete control, save as to any existing contractual rights, of the assets belonging to their organisation? One could understand the position being different if valid trusts had been declared of the assets in favour of third parties, for example charities, but that this was emphatically not the case was demonstrated by the fact that Goff J. recognised that the members could have altered the rules prior to dissolution and put the assets into their own pockets. If there was no obstacle to their doing this, it shows in my judgment quite clearly that the money was theirs all the time. Finally he purports to follow *Cunnack v Edwards* and it will be seen from the analysis which I have already made of that case that it was extremely special in its facts, resting on a curious provision of the 1829 Act which is no longer applicable. As I have already indicated, in the light of s.49(1) of the 1896 Act the case before Goff J.[10] is readily distinguishable, but I regret that, quite apart from that, I am wholly unable to square it with the relevant principles of law applicable.

5–79   "The conclusion therefore is that, as on dissolution there were members of the society here in question in existence, its assets are held on trust for such members to the total exclusion of any claim on behalf of the Crown. The remaining question under this head which falls now to be argued is, of course, whether they are simply held per capita, or, as suggested in some of the cases, in proportion to the contributions made by each. . . .

5–80   "I think that there is no doubt that, as a result of modern cases springing basically from the decision of O'Connor M.R. in *Tierney v Tough*,[11] judicial opinion has been hardening and is now firmly set along the lines that the interests and rights of persons who are members of any type of unincorporated association are governed exclusively by contract, that is to say the rights between themselves and their rights to any surplus assets. I say that to make it perfectly clear that I have not overlooked the fact that the assets of the society are usually vested in trustees on trust for the members. But that is quite a separate and distinct trust bearing no relation to the claims of the members *inter se* on the surplus funds so held on trust for their benefit.

---

[7] [1895] 1 Ch. 489 at 494.
[8] (1852) 2 De G. M. & G. 383 at 387.
[9] [1896] 2 Ch. 679.
[10] [1971 Ch. 1.
[11] [1914] I.R. 142.

"That being the case, *prima facie* there can be no doubt at all but that the **5–81** distribution is on the basis of equality, because, as between a number of people contractually interested in a fund, there is no other method of distribution if no other method is provided by the terms of the contract, and it is not for one moment suggested here that there is any other method of distribution provided by the contract. We are, of course, dealing here with a friendly society, but that really makes no difference to the principle. The Friendly Societies Acts do not incorporate the friendly society in any way and the only effect that it has is, as I pointed out in my previous judgment in this case, that there is a section which makes it crystal clear in the Friendly Societies Act 1896 that the assets are indeed held on trust for the members.

"Now the fact that the *prima facie* rule is a matter of equality has been recently **5–82** laid down, not of course for the first time, in two cases to which I need to no more than refer, *Re St Andrew's Allotment Association's Trusts*,[12] a decision of the late Ungoed-Thomas J., and *Re Sick and Funeral Society of St John's Sunday School, Golcar*,[13] a decision of Megarry J. Neither of those cases was, however, the case of a friendly society, and there are a number of previous decisions in connection with friendly societies, and, indeed *Tierney v Tough* itself is such a case, where the basis of distribution according to the subscriptions paid by the persons among whom the fund is to be distributed has been applied, and it has been suggested that perhaps those decisions are to be explained along the lines that a friendly society, or similar society, is thinking more of benefits to members, and that, thinking naturally of benefits to members, you think, on the other side of the coin, of subscriptions paid by members. But in my judgment that is not a satisfactory distinction of any description, because one is now dealing with what happens at the end of the life of the association; there are surplus funds, funds which have not been required to carry out the purposes of the association, and it does not seem to me it is a suitable method of distribution to say that one then looks to see what the purposes of the society were while the society was a going concern.

"An ingenious argument has been put up by counsel for the third and fifth **5–83** defendants, who are *ad idem* on this particular point, which runs very simply as follows: the members of the society are entitled in equity to the surplus funds which are distributable among them, therefore they are to be distributed among them according to equitable principles and those principles should, like all equitable principles, be moulded to fit the circumstances of the case, and in one case it would therefore be equitable to distribute in equal shares, in another case it might be equitable to distribute in proportion to the subscriptions that they have paid, and I suppose that in another case it might be equitable to distribute according to the length of their respective feet, following a very well known equitable precedent. Well, I completely deny the basic premise. The members are not entitled in equity to the fund: they are entitled at law. It is a matter, so far as the members are concerned, of pure contract, and, being a matter of pure contract, it is, in my judgment, as far as distribution is concerned, completely divorced from all questions of equitable doctrines. It is a matter of simple entitlement, and that entitlement, in my judgment, at this time of day must be, and can only be, in equal shares."

---

[12] [1969] 1 W.L.R. 229.
[13] [1973] Ch. 51.

Section 4. Apparent Gifts

I. WHERE RESULTING TRUSTS ARISE

(a) Purchase in the name of another

5–84　　If X buys property (real or personal) and instructs the vendor to convey the property to Y, then Y must rebut the presumption that X did not mean him to take the property beneficially for himself.[14] The most obvious way for Y to do this is to prove that X intended to make him a gift. Another way is for Y to prove that X intended to lend Y the purchase money, as in this case X must have intended Y to have beneficial ownership of the property, and to owe him a personal obligation to repay the amount of the loan. Thus, if X provides £25,000 of the £100,000 purchase price of a house in Y's name, and provides the money as purchaser, then he will be entitled to a quarter share of the house unless he intends to make Y a gift of the money, the onus being on Y to prove this.[15] But if X provides the £25,000 as a lender to Y, then he will only be entitled as Y's creditor to the repayment of the £25,000 and any agreed interest. In general, therefore, we may say that loan agreements are inconsistent with resulting trusts,[16] although in some exceptional cases where X lends Y money for a specified purpose, a resulting trust of the money may be imposed, which is defeasible by the exercise of a power vested in Y to apply the money to the specified purpose.[17]

(b) Purchase in the joint names of oneself and another

5–85　　If X purchases property (real or personal) and instructs the vendor to convey the property into the joint names of himself and Y, then Y must prove that X meant to give him a share of the property, or else X and Y will together hold the property on resulting trust for X.[18]

(c) Joint purchase

5–86　　Suppose that X *and* Y jointly purchase property (real or personal) in the name of Y alone. They both contribute towards the purchase money, but the conveyance is taken in Y's name alone. Unless Y proves that X intended a gift, he will hold the property on resulting trust for X and Y in shares proportionate to their contributions.[19]

5–87　　If X and Y purchase a yearly tenancy for £3,000 each in Y's name then Y will hold it on resulting trust in equal shares unless he can show that X meant a gift. However, if no capital sum is paid and Y alone takes on the

---

[14] *Dyer v Dyer* (1788) 2 Cox 92; *Vandervell v I.R.C.* [1967] 2 A.C. 291.
[15] *Seldon v Davidson* [1968] 1 W.L.R. 1083; *Dewar v Dewar* [1975] 1 W.L.R. 1532.
[16] *Aveling v Knipe* (1815) 19 Ves. Jun. 441; *Re Sharpe* [1980] 1 All E.R. 198 at 201; *Winkworth v Edward Baron Development Co. Ltd* [1987] 1 All E.R. 114 at 118, *per* Lord Templeman.
[17] As in *Twinsectra Ltd v Yardley* [2002] A.C. 164. See para.5–40 above.
[18] *Benger v Drew* (1721) P. Wms. 781; *Rider v Rider* (1805) 10 Ves. 360.
[19] *The Venture* [1908] P. 218; *Bull v Bull* [1955] 1 Q.B. 234.

tenancy, having arranged for X to share the rent and gas and electricity bills, and X does so, then X cannot claim a half share under a resulting trust in the tenancy, or indeed of the freehold in the event that Y purchases this on favourable terms (even if X reimburses Y half the price of the freehold).[20] Payments of a capital nature, as opposed to income, are required before a resulting trust can arise. Thus, if X and Y buy a shared home in Y's name for £100,000, and X pays £50,000 directly, and Y provides £50,000 borrowed from a lender which takes a mortgage over the property to secure repayment of the loan, Y cannot claim a greater share than half under a resulting trust. It makes no difference whether the amounts actually paid by Y to the mortgage lender amount to more or less than £50,000.

What if X and Y jointly purchase property (real or personal) as legal **5–88** joint tenants? Again, in the absence of evidence that they intended otherwise, the parties will hold the property on resulting trust for themselves in the proportions in which they contributed.[21] If X dies, then Y will take legal title to the whole by survivorship, but will be treated as a tenant in common in equity, and will hold X's share of the purchase or mortgage money on resulting trust for X's estate.[22]

(d) Joint purchase of shared homes

All of these principles apply in the case where X and Y buy a shared **5–89** home together but foolishly do not make an express written declaration of trust as to their shares.[23] Again, in the absence of clear evidence as to their intentions, it is presumed that neither intends to make a gift or loan of his or her contribution to the purchase price. Unless this presumption is rebutted, the property will then be held on resulting trust for the pair of them, the amount of their equitable interests corresponding to the contributions which they made to purchase.[24] So, for example, in the case of a house costing £100,000, if X pays £40,000 and Y pays £60,000, then X will be equitably entitled to 40 per cent and Y to 60 per cent, and the position is the same if X does not actually pay £40,000 but obtained a £40,000 discount off the market price, as a sitting tenant of the house.[25]

Nowadays, of course, most houses are purchased with the help of a **5–90** mortgage loan, the vendor receiving the whole purchase price on completion of the sale contract, but the purchaser(s) being under an obligation to

---

[20] *Savage v Dunningham* [1974] Ch. 181.
[21] *Calverley v Green* (1984) 155 C.L.R. 242; *Springette v Defoe* [1992] 2 F.L.R. 388 at 392, *per* Dillon L.J., followed in *R (on the application of Kelly) v Hammersmith & Fulham L.B.C.* [2004] EWHC 435 (Admin) at [19], *per* Richards J.
[22] *Re Jackson* (1887) 34 Ch.D. 732; *Cobb v Cobb* [1955] 2 All E.R. 696. See too Law of Property Act 1925, s.111 enabling the survivor to give a good receipt.
[23] An express written declaration of trust signed by the parties is conclusive in the absence of fraud or mistake (*Goodman v Gallant* [1986] Fam. 106) or undue influence (*Humphreys v Humphreys* [2004] EWHC 2201 (Ch)).
[24] *Pettit v Pettit* [1970] A.C. 777 at 814. *Quaere* whether acquisition costs, *e.g.* legal fees and stamp duty, are part of the purchase price? *Huntingford v Hobbs* [1993] 1 F.L.R. 736 suggests that they are, but in *Curley v Parkes* [2004] EWCA Civ 1515 at [22], Peter Gibson L.J. held otherwise. At [23] he also held that removal costs do not form part of the purchase price either.
[25] *Abbey National B.S. v Cann* (1989) 59 P. & C.R 381; *Springette v Defoe* [1992] 2 F.L.R. 388; *Mckenzie v Mckenzie* [2003] EWHC 601 (Ch) at [81]; *R (on the application of Kelly) v Hammersmith & Fulham L.B.C.* [2004] EWHC 435 (Admin). *Cf. Humphreys v Humphreys* [2004] EWHC 2201 (Ch) (decided on the basis of common intention constructive trust).

repay the mortgagee that part of the purchase price which it has provided. So what happens if X provides £40,000 and the £60,000 balance is provided by way of mortgage?

5–91   Clearly, the legal mortgage will have to be granted by the new legal owners of the house who will thereby be directly liable to the mortgagee for the amount of the mortgage loan. Where the legal title is taken in the names of X and Y this means that X and Y will be jointly and severally liable to the mortgagee, with a right of indemnity against each other for half the money unless they have agreed otherwise between themselves. Thus, if X and Y undertake liability for a £60,000 mortgage on their £100,000 house they will *prima facie* be regarded as thereby providing £30,000 of the purchase price each.[26] However, if X provides £40,000 of the purchase price in cash and agrees with Y that Y will be solely responsible for repaying the mortgage lender, who has supplied the balance of £60,000, then Y will be regarded as providing £60,000 of the purchase price.[27]

5–92   "Under a resulting trust, the existence of the trust is established once and for all at the date on which the property is acquired."[28] Because the shares of X and Y under a resulting trust crystallise at the date of acquisition, neither can subsequently claim a larger share under the resulting trust on the basis that he has paid for improvements to the property or paid a higher proportion of the mortgage instalments than the parties agreed at the time of acquisition.[29] This holds true even if the parties split up and one makes all the mortgage payments and spends money on the property while enjoying rent-free occupation, although on sale of the property, equitable accounting principles can require deductions to be made against the other party's share of the sale proceeds: *Huntingford v Hobbs*.[30] However, a party might acquire a larger share than her entitlement under the resulting trust if she can show some agreement or representation by the other party in reliance upon which she incurred detriment, as in this case she will be entitled to a (possibly larger) share of the property under the principles of proprietary estoppel and/or common intention constructive trust.[31] In this connection it is worth noting that the courts will infer the existence of a

---

[26] *Harwood v Harwood* [1991] 2 F.L.R. 274 at 292; *Springette v Defoe* (1992) 65 P. & C.R. 1; *Ammala v Savimaa* (1993) 17 Fam.L.R. 529 (Fed. Ct. of Australia).

[27] *Huntingford v Hobbs* [1993] 1 F.L.R. 736; *Ivin v Blake* (1994) 67 P. & C.R. 265; *Carlton v Goodman* [2002] 2 F.L.R. 259 at [22], *per* Mummery L.J., at [38]–[42], *per* Ward L.J.; *McKenzie v McKenzie* [2003] EWHC 601, Ch at [80]–[81]; *Trowbridge v Trowbridge* [2003] 2 F.L.R. 231.

[28] Lord Browne-Wilkinson, "Constructive Trusts and Unjust Enrichment" (1996) 10 Tru L.I. 98, 100. See too *Pettitt v Pettitt* [1970] A.C. 777 at 800, *per* Lord Morris, and at 816, *per* Lord Upjohn; *Gissing v Gissing* [1971] A.C. 886 at 900, *per* Viscount Dilhorne; *Calverley v Green* (1984) 155 C.L.R. 242 at 257, *per* Mason and Brennan JJ.; *Sekhon v Alissa* [1989] 2 F.L.R. 94 at 100; *Huntingford v Hobbs* [1993] 1 F.L.R. 736, para.5–93; *Curley v Parkes* [2004] EWCA Civ. 1515 at [14], *per* Peter Gibson L.J. In *Foskett v McKeown* [1997] 3 All E.R. 392 at 423 Morritt L.J. stated: "In most cases in which there has been found to be a resulting trust the property was acquired once and for all by simultaneous payments or assumptions of liability. But if property is acquired by a series of payments a resulting trust in respect of the due proportion may arise from the payment of one or more in the series: hire purchase or instalment transactions would be examples."

[29] The position is different in Ireland where an "extended resulting trust" analysis is used to give contributors a resulting trust interest calculated by reference to their contributions both to the purchase price and to ongoing mortgage payments: J. Mee, *The Property Rights of Cohabitees* (1999), Chap. 3.

[30] See too *Bernard v Jacobs* [1982] Ch. 391; *Re Gorman* [1990] 1 W.L.R. 616; *Re Pavlou* [1993] 1 W.L.R. 1046; *Ryan v Dries* (2002) 4 I.T.E.L.R. 829; *Re Byford* [2004] 1 F.L.R. 56.

[31] *Midland Bank v Cooke* [1995] 4 All E.R. 465; *Oxley v Hiscock* [2004] 2 F.L.R. 669; discussed at para.6–110.

common intention between the parties that each should have an equitable beneficial interest in the property from the fact that they have both contributed money towards the deposit on a house that is purchased in the name of one or both of them.[32]

HUNTINGFORD v HOBBS

Court of Appeal [1993] 1 F.L.R. 736; (1992) 24 H.L.R. 652 (Dillon and Steyn L.JJ. and Sir Christopher Slade).

Early in 1986 Mr. Huntingford and Mrs. Hobbs bought a house in their joint **5–93** names for £63,860 (£63,250 plus £610 fees). She provided £38,860 from the proceeds of her house while the £25,000 balance was provided by a joint mortgage supported by an endowment policy to produce £25,000 on maturity. She had no income and they agreed that he would pay the mortgage interest and endowment premiums. He left her in August 1988. He sought a sale under LPA 1925 s.30 and a share of the proceeds when the house was valued at £95,000 but still subject to the £25,000 mortgage, so that the equity was worth £70,000. The judge at first instance ordered that the property should be sold, that £3,500 at the proceeds should go to Mr Huntingford, and that the balance should go to Mrs Hobbs. Mr Hungtingford appealed successfully from this decision.

Sɪʀ Cʜʀɪsᴛᴏᴘʜᴇʀ Sʟᴀᴅᴇ: "There is no dispute that when the property was placed **5–94** in joint names, the two parties intended that they should each have a beneficial interest in it. The difficulty lies in establishing the extent of those beneficial interests in the absence of any declaration of trust.

"In the absence of any declaration of trust, the parties' respective beneficial **5–95** interests in the property fall to be determined not by reference to any broad concepts of justice, but by reference to the principles governing the creation or operation of resulting, implied or constructive trusts which by s.53(2) of the Law of Property Act 1925 are exempted from the general requirements of writing imposed by s.53(1).

"In *Walker v Hall* Dillon L.J. made the following statement of well-known general **5–96** principle:[33]

'. . . the law of trusts has concentrated on how the purchase money has been provided and it has been consistently held that where the purchase money for property acquired by two or more persons in their joint names has been provided by those persons in unequal amounts, they will be beneficially entitled as between themselves in the proportions in which they provided the purchase money. This is the basic doctrine of the resulting trust and it is conveniently and cogently expounded by Lord Upjohn in *Pettit v Pettit*.'[34]

"The application of this principle ordinarily gives rise to no difficulty where the **5–97** whole of the initial purchase price has been contributed by the two or more interested parties in the form of cash derived out of their respective resources without the benefit of a loan. Greater problems arise in cases such as the present

---

[32] *Midland Bank v Cooke* [1995] 4 All E.R. 465, discussed at para.6–107.
[33] [1984] F.L.R. 126 at 133.
[34] [1970] A.C. 777 at 814.

where part of the money required has been borrowed on mortgage. On the particular facts of some such cases the court, for the purpose of ascertaining the parties' proportionate interests in the property, has thought it right to impute to them the intention that their contributions to the purchase should be ascertained as at the date when the property eventually came to be sold. In *Gissing v Gissing* Lord Diplock, in the context of a case where the conveyance had been taken in the name of one spouse only, said:[35]

> 'And there is nothing inherently improbable in their acting on the understanding that the wife should be entitled to a share which was not to be quantified immediately upon the acquisition of the home but should be left to be determined when the mortgage was repaid or the property disposed of, on the basis of what would be fair having regard to the total contributions, direct or indirect, which each spouse had made by that date. Where this was the most likely inference from their conduct it would be for the court to give effect to that common intention of the parties by determining what in all the circumstances was a fair share.'

5–98   "Inferences of this nature as to the common intentions of the parties were drawn by this court on the particular facts of *Young v Young*[36] and *Passee v Passee*.[37]

5–99   "However, in a case where a purchase in the joint names of two parties has been advanced partly in the form of cash provided by one or both of them, and partly by way of a loan on mortgage, another approach open to the court is to assess the parties' contribution to the purchase, and thus their proportionate interests in the property, by reference to the time of the initial purchase, having regard to what sums each of them actually paid and what obligations each of them actually assumed in relation to the mortgage. This, for example, was the approach adopted by this court in *Crisp v Mullings*[38] and by Bush J. in *Marsh v Von Sternberg*.[39]

5–100   "In my opinion, the judge in the present case was mistaken in his view that the decision in *Young v Young* precluded him from holding that Mr. Huntingford was entitled to a share in the property ascertained by reference to the liability which he had originally assumed under the mortgage, as opposed to his actual payments towards the purchase. As appears from the passage from Lord Diplock's speech in *Gissing v Gissing* quoted above, the task of the court in cases such as this is to draw the most likely inference as to the common intention of the parties at the date of the purchase from their conduct. This must depend on the facts of the particular case. On the particular facts of *Young v Young* and *Passee v Passee*, the evidence disclosed no clear arrangement or understanding between the parties, as at the date of the purchase, in regard to the manner in which the mortgage payments were to be provided for. In the present case, in contrast, while both parties as joint proprietors had to join in the mortgage and assume joint and several liability to the mortgagee building society, there was a clear agreement or understanding that as between the two of them Mr. Huntingford would pay all the interest due under the mortgage and all the endowment policy premiums which would in due course, if the policy were duly kept up, discharge the capital debt owed to the lender. As at the date of the purchase, while Mrs. Hobbs no less than Mr. Huntingford was assuming

---

[35] [1971] A.C. 886 at 909.
[36] [1984] F.L.R. 375.
[37] (1988) 1 F.L.R. 263.
[38] [1976] 239 E.G. 119.
[39] [1986] 1 F.L.R. 526.

a liability to the lender, it was not contemplated that, as between the two of them, she would have to pay anything towards discharge of this liability.

> 'It is of course always possible to look at the subsequent conduct of the parties to see if it throws any light on what they originally agreed, but in the absence of a new or varied agreement, subsequent conduct cannot affect what was originally agreed' (*Marsh v Von Sternberg*,[40] *per* Bush J.).

"Drawing the most likely inference from the conduct of the parties in the present **5–101** case, in my judgment the proper common intention to impute to them is a common intention as at the date of purchase that Mrs. Hobbs should be treated as having contributed her cash contribution, Mr. Huntingford should be treated as having contributed the whole of the sum borrowed on mortgage, and that the property should be owned by the two of them in shares proportionate to such contributions. This approach to the problem is consistent with that of Bagnall J. in *Cowcher v Cowcher*[41] and of Vinelott J. in *Re Gorman* where he said:[42]

> 'In circumstances of this kind, the court is concerned to ascertain, so far as is possible, from the evidence, what was the intention of the parties when the property was purchased or what intention is to imputed to them. *Prima facie*, if the purchase is financed in whole or in part on mortgage, the person who assumed liability for the mortgage payments, as between the joint owners, is to be treated as having contributed the mortgage moneys.'

"I can see no sufficient grounds for not following this *prima facie* approach in the **5–102** present case. Both parties intended that the property should be purchased as a joint venture, and while Mr. Huntingford could not and would not have purchased it on his own without Mrs. Hobbs' cash contribution, the reasonable inference is that she could not and would not have purchased it on her own without the support of the commitments which he was undertaking in relation to the mortgage, both to the building society and to her personally. I would infer that if at the time of the purchase the point had been specifically put to the two parties and they had been asked in what proportions they would intend the property should be held, they would most probably have replied that it should be held in proportions corresponding with Mrs. Hobbs' cash contribution and the money raised on mortgage.

"On the basis of the parties' respective contributions and as at the date of original **5–103** completion of the purchase,

(a) Mrs. Hobbs was beneficially entitled to:

38,860/63,560 (say 61 per cent) of the property or its proceeds of sale.

(b) Mr. Huntingford was beneficially entitled to:

25,000/63,860 (say 39 per cent) of the property or its proceeds of sale.

These, I think, are the basic proportions which should govern the calculation of the sums which the parties are to receive out of the proceeds of sale of the property or the price which Mrs. Hobbs is to pay on the purchase of Mr. Huntingford's interest.

---

[40] *ibid.* at 533.
[41] [1972] 1 W.L.R. 425 at 431.
[42] [1990] 2 F.L.R. 284 at 291.

5–104   "In any such calculation Mr. Huntingford will, in my opinion, be entitled to be credited for the £2000 (approximately) paid by him for the erection of the conservatory. On either of the two alternative possible explanations of the sum of £3500 arrived at by the judge in his judgment, which will be referred to by Dillon L.J. in his judgment, it would appear that the judge at least implicitly found that this sum represented expenditure in respect of which the parties intended that Mr. Huntingford would be entitled to claim reimbursement on a subsequent sale.

5–105   "Mr. Huntingford will not in my judgment be entitled to be credited with any of the sums which he has paid either by way of interest under the mortgage or premiums due under the policy. His original 39 per cent share came into being on the footing that he would be paying all such sums.

5–106   "Correspondingly in my judgment in the course of the accounting between the parties, Mr. Huntingford should be debited with the whole of the capital debt of £25,000 still outstanding under the mortgage for the discharge of which he was to be responsible and which has not been discharged.

5–107   "If Mrs. Hobbs had not continued to occupy the property after his departure, I would have considered that he should be debited with any sums by way of mortgage interest or policy premiums which he had thereafter failed to pay and she herself had paid. However, since that date she has had the benefit of continued occupation of the property and I think that broad justice will be done if she is treated as having made these payments in place of paying an occupation rent. In short, I would propose that the calculations provided for by the order of this court should not on the one hand refer either to the mortgage interest and policy premiums paid since Mr. Huntingford left the property or on the other hand provide for any occupation rent payable by Mrs. Hobbs. . . ."

5–108   STEYN L.J.: "My Lords take the view that in all the circumstances the beneficial interests of the parties should be assessed in the proportions of 61 per cent to the woman and 39 per cent to the man. In my judgment it is impossible to infer any actual common intention as a basis for this conclusion. And the result is that the man's share will be several thousand pounds more than the sum which he would be entitled to if the actual contributions of the parties, as things turned out, were treated as decisive. . . . Reluctantly, I concur in the result."

5–109   DILLON L.J.: "If the interests of the parties are to be calculated by reference to their contributions, the interests must be calculated as per centages or fractions when the arrangements were set up and the expenditure was incurred.

5–110   ". . . [Since] the mortgage of £25,000 was only available because of the plaintiff's income, and the defendant, without the assistance of the plaintiff's acceptance of liability under the mortgage, could not have purchased the property, the plaintiff is, in my judgment, entitled to say that either a half or the whole of the liability under the mortgage is to be treated as his contribution to the purchase of the property. On the evidence at the trial however the defendant had no income out of which to make any payments in respect of the mortgage or the endowment policy. Moreover both the plaintiff and the defendant agreed in their evidence that as between themselves, he was to pay the mortgage . . .

5–111   "Basically, therefore, the plaintiff ought to have been credited with a contribution of £25,000 in respect of the mortgage loan—subject to adjustment because in the event he has not paid the full amount of the mortgage debt and the defendant has been left to pay it."

(e) Transfer from one to another

We now turn to cases where X gratuitously transfers property into Y's **5–112** name. In the cases we have considered so far, the transaction was a *purchase*; here it is a *transfer*. Property already stands in the name of X, who gratuitously transfers it into the name of Y. Here, again, there is a presumption that X does not intend to make a gift to Y, which Y must rebut if he does not wish to hold the property on resulting trust for X.

This presumption will be raised whenever the property gratuitously **5–113** transferred by X to Y is personal property (*e.g.* cash, shares, etc.).[43] Exceptionally, however, no presumption will be raised if the property is land. Under the Law of Property Act 1925, s.60(3): "In a voluntary conveyance a resulting trust for the grantor shall not be implied merely by reason that the property is not expressed to be conveyed for the use or benefit of the grantee." In *Lohia v Lohia*,[44] Nicholas Strauss Q.C., sitting as a deputy High Court judge, held that this sub-section means what it says: if X conveys land to Y and receives nothing in return, there will be no presumption in X's favour that Y must rebut if he wishes to keep the property for himself. It follows that the sub-section creates inconsistencies between the rules for real and personal property, and also between the rules for purchase of property in another's name and transferring property into another's name.

Arguably, however, these inconsistencies are justified.[45] There are many **5–114** reasons why X might buy property in Y's name without intending to make a gift to Y that do not obtain in the case of a transfer of property from X to Y: *e.g.* overlooking the need to protect X's position in the course of a complex transaction involving vendors and mortgagees.[46] Moreover, formality rules apply to conveyances of land which do not apply to transfers of personal property, increasing the likelihood that a transferor has thought carefully about whether he really wants to hand his property over to another person, and so reducing the need for a backstop rule that he should be presumed not to have intended this.

(f) Transfer into joint names of oneself and another

Suppose that property stands in the name of X, but instead of transfer- **5–115** ring it into the *sole* name of Y, as in (e) above, he gratuitously transfers it into the *joint* names of himself and Y. Again there will be a presumption that X does not intend to make a gift to Y of his share,[47] unless the property in question is land in which case there will be no such presumption, by dint of the LPA 1925, s.60(3). An example is *Young v Sealey*,[48]

---

[43] *Fowkes v Pascoe* (1875) 10 Ch. App. 343 at 348; *Hepworth v Hepworth* (1870) L.R. 11 Eq. 10; *Standing v Bowring* (1885) 16 Ch.D. 282; *Re Vinogradoff* [1935] W.N. 68; *Vandervell v I.R.C.* [1967] 2 A.C. 291 at 312–313; *Re Vandervell's Trusts (No.2)* [1974] Ch. 269; *Tinsley v Milligan* [1994] 1 A.C. 340 at 371.
[44] [2001] W.T.L.R. 101, affirmed on a different point [2001] EWCA Civ 1691, and cited with approval in *Ali v Khan* (2002) 5 I.T.E.L.R. 232 at [24] *per* Morritt V.-C.
[45] R. Chambers (2001) 15 Tru. L.I. 26, 29.
[46] *Cf. Brown v Brown* (1993) 31 N.S.W.L.R. 582.
[47] *Re Vinogradoff* [1935] W.N. 68.
[48] [1949] Ch. 278. See too *Re Reid* (1921) 50 Ont. L.R. 595; *Russell v Scott* (1936) 55 C.L.R. 440.

where X opened a joint bank account with Y, but during her life X retained complete control of the account, and Y neither paid anything into, nor drew anything out of the account. On X's death Y took the legal title by survivorship. Did he hold it on resulting trust for X's estate? Romer J. held not. A presumption arose in favour of the estate, but Y was able to rebut this with evidence of X's intentions.

5–116   What if X and Y open a joint bank account, and X provides in his will that Y should receive whatever is left in the account, X having had control of the account during his lifetime, and Y having had no sole drawing rights until X's death? Does the provision in X's will amount to a testamentary disposition? Following the lead of the High Court of Australia,[49] English courts of first instance[50] have held that no testamentary disposition is involved, there being "an immediate gift [at the time of opening the joint account] of a fluctuating asset consisting of the chose in action for the time being constituting the balance in the bank account."[51] Likewise, the Irish Supreme Court held in *Lynch v Burke*[52] that there was no testamentary disposition on similar facts, either because there was a gift subject to the contingency of surviving the donor, or because the donee had been given contractual rights under documents signed by the donee and enforceable against the bank and the donor's executor.

II. Where Resulting Trusts Do Not Arise

(a) Presumption of advancement

5–117   As we have said, where X gratuitously transfers property to Y, and there is no clear evidence of X's intentions, Equity generally presumes that X did not intend Y to take the property beneficially for himself. Exceptionally, however, Equity makes the opposite presumption when X and Y are in a special relationship such as that which exists between a father and his child. Here, a presumption of advancement is made: it is presumed that X intends Y to take the property beneficially for himself because fathers generally wish to advance their children in life by helping them financially. The principle was stated by Lord Eldon in *Murless v Franklin*[53] as follows: "The general rule is that on a purchase by one man in the name of another, the nominee is a trustee for the purchaser, is subject to exception where the purchaser is under a species of natural obligation to provide for the nominee."

5–118   The presumption of advancement is made where X is the father of Y, or stands *in loco parentis* to Y,[54] or is the husband of Y or the engaged fiancé

---

[49] *Russell v Scott* (1936) 56 C.L.R. 440.
[50] *Young v Sealey* [1943] Ch. 278; *Re Figgis* [1969] 1 Ch. 123.
[51] *Re Figgis* [1969] 1 Ch. 123 at 149 *per* Megarry J.
[52] [1995] 2 I.R. 159, discussed by D. Capper (1996) 47 N.I.L.Q. 281.
[53] (1818) 1 Swans. 13 at 17.
[54] *Hepworth v Hepworth* (1870) L.R. 11 Eq. 10; *Shephard v Cartwright* [1955] A.C. 431; *Re Cameron* [1999] *Times* April 2; *Lavelle v Lavelle* [2004] 2 F.C.R. 418 at [14], *per* Lord Phillips M.R.

of Y.[55] It does not arise where X is merely cohabiting with Y,[56] nor where X is the wife of Y.[57] The English cases are divided on the question whether the presumption arises as between a mother and her children,[58] but authorities from elsewhere in the Commonwealth say that it does.[59]

These distinctions derive from cases which date back several hundred years, and some have ceased to reflect contemporary socio-economic reality and ideas of gender equality. Specifically, there is no longer a good reason to think that fathers but not mothers have the financial wherewithal to advance their children in life, nor to think that husbands but not wives have the means to benefit their spouses. In the latter case, it seems most likely that the courts will redress the present inequality of treatment by doing away with presumptions of advancement between spouses altogether, since the strength of the presumption between husband and wife is now said to be very weak.[60] Moreover, the gender bias inherent in the rules affecting spouses probably contravenes Art.5 of the Seventh Protocol to the European Convention of Human Rights, which asserts the equality of spousal rights and responsibilities.[61]

5–119

Of the former case, it has been said that although the question whether the presumption arises between mother and child is uncertain, this is "of little practical importance, since very slight intention is sufficient to establish advancement, there being very little additional motive required beyond the mother/child relationship to induce a mother to make a gift to her child."[62] It should be borne in mind, however, that the existence of the presumption can still be crucial, and that much can still turn "upon the precise family relationship" between the parties, "so that, for example, distinctions between a wife or partner, a child or brother become central", when the courts are asked to determine "the enforceability of a transaction between two parties implicated in illegal purpose".[63]

5–120

(b) Rebutting the presumptions

In some cases, the presumption that a transferor does not intend a gift, and also the opposite presumption that a transferor intends a gift where he is in a special relationship with the transferee, can be rebutted by comparatively slight evidence,[64] but speaking generally, the strength of the

5–121

---

[55] *Tinker v Tinker* [1970] P. 136; *Silver v Silver* [1958] 1 W.L.R. 259; *Moate v Moate* [1948] 2 All E.R. 486 (intended husband: marriage afterwards solemnised); Law Reform (Miscellaneous Provisions) Act 1970, s.2(1); *Mossop v Mossop* [1988] 2 All E.R. 202.

[56] *Rider v Kidder* (1805) 10 Ves. Jun. 360; *Napier v Public Trustee* (1980) 32 A.L.R. 153 at 158; *Calverley v Green* (1984) 56 A.L.R. 483; *Lowson v Coombes* [1999] 1 F.L.R. 799.

[57] *Re Curtis* (1885) 52 L.T. 244; *Mercier v Mercier* [1903] 2 Ch. 98; *Abrahams v Trustee of Property of Abrahams* [2000] W.T.L.R. 593.

[58] Yes, at least where she is a widowed mother: *Garrett v Wilkinson* (1848) 2 De G. & Sm. 244 at 246; *Sayre v Hughes* (1886) L.R. 5 Eq. 376; *Re Grimes* [1937] I.R. 470. No: *Re De Visme* (1863) 2 De G.J. & S. 17; *Bennet v Bennet* (1879) 10 Ch.D. 474; *Sekhon v Alissa* [1989] 2 F.L.R. 94.

[59] *Re Brownlie* [1990] 3 N.Z.L.R. 243; *Brown v Brown* (1993) 31 N.S.W.L.R. 582 at 591; *Re Dreger Estate* (1994) 97 Manitoba R. (2d) 39; *Nelson v Nelson* (1995) 184 C.L.R. 538;

[60] *Pettitt v Pettitt* [1970] A.C. 777 at 793; *McGrath v Wallis* [1995] 2 F.L.R. 114 at 155, *per* Nourse L.J; *Ali v Khan* (2002) 5 I.T.E.L.R. 232 at [30], *per* Morritt V.-C.

[61] Written Answer, *Hansard* (HL) April 21, 1998, vol. 588, col. 197.

[62] *Crown Prosecution Service v Malik* [2003] EWHC 660 (Admin) at [27], *per* Richards J.

[63] *Collier v Collier* (2002) 6 I.T.E.L.R. 270, at [97], *per* Mance L.J. See paras 5–124 *et seq.*

[64] *Pettitt v Pettitt* [1970] A.C. 777 at 813, 824; *Falconer v Falconer* [1970] 1 W.L.R. 1333; *McGrath v Wallis* [1995] 2 F.L.R. 114.

evidence required to rebut either presumption will vary with the strength of the presumption, which in turn will depend on the facts and circumstances giving rise to it.[65] To give some examples: "if a young woman in her first job, not very well paid, were to raise as much as she could on mortgage in order to buy a flat, what would we make of the fact that her well-to-do uncle, a man on affable terms with her, provided a minor part of the purchase price? The most obvious explanation is not that he wanted a part of the speculation. It is more credible that it was meant to be a loan or, perhaps, a gift."[66] On the other hand, if an unmarried couple both contribute to the purchase of a shared home, and only one appears on the legal title, there is only "a fairly strong presumption" that the other does not intend to make a gift of her contribution because "modern couples usually have the property conveyed into their joint names and, if they do not, one may wonder why."[67] If a father conveys property into his child's name, but retains the title deeds and simultaneously declares that the transaction is not a gift, then that is sufficient to rebut the presumption of advancement,[68] although the retention of title deeds without such a declaration may be insufficient.[69] If land is purchased in the name of a company which is formed for the purpose and controlled by the provider of the funds, then it would be "perverse" to think that he does not wish the company to take the property beneficially for itself, since his likely intention is to use the company to deal with the property.[70]

5–122   Before the First World War, it was held that acquiescence by a child, in whose name a purchase had been made, in the receipt by his father during his life of the rents or other income from the property does not rebut the presumption of advancement,[71] at any rate where the child has not already been fully advanced to set him up in life.[72] The reason given was that if the child were an infant then it would be natural that the father should receive the profits, while if the child were an adult, then it would be an act of good manners on his part not to dispute their reception by his father. In the 2000s, however, it seems less likely that the court would regard good manners as an explanation of the child's conduct sufficient to justify his retention of the property.

5–123   In *Shephard v Cartwright*[73] Viscount Simonds held that evidence of acts subsequent to the transfer, though not admissible in favour of the party doing the acts, is admissible against him. However, this rule was abandoned

---

[65] *Vajpeyi v Yusaf* [2003] EWHC 2339 (Ch) at [71], *per* Peter Prescott Q.C. (sitting as a deputy High Court judge), following *Fowkes v Pascoe* (1875) L.R. 10 Ch. 343 at 352–3, *per* Mellish L.J.

[66] *ibid.* at [77].

[67] *ibid.* at [76].

[68] *Warren v Gurney* [1944] 2 All E.R. 472.

[69] *Scawin v Scawin* (1841) 1 Y. & C.C.C. 65.

[70] *Arab Monetary Fund v Hashim* Ch.D. 15 June 1994, *per* Chadwick J., followed in *Trade Credit Finance (No.1) Ltd v Bilgin* [2004] EWHC 2732 (Comm). *Cf. United Overseas Bank Ltd v Iwuanyanwu* Ch.D. 5 March 2001, affd. [2001] EWCA Civ 616.

[71] *Commissioner of Stamp Duties v Byrnes* [1911] A.C. 386; *cf.* Wickens V.-C. in *Stock v McAvoy* (1872) L.R. 15 Eq. 55 at 59; *Northern Canadian Trust Co. v Smith* [1947] 3 D.L.R. 135; *Re Gooch* (1890) 62 L.T. 384.

[72] *Grey v Grey* (1677) 2 Swans. 594; and see *Hepworth v Hepworth* (1870) L.R. 11 Eq. 10.

[73] [1955] A.C. 431.

in *Lavelle v Lavelle*,[74] in favour of the "less rigid" approach taken in *Pettitt v Pettitt*.[75] According to Lord Phillips M.R.[76]:

> "Equity searches for the subjective intention of the transferor. It . . . is not satisfactory to apply rigid rules of law to the evidence that is admissible to rebut the presumption of advancement. Plainly, self-serving statements or conduct of a transferor, who may long after the transaction be regretting earlier generosity, carry little or no weight. But words or conduct more proximate to the transaction itself should be given the significance that they naturally bear as part of the overall picture. Where the transferee is an adult, the words or conduct of the transferor will carry more weight if the transferee is aware of them and makes no protest or challenge to them."

(c) Illegality

When considering the evidence that may be offered to rebut the **5–124** presumptions one must also bear in mind the maxims "he who comes to equity must come with clean hands", *"ex turpi causa non oritur actio"* ("no legal action arises out of bad conduct"), and *"in pari delicto potior est conditio defendetis* (or *possidentis)"* ("when both parties are in the wrong the defendant (or the possessor of property) is in the stronger position"). These maxims may come into play when a person gratuitously transfers property to another as part of an illegal scheme, *e.g.* to defraud the Revenue, to defeat his creditors, or to defeat his wife's claims on divorce.[77]

Where the presumption of advancement applies (*e.g.* where X transfers **5–125** property to his wife W or son S) the onus is on the transferor X to produce evidence rebutting the presumption. If he honestly transfers the property to defeat his creditors then this could not lawfully be achieved without the beneficial ownership passing with the legal title, and so the presumption of advancement is strengthened that this was what he intended to accomplish, as held in *Tinker v Tinker*.[78] If he dishonestly transfers the legal title to W or S to cloak the truth from his creditors, with a view to recovering the property for himself afterwards, then he cannot usually rely on evidence of his illegal purpose to rebut the presumption of advancement.[79] However, *Tribe v Tribe* establishes that he can rely on such evidence if the creditors were not actually deceived (*e.g.* because matters were resolved without the need to resort to the relevant property): he can recover his property so long as the illegal purpose has not been "wholly or partly carried into effect".[80]

---

[74] [2004] 2 F.C.R. 418.

[75] [1970] A.C. 777.

[76] [2004] 2 F.C.R. 418 at [19].

[77] But note Insolvency Act 1986, ss.339–342, 423–425; Matrimonial Causes Act 1973, s.37; Inheritance (Provisions for Family and Dependents) Act 1975, s.10, above at para.4–132.

[78] [1970] P. 136; but note Insolvency Act 1986 ss.339–342, 423–425, above at paras 4–124 *et seq.* and at paras 4–136 *et seq.*

[79] *Gascoigne v Gascoigne* [1918] 1 K.B. 223 (where there were existing creditors and where tax was paid on the basis that the bungalow belonged to the wife); *Re Emery's Investment Trusts* [1959] Ch. 410 (where it seems that American withholding tax was evaded).

[80] *Tribe v Tribe* [1996] Ch. 107 at 134, *per* Millett L.J. See too *Symes v Hughes* (1875) L.R. 9 Eq. 475; *Petherpermal Chetty v Muniandi Servai* (1908) 24 T.L.R. 462; *Perpetual Executors Association of Australia Ltd v Wright* (1917) 23 C.L.R. 185; *Martin v Martin* (1959) 110 C.L.R. 297; *Chettiar v Chettiar* [1962] A.C. 294 at 302; *Sekhon v Alissa* [1989] 2 F.L.R. 94; *Collier v Collier* (2002) 6 I.T.E.L.R. 270, esp. [103]–[107], *per* Mance L.J.

In effect, therefore, the law provides him with a safety net if he transfers property as part of an illegal plan which later becomes unnecessary. Is this satisfactory?

5–126 According to the majority of the House of Lords in *Tinsley v Milligan*, matters are different where a presumption is made that a transferor X does not intend to make a gift (*e.g.* where X transfers property to his brother B). Here, X need not rely on evidence of his own illegal purpose. He simply needs to show that he transferred the property to B and received nothing in return for it. B must then prove that a gift was intended, or a resulting trust for X will be imposed, and B will be unable to do this where he has received property transferred to him by X for the purpose of deceiving some third party. Hence, once the coast is clear and the third party has been defrauded, X can recover the property, an iniquitous result which Millett L.J. wished to avoid in *Tribe*,[81] but which the House of Lords' decision in *Tinsley v Milligan* clearly mandates.[82]

5–127 As pointed out by the High Court of Australia,[83] the English Court of Appeal,[84] and the English Law Commission,[85] it is highly unsatisfactory to make a transferor's ability to recover property transferred for an illegal purpose turn on the essentially irrelevant question of whether or not he and the transferee are in a special relationship giving rise to a presumption of advancement. Matters are worsened by the fact that there is uncertainty as to which presumption applies to transfers from wife to husband and mother to child. Thus, the minority of the House of Lords in *Tinsley v Milligan* preferred the harsh but certain approach that "a court of equity will not assist a claimant who does not come to equity with clean hands", producing the result that the transferred property is left in the hands of the defendant.[86] All their Lordships rejected the flexible rule relied upon by the Court of Appeal,[87] which made the transferor's ability to recover the property turn upon the extent to which the public conscience would be affronted by recognising rights arising out of illegal transactions.

5–128 In principle, however, matters would be greatly improved if the law were amended in line with the Law Commission's provisional view[88] that there should be a structured statutory discretion to decide the effects of illegality. Factors to be taken into account would be "(a) the seriousness of the

---

[81] [1996] Ch. 107 at 129: "The transferor's own conduct would be inconsistent with the retention of any beneficial interest in the property" because "the only way in which a man can protect his property from his creditors is by divesting himself of all beneficial interest in it." Yet Milligan's conduct in defrauding the DHSS on the basis that she had no beneficial interest was inconsistent with her having any beneficial interest, and the Lords' majority gave no sign that Tinsley could exploit this fact against her.

[82] [1994] 1 A.C. 340 at 376, *per* Lord Browne-Wilkinson, endorsing *Gorog v Kiss* (1977) 78 D.L.R. (3d) 690.

[83] *Nelson v Nelson* (1995) 184 C.L.R. 538.

[84] *Tribe v Tribe* [1996] Ch. 107 at 118, *per* Nourse L.J. *Silverwood v Silverwood* (1997) 74 P. & C.R. 453 at 458–459, *per* Nourse L.J.; *Lowson v Coombes* [1999] Ch. 373 at 385, *per* Robert Walker L.J.; *Collier v Collier* (2002) 6 I.T.E.L.R. 270, at [105]–[106], *per* Mance L.J.

[85] Law Commission, *Illegal Transactions: The Effect of Illegality on Contracts and Trusts* (Law Com. No.154, 1999), paras 3.19–3.24.

[86] "Let the estate lie where it falls": *Muckleton v Brown* (1801) 6 Ves. Jun. 52 at 69.

[87] [1992] Ch. 310.

[88] Law Commission, *Illegal Transactions: The Effect of Illegality on Contracts and Trusts* (Law Com. No.154, 1999), para.8.63; on which see N. Enonchong, "Illegal Transactions: The Future" [2000] R.L.R. 82, 99–104.

illegality; (b) the knowledge and intent of the illegal trust beneficiary; (c) whether invalidity would tend to deter the illegality; (d) whether invalidity would further the purpose of the rule which renders the trust 'illegal'; and (e) whether invalidity would be a proportionate response to the claimant's participation in the illegality." Such statutory discretion would oust the equitable maxim "he who comes to equity must come with clean hands",[89] but views were sought on a discretion to make relief conditional on a payment or transfer of property that could come within the maxim "he who comes to equity must do equity".

Finally, it should be noted that if the transferor cannot recover then his **5–129** personal representative is in no better position.[90] Should public policy allow his trustee in bankruptcy to be in a better position?[91]

TINSLEY v MILLIGAN

House of Lords [1994] 1 A.C. 340; [1993] 3 W.L.R. 126; [1993] 3 All E.R. 65 (Lords Jauncey, Lowry, and Browne-Wilkinson, Lords Keith and Goff dissenting).

Stella Tinsley and Kathleen Milligan jointly purchased a house which they **5–130** registered only in Tinsley's name to enable Milligan (with the knowledge and assent of Tinsley) to make false social security benefit claims for the benefit of both of them cohabiting as lovers. Their relationship ended after four years, when Tinsley moved out. She claimed possession of the house as legal owner, and Milligan counterclaimed for an order for sale and a declaration that the house was held by Tinsley on trust for the two of them in equal shares. Milligan confessed her fraud to the Department of Social Security, with whom she made her peace, and thereafter was paid benefit on a lawful basis. Tinsley was prosecuted, convicted, and fined, and had to make some repayment to the Department.

LORD BROWNE-WILKINSON: "My Lords, I agree with the speech of my noble and **5–131** learned friend, Lord Goff of Chieveley, that the consequences of being a party to an illegal transaction cannot depend, as the majority in the Court of Appeal held, on such an imponderable factor as the extent to which the public conscience would be affronted by recognising rights created by illegal transactions. However, I have the misfortune to disagree with him as to the correct principle to be applied in a case where equitable property rights are acquired as a result of an illegal transaction.

"Neither at law nor in equity will the court enforce an illegal contract which has **5–132** been partially, but not fully, performed. However, it does not follow that all acts done under a partially performed contract are of no effect. In particular it is now clearly established that at law (as opposed to in equity), property in goods or land can pass under, or pursuant to, such a contract. If so, the rights of the owner of the legal title thereby acquired will be enforced, provided that the plaintiff can establish such title without pleading or leading evidence of the illegality. It is said that the property lies where it falls, even though legal title to the property was acquired as a result of the property passing under the illegal contract itself. I will first consider the

---

[89] *ibid.*, para.8.91.

[90] *Ayerst v Jenkins* (1873) L.R. 16 Eq. 275 at 281, *per* Lord Selborne L.C. The contrary view of Lord Eldon in *Mackleston v Brown* (1801) 6 Ves. Jun. 52 at 68 seems unsound.

[91] *cf. Ayerst v Jenkins* (1873) 16 Eq. 275 at 283; *Trautwein v Richardson* [1946] Argus L.R. 129 at 134, *per* Dixon J.; *Caddy v McInnes* (1995) 131 A.L.R. 277.

modern authorities laying down the circumstances under which a legal proprietary interest acquired under an illegal transaction will be enforced by the courts. I will then consider whether the courts adopt a different attitude to equitable proprietary interests so acquired. . . .

5–133   "From these authorities the following propositions emerge: (1) property in chattels and land can pass under a contract which is illegal and therefore would have been unenforceable as a contract; (2) a plaintiff can at law enforce property rights so acquired provided that he does not need to rely on the illegal contract for any purpose other than providing the basis of his claim to a property right; (3) it is irrelevant that the illegality of the underlying agreement was either pleaded or emerged in evidence: if the plaintiff has acquired legal title under the illegal contract that is enough.

5–134   "I have stressed the common law rules as to the impact of illegality on the acquisition and enforcement of property rights because it is the appellant's contention that different principles apply in equity. In particular it is said that equity will not aid Miss Milligan to assert, establish or enforce an equitable, as opposed to a legal, proprietary interest since she was a party to the fraud on the D.S.S. The house was put in the name of Miss Tinsley alone (instead of joint names) to facilitate the fraud. Therefore, it is said, Miss Milligan does not come to equity with clean hands: consequently, equity will not aid her.

5–135   "Most authorities to which we were referred deal with enforcing proprietary rights under a trust: I will deal with them in due course. But before turning to them, I must point out that if Miss Tinsley's argument is correct, the results would be far reaching and, I suggest, very surprising. There are many proprietary rights, apart from trusts, which are only enforceable in equity. For example, an agreement for a lease under which the tenant has entered is normally said to be as good as a lease, since under such an agreement equity treats the lease as having been granted and the 'lessee' as having a proprietary interest enforceable against the whole world except the *bona fide* purchaser for value without notice. . . .

5–136   "In my judgment to draw such distinctions between property rights enforceable at law and those which require the intervention of equity would be surprising. More than 100 years has elapsed since the administration of law and equity became fused. The reality of the matter is that, in 1993, English law has one single law of property made up of legal and equitable interests. Although for historical reasons legal estates and equitable estates have differing incidents, the person owning either type of estate has a right of property, a right *in rem* not merely a right *in personam*. If the law is that a party is entitled to enforce a property right acquired under an illegal transaction, in my judgment the same rule ought to apply to any property right so acquired, whether such right is legal or equitable.

5–137   "In the present case, Miss Milligan claims under a resulting or implied trust. The court below have found, and it is not now disputed, that apart from the question of illegality Miss Milligan would have been entitled in equity to a half share in the house in accordance with the principles exemplified in *Gissing v Gissing*;[92] *Grant v Edwards*;[93] and *Lloyds Bank Plc. v Rosset*.[94] The creation of such an equitable interest does not depend upon a contractual obligation but on a common intention acted upon by the parties to their detriment. It is a development of the old law of resulting trust under which, where two parties have provided the purchase money to

[92] [1971] A.C. 886.
[93] [1986] Ch. 638.
[94] [1991] 1 A.C. 107.

buy a property which is conveyed into the name of one of them alone, the latter is presumed to hold the property on a resulting trust for both parties in shares proportionate to their contributions to the purchase price. In arguments, no distinction was drawn between strict resulting trusts and a *Gissing v Gissing* type of trust.

"A presumption of resulting trust also arises in equity when A transfers **5–138** personalty or money to B.[95] Before 1925, there was also a presumption of resulting trust when land was voluntarily transferred by A to B: it is arguable, however, that the position has been altered by the 1925 property legislation.[96] The presumption of a resulting trust is, in my view, crucial in considering the authorities. On that presumption (and on the contrary presumption of advancement) hinges the answer to the crucial question 'does a plaintiff claiming under a resulting trust have to rely on the underlying illegality?' Where the presumption of resulting trust applies, the plaintiff does not have to rely on the illegality. If he proves that the property is vested in the defendant alone but that the plaintiff provided part of the purchase money, or voluntarily transferred the property to the defendant, the plaintiff establishes his claim under a resulting trust unless either the contrary presumption of advancement displaces the presumption of resulting trust or the defendant leads evidence to rebut the presumption of resulting trust. Therefore, in cases where the presumption of advancement does not apply, a plaintiff can establish his equitable interest in the property without relying in any way on the underlying illegal transaction. In this case Miss Milligan as defendant simply pleaded the common intention that the property should belong to both of them and that she contributed to the purchase price: she claimed that in consequence the property belonged to them equally. To the same effect was her evidence in chief. Therefore Miss Milligan was not forced to rely on the illegality to prove her equitable interest. Only in the reply and the course of Miss Milligan's cross-examination did such illegality emerge: it was Miss Tinsley who had to rely on that illegality.

"Although the presumption of advancement does not directly arise for considera- **5–139** tion in this case, it is important when considering the decided cases to understand its operation. On a transfer from a man to his wife, children or others to whom he stands *in loco parentis*, equity presumes an intention to make a gift. Therefore in such a case, unlike the case where the presumption of resulting trust applies, in order to establish any claim the plaintiff has himself to lead evidence sufficient to rebut the presumption of gift and in so doing will normally have to plead, and give evidence of, the underlying illegal purpose.

"Against this background, I turn to consider the authorities dealing with the **5–140** position in equity where A transferred property to B for an illegal purpose. The earlier authorities, primarily Lord Eldon, support the appellant's proposition that equity will not aid a plaintiff who has transferred property to another for an illegal purpose. . . .

[His Lordship reviewed various authorities, and then continued:] "During the **5–141** 19th century, there was originally a difference of view as to whether a transaction entered into for an illegal purpose would be enforced at law or in equity if the party had repented of his illegal purpose before it had been put into operation, *i.e.* the doctrine of *locus poenitentiae*. It was eventually recognised both at law and in equity that if the plaintiff had repented before the illegal purpose was carried through, he

---

[95] See *Snell's Equity*, 29th ed. (1990), pp.183–184; *Standing v Bowring* (1885) 31 Ch.D. 282 at 287, *per* Cotton L.J. and *Dewar v Dewar* [1975] 1 W.L.R. 1532 at 1537.
[96] See *Snell's Equity*, p.182.

could recover his property.[97] The principle of *locus poenitentiae* is in my judgment irreconcilable with any rule that where property is transferred for an illegal purpose no equitable proprietary right exists. The equitable right, if any, must arise at the time at which the property was voluntarily transferred to the third party or purchased in the name of the third party. The existence of the equitable interest cannot depend upon events occurring after that date. Therefore if, under the principle of *locus poenitentiae*, the courts recognise that an equitable interest did arise out of the underlying transaction, the same must be true where the illegal purpose was carried through. The carrying out of the illegal purpose cannot, by itself, destroy the pre-existing equitable interest. The doctrine of *locus poenitentiae* therefore demonstrates that the effect of illegality is not to prevent a proprietary interest in equity from arising or to produce a forfeiture of such right: the effect is to render the equitable interest unenforceable in certain circumstances. The effect of illegality is not substantive but procedural. The question therefore is, 'In what circumstances will equity refuse to enforce equitable rights which undoubtedly exist.'

5–142   "It is against this background that one has to assess the more recent law. Although in the cases decided during the last 100 years there are frequent references to Lord Eldon's wide principle, with one exception . . . none of the English decisions are decided by simply applying that principle. They are all cases where the unsuccessful party was held to be precluded from leading evidence of an illegal situation in order to rebut the presumption of advancement. Lord Eldon's rule would have provided a complete answer whether the transfer was made to a wife or child (where the presumption of advancement would apply) or to a stranger. Yet with one exception none of the cases in this century has been decided on that simple basis.

5–143   "The majority of cases have been those in which the presumption of advancement applied: in those authorities the rule has been stated as being that a plaintiff cannot rely on evidence of his own illegality to rebut the presumption applicable in such cases that the plaintiff intended to make a gift of the property to the transferee. Thus in *Gascoigne v Gascoigne*;[98] *McEvoy v Belfast Banking Co. Ltd*;[99] *Re Emery's Investments Trusts*;[1] *Chettiar v Chettiar*;[2] and *Tinker v Tinker*,[3] the crucial point was said to be the inability of the plaintiff to lead evidence rebutting the presumption of advancement. In each case the plaintiff was claiming to recover property voluntarily transferred to, or purchased in the name of, a wife or child, for an illegal purpose. Although reference was made to Lord Eldon's principle, none of those cases was decided on the simple ground (if it were good law) that equity would not in any circumstances enforce a resulting trust in such circumstances. On the contrary in each case the rule was stated to be that the plaintiff could not recover because he had to rely on the illegality to rebut the presumption of advancement.

5–144   "In my judgment, the explanation for this departure from Lord Eldon's absolute rule is that the fusion of law and equity has led the courts to adopt a single rule (applicable both at law and in equity) as to the circumstances in which the court will enforce property interests acquired in pursuance of an illegal transaction, *viz.*, the *Bowmakers* rule.[4] A party to an illegality can recover by virtue of a legal or equitable

---

[97] See *Taylor v Bowers* (1876) 1 Q.B.D. 291; *Symes v Hughes* (1870) L.R. 9 Eq. 475.
[98] [1918] 1 K.B. 223.
[99] [1934] N.I. 67.
[1] [1959] Ch. 410.
[2] [1962] A.C. 294.
[3] [1970] P. 136 at 141, 142.
[4] [1945] K.B. 65.

property interest if, but only if, he can establish his title without relying on his own illegality. In cases where the presumption of advancement applies, the plaintiff is faced with the presumption of gift and therefore cannot claim under a resulting trust unless and until he has rebutted that presumption of gift: for those purposes the plaintiff does have to rely on the underlying illegality and therefore fails.

"The position is well illustrated by two decisions in the Privy Council [*viz. Singh v* **5–145** *Ali*[5] and *Chettiar v Chettiar*[6]]. . . . In my judgment these two cases show that the Privy Council was applying exactly the same principle in both cases although in one case the plaintiff's claim rested on a legal title and in the other on an equitable title. The claim based on the equitable title did not fail simply because the plaintiff was a party to the illegal transaction; it only failed because the plaintiff was bound to disclose and rely upon his own illegal purpose in order to rebut the presumption of advancement. The Privy Council was plainly treating the principle applicable both at law and in equity as being that a man can recover property provided that he is not forced to rely on his own illegality.

"I therefore reach the conclusion that, although there is no case overruling the **5–146** wide principle stated by Lord Eldon, as the law has developed the equitable principle has become elided into the common law rule. In my judgment the time has come to decide clearly that the rule is the same whether a plaintiff founds himself on a legal or equitable title: he is entitled to recover if he is not forced to plead or rely on the illegality, even if it emerges that the title on which he relied was acquired in the course of carrying through an illegal transaction.

"As applied in the present case, that principle would operate as follows. Miss **5–147** Milligan established a resulting trust by showing that she had contributed to the purchase price of the house and that there was common understanding between her and Miss Tinsley that they owned the house equally. She had no need to allege or prove why the house was conveyed into the name of Miss Tinsley alone, since that fact was irrelevant to her claim: it was enough to show that the house was in fact vested in Miss Tinsley alone. The illegality only emerged at all because Miss Tinsley sought to raise it. Having proved these facts, Miss Milligan had raised a presumption of resulting trust. There was no evidence to rebut that presumption. Therefore Miss Milligan should succeed. This is exactly the process of reasoning adopted by the Ontario Court of Appeal in *Gorog v Kiss*[7] which in my judgment was rightly decided."

TRIBE v TRIBE

Court of Appeal [1996] Ch. 107; [1995] 4 All E.R. 237; [1995] 3 W.L.R. 913; [1995] 2 F.L.R. 966 (Nourse, Millett and Otton L.JJ.).

Fearful of dilapidations claims against him as the tenant of two properties, the **5–148** claimant transferred 459 out of 500 shares in the family company that operated out of the properties to one of his four children. The transfer was purportedly made in exchange for a payment of £78,030, but this payment was never made, nor was it ever intended that it should be. The presumption of advancement was allowed to be rebutted by the claimant's evidence that the purpose of the transfer was to deceive his creditors by creating the appearance that he no longer owned the shares. This

---

[5] [1960] A.C. 167.
[6] [1962] A.C. 294.
[7] (1977) 78 D.L.R. (3d) 690.

illegal purpose had never been carried into effect because, without disclosing the transfer, the claimant surrendered one lease for value and purchased the reversion on the other lease.

5–149   MILLETT L.J. reviewed a line of authorities culminating with *Tinsley v Milligan*, and then continued: "Prior to *Tinsley v Milligan* no transferor had ever succeeded in recovering his property by enforcing a resulting trust where he had transferred the property for an illegal purpose and that purpose had been carried out. In *Re Great Berlin Steamboat Co.*[8] the transferor failed to recover for this very reason; in other cases where the transferor has succeeded he did so only because the illegal purpose had not been carried out.

5–150   "In *Tinsley v Milligan* the parties, who both contributed to the purchase of a house, arranged for the conveyance to be taken in the name of the appellant alone but on the understanding that it was to belong to them jointly. The purpose of this arrangement was to enable the respondent to perpetrate frauds on the Department of Social Security, and over a number of years the respondent, with the connivance of the appellant, made false claims for benefit. Despite this the respondent was allowed to recover.

5–151   "In his dissenting speech Lord Goff refused to draw any distinction between cases where the presumption of advancement applied and cases in which the plaintiff could rely on a resulting trust. From the authorities he derived a single principle: that if one party puts property in the name of another for a fraudulent or illegal purpose neither law nor equity will allow him to recover the property. Even if he can establish a resulting trust in his favour he cannot enforce it. Given Lord Goff's opinion that there was but one principle in play, it was natural for him to describe the doctrine of the *locus poenitentiae* as an exception to that principle. Since the respondent could not bring herself within the exception, he would have allowed the appeal.

5–152   "This was not, however, the view of the majority. Lord Browne-Wilkinson expressly held that the rule was the same whether the plaintiff founded himself on a legal or an equitable title: he was entitled to succeed if he was not forced to rely on his own illegality, even if it emerged that the title on which he relied was acquired in the course of carrying through an illegal transaction. The respondent had established a resulting trust by showing that she had contributed to the purchase price and that there was a common understanding between her and the appellant that they should own the house equally. She had no need to allege or prove why she had allowed the house to be conveyed into the sole name of the appellant, since that fact was irrelevant to her claim.

5–153   "The necessary consequence of this is that where he can rely on a resulting trust the transferor will normally be able to recover his property if the illegal purpose has not been carried out. In *Tinsley v Milligan* she recovered even though the illegal purpose had been carried out. It does not, however, follow that the transferor will invariably succeed in such circumstances, so that the presence or absence of a *locus poenitentiae* is irrelevant where the transfer gives rise to a resulting trust. A resulting trust, like the presumption of advancement, rests on a presumption which is rebuttable by evidence.[9] The transferor does not need to allege or prove the purpose for which property was transferred into the name of the transferee; in equity he can rely on the presumption that no gift was intended. But the transferee cannot be

---

[8] (1884) 26 Ch.D. 616.
[9] See *Standing v Bowring* (1885) 31 Ch.D. 282 at 287.

prevented from rebutting the presumption by leading evidence of the transferor's subsequent conduct to show that it was inconsistent with any intention to retain a beneficial interest. Suppose, for example, that a man transfers property to his nephew in order to conceal it from his creditors, and suppose that he afterwards settles with his creditors on the footing that he has no interest in the property. Is it seriously suggested that he can recover the property? I think not. The transferor's own conduct would be inconsistent with the retention of any beneficial interest in the property. I can see no reason why the nephew should not give evidence of the transferor's dealings with his creditors to rebut the presumption of a resulting trust and show that a gift was intended. He would not be relying on any illegal arrangement but implicitly denying it. The transferor would have to give positive evidence of his intention to retain a beneficial interest and dishonestly conceal it from his creditors, evidence which he would not be allowed to give once the illegal purpose had been carried out.

"This analysis is not, in my view, inconsistent with a passage in Lord Browne-Wilkinson's speech where he said:[10]   **5–154**

'The equitable right, if any, must arise at the time at which the property was voluntarily transferred to the third party or purchased in the name of the third party. The existence of the equitable interest cannot depend upon events occurring after that date. Therefore if, under the principle of *locus poenitentiae*, the courts recognise that an equitable interest did arise out of the underlying transaction, the same must be true where the illegal purpose was carried through. The carrying out of the illegal purpose cannot, by itself, destroy the pre-existing equitable interest.'

"But it does not follow that subsequent conduct is necessarily irrelevant. Where   **5–155** the existence of an equitable interest depends upon a rebuttable presumption or inference of the transferor's intention, evidence may be given of his subsequent conduct in order to rebut the presumption or inference which would otherwise be drawn.

"*Tinsley v Milligan* is, in my opinion, not authority for the proposition that a party   **5–156** who transfers property for an illegal purpose in circumstances which give rise to a resulting trust can invariably enforce the trust and recover the property even though the illegal purpose has been carried into effect. I do not accept the suggestion that cases such as *Re Great Berlin Steamboat Co.* have been impliedly overruled or that the dicta in the many cases, including *Taylor v Bowers*[11] and *Singh v Ali*,[12] indicating that the result would have been otherwise if the illegal purpose had or had not been carried out, must be taken to have been overruled.

"The question in the present case is the converse: whether the transferor can   **5–157** rebut the presumption of advancement by giving evidence of his illegal purpose so long as the illegal purpose has not been carried into effect. . . .

"There is no modern case in which restitution has been denied in circumstances   **5–158** comparable to those of the present case where the illegal purpose has not been carried out. In *Tinsley v Milligan* Lord Browne-Wilkinson expressly recognised the availability of the doctrine of the *locus poenitentiae* in a restitutionary context, and cited *Taylor v Bowers* as well as *Symes v Hughes*[13] without disapproval. In my opinion

---

[10] [1994] 1 A.C. 340 at 374.
[11] (1876) 1 Q.B.D. 291.
[12] [1960] A.C. 167.
[13] (1870) L.R. 9 Eq. 475.

the weight of the authorities supports the view that a person who seeks to recover property transferred by him for an illegal purpose can lead evidence of his dishonest intention whenever it is necessary for him to do so provided that he has withdrawn from the transaction before the illegal purpose has been carried out. It is not necessary if he can rely on an express or resulting trust in his favour; but it is necessary (i) if he brings an action at law and (ii) if he brings proceedings in equity and needs to rebut the presumption of advancement. The availability of the *locus poenitentiae* is well documented in the former case. I would not willingly adopt a rule which differentiated between the rule of the common law and that of equity in a restitutionary context. . . .

5–159   "At heart the question for decision in the present case is one of legal policy. The primary rule which precludes the court from lending its assistance to a man who founds his cause of action on an illegal or immoral act often leads to a denial of justice. The justification for this is that the rule is not a principle of justice but a principle of policy.[14] The doctrine of the *locus poenitentiae* is an exception which operates to mitigate the harshness of the primary rule. It enables the court to do justice between the parties even though, in order to do so, it must allow a plaintiff to give evidence of his own dishonest intent. But he must have withdrawn from the transaction while his dishonesty still lay in intention only. The law draws the line once the intention has been wholly or partly carried into effect. . . .

5–160   "In my opinion the following propositions represent the present state of the law.

5–161   "(1) Title to property passes both at law and in equity even if the transfer is made for an illegal purpose. The fact that title has passed to the transferee does not preclude the transferor from bringing an action for restitution.

5–162   "(2) The transferor's action will fail if it would be illegal for him to retain any interest in the property.

5–163   "(3) Subject to (2) the transferor can recover the property if he can do so without relying on the illegal purpose. This will normally be the case where the property was transferred without consideration in circumstances where the transferor can rely on an express declaration of trust or a resulting trust in his favour.

5–164   "(4) It will almost invariably be so where the illegal purpose has not been carried out. It may be otherwise where the illegal purpose has been carried out and the transferee can rely on the transferor's conduct as inconsistent with his retention of a beneficial interest.

5–165   "(5) The transferor can lead evidence of the illegal purpose whenever it is necessary for him to do so provided that he has withdrawn from the transaction before the illegal purpose has been wholly or partly carried into effect. It will be necessary for him to do so (i) if he brings an action at law or (ii) if he brings proceedings in equity and needs to rebut the presumption of advancement.

5–166   "(6) The only way in which a man can protect his property from his creditors is by divesting himself of all beneficial interest in it. Evidence that he transferred the property in order to protect it from his creditors, therefore, does nothing by itself to rebut the presumption of advancement; it reinforces it. To rebut the presumption it is necessary to show that he intended to retain a beneficial interest and conceal it from his creditors.

5–167   "(7) The court should not conclude that this was his intention without compelling circumstantial evidence to this effect. The identity of the transferee and the circumstances in which the transfer was made would be highly relevant.

---

[14] See the much-quoted statement of Lord Mansfield C.J. in *Holman v Johnson* (1775) 1 Cowp. 341 at 343.

It is unlikely that the court would reach such a conclusion where the transfer was made in the absence of an imminent and perceived threat from known creditors.

"... It is impossible to reconcile all the authorities on the circumstances in which **5–168** a party to an illegal contract is permitted to withdraw from it. At one time he was allowed to withdraw so long as the contract had not been completely performed but later it was held that recovery was barred once it had been partly performed.[15] It is clear that he must withdraw voluntarily, and that it is not sufficient that he is forced to do so because his plan has been discovered. In *Bigos v Bousted*[16] this was (perhaps dubiously) extended to prevent withdrawal where the scheme has been frustrated by the refusal of the other party to carry out his part.

"... I would hold that genuine repentance is not required. Justice is not a reward **5–169** for merit; restitution should not be confined to the penitent. I would also hold that voluntary withdrawal from an illegal transaction when it has ceased to be needed is sufficient. It is true that this is not necessary to encourage withdrawal, but a rule to the opposite effect could lead to bizarre results. Suppose, for example, that in *Bigos v Bousted* exchange control had been abolished before the foreign currency was made available: it is absurd to suppose that the plaintiff should have been denied restitution."

Section 5. Why Are Resulting Trusts Imposed?

As stated in the opening section,[17] legal scholars have recently sought to **5–170** answer this question by analysing resulting trusts as "responses" to legally significant "causative events". Two main schools of thought have emerged: on one view, resulting trusts are imposed in order to give effect to the transferor's intention to create a trust for himself;[18] on another view, they are imposed in order to reverse the transferee's unjust enrichment at the transferor's expense.[19] Claims in unjust enrichment arise under English law when a defendant is enriched at the expense of a claimant in circumstances which make his enrichment unjust,[20] the question whether his enrichment is relevantly unjust being governed by "the binding authority of previous decisions", so that the courts do not have "a discretionary power to order repayment whenever it seems in the circumstance of the particular case just

---

[15] See *Kearley v Thompson* (1890) 24 Q.B.D. 742.

[16] [1951] 1 All E.R. 92.

[17] Above, paras 5–04—5–05.

[18] C. E. F. Rickett, "The Classification of Trusts" (1999) 18 N.Z Law Rev. 305; C. E. F. Rickett and R. Grantham, "Resulting Trusts: A Rather Limited Doctrine" in P. Birks and F. D. Rose (eds), *Restitution and Equity* (2000) 39. Swadling distinguishes "presumed resulting trusts" which he takes to respond to the transferor's intention, from "automatic resulting trusts", which he now regards as *sui generis*: W. J. Swadling, "A New Role for Resulting Trusts?" (1996) 16 L.S. 110; "A Hard Look at *Hodgson v Marks*" in Birks and Rose, above, 61.

[19] P. Birks, "Restitution and Resulting Trusts" in S. Goldstein (ed.), *Equity and Contemporary Legal Developments* (1992) 361; R. Chambers, *Resulting Trusts* (1997); R. Chambers, "Resulting Trusts in Canada" (2000) 38 Alberta L.R. 378, reprinted (2002) 16 Tru. L.I. 104 and 138.

[20] *Banque Financière de la Cité v Parc (Battersea) Ltd* 1999] 1 A.C. 221 at 227, *per* Lord Steyn, and 234, *per* Lord Hoffmann; *Kleinwort Benson Ltd v Lincoln CC* [1999] 2 A.C. 349 at 373, *per* Lord Goff, and 407–408, *per* Lord Hope; *Cressman v Coys of Kensington (Sales) Ltd* [2004] 1 W.L.R. 2775 at [22], *per* Mance LJ; and *Niru Battery Manufacturing Co. v Milestone Trading Ltd (No.2)* [2004] 1 All E.R. (Comm.) 289 at [28] and [41], *per* Clarke L.J.

and equitable to do so".[21] Objections can be raised to both approaches; in *Westdeutsche Landesbank Girozentrale v Islington L.B.C.*, Lord Browne-Wilkinson rejected the argument that resulting trusts respond to unjust enrichment, and favoured the view that they respond to the transferor's intention to create a trust;[22] in *Air Jamaica Ltd v Charlton*[23] and *Twinsectra Ltd v Yardley*[24] Lord Millett took the opposite view.

5–171   The main objection to the theory that resulting trusts respond to the transferor's intention to create a trust for himself is that it cannot explain cases where resulting trusts have been imposed in the teeth of evidence that the transferor never thought about it, or else formed a clear intention that he did not want to acquire a new equitable beneficial interest in the property, as in *Vandervell v I.R.C.*[25] Nor can it explain why an unwritten intention to create a trust of land takes effect as a resulting trust when it fails to take effect as an express trust because of non-compliance with the LPA 1925, s.53(1)(c), as in *Hodgson v Marks*.[26]

5–172   The main objection to the theory that resulting trusts respond to unjust enrichment is that it seems to prove too much. Pushed to its logical limits, it suggests that a resulting trust should arise whenever a claimant transfers property to a defendant, and his intention to benefit the defendant is vitiated by mistake or undue influence, or is conditional on the happening of a future event which subsequently fails to materialise. In principle, however, it seems very doubtful that claimants in these various situations should all be given proprietary rights and thus priority over the defendant's unsecured creditors, rather than a personal restitutionary remedy or a right to rescind the transfer.[27] It certainly might seem most surprising that a claimant who pays money to a defendant under a standard unsecured loan agreement should be given a proprietary remedy when the defendant defaults, although Professor Chambers would argue that even here we should distinguish between cases where the basis for the claimant's payment fails at some time after receipt of the benefit, and cases where it fails immediately, so that there is no moment at which the defendant has held the relevant asset free of any claim.[28] If that is right, then it suggests that *Sinclair v Brougham*,[29] overruled by the House of Lords in *Westdeutsche*,[30] may have been rightly decided after all, depending on whether the *ultra vires* depositors' claim to recover their money on the ground of failure of consideration was founded on the assertion that the building society had

---

[21] *Kleinwort Benson Ltd v Birmingham C.C.* [1996] 4 All E.R. 733 at 737, *per* Evans L.J. For an excellent introductory account of the circumstances which render a defendant's enrichment unjust, see A. Burrows *The Law of Restitution* 2nd ed. (2002), Chaps 3–13.
[22] See paras 5–173 *et seq.*
[23] [1999] 1 W.L.R. 1399; above at para.5–45.
[24] [2000] A.C. 164.
[25] [1967] 2 A.C. 29.
[26] [1971] Ch. 892.
[27] Lord Millett, "Restitution and Constructive Trusts" (1998) 114 L.Q.R. 399, at 416; Lord Millett, "The Law of Restitution: Taking Stock" (1999) 14 *Amicus Curiae* 1, at 7–8.
[28] R. Chambers, *Resulting Trusts* (1997) 110 and 155–170. See too P. Birks, *Unjust Enrichment* (2003) 162–178; P. Birks, "Retrieving Tied Money" in W. Swadling (ed.), *The Quistclose Trust: Critical Essays* (2004) 121, at pp.130–138.
[29] [1914] A.C. 398.
[30] See paras 5–204 to 5–212.

failed to repay their money, or on the assertion that their contracts with the building society had been void from the beginning.[31]

WESTDEUTSCHE LANDESBANK GIROZENTRALE v ISLINGTON L.B.C.

House of Lords [1996] A.C. 669; [1996] 2 All E.R. 961; [1996] 2 W.L.R. 802 (Lords Browne-Wilkinson, Slynn, and Lloyd, Lords Goff and Woolf dissenting).

The appellant bank sued the respondent council to recover £1,145,525 paid under **5–173** an interest rate swap agreement that was void because beyond the powers of the council. The Court of Appeal upheld the judge's decision that the bank was entitled to recover the money on the ground that the council had been unjustly enriched at the bank's expense, with compound interest. The council appealed against the award of compound interest, arguing that the court could only have had jurisdiction to make such an interest award if the money had been held on trust for the bank, and arguing too that no trust had arisen in the bank's favour. The House of Lords unanimously held that although the bank had a personal claim to recover the money in a common law action for money had and received, it had no proprietary equitable claim; by a 3:2 majority, it followed that only simple interest was payable (Lords Goff and Woolf dissenting on the basis that compound interest should be awarded by way of an equitable remedy in aid of the common law, so that the bank could have restitution of the user value of its money).

Lord Browne-Wilkinson reviewed the courts' jurisdiction to make awards of **5–174** compound interest, and then continued:

Was there a trust? The argument for the bank in outline

"The bank submitted that, since the contract was void, title did not pass at the **5–175** date of payment either at law or in equity. The legal title of the bank was extinguished as soon as the money was paid into the mixed account, whereupon the legal title became vested in the local authority. But, it was argued, this did not affect the equitable interest, which remained vested in the bank (the retention of title point). It was submitted that whenever the legal interest in property is vested in one person and the equitable interest in another, the owner of the legal interest holds it on trust for the owner of the equitable title: 'the separation of the legal from the equitable interest necessarily imports a trust.' For this latter proposition (the separation of title point) the bank, of course, relies on *Sinclair v Brougham*[32] and *Chase Manhattan Bank N.A. v Israel-British Bank (London) Ltd*[33]

"The generality of these submissions was narrowed by submitting that the trust **5–176** which arose in this case was a resulting trust 'not of an active character' (see *Sinclair v Brougham*,[34] *per* Viscount Haldane L.C.). This submission was reinforced, after completion of the oral argument, by sending to your Lordships Professor Peter Birks' paper 'Restitution and Resulting Trusts'.[35] Unfortunately your Lordships have

---

[31] Another example of immediate failure of basis is arguably provided by *Nesté Oy v Lloyds Bank plc* [1983] 2 Lloyd's Rep.658, where to the knowledge of the payee no performance at all could have taken place under the contract for which the payment formed the consideration. See too *Re Ames' Settlement* [1946] Ch. 217; *Criterion Properties plc v Stratford* [2004] 1 W.L.R. 1846 at [4], *per* Lord Nicholls.
[32] [1914] A.C. 398.
[33] [1981] Ch. 105.
[34] [1914] A.C. 398 at 421.
[35] Published in S. Goldstein (ed.), *Equity and Contemporary Legal Developments* (1992) 335.

not had the advantage of any submissions from the local authority on this paper, but an article by William Swadling 'A new role for resulting trusts?'[36] puts forward counter-arguments which I have found persuasive. . . .

The breadth of the submission

5–177   "Although the actual question in issue on the appeal is a narrow one, on the arguments presented it is necessary to consider fundamental principles of trust law. Does the recipient of money under a contract subsequently found to be void for mistake or as being *ultra vires* hold the moneys received on trust even where he had no knowledge at any relevant time that the contract was void? If he does hold on trust, such trust must arise at the date of receipt or, at the latest, at the date the legal title of the payer is extinguished by mixing moneys in a bank account: in the present case it does not matter at which of those dates the legal title was extinguished. If there is a trust two consequences follow: (a) the recipient will be personally liable, regardless of fault, for any subsequent payment away of the moneys to third parties even though, at the date of such payment, the 'trustee' was still ignorant of the existence of any trust;[37] (b) as from the date of the establishment of the trust (*i.e.* receipt or mixing of the moneys by the 'trustee') the original payer will have an equitable proprietary interest in the moneys so long as they are traceable into whomsoever's hands they come other than a purchaser for value of the legal interest without notice. Therefore, although in the present case the only question directly in issue is the personal liability of the local authority as a trustee, it is not possible to hold the local authority liable without imposing a trust which, in other cases, will create property rights affecting third parties because moneys received under a void contract are 'trust property'.

The practical consequences of the bank's argument

5–178   "Before considering the legal merits of the submission, it is important to appreciate the practical consequences which ensue if the bank's arguments are correct. Those who suggest that a resulting trust should arise in these circumstances accept that the creation of an equitable proprietary interest under the trust can have unfortunate, and adverse, effects if the original recipient of the moneys becomes insolvent: the moneys, if traceable in the hands of the recipient, are trust moneys and not available for the creditors of the recipient. However, the creation of an equitable proprietary interest in moneys received under a void contract is capable of having adverse effects quite apart from insolvency. The proprietary interest under the unknown trust will, quite apart from insolvency, be enforceable against any recipient of the property other than the purchaser for value of a legal interest without notice.

5–179   "Take the following example. T (the transferor) has entered into a commercial contract with R1 (the first recipient). Both parties believe the contract to be valid but it is in fact void. Pursuant to that contract: (i) T pays £1m to R1 who pays it into a mixed bank account; (ii) T transfers 100 shares in X company to R1, who is registered as a shareholder. Thereafter R1 deals with the money and shares as follows: (iii) R1 pays £50,000 out of the mixed account to R2 otherwise than for value; R2 then becomes insolvent, having trade creditors who have paid for goods not delivered at the time of the insolvency. (iv) R1 charges the shares in X company to R3 by way of equitable security for a loan from R3.

---

[36] (1996) 16 L.S. 110.
[37] A. Burrows, "Swaps and the Friction between Common Law and Equity" [1995] R.L.R. 15.

"If the bank's arguments are correct, R1 holds the £1m on trust for T once the **5–180** money has become mixed in R1's bank account. Similarly R1 becomes the legal owner of the shares in X company as from the date of his registration as a shareholder but holds such shares on a resulting trust for T. T therefore has an equitable proprietary interest in the moneys in the mixed account and in the shares.

"T's equitable interest will enjoy absolute priority as against the creditors in the **5–181** insolvency of R2 (who was not a purchaser for value) provided that the £50,000 can be traced in the assets of R2 at the date of its insolvency. Moreover, if the separation of title argument is correct, since the equitable interest is in T and the legal interest is vested in R2, R2 also holds as trustee for T. In tracing the £50,000 in the bank account of R2, R2 as trustee will be treated as having drawn out 'his own' moneys first, thereby benefiting T at the expense of the secured and unsecured creditors of R2. Therefore in practice one may well reach the position where the moneys in the bank account of R2 in reality reflect the price paid by creditors for goods not delivered by R2: yet, under the tracing rules, those moneys are to be treated as belonging in equity to T.

"So far as the shares in the X company are concerned, T can trace his equitable **5–182** interest into the shares and will take in priority to R3, whose equitable charge to secure his loan even though granted for value will *pro tanto* be defeated.

"All this will have occurred when no one was aware, or could have been aware, of **5–183** the supposed trust because no one knew that the contract was void.

"I can see no moral or legal justification for giving such priority to the right of T **5–184** to obtain restitution over third parties who have themselves not been enriched, in any real sense, at T's expense and indeed have had no dealings with T. T paid over his money and transferred the shares under a supposed valid contract. If the contract had been valid, he would have had purely personal rights against R1. Why should he be better off because the contract is void?

"My Lords, wise judges have often warned against the wholesale importation into **5–185** commercial law of equitable principles inconsistent with the certainty and speed which are essential requirements for the orderly conduct of business affairs.[38] If the bank's arguments are correct, a businessman who has entered into transactions relating to or dependent upon property rights could find that assets which apparently belong to one person in fact belong to another; that there are 'off balance sheet' liabilities of which he cannot be aware; that these property rights and liabilities arise from circumstances unknown not only to himself but also to anyone else who has been involved in the transactions. A new area of unmanageable risk will be introduced into commercial dealings. If the due application of equitable principles forced a conclusion leading to these results, your Lordships would be presented with a formidable task in reconciling legal principle with commercial common sense. But in my judgment no such conflict occurs. The resulting trust for which the bank contends is inconsistent not only with the law as it stands but with any principled development of it.

The relevant principles of trust law

"(i) Equity operates on the conscience of the owner of the legal interest. In the **5–186** case of a trust, the conscience of the legal owner requires him to carry out the purposes for which the property was vested in him (express or implied

---

[38] *Barnes v Addy* (1874) L.R. 9 Ch. App.244 at 251 at 255, and *Scandinavian Trading Tanker Co. A.B. v Flota Petrolera Ecuatoriana* [1983] 2 A.C. 694 at 703–704.

trust) or which the law imposes on him by reason of his unconscionable conduct (constructive trust).

5–187 "(ii) Since the equitable jurisdiction to enforce trusts depends upon the conscience of the holder of the legal interest being affected, he cannot be a trustee of the property if and so long as he is ignorant of the facts alleged to affect his conscience, *i.e.* until he is aware that he is intended to hold the property for the benefit of others in the case of an express or implied trust, or, in the case of a constructive trust, of the factors which are alleged to affect his conscience.

5–188 "(iii) In order to establish a trust there must be identifiable trust property. The only apparent exception to this rule is a constructive trust imposed on a person who dishonestly assists in a breach of trust who may come under fiduciary duties even if he does not receive identifiable trust property.[39]

5–189 "(iv) Once a trust is established, as from the date of its establishment the beneficiary has, in equity, a proprietary interest in the trust property, which proprietary interest will be enforceable in equity against any subsequent holder of the property (whether the original property or substituted property into which it can be traced) other than a purchaser for value of the legal interest without notice.

5–190 "These propositions are fundamental to the law of trusts and I would have thought uncontroversial. However, proposition (ii) may call for some expansion. There are cases where property has been put into the name of X without X's knowledge but in circumstances where no gift to X was intended. It has been held that such property is recoverable under a resulting trust.[40] These cases are explicable on the ground that, by the time action was brought, X or his successors in title have become aware of the facts which gave rise to a resulting trust; his conscience was affected as from the time of such discovery and thereafter he held on a resulting trust under which the property was recovered from him. There is, so far as I am aware, no authority which decides that X was a trustee, and therefore accountable for his deeds, at any time before he was aware of the circumstances which gave rise to a resulting trust.

5–191 "Those basic principles are inconsistent with the case being advanced by the bank. The latest time at which there was any possibility of identifying the 'trust property' was the date on which the moneys in the mixed bank account of the local authority ceased to be traceable when the local authority's account went into overdraft in June 1987. At that date, the local authority had no knowledge of the invalidity of the contract but regarded the moneys as its own to spend as it thought fit. There was therefore never a time at which both (a) there was defined trust property and (b) the conscience of the local authority in relation to such defined trust property was affected. The basic requirements of a trust were never satisfied. . . .

The retention of title point

5–192 "It is said that, since the bank only intended to part with its beneficial ownership of the moneys in performance of a valid contract, neither the legal nor the equitable title passed to the local authority at the date of payment. The legal title vested in the

---

[39] Editors' note: Lord Browne-Wilkinson refers here to the *personal* liability of a dishonest assistant to account in equity "as a constructive trustee"; dishonest assistants often do not hold property on constructive trust for anyone as Lord Millett makes clear in *Dubai Aluminium Co. Ltd v Salaam* [2003] 2 A.C. 366 at [141]–[142]; see too paras 6–02 and 11–06.
[40] *Birch v Blagrave* (1755) Amb. 264; *Childers v Childers* (1857) 1 De G & J 482; *Re Vinogradoff* [1935] W.N. 68; *Re Muller* [1953] N.Z.L.R. 879.

local authority by operation of law when the moneys became mixed in the bank account but, it is said, the bank 'retained' its equitable title.

"I think this argument is fallacious. A person solely entitled to the full beneficial ownership of money or property, both at law and in equity, does not enjoy an equitable interest in that property. The legal title carries with it all rights. Unless and until there is a separation of the legal and equitable estates, there is no separate equitable title. Therefore to talk about the bank 'retaining' its equitable interest is meaningless. The only question is whether the circumstances under which the money was paid were such as, in equity, to impose a trust on the local authority. If so, an equitable interest arose for the first time under that trust.   **5–193**

"This proposition is supported by *Re Cook*,[41] *Vandervell v IRC*,[42] *per* Lord Upjohn and Lord Donovan, *Commissioner of Stamp Duties v Livingston*,[43] and *Underhill and Hayton's Law of Trusts and Trustees*.[44]   **5–194**

The separation of title point

"The bank's submission, at its widest, is that if the legal title is in A but the equitable interest in B, A holds as trustee for B.   **5–195**

"Again I think this argument is fallacious. There are many cases where B enjoys rights which, in equity, are enforceable against the legal owner, A, without A being a trustee, for example an equitable right to redeem a mortgage, equitable easements, restrictive covenants, the right to rectification and an insurer's right by subrogation to receive damages subsequently recovered by the assured.[45] Even in cases where the whole beneficial interest is vested in B and the bare legal interest is in A, A is not necessarily a trustee, for example where title to land is acquired by estoppel as against the legal owner; a mortgagee who has fully discharged his indebtedness enforces his right to recover the mortgaged property in a redemption action, not an action for breach of trust.   **5–196**

"The bank contended that where, under a pre-existing trust, B is entitled to an equitable interest in trust property, if the trust property comes into the hands of a third party, X (not being a purchaser for value of the legal interest without notice), B is entitled to enforce his equitable interest against the property in the hands of X because X is a trustee for B. In my view the third party, X, is not necessarily a trustee for B: B's equitable right is enforceable against the property in just the same way as any other specifically enforceable equitable right can be enforced against a third party. Even if the third party, X, is not aware that what he has received is trust property B is entitled to assert his title in that property. If X has the necessary degree of knowledge, X may himself become a constructive trustee for B on the basis of knowing receipt. But unless he has the requisite degree of knowledge he is not personally liable to account as trustee: *Re Diplock*[46] and *Re Montagu's S.T.*[47] Therefore, innocent receipt of property by X subject to an existing equitable interest does not by itself make X a trustee despite the severance of the legal and equitable titles. *Underhill and Hayton Law of Trusts and Trustees*,[48] whilst accepting that X is under no personal liability to account unless and until be becomes aware of B's   **5–197**

---

[41] [1948] Ch. 212.
[42] [1967] 2 A.C. 291 at 311 and 317.
[43] [1965] A.C. 694 at 712.
[44] (15th ed., 1995), p.866.
[45] *Lord Napier and Ettrick v Hunter* [1993] A.C. 713.
[46] [1948] Ch. 465 at 478.
[47] [1987] Ch. 264.
[48] 15th ed., pp.369–370.

rights, does describe X as being a constructive trustee. This may only be a question of semantics: on either footing, in the present case the local authority could not have become accountable for profits until it knew that the contract was void.

Resulting trust

5–198   "This is not a case where the bank had any equitable interest which predated receipt by the local authority of the upfront payment. Therefore, in order to show that the local authority became a trustee, the bank must demonstrate circumstances which raised a trust for the first time either at the date on which the local authority received the money or at the date on which payment into the mixed account was made. Counsel for the bank specifically disavowed any claim based on a constructive trust. This was plainly right because the local authority had no relevant knowledge sufficient to raise a constructive trust at any time before the moneys, upon the bank account going into overdraft, became untraceable. Once there ceased to be an identifiable trust fund, the local authority could not become a trustee: *Re Goldcorp Exchange Ltd.*[49] Therefore, as the argument for the bank recognised, the only possible trust which could be established was a resulting trust arising from the circumstances in which the local authority received the upfront payment.

5–199   [His Lordship explained the circumstances under which resulting trusts arise, as set out at paras 5.24 to 5.27, and continued:] "Applying these conventional principles of resulting trust to the present case, the bank's claim must fail. There was no transfer of money to the local authority on express trusts: therefore a resulting trust of type (B) above could not arise. As to type (A) above, any presumption of resulting trust is rebutted since it is demonstrated that the bank paid, and the local authority received, the upfront payment with the intention that the moneys so paid should become the absolute property of the local authority. It is true that the parties were under a misapprehension that the payment was made in pursuance of a valid contract. But that does not alter the actual intentions of the parties at the date the payment was made or the moneys were mixed in the bank account. As the article by William Swadling demonstrates,[50] the presumption of resulting trust is rebutted by evidence of any intention inconsistent with such a trust, not only by evidence of an intention to make a gift.

5–200   "Professor Birks,[51] whilst accepting that the principles I have stated represent 'a very conservative form' of definition of a resulting trust, argues from restitutionary principles that the definition should be extended so as to cover a perceived gap in the law of 'subtractive unjust enrichment'[52] so as to give a plaintiff a proprietary remedy when he has transferred value under a mistake or under a contract the consideration for which wholly fails. He suggests that a resulting trust should arise wherever the money is paid under a mistake (because such mistake vitiates the actual intention) or when money is paid on a condition which is not subsequently satisfied.

5–201   "As one would expect, the argument is tightly reasoned but I am not persuaded. The search for a perceived need to strengthen the remedies of a plaintiff claiming in restitution involves, to my mind, a distortion of trust principles. First, the argument elides rights in property (which is the only proper subject matter of a trust) into

---

[49] [1995] 1 A.C. 74.
[50] "A new role for resulting trusts?" (1996) 16 L.S. 110, 133.
[51] "Restitution and Resulting Trusts" in S. Goldstein (ed.), *Equity and Contemporary Legal Developments* (1992) 335, p.360.
[52] *ibid.* at p.368.

rights in 'the value transferred'.[53] A trust can only arise where there is defined trust property: it is therefore not consistent with trust principles to say that a person is a trustee of property which cannot be defined. Second, Professor Birks' approach appears to assume (*e.g.* in the case of a transfer of value made under a contract the consideration for which subsequently fails) that the recipient will be deemed to have been a trustee from the date of his original receipt of money, *i.e.* the trust arises at a time when the 'trustee' does not, and cannot, know that there is going to be a total failure of consideration. This result is incompatible with the basic premise on which all trust law is built, *viz.* that the conscience of the trustee is affected. Unless and until the trustee is aware of the factors which give rise to the supposed trust, there is nothing which can affect his conscience. Thus neither in the case of a subsequent failure of consideration nor in the case of a payment under a contract subsequently found to be void for mistake or failure of condition will there be circumstances, at the date of receipt, which can impinge on the conscience of the recipient, thereby making him a trustee. Thirdly, Professor Birks has to impose on his wider view an arbitrary and admittedly unprincipled modification so as to ensure that a resulting trust does not arise when there has only been a failure to perform a contract, as opposed to total failure of consideration.[54] Such arbitrary exclusion is designed to preserve the rights of creditors in the insolvency of the recipient. The fact that it is necessary to exclude artificially one type of case which would logically fall within the wider concept casts doubt on the validity of the concept.

"If adopted, Professor Birks' wider concepts would give rise to all the practical **5–202** consequences and injustices to which I have referred. I do not think it right to make an unprincipled alteration to the law of property (*i.e.* the law of trusts) so as to produce in the law of unjust enrichment the injustices to third parties which I have mentioned and the consequential commercial uncertainty which any extension of proprietary interests in personal property is bound to produce.

The authorities

"Three cases were principally relied upon in direct support of the proposition that **5–203** a resulting trust arises where a payment is made under a void contract.

(A) Sinclair v Brougham[55]

"The case concerned the distribution of the assets of the Birkbeck Permanent **5–204** Benefit Building Society, an unincorporated body which was insolvent. The society had for many years been carrying on business as a bank which, it was held, was *ultra vires* its objects. The bank had accepted deposits in the course of its *ultra vires* banking business and it was held that the debts owed to such depositors were themselves void as being *ultra vires*. In addition to the banking depositors, there were ordinary trade creditors. The society had two classes of members, the A shareholders who were entitled to repayment of their investment on maturity and the B shareholders whose shares were permanent. By agreement, the claims of the ordinary trade creditors and of the A shareholders had been settled. Therefore the only claimants to the assets of the society before the court were the *ultra vires* depositors and the B shareholders, the latter of which could take no greater interest than the society itself.

"The issues for decision arose on a summons taken out by the liquidator for **5–205** directions as to how he should distribute the assets in the liquidation. In the judgments, it is not always clear whether this House was laying down general

---

[53] *ibid.* at p.361.
[54] *ibid.* at pp.356–359 and 362.
[55] [1914] A.C. 398.

propositions of law or merely giving directions as to the proper mode in which the
assets in that liquidation should be distributed. The depositors claimed, first, in
quasi-contract for money had and received. They claimed secondly, as the result of
an argument suggested for the first time in the course of argument in the House of
Lords,[56] to trace their deposits into the assets of the society.

Money had and received

5–206	"The House of Lords was unanimous in rejecting the claim by the *ultra vires*
depositors to recover in quasi-contract on the basis of moneys had and received. In
their view, the claim in quasi-contract was based on an implied contract. To imply a
contract to repay would be to imply a contract to exactly the same effect as the
express *ultra vires* contract of loan. Any such implied contract would itself be void as
being *ultra vires*.

5–207	"Subsequent developments in the law of restitution demonstrate that this
reasoning is no longer sound. The common law restitutionary claim is based not on
implied contract but on unjust enrichment: in the circumstances the law imposes an
obligation to repay rather than implying an entirely fictitious agreement to repay.[57]
In my judgment, your Lordships should now unequivocally and finally reject the
concept that the claim for moneys had and received is based on an implied contract.
I would overrule *Sinclair v Brougham* on this point.

5–208	"It follows that in *Sinclair v Brougham* the depositors should have had a personal
claim to recover the moneys at law based on a total failure of consideration. The
failure of consideration was not partial: the depositors had paid over their money in
consideration of a promise to repay. That promise was *ultra vires* and void; therefore
the consideration for the payment of the money wholly failed. So in the present
swaps case (though the point is not one under appeal) I think the Court of Appeal
were right to hold that the swap moneys were paid on a consideration that wholly
failed. The essence of the swap agreement is that, over the whole term of the
agreement, each party thinks he will come out best: the consideration for one party
making a payment is an obligation on the other party to make counter-payments
over the whole term of the agreement.

5–209	"If in *Sinclair v Brougham* the depositors had been held entitled to recover at law,
their personal claim would have ranked *pari passu* with other ordinary unsecured
creditors, in priority to the members of the society who could take nothing in the
liquidation until all creditors had been paid.

The claim in rem

5–210	"The House of Lords held that, the ordinary trade creditors having been paid in
full by agreement, the assets remaining were to be divided between the *ultra vires*
depositors and the members of the society pro rata according to their respective
payments to the society. . . .

5–211	"As has been pointed out frequently over the 80 years since it was decided,
Sinclair v Brougham is a bewildering authority: no single *ratio decidendi* can be
detected; all the reasoning is open to serious objection; it was only intended to deal
with cases where there were no trade creditors in competition and the reasoning is

[56] *ibid.* at 404.
[57] *Fibrosa Spolka Akcyjna v Fairbairn Lawson Combe Barbour Ltd* [1943] A.C. 32 at 63–64, *per* Lord Wright;
Pavey & Matthews Pty. Ltd v Paul (1987) 69 A.L.R. 577 at 579, 583, 603; *Lipkin Gorman (a firm) v
Karpnale Ltd* [1991] 2 A.C. 548 at 578; *Woolwich Building Society v I.R.C. (No.2)* [1993] A.C. 70.

incapable of application where there are such creditors. In my view the decision as to rights *in rem* in *Sinclair v Brougham* should also be overruled. Although the case is one where property rights are involved, such overruling should not in practice disturb long-settled titles. However, your Lordships should not be taken to be casting any doubt on the principles of tracing as established in *Re Diplock*.

"If *Sinclair v Brougham*, in both its aspects, is overruled the law can be established **5–212** in accordance with principle and commercial common sense: a claimant for restitution of moneys paid under an *ultra vires*, and therefore void, contract has a personal action at law to recover the moneys paid as on a total failure of consideration; he will not have an equitable proprietary claim which gives him either rights against third parties or priority in an insolvency; nor will he have a personal claim in equity, since the recipient is not a trustee.

(B) Chase Manhattan Bank N.A. v Israel-British Bank (London) Ltd[58]

"In that case Chase Manhattan, a New York bank, had by mistake paid the same **5–213** sum twice to the credit of the defendant, a London bank. Shortly thereafter, the defendant bank went into insolvent liquidation. The question was whether Chase Manhattan had a claim *in rem* against the assets of the defendant bank to recover the second payment.

"Goulding J. was asked to assume that the moneys paid under a mistake were **5–214** capable of being traced in the assets of the recipient bank: he was only concerned with the question whether there was a proprietary base on which the tracing remedy could be founded.[59] He held that, where money was paid under a mistake, the receipt of such money without more constituted the recipient a trustee: he said that the payer 'retains an equitable property in it and the conscience of [the recipient] is subjected to a fiduciary duty to respect his proprietary right'.[60]

"It will be apparent from what I have already said that I cannot agree with this **5–215** reasoning. First, it is based on a concept of retaining an equitable property in money where, prior to the payment to the recipient bank, there was no existing equitable interest. Further, I cannot understand how the recipient's 'conscience' can be affected at a time when he is not aware of any mistake. Finally, the judge found that the law of England and that of New York were in substance the same. I find this a surprising conclusion since the New York law of constructive trusts has for a long time been influenced by the concept of a *remedial* constructive trust, whereas hitherto English law has for the most part only recognised an institutional constructive trust.[61] In the present context, that distinction is of fundamental importance. Under an institutional constructive trust, the trust arises by operation of law as from the date of the circumstances which give rise to it: the function of the court is merely to declare that such trust has arisen in the past. The consequences that flow from such trust having arisen (including the possibly unfair consequences to third parties who in the interim have received the trust property) are also determined by rules of law, not under a discretion. A remedial constructive trust, as I understand it, is different. It is a judicial remedy giving rise to an enforceable equitable obligation: the extent to which it operates retrospectively to the prejudice of third parties lies in the discretion of the court. Thus for the law of New York to hold that there is a remedial constructive trust where a payment has been made

---

[58] [1981] Ch. 105.
[59] *ibid.* at 116.
[60] *ibid.* at 119.
[61] *Metall und Rohstoff AG v Donaldson Lufkin & Jenrette Inc.* [1990] 1 Q.B. 391 at 478–480.

under a void contract gives rise to different consequences from holding that an institutional constructive trust arises in English law.

5-216   "However, although I do not accept the reasoning of Goulding J., *Chase Manhattan* may well have been rightly decided. The defendant bank knew of the mistake made by the paying bank within two days of the receipt of the moneys.[62] The judge treated this fact as irrelevant,[63] but in my judgment it may well provide a proper foundation for the decision. Although the mere receipt of the moneys, in ignorance of the mistake, gives rise to no trust, the retention of the moneys after the recipient bank learned of the mistake may well have given rise to a constructive trust.[64] [His Lordship considered *Re Ames' Settlement*,[65] and then continued:]

The stolen bag of coins

5-217   "The argument for a resulting trust was said to be supported by the case of a thief who steals a bag of coins. At law those coins remain traceable only so long as they are kept separate: as soon as they are mixed with other coins or paid into a mixed bank account they cease to be traceable at law. Can it really be the case, it is asked, that in such circumstances the thief cannot be required to disgorge the property which, in equity, represents the stolen coins? Moneys can only be traced in equity if there has been at some stage a breach of fiduciary duty, *i.e.* if either before the theft there was an equitable proprietary interest (*e.g.* the coins were stolen trust moneys) or such interest arises under a resulting trust at the time of the theft or the mixing of the moneys. Therefore, it is said, a resulting trust must arise either at the time of the theft or when the moneys are subsequently mixed. Unless this is the law, there will be no right to recover the assets representing the stolen moneys once the moneys have become mixed.

5-218   "I agree that the stolen moneys are traceable in equity. But the proprietary interest which equity is enforcing in such circumstances arises under a constructive, not a resulting, trust. Although it is difficult to find clear authority for the proposition, when property is obtained by fraud equity imposes a constructive trust on the fraudulent recipient: the property is recoverable and traceable in equity. Thus, an infant who has obtained property by fraud is bound in equity to restore it.[66]

Restitution and equitable rights

5-219   "Those concerned with developing the law of restitution are anxious to ensure that, in certain circumstances, the plaintiff should have the right to recover property which he has unjustly lost. For that purpose they have sought to develop the law of resulting trusts so as to give the plaintiff a proprietary interest. For the reasons that I have given in my view such development is not based on sound principle and in the name of unjust enrichment is capable of producing most unjust results. The law of resulting trusts would confer on the plaintiff a right to recover property from, or at the expense of, those who have not been unjustly enriched at his expense at all, for example the lender whose debt is secured by a floating charge and all other third parties who have purchased an equitable interest only, albeit in all innocence and for value.

---

[62] [1981] Ch. 105 at 115.
[63] *ibid.* at 114.
[64] *Snell's Equity* (29th ed., 1991), p.193, *Pettit Equity and the Law of Trusts* (7th ed., 1993) p.168; *Metall und Rohstoff A.G. v Donaldson Lufkin & Jenrette Inc.* [1990] 1 Q.B. 391 at 473–474.
[65] [1946] Ch. 217.
[66] *Stocks v Wilson* [1913] 2 K.B. 235 at 244; *R. Leslie Ltd v Sheill* [1914] 3 K.B. 607. Moneys stolen from a bank account can be traced in equity: *Bankers Trust Co. v Shapira* [1980] 1 W.L.R. 1274 at 1282. See also *McCormick v Grogan* (1869) L.R. 4 H.L. 82 at 97.

"Although the resulting trust is an unsuitable basis for developing proprietary **5–220** restitutionary remedies, the remedial constructive trust, if introduced into English law, may provide a more satisfactory road forward. The court by way of remedy might impose a constructive trust on a defendant who knowingly retains property of which the plaintiff has been unjustly deprived. Since the remedy can be tailored to the circumstances of the particular case, innocent third parties would not be prejudiced and restitutionary defences, such as change of position, are capable of being given effect. However, whether English law should follow the United States and Canada by adopting the remedial constructive trust will have to be decided in some future case when the point is directly in issue."

QUESTIONS

1. "A resulting trust is a default mechanism to locate the beneficial **5–221** ownership of property and not a proprietary remedy for unjust enrichment." Discuss.

2. The members of the Ravers Anonymous Club, an unincorporated **5–222** association whose purposes are not charitable have dissolved the association one week after having received £10,000 from Sir Lancelot Hellfire for the purposes of the Club, and one month after having received £1,000 from various raffles and sweepstakes, along with £150 from collections taken at a public meeting held to publicise the Club. In accordance with the Club rules the members received ten days' written notice of the meeting called to dissolve the association. What should happen to the above sums?

3. Six years before her death Miss Spry opened a current account with **5–223** Barclays Bank in the joint names of herself and her nephew, Neal Smug. Both of them called on the manager when they came to open the joint account. Miss Spry told the manager that as she was getting frail her nephew would look after her banking affairs for her. She also said that if she died before her nephew then he could keep any credit balance in the account on her death. It was arranged that the bank would honour cheques drawn on the account either by Miss Spry or by Neal. Although Miss Spry kept the cheque book in her desk, all the cheques were signed by Neal. As envisaged by the parties, only Miss Spry paid money into the account. At her death a credit balance of £2,000 remained. Who is entitled to this money if Miss Spry left her estate to the RSPCA in her will?

4. Fearing that his wife might divorce him at some time, and that a new **5–224** business venture might prove financially damaging, Harold transferred legal title to his cottage to Simon, who agreed that when matters had resolved themselves so that it was safe to do so he would reconvey the cottage to Harold. The conveyance purported to be for £200,000, but in fact, as agreed, Simon paid nothing. Advise Harold who now seeks to recover the cottage. Does it matter (a) if Simon is Harold's brother or his son, or (b) if only six months have elapsed and Harold's wife is still living with him and he is sufficiently secure financially to pay his debts as they fall due?

5. "The courts should be given a statutory discretion to determine the **5–225** effects of illegality in resulting trust cases." Discuss.

Chapter 6

CONSTRUCTIVE TRUSTS

Section 1. Introduction

6–01 When a constructive trust is imposed on property, the beneficiaries acquire the same equitable proprietary rights in the trust assets as they would under an express trust or a resulting trust. The property forms no part of the trustee's estate and his creditors have no claim against it in the event of his insolvency. If the property increases in value, then the increase belongs to the beneficiaries. If the trustee uses the property to acquire new property, then the beneficiaries can trace into this new property and claim it for themselves, and if he transfers the property to anyone other than a *bona fide* purchaser for value without notice of the beneficiaries' equitable interest, then they can follow the property into the recipient's hands and claim it for themselves.[1] Until trial the beneficiaries can preserve the position by obtaining (virtually[2] as of right) an interim injunction restraining dealings with "their" property. Moreover, if a constructive trust is imposed on property and the trustee's conscience is affected with knowledge of the circumstances which have led to the imposition of the trust, then he will be personally liable as a "knowing recipient" to repay them the value of the property in the event that he is unable to pay it over at their direction.[3]

Personal liability to account as constructive trustee

6–02 Confusingly, when the courts speak of a defendant owing a claimant a personal liability to account as a constructive trustee they do not always mean the same thing. Sometimes they use this expression as it is used above, to indicate that the defendant holds property on constructive trust for the claimant, and must account to the claimant for the property in his capacity as trustee of the constructive trust. But sometimes they use the phrase differently, to describe the personal liability of a defendant who has dishonestly assisted in a breach of trust by the trustees of an express trust, without receiving trust assets into his hands. A defendant in this position does not hold trust property on constructive trust for the beneficiaries. Hence when the courts say that he is liable to account as a constructive trustee, they do not mean that he must account for property in his hands which he holds on constructive trust. Instead, they mean that he is deemed

---

[1] See Chap. 12.
[2] *Polly Peck International plc v Nadir (No.2)* [1992] 4 All E.R. 769 at 784 (claim too speculative).
[3] See paras 5–06 to 5–08, above, and 11–19 *et seq.*

to owe the same liability to the beneficiaries as the trustees whose breach of trust he has assisted: his liability derives from and duplicates theirs.[4]

Institutional and remedial constructive trusts

Under English law, constructive trusts arise as a result of legal rules **6–03** which state that they arise in particular circumstances. These rules do not give the courts a discretion to impose constructive trusts, or to refuse to do so, according to their assessment of the equities of a case: the courts' role is purely declaratory. In contrast, some other Commonwealth jurisdictions, *e.g.* Canada[5] and Australia,[6] distinguish "substantive" or "institutional" constructive trusts from "remedial" constructive trusts. Different judges and legal scholars use these terms to mean different things,[7] but most use them to distinguish constructive trusts which arise through the inflexible operation of legal rules from constructive trusts which arise following the exercise of a judicial discretion, either retrospectively or prospectively from the date of the court order.[8] It is controversial whether the courts should have a discretion to vary property rights in this way,[9] but whatever the rights and wrongs of this question in principle, it is clear that English law does not recognise "remedial" constructive trusts of this kind.[10] It remains to be seen how long this remains the case, given the current drift towards assimilating common intention constructive trusts with the doctrine of proprietary estoppel in shared homes cases.[11]

Why are constructive trusts imposed?

Constructive trusts have been imposed in a wide variety of different **6–04** circumstances. This makes it hard to understand why they are imposed, and how (if at all) they differ from resulting trusts, but a good way to approach

---

[4] See further paras 11–05 to 11–18.
[5] *Sorochan v Sorochan* [1986] 2 S.C.R. 38; *LAC Minerals Ltd v International Corona Resources Ltd*[1989] 2 S.C.R. 574; *Soulos v Korkontzilas* [1997] 2 S.C.R. 217.
[6] *Muschinski v Dodds* (1985) 160 C.L.R. 583; *Re Stevenson Nominees Pty. Ltd* (1987) 76 A.L.R. 485; *Bathurst C.C. v PWC Properties Pty. Ltd* (1998) 195 C.L.R. 566; *Giumelli v Giumelli* (1999) 196 C.L.R. 101. But *cf. Parsons v McBain* (2001) 109 F.C.R. 120; *Parianos v Melluish* (2003) 30 Fam. L.R. 524.
[7] G. Elias, *Explaining Constructive Trusts* (1990), pp.159–163; C. Rotherham, *Proprietary Remedies in Context* (2002), pp.7–32. Some judges have used the term "remedial constructive trust" to refer to the *personal* liability of strangers who dishonestly participate in a breach of trust (see para.6–02 above): *e.g. Clarke v Marlborough Fine Art (London) Ltd* [2002] 1 W.L.R. 1731 at [66], *per* Patten J.; *Kilcarne Holdings Ltd v Targetfollow (Birmingham) Ltd* [2004] EWHC 2547 (Ch) at [261], *per* Lewison J. This usage seems to have been prompted by *Paragon Finance plc v D. B. Thakerar & Co. (a firm)* [1999] 1 All E.R. 400 at 408–9, where Millett L.J. distinguished constructive trusts of property from the personal liability of dishonest participants in a breach of trust, but it is best avoided, lest this personal liability become confused with the "discretionary proprietary remedy" to which Millett L.J. also refers at 414.
[8] *e.g. Fortex Group Ltd v Macintosh* [1998] 3 N.Z.L.R. 171 at 172–3, *per* Tipping J.
[9] P. Loughlan, "No Right to the Remedy? An Analysis of Judicial Discretion in the Imposition of Equitable Remedies" (1989) 17 Melbourne L.R. 132; P. D. Finn, "Equitable Doctrine and Discretion in Remedies" in W. Cornish *et al.* (eds), *Restitution: Past, Present and Future* (1998) 251; D. Wright, *The Remedial Constructive Trust* (1998), reviewed by P. Birks (1999) 115 L.Q.R. 681; P. Birks, "Rights, Wrongs, and Remedies" (2000) 20 O.J.L.S. 1; S. Evans, "Defending Discretionary Remedialism" (2001) 23 Sydney L.R. 463; D. W. M. Waters, "Liability and Remedy: An Adjustable Relationship" (2001) 64 Sask. L.R. 426; D. M. Jensen, "The Rights and Wrongs of Discretionary Remedialism" [2003] S.J.L.S. 178; S. Gardner, *Introduction to the Law of Trusts* 2nd ed. (2003), pp.124–6.
[10] *Re Goldcorp Exchange Ltd* [1995] 1 A.C. 74 at 104, *per* Lord Mustill; *Westdeutsche Landesbank Girozentrale v Islington L.B.C.* [1996] A.C. 669 at 714–6, *per* Lord Browne-Wilkinson; *Re Polly Peck International Ltd (No.2)* [1998] 3 All E.R. 812 at 827, *per* Mummery L.J., and at 831, *per* Nourse L.J.
[11] See paras 6–119 *et seq.*; *cf.* S. Gardner, *Introduction to the Law of Trusts* 2nd ed. (2003) 123 n.24.

these questions is to consider the causative events to which they respond.[12] There is no academic consensus as to the best way to classify constructive trusts by this method, and the courts of different Commonwealth jurisdictions have varied quite widely in the approaches which they have taken, particularly in the area of shared homes. In our view, however, many constructive trusts are imposed in order to perfect the parties' intention that beneficial interest in property should be transferred, while others are imposed as a response to wrongdoing. These two types of constructive trust are considered here in turn, in sections 2 and 3 below. In section 4, we then discuss the question whether there are also constructive trusts which respond to unjust enrichment.

6–05   The discussion in this chapter is not exhaustive. There are other events to which constructive trusts might respond besides the three possibilities that we discuss. For example, a court order to convey a specific asset can lead to the imposition of a constructive trust on the property even though the order itself is not couched in these terms, and here it seems that the order is itself the event to which the constructive trust responds.[13] Again, there is authority for the proposition that a property right can be an event to which a constructive trust responds, as in cases where assets held on an express trust are transferred to a third party in breach of trust, and a constructive trust is imposed on the assets for the beneficiaries.[14] Whether such cases can be truly explained on the basis that the constructive trust vindicates the beneficiaries' pre-existing property rights is a controversial question to which we shall return in Chapter 12.[15]

Section 2. Intention

6–06   It has often been said that constructive trusts do not give effect to the parties' intentions, but are imposed "against the intentions of the trustee".[16] Nonetheless, there are good reasons for thinking that some constructive trusts are imposed on property in response to the parties' intention that beneficial ownership of the property should pass from one to the other.[17] Obviously constructive trusts are not needed in such situations unless the parties' intentions have been thwarted in some way: by failure to comply with applicable formality rules, for example, or by the property-owner's change of heart. In cases of the latter sort we could say that the constructive trust is imposed against the *current* wishes of the property-owner, and that it responds to his "wrongdoing" in denying the claimant's beneficial

---

[12] See para.5–05, above.
[13] *Mountney v Treharne* [2003] Ch. 135, affirming *Re Flint (a bankrupt)* [1993] Ch. 319.
[14] *Foskett v McKeown* [2001] 1 A.C. 102.
[15] See paras 12–107 *et seq.*
[16] *Westdeutsche Landesbank Girozentrale v Islington L.B.C* [1996] A.C. 669 at 708, *per* Lord Browne-Wilkinson. See too *Rathwell v Rathwell* [1978] 2 S.C.R. 436 at 454, *per* Dickson J.; *Air Jamaica Ltd v Charlton* [1999] 1 W.L.R. 1399 at 1412, *per* Lord Millett.
[17] R. Chambers, "Constructive Trusts in Canada" (1999) 37 Alberta L.R. 173, reprinted in (2001) 15 Tru L.I. 214 and (2002) 16 Tru. L.I. 2. A similar line is taken in the chapters on constructive trusts in *Oosterhoff on Trusts: Text, Commentary and Materials* (6th ed., 2004), of which Professor Chambers is an editor. See too S. Gardner, *Introduction to the Law of Trusts* 2nd ed. (2003), p.159 *et seq.*

interest.[18] But if we focus instead on his *original* intention, then we can say that in these cases, just as in the cases where an intended transfer has failed for non-compliance with some formality rule, the function of the constructive trust is "perfectionary": it perfects the parties' original intention that beneficial ownership should be transferred.[19]

Authorities supporting this analysis include the statement by the High **6–07** Court of Australia in *Bathurst C.C. v PWC Properties Pty. Ltd* that[20]:

> "One species of constructive trust is concerned with cases where the intent of a settlor or testator in transferring or devising property otherwise would fail for want of compliance with the formalities for creation of express trusts *inter vivos* or by will. The necessary elements are on which the question turns in many cases are 'intention, communication, and acquiescence'."[21]

Millett L.J. also held in *Paragon Finance plc v D. B. Thakerar & Co. (a firm)* that some constructive trusts arise where the trustee receives the trust property[22]:

> "by a transaction which both parties intend to create a trust from the outset and which is not impugned by the plaintiff. [The defendant's] possession of the property is coloured from the first by the trust and confidence by means of which he obtained it, and his subsequent appropriation to his own use is a breach of that trust. Well known examples of such a constructive trust are *McCormick v Grogan*[23] (a case of secret trust) and *Rochefoucauld v Boustead*[24] (where the defendant agreed to buy property for the plaintiff but the trust was improperly recorded). *Pallant v Morgan*[25] (where the defendant sought to keep for himself property which the plaintiff trusted him to buy for both parties) is another. In these cases the plaintiff does not impugn the transaction by which the defendant obtained control of the property. He alleges that the circumstances in which the defendant obtained control make it unconscionable for him thereafter to assert a beneficial interest in the property."

In the account which follows, we set out various cases in which **6–08** constructive trusts have been imposed, and which we would explain on the basis that the causative event to which the trust responded was the parties'

---

[18] *Lonrho plc v Fayed (No.2)* [1992] 1 W.L.R. 1 at 10, *per* Millett J.
[19] G. Elias, *Explaining Constructive Trusts* (1990), p.157.
[20] (1998) 195 C.L.R. 566 at [39], *per curiam*. See too *Allen v Snyder* [1977] 2 N.S.W.L.R. 685 at 693, *per* Glass J.A.; *Re Australian Elizabethan Theatre Trust* (1991) 30 F.C.R. 491 at 510, *per* Gummow J., considering *Le Compte v Public Trustee* [1983] 2 N.S.W.L.R. 109.
[21] Citing *Vosges v Monaghan* (1954) 94 C.L.R. 231 at 233, 235, and 237; *Blackwell v Blackwell* [1929] A.C. 318 at 334.
[22] [1999] 1 All E.R. 400 at 408–9.
[23] (1869) 4 App. Cas. 82.
[24] [1897] 1 Ch. 196.
[25] [1953] Ch. 43.

original intention that beneficial ownership of the trust property should be transferred from the defendant to the claimant. These cases are grouped under the following headings: (1) unauthorised fiduciary gains; (2) specifically enforceable contracts of sale; (3) assignments for value of future property; (4) purchasers' undertakings; (5) the rule in *Pallant v Morgan*; (6) incomplete transfers and the rule in *Re Rose*; (7) mutual wills and secret trusts; (8) shared homes.

6–09   If the constructive trusts imposed in these cases were perfectionary, then two questions arise.[26] First, what role does detriment play in attracting Equity's attention? One might have thought that detriment suffered by the claimant would be a necessary pre-requisite for the imposition of the constructive trust, as the element which makes it unconscionable for the defendant to act in a manner contrary to the parties' original intentions. But although this is true of some cases (*e.g.* those grouped under headings (6) and (8)) it is not true of others (*e.g.* those grouped under headings (1), (4) and (5)). Secondly, what is the significance of the parties' failure to comply with formality rules, as in *e.g.* the cases grouped under headings (5) and (6)? Should constructive trust reasoning be allowed to undermine the integrity of the statutory formality rules governing transfers of property?[27]

I. Unauthorised Fiduciary Gains

6–10 It is clearly established that a trustee or fiduciary must account to his beneficiaries or principal for unauthorised profits made in the course of his engagement, and that a constructive trust will be imposed on these profits or their traceable proceeds. However, the reason why this constructive trust is imposed is controversial. It is now often said that the constructive trust imposed in such cases is wrong-based, because the trustee or fiduciary commits a wrong when he breaches his duty "not to promote his personal interest by making or pursuing a gain in circumstances in which there is a conflict or a real or substantial possibility of a conflict between his personal interests and those of the persons whom he is bound to protect."[28] In our

---

[26] For discussion of these and other problems with the case-law, see: T. Youdan, "Formalities for Trusts of Land and the Doctrine in *Rochefoucauld v Boustead*" (1984) 43 C.L.J. 306; N. Hopkins "Acquiring Property Rights from Uncompleted Sales of Land" (1998) 61 M.L.R. 486; P. Critchley, "Instruments of Fraud, Testamentary Dispositions, and the Doctrine of Secret Trusts" (1999) 115 L.Q.R. 631; N. Hopkins "The *Pallant v Morgan* 'Equity'?" [2002] Conv. 35; S. Gardner, *Introduction to the Law of Trusts* 2nd ed. (2003), pp.86–93 and 159–162; J. Cartwright, "Formality and Informality in Property and Contract" in J. Getzler (ed.) *Rationalizing Property, Equity and Trusts* (2003) 36; B. Macfarlane, "Constructive Trusts Arising on a Receipt of Property *Sub Conditione*" (2004) 120 L.Q.R. 667; B. Macfarlane, "The Enforcement of Non-Contractual Agreements to Dispose of Interests in Land" (2005) 16 K.C.L.J.

[27] *Cf. Re Australian Elizabethan Theatre Trust* (1991) 30 F.C.R. 491 at 508, *per* Gummow J.: "constructive trusts should not readily be imposed in favour of parties which have failed in their attempts to show the necessary facts for a consensual arrangement by way of express trust."

[28] *Hospital Products Ltd v United States Surgical Corp.* (1984) 156 C.L.R. 41 at 103, *per* Mason J., citing *Aberdeen Railway Co. v Blaikie Bros.* (1854) 1 Macq. 461 at 471. For authorities which appear to support a wrong-based analysis, see *e.g. New Zealand Netherlands Society 'Oranje' Inc. v Kuys* [1973] 1 W.L.R. 1126 at 1129; *International Corona Resources Ltd v LAC Minerals Ltd* (1987) 44 D.L.R. (4th) 592 at 647, affirmed [1989] 2 S.C.R. 574; *United Pan-Europe Communications N.V. v Deutsche Bank A.G.* [2000] 2 B.C.L.C. 461 at [44]; *Walsh v Deloitte & Touche Inc.* [2001] UKPC 58 at [13]; *Glazier v Australian Men's Health Pty. Ltd (No.2)* [2001] N.S.W.S.C. 6 at [44]; *Gwembe Valley Development Co. Ltd v Koshy (No.3)* [2002] 1 B.C.L.C. 478 at [260]–[298].

view, however, the true reason is that a trustee or fiduciary binds himself at the moment when he assumes office to account to his beneficiaries or principal for any profits that he might make from his office, and the constructive trust which captures his profits responds to his original intention to turn them over as and when he receives them.

This view is supported by important authorities,[29] and it is consistent with the traditional understanding of the rules by which the behaviour of fiduciaries is governed, that these rules disable fiduciaries from acting in certain ways, rather than imposing positive duties upon them.[30] Thus, in Lord Millett's words, a fiduciary[31]: **6–11**

"is not permitted to make a profit from her position. If she does, she is accountable for it. This is a means of stripping her of her profits, but it is not a monetary award for wrongdoing. It is simply that she must be taken to have received the money for and on behalf of her principal and accordingly must account to him for it."

Who is a fiduciary?

The relationship of trustee and beneficiary is the original fiduciary relationship and provides the guidelines for determining when other persons are in a fiduciary relationship to each other by virtue of the position and power of one in respect of the other and the latter's reasonably induced expectation that the former will act exclusively in the interests of the latter or of their joint interest.[32] Trustees are persons who are under a duty to act exclusively in the interests of the trust beneficiaries, who are vulnerable, if the trustees seek to abuse their position, because the trustees have rights and powers that are capable of being exercised so as detrimentally to affect the beneficiaries. Thus, if such aspects are present in other relationships these are treated as fiduciary relationships as a matter of law, *e.g.* personal representatives and beneficiaries of deceased's estate,[33] solicitor and **6–12**

---

[29] *Furs Ltd v Tomkies* (1936) 54 C.L.R. 583 at 592; *Scott v Scott* (1963) 109 C.L.R. 649; *Regal (Hastings) Ltd v Gulliver* [1967] 2 A.C. 134 at 144. See too the American Law Institute, *Restatement of Trusts 2d* (1959), para.203, which provides that a trustee is accountable for any profit made through or arising out of the administration of the trust even though he may have committed no breach of trust. For discussion, see T. Niles, "Trustee Accountability in the Absence of Breach of Trust" (1960) 60 Columbia L.R. 141.

[30] See *e.g.* T. Lewin, *A Practical Treatise on the Law of Trusts and Trustees* (1837), p.376; J. Hill, *A Practical Treatise on the Law Relating to Trustees* (1845), pp.554–561; E. Vintner, *The History and Law of Fiduciary Relationship and Resulting Trust* 3rd ed. (1955), Chap. 1.

[31] Lord Millett, 'Book Review' (2002) 2 O.U.C.L.J. 291, 295. See too Lord Millett, "Proprietary Restitution" in S. Degeling and J. Edelman (eds), *Equity in Commercial Law* (2005).

[32] Generally see P. D. Finn, "The Fiduciary Principle" in T. G. Youdan (ed.), *Equity, Trusts and Fiduciary Relationships* (1989); P. D. Finn, "Fiduciary Law and the Modern Commercial World" in E. McKendrick (ed.), *Commercial Aspects of Trusts and Fiduciary Obligations*; P.B.H. Birks (ed.) *Privacy and Loyalty* (1997) Chapters 8, 10 and 11; P. Birks, "The Content of Fiduciary Obligation" (2002) 16 Tru. L.I. 34; L. Smith, "The Motive, Not the Deed" in J. Getzler (ed.) *Rationalizing Property, Equity and Trusts* (2003) 53; S. Worthington, *Equity* (2003), pp.117–131.

[33] *Re Diplock* [1948] Ch. 465.

client,[34] principal and agent,[39] partner and partner,[36] promoter and company,[37] director and company,[38] underwriter and Lloyds names,[39] employee and employer while the employment relationship subsists,[40] although any fiduciary obligation of confidence arising in such employment will continue until the information ceases to be confidential.[41]

6–13   As a matter of public policy, to maintain the integrity, credibility and utility of such relationships, it is vital that the fiduciary loyally serves the interests of his beneficiaries. Except with the fully-informed, freely-given consent of his beneficiaries, he cannot misuse his position of trust to his own or a third party's possible advantage and he cannot place himself in a position where there is a conflict between his duty and self-interest or between his duty to his beneficiaries and his duty to others.[42] It is thus not prescriptive but proscriptive duties that Equity imposes on a fiduciary.[43]

6–14   Separate from fiduciary relationships arising as a matter of law from status[44] are fact-based fiduciaries who become subject to fiduciary duties because of a particular factual situation where the imposition of such duties is considered appropriate in the interests of justice because of the claimant's particular vulnerability to being taken advantage of by the defendant upon whose loyalty he is reasonably relying, *e.g.* in the case of a financier using confidential information imparted by A (when seeking a loan) to help B conclude a deal to the exclusion of A and to the profit of B and the financier,[45] or of the parties to a joint venture where they were entitled to expect that the other would act in their joint interest to the exclusion of his own several interest.[46]

6–15   The distinction between fact-based fiduciaries and status-based fiduciaries is illuminated by contrasting the position of financial advisers and of discretionary portfolio managers. It seems that the latter should be regarded automatically as fiduciaries with their unilateral powers to invest

---

[34] *Clark Boyce v Mouat* [1994] 1 A.C. 428, *Nocton v Lord Ashburton* [1914] A.C. 932; *Hilton v Barker Booth & Eastwood (a firm)* [2005] All E.R. 651.

[35] *Boston Deep Sea Fishing Co. v Ansell* (1888) 39 Ch.D. 389; *Att.-Gen. of Hong Kong v Reid* [1994] 1 A.C. 324 on how *Lister v Stubbs* (1890) 45 Ch.D. 1 should have been decided. *Fyffer Group Ltd v Templeman* [2000] 2 Lloyd's Rep. 643.

[36] *Thompson's Trustee v Heaton* [1974] 1 All E.R. 1239.

[37] *Gluckstein v Barnes* [1900] A.C. 240.

[38] *Regal Hastings Ltd v Gulliver* [1942] 1 All E.R. 378.

[39] *Sphere Drake Insurance Ltd v Euro International Underwriting Ltd* [2003] EWHC 1636 (Comm) at [40]–[47].

[40] *Att.-Gen. v Blake* [1998] Ch. 439, CA; *Nottingham University v Fishel* [2000] I.C.R. 1462; *Neary v Dean of Westminster* [1999] I.R.L.R. 288.

[41] *ibid*. Since the information had ceased to be confidential, on appeal, the House of Lords held (4:1) that, very exceptionally, the Russian spy, Blake, should be subject to an account of profits as a new remedy for breach of contract: *Att.-Gen. v Blake* [2001] 1 A.C. 268.

[42] *Boardman v Phipps* [1967] 2 A.C. 46; *Warman International Ltd v Dwyer* (1995) 64 A.L.J.R. 362, 367; *Chan v Zachariah* (1984) 154 C.L.R. 178.

[43] *Breen v Williams* (1996) 70 A.L.J.R. 772, 793, 794; *Bristol & West B.S. v Mothew* [1996] 4 All E.R. 698 at 710, 712.

[44] *Hodgkinson v Simms* (1994) 117 D.L.R. (4th) 161 at 176, 215; P. D. Finn, in T. G. Youdan (ed.) *Equity, Trusts and Fiduciary Relationships*, pp.33–44; Law Commission No.124 "Fiduciary duties & Regulatory Rules" para.2.4.3.

[45] *United Pan Europe Communications N.V. v Deutsche Bank A.G.* [2000] 2 B.C.L.C. 461, CA.

[46] *Lac Minerals Ltd v International Corona Resources Ltd* (1989) 61 D.L.R. (4th) 14; *Hospital Products Ltd v U.S. Surgical Corp.* (1984) 156 C.L.R. 41; *Noranda Australia Ltd v Lachlan Resources* (1988) 14 N.W.S.L.R. 1; *John v James* [1991] F.S.R. 397 at 433; *Elliott v Wheeldon* [1993] B.C.L.C. 53 at 57; *Murad v Al-Saraj* [2004] EWHC 1235 (Ch) at [325]–[332].

and disinvest as they see fit.[47] In the case of the former it is a question of fact whether or not the parties' relationship was such as to give rise to a fiduciary duty on the part of the adviser: the circumstances can cover the whole spectrum from total reliance upon the adviser to total independence of the adviser.[48]

Scope of fiduciary duties

The scope of a defendant's fiduciary obligations depends upon the nature **6–16** and scope of his relationship with the claimant.[49] He is not to be made liable in respect of profits derived by him outside the scope of the plaintiff's business nor to be obliged to prefer the claimant's interests to his own outside such scope. "A person may be in a fiduciary position quoad a part of his activities and not quoad other parts."[50] Thus, a partner is not accountable to his partners for profits made from a business outside the scope of the partnership business.[51] A director is a fiduciary in relation to his company[52] but not to any shareholder[53] (unless exceptionally the shareholder had turned to the director so as to place special reliance on the director[54]), while the director's obligations, particularly in respect of business opportunities, depend upon the actual and prospective line(s) of business of the company.[55]

While a solicitor is a status-based fiduciary, his negligence in carrying out **6–17** his duties does not amount to a breach of fiduciary duty.[56] Such a breach requires breach of the fiduciary's obligation of loyalty, *e.g.* acting for a client in a matter that the solicitor has a personal interest without fully disclosing this or acting for both sides in a transaction without disclosing this to one of them.[57] While an agent is a status-based fiduciary, if the principal allows the agent to mix moneys paid in respect of sums due to the principal with the agent's own money and account monthly to the principal for the moneys owed to the principal, the agent is only personally liable in debt to the principal.[58] However, if the agent had agreed to hold all money received on

---

[47] *Glennie v McDougall* [1935] S.C.R. 357 at 276; *Hewson v Stock Exchange* [1968] 2 N.S.W.L.R. 245.

[48] *Hodgkinson v Simms* (1994) 117 D.L.R. (4th) 161.

[49] "To say that a man is a fiduciary only begins analysis: it gives direction to further enquiry. To whom is he a fiduciary? What obligations does he owe as a fiduciary? In what respect has he failed to discharge these obligations? And what are the consequences of his deviation from duty?" *per* Frankfurter J. in *SEC v Chenery Corp* (1943) 318 U.S. 80 at 85–86 endorsed by Lord Mustill in *Re Goldcorp Exchange Ltd* [1994] 2 All E.R. 806 at 821.

[50] *New Zealand Netherlands Society Oranje Inc. v Kuys* [1973] 2 All E.R. 1222 at 1225.

[51] *Aas v Benham* [1891] 2 Ch. 244.

[52] *Regal Hastings Ltd v Gulliver* [1967] 2 A.C. 134n; *Industrial Development Consultants v Cooley* [1972] 1 W.L.R. 443.

[53] *Percival v Wright* [1902] 2 Ch. 421; *North-west Transportation Co. Ltd v Beattry* (1887) 12 App. Cas. 589.

[54] *Coleman v Myers* [1977] 2 N.Z.L.R. 225; *Brunninghausen v Glaranics* (1999) 46 N.S.W.L.R. 538; *Peskin v Anderson* [2001] 1 B.C.L.C. 372 at [27]–[37].

[55] See para.9–00; *Queensland Mines Ltd v Hudson* (1978) 52 A.L.J.R. 394; *Canadian Aero Services Ltd v O'Malley* (1973) 40 D.L.R. (3rd) 371, *CMS Dolphin Ltd v Simonet* [2001] 2 B.C.L.C. 704; *Bhullar v Bhullar* [2003] 2 B.C.L.C. 241.

[56] *Bristol & West B. S. v Mothew* [1998] Ch. 1, CA. As Lord Mustill said in *Re Goldcorp Exchange Ltd* [1994] 2 All E.R. 806 at 821, "The essence of a fiduciary relationship is that it creates obligations of a different character from those deriving under the contract itself".

[57] *Clark Boyce v Mouat* [1994] 1 A.C. 428; *Farrington v Row McBride & Partners* [1985] 1 N.Z.L.R. 83; *Witten-Hannah v Davis* [1995] 2 N.Z.L.R. 141.

[58] *Henry v Hammond* [1953] 2 K.B. 515; *Commissioners of Customs & Excise v Richmond Theatre* [1995] S.T.C. 257; *R. v Clowes (No.2)* [1994] 2 All E.R. 316.

the principal's behalf from the principal's debtors separate from his own money for the principal's exclusive benefit, the principal would have an equitable proprietary interest in the money held by the agent as fiduciary.[59]

6–18　　In the case of fact-based fiduciary obligations imposed because of the claimant's particular vulnerability to the power of the defendant, upon whom the claimant is manifestly relying, these obligations will be restricted to the defendant's activities which result from his power and play upon the vulnerability of the claimant.[60]

6–19　　Where the fiduciary relationship arises from a contract or a partnership or trust deed or other instrument then the terms of the instrument are relevant for qualifying the scope of the fiduciary's obligations.[61] However, a fiduciary relationship can arise in the course of negotiating the terms of a contract or trust,[62] in which case abuse of such relationship or the exercise of undue influence can prevent the fiduciary relying on a clause exempting him from negligence or breach of fiduciary duties.[63]

Nature of fiduciary remedies: temptation to extend fiduciary situations

6–20　　The establishment of a fiduciary situation affords scope for an extensive range of equitable remedies for breach of fiduciary duty. The transaction with the fiduciary can be avoided[64] or equitable compensation for loss caused by the defendant's breach of fiduciary duty will be available,[65] while in respect of profits[66] the courts can impose a personal liability to account[67] or a proprietary constructive trust of the profits and their traceable product.[68] Moreover, advantages flow from suing in equity rather than common law due to the strict deterrent liability for profits imposed by equity[69] and it may be that claims in equity for negligence are governed by more claimant-friendly rules on causation, foreseeability and contributory negligence than analogous claims at common law.[70]

6–21　　The utility, and the extent, of fiduciary obligations and the remedies for breach thereof are such that claimants and courts are tempted to stretch the concept of fiduciary relationship as if it were an "accordion term"[71] However, the courts have rejected claims that treat any breach of a

---

[59] *Napier and Ettrick (Lord) v Hunter* [1993] A.C. 713 at 744 *per* Lord Goff; *Re Fleet Disposal Services Ltd* [1995] 1 B.C.L.C. 345.
[60] See "Fiduciary duties & Regulatory Rules": Law Com Consultation Paper No.124, para.2.4.8.
[61] *Kelly v Cooper* [1993] A.C. 205, *New Zealand Netherlands Society Oranje Inc. v Kuys* [1973] 2 All E.R. 1222; *Hilton v Barker Booth and Eastwood (a firm)* [2005] 1 All E.R. 651 at [30].
[62] *Swain v Law Society* [1981] 3 All E.R. 797 at 817.
[63] *Tate v Williamson* (1866) 2 Ch. App.55 at 61; *Baskerville v Thurgood* (1992) 100 Sask L.R. 214.
[64] *Wright v Morgan* [1926] A.C. 788.
[65] See paras 10–09 *et seq.*
[66] In the case of a claim for profits whether the claimant suffered any loss is altogether irrelevant because the object is to ensure that the defaulting fiduciary does not retain any profit: *Att.-Gen. v Blake* [2000] 4 All E.R. 385 at 393; *United Pan Europe Communications N.V. v Deutsche Bank A.G.* [2000] 2 B.C.L.C. 461.
[67] *Reading v Att.-Gen.* [1951] A.C. 507; *Regal Hastings Ltd v Gulliver* [1967] 2 A.C. 134n; *English v Dedham Vale Properties Ltd* [1978] 1 All E.R. 382.
[68] *Att.-Gen. of Hong Kong v Reid* [1994] 1 A.C. 324; *Boardman v Phipps* [1967] 2 A.C. 46, *Re EVTR* [1987] B.C.L.C. 646.
[69] See paras 6–24 *et seq.*
[70] See paras 10–45 *et seq.*
[71] See P. D. Finn in *Equity, Trusts and Fiduciary Relationships* (T. G. Youdan ed.), p.10.

fiduciary's obligations as a breach of fiduciary duty. As Millett L.J. stated in *Bristol & West B.S. v Mothew*[72]:

> "The expression 'fiduciary duty' is properly confined to those duties which are peculiar to fiduciaries and the breach of which attracts legal consequences differing from those consequent upon breach of other duties . . . not every breach of a duty by a fiduciary is a breach of fiduciary duty . . . It is inappropriate to apply the expression to the obligation of a trustee or other fiduciary to use proper skill and care in he discharge of his duties . . . The distinguishing obligation of a fiduciary is the obligation of loyalty . . . A fiduciary must act in good faith; he must not make a profit out of his position; he must not place himself in a position where his duty and his interest may conflict; he may not act for his own benefit or the benefit of a third person without the informed consent of his principal . . . where the fiduciary deals with his principal . . . he must prove affirmatively that the transaction is fair and that he made full disclosure of all the facts material to the transactions . . . Breach of fiduciary obligation connotes disloyaly or infidelity. Mere incompetence is not enough."

Until recently, the courts were too inclined to stretch the circumstances **6–22** giving rise to a fiduciary obligation, so converting the defendant into a fiduciary,[73] in order to enable them to make the defendant account for profits or to utilise the tracing process so as to impose an equitable lien or constructive trust against the defendant's property. Nowadays, such accounting remedy has been made available in an exceptional type of a breach of contract,[74] while the tracing rules for identifying substituted assets are now available in support of legal claims as well as equitable claims.[75] Thus there is less need to stretch the circumstances giving rise to a fiduciary obligation.

Unauthorised fiduciary gains

As Dillon L.J. stated in *Re EVTR*[76] "It is a long established principle of **6–23** equity that if a person who is a trustee receives money or property because of, or in respect of, trust property, he will hold what he receives as a constructive trustee on the trusts of the original trust property" until such money or property is duly vested in the trustees on the trusts of the trust fund. The trustees are express trustees of the fund comprising whatever happens from time to time to be duly vested in them as representing the original trust property.[77] However, the trustee will also be regarded as

---

[72] [1998] Ch. 1 at 16.
[73] A fiduciary "is not subject to fiduciary obligations because he is a fiduciary; it is because he is subject to them that he is a fiduciary": *Bristol & West B.S. v Mothew* [1998] Ch. 1, 18
[74] *Att.-Gen. v Blake* [2000] 4 All E.R. 385.
[75] *Foskett v McKeown* [2000] 3 All E.R. 97 at 106, 121.
[76] [1987] B.C.L.C. 646, 651, above para.3–50.
[77] *Re Earl of Strafford* [1979] 1 All E.R. 513 at 521.

constructive trustee of a rights issue of shares relating to a trust shareholding where he purchased them purportedly for himself with his own money, or of a lease renewed in favour of himself and not the trust,[78] or of the freehold reversion to a trust's lease,[79] or of shares in his own company formed specially to develop trust land sold by him to the company at an undervalue,[80] or of property bought in his own name with a cheque drawn on his private account containing trust money wrongfully mixed with his own money.[81] Similarly, an agent engaged to buy property for his principal will hold it on constructive trust for his principal if he buys it for himself[82] and a director diverting to himself a profitable contract which he should have taken up on behalf of the company will hold it on constructive trust for the company.[83] If a bribe is taken by a trustee or director or agent or senior employee then the bribe will forthwith be held upon a constructive trust as will property purchased therewith: *Att.-Gen. of Hong Kong v Reid*,[84] para.6–77. "That which is the fruit of trust property or of the trusteeship is itself trust property"[85] so that profits made from exploiting the fiduciary property or the position of fiduciary[86] are held on constructive trust.

Strict liability and its justification

6–24   A proprietary constructive trust (with a personal liability to account) arises as a sanction for the fundamental, strict primary obligation that a fiduciary must not place himself where his fiduciary duty does, or may sensibly, conflict with his private interest[87]—unless duly authorised by his principal or the court. It is immaterial that the fiduciary, T, acted honestly and in his principal's best interest, that the principal suffered no loss but even made a profit which he could not otherwise have obtained and that the profit was obtained through use of T's own assets and by virtue of T's skills,—though T will have a lien for his expenditure and, in exceptional circumstances, may obtain an allowance for his skills.[88] The rule is very strict in order to maintain confidence in the trust or other fiduciary relationship by deterring any slipping from the high standards required of trustees and other fiduciaries: just as a dishonest loss-causing defendant in the same situation would be liable for losses, so an honest profit-making defendant should be liable for profits. Equity has a strict prophylactic approach to ensure the defendant acts altruistically to further the beneficiaries' interests and so that nothing must be done that may enrich the

---

[78] *Keech v Sandford* (1726) 2 Eq.Cas.Abr. 741 at para.6–33.
[79] *Protheroe v Protheroe* [1968] 1 W.L.R. 519.
[80] *cf. Aberdeen Railway Co. v Blaikie Bros.* (1854) 1 Macq. 461.
[81] *cf. Re Tilley's W.T.* [1967] Ch. 1179.
[82] *Longfield Parish Council v Robson* (1913) 29 T.L.R. 357; *Lees v Nuttall* (1834) 2 My. & K. 819; *Lonrho v Fayed (No.2)* [1991] 4 All E.R. 901 at 969–970.
[83] *Cook v Deeks* [1916] 1 A.C. 554, *Industrial Developments Consultants Ltd v Cooley* [1972] 1 W.L.R. 443.
[84] [1994] 1 A.C. 324.
[85] *Swain v Law Society* [1981] 3 All E.R. 797, 813 *per* Oliver L.J.
[86] *Att.-Gen. of Hong Kong v Reid* [1994] 1 A.C. 324; *Phipps v Boardman* [1967] 2 A.C. 46.
[87] *Phipps v Boardman* [1967] 2 A.C. 46, 123, *N.Z. Netherlands Society Inc. v Kuys* [1973] 1 W.L.R. 1126, 1129. See paras 9–21 *et seq.*
[88] *Phipps v Boardman* [1967] 2 A.C. 46; *O'Sullivan v Management Agency & Music Ltd* [1985] Q.B. 428.

defendant or harm the beneficiaries. To relax standards for situations where the defendant allegedly acted "properly" cannot be allowed because most of the relevant evidence will be peculiarly within the defendant's knowledge and control, so making it very difficult for the disadvantaged claimant beneficiaries to know whether or not they have a case for saying the defendant acted "improperly." Thus, it is *per se* (in itself) improper for a defendant fiduciary to enter into transactions where there is a conflict or sensible possibility of a conflict between his fiduciary duty and his self-interest. It is up to the defendant to avoid any problems by obtaining the informed consent of his principal(s) or of the court.

He "must account . . . for any benefit or gain which has been obtained or   **6–25** received in circumstances where a conflict or significant possibility of conflict existed between his fiduciary duty and his personal interest in the pursuit or possible receipt of such a benefit or gain."[89] He also "must account . . . for any benefit or gain which was obtained or received by use or by reason of his fiduciary position or of opportunity or knowledge resulting from it" where he is "actually misusing his position for his personal advantage" rather than for the advantage of his principal(s). However, if information is acquired by a fiduciary in the course of his duties and it is not classified as confidential information he is free to use the information for the benefit of himself or of another trust of which he is trustee if there is no reasonably foreseeable possibility of his needing to use that information for his original principal(s).[90] Where information acquired by a fiduciary or his "tippee" (to whom he passes the information) is confidential so that its disclosure could be prevented by a court injunction then, although such information has insufficient "property" nature for the law of theft, it may have sufficient "property" nature for profits made by use of such information to be held on constructive trust,[91] though since then abuse of position (in addition to exploitation of fiduciary property) has been held sufficient to justify the imposition of a constructive trust on property obtained as a result of such abuse.[92]

Proprietary and/or personal liability

If there is a proprietary liability because T (a trustee or other fiduciary)   **6–26** holds specific property as constructive trustee then there is a co-extensive personal liability to account and if T is wealthy enough the claimants will usually be happy enough to rely on T's personal liability and take the cash profits from him (rather than take the property upon paying T sufficient for his lien on the property for its cost to him). Thus, a House of Lords case like *Regal Hastings Ltd v Gulliver*[93] was pleaded only as a personal claim to account and in *Phipps v Boardman*[94] counsel and judges concentrated upon

---

[89] *Chan v Zachariah* (1984) 154 C.L.R. 178 at 199 where all the citations in this para. are to be found. Also see *Warman International Ltd v Dwyer* (1995) 69 A.L.J.R. 362 at 367.
[90] *Phipps v Boardman* [1967] 2 A.C. 46, 130; see para.6–46.
[91] *Nanus Asia Co. Inc. v Standard Chartered Bank* [1990] Hong Kong L.R. 396.
[92] *Att.-Gen. for Hong Kong v Reid* [1994] 1 A.C. 324.
[93] [1967] 2 A.C. 134 at paras 6–46 *et seq*.
[94] [1967] 2 A.C. 46.

making the wealthy Boardman personally liable to account. In *Phipps v Boardman*, at para.6–46 the plaintiff with a five-eighteenths interest under a trust claimed (i) a declaration that the defendants held five-eighteenths of the shareholding obtained by them through using information acquired by them when representing the trust as constructive trustees for him, (ii) an account of the profits made by the defendants, and (iii) an order that they should transfer to him the shares held by them as constructive trustees and should pay him five-eighteenths of profits found to be due upon taking the account. Wilberforce J. gave the plaintiff the relief requested under (i) and (ii) but adjourned (iii) having ordered an inquiry as to a liberal allowance for the defendant's work. Presumably, this was to allow the taking of accounts of profits made on sale of some of the shares and the inquiry as to the proper payment to be allowed to the defendants for their skilful efforts, whereupon the balance would be due to the plaintiff, who could then consider whether to call for the remaining shares subject to reimbursing the defendants for their costs in purchasing the shares. No doubt, at the end of the day the plaintiff preferred to receive all cash rather than cash plus shares, and the defendants agreed to this.

6–27   The Court of Appeal and the House of Lords, due to counsels' concentration on personal accountability, held that the defendants were constructive trustees who were liable to account for their profits but they confirmed Wilberforce J.'s order which included a proprietary declaration of constructive trust.[95]

6–28   Where the gain emanates from property entrusted to the fiduciary it is clear that the gain should be held on a proprietary constructive trust, but three[96] of the five Law Lords held that the defendants' information obtained *qua fiduciaries* was not trust property so that the shares purchased as a result of using such information did not thereby constructively become trust property. Two Law Lords[97] thought that there was no sensible possibility of conflict of duty and interest. However, the majority[98] thought that there was: the defendant as solicitor to the trustees was not in a position to give disinterested impartial advice at the stage when he was almost about to make large profits for himself and yet when he ought, if consulted, to have been advising the trustees to obtain wider investment powers from the court so as to enable the trust (and not himself) to make large profits. Thus, the defendants had to account for their profits on the shares because they had acquired the knowledge and the opportunity to purchase the shares while purporting to represent the trust.

6–29   The Lords did not openly consider the question of a proprietary constructive trust but the court order accepts the existence of such a trust, so that the use of position as opposed to the use of trust property seemed capable of generating a proprietary constructive trust of the profit made in breach of the duty to avoid conflicts of interest, despite an earlier contrary

---

[95] See [1964] 2 All E.R. 187 at 208; [1965] Ch. 992 at 1006, 1021; [1967] 2 A.C. 46 at 99, 112.
[96] Lords Cohen and Upjohn and Viscount Dilhorne.
[97] Viscount Dilhorne and Lord Upjohn.
[98] Lords Hodson, Guest and Cohen; see at paras 6–53 *et seq.*

Court of Appeal decision, *Lister v Stubbs*,[99] rejecting any constructive trust of a bribe obtained by a fiduciary abusing his position, so that the dishonest fiduciary was only personally accountable for the bribe and his employer could not trace the bribe into assets purchased therewith. Lord Templeman, delivering the advice of the Privy Council in *Att.-Gen. for Hong Kong v Reid*,[1] rejected that decision and explained that *Boardman v Phipps* "demonstrates the strictness with which equity regards the conduct of a fiduciary and the extent to which equity is willing to impose a constructive trust on property obtained by a fiduciary by virtue of his office . . . the solicitor was held to be a constructive trustee . . . because the solicitor obtained the information . . . and the opportunity of acquiring the shares as a result of acting for certain purposes on behalf of the trustees. If a fiduciary acting honestly in good faith and making a profit which his principal could not make for himself becomes a constructive trustee of that profit, then a fiduciary acting dishonestly who accepts a bribe must also be a constructive trustee." Thus, the Attorney General could enter a *caveat* against three New Zealand properties purchased with bribes received by Reid as public prosecutor to drop prosecutions, such properties being held on constructive trust for the Crown.

It seems easier to support a proprietary constructive trust in *Lister* and **6–30** *Reid* than in *Boardman*. In a bribe case is there not an incontrovertible assumption that the victim has lost property of a value at least equal to the bribe, so that the bribe may justifiably be regarded as representing the victim's property? As between the victim and the fiduciary surely the victim has a better claim not only to the bribe but to the fruits thereof: the fiduciary would certainly be unjustly enriched if allowed to retain the bribe and its fruits. If he himself should not benefit from his dishonest wrongdoing why should his creditors be better off and receive a windfall if he is insolvent?

In *Boardman* the case for a proprietary constructive trust for profits **6–31** gained by use of position seems weaker. The profit, literally speaking, was not made at the expense of the beneficiaries, though it was made at the expense of the fiduciary not being able to give disinterested advice to the beneficiaries (if asked) and so at the risk of harming the beneficiaries' interests. Should the latter honest but wrongful breach of his duty to avoid a conflict make the fiduciary subject to a proprietary constructive trust of his profit as opposed to a mere personal liability to account?[2]

English law has an "all or nothing" approach. Boardman was unlucky **6–32** that the majority did not take the view that the remote possibility of him being asked to advise the trustees at the time of the third phase (see para.6–50 *infra*) was immaterial, particularly when, if the possibility materialised, he could have openly declared his interest or have declined to advise them, other than to seek the advice of another solicitor.

---

[99] (1890) 45 Ch.D.

[1] [1994] 1 A.C. 324, see at para.6–00. See to *Daraydan Holdings Ltd v Solland International Ltd* [2004] 3 W.L.R. 1106.

[2] Further see G. Elias, *Explaining Constructive Trusts* (OUP, 1990), at p.77; P. Birks, *Introduction to the Law of Restitution* (OUP, 1985), p.341, 388; G. H. Jones (1968) 84 L.Q.R. 472.

KEECH v SANDFORD[3]

Lord Chancellor (1726) 2 Eq.Cas.Abr. 741; Sel.Cas.Ch. 61

6–33   A person being possessed of a lease of the profits of a market devised his estate to a trustee in trust for his infant. Before the expiration of the term the trustee applied to the lessor for a renewal, for the benefit of the infant, which he refused, since the lease being only of the profits of a market, there could be no distress, and its enforcement must rest in covenant, by which the infant could not be bound. The infant sought to have the lease assigned to him, and for an account of the profits, on the principle that wherever a lease is renewed by a trustee or executor it shall be for the benefit of the *cestui que use*, which principle was agreed on the other side, though endeavoured to be differenced on account of the express proof of refusal to renew to the infant.

6–34   LORD KING L.C.: "I must consider this as a trust for the infant, for I very well see, if a trustee, on the refusal to renew, might have a lease to himself, few trust estates would be renewed to *cestui que use*. Though I do not say there is fraud in this case, yet he should rather have let it run out than to have had the lease to himself. This may seem hard, that the trustee is the only person of all mankind who might not have the lease; but it is very proper that the rule should be strictly pursued, and not in the least relaxed; for it is very obvious what would be the consequences of letting trustees have the lease on refusal to renew to *cestui que use*."

6–35   So decreed, that the lease should be assigned to the infant, and that the trustee should be indemnified from any covenants comprised in the lease, and an account of the profits made since the renewal.[4]

Note

6–36   The rule applies whether the trustee obtains a renewal by virtue of a provision in the lease to that effect or whether he obtains it by virtue of the advantage which his position as sitting tenant gives him.[5] The principle applies not only to trustees and tenants for life,[6] but also to mortgagees,[7] directors[8] and partners.[9] But unlike trustees and tenants for life the latter group of persons are not irrebuttably precluded from taking the renewal of a lease. In *Re Biss*,[10] a lease formed part of the personalty of an intestate, and after the lessor had refused to renew to the administratrix, one of her sons (helping her run the deceased's business at the premises) obtained a renewal for himself. It was held, however, to be unimpeachable, since he

---

[3] The rule in *Keech v Sandford* is derived from the principle that a trustee must not put himself in a position where his interest conflicts with his duty: in case of conflict, duty prevails over interest. Several instances of this principle occur in the administration of express trusts: at paras 9–08 to 9–38. See also Hart, "The Development of the Rule in *Keech v Sandford*" (1905) 21 L.Q.R. 258; Cretney (1969) 33 Conv.(N.S.) 161.
[4] Also, see *Re Jarvis* [1958] 1 W.L.R. 815.
[5] *Re Knowles' Will Trusts* [1948] 1 All E.R. 866.
[6] *James v Dean* (1808) 15 Ves. 236; *Lloyd-Jones v Clark-Lloyd* [1919] 1 Ch. 424; ss.16, 107 of the Settled Land Act 1925.
[7] *Rushworth's Case* (1676) Freem.Ch. 13; *Leigh v Burnett* (1885) 29 Ch.D. 231.
[8] *G. E. Smith Ltd v Smith* [1952] N.Z.L.R. 470; *Crittenden & Cowler Co. v Cowler*, 72 New York State 701 (1901).
[9] *Featherstonhaugh v Fenwick* (1810) 17 Ves. 298; *cf. Piddock v Burt* [1894] 1 Ch. 343; *John Taylors (a firm) v Masons (a firm)* [2001] EWCA Civ 2106; *Lindsley v Woodfall* [2004] 2 B.C.L.C. 131.
[10] [1903] 2 Ch. 40.

could show affirmatively that he acted bona fide and did not take advantage of the other persons interested. Romer L.J. said,[11] "where the person renewing the lease does not clearly occupy a fiduciary position" he "is only held to be a constructive trustee of the renewed lease if, in respect of the old lease, he occupied some special position and owed, by virtue of that position, a duty towards the other persons interested."

In *Protheroe v Protheroe*[12] the Court of Appeal in a one-page extempore **6–37** judgment of Lord Denning held that under the *Keech v Sandford* principle there was "a long-established rule of equity" that a trustee purchasing the reversion upon a lease held by him *automatically* held the reversion upon the same trusts as the lease. This is unsound as till then such constructive trusts of the reversion were only imposed where the lease was renewable by custom or contract (the purchase thus cutting off the right of renewal) or where the trustee obtained the reversion by virtue of his position *qua* leaseholder (*e.g.* a landlord offering enfranchisement to all his lease-holders).[13] The reason for the distinction is that "whereas in the case of a renewal the trustee is in effect buying a part of the trust property, in the case of a reversion this is not so; it is a separate item altogether."[14] However, *Protheroe* can be justified because purchasers of a reversion fall foul of the strict principles illustrated by *Boardman v Phipps*, para.6–46 especially since the trustee would personally be the landlord of the trust tenancy.

CHAN v ZACHARIA

High Court of Australia (1984) 154 C.L.R. 178 (1984) 53 A.L.R. 417

DEANE J.: "There is a wide variety of formulations of the general principle of **6–38** equity requiring a person in a fiduciary relationship to account for personal benefit or gain. The doctrine is often expressed in the form that a person 'is not allowed to put himself in a position where his interest and duty conflict' (*Bray v Ford*[15]) or 'may conflict' (*Phipps v Boardman*[16]) or that a person is 'not to allow a conflict to arise between duty and interest': *New Zealand Netherlands Society 'Oranje' Inc. v Kuys*.[17] As Sir Frederick Jordan pointed out, however (see *Chapters on Equity*, (6th ed., Stephen) (1947), p.115, reproduced in Jordan, *Select Legal Papers* (1983), p.115), this, read literally, represents 'rather a counsel of prudence than a rule of equity': indeed, even as an unqualified counsel of prudence, it may, in some circumstances, be inappropriate: see, *e.g. Hordem v Hordem*[18]; *Smith v Cock*.[19] The equitable

---

[11] *ibid.* at 61. See *Chan v Zacharia*, at para.6–38.
[12] [1968] 1 W.L.R. 519; followed in *Thompson's Trustee v Heaton* [1974] 1 W.L.R. 605. See (1968) 84 L.Q.R. 309; (1974) 38 Conv.(N.S.) 288; *Metlej v Cavanagh* [1981] 2 N.S.W.L.R. 339 at 348; *Brenner v Rose* [1973] 1 W.L.R. 443 seems erroneous.
[13] *Bevan v Webb* [1905] 1 Ch. 620; *Longton v Wilsby* (1887) 76 L.T. 770; *Randall v Russell* (1817) 3 Mer. 190; *Phillips v Phillips* (1884) 29 Ch.D. 673; *Phipps v Boardman* [1964] 1 W.L.R. 993 at 1009; *Brenner v Rose* [1973] 1 W.L.R. 443 at 448, but *cf. Thompson's Trustee v Heaton* [1974] 1 W.L.R. 605; *Popat v Shonchhatra* [1995] 4 All E.R. 646.
[14] *Phipps v Boardman (ibid.)*; *cf.* different treatment of renewals and reversions for purposes of rule against remoteness: *Woodall v Clifton* [1905] 2 Ch. 257.
[15] [1896] A.C. 44 at 51.
[16] [1967] 2 A.C. 46 at 123.
[17] [1973] 1 W.L.R. 1126 at 1129.
[18] [1910] A.C. 465 at 475.
[19] (1911) 12 C.L.R. 30 at 36 at 37.

principle governing the liability to account is concerned not so much with the mere existence of a conflict between personal interest and fiduciary duty as with the pursuit of personal interest by, for example, actually entering into a transaction or engagement 'in which he has, or can have, a personal interest conflicting . . . with the interests of those whom he is bound to protect' (*per* Lord Cranworth L.C., *Aberdeen Railway Co. v Blaikie Brothers*[20]) or the actual receipt of personal benefit or gain in circumstances where such conflict exists or has existed.

6–39		"The variations between more precise formulations of the principle governing the liability to account are largely the result of the fact that what is conveniently regarded as the one 'fundamental rule' embodies two themes. The first is that which appropriates for the benefit of the person to whom the fiduciary duty is owed any benefit or gain obtained or received by the fiduciary in circumstances where there existed a conflict of personal interest and fiduciary duty or a significant possibility of such conflict: the objective is to preclude the fiduciary from being swayed by considerations of personal interest. The second is that which requires the fiduciary to account for any benefit or gain obtained or received by reason of or by use of his fiduciary position or of opportunity or knowledge resulting from it: the objective is to preclude the fiduciary from actually misusing his position for his personal advantage. Notwithstanding authoritative statements to the effect that the 'use of fiduciary position' doctrine is but an illustration or part of a wider 'conflict of interest and duty' doctrine (see, *e.g. Phipps v Boardman*[21]: *N.Z. Netherlands Society 'Oranje' Inc. v Kuys*,[22] the two themes, while overlapping, are distinct. Neither theme fully comprehends the other and a formulation of the principle by reference to one only of them will be incomplete. Stated comprehensively in terms of the liability to account, the principle of equity is that a person who is under a fiduciary obligation must account to the person to whom the obligation is owed for any benefit or gain (i) which has been obtained or received in circumstances where a conflict-or significant possibility of conflict existed between his fiduciary duty and his personal interest in the pursuit or possible receipt of such a benefit or gain, or (ii) which was obtained or received by use or by reason of his fiduciary position or of opportunity or knowledge resulting from it. Any such benefit or gain is held by the fiduciary as constructive trustee: see *Keith Henry & Co. Pty. Ltd v Stuart Walker & Co. Pty. Ltd*[23] That constructive trust arises from the fact that a personal benefit or gain has been so obtained or received and it is immaterial that there was no absence of good faith or damage to the person to whom the fiduciary obligation was owed. In some, perhaps most, cases, the constructive trust will be consequent upon an actual breach of fiduciary duty: *e.g.* an active pursuit of personal interest in disregard of fiduciary duty or a misuse of fiduciary power for personal gain. In other cases, however, there may be no breach of fiduciary duty unless and until there is an actual failure by the fiduciary to account for the relevant benefit or gain: *e.g.* the receipt of an unsolicited personal payment from a third party as a consequence of what was an honest and conscientious performance of a fiduciary duty. The principle governing the liability to account for a benefit or gain as a constructive trustee is applicable to fiduciaries generally including partners and former partners in relation to their dealings with partnership property and the benefits and opportunities associated therewith or arising therefrom: see *Birtchnell v Equity Trustees*[24]; *Consul Development Pty. Ltd v D.P.C. Estates Pty. Ltd*[25]

---

[20] (1854) 1 Macq. 461.
[21] [1967] 2 A.C. 46 at 123.
[22] [1973] 1 W.L.R. 1126 at 1129.
[23] (1958) 100 C.L.R. 342 at 350.
[24] (1929) 42 C.L.R. 384 at 395–397, 408–409.
[25] (1975) 132 C.L.R. 373 at 394.

"In *Keech v Sandford*[26] Lord King L.C. held that it was a 'rule' that 'should be **6–40** strictly pursued, and not in the least relaxed,' that a trustee of a tenancy who obtains a renewal of the lease for himself holds the interest in the renewed lease as part of the trust estate. Lord King's admonition that the rule should be not in the least relaxed has been largely obeyed in that, in its application to the case of the ordinary trustee, the 'rule' has been accepted as being applicable regardless of whether the original lease was renewable by right or custom or whether the lessor was willing to grant a new lease for the benefit of the trust or whether there would, in the circumstances, be nothing inequitable in the trustee obtaining a renewal of the lease for his own benefit. The rule has been extended, either in its strict or in a modified form, to persons under obligations arising from certain other fiduciary relationships (*e.g.* executor or agent) and to certain other relationships which are not fiduciary but are said to be special (*e.g.* tenants for life and remaindermen: mortgagee and mortgagor). In particular, it has been applied to a member of a partnership in respect of the renewal of a lease which was held on behalf of the partnership: see *Featherstonhaugh v Fenwick*[27]; *Clegg v Edmondson*.[28] It has, in my view correctly, been accepted as being so applicable notwithstanding that the partnership has been dissolved: see *Thompson's Trustee v Heaton*.[29]

"One can point to impressive support both for the view that the rule in *Keech v* **6–41** *Sandford* is an independent doctrine of equity with no more than an 'illusory' link with the general equitable principle governing the liability of a fiduciary to account for personal benefit or gain (see the discussion of both the rule and the general equitable principle in Finn, *Fiduciary Obligations* (1977), Chs 21 and 23) and for the contrary view that that rule is no more than a manifestation of that general principle: see, *e.g., per* Dixon C.J., McTiernan and Fullagar JJ., *Keith Henry & Co. Pty. Ltd v Stuart Walker & Co. Pty. Ltd*[30] and *per* Lord Russell of Killowen, *Regal (Hastings) Ltd v Gulliver*.[31] It would plainly be futile to attempt to reconcile all that has been said in the cases as to the nature and scope of the rule in *Keech v Sandford*. It is preferable to acknowledge the existence of unresolved difficulties and differences about both the precise nature of the rule and its application to persons who are not trustees. Those difficulties and differences are, however, such as to encourage rather than preclude the search in this Court for unity of principle. With all respect to those who have expressed a contrary view, I consider that the rule should not be seen as either a completely independent principle of equity or as a mere manifestation of the general principle governing the liability of a beneficiary to account for personal benefit or gain. The case itself is an illustration of that general principle: indeed, it is one of the cases which established it. The 'rule' in *Keech v Sandford* is, however, a rule concerned with the operation of presumptions in the application of that general principle to particular types of property. 'In the case both of leases renewable by right or custom and of leases not so renewable the renewal is prima facie considered to have been obtained by virtue of the interest' under the prior lease: *per* Parker J., *Griffith v Owen*.[32]

"In its primary application to the renewal of a lease by a trustee, the rule in *Keech* **6–42** *v Sandford*[33]—'depends partly on the nature of leasehold property and partly on' the position of special opportunity which a trustee occupies: see *per* Parker J., *Griffith v*

---

[26] (1726) Sel.Cas.t.King 61 at 62.
[27] (1810) 17 Ves.Jr. 298.
[28] (1857) 8 De G.M. & G. 787 at 807.
[29] [1974] 1 W.L.R. 605.
[30] (1958) 100 C.L.R. 342 at 350.
[31] [1967] 2 A.C. 134(n) at 149–150.
[32] [1907] 1 Ch. 195 at 204.
[33] (1726) Sel.Cas.t.King 61.

Owen,[34] and *per* Collins M.R., *Re Biss*.[35] The effect of the rule in such a case is that there is an irrebuttable presumption (a presumption of law: *per* Collins M.R., *Re Biss*[36]) that the lease was obtained by use of the position of advantage which the trustee enjoyed as the tenant at law, that is to say, by the use by the trustee of his fiduciary position, with the result that he holds the new lease as constructive trustee under the general principle governing the liability of a fiduciary to account for a personal benefit or gain. The presumption which the rule creates in its application to a fiduciary other than a trustee is irrebuttable or rebuttable according to the nature of the powers and obligations of the fiduciary with respect to the leasehold property and the extent to which the interposition of the fiduciary represents, as it were, a barrier between the person to whom the fiduciary duty is owed and the lessor: *cf.* per Collins M.R., *Re Biss*. In the extension, by analogy, of the rule in *Keech v Sandford* to certain 'special' non-fiduciary relationships under which a person is under an obligation to advance or preserve the interests of another, the presumption would appear, at least ordinarily, to be a rebuttable one: see, *per* Romer L.J., *Re Biss*,[37] *cf.* Collins M.R.[38]

6–43   Notwithstanding the difficulties and differences in and between the judgments of Collins M.R. and Romer L.J. in *Re Biss*, there are clear statements in both judgments (with each of which Cozens Hardy L.J. agreed) which support the conclusion that the presumption that a partner holds a renewed lease as constructive trustee—or, as I would enunciate the primary rule in *Keech v Sandford* the presumption that the renewed lease was obtained by use of the partner's fiduciary position—is a rebuttable one. Those statements are consistent with overall authority and should be accepted as correct and applicable both to the case where the renewed lease is obtained by a partner in a subsisting partnership and the case where the renewed lease is obtained by a member of a partnership which has been dissolved but whose assets are in the course of realization: see *Clegg v Fishwick*.[39]

6–44   "Prima facie, the rule in *Keech v Sandford* has a dual operation in the present case: there is an irrebuttable presumption that any rights in respect of a new lease of the Mansfield Park premises were obtained by Dr. Chan by use of his position as a trustee of the previous tenancy and there is a rebuttable presumption of fact that any such rights were obtained by use of his position as a partner in the dissolved partnership whose assets were under receivership and in the course of realization. It follows that Dr. Chan holds and will hold any rights to or under a new lease of the premises as a constructive trustee unless there be some reason for excluding the ordinary application of the general principle.

6–45   "Many of the statements of the general principle requiring a fiduciary to account for a personal benefit or gain are framed in absolute terms—'inflexible,' 'inexorably,' 'however honest and well-intentioned,' 'universal application'—which sound some-what strangely in the ears of the student of equity and which are to be explained by judicial acceptance of the inability of the courts, 'in much the greater number of cases,' to ascertain the precise effect which the existence of a conflict with personal interest has had upon the performance of fiduciary duty: see, *per* Lord Eldon, *Ex parte James*;[44] *per* Rich, Dixon and Evatt JJ., *Furs Ltd v Tomkies*.[45] The principle is

---

[34] [1907] 1 Ch. 195 at 203.
[35] [1903] 2 Ch. 40 at 57.
[36] [1903] 2 Ch. 40 at 55.
[37] [1903] 2 Ch. 40 at 61–67.
[38] [1903] 2 Ch. 40 at 56–57.
[39] (1849) 1 Mac. & G. 294 at 298–299.
[40] (1803) 8 Ves.Jr. 337 at 345.
[41] (1936) 54 C.L.R. 583.

not however completely unqualified. The liability to account as a constructive trustee will not arise where the person under the fiduciary duty has been duly authorized, either by the instrument or agreement creating the fiduciary duty or by the circumstances of his appointment or by the informed and effective assent of the person to whom the obligation is owed, to act in the manner in which he has acted. The right to require an account from the fiduciary may be lost by reason of the operation of other doctrines of equity such as laches and equitable estoppel: see, *e.g. Clegg v Edmondson*.[42] It may still be arguable in this Court that, notwithstanding general statements and perhaps even decisions to the contrary in cases such as *Regal (Hastings) Ltd v Gulliver*[43] and *Phipps v Boardman*,[44] the liability to account for a personal benefit or gain obtained or received by use or by reason of fiduciary position, opportunity or knowledge will not arise in circumstances where it would be unconscientious to assert it or in which, for example, there is no possible conflict between personal interest and fiduciary duty and it is plainly in the interests of the person to whom the fiduciary duty is owed that the fiduciary obtain for himself rights or benefits which he is absolutely precluded from seeking or obtaining for the person to whom the fiduciary duty is owed: *cf. Peso Silver Mines Ltd (N.P.L.) v Cropper*.[45] In that regard, one cannot but be conscious of the danger that the over-enthusiastic and unnecessary statement of broad general principles of equity in terms of inflexibility may destroy the vigour which it is intended to promote in that it will exclude the ordinary interplay of the doctrines of equity and the adjustment of general principles to particular facts and changing circumstances and convert equity into an instrument of hardship and injustice in individual cases: see *Canadian Aero Service Ltd v O'Malley*[46]; Cretney, *loc. cit.*, pp.168 *et seq.*; Oakley, *Constructive Trusts* (1978), pp.57 *et seq.* There is 'no better mode of undermining the sound doctrines of equity than to make unreasonable and inequitable applications of them': *per* Lord Selborne L.C., *Barnes v Addy*."[47]

BOARDMAN v PHIPPS

House of Lords [1967] 2 A.C. 46; [1966] 3 All E.R. 721 (Lords Cohen, Hodson and Guest; Viscount Dilhorne and Lord Upjohn dissenting)

The respondent, Mr. J. A. Phipps, was one of the residuary legatees under the will **6–46** of his father, Mr. C. W. Phipps, who died in 1944. The residuary estate included 8,000 out of 30,000 issued shares in a private company, Lester & Harris Ltd By his will the testator left an annuity to his widow and subject thereto five-eighteenths of his residuary estate to each of his three sons and three-eighteenths to his only daughter. At the end of 1955 the trustees of the will were the testator's widow (who was senile and took no part in the affairs of the trust), his only daughter, Mrs. Noble, and an accountant, Mr. W. Fox. The first appellant, Mr. T. G. Boardman, was at all material times solicitor to the trustees and also to the children of the testator (other than the respondent). The second appellant, Mr. T. E. Phipps, was the younger brother of the respondent and in the transactions which gave rise to this action he was associated with and represented by the first appellant, Mr. Boardman.

---

[42] (1857) 8 De G.M. & G. at 807–810 [44 E.R. at 602].
[43] [1967] 2 A.C. 134.
[44] [1967] 2 A.C. 46.
[45] (1966) 58 D.L.R. (2d) 1 at 8.
[46] (1973) 40 D.L.R. (3d) 371.
[47] (1874) L.R. 9 Ch.App.244 at 251.

6–47   In 1956 Mr. Boardman and Mr. Fox decided that the recent accounts of Lester & Harris Ltd were unsatisfactory and with a view to improving the position the appellants attended the annual general meeting of the company in December 1956 with proxies obtained from two of the trustees, Mrs. Noble and Mr. Fox. They were not satisfied with the answers given at the meeting regarding the state of the company's affairs.

6–48   Shortly after this meeting the appellants decided with the knowledge of Mrs. Noble and Mr. Fox to try to obtain control of Lester & Harris Ltd by themselves making an offer for all the outstanding shares in that company other than the 8,000 held by the trustees. The trustees had no power to invest in the shares of the company without the sanction of the court and Mr. Fox said in evidence that he would not have considered seeking such sanction. The appellants originally offered £2 5s. per share, which they later increased to £3, but by April 1957 they had received acceptances only in respect of 2,925 shares and it was clear that as things then stood they would not go through with their offer. This ended the first phase in the negotiations which ultimately led to the acquisition by the appellants of virtually all the outstanding shares in Lester & Harris Ltd During this phase the appellants attended the annual general meeting as proxies of the two trustees and obtained information from the company as to the prices at which shares had recently changed hands; but they made the offer to purchase on their own behalf.

6–49   The second phase lasted from April 1957 to August 1958. Throughout this period Mr. Boardman carried on negotiations with the chairman of Lester & Harris Ltd with a view to reaching agreement on the division of the assets of that company between the Harris family and the directors on the one hand and the Phipps family on the other. During this phase Mr. Boardman obtained valuable information as to the value of the company's assets and throughout he purported to act on behalf of the trustees. These negotiations proved abortive.

6–50   The third phase began in August 1958 with the suggestion by Mr. Boardman that he and Mr. T. E. Phipps should acquire for themselves the outstanding shares in the company. The widow died in November 1958 and a conditional agreement for the sale of the shares was made on March 10, 1959. On May 26, 1959, the appellants gave notices making the agreements unconditional to buy 14,567 shares held by the chairman of the company and his associates at £4 10s. per share. This, in addition to the earlier agreements to purchase 2,925 shares at £3 each and the purchase of a further 4,494 shares at £4 10s. each, made the appellants holders of 21,986 shares.

6–51   Thereafter the business of the company was reorganised, part of its assets was sold off at considerable profit, and substantial sums of capital, amounting in the aggregate to £5 17s. 6d. per share, were returned to the shareholders, whose shares were still worth at least £2 each after the return of capital. The appellants acted honestly throughout.

6–52   The respondent, like the other members of the Phipps family, was asked by Mr. Boardman whether he objected to the acquisition of control of the company by the appellants for themselves; but Mr. Boardman did not give sufficient information as to the material facts to succeed in the defence of consent on the part of the respondent. At first the respondent expressed his satisfaction but later he became antagonistic and issued a writ claiming (i) that the appellants held five-eighteenths of the above-mentioned 21,986 shares as constructive trustees for him[48] and (ii) an account of the profits made by the appellants out of the said shares. Wilberforce J.

---

[48] The appellants would, of course, have a lien for their outlay on the purchase of the shares.

granted this relief[49] and his decision was affirmed by the Court of Appeal.[50] The appellants appealed to the House of Lords.

LORD COHEN: ". . . As Wilberforce J. said,[51] the mere use of any knowledge or **6–53** opportunity which comes to the trustee or agent in the course of his trusteeship or agency does not necessarily make him liable to account. In the present case had the company been a public company and had the appellants bought the shares on the market, they would not, I think have been accountable. The company, however, is a private company and not only the information but also the opportunity to purchase these shares came to them through the introduction which Mr. Fox gave them to the board of the company and, in the second phase, when the discussions related to the proposed split up of the company's undertaking, it was solely on behalf of the trustees that Mr. Boardman was purporting to negotiate with the board of the company. The question is this: when in the third phase the negotiations turned to the purchase of the shares at £4 10s. a share, were the appellant debarred by their fiduciary position from purchasing on their own behalf the 21,986 shares in the company without the informed consent of the trustees and the beneficiaries?

"Wilberforce J.[52] and, in the Court of Appeal,[53] both Lord Denning M.R. and **6–54** Pearson L.J. based their decision in favour of the respondent on the decision of your Lordships' House in *Regal (Hastings) Ltd v Gulliver*[54] I turn, therefore, to consider that case. Counsel for the respondent relied on a number of passages in the judgments of the learned Lords who heard the appeal, in particular on (i) a passage in the speech of Lord Russell of Killowen where he said.[55] 'The rule of equity which insists on those, who by use of a fiduciary position make a profit, being liable to account for that profit, in no way depends on fraud, or absence of bona fides; or upon such questions or considerations as whether the profit would or should otherwise have gone to the plaintiff, or whether the profiteer was under a duty to obtain the source of the profit for the plaintiff, or whether he took a risk or acted as he did for the benefit of the plaintiff, or whether the plaintiff has in fact been damaged or benefited by his action. The liability arises from the mere fact of a profit having, in the stated circumstances, been made'; (ii) a passage in the speech of Lord Wright where he says[56]: 'That question can be briefly stated to be whether an agent, a director, a trustee or other person in an analogous fiduciary position, when a demand is made upon him by the person to whom he stands in the fiduciary relationship to account for profits acquired by him by reason of his fiduciary position, and by reason of the opportunity and the knowledge, or either, resulting from it, is entitled to defeat the claim upon any ground save that he made profits with the knowledge and assent of the other person. The most usual and typical case of this nature is that of principal and agent. The rule in such cases is compendiously expressed to be that an agent must account for net profits secretly (that is, without the knowledge of his principal) acquired by him in the course of his agency. The authorities show how manifold and various are the applications of the rule. It does not depend on fraud or corruption.' These paragraphs undoubtedly help the respondent but they must be considered in relation to the facts of that case. In that

---

[49] [1964] 1 W.L.R. 993.
[50] [1965] Ch. 992 (Lord Denning M.R., Pearson and Russell L.JJ.).
[51] [1964] 1 W.L.R. 993 at 1011.
[52] *ibid.*
[53] [1965] Ch. 992.
[54] [1942] 1 All E.R. 378.
[55] *ibid.* at 386.
[56] *ibid.* at 392.

case the profit arose through the application by four of the directors of Regal for shares in a subsidiary company which it had been the original intention of the board should be subscribed for by Regal. Regal had not the requisite money available but there was no question of it being *ultra vires* Regal to subscribe for the shares. In the circumstances Lord Russell of Killowen said[57]: 'I have no hesitation in coming to the conclusion, upon the facts of this case, that these shares, when acquired by the directors, were acquired by reason, and only by reason, of the fact that they were directors of Regal, and in the course of their execution of that office.' He went on to consider whether the four directors were in a fiduciary relationship to Regal and concluded that they were. Accordingly, they were held accountable. Counsel for the appellants argued that the present case is distinguishable. He puts his argument thus. The question one asks is whether the information could have been used by the principal for the purpose for which it was used by his agents. If the answer to that question is no, the information was not used in the course of their duty as agents. In the present case the information could never have been used by the trustees for the purpose of purchasing shares in the company; therefore purchase of shares was outside the scope of the appellants' agency and they are not accountable.

6–55   "This is an attractive argument, but it does not seem to me to give due weight to the fact that the appellants obtained both the information which satisfied them that the purchase of the shares would be a good investment and the opportunity of acquiring them as a result of acting for certain purposes on behalf of the trustees. Information is, of course, not property in the strict sense of that word and, as I have already stated, it does not necessarily follow that, because an agent acquired information and opportunity while acting in a fiduciary capacity, he is accountable to his principals for any profit that comes his way as the result of the use he makes of that information and opportunity. His liability to account must depend on the facts of the case. In the present case much of the information came the appellants' way when Mr. Boardman was acting on behalf of the trustees on the instructions of Mr. Fox, and the opportunity of bidding for the shares came because he purported for all purposes except for making the bid to be acting on behalf of the owners of the 8,000 shares in the company. In these circumstances it seems to me that the principle of the *Regal* case applies and that the courts below came to the right conclusion.

6–56   "That is enough to dispose of the case but I would add that an agent is, in my opinion, liable to account for profits which he makes out of the trust property if there is a possibility of conflict between his interest and his duty to his principal. Mr. Boardman and Mr. Tom Phipps were not general agents of the trustees, but they were their agents for certain limited purposes. The information which they had obtained and the opportunity to purchase the 21,986 shares afforded them by their relations with the directors of the company—an opportunity they got as the result of their introduction to the directors by Mr. Fox—were not property in the strict sense but that information and that opportunity they owed to their representing themselves as agents for the holders of the 8,000 shares held by the trustees. In these circumstances they could not, I think, use that information and that opportunity to purchase the shares for themselves if there was any possibility that the trustees might wish to acquire them for the trust. Mr. Boardman was the solicitor whom the trustees were in the habit of consulting if they wanted legal advice. Granted that he would not be bound to advise on any point unless he were consulted, he would still be the person they would consult if they wanted advice. He would clearly have

---

[57] *ibid.* at 387.

advised them that they had no power to invest in shares of the company without the sanction of the court. In the first phase he would also have had to advise on the evidence then available that the court would be unlikely to give such sanction: but the appellants learnt much more during the second phase. It may well be that even in third phase the answer of the court would have been the same but, in my opinion, Mr. Boardman would not have been able to give unprejudiced advice if he had been consulted by the trustees and was at the same time negotiating for the purchase of the shares on behalf of himself and Mr. Tom Phipps. In other words, there was, in my opinion, at the crucial date (March 1959) a possibility of a conflict between his interest and his duty.

"In making these observations I have referred to the fact that Mr. Boardman was **6–57** the solicitor to the trust. Mr. Tom Phipps was only a beneficiary and was not as such debarred from bidding for the shares, but no attempt was made in the courts below to differentiate between them. Had such an attempt been made it would very likely have failed, as Mr. Tom Phipps left the negotiations largely to Mr. Boardman, and it might well be held that, if Mr. Boardman was disqualified from bidding, Mr. Tom Phipps could not be in a better position. Be that as it may, counsel for the appellants rightly did not seek at this stage to distinguish between the two. He did, it is true, say that Mr. Tom Phipps as a beneficiary would be entitled to any information that the trustees obtained. This may be so, but nonetheless I find myself unable to distinguish between the two appellants. They were, I think, in March 1959, in a fiduciary position *vis-à-vis* the trust. That fiduciary position was of such a nature that (as the trust fund was distributable) the appellants could not purchase the shares on their own behalf without the informed consent of the beneficiaries: it is now admitted that they did not obtain that consent. They are therefore, in my opinion, accountable to the respondent for his share of the net profits which they derived from the transaction.

"I desire to repeat that the integrity of the appellants is not in doubt. They acted **6–58** with complete honesty throughout, and the respondent is a fortunate man in that the rigour of equity enables him to participate in the profits which have accrued as the result of the action taken by the appellants in March 1959 in purchasing the shares at their own risk. As the last paragraph of his judgment clearly shows, the trial judge evidently shared this view. He directed an inquiry as to what sum was proper to be allowed to the appellants or either of them in respect of their or his work and skill in obtaining the said shares and the profits in respect thereof. The trial judge concluded by expressing the opinion that payment should be on a liberal scale. With that observation I respectfully agree . . ."

LORD HODSON: ". . . The proposition of law involved in this case is that no person **6–59** standing in a fiduciary position, when a demand is made on him by the person to whom he stands in the fiduciary relationship to account for profits acquired by him by reason of his fiduciary position and by reason of the opportunity and the knowledge, or either, resulting from it, is entitled to defeat the claim on any ground save that he made profits with the knowledge and assent of the other person . . .

". . . it is said on behalf of the appellants that information as such is not **6–60** necessarily property and it is only trust property which is relevant. I agree, but it is nothing to the point to say that in these times corporate trustees, *e.g.* the Public Trustee and others, necessarily acquire a mass of information in their capacity of trustees for a particular trust and cannot be held liable to account if knowledge so acquired enables them to operate to their own advantage, or to that of other trusts. Each case must depend on its own facts, and I dissent from the view that information is of its nature something which is not properly to be described as property. We are aware that what is called 'know-how' in the commercial sense is property which may be very valuable as an asset. I agree with the learned judge[58] and with the Court of Appeal[59] that the confidential information acquired in this case, which was capable of being and was turned to account, can be properly regarded as the property of the trust. It was obtained by Mr. Boardman by reason of the opportunity which he was given as solicitor acting for the trustees in the negotiations with the chairman of the company, as the correspondence demonstrates. The end result was that, out of the special position in which they were standing in the course of the negotiations, the appellants got the opportunity to make a profit and the knowledge that it was there to be made . . .

6–61   "*Regal (Hastings) Ltd v Gulliver* differs from this case mainly in that the directors took up shares and made a profit thereby, it having been originally intended that the company should buy these shares. Here there was no such intention on the part of the trustees. There is no indication that they either had the money or would have been ready to apply to the court for sanction enabling them to do so. On the contrary, Mr. Fox, the active trustee and an accountant who concerned himself with the details of the trust property, was not prepared to agree to the trustees buying the shares and encouraged the appellants to make the purchase. This does not affect the position. As *Keech v Sandford* shows, the inability of the trust to purchase makes no difference to the liability of the appellants, if liability otherwise exists. The distinction on the facts as to intention to purchase shares between this case and *Regal (Hastings) Ltd v Gulliver* is not relevant. The company (Regal) had not the money to apply for the shares on which the profit was made. The directors took the opportunity which they had presented to them to buy the shares with their own money and were held accountable. Mr Fox's refusal as one of the trustees to take any part in the matter on behalf of the trust, so far as he was concerned, can make no difference. Nothing short of fully informed consent, which the learned judge found not to have been obtained, could enable the appellants in the position which they occupied, having taken the opportunity provided by that position, to make a profit for themselves . . .

6–62   "The confidential information which the appellants obtained at a time when Mr. Boardman was admittedly holding himself out as solicitor for the trustees was obtained by him as representing the trustees, the holders of 8,000 shares of Lester & Harris Ltd As Russell L.J. put it:[60] 'The substantial trust shareholding was an asset of which one aspect was its potential use as a means of acquiring knowledge of the company's affairs, or of negotiating allocations of the company's assets, or of inducing other shareholders to part with their shares.' That aspect was part of the trust assets. Whether this aspect is properly to be regarded as part of the trust assets is, in my judgment, immaterial. The appellants obtained knowledge by reason of their fiduciary position, and they cannot escape liability by saying that they were acting for themselves and not as agents of the trustees. Whether or not the trust, or the beneficiaries in their stead, could have taken advantage of the information is immaterial, as the authorities clearly show. No doubt it was but a remote possibility that Mr. Boardman would ever be asked by the trustees to advise on the desirability of an application to the court in order that the trustees might avail themselves of the information obtained. Nevertheless, whenever the possibility of conflict is present between personal interest and the fiduciary position the rule of equity must be applied . . ."

---

[58] [1964] 1 W.L.R. 993 at 1008–1011.
[59] [1965] Ch. 992.
[60] [1965] Ch. 992 at 1031.

Lord Guest: ". . . I take the view that from first to last Mr. Boardman was acting **6–63** in a fiduciary capacity to the trustees. This fiduciary capacity arose in phase 1 and continued into phase 2, which glided into phase 3. In saying this I do not for one moment suggest that there was anything dishonest or underhand in what Mr. Boardman did. He has obtained a clean certificate below and I do not wish to sully it; but the law has a strict regard for principle in ensuring that a person in a fiduciary capacity is not allowed to benefit from any transactions into which he has entered with trust property. If Mr. Boardman was acting on behalf of the trust, then all the information that he obtained in phase 2 became trust property. The weapon which he used to obtain this information was the trust holding; and I see no reason why information and knowledge cannot be trust property . . ."

Lord Upjohn (dissenting): "On the evidence there was never any suggestion at **6–64** any subsequent stage [after 1956] that Mr Fox or any other trustee would ever have contemplated any purchase of further shares . . . In *Aberdeen Railway Co. v Blaikie Bros*[61] Lord Cranworth L.C. said, 'and it is a rule of universal application that no-one having such duties to discharge shall be allowed to enter into engagements in which he has or can have a personal interest conflicting or which possibly may conflict with the interests of those whom he is bound to protect.' The phrase "possibly may conflict" requires consideration. In my view it means that the reasonable man would think that there was a real sensible possibility of conflict; not that you could imagine some situation arising which might, in some conceivable possibility in events not contemplated as real sensible possibilities by any reasonable person, result in a conflict . . . [*Regal (Hastings) Ltd v Gulliver* and *Keech v Sandford* bear no relation to this case.]

"This case, if I may emphasise it again, is one concerned not with trust property **6–65** or with property of which the persons to whom the fiduciary duty was owed were contemplating a purchase but, in contrast to the facts in *Regal*, with property which was not trust property or property which was ever contemplated as the subject-matter of a possible purchase by the trust . . .

"This question whether the appellants were accountable requires a closer analysis **6–66** than it has received in the lower courts.

"This analysis requires detailed consideration:

1. The facts and circumstances must be carefully examined to see whether in fact a purported agent and even a confidential agent is in a fiduciary relationship to his principal. It does not necessarily follow that he is in such a position.
2. Once it is established that there is such a relationship, that relationship must be examined to see what duties are thereby imposed on the agent, to see what is the scope and ambit of the duties charged on him.
3. Having defined the scope of those duties one must see whether he has committed some breach thereof by placing himself within the scope and ambit of those duties in a position where his duty and interest may possibly conflict. It is only at this stage that any question of accountability arises.
4. Finally, having established accountability it only goes so far as to render the agent accountable for profits made within the scope and ambit of his duty.

"Before applying these principles to the facts, however, I shall refer to the **6–67** judgment of Russell L.J. which proceeded on a rather different basis. He said:

---

[61] [1843–60] All E.R. Rep. 249 at 252.

"The substantial trust shareholding was an asset of which one aspect was its potential use as a means of acquiring knowledge of the company's affairs, or of negotiating allocations of the company's assets, or of inducing other share-holders to part with their shares. That aspect was part of the trust assets."

My Lords, I regard that proposition as untenable.

6–68 "In general, information is not property at all. It is normally open to all who have eyes to read and ears to hear. The true test is to determine in what circumstances the information has been acquired. If it has been acquired in such circumstances that it would be a breach of confidence to disclose it to another, then courts of equity will restrain the recipient from communicating it to another. In such cases such confidential information is often and for many years has been described as the property of the donor, the books of authority are full of such references; knowledge of secret processes, 'know-how,' confidential information as to the prospects of a company or of someone's intention or the expected results of some horse race based on stable or other confidential information. But in the end the real truth is that it is not property in any normal sense, but equity will restrain its transmission to another if in breach of some confidential relationship.

6–69 "With all respect to the views of Russell L.J., I protest at the idea that information acquired by trustees in the course of their duties as such is necessarily part of the assets of trust property which cannot be used by the trustees except for the benefit of the trust. Russell L.J. referred to the fact that two out of three of the trustees could have no authority to turn over this aspect of trust property to the appellants except for the benefit of the trust; this I do not understand, for if such information is trust property not all the trustees acting together could do it for they cannot give away trust property.

6–70 "We heard much argument on the impact of the fact that the testator's widow was at all material times incapable of acting in the trust owing to disability. Of course trustees must act all of them and unanimously in matters affecting trust affairs, but they never performed any relevant act on behalf of the trust at all; I quoted Mr. Fox's answer earlier for this reason. At no time after going to the meeting in December 1956, did Mr. Boardman or Tom rely on any express or implied authority or consent of the trustees in relation to trust property. They understood rightly that there was no question of the trustees acquiring any further trust property by purchasing further shares in the company, and it was only in the purchase of other shares that they were interested.

"There is, in my view, and I know of no authority to the contrary, no general rule that information learnt by a trustee during the course of his duties is property of the trust and cannot be used by him. If that were to be the rule it would put the Public Trustee and other corporate trustees out of business and make it difficult for private trustees to be trustees of more than one trust. This would be the greatest possible pity for corporate trustees and others may have much information which they may initially acquire in connection with some particular trust but without prejudice to that trust can make it readily available to other trusts to the great advantage of those other trusts.

6–71 "The real rule is, in my view, that knowledge learnt by a trustee in the course of his duties as such is not in the least property of the trust and in general may be used by him for his own benefit or for the benefit of other trusts unless it is confidential information which is given to him (i) in circumstances which, regardless of his position as a trustee, would make it a breach of confidence for him to communicate to anyone, for it has been given to him expressly or impliedly as confidential; or (ii) in a fiduciary capacity, and its use would place him in a position where his duty and his interest might possibly conflict. Let me give one or two simple examples. A, as trustee of two settlements X and Y holding shares in the same small company, learns facts as trustee of X about the company which are encouraging. In the absence of special circumstances (such, for example, that X wants to buy more shares) I can see nothing whatever which would make it improper for him to tell his co-trustees of Y who feel inclined to sell that he has information that this would be a bad thing to do. Another example: A as trustee of X learns facts that make him and his co-trustees want to sell. Clearly he could not communicate this knowledge to his co-trustees of Y until at all events the holdings of X have been sold for there would be a plain conflict, reflected in the prices that might or might possibly be obtained.

"My Lords, I do not think for one moment that Lord Brougham in *Hamilton v* **6–72** *Wright*,[62] quoted in the speech of my noble and learned friend, Lord Guest, was saying anything to the contrary; one has to look and see whether the knowledge acquired was capable of being used for his own benefit *to injure* the trust (my italics). That test can have no application to the present. There was no possibility of the information being used to injure the trust. The knowledge obtained was used not in connection with trust property but to enhance the value of the trust property by the purchase of other property in which the trustees were not interested . . .

"As a result of the information the appellants acquired, admittedly by reason of **6–73** the trust holding, they found it worthwhile to offer a good deal more for the shares than in phase 1 of chapter 2. I cannot see that in offering to purchase non-trust shares at a higher price they were in breach of any fiduciary relationship in using the information which they had acquired for this purpose. I cannot see that they have, from start to finish, in the circumstances of this case, placed themselves in a position where there was any possibility of a conflict between their duty and interest.

"I have dealt with the problems that arise in this case at considerable length but it **6–74** could, in my opinion, be dealt with quite shortly. In *Barnes v Addy*,[63] Lord Selborne L.C., said:

> "It is equally important to maintain the doctrine of trusts which is established in this court, and not to strain it by unreasonable construction beyond its due and proper limits. There would be no better mode of undermining the sound doctrines of equity than to make unreasonable and inequitable applications of them."

That, in my judgment, is applicable to this case.[64]

"The trustees were not willing to buy more shares in the company. The active **6–75** trustees were very willing that the appellants should do so themselves for the benefit of their large minority holding. The trustees, so to speak, lent their name to the appellants in the course of prolonged and difficult negotiations and, of course, the appellants thereby learnt much which would have otherwise been denied to them. The negotiations were in the end brilliantly successful. How successful Tom was in his reorganisation of the company is apparent to all. They ought to be very grateful.

"In the long run the appellants have bought for themselves with their own money **6–76** shares which the trustees never contemplated buying and they did so in circumstances fully known and approved of by the trustees. To extend the doctrines of

---

[62] (1842) 9 Cl. & Fin. 111.
[63] (1874) 9 Ch.App.244 at 251.
[64] Now see *Queensland Mines v Hudson*, at para.9–28.

equity to make the appellants accountable in such circumstances is, in my judgment, to make unreasonable and inequitable applications of such doctrines."

ATT.-GEN. FOR HONG KONG v REID

[1994] 1 A.C. 324 [1993] 3 W.L.R. 1143 [1994] 1 All E.R. 1 Privy Council (Lords Templeman, Goff, Lowry, Lloyd and Sir Thomas Eichelbaum)

6–77   LORD TEMPLEMAN: "Bribery is an evil practice which threatens the foundations of any civilised society. In particular, bribery of policemen and prosecutors brings the administration of justice into disrepute. Where bribes are accepted by a trustee, servant, agent or other fiduciary, loss and damage are caused to the beneficiaries, master or principal whose interests have been betrayed. The amount of loss or damage resulting from the acceptance of a bribe may or may not be quantifiable. In the present case the amount of harm caused to the administration of justice in Hong Kong by Mr. Reid in return for bribes cannot be quantified.

6–78   "When a bribe is offered and accepted in money or in kind, the money or property constituting the bribe belongs in law to the recipient. Money paid to the false fiduciary belongs to him. The legal estate in freehold property conveyed to the false fiduciary by way of bribe vests in him. Equity however which acts in personam insists that it is unconscionable for a fiduciary to obtain and retain a benefit in breach of duty. The provider of a bribe cannot recover it because he committed a criminal offence when he paid the bribe. The false fiduciary who received the bribe in breach of duty must pay and account for the bribe to the person to whom that duty was owed. In the present case, as soon as Mr. Reid received a bribe in breach of the duties he owed to the Government of Hong Kong, he became a debtor in equity to the Crown for the amount of that bribe. So much is admitted. But, if the bribe consists of property which increases in value or if a cash bribe is invested advantageously, the false fiduciary will receive a benefit from his breach of duty unless he is accountable not only for the original amount or value of the bribe but also for the increased value of the property representing the bribe. As soon as the bribe was received it should have been paid or transferred instanter to the person who suffered from the breach of duty. Equity considered as done that which ought to have been done. As soon as the bribe was received, whether in cash or in kind, the false fiduciary held the bribe on a constructive trust for the person injured. Two objections have been raised to this analysis. First it is said that, if the fiduciary is in equity a debtor to the person injured, he cannot also be a trustee of the bribe. But there is no reason why equity should not provide two remedies, so long as they do not result in double recovery. If the property representing the bribe exceeds the original bribe in value, the fiduciary cannot retain the benefit of the increase in value which he obtained solely as a result of his breach of duty. Secondly, it is said that if the false fiduciary holds property representing the bribe in trust for the person injured, and if the false fiduciary is or becomes insolvent, the unsecured creditors of the false fiduciary will be deprived of their right to share in the proceeds of that property. But the unsecured creditors cannot be in a better position than their debtor. The authorities show that property acquired by a trustee innocently but in breach of trust and the property from time to time representing the same belong in equity to the cestui que trust and not to the trustee personally whether he is solvent or insolvent. Property acquired by a trustee as a result of a criminal breach of trust and the property from time to time representing the same must also belong in equity to his cestui que trust and not to the trustee whether he is solvent or insolvent.

"When a bribe is accepted by a fiduciary in breach of his duty then he holds that **6–79** bribe in trust for the person to whom the duty was owed. If the property representing the bribe decreases in value the fiduciary must pay the difference between that value and the initial amount of the bribe because he should not have accepted the bribe or incurred the risk of loss. If the property increases in value, the fiduciary is not entitled to any surplus in excess of the initial value of the bribe because he is not allowed by any means to make a profit out of a breach of duty . . ."

QUESTION

Tom and Trevor, holding *inter alia* a lease with two years unexpired on trust **6–80** for Brian for life, remainder for Brian's children equally, were trying to sell the lease as they were likely to receive a heavy dilapidations schedule for remedying at the expiry of the lease. They had tried to purchase the freehold reversion for the trust but the landlord had refused. Tom's friend Joe, hearing of their predicament, had relieved the trust of the lease at the proper, but low, market price. Joe happened to play golf regularly with the landlord and after persisting for four months was able to contract to purchase the freehold.

Joe, only having half the purchase price, went to see Tom and suggested **6–81** that Tom put up the other half for he had been a good friend and without him Joe would never have heard of the property and obtained the opportunity to buy the freehold. Tom was only too happy to put up half the purchase price, delighted that Joe was letting him in on the deal rather than merely borrow the money from Tom or a bank. Shortly afterwards Joe and Tom sold the property with vacant possession making £25,000 profit each.

Brian seeks your advice.

II. Specifically Enforceable Contracts of Sale

If two parties enter a specifically enforceable contract to sell land or other **6–82** property,[65] then the vendor will hold the property on constructive trust for the vendor until the contract is completed by conveyance of the property. However, as Mason J. observed in *Chang v Registrar of Titles*[66]:

"there has been controversy as to the time when the trust relationship arises and as to the character of that relationship. Lord Eldon considered that a trust arose on execution of the contract.[67] Plumer M.R. thought that until it is known whether the agreement will be performed the vendor 'is not even in the situation of constructive trustee; he is only a constructive trustee *sub modo*, and providing

---

[65] *Holroyd v Marshall* (1862) 10 H.L.C. 191 at 209, *per* Lord Westbury L.C.; *Dougan v Ley* (1946) 71 C.L.R. 142; *Oughtred v I.R.C.* [1960] A.C. 206; *Neville v Wilson* [1997] Ch. 44.
[66] (1976) 137 C.L.R. 177 at 184. See too *Martin Commercial Fueling Inc. v Virtanen* (1997) 144 D.L.R. (4th) 290, esp. at [8]–[10], *per* Newbury J.A.
[67] *Paine v Meller* (1801) 6 Ves. Jun. 349; *Broome v Monck* [1803–1813] All E.R. Rep. 631 (1805).

nothing happens to prevent it. It may turn out that the title is not good, or the purchaser may be unable to pay.'[66] Lord Hatherley said that the vendor becomes a trustee for the purchaser when the contract is completed, as by payment of the purchase money.[69] Jessel M.R. held that a trust *sub modo* arises on the execution of the contract but that the constructive trust comes into existence when title is made out by the vendor or is accepted by the purchaser.[70]"

In *Jerome v Kelly*, Lord Walker reviewed these authorities and concluded that[71]:

"It would therefore be wrong to treat an uncompleted contract for the sale of land as equivalent to an immediate, irrevocable declaration of trust (or assignment of beneficial interest) in the land. Neither the seller nor the buyer has unqualified beneficial ownership. Beneficial ownership of the land is in a sense split between the seller and buyer on the provisional assumptions that specific performance is available and that the contract will in due course be completed, if necessary by the court ordering specific performance. In the meantime, the seller is entitled to enjoyment of the land or its rental income. The provisional assumptions may be falsified by events, such as rescission of the contract (either under a contractual term or on breach). If the contract proceeds to completion the equitable interest can be viewed as passing to the buyer in stages, as title is made and accepted and the purchase price is paid in full."

6–83   Consistently with this, a vendor who enters a specifically enforceable contract to sell property must "use reasonable care to preserve the property in a reasonable state of preservation, and, so far as may be, as it was when the contract was made", or "take reasonable care that the property is not deteriorated in the interval before completion."[72] This rule may be exploited by a purchaser upon whom a vendor has served a notice to complete[73] making time of the essence of the contract: the purchaser can claim that the notice was invalid because the vendor was not ready, able and willing to complete the contract owing to breach of his equitable duty of preservation.[74] However, if the contract goes off then the vendor cannot be liable to the purchaser for failing to preserve the property.[75]

---

[66] *Wall v Bright* (1820) 1 Jac. & W 494.
[69] *Shaw v Foster* (1872) L.R. 5 H.L. 321.
[70] *Lysaght v Edwards* (1876) 2 Ch.D. 499, accepted in *Rayner v Preston* (1881) 18 Ch.D. 1.
[71] [2004] 1 W.L.R. 1409 at [32].
[72] *Clarke v Ramuz* [1891] 2 Q.B. 456 at 460 and 468; *Davron Estates Ltd v Turnshire* (1983) 133 N.L.J. 937. At law, however, risk passes to the purchaser after exchange of contracts in so far as concerns anything not caused by a breach of the vendor's duties: *Rayner v Preston* (1881) 18 Ch.D. The effect of this decision is to require both the vendor and the purchaser to insure the property, a wasteful outcome that is rightly criticized in M. Thompson, "Must the Purchaser Buy a Charred Ruin?" (1984) 48 Conv. 43, 50–52. Note though, that the parties may provide otherwise by contract: Standard Conditions of Sale, Condition 5.1 (subject to contrary agreement).
[73] Standard Conditions of Sale, Condition 6.6.
[74] Purchasers have taken this point where squatters have managed to break into the property which forms the subject-matter of the contract: so far the cases seem to have been settled without the need to spend days in court arguing whether or not the vendor's precautions were reasonable.
[75] *Plews v Samuel* [1904] 1 Ch. 464; *Ridoul v Fowler* [1904] 1 Ch. 658, [1904] 2 Ch. 93.

The vendor also has the right to protect his own interest prior to **6–84** completion.[76] He can keep the rents and profits until the date fixed for completion,[77] and retain possession of the property until the contract is completed by payment of the purchase price.[78] If he parts with possession to the purchaser before actual completion or even conveys the land he may fall back on his equitable lien over the property to ensure that he is paid.[79] If the vendor in breach of the constructive trust sells the property to a third party, then the purchaser can trace the value inherent in the property into the value inherent in the sale proceeds received by the vendor and assert a proprietary claim to these, subject to accounting to the vendor for the price agreed between them.[80] This will be useful if the contractual claim against the vendor for damages is not worthwhile, *e.g.* if the vendor is bankrupt or has generated a surplus through his dealings with the third party.[81] Note too that a vendor of shares in an unquoted company can use his votes to protect his lien for the price, but he cannot use them for any purpose that might damage the purchaser.[82]

III. ASSIGNMENTS FOR VALUE OF FUTURE PROPERTY

As Swinfen Eady L.J. stated in *Re Lind*[83]: **6–85**

> "An assignment for value of future property actually binds the property itself directly it is acquired—automatically on the happening of the event, and without any future act on the part of the assignor— and does not merely rest in, and amount to, a right in contract, giving rise to an action. The assignor, having received the consideration, becomes in equity on the happening of the event, trustee for the assignee of the property devolving upon or acquired by him, and which he had previously sold and been paid for."

Here a constructive trust arises as a result of the maxim "Equity regards **6–86** as done that which ought to be done."[84] Thus, if A makes a settlement in consideration of marriage under which he covenants to pay to trustees any money inherited from X, then such money is held on constructive trust for the trustees at the moment when A receives it.[85] Similarly, if F, for a consideration received from G, contracts to hold on trust for G any future receipts arising in respect of payments for specified future sales or services,

---

[76] *Shaw v Foster* (1872) L.R. 5 H.L. 321 at 328; *Re Watford Corporation's Contract* [1943] Ch. 82 at 85.
[77] *Cuddon v Tite* (1858) 1 Giff. 395.
[78] *Gedge v Montrose* (1858) 26 Beav. 45; *Phillips v Silvester* (1872) L.R. 8 Ch. 173.
[79] *Nives v Nives* (1880) 15 Ch. D. 649; *Re Birmingham* [1959] Ch. 523; *London & Cheshire Insurance Co. Ltd v Laplagrene* [1971] Ch. 499.
[80] *Bunny Industries Ltd v FSW Enterprises Pty. Ltd* [1982] Qd. R. 712.
[81] *Lake v Bayliss* [1974] 1 W.L.R. 1073.
[82] *Michaels v Harley House (Marylebone) Ltd* [2000] Ch. 104.
[83] [1915] 2 Ch. 354 at 360.
[84] *Palette Shoes Pty. Ltd v Krohn* (1937) 58 C.L.R. 1 at 16; *Associated Alloys Pty. Ltd v ACN 001 452 106 Pty. Ltd* (2000) 202 C.L.R. 588, above at paras 3–39 *et seq.*
[85] *Pullman v Koe* [1913] 1 Ch. 9; *Re Gillott's Settlement* [1934] Ch. 97 at 158–9.

then such payments are immediately subject to the trust when F receives them.[86] In the latter case, it is crucial that G has actually paid the consideration to F.

IV. PURCHASERS' UNDERTAKINGS

6–87 A contractual licence to occupy a house or flat is not an interest in land, and binds the contracting parties alone.[87] However, a purchaser P may undertake to a vendor V that he will take the property positively subject to the rights of a contractual licensee C. After completion of the purchase, C might be able to take advantage of a term for his benefit in V and P's contract under the Contracts (Rights of Third Parties) Act 1999. But if he cannot, then P might try to evict C by claiming that C only has contractual personal rights against V. In *Ashburn Anstalt v Arnold*,[88] the Court of Appeal held that Equity would prevent this by imposing a constructive trust on the property, compelling P to recognise C's rights under the contractual licence. However, as this case also reveals, if V conveys or contracts to convey Blackacre defensively subject to whatever rights C may happen to have, so as to satisfy V's obligation to disclose all possible incumbrances and to protect him against any possible claim by P, then P is not bound by C's rights which are merely personal and not proprietary. In other words, it is essential that P must have agreed to confer a new right on C: he must have "undertaken a new obligation, not otherwise existing, to give effect to the relevant incumbrance or prior interest. If, but only if, he has undertaken such a new obligation will a constructive trust be imposed".[89] This new right may give C the same rights against P as he would have enjoyed against V, had V never sold the land. But it may also protect C even if C had no right against V, *e.g.* because he failed to register his interest,[90] and equally if C's valid right against V was destroyed by the transfer to P.[91]

6–88 The "constructive trust" used by the courts to protect C's interests in cases of this sort is probably not a trust at all. The courts find P's conscience to be personally affected by an obligation to give effect to C's interest, and therefore treat him constructively as though he were a trustee, to the limited extent that is necessary to place him under a personal obligation to C. This does not mean that C acquires an equitable interest in the land, for otherwise his contractual licence would be a valid equitable interest binding the land, as would an unregistered void estate contract.

V. THE RULE IN *PALLANT V MORGAN*

6–89 "If A and B agree that A will acquire some specific property for the joint benefit of A and B on terms yet to be agreed and B in reliance on A's agreement is thereby induced to refrain from attempting to acquire the

---

[86] *Barclays Bank plc v Willowbank International Ltd* [1987] B.C.L.C. 717; *Associated Alloys*, above.
[87] *Ashburn Anstalt v Arnold* [1989] Ch. 1.
[88] *ibid.*
[89] *Lloyd v Dugdale* [2002] 2 P. & C. R. 13 at [52], *per* Sir Christopher Slade.
[90] *Lyus v Prowsa Developments Ltd* [1982] 1 W.L.R. 1044; *Bahr v Nicolay (No.2)* (1988) 62 A.L.J.R. 268 at 288–9, *per* Brennan J.; *IDC Group Ltd v Clark* [1992] 1 E.G.L.R. 187 at 190.
[91] *Melbury Road Properties 1995 Ltd v Kreidi* [1999] 3 E.G.L.R. 10; *Lloyd v Dugdale* [2002] 2 P. & C.R. 13.

property equity ought not to permit A when he acquires the property to insist on retaining the whole benefit for himself to the exclusion of B".[92] The source of this rule is *Pallant v Morgan*[93] where the parties both wished to buy a piece of land that was to be sold at auction. They agreed that the claimant would refrain from bidding in order to keep the price down, and that the defendant would divide the land between them after he had bought it. After the defendant bought the land, they failed to agree on the details of division and so he kept it all for himself. Harman J. held that the agreement was too uncertain to be specifically enforceable, but that the defendant should nonetheless hold the land on trust for himself and the claimant jointly because his bid had been made on the basis of an agreement for division and it would be "tantamount to sanctioning fraud" to allow him to retain all the land for himself.[94]

This decision was given a wide interpretation in *Banner Homes Group plc* **6–90** *v Luff Developments Ltd (No.2)*,[95] where Chadwick L.J. noted that the *Pallant v Morgan* equity is often triggered in cases where the claimant has suffered detriment, but held that a constructive trust can also be imposed where the claimant has suffered no detriment, but the defendant has gained an advantage by acting on the parties' arrangement. This may be the aspect of his Lordship's decision that was considered "quite difficult" by an Australian judge, Bryson J., in *Seyffer v Adamson*,[96] where he added that "what is altogether necessary, however, is that there be some agreement, arrangement or shared understanding about the way in which some interest in land will be acquired or dealt with." Consistently with this, Mummery L.J. held in *London & Regional Investments Ltd v TBI plc*[97] that a constructive trust can be imposed even though the parties have failed to enter a binding contract, but that no trust will be imposed if the parties have positively agreed not to be bound unless and until formal contracts have been exchanged: in cases where the parties have expressly negatived an intention to create legal relations, equity should follow the law in declining to place them under enforceable obligations.

VI. INCOMPLETE TRANSFERS AND THE RULE IN *RE ROSE*

A constructive trust is imposed to give effect to a donor's intentions where **6–91** he has not yet assigned the legal title to property but he has done all that is required of him to achieve this end, so that Equity will regard the intended

---

[92] *Holiday Inns of America Inc. v Broadhead* Ch. D., 19 December 1969, *per* Megarry J., quoted in *Banner Homes Group plc v Luff Developments Ltd (No.2)* [2000] Ch. 372 at 391, *per* Chadwick L.J.
[93] [1953] 1 Ch. 43.
[94] *ibid.* at 48.
[95] [2000] Ch. 372 at 396–9, followed in *Cox v Jones* [2004] EWHC 1486, Ch at [46] *per* Mann J. In both cases, the claimant suffered detriment on the facts.
[96] [2001] N.S.W.S.C. 1132.
[97] [2002] EWCA Civ 355 at [47]-[48]. See too *Thames Cruises Ltd v George Wheeler Launches Ltd* [2003] EWHC 3093 (Ch); *Kilcarne Holdings Ltd v Targetfollow (Birmingham) Ltd* [2004] EWHC 2547 (Ch). *Kinane v Mackie-Conteh* [2005] EWCA Civ 45; *Cobbe v Yeoman's Row Management Ltd* [2005] EWHC 266 (EH); discussed in B. Macfarlane "The Enforcement of Non-Contractual Agreements to Dispose of Interests in Land" (2005) 16 K.L.L.J.

recipient as beneficial owner (*e.g.* in the case of shares or land requiring registration of the intended recipient so that he becomes the new legal owner).[98] Once the constructive trust is imposed, the donor may not retain benefits such as dividends or rents from the property as these belong to the recipient in equity.

VII. MUTUAL WILLS AND SECRET TRUSTS

6–92   As we have seen,[99] under the doctrine of mutual wills the survivor of two testators is forced to observe the contract between them by the imposition of a constructive trust designed to give effect to the contract in favour of a third party. The constructive trust affecting the survivor arises on the death of the predeceasing testator leaving a will in accordance with the contract, so that she complies with her side of the bargain. As we have also seen,[1] in the case of secret trusts a deceased's informally expressed wishes are effectuated where he has made his will or died intestate on the faith of an undertaking by a legatee or the next-of-kin that his wishes would be carried out.

VIII. SHARED HOMES

6–93   Over the past forty years the courts have increasingly had to deal with the problems that can arise when two parties live together, and legal title to their shared home is vested in one party only.[2] If they both contribute, financially or in some other way, to the continuance of their ongoing relationship, and/or to the purchase and/or upkeep of their shared home, then it can be said that they have both enabled the accrual of the value inherent in the property. Hence, if their relationship comes to an end, or if the legal owner charges the property to a third-party lender and then defaults on the loan, the question can arise whether the whole of the value inherent in the property should be attributed to the legal owner, or whether equity should allot a share to the other party. To resolve this question, the courts must decide some complex and politically charged questions[3]: what kinds of contribution, made in the context of what kinds of relationship,

---

[98] *Re Rose* [1952] Ch. 499; *Mascall v Mascall* (1984) 49 P. & C.R. 119; *Corin v Patton* (1990) 169 C.L.R. 450; *Pennington v Waine* [2002] 1 W.L.R. 2075.

[99] See above, paras 2–146 *et seq.*

[1] See above, paras 2–103 *et seq.*

[2] Where legal title is taken in the name of both parties, their respective property rights will often be established by an express written declaration of trust that their lawyers should advise them to provide: *Goodman v Gallant* [1986] Fam. 106. Even where this is not done, there is plenty of scope for their shares to be decided under constructive trust principles, since the fact that the legal title is in their joint names itself reveals a common intention to share the beneficial ownership in some fashion: *Bernard v Josephs* [1982] Ch. 391; *Burns v Burns* [1984] Ch. 317; *Springette v Defoe* [1992] 2 F.L.R. 388.

[3] Various perspectives on these questions are offered by: L. Flynn and A. Lawson, "Gender, Sexuality and the Doctrine of Detrimental Reliance" (1995) 3 *Feminist Legal Studies* 105; A. Bottomley, "Women and Trust(s): Portraying the Family in the Gallery of the Law", in S. Bright and J. Dewar (eds), *Land Law: Themes and Perspectives* (1998); J. Mee, *The Property Rights of Cohabitees* (1998), chap. 1; G. Moffatt, *Trusts Law: Text and Materials*, 3rd ed. (1999), 458–463; J. Miles, "Property Law v Family Law: Resolving the Problems of Family Property" (2003) 23 J.L.S. 624.

and born of what kinds of expectation, should engender an equitable proprietary interest for the other party?

The great majority of cases in this area concern male and female **6–94** cohabitees who have lived together in a heterosexual relationship, legal title to their shared home having been vested in the man. To reflect this fact the parties will be referred to here as M and F, although this usage is inapt when applied to situations where the woman is the legal owner, and situations concerning couples in a homosexual relationship. If M and F are married and a property dispute arises between them on the breakdown of their marriage, then this will be resolved under divorce legislation[4] that does not apply in cases where the parties are unmarried, where equitable principles may come into play.[5] However, if a dispute arises between F and a third party who has taken a charge over the property from M, then F can rely on equitable principles whether or not she and M are married.

If M makes a written declaration of trust of the shared home in F's **6–95** favour which complies with the LPA 1925, s.53(1)(b), or else the parties enter a written contract under which F takes a share of the home, and which complies with the Law of Property (Miscellaneous Provisions) Act 1989, s.2, then F will be entitled to a share of the property under the trust or contract. If this has not been done—and experience indicates that very often it will not have been done, no matter how desirable it might have been for the parties to arrange their affairs more carefully[6]—then F will have to rely on alleging an equitable right under a resulting or common intention constructive trust, or else bring a proprietary estoppel claim.

If F directly contributed to the purchase of the property, or undertook **6–96** with M to contribute a proportion of the purchase price (*e.g.* using money lent on mortgage) then M will hold the legal title on resulting trust for M and F in proportion to their respective contributions or undertakings.[7] Under the resulting trust F obtains only the share she paid for (or undertook to pay for) at the outset, although if she does not fulfil an undertaking then she will have to make an equitable accounting to M in due course, even if her failure is due to her lower earnings caused by the demands of childbirth and childcare. Because of these limitations and because she may not have paid for (or have undertaken to pay for) any part of the initial purchase price, it has become preferable for F to claim instead that M holds the property on a common intention constructive trust with a view to obtaining a larger share; alternatively she may bring a proprietary estoppel claim.

---

[4] For disputes between spouses the Matrimonial Causes Act 1973, s.24 affords the courts plenty of discretion to take into account the wife's home-making and child-raising activities. Substantial contributions to improvements to M's property can enable M's spouse or fiancée to obtain a beneficial interest under the Matrimonial Property and Proceedings Act 1970, s.37.

[5] But see now the Civil Partnership Act 2004, ss.65–68.

[6] As emphasised in *Carlton v Goodman* [2002] 2 F.L.R. 259 at [44], *per* Ward L.J. See too Law Commission, *Sharing Homes: A Discussion Paper* (Law Com No.278, 2002), paras 2.41–2.44.

[7] See paras 5–89 *et seq.*, above.

Common intention constructive trusts

6–97   If F can show that she made a contribution to the accrual of wealth inherent in the shared home, in reliance on a common understanding between the parties that they would share the ownership of the property, then a constructive trust may be imposed on the basis that it would be unconscionable for M to keep the whole property for himself.

(a) Common intention

6–98   The common intention constructive trust requires a *bilateral* understanding between the parties that F should obtain a share of the property. As Lord Diplock stated in *Gissing v Gissing*[8]:

> "the relevant intention of each party is the intention which was reasonably understood by the other party to be manifested by that party's words or conduct notwithstanding that he did not consciously formulate that intention in his own mind or even acted with some different intention which he did not communicate to the other party."

6–99   It is not enough for the parties to have shared an intention to share the *use* of the property: F must show that they commonly intended to share the *ownership* of the property. Thus, in *Lloyd's Bank plc v Rosset*, Lord Bridge considered that[9]:

> "The question [is whether the parties have] entered an agreement, made an arrangement, reached an understanding or formed a common intention that the beneficial interest in the property would be jointly owned. . . . Spouses living in amity will not normally think it necessary to formulate or define their respective interests in property in any precise way. The expectation of parties to every happy marriage is that they will share the practical benefits of occupying the matrimonial home whoever owns it. But this is something quite distinct from sharing the beneficial interest in the property asset which the matrimonial home represents."

6–100   It used to be the case that the parties must also have shared an understanding that F would acquire an interest in the property in exchange for some *quid pro quo*.[10] However, in *Lloyd's Bank plc v Rosset*, Nicholls L.J. held that there is[11]:

> "no reason in principle why, if the parties' common intention is that the wife should have a beneficial interest in the property, and if

---

[8] [1971] A.C. 886, at 906.
[9] [1991] 1 A.C. 107 at 127–8.
[10] *Gissing v Gissing* [1971] A.C. 887 at 905, *per* Lord Diplock; *Austin v Keele* (1987) 61 A.L.J.R. 605 at 610, *per* Lord Oliver.
[11] [1989] Ch. 350 at 381.

thereafter to the knowledge of the husband she acts to her detriment in reliance on that common intention, the wife should not be able to assert an equitable interest against the husband just as much as she could in a case where the common intention was that, by acting in a certain way, she would acquire a beneficial interest. In each case the question is whether, having regard to what has occurred, it would be inequitable to permit the party in whom the legal estate is vested to deny the existence of the beneficial interest which they both intended should exist."

On appeal, Lord Bridge implicitly accepted this, stating that once there is a finding that there was an express common intention for the property to be shared beneficially[12]:

"It will only be necessary for the partner asserting a claim to a beneficial interest against the partner entitled to the legal estate to show that he or she has acted to his or her detriment or significantly altered his or her position in reliance on the agreement in order to give rise to a constructive trust or proprietary estoppel."

(i) Express common intention

A distinction must be made between cases based on evidence capable of establishing an *express agreement* between the parties and cases where there is no such evidence, but where there is evidence of conduct from which the court can *infer the existence of an agreement.* For a court to hold that the parties formed an express common intention, evidence of discussions is required, "however imperfectly remembered and however imprecise their terms may have been".[13] Excuses may suffice for this purpose, so that if M gives F an excuse as to why legal title to the property should be vested in his name alone, this may be interpreted as evidence that they commonly intended the beneficial ownership to be shared, as otherwise there would have been no need for an excuse.[14] A claimant must provide in her statement of claim as much particularity as possible of discussions between the parties, with the result that "the tenderest exchanges of a common law courtship may assume an unforeseen significance many years later when they are brought under equity's microscope and subjected to an analysis under which many thousands of pounds of value may be liable to turn on fine questions as to whether the relevant words were spoken in earnest or in dalliance and with or without representational intent."[15] It does not suffice that each party happened separately to form the same intention because an express common intention means one that is communicated between the parties: it is the external manifestation of intention by one

6–101

---

[12] [1991] 1 A.C. 107 at 132.
[13] *Lloyd's Bank plc v Rosset* [1991] 1 A.C. 107 at 132, *per* Lord Bridge.
[14] *Eves v Eves* [1975] 1 W.L.R. 1338; *Grant v Edwards* [1986] Ch. 638.
[15] *Hammond v Mitchell* [1991] 1 W.L.R. 1127 at 1139, *per* Waite J.

party to the other that is crucial, regardless of uncommunicated private intentions.[16]

(ii) Inferred common intention

6–102   As Lord Bridge stated in *Lloyd's Bank plc v Rosset*,[17] where there is no evidence of express discussions between the parties, however reasonable it might have been for the parties to discuss the matter and reach an arrangement on beneficial ownership, the courts will be thrown back "on the conduct of the parties both as to the basis from which to infer a common intention to share the property beneficially and as the conduct relied on to give rise to a constructive trust." In this situation, his Lordship thought that "direct contributions to the purchase price by the partner who is not the legal owner, whether initially or by payment of mortgage instalments, will readily justify the inference necessary to the creation of a constructive trust." But "it is at least extremely doubtful that anything less will do."

6–103   In the case, M and F decided to buy and renovate a semi-derelict farmhouse, which they purchased for £57,000. The purchase money was provided by the trustees of a family trust who insisted that the property be bought in M's name alone. Without F's knowledge, M mortgaged the property to Lloyds Bank to secure a £15,000 loan with interest. F spent some time supervising the builders doing renovatory works, did some preparatory cleaning work, and did some skilful painting and decorating herself. The House of Lords held that such conduct was insufficient to justify any inference that there was a common intention for her to acquire a beneficial interest in the farmhouse capable of binding the mortgagee. The value of her work in relation to a farmhouse worth about £72,000 was trifling. More significantly, their Lordships considered that[18]:

> "It would seem the most natural thing in the world for any wife, in the absence of her husband abroad, to spend all the time she could spare and to employ any skills she might have, such as the ability to decorate a room, in doing all she could to accelerate progress of the work, quite irrespective of any expectation she might have of enjoying a beneficial interest in the property. The judge's view that some of this work was work 'on which she could not reasonably have been expected to embark unless she was to have an interest in the house' [is] untenable."

Thus, the bank as mortgagee could evict her as well as M in order to be able to sell the property with vacant possession.

6–104   The authorities are clear[19] that domestic stay-at-home contributions to the welfare of the household cannot justify the inference that the parties must have shared an intention that F would obtain a share in the house. In

---

[16] *Springette v Defoe* (1992) 24 H.L.R. 552; *Mollo v Mollo* [2000] W.T.L.R. 227 at 242–243; *Lightfoot v Lightfoot-Brown* [2005] EWCA Civ 201.

[17] [1991] A.C. 107 at 132–3; at para.6–177.

[18] *ibid.* at 131.

[19] *Gissing v Gissing* [1971] A.C. 887; *Burns v Burns* [1984] Ch. 317; *Lloyds Bank plc v Rosset* [1991] 1 A.C. 107, para.6–173.

the courts' view, F's actions in bearing and rearing children, cooking and cleaning, are readily explicable on the basis that she is motivated by love for M and their children and by the desire to live in a pleasant and happy environment.[20] On this view it would be "unnatural", and would therefore require an express agreement between the parties, for F to do such things in the belief that she would thereby acquire a beneficial interest in the home.

What, then, must F have done before the court will be willing to infer the existence of a common intention from her behaviour? Lord Bridge indicated that only two things suffice for this purpose: direct contributions to the purchase money paid for the property at the outset, and direct contributions to the payment of mortgage instalments afterwards.[21] So far as the first of these is concerned, a direct contribution to the purchase money will of course give F an equitable interest under a resulting trust, the amount of her beneficial interest to be calculated by reference to the size of her contribution. However, it has been held in subsequent cases, most particularly in *Oxley v Hiscock*,[22] that F can obtain a larger share by arguing that her contribution to the purchase price was evidence from which the court can infer the existence of a common intention that she should obtain an equal share or fair share, the size of which should be calculated by reviewing the whole course of dealing between M and F relevant to their ownership and occupation of the home and their sharing of its burdens and advantages, *e.g.* contributions to mortgage instalments from pooled funds or indirect contributions. **6–105**

Are indirect contributions to mortgage payments enough in themselves to constitute evidence from which the courts can infer the existence of a common intention: *i.e.* can the courts infer the existence of a common intention from the fact that F has gone out to work and used her earnings to pay a substantial amount of the weekly household expenses, so enabling M to pay all the mortgage instalments, something that he would otherwise have been unable to do if the parties were to go on enjoying the same living standards? Lord Bridge gave a negative answer to this question,[23] but his view was out of line with previous authority to which he did not refer. In *Gissing v Gissing*, Lord Diplock implied that a court could draw the necessary inference where[24]: **6–106**

> "the wife's efforts or her earnings made it possible for the husband to raise the initial loan or the mortgage or [where] the relieving of the

---

[20] *e.g. Coombes v Smith* [1986] 1 W.L.R. 808.

[21] See para.6–102, above. It follows that there are unlikely to be many cases where F will have to argue for an inferred rather than an express common intention, since, as pointed out in *Mollo v Mollo* [2000] W.T.L.R. 227 at 236, "It is difficult in the extreme to conceive of both parties contributing to the purchase price without some form of express discussion sufficient to create an [express] agreement or understanding." But see *e.g. Midland Bank plc v Cooke* [1995] 4 All E.R. 562; and *cf. Lightfoot v Lightfoot-Brown* [2005] EWCA Civ 201 (repayment of mortgage loan).

[22] [2004] 2 F.L.R. 669, para. 6–219, disapproving *Springette v Defoe* (1992) 65 P. & C.R. 1. To like effect are *McHardy v Warren* [1994] 2 F.L.R. 388 (applied in *Halifax B.S. v Brown* (1995) 27 H.L.R. 511 at 518); *Mollo v Mollo* [2000] W.T.L.R. 227; *Midland Bank plc v Cooke* [1995] 4 All E.R. 562.

[23] See text to para.6–102, above.

[24] [1971] A.C. 886 at 910–11.

husband from the expense of buying clothing for [the wife] and for their son was undertaken in order to enable him the better to meet the mortgage instalments or to repay the loan."

Likewise Fox and May L.JJ. indicated in *Burns v Burns*[25] that the courts will infer a common intention from F's substantial financial contributions to household expenses, which are necessary to enable M alone to keep up the mortgage payments without affecting their standard of living. Reviewing these authorities in *Le Foe v Le Foe*,[26] Nicholas Mostyn Q.C. (sitting as a deputy High Court judge) concluded that it was open to him to hold that[27]:

"by virtue of her indirect contributions to the mortgage I am entitled to infer that the parties commonly intended that [F] should have a beneficial interest in the former matrimonial home."

6–107   Finally, the question arises, whether it is open to a court to infer a common intention from evidence of the parties' dealings even though they expressly state in evidence that they had never turned their minds to the question whether F should receive a beneficial interest? In *Midland Bank plc v Cooke*,[28] Waite L.J. considered that he could infer the existence of a common intention in these circumstances,[29] where crucially there was a resulting trust by virtue of a 6.7 per cent contribution to the purchase price, leading the Court of Appeal to use this as an intention spring-board to attribute to the spouses a common intention at the outset that the parties were ultimately to have the specific share as appropriately determined by the whole course of dealings of the spouses with each other. This was out of line with Lord Morris' previous statement in *Pettitt v Pettitt* that[30]:

"In reaching a decision the court does not, and, indeed, cannot find that there was some thought in the mind of a person which was never there at all. The court must find out exactly what was done or what was said and must then reach a conclusion as to what was the legal result. The court does not devise or invent a legal result."

Nevertheless, in *Oxley v Hiscock* para.6–194, the Court of Appeal has accepted the attribution approach where the parties give evidence that they had no intention at the outset but that even so, the claimant contributed to the purchase price. In such cases, the courts will treat the contribution as

---

[25] [1984] Ch. 317 at 328–329, *per* Fox L.J., and at 344, *per* May L.J.
[26] [2001] 2 F.L.R. 970.
[27] *ibid.* at [50]. *Cf.* Law Commission, *Sharing Homes: A Discussion Paper* (Law Com. No.278, 2002), paras 2.107 and 4.26, noting that the law in this area is unclear, and recommending that "an indirect contribution to the mortgage ä should be sufficient to enable the courts to infer that the parties had a common intention that the beneficial entitlement to the home be shared."
[28] [1995] 4 All E.R. 562.
[29] The parties stated that they had been "just happy, I suppose, you know": *ibid.* at 568.
[30] [1970] A.C. 777 at 804. See too Lord Hodson's comments at 810 and Lord Upjohn's comments at 816. The point was reaffirmed by the H.L. in *Gissing v Gissing* [1971] A.C. 886 at 898, *per* Lord Morris, at 900, *per* Viscount Dilhorne, and at 904, *per* Lord Diplock.

indicating an intention that the claimant is to have a share of the home, but not one limited to the proportion represented by the contributed amount: in such circumstances there is held to be an intention that the claimant is to have a fair share in the home as subsequently determined in the light of their life together.

(b) Detrimental reliance

Once a court has found that there is a common intention between the parties, the next question is whether F has acted to her detriment in reliance on the parties' agreement or arrangement in such a way that it would be unconscionable for M to deny F's beneficial interest in the property.[31] In the absence of detriment, no constructive trust will be imposed.[32] To establish detriment, F need not show that her conduct was related to M's acquisition of the property[33]: it is clearly enough for F to have made direct or indirect financial contributions to the acquisition of the property or payment of mortgage instalments,[34] but other types of conduct by F can also suffice, as can be seen from *Eves v Eves*,[35] for example, where the conduct relied on by F was painting the house, breaking up a patio with a sledgehammer, disposing of the rubble, and building a new garden shed.

6–108

In *Hyett v Stanley*,[36] Sir Martin Nourse reaffirmed his own finding in *Grant v Edwards*,[37] that F's conduct "must have been conduct on which [she] could not reasonably have been expected to embark unless she was to have an interest in the house". However, this is difficult to reconcile with Browne-Wilkinson V.-C.'s finding in the latter case that examples of detrimental reliance might include "setting up house together" and "having a baby",[38] and with his further finding that by "analogy" with the rules governing proprietary estoppel claims, the burden of proof should lie on M to show that F's conduct was attributable to mutual love and affection rather than reliance on the parties' common intention.[39]

6–109

(c) Size of F's interest

In the case of an express common intention constructive trust, the court must start by considering whether the parties have agreed what size of F's share should be.[40] For as Peter Gibson L.J. observed in *Clough v Killey*[41]:

6–110

---

[31] *Grant v Edwards* [1986] 1 Ch. 638 at 656, *per* Browne-Wilkinson V.-C; *Lloyds Bank plc v Rosset* [1991] 1 A.C. 107 at 132, *per* Lord Bridge.

[32] *H v M* [2004] 2 F.L.R. 16 at [70].

[33] *Gissing v Gissing* [1971] A.C. 886 at 805, *per* Lord Diplock; *Grant v Edwards* [1986] Ch. 638 at 647, *per* Nourse L.J and at 652, *per* Mustill L.J.; *Lloyds Bank plc v Rosset* [1991] 1 A.C. 107 at 132, *per* Lord Bridge.

[34] *Halifax B.S. v Brown* [1996] 1 F.L.R. 103 at 109, *per* Balcombe L.J.; *Grant v Edwards* [1986] 1 Ch. 638 at 650, *per* Nourse L.J.

[35] [1975] 1 W.L.R. 1338. See too *Lalani v Crump Holdings Ltd* Ch.D. June 18, 2004, at [47]: the acts alleged to give rise to detriment need not be "dealings with the property by way of contributions or by way of improvements [and other] conduct, contributions or sacrifices may suffice".

[36] [2004] 1 F.L.R. 394 at [19]. On the facts, F had acted to her detriment by rendering herself jointly and severally liable for M's debts, the repayment of which was secured by way of mortgage on their shared home.

[37] [1986] 1 Ch. 638 at 648.

[38] *ibid.* at 657.

[39] *ibid.*

[40] *Gissing v Gissing* [1971] A.C. 886 at 908, *per* Lord Diplock; *Grant v Edwards* [1986] Ch. 638 at 655, *per* Browne-Wilkinson V.-C. See too *Chan Pui Chun v Leung Kam Ho* [2003] 1 F.L.R. 23 at [40] and [99].

[41] (1996) 72 P. & C.R. D22.

"it is only common sense that where the parties form a common intention as to the specific shares they are to take, those shares *prima facie* are the shares to which the court will give effect."

Even in this case, however, the court may vary the size of F's entitlement in order to give her a "fair share" if subsequent dealings suggest that this would be appropriate, and in cases where no express agreement about the size of her share has ever been reached, the court must review the whole course of the parties' dealings in order to decide what would be fair. As Nourse L.J. put it in *Stokes v Anderson*[42]:

"all payments made and acts done by the claimant are to be treated as illuminating the common intention as to the extent of the beneficial interest. Once you get to that stage . . . there is no practical alternative to the determination of a fair share. The court must supply the common intention by reference to that which all the material circumstances have shown to be fair."

6–111   Where the parties have agreed that F should receive a particular share—say, half—in exchange for a *quid pro quo*, the courts have assumed that this will then be the size of her share if the *quid pro quo* is provided.[43] However, no court appears to have considered what should happen if F provides some but not all of the *quid pro quo*. Moreover in cases where the parties agree that F should receive a particular share, in exchange for which she need provide no *quid pro quo* at all, the further question arises whether the amount which F receives under a constructive trust should be tailored to reflect the amount of detriment which she has suffered? Should a small amount of detriment win F the same size of interest as a large amount of detriment, assuming that both are sufficient to make it unconscionable for M to deny that she should get anything at all?

6–112   The way forward must be that diffidently suggested by Browne-Wilkinson V.-C. in *Grant v Edwards*,[44] namely, following guidance in the law of proprietary estoppel, for the court to act only to the extent necessary to prevent M from acting unconscionably. Thus, in some cases, instead of the promised half share, F might only obtain a quarter share, or a charge on the property to secure a sum representing the amount of her financial contributions, or a licence to live in the property until this amount is repaid.[45]

(d) Position of third parties

6–113   Where equity confers upon F the interest she would originally have had if M's express trust had been declared in signed writing, so that the imposition of a constructive trust arguably vindicates the express oral

---

[42] [1991] 1 F.L.R. 391, at 400. See too *Midland Bank plc v Cooke* [1995] 4 All E.R. 562; *Drake v Whipp* [1996] 1 F.L.R. 826; *Oxley v Hiscock* [2004] 2 F.L.R. 669, para.6–194.

[43] *Gissing v Gissing* [1971] A.C. 887 at 905 and 908; *Midland Bank Ltd v Dobson* [1986] 1 F.L.R. 171; *Allen v Snyder* [1977] 2 N.S.W.L.R. 685; *Grant v Edwards* [1986] Ch. 638 at 657; *Savill v Goodall* [1993] 1 F.L.R. 755.

[44] [1986] Ch. 638 at 657.

[45] *Re Sharpe* [1980] 1 All E.R. 198 at 202; *Maharaj v Chand* [1986] A.C. 898; *Lim Teng Huan v Ang Jwee Chan* [1992] 1 W.L.R. 113; *Burrows v Sharp* [1989] 23 H.L.R. 82; *cf. Tanner v Tanner* [1975] 1 W.L.R. 1346.

trust,[46] the court's decree is assumed to be retrospective.[47] However, the date of the oral declaration cannot be the relevant date because the trust is then unenforceable.[48] If there is no detrimental reliance by F before M mortgages the home to X it seems that just as M is not subject to an enforceable trust so neither is X, who derives title from M. The priority of X over F crystallises at this stage[49] so as not to be affected if F subsequently acts to her detriment or subsequently persuades M to sign a memorandum evidencing the trust within the Law of Property Act 1925, section 53(1)(b).[50]

What of the case where X acquires a mortgage after F has allegedly acted **6–114** detrimentally and some years later F alleges that she has an interest that binds X? Courts assume without argument[51] that any interest established in due course by F will bind X. It will be submitted that it is correct that F's interest binds X whether on the basis that the court decree retrospectively recognises F's pre-existing proprietary interest or preferably on the same basis that would confer priority on F against X if F's interest arose only on proprietary estoppel principles.

Equitable proprietary estoppels

(a) Unilateral conduct followed by detrimental reliance. A successful **6–115** equitable estoppel claim requires only unilateral conduct by M leading F to believe that she has an interest in the family home, so that she acts to her detriment in reliance thereon and it then becomes unconscionable for M to insist on his strict legal rights.[52]

(b) Size of F's interest and its impact upon third parties. The "minimum **6–116** equity to do justice"[53] to F and prevent M's unconscionable assertion of his strict legal rights depends upon the conduct and relationship of the parties from the date of M's original conduct till the court makes its decree—the likely outcome of F's claim may fluctuate in this period.[54] The court is apparently tailoring the remedy to fit the wrong and is not upholding already-existing rights of a proprietary nature.[55] F cannot insist on having the expected interest: she is a supplicant for the court's discretionary assistance. However, the court tends to award her the promised interest but it may, instead, award her a lesser interest or even merely a sum of

---

[46] See *Allen v Snyder* [1977] 2 N.S.W.L.R. 685, *per* Glass J.A.; C. Harpum (1982) 2 O.J.L.S. 277 at 279.
[47] *Midland Bank v Dobson* [1986] 1 F.L.R. 171; *Lloyds Bank v Rosset* [1989] Ch. 350.
[48] *Gissing v Gissing* [1971] A.C. 887; *Midland Bank v Dobson* [1986] 1 F.L.R. 171.
[49] *cf. London & Cheshire Insurance Co. Ltd v Laplagrene* [1971] Ch. 499.
[50] See T. G. Youdan [1984] Camb. L.J. 306 at 321–322.
[51] See above, n.4 and *Midland Bank plc v Cooke* [1995] 4 All E.R. 562.
[52] See above, at paras 2–30 *et seq.*
[53] *Crabb v Arun D.C.* [1976] Ch. 179 at 198, *per* Scarman L.J. endorsed in *Pascoe v Turner* [1979] 1 W.L.R. 431; *Baker v Baker* (1993) 25 H.L.R. 408; *Waltons Stores (Intestate) Ltd v Maher* (1988) 164 C.L.R. 387; *Commonwealth of Australia v Verwayen* (1990) 170 C.L.R. 394.
[54] *Crabb v Arun D.C.* [1976] Ch. 179; *Williams v Staite* [1979] Ch. 291; *Dodsworth v Dodsworth* (1973) 228 E.G. 1115; *Griffiths v Williams* (1977) 248 E.G. 947; *Sledmore v Dalby* (1996) 72, P. & C.R. 196.
[55] See above paras 2–30 *et seq.* And *cf.* S. Bright and B. MacFarlane "Personal Liability in Proprietary Estoppel' (2005) 69 Conv. 14.

money,[56] to reverse her detrimental reliance, though it may be supported by granting F a licence to occupy the premises till the sum is paid or a charge on the property.

6–117   When the court puts an end to the great uncertainty[57] and the effect of its decree is that M holds the house on constructive trust[58] for F as to an equitable half share or quarter share or an equitable life interest, it seems that this should[59] only have prospective effect normally so that it is a "remedial constructive trust" that arises.[60] Thus, at first sight, if M had sold or mortgaged the house to X after some detrimental reliance of F, X should not be bound by F's rights unless he had agreed with M or F positively to take subject to F's rights so that it would be unconscionable for him to deny her rights on *Ashburn Anstalt v Arnold* principles.[61] However, if F had been in actual occupation and X had inquired, as he obviously ought to do,[62] whether F had any interest under a resulting trust or a constructive trust or protected by her co-occupation under s.70(1)(g) of the Land Registration Act 1925 or Sch.3 of the Land Registration Act 2002, this would have alerted F to what M and X were up to. If she is happy with this, but tells X she has a proprietary estoppel or a constructive or resulting trust claim or interest, then X must obtain her written consent to protect himself and, if the loan is for M's benefit (and not the joint benefit of M and F), take steps to check that her consent is not vitiated by undue influence or fraudulent misrepresentation.[63] If F is unhappy with M's plans to grant X (or other persons in the future) a mortgage with priority over her, she should take steps to have M expressly grant her a prior interest, involving the issue of a writ[64] against M if he refuses: such a writ can seek an injunction restraining him from mortgaging the property and demand that she be appointed co-trustee of the property. Thus she can fully safeguard her interests.

6–118   If X deliberately or recklessly failed to take the elementary conveyancing precaution of asking the occupier, F, whether she claims any interest in the property so that F failed to learn of M's plan and so was divested of her opportunity to take the above precautions to safeguard herself, is it not

---

[56] See As Oliver L.J. stated in *Savva v Costa* [1980] C.A. Transcript 723, Maudsley and Burn, *Land Law Cases & Materials* (5th ed.), p.556, "The expenditure gives rise to an equity to which the court will give effect in such way as may be appropriate in the circumstances giving rise to the estoppel claim. It may be by injunction, it may be by declaring a trust of the beneficial interest or it may be by a declaration of lien for monies expended."

[57] The claim is more uncertain than a mere equity to set aside a deed or rectify a deed where the ultimate court decision is predestined if the case to set aside or rectify is made out.

[58] *Yaxley v Gotts* [2000] Ch. 162, CA, para.6–182.

[59] Lord Browne-Wilkinson in 1991 Holdsworth Lecture "Constructive Trusts and Unjust Enrichment," reprinted in (1996) 10 Trust L.I. 98, though some *obiter dicta, e.g. Voyce v Voyce* (1991) 62 P. & C.R. 290 at 294 and *Campbell v Griffin* [2001] W.T.L.R. 981 at 994 assume that donees or purchasers with notice will be bound by inchoate estoppel interests, though this can be justified not only if the court decree is always retrospective but if retrospective only on grounds of conscience.

[60] *Metall und Rohstoff A.G. v Donaldson Lufkin & Jenrette Inc.* [1990] 1 Q.B. 391 at 479; *Westdeutsche Landesbank v Islington B.C.* [1996] A.C. 669 at 716.

[61] See paras 6–87 *et seq.* and *United Bank of Kuwait plc v Sahib* [1997] Ch. 107 at 142.

[62] *Kingsworth Finance Ltd v Tizard* [1986] 1 W.L.R. 119; *Williams & Glyn's Bank v Boland* [1981] A.C. 487.

[63] *Barclays Bank plc v O'Brien* [1994] 1 A.C. 180; Dixon and Harpum [1994] Conv. 421; S. Cretney [1994] R.L.R. 3.

[64] As a *lis pendens* this can be protected on the register.

clearly unconscionable for X to try to take advantage of his own lapse to claim priority over whatever interest the court decides F to have on proprietary estoppel principles? Surely, X will have to accord priority to F because X's conscience is affected[65] like that of a purchaser taking subject to a contractual licence on *Ashburn Anstalt v Arnold* principles.

The registered land position is now covered by s.116 of the Land Registration Act 2002 which indicates that a proprietary estoppel interest arises from the time of incurring detrimental reliance, which also should be the case for unregistered land once one accepts that the principles of proprietary estoppel and constructive trusts coincide in the acquisition of interests in homes.[66]

The illusory distinction between common intention constructive trusts and equitable estoppels

Consider the following three scenarios.

(1) M says to F, "This house is as much yours as mine, so long as you contribute what you can to household expenses and mortgage payments in the exigencies of our life together." F replies, "Lovely. I agree." **6–119**

(2) M says to F, "This house is as much yours as mine" when asked by her whether she has a share in the house. "I'm glad you agree," she replies.

(3) Proudly carrying F over the threshold of his house, M states, "My darling, this house is as much yours as mine from this day forth." "Oh, thank you. How wonderful!" exclaims F.

It will be seen that (1) is a common intention constructive trust with a *quid* **6–120** *pro quo*, (2) such a trust without a *quid pro quo*, while (3) is a unilateral representation upon which an estoppel claim may be based. However, all three claims hinge upon F's detrimental reliance which makes it unconscionable for M to assert his 100 per cent. formal ownership. One can see that there is not very much difference between the scenarios and that to obtain the best scenario for F there will be a heavy premium upon skilled professional assistance in the preparation of relevant evidence and in encouraging F to say that she acted not out of love and affection but out of an express or tacit understanding or expectation that she had a half share so long as she contributed what cash she could in the exigencies of their life together or so long as she was a good housekeeper.

In scenarios (2) and (3), M is making a unilateral gift of half his **6–121** ownership, so that it is his intention as donor that is the foundation for an estoppel claim, which then requires F to know of that intention, so that in

---

[65] Query whether nowadays (*e.g.* in light of Cooke P. in *Phillips v Phillips* [1993] 3 N.Z.L.R. 159 and 167 and of S. Gardmer in (1993) 109 L.Q.R. 263, 288) it could be successfully argued that M owed a particular fiduciary duty to F in respect of the house, having placed her in a vulnerable position where he had led her to expect that he would at least act in their joint interests (in respect of the legal estate) to the exclusion of his own separate interest. In breach of M's fiduciary duty X received an interest with notice, if not "Nelsonian" or "naughty" knowledge, of such breach so that it would be inequitable or unconscionable if he did not take his interest subject to F's rights as subsequently crystallised by the court.

[66] See paras 2–39 and 2–40 above and para.6–123.

reliance thereon she can act to her detriment and make it unconscionable for M to assert his strict legal rights. It follows that scenario (2) should be treated as an equitable estoppel claim.[67]

6–122　　Even in the case of scenario (1), M is making a unilateral gift, albeit conditionally, so that F knows of the condition and thus of M's intention, so that she can act detrimentally in reliance thereon. Thus in *Yaxley v Gotts*[68] and *Mollo v Mollo*[69] the courts held that express common intention *quid pro quo* constructive trusts co-existed with a proprietary estoppel interest. The key factor is what M leads F reasonably to believe so that she then acts detrimentally in reliance thereon.[70] It is the external manifestation of intention that is crucial, so that M's real intention is irrelevant where he provides an excuse for not putting the home into joint names, so leading F reasonably to believe that she is really to have some interest, though on the face of things this is not to be recorded.[71]

6–123　　Lord Oliver in *Austin v Keele*[72] states of the common intention constructive trust doctrine, "in essence, the doctrine is an application of proprietary estoppel" and Browne-Wilkinson V.-C.[73] and Nicholls[74] and Nourse L.JJ.[75] have accepted that this is so, while Lord Bridge[76] treats "constructive trust or proprietary estoppels" as if they are interchangeable terms. This has led Robert Walker L.J. to state,[77] "in the area of a joint enterprise for the acquisition of land the two concepts coincide." The proprietary estoppel approach affords extra flexibility with a broad approach to behaviour that can amount to detriment.[78] As investigated,[79] it also seems that it can afford proper protection against third parties, while producing a sensible result between the squabbling parties themselves. It is thus submitted that the way ahead is for proprietary estoppel principles (whether or not re-characterised as remedial constructive trusts) to be used to create interests with prospective effect except where it would be unconscionable for a third party to exploit such position. It is time to abandon the distorting use of the institutional constructive trust to do justice in family home situations.

---

[67] *e.g.* facts of *Lloyds Bank plc v Rosset* [1991] 1 A.C. 107.
[68] [2000] Ch. 162.
[69] [2000] W.T.L.R. 227.
[70] *Gissing v Gissing* [1971] A.C. 886 at 906 and *Mollo v Mollo* [2000] W.T.L.R. 227 at 242–243 where the claimant's contributions in money and labour were from the legal houseowner's viewpoint intended to benefit the claimant, who actually intended to benefit their children.
[71] *e.g. Eves v Eves* [1975] 1 W.L.R. 1338, *Grant v Edwards* [1986] Ch. 638.
[72] (1987) ALJR 605 at 609.
[73] *Grant v Edwards* [1986] Ch. 638 and 1991 Holdsworth Lecture, "Constructive Trusts and Unjust Enrichment" reprinted in (1996) 10 Trust L.I. 198.
[74] *Lloyds Bank v Rosset* [1989] Ch. 350.
[75] *Stokes v Anderson* [1991] 1 F.L.R. 391; and 1991 Hong Kong Law Lectures for Practitioners "Unconscionability and the unmarried Couple" discussed by Cooke P. in *Phillips v Phillips* [1993] 1 N.Z.L.R. 159 at 168.
[76] *Lloyds Bank v Rosset* [1991] A.C. 107.
[77] *Yaxley v Gotts* [2000] Ch. 162 at 176, (endorsed in *Banner Homes v Luff Developments Ltd* [2000] 2 All E.R. 126 by C.A.) and in *Birmingham Midshires v Sabherwal* (1999) 80 P. & C.R. 256 at 263. See too *Oxley v Hiscock* [2004] 2 F.L.R. 669 at [66], *per* Chadwick L.J.; para.6–208. But for the view that the two concepts are not yet one, see *Hyett v Stanley* [2004] 1 F.L.R. 394 at [27], *per* Sir Martin Nourse.
[78] "The detriment need not consist of the expenditure of money or other quantifiable financial detriment, so long as it is something substantial. The requirement must be approached as part of a broad inquiry as to whether repudiation of an assurance is or is not unconscionable in all the circumstances": *Gillett v Holt* [2000] 2 All E.R. 289 at 308.
[79] Above, paras 6–119 to 6–122.

Discretionary prevention of unconscionable conduct

Is it not time that the courts and counsel moved beyond pigeon-holing **6–124** circumstances into common intention constructive trusts and equitable estoppels and concentrated upon the basic principle of unconscionability underlying both doctrines? As Browne-Wilkinson V.-C. has pointed out,[80] in a passage endorsed by Robert Walker L.J.,[81] "In both the claimant must to the knowledge of the legal owner have acted in the belief that the claimant has or will have an interest in the property. In both the claimant must have acted to his or her detriment in reliance on such belief. In both equity acts on the conscience of the legal owner to prevent him from acting in an unconscionable manner." As Megarry V.-C. has indicated[82]: "There is today a tendency in equity to put less emphasis on detailed rules and more weight on the underlying principles that engendered those rules, treating the rules less as rules requiring complete compliance and more as guidelines to assist the court in applying the principles." Thus, the High Court of Australia in *Baumgartner v Baumgartner* in dealing with a dispute between M and F where there was insufficient evidence to establish a common intention constructive trust held[83] "the appellant's assertion, after the relationship had failed, that the Leumeah property is his property beneficially to the exclusion of any interest at all on the part of the respondent, amounts to unconscionable conduct which attracts the intervention of equity and the imposition of a constructive trust at the suit of the respondent . . . We consider that the constructive trust to be imposed [prospectively] should declare the beneficial interest of the parties in the proportion 55 per cent to the appellant and 45 per cent to the respondent."

Shortly afterwards, the Australian High Court accepted that the discre- **6–125** tionary prevention of unconscionable conduct underlies not just constructive trust claims but also estoppel claims.[84]

Whether or not M is unconscionably asserting his 100 per cent formal **6–126** ownership and so is unconscionably retaining a benefit at F's expense may be said to turn on an apparently vague standard. For this reason unconscionability factors should not affect third parties as a matter of property law but only if their consciences are affected. As has been seen, the court's decree should not recognise any pre-existing proprietary rights but should prospectively remedy the "wrong" of unconscionable conduct. The broad flexible range of remedies should just affect M and F and to the extent that any remedy confers a proprietary right on F it should not retrospectively affect X, a third party, unless in all the circumstances it would be unconscionable for X to claim priority over F.[85] Thus, the courts should not

---

[80] *Grant v Edwards* [1986] Ch. 638 at 656.
[81] *Yaxley v Gotts* [2000] Ch. 162, 177 and by Chadwick L.J. in *Banner Homes v Luff Developments Ltd* [2000] 2 All E.R. 117 at 126.
[82] *Re Montagu's Settlement* [1987] Ch. 264 at 278. Also see *Ashburn Anstalt v Arnold* [1989] Ch. 1 at 22 and 25.
[83] (1987) 164 C.L.R. 137 at 149. Subsequently, State courts have confined *Baumgartner* to unconscionability arising from financial contributions: see (1997) 113 L.Q.R. 227.
[84] *Waltons Stores (Interstate) Ltd v Maher* (1988) 164 C.L.R. 387.
[85] See above, paras 6–117 to 6–118.

be inhibited by worries about third parties in developing a flexible range of remedies as between cohabitees.

6–127   As between M and F, who have full inside knowledge of all unconscionability factors, it should matter little that there is a grey penumbra of uncertainty for which they have only themselves to blame. There should be an interpretative community of judges and lawyers who can come to a significant consensus on what is unconscionable in particular circumstances in the light of current decided cases on constructive trusts and equitable estoppels and future cases decided on unconscionability principles. Judges and lawyers already cope with whether or not a term in a mortgage[86] or a bargain with a poorly-educated member of the lower income group[87] is "unconscionable", whether it is "unconscionable" to allow a plaintiff amenable to the English jurisdiction to bring a claim against the defendant in a foreign court,[88] and whether or not a landlord is "unreasonably" withholding his consent to an assignment or sublease.[89] Indeed, they also cope with taking a spouse's domestic contributions to family life into account in arranging financial provision on divorce.[90]

6–128   A cohabitee's domestic contributions to the welfare of the family can be taken into account in the rare case where they are the *quid pro quo* of a common intention constructive trust. More commonly, M will state that the home is as much F's as his or, otherwise, lead F to believe that she is to have a fair share in the home, and F may then spend the next 15 years of her life staying at home looking after the home and M and the children they have. The key question after M and F separate is whether F would have done the acts relied upon as a detriment even if she thought she had no interest in the home: if so, she cannot successfully plead that she did the acts in reliance on her belief that she had an interest in the home and so it is not unconscionable to deny her any interest in the home.

6–129   As Browne-Wilkinson V.-C. states[91]:

> "Setting up house together, having a baby, making payments to general housekeeping expenses (not strictly necessary to enable the mortgage to be paid) may all be referable to the mutual love and affection of the parties and not specifically referable to the claimant's belief that she has an interest in the house. As at present advised, once it has been shown that there is a common intention that the claimant should have an interest in the house [or unilateral conduct of the houseowner reasonably leading the claimant to believe she should have an interest in the house],[92] any act done by her to her detriment

---

[86] *Multiservice Bookbinding Ltd v Marden* [1979] Ch. 84.
[87] *Cresswell v Potter* [1978] 1 W.L.R. 255; *Portman B.S. v Dusangh* [2000] Lloyds Rep. Banking 197.
[88] *British Airways Board v Laker Airways Ltd* [1985] A.C. 58. An equity also arises where its would be "unconscionable or inequitable" to allow one party to treat as its own property that had been acquired by it in furtherance of a pre-acquisition non-contractual arrangement with the other party: the acquiring party thereby gaining an advantage cannot act inconsistently with the arrangement, and will hold the property on constructive trust for the other party in accordance with the arrangement: *Banner Homes v Luff Developments Ltd* [2000] 2 All E.R. 117, CA.
[89] *Birkel v Duke of Westminster* [1977] Q.B. 517; *International Drilling Fluids Ltd v Louisville Investments (Uxbridge) Ltd* [1986] 1 All E.R. 321.
[90] Matrimonial Causes Act 1973, ss.23, 24, 25.
[91] *Grant v Edwards* [1986] Ch. 638 at 657. Further see *Wayling v Jones* (1993) 69 P. & C.R. 170 discussed above, para.2–36.
[92] In view of the assimilation of the two concepts: see paras 6–119 *et seq.* above.

relating to the joint lives of the parties is, in my judgment, sufficient detriment to qualify. The acts do not have to be inherently referable to the house . . . The holding out to the claimant that she had a beneficial interest in the house is an act of such a nature as to be part of the inducement to her to do the acts relied on. Accordingly, in the absence of evidence to the contrary, the right inference is that the claimant acted in reliance on such holding out and the burden lies on the legal owner to show that she did not do so: see *Greasley v Cooke*."[93]

The Privy Council and the Court of Appeal[94] have subsequently endorsed **6–130** this approach derived from proprietary estoppel and misrepresentation principles. The implication to be derived from the House of Lords in *Lloyds Bank v Rosset*[95] is that once there is a finding of an express common intention or unilateral intention made known to F by M, then F only needs to show that she acted to her detriment or significantly altered her position in reliance on the intention to establish a constructive trust or a proprietary estoppel.[96] This appears to leave unaffected the presumption that F did so act unless M can prove to the contrary.

If M does not so prove then the court has jurisdiction to grant F **6–131** whatever remedy is necessary to undo M's unconscionable behaviour such remedy usually giving effect to F's expectations rather than simply reversing F's detrimental reliance,[97] *e.g.* give F a half share, a lesser fair share, a licence to reside in the home till the children reach adulthood or until M pays her £X compensation.

Where there is no finding of an express or inferred common intention or **6–132** unilateral intention made known to F by M, then it is not unconscionable for M to assert his 100 per cent. formal ownership of the property. F's domestic conduct was clearly not induced by any beliefs encouraged by M: her domestic services were provided by way of gift out of love and of liking to live in a pleasant family environment.[98] The courts have no jurisdiction to benefit F unless it is conferred by legislation along the lines of the New South Wales De Facto Relationship Act 1984.[99]

By this Act a court can "make such order adjusting the interests of the **6–133** parties in the property as to it seems just and equitable having regard to:

(a) the financial and non-financial contributions made directly or indirectly by or on behalf of the *de facto* partners[1] to the acquisition,

---

[93] [1980] 1 W.L.R. 1306.
[94] *Maharaj v Chand* [1986] A.C. 898; *Lloyds Bank v Rosset* [1989] Ch. 350; *Wayling v Jones* (1993) P. &. C.R. 170 at 173; *Gillett v Holt* [2000] 2 All E.R. 289, 303.
[95] [1991] 1 A.C. 107 at 132.
[96] In *Gillett v Holt* [2000] 2 All E.R. 289, 308 Robert Walker L.J. states, "The detriment need not consist of the expenditure of money or other quantifiable financial detriment, so long as it is something substantial. The requirement must be approached as part of a broad enquiry as to whether repudiation of an assurance is or is not unconscionable in all the circumstances . . . whether the detriment is sufficiently substantial is to be tested by whether it would be unjust or in equitable to be disregarded—the essential test of unconscionability."
[97] See at para.2–38 above.
[98] *e.g. Coombes v Smith* [1986] 1 W.L.R. 808; *Gillies v Keogh* [1991] 2 N.Z.L.R. 327.
[99] For background see (1985) 48 M.L.R. 61.
[1] These are heterosexual partners. The Australian Capital Territory's Domestic Relationships Act 1991 extends to homosexual partners.

conservation or improvement of any of the property of the partners
of either or them; and

(b) the contributions, including any contributions made in the capacity
of homemaker or parent, made by either of the de facto partners to
the welfare of the other de facto partner or to the welfare of the
family constituted by the partners and one of more of the family,
namely (i) a child of the partners; (ii) a child accepted by the
partners or either of them into the household of the partners."

6–134 However, in the absence of such an Act, it may well be that social attitudes
in England may change so as readily to lead to expectations by those within
apparently stable and enduring *de facto* relationships that assets used by the
family, particularly the family home, are ordinarily shared and not the
exclusive property of M or of F unless it is otherwise agreed or made plain.[2]
There will thus be a presumption of a common intention to share
ownership of the family home and F's conduct will be presumed to have
been in reliance upon such intention.

GRANT v EDWARDS

Court of Appeal [1986] Ch. 638; [1986] 3 W.L.R. 114; [1986] 2 All E.R. 426 (Sir
Nicholas Browne-Wilkinson V.-C., Mustill and Nourse L.JJ.)

6–135　　NOURSE L.J.: "In order to decide whether the plaintiff has a beneficial interest in
96, Hewitt Road we must climb again the familiar ground which slopes down from
the twin peaks of *Pettitt v Pettitt* [1970] A.C. 777 and *Gissing v Gissing* [1971] A.C.
886. In a case such as the present, where there has been no written declaration or
agreement, nor any direct provision by the plaintiff of part of the purchase price so
as to give rise to a resulting trust in her favour, she must establish a common
intention between her and the defendant, acted upon by her, that she should have a
beneficial interest in the property. If she can do that, equity will not allow the
defendant to deny that interest and will construct a trust to give effect to it.

6–136　　"I must summarise the crucial facts as found, expressly or impliedly, by the judge.
They are the following. (1) The defendant told the plaintiff that her name was not
going onto the title because it would cause some prejudice in the matrimonial
proceedings between her and her husband. The defendant never had any real
intention of replacing his brother with the plaintiff when those proceedings were at
an end. Just as in *Eves v Eves* [1975] 1 W.L.R. 1338, these facts appear to me to
raise a clear inference that there was an understanding between the plaintiff and the
defendant, or a common intention, that the plaintiff was to have some sort of
proprietary interest in the house; otherwise no excuse for not putting her name onto
the title would have been needed. (2) Except for any instalments under the second
mortgage which may have been paid by the plaintiff as part of the general expenses
of the household, all the instalments under both mortgages were paid by the
defendant. Between February 1970 and October 1974 the total amount paid in

---

[2] As in New Zealand: *Gillies v Keogh* [1989] 2 N.Z.L.R. 327; *Lankon v Rose* [1995] 1 N.Z.L.R. 277. In
Canada, too, F is not presumed to be making a gift of her services: *Herman v Smith* (1984) 34 Alta L.R.
(2nd) 90; *Everson v Rich* (1988) 53 D.L.R. (4th) 470; *Peter v Beblow* (1991) 101 D.L.R. (4th) 621 at
633–634.

respect of the second mortgage was £812 at a rate of about £162 each year. Between 1972 and 1980 the defendant paid off £4,745 under the first mortgage at an average rate of £527 per year. (3) The £6 per week which the defendant admitted that the plaintiff paid to him, at least for a time after they moved into the house, was not paid as rent and must therefore have been paid as a contribution to general expenses. (4) From August 1972 onwards the plaintiff was getting the same sort of wage as the defendant, *i.e.* an annual wage of about £1,200 in 1973, out of which she made a very substantial contribution to the housekeeping and to the feeding and bringing up of the children. From June 1973 onwards she also received £5 a week from her former husband which went towards the maintenance of her two elder sons.

"As stated under (1) above, it is clear that there was a common intention that the **6–137** plaintiff was to have some sort of proprietary interest in 96, Hewitt Road. The more difficult question is whether there was conduct on her part which amounted to an acting upon that intention or, to put it more precisely, conduct on which she could not reasonably have been expected to embark unless she was to have an interest in the house.

"From the above facts and figures it is in my view an inevitable inference that the **6–138** very substantial contribution which the plaintiff made out of her earnings after August 1972 to the housekeeping and to the feeding and to the bringing up of the children enabled the defendant to keep down the instalments payable under both mortgages out of his own income and, moreover, that he could not have done that if he had had to bear the whole of the other expenses as well. For example, in 1973, when he and the plaintiff were earning about £1,200 each, the defendant had to find a total of about £643 between the two mortgages. I do not see how he would have been able to do that had it not been for the plaintiff's very substantial contribution to the other expenses. There is certainly no evidence that there was any money to spare on either side and the natural inference is to the contrary.

"In the circumstances, it seems that it may properly be inferred that the plaintiff **6–139** did make substantial indirect contributions to the instalments payable under both mortgages.

"Was the conduct of the plaintiff in making substantial indirect contributions to **6–140** the instalments payable under both mortgages conduct upon which she could not reasonably have been expected to embark unless she was to have an interest in the house? I answer that question in the affirmative. I cannot see upon what other basis she could reasonably have been expected to give the defendant such substantial assistance in paying off mortgages on his house. I therefore conclude that the plaintiff did act to her detriment on the faith of the common intention between her and the defendant that she was to have some sort of proprietary interest in the house.

"Finally, it is necessary to determine the extent of the plaintiff's beneficial interest **6–141** in 96, Hewitt Road. There is a particular feature of the present case to which we can turn for guidance. That is the crediting of the £1,037 balance of the fire insurance moneys to what the judge found was intended as a joint account. I think that this act of the defendant, when viewed against the background of the initial common intention and the substantial indirect contributions made by the plaintiff to the mortgage repayments from August 1972 onwards, is the best evidence of how the parties intended that the property should be shared. I would therefore hold that the plaintiff is entitled to a half interest in the house.

MUSTILL L.J.: "I agree. For my part, I do not think that the time has yet arrived **6–142** when it is possible to state the law in a way which will deal with all the practical problems which may arise in this difficult field, consistently with everything said in the cases. For present purposes it is unnecessary to attempt this. I believe that the following propositions, material to this appeal, can be extracted from the authorities. (For convenience it is assumed that the 'proprietor'—*viz.* the person who has the legal title—is male, and the 'claimant' who asserts a beneficial interest is female).

6–143   "(1) The law does not recognise a concept of family property, whereby people who live together in a settled relationship *ipso facto* share the rights of ownership in the assets acquired and used for the purposes of their life together. Nor does the law acknowledge that by the mere fact of doing work on the asset of one party to the relationship the other party will acquire a beneficial interest in that asset.

6–144   "(2) The question whether one party to the relationship acquires rights to property the legal title to which is vested in the other party must be answered in terms of the existing law of trusts. There are no special doctrines of equity, applicable in this field alone.

6–145   "(3) In a case such as the present the inquiry must proceed in two stages. First, by considering whether something happened between the parties in the nature of bargain, promise or tacit common intention, at the time of the acquisition. Second, if the answer is 'Yes,' by asking whether the claimant subsequently conducted herself in a manner which was (a) detrimental to herself, and (b) referable to whatever happened on acquisition. (I use the expression 'on acquisition' for simplicity. In fact, the event happening between the parties which, if followed by the relevant type of conduct on the part of the claimant, can lead to the creation of an interest in the claimant, may itself occur after acquisition. The beneficial interests may change in the course of the relationship).

6–146   "(4) For present purposes, the event happening on acquisition may take one of the following shapes. (a) An express bargain whereby the proprietor promises the claimant an interest in the property, in return for an explicit undertaking by the claimant to act in a certain way. (b) An express but incomplete bargain whereby the proprietor promises the claimant an interest in the property, on the basis that the claimant will do something in return. The parties do not themselves make explicit what the claimant is to do. The court therefore has to complete the bargain for them by means of implication, when it comes to decide whether the proprietor's promise has been matched by conduct falling within whatever undertaking the claimant must be taken to have given *sub silentio*. (c) An explicit promise by the proprietor that the claimant will have an interest in the property, unaccompanied by any express or tacit agreement as to a *quid pro quo*. (d) A common intention, not made explicit, to the effect that the claimant will have an interest in the property, if she subsequently acts in a particular way.

6–147   "(5) In order to decide whether the subsequent conduct of the claimant serves to complete the beneficial interest which has been explicitly or tacitly promised to her the court must decide whether the conduct is referable to the bargain, promise or intention. Whether the conduct satisfies this test will depend upon the nature of the conduct, and of the bargain, promise or intention.

6–148   "(6) Thus, if the situation falls into category (a) above, the only question is whether the claimant's conduct is of the type explicitly promised. It is immaterial whether it takes the shape of a contribution to the cost of acquiring the property, or is of a quite different character.

6–149   "(7) The position is the same in relation to situations (b) and (d). No doubt it will often be easier in practice to infer that the *quid pro quo* was intended to take the shape of a financial or other contribution to the cost of acquisition or of improvement, but this need not always be so. Whatever the court decides the *quid pro quo* to have been, it will suffice if the claimant has furnished it.

"(8) In considering whether there was a bargain or common intention, so as to **6–150** bring the case within categories (b) and (d) and, if there was one, what were its terms, the court must look at the true state of affairs on acquisition. It must not impute to the parties a bargain which they never made, or a common intention which they never possessed.

"(9) The conduct of the parties, and in particular of the claimant, after the **6–151** acquisition may provide material from which the court can infer the existence of an explicit bargain, or a common intention, and also the terms of such a bargain or intention. Examining the subsequent conduct of the parties to see whether an inference can be made as to a bargain or intention is quite different from examining the conduct of the claimant to see whether it amounts to compliance with a bargain or intention which has been proved in some other way. (If this distinction is not observed, there is a risk of circularity. If the claimant's conduct is too readily assumed to be explicable only by the existence of a bargain, she will always be able to say that her side of the bargain has been performed.) . . .

"Whatever the defendant's actual intention, the nature of the excuse which he **6–152** gave must have led the plaintiff to believe that she would in the future have her name on the title, and this in turn would justify her in concluding that she had from the outset some kind of right to the house. The case does not fall precisely within either of categories (b), (c) or (d) above, but the defendant's conduct must now preclude him from denying that it is sufficiently analogous to these categories to make the relevant principles apply.

"Assuming therefore that the case must be approached as if the defendant had **6–153** promised the plaintiff some kind of right to the house, or as if they had a common intention to this effect—and I do not think it matters which formula is chosen— what kind of right was this to be? In particular was it to be a right which was to arise only if the plaintiff gave something in exchange; and if so, what was that something to be? These are not easy questions to answer, especially since the judge never approached, or was asked to approach, the matter in this way. Nevertheless I consider it legitimate to hold that there must have been an assumption that the transfer of rights to the plaintiff would not be unilateral, and that the plaintiff would play her own part. Moreover, the situation of the couple was such that the plaintiff's part must have included a direct or indirect contribution to the cost of acquisition: for the defendant could not from his own resources have afforded both to buy their new home and to keep the joint household in existence.

"Finally, there remains the question whether the conduct of the plaintiff can be **6–154** regarded as referable to the bargain or intention thus construed. On the facts as analysed by Nourse L.J. I consider that it can. For the reasons given by Nourse L.J. I agree that the interest should be quantified at 50 per cent."

Sɪʀ Nɪᴄʜᴏʟᴀs Bʀᴏᴡɴᴇ-Wɪʟᴋɪɴsᴏɴ V.-C.: "I agree. In my judgment, there has been **6–155** a tendency over the years to distort the principles as laid down in the speech of Lord Diplock in *Gissing v Gissing* [1971] A.C. 886 by concentrating on only part of his reasoning. For present purposes, his speech can be treated as falling into three sections: the first deals with the nature of the substantive right; the second with the proof of the existence of that right; the third with the quantification of that right.

1. The nature of the substantive right: [1971] A.C. 886, 905ʙ–ɢ

"If the legal estate in the joint home is vested in only one of the parties ('the legal **6–156** owner') the other party ('the claimant'), in order to establish a beneficial interest, has to establish a constructive trust by showing that it would be inequitable for the legal owner to claim sole beneficial ownership. This requires two matters to be demonstrated: (a) that there was a common intention that both should have a beneficial interest; (b) that the claimant has acted to his or her detriment on the basis of that common intention.

2. The proof of the common intention

6–157   "(a) Direct evidence (p.905H). It is clear that mere agreement between the parties that both are to have beneficial interests is sufficient to prove the necessary common intention. Other passages in the speech point to the admissibility and relevance of other possible forms of direct evidence of such intention: see pp.907C and 908C.

6–158   "(b) Inferred common intention (pp.906A–908D). Lord Diplock points out that, even where parties have not used express words to communicate their intention (and therefore there is no direct evidence), the court can infer from their actions an intention that they shall both have an interest in the house. This part of his speech concentrates on the types of evidence from which the courts are most often asked to infer such intention, *viz.* contributions (direct and indirect) to the deposit, the mortgage instalments or general housekeeping expenses. In this section of the speech, he analyses what types of expenditure are capable of constituting evidence of such common intention: he does not say that if the intention is proved in some other way such contributions are essential to establish the trust.

3. The quantification of the right (pp.908D–909)

6–159   "Once it has been established that the parties had a common intention that both should have a beneficial interest *and* that the claimant has acted to his detriment, the question may still remain 'what is the extent of the claimant's beneficial interest?' This last section of Lord Diplock's speech shows that here again the direct and indirect contributions made by the parties to the cost of acquisition may be crucially important.

6–160   "If this analysis is correct, contributions made by the claimant may be relevant for four different purposes, *viz.*: (1) in the absence of direct evidence of intention, as evidence from which the parties' intentions can be inferred; (2) as corroboration of direct evidence of intention; (3) to show that the claimant has acted to his or her detriment in reliance on the common intention: Lord Diplock's speech does not deal directly with the nature of the detriment to be shown; (4) to quantify the extent of the beneficial interest.

6–161   "I have sought to analyse Lord Diplock's speech for two reasons. First, it is clear that the necessary common intention can be proved otherwise than by reference to contributions by the claimant to the cost of acquisition. Secondly, the remarks of Lord Diplock as to the contributions made by the claimant must be read in their context.

6–162   "In cases of this kind the first question must always be whether there is sufficient direct evidence of a common intention that both parties are to have a beneficial interest. Such direct evidence need have nothing to do with the contributions made to the cost of acquisition. Thus in *Eves v Eves* [1975] 1 W.L.R. 1338 the common intention was proved by the fact that the claimant was told that her name would have been on the title deeds but for her being under age. Again, in *Midland Bank Plc. v Dobson* [1986] 1 F.L.R. 171 this court held that the trial judge was entitled to find the necessary common intention from evidence which he accepted that the parties treated the house as 'our house' and had a 'principle of sharing everything.' It is only necessary to have recourse to inferences from other circumstances (such as the way in which the parties contributed, directly or indirectly, to the cost of acquisition) in cases such as *Gissing v Gissing* [1971] A.C. 886 and *Burns v Burns* [1984] Ch. 317 where there is no direct evidence of intention.

"Applying those principles to the present case, the representation made by the defendant to the plaintiff that the house would have been in the joint names but for the plaintiff's matrimonial disputes is clear direct evidence of a common intention that she was to have an interest in the house: *Eves v Eves* [1975] 1 W.L.R. 1338. Such evidence was in my judgment sufficient by itself to establish the common intention: but in any event it is wholly consistent with the contributions made by the plaintiff to the joint household expenses and the fact that the surplus fire insurance moneys were put into a joint account. **6–163**

"But as Lord Diplock's speech in *Gissing v Gissing* [1971] A.C. 886, 905D and the decision in *Midland Bank Plc. v Dobson* make clear, mere common intention by itself is not enough: the claimant has also to prove that she has acted to her detriment in the reasonable belief by so acting she was acquiring a beneficial interest. **6–164**

"There is little guidance in the authorities on constructive trusts as to what is necessary to prove that the claimant so acted to her detriment. What 'link' has to be shown between the common intention and the actions relied on? Does there have to be positive evidence that the claimant did the acts in conscious reliance on the common intention? Does the court have to be satisfied that she would not have done the acts relied on but for the common intention, *e.g.* would not the claimant have contributed to household expenses out of affection for the legal owner and as part of their joint life together even if she had no interest in the house? Do the acts relied on as a detriment have to be inherently referable to the house, *e.g.* contribution to the purchase or physical labour on the house? **6–165**

"I do not think it is necessary to express any concluded view on these questions in order to decide this case. *Eves v Eves* [1975] 1 W.L.R. 1338 indicates that there has to be some 'link' between the common intention and the acts relied on as a detriment. In that case the acts relied on did inherently relate to the house (that is the work the claimant did to the house) and from this the Court of Appeal felt able to infer that the acts were done in reliance on the common intention. So, in this case, as the analysis of Nourse L.J. makes clear, the plaintiff's contributions to the household expenses were essentially linked to the payment of the mortgage instalments by the defendant: without the plaintiff's contributions, the defendant's means were insufficient to keep up the mortgage payments. In my judgment where the claimant has made payments which, whether directly or indirectly, have been used to discharge the mortgage instalments, this is a sufficient link between the detriment suffered by the claimant and the common intention. The court can infer that she would not have made such payments were it not for her belief that she had an interest in the house. On this ground therefore I find that the plaintiff has acted to her detriment in reliance on the common intention that she had a beneficial interest in the house and accordingly that she has established such beneficial interest. **6–166**

"I suggest that in other cases of this kind, useful guidance may in the future be obtained from the principles underlying the law of proprietary estoppel which in my judgment are closely akin to those laid down in *Gissing v Gissing* [1971] A.C. 886. In both, the claimant must to the knowledge of the legal owner have acted in the belief that the claimant has or will obtain an interest in the property. In both, the claimant must have acted to his or her detriment in reliance on such belief. In both, equity acts on the conscience of the legal owner to prevent him from acting in an unconscionable manner by defeating the common intention. The two principles **6–167** have been developed separately without cross-fertilisation between them: but they rest on the same foundation and have on all other matters reached the same conclusions.

6–168   "In many cases of the present sort, it is impossible to say whether or not the claimant would have done the acts relied on as a detriment even if she thought she had no interest in the house. Setting up house together, having a baby, making payments to general housekeeping expenses (not strictly necessary to enable the mortgage to be paid) may all be referable to the mutual love and affection of the parties and not specifically referable to the claimant's belief that she has an interest in the house. As at present advised, once it has been shown that there was a common intention that the claimant should have an interest in the house, any act done by her to her detriment relating to the joint lives of the parties is, in my judgment, sufficient detriment to qualify. The acts do not have to be inherently referable to the house: see *Jones (A.E.) v Jones (F.W.)* [1977] 1 W.L.R. 438 and *Pascoe v Turner* [1979] 1 W.L.R. 431. The holding out to the claimant that she had a beneficial interest in the house is an act of such a nature as to be part of the inducement to her to do the acts relied on. Accordingly, in the absence of evidence to the contrary, the right inference is that the claimant acted in reliance on such holding out and the burden lies on the legal owner to show that she did not do so: see *Greasley v Cooke* [1980] 1 W.L.R. 1306.

6–169   "The possible analogy with proprietary estoppel was raised in argument. However, the point was not fully argued and since the case can be decided without relying on such analogy, it is unsafe for me to rest my judgment on that point. I decide the case on the narrow ground already mentioned.

6–170   "What then is the extent of the plaintiff's interest? It is clear from *Gissing v Gissing* [1971] A.C. 886 that, once the common intention and the actions to the claimant's detriment have been proved from direct or other evidence, in fixing the quantum of the claimant's beneficial interest the court can take into account indirect contributions by the plaintiff such as the plaintiff's contributions to joint household expenses: see *Gissing v Gissing* [1971] A.C. 886 at 909A and D-E. In my judgment, the passage in Lord Diplock's speech at pp.909G–910A is dealing with a case where there is no evidence of the common intention other than contributions to joint expenditure: in such a case there is insufficient evidence to prove any beneficial interest and the question of the extent of that interest cannot arise.

6–171   "Where, as in this case, the existence of some beneficial interest in the claimant has been shown, prima facie the interest of the claimant will be that which the parties intended: *Gissing v Gissing* [1971] A.C. 886 at 908G. In *Eves v Eves* [1975] 1 W.L.R. 1338 at 1345G Brightman L.J. plainly felt that a common intention that there should be a joint interest pointed to the beneficial interests being equal. However, he felt able to find a lesser beneficial interest in that case without explaining the legal basis on which he did so. With diffidence, I suggest that the law of proprietary estoppel may again provide useful guidance. If proprietary estoppel is established, the court gives effect to it by giving effect to the common intention so far as may fairly be done between the parties. For that purpose, equity is displayed at its most flexible: see *Crabb v Arun D.C.* [1976] Ch. 179. Identifiable contributions to the purchase of the house will, of course be an important factor in many cases. But in other cases, contributions by way of labour or other unquantifiable actions of the claimant will also be relevant.

6–172   "Taking into account the fact that the house was intended to be the joint property, the contributions to the common expenditure and the payment of the fire insurance moneys into the joint account, I agree that the plaintiff is entitled to a half interest in the house." *Appeal allowed with costs.*

LLOYDS BANK PLC v ROSSET

House of Lords [1991] 1 A.C. 107; [1990] 2 W.L.R. 867; [1990] 1 All E.R. 1111
    (Lords Bridge, Griffiths, Ackner, Oliver and Jauncey)

LORD BRIDGE (with whose speech the others all simply concurred) after citing the **6–173**
judge's findings on Mrs. Rosset's cleaning, painting and decorating: "It is clear from
these passages in the judgment that the judge based his inference of a common
intention that Mrs. Rossett should have a beneficial interest in the property under a
constructive trust essentially on what Mrs. Rosset did in and about assisting in the
renovation of the property between the beginning of November 1982 and the date
of completion on 17 December 1982. Yet by itself this activity, it seems to me, could
not possibly justify any such inference. It was common ground that Mrs. Rosset was
extremely anxious that the new matrimonial home should be ready for occupation
before Christmas if possible. In these circumstances, it would seem the most natural
thing in the world for any wife, in the absence of her husband abroad, to spend all
the time she could spare and to employ any skills she might have, such as the ability
to decorate a room, in doing all she could to accelerate progress of the work quite
irrespective of any expectation she might have of enjoying a beneficial interest in the
property. The judge's view that some of this work was work 'on which she could not
reasonably have been expected to embark unless she was to have an interest in the
house' seems to me, with respect, quite untenable.

"On any view the monetary value of Mrs. Rosset's work expressed as a **6–174**
contribution to a property acquired at a cost exceeding £70,000 must have been so
trifling as to be almost de minimis. I should myself have had considerable doubt
whether Mrs. Rosset's contribution to the work of renovation was sufficient to
support a claim to a constructive trust in the absence of writing to satisfy the
requirements of s.53 of the Law of Property Act 1925 even if her husband's
intention to make a gift to her of half or any other share in the equity of the
property had been clearly established or if he had clearly represented to her that
that was what he intended. But here the conversations with her husband on which
Mrs. Rosset relied, all of which took place before November 1982, were incapable
of lending support to the conclusion of a constructive trust in the light of the judge's
finding that by that date there had been no decision that she was to have any
interest in the property. The finding that the discussions 'did not exclude the
possibility' that she should have an interest does not seem to me to add anything of
significance.

"These considerations lead me to the conclusion that the judge's finding that Mr. **6–175**
Rosset held the property as constructive trustee for himself and his wife cannot be
supported and it is on this short ground that I would allow the appeal. In the course
of the argument your Lordships had the benefit of elaborate submissions as to the
test to be applied to determine the circumstances in which the sole legal proprietor
of a dwelling house can properly be held to have become a constructive trustee of a
share in the beneficial interest in the house for the benefit of the partner with whom
he or she has cohabited in the house as their shared home. Having in this case
reached a conclusion on the facts which, although at variance with the views of the
courts below, does not seem to depend on any nice legal distinction and with which,
I understand, all your Lordships agree, I cannot help doubting whether it would
contribute anything to the illumination of the law if I were to attempt an elaborate
and exhaustive analysis of the relevant law to add to the many already to be found
in the authorities to which our attention was directed in the course of the argument.
I do, however, draw attention to one critical distinction which any judge required to

resolve a dispute between former partners as to the beneficial interest in the home they formerly shared should always have in the forefront of his mind.

6–176   "The first and fundamental question which must always be resolved is whether, independently of any inference to be drawn from the conduct of the parties in the course of sharing the house as their home and managing their joint affairs, there has at any time prior to acquisition, or exceptionally at some later date, been any agreement, arrangement or understanding reached between them that the property is to be shared beneficially. The finding of an agreement or arrangement to share in this sense can only, I think, be based on evidence of express discussions between the partners, however imperfectly remembered and however imprecise their terms may have been. Once a finding to this effect is made it will only be necessary for the partner asserting a claim to a beneficial interest against the partner entitled to the legal estate to show that he or she has acted to his or her detriment or significantly altered his or her position in reliance on the agreement in order to give rise to a constructive trust or proprietary estoppel.

6–177   "In sharp contrast with this situation is the very different one where there is no evidence to support a finding of an agreement or arrangement to share, however reasonable it might have been for the parties to reach such an arrangement if they had applied their minds to the question, and where the court must rely entirely on the conduct of the parties both as the basis from which to infer a common intention to share the property beneficially and as the conduct relied on to give rise to a constructive trust. In this situation direct contributions to the purchase price by the partner who is not the legal owner, whether initially or by payment of mortgage instalments, will readily justify the inference necessary to the creation of a constructive trust. But, as I read the authorities, it is at least extremely doubtful whether anything less will do.

6–178   "The leading cases in your Lordships' House are *Pettitt v Pettitt* [1970] A.C. 777 and *Gissing v Gissing* [1971] A.C. 886. Both demonstrate situations in the second category to which I have referred and their Lordships discuss at great length the difficulties to which these situations give rise. The effect of these two decisions is very helpfully analysed in the judgment of Lord MacDermott L.C.J. in *McFarlane v McFarlane* [1972] N.I. 59.

6–179   "Outstanding examples on the other hand of cases giving rise to situations in the first category are *Eves v Eves* [1975] 1 W.L.R. 1338 and *Grant v Edwards* [1986] Ch. 638. In both these cases, where the parties who had cohabited were unmarried, the female partner had been clearly led by the male partner to believe, when they set up home together, that the property would belong to them jointly. In *Eves v Eves* the male partner had told the female partner that the only reason why the property was to be acquired in his name alone was because she was under 21 and that, but for her age, he would have had the house put into their joint names. He admitted in evidence that this was simply an 'excuse.' Similarly, in *Grant v Edwards* the female partner was told by the male partner that the only reason for not acquiring the property in joint names was because she was involved in divorce proceedings and that, if the property were acquired jointly, this might operate to her prejudice in those proceedings. As Nourse L.J. put it ([1986] Ch. 638 at 649):

> 'Just as in *Eves v Eves*, these facts appear to me to raise a clear inference that there was an understanding between the plaintiff and the defendant, or a common intention, that the plaintiff was to have some sort of proprietary interest in the house; otherwise no excuse for not putting her name onto the title would have been needed.'

The subsequent conduct of the female partner in each of these cases, which the **6–180** court rightly held sufficient to give rise to a constructive trust or proprietary estoppel supporting her claim to an interest in the property, fell far short of such conduct as would by itself have supported the claim in the absence of an express representation by the male partner that she was to have such an interest. It is significant to note that the share to which the female partners in *Eves v Eves* and *Grant v Edwards* were held entitled were one-quarter and one-half respectively. In no sense could these shares have been regarded as proportionate to what the judge in the instant case described as a "qualifying contribution" in terms of the indirect contributions to the acquisition or enhancement of the value of the houses made by the female partners.

"I cannot help thinking that the judge in the instant case would not have fallen **6–181** into error if he had kept clearly in mind the distinction between the effect of evidence on the one hand which was capable of establishing an express agreement or an express representation that Mrs. Rosset was to have an interest in the property and evidence on the other hand of conduct alone as a basis for an inference of the necessary common intention." *Appeal allowed.*

YAXLEY v GOTTS

Court of Appeal [2000] Ch. 162, [2000] 1 All E.R. 711 (Robert Walker, Clarke, and Beldam L.JJ)

ROBERT WALKER L.J.;

Proprietary estoppel and constructive trusts

"At a high level of generality, there is much common ground between the **6–182** doctrines of proprietary estoppel and the constructive trust, just as there is between proprietary estoppel and part performance. All are concerned with equity's intervention to provide relief against unconscionable conduct, whether as between neighbouring landowners, or vendor and purchaser, or relatives who make informal arrangements for sharing a home, or a fiduciary and the beneficiary or client to whom he owes a fiduciary obligation. The overlap between estoppel and part performance has been thoroughly examined in the defendants' written submissions, with a survey of authorities from *Gregory v Mighell* (1811) 18 Ves 328 to *Take Harvest Ltd v Liu* [1993] A.C. 552.

"The overlap between estoppel and the constructive trust was less fully covered in **6–183** counsel's submissions but seems to me to be of central importance to the determination of this appeal. Plainly there are large areas where the two concepts do not overlap: when a landowner stands by while his neighbour mistakenly builds on the former's land the situation is far removed (except for the element of unconscionable conduct) from that of a fiduciary who derives an improper advantage from his client. But in the area of a joint enterprise for the acquisition of land (which may be, but is not necessarily, the matrimonial home) the two concepts coincide. Lord Diplock's very well-known statement in *Gissing v Gissing* [1971] AC 886 at 905 brings this out:

"A resulting, implied or constructive trust—and it is unnecessary for present **6–184** purposes to distinguish between these three classes of trust—is created by a transaction between the trustee and the cestui que trust in connection with the acquisition by the trustee of a legal estate in land, whenever the trustee has so conducted himself that it would be inequitable to allow him to deny to the cestui que trust a beneficial interest in the land acquired. And he will be held so to have conducted himself if by his words or conduct he has induced the *cestui que trust* to act to his own detriment in the reasonable belief that by so acting he was acquiring a beneficial interest in the land."

6–185   Similarly Lord Bridge said in *Lloyds Bank plc v Rosset* [1991] 1 A.C. 107 at 132:

6–186   "The first and fundamental question which must always be resolved is whether, independently of any inference to be drawn from the conduct of the parties in the course of sharing the house as their home and managing their joint affairs, there has at any time prior to acquisition, or exceptionally at some later date, been any agreement, arrangement or understanding reached between them that the property is to be shared beneficially. The finding of an agreement or arrangement to share in this sense can only, I think, be based on evidence of express discussions between the partners, however imperfectly remembered and however imprecise their terms may have been. Once a finding to this effect is made it will only be necessary for the partner asserting a claim to a beneficial interest against the partner entitled to the legal estate to show that he or she has acted to his or her detriment or significantly altered his or her position in reliance on the agreement in order to give rise to a constructive trust or proprietary estoppel."

6–187   It is unnecessary to trace the vicissitudes in the development of the constructive trust between these two landmark authorities, except to note the important observations made by Browne-Wilkinson V-C in *Grant v Edwards* [1986] Ch 638 at 656, where he said:

"I suggest that, in other cases of this kind, useful guidance may in the future be obtained from the principles underlying the law of proprietary estoppel which in my judgment are closely akin to those laid down in *Gissing v Gissing*. In both, the claimant must to the knowledge of the legal owner have acted in the belief that the claimant has or will obtain an interest in the property. In both, the claimant must have acted to his or her detriment in reliance on such belief. In both, equity acts on the conscience of the legal owner to prevent him from acting in an unconscionable manner by defeating the common intention. The two principles have been developed separately without cross-fertilisation between them; but they rest on the same foundation and have on all other matters reached the same conclusions."

6–188   "In this case the judge did not make any finding as to the existence of a constructive trust. He was not asked to do so, because it was not then seen as an issue in the case. But on the findings of fact which the judge did make it was not disputed that a proprietary estoppel arose, and that the appropriate remedy was the grant to Mr Yaxley, in satisfaction of his equitable entitlement, of a long leasehold interest, rent free, of the ground floor of the property. Those findings do in my judgment equally provide the basis for the conclusion that Mr Yaxley was entitled to such an interest under a constructive trust. The oral bargain which the judge found to have been made between Mr Yaxley and Mr Brownie Gotts, and to have been adopted by Mr Alan Gotts, was definite enough to meet the test stated by Lord Bridge in *Lloyds Bank plc v Rosset* [1991] 1 A.C. 107 at 132.

6–189   "To recapitulate briefly: the species of constructive trust based on "common intention" is established by what Lord Bridge in *Lloyds Bank plc v Rosset* [1991] 1 AC 107 at 132 called an "agreement, arrangement or understanding" actually reached between the parties, and relied on and acted on by the claimant. A constructive trust of that sort is closely akin to, if not indistinguishable from, proprietary estoppel. Equity enforces it because it would be unconscionable for the other party to disregard the claimant's rights. Section 2(5) expressly saves the creation and operation of a constructive trust.

CLARKE LJ. . . .

(2) Constructive trust

"I entirely agree with Robert Walker LJ's analysis under this head. I also agree **6–190** that it follows from the findings of fact made by the judge that the plaintiff was entitled to a long leasehold interest under a constructive trust. I also agree with his construction of s.2(5) of the Law Reform (Miscellaneous Provisions) Act 1989. Since s.2(5) expressly provides that nothing in s.2 affects the creation or operation of a constructive trust, it follows that nothing in s.2(1) prevents the plaintiff from relying upon the constructive trust created by the facts which have been summarised by both Beldam and Robert Walker L.JJ. I agree that the appeal should be dismissed on this basis.

BELDAM LJ. . . .

"For my part I cannot see that there is any reason to qualify the plain words of **6–191** s.2(5). They were included to preserve the equitable remedies to which the Commission had referred. I do not think it inherent in a social policy of simplifying conveyancing by requiring the certainty of a written document that unconscionable conduct or equitable fraud should be allowed to prevail.

"In my view the provision that nothing in s.2 of the 1989 Act is to affect the **6–192** creation or operation of resulting, implied or constructive trusts effectively excludes from the operation of the section cases in which an interest in land might equally well be claimed by relying on constructive trust or proprietary estoppel.

"That, to my mind, is the case here. There was on the judge's findings, as I **6–193** interpret them, a clear promise made by Brownie Gotts to the plaintiff that he would have a beneficial interest in the ground floor of the premises. That promise was known to Alan Gotts when he acquired the property and he permitted the plaintiff to carry out the whole of the work needed to the property and to convert the ground floor in the belief that he had such an interest. It would be unconscionable to allow either Alan or Brownie Gotts to resile from the representations made by Brownie Gotts and adopted by Alan Gotts. For my part I would hold that the plaintiff established facts on which a court of equity would find that Alan Gotts held the property subject to a constructive trust in favour of the plaintiff for an interest in the ground floor and that that interest should be satisfied by the grant of a 99-year lease. I consider the judge was entitled to reach the same conclusion by finding a proprietary estoppel in favour of the plaintiff. I, too, would dismiss the appeal."

Appeal dismissed. Permission to appeal to the House of Lords refused.

OXLEY v HISCOCK

Court of Appeal [2004] 3 W.L.R. 715; [2004] 3 All E.R. 703; [2004] 2 F.L.R. 669 (Chadwick, Mance, and Scott Baker L.JJ.)

Mrs. Oxley, who was divorced from her husband, lived in a council house with her **6–194** children when she formed a relationship with Mr. Hiscock. Between 1985 and 1990, he lived and worked mainly in Kuwait, but he lived with Mrs. Oxley in her house during his visits to England. During this period she exercised her right to buy the council house at a discounted price using funds provided by Mr. Hiscock from the sale of his own house. In 1991 Mr. Hiscock came back to live in England and they bought a new house where they lived together with the children until 2001, when their relationship came to an end. This house cost £127,000. This was funded by the net proceeds of the sale of the council house (of which £25,000 was attributable to Mr. Hiscock's contribution, and £36,300 was attributable to Mrs. Oxley), by £35,500 cash provided by Mr. Hiscock, and by a mortgage loan of £30,000. By the time their relationship ended, the mortgage loan was repaid by roughly equal contributions from each party. Legal title to the house was vested in Mr. Hiscock against the advice of Mrs. Oxley's solicitor that she should protect her interest by joint registration. The parties went their separate ways and the house was sold for £232,000. Mrs. Oxley applied for a declaration under the Trusts of Land and Appointment of Trustees Act 1996, s.14, that the sale proceeds were held on trust for the parties in equal shares.

6–195   The trial judge made a declaration of equal ownership on the basis that the parties had evinced an intention to share the benefit and burden of the property equally, relying on *Midland Bank plc v Cooke*[3] for the proposition that she could and should look to the whole course of the parties' dealings when deciding their common intention with regard to the quantum of Mrs. Oxley's entitlement. Mr. Hiscock appealed, relying on *Springette v Defoe*[4] for the counter-proposition that because there had been no express discussion between the parties as to the extent of their shares at the time of purchase, there was no reason to displace the conclusion that he held the property on a resulting trust in proportions relative to the parties' contributions.

6–196   CHADWICK L.J. (with whom Mance and Scott Baker L.JJ. agreed, summarised the facts and continued): "The principal ground of appeal is that the judge misdirected herself in law in refusing to follow the decision of this court in *Springette v Defoe*. The basis of that decision is accurately summarised in the headnote to the report:

> 'If two or more persons purchased property in their joint names and there was no declaration of trusts on which they were to hold the property, they held the property on a resulting trust for the persons who provided the purchase money in the proportions in which they provided it, unless there was sufficient specific evidence of their common intention that they should be entitled in other proportions, that common intention being a shared intention communicated between them and made manifest at the time of the transaction itself.'

It was said that, in the present case as in *Springette v Defoe*, it was clear, notwithstanding any subjective intention each might have had, that there had been no discussion between the parties as to the extent of their respective beneficial interests at the time of the purchase of 35 Dickens Close. So it must follow that the presumption of resulting trust was not displaced and the property was held for Mr. Hiscock and Mrs. Oxley in beneficial shares proportionate to their contributions.

6–197   "That, it was said, led to the conclusion that Mrs. Oxley's share of the proceeds of sale of 35 Dickens Close was 22% or thereabouts—the proportion which her contribution to the purchase of that property (put by the appellant at £31,699, after

---

[3] [1995] 4 All E.R. 565.
[4] [1992] 2 F.L.R. 388.

deducting the costs of sale and interest on the £25,200 advanced from the proceeds of sale of 39 Page Close) bore to the whole of the acquisition cost (put by the appellant at £141,260, after adding the costs of purchase and improvements).

"There is obvious scope for debate about the figures. The appellant's approach **6–198** treats Mr. Hiscock as having contributed the whole of the monies (£30,000) advanced by the building society—no doubt on the basis that, as the person in whose sole name the property was registered, he was solely responsible for the mortgage debt. But there was no evidence as to how, in fact, the mortgage debt was discharged; and it is (at the least) arguable that, on the judge's findings, the parties should be treated as having contributed equally to the payment of that debt. But, making all assumptions in Mrs. Oxley's favour, the amount of her share (based on financial contributions) could not exceed 40%: (£36,300 + 1/2 £30,000)/£127,000.

"The first question on this appeal, therefore, is whether the judge was required, **6–199** by the decision of this court in *Springette v Defoe* to find that, in the absence of some 'shared intention [as to the proportions in which they should be entitled] communicated between them and made manifest at the time of the transaction itself', the property was held upon a resulting trust for Mr. Hiscock and Mrs. Oxley in beneficial shares proportionate to the respective financial contributions which they had made to the acquisition cost. Or was the judge entitled and required—as she plainly thought—to follow the approach adopted by this court in *Midland Bank plc v Cooke*?

[His Lordship reviewed a line of cases culminating in *Grant v Edwards*,[5] *Lloyds* **6–200** *Bank plc v Rosset*,[6] and *Stokes v Anderson*,[7] and continued:] "*Springette v Defoe* followed some 15 months later. In that case the property was purchased in the joint names of the parties. They had been living there for a short time as joint tenants of the local authority; but they were able to purchase at a substantial discount from the estimated market value because Miss Springette had, herself, been a tenant of the local authority (in another property) for 11 years or more. The property was purchased with the assistance of a building society mortgage—for the repayment of which they were both liable as covenantors. Treating the mortgage monies as provided in equal shares—and giving Miss Springette credit for the whole of the tenant's discount—her contribution to the purchase was 75% or thereabouts. It was common ground that, at the time of acquisition, they were each intended to have some beneficial interest in the property; and it was found as a fact by the trial judge that they never had any discussion at all, at or before the time of the purchase, about what their respective interests were to be. The judge held that the property was owned in equal shares; not on the basis of his finding that, although uncommunicated to each other, that was, in fact, the intention of each at the time, but because (as he put it)[8]:

'It is my judgment that there is sufficient evidence on the facts of inference of common intention or arrangement between the parties that the property should be owned in equal shares.'

"In the light of the judge's findings of fact, it might have been thought that the **6–201** case fell squarely within the first of the two categories of case identified by Lord Bridge in *Lloyds Bank plc v Rosset*.[9] There was a common intention that each should

[5] [1986] Ch. 638; above para.6–135.
[6] [1991] A.C. 107; above para.6–173.
[7] [1991] 1 F.L.R. 391.
[8] [1992] 2 F.L.R. 388 at 392.
[9] [1991] A.C. 107 at 132–3; above at para.6–176.

have some beneficial interest in the property; there was no evidence of express agreement as to what the extent of those interests should be; the court had to ask whether there was sufficient evidence from which a common intention on that latter point could be inferred.[10] That is the question which the judge asked in *Springette v Defoe*; and to which he gave the answer which he did. But the Court of Appeal reached a different conclusion.

6–202   "It is, I think, important to an understanding of the reasoning in the judgments in *Springette v Defoe* that each member of this court seems to have thought that when Lord Bridge referred, in *Lloyds Bank plc v Rosset*,[11] to the need to base a 'finding of an agreement or arrangement to share in this sense' on 'evidence of express discussions between the partners' he was addressing the secondary, or consequential, question 'what was the common intention of the parties as to extent of their respective beneficial interests?' rather than the primary, or threshold, question 'was there a common intention that each should have a beneficial interest in the property?'. That that was the basis of the reasoning in *Springette v Defoe* appears clearly from the judgments of Dillon L.J. and Steyn L.J.[12] The third member of the court, Sir Christopher Slade, agreed with that reasoning.[13]

6–203   ". . . I think that the better view is that, in the passage in *Lloyds Bank plc v Rosset* to which both Dillon and Steyn L.JJ. referred in *Springette v Defoe*, Lord Bridge was addressing only the primary question—'was there a common intention that each should have a beneficial interest in the property?': he was not addressing the secondary question—'what was the common intention of the parties as to extent of their respective beneficial interests?'. As this court had pointed out in *Grant v Edwards* and *Stokes v Anderson*, the court may well have to supply the answer to that secondary question by inference from their subsequent conduct . . . And it may be, as Nourse L.J. observed in *Stokes v Anderson* that 'once you get to that stage . . . there is no practicable alternative to the determination of a fair share. The court must supply the common intention by reference to that which all the material circumstances have shown to be fair'.[14]

6–204   [His Lordship went on to consider *Midland Bank plc v Cooke* citing Waite L.J. [1995] 4 All E.R. 562 at 574, "The general principle to be derived from *Gissing v Gissing* and *Grant v Edwards* can be summarised in this way. When the court is proceeding in cases where the partner without legal title has successfully asserted an equitable interest through direct contribution to determine (in the absence of express evidence of intention) what proportions the parties must be assumed to have intended for their beneficial ownership, the duty of the judge is to undertake a survey of the whole course of dealing between the parties relevant to their ownership and occupation of the property and their sharing of its burdens and advantages. That scrutiny will not confine itself to the limited range of acts of direct contribution of the sort that are needed to found a beneficial interest in the first place. It will take into consideration all conduct which throws light on the question what shares were intended." he then continued:] "I return, therefore, to the first question on this appeal—whether the judge was required by the decision of this court in *Springette v Defoe* to find that, in the absence of some shared intention as to the proportions in which they should be entitled to the property communicated

---

[10] See *Grant v Edwards* [1986] Ch. 638 at 651, 654 and 657; above paras 6–141, 6–153 and 6–171; *Stokes v Anderson* [1991] 1 F.L.R. 391 at 400.
[11] [1991] A.C. 107 at 132.
[12] [1992] 2 F.L.R. 388 at 393 and 395 respectively.
[13] *ibid.* at 397.
[14] [1991] 1 F.L.R. 391 at 400.

between them at the time of the purchase, the property was held upon a resulting trust for Mr. Hiscock and Mrs. Oxley in beneficial shares proportionate to the respective financial contributions which they had made to the acquisition cost. In my view the judge was not so required. For my part, I doubt whether the observations in *Springette v Defoe* upon which the appellant relies did, in truth, reflect the state of the law at the time when that appeal was decided. Be that as it may, they have not done so since the decision of this court in *Midland Bank plc v Cooke*. I reject the submission, insofar as it was pursued in argument, that *Midland Bank plc v Cooke* was wrongly decided. But I think that the law has moved on since that decision.

"The judgments of this court in *Midland Bank plc v Cooke* were handed down in July 1995. Within a few months the familiar question 'what is the interest of one unmarried cohabitee in the house purchased in the name of the other as a home in which they intend to live as husband and wife?' was before this court, again, in *Drake v Whipp*.[15] . . . [There] each party had made a financial contribution to the acquisition of the property. Mrs. Drake had provided £25,000 towards the purchase price of £61,254. The property (which had been a barn) was conveyed into the sole name of Mr. Whipp. There was no declaration of trust. The property required substantial work to convert it to a dwelling. That work cost £129,536; of which Mrs. Drake contributed £13,000. The remainder of the cost of conversion was provided by Mr. Whipp from his own resources. After they had lived together in the property as husband and wife for a few years the relationship came to an end; Mrs. Drake moved out of the property, and commenced proceedings in the county court for a declaration that she and Mr. Whipp were entitled to the property in equal shares or in such shares as the court might think fit. On the basis of their respective financial contributions, the county court judge held that Mrs. Drake was entitled to a share to the extent of 19.4%—that being the proportion which her aggregate contributions (£38,000) bore to the whole cost of acquisition and conversion (£195,790). On appeal Mrs. Drake contended for a share of 40.1%—that being the proportion which her contribution to the purchase price (£25,000) bore to the cost of acquisition (£61,250). The Court of Appeal held that a 'fair share' would be one third; and varied the county court order accordingly. It is material, in the context of the present appeal, to analyse the reasoning which led the court to that conclusion.

6–205

". . . [The Court of Appeal] in *Drake v Whipp* was in no doubt that it had been the common understanding and intention of the parties, at the time that the property was acquired, that each should have some beneficial interest. In those circumstances—notwithstanding a concession by counsel for Mrs. Drake that there had been no common intention—the court held that 'it would be artificial in the extreme to proceed to decide this appeal on the false footing that the parties' shares are to be determined in accordance with the law on resulting trusts'.[16] The case was plainly one of a constructive trust. So it was to be approached on the basis explained by this court in *Grant v Edwards*. . . . Peter Gibson L.J. went on to say this[17]:

6–206

'In the present case the judge has found what was the common intention of the parties as to their beneficial shares, but the only direct evidence in support of that finding was Mr. Whipp's evidence as to his own intention. The judge appears to have imputed the like intention to Mrs. Drake although there is nothing in her evidence to support it. Further, the judge refused to take into

---

[15] [1996] 1 F.L.R. 826.
[16] *ibid.* at 830.
[17] *ibid.* at 831.

account the contributions of the parties by way of their labour, being unquantified in monetary terms, and similarly Mrs. Drake's other contributions to the household were ignored. No doubt this was because he was not invited to consider the matter on the basis of a constructive trust.

'In my judgment the judge's finding on common intention cannot stand in the absence of any evidence that Mrs. Drake intended her share to be limited to her direct contributions to the acquisition and conversion costs. I would approach the matter more broadly, looking at the parties' entire course of conduct together. I would take into account not only those direct contributions but also the fact that Mr. Whipp and Mrs. Drake together purchased the property with the intention that it should be their home, that they both contributed their labour in 70%/30% proportions, that they had a joint account out of which the costs of conversion were met, but that that account was largely fed by his earnings, and that she paid for the food and some other household expenses and took care of the housekeeping for them both. I note that whilst it was open to Mrs. Drake to argue at the trial for a constructive trust and for a 50% share, she opted to rely solely on a resulting trust and a 40.1% share. In all the circumstances, I would hold that her fair share should be one-third.'

6–207   "It is very difficult, if not impossible, to find anything in the facts in *Drake v Whipp* to suggest that either of the parties ever gave thought to an arrangement under which the property should be shared in the proportions two-thirds and one-third; let alone that that was ever their common intention. Nor do I think that Peter Gibson L.J. approached the matter on that basis. As he said 'in constructive trust cases, the court can adopt a broad brush approach to determining the parties' respective shares'.[18] And that is what he did, as he acknowledged in the passage which I have just set out 'I would approach the matter more broadly, looking at the parties' entire course of conduct together'.[19] That approach, as it seems to me, had received the approval of the House of Lords some 35 years earlier, in *Gissing v Gissing*[20]; had been endorsed (at least by Sir Nicolas Browne-Wilkinson V.-C.) in *Grant v Edwards*[21]; and had been acknowledged and accepted by Nourse L.J. in *Stokes v Anderson.*[22] If these problems are to be solved by an analysis based on constructive trust, which requires the imputation of some common intention at the time of acquisition, then, as Nourse L.J. observed in *Stokes v Anderson*,[23] 'the court must supply the common intention by reference to that which all the material circumstances have shown to be fair'. That is, I think, what Waite L.J. had in mind when he referred, in *Midland Bank plc v Cooke*,[24] to 'equity's assistance in formulating a fair presumed basis for the sharing of the beneficial title' in a case where the parties 'had been honest enough to admit they never gave ownership a thought'.

6–208   "Once it is recognised that what the court is doing, in cases of this nature, is to supply or impute a common intention as to the parties' respective shares (in circumstances in which there was, in fact, no common intention) on the basis of that which, in the light of all the material circumstances (including the acts and conduct

---

[18] *ibid.* at 830.
[19] *ibid.* at 831.
[20] [1971] A.C. 886 at 909, *per* Lord Diplock.
[21] [1986] Ch. 638 at 657.
[22] [1991] 1 F.L.R. 391 at 399.
[23] *ibid.*
[24] [1995] 2 F.L.R. 915 at 927.

of the parties after the acquisition) is shown to be fair, it seems to me very difficult to avoid the conclusion that an analysis in terms of proprietary estoppel will, necessarily, lead to the same result; and that it may be more satisfactory to accept that there is no difference, in cases of this nature, between constructive trust and proprietary estoppel. It is clear that Sir Nicolas Browne-Wilkinson V.-C., in *Grant v Edwards* thought that there was much to be said for that view. In *Stokes v Anderson*, Nourse L.J. seems to have thought the same. More recently, in *Yaxley v Gotts*,[25] Robert Walker L.J. observed that 'in the area of a joint enterprise for the acquisition of land (which may be, but is not necessarily, the matrimonial home) the two concepts [estoppel and constructive trust] coincide'; and that 'the species of constructive trust based on "common intention" . . . is closely akin to, if not indistinguishable form, proprietary estoppel'.

". . . I have referred, in the immediately preceding paragraphs, to 'cases of this **6–209** nature'. By that, I mean cases in which the common features are: (i) the property is bought as a home for a couple who, although not married, intend to live together as husband and wife; (ii) each of them makes some financial contribution to the purchase; (iii) the property is purchased in the sole name of one of them; and (iv) there is no express declaration of trust. In those circumstances the first question is whether there is evidence from which to infer a common intention, communicated by each to the other, that each shall have a beneficial share in the property. In many such cases—of which the present is an example—there will have been some discussion between the parties at the time of the purchase which provides the answer to that question. Those are cases within the first of Lord Bridge's categories in *Lloyds Bank plc v Rosset*. In other cases—where the evidence is that the matter was not discussed at all—an affirmative answer will readily be inferred from the fact that each has made a financial contribution. Those are cases within Lord Bridge's second category. And, if the answer to the first question is that there was a common intention, communicated to each other, that each should have a beneficial share in the property, then the party who does not become the legal owner will be held to have acted to his or her detriment in making a financial contribution to the purchase in reliance on the common intention.

"In those circumstances, the second question to be answered in cases of this **6–210** nature is 'what is the extent of the parties' respective beneficial interests in the property?'. Again, in many such cases, the answer will be provided by evidence of what they said and did at the time of the acquisition. But, in a case where there is no evidence of any discussion between them as to the amount of the share which each was to have—and even in a case where the evidence is that there was no discussion on that point—the question still requires an answer. It must now be accepted that (at least in this court and below) the answer is that each is entitled to that share which the court considers fair having regard to the whole course of dealing between them in relation to the property. And, in that context, 'the whole course of dealing between them in relation to the property' includes the arrangements which they make from time to time in order to meet the outgoings (for example, mortgage contributions, council tax and utilities, repairs, insurance and housekeeping) which have to be met if they are to live in the property as their home.

"As the cases show, the courts have not found it easy to reconcile that final step **6–211** with a traditional, property-based, approach. It was rejected, in unequivocal terms, by Dillon L.J. in *Springette v Defoe* that 'The court does not as yet sit, as under a palm tree, to exercise a general discretion to do what the man in the street, on a

---

[25] [2000] Ch. 162 at 176 and 180.

general overview of the case, might regard as fair'.[26] Three strands of reasoning can be identified: (1) that suggested by Lord Diplock in *Gissing v Gissing*[27] and adopted by Nourse L.J. in *Stokes v Anderson*[28]—the parties are taken to have agreed at the time of the acquisition of the property that their respective shares are not to be quantified then, but are left to be determined when their relationship comes to an end or the property is sold on the basis of what is then fair having regard to the whole course of dealing between them. The court steps in to determine what is fair because, when the time came for that determination, the parties were unable to agree; (2) that suggested by Waite L.J. in *Midland Bank plc v Cooke*[29]—the court undertakes a survey of the whole course of dealing between the parties 'relevant to their ownership and occupation of the property and their sharing of its burdens and advantages' in order to determine 'what proportions the parties must be assumed to have intended [from the outset] for their beneficial ownership'. On that basis the court treats what has taken place while the parties have been living together in the property as evidence of what they intended at the time of the acquisition; (3) that suggested by Sir Nicolas Browne-Wilkinson V.-C. in *Grant v Edwards*[30] and approved by Robert Walker L.J. in *Yaxley v Gotts*[31]—the court makes such order as the circumstances require in order to give effect to the beneficial interest in the property of the one party, the existence of which the other party (having the legal title) is estopped from denying. That, I think, is the analysis which underlies the decision of this court in *Drake v Whipp*.[32]

6–212   "For my part, I find the reasoning adopted by this court in *Midland Bank plc v Cooke* to be the least satisfactory of the three strands. It seems to me artificial—and an unnecessary fiction—to attribute to the parties a common intention that the extent of their respective beneficial interests in the property should be fixed as from the time of the acquisition, in circumstances in which all the evidence points to the conclusion that, at the time of the acquisition, they had given no thought to the matter. The same point can be made—although with less force—in relation to the reasoning that, at the time of the acquisition, their common intention was that the amount of the respective shares should be left for later determination. But it can be said that, if it were their common intention that each should have some beneficial interest in the property -which is the hypothesis upon which it becomes necessary to answer the second question—then, in the absence of evidence that they gave any thought to the amount of their respective shares, the necessary inference is that they must have intended that question would be answered later on the basis of what was then seen to be fair. But, as I have said, I think that the time has come to accept that there is no difference in outcome, in cases of this nature, whether the true analysis lies in constructive trust or in proprietary estoppel.

Determination of the present appeal

6–213   "Her Honour Judge Hallon, directed herself that, in the light of *Midland Bank plc v Cooke*, her task was to 'look to the whole course of dealings to infer what the agreement between these parties was'. She found that 'all the evidence . . . clearly shows that both were evincing an intention to share the benefit and the burden of

---

[26] [1992] 2 F.LR. 388 at 393.
[27] [1971] A.C. 886 at 909.
[28] [1991] 1 F.L.R. 391 at 399–400.
[29] [1995] 2 F.L.R. 915 at 926.
[30] [1986] Ch. 638 at 656.
[31] [2000] Ch. 162 at 177.
[32] [1996] 1 F.L.R. 826 at 831.

this property [35 Dickens Close] jointly and equally'. But, in reaching that conclusion, she had held that that was the continuation of a 'long-term plan' which had begun before 39 Page Close, Bean, had been purchased. In my view, although the judge may have been right to identify a long-term plan, in general terms, that the parties would acquire a property 'through purchase with the advantageous discount available to a council tenant, with a view subsequently to moving on to better accommodation'; she was plainly wrong to take the view that it was a necessary incident of that plan that each property would be owned jointly or 'jointly and equally'. The grant of a charge over 39 Page Close to secure Mr. Hiscock's advance towards the purchase price of that property is inconsistent with an intention that that property should be owned jointly or in equal shares. And it is difficult to avoid the conclusion that the judge placed undue weight on the fact that (as she found) the parties regarded both 39 Page Close and 35 Dickens Close 'as their [joint] home'. It does not follow from the fact that parties live together in a house that they both regard as their home which they share the ownership of that house equally.

"If the judge had found, as was alleged by Mrs. Oxley . . . that 'it was expressly **6–214** the joint intention of the claimant and the defendant at the time of [35 Dickens Close] that they should share the beneficial ownership of that property equally', I would have taken the view that it would be wrong for this court to go behind that finding of fact. But, as I have said, she did not make that finding of fact; and we have seen no evidence upon which she could have done so. This must, I think, be seen as a case where there is no evidence of any discussion between the parties as to the amount of the share which each was to have. And, on that basis, the judge asked herself the wrong question. She should not have sought, by reference to the conduct of the parties while they were living together at 35 Dickens Close, to determine what intention both were then 'evincing'—unless, by that, she was able to find a common intention, communicated to each other, to determine, definitively, the shares which had been left undetermined at the time of acquisition. She might have asked herself whether their subsequent conduct, while living together at 35 Dickens Close, was consistent only with a common intention, at the time of the acquisition, that their shares should be equal; but she did not. The right question, in the circumstances of this case, was 'what would be a fair share for each party having regard to the whole course of dealing between them in relation to the property?'

"I think that that is a question to which this court can, and should, give an answer. **6–215** I do not think it necessary to remit the matter to the county court. In my view to declare that the parties were entitled in equal shares would be unfair to Mr. Hiscock. It would give insufficient weight to the fact that his direct contribution to the purchase price (£60,700) was substantially greater than that of Mrs. Oxley (£36,300). On the basis of the judge's finding that there was in this case 'a classic pooling of resources' and conduct consistent with an intention to share the burden of the property (by which she must, I think, have meant the outgoings referable to ownership and cohabitation), it would be fair to treat them as having made approximately equal contributions to the balance of the purchase price (£30,000). Taking that into account with their direct contributions at the time of the purchase, I would hold that a fair division of the proceeds of sale of the property would be 60% to Mr. Hiscock and 40% to Mrs. Oxley.

"I would set aside the order of 20 May 2003; declare that Mrs. Oxley is entitled to **6–216** 40% of the proceeds of sale of 35 Dickens Close; and adjust the sum payable to her by Mr. Hiscock accordingly."

QUESTIONS

6–217 1. "If legal title is taken in the names of both M and F, F is bound to obtain a fair share at the very least. Indeed, even where the legal title is taken only in M's name, if F pays part of the deposit it seems very likely that she will obtain a fair share that will be larger than an interest under a resulting trust corresponding to the proportion between the amount she paid towards the deposit and the total purchase price. It is only if she paid nothing towards the deposit and there was no agreement between M and her that she was to take responsibility to him for part of the mortgage taken on by him as sole legal owner, that the courts have difficulty preventing M from insisting on 100 per cent beneficial ownership." Discuss.

6–218 2. Kevin, a chef, lived with Sharon, a hairdresser, in a rented flat but they had separate bank accounts. Upon hearing that Sharon was pregnant, Kevin's parents gave him £1,000 to enable him to put down a deposit on a £10,000 flat of which he became registered proprietor twenty years ago subject to a registered charge for £9,000 in favour of Bigg Building Society. When the baby was born Sharon gave up her job and her separate bank account. She subsequently had two more children by Kevin.

Eight years ago Sharon returned to work, receiving a weekly pay packet. She used the money for housekeeping and holidays. This afforded Kevin the opportunity to take on and service a further loan from Bigg Building Society of £40,000 secured on the flat so that he and his mistress, Lucy, a keen gambler and cocaine user, could have a good time. She dropped him when the money was spent. Kevin took solace in alcohol and was then sacked from his job four years ago and has not worked since.

Fortunately, at this time Sharon became manageress of the hair salon where she worked. At her suggestion, "Because I love you, you silly sausage, and we have to keep the building society happy," his bank account was made into a joint account into which she had her salary paid and out of which the mortgage instalments continued to be paid. He alone monitored the monthly bank statements.

To finance his gambling habits, Kevin mortgaged the flat two years ago to Great Finance plc to secure a loan of £50,000, having forged financial references. Sharon has now discovered that all the £40,000 remaining due to Bigg Building Society represents the further loan of £40,000 of which she knew nothing, Kevin having told Bigg Building Society that he was living on his own as a bachelor and its surveyor visiting the flat when Sharon was at work. This was also the case for Great Finance plc (now owed £60,000 including interest) whose mortgage Sharon has also just discovered. The value of the flat is only £100,000.

Sharon and Kevin never discussed ownership of the flat though in conversation with friends they habitually referred to it as "our flat" or "our home".

Sharon seeks your advice as to whether she may have any interest in the flat and what considerations will determine whether any interest will bind Bigg Building Society and Great Finance plc.

To what extent would your answer differ if it was upon the marriage of Kevin and Sharon that Kevin's parents provided Kevin with the £1,000 deposit?

Section 3. Wrongs

6–219 When a defendant commits a civil wrong—*i.e.* when he breaches a pre-existing legal duty—the claimant is most likely to seek a compensatory remedy which is designed to make good his loss. In some cases, however, he may also be entitled to a remedy which is designed to make the wrongdoer restore or disgorge the benefit he has acquired through his wrongdoing.[33] Gain-based remedies of this sort can be personal—*i.e.* the defendant may be placed under a personal liability to pay over a money sum corresponding to the amount of his gain—but they can also be proprietary, in which case they can take the form of a constructive trust. One example is a constructive trust imposed on the profits of a breach of confidence, which we shall discuss in Chapter 9.[34] Another is the constructive trust imposed on trust property which comes into the hands of a trustee *de son tort*, which we shall discuss below. Constructive trusts can also be imposed on the profits of crime, as we shall also discuss below.

I. TRUSTEESHIP *DE SON TORT*

In *Mara v Browne*, A.L. Smith L.J. held that[35]:   **6–220**

"If one, not being a trustee and not having authority from a trustee, takes upon himself to intermeddle with trust matters or to do acts characteristic of the office of trustee he may thereby make himself what is called in law a trustee of his own wrong, *i.e.* a trustee *de son tort*, or as it is also termed, a constructive trustee."

A trustee *de son tort* does not purport to act for himself, but for the **6–221** beneficiaries. His conduct is equated to a declaration of himself as a trustee,[36] and like an express trustee he is expected to familiarize himself with the extent of his powers and duties on taking office, and thereafter he may be liable for a breach of these duties.[37] In the event that trust property comes into his hands he will hold it on constructive trust for the beneficiaries, to whom he will owe a duty to account for his stewardship of the property. Thus in *Blyth v Fladgate*,[38] where a sole trustee had solicitors invest trust funds in Exchequer Bills and, after his death and before appointment of any new trustees, the bills were sold by the solicitors and the proceeds invested in a loan on mortgage, the solicitors were liable for the loss arising when the security proved insufficient.

---

[33] For discussion of these two bases of gain-based relief, see J. Edelman, *Gain-Based Damages* (2002), chap. 3.
[34] See paras 9–32 to 9–34.
[35] [1896] 1 Ch. 199 at 209. See too *Blyth v Fladgate* [1891] 1 Ch. 337; *Lyell v Kennedy* (1899) 14 App. Cas. 437; *Taylor v Davies* [1920] A.C. 636 at 651; *Selangor United Rubber Ltd v Cradock (No.3)* [1968] 1 W.L.R. 1555 at 1579; *Carl Zeiss Stiftung v Herbert Smith (No.2)* [1969] 2 Ch. 276 at 289. In some circumstances an executor *de son tort* can become regarded as a trustee *de son tort*: *James v Williams* [2000] Ch. 1. In *Dubai Aluminium Co. Ltd v Salaam* [2003] 2 A.C. 366 at [138], Lord Millett preferred the term "*de facto* trustee" to the term "trustee *de son tort*", but we have adhered to the traditional terminology here to underline the point that intermeddling with other people's equitable property rights is a civil wrong. In this connection, note that constructive trusts can also be imposed on the profits of dishonest assistance in a breach of trust, another form of intermeddling discussed at paras 11–07 to 11–18: see, *e.g. Nanus Asia Co. Inc. v Standard Chartered Bank* [1990] 1 H.K.L.R. 396.
[36] *Life Association of Scotland v Siddal* (1861) 3 De G. F. & J. 58 at 72.
[37] *Pearce v Pearce* (1856) 22 Beav. 248 at 252.
[38] [1891] 1 Ch. 337. See too *Goddard v D.F.C. New Zealand Ltd* [1991] 3 N.Z.L.R. 580.

6–222   There is no need to show that a defendant has acted dishonestly in order to fix him with liability as a *de facto* trustee: he may have been honest and well intentioned, a busybody of excessive probity.[39] To show that he has relevantly "intermeddled" with trust affairs, it is not enough to show that he has attended meetings of the trustees without participating in the trustees' decision making: he must take it on himself to assume a more active management role than this.[40]

II. PROCEEDS OF CRIME

6–223 When Crippen murdered his wife her property did not on her intestacy pass to him via his will to Miss Le Neve, but passed to his wife's blood relatives.[41] Likewise, where R murdered both his parents (Mr. and Mrs. S.) who died intestate, R could not inherit their property, and neither could his son, T, so that Mr. S's sister inherited his estate and Mrs. S.'s sister's children inherited her estate.[42] If the property is not intercepted before passing to the killer it seems that he will hold it on constructive trust for those who are entitled to it by operation of the forfeiture rule.[43] Their claims will have priority if he becomes bankrupt while still owning the property, and they can also follow the property into the hands of anyone other than a *bona fide* purchaser of the legal estate for value without notice, and assert a proprietary claim against him.

6–224   If one joint tenant murders another he should hold the property on constructive trust for himself and his victim in equal shares.[44] If a remainderman murders the life tenant then the victim should be deemed to live his actuarial life-span (except for a death-bed mercy killing), so that for the period of this notional life-span the victim's interest should be held on constructive trust for his estate; thereafter, devolution should occur normally.[45] Murder and manslaughter including manslaughter by reason of diminished responsibility invoke the principle, but it does not apply to a killer who is found not guilty by reason of insanity.[46] The Forfeiture Act

---

[39] *Lyell v Kennedy* (1889) 14 App. Cas. 437 at 459; *Mara v Browne* [1896] 1 Ch. 199 at 209; *Life Association of Scotland v Siddal* (1861) 3 De G. F. & J. 58; *Baden, Delvaux v Société Générale pour Favoriser le Développement du Commerce et de l'Industrie en France SA* [1993] 1 W.L.R. 509 at 577; *Dubai Aluminium Co. Ltd v Salaam* [2003] 2 A.C. 366 at [138]
[40] *Clay v Clay* [1999] WASCA 8 at [16].
[41] *Re Crippen* [1911] P. 108. See too *Re Sigsworth* [1935] Ch. 89.
[42] *Re DWS (deceased)* [2001] Ch. 568. The reason was the intestacy rule that a child can only inherit property that would otherwise pass to his parent if the parent pre-deceases the intestate. The outcome of this case is regarded as unsatisfactory, and proposals for reform are suggested, in Law Commission, *The Forfeiture Rule and the Law of Succession* (LCCP No.172, 2004).
[43] *Schobelt v Barber* (1966) 60 D.L.R. (2nd) 519; *Re Pechar* [1969] N.Z.L.R. 574; *Rasmanis v Jurewitsch* [1970] N.S.W.L.R. 650; *Beresford v Royal Insurance Co. Ltd* [1938] A.C. 586 at 600. See further G. Virgo, *The Principles of the Law of Restitution* (1999), pp.570–588; G. Jones, "Stripping a Criminal of the Profits of Crime" (2000) 1 *Theoretical Inquiries in Law* 59.
[44] *Rasmanis v Jurewitsch* [1970] N.S.W.L.R. 650; *Re K* [1985] 1 All E.R. 403 (if A's murder of B severs their joint tenancy then A holds legal title on constructive trust for A and B's estate equally). If X, Y, and Z are joint tenants and X kills Y then X should become tenant in common of one-third and Z of two-thirds. For the destination of surplus endowment assurance moneys on the death of the murder's co-owner, see *Davitt v Titcumb* [1990] 1 Ch. 110.
[45] (1973) 89 L.Q.R. 231, 250–251 (T. G. Youdan).
[46] *Re Giles* [1972] Ch. 544; *Re Pitts* [1931] 1 Ch. 546; *Re Plaister* (1934) S.R. (N.S.W.) 547; *Permanent Trustee Co. v Gillett* (2004) 6 I.T.E.L.R. 1063 at [36] *et seq.*

1982 now enables the court to modify the effect of the forfeiture rule where the justice of the case requires it, if the killer brings proceedings within three months of conviction.[47]

Section 4. Unjust Enrichment

Claims in unjust enrichment arise under English law when a defendant is enriched at the expense of a claimant in circumstances which make his enrichment unjust.[48] Under Canadian law it was formerly held that *all* constructive trusts respond to unjust enrichment,[49] but it has now been recognised that some do not.[50] In contrast, the English and Australian courts have never subscribed to the view that *all* constructive trusts respond to unjust enrichment, but they have held in various cases that some do. Perhaps the best known English case is *Chase Manhattan Bank v. Israel-British Bank (London) Ltd*[51] in which Goulding J. held that money paid by mistake should be held on constructive trust for the payor by the recipient.[52] Constructive trusts have also been imposed on property stolen from a claimant or obtained from him by fraud,[53] and on property transferred by a claimant who has been unduly influenced by the recipient,[54] or whose ability to make decisions has otherwise been compromised by his relationship with the recipient.[55] **6–225**

These authorities are controversial for a number of reasons. Many of the Canadian cases concern shared homes, and in their wish to do justice between the parties, the courts have made awards designed to fulfil the claimant's expectations rather than to reverse a transfer of value to the defendant, riding roughshod over the requirement that a claimant in unjust **6–226**

---

[47] See, *e.g. Re K* [1986] Ch. 180; *Re H* [1990] 1 F.L.R. 441; *Jones v Roberts* [1995] 2 F.L.R. 422; *Dunbar v Plant* [1998] Ch. 412; *Dalton v Latham* [2003] EWHC 796, Ch.

[48] *Banque Financière de la Cité v Parc (Battersea) Ltd* 1999] 1 A.C. 221 at 227, *per* Lord Steyn, and 234, *per* Lord Hoffmann; *Kleinwort Benson Ltd v Lincoln CC* [1999] 2 A.C. 349 at 373, *per* Lord Goff, and 407–408, *per* Lord Hope; *Cressman v Coys of Kensington (Sales) Ltd* [2004] 1 W.L.R. 2775 at [22], *per* Mance LJ; and *Niru Battery Manufacturing Co. v Milestone Trading Ltd (No.2)* [2004] 1 All E.R. (Comm.) 289 at [28] and [41], *per* Clarke L.J.

[49] *Deglman v Guaranty Trust Co.* [1954] S.C.R. 725; *Pettkus v Becker* [1980] 2 S.C.R. 834; *Sorochan v Sorochan* [1986] 2 S.C.R 38; *Peter v Beblow* [1993] 1 S.C.R. 980.

[50] *Korkontzilas v Soulos* [1997] 2 S.C.R. 217.

[51] [1981] Ch. 105.

[52] *Chase Manhattan* remains good law in England, although its status has been diminished by Lord Browne-Wilkinson's gloss on the case in *Westdeutsche Landesbank Girozentrale v Islington L.B.C.* [1996] A.C. 669 (see paras 5–213 to 5–216, above), and by judicial reactions to this gloss in *Barclays Bank plc v Box* [1998] Lloyd's Rep. Bank. 185 at 200–201, *per* Ferris J; *Papamichael v National Westminster Bank plc* [2003] 1 Lloyd's Rep. 341 at [232]–[242] *per* Judge Chambers Q.C.; and *Shalson v Russo* [2003] EWHC 1637 (Ch) at [108]–[127], *per* Rimer J.

[53] *Westdeutsche Landesbank Girozentrale v Islington L.B.C.* [1996] A.C. 669 at 715–6, *per* Lord Browne-Wilkinson, above at para.5–218, followed in *Niru Battery Manufacturing Co. v Milestone Trading Ltd (No.1)* [2002] 2 All E.R. (Comm.) 705 at [55]–[56], *per* Moore-Bick J. See too *Black v S. Freedman & Co.* (1910) 12 C.L.R. 105 at 109; *Creak v James Moore & Sons Pty. Ltd* (1912) 15 C.L.R. 426 at 432; *Australian Postal Corp. v Lutak* (1991) 12 N.S.W.L.R. 584 at 589; *Zobory v Commissioner of Taxation* (1995) 64 F.C.R. 86 at 90–93; *Evans v European Bank Ltd* (2004) 7 I.T.E.L.R. 19 at [111].

[54] *Janz v McIntosh* (1999) 182 Sask. R. 197.

[55] *Louth v Diprose* (1992) 175 C.L.R. 621; *McCulloch v Fern* [2001] NSWSC 406; *Smith v Smith* [2004] NSWSC 663. On the Australian law governing unconscionable transactions and the law of unjust enrichment, see M. Bryan "Unjust Enrichment and Unconscionability in Australia: A False Dichotomy?" in J. W. Neyers *et al.* (eds) *Understanding Unjust Enrichment* (2004) 47.

enrichment must prove that the defendant's enrichment has been acquired at her expense.[56] More generally, some difficult questions arise, once it is accepted that at least some claimants in unjust enrichment are entitled to a proprietary rather than a personal restitutionary remedy.

6–227   First, should *all* claimants in unjust enrichment be entitled to a proprietary remedy, and if not, then how should the law distinguish those who are from those who are not? Different writers offer different answers to this question, many of them focussing on the question whether the claimant has taken the risk of the defendant's insolvency,[57] others focussing on the question whether the basis of the claimant's transfer to the defendant has immediately failed at the moment of receipt.[58] In *Westdeutsche Landesbank Girozentrale v Islington L.B.C.*,[59] Lord Browne-Wilkinson took another approach, suggesting that a claimant in unjust enrichment should be entitled to a proprietary remedy against a defendant only if his conscience is affected by knowledge of the circumstances making his enrichment unjust, at a time when the property he has received from the claimant is still identifiable in his hands. However, it is hard to see why the claimant's position relative to the defendant's other creditors should be improved by a change in the defendant's state of mind at some time between the date of receipt and the date of his insolvency.[60]

6–228   Secondly, if a trust is to be imposed on assets in a defendant's hands in order to reverse his enrichment at a claimant's expense, then is this trust a resulting trust or a constructive trust? Given that resulting trusts are always restitutionary in pattern and constructive trusts are not, then it might make sense to say that trusts imposed to reverse unjust enrichment are always resulting trusts.[61] Developing the law in this way would make it easier to understand why trusts are imposed by law, and how resulting and constructive trusts differ from one another. It would enable us to say that resulting trusts align with unjust enrichment, and that constructive trusts align with wrongdoing, intention, and other causative events.

6–229   Thirdly, should the law distinguish between consensual and non-consensual transfers? In *Twinsectra Ltd v Yardley*, Potter L.J. gave a positive answer to this question, holding that in cases where a defendant has acquired a claimant's money by fraudulent means[62]:

---

[56] J. Mee, *The Property Rights of Cohabitees* (1999), pp.213–4; J. D. McCamus, "Restitution on Dissolution of Marital and Other Intimate Relationships: Constructive Trust or *Quantum Meruit*?" in J.D. Neyers *et al.* (eds) *Understanding Unjust Enrichment* (2004) 359.

[57] *e.g.* C. Rotherham, *Proprietary Interests in Context* (2002), chaps 4, 6, 9, 11 and 12; A. Burrows, *The Law of Restitution* 2nd ed. (2002), pp.69–73.

[58] *e.g.* P. Birks, *Unjust Enrichment* (2003), pp.162–178; P. Birks, "Retrieving Tied Money" in W. Swadling (ed.), *The Quistclose Trust: Critical Essays* (2004) 121, pp.130–138.

[59] [1996] A.C. 669; above at para.5–173.

[60] *Cf.* Lord Millett, "Restitution and Constructive Trusts" (1998) 114 L.Q.R. 399, 413: "By itself notice of the existence of a ground of restitution is obviously insufficient to found a proprietary remedy; it is merely notice of a personal right to an account and payment."

[61] As mooted in *El Ajou v Dollar Land Holdings plc* [1993] 3 All E.R. 717 at 734, *per* Millett J.; *Evans v European Bank Ltd* (2004) 7 I.T.E.L.R. 19 at [112], *per* Spigelman C.J.; P. J. Millett, "Tracing the Proceeds of Fraud'" (1991) 107 L.Q.R. 71, 81; *Oosterhoff on Trusts* 6th ed. (2004), p.695; and *cf.* the discussion in paras 5–170 to 5–172, above.

[62] [1999] Lloyd's Rep. Bank. 438 at [99], considered in *Halley v Law Society* (2003) 6 I.T.E.L.R. 40 at [46]–[48].

"the distinction of importance . . . is that between non-consensual transfers and transfers pursuant to contracts which are voidable for misrepresentation. In the latter case, the transferor may elect whether to avoid or affirm the transaction and, until he elects to avoid it, there is no constructive (resulting) trust[63]; in the former case the constructive trust arises from the moment of transfer. The result, so far as third parties are concerned, is that, before rescission, the owner has no proprietary interest in the original property; all he has is the "mere equity" of his right to set aside the voidable contract."

Thus, where a claimant, C, enters a contract with a defendant, D, under which he transfers legal and beneficial[64] ownership in particular assets to D, and his intention to benefit D is vitiated by a factor such as undue influence or induced mistake, C can rescind the transaction and ask the court to exercise its discretion to restore the assets.[65] Once C elects to rescind,[66] the court can treat equitable title as retrospectively vesting in C for the purpose of allowing C to trace what happened to his assets in D's hands.[67] Since D, his trustee in bankruptcy, and his personal representatives are all bound to retransfer the original assets to C from the time when he elects to rescind and demands the return of the assets, it can be said that C enjoys a proprietary interest in the assets from that time.[68] This interest can be devised[69] or assigned,[70] but it is a mere equity rather than an equitable interest: *i.e.* it will bind a third party who is a volunteer or a purchaser with notice, but it will not bind a *bona fide* purchaser without notice of a legal *or equitable* interest in the assets.[71]

6–230

---

[63] It is unclear what his Lordship meant by "constructive (resulting) trust", but conceivably he meant to indicate that trusts imposed to reverse unjust enrichment are resulting trusts, as suggested in para.6–228, above.

[64] A case of undue influence "assumes a transfer of the beneficial interest but in circumstances which entitle the transferor to recall it": *Hodgson v Marks* [1971] Ch. 892 at 929, *per* Russell L.J. So does a case of fraudulent misrepresentation: *Shalson v Russo* [2003] EWHC 1637 (Ch) at [119], *per* Rimer J.

[65] *Lonrho plc v Fayed (No.2)* [1992] 1 W.L.R. 1 at 9, *per* Millett J.; *Re Goldcorp Exchange Ltd* [1995] 1 A.C. 74 at 103, *per* Lord Mustill; *Cheese v Thomas* [1994] 1 All E.R. 35 at 42.

[66] A claimant's action in issuing proceedings can amount to an implied election to rescind in itself: *Shalson v Russo* [2003] EWHC 1637 (Ch) at [120], *per* Rimer J., relying on *Banque Belge pour l'Etranger v Hambrouck* [1921] 1 K.B. 321 at 332, *per* Atkin L.J.

[67] *O'Sullivan v Management Agency & Music Ltd* [1985] Q.B. 428 at 475; *El Ajou v Dollar Land Holdings plc* [1993] 3 All E.R. 717 at 734, *per* Millett J.; *Bristol & West B.S. v Mothew* [1996] 4 All E.R. 698 at 716, *per* Millett L.J.

[68] *Load v Green* (1846) 15 M. & W. 216; *Re Eastgate* [1905] 1 K.B. 465; *Tilley v Bowman* [1910] 1 K.B. 745 at 750; *Banque Belge pour l'Etranger v Hambrouck* [1921] 1 K.B. 321 at 332, *per* Atkin L.J.; *Shalson v Russo* [2003] EWHC 1637 (Ch) at [122]–[126], *per* Rimer J. See generally S. Worthington, "The Proprietary Consequences of Rescission" [2002] R.L.R. 28.

[69] *Stump v Gaby* (1852) 2 De G. M. & G. 623.

[70] *Dickinson v Burrell* (1866) L.R. 1 Eq. 337; *Bruty v Edmundson* (1915) 85 L.J. Ch. 568.

[71] *Phillips v Phillips* (1861) 4 De G.F. & J. 208 at 218 and 221–3; *Lancashire Loans Ltd v Black* [1934] 1 K.B. 380; *Latec Investments Pty Ltd v Terrigal Pty. Ltd* (1965) 113 C.L.R. 265; *Blacklocks v J.B. Developments Ltd* [1981] 3 All E.R. 392 at 400. See too Lord Millett, "Restitution and Constructive Trusts" (1998) 114 L.Q.R. 399, 416.

Chapter 7

CHARITABLE TRUSTS[1]

Section 1. The Advantages of Charitable Status

Tax advantages

7–01   United Kingdom[2] charities do not pay income tax on their investment income which is applicable to charitable purposes only and is in fact applied solely for those purposes.[3] They can recover basic rate or corporation tax paid by donors in respect of four year covenants drawn up in their favour[4] or in respect of any gifts under the gift aid scheme.[5] Where trading income is concerned, however, they are only exempt from tax if either the trade is exercised in the course of the actual carrying out of a primary purpose of the charity or the work in connection with the trade is mainly carried out by beneficiaries of the charity.[6]

7–02   Charities do not pay capital gains tax in respect of gains made upon disposals by them[7] and individuals are encouraged to make *inter vivos* gifts to charities since no charge to capital gains tax arises upon such gifts.[8] Where inheritance tax is concerned transfers to charities are exempt.[9] Charities can obtain 80 per cent relief as of right in respect of non-domestic rates for premises wholly or mainly used for charitable purposes and some discretionary relief in respect of the rest.[10] Charities are also exempt in

---

[1] *Tudor on Charities* and Picarda's *The Law and Practice to Charities* are the authoritative legal works. P. Luxton, *Law of Charities* (2001) is also very useful. See too Goodman Committee: *Charity Law and Voluntary Organisations* (1976); Wolfenden Committee: *The Future of Voluntary Organisations*; Chesterman, *Charities, Trusts and Social Welfare*; F. Gladstone, *Charity Law and Social Justice*; 16th Report of Committee of Public Accounts 1987–88; *Charities: A Framework for the Future* (1989) Cm. 694; Deakin Report, *Meeting the Challenge of Change* (1996); Prime Minister's Strategy Unit, *Private Action, Public Benefit: A Review of Charities and the Wider Not-for-Profit Sector* (2002); Home Office *Charities and Not-for-Profit: A Modern Legal Framework* (2003); House of Lords and House of Commons Joint Committee on the Draft Charities Bill *The Draft Charities Bill* (HL Paper 167 and HC Paper 660, 2004).
[2] *Camille and Henry Dreyfus Foundation Inc. v I.R.C.* [1956] A.C. 39; *Civil Engineer v IRC* [2002] STC (SCD) 72.
[3] Income and Corporation Taxes Act 1988, ss.505, 506. See *I.R.C. v Educational Grants Association Ltd* [1967] Ch. 123, para.7–209.
[4] ICTA 1988, ss.660, 683, Finance Act 1989, ss.56, 59. Money can also be given (with tax relief) by employees under a payroll deduction scheme: ITEPA 2003, ss.713–715.
[5] Finance Act 1990 ss.25, 26 as amended by Finance Act 2000 s.39.
[6] ICTA 1988, s.505; G. N. Glover [1972] B.T.R. 346. If substantial trading is being carried on which is not within the exemption the charity may form a company to run the trade and have the company covenant to pay its net profits to the charity for a period capable of exceeding 3 years; the company then deducts the payment as a charge on income for the purposes of corporation tax: ICTA 1988, s.338(5)(6)(8). By concession the Revenue do not charge tax in respect of profits from occasional fund-raising bazaars, jumble sales, etc. Further see Charity Commission, CC 35: *Charities and Trading*.
[7] ICTA 1970, s.345(2); Taxation of Chargeable Gains Act 1992, s.256.
[8] TCGA 1992, s.257. The value of gifted shares is also deductible against taxable income.
[9] Inheritance Tax Act 1988, s.23.
[10] Local Government Finance Act 1988, ss.43, 47, 64.

respect of stamp duty[11] but only have a very few reliefs from value added tax[12] in prescribed circumstances, *e.g.* relating to medical supplies.

As at March 2004 there were around 189,000 charities registered with the **7–03** Charity Commission, and their total annual income was over £32 billion.[13] In the tax year 2003/4, the cost of tax reliefs to charities in terms of tax payments lost to the Treasury was approximately £2.3 billion.[14]

Trust law advantages

Charitable trusts have further advantages in that they are not subject to **7–04** the rule against inalienability[15] that applies exclusively to pure purpose trusts and, to the extent that a charity might be a company or regarded as a trust for purposes benefiting individuals with *locus standi* to sue, it enjoys one limited exemption from the rule against remoteness. At common law a gift over from one person to another that might possibly take effect outside the perpetuity period was void.[16] However, a gift over from one charity to another charity was valid, the property being treated as belonging to charity throughout so as not to be caught by the rule against remoteness,[17] if that rule be applicable as opposed to the rule against inalienability from which charities are in any event exempt.[18] If the gift were a gift over from a charity to a non-charity[19] or from a non-charity to a charity[20] then the rule against remoteness applied. Since the Perpetuities and Accumulations Act 1964 came into force it is now possible in these two latter instances to wait and see[21] when the gift over takes effect: if it takes effect within the perpetuity period then it is good; if not it is bad and the first gift becomes absolute, no longer subject to defeasance or determination.[22] Of course, the validity of gifts over from one charity to another charity is unaffected by the 1964 Act.

Furthermore, a charitable trust is valid though a pure purpose trust **7–05** because the Attorney-General can enforce it, and the trust requirement of certainty of objects is satisfied so long as the settlor manifested a general charitable intention to enable a *cy-près* scheme to be formulated for giving effect to his intention as nearly as possible.[23] Thus a trust "for world-wide

---

[11] FA 1982, s.129.
[12] Value Added Tax Act 1994, Sch.8, Group 15 and Sch. 9 Groups 7, 8, 10, 12. See too H.M. Revenue & Customs, *Charities* (Notice 701/1, May 2004 version).
[13] Charity Commission, *Annual Report for 2003/4*, 3.
[14] *Inland Revenue Statistics 2004*, Table 10.2: Costs of Tax Reliefs.
[15] *e.g. Re Banfield* [1968] 1 W.L.R. 846 compared with *Re Warre's W.T.* [1953] 1 W.L.R. 725 or *Re Gwyon* [1930] 1 Ch. 255; see n.18.
[16] *Re Frost* (1889) 43 Ch.D. 246.
[17] *Christ's Hospital v Grainger* (1849) 1 Mac. & G. 460; *Re Tyler* [1891] 3 Ch. 252.
[18] The two rules are mutually exclusive, hence the 1964 Perpetuities & Accumulations Act did not need to deal also with the rule against inalienability to save trusts for persons: see *supra*, at para.3–182.
[19] *Re Bowen* [1893] 2 Ch. 491.
[20] *Re Dalziel* [1943] Ch. 277; *Re Peel's Release* [1921] 2 Ch. 218.
[21] Perpetuities and Accumulations Act 1964, s.3.
[22] PAA 1964, s.12 treats determinable interests in the same way as conditional interests.
[23] The court has inherent jurisdiction to resolve any problems of administrative unworkability so long as the settlor has manifested a general charitable intention. If the trust is one the administration of which the court could not undertake and control and no exclusively charitable intent appears so as to found a *cy-près* scheme then the trust fails: *Re Hummultenberg* [1923] 1 Ch. 237 (legacy to the treasurer of the London Spiritualistic Alliance for the purpose of establishing a college for the training of suitable persons as mediums); *Re Koeppler's W.T.* [1984] 2 All E.R. 111 (legacy to trustees for the formation of an informed international public opinion and the promotion of greater co-operation in Europe and the West, though held charitable in the Court of Appeal [1985] 2 All E.R. 869); *Att.-Gen. of Cayman Islands v Wahr-Hansen* [2000] 3 All E.R. 642 (trust for organisations operating for the public good held void by Privy Council).

charitable purposes" or "for poor persons" or "for the following charitable religious societies" without specifying any is valid, whilst a discretionary trust for everyone in the United Kingdom is void. The *cy-près* doctrine is peculiar to charitable trusts and will be dealt with at the end of this chapter. Finally, charitable trustees can act by a majority instead of unanimously which is the position for private trusts unless the trust deed authorises majority decisions.[24]

Other legal forms

7–06   At this stage it might usefully be noted that although a charity will often take the form of a charitable trust with individual or corporate trustees,[25] it may also take a number of other forms. It may take the form of an unincorporated association, of a community benefit society,[26] or of a registered company limited by guarantee (as opposed to a registered company limited by shares, the form which is generally adopted by commercial organizations intending to distribute profits to their share-holders).[27] In the event that the Charities Bill 2005 is enacted in its current state, it will also be possible for the promoters of a charity to create a Charitable Incorporated Organisation, a new legal form which is intended to enable charities to acquire the benefits of incorporation without attracting the disadvantage of dual regulation by Companies House as well as the Charity Commission.[28] All these bodies will typically have written provisions detailing their purposes and the rules governing their administration, and for the purposes of the charities legislation these provisions count as "trusts" whether or not they take effect by way of trust.[29] By the same token, charity officers are frequently referred to as "trustees" in the legislation and in the Charity Commission regulatory literature whether or not they are actually trustees of a charitable trust. The Charities Bill 2005, clause 1(1) defines a charity as "an institution which (a) is established for charitable purposes only, and (b) falls to be subject to the control of the High Court in the exercise of its jurisdiction with respect to charities".

7–07   A gift to a registered company whose property is held for charitable purposes (without distinguishing between capital and income) without the intervention of trusts, is usually treated as intended to be held as an addition to the company's general property and not upon trusts unless the donor uses express words importing a trust.[30] Although a company can

---

[24] *Re Whiteley* [1910] 1 Ch. 600 at 608. Yet another distinction is that the six year limitation period in Limitation Act 1980, s.21(3) applies to an action by a beneficiary under a trust but not an action by the Att.-Gen.: *Att.-Gen. v Cocke* [1988] 2 All E.R. 391.

[25] Under the Charities Act 1993, ss.50–52, a group of individual trustees may collectively become a corporate body (*e.g.* to make title holding easier by avoiding the need to transfer title to individuals becoming new trustees) but the trustees will remain personally liable as though no incorporation had been effected: see s.54 of the 1993 Act. See further. Charity Commission, *CC 43: Incorporation of Charity Trustees*.

[26] A form of industrial and provident society introduced by the Co-operatives and Community Benefit Societies Act 2003.

[27] See Companies Act 1985, s.1(2)(b). See too J. Gray, "Guarantee Companies in the Voluntary Sector" in A. Dunn (ed.), *The Voluntary Sector, the State and the Law* (2000) 75.

[28] Charities Bill 2005, cl.32 and Sch.6, inserting new Charities Act 1993, Pt 8A and Sch.5A. The history of the Charities Bill 2005 is noted below at para.7–41.

[29] Charities Act 1993, s.97(1).

[30] *Re Finger's W.T.* [1972] 1 Ch. 286 and see Charity Commissioners' Report for 1971, paras 22–30.

always change its objects clause in its memorandum under section 4 of the Companies Act 1985 it cannot do so without the prior written consent of the Charity Commission.[31] Of course, where property was gifted upon express (endowment or non-endowment) trusts then the company must always give effect to those trusts unless and until a *cy-près* scheme is finalised. A charitable company's own general property is also subject to the court's *cy-près* jurisdiction, *e.g.* on its winding up.[32] In the rare case where the Commission may allow a company to change its objects so as to cease to be a charity this cannot affect the application of any property acquired other than for full consideration or any property representing property so acquired or the income from any such property.[33]

Policing and advice

Concerns over the negligent or fraudulent mismanagement of charitable **7–08** funds led to the establishment of the Charity Commission under the Charitable Trusts Acts 1853, 1855 and 1860,[34] the body which is still charged with the regulation of charity administration. Similar concerns over the past fifty years led to the enactment of the Charities Acts 1960 and 1993, statutes which progressively expanded and strengthened the Commission's powers. This process will continue if the Charities Bill 2004 is enacted in its present form, as it contains various provisions which are intended to reinforce the Commission's regulatory powers still further. In theory, the Commission is an independent regulator, a non-ministerial government department which is accountable to the Home Secretary for its efficiency, but not for the manner in which it pursues its objectives.[35] In practice, the Commission has come under political pressure at various times, from those who believe that the voluntary sector should be more heavily regulated,[36] for example, and from those who believe that the Commission should pursue a systematic programme of wealth-redistribution by forcing charitable bodies to widen access to their facilities and services on pain of losing their charitable status.[37]

Many, though not all, charities are required by statute to register with the **7–09** Charity Commission,[38] and those registered charities with a gross annual income exceeding £100,000 must submit annual accounts and returns to the

---

[31] Charities Act 1993 s.64(2); also see s.66.
[32] *Liverpool and District Hospital v Att.-Gen.* [1981] Ch. 193.
[33] Charities Act 1993 s.64(1).
[34] R. Tompson, *The Charity Commission and the Age of Reform* (1979). The Commissioners are given collective status as a body corporate by the Charities Bill 2005, cl.6 and Sch.1.
[35] For the Commission's regulatory objectives, general functions, general duties, and incidental powers, see the proposed new sections 1B–1E of the Charities Act 1993, to be inserted by the Charities Bill 2005, cl.7.
[36] See, *e.g.* Select Committee on Public Accounts, *28th Report: Charity Commission—Regulation and Support of Charities* (1998), discussed in C. Mitchell, "Reviewing the Register" in C. Mitchell and S. Moody (eds.) Foundations of Charity (2000) 174, 188–190.
[37] House of Lords and House of Commons Joint Committee on the Draft Charities Bill, *The Draft Charities Bill* (HL 167 and HC 660, 2004), 19–33. At 51–2 the Joint Committee also recommended that the Charity Commission should be required to account for itself to the Home Affairs Select Committee, and that its Annual Report should be debated in each of the Houses of Parliament every year. If implemented, these changes would be certain to erode the Commission's independence from partisan interference in its activities.
[38] Charities Act 1993, s.3.

Commission,[39] which is responsible for ensuring that they have been prepared accurately and honestly. All charities are also selectively targeted by the Inland Revenue to ensure that their accounts are in proper order, and that they are eligible for the tax exemptions to which they lay claim.[40] The Charity Commission has wide powers to institute inquiries into the administration of charities,[41] to require that people furnish them with information relevant to these inquiries,[42] and to obtain information relating to charities from the police and other public bodies.[43] In the event that misconduct or mismanagement in a charity's administration are discovered, the Commission can suspend or remove any of the charity's officers and appoint new ones as necessary.[44] It also has powers, corresponding to and concurrent with those possessed by the Attorney-General, to go directly to the courts for the enforcement of obligations against defaulting charity trustees and others.[45] It is intended that the Charities Bill 2005 will create a new Charity Appeal Tribunal to which appeals can be made from decisions, directions, and orders made pursuant to the Commission's various powers.[46] The purpose of this reform is to provide charities and their officers with a cheaper and swifter mechanism for reviewing the Commission's decisions than is currently offered by the High Court.

7–10   As well as investigating possible misconduct and abuse of charitable funds with a view to taking remedial action, the Commission also provides charities with information and advice. It provides much useful guidance in publications that can be accessed on its website: www.charity-commission.gov.uk. It is empowered to give advice to charity trustees to make the administration of their charity more effective,[47] and a charity trustee acting on such advice is deemed to have acted in accordance with the terms of the trust, provided that no court decision has been obtained on the matter, and that the trustee has not withheld material facts when seeking the Commission's directions.[48] The Commission will not advise on policy matters or legal questions concerning the charity's relationship with third parties,[49] and in practice it most often advises charities on how to simplify their administration, alter their trusts, amend their governing documents, transfer property, and appoint new trustees.[50] The Commission can also make schemes and orders to modernise the purposes and administrative machinery of charities, and to give the trustees additional powers.[51]

---

[39] *ibid.* s.42

[40] The Charity Commission and the Inland Revenue routinely pass information to one another. In 1991, around 10 per cent of the enquiries begun by the Commission were prompted by the receipt of information from the Inland Revenue: Charity Commission, *Report for 1991*, para.83.

[41] Charities Act 1993, s.8.

[42] *ibid.* s.9.

[43] *ibid.* s.10.

[44] *ibid.* s.18.

[45] *ibid.* s.32.

[46] Charities Bill 2005, cl.8, inserting new Charities Act 1993, ss.2A–2D. The history of the Charities Bill 2005 is noted below at para.7–41. Clause 8 implements a recommendation by the Prime Minister's Strategy Unit, *Private Action, Public Benefit* (2002) paras 7–71 to 7–79.

[47] Charities Act 1993, s.29.

[48] *ibid.* s.29(2).

[49] Charity Commission, *Report for 1982*, paras 24–26.

[50] Charity Commission, *Report for 1996*, paras 123–5.

[51] Charities Act 1993, s.17.

Section 2. Decision-Making Bodies

It will be seen from the foregoing discussion that trusts and organisations **7–11** with charitable status enjoy various advantages which cost the state large sums of money, in the form of foregone tax revenues and the costs of funding charity regulation.[52] This strongly suggests that decisions on entitlement to charitable status should be taken by a body with a democratic mandate, charged with deciding the question by undertaking a cost-benefit analysis of the proposed purposes of a trust or organisation to determine whether they merit the advantages flowing from charitable status.[53] However, no such body has ever been appointed, and decisions on charitable status are instead taken by various unelected bodies, whose basic approach is to decide the question as though it were a "pure" question of law divorced from fiscal considerations.

Thus, the courts are asked from time to time to decide whether **7–12** testamentary purpose trusts are charitable trusts; H.M. Revenue and Customs must frequently decide whether an institution is a "charity" for the purposes of determining its entitlement to tax reliefs; local government rating departments must decide whether institutions are entitled to rates relief; and most significantly, the Charity Commission must entertain applications by bodies to be included on the Register of Charities which it is the Commission's statutory responsibility to maintain. The effect of registration by the Commission is that for all purposes other than rectification of the Register, a body is conclusively presumed to be or to have been a charity at any time when it is or was registered.[54] Appeals from decisions by the tax authorities and Charity Commission can be made to the courts, but in practice these have been very rare as very few voluntary bodies have the resources or the inclination to incur the costs of mounting an appeal to the courts. Concern that this effectively left the development of the legal rules in this area entirely to the Charity Commission is one reason why it is proposed to establish a new Charity Appeal Tribunal, though the Charities Bill 2005, as it is contemplated that appeals from the Commission's decisions on charitable status will lie to this tribunal.

Section 3. Overview of the Rules on Charitable Status

I. METHODOLOGY

Analogising with existing charitable purposes

When deciding the question whether the purposes of a trust or organisa- **7–13** tion are charitable, the courts and the Charity Commission first consider whether such purposes have previously been held to be legally charitable. If

---

[52] The Charity Commission's costs for the year 2003/4 were around £26 million, and its agreed allocation for the years 2005–2007 is an annual £30 million: Charity Commission, *Resource Accounts 2003–04* (HC 1019, 2004).

[53] See further C. Mitchell, "Redefining Charity in English Law" (1999) 13 Tru L.I. 21, esp. at 39–41.

[54] Charities Act 1993, s.4(1). The courts are bound by this provision when considering the validity of a gift to a body which has attained or subsequently attains registration: *Re Murawski's W.T.* [1971] 1 W.L.R. 707. It also binds rating authorities: *Wynn v Skegness U.D.C.* [1967] 1 W.L.R. 52. But tax relief may be refused to registered charities who spend their money on non-charitable purposes: *I.R.C. v Educational Grants Assoc. Ltd.* [1967] Ch. 123.

they have not, then the courts and Commission move on to ask whether an analogy can be drawn between the purposes under consideration and other purposes which have previously been held to be legally charitable. This process of analogising from one purpose to another has been strongly criticised by commentators as a charade which disguises the value judgments made by the courts and Commission as to the desirability of using public money to underwrite the pursuit of particular activities.[55] An extreme example of this artificiality is furnished by the Canadian Federal Court of Appeal's decision in *Vancouver Regional FreeNet Assoc. v M.N.R.*,[56] that the provision of free public access to the "information highway", including the internet, is a charitable purpose by way of analogy to the charitable purpose of repairing bridges, ports, causeways, and highways.

Changing social and economic circumstances

7–14   In recent years, as evidenced by its publication *RR1a: Recognising New Charitable Purposes*, the Commission has laid more stress in its decisions on the question whether changes in social and economic circumstances have made it more (or less) desirable for particular purposes to be pursued— although the Commission still does not purport to decide whether one purpose is a *better* use of public money than another, nor does it attempt to co-ordinate charitable activity with government activity, save to the extent that it invariably holds that purposes which are explicitly adopted as government policy are for the public benefit.[57]

7–15   To the extent that the Commission's new approach reveals something of its policy calculations about public resource allocation, it does at least bring some transparency to the decision-making process. But the question remains, whether it is desirable for the Commission and the courts to formulate policy in this area at all? In *Dingle v Turner*, Lord Cross held that "in answering the question whether any given trust is a charitable trust the courts . . . cannot avoid having regard to the fiscal privileges accorded to charities",[58] but three other law lords in the case disassociated themselves from these remarks, considering that questions of public resource allocation are unsuited for judicial determination.[59] However, ignoring the issue does not make it go away: like it or not, the courts and the Charity Commission have effectively been left to decide such questions because successive governments have not wished to take responsibility for doing so.

Construction of trust documents

7–16   Where the purposes of a trust or body are clearly set out in a document then the question whether these purposes are charitable must be decided by sole reference to the document, and it is irrelevant to ask how the settlor or

---

[55] *e.g.* G.W. Keeton, "The Charity Muddle" (1949) 2 C.L.P. 86; N.P. Gravells, "Public Purpose Trusts" (1977) 40 M.L.R. 397: S. Gardner, *An Introduction to the Law of Trusts* (1990), pp.101–110; F. Quint, "The Rationale of Charity Law" (1994) 2 C.L.&P.R. 211.

[56] [1996] 3 F.C. 880.

[57] See, *e.g.* Charity Commission, *RR 12: The Promotion of Human Rights* (January 2005 version), paras 10– 12, noting that the U.K. government has incorporated the European Convention for the Protection of Human Rights into domestic law, in the course of holding that the promotion of human rights is a charitable purpose.

[58] [1972] A.C. 601 at 624; at para.7–166.

[59] *ibid.* at 614; at paras 7–150, 7–152, and 7–153.

founders of the organization contemplated that the purposes should be pursued.[60] If the trustees are given powers which are expressed to be incidental, but the court finds that the exercise of these powers is in substance a non-charitable purpose of the trust, then the trust will not be wholly or exclusively charitable.[61] Where a document is ambiguous, so that it is unclear whether the purposes expressed in the document are charitable, extrinsic evidence may be admitted of the manner in which the purposes have been or are capable of being carried out.[62] Some of the circumstances in which this may be needed are discussed in the Charity Commission's *Annual Report for 1966.*

CHARITY COMMISSION, *ANNUAL REPORT FOR 1966*

"36. Some of our non-legal correspondents have questioned the justification for **7–17** the importance which the law attaches to the words used rather than to the institution's activities. It is felt by such correspondents that it should be enough to examine the activities of the institution to decide whether it is a charity and that two organisations both doing the same things should be equally qualified for registration. But this fails to take account of the fact that the law must be concerned principally with the obligation imposed on the institution to pursue certain objects. It is this obligation which established it as a charity; and so long as an institution is free to pursue any activities it wishes it cannot be treated as an established charity however much its current activities may resemble those of other recognised charities.

"37. The problem of interpreting words presents a somewhat different aspect **7–18** when we are asked to consider draft documents intended to set up proposed charities. It is not unusual to find an attempt to dress up the purposes of the proposed institution in words which it is hoped will be accepted as charitable even though the purposes, so phrased, are quite remote from the true intentions of the promoters. We are convinced that this is a highly unsatisfactory course and that the governing instrument of every institution should show unequivocally what the institution really sets out to achieve. Three particular devices call for comment.

"38. The first is the over-working of the word "education". Ingenious draftsmen **7–19** have found it possible to embrace within this word a vast variety of activities, mainly propagandist, which do not come within the meaning of the "advancement of education" as it is used in charity law. A purpose which is not charitable cannot be made charitable merely by representing it to be a form of education.

"39. The second device is the use of very wide general terms. It is of course true **7–20** that there are some founders of charities, particularly those who are settling part of their own personal fortune, who genuinely expect to apply the settled property for all manner of charitable purposes; in such a case the general words are not intended

---

[60] *Keren Kayemeth Le Jisroel Ltd. v I.R.C.* [1931] 2 K.B. 465 at 484; *I.R.C. v Oldham Training and Enterprise Council* [1996] S.T.C. 1218 at 1234.
[61] *The Cowan Charitable Trust* [1976] Ch. Com. Rep. paras 45–49; *Vancouver Society of Immigrant and Visible Minority Women v M.N.R.* [1999] 1 S.C.R. 10.
[62] *Incorporated Council of Law Reporting for England and Wales v Att.-Gen.* [1972] Ch. 73 at 91; *Southwood v Att.-Gen. The Times* October 26, 1998, not considered on appeal; Charity Commission, *Decision on Application for Registration by General Medical Council* (April 2, 2001), para.8; Charity Commission, *RR1a: Recognising New Charitable Purposes* (October 2001 version) para.39; Charity Commission, *Decision on Application for Registration by Crawley Model Railway Society* (12 August 2003), para.5.

to conceal a more limited true purpose. But, nonetheless, they may be difficult to interpret and it is undesirable that they should be used in any case where the proposed charity has a more limited purpose, particularly if the charity is intending to appeal to the public and not be merely the vehicle for the founder's own benevolence.

7–21   "40. The third device is that of enumerating a number of objects, some perhaps charitable and others less obviously so, and then declaring that the institution is to be confined to carrying out such of the listed objects as are charitable. . . . This approach begs the question, prevents the real purpose of the institution from being readily recognised and quite unnecessarily introduces difficulty in construing and acting upon the documents in which it is used. If a proposed charity shows us a draft instrument incorporating such a phrase we consider ourselves entitled to enquire what are intended to be its activities, with a view to seeing whether those activities can be authorised in terms of clearly defined charitable purposes."

CHARITY COMMISSION, *RR. 1A: RECOGNISING NEW CHARITABLE PURPOSES*[63]

7–22   "1. This publication sets out briefly the legal principles that govern charitable status and the scope which the Commission has for recognising new charitable purposes.. . .

7–23   "3. In order to determine which purposes are charitable the law uses a process of precedent and analogy. The courts have decided that those purposes are charitable which fall within the objects set out in the Preamble to the Charitable Uses Act 1601 or have been held to be analogous to those objects. The Preamble contains a list of purposes which were regarded as charitable in Elizabethan times.

7–24   "4. The courts added to the list of purposes which were accepted as charitable over the years and in 1891 Lord McNaghten in the *Pemsel* case[64] classified charitable purposes under four heads:

- the relief of poverty (1st head)
- the advancement of education (2nd head)
- the advancement of religion (3rd head)
- other purposes beneficial to the community.[65]

The classification has been used since as a matter of convenience but it is not a definition.

7–25   "5. Although the courts still use the Preamble as a touchstone and refer to the *Pemsel* classification, they have long recognised that what is accepted as a charitable purpose must change to reflect current social and economic circumstances. So a purpose will be charitable not only if it is within the list in the Preamble but also if it is analogous to any purpose either within it or since held to be charitable. Nowadays many charities are set up for purposes that are not mentioned in the Preamble.

7–26   "6. In this way charitable purposes have been extended and developed, by decisions of the courts and of the Charity Commissioners, so that the development of the law has reflected changes in social and economic circumstances.

---

[63] October 2001 version.
[64] *Commissioners for Special Purposes of Income Tax v Pemsel* [1891] A.C. 531.
[65] [Editors' note: the Charities Bill 2005, cl.2(2), at para.7–43, divides this fourth head into nine.]

The Commission's powers to recognise new charitable purposes

"7. Under section 3(1) of the Charities Act 1993, the Charity Commission has an **7–27** obligation to keep a Register of institutions that are charities. In fulfilling this obligation we have the power to recognise a new purpose as charitable in circumstances where we believe the court would do so.

"8. We have the same powers as the court when determining whether an **7–28** organisation has charitable status and the same powers to take into account changing social and economic circumstances—whether to recognise a purpose as charitable for the first time or to recognise that a purpose has ceased to be charitable. We interpret and apply the law as to charitable status in accordance with the principles laid down by the courts. Faced with conflicting approaches by the courts, we take a constructive approach in adapting the concept of charity to meeting the constantly evolving needs of society. The Register of Charities is therefore a reflection of the decisions made by the courts and our decisions following the example of the courts.

"9. The courts are increasingly setting out the underlying principles when deciding **7–29** cases on charitable status and providing guidelines for future cases. The analysis by Slade J. in *McGovern v Att.-Gen.*[66] of the rules relating to political purposes is an example of this approach. In the same way, where appropriate, we will clarify the underlying principles raised by a particular application for registration in order to provide guidance for future applications. For example, the Commissioners, in reaching a decision on the charitable status of the Church of Scientology (England and Wales), considered and set out the underlying principles raised by that particular application for registration as a charity in order to reach their decision and so provide guidance for future applications.[67]

Need for a flexible legal framework

"10. The courts recognise that there is a need for a flexible legal framework by **7–30** which new charitable purposes can be recognised in the light of changing social and economic circumstances. Lord Simonds, for example, said in the case of *National Anti-Vivisection Society v I.R.C.*[68] that purposes regarded as beneficial to the public and charitable in one age may not be so regarded in a later age, and vice versa. As the courts have power, in limited circumstances, not to follow previous court decisions, so do we.

"11. The courts have stressed that the law is not static and, as Lord Hailsham **7–31** pointed out in *I.R.C. v McMullen.*[69] the law must change as ideas about social values change. This has two implications: first, new objects and purposes not previously considered charitable may be held to be so; secondly, objects and purposes previously regarded as charitable may no longer be held to be charitable. Lord Wilberforce summarised the principle to be applied in *Scottish Burial Reform and Cremation Society v Glasgow Corporation*[70] when he said that the court's decisions 'have to keep the law as to charities moving according as new ideas arise or old ones become obsolete or satisfied.'

---

[66] [1982] Ch. 321.
[67] See report of the decision of the Commissioners on the application for registration by the Church of Scientology (England and Wales) which can be found on our website (www.charity-commission.gov.uk). [Editors' note: the text of this decision is reproduced at paras 7–243 *et seq.*]
[68] [1948] Ch. 31 at 74.
[69] [1981] A.C. 1 at 15.
[70] [1968] A.C. 138 at 154.

7–32   "12. The courts have clearly indicated that they will not be rigidly bound by precedent and that a particular purpose may cease to be charitable as social circumstances change. Thus, in *National Anti-Vivisection Society v I.R.C.*, Lord Wright said that:[71]

> '. . . trusts [providing particular remedies thought to relieve the distress caused by advanced age, sickness, disability or poverty] may, as economic ideas and conditions and ideas of social service change, cease to be regarded as being for the benefit of the community. And trusts for the advancement of learning or education may fail to secure a place as charities, if it is seen that the learning or education is not of public value.'

Changing social circumstances

7–33   "13. We also recognise the need to apply the law in changing social circumstances, although we are only able to determine which purposes are charitable in the way that the courts have done or in a way that we anticipate the courts would do. In deciding whether novel purposes are charitable or not, we seek to predict the decision the court would reach if it were to consider the matter.

7–34   "14. The Commission is the first level at which an organisation may obtain a decision as to whether or not it is charitable in law. Given our predictive role in assessing whether an organisation may be charitable in anticipation of what a court itself might decide when faced with a novel charitable purpose, we may be able to recognise a new charitable purpose where the legal framework permits. It may be the case that we could also depart from previous contrary legal precedent where there has been a significant change in circumstances from when those court decisions were taken . . .

THE NEED FOR AN ANALOGY TO AN EXISTING CHARITABLE PURPOSE

7–35   "23. In 1985 we reviewed our policy for deciding whether novel purposes are charitable.[72] Having examined the legal authorities, the Commissioners concluded that they must follow the courts' approach in seeking an analogy.[73] An up to date interpretation of that policy is as follows:

> 'The Commission will take a constructive approach in adapting the concept of charity to meet constantly evolving social needs and new ideas through which those needs can be met. Acting within the legal framework which governs the recognition of new charitable purposes, we would aim to act constructively and imaginatively.
>
> 'In considering new purposes as charitable we will look closely at those purposes which have already been recognised as charitable either under the Preamble or in subsequent decisions of the court or the Commission. We will also look at contemporary needs of society and relevant legislation passed by Parliament and, where Convention rights are in issue, to the European Convention on Human Rights and decisions of the European Court of Human Rights and the European Commission of Human Rights.

---

[71] [1948] A.C. 31 at 42.
[72] See Commissioners' *Annual Report for 1985*, paras 24–27.
[73] *Barralet v Att.-Gen.* [1980] All E.R. 918 at 926–927, *per* Dillon J.

'In identifying a new purpose as charitable we will, following the legal framework, need to be clear that there exists a sufficient correlation between those new purposes and purposes already accepted as charitable. While in most cases a sufficiently close analogy may be found, in others an analogy may be found by following the broad principles which may be derived from the scope of the Preamble or from decided cases of the court or the Commission.

'In addition we will need to be clear that the purpose is not a political purpose as understood in charity law and that the purposes are expressed with clarity and certainty to facilitate monitoring by us and any subsequent control by the court should that be necessary.'

"24. In effect, our view is that we will look for a suitable analogy in order to **7–36** confirm whether or not the way in which a purpose will benefit the public is charitable. We also believe it will nearly always be possible to find an analogy, if the nature of the benefit is really of a kind that ought to be recognised as charitable.

"25. Other legal authorities suggest that analogy with specific purposes already **7–37** accepted as charitable is not strictly needed but that a broader analogy with the kinds of purposes already accepted as charitable is sufficient . . . We will adopt this approach where there is clear benefit to the public . . ."

II. Charitable Purposes

Before the Statute of Charitable Uses 1601, the Court of Chancery **7–38** exercised jurisdiction in matters relating to charity (although in administering deceaseds' estates of personalty the ecclesiastical courts exercised a significant jurisdiction sanctioned by fines and excommunication), but notions of what was a charity were imprecise. The preamble to that statute contained a list of charitable objects which the courts used as "an index or chart" for the decision of particular cases, with the result that, in addition to the objects enumerated in the preamble, other objects analogous to them or within the spirit and intendment of the preamble came to be regarded as charitable. So for example, in *Scottish Burial Reform and Cremation Society v Glasgow Corporation* the House of Lords held the provision of crematoria charitable by analogy with the provision of burial grounds by analogy with the upkeep of churchyards by analogy with the repair of churches.[74] This enables the courts to avoid direct assessment of the social worth of putative charitable trusts and to avoid overt value judgments.

The 1601 statute was enacted as part of a comprehensive poor law code **7–39** and provided for commissioners to be appointed to investigate misappropriations of charity property. Its preamble commenced:

"Whereas lands, chattels, money have been given by sundry well disposed persons: some for the relief of aged, impotent and poor people; the maintenance of sick and maimed soldiers and mariners, schools of learning, free schools, and scholars in universities; the repair of bridges, ports, havens, causeways, churches, sea banks and highways;

---

[74] [1968] A.C. 138.

the education and preferment of orphans; the relief, stock, or maintenance for houses of correction; the marriage of poor maids; the supportation aid and help of young tradesmen, handicraftsmen and persons decayed; the relief or redemption of prisoners or captives; the aid or ease of any poor inhabitants concerning payment of fifteens, setting out of soldiers and other taxes; which lands, chattels and money have not been employed according to the charitable intent of the givers by reason of frauds, breaches of trust and negligence."

7–40   The Statute of Charitable Uses 1601 was repealed by the Mortmain and Charitable Uses Act 1888, but section 13(2) of the latter Act expressly preserved the preamble to the former statute, and on the basis of its continued existence Lord Macnaghten in *Commissioners of Income Tax v Pemsel* enunciated his famous fourfold classification of charity:

"Charity in its legal sense comprises four principal divisions: trusts for the relief of poverty; trusts for the advancement of education; trusts for the advancement of religion; and trusts for other purposes beneficial to the community, not falling under any of the preceding heads."

7–41   The Mortmain and Charitable Uses Act 1888, and with it the preamble to the Statute of Charitable Uses 1601, were repealed by the Charities Act 1960, section 38(4). Nonetheless the classification to which the Preamble gave rise has continued to form the starting-point for the courts and the Charity Commission when they are called upon to decide whether a purpose is charitable. It remains to be seen how long this remains the case. Recently moves have been made to enact a statutory restatement of the law of charitable status through clause 2 of the Charities Bill 2005. This Bill was originally introduced in December 2004 and had passed its second reading and amendment by the House of Lords Grand Committee when it was dropped prior to the general election in May 2005. It was reintroduced in an amended form in May 2005, and at the time of writing it seems likely that the bill will be enacted before the year is out. It will be seen that clause 2 retains the first three *Pemsel* heads, and sub-divides the fourth head into nine new heads, including a residual category of purposes which are "within the spirit" of any purposes which have been previously recognised as charitable. This residual category sweeps in all the existing charitable purposes which do not fall under any of the other eleven heads, and also allows for the recognition of new charitable purposes by a statutory version of the analogising process familiar from the case-law. Note that the terms in which the statutory heads are expressed—*e.g.* "the advancement of religion"—are to be read in line with their meanings at common law under clause 2(5).

Charities Bill 2005

Meaning of "charitable purpose"

"2.—(1) For the purposes of the law of England and Wales, a charitable purpose **7–42** is a purpose which:

   (a) falls within subsection (2), and
   (b) is for the public benefit (see section 3).

"(2) A purpose falls within this subsection if it falls within any of the following **7–43** descriptions of purposes:

   (a) the prevention or relief of poverty;
   (b) the advancement of education;
   (c) the advancement of religion;
   (d) the advancement of health or the saving of lives;
   (e) the advancement of citizenship or community development;
   (f) the advancement of the arts, culture, heritage or science;
   (g) the advancement of amateur sport;
   (h) the advancement of human rights, conflict resolution or reconciliation or the promotion of religious or racial harmony or equality and diversity;
   (i) the advancement of environmental protection or improvement;
   (j) the relief of those in need by reason of youth, age, ill-health, disability, financial hardship or other disadvantage;
   (k) the advancement of animal welfare;
   (l) any other purposes within subsection (4).

"(3) In subsection (2):   **7–44**

   (a) in paragraph (c) "religion" includes—

      (i) a religion which involves belief in more than one god, and
     (ii) a religion which does not involve belief in a god;

   (b) in paragraph (d) "the advancement of health" includes the prevention or relief of sickness, disease or human suffering;
   (c) paragraph (e) includes:

      (i) rural or urban regeneration, and
     (ii) the promotion of civic responsibility, volunteering, the voluntary sector or the effectiveness or efficiency of charities;

   (d) in paragraph (g) "sport" means sport which involves physical skill and exertion; and
   (e) paragraph (j) includes relief given by the provision of accommodation or care to the persons mentioned in that paragraph.

"(4) The purposes within this subsection (see subsection (2)(l)) are: **7–45**

   (a) any purposes not within paragraphs (a) to (k) of subsection (2) but recognised as charitable purposes under existing charity law or by virtue of section 1 of the Recreational Charities Act 1958 (c. 17);

(b) any purposes that may reasonably be regarded as analogous to, or within the spirit of, any purposes falling within any of those paragraphs or paragraph (a) above; and

(c) any purposes that may reasonably be regarded as analogous to, or within the spirit of, any purposes which have been recognised under charity law as falling within paragraph (b) above or this paragraph.

7–46   "(5) Where any of the terms used in any of paragraphs (a) to (k) of subsection (2), or in subsection (3), has a particular meaning under charity law, the term is to be taken as having the same meaning where it appears in that provision.

7–47   "(6) In this section:

'charity law' means the law relating to charities in England and Wales; and 'existing charity law' means charity law as in force immediately before the day on which this section comes into force."

III. Public Benefit

7–48   A valid charitable trust must also provide some identifiable and definable benefit[75] directly or indirectly for at least a section of the public, as opposed to a private class of individuals. In theory, a presumption was formerly made that trusts for the relief of poverty, the advancement of religion, and the advancement of education would all be for the public benefit,[76] although in practice the Charity Commissioners have applied a public benefit test to all new applicants for registration in recent years. It is intended that the presumption will be removed by clause 3(2) of the Charities Bill 2005. In the event that this clause is enacted in its present form, some older organisations which were granted charitable status by operation of the presumption will have to be revisited by the Commission and their public benefit credentials subjected to scrutiny.[77]

7–49   It is clear that a trust need not benefit every person in the country to be charitable, but the courts have struggled to articulate a clear test to distinguish between charitable trusts which benefit a group of people *qua* members of the public, from private trusts which benefit a group of people *qua* private individuals. The House of Lords in *Oppenheim v Tobacco Securities Trust Co. Ltd*, at para.7–194, used the personal nexus test put forward in *Re Compton* to distinguish between charitable trusts and private trusts: they held that except in "poverty" cases no class of beneficiaries can constitute a section of the public if the distinguishing quality which links them together is a relationship to a particular person either through a common ancestor or a common employer. Thus a trust for the education of the children of employees of British American Tobacco Co. Ltd or any of its subsidiary or allied companies was not a valid charitable trust though

---

[75] *Gilmour v Coats* [1949] A.C. 426; *Re Pinion* [1965] Ch. 85.
[76] *National Anti-Vivisection Society v I.R.C.* [1948] A.C. 31 at 42.
[77] The Charity Commission has issued provisional guidance on the approach which it expects to take to such bodies in its paper *Public Benefit: The Charity Commission's Approach* (January 2005 version).

there were over 110,000 current employees. If the trust had been for the education of those employed or formerly employed in the tobacco industry it would have been valid as it would if it had been confined to children of those engaged in the tobacco industry in a particular county or town.

The weaknesses of the personal nexus test are revealed in the dissenting **7–50** speech of Lord MacDermott in *Oppenheim*, at para.7–199, with whose broad approach the House of Lords were in *obiter* agreement in *Dingle v Turner*, at para.7–165. There, Lord Cross indicated that whether or not the potential beneficiaries of a trust can fairly be said to constitute a section of the public is a question of degree in all the circumstances of the case, and that much must depend on the purposes of the trusts. If that is correct, then it means that there can be no universal test of public benefit because the question whether a purpose is charitable, and the question whether the pursuit of the purpose is for the public benefit, are not separate but interrelated questions.

Owing to the conflicting views expressed in the Lords in *Oppenheim* and **7–51** *Dingle*, the lower courts and the Charity Commission face a dilemma when cases arise that compel a choice between the two views. The narrow personal nexus approach, though conducive to certainty, also leads to artificial manipulation of the legal forms so as to obtain fiscal advantages, *e.g.* in the case of a trust for the education of children of inhabitants of Bournville, which might be invalidated under the broad approach as being in substance a trust benefiting employees of Cadbury Schweppes plc. The broad approach, though less predictable in outcome, at least concerns itself with the substance of the matter and is not unduly preoccupied with form. The Charity Commission currently tries to steer a middle course, stating in its paper, *Public Benefit: The Legal Principles*, that "whilst the Commission must apply the law as set out in the *Oppenheim* decision . . . it should be both cautious and flexible in the application of the test."[78] This seems to mean that in practice the Commission will not necessarily refuse charitable status to a trust for the benefit of a class defined by a personal nexus with the settlor and/or one another, provided that "on a general survey of the circumstances and considerations regarded as relevant it is clear that a public class is intended . . . [and the class can be] described otherwise than by relation to kin or contractual relationship."[79]

Charging for services

The fact that an organization charges for its services does not prevent it **7–52** from being charitable, so long as profits are not distributed to individuals, and are instead used to further the organization's charitable purposes.[80]

---

[78] Appendix A, para.A11.
[79] *ibid.* at para.A13.
[80] *ibid.* at paras A20 *et seq.* See too *Re Resch's W.T.* [1969] 1 A.C. 514; *Re Rowntree Memorial Housing Assoc. Ltd* [1983] Ch. 159; *C. & E. Commissioners v Bell Concord Educational Trust Ltd* [1989] 2 All E.R. 217.

Charities Bill 2005

The "public benefit" test

7–53   "3.—(1) This section applies in connection with the requirement in section 2(1)(b) that a purpose falling within section 2(2) must be for the public benefit if it is to be a charitable purpose.

7–54   "(2) In determining whether that requirement is satisfied in relation to any such purpose, it is not to be presumed that a purpose of a particular description is for the public benefit.

7–55   "(3) In this Part any reference to the public benefit is a reference to the public benefit as that term is understood for the purposes of the law relating to charities in England and Wales.

7–56   "(4) Subsection (3) applies subject to subsection (2)."

CHARITY COMMISSION, PUBLIC BENEFIT: *THE LEGAL PRINCIPLES*[81]

What is public benefit?

7–57   "3. There are five main principles which show whether an organisation provides benefit to the public. These are:

The Benefit   (i)   There must be an identifiable benefit, but this can take many different forms.
                   (ii) Benefit is assessed in the light of modern conditions.
The Public   (iii) The benefit must be to the public at large, or to a sufficient section of the public.
                   (iv) Any private benefit must be incidental.
                   (v)   Those who are less well off must not be entirely excluded from benefit.

The Benefit

7–58   "4. The following principles apply when deciding whether a purpose is beneficial in a way that the law regards as charitable.

There must be an identifiable benefit, but this can take many different forms

7–59   "5. Every charity must be set up for the benefit of the public, but the law does not adopt the same practical measures to assess public benefit in every type of case. This means that the ways in which benefit can be demonstrated can differ for different charitable purposes.

7–60   "6. 'Benefit' in this context means the overall benefit to the public. It is not simply a question of showing that some benefit may result. The achievement of a particular purpose may provide a measure of benefit to the public but, in achieving that benefit, may also cause harm. If the harm outweighs the benefits, the overall result is that the purpose would not be charitable.

---

[81] January 2005 version.

Tangible and intangible benefit

"7. The benefit to the public should be capable of being identified and defined, **7–61** whether the nature of that benefit is tangible or intangible. In some cases a purpose may be so clearly beneficial to the public that there would be no need for further proof of public benefit to be provided. In other cases, the element of benefit to the public may be more debatable and will need to be shown.

"8. Tangible benefits are usually material or measurable. For example, if a charity **7–62** relieves a person's sickness or financial hardship, the person's health or financial circumstances are measurably improved. In such cases, the benefit is normally obvious.

"9. The general rule is to look for tangible benefits first. Where there are no **7–63** tangible benefits, intangible benefits will suffice provided that the benefit is clear. Intangible benefits may be more difficult to measure, but are nonetheless identifiable. They can include, for example, many of the benefits of education, or the appreciation of a historic building or a beautiful landscape. When considering intangible benefits, the Charity Commission, court or tribunal will take into account the general consensus of fair-minded and unprejudiced opinion. But public opinion cannot by itself determine what is and is not charitable.

Direct and indirect benefit

"10. A direct benefit is one which arises as a direct consequence of carrying out **7–64** the particular charitable purpose. For example, there is a direct benefit to the people who receive medical care if they are sick; to the people whose conditions in life have been improved by taking part in recreational activities; or to the people whose skills have been developed by taking part in a training programme. Most charitable purposes will involve direct benefits.

"11. However, indirect as well as direct benefits may be taken into account in **7–65** assessing whether an organisation provides sufficient benefit to the public.

"12. An indirect benefit is one where the benefit can be said to extend beyond the **7–66** immediate beneficiaries, in many cases to the public generally. Examples include:—

- the indirect benefit to patients where a charity provides accommodation or recreational facilities for nurses in order to improve their efficiency and performance;
- the indirect benefit to the public where one charity provides services to other charities in order to improve their efficiency and effectiveness and make the best use of their resources to the advantage of their beneficiaries and donors; and
- providing a scanner in a hospital, which (as well as providing direct benefits to those who use it) indirectly benefits other patients in the hospital and the public at large by enabling the hospital to use its resources in other ways.

Benefit is assessed in the light of modern conditions

"14. The courts develop charity law to take into account modern needs and **7–67** circumstances. This means that perceptions of public benefit can change over time, and those changes are influenced (among other things) by social and economic conditions, by increasing knowledge and understanding and by changes in social values.

"15. Purposes that may not have been regarded as beneficial years ago may, in the **7–68** light of changing circumstances, be regarded as beneficial now, and vice versa.

7–69   "16. For example, in recent years we have recognised the promotion of urban and rural regeneration, the promotion of community capacity building, the promotion of equality and diversity, conservation of the environment and the promotion of sustainable development as charitable purposes in the light of modern circumstances.

Public

7–70   "17. The following principles apply when deciding whether an organisation with charitable purposes benefits the public or a sufficient section of it . . .

The benefit must be to the public at large, or to a sufficient section of the public

7–71   "18. This is not a simple matter of numbers. What is 'sufficient' will vary from case to case depending upon the organisation's purposes.

7–72   "19. Beneficiaries may be defined by reference to qualifications of charitable need (such as sickness or financial hardship for example), by a particular geographical area, or other criteria, provided that the resulting number of beneficiaries is sufficiently large or open in nature and is consistent with the charitable purpose being pursued.

7–73   "20. If the organisation's benefits are available to anyone who, being suitably qualified, chooses to take advantage of them, it provides benefit to the public, even though in some cases the actual number of beneficiaries may be quite small. For example, an organisation may offer only a small number of places for the services it provides, such as a small number of available rooms in an almshouse or care home, but those places are open to a sufficient section of the public to apply for them.

7–74   "21. Generally, it will not be a sufficient section of the public if those who make up the section of the public who could benefit are numerically negligible. However, in some cases, it might be possible to show that a benefit to a small section of the public benefits the public as a whole. For example, an organisation directed towards relieving the suffering caused by a very rare disease will provide benefit to the public even though few people need to avail themselves of its services.

7–75   "22. Similarly, there may be some groups of people within society which, though numerically small, are suffering some common disadvantage. For example, there are many registered charities designed to cater for the educational, social and personal safety needs of vulnerable people in particular circumstances. What must be considered in each case is whether any limitations placed upon who benefits are justifiable and reasonable given the nature of the charitable purpose being pursued and whether those who can benefit constitute overall a sufficient section of the public.

7–76   "23. Those who benefit from the charity should not be defined by a connecting link which either:

- involves a personal connection, such as family relationship or common employer (although this does not apply to charities for the prevention or relief of poverty where beneficiaries can be defined by reference to family or employer connections); or is
- irrational, *i.e.* the qualities used to define its beneficiaries should be related to the organisation's purpose (*e.g.* in most cases beneficiaries cannot be determined by hair colour or support for a particular football team); the beneficiaries must be rationally identified.

Restrictions on public access

"24. Where an organisation is set up to provide or maintain particular facilities **7–77** for the benefit of the public, any restrictions on public access (such as limited opening hours or limitations on what areas people have physical access to) must be reasonable and appropriate in the circumstances. In such cases, the degree of public access (however that is provided) must be sufficient overall for the organisation to claim that it provides public benefit.

Membership

"25. Some charities have a membership structure under which the members are **7–78** also the charity's beneficiaries. In this case, any restrictions placed on who may join as a member must be reasonable and justifiable in the circumstances if the public benefit of the organisation is not to be compromised.

"26. However, where members are beneficiaries, access to membership may, in **7–79** certain circumstances, be properly limited where this is linked to the charity's purpose. For example:

- it may be limited to the inhabitants of a particular geographical area;
- where, in order to deliver benefit to the public, it is reasonable to expect the members to have reached a certain standard of skill or knowledge or possess particular qualifications (such as a performing orchestra or choir);
- where a particular membership structure is appropriate for the better delivery of benefits (provided that all those who might benefit can join and there are objective criteria for deciding membership);
- where practical reasons (such as limited space) dictate a limit upon membership numbers. (In such cases it is reasonable to have a waiting list for membership provided the next available membership is offered on a first come first served basis.)

Any private benefit must be incidental

"27. Any benefit to an individual or organisation must either: **7–80**

- directly further the charity's purposes (*e.g.* a grant to relieve financial hardship); or
- be incidental to the pursuit of the charity's purposes (e.g. paying reasonable salaries to its staff or limited profit to businesses as a result of urban regeneration projects).

"28. In general, a private benefit is legitimately incidental if: **7–81**

- it arises as a necessary, but secondary, consequence of a decision by the trustees; and
- that decision is directed only at furthering the organisation's charitable purposes (as opposed to a separate purpose of in effect providing private benefit); and
- the amount of benefit is reasonable in the circumstances.

"29. If it is necessary and desirable to confer special benefits on the members of **7–82** an organisation in order to carry out its charitable purposes, generally the private benefit to the members can be regarded as incidental. However, an association which is supported by its members for the purpose of providing benefits for themselves cannot usually be a charity. It is a question of degree; does the organisation exist primarily for the advantage of its members or has the membership structure been adopted solely as an effective way of delivering charitable benefits or for administrative convenience? . . .

Those who are less well off must not be entirely excluded from benefit

7–83   "31. Generally speaking, charities may charge their users for access to their services and facilities and indeed many do. These include, for example:

- Educational organisations (such as schools and universities);
- Private hospitals;
- Care homes;
- Recreational charities (such as sports centres, recreation grounds or village halls) that charge for hire of facilities;
- Artistic, preservation and conservation charities (such as theatres, museums and stately homes) which charge entry to view performances, exhibits, land or properties;
- Charities that charge for membership (whether annual, seasonal or daily); and
- Charities that charge for publications.

7–84   "32. A charity may charge fees which more than cover the cost of the services or facilities it provides. This is acceptable provided that the charges are reasonably and necessarily applied in furtherance of the charity's purposes, for example in maintaining or developing the service being provided.

7–85   "33. However, where the charges are so high that they effectively exclude the less well off, this can affect public benefit.

7–86   "34. In considering the extent to which charging by a charity might affect its ability to demonstrate benefit to the public, the following broad principles apply:

- Both direct and indirect benefits to the public, or a sufficient section of the public, may be taken into account in deciding whether an organisation is set up and operates for the benefit of the public;
- The fact that the charitable facilities or services will be charged for, and will be provided mainly to people who can afford to pay the charges, does not necessarily mean that the organisation is not set up for and does not operate for the benefit of the public;
- However, an organisation which wholly excluded less well off people from any benefits, direct or indirect, would not be set up and operate for the benefit of the public and therefore would not be a charity.

7–87   "35. Applying this approach in cases where high fees are charged for services or facilities provided, the following issues will be considered:-

1. Does the level at which fees are set have the effect of preventing or deterring the less well off from accessing the services or facilities?
2. If this is the case, is it possible to show that the less well off are not wholly excluded from any possible benefits, direct or indirect?

7–88   "36. The following general factors may be relevant:-

- Whether and how the less well off may otherwise access those services. This is likely to vary from charity to charity and for different charitable purposes but may include considering:

  - The provision of concessions, subsidised or free places (for example, in the case of schools by offering scholarships, bursaries or assisted places, or in the case of theatres by offering concessionary tickets);
  - The existence of accessible insurance or other benefit schemes (for example, medical insurance schemes);
  - The provision of wider access to charitable facilities or services. For example some charities may provide additional facilities or services for the less well off people who would otherwise be excluded. Some charities may lend equipment or staff out to other charities or groups which provide the same facilities or services to the less well off. For example, a charitable independent school allowing a state maintained school to use its educational facilities.

- What is the nature and extent of the benefit provided? This may include considering how far the type of service or facility provided is one for which there is a public need, and how far the service or facility provided in the particular case contributes towards meeting that need. For example, a hospital not run by the NHS may provide specialised scanning equipment which is not available in the local NHS hospital, or an elderly person in a home might be provided with care for longer than he or she would have received it from the public service provider.
- The nature and extent of any indirect public benefit. This may take various forms. For example, a care home not run by the state working alongside state run homes may be able to meet local needs for the provision of care which the state run homes alone would be unable to do."

IV. TRUSTS WITH POLITICAL PURPOSES

Trusts for political purposes are non-charitable trusts on the basis that **7–89** the courts have no means of judging whether a proposed change in the law would or would not be for the public benefit,[82] and the law could not stultify itself by holding that it was for the public benefit that the law itself should be changed.[83] Political purposes comprise not only attempts to change the law by legislation or to oppose proposed changes but also attempts to influence local or national government home or foreign policy. Thus a university student union cannot indulge in a campaign against the Government ending free milk for school children or against the Government's support of a foreign war like that in the Gulf between Iraq and Kuwait.[84]

---

[82] *Bowman v Secular Society* [1917] A.C. 406 at 442, *per* Lord Parker.
[83] *National Anti-Vivisection Society v I.R.C.*, [1948] A.C. 31 at 49, 62, para.7–281. See also *Bonar Law Memorial Trust v I.R.C.* (1933) 49 T.L.R. 220 (Conservative); *Re Ogden* [1933] Ch. 678 (Liberal); *Re Hopkinson* [1949] W.N. 29 (Socialist); *Re Strakosch* [1949] Ch. 529 (appeasing racial feeling); *Re Bushnell* [1975] 1 All E.R. 721; (1975) 38 M.L.R. 471 (furthering socialised medicine in a socialist state); C.J. Forder [1984] Conv. 263.
[84] See *Baldry v Feintuck* [1972] 2 All E.R. 81; *Webb v O'Doherty* (1991) 3 Admin. L.R. 731, and also *Re Koeppler's W.T.* [1984] Ch. 243. In *Southwood v Att.-Gen.* [2000] W.T.L.R. 1199 the Court of Appeal held that a trust to educate the public to accept that peace is best secured by demilitarisation and disarmament is political and non-charitable.

The following bodies are not registered as charities: the National Anti-Vivisection Society, National Council for Civil Liberties, Campaign against Racial Discrimination, Martin Luther King Fund, United Nations Association, Animal Abuse, and the Disablement Income Group.

7–90 However, if a body, particularly a long established one, which exists for much wider charitable purposes,[85] incidentally indulges in political activity so as to put pressure on the public and politicians this does not affect the charitable status of the body, *e.g.* the RSPCA fighting vivisection, the British Legion fighting for better pensions for ex-servicemen, Guide Dogs for the Blind resisting VAT on dog food, the National Association for Mental Health in their MIND campaign organising and presenting a petition to Parliament. Certain registered charities such as the Child Poverty Action Group and Shelter have been walking the tightrope so precariously as to lead the Charity Commissioners to publish guidance on this issue which they have recently updated, in response to the recommendation by the Prime Minister's Strategy Unit, that they should highlight the benefits to be had from charities playing an advocacy and campaigning role.

CHARITY COMMISSION, *CC 9: CAMPAIGNING AND POLITICAL ACTIVITIES BY CHARITIES*[86]

Meaning of words and expressions used

7–91 "3. In this guidance . . .

Political purpose means in essence any purpose directed at:

- furthering the interests of any political party; or
- securing, or opposing, any change in the law or in the policy or decisions of central government or local authorities, whether in this country or abroad.

Campaigning covers a wide range of activities. It is used to refer to:

- public awareness raising and education on a particular issue;
- influencing and changing public attitudes; and
- political activities which are intended to influence Government policy or legislation, and which may involve contact with political parties.

Much campaigning work by charities involves acting as an advocate for their service users or beneficiaries. Like campaigning, advocacy covers a wide range of activities, which can range from general awareness raising activities through to direct engagement in political activities. It may, or may not, involve political campaigning.

---

[85] These purposes do not in practice have to be much wider in the case of respectable long established charities like the Anti-Slavery Society, the Lords Day Observance Society and the Howard League for Penal Reform. By way of contrast the Humanist Trust, the National Secular Society and the Sexual Law Reform Society are not charities. The Upper Teesdale Defence Fund was registered as a charity, though its *raison d'être* seemed to be to oppose a private Bill in Parliament, since the Commissioners take the view that virtually all private Bills are free from the taint of political activity: see 1969 Annual Report, para.15.

[86] September 2004 version.

Political activity means any activity that is directed at securing, or opposing, any change in the law or in the policy or decisions of central government or local authorities, whether in this country or abroad.

Introduction

"4. Since the Charity Commission's guidance, *Political Activities and Campaigning*   **7–92** *by Charities*, was first published in 1995, there have been significant changes to the ways in which campaigning and political activities are carried out, both in the sophistication of the methods used by charities, and within the environment in which these activities take place.

"5. More recently, the Government's Strategy Unit report, *Private Action, Public*   **7–93** *Benefit* (September 2002), has highlighted the benefits to be had if charities are encouraged, rather than restricted, from playing an advocacy and campaigning role. The report suggested that charities are well placed to carry out this role because of:

- their strong links into local communities which means that charities are well placed to monitor, evaluate and comment upon policies as they are implemented;
- the high levels of public trust and confidence they command means that charities are well placed to offer alternative ways of engaging with the public policy debate and the processes of democracy; and
- the diversity of causes they represent, enabling charities to give voice to a far wider range of political perspectives, including those of minority groups or interests, than might otherwise be heard by government.

"6. The report recommends that the Charity Commission's guidance on political   **7–94** campaigning should reflect these benefits, by placing a greater emphasis on the campaigning activities that charities can undertake, as opposed to the restrictions. The Charity Commission accepts the Strategy Unit's recommendation, and this revised guidance implements the recommendation . . .

The legal and regulatory framework

The scope of charity

"12. Although organisations that are established to pursue political purposes   **7–95** cannot be charities, campaigning and political activity may be carried out by recognised charities as a means of furthering their charitable purposes.

"13. Consequently, an organisation set up for a purpose (or which includes a   **7–96** purpose) of advocating or opposing changes in the law or public policy (in this country or abroad) or supporting a political party cannot be a charity. This is because the question of whether the organisation is established for the benefit of the public, an essential feature of all charities, cannot be assessed by the Charity Commission.

"14. Organisations established for exclusively charitable purposes may carry out   **7–97** campaigning and political activities to the extent outlined below, provided that the activities pursued are a legitimate means of furthering those purposes. A charity may quite properly be established with charitable purposes which can be carried out either wholly or partly by campaigning methods.

"15. Campaigning and political campaigning are distinct activities—the latter   **7–98** confined only to campaigns and activities which advocate or oppose changes in the law or public policy. Apart from the question of the proportion of charitable resources which may be applied (see below), expenditure on both are governed by the same legal rules.

The decision-making framework

7–99   "16. As with any other area of charitable activity, when considering whether to engage in campaigning or political activities charity trustees must be satisfied on reasonable grounds that :

- the activities will be an effective means of furthering the purposes of the charity; and
- they will do so to an extent justified by the resources applied.

7–100   "17. Trustees should also have regard to the following key points:

- the activities must be permitted under the governing document;
- the trustees must weigh the possible benefits for their charity and beneficiaries, against any possible reputational or other risks; and
- the charity must comply with the general law and with any other regulatory requirements.

What proportion of its resources can a charity properly devote to campaigning and political activity?

7–101   "22. As noted above, campaigning is a broad term that can include public awareness raising and education, or seeking to influence and change public attitudes. Provided it complies with the requirements set out above, a charity may choose to devote up to all its resources to non-political campaigning to further its purposes.

7–102   "23. However, where the campaign or other activity is of a political nature (*i.e.* seeking to advocate or oppose a change in the law or public policy), charity trustees must ensure that these activities do not become the dominant means by which they carry out the purposes of the charity. These activities must remain incidental or ancillary to the charity's purposes. What is dominant is a question of scope and degree upon which trustees must make a judgement. In making this judgement trustees should take into account factors such as the amount of resources applied and the period involved, the purposes of the charity and the nature of the activity.

7–103   "24. Where political activities do begin to dominate the activities of the charity, an issue will arise as to whether the charity trustees are acting outside their trusts. In exceptional cases this might also lead us to reconsider whether the organisation should ever have been registered as a charity, or whether it was in fact established for non-charitable political purposes . . .

Campaigning

7–104   "33. There are many forms of activity that charities use to deliver campaigns, and these are changing and developing all the time. This section covers some of the issues that charities should consider, and provides guidance on some of the methods used.

Use of campaign materials

7–105   "34. Irrespective of whether a charity is engaging the support of the general public, or a local community, it is free to use whatever method of communication it believes to be appropriate to its campaign.

"35. Whilst sometimes a charity will choose to set out a full explanation of its **7–106** position and reasons for the campaign, in order to gain support for it, there is no specific legal or regulatory requirement for the full position to be set out in all campaign materials. Indeed many forms of communication used for campaigning work, for example a newspaper advertisement limited by its size, or a restricted time slot on television or radio, will make it impractical to do so. However, as part of its assessment of the overall risks and benefits of the activity, a charity should consider:

- the benefits of engaging in a particular campaign;
- ways of approaching the campaign;
- the risks attached to the campaign, and how these might best be managed;
- the strategy for delivering the campaign; and
- how best to evaluate the campaign's success and impact.

"36. Charity trustees should also be prepared to properly explain and defend their **7–107** charity's decision to campaign, if asked to do so.

Use of emotive materials in campaigns

"37. Many charities, by the nature of their work and the issues they deal with, will **7–108** raise issues which are emotive for the public, and such charities' campaign materials will frequently have an emotive content. It is perfectly acceptable for a charity to decide to seek to raise awareness or to influence by means of using an argument or material which evokes strong emotions, without also providing the full rationale for carrying out the campaign. However, such charities need to consider the particular risks of using emotive materials, which may be significant because such materials can be controversial and potentially adversely affect the public's perception and attitude towards the charity. These risks will need to be weighed up against the potential benefits which might include enhanced public understanding and a change in attitude towards an issue.

Charities' involvement in demonstrations and direct action

"38. As part of a campaign, charities may wish to organise, promote or participate **7–109** in some kind of demonstration or direct action. This might involve simply the provision of information in a public place, such as handing out leaflets in order to raise awareness, in which case the guidance on the use of campaign materials outlined above will apply.

"39. Further considerations apply if a charity wishes to participate in an event and **7–110** do more than simply provide information. Such events might include participation in marches, rallies, or peaceful picketing. Such participation might offer significant opportunities for publicising a charity's position on an issue, and further its purposes, or show the extent of public support for the issue. Equally, a charity will also need to balance these potential benefits against any possible risks from engaging in the event. For example, there will always be some people who regard any involvement by a charity in events of this kind as inappropriate, and this view could pose risks for the reputation of the charity. Therefore, at the outset it is important to assess the likelihood and scale of any risk of damaging public support for the charity,

"40. Events such as demonstrations and rallies can also present real problems of **7–111** control for a charity, because of the complexities of public order legislation. These complexities mean that there is increased potential for the commission of an offence by the charity, its officers, or those taking part, compared with other campaigning activities. For this reason the charity should consider carefully what steps it can take to minimise or mitigate the risk of these offences occurring, for example through careful preparation and good liaison with the police or other authorities.

7–112   "41. Charities taking part in events involving a number of organisations should consider and manage the risks of participating alongside organisations who do not share the aims of the event organisers. A charity should also seek to ensure that any event is fully under the control of the organiser (whether or not this is the charity itself) and peaceful.

Acting with other bodies

7–113   "42. As well as working with another organisation and with individuals, a charity can work with and affiliate to a campaigning alliance, sometimes referred to as a 'coalition' or a 'consortium' of charities.

7–114   "43. It is not realistic to expect that everything that a campaigning alliance does, particularly if it has a large membership, will fit with every one of its members' charitable purposes.

7–115   "44. A charity wishing to participate in such an alliance should consider whether:

- there is a reasonable expectation that the arrangement will help to further the charity's purposes
- any expenditure can be justified; and
- the risks of participating are outweighed by the benefits. In particular, if some of the political activities that an alliance is engaging in do not fit with a charity's own charitable purposes, the charity will need to consider how best to manage any risks to its reputation, and its work. There may also be times when a charity is not able to support an alliance on a particular issue, but does not want to damage its relations with the alliance and, again, the charity will need to consider the best means of managing the risk.

7–116   "45. There may be some issues which generate interest and support from a range of different bodies, not all of them charitable, and sometimes alliances will consist of representatives from a number of charities, non-charitable organisations, individuals and perhaps representatives of a political party. In these circumstances, the considerations outlined above also apply . . .

Contact with political parties

7–117   "47. The principles which apply to charities' involvement in campaigning and political activities, apply equally to charities' contact with political parties and their representatives. Such contact is a natural and integral part of some campaigns. However, the value which the public attach to the independence of charities, and the confidence the public have in charities' work, means that charities need to pay particular consideration to the consequences of working with political parties and their representatives.

7–118   "48. Following the principles, it is acceptable for a charity to advocate support for a particular policy, even if that policy solution is advocated by a political party or candidate, providing the policy is in furtherance of the charity's purposes. However a charity must not support a political party or candidate.

7–119   "49. There are a number of ways in which charities might have contact with political parties or their representatives. A few examples are considered in Part B below, along with some other illustrative examples of campaigning and political activities.

Campaigning and political activities—some practical examples

"50. This list is not exhaustive or exclusive, and does not mean or imply that **7–120** charities are prevented from engaging in other types of political activity.

Influencing Government or local authorities

"51. A charity can seek to influence Government, local authorities, or public **7–121** opinion on issues either relating to the achievement of the charity's own stated purposes, or on issues of relevance to the well-being of the charitable sector.

"52. A charity can provide information to its supporters or the public on how **7–122** individual Members of Parliament, local councillors or parties have voted on an issue, in order to seek to persuade those Members, councillors, or parties to change their position, provided it can explain its reasons for doing so if requested.

"53. A charity can provide its supporters, or members of the public, with material **7–123** to send to Members of Parliament, councillors, central government, or the local authority, provided that—if requested—it can justify and demonstrate that a considered decision was made to engage in the activity and there is a rationale for using the chosen material.

"54. A charity is able to organise and present a petition to either House of **7–124** Parliament or to national or local government. The petition, or supporting material provided by the charity, should make it clear what the purpose of the petition is, so that those individuals considering supporting it know what they are signing up to. The charity should also be able to demonstrate, on request, that the petition's authenticity can be verified.

Responding to proposed legislation

"55. A charity may provide and publish comments on possible or proposed **7–125** changes in the law or government policy, whether contained in a Green or White Paper, draft Parliamentary Bill or elsewhere. A charity may also supply to Members of either House relevant information about the implications of a Parliamentary Bill, for use in debate.

Supporting, opposing and promoting new legislation and public policy, and changes to existing legislation and public policy

"56. A charity can support or oppose the passage of a Parliamentary Bill if such **7–126** support or opposition can reasonably be expected to further its charitable purposes. On the same basis a charity can also promote the need for a particular piece of legislation.

"57. These principles apply both to consideration of new and to existing public **7–127** policy. They also apply at both a national and a local level. For example:

- A local charity for homeless people could provide assistance in connection with an appeal against a decision of a local authority not to award accommodation;
- A national charity for homeless people could promote the need for a change in public policy or legislation relating to the way in which decisions are made in allocating accommodation;
- A civic trust could seek to influence decisions by a local authority concerning the listing of buildings of architectural merit; and
- A national conservation charity could seek to influence decisions by the body responsible for the listing of buildings.

7–128   "58. A national charity is free to influence on a local issue and a local charity is free to influence on a national issue, providing these principles are adhered to.

7–129   "59. In seeking to influence legislation or public policy a charity may wish to consider consulting with its key stakeholders, and possibly with members of the public. It might, for example, arrange consultative meetings in order to test the views of its beneficiaries and, when appropriate, the views of the general public, before supporting, opposing or promoting changes to legislation and public policy. Such consultation is not, however, a prerequisite when engaging in political activity. The main consideration for charity trustees is that they have a clear understanding of the ways in which the activity will further the interests of their beneficiaries.

7–130   "60. In circumstances where a charity is working internationally, and is seeking to promote any change in legislation or public policy, it must satisfy itself that such a change is in furtherance of its charitable purpose. Our guidance *Charities Working Internationally*, sets out specific legal requirements and recommended good practice for charities whose work is either wholly or partly international or overseas based.

Commenting on public issues

7–131   "61. A charity can make public comment on social, economic and political issues if these relate to its purpose or the way in which the charity is able to carry out its work.

Supporting political parties

7–132   "62. As explained in paragraphs 47–49, to support a political party, or its doctrine, is not, in itself, a charitable purpose. However, it may further a charity's purposes to support a policy which is also advocated by a political party. In supporting a policy that a political party also advocates the charity should seek to stress and make clear its independence, both to its supporters and to those people whose views its is seeking to influence.

Publishing the views of politicians and other contact with politicians

7–133   "63. A charity, whether local or national, may publish in its newsletter or other publications the views of local councillors, Members of Parliament and opposition candidates, where these views relate to the charity's purposes. The charity should consider the impact of the range and scope of the views, and how they are expressed, for the charity's work overall; as part of this consideration the trustees should assess whether the views represent any risks to the charity's reputation.

7–134   "64. A charity can invite a politician to speak on behalf of its cause, for example at a reception to launch a national campaign. Whilst ideally a charity enlisting the support of politicians should, for reasons of independence, seek cross party representation, some forms of campaign methods might make this impractical. The Charity Commission would however be concerned if a charity consistently enlisted the support of politicians from one political party only. In summary, due consideration should be given by a charity to ensuring that the methods chosen for delivering a campaign are part of a well thought through strategy and do not inadvertently result in any form of partisan support . . ."

V. No Unlawful Discrimination

Race Relations Act 1967

It is not against public policy or unlawful in a private trust to discriminate **7–135**
on grounds of race, religion, nationality or colour.[87] However the Race
Relations Act 1976 prohibits discrimination *against* persons on ground of
colour, race, nationality, or ethnic or national origins in the case of
charitable trusts, though it allows discrimination in *favour* of persons of a
class defined by reference to race, nationality or ethnic or national origins,[88]
though not by reference to colour. The colour qualification is disregarded
even where favourable discrimination is concerned.[89] Thus, a trust to
educate "black youngsters of West Indian origin in Brixton" would have the
word "black" deleted. In exceptional circumstances the removal of any
discriminatory provision unacceptable to the original trustees is possible
under the *cy-près* jurisdiction.[90]

Sex Discrimination Act 1975

Sexually discriminating provisions in private trusts are valid. Where a **7–136**
charitable trust contains a provision for benefiting persons of one sex only it
is valid,[91] *e.g.* Boy Scouts, Girl Guides, retired schoolmasters, research
fellowships available for men only.[92] In the case of an educational charity,
however, the trustees can apply to the Secretary of State for Education to
make the trust's benefits open to both sexes. He will make the order if
satisfied that to do so would conduce to the advancement of education
without sex discrimination and 25 years have elapsed since creation of the
trust, unless the donor (or his personal representatives) or the personal
representatives of the testator have consented in writing.[93]

Disability Discrimination Act 1995

Discrimination against the disabled is prescribed except that charities can **7–137**
treat some categories of disabled more favourably than others[94] *e.g.* so the
Royal National Institute for the Blind can prefer employing visually
impaired persons. Discrimination in favour of the disabled against the able
is authorised.[95]

VI. The Purpose of the Trust must be Exclusively Charitable

If, consistently with its terms, a trust may be applied exclusively for **7–138**
purposes which are not charitable, it is a non-charitable trust notwithstanding that, consistently with its terms, it may be applied exclusively for

---

[87] *Re Lysaght* [1986] Ch. 191: *Re Dominion Students' Hall Trusts* [1947] Ch. 183; *Blathwayt v Lord Cawley*
   [1967] A.C. 397. The Human Rights Act 1998 may affect religious conditions.
[88] s.34(2)(3).
[89] s.34(1).
[90] See Lysaght [1966] Ch. 191; *Re Woodhams* [1981] 1 W.L.R. 493; see para.7–321, n.41.
[91] Sex Discrimination Act 1975, s.43.
[92] *Hugh-Jones v St. John's College Cambridge* (1979) 123 So. Jo. 603.
[93] 1975 Act, s.78.
[94] Disability Discrimination Act 1995 s.10.
[95] *ibid.*, s.19(5)(K).

purposes which are charitable. Thus a trust to apply income to "registered charities or to such bodies as in the opinion of the trustees have charitable objects" is not charitable since the final clause does not state *"exclusively* charitable objects" and, even if it did, bodies *in the opinion of the trustees* having exclusively charitable objects might not be regarded by the courts as having exclusively charitable objects.[96] More obviously, the following trusts are not exclusively charitable and so are void: "for worthy causes," "for benevolent purposes," for "charitable or benevolent purposes,[97] for purposes[98] "connected with the education and welfare of children" or "for the public good".[99] However, a benignant construction may save a charitable trust as in *Guild v I.R.C.*[1] where the trust deed required funds to be used for a Sports Centre in North Berwick qualifying as a valid recreational charity under the 1958 Recreational Charities Act "or some similar purpose in connection with sport", where the House of Lords held such "similar purpose" must likewise be a charitable purpose.

Exceptions

7–139	There are some exceptions to the rule that a trust cannot be charitable unless its purposes are exclusively charitable.

(i) Incidental Purposes

7–140	If the main purpose of a corporation or trust is charitable and the only elements in its constitution and operations, which are non-charitable, are merely incidental to the effective promotion of that main purpose, the corporation and trust are established for charitable purposes only.[2] If the non-charitable object is itself a main object, neither the corporation nor the trust is established for charitable purposes only; but there is this difference between them: the corporation remains validly constituted, but the trust is void.[3] As Slade J. states,[4] "The distinction is between (a) those non-charitable activities authorised by the trust instrument which are merely incidental or subsidiary to a charitable purpose and (b) those non-charitable activities so authorised which themselves form part of the trust purpose. In the latter but not the former case the reference to non-charitable activities will deprive the trust of its charitable status."

---

[96] *Re Wootton's W.T.* [1968] 2 All E.R. 618. In poverty cases the courts seem ready to restrict the opinion of trustees as to persons in needy circumstances or special need to such persons that the law recognises as within the poverty head of charity: *Re Scarisbrick* [1951] Ch. 622; *Re Cohen* [1973] 1 All E.R. 889.

[97] *Chichester Diocesan Fund v Simpson* [1944] A.C. 341; *Latimer v C.I.R.* [2004] 4 All E.R. 558 at [32].

[98] *Att.-Gen. of the Bahamas v Royal Trust Co.* [1986] 1 W.L.R. 1001 (welfare purposes not restricted to educational welfare purposes so as to qualify as charitable).

[99] *Att.-Gen. of Cayman Islands v Wahr-Hansen* [2000] 3 All E.R. 642.

[1] [1992] 2 A.C. 310, at para.7-305. See too *Armenian Patriarch of Jerusalem v Sorsino* (2002) 5 I.T.E.L.R. 125 (trust for "education and advancement in life of Armenian children" construed conjunctively and so for charitable purpose of education).

[2] *Royal College of Surgeons of England v National Provincial Bank Ltd* [1952] A.C. 631; *Re Coxen* [1948] Ch. 747; *London Hospital Medical College v I.R.C.* [1976] 1 W.L.R. 613; N. Gravells [1978] Conv. 92.

[3] *Oxford Group v I.R.C.* [1949] W.N. 343; *Chichester Diocesan Fund and Board of Finance (Incorporated) v Simpson* [1944] A.C. 341; *Associated Artists Ltd v I.R.C.* [1956] 1 W.L.R. 752.

[4] *McGovern v Att.-Gen.* [1981] 3 All E.R. 493 at 510.

(ii) Apportionment

Where a trustee is directed to apportion between charitable and non- **7–141**
charitable objects the trust is always good as to the charitable objects. The
trust will be valid *in toto* if the non-charitable objects are certain and valid,[5]
and, in the absence of apportionment by the trustee, the court will divide
the fund equally between both classes of objects in accordance with the
maxim that "equality is equity."[6] If the non-charitable objects are uncertain,
the trust will be good as to the charitable objects only[7] so long as they are
sufficiently defined to reveal a general charitable intention.[8]

If there is no direction to apportion, and if the trust is partly for a non- **7–142**
charitable purpose, and then to apply the remainder to a charitable
purpose, some cases decide that where the court is satisfied that an inquiry
is practicable as to the portion required for the non-charitable purpose, it
will direct such an inquiry and uphold the charitable part of the gift.[9] If, on
the other hand, such an inquiry is impracticable, it will divide the fund into
equal shares, the share applicable to non-charitable purposes falling into
residue.[10] Other cases, however, have held that the whole of the gift goes to
charity, independently of the question whether the portion which would
otherwise have been required for the non-charitable purpose is ascertainable.[11] Yet another case decides that if the non-charitable part of the gift
cannot be carried out without also performing the charitable part the whole
gift will be valid.[12]

In *Re Coxen*,[13] Jenkins J. (as he then was) emphasised that, where the **7–143**
amount applicable to the non-charitable purpose cannot be quantified, the
whole gift fails for uncertainty. He pointed out, however, that there were
two exceptions to this general rule: first, an exception of a general character
to the effect that, where, as a matter of construction, the gift to charity was
a gift of the entire fund subject to the payments thereout required for the
non-charitable purpose, the amount set free by the failure of the non-
charitable gift was caught by, and passed under, the charitable gift;[14] and,
secondly, an exception of a more limited character, applicable in the
"tomb" cases, to the effect that where there is a primary trust (imposing a
merely honorary obligation[15]) to apply the income in perpetuity to the

---

[5] *Re Douglas* (1887) 35 Ch.D. 472.
[6] *Salusbury v Denton* (1857) 3 K. & J. 529.
[7] *Re Clarke* [1923] 2 Ch. 407.
[8] The *cy-près* doctrine is available if required.
[9] *Re Rigley* (1867) 36 L.J.Ch. 147; *Re Vaughan* (1886) 33 Ch.D. 187. The distinction between the invalid
"charitable or benevolent purposes" cases and the apportionment cases is made by Page-Wood V.-C. in
Salusbury v Denton (1857) 3 K. & J. 529 at 539. "It is one thing to direct a trustee to give a *part* of a fund
to one set of objects and the *remainder* to another, and it is a distinct thing to direct him to give either to
one set of objects or to another."
[10] *Adnam v Cole* (1843) 6 Beav. 353; *Hoare v Osborne* (1866) L.R. 1 Eq. 585; *cf. Fowler v Fowler* (1864) 33
Beav. 616, where the whole gift failed.
[11] *Fisk v Att.-Gen.* (1867) L.R. 4 Eq. 521; *Hunter v Bullock* (1872) L.R. 14 Eq. 45; *Dawson v Small* (1874)
L.R. 18 Eq. 114; *Re Williams* (1877) 5 Ch.D. 735; *Re Birkett* (1878) 9 Ch.D. 576; *Re Rogerson* [1901] 1 Ch.
715; *cf. Re Porter* [1925] Ch. 746.
[12] *Re Eighmie* [1935] Ch. 524.
[13] [1948] Ch. 747 at 752.
[14] *cf. Hancock v Watson* [1902] A.C. 14; above, para.5–41.
[15] *Re Morton's W.T.* [1948] 2 All E.R. 842; *Re Dalziel* [1943] Ch. 277 at 278; above, para.3–000; *Picarda on
Charities*, (3rd ed.), p.218.

repair of a tomb not in a church, followed by a charitable trust in terms extending only to the balance of the income, the established rule is to ignore the invalid trust for the repair of the tomb and treat the whole income as given to charity.

(iii) The Charitable Trusts (Validation) Act 1954

7–144   This Act only applies to the terms of a trust which took effect before December 16, 1952[16] and so nowadays will apply to few trusts. Consideration of this complex Act is therefore omitted.

Section 4. The Twelve Heads of Charity

In the following discussion we have adopted the classificatory scheme used in clause 2(2) of the Charities Bill 2005 (for which see paras 7–42ff. above). As noted in para.7–41, this Bill was introduced in May 2005, and it seems likely that it will be enacted before the end of the year.

I. RELIEF OF POVERTY

7–145   This group of charitable trusts has its origins in that part of the preamble to the Statute of Charitable Uses 1601 which speaks of "the relief of aged, impotent and poor people." It has been held that these words must be read disjunctively so that a trust is charitable if the beneficiaries are either elderly or ill or poor.[17] The word "relief" implies that the persons in question have a need attributable to their condition as aged, ill or poor persons which requires alleviating and which those persons could not alleviate or would find difficulty in alleviating themselves from their own resources. The word "relief" is not synonymous with "benefit."[18] A trust for aged millionaires of Mayfair would thus not be charitable.

7–146   "Poverty" is a relative term and the expression "poor people" is not necessarily confined to the destitute poor: it includes persons who have to "go short" in the ordinary acceptation of that term, due regard being had to their station in life and so forth.[19] Thus, a trust fund for "poor and needy" relatives could be used to assist those who may need a helping hand from time to time in order to overcome an unforeseen crisis: the failure of a business venture, urgent repairs to a dwelling house or expenses brought on by reason of failing health, while the "working classes" do not *ipso facto*

---

[16] The date on which the Report of the Nathan Committee on Charitable Trusts was presented to Parliament. The Act gives effect to certain recommendations of that Committee (Cmnd. 8710 Chap. 12).

[17] Age: *Re Robinson* [1951] Ch. 198; *Re Glyn's W.T.* [1950] 2 All E.R. 1150n.; *Re Bradbury* [1950] 2 All E.R. 1150n.; *Rowntree Memorial Trust Housing Association v Att.-Gen.* [1983] Ch. 159; impotence: *Re Elliott* (1910) 102 L.T. 528; *Re Hillier* [1944] 1 All E.R. 480; *Re Lewis* [1955] Ch. 104.

[18] *Rowntree Memorial Trust* [1983] Ch. 159 at 171, *per* Peter Gibson J.

[19] *Re Segelman* [1996] Ch. 171; *Re Coulthurst* [1951] Ch. 661 at 666; *Re Young* [1953] 3 All E.R. 689: Charity Commission. *Decision to Register the A.I.T.C. Foundation* (February 19, 2004). For general discussion of the types of assistance which can be given to people in need, see Charity Commission *CC 4: Charities for the Relief of Financial Hardship* (August 2003 version).

constitute a section of the poor.[20] In *Re Niyazi's W.T.*[21] a gift of residue worth about £15,000 for "the construction of or as a contribution towards the construction of a working men's hostel" in Famagusta was held charitable. The size of the gift, the grave housing shortage in Famagusta, and the term "working men's hostel" provided a sufficient connotation of poverty to make the gift charitable.

If a trust may be brought under any of the other three heads, then it is no **7–147** objection that it may incidentally benefit the rich as well as the poor; but if it cannot be brought under any head save that of the relief of poverty, then the benefits contemplated by the trust must be directed exclusively to that end: *Re Gwyon*,[22] where clothing for boys would benefit rich and poor boys.

Trusts for the relief of poverty (but not for the relief of elderly[23] or ill **7–148** persons[24]) form an exception to the principle that because every charitable trust must be for the public benefit the beneficiaries must not be a private class defined by reference to a personal nexus with a particular person. The exception covers both the poor relations of a named individual[25] and the poor employees of a particular employer and their families: *Dingle v Turner*. However, there must be a primary intent to relieve poverty, though amongst a particular class of person. If the primary intent is to benefit particular persons (*e.g.* A, B, C and their children for their relief in needy circumstances) the trust is a private one and not charitable.[26]

DINGLE v TURNER

House of Lords [1972] A.C. 601; [1972] 2 W.L.R. 523; [1972] 1 All E.R. 878.

VISCOUNT DILHORNE: "My Lords, I agree with Lord Cross that this appeal should **7–149** be dismissed and with the reasons he gives for the conclusion.

"With Lord MacDermott, I too do not wish to extend my concurrence to what my **7–150** noble and learned friend Lord Cross has said with regard to the fiscal privileges of a legal charity. Those privileges may be altered from time to time by Parliament and I doubt whether their existence should be a determining factor in deciding whether a gift or trust is charitable."

LORD MACDERMOTT: "My Lords, the conclusion I have reached on the facts of **7–151** this case is that the gift in question constitutes a public trust for the relief of poverty which is charitable in law. I would therefore dismiss the appeal.

"I do not find it necessary to state my reasons for this conclusion in detail. In the **7–152** first place, the views which I have expressed at some length in relation to an educational trust in *Oppenheim v Tobacco Securities Trust Co. Ltd*[27] seem to me to

---

[20] *Re Sanders' W.T.* [1954] Ch. 265, ("dwellings for the working classes and their families resident in the area of Pembroke Dock or within a radius of 5 miles therefrom" held not charitable).

[21] [1978] 3 All E.R. 785. Also see *Cresswell v Potter* [1978] 1 W.L.R. 255 at 257 treating "poor" as a member of the lower income group," covering post office telephonists.

[22] [1930] 1 Ch. 255.

[23] *Re Dunlop* [1984] N.I. 408 (trust to found a home for old Presbyterian persons held to be for sufficient section of public to be charitable under fourth head of charity).

[24] *Re Resch's W.T.* [1969] 1 A.C. 514.

[25] *Re Scarisbrick* [1951] Ch. 662.

[26] *Re Scarisbrick* [1951] Ch. 662; *Re Cohen* [1973] 1 W.L.R. 415; *Re Segelman* [1995] 3 All E.R. 676 at 687–692 (26 persons in class which would increase with birth of further members).

[27] [1951] A.C. 297. See at para.7–199 *et seq.*

apply to this appeal and to mean that it fails. And, secondly, I have had the advantage of reading the opinion prepared by my noble and learned friend, Lord Cross of Chelsea, and find myself in agreement with his conclusion for the reasons he has given. But I would prefer not to extend my concurrence to what my noble and learned friend goes on to say respecting the fiscal privileges of a legal charity. This subject may be material on the question whether what is alleged to be a charity is sufficiently altruistic in nature to qualify as such, but beyond that, and without wishing to express any final view on the matter, I doubt if these consequential privileges have much relevance to the primary question whether a given trust or purpose should be held charitable in law."

7–153   LORD HODSON: "My Lords, I agree with my noble and learned friend, Lord Cross of Chelsea, that this appeal should be dismissed and with his reasons for that conclusion. With this reservation: that I share the doubts expressed by my noble and learned friends, Lord MacDermott and Viscount Dilhorne, as to the relevance of fiscal considerations in deciding whether a gift or trust is charitable."

7–154   LORD SIMON OF GLAISDALE: "My Lords, I have had the advantage of reading the opinion of my noble and learned friend, Lord Cross of Chelsea, with which I agree."

7–155   LORD CROSS OF CHELSEA: "My Lords, . . . Clause 8(*e*) was in the following terms:

> '(*e*) To invest the sum of ten thousand pounds in any of the investments for the time being authorised by law for the investment of trust funds in the names of three persons (hereinafter referred to as "the Pension Fund Trustees") to be nominated for the purpose by the persons who at the time at which my Executors assent to this bequest are directors of E. Dingle & Company Limited and the Pension Fund Trustees shall hold the said sum and the investments for the time being representing the same (hereinafter referred to as "the Pensions Fund") UPON TRUST to apply the income thereof in paying pensions to poor employees of E. Dingle & Company Limited or of any other company to which upon any reconstruction or amalgamation the goodwill and the assets of E. Dingle & Company Limited may be transferred who are of the age of Sixty years at least or who being of the age of Forty five years at least are incapacitated from earning their living by reason of some physical or mental infirmity PROVIDED ALWAYS that if at any time the Pension Fund Trustees shall for any reason be unable to apply the income of the Pension Fund in paying such pensions to such employees as aforesaid the Pension Fund Trustees shall hold the Pensions Fund and the income thereof UPON TRUST for the aged poor in the Parish of St. Andrew, Plymouth.'

Finally by clause 8(*g*) the testator directed his trustees to hold the ultimate residue of his estate on the trusts set out in clause 8(*e*).

7–156   "The testator died on January 10, 1950. His widow died on October 8, 1966, having previously released her testamentary power of appointment over her husband's shares in E. Dingle & Co. Ltd, which accordingly fell into the residuary estate. When these proceedings started in July 1970, the value of the fund held on the trusts declared by clause 8(*e*) was about £320,000 producing a gross income of about £17,800 per annum.

7–157   "E. Dingle and Co. Ltd was incorporated as a private company on January 20, 1935. Its capital was owned by the testator and one John Russell Baker and it carried on the business of a departmental store. At the time of the testator's death the company employed over 600 persons and there was a substantial number of ex-employees. On October 23, 1950, the company became a public company. Since the testator's death its business has expanded and when these proceedings started it had 705 full-time and 189 part-time employees and was paying pensions to 89 ex-employees.

"The trustees took out an originating summons asking the court to determine **7–158** whether the trust declared by clause 8(e) were valid and if so to determine various subsidiary questions of construction—as, for example, whether part-time employees or employees of subsidiary companies were eligible to receive benefits under the trust. To this summons they made defendants (1) representatives of the various classes of employees or ex-employees, (2) those who would be interested on an intestacy if the trusts failed, and (3) Her Majesty's Attorney-General. It has been common ground throughout that the trust at the end of clause 8(e) for the aged poor in the Parish of St. Andrew Plymouth is dependent on the preceding trust for poor employees of the company so that although it will catch any surplus income which the trustees do not apply for the benefit of poor employees it can have no application if the preceding trust is itself void.

"The contentions of the appellant and the respondents may be stated broadly as **7–159** follows. The appellant says that in the *Oppenheim* case this House decided that in principle a trust ought not to be regarded as charitable if the benefits under it are confined either to the descendants of a named individual or individuals or the employees of a given individual or company and that although the 'poor relations' cases may have to be left standing as an anomalous exception to the general rule because their validity has been recognised for so long, the exception ought not to be extended to 'poor employees' trusts which had not been recognised for long before their status as charitable trusts began to be called in question. The respondents, on the other hand, say, first, that the rule laid down in the *Oppenheim* case with regard to educational trusts ought not to be regarded as a rule applicable in principle to all kinds of charitable trust and, secondly, that in any case it is impossible to draw any logical distinction between 'poor relations' trusts and 'poor employees' trusts, and, that as the former cannot be held invalid today after having been recognised as valid for so long, the latter must be regarded as valid also.

"By a curious coincidence within a few months of the decision of this House in **7–160** the *Oppenheim* case the cases on gifts to 'poor relations' had to be considered by the Court of Appeal in *Re Scarisbrick*.[28] Most of the cases on this subject were decided in the eighteenth or early nineteenth centuries and are very inadequately reported but two things at least were clear. First, that it never occurred to the judges who decided them that in the field of 'poverty' a trust could not be a charitable trust if the class of beneficiaries was defined by reference to descent from a common ancestor. Secondly, that the courts did not treat a gift or trust as necessarily charitable because the objects of it had to be poor in order to qualify, for in some of the cases the trust was treated as a private trust and not a charity. The problem in *Re Scarisbrick* was to determine on what basis the distinction was drawn. The Court of Appeal held that in this field the distinction between a public or charitable trust and a private trust depended on whether as a matter of construction the gift was for the relief of poverty amongst a particular description of poor people or was merely a gift to particular poor persons. The fact that the gift took the form of a perpetual trust would no doubt indicate that the intention of the donor could not have been to confer private benefits on particular people whose possible necessities he had in mind; but the fact that the capital of the gift was to be distributed at once did not necessarily show that the gift was a private trust.

---

[28] [1951] Ch. 622.

7–161   [His Lordship then reviewed the earlier cases leading up to *Gibson v S. American Stores and continued:*.] "The facts in *Gibson v South American Stores (Gath & Chaves) Ltd*[29]—the case followed by Megarry J. in this case—were that a company had vested in trustees a fund derived solely from its profits to be applied at the discretion of the directors in granting gratuities, pensions or allowances to persons—

> 'who . . . are or shall be necessitous and deserving and who for the time being are or have been in the company's employ . . . and the wives widows husbands widowers children parents and other dependants of any person who for the time being is or would if living have been himself or herself a member of the class of beneficiaries.'

7–162   The Court of Appeal held that this trust was a valid charitable trust but it did so without expressing a view of its own on the question of principle involved, because the case of *Re Laidlaw*[30] which was unearthed in the course of the hearing showed that the Court of Appeal had already accepted the decision in *Re Gosling*[31] as correct.

7–163   "In *Oppenheim v Tobacco Securities Trust Co. Ltd*[32] this House had to consider the principle laid down by the Court of Appeal in *Re Compton*.[33] There the trustees of a fund worth over £125,000 were directed to apply its income and also if they thought fit all or any part of the capital—

> "in providing for or assisting in providing for the education of children of employees or former employees of British-American Tobacco Co., Ltd . . . or any of its subsidiary or allied companies . . .'

7–164   "There were over 110,000 such employees. The majority of your Lordships—namely Lord Simonds (in whose judgment Lord Oaksey concurred), Lord Normand and Lord Morton of Henryton—in holding that the trust was not a valid charitable trust gave unqualified approval to the *Compton* principle. They held, that is to say, that although the 'poverty' cases might afford an anomalous exception to the rule, it was otherwise a general rule applicable to all charitable trusts that no class of beneficiaries can constitute a 'section of the public' for the purpose of the law of charity if the distinguishing quality which links them together is relationship to a particular individual either through common descent or common employment. My noble and learned friend, Lord MacDermott, on the other hand, in his dissenting speech, while not challenging the correctness of the decisions in *Re Compton* or in the *Hobourn Aero* case[34] said that he could not regard the principle stated by Lord Greene M.R. as a criterion of general applicability and conclusiveness. He said:[35]

> '. . . I see much difficulty in dividing the qualities or attributes which may serve to bind human beings into classes into two mutually exclusive groups, the one involving individual status and purely personal, the other disregarding such status and quite impersonal. As a task this seems to me no less baffling and

---

[29] [1950] Ch. 177.
[30] (January 11, 1935) unreported, the decision (and not the reasoning) only being available.
[31] (1900) 48 W.R. 300.
[32] [1951] A.C. 297.
[33] [1945] Ch. 123.
[34] [1946] Ch. 194.
[35] [1951] A.C. 297 at 317.

elusive than the problem to which it is directed, namely, the determination of what is and what is not a section of the public for the purposes of this branch of the law.'

He thought that the question whether any given trust was a public or a private trust was a question of degree to be decided in the light of the facts of the particular case and that viewed in that light the trust in the *Oppenheim* case was a valid charitable trust . . .

"The *Oppenheim* case was a case of an educational trust and although the **7–165** majority evidently agreed with the view expressed by the Court of Appeal in the *Hobourn Aero* case,[36] that the *Compton* rule was of universal application outside the field of poverty, it would no doubt be open to this House without overruling *Oppenheim* to hold that the scope of the rule was more limited. If ever I should be called on to pronounce on this question—which does not arise in this appeal—I would as at present advised be inclined to draw a distinction between the practical merits of the *Compton* rule and the reasoning by which Lord Greene M.R. sought to justify it. That reasoning—based on the distinction between personal and impersonal relationships—has never seemed to me very satisfactory and I have always—if I may say so—felt the force of the criticism to which my noble and learned friend Lord MacDermott subjected it in his dissenting speech in the *Oppenheim* case.[37] For my part I would prefer to approach the problem on far broader lines. The phrase 'a section of the public' is in truth a phrase which may mean different things to different people. In the law of charity judges have sought to elucidate its meaning by contrasting it with another phrase 'a fluctuating body of private individuals.' But I get little help from the supposed contrast for as I see it one and the same aggregate of persons may well be describable both as a section of the public and as a fluctuating body of private individuals. The ratepayers in the Royal Borough of Kensington and Chelsea, for example, certainly constitute a section of the public; but would it be a misuse of language to describe them as a 'fluctuating body of private individuals'? After all, every part of the public is composed of individuals and being susceptible of increase or decrease is fluctuating. So at the end of the day one is left where one started with the bare contrast between 'public' and 'private.' No doubt some classes are more naturally describable as sections of the public than as private classes while other classes are more naturally describable as private classes than as sections of the public. The blind, for example, can naturally be described as a section of the public; but what they have in common—their blindness—does not join them together in such a way that they could be called a private class. On the other hand, the descendants of Mr. Gladstone might more reasonably be described as a 'private class' than as a section of the public, and in the field of common employment the same might well be said of the employees in some fairly small firm. But if one turns to large companies employing many thousands of men and women most of whom are quite unknown to one another and to the directors the answer is by no means so clear. One might say that in such a case the distinction between a section of the public and a private class is not applicable at all or even that the employees in such concerns as ICI or GEC are just as much 'sections of the public' as the residents in some geographical area. In truth the question whether or not the potential beneficiaries of a trust can fairly be said to constitute a section of the public is a question of degree and cannot be by

---

[36] [1946] Ch. 194.
[37] [1951] A.C. 297. (See also G. Cross, as Lord Cross then was, (1956) 72 L.Q.R. 187.)

itself decisive of the question whether the trust is a charity. Much must depend on the purpose of the trust. It may well be that, on the one hand, a trust to promote some purpose, prima facie charitable, will constitute a charity even though the class of potential beneficiaries might fairly be called a private class and that, on the other hand, a trust to promote another purpose, also prima facie charitable, will not constitute a charity even though the class of potential beneficiaries might seem to some people fairly describable as a section of the public.

7–166   "In answering the question whether any given trust is a charitable trust the courts—as I see it—cannot avoid having regard to the fiscal privileges accorded to charities. As counsel for the Attorney-General remarked in the course of the argument the law of charity is bedevilled by the fact that charitable trusts enjoy two quite different sorts of privilege. On the one hand, they enjoy immunity from the rules against perpetuity and uncertainty and although individual potential beneficiaries cannot sue to enforce them the public interest arising under them is protected by the Attorney-General. If this was all there would be no reason for the courts not to look favourably on the claim of any 'purpose' trust to be considered as a charity if it seemed calculated to confer some real benefit on those intended to benefit by it whoever they might be and if it would fail if not held to be a charity. But that is not all. Charities automatically enjoy fiscal privileges which with the increased burden of taxation have become more and more important and in deciding that such and such a trust is a charitable trust the court is endowing it with a substantial annual subsidy at the expense of the taxpayer. Indeed, claims of trusts to rank as charities are just as often challenged by the Revenue as by those who would take the fund if the trust was invalid. It is, of course, unfortunate that the recognition of any trust as a valid charitable trust should automatically attract fiscal privileges, for the question whether a trust to further some purpose is so little likely to benefit the public that it ought to be declared invalid and the question whether it is likely to confer such great benefits on the public that it should enjoy fiscal immunity are really two quite different questions. The logical solution would be to separate them and to say—as the Radcliffe Commission proposed—that only some charities should enjoy fiscal privileges. But as things, are, validity and fiscal immunity march hand in hand and the decisions in the *Compton*[38] and *Oppenheim*[39] cases were pretty obviously influenced by the consideration that if such trusts as were there in question were held valid they would enjoy an undeserved fiscal immunity. To establish a trust for the education of the children of employees in a company in which you are interested is no doubt a meritorious act; but however numerous the employees may be the purpose which you are seeking to achieve is not a public purpose.[40] It is a company purpose and there is no reason why your fellow taxpayers should contribute to a scheme which by providing 'fringe benefits' for your employees will benefit the company by making their conditions of employment more attractive. The temptation to enlist the assistance of the law of charity in private endeavours of this sort is considerable—witness the recent case of the Metal Box scholarships—*Inland Revenue Comrs. v Educational Grants Association Ltd.*[41]—and the courts must do what they can to discourage such attempts. In the field of poverty the danger is not so great as in the field of education—for while people are keenly alive to the need to give their children a good education and to the expense of doing so, they are generally optimistic enough not to entertain serious fears of falling on evil days

---

[38] [1945] Ch. 123.
[39] [1951] A.C. 297.
[40] For a critical view of this approach see T. G. Watkin [1978] Conv. 277.
[41] [1967] Ch. 993, para.7–209.

much before they fall on them. Consequently the existence of company 'benevolent funds,' the income of which is free of tax does not constitute a very attractive 'fringe benefit.' This is a practical justification—although not, of course, the historical explanation—for the special treatment accorded to poverty trusts in charity law. For the same sort of reason a trust to promote some religion among the employees of a company might perhaps safely be held to be charitable provided that it was clear that the benefits were to be purely spiritual. On the other hand, many 'purpose' trusts falling under Lord Macnaghten's fourth head if confined to a class of employees would clearly be open to the same sort of objection as educational trusts. As I see it, it is on these broad lines rather than for the reasons actually given by Lord Greene M.R. that the *Compton* rule can best be justified.

"My Lords, I would dismiss this appeal." *Appeal dismissed*.   **7–167**

II. The Advancement of Education

Educational purposes

This group of charitable trusts has its origins in those parts of the **7–168** preamble to the Statute of Charitable Uses 1601 which speak of "the maintenance of schools of learning, free schools and scholars in universities" and "the education and preferment of orphans." It is now clear that trusts endowing fee-paying schools are charitable if the school is non-profit-making or if, though profit-making, its profits are used for school purposes only.[42] Similarly, the Incorporated Council of Law Reporting is a charity because its charges are retained for its purposes and do not enure for the benefit of its members: it provides essential material for the study of law so as to be for the advancement of education, it being immaterial that thereby lawyers are able to make money because one must not confuse the results flowing from the achievement of the purpose with the purpose itself.[43]

Education is not confined to matters formally taught in schools and **7–169** universities. It includes the promotion or encouragement of the arts and graces of life: see *Re Shaw's Will Trusts*[44] ("the teaching, promotion and encouragement in Ireland of self-control, elocution, oratory, deportment, the arts of personal contact, of social intercourse, and the other arts of public, private, professional and business life"); *Royal Choral Society v I.R.C.*[45] (choral singing in London); *Re Levien*[46] (organ music); *Re Delius*[47] (the music of the composer Delius); *Re Dupree's Deed Trusts*[48] (encouragement of chess-playing among young people in Portsmouth); and *Re South Place Ethical Society*[49] (the study and dissemination of ethical principles and

---

[42] *Abbey Malvern Wells Ltd v Ministry of Local Government* [1951] Ch. 728; *Customs & Excise Commissioners v Bell Concord Education Trust* [1989] 2 All E.R. 217.

[43] *Incorporated Council of Law Reporting v Att.-Gen.* [1972] Ch. 73 where two L.JJ. held the Council to fall within the educational head of charity and all three L.JJ. held it within the fourth head.

[44] [1952] Ch. 163.

[45] [1943] 2 All E.R. 101; contrast *Associated Artists Ltd v I.R.C.* [1956] 1 W.L.R. 752 (production of artistic dramatic works).

[46] [1955] 1 W.L.R. 964.

[47] [1957] Ch. 299; contrast *Re Pinion* [1965] Ch. 85 (bequest of worthless works of art to found a museum); *Sutherland's Trustees v Verschoyle*, 1968 S.L.T. 43.

[48] [1945] Ch. 16.

[49] [1980] 1 W.L.R. 1565.

the cultivation of a rational religious sentiment). Indeed, the Charity Commissioners have upheld as charitable[50] a Cult Information Centre (researching into and making people aware of movements concerned with the exploration of spiritual life) and Public Concern at Work (concerned with promoting business ethics and advising and protecting employees faced with ethical dilemmas at work).

7–170   The decision of Harman J. in *Re Shaw*[51] (denying charitable status where George Bernard Shaw had bequeathed funds for pursuing inquiries into a new 40 letter alphabet) appeared to render doubtful the validity of trusts for the advancement of research, at any rate where no element of teaching was involved; but the decision of Wilberforce J. in *Re Hopkins' Will Trusts*[52] removes most of the doubts. Wilberforce J. held "that the word 'education', as used by Harman J, must be used in a wide sense, certainly extending beyond teaching, and that the requirement is that, in order to be charitable, research must either be of educational value to the researcher or must be so directed as to lead to something which will pass into the store of educational material or so as to improve the sum of communicable knowledge in an area which education may cover . . . research of a private character, for the benefit only of the members of a society, would not normally be educational or otherwise charitable but I do not think that the research in the present case [into the works of Francis Bacon and whether he might have been the author of plays ascribed to Shakespeare] can be said to be of private character, for it is inherently inevitable and manifestly intended that the result of any discovery should be published to the world."

7–171   In *McGovern v Att.-Gen.*[53] Slade J. summarised the principles as follows:

> "(1) A trust for research will ordinarily qualify as a charitable trust if, but only if (a) the subject matter of the proposed research is a useful subject of study; and (b) it is contemplated that knowledge acquired as a result of the research will be disseminated to others; and (c) the trust is for the benefit of the public, or a sufficiently important section of the public. (2) In the absence of a contrary context, however, the court will be readily inclined to construe a trust for research as importing subsequent dissemination of the results thereof. (3) Furthermore, if a trust for research is to constitute a valid trust for the advancement of education, it is not necessary either (a) that a teacher/pupil relationship should be in contemplation, or (b) that the persons to benefit from the knowledge to be acquired should be persons who are already in the course of receiving 'education' in the conventional sense."

7–172   Until recently, the promotion of sport as such was not a charitable object but the law in this area has now changed: see paras 7–273 *et seq.* In *I.R.C. v McMullen*, para 7–178, the House of Lords held that it is charitable to

---

[50] See respectively Decisions Vol. 1, p.1 and Vol. 2, p.5.
[51] [1965] Ch. 699; [1957] 1 W.L.R. 729.
[52] See (1965) 29 Conv. (N.S.) 368 (Newark and Samuels).
[53] [1982] Ch. 321 at 352.

provide sports facilities for children and young people at school and university because physical education and development are an integral part of the education of the young.

Public benefit

The promotion of a particular type of political education[54] is not **7–173** charitable; and some other forms of education may also not be for the public benefit: *Re Hummeltenberg*[55] (training of spiritualistic mediums). In *Southwood v Attorney–General*[56] the Court of Appeal held that a trust to educate the public that peace is best secured by disarmament and pacifism was not charitable because "the court cannot determine whether or not it promotes the public benefit for the public to be" so educated: "there are differing views as to how best to secure peace and avoid war . . . on the one hand it can be argued that war is best avoided by bargaining through strength; on the other hand it can be argued that peace is best secured through disarmament—if necessary, by unilateral disarmament." The court and not the settlor determines whether public benefit is present so that a testator cannot set up a charitable museum of his artistic collection if it has no artistic merit.[57] The fact that it is by means of an educational process that non-charitable purposes are to be achieved does not render such purposes charitable.[58]

A trust for the education of beneficiaries who are ascertained by **7–174** reference to some personal tie (*e.g.* of blood or contract), such as the relations of a particular individual, the members of a particular family, the employees of a particular firm, or the members of a particular trade union, lacks the element of public benefit and is not charitable: *Oppenheim v Tobacco Securities Trust Co. Ltd*, para.7–194, though this may require reconsideration in the light of *Dingle v Turner*[59] where large-scale trusts are concerned. A trust to educate residents of a town[60] or children of members of a particular profession[61] or to provide "closed" scholarships from a specified school to a specified Oxbridge College will be valid.[62]

Merely creating a clearly valid charitable trust, *e.g.* "for the advancement **7–175** of the education of children in the United Kingdom" will not confer tax advantages if the trustees run the trust as a private trust for certain associated persons: *I.R.C. v Educational Grants Association*, para.7–209.

---

[54] *Bonar Law Memorial Trust v I.R.C.* (1933) 49 T.L.R. 220; *Re Hopkinson* [1949] 1 All E.R. 346; *cf. Re Scowcroft* [1898] 2 Ch. 638 which nowadays should be regarded as of doubtful authority; and see *Re McDougall* [1957] 1 W.L.R. 81 (study of methods of government is a charitable object).
[55] [1923] 1 Ch. 237. *Cf. Funnel v Stewart* [1996] 1 All E.R. 715.
[56] [2000] W.T.L.R. 1199 at 1217.
[57] *Re Pinion* [1965] Ch. 85.
[58] *Re Koeppler's W.T.* [1984] 2 All E.R. 111 though reversed by the Court of Appeal [1985] 2 All E.R. 869 since the purpose was held charitable.
[59] [1972] A.C. 601, set out above at para.7–149. However the majority there seemed to favour the result in *Oppenheim*, tax advantages preventing the trust being sufficiently altruistic.
[60] *Re Tree* [1945] Ch. 325: a restriction to Methodists or members of the Church of England would seem valid.
[61] *Hall v Derby Sanitary Authority* (1885) 16 Q.B.D. 163 approved in *Oppenheim v Tobacco Securities Trust Co.* [1951] A.C. 297.
[62] Picarda *Law & Practice Relating to Charities* (2nd ed.), p.49.

Indeed, the trustees will be acting beyond their powers and so be liable for breach of trust.

7–176   If a trust for a broad charitable class of beneficiaries gives the trustees a power, without being under any duty, to prefer a certain private class within the broader public class this does not vitiate the validity of the trust as a charitable trust.[63] However, payments to members of the private class will have unfortunate tax consequences if regarded as of such significance that they ought fairly to be considered as misuse of public funds for a private purpose. Rather than put the tax inspector on his mettle some settlors may omit the preference from the trust deed and rely on the sensible selection of beneficiaries by trustees.

7–177   If the trust for the broad charitable class imposes a duty upon the trustees to use the whole, if possible, or an uncertain part of the funds for a specified private class then the trust cannot be a valid charitable trust.[64] If only a maximum specified part of the fund is directed to be used for the private class then whilst such part should not be charitable the remainder, presumably, should be severed as charitable since it can be used for exclusively charitable purposes. However, in *Re Koettgen*[65] (doubted in *I.R.C. v Educational Grants Association*[66], at para. 7–209). Upjohn J. in a brief extempore judgment held that if there was a broad primary class that was charitable the trust remained charitable despite an imperative direction imposing a duty to prefer a private class for up to a maximum of 75 per cent. of the trust income. This is difficult to justify logically, but pragmatically it validates the trust, whilst leaving it open to the Revenue to charge tax if the trust is operated as a private trust and enabling charitable purposes to be carried out to the extent it is impossible or impracticable to benefit the preferred class. The Charity Commissioners have accepted *Re Koettgen* as good law.[67]

INLAND REVENUE COMMISSIONERS v MCMULLEN

House of Lords [1981] A.C. 1; [1980] 1 All E.R. 884.

7–178   LORD HAILSHAM: "Four questions arose for decision below. In the first place neither the parties nor the judgments below were in agreement as to the proper construction of the trust deed itself. Clearly this is a preliminary debate which must be settled before the remaining questions are even capable of decision. In the second place the trustees contend and the Crown disputes that, on the correct construction of the deed, the trust is charitable as being for the advancement of

---

[63] *Re Koettgen* [1954] Ch. 252; *Caffoor v Comr. of Income Tax, Colombo* [1961] A.C. 584; *I.R.C. v Educational Grants Association* [1967] Ch. 123, dealing with above cases, para.7–209.
[64] *Re Martin* (1977) 121 Sol. J. 828, *The Times*, November 17, 1977. An anomalous exception exists for the ancient English institution of educational provision for Founder's Kin in certain schools and colleges "though there seems to be virtually no direct authority as to the principle on which they rested and they should probably be regarded more as belonging to history than to doctrine": *Caffoor v Comr. of Income Tax* [1961] A.C. 584 at 602.
[65] [1954] Ch. 252.
[66] [1967] Ch. 123.
[67] [1978] Annual Report, paras 86, 89.

education. Thirdly, the trustees contend and the Crown disputes that if they are wrong on the second question the trust is charitable at least because it falls within the fourth class of Lord Macnaghten's categories as enumerated in *Income Tax Special Purposes Comrs. v Pemsel*[68] as a trust beneficial to the community within the spirit and intendment of the preamble to the statute 43 Eliz. I, c.4.[69] Fourthly, the trustees contend and the Crown disputes that, even if not otherwise charitable, the trust is a valid charitable trust as falling within section I of the Recreational Charities Act 1958, that is as a trust to provide or to assist in the provision of facilities for recreation or other leisure time occupation provided in the interests of social welfare.

"Since we have reached the view that the trust is a valid educational charity their **7–179** Lordships have not sought to hear argument nor, therefore, to reach a conclusion on any but the first two disputed questions in the dispute. Speaking for myself, however, I do not wish my absence of decision on the third or fourth points to be interpreted as an indorsement of the majority judgments in the Court of Appeal nor as necessarily dissenting from the contrary views contained in the minority judgment of Bridge L.J. For me at least the answers to the third and fourth questions are still left entirely undecided.

"I now turn to the question of construction, for which it is necessary that I **7–180** reproduce the material portions of the deed . . . "The objects of the Trusts are:—

'(a) to organise or provide or assist in the organisation and provision of facilities which will enable and encourage pupils of Schools and Universities in any part of the United Kingdom to play Association Football or other games or sports and thereby to assist in ensuring that due attention is given to the physical education and development of such pupils as well as to the development and occupation of their minds and with a view to furthering this object (i) to provide or assist in the provision of Association Football or games or sports equipment of every kind for the use of such pupils as aforesaid (ii) to provide or assist in the provision of courses lectures demonstrations and coaching for pupils of Schools and Universities in any part of the United Kingdom and for teachers who organise or supervise playing and coaching of Association Football or other games or sports at such Schools and Universities as aforesaid (iii) to promote provide or assist in the promotion and provision of training colleges for the purpose of training teachers in the coaching of Association Football or other games or sports at such Schools and Universities as aforesaid (iv) to lay out manage equip and maintain or assist in the laying out management equipment and maintenance of playing fields or appropriate indoor facilities or accommodation (whether vested in the Trustees or not) to be used for the teaching and playing of Association Football or other sports or games by such pupils as aforesaid.

'(b) to organise or provide or assist in the organisation or provision of facilities for physical recreation in the interests of social welfare in any part of the United Kingdom (with the object of improving the conditions of life for the boys and girls for whom the same are provided) for boys and girls who are under the age of twenty-one years and who by reason of their youth or social and economic circumstances have need of such facilities.'

"I pause here only to say that no question arises as to clause 3(b) above which **7–181** clearly corresponds to the language of the Recreational Charities Act 1958. Controversy therefore revolves solely around clause 3(a), since it is obvious that, if

---

[68] [1891] A.C. 531 at 583: [1891–94] All E.R. Rep.28 at 55.
[69] Charitable Uses Act 1601.

this cannot be shown to be solely for charitable purposes, the whole trust ceases to be a charitable trust . . .

7–182   "I agree with [the judgment of Bridge L.J.] . . . that what the deed means is that the purpose of the settlor is to promote the physical education and development of pupils at schools and universities as an addition to such part of their education as relates to their mental education by providing the facilities and assistance to games and sports in the manner set out at greater length and in greater detail in the enumerated sub-clauses of clause 3(a) of the deed . . .

7–183   "On a proper analysis, therefore, I do not find clause 3(a) ambiguous. But, before I part with the question of construction, I would wish to express agreement with a contention made on behalf of the trustees and of the Attorney-General, but not agreed to on behalf of the Crown, that in construing trust deeds the intention of which is to set up a charitable trust, and in others too, where it can be claimed that there is an ambiguity, a benignant construction should be given if possible. This was the maxim of the civil law: semper in dubiis benigniora praeferenda sunt. There is a similar maxim in English law: ut res magis valeat quam pereat. It certainly applies to charities when the question is one of uncertainty (*Weir v Crum-Brown*[70]) and, I think, also where a gift is capable of two constructions one of which would make it void and the other effectual (*cf. Bruce v Deer Presbytery,*[71] *Houston v Burns*[72] and *Bain, Public Trustee v Ross*[73]). In the present case I do not find it necessary to resort to benignancy in order to construe the clause, but, had I been in doubt, I would certainly have been prepared to do so . . .

7–184   "I must now turn to the deed, construed in the manner in which I have found it necessary to construe it, to consider whether it sets up a valid charitable trust for the advancement of education.

7–185   "It is admitted, of course, that the words 'charity' and 'charitable' bear, for the purposes of English law and equity, meanings totally different from the senses in which they are used in ordinary educated speech, or for instance, in the Authorised Version of the Bible But I do not share the view, implied by Stamp and Orr L.JJ. in the instant case,[74] that the words 'education' and 'educational' bear, or can bear, for the purposes of the law of charity, meanings different from those current in present day educated English speech. I do not believe that there is such a difference. What has to be remembered, however, is that, as Lord Wilberforce pointed out in *Re Hopkins' Will Trusts*[75] and in *Scottish Burial Reform and Cremation Society Ltd v Glasgow City Corpn,*[76] both the legal conception of charity, and within it the educated man's ideas about education are not static, but moving and changing. Both change with changes in ideas about social values. Both have evolved with the years. In particular in applying the law to contemporary circumstances it is extremely dangerous to forget that thoughts concerning the scope and width of education differed in the past greatly from those which are now generally accepted.

7–186   "In saying this I do not in the least wish to cast doubt on *Re Nottage,*[77] which was referred to in both courts below and largely relied on by the Crown here. Strictly speaking *Re Nottage* was not a case about education at all. The issue there was

---

[70] [1908] A.C. 162 at 167.
[71] (1867) L.R. 1 Sc. & Div. 96 at 97.
[72] [1918] A.C. 337 at 341–342.
[73] [1930] 1 Ch. 224 at 230.
[74] [1979] 1 W.L.R. 130 at 135, 139.
[75] [1965] Ch. 669 at 678.
[76] [1968] A.C. 138 at 154.
[77] [1895] 2 Ch. 649.

whether the bequest came into the fourth class of charity categorised in Lord Macnaghten's classification of 1891.[78] The mere playing of games or enjoyment of amusement or competition is not per se charitable, nor necessarily educational, though they may (or may not) have an educational or beneficial effect if diligently practised. Neither am I deciding in the present case even that a gift for physical education per se and not associated with persons of school age or just above would necessarily be a good charitable gift. That is a question which the courts may have to face at some time in the future. But in deciding what is or is not an educational purpose for the young in 1980 it is not irrelevant to point out what Parliament considered to be educational for the young in 1944 when, by the Education Act of that year in sections 7 and 53 (which are still on the statute book), Parliament attempted to lay down what was then intended to be the statutory system of education organised by the state, and the duties of the local education authorities and the Minister in establishing and maintaining the system. Those sections are so germane to the present issue that I cannot forbear to quote them both. Section 7 provides (in each of the sections the emphasis being mine):

'The statutory system of public education shall be organised in three progressive stages to be known as primary education, secondary education, and further education; and it shall be the duty of the local education authority for every area, so far as their powers extend, to contribute towards *the spiritual, moral, mental, and physical development of the community by securing that efficient education throughout those stages shall be available to meet the needs of the population of their area*'

and in section 53 of the same Act it is said:

'(1) It shall be the duty of every local education authority to secure that the facilities for primary, secondary and further education provided for their area include adequate facilities for recreation d social and physical training, and for that purpose a local education authority, with the approval of the Secretary of State, may establish maintain and manage, or assist the establishment, maintenance, and management of *camps, holiday classes, playing fields, play centres and other places (including playgrounds, gymnasiums, and swimming baths not appropriated to any school or college), at which facilities for recreation and for such training as aforesaid are available for persons receiving primary, secondary or further education, and may organise games, expeditions and other activities for such persons, and may defray or contribute towards the expenses thereof.*

"I find the first instance case of *Mariette*,[79] a decision of Eve J., both stimulating **7–187** and instructive. Counsel for the Crown properly reminded us that this concerned a bequest effectively tied to a particular institution. Nevertheless, I cannot forbear to quote a phrase from the judgment, always bearing in mind the danger of quoting out of context. Eve J. said[80]:

"No one of sense could be found to suggest that between those ages [10 to 19] any boy can be properly educated unless at least as much attention is given to the development of his body as is given to the development of his mind."

---

[78] See *Income Tax Special Purposes Comrs. v Pemsel* [1891] A.C. 531 at 583.
[79] [1915] 2 Ch. 284.
[80] [1915] 2 Ch. 284 at 288.

7–188   "Apart from the limitation to the particular institution I would think that these words apply as well to the settlor's intention in the instant appeal as to the testator's in *Re Mariette*, and I regard the limitation to the pupils of schools and universities in the instant case as a sufficient association with the provision of formal education to prevent any danger of vagueness in the object of the trust or irresponsibility or capriciousness in application by the trustees. I am far from suggesting either that the concept of education or of physical education even for the young is capable of indefinite extension. On the contrary, I do not think that the courts have as yet explored the extent to which elements of organisation, instruction or the disciplined inculcation of information, instruction or skill may limit the whole concept of education. I believe that in some ways it will prove more extensive, in others more restrictive than has been thought hitherto. But it is clear at least to me that the decision in *Re Mariette*[81] is not to be read in a sense which confines its application for ever to gifts to a particular institution. It has been extended already in *Re Mellody*[82] to gifts for annual treats for schoolchildren in a particular locality (another decision of Eve J), to playgrounds for children (*Re Chester*,[83] possibly *not* educational, but referred to in *Inland Revenue Comrs. v Baddeley*[84]); to a children's outing (*Re Ward's Estate*[85]), to a prize for chess to boys and young men resident in the City of Portsmouth (*Re Dupree's Deed Trusts*,[86] a decision of Vaisey J.) and for the furthering of the Boy Scouts' movement by helping to purchase sites for camping, outfits, etc. (*Re Webber*,[87] another decision of Vaisey J.).

7–189   "It is important to remember that in the instant appeal we are dealing with the concept of physical education and development of the young deliberately associated by the settlor with the status of pupillage in schools or universities (of which, according to the evidence, about 95 per cent are within the age-group 17 to 22). We are not dealing with adult education, physical or otherwise, as to which some considerations may be different.

7–190   "I am at pains to disclaim the view that the conception of this evolving, and therefore not static, view of education is capable of infinite abuse or, even worse, proving void for uncertainty. Quite apart from the doctrine of the benignant approach to which I have already referred, and which undoubtedly comes to the assistance of settlors in danger of attack for uncertainty, I am content to adopt the approach of my predecessor Lord Loreburn L.C. in *Weir v Crum-Brown*,[88] to which attention was drawn by counsel for the Attorney-General, that if the bequest to a class of persons, is as here capable of application by the trustees, or, failing them, the court, the gift is not void for uncertainty. Lord Macnaghten also said[89]:

> "The testator has taken pains to provide competent judges. It is for the trustees to consider and determine the value of the service on which a candidate may rest his claim to participate in the testator's bounty."

7–191   "*Mutatis mutandis*, I think this kind of reasoning should apply here. Granted that the question of application may present difficulties for the trustees, or, failing them, for the court, nevertheless it is capable of being applied, for the concept in the mind

---

[81] [1915] 2 Ch. 284.
[82] [1918] 1 Ch. 228.
[83] (July 25, 1934) unreported.
[84] [1955] A.C. 572 at 596.
[85] [1937] 81 SJ. 397.
[86] [1945] Ch. 16.
[87] [1954] 1 W.L.R. 1500.
[88] [1908] A.C. 162 at 167.
[89] [1908] A.C. 162 at 169.

of the settlor is an object sufficiently clear, is exclusively for the advancement of education, and, in the hands of competent judges, is capable of application.

"My Lords, for these reasons I reach the conclusion that the trust is a valid **7–192** charitable gift for the advancement of education, which, after all, is what it claims to be. The conclusion follows that the appeal should be allowed."

Lords Diplock and Salmon merely concurred while Lords Russell and Keith, **7–193** concurred and gave brief speeches.

OPPENHEIM v TOBACCO SECURITIES TRUST CO. LTD

House of Lords [1951] A.C. 297; [1951] 1 T.L.R. 118; [1951] 1 All E.R. 31 (Lord Simonds, Normand, Oaksey and Morton; Lord MacDermott dissenting)[90]

Investments were held by the respondents, Tobacco Securities Trust Co. Ltd, on **7–194** trust to apply the income in providing for the education of children of employees or former employees of British-American Tobacco Co. Ltd . . . or any of its subsidiary or allied companies without any limit of time being specified. The High Court and Court of Appeal held the trust void for perpetuity because it was not charitable on the ground that it lacked public benefit.

LORD SIMONDS: "In the case of trusts for educational purposes the condition of the **7–195** public benefit must be satisfied. The difficulty lies in determining what is sufficient to satisfy the test, and there is little to help your Lordships to solve it.

"If I may begin at the bottom of the scale, a trust established by a father for the **7–196** education of his son is not a charity. The public element, as I will call it, is not supplied by the fact that from that son's education all may benefit. At the other end of the scale the establishment of a college or university is beyond doubt a charity. 'Schools of learning and free schools, and scholars of universities' are the very words of the preamble to the [Charitable Uses Act 1601 (43 Eliz. I, c.4)]. So also the endowment of a college, university or school by the creation of scholarships or bursaries is a charity, and nonetheless because competition may be limited to a particular class of persons. It is on this ground, as Lord Greene M.R. pointed out in *Re Compton*,[91] that the so-called 'founder's kin' cases can be rested. The difficulty arises where the trust is not for the benefit of any institution either then existing or by the terms of the trust to be brought into existence, but for the benefit of a class of persons at large. Then the question is whether that class of persons can be regarded as such a 'section of the community' as to satisfy the test of public benefit. These words 'section of the community' have no special sanctity, but they conveniently indicate (1) that the possible (I emphasise the word 'possible') beneficiaries must not be numerically negligible, and (2) that the quality which distinguishes them from other members of the community, so that they form by themselves a section of it, must be a quality which does not depend on their relationship to a particular individual. It is for this reason that a trust for the education of members of a family or, as in *Re Compton*, of a number of families cannot be regarded as charitable. A group of persons may be numerous, but, if the nexus between them is their personal relationship to a single *propositus* or to several *propositi*, they are neither the community nor a section of the community for charitable purposes.

---

[90] See also *Davies v Perpetual Trustee Co.* [1959] A.C. 439; 75 L.Q.R. 292. These broad employee benefit discretionary trusts were usually void as private trusts before *McPhail v Doulton* [1971] A.C. 424 liberalised the test for certainty of beneficiaries.
[91] [1945] Ch. 123.

7–197   "I come, then, to the present case where the class of beneficiaries is numerous, but the difficulty arises in regard to their common and distinguishing quality. That quality is being children of employees of one or other of a group of companies. I can make no distinction between children of employees and the employees themselves. In both cases the common quality is found in employment by particular employers. The latter of the two cases, by which the Court of Appeal held itself to be bound, the *Hobourn* case, is a direct authority for saying that such a common quality does not constitute its possessors a section of the public for charitable purposes. In the former case, *Re Compton*, Lord Greene M.R. had by way of illustration placed members of a family and employees of a particular employer on the same footing, finding neither in common kinship nor in common employment the sort of nexus which is sufficient. My Lords, I am so fully in agreement with what was said by Lord Greene in both cases, and by my noble and learned friend, then Morton L.J., in the *Hobourn* case, that I am in danger of repeating without improving upon their words. It appears to me that it would be an extension [of the legal definition of charity], for which there is no justification in principle or authority, to regard common employment as a quality which constitutes those employed a section of the community. It must not, I think, be forgotten that charitable institutions enjoy rare and increasing privileges, and that the claim to come within that privileged class should be clearly established. With the single exception of *Re Rayner*,[92] which I must regard as of doubtful authority, no case has been brought to the notice of the House in which such a claim as this has been made, where there is no element of poverty in the beneficiaries, but just this and no more, that they are the children of those in a common employment.

7–198   "Learned counsel for the appellant sought to fortify his case by pointing to the anomalies that would ensue from the rejection of his argument. For, he said, admittedly those who follow a profession or calling—clergymen, lawyers, colliers, tobacco-workers and so on—are a section of the public; how strange then it would be if, as in the case of railwaymen, those who follow a particular calling are all employed by one employer. Would a trust for the education of railwaymen be charitable,[93] but a trust for the education of men employed on the railways by the Transport Board not be charitable? And what of service of the Crown, whether in the civil service or the armed forces? Is there a difference between soldiers and soldiers of the King? My Lords, I am not impressed by this sort of argument and will consider on its merits if the occasion should arise, the case where the description of the occupation and the employment is in effect the same, where in a word, if you know what a man does, you know who employs him to do it. It is to me a far more cogent argument, as it was to my noble and learned friend in the *Hobourn* case, that, if a section of the public is constituted by the personal relation of employment, it is impossible to say that it is not constituted by a thousand as by 100,000 employees, and if by a thousand, then by a hundred, and, if by a hundred, then by ten. I do not mean merely that there is a difficulty in drawing the line, though that, too, is significant. I have it also in mind that, though the actual number of employees at any one moment might be small, it might increase to any extent, just as, being large, it might decrease to any extent. If the number of employees is the test of validity, must the court take into account potential increase or decrease, and, if so, as at what date?

---

[92] (1920) 89 L.J.Ch. 369.
[93] As to this see *Hall v Derby Sanitary Authority* (1885) 16 Q.B.D. 163.

LORD MACDERMOTT (dissenting)[94]: ". . . The question is whether it is of a public **7–199** nature, whether, in the words of Lord Wrenbury in *Verge v Somerville*,[98] 'it is for the benefit of the community or of an appreciably important class of the community.' The relevant class here is that from which those to be educated are to be selected. The appellant contends that this class is public in character; the respondent bank (as personal representative of the last surviving settlor) denies this and says that the class is no more than a group of private individuals.

"Until comparatively recently the usual way of approaching an issue of this sort, **7–200** at any rate where educational trusts were concerned, was, I believe, to regard the facts of each case and to treat the matter very much as one of degree. No definition of what constituted a sufficient section of the public for the purpose was applied, for none existed; and the process seems to have been one of reaching a conclusion on a general survey of the circumstances and considerations regarded as relevant rather than of making a single, conclusive test. The investigation left the course of the dividing line between what was and what was not a section of the community unexplored, and was concluded when it had gone far enough to establish to the satisfaction of the court whether or not the trust was public; and the decision as to that was, I think, very often reached by determining whether or not the trust was private.

"If it is still permissible to conduct the present inquiry on these broad if imprecise **7–201** lines, I would hold with the appellant. The numerical strength of the class is considerable on any showing. The employees concerned number over 110,000, and it may reasonably be assumed that the children, who constitute the class in question, are no fewer. The large size of the class is not, of course, decisive but in my view it cannot be left out of account when the problem is approached in this way. Then it must be observed that the *propositi* are not limited to those presently employed. They include former employees (not reckoned in the figure I have given) and are, therefore, a more stable category than would otherwise be the case. And, further, the employees concerned are not limited to those in the service of the 'British American Tobacco Co. Ltd or any of its subsidiary or allied companies'—itself a description of great width—but include the employees, in the event of the British American Tobacco Co. Ltd being reconstructed or merged on amalgamation, of the reconstructed or amalgamated company or any of its subsidiary companies. No doubt the settlors here had a special interest in the welfare of the class they described, but, apart from the fact that this may serve to explain the particular form of their bounty, I do not think it material to the question in hand. What is material, as I regard the matter, is that they have chosen to benefit a class which is, in fact, substantial in point of size and importance and have done so in a manner which, to my mind, manifests an intention to advance the interests of the class described as a class rather than as a collection or succession of particular individuals . . .

"The respondent bank, however, contends that the inquiry should be of quite a **7–202** different character to that which I have been discussing. It advances as the sole criterion a narrower test derived from the decisions of the Court of Appeal in *Compton*,[96] and in *Hobourn*.[97] The basis and nature of this test appear from the passage in the judgment of the court in *Compton*,[98] where Lord Greene M.R., says:

---

[94] See (1951) 67 L.Q.R. 162 (R.E.M.); *ibid.* 164 (A. L. G.) and the support in *Dingle v Turner* [1972] A.C. 601 set out above, at para.7–165.
[95] [1924] A.C. 496 at 499.
[96] [1945] Ch. 123.
[97] [1946] Ch. 194.
[98] [1945] Ch. 123 at 129–30.

'In the case of many charitable gifts it is possible to identify the individuals who are to benefit, or who at any given moment constitute the class from which the beneficiaries are to be selected. This circumstance does not, however, deprive the gift of its public character. Thus, if there is a gift to relieve the poor inhabitants of a parish the class to benefit is readily ascertainable. But they do not enjoy the benefit, when they receive it, by virtue of their character as individuals but by virtue of their membership of the specified class. In such a case the common quality which unites the potential beneficiaries into a class is essentially an impersonal one. It is definable by reference to what each has in common with the others, and that is something into which their status as individuals does not enter. Persons claiming to belong to the class do so not because they are A.B., C.D. and E.F., but because they are poor inhabitants of the parish. If, in asserting their claim, it were necessary for them to establish the fact that they were the individuals A.B., C.D. and E.F., I cannot help thinking that on principle the gift ought not to be held to be a charitable gift, since the introduction into their qualification of a purely personal element would deprive the gift of its necessary public character. It seems to me that the same principle ought to apply when the claimants, in order to establish their status, have to assert and prove, not that they themselves are A.B., C.D., and E.F., but that they stand in some specified relationship to the individuals A.B., C.D., and E.F., such as that of children or employees. In that case, too, a purely personal element enters into and is an essential part of the qualification, which is defined by reference to something, *i.e.*, personal relationship to individuals or an individual which is in its essence non-public.'

7–203   "The test thus propounded focuses upon the common quality which unites those within the class concerned and asks whether that quality is essentially impersonal or essentially personal. If the former, the class will rank as a section of the public and the trust will have the element common to and necessary for all legal charities; but, if the latter, the trust will be private and not charitable. It is suggested in the passage just quoted, and made clear beyond doubt in *Hobourn*,[99] that in the opinion of the Court of Appeal employment by a designated employer must be regarded for this purpose as a personal and not as an impersonal bond of union. In this connection and as illustrating the discriminating character of what I may call 'the *Compton*[1] test' reference should be made to that part of the judgment of the learned Master of the Rolls in *Hobourn*,[2] in which he speaks of the decision in *Hall v Derby Borough Urban Sanitary Authority*.[3] The passage runs thus:

'That related to a trust for railway servants. It is said that if a trust for railway servants can be a good charity, so too a trust for railway servants in the employment of a particular railway company is a good charity. That is not so. The reason, I think, is that in the one case the trust is for railway servants in general and in the other case it is for employees of a particular company, a fact which limits the potential beneficiaries to a class ascertained on a purely personal basis.'

7–204   "My Lords, I do not quarrel with the result arrived at in the *Compton* and *Hobourn* cases, and I do not doubt that the *Compton* test may often prove of value and lead to a correct determination. But, with the great respect due to those who

---

[99] [1946] Ch. 194.
[1] [1945] Ch. 123.
[2] [1946] Ch. 194 at 206.
[3] (1885) 16 Q.B.D. 163

have formulated this test, I find myself unable to regard it as a criterion of general applicability and conclusiveness. In the first place I see much difficulty in dividing the qualities or attributes, which may serve to bind human beings into classes, into two mutually exclusive groups, the one involving individual status and purely personal, the other disregarding such status and quite impersonal. As a task this seems to me no less baffling and elusive than the problem to which it is directed, namely, the determination of what is and what is not a section of the public for the purposes of this branch of the law. After all, what is more personal than poverty or blindness or ignorance? Yet none would deny that a gift for the education of the children of the poor or blind was charitable; and I doubt if there is any less certainty about the charitable nature of a gift for, say, the education of children who satisfy a specified examining body that they need and would benefit by a course of special instruction designed to remedy their educational defects.

"But can any really fundamental distinction, as respects the personal or imperso- **7–205** nal nature of the common link, be drawn between those employed, for example, by a particular university and those whom the same university has put in a certain category as the result of individual examination and assessment? Again, if the bond between these employed by a particular railway is purely personal, why should the bond between those who are employed as railway men be so essentially different? Is a distinction to be drawn in this respect between those who are employed in a particular industry before it is nationalized and those who are employed therein after that process has been completed and one employer has taken the place of many? Are miners in the service of the National Coal Board now in one category and miners at a particular pit or of a particular district in another? Is the relationship between those in the service of the Crown to be distinguished from that obtaining between those in the service of some other employer? Or, if not, are the children of, say, soldiers or civil servants to be regarded as not constituting a sufficient section of the public to make a trust for their education charitable?

"It was conceded in the course of the argument that, had the present trust been **7–206** framed so as to provide for the education of the children of those engaged in the tobacco industry in a named county or town, it would have been a good charitable disposition, and that even though the class to be benefited would have been appreciably smaller and no more important than is the class here. That concession follows from what the Court of Appeal has said. But if it is sound and a personal or impersonal relationship remains the universal criterion I think it shows, no less than the queries I have just raised in indicating some of the difficulties of the problem, that the *Compton* test is a very arbitrary and artificial rule. This leads me to the second difficulty that I have regarding it. If I understand it aright it necessarily makes the quantum of public benefit a consideration of little moment; the size of the class becomes immaterial and the need of its members and the public advantage of having that need met appear alike to be irrelevant. To my mind these are considerations of some account in the sphere of educational trusts for, as already indicated, I think the educational value and scope of the work actually to be done must have a bearing on the question of public benefit.

"Finally, it seems to me that, far from settling the state of the law on this **7–207** particular subject, the *Compton* test is more likely to create confusion and doubt in the case of many trusts and institutions of a character whose legal standing as charities has never been in question. Take, for instance, a trust for the provision of university education for boys coming from a particular school. The common quality binding the members of that class seems to reside in the fact that their parents or guardians all contracted for their schooling with the same establishment or body. That the school in such a case may itself be a charitable foundation seems altogether beside the point and quite insufficient to hold the *Compton* test at bay if it is well founded in law.

7–208   "I therefore return to what I think was the process followed before the decision in *Compton's* case, and, for the reasons already given, I would hold the present trust charitable and allow the appeal. I have only to add that I recognize the imperfections and uncertainties of that process. They are as evident as the difficulties of finding something better. But I venture to doubt if it is in the power of the courts to resolve those difficulties satisfactorily as matters stand. It is a long cry to the age of Elizabeth and I think what is needed is a fresh start from a new statute." *Appeal dismissed.*

I.R.C. v EDUCATIONAL GRANTS ASSOCIATION LTD

Chancery Division [1967] Ch. 123; [1966] 3 W.L.R. 724; [1966] 3 All E.R. 708

7–209   The Revenue appealed from a decision of the Special Commissioners of Income Tax that the respondents were a charity entitled to exemption from income tax under section 447(1)(*b*) of the Income Tax Act 1952 (now section 505 of the Income and Corporation Taxes Act 1988). The respondents were a company limited by guarantee formed for the advancement of education. However, the promoters of the company and its management were very much connected with Metal Box Ltd Virtually all the income came from a seven-year deed of covenant executed by Metal Box Ltd Care was taken that details of the company's objects did not leak out except to the higher ranks of Metal Box employees and their associates. Between 75 and 85 per cent. of payments were for the benefit of children of Metal Box employees. The Revenue conceded that the respondents were established for charitable purposes only and so the case turned upon whether or not the payments had been applied to charitable purposes only.

7–210   Pennycuick J. allowed the appeal holding that the absence of public benefit had the consequence that the payments had not been applied to charitable purposes only. The Court of Appeal[4] in short extempore judgments affirmed his decision but without pursuing his doubts over *Re Koettgen*. The reserved judgment of Pennycuick J. appears below as illuminating the issues more clearly than the Court of Appeal decision.

7–211   PENNYCUICK J.: "I will next read the relevant part of section 447 of the Income Tax Act 1952.[5]

> '(1) Exemption shall be granted . . . (*b*) . . . from tax chargeable under Sch. D in respect of any yearly interest or other annual payment, forming part of the income of any body of persons or trust established for charitable purposes only, or which, according to the rules or regulations established by Act of Parliament, charter, decree, deed of trust or will, are applicable to charitable purposes only, and so far as the same are applied to charitable purposes only.'

7–212   "It will be observed that the subsection imposes two distinct requirements: (i) the income must form part of the income of a body of persons or trust established for charitable purposes only, or must, according to the rules established by the relevant

---

[4] [1967] Ch. 993.
[5] See now Income and Corporation Taxes Act 1988, s.505, replacing ICTA 1970, s.360.

instrument, be applicable to charitable purposes only; and (ii) the exemption is available only so far as the income is applied to charitable purposes only. The first requirement depends on the construction of the relevant instrument; the second requirement depends on what is in fact done with the income as it arises from time to time. I will, for convenience, consider these requirements in their application to a corporate body, since that is the case now before me. They apply equally, mutatis mutandis, in the case of a trust created by a will or settlement.

"The objects of the corporation, in order that they may be exclusively charitable, **7–213** must be confined to objects for the public benefit. Equally, the application of the income, if it is to be within those objects, must be for the public benefit. Conversely, the application of income otherwise than for the public benefit must be outside the objects and *ultra vires*. For example, under an object for the advancement of education, once that is accepted as an exclusively charitable object, the income must be applied for the advancement of education by way of public benefit. An application of income for the advancement of education by way of private benefit would be *ultra vires*, and nonetheless so by reason that, in the nature of things, the members of a private class are included in the public as a whole. This may perhaps explain the repetition of the words 'for charitable purposes only' in the second requirement of the subsection.

"Counsel for the taxpayers advanced a simple and formidable argument: *viz.* (i) **7–214** the taxpayers are established for specified educational purposes; (ii) those purposes are admittedly charitable purposes, so the first requirement is satisfied; (iii) the income has been applied for the specified educational purposes; and (iv) therefore the income has been applied for charitable purposes, and the second requirement is satisfied. It seems to me that this argument leaves out of account the element of public benefit. It is true that it is claimed by the taxpayers and admitted by the Crown that the educational purposes specified in the taxpayers' memorandum are charitable purposes, but this by definition implies that the purposes are for the public benefit. In order that the second requirement may be satisfied, it must equally be shown that their income has been applied not merely for educational purposes as expressed in the memorandum but for those educational purposes by way of public benefit. An application of income by way of private benefit would be *ultra vires*. It is not open to the taxpayers first to set up a claim which can only be sustained on the basis that the purposes expressed in the memorandum are for the public benefit, and then, when it comes to the application of the income, to look only to the purposes expressed in the memorandum, leaving the element of public benefit out of account. This point may be illustrated by considering the familiar example of a case in which a fund is settled on trust for the advancement of education in general terms and the income is applied for the education of the settlor's children. Counsel for the taxpayer does not shrink from the conclusion that such an application comes within the terms of the trust and satisfies the second requirement of the subsection. I think that it does neither.

"Counsel for the Crown based his argument on construction broadly on the lines **7–215** which I have indicated above as being correct. He devoted much of his argument to repelling the application of the *Koettgen* case to the present one. In the *Koettgen*[6] case a testatrix bequeathed her residuary estate on trust 'for the promotion and furtherance of commercial education . . .' The will provided that

'The persons eligible as beneficiaries under the fund shall be persons of either sex who are British born subjects and who are desirous of educating themselves

---

[6] [1954] Ch. 252.

or obtaining tuition for a higher commercial career but whose means are insufficient or will not allow of their obtaining such education or tuition at their own expense . . .'

The testatrix further directed that in selecting the beneficiaries

'It is my wish that the . . . trustees shall give a preference to any employees of J.B. & Co. (London), Ltd, or any members of the families of such employees; failing a sufficient number of beneficiaries under such description then the persons eligible shall be any persons of British birth as the . . . trustees may select provided that the total income to be available for benefiting the preferred beneficiaries shall not in any one year be more than seventy-five per cent. of the total available income for that year.'

In the event of the failure of those trusts there was a gift over to a named charity. It was admitted that the trust was for the advancement of education, but it was contended for the charity that having regard to the direction to prefer a limited class of persons the trusts were not of a sufficiently public nature to constitute valid charitable trusts. It was held that the gift to the primary class from whom the trustees could select beneficiaries contained the necessary element of benefit to the public, and that it was when that class was ascertained that the validity of the trust had to be determined; so that the subsequent direction to prefer, as to 75 per cent. of the income, a limited class did not affect the validity of the trust, which was accordingly a valid and effective charitable trust. *Oppenheim v Tobacco Securities Trust Co. Ltd*,[7] was distinguished.

7–216   "The other case considered by the Special Commissioners was *Caffoor (Trustees of the Abdul Gaffoor Trust) v Comr. of Income Tax, Colombo*[8] in the Privy Council. In that case by the terms of a trust deed executed in Ceylon in 1942 the trust income after the death of the grantor was to be applied by the board of trustees, the appellants, in their absolute discretion for all or any of a number of purposes, which included '(2)(b) the education instruction or training in England or elsewhere abroad of deserving youths of the Islamic Faith' in any department of human activity. The recipients of the benefits were to be selected by the board 'from the following classes of persons and in the following order: (i) male descendants along either the male or female line of the grantor or of any of his brothers or sisters' failing whom youths of the Islamic Faith born of Muslim parents of the Ceylon Moorish community permanently resident in Colombo or elsewhere in Ceylon. It was held that in view of what was in effect the absolute priority to the benefit of the trust income which was conferred on the grantor's own family by clause 2(b)(i) of the trust deed this was a family trust and not a trust of a public character solely for charitable purposes, and the income thereof was accordingly not entitled to the exemption claimed. In his speech, Lord Radcliffe, giving the decision of the Privy Council, made the following comments[9] on the *Koettgen* case:

'It was argued with plausibility for the appellants that what this trust amounted to was a trust whose general purpose was the education of deserving young people of the Islamic Faith, and that its required public character was not destroyed by the circumstances that a preference in the selection of deserving

---

[7] [1951] A.C. 297.
[8] [1961] A.C. 584.
[9] [1961] A.C. 297 at 603.

recipients was directed to be given to members of the grantor's own family. Their Lordships go with the argument so far as to say that they do not think that a trust which provides for the education of a section of the public necessarily loses its charitable status or its public character merely because members of the founder's family are mentioned explicitly as qualified to share in the educational benefits or even, possibly, are given some kind of preference in the selection. They part with the argument, however, because they do not consider that the trust which is now before them comes within the range of any such qualified exception.'

"Lord Radcliffe went on to say that, there, the grantor's own family had, in effect, absolute priority. Then he said of the *Koettgen* case[10]:   **7–217**

'It is not necessary for their Lordships to say whether they would have put the same construction on the will there in question as the learned judge did, or whether they regard the distinction which he made as ultimately maintainable. The decision edges very near to being inconsistent with *Oppenheim's* case, but it is sufficient to say that the construction of the gift which was there adopted does not tally with the construction which their Lordships are bound to place on the trust which is now before them. Here, the effect of the wording of para.2(b)(i) is to create a primary disposition of the trust income in favour of the family of the grantor.'

"I am not concerned with the construction placed by Upjohn J. on the particular will   **7–218**
before him in the *Koettgen* case. I will assume that the effect of the will was as he construed it, *i.e.*, that it constituted a primary public class and then directed that the trustees should give preference to employees of a named company and their families, those employees being necessarily members of the whole public class. Upjohn J., held the trust to be charitable. In the *Caffoor* case, Lord Radcliffe gave a very guarded and qualified assent to that principle. The decision in *Koettgen's* case is concerned with the character of a trust on the construction of the relevant instrument, and not with the application of income. Its relevance in the latter connection is presumably that, if in the instrument creating a trust for a public class a private class whose members are included in the public class can be mentioned specifically and accorded a preference, then a preferential application of income for the benefit of a private class whose members are comprised in a public class is a proper execution of a trust for the public class. This is a long step, and I do not feel obliged to take it.

"For myself I find considerable difficulty in the *Koettgen* decision. I should have   **7–219**
thought that a trust for the public with preference for a private class comprised in the public might be regarded as a trust for the application of income at the discretion of the trustees between charitable and non-charitable objects. However, I am not concerned here to dispute the validity of the *Koettgen* decision. I only mention the difficulty which I feel as affording some additional reason for not applying the *Koettgen* decision by analogy in connection with the second requirement of the subsection.

"I return now to the present case. The taxpayers have claimed that the purposes   **7–220**
of the taxpayers are exclusively charitable, which imports that the purposes must be for the public benefit. The Crown have admitted that claim. I have then to consider

---

[10] [1961] A.C. 297 at 604.

whether the taxpayers have applied their income within their expressed objects and by way of public benefit. There is no doubt that the application has been within their expressed objects, but has it been by way of the public benefit? In order to answer this question, I must, I think, look at the individuals and institutions for whose benefit the income has been applied, and seek to discern whether these individuals and institutions possess any, and if so, what, relevant characteristics by virtue of which the income has been applied for their benefit. One may for this purpose look at the minutes of the council, circular letters and so forth. Counsel for the Crown at one time appeared to suggest that one might look at the actual intention of the members of the council. I do not think that is so.

7–221   "When one makes this enquiry, one finds that between 75 per cent and 85 per cent of the income of the taxpayers has been expended on the education of children connected with Metal Box Co. Ltd. The taxpayers are intimately connected with Metal Box Co. Ltd, in the many respects found in the Case Stated. They derive most of their income from Metal Box Co. Ltd. The council of management, as the Special Commissioners found, has followed a policy of seeking applications for grants from employees and ex-employees of Metal Box Co. Ltd, though these applications are not, of course, always successful. The inference is inescapable that this part of the taxpayer's income—*i.e.* 75 per cent to 85 per cent—has been expended for the benefit of these children by virtue of a private characteristic: *i.e.*, their connection with Metal Box Co. Ltd Such an application is not by way of public benefit. It is on all fours with an application of 75 per cent to 85 per cent. of the income of a trust fund on the education of a settlor's children. It follows, in my judgment, that, as regards the income which has been applied for the education of children of Metal Box Co. Ltd's employees, the taxpayers have failed to satisfy the second requirement in the subsection, and that the claim for relief fails. No reason has been suggested why the taxpayers should not obtain relief in respect of income applied for the benefit of institutions and outside individuals; see the words 'so far as' in the section.

7–222   "I recognise that this conclusion involves a finding that the council of management has acted *ultra vires* in applying the income of the taxpayers as it has done, albeit within the expressed objects of the taxpayers' memorandum. This conclusion follows from the basis on which the taxpayers have framed their objects and based their claim. It is of course open to a comparable body to frame its objects so as to make clear that its income may be applied for private as well as public purposes, but in that case it may not obtain tax relief. It does not seem to me that such a body can have it both ways. I propose, therefore, to allow this appeal." *Appeal allowed*.

III. THE ADVANCEMENT OF RELIGION

Religious purposes

7–223   This category of charitable trusts has its origin in the preamble to the 1601 Statute which speaks of "the repair of churches" but the courts soon held that the equity of the Statute extended to trusts advancing orthodox religion. With increasing religious toleration "the present position is that any religious body is entitled to charitable status so long as its tenets are not morally subversive and so long as its purposes are directed to the benefit of the public."[11] In rejecting the claim of an ethical society to be a charity for the advancement of religion Dillon J. said[12]:

---

[11] *Charities: A Framework for the Future* (1989) Cm. 694, para.2.20.
[12] *Re South Place Ethical Society* [1980] 1 W.L.R. 1565 at 1571. The society was charitable under the second and fourth heads of charity.

"Religion is concerned with man's relations with God, and ethics are concerned with man's relations with man. The two are not the same, all are not made the same by sincere inquiry into the question: what is God? If reason leads people not to accept Christianity or any known religion, but they do believe in the excellence of qualities, such as truth, beauty and love, or believe in the platonic concept of the ideal, their beliefs may seem to them to be the equivalent of a religion, but viewed objectively they are not religion . . . It seems to me that two of the essential attributes of religion are faith and worship: faith in a god and worship of that god. The Oxford English Dictionary gives as one of the definitions of religion: 'A particular system of faith and worship.' Then: 'Recognition on the part of man of some higher unseen power as having control of his destiny, and as being entitled to obedience, reverence and worship.'"

No distinction is drawn between monotheistic and polytheistic religions. **7–224** Charitable trusts have been registered for the advancement of the Church of England, Catholic,[13] Baptist,[14] Quaker,[15] Exclusive Brethren,[16] Jewish,[17] Sikh, Islamic, Hindu[18] and Spiritualist[19] religions. Various Buddhist groups also have registered charitable status,[19a] as does the Unification Church (the "Moonies")[20] but not the Church of Scientology. The Charity Commission[21] rejected its application for registration because although it believed in a supreme being such belief did not find expression in conduct indicative of reverence or veneration for the supreme being: study and therapy or counselling did not amount to such worship. However, in Australia[22] Scientology (as exemplified by the Church of New Faith) has been accepted as a charitable religion.

Mason A.C.J. and Brennan J. in the Australian High Court said[23]:

---

[13] *Bradshaw v Tasker* (1834) 2 Myl. & K. 221.
[14] *Re Strickland's W.T.* [1936] 3 All E.R. 1027.
[15] *Re Manser* [1905] 1 Ch. 68.
[16] *Holmes v Att.-Gen., The Times*, February 12, 1981.
[17] *Neville Estates Ltd v Madden* [1962] Ch. 832 but not a trust for the settlement of Jews in Palestine: *Keren Kayemeth Le Jisroel v I.R.C.* [1932] A.C. 650.
[18] See (1989) Cm. 694, para.2.19, S.I. 1962/1421, S.I. 1963/2074; *Varsani v Jesani* [1998] 3 All E.R. 273.
[19] Charity Commission, *Decision on the Application for Registration of the Sacred Hands Spiritual Centre* (September 5, 2003).
[19a] See, *e.g. Muman v Nagasena* [2001] 1 W.L.R. 299. *Quare* whether Buddhism recognises a supreme being? In *R. v Registrar General, ex parte Segerdal* [1970] 2 Q.B. 697 at 707, Lord Denning M.R. assumed that it does not, but in *Re South Place Ethical Society* [1980] 1 W.L.R. 1565 at 1573, Dillon J. left the point open. The Charities Bill 2005, cl.2(3)(a)(ii) is designed to bring Buddhism within the statutory definition of charitable religion by deeming "religion" to include "religion which does not involve belief in a god". But where does this leave Dillon J's dicta quoted above in the text to n.12?
[20] [1982] Charity Commissioners Annual Report paras 36–38. The Att.-Gen. dropped his action to deprive them of charitable status: Hansard February 3, 1988, p.977.
[21] Decision of November 17, 1999 taking account of *R. v Registrar General Ex p. Segerdal* [1970] 2 Q.B. 697. Its creed was more of a philosophy of the existence of man rather than a religion; such creed was described as "dangerous material" (*per* Lord Denning in *Hubbard v Vosper* [1972] 2 Q.B. 84 at 96) and as "pernicious nonsense" (*per* Goff J. in *Church of Scientology v Kaufman* [1973] R.P.C. 635 at 658).
[22] *Church of the New Faith v Commissioner of Pay-roll Tax* [1982–1983] 154 C.L.R. 120. The broad Australian view has been applied in New Zealand: *Centrepoint Community Growth Trust v I.R.C.* [1985] 1 N.Z.L.R. 673.
[23] [1982–1983] 154 C.L.R. 120 at 136.

7–225   "We would hold that the criteria of religion are twofold: first, belief in a supernatural Being, Thing or Principle; and, second, the acceptance of canons of conduct in order to give effect to that belief, though canons of conduct which offend against the ordinary law are outside the area of any immunity, privilege or right conferred on the grounds of religion. Those criteria may vary in their comparative importance, and there may be a different intensity of belief or of acceptance of canons of conduct among religions or among the adherents to a religion . . . Variations in emphasis may distinguish one religion from other religions, but they are irrelevant to the determination of an individual's or a group's freedom to profess and exercise the religion of his or their choice."

7–226   Wilson and Deane JJ. stated[24]:

"One of the more important indicia of 'religion' is that the particular collection of ideas and/or practices involves belief in the supernatural, that is to say, belief that reality extends beyond that which is capable of perception by the senses. If that be absent it is unlikely that one has a 'religion.' Another is that the ideas relate to a man's nature and place in the universe and his relation to things supernatural. A third is that the ideas are accepted by adherents as requiring or encouraging them to observe particular standards or codes of conduct or to participate in specific practices having supernatural significance. A fourth is that, however loosely knit and varying in beliefs and practices adherents may be, they constitute an identifiable group or groups. A fifth, and perhaps more controversial, indicium is that the adherents themselves see the collection of ideas and/or practices as constituting a religion. . . . No one of the above indicia is necessarily determinative of the question whether a particular collection of ideas of and/or practices should be objectively characterised as a 'religion.' They are no more than aids in determining that question. . . . All of those indicia are, however, satisfied by most or all leading religions."

7–227   Public anxiety has been expressed about some religious movements that may cause dissension in, and a break-up of, family life, but the question is usually not whether their *objects* are contrary to morality or the public interest but whether *conduct* of the movement causes harm. Here the Government has emphasised that the Charity Commissioners have powers of inquiry available to them under s.6 of the 1960 Charities Act (now s.8 of the 1993 Act) and stated[25]:

"Where conduct is in breach of trust or is marginal to the pursuit of an organisation's objects, action can generally be taken to restrain the

---

[24] *ibid.* at 174.
[25] (1989) Cm. 694, para.2.32.

trustees or their agents. Action of this kind does not affect an organisation's charitable status. But in exceptional circumstances where from a careful examination of all the circumstances the activities complained of appeared to them to be directly and essentially expressive of the objects and tenets of a particular movement, the Commissioners might conclude that the pursuit of those objects was not beneficial, and hence not therefore being directed to charitable purposes. Should they reach this conclusion the Commissioner could remove the organisation from the register of charities under section 4(3) of the 1960 Act [now s.3(4) of 1993 Act]. Under section 5(3) (now s.4(3) of 1993 Act) the Att.-Gen. can appeal against any decision of the Commissioners to remove or not to remove an organisation from the register."

The Freemasons[26] and the Oxford Group[27] (as originally formed) are not **7–228** religious charities, though a trust for the publication of the writings of Joanna Southcott (who claimed to be with child by the Holy Ghost and so about to give birth to a new Messiah) was held to be charitable[28] (and so void under the 1736 Mortmain and Charitable Uses Act). Indeed, a trust "for the continuance of the work of God as it has been maintained by H and myself since 1942" was held charitable[29] where the work consisted mainly in the free distribution of fundamentalist Christian tracts written by H, though the tracts were of no intrinsic merit except in confirming the beliefs of H's circle.

Trusts for adding to or repairing the fabric of a church[30] or for the **7–229** upkeep of a churchyard[31] are charitable but not for the erection or upkeep of a particular tomb in a churchyard.[32] If a gift is made to an ecclesiastic in his official name and by virtue of his office then if no purposes are expressed in the gift the gift is for charitable religious purposes inherent in the office.[33] However, if the purposes are expressed in terms not confining them to exclusively charitable purposes then the charitable character of the trustee will not make the gift charitable.[34] A trust for religious purposes will be treated as for charitable religious purposes[35] but a trust for religious institutions will not be a charitable trust because some religious institutions (like a purely contemplative order of nuns) lack the necessary public benefit for a charitable trust.[36]

[26] *United Grand Lodge of Freemasons v Holborn B.C.* [1957] 1 W.L.R. 1080.
[27] *Re Thackrach* [1939] 2 All E.R. 4, *Oxford Group v I.R.C.* [1949] 2 All E.R. 537.
[28] *Thornton v Howe* (1862) 31 Beav. 14.
[29] *Re Watson* [1973] 1 W.L.R. 1472.
[30] *Re Raine* [1956] Ch. 417; *Hoare v Osborne* (1866) L.R. 1 Eq. 585.
[31] *Re Douglas* [1905] 1 Ch. 279; *Re Vaughan* (1866) 33 Ch.D. 187 at 192.
[32] *Lloyd v Lloyd* (1852) 2 Sim. (N.S.) 225; *Re Hooper* [1932] 1 Ch. 38; see Parish Councils and Burial Authorities Miscellaneous Provisions Act 1970, s.1 (a burial or local authority may contract to maintain a grave or memorial for not exceeding 99 years).
[33] *Re Rumball* [1956] Ch. 105.
[34] *Re Simson* [1946] Ch. 299 (gift to vicar "for his work in the parish" charitable); *Farley v Westminster Bank* [1939] A.C. 430 (gift to vicar "for parish work" not charitable) applying *Dunn v Byrne* [1912] A.C. 407.
[35] *MacLaughlin v Campbell* [1906] I.R. 588 to trustees "for such Roman Catholic purposes in the parish of Coleraine or elsewhere as they deem fit" void because possibility of Catholic political economic or social purposes, while there and in *Re White* [1893] 2 Ch. 41 it was accepted that a gift for "religious purposes" means impliedly "charitable religious purposes."
[36] *Gilmour v Coats* [1949] A.C. 426.

Public benefit

7–230　　The courts are generally reluctant to enter into questions of the comparative worth of different religions. However, in *Gilmour v Coats*, at para.7–236 the House of Lords held that a trust for a contemplative order of nuns who did not leave their cloisters nor allow the public into them was not charitable. The benefits of their edifying example and their intercessory prayers were too vague and incapable of being proved to be of tangible benefit for the public. The court does not have to accept as proved whatever a particular religion believes. Nonetheless, in *Neville Estates Ltd v Madden*[37] Cross J. upheld as charitable a trust for the members from time to time of the Catford Jewish Synagogue because[38] "the court is entitled to assume that some benefit accrues to the public from the attendance at places of worship of persons who live in this world and mix with their fellow citizens." Moreover, the Charity Commissioners[39] registered as charitable The Society of the Precious Blood. This was an enclosed contemplative society of Anglican Nuns but their activities included within their walls public religious services, religious and secular education of the public and the relief of suffering, sickness, poverty and distress through their counselling service.

7–231　　A further issue is whether or not the saying of Catholic Masses for the repose of particular souls is for the public benefit. The benefit of intercessory prayer is incapable of legal proof, but if Masses are said in public this has an edifying and improving effect on members of the public who happen to be in attendance, Masses held in private only edifying a private and not a public class of people. In both cases, however, one can argue that the money paid to the priest for saying Masses relieves the Catholic Church to that extent of its liability to provide stipends for priests and so benefits the Catholic Church and its members. In *Re Hetherington*[40] it was held that this in itself is not enough, so that the trust for Masses for the repose of particular souls was held to be charitable only by implicitly restricting it to Masses that had to be held in public.

7–232　　On this basis, the Charity Commissioners, in rejecting the application for registration as a charity of the Church of Scientology (para.7–243), held that it is the public nature of the religious practice which is essential to the trust being charitable. The Commissioners also considered that it was clearly possible that the European Convention on Human Rights, as applied in the United Kingdom by the Human Rights Act 1999, could apply to their decisions so that they needed to interpret the case law consistently with the Convention.

7–233　　In particular under Art.9 (1) "everyone has the right to freedom of thought, conscience and religion; this right includes freedom to change his religion or belief and freedom either alone or in community with others

---

[37] *Neville Estates Ltd v Madden* [1962] Ch. 832. Clearly, the benefited class was small, and in *Dingle v Turner* [1972] A.C. 601 at 625 Lord Cross said, "A trust to promote some religion among the employees of a company might perhaps be held to be charitable, provided it was clear that the benefits were to be purely spiritual."

[38] *ibid.* 853; *Re Warre's W.T.* [1953] 1 W.L.R. 725 (retreat house not charitable) is of dubious authority.

[39] [1989] Annual Report paras 56–62, *Decisions*, Vol. 3, p.11.

[40] [1990] Ch.1 criticised by C. Rickett [1990] Conv. 34; further see *Nolan v Downes* (1917) 23 C.L.R. 546 and *Carrigan v Redwood* (1910) 30 N.Z.L.R. 244.

and in public or private to manifest his religion or belief in worship, teaching, practice and observance", while by Art.9(2) "Freedom to manifest one's religion or beliefs shall be subject only to such limitations as are prescribed by law and are necessary in a democratic society in the interests of public safety, for the protection of public order, health or morals, or for the protection of the rights or freedoms of others".

Art.14 may be used in conjunction with Art.9: "The enjoyment of the **7–234** rights and freedoms set forth in this Convention shall be secured without discrimination on any ground such as sex, race, colour, language, religion, political or other opinion, national or social origin, association with a national minority, property, birth or other status."

A reasonable case can be made that to decline registration of a body as a **7–235** charity, with the fiscal privileges attaching thereto, would impair protected freedoms as it limits the body's ability to manifest its beliefs through teaching and evangelical activities designed to encourage persons to change their religious affiliations.[41] Nevertheless, the Commissioners held that the Church of Scientology failed the public benefit test as prescribed by English cases that satisfied the requirements of the Convention. Moreover, as Strayer J.A. held in the Canadian Federal Court of Appeal in *Human Life International of Canada Inc. v M.N.R.*,[42] a guarantee of human rights such as freedom of expression is not the same thing as "a guarantee of public funding through tax exemptions for the propagation of opinions no matter how good or sincerely held."

GILMOUR v COATS

House of Lords [1949] A.C. 426; [1949] 1 All E.R. 848 (Lords Simonds, du Parcq, Normand, Morton and Reid)

The income of a trust fund was to be applied to the purposes of a Carmelite **7–236** convent, if those purposes were charitable. The convent was comprised of an association of strictly cloistered and purely contemplative nuns who were concerned with prayers and meditation, and who did not engage in any activities for the benefit of people outside the convent. In the view of the Roman Catholic Church, however, their prayers and meditation caused the intervention of God for the benefit of members of the public, and their life inside the convent provided an example of self-denial and concentration on religious matters which was beneficial to the public. All courts held that the trust was not a charitable one.

LORD SIMONDS: ". . . I need not go back beyond the case of *Cocks v Manners*,[43] **7–237** which was decided nearly eighty years ago by Wickens V.-C. In that case the testatrix left her residuary estate between a number of religious institutions, one of them being the Dominican convent at Carisbrooke, a community not differing in any material respect from the community of nuns now under consideration. The

---

[41] *Kokkinakis v Greece* (1997) 24 EHRR (C.D.) 52. In other respects the recognition or non-recognition as a charity does not appear to interfere with the manifestation of a person's belief, so that the State's declining to confer a privilege would not breach Art.9.
[42] [1998] 3 F.C. 202 at 220–221.
[43] (1871) L.R. 12 Eq. 574.

learned judge used these words,[44] which I venture to repeat, though they have already been cited in the courts below: 'On the Act [the statute of Elizabeth] unaffected by authority I should certainly hold that the gift to the Dominican convent is neither within the letter nor the spirit of it; and no decision has been referred to which compels me to adopt a different conclusion. A voluntary association of women for the purpose of working out their own salvation by religious exercises and self-denial seems to me to have none of the requisites of a charitable institution, whether the word 'charitable' is used in its popular sense or in its legal sense. It is said, in some of the cases, that religious purposes are charitable, but that can only be true as to religious services tending directly or indirectly towards the instruction or the edification of the public; an annuity to an individual, so long as he spent his time in retirement and constant devotion, would not be charitable, nor would a gift to ten persons, so long as they lived together in retirement and performed acts of devotion, be charitable. Therefore the gift to the Dominican convent is not, in my opinion, a gift on a charitable trust.'

7–238 "Apart from what I have called the final argument, which I will deal with later, the contention of the appellant rests, not on any change in the lives of the members of such a community as this, nor, from a wider aspect, on the emergence of any new conception of the public good, but solely on the fact that for the first time certain evidence of the value of such lives to a wider public together with new arguments based on that evidence has been presented to the court. Never before, it was urged, has the benefit to be derived from intercessory prayer and from edification been brought to the attention of the court; if it had been, the decision in *Cocks v Manners* would, at least should, have been otherwise.

7–239 "My Lords, I would speak with all respect and reverence of those who spend their lives in cloistered piety, and in this House of Lords spiritual and temporal, which daily commences its proceedings with intercessory prayers, how can I deny that the Divine Being may in His Wisdom think fit to answer them? But, my Lords, whether I affirm or deny, whether I believe or disbelieve, what has that to do with the proof which the court demands that a particular purpose satisfies the test of benefit to the community? Here is something which is manifestly not susceptible of proof. But, then it is said, this is a matter not of proof but of belief, for the value of intercessory prayer is a tenet of the Catholic faith, therefore, and in such a prayer there is benefit to the community. But it is just at this 'therefore' that I must pause. It is, no doubt, true that the advancement of religion is, generally speaking, one of the heads of charity, but it does not follow from this that the court must accept as proved whatever a particular church believes. The faithful must embrace their faith believing where they cannot prove: the court can act only on proof. A gift to two or ten or a hundred cloistered nuns in the belief that their prayers will benefit the world at large does not from that belief alone derive validity any more than does the belief of any other donor for any other purpose. The importance of this case leads me to state my opinion in my own words but, having read again the judgment of the learned Master of the Rolls, I will add that I am in full agreement with what he says on this part of the case.

7–240 "I turn to the second of the alleged elements of public benefit, edification by example, and I think that this argument can be dealt with very shortly. It is, in my opinion, sufficient to say that this is something too vague and intangible to satisfy the prescribed test. The test of public benefit has, I think, been developed in the last two centuries. Today it is beyond doubt that that element must be present. No court

---

[44] *ibid.* at 585.

would be rash enough to attempt to define precisely or exhaustively what its content must be. But it would assume a burden which it could not discharge if now for the first time it admitted into the category of public benefit something so indirect, remote, imponderable and, I would add, controversial as the benefit which may be derived by others from the example of pious lives.

"I must now refer to certain cases on which the appellant relied. They consist of a number of cases in the Irish courts and *Re Caus*,[45] a decision of Luxmoore J. A consideration of the Irish cases shows that it has there been decided that a bequest for the saying of masses, whether in public or in private, is a good charitable bequest: see, *e.g.*, *Att.-Gen. v Hall*[46] and *O'Hanlon v Logue*.[47] And in *Re Caus* Luxmoore J. came to the same conclusion. I would expressly reserve my opinion on the question whether these decisions should be sustained in this House. So important a matter should not be decided except on a direct consideration of it. It is possible that, particularly in regard to the celebration of masses in public, good reason may be found for supporting a gift for such an object as both a legal and a charitable purpose. But it follows from what I have said in the earlier part of this opinion that I am unable to accept the view, which at least in the Irish cases is clearly expressed, that in intercessory prayer and edification that public benefit which is the condition of legal charity is to be found. Of the decision of Luxmoore J. in *Re Caus*, I would only say that his *ratio decidendi* is expressly stated to be,[48] 'first, that it (*i.e.*, a gift for the saying of masses) enables a ritual act to be performed which is recognised by a large proportion of Christian people to be the central act of their religion, and, secondly, that it assists in the endowment of priests whose duty it is to perform the ritual act.' The decision, therefore, does not assist the appellant's argument in the present case and I make no further comments on it.[49]

"It remains, finally, to deal with the argument that the element of public benefit is supplied by the fact that qualification for admission to membership of the community is not limited to any group of persons but is open to any woman in the wide world who has the necessary vocation. Thus, it is said, just as the endowment of a scholarship open to public competition is a charity, so also a gift to enable any woman (or, presumably, any man) to enter a fuller religious life is a charity. To this argument, which, it must be admitted, has a speciously logical appearance, the first answer is that which I have indicated earlier in this opinion. There is no novelty in the idea that a community of nuns must, if it is to continue, from time to time obtain fresh recruits from the outside world. That is why a perpetuity is involved in a gift for the benefit of such a community, and it is not to be supposed that, to mention only three masters of this branch of the law, Wickens V.-C., Lord Lindley or Lord Macnaghten failed to appreciate the point. Yet, by direct decision or by way of emphatic example, a community such as this is by them regarded as the very type of religious institution which is not charitable. I know of no consideration applicable to this case which would justify this House in unsettling a rule of law which has been established so long and by such high authority. But that is not the only, nor, indeed, the most cogent reason why I cannot accede to the appellant's argument. It is a trite saying that the law is life, not logic. But it is, I think, conspicuously true of the law of charity that it has been built up, not logically, but empirically. It would not, therefore, be surprising to find that, while in every category of legal charity some

7–241

7–242

---

[45] [1934] Ch. 162.
[46] [1897] 2 I.R. 426.
[47] [1906] 1 I.R. 247.
[48] [1934] Ch. 162 at 170.
[49] See *Re Hetherington* [1990] Ch 1 on *Re Caus*.

element of public benefit must be present, the court had not adopted the same measure in regard to different categories, but had accepted one standard in regard to those gifts which are alleged to be for the advancement of religion, and it may be yet another in regard to the relief of poverty. To argue by a method of syllogism or analogy from the category of education to that of religion ignores the historical process of the law. Nor would there be lack of justification for the divergence of treatment which is here assumed. For there is a legislative and political background peculiar to so-called religious trusts, which has, I think, influenced the development of the law in this matter."[50] *Appeal dismissed*.

CHARITY COMMISSIONERS' DECISION ON APPLICATION FOR REGISTRATION OF THE CHURCH OF SCIENTOLOGY

The legal test of public benefit under the third head of charity

7–243   "The **Commissioners** noted that it is clear (from the dicta of Lord Greene M.R. in *Coats v Gilmour*) that the burden is upon the religious organisation in question to demonstrate both its impact upon the community and that the impact is beneficial, if public benefit is to be demonstrated.

7–244   "Some clear principles emerge from the decided cases:

- a gift for the advancement of religion must be beneficial to the public (or a sufficient section of the public)[51] and not simply for the benefit of the adherents of the particular religion themselves.[52]
- It is settled law that the question whether a particular gift satisfies the requirement of public benefit must be determined by the court and the opinion of the donor or testator is irrelevant.[53]
- The court must decide whether or not there is a benefit to the community in the light of evidence of a kind cognisable by the court[54]

7–245   "The presence or absence of the necessary element of public benefit has also been considered in a number of cases. The essential distinguishing feature seems to be whether or not the practice of the religion is essentially public. The case **In re Hetherington decd. [1990] Ch. 1** focused on the question of public benefit in relation to religion. In that case the Judge summarised the principles established by the legal authorities. In concluding that a gift for the celebration of masses (assumed to be in public) was charitable he drew upon cases concerning a variety of religious practices and concluded as follows:

1. A trust for the advancement of education, the relief of poverty or the advancement of religion is charitable and assumed to be for the public benefit. The assumption can be rebutted by showing that in fact the particular trust in question cannot operate so as to confer a legally recognised benefit on the public—as in *Gilmour v Coats*;

---

[50] The Nathan Committee on Charitable Trusts rejected the suggestion of the representatives of the Roman Catholic Church that trusts for the advancement of religion should be defined to include "the advancement of religion by those means which that religion believes and teaches are means by which it does advance it": (1952) Cmnd.8710, paras 129–130.
[51] *National Anti-Vivisection Society v IRC* [1948] A.C. 31.
[52] *Holmes v Att.-Gen.; The Times*, February 12, 1981.
[53] *Re Hummeltenberg* [1923] 1 Ch. 237 and *National Anti-Vivisection Society v IRC* (above).
[54] *Gilmour v Coats* [1949] A.C. 426.

2. The celebration of a religious rite in public does confer sufficient public benefit because of the edifying and improving effect of such celebration on the members of the public who attend; and

3. The celebration of a religious rite in private does not contain the necessary element of public benefit since any benefit of prayer or example is incapable of proof in the legal sense and any element of edification is limited to a private not public class of those present at the celebration. Following *Gilmour v Coats*,[55] *Yeap Cheah Neo v Ong Cheng Neo*[56] and *Hoare v Hoare*[57]; and

4. Where there is a gift for a religious purpose which could be carried out in a way which is beneficial to the public, (*i.e.* by public masses) but could also be carried out in a way which would not have a sufficient element of public element (ie by private masses) the gift is to be construed as a gift to be carried out by methods that are charitable, all non charitable methods being excluded.

It is clear from **In re Hetherington decd**.[58] and the cases cited there that it is the public nature of the religious practice which is essential to the gift being charitable.

"The **Commissioners** concluded that the decided cases indicated that where the practice of the religion is essentially private or is limited to a private class of individuals not extending to the public generally, the element of public benefit will not be established.[59]

7–246

The legal test of public benefit under the fourth head

"The **Commissioners** turned next to the legal test of public benefit under the fourth head of charity and considered the test to be that set out by Lord Wright in *National Anti-Vivisection Society v IRC*.[60] Lord Wright said that:

7–247

'I think the whole tendency of the concept of charity in a legal sense under the fourth head is towards tangible and objective benefits, and at least, that approval by the common understanding of enlightened opinion for the time being, is necessary before an intangible benefit can be taken to constitute a sufficient benefit to the community to justify admission of the object into the fourth class.'

"It seemed to the **Commissioners** that the benefit that arises from the moral or spiritual welfare or improvement of the community is likely to be an intangible rather than a tangible one. The **Commissioners** considered the test in respect of an intangible benefit to mean a common consensus of opinion amongst people who were fair minded and free from prejudice or bias.

7–248

"The **Commissioners** considered in particular whether the representations which it had received about Scientology generally and **CoS** in particular, both favourable and unfavourable amounted to such "common understanding" and concluded that they did not. The representations were not easily substantiated and in effect

7–249

---

[55] [1949] A.C. 426.
[56] [1875] L.R. 6 P.C. 381.
[57] [1886] 56 L.T. 147.
[58] [1990] Ch. 1.
[59] *In re Hetherington decd.*, (above) *Coats v Gilmour* [1948] Ch. 340, 347 *per* Lord Evershed.
[60] [1948] A.C. 31 at 49.

represented opposing ends of the spectrum of opinion about **CoS** or Scientology generally.

7–250   "The **Commissioners** further indicated that a key factor in assessing whether the test in that case was met (ie whether there was a common understanding of enlightened opinion that public benefit flowed from the advancement of Scientology by **CoS**), was the extent to which the core practices of Scientology were readily accessible by the public generally.

7–251   "Accordingly, the **Commissioners** would need to consider whether there was approval by the common understanding of enlightened opinion that pursuit of Scientology doctrines and practices is beneficial to the community such that **CoS** may be regarded as charitable under the fourth head.

Consideration of CoS's arguments as to public benefit under the fourth head of charity

7–252   "The **Commissioners** noted **CoS**'s arguments in this respect. One interpretation of **CoS**'s legal arguments was to the effect that public benefit under the fourth head of charity does not have to be *proved*, but that it is only necessary to *show* that the organisation's activities *may* have that result.

7–253   "The **Commissioners** considered CoS's argument apparently based upon *Berry v St Marylebone Corporation* [1959] Ch 406 concerning the Theosophical Society in England seeking relief from paying rates under section 8 of the Ratings and Valuation (Miscellaneous Provisions) Act 1955. The **Commissioners** noted that **CoS** appeared to rely on dicta of Romer L.J. in that case as support for the proposition that public benefit under the fourth head of charity need not be proven but should only be shown.

7–254   "The **Commissioners** did not accept this argument, as it was not clear to them that the case cited—*Berry v St Marylebone Corporation*—was authority for this proposition, rather it seemed to the **Commissioners** that it was authority for the proposition that it was necessary to show that the purpose (in that case the advancement of religion) may be likely to be advanced. This they had considered above. In any event the case related specifically to the requirements of section 8 of the Ratings and Valuation (Miscellaneous Provisions) Act 1955 and was not a discussion about charitable status such that the judge's comments were not directly applicable to charity law.

7–255   "In relation to the question of public benefit it seemed clear to the Commissioners from the dicta of Lord Wright in *National Anti-vivisection Society v IRC* that public benefit must positively be shown under the fourth head of charity. Lord Wright's comments in that case that the whole tendency of the concept of charity under the fourth head is towards tangible and objective benefits, seemed to the **Commissioners** to indicate quite clearly that the benefits must be identifiable and demonstrable, and that a common consensus of approval is necessary before an intangible benefit can be regarded as sufficient to satisfy the requirement of public benefit.

Whether CoS is established for the public benefit, whether under the third or fourth heads of charity

7–256   "The **Commissioners** next sought to address the question of whether **CoS** had shown itself to be established for the public benefit. The **Commissioners** considered the considerable volume of evidence supplied by **CoS** in support of its arguments that **CoS** was established for the public benefit whether under the third or fourth heads of charity because

- Individual churches of Scientology conduct numerous religious services freely accessible by members of the public.
- CoS sufficiently benefits the public through extensive charitable and public benefit programmes including anti drug campaigns, eradicating illiteracy, disaster relief and raising public morality.
- The Company (CoS) is limited by guarantee and its members make no profit.
- It is of the essence of Scientology "like most other religions" to seek to make itself available to all.
- Many of Mr Hubbard's teachings are already recognised as charitable and applied by existing registered charities.
- The Scientology movement engages in other activities which could potentially give rise to public benefit eg volunteer and relief programmes; rituals and practices such as "assists" (described as a form of healing); work in the field of criminal rehabilitation; observance of a moral code by individual Scientologists and promulgation of that moral code through the "Way to Happiness Foundation".

"The **Commissioners** *considered* that the evidence and arguments supplied by **7–257** CoS may indicate ways in which Scientology organisations, and individual Scientologists, seek to benefit the wider community. They noted that in terms of English charity law some of that work may potentially be charitable in its own right, albeit not as promoting the moral or spiritual welfare or improvement of the community nor as advancing religion.[61] However, the **Commissioners** noted that the evidence and argument put to them by **CoS** did not address the central question of whether the advancement of Scientology (whether as a religion or as a non-religious belief system) confers recognisable benefit upon the public in English charity law. **CoS** states that its principal activities are auditing and training and that it is through these core activities that Scientology is advanced. In the **Commissioners** view it therefore had to be demonstrated that the advancement of Scientology through auditing and training is beneficial to the public. The **Commissioners** considered that it is to the central activities of auditing and training that the question of public benefit should be addressed.

"The **Commissioners** went on to consider whether it was demonstrated that **7–258** public benefit flowed from the core practices of Scientology. The **Commissioners** again noted that the test of public benefit was slightly different in relation to the third and fourth heads of charity. In relation to the third head the decided cases indicated that the public or private nature of the "religious practice" of the organisation in question was central to determining the presence or absence of public benefit. In relation to the purpose of promoting the moral or spiritual welfare or improvement of the community under the fourth head of charity the legal test was that set out by Lord Wright in the *National Vivisection Society v IRC* case.

In relation to the test of public benefit for the advancement of religion the **Commissioners** *concluded that*

(1) The central "religious" practices of Scientology are conducted in private and not in public.

---

[61] Much Scientology activity appeared to the Commissioners to be in the fields of education and what might broadly be termed "relief in need".

7–259   "The "religious practices" of Scientology are auditing and training. Scientologists regard these as worship. Auditing is conducted in private on a one to one basis. It appears akin to a form of counselling and is described by Scientologists as such.[62] Training is essentially a private activity requiring the study of specialist material and access to specialist trainers. Whilst members of the public may sign up for a course of auditing and training, generally upon payment of the appropriate requested donation, these activities are not carried out "in public". Further, progression beyond introductory or initial levels of auditing and training necessitated membership of the Church.

7–260   "Attendance at a session of auditing or training by members of the public generally does not appear to be a possibility. The **Commissioners** found it difficult therefore to see how any edifying and improving effects upon the public generally might flow from the "religious" practices of Scientology.

7–261   "In relation to the fourth proposition in In *re Hetherington* decd., there was no suggestion that auditing and training could be carried out in a way that was public rather than private. It did not seem possible to construe auditing and training as religious rites which could be conducted in public rather than in private such as to render them charitable.

(2) Auditing and training are in their nature private rather than public activities

7–262   "The **Commissioners** considered that even if a member of the public could attend an auditing and/or training session other than as a participant but rather as an observer, these Scientology services are by their very nature directed to the particular individual receiving them. Auditing appears akin to a form of counselling and is described by Scientologists who receive it as "counselling". It is directed to the private needs of the individual receiving it. The **Commissioners** found it difficult to see how the public could be edified or otherwise benefited by attending and observing at such a session.

7–263   "Both the above factors—that Scientology services are conducted in private, and are in their nature private being directed to the needs of the private individual in receipt of them seemed to the **Commissioners** to indicate that these actual activities are of a private rather than a public kind. In any event it seemed to the **Commissioners** that any benefit to the public that may flow from auditing and training is incapable of proof, any edification or improving effect being limited to the private individual engaging in the auditing or training. Accordingly, the **Commissioners** concluded that these activities conferred no legally recognised benefit on the public.

7–264   "**In addition** the **Commissioners** noted that the apparent dependence of participation in those activities upon payment of the requested donation referred to by **CoS** strengthened their perception that these activities were of a private rather than a public kind. Whilst **CoS** states that there are ways in which adherents can and do participate in auditing and training without making any form of monetary contribution, so that a lack of financial means is no bar to a member's progress in Scientology, access to auditing and training through requested donations is the norm. The **Commissioners** noted that the fact that a practice existed of requesting and making these payments strengthened the **Commissioners** in their perception that the activities were of a private rather than a public kind.

---

[62] Video presentation "The Church of Scientology at Saint Hill—A Special presentation to the Charity Commission of England and Wales".

"The **Commissioners** further noted that in its published and promotional **7–265** literature, including the book "What is Scientology?", Scientology on balance presented its benefits in private rather than public terms.

"In addition the **Commissioners** noted that a not insignificant number of **7–266** individual Scientologists described the benefits of Scientology in private and personal terms this being borne out both by a number of the statements printed in Scientology's published literature and by a significant proportion of the letters of support for **CoS** received from individual Scientologists.

"The fact that Scientology describes its benefits in private rather than public **7–267** terms in its published and promotional literature, and that individual Scientologists described the benefits of Scientology to them in private and personal terms confirmed the **Commissioners** conclusion that **CoS** is not established for the public benefit.

In relation to the test of public benefit under the fourth head of charity law for the moral or spiritual welfare or improvement of the community the **Commissioners** *concluded that:*

"The question of accessibility by the public was key to the existence of public **7–268** benefit. As indicated above, the **Commissioners** had already concluded that the central practices of Scientology (auditing and training) were conducted in private rather than in public, and were in their nature private rather than public activities. In addition there was the practice of requesting donations in advance of receipt of those services. This led the **Commissioners** to conclude that the restricted access to those practices meant that any benefit flowing from Scientology as advanced by **CoS** is of a private rather than a public kind. In addition the description of the benefits of Scientology, both in Scientology published and promotional literature and by individual Scientologists, as already acknowledged by the **Commissioners**, confirmed them in this conclusion.

"The **Commissioners** concluded that it could not be said that **CoS** had demon- **7–269** strated that it was established for the public benefit so as to satisfy the legal test of public benefit of a charitable purpose for the advancement of religion or for the moral or spiritual welfare or improvement of the community."

IV. THE ADVANCEMENT OF HEALTH OR SAVING OF LIVES

This head includes the prevention or relief of sickness, disease or human **7–270** suffering,[63] the promotion of health by the provision of items, services and facilities both for patients and for health professionals,[64] and the saving of lives by rescue services such as those provided by the R.N.L.I.[65] and mountain rescue teams.[66] So far as the advancement of health is concerned, the Charity Commission has stated that:[67]

---

[63] *Cf.* Charities Bill 2005, cl.2(3)(b). See too *Re Resch's W.T.* [1969] 1 A.C. 514; Charity Commission, *CC 6: Charities for the Relief of Sickness* (March 2000 version).

[64] Including the promulgation and enforcement of professional standards: *C.I.R. v Medical Council of New Zealand* [1997] 2 N.Z.L.R. 297; Charity Commission, *Decision on the Application for Registration as a Charity by the General Medical Council* (April 2, 2001), declining to follow two previous court decisions to the contrary, on the ground of changed social circumstances: *General Medical Council v I.R.C.* [1928] 1 All E.R. 252 and *General Nursing Council v St. Marylebone B.C.* [1959] A.C. 540 (where the G.M.C. and G.N.C. were thought to be bodies established for the benefit of their members rather than the public at large).

[65] *Thomas v Howell* (1874) L.R. 18 Eq. 198; *Re David* (1889) 43 Ch.D. 27.

[66] See too *Re Wokingham Fire Brigade Trusts* [1951] Ch. 373 (provision for local fire brigade); *The League of Highway Safety and Safe Drivers Ltd* [1965] Ch. Com. Rep. 27 (promotion of road safety).

[67] Charity Commission, *Commentary on the Descriptions of Charitable Purposes in the Charities Bill* (January 2005 version) para.12.

"It includes conventional methods as well as complementary, alternative or holistic methods which are concerned with healing mind, body and spirit in the alleviation of symptoms and the cure of illness. To be charitable there needs to be sufficient evidence of the efficacy of the method used. Assessing the efficacy of different therapies will depend upon what benefits are claimed for it (*i.e.* whether it is diagnostic, curative, therapeutic and/or palliative) and whether it is offered as a complement to conventional medicine or as an alternative. Each case is considered on its merits but the House of Lords Report on complementary and alternative medicine is a useful guide."[68]

V. The Advancement of Citizenship or Community Development

7–271   This head takes in a broad group of charitable purposes which are directed towards support for community and social infrastructure and whose focus is on the community rather than the individual. These include the promotion of urban and rural regeneration,[69] the promotion of community capacity building,[70] and promotion of the voluntary sector.[71]

VI. The Advancement of the Arts, Culture, Heritage, or Science

7–272   Charities concerned with the advancement of art, such as museums[72] and art galleries,[73] must satisfy a criterion of educational or artistic merit.[74] The advancement of "heritage" takes in the preservation and conservation of historic land and buildings,[75] as well as the preservation of historical traditions by folk clubs, country dancing societies, eisteddfods, etc. The advancement of science includes scientific research projects and charities connected with learned societies and institutions, *e.g.* the Royal College of Surgeons[76] and the Royal Geographical Society.[77]

---

[68] *6th Report of the House of Lords Select Committee on Science and Technology, Session 1999–2000.* See too the discussion in Charity Commission, *Decision on the Application for Registration of N.S.F.H. Charitable Trust Ltd.* (15 August 2002) (promotion of spiritual healing a charitable purpose).

[69] Charity Commission, *RR 2: Promotion of Rural and Urban Regeneration* (March 1999 version). *Cf. Re Tenant* [1996] 2 N.Z.L.R. 633 (provision of creamery).

[70] Charity Commission, *RR 5: The Promotion of Community Capacity Building* (November 2000 version).

[71] Charity Commission, *RR 13: Promotion of the Voluntary Sector for the Benefit of the Public* (September 2004 version). See too Charity Commission, *Decision on the Application for Registration of the Charity Bank Ltd.* (April 17, 2002); Charity Commission, *Decision on the Application for Registration of Guidestar U.K.* (March 7, 2003); Charity Commission, *RR 14: Promoting the Efficiency and Effectiveness of Charities and the Effective Use of Charitable Resources for the Benefit of the Public* (September 2004 version).

[72] *Trustees of the British Museum v White* (1826) 2 Sim. & St. 594; *Re Holburne* (1885) 53 L.T. 212.

[73] *Abbott v Fraser* (1874) L.R. 6 P.C. 96.

[74] Charity Commission, *RR 10: Museums and Art Galleries*, paras 7–12 and Annex A.

[75] *Re Verrall* [1916] 1 Ch. 100 (National Trust); *Re Cranstoun* [1932] 1 Ch. 537 (Elizabethan cottages); *Settle & Carlisle Railway Trust* [1990] Ch. Com. Rep. 23-26 (railway line). See too Charity Commission, *RR 9: Preservation and Conservation* (February 2001 version).

[76] *Royal College of Surgeons of England v National Provincial Bank Ltd* [1952] A.C. 631.

[77] *Beaumont v Oliviera* (1869) L.R. 4 Ch. 309.

VII. The Advancement of Amateur Sport

For many years, the promotion of sport has been upheld as charitable **7–273** where it has been ancillary to the pursuit of a charitable purpose: *Re Mariette*[78] (sport in a school—educational); *Re Gray*[79] (sport in an army regiment—general public benefit in promoting the efficiency of the Army); *London Hospital Medical College v I.R.C.*[80] (athletic, cultural and social activities of Students Union—furthering educational purposes of medical school); *I.R.C. v McMullen*, para.7–178 (soccer and other sports in schools and universities—educational). Until recently, however, the promotion of sport as such was not a charitable object: *Re Nottage*[81] (yacht racing); *Re Clifford*[82] (angling); *Re Patten*[83] (cricket); *Re King*[84] (general sport); *Re Birchfield Harriers*[85] (competitive athletics).

In 2003, the law was changed by the Charity Commission's decision to **7–274** recognise as charitable "the promotion of community participation in healthy recreation by providing facilities for playing particular sports".[86] In this context, "facilities" means not just lands, building, and equipment, but also the organising of sporting activity such as that undertaken by community amateur sports clubs (C.A.S.C.s). In practical terms, a C.A.S.C. can therefore be a charity provided that: (1) the sport in question is capable of improving physical health and fitness, and (2) the club has an open membership; *i.e.* access to the club's facilities are genuinely available to anyone who wishes to take advantage of them.[87] The Commission does not currently regard the following sports as constituting "healthy recreation": angling, ballooning, billiards, pool and snooker, crossbow, rifle and pistol shooting, flying, gliding, motor sports, and parachuting.[88] Some restrictions on club membership are tolerated, *e.g.* limited facilities and health of applicants,[89] but others are not, *e.g.* tests of skill for admission and membership subscriptions which are unaffordable for most of the community served by the club.[90]

---

[78] [1915] 2 Ch. 284. See too *Re Geere's W.T.* [1954] C.L.Y. 388 (swimming pool at Marlborough College).
[79] [1925] Ch. 362; but doubted in *I.R.C. v City of Glasgow Police Athletic Assoc.* [1953] A.C. 380 at 391 and 401.
[80] [1976] 2 All E.R. 113. See too *Att.-Gen. v Ross* [1985] 3 All E.R. 334 (North London Polytechnic Students' Union).
[81] [1885] 2 Ch. 649.
[82] (1911) 106 L.T. 14.
[83] [1929] 2 Ch. 276.
[84] [1931] W.N. 232.
[85] [1989] Ch. Com. Rep. paras 48–52.
[86] Charity Commission, *RR 11: Charitable Status and Sport* (April 2003 version).
[87] *ibid.* at para.7.
[88] *ibid.* at para.11. *Cf.* the Charities Bill 2005, cl.2(3)(d): "sport" means "sport which involves physical skill and exertion".
[89] *ibid.* at paras 16–17.
[90] *ibid.* at paras 18–19.

VIII. The Advancement of Human Rights, Conflict Resolution or Reconciliation, or the Promotion of Religious or Racial Harmony or Equality and Diversity

7–275   The promotion of human rights can be accomplished in various ways including monitoring human rights abuses, obtaining redress for the victims of such abuses, and campaigning in favour of the recognition of human rights, to the extent that political activity of this kind is ancillary to the charity's main purposes.[91] The advancement of conflict resolution or reconciliation includes the resolution of international conflicts, the promotion of international co-operation,[92] and relieving the suffering and distress arising through conflict on a national and international scale. It also includes mediation and conciliation services,[93] and the promotion of restorative justice, where all the parties affected by a particular criminal offence come together to resolve collectively how to deal with its aftermath.[94]

7–276   The appeasement of racial feelings between Dutch- and English-speaking South Africans was held not to be a charitable purpose in *Re Strakosch*,[95] essentially because the court considered it to be a political purpose. Social attitudes subsequently underwent a considerable shift, however, and the enactment of the Race Relations Act 1968 indicated that Parliament considered the promotion of harmonious race relations to be for the public benefit. For this reason, the Charity Commissioners refused to follow *Re Strakosch* in 1983, when they stated that "promoting race relations, endeavouring to eliminate discrimination on grounds of race, and encouraging equality of opportunity" are charitable purposes.[96]

IX. The Advancement of Environmental Protection or Improvement

7–277   This head includes the conservation of particular species of flora and fauna, of particular geographical areas,[97] and of the environment more generally,[98] along with the promotion of sustainable development and biodiversity and the promotion of recycling and renewable energy resources.[99] Charities for the conservation of species or of particular land must produce

---

[91] See further Charity Commission, *RR 12: The Promotion of Human Rights* (January 2005 version). For discussion of political activities, see paras 7–91 *et seq.*, above.

[92] *Cf. Re Koeppler's W.T.* [1986] Ch. 423 (trust to fund conferences to promote co-operation in Europe charitable as for the advancement of education).

[93] *Mediation in Divorce (Richmond-upon-Thames); The National Family Conciliation Council* [1983] Ch. Com. Rep. paras 28–34.

[94] Charity Commission, *Decision on Application for Registration by Restorative Justice Consortium Ltd.* (January 15, 2003).

[95] [1949] Ch. 529.

[96] [1983] Ch. Com. Rep. paras 15–20. See too *Community Security Trust* (1995) 4 *Decisions of the Charity Commissioners* 8. Note that the promotion of gender equality is also a charitable purpose: *Halpin v Seear* Ch.D. 27 February 1976; *Women's Service Trust* [1977] Ch. Com. Rep. paras 34–36.

[97] *The Upper Teesdale Defence Fund* [1969] Ch. Comm. Rep. paras 23–24 (fund for preservation of flora and fauna of Upper Teesdale).

[98] Charity Commission, *Decision on the Application for Registration of Environment Foundation* (January 24, 2003).

[99] Charity Commission, *Decision on the Application for Registration of Recycling in Ottery* (April 2002).

independent expert evidence that the species or land in question are worthy of conservation.[1]

In *Re Grove-Grady*,[2] the Court of Appeal struck down a trust to establish **7–278** a sanctuary for wild birds and animals from which the public would be excluded, because the court could perceive no benefit to mankind in leaving the animals to their own devices in this way. However, ideas about environmental protection and the survival of endangered species have moved on. The Charity Commission's current approach to wildlife sanctuaries is to presume that they are not for the public benefit unless the public is given physical access to the site, but to take a flexible approach to the level of access needed, acknowledging that access "needs to be consistent with the aims of the charity so that visitors should not be allowed access at the expense of deterioration of a fragile . . . environment".[3] If an organisation can make out a case for limiting or excluding public access, it may still be able to satisfy the public benefit requirement by other means, *e.g.* restricting access to parts of the site, publishing books and videos about their activities, etc.[4]

X. The Relief of Those in Need, by Reason of Youth, Age, Ill-Health, Disability, Financial Hardship or Other Disadvantage

As previously noted,[5] "the relief of aged, impotent and poor people" was **7–279** specified as charitable in the Preamble to the Statute of Charitable Uses 1601, but because these words are to be construed disjunctively,[6] the relief of those in need by reason of age,[7] and the relief of those in need by reason of ill-health[8] or disability,[9] are stand-alone charitable purposes. The Preamble also mentions "the education and preferment of orphans", and by analogy with this purpose, the promotion of the welfare of children generally is also a charitable purpose.[10]

---

[1] Charity Commission, *RR 9: Preservation and Conservation* (February 2001 version), paras A10–A15.
[2] [1929] 1 Ch. 557.
[3] Charity Commission, *RR 9: Preservation and Conservation* (February 2001 version) para.A19.
[4] *ibid.* para.A20. *Cf. Att.-Gen. for New South Wales v Sawtell* [1978] 2 N.S.W.L.R. 200.
[5] See para.7–145, above.
[6] *Re Robinson* [1951] Ch. 198; *Joseph Rowntree Memorial Trust Housing Assoc. Ltd v Att.-Gen.* [1983] Ch. 159.
[7] *Re Dunlop* [1984] N.I. 408 (home for elderly Presbyterians); *Joseph Rowntree Memorial Trust Housing Assoc. Ltd. v Att.-Gen.* [1983] Ch. 159 (sheltered accommodation for the elderly). The Charities Bill 2004, clause 2(3)(d) specifies that "relief" of those in need under this head includes the provision of accommodation or care.
[8] *Re Resch's W.T.* [1969] 1 A.C. 514 (private hospital).
[9] *Re Lewis* [1955] Ch. 104 (the blind); *Motability* [1977] Ch. Com. Rep. paras 51–56 (personal transport for the disabled); *The Royal Association for Disability and Rehabilitation* [1977] Ch. Com. Rep. para.57 (promotion of understanding of the causes of disablement and the ways in which these may be reduced or eliminated); *Sarah Mary Collard Fund for the Provision of Guide Dogs* [1983] Ch. Com. Rep. paras 57–8.
[10] *D v N.S.P.C.C.* [1978] A.C. 171 at 228. See too *Re Sahal's W.T.* [1958] 1 W.L.R. 1243 (gift of house as children's home); Charity Commission, *Decision on the Application for Registration of the Internet Content Rating Association* (September 12, 2002) (protection of children and young people from harm arising from contact with unsuitable material on the internet).

XI. The Advancement of Animal Welfare

7–280   Trusts for the protection or welfare of animals have been upheld as charitable provided that they benefit, or promote the moral improvement of, the community.[11] However, in *National Anti-Vivisection Society v I.R.C.*, the House of Lords held inter alia that anti-vivisection is not a charitable purpose because the benefits to mankind of retaining vivisection outweighed the moral benefits of abolishing it.

NATIONAL ANTI-VIVISECTION SOCIETY v INLAND REVENUE COMMISSIONERS

House of Lords [1948] A.C. 31; (1947) 177 L.T. 226; [1947] 2 All E.R. 217 (Lords Simon, Wright, Simonds and Normand; Lord Porter dissenting)

7–281   The question was whether the appellant society was a body established for charitable purposes only, within the meaning of the Income Tax Act 1918, s.37, and accordingly entitled to exemption from income tax upon the income which it derived from its investments. The Special Commissioners for the Purposes of Income Tax held that the society was so entitled, but this decision was reversed by Mcnaghten J.,[12] whose judgment was upheld by the Court of Appeal.[13] The society appealed unsuccessfully.

7–282   LORD SIMONDS: " . . The first and shorter point is whether a main purpose of the society is of such a political character that the court cannot regard it as charitable. To this point little attention was directed in the courts below. . . . As will appear in the course of this opinion, it is worthy of more serious debate. The second point . . . is whether the court, for the purpose of determining whether the object of the society is charitable may disregard the finding of fact that any assumed public benefit in the direction of the advancement of morals and education was far outweighed by the detriment to medical science and research, and, consequently, to the public health, which would result if the society succeeded in achieving its object, and that, on balance, the object of the society, so far from being for the public benefit, was gravely injurious thereto. The society says that the court must disregard this fact, arguing that evidence of disadvantages or evils which would or might result from the stopping of vivisection is irrelevant and inadmissible.

7–283   "My Lords, on the first point the learned Master of the Rolls cites in his judgment[14] a passage from the speech of Lord Parker in *Bowman v Secular Society Ltd.*:[15] ' . . . a trust for the attainment of political objects has always been held invalid, not because it is illegal I . . . but because the court has no means of judging whether a proposed change in the law will or will not be for the public benefit . . .' Lord Parker is here considering the possibility of a valid charitable trust, and nothing else, and when he says 'has always been held invalid' he means 'has always been held not to be a valid charitable trust.' The learned Master of the Rolls found

---

[11] *Re Wedgwood* [1915] 1 Ch. 113 (promotion of humane methods of slaughtering livestock); *Re Moss* [1949] 1 All E.R. 495 (welfare of cats and kittens); *Re Green's W.T.* [1985] 3 All E.R. 455 (rescue, maintenance, and benefit of cruelly treated animals).
[12] [1945] 2 All E.R. 529.
[13] [1946] K.B. 185.
[14] [1946] K.B. 185 at 207.
[15] [1917] A.C. 406 at 442.

this authoritative statement upon a branch of the law, with which no one was more familiar than Lord Parker, to be inapplicable to the present case for two reasons, first, because he felt difficulty in applying the words to 'a change in the law which is in common parlance a "non-political" question," and, secondly, because he though they could not in any case apply when the desired legislation is 'merely ancillary to the attainment of what is *ex hypothesi* a good charitable object.'

"My Lords, if I may deal with this second reason first, I cannot agree that in this case an alteration in the law is merely ancillary to the attainment of a good charitable object. In a sense, no doubt, since legislation is not an end in itself, every law may be regarded as ancillary to the object which its provisions are intended to achieve. But that is not the sense in which it is said that a society has a political object. Here the finding of the commissioners is itself conclusive. 'We are satisfied,' they say, 'that the main object of the society is the total abolition of vivisection . . . and (for that purpose) the repeal of the Cruelty to Animals Act 1876, and the substitution of a new enactment prohibiting vivisection altogether.' This is a finding that the main purpose of the society is the compulsory abolition of vivisection by Act of Parliament. What else can it mean? And how else can it be supposed that vivisection is to be abolished? **7–284**

"Abolition and suppression are words that connote some form of compulsion. It can only be by Act of Parliament that that element can be supplied. . . . Coming to the conclusion that it is a main object, if not the main object, of the society, to obtain an alteration of the law, I ask whether that can be a charitable object, even if its purposes might otherwise be regarded as charitable. **7–285**

"My Lords, I see no reason for supposing that Lord Parker, in the cited passage, used the expression 'political objects' in any narrow sense or was confining it to objects of acute political controversy. On the contrary, he was, I think, propounding familiar doctrine, nowhere better stated than in a text book, which has long been regarded as of high authority, but appears not to have been cited for this purpose to the courts below (as it certainly was not to your Lordships), *Tyssen on Charitable Bequests*. The passage[16] is worth repeating at length: **7–286**

> 'It is a common practice for a number of individuals amongst us to form an association for promoting some change in the law, and it is worth our while to consider the effect of a gift to such an association. It is clear that such an association is not of a chartable nature. However desirable the change may really be, the law could not stultify itself by holding that it was for the public benefit that the law itself should be changed. Each court in deciding on the validity of a gift must decide on the principle that the law is right as it stands. On the other hand, such a gift could not be held void for illegality.

"Lord Parker uses slightly different language, but means the same thing, when he says that the court has no means of judging whether a proposed change in the law will or will not be for the public benefit. It is not for the court to judge and the court has no means of judging. The same question may be looked at from a slightly different angle. One of the tests, and a crucial test, whether a trust is charitable, lies in the competence of the court to control and reform it. I would remind your Lordships that it is the King as *parens patriae* who is the guardian of charity, and that it is the right and duty of his Attorney-General to intervene and inform the court, if the trustees of a charitable trust falls short of their duty. So too is his duty **7–287**

---

16 (1st ed., 1898). p.176.

to assist the court, if need be, in the formulation of a scheme for the execution of a charitable trust. But, my Lords, is it for a moment to be supposed that it is the function of the Attorney-General, on behalf of the Crown, to intervene and demand that a trust shall be established and administered by the court, the object of which is to alter the law in a manner highly prejudicial, as he and His Majesty's Government may think, to the welfare of the State? This very case would serve as an example, if upon the footing that it was a charitable trust it became the duty of the Attorney-General on account of its maladministration to intervene. There is, undoubtedly, a paucity of judicial authority on this point. . . . But in truth the reason of the thing appears to me so clear that I neither expect nor require much authority. I conclude upon this part of the case that a main object of the society is political and for that reason the society is not established for charitable purposes only. I would only add that I would reserve my opinion upon the hypothetical example of a private enabling Act, which was suggested in the course of the argument . . .

7–288   "The second question raised in this appeal, which I have already tried to formulate, is of wider importance, and I must say at once that, I cannot reconcile it with my conception of a court of equity, that it should take under its care and administer a trust, however well-intentioned its creator, of which the consequence would be calamitous to the community. [His Lordship undertook a brief review of the origin of the equitable jurisdiction in matters of charity, and continued:]

7–289   "My Lords, this then being the position, that the court determined 'one by one' whether particular named purposes were charitable, applying always the overriding test whether the purpose was for the public benefit, and that the King as *parens patriae* intervened *pro bono publico* for the protection of charities, what room is there for the doctrine, which has found favour with the learned Master of the Rolls, and has been so vigorously supported at the Bar of the House, that the court may disregard the evils that will ensue from the achievement by the society of its ends? It is to me a strange and bewildering idea that the court must look so far and no farther, must see a charitable purpose in the intention of the society to benefit animals, and thus elevate the moral character of men, but must shut its eyes to the injurious results to the whole human and animal creation. I will readily concede, that, if the purpose is within one of the heads of charity forming the first three classes in the classification which Lord MacNaghten borrowed from Sir Samuel Romilly's argument in *Morice v Bishop of Durham*,[17] the court will easily conclude that it is a charitable purpose. But even here to give the purpose the name of 'religious' or 'educational' is not to conclude the matter. It may yet not be charitable, if the religious purpose is illegal or the educational purpose is contrary to public policy. Still there remains the overriding question: Is it *pro bono publico*? It would be another strange misreading of Lord MacNaghten's speech in *Pemsel's case*[18] . . to suggest that he intended anything to the contrary. I would rather say that, when a purpose appears broadly to fall within one of the familiar categories of charity, the court will assume it to be for the benefit of the community and therefore charitable unless the contrary is shown, and further that the court will not be astute in such a case to defeat upon doubtful evidence the avowed benevolent intention of a donor. But, my Lords, the next step is one that I cannot take. Where upon the evidence before it the court concludes that, however well-intentioned the donor, the achievement of his object will be greatly to the public disadvantage, there can be no justification for saying that it is a charitable object. If and so far as there is any

---

[17] (1805) 10 Ves. Jun. 522.
[18] [1891] A.C. 531.

judicial decision to the contrary, it must, in my opinion, be regarded as inconsistent with principle and be overruled . . ." *Appeal dismissed*.

XII. OTHER PURPOSES

This final head includes existing charitable purposes which do not fall **7–290** under any other head, and any new charitable purposes which are recognised in the future by analogising from existing charitable purposes.[19] Existing purposes falling under this head include: the defence of the realm;[20] the payment of rates and taxes;[21] the provision of public works and public amenities;[22] the promotion of agriculture,[23] and of industry and commerce,[24] provided that the public benefit outweighs any private benefits derived by those involved;[25] the relief of unemployment;[26] the promotion of moral or spiritual welfare;[27] the relief of refugees;[28] and the relief of victims of accidents and disasters.[29]

It also includes the provision of facilities for public recreation. Trusts of **7–291** land for public use as a recreation ground have long been charitable,[30] but problems were then created by the House of Lords' decision in *I.R.C. v Baddeley*, para.7–293.[31] This concerned a trust to promote the moral, social, and physical well-being of Methodists resident in West Ham and Leyton by the provision of facilities for moral, social, and physical training and recreation. The court held that this was not charitable, first, because the intended beneficiaries did not comprise a sufficient section of the community, and, secondly, because the promotion of social well-being was not a

---

[19] *Cf.* Charities Bill 2005, clause 2(4)(b) and (c), which clearly contemplate that new purposes should be recognised by means of the analogising process familiar from the case-law.

[20] *Re Stratheden* [1895] 3 Ch. 265; *Re Corbyn* [1941] Ch. 400. Note, however, that although various gun and rifle associations were formerly registered as charities in line with *Re Stephens* (1895) 2 T.L.R. 792 (teaching of shooting a charitable purpose), they have now all been deregistered, following the Charity Commissioners' decision that changing social circumstances have rendered *Re Stephens* obsolete: *The City of London Rifle and Pistol Club; The Burney Rifle Club* (1993) 1 Decisions of the Charity Commissioners 4.

[21] Dating back to the Preamble which refers to the "aid or ease of any poor inhabitants concerning payment of fifteens, setting out of soldiers and other taxes." See *e.g. Nightingale v Goulburn* (1848) 2 Ph. 594.

[22] *Att.-Gen. v Heelis* (1824) 2 Sim. & St. 67 (town lighting, paving, drains and sewers); *Att.-Gen. v Shrewsbury Corp.* (1843) 6 Beav. 220 (repair and improvement of town's bridges, towers and walls); *Scottish Burial Reform and Cremation Soc. v Glasgow Corp.* [1968] A.C. 138 (crematorium); *Oxford Ice-Skating Assoc. Ltd.* [1984] Ch. Com. Rep. paras 19–25 (ice-rink). Because the provision of amenities and services of this kind is nowadays frequently undertaken by public authorities, many trusts for their provision have been made the subject of schemes under the Charities Act 1993, s.13. See further "Charities for the Maintenance of Highways, Bridges, and Similar Works" [1968] Ch. Com. Rep. paras 67–72.

[23] *I.R.C. v Yorkshire Agricultural Soc.* [1928] 1 K.B. 611.

[24] *I.R.C. v White* (1980) 55 T.C. 61 (improvement of standards of craftsmanship); *Business in the Community* [1987] Ch. Com. Rep. paras 16–19. Note that the regulation of a trade is not a charitable purpose: *Wine Standards Board of the Vintners' Company* [1978] Ch. Com. Rep. paras 95–98.

[25] *I.R.C. v Oldham Training and Enterprise Council* [1996] S.T.C. 1218.

[26] *ibid.* at 1234; Charity Commission, *RR 3: Charities for the Relief of Unemployment* (March 1999 version).

[27] *Re South Place Ethical Society* [1980] 1 W.L.R. 1565; *Public Concern at Work* (1994) 2 Decisions of the Charity Commissioners 5 (assistance to employees faced with moral and ethical issues of whistle-blowing).

[28] *Re Morison* (1967) 117 N.L.J. 757.

[29] *Re Hartley Colliery Accident Relief Fund* (1908) 102 L.T. 165n.; *Re North Devon and Somerset Relief Fund Trusts* [1953] 1 W.L.R. 1260. Disaster funds are entitled to charitable status only if the help is given to those in need: Charity Commission, *CC 40: Disaster Appeals* (January 2002 version).

[30] *Re Hadden* [1932] 1 Ch. 133 (park); *Re Morgan* [1955] 1 W.L.R. 738 (recreation ground); *Brisbane C.C. v Att.-Gen. for Queensland* [1979] A.C. 411 (park); *Bath and North Eastern Somerset Council v Att.-Gen.* (2002) 5 I.T.E.L.R. 274 (recreation ground).

[31] See too *Londonderry Presbyterian Church House Trustees v I.R.C.* [1946] N.I. 178; *Williams Trustees v I.R.C.* [1947] A.C. 447.

charitable purpose. It was then feared that village halls and similar institutions which had previously been considered charitable might not be charitable after all, and so the Recreational Charities Act 1958, was passed to remove any doubt on this point.

7–292   The 1958 Act establishes two criteria for the validity of a recreational charity: first, the trust must be for the public benefit; and, secondly, the facilities must be provided in the interests of social welfare. The second criterion itself has two elements: the first is constant, namely, that the object of providing the facilities must be to improve the intended beneficiaries' conditions of life; but the second may be satisfied in alternative ways—by showing *either* that the beneficiaries have need of the facilities by reason of the factors enumerated in the Act, *or* that the facilities are available to the members or female (but not male) members of the public at large. The proper interpretation of these provisions is considered by the House of Lords in *Guild v I.R.C.*, para.7–305.[32]

INLAND REVENUE COMMISSIONERS v BADDELEY

House of Lords [1955] A.C. 572; [1955] 1 All E.R. 525

7–293   Land was conveyed to trustees on trust to be used by certain Methodist leaders "for the promotion of the religious social and physical well-being of persons resident in . . . West Ham and Leyton . . . *by the provision of facilities for religious services and instruction and for the social and physical training and recreation of such aforementioned persons* who for the time being are in the opinion of such leaders members or likely to become members of the Methodist Church and of insufficient means otherwise to enjoy the advantages provided by these presents and by the provision of facilities for religious social and physical training and education and by promoting and encouraging all forms of such activities as are calculated to contribute to the health and well-being of such persons." A second conveyance was in the same terms but with the omission of the italicized words. The conveyances were held not to be charitable and so not exempt from stamp duty.

7–294   VISCOUNT SIMONDS: "This brings me to another aspect of the case, which was argued at great length and to me at least presents the most difficult problems in this branch of the law. Suppose that, contrary to the view that I have expressed that the social element prevented the trust being charitable, the trust would be a valid charitable trust, if the beneficiaries were the community at large or a section of the community defined by some geographical limits, is it the less a valid trust if it is confined to members or potential members of a particular church within a limited geographical area?

7–295   "The starting point of the argument must be, that this charity (if it be a charity) falls within the fourth class in Lord Macnaghten's classification. It must therefore be a trust which is, to use the words of Sir Samuel Romilly in *Morice v Bishop of Durham* (1805) 10 Ves. 522 at 532, of 'general public utility,' and the question is what these words mean. It is, indeed, an essential feature of all 'charity' in the legal

---

[32] See too Charity Commission, *RR 4: The Recreational Charities Act 1958* (August 2000 version); Charity Commission, *Decision on Application for Registration of Community Server* (September 15, 2003).

sense that there must be in it some element of public benefit, whether the purpose is educational, religious or eleemosynary . . . and, as I have said elsewhere, it is possible, particularly in view of the so-called 'poor relations' cases,' the scope of which may one day have to be considered, that a different degree of public benefit is requisite according to the class in which the charity is said to fall. But it is said that if a charity falls within the fourth class, it must be for the benefit of the whole community or at least of all the inhabitants of a sufficient area. And it has been urged with much force that, if, as Lord Greene said in *Re Strakosch* [1949] Ch. 529, this fourth class is represented in the preamble to the Statute of Elizabeth by the repair of bridges, etc., and possibly by the maintenance of Houses of Correction, the class of beneficiaries or potential beneficiaries cannot be further narrowed down. Some confusion has arisen from the fact that a trust of general public utility, however general and however public, cannot be of equal utility to all and may be of immediate utility to few. A sea wall, the prototype of this class in the preamble, is of remote, if any, utility to those who live in the heart of the Midlands. But there is no doubt that a trust for the maintenance of sea walls generally or along a particular stretch of coast is a good charitable trust. Nor, as it appears to me, is the validity of a trust affected by the fact that by its very nature only a limited number of people are likely to avail themselves, or are perhaps even capable of availing themselves, of its benefits. It is easy, for instance, to imagine a charity which has for its object some form of child welfare, of which the immediate beneficiaries could only be persons of tender age. Yet this would satisfy any test of general public utility. It may be said that it would satisfy the test because the indirect benefit of such a charity would extend far beyond its direct beneficiaries, and that aspect of the matter has probably not been out of sight. Indirect benefit is certainly an aspect which must have influenced the decision of the 'cruelty to animal' cases. But, I doubt whether this sort of rationalization helps to explain a branch of the law which has developed empirically and by analogy upon analogy.

"It is, however, in my opinion, particularly important in cases falling within the **7–296** fourth category to keep firmly in mind the necessity of the element of general public utility, and I would not relax this rule. For here is a slippery slope. In the case under appeal the intended beneficiaries are a class within a class; they are those of the inhabitants of a particular area who are members of a particular church: the area is comparatively large and populous and the members may be numerous. But, if this trust is charitable for them, does it cease to be charitable as the area narrows down and the numbers diminish? Suppose the area is confined to a single street and the beneficiaries to those whose creed commands few adherents: or suppose the class is one that is determined not by religious belief but by membership of a particular profession or by pursuit of a particular trade. These were considerations which influenced the House in the recent case of *Oppenheim*. That was a case of an educational trust, but I think that they have even greater weight in the case of trusts which by their normal classification depend for their validity upon general public utility.

"It is pertinent, then, to ask how far your Lordships might regard yourselves **7–297** bound by authority to hold the trusts now under review valid charitable trusts, if the only question in issue was the sufficiency of the public element . . .

"In *[Verge v Somerville* [1924] A.C. 496 at 499] in which the issue was as to the **7–298** validity of a gift 'to the trustees of the Repatriation Fund or other similar fund for the benefit of New South Wales returned soldiers,' Lord Wrenbury, delivering the judgment of the Judicial Committee, said that, to be a charity, a trust must be 'for the benefit of the community or of an appreciably important class of the community.' The inhabitants,' he said, 'of a parish or town or any particular class of such inhabitants, may, for instance, be the objects of such a gift, but private individuals, or a fluctuating body of private individuals, cannot.' Here, my Lords, are two expressions: 'an appreciably important class of the community' and 'any particular class of such inhabitants,' to which in any case it is not easy to give a precise quantitative or qualitative meaning. But I think that in consideration of them the difficulty has sometimes been increased by failing to observe the distinction, at which I hinted earlier in this opinion, between a form of relief accorded to the whole community yet by its very nature advantageous only to the few and a form of relief accorded to a selected few out of a larger number equally willing and able to take advantage of it. Of the former type repatriated New South Wales soldiers would serve as a clear example. To me it would not seem arguable that they did not form an adequate class of the community for the purpose of the particular charity that was being established. It was with this type of case that Lord Wrenbury was dealing, and his words are apt to deal with it. Somewhat different considerations arise if the form, which the purporting charity takes, is something of general utility which is nevertheless made available not to the whole public but only to a selected body of the public—an important class of the public it may be. For example, a bridge which is available for all the public may undoubtedly be a charity and it is indifferent how many people use it. But confine its use to a selected number of persons, however numerous and important: it is then clearly not a charity. It is not of general public utility: for it does not serve the public purpose which its nature qualifies it to serve.

7–299   "Bearing this distinction in mind, though I am well aware that in its application it may often be very difficult to draw the line between public and private purposes, I should in the present case conclude that a trust cannot qualify as a charity within the fourth class . . . if the beneficiaries are a class of persons not only confined to a particular area but selected from within it by reference to a particular creed. The Master of the Rolls in his judgment cites a rhetorical question asked by Mr. Stamp in argument [1953] Ch. 504 at 519: 'Who has ever heard of a bridge to be crossed only by impecunious Methodists?' The *reductio ad absurdum* is sometimes a cogent form of argument, and this illustration serves to show the danger of conceding the quality of charity to a purpose which is not a public purpose. What is true of a bridge for Methodists is equally true of any other public purpose falling within the fourth class and of the adherents of any other creed.

7–300   LORD REID [dissenting, and disagreeing with Viscount Simonds on the "public" point] "But your Lordships are bound by a previous decision in this House, and it appears to me to be unquestionable that in *Goodman v Mayor of Saltash* (1882) 7 App. Cas. 633 this House decided that there was a valid charitable trust where there was no question of poverty or disability or of education or religion, and where the beneficiaries were not by any means all the inhabitants of any particular area . . . [If] the members of a religious denomination do not constitute a section of the public (or the community) then a trust solely for the advancement of religion or of education would not be a charitable trust if limited to members of a particular church. Of course, the appellants do not contend that that is right: they could not but admit that the members of a church are a section of the community for the purpose of such trusts. But they maintain that they cease to be a section of the community when it comes to trusts within the fourth class . . . Poverty may be in a special position but otherwise I can see no justification in principle or authority for holding that when dealing with one deed for one charitable purpose the members of the Methodist or any other church are a section of the community, but when dealing with another deed for a different charitable purpose they are only a fluctuating body of private individuals. I therefore reject this argument and on the whole matter I am of opinion that this appeal ought to be dismissed."

LORD SOMERVELL OF HARROW: "I agree with the Court of Appeal in rejecting the **7–301** argument that as a matter of law a trust to qualify under Lord Macnaghten's fourth class must be analgous to the repair of 'bridges portes havens causwaies seabankes and highewaies,' being the examples given in the preamble outside the three main categories of poverty, religion and education . . . I think, however, that a trust to be valid under this head would normally be for the public or all members of the public who needed the help or facilities which the trust was to provide. The present trust is not for the public.

"I cannot accept the principle submitted by the respondents that a section of the **7–302** public sufficient to support a valid trust in one category must as a matter of law be sufficient to support a trust in any other category. I think that difficulties are apt to arise if one seeks to consider the class apart from the particular nature of the charitable purpose. They are, in my opinion, interdependent. There might well be a valid trust for the promotion of religion benefiting a very small class. It would not at all follow that a recreation ground for the exclusive use of the same class would be a valid charity, though it is clear from the Mortmain and Charitable Uses Act 1888, that a recreation ground for the public is a charitable purpose."

[LORDS PORTER AND TUCKER expressed no opinion on the "public" point.]

The Recreational Charities Act 1958[33]

Section 1.—(1) Subject to the provisions of this Act, it shall be and be deemed **7–303** always to have been charitable to provide, or assist in the provision of, facilities for recreation or other leisure-time occupation, if the facilities are provided in the interests of social welfare:

Provided that nothing in this section shall be taken to derogate from the principle that a trust or institution to be charitable must be for the public benefit.

(2) The requirement of the foregoing subsection that the facilities are provided in the interests of social welfare shall not be treated as satisfied unless—

    (a) the facilities are provided with the object of improving the conditions of life for the persons for whom the facilities are primarily intended; and

    (b) either—

        (I) Those persons have need of such facilities as aforesaid by reason of their youth, age, infirmity or disablement, poverty or social and economic circumstances; or

        (ii) The facilities are to be available to the members or female members of the public at large.

(3) Subject to the said requirement, subsection (1) of this section applies in **7–304** particular to the provision of facilities at village halls, community centres and women's institutes, and to the provision and maintenance of grounds and buildings to be used for purposes of recreation or leisure-time occupation, and extends to the provision of facilities for those purposes by the organising of any activity.

[Section 2 makes special provision for trusts for miners' welfare; section 3 makes it clear that the Act does not restrict the purposes which are charitable independently of the Act.]

---

[33] See S. G. Maurice, "Recreational Charities" (1959) 23 Conv.(N.S.) 15; (1958) 21 M.L.R. 534 (L. Price). There is a Northern Ireland Recreational Charities Act 1958 in similar terms.

GUILD v I.R.C.

House of Lords [1992] 2 A.C. 310.

7–305   Lord Keith of Kinkel.[34] "My Lords, the late James Young Russell (the testator), who resided in North Berwick, died on September 11, 1982 leaving a will dated April 7, 1971 in which, after bequeathing a number of pecuniary legacies, he provided as follows:

> 'And I leave the whole, rest, residue and remainder of my said means and estate to the Town Council of North Berwick for the use in connection with the Sports Centre in North Berwick or some similar purpose in connection with sport and the receipt of the Treasurer for the time being of the Burgh of North Berwick shall be a sufficient receipt and discharge for my Executor.'

7–306   "In the course of his argument in relation to the first branch of the bequest counsel for the Crown accepted that it assisted in the provision of facilities for recreation or other leisure-time occupation within the meaning of sub-s (1) of s.1 of the 1958 Act, and also that the requirement of public benefit in the proviso to the subsection was satisfied. It was further accepted that the facilities of the sports centre were available to the public at large so that the condition of sub-s (2)(b)(ii) was satisfied. It was maintained, however, that these facilities were not provided 'in the interests of social welfare' as required by sub-s (1), because they did not meet the condition laid down in sub-s (2)(a), namely that they should be 'provided with the object of improving the conditions of life for the persons for whom the facilities are primarily intened'. The reason why it was said that this condition was not met was that on a proper construction it involved that the facilities should be provided with the object of meeting a need for such facilities in people who suffered from a position of relative social disadvantage. Reliance was placed on a passage from the judgment of Walton J. in *I.R.C. v McMullen* [1978] 1 W.L.R. 664 at 675. He said in relation to the words 'social welfare' in sub-s(1):

> 'In my view, however, these words in themselves indicate that there is some sort of deprivation, not, of course, by any means necessarily of money, which falls to be alleviated; and I think that this is made even clearer by the terms of s.1(2)(a) of the 1958 Act. The facilities must be provided with the object of improving the conditions of life for persons for whom the facilities are primarily intended. In other words, they must be to some extent and in some way deprived persons.'

7–307   "When the case went to the Court of Appeal (see [1979] 1 W.L.R. 130) the majority (Stamp and Orr L.JJ.) affirmed the judgment of Walton J. on both points, but Bridge L.J. dissented. As regards the 1958 Act point he said [1979] 1 W.L.R. 130 at 142–143):

> 'I turn therefore to consider whether the object defined by cl. 3(a) is charitable under the express terms of s.1 of the Recreational Charities Act 1958. Are the facilities for recreation contemplated in this clause to be "provided in the interests of social welfare" under s.1(1)? If this phrase stood without further

---

[34] Lords Roskill, Griffiths, Jauncey and Lowry simply concurred with Lord Keith.

statutory elaboration, I should not hesitate to decide that sporting facilities for persons undergoing any formal process of education are provided in the interests of social welfare. Save in the sense that the interests of social welfare can only be served by the meeting of some social need, I cannot accept the judge's view that the interests of social welfare can only be served in relation to some "deprived" class. The judge found this view reinforced by the require- ment of s.1(2)(a) that the facilities must be provided "with the object of improving the conditions of life for the persons for whom the facilities are primarily intended". Here again I can see no reason to conclude that only the deprived can have their conditions of life improved. Hyde Park improves the conditions of life for residents in Mayfair and Belgravia as much as for those in Pimlico or the Portobello Road, and the village hall may improve the conditions of life for the squire and his family as well as for the cottagers. The persons for whom the facilities here are primarily intended are pupils of schools and universities, as defined in the trust deed, and these facilities are in my judgment unquestionably to be provided with the object of improving their conditions of life. Accordingly the ultimate question on which the application of the statute to this trust depends, is whether the requirements of s.1(2)(b)(i) are satisfied on the ground that such pupils as a class have need of facilities for games or sports which will promote their physical education and development by reason either of their youth or of their social and economic circumstances, or both. The overwhelming majority of pupils within the definition are your persons and the tiny majority of mature students can be ignored as *de minimis*. There cannot surely be any doubt that young persons as part of their education do need facilities for organised games and sports both by reason of their youth and by reason of their social and economic circumstances. They cannot provide such facilities for themselves but are dependent on what is provided for them.'

"In the House of Lords the case was decided against the Crown upon the ground **7–308** that the trust was one for the advancement of education, opinion being reserved on the point under the 1958 Act. Lord Hailsham of St Marylebone L.C. said [1981] A.C. 1 at 11):

'. . . I do not wish my absence of decision on the third or fourth points to be interpreted as an indorsement of the majority judgments in the Court of Appeal nor as necessarily dissenting from the contrary views contained in the minority judgment of Bridge L.J.'

"Counsel for the executor, for his part, relied on part of the judgment of Lord **7–309** MacDermott L.C.J. in *Valuation Comr. for Northern Ireland v Lurgan B.C.* [1968] N.I. 104. A local authority which was the owner and occupier of an indoor swimming pool claimed exemption from rates in respect of it under s.2 of the Valuation (Ireland) Act 1854 on the ground, inter alia, that it was used exclusively for the purposes of a recreational charity under the Recreational Charities Act (Northern Ireland) 1958. A majority of the Court of Appeal held that this ground of exemption was established.

"Lord MacDermott L.C.J. makes the point that s.1(2) of the 1958 Act does not **7–310** exactly contain a definition but that it does state the essential elements which must be present if the requirements that the facilities should be provided in the interests of social welfare is to be met. It is difficult to envisage a case where, although these essential elements are present, yet the facilities are not provided in the interests of social welfare. Nor do I consider that the reference to social welfare in sub-s (1) can properly be held to colour sub-s (2)(a) to the effect that the persons for whom the facilities are primarily intended must be confined to those persons who suffer from some form of social deprivation. That this is not so seems to me to follow from the alternative conditions expressed in sub-s (2)(b). If it suffices that the facilities are to be available to the members of the public at large, as sub-para (ii) provides, it must necessarily be inferred that the persons for whom the facilities are primarily intended are not to be confined to those who have need of them by reason of one of the forms of social deprivation mentioned in sub-para. (1).

7–311   "The fact is that persons in all walks of life and all kinds of social circumstances may have their conditions of life improved by the provision of recreational facilities of suitable character. The proviso requiring public benefit excludes facilities of an undesirable nature. In my opinion the view expressed by Bridge L.J. in *I.R.C. v McMullen* is clearly correct and that of Walton J. in the same case is incorrect. Lord MacDermott L.C.J. in the *Lurgan B.C.* case plainly did not consider that the category of persons for whom the facilities were primarily intended was subject to any restriction. I would therefore reject the argument that the facilities are not provided in the interests of social welfare unless they are provided with the object of improving the conditions of life for persons who suffer from some form of social disadvantage. It suffices if they are provided with the object of improving the conditions of life for members of the community generally. The Lord President, whose opinion contains a description of the facilities available at the sports centre which it is unnecessary to repeat, took the view that they were so provided (see [1991] S.T.C. 281 at 288–289). I respectfully agree, and indeed the contrary was not seriously maintained.

7–312   "It remains to consider the point upon which the executor was unsuccessful before the First Division, namely whether or not the second branch of the bequest of residue, referring to 'some similar purpose in connection with sport', is so widely expressed as to admit of the funds being applied in some manner which falls outside the requirements of s.1 of the 1958 Act. Counsel for the executor invited your Lordships, in construing this part of the bequest, to adopt the benignant approach which has regularly been favoured in the interpretation of trust deeds capable of being regarded as evincing a charitable intention. That approach is appropriate where the language used is susceptible of two constructions one of which would make it void and the other effectual (see *I.R.C. v McMullen* [1980] 1 All E.R. 884 at 890; [1981] A.C. 1 at 14 per Lord Hailsham of St Marylebone L.C. and *Weir v Crum-Brown* [1908] A.C. 162 at 167 per Lord Loreburn L.C.). It was argued for the Crown that the benignant approach was not apt in the present case, since the question was not whether the trust was valid or invalid, but whether it qualified for exemption from tax by virtue of the 1958 Act. But the importation into Scots law, for tax purposes, of the technical English law of charities involves that a Scottish judge should approach any question of construction arising out of the language used in the relevant instrument in the same manner as would an English judge who had to consider its validity as a charitable gift. The English judge would adopt the benignant approach in setting about that task, and so the Scottish judge dealing with the tax consequences should do likewise.

7–313   "The matter for decision turns upon the ascertainment of the intention of the testator in using the words he did. The adjective 'similar' connotes that there are points of resemblance between one thing and another. The points of resemblance here with the sports centre cannot be related only to location in North Berwick or to connection with sport. The first of these is plainly to be implied from the fact of the gift being to the town council of North Berwick and the second is expressly stated in the words under construction. So the resemblance to the sports centre which the testator had in mind must be ascertained by reference to some other characteristics possessed by it. The leading characteristics of the sports centre lie in the nature of the facilities which are provided there and the fact that those facilities are available to the public at large. These are the characteristics which enable it to satisfy s.1 of the 1958 Act. Adopting so far as necessary a benignant construction, I infer that the intention of the testator was that any other purpose to which the town council might apply the bequest or any part of it should also display those characteristics. In the result I am of opinion, the first part of the bequest having been found to be charitable within the meaning of s.1 of the 1958 Act, that the same is true of the second part, so that the funds in question qualify for exemption from capital transfer tax.

"My Lords, for these reasons I would allow the appeal and set aside the **7–314** determination of the commissioners."

Section 5. The Cy-près Doctrine[35]

As already seen in Chapter 5 where a private trust is initially ineffective **7–315** or subsequently fails there arises a resulting trust for the settlor or his estate if he is dead. If a charitable trust is *initially* impracticable or impossible it is presumed that there is a resulting trust in favour of the settlor or, if he is dead, his estate (thereby normally benefiting his family[36]) unless the settlor had a general charitable intention.[37] If he had such an intention, then the trust property will be applied *cy-près* under a scheme formulated by the Charity Commissioners or the court, *i.e.* it will be applied to some other charitable purposes as nearly as possible resembling the original purposes. If an effective charitable trust *subsequently* becomes impracticable or impossible then the trust property will be applied *cy-près* irrespective of the question of general charitable intention[38]: the settlor or, if he is dead, his residuary legatee or next of kin are forever excluded once the property has been effectually dedicated to charity absolutely.

It is the duty of trustees to secure the effective use for charity of trust **7–316** property by a *cy-près* application where appropriate,[39] although the Commissioners may make a scheme of their own volition if satisfied that the trustees "ought in the interests of the charity to apply for a scheme but have unreasonably refused or neglected to do so" after being approached by the Commissioners.[40]

As the law currently stands, when the courts and the Commissioners **7–317** make a scheme to change the charitable purposes for which particular property is held, they must choose new purposes which are as close as

---

[35] See *Tudor on Charities*, Chap. 11; *Picarda on Charities*, Chap. 24; 1989 Annual Report of the Ch. Commrs., paras 73–80.
[36] This presumption in favour of a testator's family seems less strong than it used to be, particularly when disinherited family members can make a claim that the charitable bequest be reduced in their favour under the Inheritance (Provision for Family and Dependants) Act 1975 replacing the 1938 Family Provisions Act.
[37] *Re Rymer* [1895] 1 Ch. 19; *Re Stemson* [1970] Ch. 16. Gifts to particular Churches or to augment particular vicars' stipends may be saved under special legislation, *e.g.* Methodist Church Act 1976, s.15 or Endowments and Glebe Measures 1976 of the Church of England.
[38] Assuming the gift is an absolute one or made absolute by Perpetuities and Accumulations Act 1964, s.12.
[39] Section 13(5) Charities Act 1993.
[40] Section 16(6).

possible to the original purposes. Under the Charities Bill 2005, clause 18,[41] this requirement is to be relaxed: the nearness of the new purposes to the old will remain, but equal weight given to two other matters, namely the spirit of the gift by which the property came to the charity, and the need to ensure that, once the scheme has been made, the property can be used to make a significant social or economic impact.

7–318   Section 14 of the Charities Act 1993 may be relied upon if need be in special circumstances to establish general charitable intention and s.13 has relaxed the requirements of impracticability or impossibility. Such provisions have been in force since the 1960 Charities Act.

7–319   One must appreciate that the case law reveals how much leeway a court has in determining whether there has been an initial failure of charitable purposes and, if so, whether there was a general charitable intention manifested by the testator or donor.

Whether or Not There is Initial Lapse or Failure

7–320   There are three basic ways in which a testator might bequeath property: (1) for the relief of the blind in Batley; (2) for Batley Blind Home, High Street, Batley, the receipt of the treasurer for the time being to be sufficient discharge to the executors; (3) for Batley Blind Home Ltd [a company limited by guarantee under the Companies Act 1985], High Street, Batley.

7–321   No problem arises in the *first case* since the purpose is not initially impracticable or impossible and purposes live for ever, though particular institutions carrying out purposes may die. If the purpose had been more specific such as building a blind home at a particular site, where there was no reasonable chance of such a blind home being erected whether because of planning permission problems or lack of cash so the purpose failed *ab initio* then the legacy would lapse unless a general charitable intention was present[42] to enable a *cy-près* application to be made. However, if the site for the testator's project is merely incidental to his charitable intention and the preservation or use of that site is not an original purpose of the charitable gift then an alternative site may be used without the need for a *cy-près* scheme.[43] The time for determining whether failure has occurred is the date

---

[41] Inserting a new Charities Act 1993, s.14B.

[42] *Re Wilson* [1913] 1 Ch. 314 (to endow a school at a particular place where there was no reasonable chance of such a school being established); *Re Good's W.T.* [1950] 2 All E.R. 653 (funds insufficient for erection and upkeep of rest-homes); *Re Ulverston and District New Hospital Building Trusts* [1956] Ch. 622 (funds always insufficient for required purpose); *Re Mackenzie* [1962] 2 All E.R. 890 (trust to provide bursaries for education at secondary schools rendered impossible by provision of free education by state); *Re Lysaght* [1966] Ch. 191 (gift to Royal College of Surgeons on trust to provide studentships for persons not of Jewish or Catholic faith failed as the college was not prepared to act as trustees of such a trust and Buckley J., rather remarkably, held that this was the rare type of case where the identity of the trustees was vital to the trust. He further held that a paramount charitable intent was present so that a *cy-près* scheme could be directed omitting the offending religious conditions. This reveals the flexibility of *cy-près* applications which can even provide remedies in special circumstances); *Re Woodhams* [1981] 1 W.L.R. 493 (music scholarship for British boys restricted to orphans from two institutions but the trustee, the London College of Music, would not accept the trust as so restricted so Vinelott J. removed the restrictions by *cy-près* scheme).

[43] *Oldham B.C. v Att.-Gen.* [1993] Ch. 210. The council was trustee of The Clayton Playing Fields "for the benefit and enjoyment of the inhabitants of Oldham, Chatterton and Rayton" and was allowed to sell the land for supermarket development and purchase an alternative site for playing fields to benefit such inhabitants. Nothing could have been done if the purpose of the original gift was that the particular land conveyed should be used for ever as playing fields, none of the section 13 criteria for a *cy-près* application being applicable.

of the *inter vivos* gift or, in the case of a testamentary gift, the date of the testator's death,[44] *i.e.* when the gift vests in interest not when it vests in possession, *e.g.* after a life interest. If need be, an inquiry will be directed "whether at the date of the death of the testator it was practicable to carry his intentions into effect or whether at the said date there was any reasonable prospect that it would be practicable to do so at some future time."[45] Where a future gift is defeasible an inquiry as to its practicability should be undertaken on the basis that the gift will not be defeated but will take effect at some future time as an interest in possession.[46] The onus of proving impracticability is on the person who is asserting it.[47]

Problems arise in the *second case*, where an unincorporated charitable **7-322** association runs the home, if the home has ceased to exist by the testator's death. Since the association is unincorporated and charitable (not being a private members' club) the gift must necessarily be construed as a gift on trust for purposes: *Re Vernon's W.T.*, para.7–340. The purposes may be (a) the relief of the blind from time to time in the Batley Blind Home and nothing more (b) the relief of the Blind in Batley (c) the augmentation[48] of the endowed trust funds of the Batley Blind Home for whatever purposes such endowed trust funds might become held, *e.g.* if amalgamated with the Bury Blind Home and the Dewsbury Deaf Home.

In (a) where the gift is construed as a gift to a particular charitable **7-323** institution just for its particular purposes then the gift lapses if the institution ceases to exist before the testator's death[49] unless, which is most unlikely,[50] a general charitable intention can be found to justify a *cy-près* application.[51]

In (b) where the gift is construed as a gift for a charitable purpose in **7-324** circumstances where the existence of the particular institution carrying out the purpose is not material to the gift's validity, the gift does not lapse so long as the purpose can be carried out by other means which are to be determined by the court in cases of doubt.[52]

Construction (c) ensures that so long as there are endowment funds held **7-325** in trust for the named charity's purposes the gift augments such funds despite any alteration in its name or constitution or any amalgamation with other charities.[53] Thus the bequest in (c) unlike (b) could be used for the Bury Blind Home and the Dewsbury Deaf Home. However, if the

---

[44] *Re Wright* [1954] Ch. 347, *Harris v Sharp* (unreported, CA March 21, 1989).
[45] *Re Wright* [1954] Ch. 347; *Re White* [1955] Ch. 188; *Re Martin* (1977) 121 Sol. J. 828.
[46] *Re Tacon* [1958] Ch. 447.
[47] *ibid. Harris v Sharp* (unreported, CA March 21, 1989).
[48] *cf.* accretion to funds of unincorporated members' club: *Re Recher's W.T.* [1972] Ch. 526, above, para.3–237.
[49] *Re Rymer* [1895] 1 Ch. 19, *Re Slatter's W.T.* [1964] Ch. 512. *Re Spence's W.T.* [1979] Ch. 483. On the possible constructions see J.B.E. Hutton (1969) 32 M.L.R. 283; R.M.B. Cotterell (1972) 36 Conv. 198; J. Martin (1974) 38 Conv. 187.
[50] *Re Harwood* [1936] Ch. 285; *Re Stemson* [1970] Ch. 16 at 21.
[51] As happened in *Re Finger's W.T.* [1972] 1 Ch. 286 on which Megarry V.-C. had some reservations in *Re Spence's W.T.* [1978] 3 All E.R. 92, see para.7–363.
[52] *Re Watt* [1932] 2 Ch. 243; *Re Roberts* [1963] 1 W.L.R. 406; *Re Finger's W.T.* [1972] 1 Ch. 286; *Re Broadbent* [2001] EWCA Civ 714.
[53] *Re Lucas* [1948] Ch. 424 (on which see *Re Spence's W.T.* [1978] 3 All E.R. 92); *Re Faraker* [1912] 2 Ch. 488; *Re Bagshaw* [1954] 1 W.L.R. 238.

constitution of the named charity does not provide for there to be a fund in existence for ever devoted to charity so that the charity is liable to dissolution under its own constitution and chooses to dissolve itself, whereupon its surplus funds on its winding up are transferred to some other charity, the gift will lapse on the basis that the charity has ceased to exist.[54]

7–326   In the *third case* where the bequest is to the Batley Blind Home Ltd, High Street, Batley the bequest is presumed to be an out and out gift to the corporate institution beneficially as part of its general funds, unless there is something positive in the will to justify the bequest being treated as on trust for the purposes of the company's charitable objects. In the former case the gift will lapse if the company is would up before the testator dies unless, which is most unlikely, a general charitable intention can be found to justify a *cy-près* application.[55] In the latter case the trust purposes will be (a) the relief of the blind from time to time in the Batley Blind Home, High Street, Batley, as run by the Batley Blind Home Ltd, or (b) the relief of the blind from time to time in premises run by the Batley Blind Home Ltd, or (c) the relief of the blind in Batley. In (a) lapse will occur if such home ceases to exist before the testator's death, in (b) lapse will occur if the company is wound up before the testator's death whilst in (c) lapse will not occur.[56]

Where There is Initial Lapse or Failure

7–327   If matters of construction cannot save the gift then the gift lapses unless the court can find a general charitable intention present. There have been many judicial statements on the meaning of the phrase: *e.g.* Kay J. in *Re Taylor*[57] "If upon the whole scope and intent of the will you discover the paramount object of the testator was to benefit not a particular institution but to effect a particular form of charity independently of any special institution or mode, then, although he may have indicated the mode in which he desires that to be carried out, you are to regard the primary paramount intention chiefly, and if the particular mode for any reason fails, to use the phrase familiar to us, execute that *cy-près*, that is, carry out the general paramount intention indicated without which his intention itself cannot be effected." Also Buckley J. in *Re Lysaght*[58]: "A general charitable intention . . . may be said to be a paramount intention on the part of a donor to effect some charitable purpose which the court can find a method of putting into operation, notwithstanding that it is impracticable to give effect to some direction by the donor which is not an essential part of his true intention—not, that is to say, of his paramount intention.

7–328   "In contrast, a particular charitable intention exists when the donor means his charitable disposition to take effect if, but only if, it can be carried into effect in a particular specified way, for example, in connection

---

[54] *Re Stemson's W.T.* [1970] Ch. 16.
[55] *ibid.*
[56] *Re Meyers* [1951] Ch. 534.
[57] (1888) 58 L.T. 538 at 543.
[58] [1966] Ch. 191 at 202, approved in *Re Woodhams* [1981] 1 All E.R. 202 at 209.

with a particular school to be established at a particular place,[59] or by establishing a home in a particular house . . ."[60]

Where the gift is to an institution described by a particular name and the **7–329** institution has never existed, a general charitable intent is presumed if the name imports a charitable object[61]; but the presumption may be easily rebutted if the will also includes a residuary gift in favour of charity.[62] On the other hand, the court is assisted in discovering a general charitable intention if the gift to the non-existent institution is of a share of residue and the other residuary legatees are charities.[63]

Subsequent Failure

If at the testator's death the designated charity existed or it was not then **7–330** impossible or impracticable to carry out the designated charitable purposes then the gifted property has become charitable property to the perpetual exclusion of the testator's residuary legatee or next of kin.[64] Accordingly, the *cy-près* doctrine is available upon any subsequent failure[65]: there is no need to prove any general charitable intent.[66]

The position is the same for *inter vivos* gifts effectively dedicated to **7–331** charity, whether the surplus funds are general assets of a charitable company that has been wound up[67] or assets held on charitable trusts by trustees for an unincorporated association that has been dissolved or for purposes that have been carried out.[68] As Jenkins L.J. remarked,[69] "Once the charity for which the fund was raised had been effectively brought into action the fund was to be regarded as permanently devoted to charity to the exclusion of any resulting trust" for the subscribers. He endorsed[70] the decision of Danckwerts J.[71] that no general charitable intention need be

---

[59] *Re Wilson* [1913] 1 Ch. 314.
[60] *Re Packe* [1918] 1 Ch. 437.
[61] *Re Davis* [1902] 1 Ch. 876; *Re Harwood* [1936] Ch. 285 (though Peace Societies are probably not charitable: *Re Koeppler's W.T.* [1984] 2 All E.R. 111 at 122, 124); but *cf. Att.-Gen. for N.S.W. v Public Trustee* (1987) 8 N.S.W.L.R. 550.
[62] *Re Goldschmidt* [1957] 1 W.L.R. 524; 73 L.Q.R. 166 (V.T.H. Delany).
[63] *Re Knox* [1937] Ch. 109. See also *Re Satterthwaite's W.T.* [1966] 1 W.L.R. 277, where a misanthropic testatrix left her residuary estate in nine shares to nine named institutions, seven of which were animal charities, an anti-vivisection society (once thought charitable but now in law not charitable) and the London Animal Hospital (not ascertainable): a general charitable intent was found to infect the latter two shares of residue. In *Re Jenkin's W.T.* [1966] Ch. 249 residue was divided into sevenths, six for charitable institutions and one for "the British Union for the Abolition of Vivisection to do all in its power to urge and get an Act passed prohibiting atrocious unnecessary cruelty to animals": no general charitable intent was found since there was such a clearly expressed non-charitable purpose.
[64] Assuming the gift is an absolute one or made absolute by Perpetuities and Accumulations Act 1964, s.12.
[65] Assuming the gift is an absolute one or made absolute by Perpetuities and Accumulations Act 1964, s.12.
[66] *Re Slevin* [1891] 2 Ch. 236; *Re Moon's W.T.* [1948] 1 All E.R. 300; *Re Wright* [1954] Ch. 347; *Re King* [1923] 1 Ch. 243; *Re Raine* [1956] Ch. 417; *Re Tacon* [1958] Ch. 447. Peter Luxton [1983] Conv. 107 accepts the position for simple legacies to bodies corporate or unincorporate, but submits it is open to the House of Lords to deal differently with legacies on trust for purposes which should be regarded as only disposing of the testator's equitable interest to the extent that the stated purposes are achieved. Thus, failure of the purposes after as well as before, the testator's death, should be capable of giving rise to a resulting trust unless ousted by a general charitable intention.
[67] *Liverpool & District Hospital v Att.-Gen.* [1981] Ch. 193.
[68] *Re Wokingham Fire Brigade Trusts* [1951] Ch. 373.
[69] *Re Ulverston & District New Hospital Building Trusts* [1956] Ch. 622 at 636. To similar effect see Upjohn J. in *Re Coopers Conveyance* [1956] 1 W.L.R. 1096.
[70] *ibid.* at 637.
[71] *Re Wokingham Fire Brigade Trusts* [1951] Ch. 373.

proved in such cases, though there are some illogical cases[72] where the courts have gone to the lengths of excluding any resulting trust by holding that the subscribers intended to give their money out and out under a general charitable intention.

Cy-près under Charities Act 1993, s.14

7–332   In the case of initial failure of charitable purposes section 14 (replacing section 14 of the 1960 Act) permits a *cy-près* application as if a general charitable intention had been present. It is necessary to show that the donors cannot be traced or have executed written disclaimers.[73] The idea is to prevent resulting trusts arising in favour of anonymous donors contributing in the course of street collections, etc., to specific charitable appeals. However, the section seems to be superfluous as pointed out by David Wilson.[74]

7–333   The problem is that the section only applies where[75] "any difficulty in applying property to those purposes makes that property or the part not applicable *cy-près* available to be returned to the donors." Thus, it applies only where under the general law the property is held on a resulting trust for donors. It does not apply where the property passes to the Crown as *bona vacantia*, as an out and out gift without any general charitable intention, nor where the property is in any event applicable *cy-près* as an out and out gift under a general charitable intention. Since 1970 it has been clear that cash put into collection boxes is by way of out and out gift[76] so there is no scope for s.14 to apply to such cash collections.

7–334   At face value, the section purports to cover the proceeds of lotteries, competitions, entertainments or sales, but in most cases the so-called donors will have provided contractual consideration for their tickets, so there is no question of returning their money to them by way of a resulting trust,[77] so the section is inapplicable to such proceeds. If the money paid is *ex gratia* and not contractual then this will be by way of out and out gift[78] so that the section will be inapplicable.

7–335   In the case of supervening failure of charitable purposes where the property has been given out and out to charity then such property is regarded as permanently devoted to charity to the exclusion of any resulting trust[79] so that s.14 can have no scope.

---

[72] *Re Welsh Hospital (Netley) Fund* [1921] 1 Ch. 655; *Re North Devon & West Somerset Relief Fund Trusts* [1953] 1 W.L.R. 1260; *Re British School of Egyptian Archaeology* [1954] 1 W.L.R. 546; *Picarda on Charities*, (2nd ed.) pp.299–301.

[73] *Cf.* Charities Bill 2005. cl.17, which permits *cy-près* applications where a charity has told the donors at the time of soliciting their payments that these will be applied *cy-près* if the purposes for which the money was solicited fail.

[74] [1983] Conv. 40, but *cf. Beggs v Kirkpatrick* [1961] V.R. 764.

[75] Charities Act 1993, s.14(7).

[76] *Re West Sussex Constabulary's Benevolent Fund Trusts* [1971] Ch. 1, above at para.5–58; *Re Hillier* [1954] 1 W.L.R. 700 (out-and-out gift and general charitable intention imputed); *Re Ulverston & District New Hospital Building Fund* [1956] 1 Ch. 622 (out-and-out gift but *bona vacantia* since no general charitable intention imputed). In *bona vacantia* cases the Att.-Gen. normally waives the Crown's rights and has the property applied *cy-près* as emerges from *Re Ulverston* [1956] 1 Ch. 622 at 634.

[77] *Re West Sussex Constabulary's Benevolent Fund Trust* [1971] Ch. 1, above at para.5–58. Previously, the courts had overlooked this and so too, naturally, did the 1960 Act.

[78] See above, para.5–13, n.33.

[79] *Re Wright* [1954] Ch. 347; *Re Ulverston* [1956] 1 Ch. 622 at 636; *Re Wokingham Fire Brigade Trusts* [1951] Ch. 373.

Extension of Cy-près under Charities Act 1993, s.13

Before s.13 of the 1960 Act (replaced by the 1993 Act) was enacted **7–336** failure justifying *cy-près* occurred when the purposes of a trust became impossible or impracticable or there was a surplus after the purposes had been carried out. "Impracticable" came to be liberally interpreted over the years so as to include "highly undesirable,"[80] but failure did not occur just because performance in another way would be more suitable or more beneficial.[81] Section 13 now extends the occasions when *cy-près* may be available but in cases of initial failure it is still necessary to show general charitable intention.[82] The section deals with difficulties over the original purposes of the trust (*e.g.* where £3 p.a. for clergyman and rest to poor when total income was £5 in 1716 and the income then rose to £800 p.a.)[83] and not over provisions as to administration of the trust (*e.g.* a provision for distribution of all capital for charitable purposes within 10 years of the settlor's death).[84] However, matters relating to administration of the trust may be dealt with under the court's inherent jurisdiction.[85]

Section 13 has no application of course, if there would have been no **7–337** need for a scheme before s.13 of the 1960 was enacted, as appears from *Oldham B.C. v Att.-Gen.*[86] where the Council held land "upon trust to preserve and manage the same at all times hereafter as playing fields for the benefit and enjoyment of" local inhabitants. The Council wanted to sell the land to developers and use the proceeds to buy other land with better facilities. The Court of Appeal held that this did not involve an alteration of the "original purposes" of the charitable gift so that the sale could proceed without the need for a *cy-près* scheme.

For s.13 to apply the circumstances must be fitted into one or other of **7–338** the "pigeonholes" in paragraphs (a) to (e), the largest pigeonhole being (e)(iii) "where the original purposes, in whole or in part, have, since they were laid down ceased to provide a suitable and effective method of using the property available by virtue of the gift, regard being had to the "spirit of the gift". This requires the court to make a value judgment taking account of "the basic intention underlying the gift or the substance of the gift"[87]: "to look beyond the original purposes as defined by the objects specified in the declaration of trust and to seek to identify the spirit in which the donors gave property upon trust for those purposes . . . with the assistance of the document as a whole and any relevant evidence as to the circumstances in which the gift was made."[88]

---

[80] *Re Dominion Students' Hall Trust* [1947] Ch. 183 (scheme removing provision restricting Hall for Dominion students to students of European origin, *i.e.* white students).

[81] *Re Weir Hospital* [1910] 2 Ch. 124.

[82] Charities Acts 1960 and 1993, s.13(2). In *Re J. W. Laing Trust* [1984] 1 All E.R. 50 at 53 counsel surprisingly (and erroneously) conceded that general charitable intent was necessary for property effectively dedicated to charity in 1922.

[83] *Re Lepton's Charity* [1972] Ch. 276.

[84] *Re J. W. Laing Trust* [1984] 1 All E.R. 50.

[85] *ibid. Att.-Gen. v Dedham School* (1857) 23 Beav. 350.

[86] [1993] Ch. 210. Before ss.36–38 of the Charities Act 1993 the Commissioners' consent was still needed to dispose of charity land.

[87] *Varsani v Jesani* [1998] 3 All E.R. 273 at 283.

[88] *ibid*, 288. *Cf.* Charities Bill 2005, cl.15(3), permitting the court or Commission to have regard to the "social and economic circumstances prevailing at the time of the proposed alteration" in addition to "the spirit of the gift".

7–339   In *Varsani v Jesani*[89] a group of Hendon Hindus in 1967 set up a trust to promote the faith of Swaminarayan as practised in accordance with the teaching and tenets of Muktajivandasji, to provide facilities for a small united community of his followers in the Hendon area of London. After his death problems arose over his successor as divine leader of the sect so that the community divided into two factions, each claiming that it adhered to the true faith while the other did not. The Court of Appeal held that to appropriate the property to one faction to the exclusion of the other would be contrary to the spirit in which the gift to the charitable trust was made, and that the impasse between the two factions with the majority faction excluding the minority faction meant that a *cy-près* scheme could be made under paragraph (e)(iii) to divide the trust property between the two factions.

RE VERNON'S WILL TRUSTS

[1972] Ch. 300n., 303

7–340   BUCKLEY J.: "Every [charitable] bequest to an unincorporated charity by name without more must take effect as a gift for a charitable purpose. No individual or aggregate of individuals could claim to take such a bequest beneficially. If the gift is to be permitted to take effect at all, it must be as a bequest for a purpose, *i.e.*, that charitable purpose which the named charity exists to serve. A bequest which is in terms made for a charitable purpose will not fail for lack of a trustee but will be carried into effect either under the sign manual or by means of a scheme. A bequest to a named unincorporated charity, however, may on its true interpretation show that the testator's intention to make the gift at all was dependent on the named charitable organisation being available at the time when the gift takes effect to serve as the instrument for applying the subject-matter of the gift to the charitable purpose for which it is by inference given. If so and the named charity ceases to exist in the lifetime of the testator, the gift fails (*Re Ovey*[90]). A bequest to a corporate body, on the other hand, takes effect simply as a gift to that body beneficially, unless there are circumstances which show that the recipient is to take the gift as a trustee. There is no need in such a case to infer a trust for any particular purpose. The objects to which the corporate body can properly apply its funds may be restricted by its constitution, but this does not necessitate inferring as a matter of construction of the testator's will a direction that the bequest is to be held in trust to be applied for those purposes: the natural construction is that the bequest is made to the corporate body as part of its general funds, that is to say, beneficially and without the imposition of any trust. That the testator's motive in making the bequest may have undoubtedly been to assist the work of the incorporated body would be insufficient to create a trust."

Note

7–341   This dictum was applied by Goff J. in *Re Finger's W.T.*[91] so as to hold a gift to a dissolved unincorporated charity, the National Radium Commission, to be a purpose trust for the sort of work carried on by the

---

[89] [1998] 3 All E.R. 273.
[90] (1885) 29 Ch.D. 560.
[91] [1972] Ch. 286; and also see *Re Koeppler's W.T.* [1986] Ch. 423 at 434, taking the *Re Vemon's W.T.* [1972] Ch. 300 approach.

Commission so as not to lapse, whilst a gift to a dissolved corporate charity, the National Council for Maternity and Child Welfare, he held to be for such charity absolutely beneficially, so as to lapse unless a general charitable intention could be found to justify a *cy-près* application: he found such an intention enabling the gift to pass to the National Association for Maternity and Child Welfare. Earlier he had said,[92] "If the matter were *res integra* I would have thought there would be much to be said for the view that the status of the donee, whether corporate or unincorporate, can make no difference to the question whether as a matter of construction a gift is absolute or on trust for purposes. Certainly drawing such a distinction produces anomalous results."

Nevertheless, the dictum of Buckley J. was applied in *Re ARMS (Multiple Sclerosis Research) Ltd*[93] where the recipient company went into compulsory insolvent liquidation after the testator's will was made but before the testator's death, by which date the company had not been formally dissolved. Neuberger J. held that the company took the money as part of its general assets available for its creditors.   **7–342**

RE SPENCE'S WILL TRUSTS

[1979] Ch. 483; [1978] 3 All E.R. 92; [1978] 3 W.L.R. 483

MEGARRY V.-C. read the following judgment: "The testatrix, Mrs. Spence, . . .   **7–343**
made her will on December 4, 1968, and died on May 30, 1972 . . . She gave her residuary estate to her trustees on trust to sell it and to pay her funeral and testamentary expenses and debts, and then:

> 'to pay and divide the residue thereof equally between The Blind Home, Scott Street, Keighley and the Old Folks Home at Hillworth Lodge, Keighley for the benefit of the patients.'

The will next provided that the receipt of the treasurer for the time being of 'each of the above-mentioned institutions' should be a sufficient discharge to her trustees. Subject to the expenses of administration and to the costs of these proceedings, the net residue is now worth some £17,000 . . .

"I shall first consider the gift to 'The Blind Home, Scott Street, Keighley . . . for   **7–344**
the benefit of the patients.' I think it is clear that these last six words apply to the gift to the Blind Home as they apply to the gift to the Old Folks Home; and nobody contended to the contrary. The question is whether this gift carries a moiety of residue to the Keighley and District Association for the Blind and, if so, on what terms. That charity was founded in 1907 and, over the years, it has changed its name thrice. It has borne its present name for nearly 20 years and is at present governed by a trust deed dated October 25, 1963. For over 25 years it has been running a blind home at 31 Scott Street, Keighley, which provides permanent accommodation for the blind in Keighley and district. Since 1907 there have been no other premises

---

[92] [1972] Ch. 286 at 294. See also *Montefiore Jewish Home v Howell* [1984] 2 N.S.W.L.R. 407, for treating corporate and unincorporated charities similarly.
[93] [1997] 1 W.L.R. 877.

or associations connected with the blind in Keighley. The premises in Scott Street are often called 'The Blind Home'; and a memorandum of the appointment of new trustees made on June 9, 1970, refers to the meeting for that purpose held at 'The Blind Home, Scott Street, Keighley.' Other names are used. A board on the building calls it 'The Keighley and District Home for the Blind,' and a brochure in evidence calls it 'Keighley Home for the Blind.' It seems clear beyond a peradventure that the language of the will fits the home run by the charity at these premises.

7–345   "In those circumstances, counsel for the plaintiff felt unable to advance any argument that the gift of this moiety failed and passed as on intestacy; and in this I think he was right. That, however, does not dispose of the matter, since the charity also carries on a home for the blind at Bingley, and may of course expend some or all of its funds on this or other purposes within its objects. There is therefore the question whether the moiety should go to the charity as an accretion to its endowment, and so be capable of being employed on any of its activities, or whether it is to be confined to the particular part of the charity's activities that are carried on at The Blind Home in Scott Street, Keighley. I confess that but for the decision of the Court of Appeal in *Re Lucas*[94] I should have had little hesitation in resolving this question in the latter and narrower sense, confining the moiety to the particular Blind Home in Scott Street, Keighley.

7–346   "In *Re Lucas* the testatrix made her will on October 12, 1942, and died on December 18, 1943. The will made gifts to 'the Crippled Children's Home, Lindley Moor, Huddersfield'; and it provided that the receipt of the treasurer or other officer for the time being should be a sufficient discharge. From 1916 there had been an establishment called 'The Huddersfield Home for Crippled Children' at Lindley Moor, governed by the charitable trusts established by a deed dated March 29, 1915; but according to the statement of facts in the report[95] 'On October 17, 1941, this home was closed and a scheme for the future administration of its assets was made by the charity commissioners.' Under that scheme the charity thereby created was to be known as 'The Huddersfield Charity for Crippled Children,' and the income was to be applied in sending poor crippled children to holiday or convalescent homes.

7–347   In the All England Law Reports,[96] passages in the judgments which are omitted from the Law Reports explicitly state that the scheme of the Charity Commissioners was sealed on October 17, 1941. They also show that the home had been closed not on that day but some two-and-a-half years before, on April 6, 1939, when the lease had run out. The statement of facts in the Law Reports is thus wrong in this respect. When the testatrix came to make her will on October 12, 1942, the home had been closed for some three-and-a-half years, and the charity had for almost a year had a name which, in accord with its new objects, had had the word 'Home' in it replaced by 'Charity.' The All England Law Reports also show that the original name, 'The Huddersfield Home for Crippled Children,' had been given to the charity by the trust deed. The question for resolution in *Re Lucas* was thus whether the gifts to 'the Crippled Children's Home, Lindley Moor, Huddersfield' took effect as gifts to 'The Huddersfield Charity for Crippled Children,' or whether they were gifts for the upkeep of a particular home for crippled children which had ceased to exist before the will had been made, so that they failed.

7–348   "At first instance, Roxburgh J. held that the latter was the correct view: *Re Lucas.*[97] On appeal, Lord Greene M.R. delivered the reserved judgment of himself, Somervell L.J. and Jenkins J. This reversed the decision below, and held that the

---

[94] [1948] Ch. 424.
[95] [1948] Ch. 424 at 425.
[96] [1947] 2 All E.R. 773 at 774; [1948] 2 All E.R. 22 at 24.
[97] [1948] Ch. 175.

gifts were gifts which contributed to the endowment of the charity, and so did not fail. I have found the judgment puzzling in places. Lord Greene M.R. discussed the misdescription in the will as follows.[98]

> 'As to the misdescription (*i.e.* "The Crippled Children's Home" for "the Huddersfield Home for Crippled Children") the description given by the testatrix was no more an accurate description of the particular home than it was of the charity.'

Later the judgment considers the position if the testatrix 'did know the correct name of the charity (*i.e.* "The Huddersfield Home for Crippled Children").'

"I find this puzzling. My difficulty is this. Nearly a year before the will was made, **7–349** the correct name of the charity had ceased to be what the judgment says it was. The 'description given by the testatrix' was 'the Crippled Children's Home, Lindley Moor, Huddersfield.' This, said the judgment, was 'no more an accurate description of the particular home [that is, the Huddersfield Home for Crippled Children which was at Lindley Moor] than it was of the charity.' Yet when the will was made the name of the charity had for nearly a year been 'The Huddersfield Charity for Crippled Children,' a name which did not include the word 'Home.' I find it difficult to see why a gift to a 'Home' does not fit an entity with 'Home' in its title better than it fits an entity without the word 'Home' in its title, but the word 'Charity,' instead. If in referring to the 'correct name' of the charity the judgment intends to refer to what had once been the correct name of the charity, I cannot see what it was that made the court reject the state of affairs when the will was made in favour of the past, particularly when there appears to have been no evidence about what the testatrix knew about the charity. I say what I say with all due humility, and a ready recognition that the fault may be an inability on my part to see what is plain to others; but, though humble, I remain puzzled.

"The main factors in the decision of the Court of Appeal seem to have been that **7–350** the words used in the will fitted the home that had been closed down no better than the charity which continued in existence, and that the will had omitted to make any specific reference to the upkeep or maintenance of the home which would indicate that the gifts were to be confined to the upkeep of the home. The gifts were accordingly gifts to the charity, and so did not fail. The question for me is whether on the case before me there ought to be a similar result, so that the moiety of residue would go to the Keighley, and District Association for the Blind as an addition to its endowment generally, and would not be confined to the Blind Home in Scott Street, Keighley, carried on by the association.

"Counsel for the first defendant submitted that there were two substantial points **7–351** of distinction between the present case and *Re Lucas*.[99] First, the words of the will fitted the Blind Home far better than they fitted the association. Indeed, although the Blind Home was from time to time described by different names, all the names used included both 'Blind' and 'Home': and, as I have mentioned, the appointment of new trustees in June 1970 uses the name 'The Blind Home, Scott Street, Keighley,' which is the precise expression used in the will. The title of the charity, 'The Keighley and District Association for the Blind,' is very different. True, it has the word 'Blind' in common with the title used in the will. There is also the word 'Keighley,' though this is used adjectivally and not as part of the address. But

---

[98] [1948] Ch. 424 at 428.
[99] [1948] Ch. 424.

otherwise there is nothing in common. In particular, there is not the use of the word 'Home' in both titles which the Court of Appeal in *Re Lucas* said was present in that case; and I think the words 'Home' and 'Association' are different in a real and significant sense.

7–352   "Secondly, in the case before me, there are the words 'for the benefit of the patients' which follow and govern the expression 'The Blind Home, Scott Street, Keighley.' In *Re Lucas* there was no counterpart to this. Indeed, the absence of any reference to the upkeep or maintenance of the home in that case was, as I have indicated, one of the grounds on which the decision was based. Here, there is no reference to upkeep or maintenance as such: but I think 'patients' must mean 'patients of the Blind Home,' and the upkeep and maintenance of the home is an obvious means of providing a benefit for the patients in it.

7–353   "In my judgment both these distinctions are valid and substantial. It therefore seems to me that the case before me is distinguishable from *Re Lucas*, so far as I have correctly understood that case. The testatrix was making provision for the benefit of the patients for the time being at a particular home, namely, the home usually known as The Blind Home at Scott Street, Keighley. She was giving the money not to augment generally the endowment of the charity which runs that home, with the consequences that the money might be used for purposes other than the benefit of the patients at that home, but was giving the money so that it would be used exclusively for the benefit of those patients. The only way in which this can conveniently be done is to give the money to the charity but to confine its use to use for the benefit of the patients for the time being at the home. That, I think, requires a scheme; but I see no need to direct that a scheme should be settled in chambers. Instead, I think that I can follow the convenient course taken by Goff J. in *Re Finger's Will Trusts*.[1] I shall therefore order by way of scheme (the Attorney-General not objecting) that the moiety be paid to the proper officer of the charity to be held on trust to apply it for the benefit of the patients for the time being of the home known as The Blind Home, Scott Street, Keighley.

7–354   "I now turn to the other moiety of residue, given by the will to 'the Old Folks Home at Hillworth Lodge, Keighley for the benefit of the patients.' Hillworth Lodge was built as a workhouse in 1858. Shortly before the outbreak of war in 1939 the West Riding Country Council, in whom it had become vested, closed it down: but during the war it was used to house what were generally but inelegantly called 'evacuees.' In 1948 it became an aged persons' home under the National Assistance Act 1948, and it continued as such until January 28, 1971, when it was finally closed down. There had been between 120 and 140 residents in it as late as 1969, but the numbers were then progressively run down, until in January 1971, just before it closed, only ten residents were left; and these were transferred to another establishment in Pudsey. The aged of the area had over the years been increasingly accommodated in purpose-designed old people's homes which provided better accommodation for the aged than could the old workhouse, despite many improvements to it. Since the building ceased to house old people it has been used as Divisional Social Services Offices.

7–355   "When the testatrix made her will in 1968 the building was accordingly still in use as an old people's home run by the local authority in accordance with their duty under the National Assistance Act 1948. As an old people's home it had no assets of its own, and residents contributed towards their maintenance in accordance with the Ministry of Social Security Act 1966, Part III. When the testatrix died on May 30,

---

[1] [1972] 1 Ch. 286 at 300.

1972, the building was no longer used as an old people's home, and was being used, or was soon to be used, as offices. The home had been run neither as nor by a charity. It formerly provided homes for those living in a large area of the West Riding, and not merely Keighley; and it has not been replaced by any one home. Instead, there are many old people's homes serving the area.

"Now without looking at the authorities I would have said that this was a fairly **7–356** plain case of a will which made a gift for a particular purpose in fairly specific terms. The gift was for the benefit of the patients at a particular home, namely the Old Folks Home at Hillworth Lodge, Keighley. At the date of the will there were patients at that home. When the testatrix died, there was no longer any home there, but offices instead; and so there were no longer any patients there, or any possibility of them. The gift was a gift for a charitable purpose which at the date of the will was capable of accomplishment and at the date of death was not. Prima facie, therefore, the gift fails unless a general charitable intention has been manifested so that the property can be applied *cy-près*. Buttressed by authority, counsel for the plaintiff contended that the court would be slow to find a general charitable intention where the object of the gift is defined with some particularity, as it was here.

"Against that, counsel for the Attorney-General advanced two main contentions. **7–357** First, he said that as a matter of construction it was wrong to construe the gift as being merely for the benefit of patients who were actually at the Old Folks Home at Hillworth Lodge; admittedly, of course, there are none of these. Instead, those who were intended to benefit included all those who would have been sent to that home if it had still existed, irrespective of the type of home in which in fact they are being or will be accommodated. He emphasised that the gift was essentially a gift for old people in Keighley, and the home was merely a means of providing a benefit for them.

"I do not think that this argument can be right. When the testatrix made her will **7–358** there were patients at the Old Folks Home at Hillworth Lodge. The gift to that home 'for the benefit of the patients' is, on this construction, to be treated as being a gift for the benefit not only of the patients who successively were for the time being at the home, but of others who never go near the home but who might or would have been sent to it in certain circumstances. The words of the will were perfectly capable of being satisfied by confining their meaning to their natural sense, namely, as relating to those who are or will in the future be patients at the home. Why is there to be forced on to those words a notional extension of uncertain effect? If at the time they were being written those words could not have their natural effect, one might indeed look round for a secondary meaning; but that is not the case.

"There are further difficulties. If the notional extension is made, who are within **7–359** it? As I have said, the defunct home provided for a large area of the West Riding, and not merely Keighley. How is it to be determined who can hope to benefit under the gift? Which of the occupants of the other old people's homes in such an area (the extent of which is undefined) can claim to be objects of the testatrix's bounty? Who is to decide whether any particular individual could (or would) have been sent to the defunct home had it still existed, and so would fall within the scope of the gift? I do not see how such an extension of meaning can fairly be placed on the words of the will. No doubt a scheme could cure much, but my difficulty is in seeing what on this footing, was the intention of the testatrix. For the reasons that I have given, I reject this contention.

7–360   "Counsel's other contention for the Attorney-General was that the will displayed
a sufficient general charitable intention for the moiety to be applied *cy-près*. In
doing this he had to contend with *Re Harwood*.[2] This, and cases which apply to it,
such as *Re Stemson's Will Trusts*[3] establish that it is very difficult to find a general
charitable intention where the testator has selected a particular charity, taking some
care to identify it, and the charity then ceases to exist before the testator's death.
This contrasts with cases where the charity described in the will has never existed,
when it is much easier to find a general charitable intention.

7–361   "These cases have been concerned with gifts to institutions, rather than gifts for
purposes. The case before me, on the other hand, is a gift for a purpose, namely, the
benefit of the patients at a particular old folks home. It therefore seems to me that I
ought to consider the question, of which little or nothing was said in argument,
whether the principle in *Re Harwood*, or a parallel principle, has any application to
such a case. In other words, is a similar distinction to be made between, on the one
hand, a case in which the testator has selected a particular charitable purpose,
taking some care to identify it, and before the testator dies that purpose has become
impracticable or impossible of accomplishment, and on the other hand a case where
the charitable purpose has never been possible or practicable?

7–362   "As at present advised I would answer yes to that question. I do not think that the
reasoning of the *Re Harwood* line of cases is directed to any feature of institutions as
distinct from purposes. Instead, I think the essence of the distinction is in the
difference between particularity and generality. If a particular institution or purpose
is specified, then it is that institution or purpose, and no other, that is to be the
object of the benefaction. It is difficult to envisage a testator as being suffused with a
general glow of broad charity when he is labouring, and labouring successfully, to
identify some particular specified institution or purpose as the object of his bounty.
The specific displaces the general. It is otherwise where the testator has been unable
to specify any particular charitable institution or practicable purpose, and so,
although his intention of charity can be seen, he has failed to provide any way of
giving effect to it. There, the absence of the specific leaves the general undisturbed.
It follows that in my view in the case before me, where the testatrix has clearly
specified a particular charitable purpose which before her death became impossible
to carry out, counsel for the Attorney-General has to face that level of great
difficulty in demonstrating the existence of a general charitable intention which was
indicated by *Re Harwood*.

7–363   "One way in which counsel sought to meet that difficulty was by citing *Re Finger's
Will Trusts*.[4] There, Goff J. distinguished *Re Harwood* and held that the will before
him displayed a general charitable intention. He did this on the footing that the
circumstances of the case were 'very special.' The gift that failed was a gift to an
incorporated charity which had ceased to exist before the testatrix died. The 'very
special' circumstances were, first, that apart from a life interest and two small
legacies, the whole estate was devoted to charity, and that this was emphasised by
the direction to hold the residue in trust for division 'between the following
charitable institutions and funds.' Secondly, the charitable donee that had ceased
was mainly, if not exclusively, a co-ordinating body, and the judge could not believe
that the testatrix meant to benefit that body alone. Thirdly, there was evidence that
the testatrix regarded herself as having no relatives.

---

[2] [1936] Ch. 285.
[3] [1970] Ch. 16.
[4] [1972] 1 Ch. 286.

"In the case before me neither of these last two circumstances applies, nor have **7–364** any substitute special circumstances been suggested. As for the first, the will before me gives 17 pecuniary legacies to relations and friends, amounting in all to well over one-third of the net estate. Further, in *Re Rymer*,[5] which does not appear to have been cited, the will had prefaced the disputed gift by the words 'I give the following charitable legacies to the following institutions and persons respectively.' These words correspond to the direction which in *Re Finger's Will Trusts* was regarded as providing emphasis, and yet they did not suffice to avoid the conclusion of Chitty J. and the Court of Appeal that a gift to an institution which had ceased to exist before the testator's death lapsed and could not be applied *cy-près*. I am not sure that I have been able to appreciate to the full the cogency of the special circumstances that appealed to Goff J.; but however that may be I can see neither those nor any other special circumstances in the present case which would suffice to distinguish *Re Harwood*.

"The other way in which counsel for the Attorney-General sought to meet his **7–365** difficulty was by relying on *Re Satterthwaite's Will Trusts*[6] and on *Re Knox*.[7] The doctrine may for brevity be described as charity by association. If the will gives the residue among a number of charities with kindred objects, but one of the apparent charities does not in fact exist, the court will be ready to find a general charitable intention and so apply the share of the non-existent charity *cy-près*. I have not been referred to any explicit statement of the underlying principle, but it seems to me that in such cases the court treats the testator as having shown the general intention of giving his residue to promote charities with that type of kindred objects, and then, when he comes to dividing the residue, as casting round for particular charities with that type of objects to name as donees. If one or more of these are non-existent, then the general intention will suffice for a *cy-près* application. It will be observed that, as stated, the doctrine depends, at least to some extent, on the detection of 'kindred objects' (a phrase which comes from the judgment of Luxmoore J. in *Re Knox*[8]) in the charities to which the shares of residue are given; in this respect the charities must in some degree be *ejusdem generis*.

"In *Re Satterthwaite's Will Trusts*[9] the residuary gift was to nine charitable bodies **7–366** which were all concerned with kindness to animals; but the gifts to two of them failed as no bodies could be found which sufficiently answered the descriptions in the will. Harman L.J. said[10] that he 'felt the gravest doubts' whether a general charitable intent had been shown. However, at first instance the judge had held that in respect of one of the bodies a sufficient general charitable intention had been displayed, and as there had been no appeal as to that share, he (Harman L.J.) would reach the same conclusion in respect of the other share, which was the subject of the appeal. On the other hand, Russell L.J. had no doubt that a general charitable intention had been shown.[11] Diplock L.J. delivered a single-sentence judgment agreeing with both the other judgments. The support which this case provides for counsel for the Attorney-General accordingly seems to me to be a trifle muted.

"In *Re Knox* Luxmoore J. distilled a general charitable intention out of a **7–367** residuary gift in quarters to two named infirmaries, a named nursing home and Dr. Barnardo's Homes. No institution existed which correctly answered the description

---

[5] [1895] 1 Ch. 19.
[6] [1966] 1 W.L.R. 277.
[7] [1937] Ch. 109.
[8] [1937] Ch. 109 at 113.
[9] [1966] 1 W.L.R. 277.
[10] [1966] 1 W.L.R. 277 at 284.
[11] [1966] 1 W.L.R. 277 at 286.

of the nursing home, and it was held that the quarter share that had been given to it should be applied *cy-près*. I am not entirely sure what genus the judge had in mind as embracing the infirmaries and Dr. Barnardo's Homes when he said that 'the object of each of the other charities is a kindred object to that which is to be inferred from the name' of the nursing home: perhaps it was the provision of residential accommodation for those in need. "It will be observed that these are all cases of gifts to bodies which did not exist. In such cases, the court is ready to find a general charitable intention: see *Re Davis*.[12] The court is far less ready to find such an intention where the gift is to a body which existed at the date of the will but ceased to exist before the testator died, or, as I have already held, where the gift is for a purpose which, though possible and practicable at the date of the will, has ceased to be so before the testator's death. The case before me is, of course, a case in this latter category, so that counsel for the Attorney-General has to overcome this greater difficulty in finding a general charitable intention. Not only does counsel have this greater difficulty: he also has, I think, less material with which to meet it. He has to extract the general charitable intention for the gift which fails from only one other gift: the residue, of course, was simply divided into two. In *Re Knox* and *Re Hartley (deceased)*[13] the gifts which failed were each among three other gifts, and in *Re Satterthwaite's Will Trusts* there were seven or eight other gifts. I do not say that a general charitable intention or a genus cannot be extracted from a gift of residue equally between two: but I do say that larger numbers are likely to assist in conveying to the court a sufficient conviction both of the genus and of the generality of the charitable intention.

7–368   "A further point occurred to me which I think that I should mention. There are, of course, cases where there is merely a single gift, but the court is nevertheless able to see a clear general charitable intention underlying the particular mode of carrying it out that the testator has laid down. Thus in the well known case of *Biscoe v Jackson*,[14] which I read in the light of *Re Wilson*,[15] the gift was to provide a soup kitchen and cottage hospital 'for the parish of Shoreditch.' Despite a considerable degree of particularity about the soup kitchen and the cottage hospital that were to be provided, the court found a general charitable intention to provide a benefit for the sick and poor of the parish. In that case, of course, there would have been no real difficulty in ascertaining those who were intended to benefit. Whatever the practical difficulties, at least the concept of those who were to be included is clear enough. The only real difficulty or impossibility lay in the particular method of carrying out that intention which the testator had specified. In the present case, on the other hand, the difficulty lies not only in the particular method but also in the very nature of the general charitable intention that is said to underlie that method. For the reasons that I have already given, I find it far from clear which 'patients' are intended to benefit once the touchstone of the Old Folks Home at Hillworth Lodge is removed. There is no geographical or other limitation to provide a guide. Where the difficulty or impossibility not only afflicts the method but also invades the concept of the alleged general charitable intention, then I think that the difficulty of establishing that the will displays any general charitable intention becomes almost insuperable.

7–369   "From what I have said it follows that I have been quite unable to extract from the will, construed in its context, any expression of a general charitable intention which would suffice for the moiety to be applied *cy-près*. Instead, in my judgment,

---

[12] [1902] 1 Ch. 876 at 884.
[13] March 15, 1978 (unreported decision of Megarry J.).
[14] (1887) 35 Ch.D. 460.
[15] [1913] 1 Ch. 314.

the moiety was given for a specific charitable purpose which, though possible when the will was made, became impossible before the testatrix died. The gift of the moiety accordingly fails, and it passes as on intestacy."

Charities Act 1993

Occasions for applying property cy-près

13.—(1) Subject to subsection (2) below, the circumstances in which the original **7–370** purposes of a charitable gift can be altered to allow the property given or part of it to be applied *cy-près* shall be as follows.[16]

(a) where the original purposes, in whole or in part,—
  (i) Have been as far as may be fulfilled; or
  (ii) Cannot be carried out, or not according to the directions given and to the spirit of the gift; or
(b) Where the original purposes provide a use for part only of the property available by virtue of the gift; or
(c) where the property available by virtue of the gift and other property applicable for similar purposes can be more effectively used in conjunction, and to that end can suitably, regard being had to the spirit of the gift, be made applicable to common purposes; or
(d) where the original purposes were laid down by reference to an area which then was but has since ceased to be a unit for some other purpose, or by reference to a class of persons or to an area which has for any reason since ceased to be suitable, regard being had to the spirit of the gift, or to be practical in administering the gift; or
(e) where the original purposes,[17] in whole or in part, have, since they were laid down,—
  (i) been adequately provided for by other means; or
  (ii) ceased,[18] as being useless or harmful to the community or for other reasons, to be in law charitable; or
  (iii) ceased in any other way to provide a suitable and effective method of using the property available by virtue of the gift, regard being had to the appropriate consideration.

(2) Subsection (1) above shall not affect the conditions which must be satisfied in order that property given for charitable purposes may be applied *cy-près*, except in so far as those conditions require a failure of the original purposes.

(3) References in the foregoing subsections to the original purposes of a gift shall be construed, where the application of the property given has been altered or regulated by a scheme or otherwise, as referring to the purposes for which the property is for the time being applicable.

(5) It is hereby declared that a trust for charitable purposes places a trustee under a duty, where the case permits and requires the property or some part of it to

---

[16] The section is available for initial and subsequent failure, subs. (2) preserving the requirement of general charitable intention for cases of initial failure.
[17] "The original purposes" are apt to apply to the trusts as a whole where the trust is for payment of a fixed annual sum out of the income of a fund to charity A and payment of the residue of the income to charity B: the phrase is not read severally in relation to the trust for payment of the fixed annual sum and the trust for payment of residuary income: *Re Lepton's Charity* [1972] 1 Ch. 276.
[18] See Lord Simonds in *National Anti-Vivisection Society v I.R.C.* [1948] A.C. 31 at 64, 65.

be applied *cy-près*, to secure its effective use for charity by taking steps to enable it to be so applied.

Application cy-près of gifts of donors unknown or disclaiming

7–371   **14.**—(1) Property given for specific charitable purposes which fail shall be applicable *cy-près* as if given for charitable purposes generally, where it belongs—

(a) to a donor who, after—
   (i) the prescribed advertisements and inquiries have been published and made, and
   (ii) the prescribed period beginning with the publication of those advertisements has expired,
   cannot be identified or cannot be found; or
(b) to a donor who has executed a disclaimer in the prescribed form of his right to have the property returned.

(2) Where the prescribed advertisements and inquiries have been published and made by or on behalf of trustees with respect to any such property, the trustees shall not be liable to any person in respect of the property if no claim by him to be interested in it is received by them before the expiry of the period mentioned in subsection (1)(a)(ii) above.

(3) For the purpose of this section property shall be conclusively presumed (without any advertisement or inquiry) to belong to donors who cannot be identified, in so far as it consists—

(a) of the proceeds of cash collections made by means of collecting boxes or by other means not adapted for distinguishing one gift from another; or
(b) of the proceeds of any lottery, competition, entertainment, sale or similar money-raising activity, after allowing for property given to provide prizes or articles for sale or otherwise to enable the activity to be undertaken.

(4) The court may be order direct that property not falling within subsection (3) above shall for the purposes of this section be treated (without any advertisement or inquiry) as belonging to donors who cannot be identified where it appears to the court either—

(a) that it would be unreasonable, having regard to the amounts likely to be returned to the donors, to incur expense with a view to returning the property; or
(b) that it would be unreasonable, having regard to the nature, circumstances and amounts of the gifts, and to the lapse of time since the gifts were made, for the donors to expect the property to be returned.

7–372   (5) Where property is applied *cy-près* by virtue of this section, the donor shall be deemed to have parted with all his interest at the time when the gift was made; but where property is so applied as belonging to donors who cannot be identified or cannot be found, and is not so applied by virtue of subsection (3) or (4) above—

(a) the scheme shall specify the total amount of that property; and
(b) the donor of any part of that amount shall be entitled, if he makes a claim not later than six months after the date on which the scheme is made, to

recover from the charity for which the property is applied a sum equal to that part, less any expenses properly incurred by the charity trustees after that date in connection with claims relating to his gift; and

(c) the scheme may include directions as to the provisions to be made for meeting any such claim.

(6) Where—

(a) any sum is, in accordance with any such directions, set aside for meeting any such claims, but

(b) the aggregate amount of any such claims actually made exceeds the relevant amount,

then, if the Commissioners so direct, each of the donors in question shall be entitled only to such proportion of the relevant amount as the amount of his claim bears to the aggregate amount referred to in paragraph (b) above; and for this purpose "the relevant amount" means the amount of the sum so set aside after deduction of any expenses properly incurred by the charity trustees in connection with claims relating to the donor's gifts.

(7) For the purposes of this section, charitable purposes shall be deemed to "fail" where any difficulty in applying property to those purposes makes that property or the part not applicable *cy-près* available to be returned to the donors.

(8) In this section "prescribed" means prescribed by regulations made by the **7–373** Commissioners; and such regulations may, as respects the advertisements which are to be published for the purposes of subsection (1)(a) above, make provision as to the form and content of such advertisements as well as the manner in which they are to be published.

(9) Any regulations made by the Commissioners under this section shall be published by the Commissioners in such manners as they think fit.

(10) In this section, except in so far as the context otherwise requires, references to a donor include persons claiming through or under the original donor, and references to property given include the property for the time being representing the property originally given or property derived from it.

(11) This section shall apply to property given for charitable purposes, notwithstanding that it was so given before the commencement of this Act.

QUESTIONS

1. Are the following trusts charitable, and, if not, are they otherwise **7–374** valid?

(i) To apply the income from £500,000 amongst such persons having the surnames Smith or Hayton, with preference so far as practicable for 50 per cent of the income to be used for the relatives of David Hayton, as my trustees may consider to merit educational assistance.

(ii) £400,000 to my trustees to invest and apply the income therefrom in educating the children of needy employees or ex-employees of London Transport for 21 years whereupon the income shall be used to provide an English Public School education for such children of European origin living in Oxford as my trustees shall determine provided that in either case no person of the Roman Catholic faith shall be so assisted.

(iii) A £10 million trust set up by I.C.I. plc and Barclays Bank plc for the income to be used at the trustees' discretion in assisting towards the education of the children or grandchildren of any persons employed or formerly employed by I.C.I. or Barclays Bank or any of their subsidiary or associated companies.

7–375   2. In 2000 a public appeal for funds to establish a recreation and sports centre for the City of London Police was launched. £200,000 was donated by Hank Badman, £80,000 was obtained from street collections, £110,000 profit was made out of a pop festival in aid of the appeal and £20,000 was donated anonymously. It has now proved completely impossible in view of the size of the fund to obtain any suitable site. What should be done with the moneys?

7–376   3. By his will dated April 1, 1999, Oscar O'Flaherty (who died three months ago) bequeathed £60,000 to his executors to use part thereof for benevolent purposes and the remainder for charitable purposes and £50,000 to the "Torquay Home for Distressed Gentlefolk for the benefit of the needy who happen to be there." The Home, an unincorporated body, closed down six months before Oscar's death, its funds and many of its inhabitants going to the Bournemouth Home for the Handicapped. Advise Oscar's executors. Would your answer differ at all if the gift had been to the Torquay Home for Distressed Gentlefolk Ltd which had gone into compulsory insolvent liquidation six months before Oscar's death although it had not been formally dissolved by his death?

7–377   4. By his will Alan left his residuary estate to Tim and Tom "upon trust to apply the income therefrom for such of the adult residents of Greater London as my Trustees in their absolute discretion shall think fit having due regard to the need to combat the stress, squalor and expense of residing in Greater London provided that my Trustees shall have power to add as further possible beneficiaries adult residents of any other city in the United Kingdom where the stress, squalor and expense are in my Trustees' absolute discretion comparable to that of Greater London provided further that one day before the expiration of the period of eighty years from my death (which period I hereby specify as the perpetuity period applicable hereto) the aforesaid Trust shall determine and the capital shall be distributed equally between United Reform Churches in West Ham and Leyton to use the income therefrom to assist in the burial or cremation of members of their congregations."

Alan has just died and Tim and Tom seek advice on the validity of the Trust.

7–378   5. During a motor race in Birmingham a car spun out of control killing the driver, a marshal and four mechanics. The Lord Mayor wants to appeal for funds for the families of the deceased and for the distressed surviving drivers, marshals, mechanics and spectators. Advise him.

6. "In assessing the merits of putative charitable trusts the judges and the **7–379** Charity Commissioners make the best of a bad job: the alternative is to go back to first principles and have a special tribunal concerned with cost-benefit analyses and value-judgments on social merits and whose decisions could not be overturned unless no reasonable person could have made such a decision." Discuss.

Chapter 8

APPOINTMENT, RETIREMENT AND REMOVAL OF TRUSTEES

It is vital to ensure that appointment, retirement and removal of trustees is correctly carried out. If not, the dispositions of trust property will not be made by the proper legal owners, while the old trustees will remain liable as trustees and the new "trustees" become liable as trustees *de son tort* (or *de facto* trustees).

Section 1. Appointment of Trustees

I. APPOINTMENT UNDER THE STATUTORY POWER

The Trustee Act 1925

8–01 Section 36.[1]—(1) Where a trustee,[2] either original or substituted, and whether appointed by a court or otherwise, is dead, or remains out of the United Kingdom for more than twelve months,[3] or desires to be discharged from all or any of the trusts or powers reposed in or conferred on him, or refuses or is unfit to act therein, or is incapable of acting therein, or is an infant, then, subject to the restrictions imposed by this Act on the number of trustees[4]—

    (a) the person or persons nominated for the purpose of appointing new trustees by the instrument, if any, creating the trust;[5] or

---

[1] This section reproduces, with amendments and additions, the Trustee Act 1893, s.10(1), (3) and (4). Wolstenholme & Cherry's *Conveyancing Statutes* (13th ed.), by J. T. Farrand, Vol. 4, provides a most useful commentary on all sections of the Trustee Act.

[2] "Trustee" is used as to exclude personal representatives. Accordingly, no power is conferred to appoint executors. By the Administration of Estates Act 1925, s.7, an executor of a sole or last surviving executor of a testator is the executor by representation of that testator.

[3] It does not follow that there is an absolute bar to the appointment of non-resident trustees: *Re Whitehead's W.T.* [1971] 1 W.L.R. 833. Further see *Richard v Mackay* (1997) 11 Trust L-I(1),22 discussed by R. Bramwell O.C. in (1990) 1 OTPR 1: para.8–08, below.

[4] Maximum of four trustees except for charities: Trustee Act 1925, s.34 and see s.36(5).

[5] See *Re Wheeler* [1896] 1 Ch. 315: a decision on s.10(1) of the Trustee Act of 1893, which is re-enacted by s.36(1) of the Act of 1925. In that case the settlor, instead of nominating X the person to appoint new trustees generally—as in *Re Walker and Hughes* (1883) 24 Ch.D. 698—nominated X to appoint new trustees in certain specified events. One of the trustees became bankrupt and absconded, whereupon he became "unfit" to act, but not "incapable" of acting. The events specified by the settlor included the event of a trustee becoming "incapable," but not that of a trustee becoming "unfit." The question was whether the proper person to nominate a new trustee was X, as being "the person or persons nominated for the purpose of appointing new trustees by the instrument, if any, creating the trust"—s.36(1)(a)—or whether the proper person was the surviving or continuing trustees or trustee under s.36(1)(b). Kekewich J. held that if a power of appointment contained in the instrument of trust is a limited one, and the event which has actually happened is not one of the events contemplated by that power, then the nominee is not "the person or persons nominated for the purpose of appointing new trustees by the instrument, if any, creating the trust." Hence the proper person to appoint a new trustee in *Re Wheeler* was to be found in s.36(1)(b). *Re Wheeler* was followed, with reluctance, by Neville J. in *Re Sichel* [1916] 1 Ch. 358. The Act of 1925 does not seem to alter the position.

(b) if there is no such person, or no such person able and willing to act, then the surviving or continuing[6] trustees or trustee for the time being, or the personal representatives of the last surviving or continuing trustee[7]:

may, by writing,[8] appoint one or more other persons (whether or not being the persons exercising the power) to be a trustee or trustees *in the place of*[9] the trustee so deceased, remaining out of the United Kingdom, desiring to be discharged, refusing, or being unfit or being incapable, or being an infant, as aforesaid.

(2) Where a trustee has been removed under a power contained in the instrument creating the trust, a new trustee or new trustees may be appointed in the place of the trustee who is removed, as if he were dead, or, in the case of a corporation, as if the corporation desired to be discharged from the trust, and the provisions of this section shall apply accordingly, but subject to the restrictions imposed by this Act on the number of trustees. **8–02**

(3) Where a corporation being a trustee is or has been dissolved, either before or or after the commencement of this Act, then, for the purposes of this section and of any enactment replaced thereby, the corporation shall be deemed to be and to have been from the date of the dissolution incapable of acting in the trusts or powers reposed in or conferred on the corporation.

(4) The power of appointment given by subsection (1) of this section or any similar previous enactment to the personal representatives of a last surviving or continuing trustee shall be and shall be deemed always to have been exercisable by the executors for the time being (whether original or by representation) of such surviving or continuing trustee who have proved the will of their testator or by the administrators for the time being of such trustee without the concurrence of any executor who has renounced or has not proved.

(5) But a sole or last surviving executor intending to renounce, or all the executors where they all intend to renounce, shall have and shall be deemed always to have had power, at any time before renouncing probate, to exercise the power of appointment given by this section, or by any similar previous enactment, if willing to act for the purpose and without thereby accepting the office of executor. **8–03**

(6) Where, in the case of any trust, there are not more than three trustees[10]

(a) the person or persons nominated for the purpose of appointing new trustees by the instrument, if any creating the trust; or

(b) if there is no such person, or no such person able and willing to act, then the trustee or trustees for the time being;

may, by writing, appoint another person or other persons[11] to be an additional trustee or additional trustees, but it shall not be obligatory to appoint any additional

---

[6] A continuing trustee is one who is to continue to act after completion of the intended appointment: *Re Coates to Parsons* (1886) 34 Ch.D. 370.

[7] Persons appointed executors and trustees of wills of land must formally assent in favour of themselves *qua* trustees so as to take advantage of s.40: *Re King's W.T.* [1964] Ch. 542 discussed *supra*, at para.1–128. An executor who has not proved his testator's will can exercise the power but the trustee appointed in such circumstances can only prove his title by reference to a proper grant of representation so that such a grant is, in practice, vital: *Re Crowhurst Park* [1974] 1 W.L.R. 583. If a will creates trusts but the trustees predecease the testator then s.36 is inapplicable: *Nicholson v Field* [1893] 2 Ch. 511.

[8] For the desirability of making the appointment by deed, see s.40 of the Trustee Act 1925, para.8–23.

[9] See *Adam Co. International Trustee Ltd v Theodore Goddard* [2000] W.T.L.R. 349 at 355.

[10] This broad provision was inserted by the Trusts of Land and Appointment of Trustees Act 1996 Sch.3 para.3(11).

[11] An appointor cannot appoint himself additional trustee: *Re Power's S.T.* [1951] Ch. 1074.

trustee, unless the instrument, if any, creating the trust, or any statutory enactment provides to the contrary, nor shall the number of trustees be increased beyond four by virtue of any such appointment.

[(6)A to (6)D deal with the position of an attorney for a trustee making an appointment on behalf of the trustee: added by Trustee Delegation Act 1999, s.8].

8–04   (7)   Every new trustee appointed under this section as well before as after all the trust property becomes by law, or by assurance, or otherwise, vested in him, shall have the same powers, authorities, and discretions, and may in all respects act as if he had been originally appointed a trustee by the instrument, if any, creating the trust.

(8)   The provisions of this section relating to a trustee who is dead include the case of a person nominated trustee in a will but dying before the testator, and those relative to a continuing trustee include a refusing or retiring trustee, if willing to act in the execution of the provisions of this section.[12]

(9)   Where a trustee lacks capacity to exercise his functions as trustee and is also entitled in possession to some beneficial interest in the trust property, no appointment of a new trustee in his place shall be made by virtue of paragraph (b) of subsection (1) of this section unless leave to make the appointment has been given by the Court of Protection.[13]

8–05   Section 37.—(1)   On the appointment of a trustee for the whole or any part of trust property—

(a)   the number of trustees may, subject to the restrictions imposed by this Act on the number of trustees, be increased; and

(b)   a separate set of trustees, not exceeding four, may be appointed for any part of the trust property held on trusts distinct from those relating to any other part or parts of the trust property, notwithstanding that no new trustees or trustee are or is to be appointed for other parts of the trust property, and any existing trustee may be appointed or remain one of such separate set of trustees, or, if only one trustee was originally appointed, then, save as hereinafter provided, one separate trustee may be so appointed; and

(c)   it shall not be obligatory, save as hereinafter provided, to appoint more than one new trustee where only one trustee was originally appointed, or to fill up the original number of trustees where more than two trustees were originally appointed, but, except where only one trustee was originally appointed, and a sole trustee when appointed will be able to give valid receipts for all capital money, a trustee shall not be discharged from his trust unless there will be either a trust corporation[14] or at least two persons[15] to act as trustees to perform the trust; and

---

[12] In *Re Stoneham's Settlement Trusts* [1953] Ch. 59, X and Y were the trustees of a settlement. Y remained out of the United Kingdom for a period longer than 12 months. X executed a deed retiring from the trust and appointing C and D to be trustees in place of himself and Y. Y challenged the validity of the new appointments on the ground that he was entitled to participate in making them. Danckwerts J. rejected his contention, first because he had been validly removed from the trust owing to his continuous absence from the United Kingdom for more than 12 months, even though the removal might have been against his will, and secondly because he was not a "continuing trustee" within the meaning of s.36(8) of the Act of 1925. He was not a "refusing or retiring" trustee but a trustee who had been compulsorily removed from the trust and so his concurrence in the new appointments could be dispensed with: *Re Coates to Parsons* (1886) 34 Ch.D. 370 explained.
[13] As amended by the Mental Capacity Act 2005.
[14] See limited meaning of "trust corporation" para.8–36.
[15] "Persons" replaced "individuals" under Trusts of Land and Appointment of Trustees Act 1996, Sch.3 para.3(12).

(d) any assurance or thing requisite for vesting the trust property, or any part thereof, in a sole trustee, or jointly in the persons who are the trustees, shall be executed or done.

(2) Nothing in this Act shall authorise the appointment of a sole trustee, not **8–06** being a trust corporation where the trustee, when appointed, would not be able to give valid receipts for all capital money arising under the trust.

It should be noted that the power of appointment of trustees is a fiduciary power[16] exercisable by the current trustees having due regard to the interests of the trust and of the conflicting interests of the beneficiaries. Indeed, the trustees' function is a paternalistic one requiring them to protect the beneficiaries from themselves.[17] Thus, before 1996 if the beneficiaries were all of full capacity and between them absolutely entitled they could not compel the trustees under s.36 to appoint their nominee: the trustees were entitled to exercise their independent judgment.[18] All that the beneficiaries could do was put an end to the existing settlement under the rule in *Saunders v Vautier*[19] and then create a new settlement of which, as settlors, they were be able to appoint new trustees—but this had fiscal disadvantages.

However, after s.19 of the Trusts of Land and Appointment of Trustees Act 1996 if all the beneficiaries are ascertained and of full age and capacity they have a right to require the trustees to retire and to direct the trustees to appoint specified persons to be new trustees, such right not existing where a person nominated in the trust instrument (not the current trustees) has the power to appoint new trustees.[20]

Appointment of foreign trustees

The provision in Trustee Act 1925, s.36(1) which enables a trustee who **8–07** remains out of the United Kingdom for more than 12 months to be replaced does not make persons resident abroad ineligible to be appointed as trustees, as held by Pennycuick V.-C. in *Re Whitehead's W.T.*[21] However, while accepting that the appointment of non-resident trustees had been a proper valid one in the case before him, he went on to say that in the absence of special circumstances (*e.g.* the beneficiaries having taken up permanent residence in a foreign country where the newly-appointed trustees reside) the appointment of non-residents was improper (though neither void nor illegal) so that the court would be likely to interfere at the instance of the beneficiaries.[22]

---

[16] Indeed, even if the power of appointing new trustees is reserved to the settlor while alive it will be presumed to be a fiduciary power: *IRC v Schroder* [1983] S.T.C. 480; *Re Osiris Trustees Ltd* [2000] W.T.L.R. 933. The settlor needs to act in altruistic good faith.
[17] *Head v Gould* [1898] 2 Ch. 250.
[18] *Re Brockbank* [1948] Ch. 206.
[19] See para.9–123.
[20] Section 19(1)(a). Section 19 is inapplicable to a pre-Act trust if the settlor subsequently executes a deed stating it is to be inapplicable: s.21(6).
[21] [1971] 1 W.L.R. 833.
[22] It thus seems that the appointment is voidable by the beneficiaries: the Revenue will have no *locus standi* to object unless the appointment was void as part of a criminal conspiracy to defraud the Revenue.

8–08   This approach is now out of date where the trustees are exercising their discretion to appoint foreign trustees and are merely seeking the declaratory authorisation of the court for their own protection. In *Richard v Mackay*[23] Millett J. stated:

> "The appropriateness is for the trustees to decide, and different minds may have different views on what is appropriate in particular circumstances. Certainly, in the conditions of today when one can have an international family with international interests and where they are as likely to make their home in one country as in another and as likely to choose one jurisdiction as another for the investment of their capital, I doubt that the language of Sir John Pennycuick is really in tune with the times. In my judgment, where the trustees retain their discretion, as they do in the present case, the court should need to be satisfied only that the proposed transaction is not so inappropriate that no reasonable trustee could entertain it."

8–09   Thus, the trustees (in case United Kingdom exchange control was reintroduced) could properly transfer part of the trust fund to the trustees of a trust to be established in Bermuda with Bermudan resident trustees, Bermuda having a stable English system of law and very experienced corporate trustees, even though the beneficiaries had no connection with Bermuda. Although the proposal was not to appoint new trustees of an existing trust nothing turns on the distinction, as recognised in *Re Whitehead's W.T.*[24]

However, Millett J. contrasted cases where the court is asked to exercise a discretion of its own (*e.g.* under the Variation of Trusts Act 1958[25] or s.41[26] of the Trustee Act 1925) with cases where the trustees are exercising their own discretion. In the former situation the applicants have to make out a positive case for the court's exercise of its discretion "and the court is unlikely to assist them where the scheme is nothing more than a device to avoid tax and has no other advantages of any kind."

8–10   Tax-saving is, of course, a proper consideration for trustees[27] and where it is clear that the proposed transaction is not so inappropriate that no reasonable trustee could entertain it the appointment of foreign trustees can now proceed without seeking any confirmation from the court.

The foreign trust corporation trap

Under Trustee Act 1925, s.37(1)(c) "a trustee shall not be discharged from his trust unless there will be either a trust corporation or at least two persons to act as trustees to perform the trust." It is important to notice that the broader expression "persons" (including companies) has replaced

---

[23] (1997) ll Trust L. I. (1) 22 noted by R. Bramwell Q.C. in (1990) 1 O.T.P.R. 1 and followed in *Re Beatty's W.T. (No.2)* (1997) 11 Trust L.I. (3) 77.
[24] [1971] 1 W.L.R. 833 at 838.
[25] See para.9–135, *Re Weston's Settlements* [1969] 1 Ch. 223, though in *Re Chamberlain* (1976) 126 New L.J. 1034 the Court approved Guernsey trustees where the primary beneficiaries were domiciled in France and the remaindermen in Indonesia.
[26] See at para.8–13.
[27] [1971] 1 W.L.R. 833 at 839.

"individuals" and that "trust corporation" cannot cover a company that is not incorporated in a Member State of the European Union.[28] If a sole corporate trustee is appointed then the purportedly replaced trustees remain as trustees if such trustee does not rank as a "trust corporation."[29]

However, it seems that section 37(1)(c) is subject to express contrary **8–11** intention so that the trust instrument can expressly authorise the discharge of trustees from the trusts by replacing them with the appointment as sole trustee of a corporation ranking as a trust corporation by the law of the State of its incorporation, except for trust property consisting of land in England and Wales.[30] After all, a valid receipt for the proceeds of sale of such land can only be given by a trust corporation or two persons acting as trustees.[31]

II. APPOINTMENT BY THE COURT

The court has power to appoint new trustees under section 41[32] of the **8–12** Trustee Act 1925, but application should not be made to the court if the power of appointing new trustees contained in section 36(1) of the Act, can be exercised: *Re Gibbon's Trusts*.[33] The principles which guide the court in making an appointment are set out in *Re Tempest, infra*. If non-resident trustees are to be appointed the beneficiaries must usually[34] have a real and substantial connection with the country where the proposed trustees are resident.

The Trustee Act 1925

Section 41—(1) The court, may, whenever it is expedient to appoint a new **8–13** trustee or new trustees, and it is found inexpedient, difficult or impracticable so to do without the assistance of the court, make an order appointing a new trustee or trustees either in substitution for or in addition to any existing trustee or trustees, or although there is no existing trustee.

In particular and without prejudice to the generality of the foregoing provision, the court may make an order appointing a new trustee in substitution for a trustee who is lacks capacity to exercise his functions as trustee, or is a bankrupt, or is a corporation which is in liquidation or has been dissolved.

RE TEMPEST

Court of Appeal in Chancery (1866) L.R. 1 Ch. 485; 35 L.J.Ch. 632; 14 L.T. 688; 12 Jur.(N.S.) 539; 14 W.R. 850 (Turner and Knight-Bruce L.JJ.)

---

[28] See Trustee Act 1925, s.68(18) and at para.8–36.
[29] *e.g. Adam & Company International Trustees Ltd v Theodore Goddard* (2000) 2 I.T.E.L.R. 634, [2000] W.T.L.R. 349.
[30] Trustee Act 1925, ss.69(2), 71(3); *London Regional Transport Pension Fund Trust Co. v Hatt* [1993] P. L.R. 227, 260, accepted in *Adam & Co. International Trustee Ltd v Theodore Goddard* [2000] W.T.L.R. 349.
[31] *ibid.* s.14(2), (3); Law of Property Act 1925, s.27(2).
[32] Under the section a trustee may be displaced against his will: *Re Henderson* [1940] Ch. 764. The section authorises removal of trustees by replacement but not otherwise: *Re Harrison's S.T.* [1965] 3 All E.R. 795 at 799.
[33] (1882) 30 W.R. 287; 45 L.T. 756. Otherwise, if it is uncertain whether the power under s.36(1) of the Act is exercisable: *Re May's Will Trusts* [1941] Ch. 109.
[34] In *Re Chamberlain* [1976] 126 New Law Jo. 1034 (reported in article by J. B. Morcom) the court approved Guernsey trustees where the beneficiaries were domiciled and resident some in France some in Indonesia. See above, paras 8–07 to 8–09.

8–14   Turner L.J.: " In making such appointments the court acts upon and exercises its discretion; and this, no doubt, is generally true; but the discretion which the court has and exercises in making such appointments is not, as I conceive, a mere arbitrary discretion, but a discretion in the exercise of which the court is, and ought to be, guided by some general rules and principles, and, in my opinion, the difficulty which the court has to encounter in these cases lies not so much in ascertaining the rules and principles by which it ought to be guided, as in applying those rules and principles to the varying circumstances of each particular case. The following rules and principles may, I think, safely be laid down as applying to all cases of appointments by the court of new trustees.

"First, the court will have regard to the wishes of the persons by whom the trust has been created, if expressed in the instrument creating the trust, or clearly to be collected from it.[35] I think this rule may be safely laid down, because if the author of the trust has in terms declared that a particular person, or a person filling a particular character, should not be a trustee of the instrument, there cannot, as I apprehend, be the least doubt that the court would not appoint to the office a person whose appointment was so prohibited, and I do not think that upon a question of this description any distribution can be drawn between express declarations and demonstrated intention. The analogy of the course which the court pursued in the appointment of guardians affords, I think, some support to this rule. The court in those cases attends to the wishes of the parents, however informally they may be expressed.

8–15   "Another rule which may, I think, safely be laid down is this—that the court will not appoint a person to be trustee with a view to the interest of some of the persons interested under the trust, in opposition either to the wishes of the testator or to the interests of others of the *cestuis que trust*. I think so for this reason, that it is of the essence of the duty of every trustee to hold an even hand between the parties interested under the trust. Every trustee is in duty bound to look to the interests of all, and not of any particular member or class of members of his *cestuis que trust*.

"A third rule which, I think, may safely be laid down is that the court in appointing a trustee will have regard to the question whether his appointment will promote or impede the execution of the trust, for the very purpose of the appointment is that the trust may be better carried into execution . . .[36]

8–16   "There cannot, I think, be any doubt that the court ought not to appoint a trustee whose appointment will impede the due execution of the trust; but, on the other hand, if the continuing or surviving trustee refuses to act with a trustee who may be proposed to be appointed . . . I think it would be going too far to say that the court ought, on that ground alone, to refuse to appoint the proposed trustee; for this would, as suggested in the argument, be to give the continuing or surviving trustee a veto upon the appointment of the new trustee. In such a case, I think it must be the duty of the court to inquire and ascertain whether the objection of the surviving or continuing trustee is well founded or not, and to act or refuse to act upon it accordingly. . . ."[37]

---

[35] See also *Re Badger* [1915] W.N. 166; 84 L.J. Ch. 567: the court will not appoint an additional trustee against the wishes of a sole trustee appointed by the settlor, in the absence of allegations against his honesty, even at the unanimous request of the beneficiaries of full capacity (not between them absolutely entitled to the whole beneficial interest so as to be able to invoke s.19 of the 1996 Trusts of Land and Appointment of Trustees Act), except where land is trust property since a valid receipt cannot be given by less than two trustees or a trust corporation: Law of Property Act 1925, s.27(2).

[36] A person will thus not be appointed if so to do would place him in a position in which his interest and duty would be likely to conflict: *Re Parsons* [1940] Ch. 973.

[37] The court may postpone an order for appointment of new trustees in order to protect the interests of the existing trustees, *e.g. Re Pauling S.T. (No.2)* [1963] Ch. 576.

III. APPOINTMENT INDIRECTLY BY BENEFICIARIES

Trusts of Land and Appointment of Trustees Act 1996

19.—(1) This section applies in the case of a trust where—

(a) there is no person nominated for the purpose of appointing new trustees by **8–17** the instrument, if any, creating the trust, and
(b) the beneficiaries under the trust are of full age and capacity and (taken together) are absolutely entitled to the property subject to the trust.

(2) The beneficiaries may give a direction or directions of either or both of the following descriptions—

(a) a written direction to a trustee or trustees to retire from the trust, and
(b) a written direction to the trustees or trustee for the time being (or, if there are none, to the personal representative of the last person who was a trustee) to appoint by writing to be a trustee or trustees the person or persons specified in the direction.

(3) Where—

(a) a trustee has been given a direction under subsection (2)(a),   **8–18**
(b) reasonable arrangements have been made for the protection of any rights of his in connection with the trust,
(c) after he has retired there will be either a trust corporation or at least two persons to act as trustees to perform the trust, and
(d) either another person is to be appointed to be a new trustee on his retirement (whether in compliance with a direction under subsection (2)(b) or otherwise) or the continuing trustees by deed consent to his retirement,

he shall make a deed declaring his retirement and shall be deemed to have retired and be discharged from the trust.

(4) Where a trustee retires under subsection (3) he and the continuing trustees (together with any new trustee) shall (subject to any arrangements for the protection of his rights) do anything necessary to vest the trust property in the continuing trustees (or the continuing and new trustees).

(5) This section has effect subject to the restrictions imposed by the Trustee Act **8–19** 1925 on the number of trustees.

20.—(1) This section applies where—

(a) a trustee lacks capacity (within the meaning of the Mental Capacity Act 2005) to exercise his functions as trustee,
(b) there is no person who is both entitled and willing and able to appoint a trustee in place of him under section 36(1) of the Trustee Act 1925, and
(c) the beneficiaries under the trust are of full age and capacity and (taken together) are absolutely entitled to the property subject to the trust.

(2) The beneficiaries may give to—

(a) deputy appointed for the trustee by the Court of Protection,

(b) an attorney acting for him under the authority of an enduring power of attorney or lasting power of attorney registered under the Mental Capacity Act 2005, or

(c) a person authorised for the purpose by the Court of Protection under Part VII of the Mental Health Act 1983.

a written direction to appoint by writing the person or persons specified in the direction to be a trustee or trustees in place of the incapable trustee.

8–20   21.—(1)   For the purposes of s.19 or 20 a direction is given by beneficiaries if—

(a) a single direction is jointly given by all of them, or

(b) (subject to subsection (2)) a direction is given by each of them (whether solely or jointly with one or more, but not all, of the others),

and none of them by writing withdraws the direction given by him before it has been complied with.

(2)   Where more than one direction is given each must specify for appointment or retirement the same person or persons.

(3)   Subsection (7) of section 36 of the Trustee Act 1925 (powers of trustees appointed under that section) applies to a trustee appointed under section 19 or 20 as if he were appointed under that section.

(4)   A direction under section 19 or 20 must not specify a person or persons for appointment if the appointment of that person or those persons would be in contravention of section 35(1) of the Trustee Act 1925 or section 24(1) of the Law of Property Act 1925 (requirements as to identity of trustees).

(5)   Sections 19 or 20 do not apply in relation to a trust created by a disposition in so far as provision that they do not apply is made by the disposition.

8–21   (6)   Sections 19 and 20 do not apply in relation to a trust created before the commencement of this Act by a disposition in so far as provision to the effect that they do not apply is made by a deed executed—

(a) in a case in which the trust was created by one person and he is of full capacity, by that person, or

(b) in a case in which the trust was created by more than one person, by such of the persons who created the trust as are alive and of full capacity.

(7)   A deed executed for the purpose of subsection (6) is irrevocable.

(8)   Where a deed is executed for the purposes of subsection (6)—

(a) it does not affect anything done before its execution to comply with a direction under section 19 or 20, but

(b) a direction under section 19 or 20 which has been given but not complied with before its execution shall cease to have effect.

IV. Protection of a Purchaser of Land of which New Trustees Have Been Appointed

The Trustee Act 1925

8–22   Section 38.—(1) A statement, contained in any instrument coming into operation after the commencement of this Act by which a new trustee is appointed for any purpose connected with land, to the effect that a trustee has remained out of the

United Kingdom for more than twelve months or refuses or is unfit to act, or is incapable of acting, or that he is not entitled to a beneficial interest in the trust property in possession, shall, in favour of a purchaser of a legal estate, be conclusive evidence of the matter stated.

(2) In favour of such purchaser any appointment of a new trustee depending on that statement, and any vesting declaration, express or implied, consequent on the appointment, shall be valid.

Where an appointment is invalid the general rule is that the old trustee remains trustee with the powers and liabilities of a trustee[38] though the invalidly appointed new trustee will become liable as trustee *de son tort* if he intermeddles with the property.[39]

V. Vesting of Trust Property in New or Continuing Trustees

The Trustee Act 1925

Section 40.—(1) Where by a deed a new trustee is appointed to perform any trust, then— **8–23**

(a) if the deed contains a declaration by the appointor to the effect that any estate or interest in any land subject to the trust, or in any chattel so subject, or the right to recover or receive any debt or other thing in action so subject, shall vest in the persons who by virtue of the deed become or are the trustees for performing the trust, the deed shall operate,[40] without any conveyance or assignment, to vest in those persons as joint tenants and for the purposes of the trust the estate interest or right to which the declaration relates; and

(b) if the deed is made after the commencement of this Act and does not contain such a declaration, the deed shall, subject to any express provision to the contrary therein contained, operate as if it had contained such a declaration by the appointor extending to all the estates interests and rights with respect to which a declaration could have been made.

(2) Where by a deed a retiring trustee is discharged under the statutory power without a new trustee being appointed, then— **8–24**

(a) if the deed contains such a declaration as aforesaid by the retiring and continuing trustees, and by the other person, if any, empowered to appoint trustees, the deed shall, without any conveyance or assignment, operate to vest in the continuing trustees alone, as joint tenants, and for the purposes of the trust, the estate, interest, or right to which the declaration relates; and

---

[38] *Adam & Company International Trustees Ltd v Theodore Goddard* (2000) 2 I.T.E.L.R. 634, [2000] W.T.L.R. 389.

[39] *Pearce v Pearce* (1856) 22 Beav. 248.

[40] Even when the estate, interest or right is not vested in the person making the appointment. *cf.* s.9 of the Law of Property Act 1925; but not as in *Re King's W.T.* [1964] Ch. 542, above, at para.1–128, where the legal estate is held by the appointor in his capacity as personal representative, not having executed an assent in his favour as trustee. Entry on the register is needed for registered land. The practice is for the current registered proprietor(s) to execute a transfer to the new trustees as new registered proprietors: this saves the Registrar from having to check on the validity of the deed of appointment and then altering the register.

(b) if the deed is made after the commencement of this Act and does not contain such a declaration, the deed shall, subject to any express provision to the contrary therein contained, operate as if it had contained such a declaration by such persons as aforesaid extending to all the estates, interests and rights with respect to which a declaration could have been made.

8–25 (3) An express vesting declaration, whether made before or after the commencement of this Act, shall, notwithstanding that the estate, interest or right to be vested is not expressly referred to, and provided that the other statutory requirements were or are complied with, operate and be deemed always to have operated (but without prejudice to any express provision to the contrary contained in the deed of appointment on discharge) to vest in the persons respectively referred to in subsections (1) and (2) of this section, as the case may require, such estates, interests and rights as are capable of being and ought to be vested in those persons.

(4) This section does not extend—

(a) to land conveyed by way of mortgage for securing money subject to the trust, except land conveyed on trust for securing debentures or debenture stock;

(b) to land held under a lease which contains any covenant, condition or agreement against assignment or disposing of the land without licence or consent, unless, prior to the execution of the deed containing expressly or impliedly the vesting declaration, the requisite licence or consent has been obtained, or unless, by virtue of any statute or rule of law, the vesting declaration, express or implied, would not operate as a breach of covenant or give rise to a forfeiture;

(c) to any share, stock, annuity or property which is only transferable in books kept by a company or other body, or in manner directed by or under an Act of Parliament.

8–26 In this subsection "lease" includes an underlease and an agreement for a lease or underlease.

(5) For purposes of registration of the deed in any registry, the person or persons making the declaration expressly or impliedly, shall be deemed the conveying party or parties, and the conveyance shall be deemed to be made by him or them under a power conferred by this Act.

(6) This section applies to deeds of appointment or discharge executed on or after the first day of January, eighteen hundred and eighty-two.

Section 2. Retirement of Trustees

8–27 Where a trustee retires and a new trustee is appointed[41] to fill the vacancy, the retirement and new appointment are effected under s.36(1) of the Trustee Act 1925, above. Where all the beneficiaries require retirement under section 19 of the 1996 Act, the retiring trustee must execute a deed discharging himself or herself under s.19(3). Where a new trustee is not appointed to fill the vacancy, the retirement is effected under s.39.

---

[41] If no one else can be found the Public Trustee will usually be willing to act.

The Trustee Act 1925

Section 39.[42]—(1) Where a trustee is desirous of being discharged from the trust, and after his discharge there will be either a trust corporation or at least two individuals to act as trustees to perform the trust, then, if such trustee as aforesaid by deed declares that he is desirous of being discharged from the trust, and if his co-trustees and such other person, if any, as is empowered to appoint trustees, by deed consent to the discharge of the trustee, and to the vesting in the co-trustees alone of the trust property, the trustee desirous of being discharged shall be deemed to have retired from the trust, and shall, by the deed, be discharged therefrom under this Act, without any new trustee being appointed in his place.

(2) Any assurance or thing requisite for vesting the trust property in the continuing trustees alone shall be executed or done.

Section 3. Disclaimer by Trustees

A person appointed trustee may naturally *disclaim*, for "a man cannot have an estate put into him in spite of his teeth." The disclaimer of a trust by a person appointed trustee— **8–28**

 (i) ought to be in writing (or by deed); but it may be

   (a) oral[43];
   (b) by conduct[44];
   (c) by mere inactivity (it seems)[45];
   (d) signified on behalf of the person appointed trustee by counsel at the Bar[46];

 (ii) must be a disclaimer of the whole trust; it cannot be partial.[47]

If a person is appointed both executor and trustee and he proves the will, he thereby accepts the trust. But if he renounces probate, he does not thereby necessarily disclaim the trust.[48]

Section 4. Removal of Trustees

If the conditions in s.36(1) for replacing a trustee with another person cannot be satisfied for removal of such trustee, then removal will require an **8–29**

---

[42] Independently of statute a trustee may retire (i) under a power of retirement contained in the trust instrument: *Camoys v Best* (1854) 19 Beav. 414; (ii) by the consent of all the beneficiaries, the latter being of full capacity: *Wilkinson v Parry* (1828) 4 Russ. 472 at 476; (iii) by authority of the court, to which the trustee has a right to apply to be discharged from the trust; but costs will depend on whether he has reasonable grounds for desiring to be discharged: *Gardiner v Dounes* (1856) 22 Beav. 395; *Barker v Peile* (1865) 2 Dr. & Sm. 340; *Re Chetwynd* [1902] 1 Ch. 692. Section 39 like s.37(1)(c) is subject to contrary intention *e.g.* if the trust instrument authorises retirement if a non European Union trust corporation remains a trustee: *Adam & Company International Trustee Ltd v Theodore Goddard* (2000) 2 I.T.E.L.R. 634, [2000] W.T.L.R. 349.
[43] *Bingham v Clanmorris* (1828) 2 Moll. 253; doubted by Wood V.-C. in *Re Ellison* (1856) 2 Jur. 62.
[44] *Stacey v Elph* (1883) 1 My. & K. 195; *Re Birchall* (1889) 40 Ch.D. 436.
[45] *Re Clout and Frewer* [1924] 2 Ch. 230.
[46] *Landbroke v Bleaden* (1852) 16 Jur.(o.s.) 630; *Foster v Dawber* (1860) 8 W.R. 646.
[47] *Re Lord and Fullerton* [1896] 1 Ch. 228.
[48] *Mucklow v Fuller* (1821) Jac. 198; *Ward v Butler* (1824) 2 Moll. 533; Romilly M.R. in *Dix v Burford* (1854) 19 Beav. 409 at 412.

express power in the trust instrument or an application to the court. The trust instrument may confer a power of removal,[49] though if it is conferred on a majority of the trustees and they are not unanimous then a meeting will need to be held.[50] It needs to be borne in mind that the benefit of property passing from the old trustees to the new trustees under section 40 only applies if a new trustee is appointed in place of the old trustee and not if the old trustee is simply removed.

The court has a jurisdiction, independent of statute, to remove trustees (*Letterstedt v Broers*, below) and under section 41 on appointing a new trustee it may remove a trustee.[51] On appointment of a new trustee under s.36 the appointors may remove a trustee. If hostility between trustees prevents them from acting unanimously (as they must do unless the trust instrument authorises otherwise) then one or all should be removed and replaced.[52]

In an emergency, trustees may be removed on an *ex parte* interlocutory application and a receiver appointed of the trust assets until appointment of new trustees at an *inter partes* hearing.[53]

The Occupational Pensions Regulatory Authority has power under ss.4 to 9 of the Pensions Act 1995 to suspend or remove trustees and appoint new trustees in the case of pension trust schemes, while the Charity Commissioners have similar powers under s.18 of the Charities Act 1993.

LETTERSTEDT v BROERS

8–30   Privy Council (1884) 9 App.Cas. 371; 51 L.T. 169 (Lord Blackburn, Sir Robert P. Collier, Sir Richard Couch and Sir Arthur Hobhouse)

The Board of Executors of Cape Town were the sole surviving executors and trustees of a will under which the appellant was a beneficiary. The appellant alleged misconduct in the administration of the trust, and claimed that the Board were unfit to be entrusted with the management of the estate and should be removed in favour of a new appointment. The Supreme Court of the Cape of Good Hope had refused the application to remove the Board. The beneficiary appealed successfully.

8–31   LORD BLACKBURN: ". . . the whole case has been argued here, and, as far as their Lordships can perceive, in the court below, as depending on the principles which should guide an English court of equity when called upon to remove old trustees and substitute new ones. It is not disputed that there is a jurisdiction 'in cases requiring such a remedy,' as is said in Story's *Equity Jurisprudence*, s.1287, but there is very little to be found to guide us in saying what are the cases requiring such a

---

[49] A power of removal, *e.g.* vested in a protector, will be presumed a fiduciary power not to be exercised for the personal benefit of the power-holder but for the beneficiaries as a whole or perhaps even for the benefit of the settlor (although the trust instrument should spell this out): *Von Knierem v Bermuda Trust Co.* (1994) Butts, O.C.M. Vol. 1 at 116; *Re Osiris* [2000] W.T.L.R. 933.

[50] *Att.-Gen. v Scott* (1750) 1 Ves. Sen. 413.

[51] If there is a dispute as to fact then instead of taking out a summons under s.41 a writ should be issued for administration or execution of the trusts invoking the inherent jurisdiction to remove trustees: *Re Henderson* [1940] Ch. 764.

[52] *Re Consiglis' Trusts (No.1)* (1973) 36 D.L.R. (3d) 658. On exercise of court's jurisdiction see *Monty v Delmo* [1996] 1 VR 65 and *Titterton v Oates* [2001] W.T.L.R. 319.

[53] *Clarke v Heathfield* (1985) 82 Law Soc. Gaz. 599; [1985] I.C.R. 203.

remedy; so little that their Lordships are compelled to have recourse to general principles.

"Story says, section 1289: 'But in cases of positive misconduct, courts of equity **8–32** have no difficulty in interposing to remove trustees who have abused their trust; it is not indeed every mistake or neglect of duty, or inaccuracy of conduct of trustees, which will induce courts of equity to adopt such a course. But the acts or omissions must be such as to endanger the trust property or to show a want of honesty, or a want of proper capacity to execute the duties, or a want of reasonable fidelity.'

"It seems to their Lordships that the jurisdiction which a court of equity has no difficulty in exercising under the circumstances indicated by Story is merely ancillary to its principal duty, to see that the trusts are properly executed. This duty is constantly being performed by the substitution of new trustees in the place of original trustees for a variety of reasons in non-contentious cases. And therefore, though it should appear that the charges of misconduct were either not made out, or were greatly exaggerated, so that the trustee was justified in resisting them, and the court might consider that in awarding costs, yet if satisfied that the continuance of the trustee would prevent the trusts being properly executed, the trustee might be removed. It must always be borne in mind that trustees exist for the benefit of those to whom the creator of the trust has given the trust estate.

"The reason why there is so little to be found in the books on this subject is **8–33** probably that suggested by Mr. Davey in his argument. As soon as all questions of character are as far settled as the nature of the case admits, if it appears clear that the continuance of the trustee would be detrimental to the execution of the trusts, even if for no other reason than that human infirmity would prevent those beneficially interested, or those who act for them, from working in harmony with the trustee, and if there is no reason to the contrary from the intentions of the framer of the trust to give this trustee a benefit or otherwise, the trustee is always advised by his own counsel to resign, and does so. If, without any reasonable ground, he refused to do so, it seems to their Lordships that the court might think it proper to remove him; but cases involving the necessity of deciding this, if they ever arise, do so without getting reported. It is to be lamented that the case was not considered in this light by the parties in the court below, for, as far as their Lordships can see, the Board would have little or no profit from continuing to be trustees, and as such coming into continual conflict with the appellant and her legal advisers, and would probably have been glad to resign, and get out of an onerous and disagreeable position. But the case was not so treated.

"In exercising so delicate a jurisdiction as that of removing trustees, their Lords **8–34** do not venture to lay down any general rule beyond the very broad principle above enunciated, that their main guide must be the welfare of the beneficiaries. Probably it is not possible to lay down any more definite rule in a matter so essentially dependent on details often of great nicety.[54] . . .

"It is quite true that friction or hostility between trustees and the immediate possessor of the trust estate is not of itself a reason for the removal of the trustees. But where the hostility is grounded on the mode in which the trust has been administered, where it has been caused wholly or partially by substantial over-charges against the trust estate, it is certainly not to be disregarded.

---

[54] "You must find," said Warrington J. in *Re Wrightson* [1908] 1 Ch. 789 at 803, "something which induces the court to think either that the trust property will not be safe, or that the trust will not properly be executed in the interests of the beneficiaries." In *Miller v Cameron* (1936) 54 C.L.R. 572 at 580 Dixon C.J. stated: "The jurisdiction to remove a trustee is exercised with a view to the interests of the beneficiaries, to the security of the trust property and to an efficient and satisfactory execution of the trusts and a faithful and sound exercise of the powers conferred upon the trustee."

"Looking, therefore, at the whole circumstances of this very peculiar case, the complete change of position, the unfortunate hostility that has arisen, and the difficult and delicate duties that may yet have to be performed, their Lordships can come to no other conclusion than that it is necessary, for the welfare of the beneficiaries, that the Board should no longer be trustees.

"Probably if it had been put in this way below they would have consented. But for the benefit of the trust they should cease to be trustees, whether they consent or not . . ."

The charge of misconduct was not proved: no costs were awarded.

Section 5. Special Types of Trustee

Custodian trustees[55]

8–35 These are distinct from the usual managing trustees. They hold the trust property and the trust documents of title (*e.g.* title deeds, share certificates) and all sums payable to or out of the income or capital of the trust property are paid to or by them except that dividends and other income derived from the trust property may be paid to such other persons as they direct, *e.g.* the managing trustees or a beneficiary.[56] The day-to-day running of the trust is left to the managing trustees whose instructions must be obeyed by the custodian trustee unless aware that they involve a breach of trust.[57] The following may be appointed custodian trustees: the Public Trustee, the Official Custodian for Charities and trust corporations.[58] A trustee cannot be custodian trustee and managing trustee of the same trust.[59]

Trust corporations

8–36 A trust corporation can act alone where otherwise two trustees would be required, *e.g.* receipt of capital moneys on a sale of land. The following are trust corporations[60]: the Public Trustee, the Treasury Solicitor, the Official Solicitor, certain charitable corporations and corporations either appointed by the court in any particular case or entitled to act as custodian trustees under the Public Trustee Act 1906. Corporations so entitled include those constituted under United Kingdom law or the law of an EU state and having a place of business in the United Kingdom and empowered to undertake trust business, which are either incorporated by special Act or Royal Charter or else registered United Kingdom or other European Union state companies with an issued capital of at least £250,000 (or its

---

[55] Generally see S. G. Maurice (1960) 24 Conv.(N.S.) 196; P. Pearce (1972) 36 Conv.(N.S.) 260–261; Keeton's *Modern Developments in the Law of Trusts*, Chap.3.
[56] Public Trustee Act, s.4(2).
[57] *ibid.* Exceptionally, in the case of an authorised unit trust, the trustee, which must be a corporate E.U. trustee independent of the manager of the unit trust, has to take reasonable care to ensure that the manager acts within its powers, keeps adquate records and manages the scheme in accordance with the Financial Service Authority's Regulations for Collective Investment Schemes.
[58] Public Trustee Rules 1912 r. 30, as substituted by the Public Trustee (Custodian Trustees) Rules 1975, SI 1975 No. 1189 and amended by SI 1976/836, SI 1981/358, SI 1984/109, SI 1985/132; SI 1987/1891.
[59] *Forster v Williams Deacon's Bank Ltd* [1935] Ch. 359; *Arning v James* [1936] Ch. 58.
[60] See above n.58 and Law of Property Act 1925 s.205(1)(xxviii); Trustee Act 1925, s.68(18); Law of Property (Amendment) Act 1925, s.3 (including trustees in bankruptcy).

foreign equivalent) of which at least £100,000 (or its equivalent) has been paid up in cash.

The Public Trustee[61] in the Official Solicitor's Office

The Public Trustee was established in 1906 as a corporation sole **8–36A** available to deal with the difficulty persons might have in finding someone willing to act as trustee especially of low value trusts. However, it cannot accept charitable trusts, insolvent estates or, normally, trusts involving the carrying on of a business. It can act as personal representative, ordinary managing trustee, custodian trustee or judicial trustee. Since April 1, 2001 the Official Solicitor is also the Public Trustee.

Judicial trustee

The Judicial Trustees Act 1896 established judicial trustees in order "to **8–37** provide a middle course in cases where the administration of the estate by the ordinary trustees had broken down and it was not desired to put the estate to the expense of a full administration" by the court.[62] Judicial trustees can only be appointed by the court upon a claim in existing proceedings or an original Part 8 claim. Trouble-shooting accountants are often appointed to sort out the muddled situation. The judicial trustee is an officer of the court so that he can at any time obtain the court's directions as to the way in which he should act without the necessity of a formal application by summons though he has as much authority as ordinary trustees to act on his own initiative, and, for example, compromise claims.[63]

Can there be a controlling trustee?

The basic position is that all trustees are equal and must act unan- **8–38** imously, trusteeship being a joint office *par excellence*, so one trustee cannot be "controlling" or "managing" trustee whom the other trustees can safely[64] leave on his or her own to deal with all trust matters. However, as where two trustees are needed to give a good receipt for capital moneys derived from land, the trust instrument can effectively provide for T2 always to do whatever T1 decides without being liable in any way for any breach of trust unless T2 was aware that he was assisting T1 to commit a breach of trust.[65] Similarly, there is no reason why a trust instrument might not effectively provide for T1 to have a casting vote if T1 and T2 cannot agree on a trust matter.[66]

---

[61] The Hutton Committee of Enquiry into the Public Trustee Office (1972) Cmnd. 4913 recommended that it be wound up and merged with the Official Solicitor's Department but the government did not take any action on the Committee's recommendations. By Public Trustee and Administration of Funds Act 1986 the Public Trustee was given the powers of a judge of the Court of Protection concerned with mental patients' property and affairs, but since April 1, 2001 the mental health functions were taken from the Public Trustee by the Public Guardian's Office now see Mental Capacity Act 2005 ss.57–60.

[62] *per* Jenkins J. in *Re Ridsdell* [1947] Ch. 597 at 605. See Judicial Trustee Rules 1983 and *Practice Note* [2003] 3 All E.R. 974.

[63] *Re Ridsdell* [1947] Ch. 597.

[64] It is a breach of trust to leave matters to a co-trustee: all co-trustees must positively involve themselves with all trust matters; see at para.10–02.

[65] *Re Arnott* [1899] I.R. 201.

[66] After all, the settlor can provide for trustees, to act by majority decisions, but if only an even number of trustees subsists then the chairman of the trustees is to have a casting vote where the trustees are equally divided.

Section 6. Trusts do not Fail for want of Trustees

8–39   If the testator failed to appoint trustees or if the trustees appointed refuse or are unable to act or have ceased to exist the trust does not fail[67] (unless its operation was conditional upon a specific trustee undertaking the trust[68]) nor does it fail if the intended trustees disclaim ownership of shares or land secretly transferred into their names by a settlor. The property or the beneficial interest therein remains in the settlor or the personal representatives of the testator to be held upon the trusts of the settlement or the will as the case may be.[69]

On the death of a sole or sole surviving trustee the trust property vests in his personal representatives subject to the trusts and by the Trustee Act 1925, s.18(2), they are capable of exercising or performing any power or trust which the deceased trustee could have exercised or performed. They are not bound to accept the position and duties of trustees and may exercise their power of appointing new trustees under s.36 with a right to payment of the costs thereof from the trust moneys.[70] If need be the court may appoint new trustees under section 41[71] or itself execute the trust.[72]

8–40   Where a deceased trustee's powers have devolved upon his personal representative who then dies (without having appointed new trustees) it seems that if he accepted the trustee role under s.18(2) then he should himself be treated as a trustee for his powers to devolve under s.18(2) to his own personal representative.[73] If he was executor of the deceased trustee and himself appointed an executor then his executor would be executor by representation of the trustee[74] and so have the s.18(2) powers in any event.

---

[67] *Re Willis* [1921] 1 Ch. 44; *Re Armitage* [1972] Ch. 438; *Re Morrison* (1967) 111 S.J. 758.

[68] *Re Lysaght* [1966] 1 Ch. 191.

[69] *Mallot v Wilson* [1903] 2 Ch. 494, accepted as good law by the Court of Appeal in *Harris v Sharp* [2003] W.T.L.R. 1541. P. Matthews [1981] Conv. 141 contends that disclaimer of an *inter vivos* transfer to a trustee should make the transfer void and the trust fail; but one may treat the transferor as constructive trustee by *Re Rose* [1952] Ch. 499 principles and *Tett v Phoenix* [1984] B.C.L.C. 599: above, para.4–29. See also *Standing v Bowring* (1885) 31 Ch.D. 282 at 288. On the unilateral and bilateral nature of gifts see J. Hill (2001) 117 L.Q.R. 127.

[70] *Re Benett* [1906] 1 Ch. 216.

[71] *Jones v Jones* (1874) 31 L.T. 538.

[72] *McPhail v Doulton* [1971] A.C. 424 at 457, *supra*, at para.3–124; (A. J. Hawkins) (1967) 31 (Conv. (N.S.) 117).

[73] P. W. Smith (1977) 41 Conv. 423; *Williams on Title* (4th ed.), p.490.

[74] Administration of Estates Act 1925, s.7.

Chapter 9

THE OBLIGATIONS OF TRUSTEESHIP

Section 1. General Introduction

THE office of trustee is onerous unless lightened by the terms of the trust **9–01** instrument. Equity, supplemented by the Trustee Act 2000, imposes many duties upon a trustee. A trustee has two roles to fulfil: a distributive role, concerned with distributing income and capital to appropriate beneficiaries, and an administrative or managerial role, concerned with safeguarding and developing the value of the trust fund.

In exercising these roles, a trustee is subject to the proscriptive obligations of keeping within the terms of the trust and of exhibiting undivided loyalty to the beneficiaries and in the managerial role, to prescriptive equitable duties of skill and care. A trustee is under fiduciary obligations not to act in bad faith and not (without authorisation) to profit from the trust, nor place himself in a position where his or her duty as trustee may conflict with his or her personal interest, nor to act for his or her own benefit or benefit of a third party.[1] As Millett L.J. states[2]:

> "The various obligations of a fiduciary merely reflect different aspects of his core duties of loyalty and fidelity. Breach of fiduciary obligation, therefore, connotes disloyalty or infidelity. Mere incompetence is not enough."

Incompetence is a breach of the equitable duty of skill and care in the administration or management of the trust property.

The distributive rule

In carrying out the distributive role the trustee does not have to afford **9–02** individual beneficiaries or objects of powers the opportunity to make their case[3] but must ensure that trust money or other property is not distributed to a person who is not entitled to benefit under the trust instrument[4]; he must exercise any discretionary power in responsible fashion only for the purposes intended by the settlor (not capriciously or perverse to any sensible expectation of the settlor),[5] while taking account in disinterested or

---

[1] *Bristol & West B.S. v Mothew* [1998] Ch. 1 at 18.
[2] *ibid.*
[3] *R v Charity Commissioners, Ex p Baldwin* [2001] W.T.L.R. 137; *Re B* [1987] 2 All E.R. 475 at 478.
[4] Equity does not allow the trustee's accounts to show that he transferred property to X not entitled to receive such property; the property is treated as still trust property in the accounts, so the trustee must replace the property wrongfully transferred to X: see para.10–10 to 10–11.
[5] *Re Hay's S.T.* [1981] 3 All E.R. 786 at 792; *Re Beatty's W.T.* [1990] 3 All E.R. 844 at 846; *McPhail v Doulton* [1971] A.C. 424 at 449, *Re Manisty's Settlement* [1994] Ch. 17 at 26.

impartial fashion[6] of all relevant factors and ignoring all irrelevant factors, so that any decision cannot be vitiated on the basis that the trustee would have decided otherwise if he had taken account of all relevant factors and ignored all irrelevant factors.[7] There is a modern trend[8] to introduce issues of public law *Wednesbury*[9] unreasonableness into the private law of trusts where application of the traditional principles just described seems to cover the same ground and so ought to make it unnecessary to ask the question "is this decision so unreasonable that no properly informed body of trustees could have reached such decision?" in which event the decision can be set aside for the body to reconsider when it is properly informed.

The managerial duty of care

9–03 In administering and managing the trust property Lord Watson said,[10] "As a general rule, the law requires of a trustee no higher degree of diligence than a man of ordinary prudence would exercise in the management of his own private affairs". However, in the investment sphere Lindley L.J. stated[11] in a much-endorsed[12] passage, "The duty of a trustee is not to take such care only as a prudent man would take if he had only himself to consider; the duty rather is to take such care as an ordinary prudent man would take if he were minded to make an investment for the benefit of other people for whom he felt morally bound to provide". With the advent of professional paid trustees and trust companies it became established that a higher degree of care was expected of them so that they were to be judged on the standards they professed and which had led to their appointment.[13] This equitable duty of care has now been replaced by a statutory duty of care covering most, but not all, activities of trustees from February 1, 2001.

Section 1 of the Trustee Act 2000 lays down "the duty of care" applicable to the activities mentioned in schedule 1 relating to investments, using agents, nominees and custodians, compounding liabilities, insuring, valuing and auditing—but the duty does not apply so far as it appears from the trust instrument that it is not meant to apply.[14] Thus, as concerns such activities, a trustee:

9–04		"must exercise such care and skill as is reasonable in the circumstances, having regard in particular—

		(a) to any special knowledge or experience that he has or holds himself out as having, and

---

[6] *Edge v Pensions Ombudsman* [2000] Ch. 602 (disinterested discrimination fine).
[7] *Re Hastings-Bass* [1975] Ch. 25, 41; *Mettoy Pensions Trustees Ltd v Evans* [1991] 2 All E.R. 513 at 553; *Abacus Trustees Ltd v Barr* [2000] Ch. 409.
[8] *Edge v Pensions Ombudsman* [1998] Ch. 512, 534, on appeal [1999] 4 All E.R. 546 at 569–570, *Scott v National Trust* [1998] 2 All E.R. 705, 718.
[9] *Associated Picture House v Wednesbury Corporation* [1948] 1 K.B. 223.
[10] *Learoyd v Whiteley* (1887) 12 A.C. 727 at 733.
[11] *Re Whiteley* (1886) 33 Ch.D. 347, 355.
[12] *e.g. Cowan v Scargill* [1985] Ch. 270, 289. *Nestlé v National Westminster Bank* [1994] 1 All E.R. 118, 126, 140.
[13] *Bartlett v Barclays Bank Trust Co.* [1980] 1 All E.R. 139 at 152; Lord Nicholls (1995) 9 Trust L.I. 71 at 73.
[14] Trustee Act 2000, Sch.1, para.7.

(b) if he acts as a trustee in the course of a business or profession, to any special knowledge or experience that it is reasonable to expect of a person acting in the course of that kind of business or profession".

It will be noted that (a) involves a subjective element relating to any extra knowledge or experience of the trustee personally, while (b) objectively relates to persons engaged in the trustee's business or profession generally. In (b) there is a distinction between a trustee who carries on trust business in the course of practising generally as a solicitor or accountant and a trustee who specialises in trust work in the course of the specific business of being a trustee: the latter will normally be governed by a higher standard.

If the appropriate standard of care is honestly taken but loss occurs the trustee will not be liable (*e.g.* for the dramatic depreciation of a trust holding in apparently safe companies like Rolls-Royce or Polly Peck) nor will he be liable for profits that the trust would have made if he had been more dynamic and skilful (*e.g.* in more actively selling and buying shares or in manipulating a significant minority shareholding in a private company so as either to sell at a very high price or to take over the company and strip it of its assets). In making decisions (*e.g.* on selling or buying particular investments) that are alleged to be negligent breaches of trust the position of a trustee is equated[15] with that of other professionals facing a claim for professional negligence who can only be "liable for damage caused by their advice, acts or omissions in the course of their professional work which no member of the profession who was reasonably well-informed and competent would have given or done or omitted to do."[16]

Protection by court applications

If any doubts arise then the trustee should apply to the Chancery Division **9–05** for directions to guide and protect him. As a last resort the court may under section 61 of the Trustee Act excuse the trustee from liability wholly or partly for breach of trust if he acted "honestly and reasonably, and ought fairly to be excused for the breach of trust *and* for omitting to obtain the directions of the court in the matter in which he committed such breach." A paid trustee will be much less likely to be excused than an unpaid trustee.[17]

Co-trustees

Where there is more than one trustee, as is usually the case, each trustee is **9–06** personally responsible for the acts performed in the administration of the trust and so should personally consider each act requiring to be done: it is

---

[15] *Wight v Olswang (No.2)* (2000) 2 I.T.E.L.R 689; [2000] W.T.L.R. 783, and on appeal [2001] W.L.T.R. 291, applying *dicta* in *Bristol & West B.S. v Mothew* [1998] Ch. 1 at 17–18.
[16] Per Lord Diplock in *Saif Ali v Sydney Mitchell & Co* [1980] A.C. 198 at 218, applied in *Wight v Olswang (No.2) above.*
[17] *Re Rosenthal* [1972] 1 W.L.R. 1273; *Re Pauling's S.T.* [1964] Ch. 303 at 338 and 339; *National Trustee Co. of Australasia v General Finance Co.* [1905] A.C. 373. See para.10–111.

no defence that one was a "sleeping trustee" blindly relying on one's co-trustees.[18] It is not possible for the trustees collectively to delegate their duties except where authorised under the trust instrument or by the Trustee Act 2000 which confers broad powers of delegation of managerial, but not distributive, functions.[19] The trustees must act unanimously except where the settlement or the court otherwise directs or, in the case of charitable trusts or pension trusts, where the trustees may act by a majority.[20] It follows that normally, if there is a trust to sell with power to postpone sale then the power is only effective so long as all trustees wish to postpone sale: once one wishes a sale the trust to sell must be carried out, all the trustees being under a duty to sell so long as the power to postpone sale is not effectively exercised unanimously.[21] Where the trust is to hold land with power to sell it,[22] then sale requires the agreement of all trustees or an application to the court.[23]

New trustees

9–07 Upon accepting[24] trusteeship in order to safeguard himself against claims for breach of trust the new trustee should ascertain the terms of the trust and check that he has been properly appointed. He should inspect all trust documents and ensure that all trust property is properly invested and is in the joint names of himself and his co-trustees[25] or in the name of a duly authorised nominee or custodian.[26] It is often best to have title deeds or share certificates deposited at a bank in the joint names but in the absence of special circumstances the court will not order one trustee who has possession of the documents so to deposit them.[27] If appointed new trustee of an existing trust then it is necessary to investigate any suspicious circumstances which indicate a prior breach of trust so that action may be taken to recoup the trust fund if necessary.[28]

---

[18] *Bahin v Hughes* (1886) 31 Ch.D. 390; *Munch v Cockerell* (1840) 5 Myl. & Cr. 178; *Re Turner* [1897] 1 Ch. 536; *Head v Gould* [1898] 2 Ch. 250. There is no automatic vicarious liability for co-trustees' breaches, *e.g. Re Lucking's W.T.* [1968] 1 W.L.R. 866; just personal liability for a trustee's own conduct.

[19] Trustee Art 2000 Pt IV. An individual trustee may delegate his own functions, including distributive functions, under the Trustee Delegation Act 1999. Further see paras 9–117 *et seq.*

[20] *Luke v South Kensington Hotel Ltd* (1879) 11 Ch.D. 121; *Re Whiteley* [1910] 1 Ch. 600, 608 (Charities); Pensions Act 1995, s.32; *Re Butlin's S.T.* [1976] Ch. 251 (rectification to allow majority decisions). If decision by majority is allowed it is not enough that a majority sign a paper recording the decision: the trustees must meet (*Att.-Gen. v Scott* (1750) 1 Ves. Sen. 413).

[21] *Re Mayo* [1943] Ch. 302. However, the letter of the trust will not be enforced if so to do would defeat the spirit of the trust: *Jones v Challenger* [1961] 1 Q.B. 176.

[22] As normal for co-ownership under Trusts of Land and Appointment of Trustees Act 1996.

[23] Trusts of Land and Appointment of New Trustees Act 1996, ss.14, 15.

[24] Of course, no one is bound to accept office as trustee and office should be refused if one wishes to buy property owned by the trust, or run a business likely to compete with a business owned by the trust, or if one is likely to be in a position where it might be said that profits had been made through advantage being taken of the office.

[25] *Hallows v Lloyd* (1888) 39 Ch.D. 686 at 691; *Harvey v Olliver* (1887) 57 L.T. 239; *Tiger v Barclays Bank* [1952] W.N. 38; *Lewis v Nobbs* (1878) 8 Ch.D. 591. For those classes of property not vesting in the new trustee under Trustee Act 1925, s.40, the ordinary modes of transferring the property will have to be utilised.

[26] Trustee Act 2000, ss.16–23.

[27] *Re Sisson's Settlements* [1903] 1 Ch. 262. Bearer securities have to be deposited with a custodian unless otherwise authorised by the trust instrument: Trustee Act 2000, s.18.

[28] *Re Strahan* (1856) 8 De G.M. & G. 291; *Re Forest of Dean Coal Co.* (1878) 10 Ch.D. 250.

Equity is seen at its strictest in the duty it imposes upon a trustee not to allow himself to be put in a position where there may be a conflict between his position as trustee and his personal interest—as the next section shows. This overriding duty of loyalty to the trust must always be borne in mind by trustees.

Section 2. Conflict of Interest and Duty

1. PURCHASE OF TRUST PROPERTY BY TRUSTEES

Of course, at law and in equity T cannot sell, lease or contract to sell or lease property to himself or herself,[29] but often there is more than one trustee. The rule is that a purchase of trust property by a trustee is voidable *ex debito justitiae*, however fair the price, at the instance of any beneficiary, unless authorised by the trust instrument expressly or by necessary implication,[30] or by the court, or by section 68 of the Settled Land Act 1925 (purchases by tenant for life), or made pursuant to a contract or option[31] arising before the trusteeship arose, or acquiesced in by the beneficiary or very special circumstances exist that would make the application of the strict rule unfair as in *Holder v Holder* [1968] Ch. 353. Here it was held by the Court of Appeal, boldly examining the mischief underlying the supposed arbitrary rule, that a renouncing executor who remained executor owing to technical acts of intermeddling (by earlier signing some cheques for trivial amounts) and who acquired no special knowledge as executor and who took no part in preparing for a sale by public auction took a valid title as the highest bidder for a farm of which he was the sitting tenant. He had never acted as executor in a way which could be taken to amount to acceptance of a duty to act in the interests of the beneficiaries under the will, who had never looked to him to protect their interests.

9–08

The Width of the "Self-dealing" Rule

In *Movitex Ltd v Bulfield*[32] Vinelott J. stated, "The self-dealing rule is founded on and exemplifies the wider principle that 'no one who has a duty to perform shall place himself in a situation to have his interests conflicting with that duty.'[33] To that should be added for completeness 'nor to have his duty to one conflicting with his duty to another.'[34] So, the fiduciary owes a duty to the person whose interest he is bound to protect not to place himself in a position in which duty and interest or duty and duty are in conflict."[35]

9–09

---

[29] *Rye v Rye* [1962] A.C. 496, *Ingram v I.R.C.* [2000] 1 A.C. 293 as affected by s.72 Law of Property Act 1925. Further see McPherson J. in Chapter 6, *Trends in Contemporary Trust Law* (ed. A. J. Oakley) (1996).
[30] *Sargeant v National Westminster Bank* (1990) 61 P & C.R. 518; *Edge v Pensions Ombudsman* [1998] Ch. 512, affirmed [2000] Ch. 602.
[31] *Re Mulholland's W.T.* [1949] 1 All E.R. 460.
[32] [1988] B.C.LC 104 at 117.
[33] *Broughton v Broughton* (1855) 5 De G.M. & G. 160 at 164.
[34] *Re Haslam & Hier-Evans* [1902] 1 Ch. 765.
[35] See also *Chan v Zachariah* (1984) 154 C.L.R. 178, see above, at para.6–38.

9–10   The prohibition against purchase by the trustee applies whether or not he himself fixes the price. Thus in *Wright v Morgan*,[36] a testator left land on trust for sale with power to postpone sale for seven years and provided that it should be offered at a price to be fixed by valuers to one of his sons, X, who was one of the trustees. X assigned his right (which was treated as an option and not a right of pre-emption) to his brother, Y, who was also one of the trustees but who was not authorised to purchase by the terms of the will. Y arranged for the sale to himself, retired from the trust and purchased at a price fixed by the valuers, and it was held that the sale could be set aside. After all, Y as a trustee was one of those responsible for determining when the land was first to be offered for sale (and prices could fluctuate over the years) and for determining the terms of payment, *e.g.* cash or instalments with interest payable. If X had assigned to a stranger, Z, then assuming the right was assignable and not personal to X, Z could quite properly have purchased the land. Of course, if X had exercised his right and had the land conveyed to him, then a subsequent conveyance to Y would have been proper.

9–11   The prohibition against purchase by the trustee is applicable where the sale is conducted at an auction held by the trustee himself,[37] since the trustee is in a position to discourage bidders. Further, where the sale is conducted, not by the trustee, but a third party, as, for example, where a trustee holds trust property subject to a mortgage and the mortgagee sells under his power of sale, the trustee is nevertheless not allowed to buy the property, since to hold otherwise might be to permit him to prefer his own interest to his duty,[38] and this is so whether or not he could have prevented the sale.[39] The rule is a strong one and is not circumvented by the device of the trustee selling to a third party to hold on trust for him.[40] But if there is no prior agreement and the sale is in all respects bona fide there is no objection to the trustee subsequently buying the trust property from the person to whom he sold it,[41] though if the trustee contracts to sell the property to X, a stranger, and before the conveyance is made he purchases the benefit of the contract from X, the contract can be set aside.[42] Further, if the trustee has retired from the trust with a view to purchasing the property the sale can be avoided,[43] but it is otherwise if at the date of his retirement he had no idea of making the purchase, unless the circumstances show that when he made the purchase he used information acquired by him while a trustee.[44] But a trustee who has disclaimed is not caught by the rule.[45]

---

[36] [1926] A.C. 788.
[37] *Whelpdale v Cookson* (1747) 1 Ves.Sen. 9; *Campbell v Walker* (1800) 5 Ves. 678 at 682.
[38] A. W. Scott, "The Trustee's Duty of Loyalty" (1936) 49 H.L.R. 521 at 529–530.
[39] *Griffith v Owen* [1907] 1 Ch. 195, where it was held that the tenant for life of an equity of redemption could not purchase the property for himself from the mortgagee selling under his power of sale.
[40] *Michoud v Girod* (1846) 4 How. 503 (U.S.).
[41] *Re Postlethwaite* (1888) 37 W.R. 200.
[42] *Williams v Scott* [1900] A.C. 499.
[43] *Wright v Morgan* [1926] A.C. 788.
[44] *Re Boles and British Land Co.'s Contract* [1902] 1 Ch. 244.
[45] *Stacey v Elph* (1833) 1 Myl. & K. 195; *cf.* Clark v Clark (1884) 9 App.Cas. 733 at 737, PC.

Moreover, the rule is sufficiently strong and elastic to prevent a trustee **9–12** from selling the trust property to a company of which he is the principal shareholder,[46] managing director or other principal officer,[47] or to a partnership of which he is a member.[48] Of course, the rule applies to corporate trustees, so that a trust corporation cannot in the absence of authorisation by the trust instrument or consent of the beneficiaries or approval of the court sell the trust property either to itself or to its subsidiaries.[49]

Where a sale takes place in breach of the rules outlined above, the **9–13** beneficiaries have a number of remedies open to them. Thus they may claim any profit made by the trustee on a resale of the property. If the property has not been resold they can insist on a reconveyance or alternatively they can demand that it be offered for sale again. If on this occasion a higher price is bid than which the trustee paid, it will be sold at that price. If not, the trustee may at the option of the beneficiaries be allowed to retain the property, and in the nature of things the beneficiaries will confer this doubtful favour upon him where the property has fallen in value since he purchased it.[50] The right which the beneficiaries have to avoid the sale is an equitable one, and as such is liable to be lost through laches, but for laches to apply the beneficiaries must have full knowledge of the facts and must acquiesce in the situation for an unreasonably long period.[51] Further, the right to have the sale set aside may be lost if the court in the exercise of its inherent jurisdiction sets the seal of its approval on the transaction, and it seems that not only may the court authorise a sale which is about to take place, but in a suitable case it may ratify one which has already occurred.[52]

The above presupposes that the sale has taken place without the consent **9–14** of the beneficiaries. Where, however, the beneficiaries are of full capacity they may authorise the sale, which will then stand, provided that the trustee made a full disclosure, and did not induce the sale by taking advantage of his relation to the beneficiaries or by other improper conduct, as evidenced by the fact that the transaction was apparently fair and reasonable.[53] The

---

[46] *Silkstone & Haigh Moor Coal Co. v Edey* [1900] 1 Ch. 167; *Farrars v Farrars Ltd* (1888) 40 Ch.D. 395. Sale to a trustee's wife is risky (see *Ferraby v Hobson* (1847) 2 Ph. 255 at 261) but perhaps not absolutely prohibited (see *Burrell v Burrell's Trustees*, 1915 S.C. 33; (1949) 13 Conv.(N.S.) 248; *Re King's W.T.* (1959) 173 Est.Gaz. 627; *Tito v Waddell (No.2)* [1977] 3 All E.R. 129 at 241) though see *Re McNally* [1967] N.Z.L.R. 521. A mortgagee can exercise his power of sale in favour of a company in which he is interested only if he shows he acted in good faith and took all reasonable steps to obtain the best price reasonably obtainable: *Tse Kwong Lam v Wong Chit Sen* [1983] 3 All. E.R. 54.

[47] *Eberhardt v Christiana Window Glass Co.* (1911) 9 Del.Ch. 284 (U.S.).

[48] *Colgate's Executor v Colgate* (1873) 23 N.J.Eq. 372 (U.S.). The self-dealing rule extends to cases where a trustee concurs in a transaction which cannot be effected without his consent and where he also has an interest in, or holds a fiduciary duty to another in relation to, the same transaction: *Re Thompson* [1985] 2 All E.R. 720.

[49] *Purchase v Atlantic Safe Deposit and Trust Co.* (1913) 81 N.J.Eq. 334 (U.S.).

[50] For further details, see *Holder v Holder* [1966] 2 All E.R. 116 at 130, *per* Cross J.

[51] Para.10–141; *Holder v Holder* [1968] Ch. 353.

[52] *Farmer v Dean* (1863) 32 Beav. 327; *Campbell v Walker* (1800) 5 Ves. 678.

[53] *Coles v Trecothick* (1804) 9 Ves. 234; *Morse v Royal* (1806) 12 Ves. 355; *Gibson v Jeyes* (1801) 6 Ves. 266; *cf. Fox v Mackreth* (1788) 2 Bro.C.C. 400. These factors can make it difficult for the trustee to find a purchaser when he himself wishes to sell, as a purchaser will be bound by a beneficiary's equity to set aside the transaction if he has actual or constructive notice.

onus of proof is on the trustee to show affirmatively that these conditions existed, but there is no objection to the consent of the beneficiaries being obtained after the sale to the trustees.[54]

The "fair dealing" rule

9–15 Of course, a trustee may purchase his beneficiary's equitable interest under the trust (subject to making full disclosure and negativing undue influence) so as to acquire the trust property itself when he has acquired all the equitable interests. In *Tito v Waddell (No. 2)*[55] Megarry V.-C. categorised this as subject to the "fair-dealing" rule that "if a trustee purchases the beneficial interest of any of his beneficiaries, the transaction is not voidable *ex debito justitiae*, however fair the transaction, [as under the 'self-dealing' rule] but can be set aside by the beneficiary unless the trustee can show that he has taken no advantage of his position and has made full disclosure to the beneficiary, and that the transaction is fair and honest."

9–16 This seems little different from the "self-dealing" rule under which the self-dealing will be set aside unless the trustee can show that he took no advantage of his position in obtaining a fully informed consent from all the beneficiaries, as evidenced by the transaction appearing to be a fair and honest transaction.

Plenty of scope for authorised self-dealing

9–17 A trust instrument, for example, may authorise a trustee which is a bank or is associated with a bank to lend trust money on deposit with itself[56] or its associate. It may authorise a distribution of trust assets to a trustee, usually so long as there is more than one trustee, but, if a settlor or testator wishes, he can even authorise a sole executor to appoint income or capital to himself.[57] A trustee that is trustee of ten trusts for the settlor's ten grandchildren may be authorised to transfer assets from any one of those trusts to any other one or more of them, thereby creating new equitable interests in respect of the assets that, of course, remain owned by the trustee[58]: such authority, essentially, confers upon the trustee a power of appointing or declaring new trusts, which could be gratuitously[59] or for a market price consideration (*e.g.* fixed by an independent valuer) provided out of the recipient trust's assets, so as to maintain the equilibrium between the transferor trust and the recipient trust.

II. Profits Incidental to Trusteeship

9–18 In order to maintain confidence in the trust institution by ensuring that the trustee acts to further the beneficiaries' interests and not his own Equity has developed the rule that a trustee may not place himself in a position

---

[54] T. B. Ruoff, "Purchases in Breach of Trust: A Suggested Cure" (1954) 18 Conv.(N.S.) 528.

[55] [1977] 3 All E.R. 129 at 241. A mortgagee may purchase the mortgagor's equity of redemption by a subsequent transaction independent of and separate from the mortgage: *Alec Lobb Garages Ltd v Total Oil* [1983] 1 All E.R. 944 at 965.

[56] *Space Investments Ltd v Canadian Imperial Bank of Commerce Trust Co. (Bahamas) Ltd* [1986] 1 W.L.R. 1072, PC.

[57] *Re Beatty's W.T.* [1990] 1 W.L.R. 1503 at 1506.

[58] *Re Vandervell's Trusts (No.2)* [1974] Ch 269.

[59] *ibid.*

where his trusteeship duties and his personal interest may possibly conflict[60] or, if he does, he must prefer his beneficiaries' interests; and the allied rule that, unless authorised,[61] he is strictly liable to account for any profit made by using trust property or his position as trustee. Thus, there is no point in trying to make a profit for himself. Indeed, the court, if required, will be prepared to find that the property acquired by such use is held on constructive trust for the trust beneficiaries, the purpose being to ensure that the defaulting fiduciary does not retain such property for herself and not to compensate the beneficiaries for any losses.[62] Of course, an injunction may also lie against any trustee who is in breach of or is about to break his duties to the trust.

The rules applicable to trustees have been extended to all persons in a **9–19** status-based fiduciary relationship.[63] These include director,[64] promoter[65] and the company; solicitor and client[66]; agent (including a self-appointed agent[67]) and principal[68]; partner and co-partner[69]; mortgagee and mortgagor.[70] Once a fiduciary relationship has been established it is necessary to ascertain the scope and ambit of the fiduciary's duties, which will be affected by the terms of any contract between the parties.[71] Then one can examine whether or not the fiduciary has placed himself in a position where his personal interest may possibly conflict with those duties. If so, then he is accountable for all profits made from acting within the scope and ambit of those duties[72] whether the profit arises before or after his resignation, retirement or dismissal from his fiduciary post, *e.g.* where information concerning certain economic opportunities has been gained *qua* fiduciary which leads to the fiduciary resigning his post so that *he* can profit from the opportunity rather than his principal.[73]

---

[60] See above para.6–24, *Bray v Ford* [1896] A.C. 44 at 51; *Parker v McKenna* (1874) L.R. 10 Ch.App. 96 at 124–125; *Boardman v Phipps* [1967] 2 A.C. 46. Generally see Goff & Jones, *Law of Restitution*, Chap.33; Oakley, *Constructive Trusts*, Chap.3. In *Swain v Law Society* [1981] 3 All E.R. 797 at 813 Oliver L.J. preferred to consider the rule "as an application of the principle that that which is the fruit of trust property or of the trusteeship is itself trust property." In *Movitex Ltd v Bulfield* [1988] B.C.L.C 104 at 117, Vinelott J. pointed out that "the fiduciary owes a duty to the person whose interest he is bound to protect not to place himself in a position in which duty and interest *or duty and duty* are in conflict."
[61] See at para.9–29.
[62] See Chap.6, s.1, above, at para.6–24 and *United Pan-Europe Communications NV v Deutsche Bank AG* [2000] 2 B.C.L.C. 461, C.A.
[63] Generally see Law Commission No.124, "Fiduciary Duties and Regulatory Rules" and para.6–21 above.
[64] *Regal (Hastings) Ltd v Gulliver* [1967] 2 A.C. 134; L. S. Sealy [1967] C.L.J. 83.
[65] *Lydney Iron Ore Co. v Bird* (1886) 33 Ch.D. 85 at 94.
[66] *McMaster v Byrne* [1952] 1 All E.R. 1362.
[67] *English v Dedham Vale Properties Ltd* [1978] 1 All E.R. 382.
[68] *Lowther v Lowther* (1806) 13 Ves. 95 at 103; *Parker v McKenna* (1874) 10 Ch.App. 96 at 124–125. To the extent the agent-principal relationship is a debtor-creditor relationship no constructive trusteeship or tracing can be allowed: *Halifax B.S. v Thomas* [1995] 4 All E.R. 673.
[69] *Bentley v Craven* (1853) 18 Beav. 75.
[70] *Farrars v Farrars Ltd* (1888) 40 Ch.D. 395.
[71] *Kelly v Cooper* [1993] A.C. 205.
[72] *Boardman v Phipps* [1967] 2 A.C. 46 at 128–129, *per* Lord Upjohn; *Patel v Patel* [1982] 1 All E.R. 68 (no breach of trust and so no accountability where trustees live in a house held on trust for young children adopted by trustees on death of their parents). Further see *Warman International Ltd v Dwyer* (1995) 69 A.L.J.R. 362.
[73] *Industrial Development Consultants Ltd v Cooley* [1972] 1 W.L.R. 443; *Canadian Aero Services Ltd v O'Malley* (1973) 40 D.L.R. (3d) 371; *Abbey Glen Pty. Co. v Stumborg* (1978) 85 D.L.R. (3d) 35. Contrast *Queensland Mines v Hudson* (1978) 18 A.L.R. 1.

9–20   The courts have also been prepared to find that special factual circumstances may create a fact-based fiduciary relationship in respect of the particular circumstances.[74] These circumstances include a claimant led to believe by the defendant that the defendant will exercise his power exclusively for the benefit of the claimant (or of the claimant and the defendant) but not in the selfish interest of the defendant, where the claimant is particularly vulnerable to exploitation by the defendant.

9–21   The English courts have retained a strict deterrent approach to fiduciaries. *Boardman v Phipps* (above, at para.6–46) establishes that the fiduciary must disgorge any benefit obtained by him "even though he acted honestly and in his principal's best interest, even though his principal benefited as well as he from his conduct, even though his principal could not otherwise have obtained the benefit and even though the benefit was obtained through the use of the fiduciary's own assets and in consequence of his personal skill and judgment."[75]

9–22   As will be seen from reading *Boardman v Phipps* the majority thought there was a feasible possibility of conflict: since the trustees might possibly have changed their minds and have sought Boardman's advice on an application to the court to acquire power to purchase the outstanding shares in the company, when there would be required not just legal advice but practical advice as to the likelihood of the assured success of the proposed takeover and reorganisation of the company. Boardman would hardly have been able to give unprejudiced advice if, when his plans were well advanced, he had been consulted by the trustees as to whether they should then try to take advantage of what he had done so as to obtain profits otherwise passing to him. However, the minority considered that a reasonable man would not think there was a real sensible possibility of conflict when there seemed virtually no chance the trustees would have changed their minds and so consult Boardman: indeed, in that exceptionally unlikely event, Boardman could have declined to advise and have referred them to another solicitor.

9–23   More recently, in *Industrial Development Consultants v Cooley*[76] the managing director of the plaintiff company was held constructive trustee of the benefit of a contract with the Eastern Gas Board and made liable to account for the profits thereof. The Gas Board had privately told him he would not obtain a contract from them for the benefit of his company but that he would have a good chance of privately obtaining the contract for himself if he left the company. Pretending poor health and concealing his true reason, he secured his release from his employment with the company. He then personally obtained the contract with the Gas Board which he had tried unsuccessfully to obtain for the company. He was held liable to

---

[74] *Hodgkinson v Simms* (1994) 117 D.L.R. 4th 161 (investment advisor on real estate tax shelters held liable as fiduciary—though for all consequential losses).

[75] (1968) 84 L.Q.R. 472 at 474, Prof. G. H. Jones. The prophyllactic approach is reflected in *Guinness plc v. Saunders* [1990] 2 A.C. 663.

[76] [1972] 1 W.L.R. 443. For Canadian cases where directors were liable see *Canadian Aero Services Ltd v O'Malley* (1973) 40 D.L.R. (3d) 371 noted (1974) 37 M.L.R. 464; *Abbey Glen Pty. Co. v Stumborg* (1978) 85 D.L.R. (3d) 35 noted (1979) 42 M.L.R. 215; (1975) 51 Can.B.R. 771 (Beck).

account for all the profit, though the chance of his persuading the Gas Board to contract with the company was estimated by the judge as no greater than 10 per cent.

In *English v Dedham Vale Properties*[77] self-appointed agents were held **9–24** liable to account for profits. The plaintiff sold her property to the defendant for £7,750. However, seven days before contracts were exchanged the defendant had applied for planning permission, making the application in the plaintiff's name and signed by the defendant as agent for the plaintiff. Under the Planning Acts the plaintiff did not then need to be notified of the application or informed of its outcome. Planning permission was granted after exchange of contracts but before completion. When, after completion, the plaintiff discovered the position she successfully claimed an account of profits since Slade J. was prepared to treat the defendant as a fiduciary who should have disclosed the planning application to the plaintiff before the contract and the price had been concluded.

In *Re Gee*[78] the issue arose as to whether an executor-trustee involved in **9–25** his own appointment as managing director of a company, in which he held some shares in his capacity as executor-trustee, was liable to account for his remuneration as managing director. It was held that if using his own shares in his favour but voting the trust shares against himself he was still able to secure his appointment, then he was not accountable for his remuneration from the appointment.

In *Swain v Law Society*[79] a solicitor sought to make the Law Society **9–26** accountable for commission received by it from an insurance company in respect of premiums paid by solicitors under the Solicitors' Indemnity Insurance Scheme which the Law Society had negotiated with the company. Oliver L.J. stated[80]:

> "What one has to do is to ascertain first of all whether there was a fiduciary relationship and, if there was, from what it arose and what, if there was any, was the trust property; and then to inquire whether that of which an account is claimed either arose, directly or indirectly, from the trust property itself or was acquired not only in the course of, but by reason of, the fiduciary relationship."

On appeal, Lord Brightman (with whom the other Law Lords agreed) **9–27** endorsed[81] this approach but held that no fiduciary relationship existed since the Law Society was performing a public duty under section 37 of the Solicitors Act 1974.

In *Queensland Mines Ltd v Hudson*[82] the Privy Council took a liberal view **9–28** on a case of unusual merits to produce a decision that is out of line with earlier strict cases. Queensland was formed to exploit the anticipated award

---

[77] [1978] 1 All E.R. 382. Exploitation of maturing business opportunities of a company or partnership after retirement therefrom leads to accountability for profits, though they may be limited to a particular period: *CMS Dolphin Ltd v Simonet* [2001] 2 B.C.L.C. 704; *Kao Lee and Yup v Koo* [2003] W.T.L.R. 1283.
[78] [1948] Ch. 284.
[79] [1982] 1 W.L.R. 17; reversed [1982] 2 All E.R. 827; [1983] 1 A.C. 598.
[80] [1982] 1 W.L.R. 17 at 37.
[81] [1982] 2 All E.R. 827 at 838; [1983] A.C. 598 at 619.
[82] (1978) 18 A.L.R. 1, well criticised by G. R. Sullivan (1979) 42 M.L.R. 711.

of mining licences: its managing director was Hudson. At the last minute Queensland's financial backing collapsed so Hudson took the licences in his own name in 1961 and resigned as managing director, though remaining a director for a further 10 years. At a 1962 board meeting Hudson admitted he held the licences for Queensland and candidly warned of the risks attendant on exploiting the licences. So the board resolved Queensland would not pursue the matter further, so Hudson was free to go it alone. It was held that Hudson was not liable for his profits for either of two reasons since the board had (1) given their fully informed consent, and (2) placed the licences venture outside the scope of the fiduciary relationship of director and company. As to (1) the consent of the board is not enough: one needs the consent of the majority vote of shareholders at a general meeting at the very least,[83] if not the consent of all the shareholders.[84] As to (2) to allow fiduciary managers to define the scope of their own fiduciary obligations, and so immunise themselves from liability, is startling when there will be such a conflict of interest involved if the directors can then acquire for themselves what they have rejected on behalf of the company. The decision seems rather weak when contrasted with the House of Lords decisions in *Regal (Hastings) Ltd v Gulliver*[85] and in *Boardman v Phipps*.[86] The Privy Council were over-influenced by the fact that Hudson seemed a good chap who had worked hard and risked all, while Queensland had risked nothing, and watched him becoming very successful and then had tried to take away everything he had worked for.

Defences

9–29 It will be a defence to show that the conduct generating the profit was authorised by the trust instrument expressly or by necessary implication,[87] or by the contract of agency,[88] or the deed of partnership, or the articles of a company,[89] or by the court.[90] A further defence is to show the informed consent of all the beneficiaries being each of full capacity and between them absolutely entitled to the trust property.[91] A partner will need the consent of the other partners; a director the consent of all the members of the company for it will be a fraud on the minority to expropriate property held on a constructive trust for the company.[92] It would seem that someone employed by trustees in a fiduciary position (*e.g.* a solicitor or accountant)

---

[83] *Imperial Credit Association v Coleman* (1871) 6 Ch.App. 556 at 557; *Regal (Hastings) Ltd v Gulliver* [1967] 2 A.C. 134 at 150, 154; *Prudential Assurance Co. v Newman Industries (No.2)* [1980] 2 All E.R. 841 at 862.
[84] *Cook v Deeks* [1916] 1 A.C. 554; *Daniels v Daniels* [1978] 2 All E.R. 89 at 95.
[85] [1967] 2 A.C. 134.
[86] [1967] 2 A.C. 46.
[87] *Re Llewellin* [1949] Ch. 225. *Sargeant v National Westminister Bank* (1990) 61 P. & C.R. 518, *Edge v Pensions Ombudsman* [1998] Ch. 512.
[88] *Kelly v Cooper* [1993] A.C. 205.
[89] *Movitex Ltd v Bulfield* [1988] B.C.L.C. 104; *Guiness plc v Saunders* [1990] 2 A.C. 663.
[90] *e.g.* Trustee Act, s.42; C.P.R., pt 64.
[91] *Boardman v Phipps* [1967] 2 A.C. 46.
[92] *Cook v Deeks* [1916] 1 A.C. 554; *Borland's Trustees v Steel Bros. Ltd* [1901] Ch. 279. In contrast a majority by resolution in general meeting may waive a director's personal liability to account if they consider he acted in the company's best interests: *Regal (Hastings) Ltd v Gulliver* [1967] 2 A.C. 134.

or a beneficiary acquiring special information while purportedly representing the trust so as to be treated as a fiduciary, may have a defence if obtaining the informed consent of independent trustees.[93]

Where a fiduciary in his professional capacity may have clients with **9–30** differing interests he has to cope with his need not to have his fiduciary duty to one conflicting with his duty to another. He can take advantage of the principle that the scope of the fiduciary duties owed by him to his clients is to be defined by the express or implied terms of his contract with each of them.[94] Indeed, "it is the contractual foundation which is all-important . . . The fiduciary relationship, if it is to exist at all, must accommodate itself to the terms of the contract so that it is consistent with, and conforms to, them."[95]

The fact that a fiduciary could have avoided problems by an apt contractual term or by obtaining an informed consent or court approval before entering into the profit-making situation and the practical problems in the way of the principal finding out for himself what exactly the fiduciary was involved in, combine to indicate that the strict deterrent approach is likely to be maintained.

Allowance for fiduciary's services

In an exceptional case, like *Boardman v Phipps*, the court can grant the **9–31** defendant an allowance for his valuable services and, perhaps, even an element of the profit, though the court should be very cautious in this: it does not want to encourage trustees or other fiduciaries to put themselves in a position where their interests conflict with their duties.[96]

The equitable obligation of confidence

This equitable right of confidentiality is still in course of development. It is **9–32** usually protected by the grant of an injunction to prevent disclosure of the confidence or by damages in lieu of an injunction under Lord Cairns's Act or by making the confidant liable to account to the confider for profits made from exploiting the confidence or, perhaps, by making a *quantum meruit* award. The right "depends on the broad principle of equity that he

---

[93] *Regal (Hastings) Ltd v Gulliver* [1967] 2 A.C. 134 (solicitor not liable though closely involved with the directors as emerges from *Luxor (Eastbourne) Ltd v Cooper* [1941] A.C. 108, especially [1939] 4 All E.R. 411 at 414–417); *Boardman v Phipps* [1967] 2 A.C. 46 at 93, 117 and implicit in Lord Upjohn's speech 130–133; *Anson v Potter* (1879) 13 Ch.D. 141. The trustees should be independent just like company directors must be if disclosure to them is to protect a promoter: *Gluckstein v Barnes* [1900] A.C. 240. If to the fiduciary's knowledge a fund is distributable under a bare trust because the beneficiaries are each of full capacity and between them absolutely entitled to call for the capital then according to Lord Cohen in *Boardman v Phipps* [1967] 2 A.C. 46 at 104, the informed consent of the beneficiaries is required. Presumably, trustees can employ an agent to exploit information on terms he receives as fee a per centage of the profit.
[94] *Kelly v Cooper* [1993] A.C. 205, *Clark Boyce v Mouat* [1994] 1 A.C. 428.
[95] *Hospital Products Ltd v United States Surgical Corporation* (1984) 156 C.L.R. 41 at 97 endorsed in *Kelly v Cooper*, above.
[96] See Lord Goff in *Guinness plc v Saunders* [1990] 2 A.C. 663 at 701, though the Court of Appeal were flexible in *O'Sullivan v Management Agency and Music Ltd* [1985] Q.B. 428 at 468. Indeed, in *Re Badfinger* [2001] W.T.L.R. 1 the High Court held that not only a flat fee but a fee based on a per centage of profits could and would be allowed to the sound-engineer hired by the fiduciary: it was open to allow a per centage fee to the fiduciary himself but in the circumstances only a flat fee would be allowed.

who has received information in confidence shall not take unfair advantage of it. He must not make use of it to the prejudice of him who gave it without obtaining his consent": *Seager v Copydex*.[97] Thus the information must have the necessary quality of confidentiality, must have been imparted in circumstances importing an obligation of confidence, and there must have been unauthorised use of the information.[98] If the circumstances are such that any reasonable man, standing in the shoes of the recipient of the information, would have realised upon reasonable grounds that the information was being given to him in confidence, then this should suffice to impose upon him the equitable obligation of confidence.[99] Indeed, Lord Goff[1] has stated that:

"a duty of confidence arises when confidential information comes to the knowledge of a person (the confidant) in circumstances where he has notice, or is held to have agreed, that the information is confidential, with the effect that it would be just in all the circumstances that he should be precluded from disclosing the information to others."

It will be a defence to show that disclosure was in the public interest[2] or that the obligation of confidentiality was at an end at the relevant time because the information was in the public domain available to all on reasonable inquiry.[3]

9–33   If the confidant consciously breaks the claimant's confidence the court will grant an injunction and direct an account of profits, treating the confidant as constructive trustee of the profits or any patent or copyright which is the product of the confidential information.[4] Indeed in *LAC Minerals Ltd v International Corona Resources Ltd*[5] the Supreme Court of Canada held that LAC was constructive trustee of land it had bought for itself, because told in confidence by a potential joint-venturer that it could well contain gold deposits. If the confidant acted honestly but foolishly in

---

[97] [1967] 1 W.L.R. 923 at 931; See *Malone v Commissioner of Police (No.2)* [1979] 2 All E.R. 620 at 633; Goff & Jones, Chap.36; Law Commission *Breach of Confidence*, Law. Com. No.110; Meagher, Gummow & Lehane, Chap.41.

[98] See *Coco v Clark (Engineers) Ltd* [1969] R.P.C. 41 at 47 endorsed by CA in *Murray v Yorkshire Fund Managers* [1998] 2 All E.R. 1015 at 1020; *Att.-Gen. v Jonathan Cape* [1975] 3 All E.R. 484 at 494; *Dunford & Elliott Ltd v Johnson* [1977] 1 Lloyd's Rep.505; *Fraser v Thames Television* [1983] 2 All E.R. 101 at 116. See also Braithwaite (1979) 42 M.L.R. 94.

[99] *Coco v Clark (Engineers) Ltd* [1969] R.P.C. 41 at 48; *Att.-Gen. v Guardian Newspapers (No.2)* [1988] 3 All E.R. 545.

[1] *Att.-Gen. v Guardian Newspapers Ltd (No.2)* [1990] 1 A.C. 109 at 281. In *A v B* [2003] Q.B. 195 at 207 the Court of Appeal stated: "A duty of confidence will arise whenever the party subject to the duty is in a situation where he either knows or ought to know that the other person can reasonably expect his privacy to be protected."

[2] *Initial Services Ltd v Putterill* [1968] 1 Q.B. 396 at 405; *Lion Laboratories Ltd v Evans* [1984] 2 All E.R. 417; *Francome v Mirror Group Newspapers* [1984] 2 All E.R. 408.

[3] *Satnam Investments Ltd v Dunlop Heywood & Co. Ltd* [1999] 3 All E.R. 652 at 672; *Bunn v BBC* [1998] 3 All E.R. 552.

[4] *Peter Pan Manufacturing Co. v Corsets Silhouette Ltd* [1964] 1 W.L.R. 96; *British Syphon Co. v Homewood* [1956] 1 W.L.R. 1190; *Att.-Gen. v Guardian Newspapers (No.2)* [1988] 3 All E.R. 545; *Nanus Asia Co. Inc. v Standard Chartered Bank* [1990] Hong Kong L.R. 396 holding that even a tippee may be constructive trustee of his profits.

[5] (1989) 61 D.L.R. (4th) 14.

believing that he was not breaching confidence then damages[6] under Lord Cairns's Act[7] or a *quantum meruit*[8] will be awarded, at least if the information had only partially contributed to the product marketed to produce the profits. If the information were the *sine qua non* and the confidant was foolish in thinking he was not breaching the plaintiff's confidence the confidant should be liable to account for his unjust enrichment.[9] If a person uses information without having reason to think that it had been imparted to him in breach of another's confidence, and later discovers the truth of the matter, he should not be liable for use of the information in the prior period.[10] Thereafter he should be liable whether he be a volunteer or a purchaser,[11] so that if he continues with a project with the informant he should be liable to be restrained as participating in a dishonest design in breach of confidence.[12] The general defence of change of position will be available in appropriate circumstances.[13]

Recently, the Court of Appeal[14] in developing English law consistently **9–34** with the European Convention on Human Rights, implemented by the Human Rights Act 1999, has recognised a right of privacy grounded in the equitable doctrine of breach of confidence, without any longer needing to construct an artificial relationship of confidentiality between intruder and victim. Thus, injunctions may also be obtained against surreptitious photographers and industrious eavesdroppers without the need to decide whether there exists a new candues of action in tort which protects privacy. Balancing the right to respect for private and family life with the right of the press to freedom of expression in respect of individuals in the public eye is very difficult.[15]

---

[6] For principles of assessment see *Seager v Copydex (No.2)* [1969] 1 W.L.R. 809 and *Dowson & Mason Ltd v Potter* [1986] 2 All E.R. 418. If the plaintiff is a manufacturer loss of manufacturing profits is an appropriate basis but not if the plaintiff instead intended to exploit the information by licensing it to others when the value to the plaintiff of the information is an appropriate basis.

[7] The damages were treated as in lieu of an injunction under Lord Cairns's Act 1858 by Slade J. in *English v Dedham Vale Properties Ltd* [1978] 1 All E.R. 382 at 399, and Megarry V.-C. in *Malone v Commissioner of Police (No.2)* [1979] 2 All E.R. 620 at 633; and Lord Goff in *Att.-Gen. v Guardian Newspapers Ltd (No.2)* [1990] 1 A.C. 109 at 286. It is probable that Lord Cairns's Act is concerned purely with damages in aid of legal rights and that where the plaintiff has suffered a loss and seeks relief within the exclusive jurisdiction of equity he is entitled to equitable compensation (see, paras 10–09 *et seq.*) so that the court should award this restorative remedy and not damages: Meagher, Gummow & Lehane, *Equity* (3rd ed.), pp.888–889.

[8] See Goff & Jones, on remedies Chapter 34.

[9] Prof. G. H. Jones (1970) 86 L.Q.R. 463 at 476.

[10] "It may be a reason for limiting the account of profits to the period subsequent to the date at which he becomes aware of the true facts": *Att.-Gen. v Spalding* (1915) 32 R.P.C. 273 at 283.

[11] The defence of bona fide purchaser for value without notice does not apply since the equitable obligation is not a property right, *e.g. Oxford v Moss* (1978) 68 Cr.App.R. 183; [1979] Crim. L.R. 119. Even if the property analogy were adopted the equitable nature of the right would mean that the confider's claim would prevail as being the equitable right first in time.

[12] *cf.* the constructive trusteeship imposed on strangers to a trust to make them accountable: below, Chap.11, section 2; *Wheatley v Bell* [1982] 2 N.S.W.L.R. 544; [1984] F.S.R. 16; J. D. Davies (1984) 4 Ox.J.L.S. 142; *Malone v Commissioner of Police* [1979] 2 All E.R. 620 at 634.

[13] See paras 11–28 *et seq.*

[14] *Douglas v Hello Ltd* [2001] QB 967 applied in *Venables v News Group Newspapers* [2001] 1 All E.R. 908; also *A v B plc* [2003] Q.B. 195, para.11(vi).

[15] *Campbell v MGN Ltd* [2004] UKHL 22, [2004] 2 A.C. 457, HL by 3:2 reversing CA, and the CA in *Douglas v Hello Ltd (No. 2)* [2005] EWCA Civ 395 at paras 54 *et seq* further developing privacy protection within the law of confidence and at paras 251 *et seq* finding the refusal of the interlocutory injunction in *Douglas v Hello Ltd* [2001] Q.B. 967 to have been wrong.

Use of information acquired qua fiduciary

9–35   Information acquired by a trustee in the course of his duties as such may be used by him for his own benefit or for the benefit of other trusts unless its use would place him in a position where his duty and his interest might possibly conflict or it was imparted to him in circumstances placing an obligation of confidence upon him.[16] Thus if A is trustee of S1 and of S2 and as trustee of S1 learns facts that make him and his co-trustees wish to sell X Co. shares he cannot use this knowledge for S2 until S1's X Co. shares have been sold, for a prior sale of S2's shares could well drive down the price of X Co. shares. If A as trustee of S1 learnt encouraging facts about Y Co. shares and his S2 co-trustees were thinking of selling Y Co. shares then A could tell them this would be unsatisfactory unless S1 was thinking of purchasing more Y Co. shares. If A obtains as trustee of S2 information subject to the equitable obligation of confidence then he cannot use it for the benefit of S1 and, it seems, even if he became trustee of S1 before he became trustee of S2, he cannot be sued by the S1 beneficiaries for breach of trust for failing to take advantage of the confidential information obtained *qua* S2 trustee.[17]

9–36   A partner may make a profit from information obtained in the course of the partnership business where he does so in another firm with business outside the scope of the partnership business.[18] As Lord Hodson stated in *Boardman v Phipps*,[19] "Partnership is special in that a partner is the principal as well as the agent of the other partners and works in a defined area of business so that it can normally be determined whether the particular transaction is within or without the scope of the partnership. It is otherwise in the case of a general trusteeship or fiduciary position such as was occupied by Mr. Boardman the limits of which are not readily defined."

The scope of a trustee's duties to the trust is unclear where he acquired useful information privately but not in circumstances placing him under the equitable obligation of confidence. Obviously, he can first make as much use of the information for himself as he likes. If he uses the information to make a profit for himself should he not also go on to use it for the benefit of the trust if a trustee with his special knowledge should be expected so to act?[20] If use of the information could enable the shares to be sold quickly before the share price drops dramatically should he not use such information to save the trust suffering a loss?

---

[16] *Boardman v Phipps* [1967] 2 A.C. 46 at 128–129, *per* Lord Upjohn who also provides the next two examples. Further see *Kelly v Cooper* [1993] A.C. 205; *Mortgage Express Ltd v Bowerman* [1996] 2 All E.R. 836, C.A.

[17] *cf. North & South Trust Co. v Berkeley* [1971] 1 W.L.R. 470 and see B. A. K. Rider [1978] Conv. 114.

[18] *Aas v Benham* [1891] 2 Ch. 244.

[19] [1967] 2 A.C. 46 at 108. For companies see *Queensland Mines*, above, para.9–28. On the position of an agent acting for two principals (*e.g.* a solicitor acting for a purchaser and the purchaser's prospective mortgagee) see *Bristol & West B.S. v Mothew* [1998] Ch. 1, CA.

[20] See what approximates to a trustee's duty to gazump in *Buttle v Saunders* [1950] 2 All E.R. 193. Is there a distinction between a profit-making situation when there are so many different ways of investing money for profit and a loss-making situation when there is only one way of avoiding the loss, *viz.* selling the shares as soon as possible?

III. COMPETITION WITH THE TRUST

The general rule is that a trustee may not, after accepting a trust which **9–37** comprises a business, set up a private business which competes or may compete with the business of the trust since, if he did so, his interest would conflict with his duty. Thus in *Re Thomson*,[21] the testator's estate included a yachtbroker's business which he bequeathed to his executors on trust to continue it. One of the executors claimed the right to set up a similar business in competition with the trust, but the court granted an injunction to restrain him.[22] On the other hand, in the Irish case of *Moore v M'Glynn*,[23] the court refused to restrain a trustee from setting up a competing business, but considered that it would be a good ground for removing him from his trusteeship. Chatterton V.-C. observed[24]: "I have not been referred to, nor am I aware of, any case deciding that an executor or trustee of a will carrying on the business of his testator is disabled from setting up a similar business in the same locality on his own account. . . . I am not prepared to hold that a trustee is guilty of a breach of trust in setting up for himself in a similar line of business in the neighbourhood, provided that he does not resort to deception or solicitation of custom from persons dealing at the old shop." A distinction between this case and *Re Thomson* is that in the latter the business was highly specialised and the locality was very small so that the competition was inevitable whether or not there was solicitation of custom.

Any profits made in breach of duty should be held on trust for the **9–38** beneficiaries as the profits are their profits which have been lost by the trustee's competition.[25] Whilst partners are under a statutory obligation[26] not to engage in a competing business it seems that non-service directors are not so obliged (unless their contract so provides) but they must be very careful as to the information they disclose to rival companies[27] since confidential information must not be disclosed.

IV. GRATUITOUS ADMINSTRATION OF TRUST UNLESS OTHERWISE AUTHORISED

Trustees must, in the absence of some special dispensation, administer the **9–39** trust gratuitously for otherwise "the trust estate might be loaded and made of little value."[28] There is an obvious conflict between their self-interest and

---

[21] [1930] 1 Ch. 203. Where at 215 Clauson J. said, "An executor and trustee having duties to discharge of a fiduciary nature towards the beneficiaries under the will shall not be allowed to enter into any engagement in which he has or can have a personal interest conflicting or which possibly may conflict with the interests of those whom he is bound to protect."

[22] For the grant of an injunction against a business competitor allegedly taking advantage of confidential financial information see *United Pau-Europe Communications NV. v Deutsche Bank A.G.* [2000] 2 B.C.L.C. 461 C.A.

[23] [1894] 1 I.R. 74.

[24] *ibid.* at 89.

[25] *Somerville v Mackay* (1810) 16 Ves. 382; *Dean v MacDowell* (1877) 8 Ch.D. 345 at 353; *Trimble v Goldberg* [1906] A.C. 494; Restatement of Restitution, para.199.

[26] Partnership Act 1890, s.30.

[27] *London & Mashonaland Exploration Co. v New Mashonaland Exploration Co.* [1891] W.N. 165 approved by Lord Blanesburgh in *Bell v Lever Bros.* [1932] A.C. 161, 195; *Aubanei & Atabaster Ltd v Aubanel* (1949) 66 R.P.C. 343.

[28] *Robinson v Pett* (1734) 3 P. Wms, 249 at 251.

their fiduciary duty, but the position has been much liberalised and modernised by the Trustee Act 2000.

The cases in which the trustee is entitled to payment for his services are as follows.

First, in a suitable case the court has an inherent jurisdiction to be excercised sparingly to authorise a trustee to receive remuneration prospectively or retrospectively and it may increase the remuneration authorised by the trust instrument. In order to do so the court must be satisfied that the services of the particular trustee will be or have been of exceptional benefit to the estate.[29] The court, when appointing a *corporation* (other than the Public Trustee) to act, also has a statutory jurisdiction[30] under section 42 of the Trustee Act 1925 to authorise it to charge for its services.

9–40 Second, if the settlement authorises the trustee to charge for his services he is entitled to be paid, but charging clauses used to be construed strictly with the onus on the trustee to show that the charge which he proposes to make is covered by the terms of the settlement. Thus, where a solicitor-trustee was authorised to make "professional charges," and even where the words "for his time and trouble" were added, he was not be allowed to charge for time and trouble expended other than in his position as solicitor.[31] But where a will authorised the solicitor-trustee to make "the usual professional or *other proper and reasonable* charges for all business done and time expended in relation to the trusts of the will, *whether such business is usually within the business of a solicitor or not*," the solicitor was permitted to charge for business not strictly of a professional nature transacted by him in relation to the trust,[32] though, apparently, not for work altogether outside his professional vocation that a layman could do.[33]

9–41 However, in radical fashion s.28(2) of the Trustee Act 2000 treats a trustee entitled under the trust instrument to charge for services provided by him as entitled to receive payment "in respect of services even if they are services which are capable of being provided by a lay trustee", so long as the trustee is "a trust corporation or is acting in a professional capacity"— and the services were provided after January 2001.[34] A trustee acts in a professional capacity[35] "if he acts in the course of a profession or business which consists of or includes the provision of services in connection with (a) the management or administration of trusts generally or a particular kind of trust, or (b) any particular aspect of the management or administration of

---

[29] *Re Duke of Norfolk's S.T.* [1982] Ch. 61; *Marshall v Holloway* (1820) 2 Swans. 432; *Docker v Somes* (1834) 2 My. & K. 655; *Re Freeman* (1887) 37 Ch.D. 148; *Re Masters* [1953] 1 W.L.R. 81; *Re Macadam* [1946] Ch. 73; *Boardman v Phipps* [1967] 2 A.C. 46; *Re Barbour's Settlement* [1974] 1 All E.R. 1188, 1192; *Re Keeler's S.T.* [1981] 1 All E.R. 888 (though it overlooks *Re Llewellin's W.T.* [1949] Ch. 225); *Foster v Spencer* [1996] 2 All E.R. 672. Even a wrongdoer may benefit: *O'Sullivan v Management Agency & Music Ltd* [1985] 3 All E.R. 351; *John v James* [1986] S.T.C. 352 at 358; *Re Badfinger* [2001] W.T.L.R. 1, *Kao Lee and Yup v Koo* [2003] W.T.L.R. 1283..
[30] The Public Trustee has a statutory right to charge under the Public Trustee Act 1906, s.9, as have custodian trustees acting as custodian trustees *only* under the Public Trustee Act 1906, s.4: *Forster v Williams Deacon's Bank* [1935] Ch. 359. Judicial trustees may charge under Judicial Trustees Act 1896, s.1.
[31] *Re Chapple* (1884) 27 Ch.D. 584; *Re Orwell* [1982] 3 All E.R. 177.
[32] *Re Ames* (1883) 25 Ch.D. 72.
[33] *Clarkson v Robinson* [1900] 2 Ch. 722.
[34] Section 33(1) Trustee Act 2000.
[35] s.28(5) *ibid.*

trusts generally or a particular kind of trust." A person acts as a "lay trustee" if he does not act in a professional capacity and is not a trust corporation.[36] For deaths after January 2001 payments of remuneration to a personal representative who (or whose spouse) witnesses the will will not be treated as legacies that fail due to such witnessing and will not abate with other legacies if the estate is unable to pay all legacies in full but will be paid in priority thereto.[37]

Third, by s.29 of the Trustee Act 2000 (unless provision as to entitlement **9–42** to remuneration has been made by the trust instrument or by primary or subordinate legislation[38]—and unless the trust is a charitable trust[39]) a trustee which is a trust corporation is entitled to "reasonable remuneration",[40] while a trustee who acts in a "professional capacity" (as defined in the last paragraph) and is not a sole trustee, is also entitled to reasonable remuneration if each other trustee has agreed in writing that he may be remunerated for the services he provides to the trust,[41] including services capable of being provided by a lay trustee.[42] The power for a trustee to agree that another trustee be remunerated for her services is a power to be exercised in the interests of the beneficiaries as a whole and not for the personal benefit of the trustee to be remunerated or of the power-exerciser,[43] hoping perhaps for a reciprocal agreement for him to be remunerated. However, because it is the legislation that has placed a trustee in an invidious position where there is a sensible possibility of a conflict between self-interest and fiduciary duty, the exercise of the power to agree remuneration of a trustee is not impeachable by reason only that a conflict situation has arisen.[44] Where T_1 and T_2 are to be trustees it is better not to rely on section 29 but on an express remuneration clause: in the absence of the latter, T_1 and T_2 agreeing to each other being remunerated would be vulnerable to attack by disaffected beneficiaries so that to protect themselves T_1 and T_2 would want to obtain the prior consent of adult beneficiaries[45] or the authorisation of the court.[46]

Fourth, if the beneficiaries are all of full capacity and between them **9–43** absolutely entitled to the trust estate, they may authorise the trustee to be paid. If the beneficiaries then sue the trustee for breach of trust in paying trust moneys to himself the trustee has their authorisation as a defence unless undue influence was exercised by him.

Fifth, the general rule of gratuitous service was particularly severe in the case of solicitor-trustees. Thus in *Christophers v White*,[47] it was held that a

---

[36] s.28(6) *ibid.*
[37] s.33(2) *ibid.*
[38] s.29(5) *ibid.*
[39] s.29(1)(b), (2)(b) *ibid.* By s.30 the Secretary of State can make regulations for remuneration of trustees of charitable trusts who are trust corporations or act in a professional capacity.
[40] As defined in s.29(3).
[41] s.29(2).
[42] s.29(4).
[43] See Report on Trustees' Powers and Duties, Law Com No.260 (1999) para.7.10 and Explanatory Note to Trustee Act 2000, para.103.
[44] Cp. *Edge v Pensions Ombudsman* [1998] Ch. 512.
[45] A trustee can invoke s.62 of the Trustee Act 1925 to claim an indemnity from a beneficiary who consented to a breach of trust, so inhibiting action by a descendant of such a beneficiary.
[46] See *Lewin on Trusts* (17th ed.), para.20–149D.
[47] (1847) 10 Beav. 523.

solicitor-trustee's firm was not entitled to charge for professional services rendered to the trust by a partner in the firm even though the partner was not one of the trustees.[48] But where a solicitor-trustee employed his partner, as distinct from his firm, under an *express* agreement that the partner should be individually entitled to charges, these were allowed on the ground that where such an agreement is carried out there is no infringement of the rule that a trustee may not make his office a source of remuneration.[49] Moreover, the severity of the rule was relaxed by the case of *Cradock v Piper*,[50] in which a solicitor-trustee acted as solicitor for himself and his co-trustees in legal proceedings relating to the trust, and was held to be entitled to his usual charges. The rule is that unlike a sole trustee acting as solicitor to the trust, a solicitor-trustee acting in legal proceedings[51] for a body of trustees, of whom he himself is one, is entitled to his usual charges if the fact of his appearing for himself and his co-trustees jointly has not increased the costs which would have been incurred if he had appeared for those co-trustees only.

9–44   Sixth, where the trust property is situate abroad and the law of the foreign country permits payment, the trustee is entitled to keep any remuneration which he has received. Thus in *Re Northcote*,[52] a testator who left assets both in this country and in the United States died domiciled in England, and the principal forum of administration was therefore English. The executors took out an English grant, and on doing so they were put on terms by the Revenue, the English effects being insufficient to pay the English duty, to undertake themselves personally to obtain a grant in New York in respect of the American assets. In due course they obtained such a grant, and got in the assets. Under the law of New York they were entitled to commission for so doing, and Harman J. held that they were under no duty to account for it to the beneficiaries.

Trustee Act 2000

REMUNERATION & EXPENSES

9–45   **28.**—(1) Except to the extent (if any) to which the trust instrument makes inconsistent provision, subsections (2) to (4) apply to a trustee if—

(a) there is a provision in the trust instrument entitling him to receive payment out of trust funds in respect of services provided by him to or on behalf of the trust, and

(b) the trustee is a trust corporation or is acting in a professional capacity.

(2) The trustee is to be treated as entitled under the trust instrument to receive payment in respect of services even if they are services which are capable of being provided by a lay trustee.

---

[48] See also *Re Gates* [1933] Ch. 913 and *Re Hill* [1934] Ch. 623.
[49] *Clack v Carlon* (1861) 30 L.J.Ch. 639.
[50] (1850) 1 Mac. & G. 664.
[51] Legal proceedings need not necessarily be hostile litigation but may be friendly proceedings in chambers: *Re Corsellis* (1887) 34 Ch.D. 675. It must be work in connection with a writ or an originating summons rather than general advisory work not relating to legal proceedings.
[52] [1949] 1 All E.R. 442; see also *Chambers v Goldwin* (1802) 9 Ves. 271.

(3) Subsection (2) applies to a trustee of a charitable trust who is not a trust corporation only—

(a) if he is not a sole trustee, and
(b) to the extent that a majority of the other trustees have agreed that it should apply to him.

(4) Any payments to which the trustee is entitled in respect of services are to be treated as remuneration for services (and not as a gift) for the purposes of—

(a) section 15 of the Wills Act 1837 (gifts to an attesting witness to be void), and
(b) section 34(3) of the Administration of Estates Act 1925 (order in which estate to be paid out).

(5) For the purposes of this Part, a trustee acts in a professional capacity if he acts in the course of a profession or business which consists of or includes the provision of services in connection with—

(a) the management or administration of trusts generally or a particular kind of trust, or
(b) any particular aspect of the management or administration of trusts generally or a particular kind of trust,

and the services he provides to or on behalf of the trust fall within that description.

(6) For the purposes of this Part, a person acts as a lay trustee if he—

(a) is not a trust corporation, and
(b) does not act in a professional capacity.

9–46

29.—(1) Subject to subsection (5), a trustee who—

(a) is a trust corporation, but
(b) is not a trustee of a charitable trust,

is entitled to receive reasonable remuneration out of the trust funds for any services that the trust corporation provides to or on behalf of the trust.

(2) Subject to subsection (5), a trustee who—

(a) acts in a professional capacity, but
(b) is not a trust corporation, a trustee of a charitable trust or a sole trustee,

is entitled to receive reasonable remuneration out of the trust funds for any services that he provides to or on behalf of the trust if each other trustee has agreed in writing that he may be remunerated for the services.

(3) "Reasonable remuneration" means, in relation to the provision of services by a trustee, such remuneration as is reasonable in the circumstances for the provision of those services to or on behalf of that trust by that trustee and for the purposes of subsection (1) includes, in relation to the provision of services by a trustee who is an authorised institution under the Banking Act 1987 and provides the services in that capacity, the institution's reasonable charges for the provision of such services.

(4) A trustee is entitled to remuneration under this section even if the services in question are capable of being provided by a lay trustee.

(5) A trustee is not entitled to remuneration under this section if any provision about his entitlement to remuneration has been made—

(a) by the trust instrument, or
(b) by any enactment or any provision of subordinate legislation.

(6) This section applies to a trustee who has been authorised under a power conferred by Part IV or the trust instrument—

(a) to exercise functions as an agent of the trustees, or
(b) to act as a nominee or custodian,

as it applies to any other trustee.

9–47   30.—(1) The Secretary of State may by regulations make provision for the remuneration of trustees of charitable trusts who are trust corporations or act in a professional capacity.

(2) The power under subsection (1) includes power to make provision for the remuneration of a trustee who has been authorised under a power conferred by Part IV or any other enactment or any provision of subordinate legislation, or by the trust instrument—

(a) to exercise functions as an agent of the trustees, or
(b) to act as a nominee or custodian.

9–48   31.—(1) A trustee—

(a) is entitled to be reimbursed from the trust funds, or
(b) may pay out of the trust funds,

expenses properly incurred by him when acting on behalf of the trust.

(2) This section applies to a trustee who has been authorised under a power conferred by Part IV or any other enactment or any provision of subordinate legislation, or by the trust instrument—

(a) to exercise functions as an agent of the trustees, or
(b) to act as a nominee or custodian,

as it applies to any other trustee.

9–49   32.—(1) This section applies if, under a power conferred by Part IV or any other enactment or any provision of subordinate legislation, or by the trust instrument, a person other than a trustee has been—

(a) authorised to exercise functions as an agent of the trustees, or
(b) appointed to act as a nominee or custodian.

(2) The trustees may remunerate the agent, nominee or custodian out of the trust funds for services if—

(a) he is engaged on terms entitling him to be remunerated for those services, and

(b) the amount does not exceed such remuneration as is reasonable in the circumstances for the provision of those services by him to or on behalf of that trust.

(3) The trustees may reimburse the agent, nominee or custodian out of the trust funds for any expenses properly incurred by him in exercising functions as an agent, nominee or custodian.

33.—(1) Subject to subsection (2), sections 28, 29, 31 and 32 apply in relation to **9–50** services provided to or on behalf of, or (as the case may be) expenses incurred on or after their commencement on behalf of, trusts whenever created.
(2) Nothing in section 28 or 29 is to be treated as affecting the operation of—

(a) section 15 of the Wills Act 1837, or
(b) section 34(3) of the Administration of Estates Act 1925,

in relation to any death occurring before the commencement of section 28 or (as the case may be) section 29.

Section 3. Investment of Trust Funds

A fundamental function of the trustees is to invest and manage the trust **9–51** fund so that there is adequate income and capital available for the beneficiaries when the trustees come to exercise their other fundamental function, their distributive function. First, the trustees must familiarise themselves with their powers of investment so that they know which investments are within or outside their powers. Second, in deciding whether to sell or purchase investments within the authorised range of investments, the trustees must comply with further duties.

I. THE RANGE OF AUTHORISED INVESTMENTS

Trustees are under a fundamental duty to invest the trust funds in **9–52** investments authorised expressly or impliedly by the trust instrument or by the court[53] or in default by the Trustee Act 2000. A properly drafted trust instrument will contain very extensive powers of investment so that there is no need to apply to the court for wider powers or otherwise rely upon the Trustee Act 2000 which applies to pre-existing trusts (from February 1, 2001) as well as new trusts. If a testator by specific gift leaves certain investments (*e.g.* my apartments in Tenerife) to trustees for A for life, then B absolutely, this impliedly authorises the trustees to retain such investments but not to purchase any more.[54] If personal representatives appropriate property to trustees under section 41 of the Administration of Estates

---

[53] The court's powers are in Trustee Act 1925, s.57 and the Variation of Trusts Act 1958.
[54] *Re Pugh* [1887] W.N. 143; *Re Whitfield* (1920) 125 L.T. 61.

Act 1925, then such property is by such section thereafter treated as an authorised investment for purposes of retention but not for purchasing more of the same.

If an express investment power is void for uncertainty[55] (*e.g.* to invest in blue chip shares and such other investments as my trustees know I would approve of) then the trustees are relegated to the powers under the 2000 Act unless they obtain wider powers from the court.

II. Duties when Investing

To exhibit the statutory duty of care like a prudent person conducting another's affairs

9–53   Trustees must exhibit the statutory duty of care[56] like a prudent person, investing not for himself but for others, when they are exercising their powers of investment, reviewing investments in the light of the standard investment criteria and obtaining and considering proper advice.[57] It is considered that "such care and skill as is reasonable in the circumstances" must take account of the fact, as old case law did,[58] that prudent business persons may reasonably select some speculative investments for themselves, which they should avoid if investing for the future of someone who is depending on the trust fund as a safe and sound basis for securing her future. Thus, the Trustee Act 2000 has not affected the following risk averse approach summarised by Lord Nicholls.[59] "It is not enough that a trustee should act honestly. Promotion of the trust purpose requires a trustee to be prudent and exercise the degree of care he would in conducting his own affairs but mindful, when making investment decisions, that he is dealing with another's property. The classic formulation of this standard of conduct was enunciated by Lindley L.J. in *Re Whiteley*[60] The duty of a trustee is not to take such care only as a prudent man would take if he had only himself to consider; the duty is rather to take such care as an ordinary prudent man would take if he were minded to make an investment for the benefit of other people for whom he felt morally bound to provide. . . . This 'ordinary prudent person conducting another's affairs' is the equitable counterpart of the reasonable man who is so ubiquitous in the common law . . . A comment is needed here on the ordinary prudent person. His standards are the minimum standards expected of trustees. If the trustee is a person professing particular expertise in the management of trusts, and he has been appointed for that reason, his conduct will be judged by the standards he professes. A professional person, a trust

---

[55] *Re Kolb's W.T.* [1962] Ch. 531.
[56] Set out at para.9–41 above; it may be excluded or modified by the trust instrument: Trustee Act 2000 Sch.1, para.7.
[57] Trustee Act 2000, Sch.1 paras 1 and 2.
[58] *Re Whiteley* (1886) 33 Ch.D. 347 at 355 endorsed thereafter in every case involving trustees' alleged breaches of their investment duties.
[59] (1995) 9 Trust L.I. 71 at 73.
[60] (1886) 33 Ch.D. 347 at 355.

corporation, held out as an expert, will be expected to display the degree of skill and care and diligence such an expert would have."

Lord Nicholls went on to endorse the view of Hoffmann J. (as he then was) who had stated[61] "Modern trustees acting within their investment powers are entitled to be judged by the standards of current portfolio theory, which emphasises the risk level of the entire portfolio rather than the risk attaching to each investment taken in isolation." After all, as Dillon L.J. has emphasised,[62] "What the prudent man should do at any time depends on the economic and financial conditions of that time not on what judges of the past, however eminent, have held to be the prudent course in the conditions of 50 or 100 years before . . . when investment conditions were very different." **9–54**

As Lord Nicholls states,[63] "Investment policy is aimed at producing a portfolio of investments which is balanced overall and suited to the needs of the particular trust. Different investments are accompanied by different degrees of risk, which are reflected in the expected rate of return. A large fund with a widely diversified portfolio of securities might justifiably include modest holdings of high risk securities which would be imprudent and out of place in a smaller fund. In such a case it would be inappropriate to isolate one particular investment out of a vast portfolio and enquire whether that can be justified as a trust investment. Such a "line by line" approach is misplaced. The inquiry, rather, should be to look at a particular investment and enquire whether that is justified as a holding in the context of the overall portfolio. Traditional warnings against the need for trustees to avoid speculative or hazardous investments are not to be read as inhibiting trustees from maintaining portfolios of investments which contain a prudent and sensible mixture of low risk and higher risk securities. They are not to be so read, because they were not directed at a portfolio which is a balanced exercise in risk management." **9–55**

This requires portfolio securities having a low co-variance with each other where a positive co-variance means the values of two assets are likely to move in the same direction and a low co-variance means the values are likely to move in opposite directions. Having dissimilar investments is not sufficient: real estate and government bonds are different, but when interest rates increase both types of investment suffer and *vice versa*. The proportions of different types of asset within the portfolio are crucial for achieving the purposes of the fund, the most basic proportion being that between equity and debt, *viz.* between stocks and shares and fixed interest securities, *e.g.* 60 per cent to 40 per cent or *vice versa*. **9–56**

The ordinary prudent person conducting another's affairs will of course review the portfolio of investments regularly[64] and if lacking investment knowledge will of course seek professional advice and consider such advice before acting upon it.[65] **9–57**

---

[61] *Nestlé v National Westminster Bank plc* June 29, 1988, [2000] W.T.L.R. 795 at 802.
[62] *Nestlé v National Westminster Bank plc* [1994] 1 All E.R. 118 at 126.
[63] Article cited in n.59 above. On modern portfolio theory see J. Langbein (1996) 81 Iowa L.R. 641 and I. N. Legair (2000) 14 Trust L.I. 75.
[64] *Nestlé v National Westminster Bank plc* [1994] 1 All E.R. 118.
[65] *Cowan v Scargill* [1985] Ch. 270; *Jones v AMP Perpetual Trustee Co. N.Z. Ltd* [1994] 1 N.Z.L.R. 690.

9–58   Sections 4 and 5 of the Trustee Act 2000 now expressly impose such duties upon trustees as follows:

Section 4:

> "(1) In exercising any power of investment, whether arising under this Part *or otherwise*, a trustee must have regard to the standard investment criteria.
>
> (2) A trustee must from time to time review the investments of the trust and consider whether, having regard to the standard investment criteria, they should be varied.
>
> (3) The standard investment criteria, in relation to a trust, are—
>
> > (a) the suitability to the trust of investments of the same kind as any particular investment proposed to be made or retained and of that particular investment as an investment of that kind, and
> >
> > (b) the need for diversification of investments of the trust, *in so far as is appropriate* to the circumstances of the trust."[66]

Section 5:

9–59   "(1) Before exercising any power of investment, whether arising under this Part *or otherwise*, a trustee must (unless the exception applies) obtain and consider proper advice about the way in which, having regard to the standard investment criteria, the power should be exercised.

> (2) When reviewing the investments of the trust, a trustee must (unless the exception applies) obtain and consider proper advice about whether, having regard to the standard investment criteria, the investments should be varied.
>
> (3) The exception is that a trustee need not obtain such advice if he reasonably concludes that in all the circumstances it is unnecessary or inappropriate to do so.
>
> (4) Proper advice is the advice of a person who is reasonably believed by the trustee to be qualified to give it by his ability in and practical experience of financial and other matters relating to the proposed investment."

9–60   It will be seen that proper advice is not needed if the trustee reasonably concludes (an objective test) that in all the circumstances it is unnecessary or inappropriate (*e.g.* the investment seems a safe one and a small one or the trustee is an experienced knowledgeable investor), while it would seem proper advice could be that of a co-trustee or employee reasonably believed by the trustee to be qualified to give it.[67] It will be advisable to have the

---

[66] The duty to diversify may be ousted expressly or by necessary implication, *e.g.* where the settler intended the trustee to retain a majority shareholding in a family company comprising by far the greatest valued part of the trust fund.

[67] See subsections (3) and (4) between which there may be an overlap.

advice in writing and also to record in writing when advice is considered unnecessary or inappropriate.

Often trustees will delegate their asset management functions[68] to a land agent or a discretionary portfolio manager and have investments held by a nominee or custodian.[69] There must be a written agreement as to the terms of asset management delegation coupled with a policy statement, while there is a duty to keep the delegation arrangements and the policy statement under regular review—as is considered para.9–110.

To act fairly

A "trustee must act fairly in making investment decisions which may have **9–61** different consequences for differing classes of beneficiaries,"[70] *e.g.* life tenant and remainderman. As Hoffmann J. stated[71]:

> "The trustees have a wide discretion. They are, for example, entitled to take into account the income needs of the tenant for life or the fact that the tenant for life was a person known to the settlor and a primary object of the trust whereas the remainderman is a remoter relative or stranger. Of course, these cannot be allowed to become the overriding considerations but the concept of fairness between classes of beneficiaries does not require them to be excluded. It would be an inhuman rule which required trustees to adhere to some mechanical rule for preserving the real value of the capital when the tenant for life was the testator's widow who had fallen upon hard times and the remainderman was young and well-off."

On appeal Staughton L.J. stated[72]:

> "A life tenant may be anxious to receive the highest possible income **9–62** while the remainderman will wish the real value of the fund to be preserved. If the life tenant is living in penury and the remainderman already has ample wealth common sense suggests that a trustee should be able to take that into account, not necessarily by seeking the highest possible income at the expense of capital but by inclining in that direction. However, before adopting that course a trustee should require some verification of the facts . . . Similarly, I would not regard it as a breach of trust for the trustees to pay some regard to the relationship between Mr. George Nestlé and Miss Nestlé. He was merely her uncle and she would have received nothing from his share of the fund if he had fathered a child who survived him. The trustees would be entitled to incline towards income during his life tenancy . . . I do not think it would be a breach of the duty to act fairly or impartially."

---

[68] Trustee Act 2000, ss.11, 12, 13, 14, 15.
[69] *ibid.*, ss.16, 17, 19, 20. Pension trustees are governed by Pensions Act 1995 and 2004 at paras 9–327 to 9–335.
[70] *Nestlé v National Westminster Bank*, June 29, 1988, [2000] W.T.L.R. 795 at 803.
[71] *ibid.*
[72] *Nestlé v National Westminster Bank plc* [1994] 1 All E.R. 118 at 137.

9–63   Where there is a life tenant the distinction between income and capital is crucial because the life tenant is only entitled to income, though in selecting investments, as Hoffmann J. and Staughton L.J. make clear, the trustees have a discretion in appropriate circumstances to favour income-producing investments at the expense of the remainderman (or capital-growth investments at the expense of the life tenant). Where, as will almost always be the case for a well-drafted trust, there is a power to appoint capital to the life tenant, the trustees will have the flexibility to invest a greater part than otherwise would be possible in assets yielding little or no income but where much capital growth is expected, so that they can then sell some of such assets and appoint the proceeds (capital) to the life tenant to make up for the income lost by investing in fewer assets yielding a good income.

9–64   After all, economists and investors are concerned with the concept of total return, *i.e.* income yield plus capital growth. The legal concept of capital based on land settled on persons in succession regards capital as the tree and income as the fruit of the tree,[73] though the economist's view of income is exemplified by the well-known definition of Hicks[74]: "Income is the maximum amount the individual can consume in a week and still expect to be as well-off at the end of the week as he was at the beginning." Thus, if £1 million of trust assets appreciate to be worth £1,100,000 at the end of the year and yield income of £40,000 then the total return of £140,000 less an amount for inflation can be spent without the trust fund being any worse off than it was at the outset. To make allowance for annual ups and downs of the stock market it may be advisable to have a policy, if the terms of the trust allow it, to pay out the equivalent of five per cent of the value of the fund at the end of the year including the income produced that year. This can be done not just for many charitable[75] and pension trusts but also for well-drafted discretionary trusts or even well-drafted fixed interest trusts where the trustees have power to appoint capital to any beneficiary.[76]

9–65   Judges nowadays emphasise the total return. Megarry V.-C. stated[77] that the power of investment "must be exercised so as to yield the best return for the beneficiaries, judged in relation to the risks of the investments in question; and the prospects of the yield of income and of capital appreciation both have to be considered in judging the return from the investment" while Nicholls V.-C. stated[78] that charity trustees should seek:

> "the maximum return, whether by income or capital growth, which is consistent with commercial prudence . . . having due regard to the need to diversify, the need to balance income against capital growth and the need to balance risk against return."

---

[73] L. H. Seltzer, *The Nature and Tax Treatment of Capital Gains and Losses* 1951, Chap.2.
[74] J. R. Hicks, *Value and Capital*, (1938), p.172. Further see J. Flower, A Note on Capital and Income in the Law of Trusts in Edey & Yamey (eds.) *Debits, Credits, Finance and Profits* (1974), pp.85–87.
[75] But not in respect of endowment capital providing the permanent base for the charity's activities.
[76] The Law Commission in its Consultation Paper No.175, "Capital and Income in Trusts: Classification and Apportionment", supports the total return approach, going so far as to recommend trustees having a statutory power of allocation of receipts into income and capital regardless of whether the receipt is fruit of the tree or the tree itself: see paras 5.41 to 5.48 thereof.
[77] *Cowan v Scargill* [1985] Ch. 270 at 287.
[78] *Harries v Church Commissioners* [1992] 1 W.L.R. 1241 at 1246.

To do the best they can financially for the beneficiaries as a whole

The last two quotations of Megarry V.-C. and Nicholls V.-C. make plain **9–66** the fundamental duty of trustees to do the best they can financially for the beneficiaries. Indeed, if trustees have agreed to sell Blackacre so as to be morally bound but not yet legally bound by a contract, they are under a duty to gazump (*i.e.* negotiate with someone putting in a serious higher offer) so as to obtain a higher price for the beneficiaries, even if as honourable men they would prefer to implement the bargain to which they felt in honour bound: *Buttle v Saunders*.[79] If they have strong opinions against alcohol or investment in "Genocidia" then if such investments would be likely to be more beneficial financially than other proposed investments they must purchase those investments despite finding them disagreeable.[80] However, if trustees obtain professional advice that particular investments other than in alcohol or in Genocidia are equally satisfactory for the portfolio from the financial point of view then, of course, they can proceed to purchase those other investments. Thus, "all things being equal," trustees can refuse to invest in companies whose products or policies they find disagreeable.[81] Indeed Lord Nicholls has concluded,[82]

> "In practice in these cases where trustees or [beneficiaries] have strong **9–67** views about particular investments on non-financial grounds it should be possible for trustees to exercise their investment powers in a manner avoiding embarrassment to all concerned without upsetting the balance of the portfolio . . . The range of investment is so extensive that there is scope for trustees to give effect to moral considerations without thereby prejudicing beneficiaries' financial interests."

A settlor, of course, can always restrict the trustees' powers of investment **9–68** by excluding certain types of investments and can always reduce the duties owed by the trustees, *e.g.* by permitting or directing the trustees to invest only in companies whose products or policies are ecologically more beneficial than those of other competing companies in the opinion of the trustees and by exempting[83] the trustees from any liability so long as they acted in good faith.

In the case of charitable trusts, the trustees must consider whether a **9–69** particular investment is consistent with its charitable purposes so that, for example, it would not be proper for a trust concerned to rehabilitate alcoholics and prevent alcoholism to invest in companies manufacturing and distributing alcoholic drinks or for a trust for the Society of Friends to invest in shares in companies engaged in the armaments industry.[84]

---

[79] [1950] 2 All E.R. 193.
[80] *Cowan v Scargill* [1985] Ch. 270.
[81] See Sir Robert Megarry in *Equity, Fiduciaries and Trusts* (T. G. Youdan ed.), pp.149–159.
[82] In "Trustees and Their Broader Community: Where Duty, Morality and Ethics Converge" (1995) 9 Trust L.I. 71 at 75.
[83] On exemption clauses see at paras 9–250 *et seq.*
[84] *Martin v Edinburgh D.C.* [1989] I Pensions L.R. 9; *Harries v Church Commissioners* [1992] 1 W.L.R. 1241. Trustees should shun holdings of investments which might hamper a charity's work by making potential receipients of aid unwilling to be helped or by alienating some of those who support the charity financially or by voluntary work.

American guidance on investment considerations

The American Uniform Prudent Investor Act seems to reflect the English position when it states in section 2(c) "Among circumstances that a trustee shall consider in investing and managing trust assets are such of the following as are relevant to the trust or its beneficiaries:

(1) general economic conditions;
(2) the possible impact of inflation or deflation;
(3) the expected tax consequences[85] of investment decisions or strategies;
(4) the role that each investment or course of action plays within the overall trust portfolio;
(5) the expected total return from income and the appreciation of capital;
(6) other resources of the beneficiaries;
(7) needs for liquidity, regularity of income, and preservation or appreciation of capital; and
(8) an assets special relationship or special value, if any, to the purposes of the trust or to one or more of the beneficiaries."

This is buttressed by section 2(d), "A trustee shall make a reasonable effort[86] to verify facts relevant to the investment and management of the trust assets." In England, statute[87] only provides detailed guidance for pensions trustees, as discussed, paras 9–324 *et seq.*

Extent of liability

9–70	Liability will normally be to account for a *loss* caused by purchasing an unauthorised investment or by recklessly or negligently purchasing a wholly inappropriate authorised investment.[88] Exceptionally, it may be possible to make out a case that the trustee should be liable to account for a *profit* that ought to have been made, *e.g.* fair compensation taking account of the proper per centage that should have been invested in shares and not just interest-yielding gilts or bonds, and of the average performance of shares in the period.[89] However, as Hoffmann J. said,[90] "In reviewing the conduct of trustees over a period of more than 60 years, one must be careful not to endow the prudent trustee with prophetic vision or expect him to have ignored the received wisdom of his time," *e.g.* as to the balance between gilt-edged securities and company shares. Where trustees invest in authorised investments it is difficult to make them liable for negligent breach of their equitable and statutory duties of care. It has to be proved that the

---

[85] See *Nestlé v National Westminster Bank plc* [1993] 1 W.L.R. 1260.
[86] *ibid.*
[87] Pensions Act 1995, ss.35, 36.
[88] See paras 10–09 *et seq.*
[89] *Nestlé v National Westminster Bank plc* [1993] 1 W.L.R. 1260 at 1268 and 1280 applied in *Re Mulligan* [1998] 1 N.Z.L.R. 481.
[90] *Nestlé v National Westminster Bank*, June 29, 1988, [2000] W.T.L.R. 795.

trustees' course of conduct was a course which no properly informed[91] prudent trustee could have followed, so affording trustees plenty of leeway.[92]

COWAN v SCARGILL

Chancery Division [1985] Ch. 270; [1984] 2 All E.R. 750; [1984] 3 W.L.R. 501

MEGARRY V.-C.: "I turn to the law. The starting point is the duty of trustees to **9–71** exercise their powers in the best interests of the present and future beneficiaries of the trust, holding the scales impartially between different classes of beneficiaries. This duty of the trustees towards their beneficiaries is paramount. They must, of course, obey the law; but subject to that, they must put the interests of their beneficiaries first. When the purpose of the trust is to provide financial benefits for the beneficiaries, as is usually the case, the best interests of the beneficiaries are normally their best financial interests. In the case of a power of investment, as in the present case, the power must be exercised so as to yield the best return for the beneficiaries, judged in relation to the risks of the investments in question; and the prospects for the yield of income and capital appreciation both have to be considered in judging the return from the investment.

"The legal memorandum that the union obtained from their solicitors is generally **9–72** in accord with these views. In considering the possibility of investment for 'socially beneficial reasons which may result in lower returns to the fund,' the memorandum states that 'the trustees' only concern is to ensure that the return is the maximum possible consistent with security'; and then it refers to the need for diversification. However, it continues by saying that:

> 'Trustees cannot be criticised for failing to make a particular investment for social or political reasons, such as in South African stock for example, but may be held liable for investing in assets which yield a poor return or for disinvesting in stock at inappropriate times for non-financial criteria.'

This last sentence must be considered in the light of subsequent passages in the **9–73** memorandum which indicate that the sale of South African securities by trustees might be justified on the ground of doubts about political stability in South Africa and the long-term financial soundness of its economy, whereas trustees could not properly support motions at a company meeting dealing with pay levels in South Africa, work accidents, pollution control, employment conditions for minorities, military contracting and consumer protection. The assertion that trustees could not be criticised for failing to make a particular investment for social or political reasons is one that I would not accept in its full width. If the investment in fact made is equally beneficial to the beneficiaries, then criticism would be difficult to sustain in practice, whatever the position in theory. But if the investment in fact made is less beneficial, then both in theory and in practice the trustees would normally be open to criticism.

---

[91] Taking account of relevant considerations like those set out in the American Uniform Prudent Investor Act. Further see J. Dobris, "Speculations on the idea of 'Speculation' in Trust Investing" (2004) 39 *Real Property, Probate and Trust Journal* 439.

[92] *Wight v Olswang (No.2)* (2000) 2 I.T.E.L.R. 689, [2000] W.T.L.R. 783 reversed (on other grounds) on appeal [2001] W.T.L.R. 291, *Nestlé v National Westminster Bank* [1993] 1 W.L.R. 1260 at 1281 *per* Staughton L.J. "I cannot accept that failure to diversify in that decade was a course which no prudent trustee would have followed."

9–74   "This leads me to the second point, which is a corollary of the first. In considering what investments to make trustees must put on one side their own personal interests and views. Trustees may have strongly held social or political views. They may be firmly opposed to any investment in South Africa or other countries, or they may object to any form of investment in companies concerned with alcohol, tobacco, armaments or many other things. In the conduct of their own affairs, of course, they are free to abstain from making any such investments. Yet under a trust, if investments of this type would be more beneficial to the beneficiaries than other investments, the trustees must not refrain from making the investments by reasons of the views that they hold.

"Trustees may even have to act dishonourably (though not illegally) if the interests of their beneficiaries require it. Thus where trustees for sale had struck a bargain for the sale of trust property but had not bound themselves by a legally enforceable contract, they were held to be under a duty to consider and explore a better offer that they received, and not to carry through the bargain to which they felt in honour bound: see *Buttle v Saunders* [1950] 2 All E.R. 193. In other words, the duty of trustees to their beneficiaries may include a duty to 'gazump,' however honourable the trustees. As Wynn-Parry J. said (at 195), trustees 'have an overriding duty to obtain the best price which they can for their beneficiaries.' . . .

Powers must be exercised fairly and honestly for the purposes for which they are given and not so as to accomplish any ulterior purpose, whether for the benefit of the trustees or otherwise: see *Duke of Portland v Topham* (1864) 11 H.L. Cas. 32 a case on a power of appointment that must apply a fortiori to a power given to trustees as such.

9–75   "Third, by way of a caveat I should say that I am not asserting that the benefit of the beneficiaries which a trustee must make his paramount concern inevitably and solely means their financial benefit, even if the only object of the trust is to provide financial benefits. Thus if the only actual or potential beneficiaries of a trust are all adults with very strict views on moral and social matters, condemning all forms of alcohol, tobacco and popular entertainment, as well as armaments, I can well understand that it might not be for the "benefit" of such beneficiaries to know that they are obtaining rather larger financial returns under the trust by reason of investments in those activities than they would have received if the trustees had invested the trust funds in other investments. The beneficiaries might well consider that it was far better to receive less than to receive more money from what they consider to be evil and tainted sources. 'Benefit' is a word with a very wide meaning, and there are circumstances in which arrangements which work to the financial disadvantage of a beneficiary may yet be for his benefit: see, for example, *Re Towler's Settlement Trusts* [1964]Ch. 158; *Re C L* [1969] 1 Ch. 587. But I would emphasise that such cases are likely to be very rare, and in any case I think that under a trust for the provision of financial benefits the burden would rest, and rest heavy, on him who asserts that it is for the benefit of the beneficiaries as a whole to receive less by reason of the exclusion of some of the possibly more profitable forms of investment. Plainly the present case is not one of this rare type of case. Subject to such matters, under a trust for the provision of financial benefits, the paramount duty of the trustees is to provide the greatest financial benefits for the present and future beneficiaries.

9–76   "Fourth, the standard required of a trustee in exercising his powers of investment is that he must—

'. . . take such care as an ordinary prudent man would take if he were minded to make an investment for the benefit of other people for whom he felt morally bound to provide.'

See *Re Whiteley* (1886) 33 Ch.D. 347 at 355 *per* Lindley L.J. and see also at 350, 358; *Learoyd v Whiteley* (1887) 12 App. Cas. 727. That duty includes the duty to seek advice on matters which the trustee does not understand, such as the making of investments, and on receiving that advice to act with the same degree of prudence. This requirement is not discharged merely by showing that the trustee has acted in good faith and with sincerity. Honesty and sincerity are not the same as prudence and reasonableness. Some of the most sincere people are the most unreasonable; and Mr. Scargill told me that he had met quite a few of them. Accordingly, although a trustee who takes advice on investments is not bound to accept and act on that advice, he is not entitled to reject it merely because he sincerely disagrees with it, unless in addition to being sincere he is acting as an ordinary prudent man would act.

"Fifth, trustees have a duty to consider the need for diversification of investments. **9–77** By section 6(1) of the Trustee Investments Act 1961[93]:

'In the exercise of his powers of investment a trustee shall have regard—(a) to the need for diversification of investments of the trust, in so far as is appropriate to the circumstances of the trust; (b) to the suitability to the trust of investments of the description of investment proposed and of the investment proposed as an investment of that description."

The degree of diversification that is practicable and desirable for a large fund may plainly be impracticable or undesirable (or both) in the case of a small fund. "In the case before me, it is not in issue that there ought to be diversification of **9–78** the investments held by the fund. The contention of the defendants, put very shortly, is that there can be a sufficient degree of diversification without any investment overseas or in oil, and that in any case there is no need to increase the level of overseas investments beyond the existing level. Other pension funds got on well enough without overseas investments, it was said, and in particular the NUM's own scheme had, in 1982, produced better results than the scheme here in question. . . "I shall not pursue this matter. Even if other funds in one particular year, or in many years, had done better than the scheme which is before me, that does not begin to show that it is beneficial to this scheme to be shorn of the ability to invest overseas. . . .

"Sixth, there is the question whether the principles that I have been stating apply, **9–79** with or without modification, to trusts of pension funds. Counsel for the plaintiffs asserted that they applied without modification, and that it made no difference that some of the funds came from the members of the pension scheme, or that the funds were often of a very substantial size. Mr. Scargill did not in terms assert the contrary. He merely said that this was one of the questions to be decided, and that pension funds may be subject to different rules. I was somewhat unsuccessful in my attempts to find out from him why this was so, and what the differences were. What it came down to, I think, was that the rules for trusts had been laid down for private and family trusts and wills a long time ago; that pension funds were very large and affected large numbers of people; that in the present case the well-being of all within the coal industry was affected; . . .

"I can see no reason for holding that different principles apply to pension fund **9–80** trusts[94] from those which apply to other trusts. Of course, there are many provisions in pension schemes which are not to be found in private trusts, and to these the

---

[93] Replaced by Trustee Act 2000, s.4(3), at para.9–58 above.
[94] For detailed investment criteria now see Pension Act 1995, s.35 para.9–332.

general law of trusts will be subordinated. But subject to that, I think that the trusts of pension funds are subject to the same rules as other trusts. The large size of pension funds emphasises the need for diversification, rather than lessening it, and the fact that much of the fund has been contributed by members of the scheme seems to me to make it even more important that the trustees should exercise their powers in the best interests of the beneficiaries. In a private trust, most, if not all, of the beneficiaries are the recipients of the bounty of the settlor, whereas under the trusts of a pension fund many (though not all) of the beneficiaries are those who, as members, contributed to the funds so that in due time they would receive pensions. It is thus all the more important that the interests of the beneficiaries should be paramount, so that they may receive the benefits which in part they have paid for. I can see no justification for holding that the benefits to them should run the risk of being lessened because the trustees were pursuing an investment policy intended to assist the industry that the pensioners have left, or their union . . .

9–81   "I reach the unhesitating conclusion that the trusts of pension funds are in general governed by the ordinary law of trusts, subject to any contrary provision in the rules or other provisions which govern the trust. In particular, the trustees of a pension fund are subject to the overriding duty to do the best that they can for the beneficiaries, the duty that in the United States is known as 'the duty of undivided loyalty to the beneficiaries' (see *Blankenship v Boyle* 329 F.Supp.1089 at 1095).

"In considering that duty, it must be remembered that very many of the beneficiaries will not in any way be directly affected by the prosperity of the mining industry or the union. Miners who have retired, and the widows and children of deceased miners, will continue to receive their benefits from the fund even if the mining industry shrinks: for the scheme is fully funded, and the fund does not depend on further contributions to it being made. I cannot regard any policy designed to ensure the general prosperity of coal mining as being a policy which is directed to obtaining the best possible results for the beneficiaries, most of whom are no longer engaged in the industry, and some of whom never were. The connection is far too remote and insubstantial. Further, the assets of even so large a pension fund as this are nowhere near the size at which there could be expected to be any perceptible impact from the adoption of the policies for which Mr. Scargill contends . . ."

NESTLÉ v NATIONAL WESTMINSTER BANK PLC

Court of Appeal (Dillon, Staughton and Leggatt L.JJ.) [1995] 1 W.L.R. 1260; [1994] 1 All E.R. 118.

9–82   STAUGHTON L.J.: "When Mr. William Nestlé died in 1922, the value of his trust fund (after payment of debts, legacies and estate duty) was about £50,000. In November 1986, when the plaintiff, his granddaughter Miss Georgina Nestlé, became absolutely entitled after the death of the last life tenant, it was worth £269,203. That, it might be thought, was a substantial improvement. But during the same period the cost of living had multiplied by a factor of 20, so that it would have required £1m. to provide equivalent wealth: see the B.Z.W. equity-gilt study of 1988. The same source shows that an equity price index rose by 5203 per cent. in that period. An equivalent appreciation in the value of the trust fund would have left it worth £2.6m. in 1986. It is true that a small portion of the fund was advanced to life tenants, that some capital was used to supplement income for an annuity, and that there were no doubt transaction costs; against that, a sum of about £5,000 was added to the fund in

1959 when Mr. Nestlé's house and contents were sold. Nevertheless, it is apparent that the investments retained or made by the trustees fell woefully short of maintaining the real value of the fund, let alone matching the average increase in price of ordinary shares.

"Of course it is not a breach of trust to invest the trust fund in such a manner that **9–83** its real value is not maintained. At times that will be impossible, and at others it will require extraordinary skill or luck. The highest that even the plaintiff puts her claim is that, if the equity portion in the fund as it stood in 1922 (74 per cent) had been invested so as to achieve no more than the index, the fund as a whole would have been worth over £1.8m. in 1986 . . .

"In the experts' reports and during the course of the trial it appeared that there were four main strands to the plaintiff's case. (1) The trustees misunderstood the investment clause in the will. (2) The trustees failed to conduct a regular and periodic review of the investments. (3) Throughout the trust period, but in particular in the later stages when there were life tenants domiciled abroad, they retained or bought too high a proportion of fixed interest securities and too few ordinary shares. (4) To the extent that the trustees did invest in ordinary shares, they concentrated too heavily on shares in banking and insurance companies, to the exclusion of other sectors.

Misunderstanding, and failure to review

"In my judgment the first two charges were proved. It was admitted that at times the **9–84** trustees misunderstood the investment clause; but the evidence showed that they continually misunderstood it, and there is nothing to show that they ever understood it correctly. To a novice in these matters it seems that they might deserve to be forgiven, since only among much other detail are to be found the words 'stocks shares bonds debentures or securities of any railway or other company.' But there is authority which shows plainly that the word 'company' in such a clause is not limited by its context. Trustees are not allowed to make mistakes in law; they should take legal advice, and if they are still left in doubt they can apply to the court for a ruling. Either course would have revealed their mistake in this case.

"I also consider that, for a substantial period, the trustees failed to conduct **9–85** regular periodic reviews of the investments. From 1922 to 1959 there was only one change of an investment, other than changes which were forced on the trustees by rights issues or because a security reached its redemption date . . .

"However, the misunderstanding of the investment clause and the failure to conduct periodic reviews do not by themselves, whether separately or together, afford the plaintiff a remedy. They were symptoms of incompetence or idleness— not on the part of National Westminster Bank but of their predecessors; they were not, without more, breaches of trust. The plaintiff must show that, through one or other or both of those causes, the trustees made decisions which they should not have made or failed to make decisions which they should have made. If that were proved, and if at first sight loss resulted, it would be appropriate to order an inquiry as to the loss suffered by the trust fund.

"It may be difficult to discharge that burden, and particularly to show that decisions were not taken when they should have been. But that does not absolve a plaintiff from discharging it, and I cannot find that it was discharged in this case . . .

The balance of the fund between equities and gilts

"That brings me to what I regard as the substance of the case, the failure to invest a **9–86** higher proportion of the trust fund in ordinary shares. Here one must take care to avoid two errors. First, the trustees' performance must not be judged with hindsight:

after the event even a fool is wise, as a poet said nearly 3,000 years ago. Secondly (unless this is the same point), one must bear in mind that investment philosophy was very different in the early years of this trust from what it became later. Inflation was non-existent, overall, from 1921 to 1938. It occurred in modest degree during the war years, and became a more persistent phenomenon from 1947 onwards. Equities were regarded as risky during the 1920s and 1930s, and yielded a higher return then gilt-edged securities. It was only in 1959 that the so-called reverse yield gap occurred.

9–87   "During the period from 1922 until the death of Mrs. Barbara Nestlé in 1960, the proportion of ordinary shares in the trust fund as a whole varied between 46 and 82 per cent. Until 1951 it never rose above 57 per cent.; there was then quite a sharp rise until 1960, not caused by any change in investment policy but presumably by a general rise in the value of ordinary shares (183 per cent., according to the index, between 1950 and 1960).

"In my judgment the trustees are not shown to have failed in their duties at any time up to 1959 in this respect. I cannot say that, in the light of investment conditions then prevailing, they were in breach of trust by not holding a higher proportion of ordinary shares. In addition, they were charged with the duty of providing an annuity of £1,500 after tax for the widow of Mr. William Nestlé, and of setting aside a fund for that purpose. The plaintiff's expert witnesses were themselves disinclined to criticise the balance of the fund, as between fixed interest and ordinary shares, in that period.

"After 1959 the situation had changed. Mrs. Barbara Nestlé died in October 1960, and the trustees were relieved of the task of providing for her annuity. The cult of the equity had begun by then, if not some years before. From that date I would accept the evidence of the plaintiff's experts that, all other things being equal, there should be at least 50 per cent. of the fund in ordinary shares.

9–88   "The trustees' experts countered that on two grounds. First, they pointed to evidence that pension funds and life assurance companies continued to invest less than half their funds in equities, and a substantial proportion in gilt-edged securities. Counsel for the plaintiff provided us with a calculation which was said to disprove this in the case of pension funds. But it had not been made in the court below or put to witnesses, and was incomplete for this purpose . . .

"There is in my opinion a better answer to this comparison. Life assurance companies and pension funds have as their primary duty an obligation to pay at some future date a sum that is fixed in monetary terms. No doubt they offer profits, or an increase on the promised pension; and it may be that even in 1959 there was competition between companies by reference to their past records of success. But I am convinced that they could be expected to follow a policy of considerable caution in order to ensure that, come what may, their minimum obligations in monetary terms were fulfilled. I do not regard them as a reliable guide to what would have been done by private investors, or should have been done by trustees of a private family trust.

"The second point is this, Professor Briston, who gave evidence for the plaintiff, made a calculation on the basis that the part of the trust fund which was invested in ordinary shares initially remained in ordinary shares throughout. His calculation shows that, if one takes the 74 per cent proportion of equities when Mr. William Nestlé died, the fund as a whole would have grown to £1.8m. in 1986. Alternatively, the portfolio had a proportion of 54 per cent in equities after the setting up of the annuity fund and some restructuring between 1922 and 1924; if that part of the fund had remained in ordinary shares, the value of the fund as a whole would in 1986 have been £1.36m.

"I have already expressed the view that, in the light of investment conditions then **9–89** prevailing, the trustees are not to be criticised over the balance of the fund between fixed interest and equities in the period from 1922 to 1959. It follows that I do not accept the evidence of Professor Briston that they ought to have acted differently in that period. Neither did he persist in it when cross-examined . . .

"In my judgment they should, in the investment climate prevailing from 1960 onwards, have followed Professor Briston's policy, subject only to one important consideration—the overseas domicile of life tenants. If all the beneficiaries had been subject to United Kingdom tax, they should have regarded the 76.8 per cent. of the fund that was in ordinary shares in 1959 (or even the 82.6 per cent. in 1960) as devoted to equity investment, and only the balance as available for fixed interest securities. No doubt there were times during the period from 1960 to 1986 when it would not have been a breach of trust, and may even have been wise, to depart temporarily from that policy. But in the main I am convinced that it is the policy which they should have followed. With hindsight, one can see that the B.Z.W. Equity Index rose from 789.9 to 6353.2 in that period; the gilt index fell from 74.6 to 48.4. But my conclusion is based on the evidence of Professor Briston and Mr. Harris, not on hindsight.

"That, however, assumes that all the beneficiaries were subject to United **9–90** Kingdom tax, which they were not. George Nestlé lived in Tanganyika from 1933 to 1963, when he moved to Malta and lived there until he died in 1972. Elsie, his widow, continued to live there until 1980, when she returned to England. She died in 1982. John Nestlé went to live in Cyprus in 1969, and died there in 1986. The fiscal effects of residence/ordinary residence/domicile overseas were, as I understand it, twofold: first, the life tenant would not be liable for United Kingdom income tax on investments outside the United Kingdom, or (more significantly) on the income from gilt-edged securities which were tax exempt; secondly, neither estate duty nor capital transfer tax would be payable on the death of a life tenant in respect of such securities.

"The obligation of a trustee is to administer the trust fund impartially, or fairly (I can see no significant difference), having regard to the different interests of beneficiaries. Wilberforce J. said in *Re Pauling's Settlement Trusts (No. 2)* [1963] Ch. 576, 586:

> 'The new trustees would be under the normal duty of preserving an equitable balance, and if at any time it was shown they were inclining one way or the other, it would not be a difficult matter to bring them to account.'

"At times it will not be easy to decide what is an equitable balance. A life tenant **9–91** may be anxious to receive the highest possible income, whilst the remainderman will wish the real value of the trust fund to be preserved. If the life tenant is living in penury and the remainderman already has ample wealth, common sense suggests that a trustee should be able to take that into account, not necessarily by seeking the highest possible income at the expense of capital but by inclining in that direction. However, before adopting that course a trustee should, I think, require some verification of the facts. In this case the trustees did not, so far as I am aware, have any reliable information as to the relative wealth of the life tenants and the plaintiff. They did send an official to interview Mr. John Nestlé in Cyprus on one occasion; but the information which they obtained was conflicting and (as it turned out) incomplete.

"Similarly I would not regard it as a breach of trust for the trustees to pay some regard to the relationship between Mr. George Nestlé and the plaintiff. He was merely her uncle, and she would have received nothing from his share of the fund if he had fathered a child who survived him. The trustees would be entitled, in my view, to incline towards income during his life tenancy and that of his widow, on that ground. Again common sense suggests to me that such a course might be appropriate, and I do not think that it would be a breach of the duty to act fairly, or impartially.

9–92   "The dominant consideration for the trustees, however, was that George's fund from 1960, and John's from 1969, would not be subject to United Kingdom income tax in so far as it was invested in exempt gilts. That was a factor which the trustees were entitled—and I would say bound—to take into account. A beneficiary who has been left a life interest in a trust fund has an arguable case for saying that he should not be compelled to bear tax on the income if he is not lawfully obliged to do so.

"It was no more than a factor for the trustees to bear in mind, and would rarely justify more than a modest degree of preference for income paid gross over capital growth.

"A trustee should also bear in mind, as these trustees did, that estate duty or capital transfer tax is likely to be reduced in such a case if part of the fund is invested in tax-exempt gilts. That may provide a compensating benefit for the remainderman. Of course it is by no means certain that the benefit will materialise; the life tenant may return to this country, as happened in the case of Mrs. Elsie Nestlé. It has been said that nothing in this world is certain except death and taxes. But even the tax benefit was imponderable, since it could not be forecast what rate of tax would be applicable on the death of a life tenant.

9–93   "It is said that the trustees should have anticipated that Elsie would return to the United Kingdom, or at least have made inquiries as to her intentions. I can see some force in the second part of that argument. It would have been prudent to ask her to let them know if she planned to come back to this country. But this was never put to the bank's witnesses. And I cannot find that any loss to the trust fund resulted from failure to request information from Elsie. From time to time during her life tenancy there were indications that she might return, but it was only at a late stage that this attained any degree of probability; and I doubt whether even then it would have been right for the trustees to switch investments, thus reducing her income and foregoing any prospect of a saving in capital transfer tax.

"I do not consider it necessary to examine separately the balance of the two different funds from 1961 to 1986. From the point of view of the plaintiff, what mattered was the balance of the fund as a whole. The proportion in ordinary shares varied between 59.55 per cent. and 35.9 per cent. On occasion the lower figure may be attributable not to a change in investments but to a fall in the value of equities, for example in 1974 when there was a catastrophic fall. But there can be no doubt that there were other occasions when money was switched from ordinary shares to gilt-edged securities.

9–94   "The policy of the trustees during this period was to achieve a 50/50 split between equities and fixed-interest. This was not to be an initial division of the kind favoured by Professor Briston, which would have resulted in a much higher proportion of equities by 1986; it was to be a division that was rebalanced from time to time, as envisaged by Professor Brealey. Whilst I much prefer Professor Briston's method in general for trust funds during this period, I consider that the circumstances of this trust and in particular the overseas life tenants, justified the policy which the trustees adopted. They did not fail to act fairly or impartially by adopting it.

9–95   "But it is said that the trustees failed to implement their own policy: the proportion of ordinary shares fell on one occasion to 35.9 per cent, and in six years it was below 40 per cent. In my judgment the trustees were not obliged to rebalance the fund annually, still less at more frequent intervals. It would have been questionable to switch immediately into equities when they fell through the floor in 1974, merely because the ordinary shares then held were only 36.37 per cent of the fund. There was evidence that it is not a wise policy for trustees to be changing investments continually; and whilst I would not regard that as a justification for sheer inertia, I accept that an ordinary fund manager who has no special expertise should not busy himself with constant changes. The equity content started as 59.55 per cent in 1961 and ended as 51.31 per cent in 1986. Over those 26 years the average; according to my arithmetic, was 44.56 per cent. I would not regard that as revealing a serious departure from the trustees' policy, or a failure to act fairly and impartially. But I should add that, if I had found a breach of trust in this respect I would have been reluctant to accept that compensation should be measured by the difference between the actual performance of the fund and the very least that a prudent trustee might have achieved. There is said to be 19th century authority to that effect; but I would be inclined to prefer a comparison with what a prudent trustee was likely to have achieved—in other words, the average performance of ordinary shares during the period.

Diversification

"The complaint here is that there was undue emphasis on the shares of banks and **9–96** insurance companies during the period from 1922 to 1960. Indeed the equities in the annuity fund when it was set up in 1922 were entirely of that description.

"However, there was evidence from the experts on both sides that bank and insurance shares were regarded as safest in the earlier period of this trust, 'a low risk portfolio.' I am inclined to agree with Professor Briston that there should have been diversification in the 1950s, rather than from 1960 onwards. But I cannot accept that failure to diversify in that decade was a course which no prudent trustee would have followed . . .

"I would dismiss the appeal. . . . It is not shown that there was loss arising from a breach of trust for which the trustees ought to compensate the trust fund . . .

III. THE TRUSTEE ACT 2000 DEFAULT POWERS

In the absence of wider express powers in the trust instrument and subject **9–96A** to any restriction or exclusion in such instrument or in primary or subordinate legislation,[95] the Trustee Act 2000 (after repealing most of the Trustee Investments Act 1961) confers on trustees of old or new trusts[96] first, a "general power of investment", extending to loans secured on land (whether by way of legal or equitable mortgage or charge) but not to acquiring land, and second, a power to acquire legal estates in freehold or leasehold land in the UK as an investment or for occupation by a beneficiary or for any other reason.

By s.3(1) "a trustee may make any kind of investment that he could make if he[97] were absolutely entitled to the assets of the trust", but by subsection

---

[95] Pension fund investment is dealt with in the Pensions Act 1995, at para.9–332.
[96] Trustee Act 2000 ss.7(1), 10(2).
[97] If the trustee were a corporation with powers less than those of an absolute beneficial owner this would limit the range of investments to that permitted to that corporation.

(3) "the general power of investment does not permit a trustee to make investments in land other than in loans secured on land." Investments can thus properly be made in assets anywhere in the world, including loans secured on foreign land, so long, of course, as the various equitable and statutory duties of care are observed. An "investment" was originally considered to be an asset acquired for the sake of the income it was expected to yield[98] but, nowadays, with the emphasis on "total return",[99] taking account of income yield and capital appreciation in accordance with modern portfolio theory, an investment is considered to cover an asset acquired for the sake of either or both an income yield or a likely capital profit.[1] It follows, for example, that the purchase of depreciating chattels for a villa owned by the trustees or of a depreciating vehicle for use by a beneficiary or of a lottery ticket fall outside the general power of investment, so that the beneficiary will need to have trust income or capital properly distributed to him or her and then use it to purchase the chattels or vehicle or lottery ticket for himself or herself.

9–96B   By s.8(1) "a trustee may acquire freehold or leasehold land in the United Kingdom (a) as an investment, (b) for occupation by a beneficiary, or (c) for any other reason." In England and Wales "freehold or leasehold land"[2] means a legal estate in land and, particularly in purchasing leases, the trustees will need to ensure that they observe their equitable and statutory duties of care. Then, by s.8(3), "for the purpose of exercising his functions as a trustee, a trustee who acquires land under this section has all the powers of an absolute owner in relation to the land." For trustees who have acquired land other than under s.8(3), *e.g.* because the settlor settled land[3] on the trustees, s.6(3) of the Trusts of Land and Appointment of Trustees Act 1996 (as amended by the Trustee Act 2000) provides, "The trustees of land have power to acquire land under the power conferred by section 8 of the Trustee Act 2000." Under section 8(3) it seems that the use of the present tense enables trustees to acquire the land with the assistance of a mortgage thereon and, to that extent, "gear up" the value of the trust fund. Otherwise, gearing up by money borrowed on the security of existing assets to acquire new assets needs express authorisation.[4]

IV. EXPRESS INVESTMENT CLAUSES

9–97   Express investment clauses are found in virtually all trusts (other than those arising on a person's death intestate or those arising without the assistance of legal advice), although clauses in trust instruments more than 40 or 50

---

[98] *Re Wragg* [1919] 2 Ch. 58 at 64, 65, *Re Power's W.T.* [1947] Ch. 576, *Tootal Broadhurst Lee Co. Ltd v I.R.C.* [1949] 1 Al E.R. 261, 265.

[99] See para.9–65, above.

[1] In *Cook v Medway Housing Society* [1997] S.T.C. 90, 98 "investment" was said to amount to the "laying out of moneys in anticipation of a profitable capital or income return". See also *Marson v Morton* [1986] 1 W.L.R. 1363 at 1350 and Explanatory Notes to Trustee Act 2000, paras 22 and 23 and Law Com No.260 at p.22 n.56.

[2] Trustee Act 2000, s.8(2). Interests in foreign land may be acquired via acquiring shares in a company that owns foreign land.

[3] But land that is within the Settled Land Act 1925 is governed exclusively by such Act: Trustee Act 2000, s.10(1).

[4] *Re Suenson-Taylor's S.T.* [1974] 1 W.L.R. 1280.

years old will usually be much more limited than modern clauses drafted in the light of the variety of financial products now on offer. Powers (to acquire investments in a safe list of authorised investments) in default of express powers of investment were conferred by the Trustee Act 1925 and then the Trustee Investments Act 1961, but such powers soon became increasingly out-dated and ineffective in safeguarding and developing the value of the trust fund.

Draftspersons have developed their own sophisticated investment clauses and will continue to use them (rather than rely on the default powers in the Trustee Act 2000) so as to confer the broadest possible powers on the trustees who, however broad their powers, have their opportunities much narrowed by the equitable and statutory duties of care imposed upon them (except to the extent expressly modified or excluded by the trust instrument). To confer the broadest possible powers, draftspersons will often employ clauses like "to apply or invest in the purchase or acquisition of assets or investments of whatsoever nature and wherever situated, and whether or not yielding income or being appreciating or depreciating assets, and including the acquisition of derivatives but only for the purpose of limiting risks and not for the purpose of speculation." However, if most exceptionally, speculation is desired, the draftsperson can insert "or speculate" after "or invest" and omit the limitation on the acquisition of derivatives, while providing that in exercising such flexible powers the trustees "are under a duty to speculate with the trust fund as would an absolute beneficial owner who could afford to lose an amount equivalent to the value of the trust fund without it affecting his standard of living in any way whatever" and "are not to be liable for any conduct unless acting dishonestly."[5] The draftsperson can also confer express power to "gear up" the trust fund by borrowing on the security of existing trust property in order to acquire further property for the trust[6] and express power to lend merely on the security of a personal promise of the borrower to repay,[7] when a high interest rate will of course be payable because a personal promise provides no security at all in the event of non-payment.

At one stage the courts took a narrow restrictive approach to the **9–98** interpretation of investment clauses as extending the default powers as little as possible, but for the last fifty years the courts[8] have been interpreting investment clauses[9] according to the natural and proper meaning of the words used in their context so as to empower investment in a fairly-construed wide range of investments. However, the courts have been strict in refusing to treat conferment of a power for the trustee to invest in his absolute discretion in all respects as if he were the absolute beneficial

---

[5] Such exemption clauses are valid if known of and approved by the settlor: *Armitage v Nurse* [1998] Ch. 241, *Bogg v Roper* (1998) 1 I.T.E.L.R. 267.
[6] Otherwise not permitted: *Re Suenson–Taylor's S.T.* [1974] 1 W.L.R. 1280.
[7] Otherwise not permitted: *Khoo Tek Keong v Ch'ng Joo Tuan Neoh* [1934] A.C. 529.
[8] *Re Harari's S.T.* [1949] 1 All E.R. 430, *Re Peczenik's settlement* [1964] 1 W.L.R. 720, *Re Douglas' W.T.* [1959] 1 W.L.R. 744.
[9] In *R v Clowes* (*No.2*) [1994] 2 All E.R. 316 at 327–330 the Court of Appeal held that a clause "to place any uninvested funds with any body on such terms and conditions as you see fit" was not an investment clause to be treated liberally: it merely allowed money to be placed temporarily pending investment.

owner of the trust fund as exempting such trustee from the need to exhibit the appropriate duties of care.[10]

Section 4. Delegation by a Trustee

I. INTRODUCTION

9–99   The general rule of equity is *delegatus non potest delegare* ("a delegate is not able to delegate") "I must observe," said Langdale M.R. in *Turner v Corney*[11] "that trustees who take on themselves the management of property for the benefit of others have no right to shift their duty on other persons; and if they employ an agent, they remain subject to the responsibility towards their *cestuis que trust*, for whom they have undertaken the duty". If, in breach of trust, trustees employed an agent then they were automatically liable for all losses that flowed from the unauthorised agent's activities in respect of the trust.[12] The trustees were, however, justified in delegating if authorised in the trust instrument or if, in the circumstances, delegation was either reasonably necessary or in the ordinary course of affairs.[13] Such delegation was normally permissible only in respect of the trustees employing agents to do things decided upon by the trustees,[14] but in the case of property situated abroad in the far-flung British Empire trustees could confer discretionary management powers (*e.g.* to sell, lease or buy property and to employ agents).[15]

9–100   However, where the employment of an agent to do specific acts was justified, the trustee had to be prudent in his selection and supervision of his agent. He had to exercise the care of a prudent man of business in his choice of the agent and he could not employ an agent to do an act outside the scope of the agent's business.[16] If these conditions were satisfied the trustee would not be responsible for a loss arising through the default of the agent, provided he exercised a proper supervision over the agent.[17] In this respect an express or statutory provision[18] authorising a wide use of agents in ministerial matters and exempting a trustee from liability for loss caused by the acts or defaults of an agent unless the loss occurred through

---

[10] *Barlett v Barclays Bank Trust Co.* [1980] Ch. 515 at 536; also see *Re Maberly* (1886) 33 Ch.D. 455 at 458.
[11] (1841) 5 Beav. 515 at 517.
[12] *Att.-Gen. v Scott* (1749) 1 Ves. Sen 413,417; *Rowland v Witherden* (1851) 3 Mac & Cr 568; *Clough v Bond* (1838) 3 My & Cr 440, 496–497; *Re Dewar* (1885) 54, L.J.Ch. 830 at 832.
[13] *Ex p. Belchier* (1754) Amb. 218, applied in *Speight v Gaunt* (1883) 22 Ch.D. 727; 9 App.Cas. 1.
[14] Trustees' discretions could not be delegated (unless authorised by the trust deed); *Robson v Flight* (1865) 4 De G.J. & S. 608, 613, *Re Airey* [1897] 1 Ch. 164, 170.
[15] In those days post took a long time to arrive by boat; there were no telephones or fax machines or e-mails. See *Stuart v Norton* (1860) 14 M 00, P.C. In *Re Muffet* (1887) 56 L.J.Ch. 600 the Court of Appeal even assumed that trustees with 80 English rented properties to manage could delegate collecting rents and seeing to repairs and to re-letting of vacated premises; presumably in such a case such delegation in the 1880s, could be reasonably necessary.
[16] *Fry v Tapson* (1884) 28 Ch.D. 268; *Rowland v Witherden* (1851) 3 Mac. & Cr. 508.
[17] *Matthews v Brise* (1845) 10 Jur.(o.s.) 105.
[18] *Underwood v Stevens* (1816) 1 Mer. 712; s.30(1) of the Trustee Act 1925, replacing s.24 of the Trustee Act 1893, replacing s.31 of the Law of Property Amendment Act 1859. Section 23 of the Trustee Act 2000 now governs the position.

the trustee's 'wilful default' did not relieve the trustee of his duty to show the care of the prudent man of business both in the selection and in the supervision of agents.[19] A trustee was thus only liable for his *own* acts or defaults, *e.g.* negligent selection, or negligent supervision. There was no automatic liability for the agent's acts or defaults in those cases where delegation to agents was permissible.

The Trustee Act 1925 radically enlarged trustees' collective powers to delegate implementation of their decisions to an agent because s.23(1) enabled them to delegate whether or not there was any reasonable need for this, and lazy trustees could even so delegate matters they could have seen to personally. However, they could not delegate the exercise of their own discretion to decide what should be done except as before in the case of managing overseas property, although under s.23(2) they could now do this whether or not there was any reasonable necessity for it.

9–101

While it was clear that, as before, trustees were not to be automatically liable for the acts of agents employable under the general law or under the s.23 extension thereof after 1925, it was uncertain whether trustees still owed a duty to select and supervise such agents with the care of the prudent business person. Traditionalists considered such duty continued after 1925, so that trustees would still be liable if personally guilty of wilful default in the traditional equitable sense which covered deliberate, reckless and negligent conduct.[20] Modernists believed in a literal, rather than a history-based, interpretation of section 23(1) so that in cases where use of agents was permissible trustees should not only never be automatically responsible but should not be personally "responsible for the default of any such agent if employed in good faith", although there could be personal liability for trustees guilty of wilful default in the common law sense of deliberate or reckless conduct.[21] In *Armitage v Nurse* in *obiter dicta*[22] the Court of Appeal, without full consideration of the arguments favouring the traditional approach, accepted the modernists' interpretation. It has to be said, however, that in modern times it does seem unsatisfactory that the default rule, in the absence of a higher duty imposed in the trust instrument, protects trustees unless not acting in good faith by being guilty of deliberate or reckless conduct. Hence the Trustee Act 2000 imposes the statutory duty of care in the employment and supervision of agents, nominees and custodians.[23]

---

[19] *Re Brier* (1884) 26 Ch.D. 238 at 243 (*per* Lord Selborne L.C.). Also *Re Chapman* [1896] 2 Ch. 763 at 776, *per* Lindley L.J., "Wilful default which includes want of ordinary prudence on the part of the trustees must be proved"; and in *Speight v Gaunt* (1883) 9 App.Cas. 1 at 13–15, 22–23 the Lords treated wilful default as including want of ordinary prudence.

[20] G. H. Jones (1959) 22 M.L.R 381, J. E. Stannard [1979] Conv. 345.

[21] *Re Vickery* [1931] 1 Ch. 572.

[22] [1998] Ch. 241.

[23] Generally see Law Com. No.260 (1999) "Trustees' Powers and Duties" upon which the Trustee Act 2000 is based.

II. COLLECTIVE DELEGATION UNDER TRUSTEE ACT 2000

9–102   In addition to powers conferred on trustees other than by the Trustee Act 2000, but subject to any restriction or exclusion imposed by the trust instrument or by any primary or subordinate legislation,[24] Part IV (ss.11 to 27) of the Trustee Act 2000 confers the following powers on trustees collectively subject to the following duties.

1. Agents

(a) Power to employ agents

9–103   By s.11 of the Trustee Act 2000:

"(1) Subject to the provisions of this Part, the trustees of a trust may authorise any person to exercise any or all of their delegable functions as their agent.

(2) In the case of a trust other than a charitable trust, the trustees' delegable functions consist of any function other than—

(a) any function relating to whether or in what way any assets of the trust should be distributed,

(b) any power to decide whether any fees or other payment due to be made out of the trust funds should be made out of income or capital,

(c) any power to appoint a person to be a trustee of the trust, or

(d) any power conferred by any other enactment or the trust instrument which permits the trustees to delegate any of their functions or to appoint a person to act as a nominee or custodian.

(3) In the case of a charitable trust, the trustees' delegable functions are—

(a) any function consisting of carrying out a decision that the trustees have taken;

(b) any function relating to the investment of assets subject to the trust (including, in the case of land held as an investment, managing the land and creating or disposing of an interest in the land);

(c) any function relating to the raising of funds for the trust otherwise than by means of profits of a trade which is an integral part of carrying out the trust's charitable purpose;

(d) any other function prescribed by an order made by the Secretary of State.

9–104   (4) For the purposes of subsection (3)(c) a trade is an integral part of carrying out a trust's charitable purpose if the profits are applied solely to the purposes of the trust and either—

(a) the trade is exercised in the course of the actual carrying out of a primary purpose of the trust, or

(b) the work in connection with the trade is mainly carried out by beneficiaries of the trust."

It will be seen that the section is concerned with trustees' management or administrative functions, not their discretionary distributive functions. It

---

[24] Trustee Act 2000, s.26.

extends to a sole trustee[25] but not to trustees of authorised unit trusts[26] nor to enable pension trustees to delegate investment functions which are dealt with by ss 34 to 36 of the Pensions Act 1995.

(b) Persons eligible to be agents

By s.12 of the Trustee Act 2000:   **9–105**

"(1) Subject to subsection (2), the persons whom the trustees may under section 11 authorise to exercise functions as their agent include one or more of their number.

(2) The trustees may not authorise two (or more) persons to exercise the same function unless they are to exercise the function jointly.

(3) The trustees may not under section 11 authorise a beneficiary to exercise any function as their agent (even if the beneficiary is also a trustee)

(4) The trustees may under section 11 authorise a beneficiary to exercise any function as their agent even though he is also appointed to act as their nominee or custodian (whether under section 16, 17 or 18 or any other power)."

It is important that the trustees can employ one of themselves for particular tasks so long as such trustee is not a beneficiary, there then being conflict of interest possibilities with a beneficiary-agent being vulnerable to the charge of preferring his or her own interests to those of other beneficiaries. Exceptionally under section 9(1) of the Trusts of Land and Appointment of Trustees Act 1996, "The trustees of land may, by power of attorney, delegate to any beneficiary or beneficiaries of full age and beneficially entitled to an interest in possession in land subject to the trust any of their functions as trustees which relate to the land." This power of attorney may be for any period or indefinite,[27] must be given by all the trustees jointly, may be revoked by any one or more of them and will be revoked by the appointment of a new trustee.[28] Such power can be exercised to enable a life tenant to decide upon sale or lease of the land but cannot enable the life tenant to receive or give receipts for capital money,[29] two trustees being required for this purpose[30] (considering the practical danger of permitting an income beneficiary to receive capital moneys). Beneficiaries exercising delegated functions are in the same position as trustees (with the same duties and liabilities) but are not regarded "as trustees for any other purposes (including the purposes of any enactment permitting the delegation of functions by trustees or imposing requirements relating to the payment of capital money)."[31]

---

[25] *ibid*, s.25.
[26] *ibid*, s.37.
[27] Trusts of Land Appointment of Trustees Act 1996, s.9(5).
[28] *ibid*, s.9(3).
[29] *ibid*, s.9(7).
[30] Law of Property Act 1925, s.27, Trustee Act 1925, s.14.
[31] T. L. A. T. A. 1996, s.9(7).

(c) Agent subject to duties and restrictions linked to function delegated

9–106   As to be expected if an agent is employed under s.11 to carry out a function (like investment) he is subject to the duties and restrictions attached to such function (like having regard to the standard investment criteria) if the trustees themselves were exercising such function.[32]

(d) Asset management restrictions

9–106A   By s.15 of the Trustee Act 2000:

"(1) The trustees may not authorise a person to exercise any of their asset management functions as their agent except by an agreement which is in or evidenced in writing.
(2) The trustees may not authorise a person to exercise any of their asset management functions as their agent unless—

(a) they have prepared a statement that gives guidance as to how the functions should be exercised ("a policy statement"), and
(b) the agreement under which the agent is to act includes a term to the effect that he will secure compliance with—
    (i) the policy statement, or
    (ii) if the policy statement is revised or replaced under section 22, the revised or replacement policy statement.

(3) The trustees must formulate any guidance given in the policy statement with a view to ensuring that the functions will be exercised in the best interests of the trust.
(4) The policy statement must be in or evidenced in writing.
(5) The asset management functions of trustees are their functions relating to—

(a) the investment of assets subject to the trust,
(b) the acquisition of property which is to be subject to the trust, and
(c) managing property which is subject to the trust and disposing of, or creating or disposing of an interest in, such property."

Clearly, this authorises the common useful, if not necessary, practice of employing a discretionary portfolio manager, but it extends to employing an estate agent to sell a trust property at the best price. It is noteworthy that the section applies to all asset management delegations, whether under the Act or otherwise (*e.g.* under the terms of the trust instrument).

(e) Terms of engagement

9–107   By s.14 of the Trustee Act 2000:

"(1) Subject to subsection (2) and sections 15(2) and 29 to 32, the trustees may authorise a person to exercise functions as their agent on such terms as to remuneration and other matters as they may determine.

---

[32] T. A. 2000, s.13.

(2) The Trustees may not authorise a person to exercise functions as their agent on any of the terms mentioned in subsection (3) unless it is reasonably necessary for them to do so.

(3) The terms are—

(a) a term permitting the agent to appoint a substitute;

(b) a term restricting the liability of the agent or his substitute to the trustees or any beneficiary;

(c) a term permitting the agent to act in circumstances capable of giving rise to a conflict of interest."

It will be seen that an objective test of what is "reasonably necessary" in **9–108** all the circumstances applies to use of s.14 to authorise the potentially detrimental terms specified in s.4(3). An express power may liberally permit trustees to authorise any terms if the trustees subjectively bona fide believe such terms to be reasonably necessary in the best interests of the beneficiaries. It is doubtful whether a term ousting the liability of an agent (*e.g.* by excluding some otherwise applicable duty) is covered as "a term restricting the liability of" an agent[33] although, in any event, it may be difficult to justify any such ouster as "reasonably necessary".

In engaging a discretionary portfolio manager[34] it may well be reasonably necessary to permit it to appoint a substitute for a foreign portfolio of shares, to permit it to exclude liability for negligence, to permit it as a market-maker in shares in a particular company to sell such shares to the trustees and to permit it to place business with a subsidiary or associated company entitled to charge for its services. At the time of the engagement it will be good practice for the trustees to record the factors making them consider that particular terms were reasonably necessary.

(f) Remuneration

Where a person other than a trustee has been appointed an agent (or a **9–109** nominee or custodian) s.32 of the Trustee Act 2000 provides:

"(1) This section applies if, under a power conferred by Part IV or any other enactment or any provision of subordinate legislation, or by the trust instrument, a person other than a trustee has been—

(a) authorised to exercise functions as an agent of the trustees, or

(b) appointed to act as a nominee or custodian.

(2) The trustees may remunerate the agent, nominee or custodian out of trust funds for services if—

(a) he is engaged on terms entitling him to be remunerated for those services, and

---

[33] Ouster of one particular duty, however, may be said to reduce or restrict the overall possible liability of the agent.

[34] See D. J. Hayton (1990) 106 L.Q.R. 89–93.

(b) the amount does not exceed such remuneration as is reasonable in the circumstances for the provision of those services by him to or on behalf of that trust.

(3) The trustees may reimburse the agent, nominee or custodian out of the trust funds for any expenses properly incurred by him in exercising functions as an agent, nominee or custodian."

If a trustee has been appointed agent, nominee or custodian, then he can claim properly incurred expenses out of the trust fund, but entitlement to remuneration for his services will be based on a clause in the trust instrument or, otherwise, s.29 of the Trustee Act 2000 (para.9-46 above).

(g) Duty of care in appointing and supervising agents

9–110 Trustees are under the statutory duty of care[35] when selecting the person who is to act, when determining any terms on which that person is to act, and, if such person is to exercise asset management functions, when preparing a policy statement under s.15, such duty applying whether the appointment is made under the Trustee Act 2000 or otherwise[36] (*e.g.* under the terms of the trust instrument except, of course, to the extent the statutory duty is modified or excluded in the trust instrument[37]).

Under s.22 of the Trustee Act 2000, while the agent continues to act for the trustees (a) they must keep under review the arrangements under which the agent acts and how those arrangements are being put into effect, (b) if circumstances make it appropriate to do so, they must consider whether there is a need to exercise any power of intervention that they have (*e.g.* a power to revoke the appointment or to give directions to the agent) and (c) if they consider that there is a need to exercise such a power, they must do so. The position is the same[38] where trustees of land delegate their functions under s.9 of the Trusts of Land and Appointment of Trustees Act 1996. In the case of an agent authorised to exercise asset management functions, the trustees' duties include a duty to consider whether there is any need to revise or replace the s.15 policy statement, a duty to revise or replace it if they consider that there is such a need, and a duty to assess whether the current policy statement is being complied with.[39] The revision or replacement must be in, or evidenced in, writing and must be formulated with a view to ensuring that the delegated functions will be exercised in the best interests of the trust beneficiaries as a whole.[40] The statutory duty of care applies to the exercise of these supervisory duties under s.22 of the Trustee Act 2000[41] and s.9A (3) of the Trusts of Land and Appointment of Trustees Act 1966,[42] but delegations made under s.9 before February 2001

---

[35] See para.9–04 above.
[36] T.A. 2000, Sch.1, para.3 and s.21(3).
[37] *ibid*, para.7.
[38] T. L. A. T. A. 1996, s.9A(2) to (5) inserted by TA 2000, Sch.2, para.47.
[39] T. A. 2000, s.22(2).
[40] *ibid*, s.15.
[41] *ibid*, Sch.1, para.3(1)(e).
[42] T. L. A. T. A. 1996, s.9A(5).

remain subject to the old law, including the prospectively repealed s.9(8).[43] Breach of the duty of care will, of course, lead to liability for losses directly flowing from such breach.

(h) No duty of care in deciding whether or not to delegate (except for delegations under s.9 Trusts of Land and Appointment of Trustees Act 1996)

In deciding whether or not to exercise their powers of delegation under the Trustee Act 2000 the trustees can suit themselves and do not need to prove it was reasonably necessary to exercise the power or that exercise of the power was in the best interests of the trust beneficiaries, although they cannot, of course, commit a fraud on the power[44] by exercising it for some ulterior purpose. However, the statutory duty of care applies to trustees of land in deciding whether or not to delegate any of their extensive functions under s.9 of the Trusts of Land and Appointment of Trustees Act 1996 to a beneficiary with an interest in possession[45]—because the extensive powers conferred upon such a beneficiary can be exercised with little constraint and much impact. **9–111**

(i) Trustees exceeding their powers

If trustees fail to act within the limits of their powers under the Trustee Act 2000 in authorising a person to act as their agent this does not invalidate the authorisation.[46] The Trustees, of course, will still be liable for losses flowing from the improper authorisation, while the agent may perhaps be liable as a trustee *de son tort*. **9–112**

2. Nominees and Custodians

The need for speedy settlement of share dealings within 3 days, the introduction of dematerialised holding and transfer of shares via the London Stock Exchange CREST system, and the use of computerised clearing systems in other financial markets make it vital that there are broad powers to use nominees and custodians. These broad powers are contained in ss.16, 17 and 18 of the Trustee Act 2000: **9–113**

However, by s.19 of the Trustee Act 2000:

"(1) A person may not be appointed under section 16, 17 or 18 as a nominee or custodian unless one of the relevant conditions is satisfied.
  (2) The relevant conditions are that—

  (a) the person carries on a business which consists of or includes acting as a nominee or custodian;

---

[43] T. L. A. T. A. 1996, s.9A(7).
[44] For fraud on a power see para.9–234.
[45] T. L. A. T. A. 1996, s.9A(1).
[46] T. A. 2000, s.4(a).

(b) the person is a body corporate which is controlled by the trustees;
(c) the person is a body corporate recognised under section 9 of the Administration of Justice Act 1985.

9–114   (5) Subject to subsections (1) and (4), the persons whom the trustees may under section 16, 17 or 18 appoint as a nominee or custodian include—

(a) one of their number, if that one is a trust corporation, or
(b) two (or more) of their number, if they are to act as joint nominees or joint custodians.

(6) The trustees may under section 16 appoint a person to act as their nominee even though he is also—

(a) appointed to act as their custodian (whether under section 17 or 18 or any other power), or
(b) authorised to exercise functions as their agent (whether under section 11 or any other power).

(7) Likewise, the trustees may under section 17 or 18 appoint a person to act as their custodian even though he is also—

(a) appointed to act as their nominee (whether under section 16 or any other power), or
(b) authorised to exercise functions as their agent (whether under section 11 or any other power)."

(a) Terms of engagement

9–115   By s.20 of the Trustee Act 2000:

(1) Subject to subsection (2) and sections 29 to 32, the trustees may under section 16, 17 and 18 appoint a person to act as a nominee or custodian on such terms as to remuneration and other matters as they may determine.
(2) The trustees may not under section 16, 17 or 18 appoint a person to act as a nominee or custodian on any of the terms mentioned in subsection (3) unless it is reasonably necessary for them to do so.
(3) The terms are—

(a) a term permitting the nominee or custodian to appoint a substitute;
(b) a term restricting the liability of the nominee or custodian or his substitute to the trustees or to any beneficiary;
(c) a term permitting the nominee or custodian to act in circumstances capable of giving rise to a conflict of interest."

(b) Remuneration

9–116   The position is set out in s.32 of the Trustee Act 2000 as discussed earlier[47] in relation to agents.

---

[47] See para.9–109 above.

(c) Duty of care in appointing and supervising nominees and custodian

Trustees are under the statutory duty of care when selecting the nominee **9–116A**
or custodian and determining the terms of engagement thereof, whether
under the Trustee Act 2000 or otherwise[48] (*e.g.* under the trust instrument,
except to the extent there is a contrary intention therein). They also need to
keep under review the arrangements under which the nominee or custodian
acts and how those arrangements are being put into effect, considering
whether any power of intervention needs to be exercised and then
exercising it if called for.[49] The statutory duty of care applies to this
reviewing duty[50] but not to deciding whether or not to exercise the powers
to utilise the services of custodians or nominees.

(d) Trustees exceeding their powers

If trustees exceed their powers under the Trustee Act 2000 in appointing **9–116B**
a person to act as nominee or custodian this does not invalidate the
appointment.[51]

III DELEGATION BY INDIVIDUAL TRUSTEES

Section 25 of the Trustee Act 1925 for the first time allowed an individual **9–117**
trustee to delegate all or any of his discretionary functions, whether
distributive functions or administrative functions, if he would be absent
from the UK for more than a month. The Powers of Attorney Act 1971
then amended s.25 of the 1925 Act so that the facility was generally
available to a trustee (whether or not absent abroad for a period) but the
period for delegation was confined to 12 months, although another power
of attorney could then forthwith be created for another 12 months and so
on, if appropriate. The Trustee Delegation Act 1999 slightly further
amended s.25 and repealed s.3 (3) of the Enduring Powers of Attorney Act
1985. This subsection had been a last-minute amendment to the 1985 Act,
to reverse a particular recent case involving co-owners of land[52] but it
accidentally had the vastly greater effect of enabling a trustee by an
enduring power of attorney to delegate all her trusteeships to another
person for an unlimited period. The 1999 Act further made special
provision[53] for co-owners of land so that a trustee who also has a beneficial
interest in trust land (or the proceeds thereof) can simply grant an ordinary
power of attorney under the Powers of Attorney Act 1971 to his co-owner,
enabling such co-owner to make a valid overreaching sale of the land.

The amended s.25 of the Trustee Act 1925 reads as follows.

---

[48] T. A. 2000, s.21(3) and Sch.1, para.3.
[49] *ibid*, s.22.
[50] *ibid.*, Sch.1, para.3.
[51] T. A. 2000, s.24(b).
[52] *Walia v Michael Naughton Ltd* [1985] 1 W.L.R. 1115; Hansard (HL) Vol. 465, June 24, 1985 cols. 548–549.
[53] Sections 1, 2, 3 Trustee Delegation Act 1999.

9–118   "(1) Notwithstanding any rule of law or equity to the contrary, a trustee may, by power of attorney, delegate the execution or exercise of all or any of the trusts, powers and discretions vested in him as trustee either alone or jointly with any other person or persons.

(2) A delegation under this section—

(a) commences as provided by the instrument creating the power or, if the instrument makes no provision as to the commencement of the delegation, with the date of the execution of the instrument by the donor; and

(b) continues for a period of twelve months or any shorter period provided by the instrument creating the power.

(3) The persons who may be donees of a power of attorney under this section include a trust corporation.

9–119   (4) Before or within seven days after giving a power of attorney under this section the donor shall give written notice of it (specifying the date on which the power comes into operation and its duration, the donee of the power, the reason why the power is given and, where some only are delegated, the trusts, powers and discretions delegated) to—

(a) each person (other than himself), if any, who under any instrument creating the trust has power (whether alone or jointly) to appoint a new trustee; and

(b) each of the other trustees, if any; but failure to comply with this subsection shall not, in favour of a person dealing with the donee of the power, invalidate any act done or instrument executed by the donee.

(5) A power of attorney given under this section by a single donor—

(a) in the form set out in subsection (6) of this section; or

(b) in a form to the like effect but expressed to be made under this subsection, shall operate to delegate to the person identified in the form as the single donee of the power the execution and exercise of all the trusts, powers and discretions vested in the donor as trustee (either alone or jointly with any other person or persons) under the single trust so identified.

9–120   (6) The form referred to in subsection (5) of this section is as follows—"THIS GENERAL TRUSTEE POWER OF ATTORNEY is made on [date] by [name of one donor] of [address of donor] as trustee of [name or details of one trust]. I appoint [name of one donee] of [address of donee] to be my attorney [if desired, the date on which the delegation commences or the period for which it continues (or both)] in accordance with section 25 (5) of the Trustee Act 1925. [To be executed as a deed]".

(7) The donor of a power of attorney given under this section shall be liable for the acts or defaults of the donee in the same manner as if they were the acts or defaults of the donor.

(8) For the purpose of executing or exercising the trusts or powers delegated to him, the donee may exercise any of the powers conferred on the donor as trustee by statute or by the instrument creating the trust, including power, for the purpose of the transfer of any inscribed stock, himself to delegate to an attorney power to transfer, but not including the power of delegation conferred by this section."

9–121   This amended s.25 applies to powers of attorney created from March 1 2000 onwards.[54] The duration of the delegation cannot exceed 12 months reckoned from the specified date or, in default, from the date of execution

---

[54] Trustee Delegation Act 1999 Commencement Order 2000, SI 2000/216.

of the power.[55] It is now possible to delegate to a sole co-trustee[56] but, unless this be a trust corporation, such sole attorney-co-trustee can give no valid overreaching receipt for capital moneys arising from a disposition of land.[57] Sub-delegation by the attorney is still prohibited.[58] A statutory short form of power of attorney is available for use but, if used, a separate one has to be used for each trust fund to which the delegation is to apply.[59] However, there is nothing to stop a partner in a firm of solicitors who is trustee of ten trusts from executing one power of attorney delegating to a fellow partner the trusteeship powers of all ten trusts while enjoying six months sabbatical leave.

Delegation under s.25 is intended as a temporary measure, the donor of **9–122** the power being automatically liable for the acts and defaults of the donee as if the donor's[60] and also having to give written notification to the person, if any, having power to appoint new trustees *and* to the donor's co-trustees,[61] who have the same power in default of any such person.[62] They might then consider it more appropriate to replace the donor as trustee. If not, the delegation lasts till the expiry of the 12 months (or lesser specified period) unless the donor earlier dies or becomes mentally incompetent, except that if the power was executed as an enduring power of attorney then mental incapacity will not vitiate the delegation.[63]

Section 5. Deviations from the Terms of a Trust

In case it is overlooked it is, of course, possible to change the structure of **9–122A** fixed or discretionary interests under a settlement or the terms of a trust if there is an overriding power of appointment in this behalf conferred by the settlement[64] (*e.g.* upon the trustees, or the life-tenant or settlor) or an overriding power of advancement of capital vested in the trustees.[65] Indeed, there can also be an overriding power of amendment of the trust vested in the trustees or the settlor (*e.g.* of a pension trust or of an insurance premiums trust deed), but the latter power is confined to such amendments as can reasonably be considered to have been within the contemplation of the parties and trustees are constrained to observe their undivided duty of loyalty.[66]

---

[55] Trustee Act 1925 s.25(2) (as substituted by Trustee Delegation Act 1999 s.5).
[56] *ibid.*, s.25(3), contrast previous s.25(2).
[57] Trustee Delegation Act 1999, s.7.
[58] Trustee Act 1925 s.25(8).
[59] *ibid*, s.25(5)(6).
[60] *ibid*, s.25(7).
[61] *ibid*, s.25(4).
[62] Trustee Act 1925, s.36.
[63] Trustee Delegation Act 1999, ss.6 and 9.
[64] For capital gains tax purposes it is vital whether the power is exerciseable and exercised to create a re-settlement (as a separate settlement occasioning a charge to tax) or merely a sub-settlement (no charge): *Roome v Edwards* [1982] A.C. 279; *Swires v Renton* [1991] S.T.C. 490.
[65] *Pilkington v I.R.C.* [1966] A.C. 612.
[66] *Napier and Ettrick v Kershaw Ltd* (No.2) [1999] 1 W.L.R. 756; *Hillsdown Holdings plc v Pensions Ombudsman* [1997] 1 All E.R. 862.

I. WHERE THE BENEFICIARIES ARE OF FULL CAPACITY

9–122B If property is given not contingently but absolutely to a person of full age *any* restriction on his enjoyment of it is inconsistent with his absolute interest.[67] Hence a beneficiary of full capacity and entitled *absolutely* can call for a transfer: *Saunders v Vautier, infra*; and he may do so even if the settlor purports to remove this right.[68] As a matter of property law the absolute owner(s) of property can do whatever be desired, irrespective of any material purpose that the donor might have had in mind. So also *several* beneficiaries and any objects of a power of appointment[69] who are all of full capacity and between them entitled absolutely may call for a transfer, if they act together.[70] Even beneficiaries who are entitled *in succession* can combine to call for a transfer, provided they are of full capacity and are collectively entitled absolutely.[71] Thus a fluctuating body of beneficiaries from time to time within a class cannot exercise *Saunders v Vautier* rights.[72] However the rule in *Saunders v Vautier, infra*, operates also in favour of a charity.[73] But it does not apply where other persons have an interest in the accumulations of income which the beneficiaries are seeking to stop.[74] However, it does not give beneficiaries the right to control the trustee in the exercise of any discretion conferred upon him by statute or the trust instrument,[75] except[76] that where property is held on trust for beneficiaries all of whom are ascertained and of full age and capacity all such beneficiaries may force the trustees to retire in favour of new trustees nominated unanimously by the beneficiaries.

9–123 In the case of income accruing to a closed class of discretionary trust beneficiaries the sole member of the class for the time being can claim an entitlement to that income. If such class were open such sole member cannot claim such entitlement so long as it is possible for another member of the class to come into existence before a reasonable time for the distribution of the accrued income has elapsed.[77]

Where trusts arise out of contractual relationships it is possible for the parties who are beneficiaries to contract out of their *Saunders v Vautier* rights *e.g.* so that unit-holders in a unit trust cannot terminate the trust and claim the trust property while the trust is operating as a going concern and before it is wound up as agreed pursuant to the trust deed.

One must distinguish between the rights of the beneficial interest holders collectively and the rights of one of the co-owners: the latter are much more restricted as is made clear in *Stephenson v Barclays Bank*, below.

---

[67] *Weatherall v Thornburgh* (1978) 8 Ch.D. 261 at 270 (Cotton L.J.).
[68] *Stokes v Cheek* (1860) 28 Beav. 620.
[69] *Schmidt v Rosewood Trust Ltd* [2003] 2 A.C. 709, para.41.
[70] *Re Sandeman* [1937] 1 All E.R. 368; *Re Smith* [1928] Ch. 915.
[71] *Anson v Potter* (1879) 13 Ch.D. 141; *Re White* [1901] 1 Ch. 570; *Re Bowes* [1896] 1 Ch. 507.
[72] *Re Westphal* [1972] N.Z.L.R. 792 at 794–795, *Re Levy* [1960] Ch. 346 at 363.
[73] *Wharton v Masterman* [1895] A.C. 186; but see *Re Levy* [1960] Ch. 346. Whilst an indefinite gift of income to an individual carries the right to the capital, this is not necessarily so in the case of a similar gift to charity, for such a gift can be enjoyed by the charity in perpetuity.
[74] *Berry v Geen* [1938] A.C. 575.
[75] *Re Brockbank* [1948] Ch. 206; *Holding and Management Ltd v Property Holdings plc* [1990] 1 All E.R. 938 at 948; *Re George Whichelow Ltd* [1954] 1 W.L.R. 5; *cf. Butt v Kelson* [1952] Ch. 197 at 207.
[76] Trusts of Land and Appointment of Trustees Act 1996, ss.19, 20. where no-one else has the power to nominate new trustees.
[77] *Re Trafford's Settlement* [1984] 1 All E.R. 1108; *Re Weir's Settlement* [1971] Ch. 145.

SAUNDERS v VAUTIER

Master of the Rolls (1841) 4 Beav. 115; Cr. & Ph. 240; 10 L.J.Ch. 354

A testator bequeathed his stock on trust to accumulate the dividends until V. **9–124** should attain the age of twenty-five, and then to transfer the principal, together with the accumulated dividends, to V. V., having attained twenty-one, claimed to have the fund transferred to him. It was contended for him that he had "a vested interest, and that as the accumulation and postponement of payment was for his benefit alone, he might waive it and call for an immediate transfer of the fund."

LORD LANGDALE M.R.: "I think that principle has been repeatedly acted upon; and where a legacy is directed to accumulate for a certain period, or where the payment is postponed the legatee, if he has an absolute indefeasible interest in the legacy, is not bound to wait until the expiration of that period, but may require payment the moment he is competent to give a valid discharge."

On a question raised, with reference to a previous order for maintenance, as to whether there was a vested interest in V. before he attained twenty-five, the petition stood over, with liberty to apply to the Lord Chancellor.

Held, by the Lord Chancellor, the fund was intended wholly for the benefit of V., although the enjoyment of it was postponed: it vested immediately, and he could now claim the transfer.[78]

STEPHENSON v BARCLAYS BANK

Chancery Division [1975] 1 All E.R. 625; [1975] 1 W.L.R. 88

WALTON J.: "I think it may be desirable to state what I conceive to be certain **9–125** elementary principles. (1) In a case where the persons who between them hold the entirety of the beneficial interests in any particular trust fund are all *sui juris* and acting together ('the beneficial interest holders'), they are entitled to direct the trustees how the trust fund may be dealt with. (2) This does not mean, however, that they can at one and the same time override the pre-existing trusts and keep them in existence. Thus, in *Re Brockbank*[79] itself the beneficial interest holders were entitled to override the pre-existing trusts by, for example, directing the trustees to transfer the trust fund to X and Y, whether X and Y were the trustees of some other trust or not, but they were not entitled to direct the existing trustees to appoint their own nominee as a new trustee of the existing trust. By so doing they would be pursuing inconsistent rights. (3) Nor, I think, are the beneficial interest holders entitled to direct the trustees as to the particular investment they should make of the trust fund. I think this follows for the same reasons as the above. Moreover, it appears to me that once the beneficial interest holders have determined to end the trust they are not entitled, unless by agreement, to the further services of the trustees. Those trustees can of course be compelled to hand over the entire trust assets to any person or persons selected by the beneficiaries against a proper discharge, but they cannot be compelled, unless they are in fact willing to comply with the directions, to do anything else with the trust fund which they are not in fact willing to do. (4) Of course, the rights of the beneficial interest holders are always subject to the right of

---

[78] Joyce J., in *Re Couturier* [1907] 1 Ch. 470 at 473, points out the distinction between giving a person a *vested* interest and postponing the enjoyment to a certain age, and giving him an interest *contingent* on his attaining a certain age. Also see *Gosling v Gosling* (1859) John 265.
[79] [1948] Ch. 206.

the trustees to be fully protected against such matters as duty, taxes, costs or other outgoings; for example, the rent under a lease which the trustees have properly accepted as part of the trust property.

9–126   "So much for the rights of the beneficial interest holders collectively. When the situation is that a single person who is *sui juris* has an absolutely vested beneficial interest in a share of the trust fund, his rights are not, I think, quite as extensive as those of the beneficial interest holders as a body. In general, he is entitled to have transferred to him (subject, of course, always to the same rights of the trustees as I have already mentioned above) an aliquot share of each and every asset of the trust fund which presents no difficulty so far as division is concerned. This will apply to such items as cash, money at the bank or an unsecured loan, stock exchange securities and the like. However, as regards land, certainly, in all cases, as regards shares in a private company in very special circumstances (see *Re Weiner's Will Trusts*[80]) and possibly (although the logic of the addition in facts escapes me[81]) mortgage debts (see *Re Marshall*[82] *per* Cozens-Hardy M.R.) the situation is not so simple, and even a person with a vested interest in possession in an aliquot share of the trust fund may have to wait until the land is sold, and so forth, before being able to call on the trustees as of right to account to him for his share of the assets."

II. Where the Beneficiaries are not of Full Capacity

A. Introduction[83]

9–127   The decision of the House of Lords in *Chapman v Chapman*[84] in 1954 made it clear that the court did not possess plenary powers to alter a trust because alteration was thought to be advantageous to infant or unborn beneficiaries except in certain limited cases. Some of these exceptions related to acts done by the trustees in regard to the trust property in the administration of the trust, while others went beyond this and conferred a limited power to remould the beneficial interests when this was to the advantage of the beneficiaries.

(a) Exceptions relating to acts done in administration of trust

9–127A   (i) *Salvage.* This group of cases involved the alienation of infants' property and established the proposition that the court could sanction a mortgage or sale of part of an infant's beneficial interest for the benefit of the part retained in cases of absolute necessity.[85]

---

[80] [1956] 1 W.L.R. 579. Now see *Lloyds Bank v Duker* [1987] 1 W.L.R. 1324 where a beneficiary entitled to 46/80 of the testator's residuary estate claimed therefore to have 574 of 999 shares in a private company transferred to her. Such a majority shareholding was worth much more than 46/80 of the proceeds of sale of the whole 999 shares. It was held that the duty to maintain an even hand or fair balance between the beneficiaries prevailed so that the shares must be sold and the claimant beneficiary receive 46/80 of the proceeds.

[81] In *Crowe v Appleby* [1975] 3 All E.R. 529 at 537, Goff J. endorsed Walton J.'s views and pointed out "the logic of the addition of mortgages is that they include not only the debt but the estate and powers of the mortgagee."

[82] [1914] 1 Ch. 192 at 199.

[83] See O. R. Marshall (1954) 17 M.L.R. 420; (1957) 21 Conv.(N.S.) 448.

[84] [1954] A.C. 429. The variation of the trust in that case was later effected under the Variation of Trusts Act 1958, at para.9–135; see *Re Chapman's Settlement Trusts (No.2)* [1959] 1 W.L.R. 372.

[85] See *Re Jackson* (1882) 21 Ch.D. 786; *Conway v Fenton* (1888) 40 Ch.D. 512; *cf. Re De Teissier* [1893] 1 Ch. 153; *Re Montagu* [1897] 2 Ch. 8.

(ii) *Emergency.* This exception can be regarded as an extension of the **9–128** salvage cases. The salvage cases required proof of absolute necessity. The principle of the emergency cases was somewhat wider and enabled the court to sanction departure from the terms of a trust where an emergency had arisen which the settlor had not foreseen and which required to be dealt with by the conferment of extraordinary powers on the trustees.[86]

(iii) *Expediency*—Section 57 of the Trustee Act 1925. Section 57 of the **9–128A** Trustee Act 1925 rested the jurisdiction on expediency—a basis which, it is conceived, is wider than that of salvage or emergency. The section provides:

"Where in the management or administration of any property vested in trustees, any sale, lease, mortgage, surrender, release or other disposition or any purchase, investment, acquisition, expenditure, or other transaction is in the opinion of the court expedient, but the same cannot be effected by reason of the absence of any power for that purpose vested in the trustees by the trust instrument, if any, or by law, the court may by order confer upon the trustees, either generally or in any particular instance, the necessary power for the purpose, in such terms, and subject to such provisions and conditions, if any, as the court may think fit and may direct in what manner any money authorised to be expended, and the costs of any transaction, are to be paid or borne as between capital and income."

The object of the section is to enable the court to authorise specific **9–129** dealings with the trust property which it might not have been able to do on the basis of salvage or emergency, but it was no part of the legislative aim to disturb the rule that the court will not rewrite a trust.[87]

This is an overriding section, the provisions of which are read into every settlement.[88] The powers of the court are limited only by expediency, though the proposed transaction must be for the benefit not of one beneficiary but of the whole trust.[89] The power has been used to authorise the sale of chattels settled on trusts which prevent sale,[90] the sale of land where a consent requisite to sale has been refused,[91] the partitioning of land where there was no power to partition,[92] and the blending of two charitable funds into one.[93] In 1990, the powers of the court under s.57 were utilised to enable efficient investment management of a trust. In *Anker-Petersen v Anker-Petersen*[94] the trustees were given power to invest in assets of any kind as if they were beneficial owners subject to obtaining advice from an

---

[86] *Re New* [1901] 1 Ch. 534; *Re Tollemache* [1903] 1 Ch. 457. The jurisdiction has been used to resolve a retention trust fund problem in a construction contract: *Rafidain Bank v Saipem* (unreported March 2, 1994, Underhill & Hayton, *Law of Trusts & Trustees* (16th ed.), p.524).
[87] *Re Downshire* [1953] Ch. 218.
[88] *Re Mair* [1935] Ch. 562.
[89] *Re Craven's Estate (No.2)* [1937] Ch. 431.
[90] *Re Hope's Will Trust* [1929] 2 Ch. 136.
[91] *Re Beale's Settlement Trusts* [1932] 2 Ch. 15.
[92] *Re Thomas* [1930] 1 Ch. 194. Now see *Rodway v Landy* [2001] Ch. 703 for such power under Trusts of Land and Appointment of Trustees Act 1999, s.13.
[93] *Re Harvey* [1941] 3 All E.R. 284; for other cases on s.57, see *Municipal and General Securities Ltd v Lloyds Bank Ltd* [1950] Ch. 212; *Re Pratt* [1943] 2 All E.R. 375.
[94] (1991) 88 Law Soc. Gaz. Part 16, p.32, [2000] W.T.L.R. 581.

"Investment Adviser" as defined, power to use an Investment Adviser as a discretionary portfolio manager, power to hold investments in the names of nominees and power to borrow money.

(b) Exceptions relating to the remoulding of the beneficial interests

9–130　　(i) *Maintenance.*[95] Where a settlor made a provision for a family but postponed the enjoyment, either for a particular purpose or generally for the increase of the estate, it was assumed that he did not intend that the children should be left unprovided for, or in a state of such moderate means that they could not be educated properly for the position which he intended them to have, and the court accordingly broke in upon the accumulation and provided maintenance for the children. The exercise of this jurisdiction resulted in an alteration of beneficial interests since income was applied in maintaining beneficiaries notwithstanding the fact that the settlor had directed that it should be accumulated or applied in reduction of incumbrances. The jurisdiction was not confined to cases of emergency or necessity.[96]

9–131　　(ii) *Compromise.* It has long been clear that where the rights of the beneficiaries under a trust are the subject of doubt or dispute, the court has jurisdiction on behalf of all interested parties, whether adult, infant or unborn, to sanction a compromise by substituting certainty for doubt.[97] The issue in *Re Downshire*, *Re Blackwell* and *Re Chapman* before the Court of Appeal,[98] and in the last-named case[99] before the House of Lords, was whether the court had jurisdiction to do the same with regard to rights which were admittedly not in dispute. Their Lordships emphatically rejected the view that the courts had so ample a jurisdiction.

9–132　　(iii) *Section 64 of the Settled Land Act* 1925. Section 64(1) of the Settled Land Act 1925 provides that any transaction affecting or concerning the settled land, or any part thereof, or any other land (not being a transaction otherwise authorised by the Act, or by the settlement) which in the opinion of the court would be for the benefit of the settled land, or any part thereof, or the persons interested under the settlement, may, under an order of the court, be effected by a tenant for life, if it is one which could have been validly effected by an absolute owner. "Transaction" is defined by subsection (2) to include "any sale, extinguishment of manorial incidents, exchange, assurance, grant, lease, surrender, reconveyance, release, reservation or other disposition, any purchase or other acquisition, any covenant, contract, or option, and any *application of capital money . . . and any compromise or other dealing or arrangement. . . ."*

---

[95] *Havelock v Havelock* (1880) 17 Ch.D. 807; *Re Collins* (1886) Ch.D. 229; *Re Walker* [1901] 1 Ch. 879; *Greenwell v Greenwell* (1800) 5 Ves. 194; *Errat v Barlow* (1807) 14 Ves. 202.
[96] See *Haley v Bannister* (1820) 4 Madd. 275.
[97] *Brooke v Mostyn* (1864) 2 De G.J. & S. 415; *Re Barbour's Settlement* [1974] 1 All E.R. 1188.
[98] [1953] Ch. 218.
[99] [1954] A.C. 429. In *Mason v Farbrother* [1983] 2 All E.R. 1078 it was held that doubts over the scope of narrow investment powers should not be compromised in the court's discretion by insertion of a new wide investment clause.

"Transaction" is a word of very wide import, and enables beneficial **9–133** interests to be altered even without the consent of beneficiaries of full age and capacity. Section 64 has been held wide enough to enable trustees to transfer part of their trust property to another settlement of which they were trustees even though benefiting some other persons,[1] and to enable the Eleventh Duke of Marlborough to convey the Blenheim estate to trustees of a new settlement giving his troublesome son a protected life interest instead of a fee tail, such interest being under a trust for sale and not under a SLA trust so that the son had no power as tenant for life.[2]

(iv) *Section 53 of the Trustee Act 1925.* Section 53 of the Trustee Act **9–134** provides that where an infant is beneficially entitled to *any* property the court may with a view to the *application* of the capital or income thereof for the maintenance, education or *benefit* of the infant make an order appointing a person to convey such property upon such terms as the court may think fit. The effect of this section may be summarised as follows: Where:

(a) an infant is beneficially entitled to any interest in property, whether real or personal;

(b) the interest itself is not under the settlement applicable for his maintenance, education or benefit, nor is it producing any income which is so applicable;

(c) a proposal is made that the court should authorise a "conveyance"[3] of the infant's interest with a view to the application of the capital or income, arising out of such conveyance, for the maintenance, education or benefit of the infant;

then the court has jurisdiction to sanction the proposal upon such terms as it thinks fit. Thus the sale of an infant's contingent reversionary interest to the life-tenant in order to minimise liability to estate duty was made with a view to, and was, an application of the proceeds of sale for the infant's benefit, where they amounted to more than he would have been likely to receive if no sale had taken place, and they were to be settled upon[4] and not paid outright to him.[5]

B. The Variation of Trusts Act 1958

The decision in *Chapman v Chapman*[6] was criticised by the Law Reform **9–135** Committee whose report[7] led to the passing of the Variation of Trusts Act 1958.

---

[1] *Raikes v Lygon* [1988] 1 W.L.R. 28.
[2] *Hambro v Duke of Marlborough* [1994] Ch. 158.
[3] Including a mortgage: *Re Gower's Settlement* [1934] Ch. 365; *Re Bristol's Settled Estates* [1965] 1 W.L.R. 469.
[4] *Re Meux's Will Trusts* [1957] 3 W.L.R. 377; *Re Lansdowne's W.T.* [1967] 1 All E.R. 888.
[5] *Re Heyworth's Contingent Reversionary Interest* [1956] Ch. 364. Other exceptions under this head which are outside the scope of this note are the *cy-près* jurisdiction of the court in relation to charitable trusts, the statutory jurisdiction of the court in regard to mental patients' settlements under the Mental Health Act 1983, s.96, and the statutory jurisdiction of the Family Division of the High Court to vary ante-nuptial and post-nuptial settlements. See Matrimonial Causes Act 1973, ss.24, 31.
[6] [1954] A.C. 429.
[7] (1957) Cmnd. 310; [1958] C.L.J. 1 (S. J. Bailey).

Essentially, the Act enables the court on behalf of persons who cannot themselves give their approval (*e.g.* because unborn, unascertainable or minors) to approve arrangements varying or revoking beneficial and administrative provisions under trusts so long as such arrangements are for the benefit of the individual persons in question. Exceptionally, in the case of persons with contingent discretionary interests under protective trusts, where the interest of the protected beneficiary has not failed or determined, the court can give an approval on behalf of (and against the will of) ascertained adults and no benefit to them is required.[8] Jurisdiction extends to foreign settlements where the property and the trustees are within the physical jurisdiction[9] and the foreign law governing validity of the trust allows variation of the trust.[10] It also extends to the approval of an arrangement substituting a foreign settlement for an English one[11] but the court in its discretion may require that the beneficiaries have a genuine foreign connection.[12] The Act has been useful for saving tax by exporting trusts and by a partition of the trust fund between the life tenant (who might have a protected interest) and the remaindermen (who might be minors, unborn or unascertained). Where new administrative provisions are needed it is simpler and cheaper to invoke s.57 of the Trustee Act which also obviates the need to obtain the consent of every adult beneficiary.

Variation cannot be resettlement

9–136 It is often said that the Act does not extend beyond a variation to a completely new resettlement.[13] However, in *Re Ball's Settlement* Megarry J. stated[14]: "If an arrangement changes the whole substratum of the trust, then it may well be that it cannot be regarded merely as varying that trust. But if, an arrangement, whilst leaving the substratum, effectuates the purpose of the trust by other means, it may still be possible to regard that arrangement as merely varying the original trusts, even though the means employed are wholly different and even though the form is completely changed . . . in essence the court is merely contributing on behalf of infants and unborn and unascertained persons the binding assets which they, unlike an adult beneficiary, cannot give. So far as is proper, the power of the court to give that consent should be assimilated to the wide powers which the ascertained adults have." In the case a settlement conferred a life interest on the

---

[8] s.1(1)(d) and proviso thereto in Variation of Trusts Act 1958. Here the settlor's intentions have much significance: *Re Steed's W.T.* [1960] Ch. 407 *Goulding v James* [1997] 2 All E.R. 239, 250.

[9] *Re Ker's S.T.* [1963] Ch. 553; *Re Paget's Settlement* [1965] 1 W.L.R. 1046 at 1050.

[10] Recognition of Trusts Act 1987 incorporating Art.8 of The Hague Convention on The Law Applicable to Trusts and on their Recognition, para.13–31. The safest course is to vary the trust in the jurisdiction of the governing law.

[11] *Re Seale's Settlement* [1961] Ch. 574; *Re Windeat's W.T.* [1969] 1 W.L.R. 692.

[12] *Re Weston's Settlement* [1969] 1 Ch. 224 where the Court of Appeal refused to make the settlement a Jersey settlement for the reason *inter alia* that it doubted whether the beneficiaries, having only moved to Jersey three months before making the application, would stay in Jersey very long after the approval of the arrangement, if approved, and the saving of the liability to capital gains tax of £163,000. Also see *Re Chamberlain* unreported but discussed in (1976) 126 N.L.J. 1034 (J. B. Morcom): see above, para.8–09. Nowadays the courts are likely to take a move relaxed attitude, given the free choice of law permitted by the Recognition of Trusts Act 1987: see *Richard v Mackay* (1997) 11 Trust L.I. 123.

[13] *Re T's S.T.* [1964] Ch. 158 at 162, *Re Holts Settlement* [1969] 1 Ch. 100 at 117.

[14] [1968] 2 All E.R. 438 at 442.

settlor (subject to a power of appointment in favour of his sons and grandchildren) and the capital was in default of appointment to be divided between the two sons of the settlor or their issue *per stirpes* if either son predeceased the settlor. The approved arrangement revoked the beneficial and administrative provisions of the settlement and replaced them with new provisions whereby each half of the trust fund was held on trust for one of the sons for life and, subject thereto, for such of that son's children equally as were born before a certain date. This jurisdictional limit is thus unlikely in practice to cause much difficulty.

Indeed it has been held[15] to be for the benefit of a minor, becoming absolutely entitled to capital on attaining majority, to convert such interest into an interest under a discretionary trust where the trustee would be unlikely to refuse any reasonable proposal or request from the beneficiary.

Benefit

"Benefit" may be financial, moral or social[16] or the facilitation of the **9–137** administration of the settlement.[17] Unfortunately, the reported cases all too often show, as one commentator puts it,[18] "that benefit and the measure of it is simply what the court says it is." An extreme case is *Re Remnant's W.T.*[19] where the children of two sisters, Dawn and Merrial, had contingent interests under a testamentary trust which contained a forfeiture provision in respect of any child who practised Roman Catholicism or was married to a Catholic at the time of vesting, with an accruer provision in favour of the children of the other sister. Dawn's children were Protestant whilst Merrial's children were Catholic. In the interests of family harmony an application was made *inter alia* for deletion of the forfeiture provision. Pennycuick J. acceded to the application in the interests of family harmony and freedom of marital choice, though defeating the testator's clear intentions and though financially disadvantageous to Dawn's children who otherwise had a good chance of gaining under the accruer clause. *Re Tinker's Settlement*[20] was not cited where Russell J. had refused approval to inserting a provision (omitted in error) which would have taken away a sister's children's chance of obtaining property under an accruer clause on the brother's death under 30. Further, Pennycuick J. did not consider whether the Protestant children, when adult, would in all probability be happy to forgo a larger share in the trust fund resulting from their cousins' Catholicism, this being the test taken by Cross J. in *Re C.L.*[21] to distinguish *Re Tinker* from *Re C.L.*, where he approved a mental patient giving up

---

[15] *Re Estate Trust* [2001] W.T.L.R. 571; deferment of entitlement to capital is the normal acceptable variation. In a small trust, the statutory power of advancement for the benefit of a beneficiary may be extended from half to the whole fund in order to enable a child to complete her education at a fee-paying school: *CD v O* [2004] 3 All E.R. 780.
[16] *Re Towler's S.T.* [1964] Ch. 158; *Re Holt's Settlement* [1969] 1 Ch. 100; *Re Weston's Settlement* [1969] 1 Ch. 224; *Re Remnant's S.T.* [1970] 1 Ch. 560, but cf. *Re Tinker's Settlement* [1960] 1 W.L.R. 1011.
[17] *Re University of London Charitable Trusts* [1964] Ch. 282; *Re Seale's Marriage Settlement* [1961] Ch. 574.
[18] R. B. M. Cotterell (1971) 34 M.L.R. 98.
[19] [1970] 1 Ch. 560.
[20] [1960] 1 W.L.R. 1011.
[21] [1969] 1 Ch. 587.

certain life interests in favour of her adopted daughters with interests in remainder. Perhaps one may artificially reconcile *Re Remnant's W.T.* with *Re Tinker's Settlement* on the basis that in the former both sides of the family could benefit in theory while in the latter only one side of the family could benefit.[22]

9–138   So long as the arrangement is for the benefit of the incapable or unborn beneficiaries it does not matter that it is contrary to the settlor's wishes,[23] the operation of the rule in *Saunders v Vautier* entitling the beneficiaries collectively to deal with their property as they want and the court's approval operating as the collective consent of the unborn or incapable beneficiaries. Exceptionally, in the case of protective trust cases under s.1(1)(d) of the 1958 Act where it is immaterial that there is no benefit for the class of contingent beneficiaries the settlor's purpose to protect the protected life tenant from improvident dealings is a significant consideration.[24]

The court may sanction a proposed arrangement which involves an element of risk to infant or unborn beneficiaries if the risk is one which an adult might well be prepared to take.[25] It will not sanction an arrangement involving an appointment made under a special power considered to be a fraud on the power. Thus, if a life tenant exercises a power to appoint capital to his two minor children to the exclusion of any of his future children, with the ulterior intent of receiving a larger share of the capital than otherwise would be possible this can be invalidated.[26]

Parties to the application

9–139   Application is by claim form (under Pt 8 of the Civil Procedure Rules) supported by affidavits to which a draft scheme of arrangement will be exhibited. The proper claimants are the adult beneficiaries and not the trustees.[27] The trustees are supposed to be "watch-dogs" concerned with the interests of those who may possibly be adversely affected by the arrangement proposed. The defendant should be the trustees, the settlor, any beneficiary not a claimants, and any person who may become entitled to an interest under the trusts as being at a future date or on the happening of a future event a person of any specified description or a member of any specified class (*e.g.* next-of-kin of S, still alive) who would be of that description or of that class if the said date had fallen or the said event had happened (*e.g.* S's death) at the date of the application to the court, being the date of issue of the claim form.[28] No other persons who might

---

[22] P. J. Clarke [1987] Conv. 69.

[23] *Goulding v James* [1997] 2 All E.R. 239; CA. Four fifths of the costs of affidavits filed by the trustee relating to the testator's wishes of "little if any relevance or weight" were disallowed.

[24] *ibid*, pp 249–251, based on *Re Steed's W.T.* [1960] Ch. 407 CA.

[25] *Re Cohen's W.T.* [1959] 1 W.L.R. 865; (1960) 76 L.Q.R. (R.E.M.); *Re Holt's Settlement* [1969] 1 Ch. 100; *Re Robinson's S.T.* [1976] 1 W.L.R. 806.

[26] *Re Brook's Settlement* [1968] 1 W.L.R. 1661, on which see S. M. Cretney (1969) 32 M.L.R. 317, contrasting this with *Re Wallece's Settlements* [1963] 1 W.L.R. 711.

[27] *Re Druce's S.T.* [1962] 1 W.L.R. 363; trustees should only act as claimants where they are satisfied that the proposed arrangement is beneficial and that no beneficiary is willing to make the application.

[28] *Knocker v Youle* [1986] 1 W.L.R. 934 at 938. For infants or unborn beneficiaries evidence in a witness statement verified by a statement of truth or in an affidavit must show that their litigation friends and the trustees support the arrangement as in their interests and exhibit counsel's opinion to this effect; See CPR 64.2(c).

eventually fulfil that description or be members of that class (*e.g.* distant relatives who might be next-of-kin if the nearer relatives conveniently died) need be made parties, nor need possible objects of a power of appointment which has not actually been exercised in their favour, or persons whose only interest is under discretionary trusts in a protective trust where the interest of the protected beneficiary has not failed or determined. However, a person who has an actual interest conferred directly on him by a settlement, however remote or contingent, has been held not to be a person who *may* become entitled to an interest so the court cannot approve on his behalf: *Knocker v Youle*, para.9–145.

The effect of approval by the court

The variation takes effect as soon as the order of the court is made without **9–140** any further instrument,[29] and the order may be liable to stamp duty.[30]

A fundamental question is whether it is the order of the court or the arrangement which that order approves which has the effect of varying the trusts. The former view was taken in *Re Hambleden's W.T.*[31] The latter view is supported by dicta of Lords Reid and Wilberforce in *Re Holmden's Settlement.*[32]

In *Re Holt's Settlement*,[33] decided before *Re Holmden's Settlement* was **9–141** reported, Megarry J. rejected the view taken in *Re Hambleden's W.T.*, canvassed the difficulties arising from such rejection and accepted counsel's submission that,[34] "when the adults by their counsel assented to the arrangement and the court on behalf of the infants by order approved the arrangement then there was an arrangement which varied the trusts." The variation is thus effected by the consent of all parties on *Saunders v Vautier*[35] principles, the court supplying the consents of the unborn, the unascertained and infants, and new trusts replace the old so that since July 16, 1964, the Perpetuities and Accumulations Act 1964 has been available to provide new perpetuity and accumulation periods for trusts varied under the Variation of Trusts Act.[36]

This was endorsed in *Goulding v James* by Mummery L.J.[37]: "The court is merely contributing on behalf of infants and unborn and unascertained persons the binding assents to the arrangements which they, unlike an adult beneficiary, cannot give. The 1958 Act has thus been viewed by the courts as a statutory extension of the consent principle embodied in the rule in

---

[29] *Re Holmden's Settlement* [1968] A.C. 685; *Re Holt's Settlement* [1969] 1 Ch. 100.
[30] Practice Note [1966] 1 W.L.R. 345; *Re Holt's Settlement*, above *Thorn v I.R.C.* [1976] 1 W.L.R. 915, though *ad valorem* duty on gifts abolished by Finance Act 1985, s.82.
[31] [1960] 1 W.L.R. 82.
[32] [1968] A.C. 685 at 701, 702, 710, 713.
[33] [1969] 1 Ch. 100.
[34] [1969] 1 Ch. 100 at 115.
[35] Above, para.9–123.
[36] So held in *Re Holt's Settlement* [1969] 1 Ch. 100. It is thought that as it is the court that orders variations under Matrimonial Causes Act 1973, s.24 such orders in the Family Division, like the exercise of special powers, are subject to the periods laid down in the original settlement.
[37] [1997] 2 All E.R. 239, 247.

Saunders v Vantier. The principle recognises the rights of beneficiaries who are *sui juris* and together absolutely entitled to the trust property, to exercise their proprietary rights to overbear and defeat the intention of a testator or settlor."

9–142   Adult beneficiaries who give their own consents to the variation would seem to be *pro tanto* disposing of their subsisting equitable interests so that signed writing is required by s.53(1)(*c*) of the Law of Property Act 1925. However, in *Re Holt's Settlement*[38] Megarry J. held that the court's power under the 1958 Act was to approve arrangements that actually did vary the trusts effectively so the court's order approving the arrangement makes it effective irrespective of whether there is any signed writing provided by the consenting adults. The 1958 Act by implication ousted s.53(1)(*c*). Furthermore, where the arrangement consisted of a specifically enforceable contract the beneficial interests would have passed under a constructive trust to the purchasers, such a trust being effective under section 53(2) without signed writing.

Variation of Trusts Act 1958

9–143   **Section 1.**—(1) Where property, whether real or personal, is held on trusts arising, whether before or after the passing of this Act, under any will, settlement or other disposition, the court may if it thinks fit by order approve on behalf of—

    (a) any person having, directly or indirectly, an interest, whether vested or contingent, under the trusts who by reason of infancy or other incapacity is incapable of assenting,[39] or

    (b) any person (whether ascertained or not) who may[40] become entitled, directly or indirectly, to an interest under the trusts as being at a future date or on the happening of a future event a person of any specified description[41] or a member of any specified class of persons, so however that this paragraph shall not include any person[42] who would be of that description, or a member of that class, as the case may be, if the said date had fallen or the said event had happened at the date of the application to the court,[43] or

    (c) any person unborn, or

    (d) any person[44] in respect of any discretionary interest of his under protective trusts where the interest of the principal beneficiary has not failed or determined,

any arrangement (by whomsoever proposed,[45] and whether or not there is any other person beneficially interested who is capable of assenting thereto) varying or

---

[38] [1969] 1 Ch. 100 at 115–116.

[39] Objects of a discretionary trust are treated as included (*Re Clitheroe's S.T.* [1959] 3 All E.R. 784) but not objects of a power of appointment (*Knocker v Youle* [1986] 2 All E.R. 114).

[40] See *Knocker v Youle* [1986] 2 All E.R. 914, para.9–145.

[41] Unascertained future spouses are included: *Re Steed's W.T.* [1960] Ch. 407.

[42] This is tacitly assumed to cover only "ascertained" persons so as not to cover all females who may possibly marry a bachelor beneficiary and so become a beneficiary.

[43] This refers *inter alia* to the potential next-of-kin of a living person, who must make up their own minds whether or not to give their consent: *Re Suffert's Settlement* [1961] Ch. 1. The relevant date is the date of issue of the claim form; *Knocker v Youle* [1986] 1 W.L.R. 934 at 938.

[44] Including an unascertained or unborn person: *Re Turner's Will Trusts* [1960] Ch. 122; (1959) 75 L.Q.R. 541 (R.E.M.). This approval may be given without the need to show "benefit."

[45] The arrangement need not be in the nature of a contract between parties: *Re Steed's W.T.* [1959] Ch. 354; but must not amount to a completely new settlement: *Re T's S.T.* [1964] Ch. 158; *Re Ball's S.T.* [1968] 1 W.L.R. 899; and it must be practical and businesslike: *Re Van Jenisen's W.T.* [1964] 1 W.L.R. 449.

revoking all or any of the trusts, or enlarging[46] the powers of the trustees of managing or administering any of the property subject to the trusts:

Providing that except[47] by virtue of paragraph (d) of this subsection the court shall not approve an arrangement on behalf of any person unless the carrying out thereof would be for the benefit[48] of that person. **9–144**

(2) In the foregoing subsection "protective trusts" means the trusts specified in paragraphs (i) and (ii) of subsection (1) of section thirty-three of the Trustee Act 1925 or any like trusts, "the principal beneficiary" has the same meaning as in the said subsection (1) and "discretionary interest" means an interest arising under the trust specified in paragraph (ii) of the said subsection (1) or any like trust.[49]

(3) The jurisdiction conferred by subsection (1) of this section shall be exercisable by the High Court, except that the question whether the carrying out of any arrangement would be for the benefit of a person falling within paragraph (a) of the said subsection (1) who lacks capacity (within the meaning of the Mental Capacity Act 2005) to give his assent is to be determined by the Court of Protection.

(5) Nothing in the foregoing provisions of this section shall apply to trusts affecting property settled by Act of Parliament.

(6) Nothing in this section shall be taken to limit the powers conferred by section sixty-four of the Settled Land Act 1925, section fifty-seven of the Trustee Act 1925, or the powers of the Court of Protection.

KNOCKER v YOULE[50]

Chancery Division [1986] 2 All E.R. 914; [1986]1 W.L.R. 934

WARNER J.: "A problem has arisen which particularly affects the second settlement, that dated 22 December 1937. The trusts of that settlement were unusual and are now effectively these. In the case of a share of the trust fund settled on Mrs Youle (referred to in the settlement as 'Augusta') cl. 3(2) provides: **9–145**

'*If* Augusta shall attain the age of twenty-one years [which of course she did long ago] the Trustees shall thereafter pay the income of the first share to

---

[46] *e.g.* conferring wider investment powers: see *Re Coates's Trusts* [1959] 1 W.L.R. 375; *Re Byng's Will Trusts* [1959] 1 W.L.R. 375; *Re Allen's Settlement Trusts* [1960] 1 W.L.R. 6; *Re Royal Naval and Royal Marine Children's Homes, Portsmouth* [1959] 1 W.L.R. 755. Where no alteration of beneficial interests is sought, only larger administrative powers, it is more convenient to use Trustee Act 1925, s.57: the advantages of s.57 are that the trustees are normally the applicants, the consent of each *sui juris* beneficiary is not required, the court considers the interest of the beneficiaries collectively not individually: *Anker-Petersen v Anker-Petersen* [2000] W.T.L.R 581.

[47] Even in the excepted case the court must exercise its discretion judicially: *Re Burney's Settlement* [1961] 1 W.L.R. 545; *Re Baker's S.T.* [1964] 1 W.L.R. 336.

[48] In *Re Cohen's W.T.* [1959] 1 W.L.R. 865 at 868 Danckwerts J. said that the court could take a risk on behalf of an infant if it was a risk an adult would be prepared to take. This was criticised at (1960) 76 L.Q.R. 22 (R. E. M.). In a case of the same name [1965] 1 W.L.R. 1229, Stamp J. stressed, however, that (i) the court had to be satisfied that there was a benefit in the case of each individual infant and not merely of the whole class to which the infant belonged; and (ii) while the court need not be satisfied that each individual infant is bound to be better off than he would otherwise have been, it must be sure that he is making a bargain which is a reasonable one which an adult would be prepared to make. The court may take a broad reasonable view but not a galloping gambling view: *Re Robinson's S.T.* [1976] 1 W.L.R. 806. The court will not approve an arrangement which is a fraud on a power (*Re Robertson's W.T.* [1960] 1 W.L.R. 1050) or is contrary to public policy (*Re Michelham's W.T.* [1964] Ch. 550). Nor will the court use the Act as a justification for rectifying a settlement on the basis of mistake (*Re Tinker's Settlement* [1960] 1 W.L.R. 1011) or for making an order which can be made without the aid of the Act (*Re Pettifor's W.T.* [1966] Ch. 257 where the female beneficiary was 70 years old and so well past child-bearing age.)

[49] For "like" trusts, see *Re Wallace's Settlement* [1968] 1 W.L.R. 711 at 716.

[50] Endorsed by British Columbia Court of Appeal in *Buschau v Rogers Communications* (2004) 6 I.T.E.L.R. 919.

Augusta during the reminder of her life and after her death shall hold such share and the future income thereof in trust for such person or persons for such purposes and in such manner as Augusta shall by Will or Codicil appoint.'

"In default of appointment there is an accruer clause to a share of the trust fund settled on Mr Knocker. The trusts of that share are, *mutatis mutandis*, the same. Then there is, in cl. 7, an ultimate trust in these terms:

'IN the event of the failure or determination of the trusts hereinbefore declared concerning the Trust Fund and subject to the trusts powers and provisions hereinbefore declared and contained concerning the same and to every or any exercise of such powers and to any statutory provisions which may be applicable the Trustees shall hold the Trust Fund upon trust to pay the income thereof to the Settlor's Wife Mildred Alice Knocker for her life or until she remarries and subject thereto shall hold the Trust Fund and the income thereof in trust for such of the Settlor's four sistérs Emily Mills the said Ada Florence Potter Annie Maude Leveaux and Alice Augusta Baker as shall be living at the time of such failure or determination and the issue then living and attaining the age of twenty-one years of such of the said four sisters as shall then be dead in equal shares per stirpes.'

9–146   "The settlor's wife, Mildred Alice Knocker, and his four named sisters have all long since died. The problem is this. None of the issue of the four sisters, whom I will call, for convenience, 'the cousins,' has been made a party to any of these originating summonses. They are very numerous and some of them live in Australia. It is not practicable to get their approval of the proposed arrangement. There are 17 of them who, if the failure or determination of the prior trusts had occurred at the date of the issue of the originating summonses, would have been members of the class of issue entitled to take under the ultimate trust in cl. 7 of the settlement.

"What is said by counsel is that I have power under s.1(1)(b) of the Variation of Trusts Act 1958 to approve the arrangement on behalf of the cousins.

"There are two difficulties. First, it is not strictly accurate to describe the cousins as persons 'who may become entitled . . . to an interest under the trusts.' There is no doubt of course that they are members of a 'specified class.' Each of them is, however, entitled now to an interest under the trusts, albeit a contingent one (in the case of those who are under 21, a doubly contingent one) and albeit also that it is an interest that is defeasible on the exercise of the general testamentary powers of appointment vested in Mrs Youle and Mr Knocker. None the less, it is properly described in legal language as an interest, and it seems to me plain that in this Act the word 'interest' is used in its technical, legal sense. Otherwise, the words 'whether vested or contingent' in para. (a) of s.1(1) would be out of place.

9–147   "What counsel invited me to do was in effect to interpret the word 'interest' in s.1(1) loosely, as a layman might, so as not to include an interest that was remote. I was referred to two authorities: *Re Moncrieff's Settlement Trusts* [1962] 1 W.L.R. 1344 and the earlier case of *Re Suffert's Settlement* [1961] Ch. 1. In both those cases, however, the class in question was a class of prospective next of kin, and, of course it is trite law that the prospective or presumptive next of kin of a living person do not have an interest. They have only a *spes successionis*, a hope of succeeding, and quite certainly they are the typical category of persons who fall within s.1(1)(b). Another familiar example of a person falling within that provision is a potential future spouse. It seems to me, however, that a person who has an actual interest directly conferred on him or her by a settlement, albeit a remote interest, cannot properly be described as one who 'may become' entitled to an interest.

"The second difficulty (if one could think of a way of overcoming the first) is that there are, as I indicated earlier, 17 cousins who, if the failure or determination of the earlier trusts declared by the settlement had occurred at the date of the application to the court, would have been members of the specified class, in that they were then living and over 21. Therefore, they are *prima facie* excluded from s.1(1)(b) by what has been conveniently called the proviso to it, that is to say the part beginning 'so however that this paragraph shall not include . . .' They are in the same boat, if I may express it in that way, as the first cousins in *Re Suffert's Settlement* and the adopted son in *Re Moncrieff's Settlement Trusts*. The court cannot approve the arrangement on their behalf; only they themselves can do so.

"Counsel for the plaintiffs suggested that I could distinguish *Re Suffert's Settle-* **9–148** *ment* and *Re Moncrieff's Settlement Trusts* in that respect for two reasons.

"First, he suggested that the proviso applied only if there was a single event on the happening of which one could ascertain the class. Here, he said, both Mr Knocker and Mrs Youle must die without exercising their general testamentary powers of appointment to the full before any of the cousins could take anything. But it seems to me that what the proviso is referring to is the event on which the class becomes ascertainable, and that that is a single event. It is, in this case, the death of the survivor of Mrs Youle and Mr Knocker, neither of them having exercised the power to the full; in the words of cl. 7 of the settlement, it is 'the failure or determination of the trusts hereinbefore declared concerning the trust fund.'

"The second reason suggested why I should distinguish the earlier authorities was that the event hypothesised in the proviso was the death of the survivor of Mr Knocker and Mrs Youle on the date when the originating summonses were issued, that is to say on 6 January 1984. There is evidence that on that day there were in existence wills of both of them exercising their testamentary powers to the full. The difficulty about that is that the proviso does not say '. . . so however that this paragraph shall not include any person who would have become entitled if the said event has happened at the date of the application to the court.' It says:

'. . . so however that this paragraph shall not include any person who would be of that description, or a member of that class, as the case may be, if the said date had fallen or the said event had happened at the date of the application to the court.'

"So the proviso is designed to identify the presumptive members of the class at the **9–149** date of the application to the court and does not advert to the question whether at that date they would or would not have become entitled.

"I was reminded by counsel of the principle that one must construe Acts of Parliament having regard to their purpose, and it was suggested that the purpose here was to exclude the need to join as parties to applications under the Variation of Trusts Act 1958 people whose interests were remote. In my view, however, that principle does not enable me to take the sort of liberty with the language of this statute that I was invited to take. It is noteworthy that remoteness does not seem to be the test if one thinks in terms of presumptive statutory next of kin. The healthy issue of an elderly widow who is on her deathbed, and who has not made a will, have an expectation of succeeding to her estate; that could hardly be described as remote. Yet they are a category of persons on whose behalf the court could, subject of course to the proviso, approve an arrangement under this Act. On the other hand, people in the position of the cousins in this case have an interest that is extremely remote. None the less, it is an interest, and the distinction between an expectation and an interest is one which I do not think that I am entitled to blur. So, with regret, having regard to the particular circumstances of this case, I have to say that I do not think that I have jurisdiction to approve these arrangements on behalf of the cousins."

C. The Matrimonial Causes Act 1973

9–149A Under ss.21(2)(c) and 24(1)(c) of the Matrimonial Causes Act 1973 the court has very extensive powers to make an order varying any "ante-nuptial or post-nuptial"[51] settlement made on the parties to the marriage for the benefit of the parties and/or the children of the marriage, so long as it is for the benefit of some of them. An order extinguishing or reducing the interest of either of the spouses may even be made under s.24(1)(d). The trustees should be made parties and may be replaced, while the terms of the settlement may be completely rewritten.[52]

Section 6. Capital and Income: The Trustee's Duty of Impartiality

9–150 It is the trustees' duty to balance the conflicting interests of life-tenants interested in income and remaindermen interested in capital[53] and certain rules have evolved to guide trustees and, in some cases, to provide what is to be done if the rules have been broken.[54] In an exceptional case it may even be necessary for the trustees to balance fairly the interests of beneficiaries entitled to capital. Thus, they can reject the claim of a beneficiary entitled to 46/80 of a trust fund to have 574 of the 999 shares in a private company owned by the trust where such majority shareholding is worth much more than 46/80 of the proceeds of sale of the 999 shares.[55] To maintain an even hand or fair balance between the beneficiaries the shares should be sold and the proceeds divided in the relevant fractions between the beneficiaries. In making investments we have already seen[56] that the trustees must act fairly in making decisions which may have different consequences for different classes of beneficiaries.

1. RECEIPTS AND EXPENSES

9–151 Property which can be categorised as the "tree" is capital and the "fruit" it produces is income, *e.g.* rents, interest payments, dividends from shares. However, receipts by trustees from companies raise special problems.

   Except for the purposes of taxation, no distinction is made between a company's trading profits (being the excess of trading receipts over the

---

[51] *Brooks v Brooks* [1996] A.C. 375 but pension schemes that amount to nuptial settlements are now outside the MCA 1973 because pension-splitting is now possible under the Welfare Reform and Pensions Act 1999.

[52] *E v E (Financial Provision)* [1990] 2 F.L.R. 233, *T v Y (Joinder of Third Parties)* [1996] 2 F.L.R. 357.

[53] In the case of charitable trusts which have an endowment, which must be kept intact as capital, a balance also needs to be kept between capital and income.

[54] See now Commission C.P. No.175 "Capital and Income in Trusts: Classification and Apportionment".

[55] *Lloyds Bank plc v Duker* [1987] 1 W.L.R. 1324.

[56] See above, para.9–61.

costs of trading) and a company's capital profits (arising from selling an asset in excess of its balance sheet value). Both sorts are available for distribution to shareholders, but the company's capital itself can only be distributed to shareholders[57] on liquidation of the company or under an authorised reduction of share capital (or a payment out of a special share premium account[58]) or a bonus issue of stock or shares which capitalises company profits. What is paid out by the company as capital goes to benefit remaindermen: what is paid out as dividend goes to the life tenant.

Distributions of capital profits can cause great unfairness. Thus, when Thomas Tilling & Co. Ltd was nationalised, being obliged to sell its road transport interests to the British Transport Commission in return for BTC stock, it decided to distribute £5 of BTC stock for each £1 of stock held by its shareholders. This led to a 75 per cent drop in the value of its shares. The life tenant was held to be entitled to the distribution as income,[59] thus receiving much more than was fair in view of the drastic diminution in value of the capital for the remaindermen.

In *Sinclair v Lee*[60] ICI plc had hived off its bioscience activities to its **9–152** subsidiary Zeneca Ltd and then transferred the shares in Zeneca Ltd to Zeneca Group plc, the shares in which were then distributed to ICI shareholders. This indirect, as opposed to direct, demerger halved the value of the ICI shares. Nicholls V.-C. boldly, but artificially, distinguished this from the direct demerger cases like the Thomas Tilling case, so that the Zeneca Group plc shares were held to be capital for the benefit of the remaindermen, thereby preventing the life tenant from obtaining an unfair windfall and preserving the value of capital for the remaindermen.

In the case of ordinary scrip dividends, where a company declares a dividend but affords shareholders the option to take the dividend either as cash or as bonus shares, the receipt is income even if the shares are taken instead of cash: the company's intention is to pay a dividend and not to capitalise its profits.

In the case of enhanced scrip dividends the bonus shares are issued at a price below market value in circumstances where the company has a third party lined-up ready to pay the market price for the shares. Shareholders are thus better off if taking and then selling the bonus shares, so the company's intention prima facie seems to be to capitalise the profits. However, so long as the trustee's decisions on what the trustee believed to be the company's intention were consistent, the Revenue[61] was prepared to accept the trustee's decision that the bonus shares and their proceeds were wholly capital or wholly income or, indeed, capital subject to a lien in favour of the life tenant for the amount of the cash dividend[62] (such lien being satisfied out of the proceeds of sale of the bonus shares).

---

[57] *Hill v Permanent Trustee Company of New South Wales Ltd* [1930] A.C. 720.
[58] Tantamount to an authorised reduction of capital: *Re Duff's Settlements* [1951] Ch. 923.
[59] *Re Sechiari* [1950] 1 All E.R. 417 based on the rule in *Bouch v Sproule* (1885) 12 App. Cas. 385.
[60] [1993] Ch. 497.
[61] Statement of Practice 4/94 in the days when companies had to pay advance corporation tax on cash dividends, something they wished to avoid.
[62] As permitted in *Re Malam* [1894] 3 Ch. 578.

9–153   The Law Commission has provisionally proposed[63] that companies' cash distributions (excluding payments on liquidation or in the nature of authorised reductions of capital)to trustee-shareholders or distributions which trustees could have taken in cash, should be classified as income and all other distributions from companies should be classified as capital: the existing rules should be abolished.

However, this general new rule is subject to the trustee's established duty fairly to balance the interests of income and capital beneficiaries.[64] After all, take the case of a trustee which owns an underlying investment company that owns a portfolio of shares worth £10 million and happens to sell in one year shareholdings that cost £1 million for a capital profit of £2 million. If this is distributed by way of cash dividend to the trustee then prima facie the life tenant receives this £2 million, whereas if the trustee had directly owned the shares and made a capital profit of £2 million, this would have remained part of the trust capital for the benefit of the remainderman.

Distribution of the £2 million to the life tenant clearly imbalances the relationship between him and the remainderman, now interested only in a fund worth £8 million. Normally, a well-drafted trust deed frees the trustee from the obligation as owner-controller of the underlying company to exercise its control so as to cause the company to distribute all its profits by way of dividend to the trustee. However, it seems likely that the equitable obligation to hold a fair balance between life tenant and remainderman should justify a trustee's refusal to exercise its control to pass all the company's capital profits up to the trustee to be held as income for distribution to the life tenant.[65]

9–154   The Law Commission further provisionally proposes[66] that trustees should have a statutory power of allocation of income and capital so as to achieve a fair balance between the interests of life tenant and remainderman, such power, indeed, enabling emphasis to be put on total return investment policies as opposed to the unsatisfactory "tree" and "fruit of the tree" approach.[67]

So far as concerns payment of expenses, Lord Templeman in *Carver v Duncan*[68] stated, "The general rule is that income must bear all ordinary outgoings of a recurrent nature, such as rates and taxes, and interest on charges and incumbrances. Capital must bear all costs, charges and expenses incurred for the benefit of the whole estate"—subject, of course, to any contrary provisions in the trust instrument. Thus, annual premiums on insurance policies to protect the value of the trust fund are a capital expense, as are the annual fees of investment advisers or portfolio managers. The trustee's fees appear to benefit the whole estate though, in so far as connected with providing income benefits, they can be regarded as having an income nature: no case decides the issue, and an apportionment

---

[63] C.P. No.175 para.5.12.
[64] See para 9–150 above.
[65] See e.g. *JW v Morgan Trust Co. of the Bahamas* (2002) 4 I.T.E.L.R. 541.
[66] C.P. No.175 para.5.48 (and see paras 5.45 and 3.74).
[67] See para.9–64 above.
[68] [1985] A.C. 1082 at 1120.

of the fees may be appropriate e.g. 95 per cent borne by capital, 5 per cent by income.

Indeed, since the Trustee Act 2000, expenses properly incurred by a trustee acting on behalf of the trust can be taken out of the trust funds[69] defined[70] as "income or capital funds of the trust". A trustee has always had a right initially to pay expenses out of whatever income or capital is to hand[71] before ultimately in the trust accounts adjusting the accounts to allocate payments to income or capital, while the Law Commission clearly intended that the definition of trust funds would give the trustee a flexible discretion as to the ultimate incidence of insurance premiums[72] and the costs of employing a custodian or nominee or agent.[73] There is thus much to be said for taking the definition at its face value as conferring a flexible discretion as to the ultimate incidence on income or capital of all types of expenses, rather than merely initially enabling the trustee to pay expenses out of income or capital before ultimately determining the incidence of such expenses in accordance with old case law.[74] However, the flexible discretion needs to be exercised so as to balance fairly the interests of life tenants and of remaindermen.

II. THE APPORTIONMENT RULES.

Particular apportionment rules have developed to deal with a testator's **9–155** residuary estate left on trust for A for life, remainder to B absolutely. Debts, expenses and legacies have to be paid out of residue in the course of the year traditionally allowed to the executor to wind up distribution of the deceased's estate. These payments are treated under the rule in *Allhusen v Whittell*[75] as coming partly from income and partly from capital. One must ascertain that sum which together with interest for the year would amount to the total expended on debts, expenses and legacies: such sum is borne by B as out of capital, while the excess of the total expenditure over that sum is borne by A. The rate of interest is based on the ratio subsisting between the actual net income after tax for the year and the gross capital value of the estate.[76]

Once the net residue has been ascertained there are problems if A is receiving too high an income from unauthorised investments of a wasting or hazardous nature or if A is receiving too little income because some assets are non-income-producing (*e.g.* an equitable reversionary interest under another trust where the income is going to the prior life tenant).

---

[69] Trustee Act 2000, s.31(1).
[70] Trustee Act 2000, s.39.
[71] *Stott v Milne* (1884) 25 Ch.D. 710 at 715, *Carver v Duncan* [1985] A.C. 1082 at 1120.
[72] Law Com Report No.260 "Trustees' Powers and Duties" at paras 6.6 and 8.39 and at p.119 note on clause 34 of draft Bill.
[73] *ibid* at paras 5.13 and 8.33 and at p.117 note on clauses 31 and 32 of draft Bill.
[74] As believed by *Lewin on Trusts* (17th ed.), para.25–26B.
[75] (1867) 4 Eq 295, *Re Wills* [1915] 1 Ch. 769.
[76] *Re Oldham* [1927] W.N. 113.

Under the rule in *Howe v Dartmouth*[77] the unauthorised[78] investments must be sold and the life tenant only receives an income of 4 per cent[79] of the value of the property, excess income having to be invested in authorised securities. Under the rule in *Re Earl of Chesterfield's Trusts*[80] once a capital value has materialised for the non-income-producing asset, whether by selling it or waiting until the death of the life tenant in the case of a reversionary interest, then the capital is apportioned between income and capital. One must ascertain that sum which, invested at 4 per cent from the date of the testator's death and accumulating at compound interest with yearly rests, would, with the accumulations, have produced the amount of capital to be apportioned: that ascertained sum is treated as capital and the excess as income.

9–156   A need for an apportionment also arises if a trustee lends money on a security that turns out to be insufficient to repay principal and arrears of interest. Where this was an authorised investment the sum realised from the security is apportioned between life tenant and remainderman by reference to the ratio of the arrears of interest to the amount of outstanding principal.[81] Where the investment was unauthorised, then the proceeds of realisation of the investment plus any income from such investment must be apportioned between the life tenant and remainderman in the proportion which the income which the life tenant ought to have received had the unauthorised investment not been made bears to the value of the sum wrongly invested, but the life tenant must bring into hotchpot all the income actually received during the currency of the unauthorised investment.[82]

In the case of a purchase or sale of shares "cum" (with) or "ex" (without) dividend the trustees may prefer capital or income beneficiaries as the case may be. However, no apportionment is made unless a really glaring injustice would otherwise be caused.[83]

9–157   Finally, s.2 of the Apportionment Act 1870 requires payments in the nature of income to be treated as accruing from day to day and be apportioned accordingly, which creates difficulties for a testator's life tenant (when payments received after death are apportioned to the pre-death period) as well as for classes of beneficiaries benefiting under s.31 of the Trustee Act as made clear in *Re Joel's WT*.[84] It is routinely excluded by draftspersons.

---

[77] (1802) 7 Ves. Jr. 137.
[78] After the Trustee Act 2000, unless there is a contrary intention in the testator's will, the executor and trustee will be treated as being authorised to invest in any kind of investment other than land outside the UK. However, it may well be that an investment may be regarded as an unauthorised one from the date of the testator's death if after complying with the core duty to obtain and consider proper advice the executor decides it is not proper to retain the investment: see Underhill & Hayton, *Law of Trusts and Trustees* (16th ed.), p.550.
[79] The percentage figure is supposed to represent a fair current rate: *Re Fawcett* [1940] Ch. 402, *Re Parry* [1947] Ch. 23, *Re Berry* [1962] Ch.97.
[80] (1883) 24 Ch.D. 643.
[81] *Re Atkinson* [1904] 2 Ch. 160.
[82] *Re Bird* [1901] 1 Ch. 916.
[83] *Bulkeley v Stephens* [1896] 2 Ch. 241, and *Hitch v Ruegg* [1986] T.L. & P. 62 disapproving *Re Winterstoke's W.T.* [1938] Ch. 158.
[84] [1967] Ch. 14.

The Law Commission has provisionally proposed that all existing equitable rules of apportionment should be abrogated[85] and the statutory apportionment rule should not apply to trusts (unless the terms of the trust indicate a contrary intention).[86] It also provisionally proposes that a broad statutory power of allocation should be made available to enable trustees of private trusts retrospectively to keep a fair balance between the interests of income and of capital beneficiaries, so that they will also have much greater freedom to select investments without worrying whether the form of the return will be that of income or capital.[87]

As matters stand, as seen below, there is an overriding duty upon trustees prospectively to act fairly and prudently where there are income and capital beneficiaries with conflicting interests, but a return in the nature of income can only be distributed to a beneficiary interested in income and a return in the nature of capital can only be distributed to a beneficiary interested in capital (or an object of a power of appointment of capital).

III. Overriding Duty to Act Fairly, Maintaining an Equitable Balance

In case it might be thought that s.8 of the Trustee Act 2000 scandalously **9–158** enables trustees to purchase or retain a short lease of premises leased out so that the life-tenant can receive all rents during the last 10 or 12 years of the authorised lease, leaving nothing for the remainderman, it should be remembered that the trustees have an overriding duty to keep an even hand between the beneficiaries and also have a duty to invest prudently.[88] They would be in breach of this duty[89] if they retained the leases till they expired or for any longer period than reasonably necessary to sell the depreciating leases, while purchasing such a lease would not be prudent.[90] It would also seem that the remainderman could specifically invoke ss.14 and 15 of the Trusts of Land and Appointment of Trustees Act 1996 for the court to compel the trustees to sell or he could take advantage of his inherent right to call for conversion if the land was held on trust for sale.[91]

Hoffmann J. has pointed out[92] that the duty to keep an even hand **9–159** between the beneficiaries in making or retaining investments is more appropriately the less mechanical duty to act fairly. His approach indicates

---

[85] CP. No.175 para.5.85.
[86] *ibid.* para.5.87.
[87] *ibid.* para.5.48.
[88] See above, para.9–53. The duty can be ousted expressly or by necessary implication.
[89] *e.g. Beauclerk v Ashburnham* (1845) 8 Beav. 322; 14 L.J.Ch. 241 where trustees were *authorised and required* by and with the consent and direction in writing of the life-tenant to invest in leaseholds. Obviously, the trustees could not object to investment in leaseholds as such, but they had a discretion whether or not to agree to a particular investment proposed "because it must be agreed at once that it would not be fit for them to lay out the trust moneys in a low, bad and deteriorating situation," *per* Lord Langdale M.R. at 8 Beav. 328.
[90] *e.g. Re Maberly* (1886) 33 Ch.D. 455 (should not invest as directed in Irish land but in statutorily authorised investments).
[91] *Thornton v Ellis* (1852) 15 Beav. 193; *Wightwick v Lord* (1857) 6 H.L.C. 217.
[92] *Nestlé v National Westminster Bank* [2000] W.T.L.R. 795 at 803. Also see Staughton L.J. in *Nestlé v National Westminster Bank* [1994] 1 All E.R. 118 at 137 and Wilberforce J. in *Re Pauling's S.T. (No.2)* [1963] Ch. 576 at 586 referring to "the normal duty of preserving an equitable balance".

that English courts would reach the same result as the Ontario Court of Appeal in *Re Smith*[93] circumstances. The authorised trust property comprised only Imperial Oil Co. stock held on trust for S's mother for life, remainder to S. From the outset there was only an average dividend of 2 1/2 per cent when returns of 8 to 10 per cent were available in respect of good quality bonds and mortgages. S did not want the stock sold and the trustee felt bound to agree with this and ignore the life tenant's requests to obtain a higher income for her. The Court of Appeal upheld the judge's finding that the trustee was in breach of trust and should be removed and replaced by a new trustee.

Section 7. The Trust Property

I. Reduction of Trust Property into Possession

9–159A The position upon accepting trusteeship has been considered at para.9–07 above but one needs also to be aware of the following statutory powers.

The Trustee Act 1925

Power to compound liabilities

9–160 Section 15. A personal representative or two or more trustees acting together, subject to the restrictions[94] imposed in regard to receipts by a sole trustee not being a trust corporation, a sole acting trustee where by the instrument, if any, creating the trust, or by statute, a sole trustee is authorised to execute the trusts and powers reposed in him, may, if and as he or they think fit—

(a) accept any property, real or personal, before the time at which it is made transferable or payable; or

(b) sever and apportion any blended trust funds or property; or

(c) pay or allow any debt or claim on any evidence that he or they think sufficient; or

(d) accept any composition or any security, real or personal, for any debt or for any property, real or personal, claimed; or

(e) allow any time of payment of any debt; or

(f) compromise, compound, abandon, submit to arbitration, or otherwise settle any debt, account, claim or thing whatever relating to the testator's or intestate's estate or to the trust[95];

and for any of those purposes may enter into, give, execute, and do such agreements, instruments of composition or arrangement, releases, and other things as to him or them seem expedient, without being responsible for any loss occasioned by any act or thing so done by him or them if he has or they have discharged the duty of care set out in section 1(1) of the Trustee Act 2000.[96]

---

[93] (1971) 16 D.L.R. (3d) 130; 18 D.L.R. (3d) 405. Also see *Re Mulligan* [1998] 1 N.Z.L.R. 481 (where it was the life tenant who was unfairly benefited).

[94] See s.27 of the Law of Property Act 1925; s.14 of the Trustee Act 1925.

[95] See *Re Strafford (Earl of)* [1980] Ch. 28 for a useful examination of the scope of this.

[96] Before February 1, 2001 trustees only needed to have acted "in good faith".

[This section replaces, with amendments and additions, section 21 of the Trustee **9–161** Act 1893 which replaced section 37 of the Conveyancing Act 1881. In *Re Brogden*[97] the Court of Appeal laid it down that trustees must demand payment of funds due to the trust, and take legal proceedings, if necessary, to enforce payment if the demand is not complied with within a reasonable time, unless they reasonably believe that such action would be fruitless. In this case the breach of trust occurred before the Conveyancing Act 1881 came into force. Where trustees of a pension trust are desirous of ensuring that a s.15 compromise of their claim against the employer to add funds to the trust will be a proper exercise of their powers they can obtain confirmation from the court.[98]]

Reversionary interests, valuations and audit

Section 22.—(1) Where trust property includes any share or interest in property **9–162** not vested in the trustees, or the proceeds of the sale of any such property, or any other thing in action, the trustees on the same falling into possession, or becoming payable or transferable may—

(a) agree or ascertain the amount or value thereof or any part thereof in such manner as they may think fit;

(b) accept in or towards satisfaction thereof, at the market or current value, or upon any valuation or estimate of value which they may think fit, any authorised investments;

(c) allow any deductions for duties, costs, charges and expenses which they may think proper or reasonable;

(d) execute any release in respect of the premises so as effectually to discharge all accountable parties from all liability in respect of any matter coming within the scope of such release;

without being responsible in any such case for any loss occasioned by any act or thing so done by them if they have discharged the duty of care set out in section 1(1) of the Trustee Act 2000.[99]

(2) The trustees shall not be under any obligation and shall not be chargeable **9–163** with any breach of trust by reason of any omission—

(a) to place any distringas notice or apply for any stop or other like order upon any securities or other property out of or on which such share or interest or other thing in action as aforesaid is derived, payable or charged; or

(b) to take any proceedings on account of any act, default, or neglect on the part of the persons in whom such securities or other property or any of them or any part thereof are for the time being, or had at any time been, vested;

unless and until required in writing so to do by some person, or the guardian of some person, beneficially interested under the trust, and unless also due provision is made to their satisfaction for payment of the costs of any proceedings required to be taken:

Provided that nothing in this subsection shall relieve the trustees of the obligation to get in and obtain payment or transfer of such share or interest or other thing in action on the same falling into possession.

---

[97] (1888) 38 Ch.D. 546.
[98] *Bradstock Group Pension Scheme Trustees Ltd v Bradstock Group plc* [2003] W.T.L.R. 1281; [2002] Pens. L.R. 327.
[99] Before February 1, 2001 trustees only needed to have acted "in good faith".

9–164   (3) Trustees may, for the purpose of giving effect to the trust, or any of the provisions of the instrument, if any, creating the trust or of any statute, from time to time (by duly qualified agents) ascertain and fix the value of any trust property in such manner as they think proper, and any valuation so made shall be binding upon all persons interested under the trust if the trustees have discharged the duty of care set out in section 1(1) of the Trustee Act 2000.

(4) Trustees may, in their absolute discretion, from time to time, but not more than once in every three years unless the nature of the trust or any special dealings with the trust property make a more frequent exercise of the right reasonable, cause the accounts of the trust property to be examined or audited by an independent accountant, and shall, for that purpose, produce such vouchers and give such information to him as he may require; and the costs of such examination or audit, including the fee of the auditor, shall be paid out of the capital or income of the trust property, or partly in one way and partly in the other, as the trustees, in their absolute discretion, think fit, but, in default of any direction by the trustees to the contrary in any special case, costs attributable to capital shall be borne by capital and those attributable to income by income.

Public Trustee Act 1906

Investigation and audit of trust accounts

9–165   **Section 13.**—(1) Subject to rules under this Act and unless the court otherwise orders, the condition and accounts of any trust shall, on an application being made and notice thereof given in the prescribed manner by any trustee or beneficiary, be investigated and audited by such solicitor or public accountant as may be agreed on by the applicant and the trustees or, in default of agreement, by the public trustee or some person appointed by him:

Provided that (except with the leave of the court) such an investigation or audit shall not be required within twelve months after any such previous investigation or audit, and that a trustee or beneficiary shall not be appointed under this section to make an investigation or audit.

9–166   (2) The person making the investigation or audit (hereinafter called the auditor) shall have a right of access to the books, accounts, and vouchers of the trustees, and to any securities and documents of title held by them on account of the trust, and may require from them such information and explanation as may be necessary for the performance of his duties and upon the completion of the investigation and audit shall forward to the applicant and to every trustee a copy of the accounts, together with a report thereon, and a certificate signed by him to the effect that the accounts exhibit a true view of the state of the affairs of the trust and that he has had the securities of the trust fund investments produced to and verified by him (or as the case may be) that such accounts are deficient in such respects as may be specified in such certificate.

(3) Every beneficiary under the trust shall, subject to rules under this Act, be entitled at all reasonable times to inspect and take copies of the accounts, report, and certificate, and, at his own expense, to be furnished with copies thereof or extracts therefrom.

[The Law Reform Committee (Cmnd. 8733, para.4.48) recommend that Public Trustee Act 1906, s.13 be repealed: there are no powers to enforce the Public Trustee's findings and Trustee Act 1925, s.22(4) provides adequate protection.]

II. DUTY TO NOTIFY BENEFICIARIES AND ACCOUNT TO THEM

As Millett L.J. (as he then was) stated in *Armitage v Nurse*[1] "there is an **9–167** irreducible core of obligations owed by the trustees to the beneficiaries and enforceable by them which is fundamental to the concept of a trust. If the beneficiaries have no rights enforceable against the trustees there are no trusts" [for beneficiaries, only a resulting trust for the settlor]. The rights of a beneficiary to obtain accounts from the trustee[2] so that they can then be falsified or surcharged[3] is at the heart of the trust concept. To give substance to this right, a beneficiary of full age or a primary object of a power of appointment has a right to be told by the trustee that she is a beneficiary[4] and, indeed, a right to be told by the settlor the name and address of the trustee to whom a request can then be made for a discretionary distribution.[5]

"Every beneficiary is entitled to see the trust accounts, whether his interest is in possession or not."[6] Thus, any beneficiary with a future interest,[7] including (so far as practicable) a person who is merely the likely object of a discretionary trust or power[8] which may never be exercised in his favour, has the means to discover a breach of trust, although time does not begin to run against him till he obtains a present interest in trust property because "he should not be compelled to litigate (at considerable personal

---

[1] [1998] Ch. 241, 253 and D. J. Hayton, "The Irreducible Core Content of Trusteeship", Chap.3 of A. J. Oakley (ed.) *Trends in Contemporary Trust Law*, (1996, Oxford). Also see *Raak v Raak* 428 NW 2d 778, 780 (1988), Michigan CA.

[2] Trustees are under a duty to keep proper accounts and be ready to provide them and supporting oral or documentary information: *White v Lady Lincoln* (1803) 8 Ves Jr 363; *Pearse v Green* (1819) 1 Jac. & W. 135, 140, *Eglin v Sanderson* (1862) 3 Giff 434, 440; but legacies to parents for maintaining and educating their infant children do not create trusts: *Re Rogers* [1944] Ch. 297. Defaulting trustees will have to pay for expenses and costs arising from such default: *Re Skinner* [1904] 1 Ch. 289, *Re Den Haag Trust* (1997/98) 1 O.F.L.R. 495.

[3] See paras 10–69 *et seq.* In the case of charitable trusts (or foreign non charitable purpose trusts) one needs the Attorney–General (or an appointed enforcer) to have the right to make the trustees account.

[4] The right to make trustees account is meaningless unless the beneficiaries know they are beneficiaries: *Foreman v Kingston* (2004) 6 I.T.E.L.R. 841 para.85. *Hawkesley v May* [1956] 1 Q.B. 304, *Brittlebank v Goodwin* (1868) L.R.5 Eq. 541, 550; cp. *Scally v Southern Health & Social Services Board* [1992] 1 A.C. 294, 306–307. In the case of a testamentary trust or the statutory intestacy trust, the executor is under no duty to disclose the gift to the specified beneficiaries (*Re Lewis* [1904] Ch. 656) until the estate has been fully administered and the net trust fund ascertained in which the beneficiaries for the first time acquire an equitable proprietary interest (different from the equitable chose in action to have the estate duly administered): see para.1–127 above).

[5] *Re Murphy's Settlement* [1998] 3 All E.R. 1 where from p.3 and the p.9 reference to *Re Manisty's Settlement* [1974] Ch. 17 it appears the judge treated the claimant as a primary object of a power of appointment in a discretionary trust.

[6] *Armitage v Nurse* [1998] Ch. 241, 261 per Millett L.J. Unless there is a possibility of income being accumulated and added to capital it seems that a capital beneficiary is, however, not entitled to see the income accounts disposing of income to income beneficiaries: *Nestlé v National Westminster Bank* [2000] W.T.L.R. 795, 822; but he must be entitled to check that the investment policy keeps an equitable balance between income and capital beneficiaries: see para.9–150 above.

[7] Including contingent interests: *Re Tillott* [1892] 1 Ch. 86; *Att-Gen of Ontario v Stavro* (1995) 119 DLR (4th) 750.

[8] *Schmidt v Rosewell Trust Ltd* [2003] 2 A.C. 709; *Chaine-Nickson v Bank of Ireland* [1976] I.R. 393; *Spellson v George* (1987) 11 N.S.W.L.R. 300, 315–316; *Hartigan Nominees Pty. Ltd v Rydge* (1992) 29 N.S.W.L.R. 405; *Lemos v Coutts* [1992–93] C.I.L.R. 460; *Re Rabbaiotti's 1989 Settlement* [2000] W.T.L.R. 953. The trustee's duty to inform is only so far as this is reasonably practicable: *Re Hay's Settlement* [1981] 3 All E.R. 786, 793, while if objects of a power consist of more than one category of person, *e.g.* for issue, relatives and employees of the settlor the court is likely to consider that by necessary implication the settlor only intended the first category as the prime object of his bounty to be informed: *Re Manisty's Settlements* [1974] Ch. 17 at 25.

expense) in respect of an injury to an interest which he may never live to enjoy".[9]

9–168   Recently in *Schmidt v Rosewood Trust Ltd*[10] Lord Walker, on behalf of the Privy Council, emphasised that no bright-line distinction[11] should be made between beneficiaries under discretionary trusts and objects of discretionary powers of appointment. The nub of the matter is the strength of the claimant's claim to benefit, depending upon whether such persons are intended to receive significant bounty from the settlor via his trustees. In the case of a discretionary trust for the settlor's descendants, his other relatives known to his trustees, employees of X Co. Ltd founded by the settlor and ex-employees, the latter two classes are peripheral and should not have as extensive rights as the former two classes, while, if there was also a power of appointment vested in the trustees of such trust in favour of English charities benefiting children or of any charity in Vanuatu, such charities' interests should also be considered peripheral. On the other hand, if there is a discretionary trust to accumulate income for the trust period and then distribute the capital between such English charities as the trustees then see fit in their discretion but with a power, instead, to appoint income or capital from time to time to the descendants of the settlor and their spouses or cohabitants, the descendant-objects are likely to be the primary focus of the settlor's bounty with charities only having a peripheral interest in the capital, if any, left at the end of the period.

Matters therefore turn not on technicalities but on the substance of the matter, questions of fact and of degree in all the circumstances which would seem to include the contents of any letter of wishes.[12] The court may then consider that a discretionary object or some beneficiary with only a remote or wholly defeasible interest should not be afforded any relief at all in the exercise of the court's inherent jurisdiction to supervise and if necessary to intervene in the administration of trusts.[13]

9–169   However, it still seems that such discretionary object or beneficiary with a remote interest should be informed of his or her interest, so that there is an opportunity to apply to the court even if the application[14] for relief is ultimately rejected. Although the interest is a remote or peripheral one, the settlor by conferring the interest envisaged some extreme or remote circumstances in which it might be appropriate for the trustees in their discretion to benefit the claimant. For the trustees to be in a position to be adequately informed to consider a claim and for the claimant to have any meaningful right to have his claim considered, the trustees need to take whatever steps are practicable[15] (in the light of the value of the trust fund

---

[9] *Armitage v Nurse* [1988] Ch. 241 at 261.
[10] [2003] 2 A.C. 709, para.3–155.
[11] [2003] 2 A.C. 709, para.66.
[12] See D. J. Hayton, "Beneficiaries' and Objects' Rights to Information" (2003) 10 J.Int. Trust & Corp. P.139.
[13] [2003] 2 A.C. 709 paras 51, 54, 67.
[14] It may be that the claimant's interest amounts to a "possession" (within Art.1 of Protocol No.1 of March 20, 1952 to the Human Rights Convention) in respect of which they must have locus standi to apply to the court for protection.
[15] *Re Hay's S.T.* [1981] 3 All E.R. 786 at 793.

and the extent and number of claims of persons primarily intended by the settlor to benefit from his bounty) to make persons within the class of potential claimants become aware of this. Only then are such persons in a position to be able to make a claim that falls within the extreme or remote circumstances envisaged by the settlor, so that the trustees are then aware of the claim and can further the settlor's purposes and expectations.[16]

If the settlor does not want discretionary objects of a power of appointment to be informed that they are such or, if becoming aware of their status, are to have no right to see the trust accounts and supporting documents and so no right to make the trustees account for their trusteeship (such right being exclusively reserved to beneficiaries and to objects of a fiduciary power of appointment[17]), then he should make them objects of a personal power of appointment, only having the right to retain whatever might happen to be appointed them. To ensure that a power conferred on a trustee (as opposed to some other person) is merely a personal power, it should be expressly stated that the exercise or non-exercise of the power is to be unchallengeable in the courts unless amounting to a fraud on the power.[18]

The right to inspect trust documents and take copies at own expense

A person who has the right to see trust accounts, so that he or she can **9–170** falsify or surcharge the accounts and have the trustee top up the trust fund by the amount due on finalising a proper account, has a right at all reasonable times to inspect documents concerning stewardship of the trust fund,[19] and at his or her own expense[20] to make copies thereof or to pay the trustee for copies provided by the trustee for an agreed sum representing the cost to the trustee.

In *Re Londonderry's Settlement*, the Court of Appeal held that correspondence between the trustees themselves or between the trustees and beneficiaries and the agenda for trustees' meeting were not to be treated as trust documents that could be inspected by a beneficiary. However, minutes of trustees' meetings and other documents of the trustees[21] disclosing their deliberations on the exercise of their discretions or their reasons for any particular exercise of their discretions or "the material upon which such reasons were or might have been based," were exempt from the beneficiaries' right to inspect trust documents because, otherwise, the right of trustees not to be obliged to give reasons for the exercise of their discretionary distributive functions[22] would be undermined. This still enabled beneficiaries to see a factual aide-memoire on the state of the

---

[16] The trustee's fundamental function is to further the settlor's purposes and expectations: see para.9–233.
[17] Lord Walker so confined himself in *Schmidt v Rosewood Trust Ltd* [2003] 2 A.C. 709.
[18] Further see para.9–234.
[19] *Re Cowin* (1886) 33 Ch.D. 179; *Re Rabaiotti's 1989 Settlement* [2000] W.T.L.R. 953; *Schmidt v Rosewell Trust Ltd* [2003] 2 A.C. 709.
[20] *Re Watson* (1904) 49 S.J. 54; *Kemp v Burn* (1863) 4 Giff. 348.
[21] A letter of wishes, like the trust instrument, is a document of the letter.
[22] *Re Beloved Wilkes' Charity* (1851) 3 Mac. 8 G. 440; *Wilson v Law Debenture Trust Corp.* [1995] 2 All E.R. 337.

fund, past distributions and future possibilities, and legal advice as to the law relating to the manner in which trustees are entitled to exercise their discretions; but there is no right to see legal advice obtained by a trustee (which should be at his own expense) for his own protection when aware of likely proceedings against him[23] or to any evidence on a *Beddoe's* application by trustees for directions whether to take proceedings against a beneficiary.[24]

In view of *Schmidt v Rosewood Trust Ltd*[25] it now seems futile to try to distinguish "trust documents" from other documents that a beneficiary or an object of a power seeks to inspect. The court in its inherent equitable jurisdiction to supervise, and if appropriate intervene in, the administration of trusts can order the trustee to give the claimant access to such documents and other information relating to the trusteeship functions as to the court seems appropriate in all the circumstances.

Once the claimant has satisfied the court that he or she has more than a theoretical possibility of benefiting, not having a remote or peripheral or likely defeasible interest, then the court will order disclosure subject, where there are issues as to personal[26] or commercial[27] confidentiality, to balancing the competing interests of different beneficiaries, the trustees themselves and third parties.[28] It may be that some documents will be disclosed in redacted form or with parts obliterated, while safeguards may be imposed (whether by undertakings to the court or arrangements for inspection only by the claimant's professional advisers or otherwise) to limit the use which may be made of documents or information disclosed under the order of the court.[29]

In particular, discretionary beneficiaries and objects are not entitled to the reasons for the exercise by trustees of their discretion but must respect the autonomy of the trustees in exercising their discretionary distributive functions,[30] except perhaps in the context of pension trusts where the beneficiaries may well have earned more extensive rights.[31]

Beneficiaries' rights to disclosure in course of civil litigation

9–171   So far, one has been concerned with the rights of a beneficiary or object of a fiduciary power, to whom the trustee must account for the trusteeships to obtain disclosure of trust documents and supporting information under the law of trusts. Quite separately, under the Civil Procedure Rules governing civil litigation,[32] if a beneficiary can make out a properly

---

[23] *Talbot v Marshfield* (1865) 2 Dr. & Sm. 549; *Bacon v Bacon* (1876) 3 4 L.T. 349.
[24] *Re Eaton* [1964] 1 W.L.R. 1269; *Midland Bank Trust Co. Ltd v Green* [1980] Ch. 590 at 604–609.
[25] [2003] 2 A.C. 709 set out para.3–155 above.
[26] *E.g.* as to a beneficiary's needs as a drug-addict or a person HIV positive.
[27] *E.g.* where a rival businessman or litigant against the trustees purchases an equitable interest under a trust to discover more about trust matters: *Rouse v 100F Australia Trustees Ltd* [2002] W.T.L.R. 111 at 128–129.
[28] *ibid.*, para.67.
[29] *ibid.* para.54.
[30] *Foreman v Kingston* [2004] 1 N.Z.L.R. 841, para.99, *Re Londonderry's Settlement* [1965] Ch. 918.
[31] See para.9–289.
[32] Part 31 and Practice Direction thereon. It is also possible to obtain pre-action disclosure of specific documents discoverable under standard disclosure post-action: see CPR 31.16 and *Black v Sumitomo Corp* [2003] 3 All E.R. 643 (if desirable to save costs or dispose fairly of the proceedings or assist the dispute to be resolved without proceedings).

particularised claim (so that it cannot be struck down as a mere "fishing expedition" to see if material can be found to support a claim) then this triggers standard disclosure of documents that can advance or hinder either party's case and subsequent applications can be made in relation to specific disclosure of documents not disclosed pursuant to standard disclosure. Previously, a similar procedure was known as "discovery", and the order in *Re Londonderry's Settlement* was expressly "without prejudice to any right of the defendant to discovery in separate proceedings against the plaintiffs." As Robert Walker J. has pointed out.[33] "If a decision taken by trustees is directly attacked in legal proceedings, the trustees may be compelled either legally (through discovery or subpoena) or practically (in order to avoid adverse inferences being drawn) to disclose the substance of the reasons for their decision".

Letters of wishes

Finally, difficult issues arise in respect of a letter of wishes which a settlor **9–172** provides for the trustee to have some legal significance in guiding the trustee as to the purposes for which broad discretionary powers were conferred by the settlor on the trustee. The letter has special significance after the settlor's death, because while alive the settler should in any event be consulted by the trustees before a significant exercise of their discretionary distributive functions.[34] Such a letter, brought into existence for the purposes of the operation of the trust, needs to be handed on from a retiring trustee to the new trustee, some regard needing to be had to it before a discretionary decision is taken on a matter referred to in the letter of wishes, even if the trustee exercising its independent discretion then decides to ignore a particular wish.[35] Thus, the letter is a trust document that is *legally significant*, although not so significant as the trust deed itself unless, exceptionally, the settlor intended the letter to be *legally binding* so as to override the trust deed to the extent necessary to give effect to what was laid down in the letter.[36]

However, in *Re Rabaiotti's 1989 Settlement*,[37] the Jersey Royal Court held a beneficiary had no right to see a letter of wishes because it was "material upon which reasons were or might have been based" within the terms of the Court order in *Re Londonderry's Settlement*,[38] and in any event, "to require disclosure of a letter of wishes would be likely in practice to undermine the immunity from the provision of reasons and to lead to just the sort of problems which the immunity was designed to avoid."[39]

---

[33] *Scott v National Trust* [1998] 2 All E.R. 705 at 719, and to similar effect Buxton L.J. in *Taylor v Midland Bank Trust Co.* (2000) 2 I.T.E.L.R. 439 at 459–461.
[34] *Abacus Trust Co. v Barr* [2003] Ch. 409. paras 23–25.
[35] *Bank of Nova Scotia Trust Co.(Bahamas) Ltd v Ricart de Barletta* 1 Butterworths Offshore Cases & Materials 5 discussed by H. Thompson in (1994) 3 Jo. Int. Tr. & Corp. Pl 35. Further see D. J. Hayton (1999) 32 Vanderbilt Jo. of Transnat. Law 555, 573–576.
[36] *Chase Manhattan Equities Ltd v Goodman* [191] B.C.L.C. 897 at 823.
[37] [2000] W.T.L.R. 953.
[38] [1965] Ch. 918 at 938, though it was letters of the trustees here that provided such material, not the guidance of the settlor.
[39] *Re Rabbaiotti's 1989 Settlement* [2000] W.T.L.R. 953 at 968.

Furthermore, "as an additional ground", "the letter of wishes need not be disclosed on the ground of confidentiality": although the letter was not expressed to be confidential, "the fact that the settlor writes a separate letter addressed privately to trustees raises a strong implication that he intended the document to be confidential."[40]

9–173 As pointed out in *Lewin on Trusts*,[41] because the letter is given by the settlor to provide guidance to the trustees on the sound administration of the trust and the exercise of their discretions, the obligation of confidence to the settlor should permit the trustees to disclose the contents of the letter to the extent they consider it appropriate for the sound administration of the trust and the proper exercise of their discretions. Upon reaching this stage, one wonders why the beneficiaries should not have a right to see the letter of wishes where it concerns a matter of which the beneficiary complains involving the sound administration of the trust and the proper exercise of the trustees' discretions. After all, the trustees' discretions can only be exercised in a responsible manner for the purposes for which they were conferred upon the trustees[42] as indicated by the settlor in his legally significant letter of wishes. How can a beneficiary take advantage of the accountability to him of the trustees in exercising their discretions unless he knows the purposes for which such were conferred upon the trustees? Without knowing such purposes how can there be any meaningful substance to the fundamental right to make the trustees account for their trusteeship? In essence, in trying to establish a *prima facie* case the beneficiary is fighting the trustee in circumstances where the beneficiary is blind-folded and has one arm tied behind his back.

9–174 Consider the case of a discretionary trust for A, B, C, D, E and F where the trustees are directed not to inform D, E and F that they are beneficiaries, and so are not to show them the trust deed, and that the settlor's letter of wishes is expressly confidential to the trustees and A, B and C. Should the Court not hold that not only are D, E and F entitled to be told they are beneficiaries, and to see the trust deed but they are also entitled to see the letter of wishes. The first two restrictions, amounting to keeping the trust deed confidential, are repugnant to, or inconsistent with the trust concept which requires the beneficiaries having an irreducible core of rights against the trustees.[43] Is not a confidentiality restriction in a letter of wishes similarly repugnant to the trust concept because, if it prevents a beneficiary from knowing what is the purpose behind a particular discretionary power, how can he possibly allege the trustee is not responsibly exercising the power for the purpose for which it was conferred on the trustee by the settlor? Thus, the beneficiary has no meaningful right to make the trustee account for the trusteeship.

---

[40] This was also the majority view in *Hartigan Nominees Pty. Ltd v Rydge* (1992) 29 N.S.W.L.R 405, but the dissenting judgment of Kirby P. (later promoted to the High Court of Australia) has much to commend it in modern circumstances, when the court has the discretion expounded in *Schmidt v Rosewood Trust Ltd* [2003] 2 A.C. 709.

[41] 17th ed. (2000) at 632.

[42] *Re Hay's S.T.* [1981] 3 All E.R. 786 at 792; *Re Beatty's W.T.* [1990] 3 All E.R. 844 at 846; *McPhail v Doulton* [1971] A.C. 424 at 449.

[43] *Armitage v Nurse* [1998] Ch. 241 at 253; D. J. Hayton, "The Irreducible Core Content of Trusteeship", Chapter 3 of A. J. Oakley (ed.) *Trends in Contemporary Trust Law*.

What if the letter of wishes was expressed to be confidential between the settlor and the trustee so as not to be disclosed to A, B, C, D, E or F? Is the position the equivalent of the trust deed being expressed to be similarly confidential, which would clearly be ignored as repugnant to the trust concept unless one accepted it as forming the basis of a claim that the trust was a sham? **9–175**

Such argument has a logical attraction which may well appeal to a court taking account of its broad inherent jurisdiction expounded in *Schmidt v Rosewood Trust Ltd*.[44] To avoid problems, the letter of wishes should provide for it to be disclosed to, say, two responsible members of the class of beneficiaries or if, as yet, there are no ascertained beneficiaries of full capacity to, say, two members of a class of objects of the power who have a right to make the trustees account; or, if there are none yet ascertained of full capacity, then to a person designated as a protector until there is an ascertained person of full capacity with a right to make the trustees account. However, it would be open to a court to require the letter to be made generally available to beneficiaries or objects subject to deletion of any personal or commercial confidential information.

Thus, a settlor could rely upon a morally binding letter of wishes which is not treated as of any legal significance: "This letter is not to be regarded as indicating in a legally significant way the purposes for which the powers in my trust deed have been conferred on my trustees because I do not want my trustees to have any extra legal obligations placed upon them by this letter so as to have to go out of their way to justify the exercise of their powers. I believe the imposition of such extra legal obligations would cause more difficulties than benefits to accrue, creating greater cost burdens and proving likely to upset relationships between my beneficiaries. Thus, my trustees are only to be under a moral obligation to take into account the following wishes of mine and shall not be accountable before the courts in relation to taking into account or failing to take into account such wishes. I accept that if they wish my trustees may destroy this letter and not pass it on to any successor trustees." There is no case law on this but, in principle, there is no reason why facilitative effect should not be given by the courts to the settlor's genuine intention to create a merely morally binding letter of no legal significance even if it omitted the last sentence. **9–176**

"Blind trusts"

Exceptionally, legally binding restrictions on a particular beneficiary for a limited period may prevent such beneficiary from discovering how the trustees have performed their investment role. Thus, the Prime Minister or the Chancellor of the Exchequer or the Director of the Serious Fraud Office can place their investments in a "blind trust" so as to be free from allegations that they abused their inside information for their own ends while in office. **9–177**

---

[44] [2003] 2 A.C. 709, para.3–155 above.

III. Distribution of Trust Property

A. Maintenance

The statutory power of maintenance in the Trustee Act 1925, s.31 is of fundamental importance in the administration of trusts for the assistance it may provide to minors, for the taxation repercussions flowing from the way in which it can convert what are vested interests under the terms of the trust into contingent interests and also flowing from a beneficiary's entitlement to income at eighteen years of age, and for the apportionment problems it creates where there is a class of beneficiaries.

9–178   The trustees must be aware of these points and they must consciously exercise their discretion. In *Wilson v Turner*[45] they automatically paid over the income to the minor's father without any request from him and without any attempt to ascertain whether any income was required for the minor's maintenance: the father was ordered to repay the income. Trustees should particularly review the situation a month or two before the minor attains eighteen years since the statutory power to apply income and its accumulations over the years expires on his eighteenth birthday.

Under the statutory power, so long as income is legally available,[46] there is a *duty* to accumulate the income, so far as not used under a *power* to apply it for the maintenance education or benefit of the beneficiary, for the period of the beneficiary's minority. During such period accumulations may be used as if they were current income despite having accrued to the capital.[47] Once the beneficiary attains eighteen the trustees *must* pay the income from the capital (including the accumulations which become part of the capital) to the beneficiary even if the beneficiary's interest is still contingent under the trust terms, *e.g.* to B if he attains 25 years.[48]

9–179   Section 31(2) may convert what appear to be indefeasible vested interests into defeasible or contingent interests[49] since accumulations of income will not pass to a beneficiary with a vested interest in income under the terms of the trust unless he satisfies a contingency within s.31(2)(i) or unless he is entitled not just to income but also to the capital to which the accumulations automatically accrue, as where personalty is settled on a minor not for life but absolutely (s.31(2)(ii)). The contingencies within s.31(2)(i) are (a) attaining the age of eighteen or marrying thereunder when having a vested interest in income during his infancy and (b) attaining the age of eighteen or marrying thereunder when thereupon becoming entitled to the capital from which the income arose in fee simple absolute or determinable[50]

---

[45] (1883) 22 Ch.D. 521.

[46] A trust instrument may oust s.31 expressly or by necessary implication and s.31 only applies in the case of a contingent interest if the interest carries the intermediate income: see para.9–184.

[47] s.31(2).

[48] This gives the beneficiary an interest in possession which has much significance for inheritance tax purposes: Inheritance Tax Act 1984, ss.49–53 and above para.1–108. Also see *Swales v I.R.C.* [1984] 3 All E.R. 16 at 24.

[49] Thus making 40 per cent tax payable under Income and Corporation Taxes Act 1988 ss.686, 687, see above para.1–101.

[50] *Re Sharp's S.T.* [1973] Ch. 331 treats this as a determinable fee in the strict sense distinct from a fee simple on condition though the Settled Land Act 1925, s.117(1)(iv) (not cited) treats "determinable fee" as meaning a fee determinable whether by limitation or condition. Consider Trustee Act 1925, s.68(1)(18).

(realty) or absolutely and indefeasibly[51] (personalty) or for an entailed interest (realty and personalty). Thus, if B is an unmarried minor and under a trust an apparently indefeasible vested interest is conferred on him (*e.g.* to B for life) in substance B's interest in income is defeasible or contingent[52] since he has no right to income as it arises (the trustees being under a duty to accumulate it in so far as not exercising their power to use it if they see fit for B's maintenance, education or benefit) and he has no right to accumulated income unless he attains eighteen or marries thereunder.[53]

The Apportionment Act 1870 requiring apportionment of income on a day to day basis has an odd effect when a beneficiary attains eighteen. Take dividends received after the eighteenth birthday in respect of a period before and after the birthday. The income apportioned to the pre-birthday period "cannot be applied for maintenance, etc., because the trustees cannot exercise their discretion in advance so as to affect the income when it is received and they cannot apply it in arrear because the infancy will have ceased."[54]

9–180

The 1870 Act also applies when a class member dies or is born. So much of a particular beneficiary's share of income that is not used for his maintenance but accumulated must be allocated to him and kept separate from the other beneficiaries' allocations. The particular share of income will vary with births or deaths of class members. If a minor dies before obtaining a vested interest the income provisionally accumulated and allocated to him is treated as an accretion to the capital of the whole fund, divisible among all beneficiaries ultimately becoming entitled to capital even if not alive during the period when such accumulation occurred.[55]

Section 31 may be ousted wholly or partly by a contrary intention expressed directly or indirectly in the trust instrument. Its provisions will be inapplicable if on a fair reading of the instrument in question one can say that such application would be inconsistent with the purport of the instrument.[56]

The Trustee Act 1925

Power to apply income for maintenance and to accumulate surplus income during a minority

Section 31.—(1) Where any property is held by trustees in trust for any person for any interest whatsoever, whether vested or contingent, then, subject to any prior interests[57] or charges affecting that property—

9–181

---

[51] The interest will not be absolute if defeasible by an overriding power or a condition: *Re Sharp's S.T.*, above.

[52] *Stanley v I.R.C.* [1944] K.B. 255, *Re Delamere's S.T.* [1984] 1 All E.R. 584.

[53] The Income and Corporation Taxes Act 1988 s.686 applies to tax the income at 10 per cent above the standard rate.

[54] *Re Joel's W.T.* [1967] Ch. 14 at 29. The Law Commission C.P. No.175 Para.5.87 recommend replacing time apportionment by apportionment between the class of beneficiaries as constituted on the date the income is received by the trustees.

[55] *Re Joel's W.T.* [1967] Ch. 14. If trustees hold property on discretionary trusts and allocate income absolutely to a minor beneficiary such income does not fall within s.31 (though income arising from such income will): *Re Vestey's Settlement* [1951] Ch. 209.

[56] *I.R.C. v Bernstein* [1961] Ch. 399 at 412; *Re Delamere's S.T.* [1984] 1 All E.R. 584 at 588.

[57] If there is a prior direction to set apart and accumulate income, the trustees have no power to apply intermediate income for maintenance under this section: *Re Reade-Revell* [1930] 1 Ch. 52, but the court may do so under its inherent jurisdiction: *Re Walker* [1901] 1 Ch. 879; above, para.9–130.

(i) during the infancy of any such person, if his interest so long continues, the trustees may, at their sole discretion, pay to his parent or guardian, if any, or otherwise apply for or towards his maintenance, education, or benefit, the whole or such part, if any, of the income of that property as may, in all the circumstances, be reasonable, whether or not there is—

   (a) any other fund applicable to the same purpose; or
   (b) Ny person bound by law to provide for his maintenance or education; and

(ii) if such person on attaining the age of [eighteen][58] years has not a vested[59] interest in such income, the trustees shall[60] thenceforth pay the income of that property and of any accretion thereto under subsection (2) of this section to him, until he either attains a vested interest therein or dies, or until failure of his interest:

9–182   Provided that, in deciding whether the whole or any part of the income of the property is during a minority to be paid or applied for the purposes aforesaid, the trustees shall have regard to the age of the infant and his requirements and generally to the circumstances of the case, and in particular to what other income, if any, is applicable for the same purposes; and where trustees have notice that the income of more than one fund is applicable for those purposes, then, so far as practicable, unless the entire income of the funds is paid or applied as aforesaid or the court otherwise directs, a proportionate part only of the income of each fund shall be so paid or applied.

(2) During the infancy of any such person, if his interest so long continues, the trustees shall accumulate[61] all the residue of that income by investing it, and any profits from so investing it[62] from time to time in authorised investments, and shall hold those accumulations as follows:

(i) If any such person—
   (a) attains the age of [eighteen][63] years, or marries under that age, and his interest in such income during his infancy or until his marriage is a vested interest; or
   (b) on attaining the age of [eighteen][64] years or on marriage under that age becomes entitled to the property from which such income arose in

---

[58] Substituted by the Family Law Reform Act 1969, s.1(3), Sch.1, Pt. 1. For interests under any instruments made before Jan. 1, 1970, 21 years remain the relevant age: Sch.III, para.5(1). In such a case money may be paid direct to the beneficiary once he attains 18 instead of to his parent or guardian, Sch.III, para.5(2). For appointments made after 1969 under a pre-1970 settlement the relevant age is 18: *Re Delamere's S.T.* [1984] 1 All E.R. 584 at 588 *Begg-McBrearty v Stilwell* [1996] 4 All E.R. 205.

[59] The section does not apply if the person has a vested interest, even if it is liable to be divested: *Re McGeorge* [1963] Ch. 544.

[60] The word "shall" prima facie imports a "duty" as distinct from a "power." In this context, however, it imports a "power" which can be overriden by the expression of a contrary intention: see s.69(2) of the Trustee Act 1925; *Re Turner's Will Trusts* [1937] Ch. 15. Provisions made by the settlor or testator if inconsistent with the statutory power amount to contrary intention, *e.g.* a direction to accumulate; *Re Erskine's S.T.* [1971] 1 W.L.R. 162; *Re Henderson's Trusts* [1969] 1 W.L.R. 651 at 659. But if there is no contrary intention the trustees are under a duty to pay the income to the beneficiary on his attaining the age of 18; *Re Jones' Will Trusts* [1947] Ch. 48. Even though the beneficiary may not be entitled to the capital till attaining 30 years of age the fact that he is entitled to the income will give him an interest in possession for inheritance tax purposes.

[61] See A. M. Prichard [1973] C.L.J. 246.

[62] These last 10 words substituted by Trustee Act 2000, Sch.2 para.25.

[63] See above, n.58.

[64] See above, n.58.

fee simple, absolute or determinable,[65] or absolutely,[66] for an entailed interest;

the trustees shall hold the accumulations in trust for such person absolutely, but without prejudice to any provision with respect thereto contained in any settlement by him made under any statutory powers during his infancy, and so that the receipt of such person after marriage, and though still an infant, shall be a good discharge; and

(ii) In any other case the trustees shall,[67] notwithstanding that such person had a vested interest in such income, hold the accumulations as an accretion to the capital of the property from which such accumulations arose,[68] and as one fund with such capital for all purposes, and so that, if such property is settled land, such accumulations shall be held upon the same trusts as if the same were capital money arising therefrom;

but the trustees may, at any time during the infancy of such person if his interest so long continues, apply those accumulations, or any part thereof, as if they were income arising in the then current year.

(3) This section applies in the case of a contingent interest only if the limitation **9–183** or trust carries the intermediate income[69] of the property, but it applies to a future or contingent legacy by the parent of, or a person standing in *loco parentis* to, the legatee, if and for such period as, under the general law, the legacy carries interest for the maintenance of the legatee, and in any such case as last aforesaid the rate of interest shall (if the income available is sufficient, and subject to any rules of court to the contrary[70]) be five pounds per centum per annum.

(4) This section applies to a vested annuity in like manner as if the annuity were the income of property held by trustees in trust to pay the income thereof to the annuitant for the same period for which the annuity is payable, save that in any case accumulations made during the infancy of the annuitant shall be held in trust for the annuitant or his personal representatives absolutely.

(5) This section does not apply where the instrument, if any, under which the interest arises came into operation before the commencement of this Act.[71]

The Law of Property Act 1925

Contingent and future testamentary gifts carry intermediate income

Section 175.—(1) A contingent or future specific devise or bequest of property, **9–184** whether real or personal, and a contingent residuary devise of freehold land, and a specific or residuary devise of freehold land to trustees upon trust for persons whose

---

[65] See above, n.50.
[66] This applies exclusively to personalty and requires the interest in personalty to be indefeasible so that there is an odd distinction between realty and personalty: *Re Sharp's S.T.* [1973] Ch. 331.
[67] This may be excluded if its application would be inconsistent with the purport of the instrument in question, *e.g.* where an appointment of income to six minors "in equal shares *absolutely*" reveals in context an intention that each was to take an indefeasible share even if dying before attaining 18: *Re Delamere's S.T.* [1984] 1 All E.R. 584.
[68] Thus accumulation subject to an overriding power of appointment form an accretion to the respective shares of the beneficiaries subject to the overriding power. *Re Sharp's S.T.* [1973] Ch. 331 following *Re Joel's W.T.* [1967] Ch. 14.
[69] As to this, see s.175 of the Law of Property Act 1925, para.9–184; (1963) 79 L.Q.R. 184 (PVB).
[70] 4 per cent is now prescribed pursuant to CPR Practice Direction 40.15.
[71] The section applies to an appointment made after 1925 under a power created before 1926: *Re Dickinson's Settlements* [1939] Ch. 27. S. 43 of the Conveyancing Act 1881, which was more limited in its scope than the present section, applies to instruments coming into operation before 1926.

interests are contingent or executory shall, subject to the statutory provisions relating to accumulations, carry the intermediate income of that property from the death of the testator, except so far as such income, or part thereof, may be otherwise expressly disposed of.

(2) This section applies only to wills coming into operation after the commencement of this Act.

Need for available income or interest

9–185 In the case of an infant with a vested interest s.31 of the Trustee Act 1925, above, requires income to be accumulated except so far as it is applied for the maintenance of the infant unless the income is disposed of in favour of someone else or directed only to be accumulated.[72] But if the infant's interest is contingent, by s.31(3) income is not so required to be dealt with unless the limitation or trust carries the intermediate income. The rules in regard to this are as follows (subject to any contrary intention):

1. A contingent gift by will of residuary personalty carries with it all the income which it produces after the testator's death: *Re Adams*.[73] If the income is accumulated until the contingency occurs, the rules in ss.164–166 of the Law of Property Act 1925, and section 13 of the Perpetuities and Accumulations Act 1964, which limit the period of accumulation, must be complied with: *Countess of Bective v Hodgson*.[74] On the other hand, a residuary bequest, whether vested or contingent, which is expressly deferred to a future date does not carry intermediate income: *Re Oliver*[75]; *Re Gillett's Will Trusts*[76]; *Re Geering*.[77]

2. A contingent residuary devise of freehold land and a residuary devise of freehold land to trustees upon trust for persons, whose interests are contingent, carry the intermediate income which they produce: s.175 of the Law of Property Act 1925, above.

3. A contingent or future specific bequest of personalty carries the intermediate income: *ibid*.

4. So does a contingent or future specific devise of realty.[78]

5. An *inter vivos* contingent interest will be of specific property and will carry the intermediate income (unless the income is disposed of in favour of someone else or directed to be accumulated).

6. Where a testator directs that a general or pecuniary contingent legacy (*e.g.* "a thousand ICI plc shares" or "£15,000") be set apart from the rest of his estate for the benefit of the minor contingent legatee this will carry the intermediate income produced by such separate fund.[79]

---

[72] *Re Turner's W.T.* [1937] Ch. 15; *Re Ransome* [1957] Ch. 348; *Re Reade-Revell* [1930] 1 Ch. 52; *Re Stapleton* [1946] 1 All E.R. 323.
[73] [1893] 1 Ch. 329 at 334.
[74] (1864) 10 H.L.C. 656.
[75] [1947] 2 All E.R. 162 at 166.
[76] [1950] Ch. 102.
[77] [1964] Ch. 136.
[78] *Re McGeorge* [1963] Ch. 544.
[79] *Re Medlock* (1886) 55 L.J.Ch. 738; *Re Woodin* [1895] 2 Ch. 309; *Re Couturier* [1907] 1 Ch. 470. Income will be carried from the end of the executor's year unless intended to provide for the maintenance of a minor legatee as from the testator's death.

Section 31(3) further makes section 31 apply to a future or contingent **9–186** legacy by a parent or person *in loco parentis* so far as under the general law the legacy *carries interest* for the maintenance of the legatee. Where a future or contingent legacy has not been directed to be set apart so as itself to produce intermediate income, it will be paid in due course at the appropriate time out of the residuary estate, and usually the legatee just receives the legacy without being allowed any interest for the period before the legacy became payable.[80] Exceptionally, a legacy carries 4 per cent interest[81] payable from the testator's death out of the residuary estate income if the testator was the parent or *in loco parentis* to the minor legatee, the legacy was direct to the minor and not to trustees for him,[82] no other fund was set aside for the maintenance of the minor,[83] and, if the legacy was contingent, the contingency related to the legatee's minority and so was not the attaining of an age greater than the age of majority.[84] In this exceptional case the provisions of section 31 apply.

There is a further exceptional case where a contingent legacy carries 6 **9–187** per cent interest before it becomes payable: where the testator's will reveals an intention that the legacy should carry interest from the testator's death for the maintenance of the minor.[85] Here the testator need not be the parent of or *in loco parentis* to the minor and the contingency may be the attainment of an age exceeding majority.[86] It would seem that this was overlooked so that, strictly, section 31 is inapplicable, so that there must be used for the maintenance of the legatee interest at 4 per cent. rather than the higher actual income produced if, on winding up the testator's estate, the executors for convenience sake set aside the capital to which the legatee will be entitled on attaining, say, 25 years of age. It will be troublesome that the balance of income over the sum representing 4 per cent. interest will fall into residue. However, it would probably strain section 31(3) too much to construe "contingent interest" which "carries the intermediate income" to include contingent legacies to the extent they indirectly (via interest payable out of the residuary estate income) carry intermediate income so as to cover this further exceptional case,[87] especially when the latter half of the subsection deals with legacies which carry interest for maintenance.

Tax considerations should always be borne in mind. Income applied for **9–188** an infant unmarried child of the settlor is treated as the settlor's income.[88] Moreover, any sum paid out of trust funds to the settlor's child is treated as income and not capital to an amount equal to the total undistributed income of the trust to that date.[89]

---

[80] *Re Raine* [1929] 1 Ch. 716.
[81] Trustee Act 1925, s.31(3); CPR Practice Direction 40.15.
[82] *Re Pollock* [1943] Ch. 338.
[83] *Re West* [1913] 2 Ch. 345.
[84] *Re Abrahams* [1911] 1 Ch. 108.
[85] *Re Churchill* [1909] 2 Ch. 431 (intention implied from a power to apply the whole or any part of the contingent legacy for the advancement or otherwise for the benefit of the legatee at any time before attaining 21 years of age, which clearly authorised payments for the minor's maintenance), *Re Selby Walker* [1949] 2 All E.R. 178.
[86] *Re Jones* [1932] 1 Ch. 108 (beware the incorrect headnote).
[87] But see B. S. Ker (1953) 17 Conv. 273 at 279, 283–284.
[88] The Income and Corporation Taxes Act 1988, ss.663, 664.
[89] *ibid.* s.664(2)(3), and see above, para.1–99.

B. Advancement

9–189 Trustees must be particularly careful in exercising the statutory power of advancement in order to "benefit" a beneficiary, for a mistake will mean that both capital and income disappear, probably for good. Danckwerts J. has said,[90] " 'benefit' is the widest possible word one could have and it must include payment direct to the beneficiary but that does not absolve the trustees from making up their minds whether the payment in the particular manner which they contemplate is for the benefit of the beneficiary." Viscount Radcliffe has said,[91] it "means any use of money which will improve the material situation of the beneficiary." In *Re Clore's S.T.*[92] making a donation to a charity at a wealthy beneficiary's request to discharge what he felt to be a moral obligation was held an advancement for his benefit. In *Re Hampden*[93] a transfer to trustees for the benefit of the beneficiary's children was held authorised by an express power to benefit the beneficiary.

9–190   *Re Pauling's S.T.*[94] provides a sorry, salutary story for compulsory reading before trustees exercise their power of advancement. It is a fascinating but overlengthy case to set out in any detail. Essentially, the father of the beneficiaries was so charming and forceful that the trustees frittered away much of the capital in ways that enabled the wife's overdraft to be paid off, a house to be bought for the father and his wife absolutely and an overly high standard of living to be maintained for the family. The lessons to be drawn are that requests for advancements from young adults unemancipated from the undue influence of their parents must be treated with caution and the moneys requested applied by the trustees themselves for a particular purpose if previous experience indicates that otherwise the purported purpose is unlikely to be effected.

9–191   An advancement may be by way of settlement that benefits someone other than the beneficiary so long as the beneficiary receives significant benefit,[95] *e.g.* receiving a life interest in the advanced moneys, remainder to his widow for life, remainder to his children equally. To deal with a dictum of Upjohn J.[96] and cases narrowly construing powers of appointment in outdated fashion the power of advancement has often been expressly extended to permit delegation of duties and discretions to make clear that a re-settlement may be by way of discretionary trusts or by way of protective trusts which may end up after forfeiture as discretionary trusts. However, the modern consensus,[97] supported by Viscount Radcliffe in *Pilkington v I.R.C.*,[98] is that no question of delegation of the trustees' functions arises

---

[90] *Re Moxon's W.T.* [1958] 1 W.L.R. 165. For "benefit" under an express clause see *Re Buckinghamshire's S.T., The Times*, March 29, 1977.
[91] *Pilkington v I.R.C.* [1964] A.C. 612 at 635.
[92] [1966] 1 W.L.R. 955.
[93] [1977] T.R. 177, [2001] W.T.L.R. 195; *Re Esteem Settlement* [2001] W.T.L.R. 641.
[94] [1964] Ch. 303.
[95] *Pilkington v I.R.C.* [1964] A.C. 612, *Re Hampden* [1977] T.R. 177, [2001] W.T.L.R. 195.
[96] *Re Wills' Trusts* [1959] Ch. 1, 13.
[97] See J. Kessler, *Drafting Trusts and Will Trusts* (7th ed.), paras 10.5 and 10.11; Parker & Mellows, *The Modern Law of Trusts* (7th ed. by A. J. Oakley), pp.626–627; *Lewin on Trusts* (17th ed.), para.32.18.
[98] [1964] A.C. 612 at 639.

where they transfer property to be held on new trusts which may contain discretionary trusts and powers, because the new trustees are not exercising delegated functions but are exercising new original functions of their own as a result of the outright advancement.

It is necessary to ensure that the rule against remoteness is not infringed, **9–192** for the perpetuity period relevant to the exercise of the power of advancement runs from the date of the settlement and not from the date of the exercise of the power[99]: *Pilkington v I.R.C.*, para.9–198. If part of the exercise of the power of advancement is void for remoteness *and* the resultant effect of the intended advancement is such that it could not **9–193** reasonably be regarded as being beneficial to the beneficiary intended to be advanced, then the advancement fails for it cannot be authorised as within the powers of the trustees under s.32: otherwise the part of the advancement not void for remoteness will stand as within the trustees' powers,[1] *e.g.* C's life interest stands where the advancement is to trustees for C for life with remainders to his issue where the remainders are void for remoteness. The fact that in such a case no effective beneficial trusts of capital are created does not mean that there has been no payment or application of capital as required by s.32: the transfer of capital to the trustees of the settlement for C for life is an application of capital within section 32.[2] A capital gains tax charge arises not only on an advance to a beneficiary absolutely but also where the advancement is on new trusts even where T1 and T2 appropriate the property on new trusts and are themselves trustees of the appropriated property. No capital[3] gains tax charge will arise if the trustees instead of creating a new separate settlement (though tied to the old settlement by an umbilical cord"[4] so the old settlement's perpetuity period sets the limits to the new settlement) merely sub-settle some trust assets. To help distinguish between a new settlement and a sub-settlement the Revenue issued a Statement of Practice as follows:

> "It is now clear that a deemed disposal under C.G.T.A. 1979, section 54(1) **9–194** (now T.C.G.A. 1992, s.71) cannot arise unless the power exercised by the trustees, or the instrument conferring the power, expressly or by necessary implication, confers on the trustees authority to remove assets from the original settlement by subjecting them to the trusts of a different settlement. Such powers (which may be powers of advancement or appointment) are

---

[99] The exercise of a power of advancement is treated as the exercise of a special power so that the Perpetuities and Accumulations Act 1964 is of no avail unless the original settlement was created after July 15, 1964: s.15(5) of the Perpetuities and Accumulations Act 1964.
[1] *Re Abraham's W.T.* [1969] 1 Ch. 463 as cut down by the interpretation of the Court of Appeal in *Re Hastings-Bass* [1975] Ch. 25 explored in *Mettoy Pension Trustees v Evans* [1991] 2 All E.R. 513.
[2] *Re Hastings-Bass* [1975] Ch. 25. At 40 the court laid down the general proposition, "where by the terms of a trust (as under s.32) a trustee is given a discretion as to some matter under which he acts in good faith, the court should not interfere with his action notwithstanding that it does not have the full effect intended unless (1) what he has achieved is unauthorised by the power conferred on him or (2) it is clear that he would not have acted as he did (a) had he not taken into account considerations which he should not have taken into account or (b) had he not failed to take into account considerations which he ought to have taken into account."
[3] *Hart v Briscoe* [1979] Ch. 110; *Roome v Edwards* [1981] 1 All E.R. 736; *Bond v Pickford* [1983] S.T.C. 517; Taxation of Chargeable Gains Act 1992, s.71.
[4] See Lord Walker in *Trennery v West* [2005] UKHL 5, para.41.

referred to by the Court of Appeal as 'powers in the wider form.' However, the Board considers that a deemed disposal will not arise when such a power is exercised and trusts are declared in circumstances such that:
  (a) the appointment is revocable, or
  (b) the trusts declared of the advanced or appointed funds are not exhaustive so that there exists a possibility at the time when the advancement or appointment is made that the funds covered by it will on the occasion of some event cease to be held upon such trusts and once again come to be held upon the original trusts of the settlement.

9–195   Further, when such a power is exercised the Board considers it unlikely that a deemed disposal will arise when trusts are declared if duties in regard to the appointed assets still fall to the trustees of the original settlement in their capacity as trustees of that settlement, bearing in mind the provision in CGTA 1979 section 52(1) (now T.C.G.A. 1992, s.69(1)) that the trustees of a settlement form a single and continuing body (distinct from the persons who may from time to time be the trustees).

Finally, the Board accept that a power of appointment or advancement can be exercised over only part of the settled property and that the above consequences would apply to that part."

When advances are brought into account they are accounted for at their value at the time of the advance and not at their value prevailing at the time of the final distribution.[5] This is unjust in these inflationary times so the Law Reform Committee (Cmnd. 8733, para.4.47) recommended that advances should be accounted for at their value at the time of the advance multiplied by any increase in the retail price index up to the time of the final distribution.

The Trustee Act 1925

9–196   **Section 32.**—(1) Trustees may[6] at any time or times pay or apply any capital money[7] subject to a trust, for the advancement or benefit, in such manner as they may, in their absolute discretion, think fit, of any person entitled to the capital[8] of the trust property or of any share thereof, whether absolutely or contingently on his attaining any specified age or on the occurrence of any other event, or subject to a gift over on his death under any specified age or on the occurrence of any other event, and whether in possession or in remainder or reversion, and such payment or application may be made notwithstanding that the interest of such person is liable to be defeated by the exercise of a power of appointment or revocation, or to be diminished by the increase of the class to which he belongs:

---

[5] *Re Gollins' Declaration of Trust* [1969] 3 All E.R. 1591, but trustees may get a beneficiary to consent to his advancement being treated as of a fraction of the fund: *Re Leigh's S.T.* [1981] C.L.Y. 2453.

[6] The section confers a power; it does not impose a duty: hence it cannot be utilised if the settlement contains a contrary intention: see *Inland Revenue Commissioners v Bernstein* [1960] Ch. 444 (Danckwerts J.); [1961] Ch. 399, CA; *Re Henderson's Trusts* [1969] 1 W.L.R. 651; *Re Evans' Settlement* [1967] 1 W.L.R. 1294. Whilst a duty to accumulate is necessarily inconsistent with the power of maintenance it is not necessarily inconsistent with the power of advancement: *I.R.C. v Bernstein* [1961] Ch. 399. S.32 is not excluded by the accumulation trust in s.31 nor by express accumulation and maintenance trusts in similar form to s.31.

[7] Assets can be transferred *in specie*: *Re Collard's W.T.* [1961] Ch. 293 noted (1961) 77 L.Q.R. 161. When brought into account on final distribution of the trust property they will be taken into account as of their cash value when originally received: *Re Gollins' Declaration of Trust* [1969] 3 All E.R. 1591.

[8] The section does not apply where the beneficiary is given only an interest in income: *Re Winch's Settlement* [1917] 1 Ch. 633.

Provided that—

(a) the money so paid or applied for the advancement or benefit of any person **9–197**
shall not exceed altogether in amount *one-half*[9] of the presumptive or vested
share or interest of that person in the trust property; and

(b) if that person is or becomes absolutely and indefeasibly entitled to a share in
the trust property the money so paid or applied shall be brought into
account as part of such share; and

(c) *no such payment or application shall be made so as to prejudice any person
entitled to any prior life or other interest,*[10] whether vested or contingent, in
the money paid or applied *unless* such person is in existence and of full age
and *consents in writing* to such payment or application.

(2) This section applies only where the trust property consists of money or
securities or of property held upon trust for sale calling in and conversion, and such
money or securities, or the proceeds of such sale calling in and conversion are not
by statute or in equity considered as land, or applicable as capital money for the
purposes of the Settled Land Act 1925.

(3) This section does not apply to trusts constituted or created before the
commencement of this Act.

PILKINGTON AND ANOTHER v INLAND REVENUE COMMISSIONERS

House of Lords [1964] A.C. 612; [1962] 3 W.L.R. 1051; [1962] 3 All E.R. 622; 40
T.C. 416 (Viscount Radcliffe, Lords Reid, Jenkins, Hodson and Devlin)

By will the testator left his residuary estate to trustees on trust, for his nephew, **9–198**
Richard Godfrey Pilkington ("Richard"), upon protective trusts during his life with
a provision that any consent which he might give to the exercise of any applicable
form of advancement should not cause a forfeiture of his life interest. After
Richard's death the trustees were to hold the residuary estate upon trust for such of
Richard's children or remoter issue at such age in such shares and with such trusts
for their respective benefit and such provisions for their respective advancement and
maintenance and education as Richard should by deed or will without transgressing
the rule against perpetuities appoint. In default of appointment the trustees were to

---

[9] If A and B are the two beneficiaries contingently equally entitled to a trust fund of £200,000 and B
receives the maximum advancement of £50,000 does this mean that the power can no longer be exercised
in his favour or, if the fund remaining appreciates to £250,000, can B maintain that the fund is now
notionally worth £250,000 plus his advanced £50,000 so that an advancement of half of half of £300,000,
i.e., £75,000, may be made to him so that he may receive a further £25,000 on top of the £50,000 he has
already received? Consider s.32(1) proviso (b) and *Re Marquess of Abergavenny's Estate Act Trusts* [1981] 2
All E.R. 643 (trustees had express power to advance to the life tenant "any part or parts not exceeding in
all one half in value of the settled fund." Goulding J. held an advance of half the value of the settled fund
exhausted the exercise of the power so that it ceased to be exercisable in the future even though the
retained assets had later increased in value).

[10] A beneficiary under a discretionary trust is not entitled to such a prior interest as to render his consent
requisite: *Re Beckett's Settlement* [1940] Ch. 279 but where income is held on the protective trusts in
Trustee Act 1925, s.33, and there has been no forfeiture the "principal beneficiary" has a prior interest
within para. (c) his consent not incurring a forfeiture: *Re Harris' Settlement* (1940) 162 L.T. 358; *Re Rees'
W.T.* [1954] Ch. 202. Further see *I.R.C. v Bernstein* [1960] Ch. 444; [1961] Ch. 399. Often the power to
advance is extended to the whole, rather than half, of the prospective share but the life tenant's consent
remains requisite: *Henley v Wardell, The Times*, January 29, 1988. In the case of a small trust fund for a
minor the half may be extended to the whole under the Variation of Trusts Act 1958: *CD v O* [2004] 3 All
E.R. 780.

hold the residuary estate on trust for such of Richard's children as, being male, attained the age of twenty-one, or, being female, attained that age or married under it, and, if more than one, in equal shares.

The testator's will did not confer any express power of advancement upon the trustees, but, by implication, the power of advancement under s.32 of the Trustee Act 1925, above, was applicable.

Richard had three children, of whom the defendant Penelope Margaret Pilkington ("Penelope") was one.

9–199		Richard's father, Guy Reginald Pilkington ("the settlor"), proposed to make a settlement, to be executed by himself, Richard and the trustees of the testator's will, upon the following trusts: (i) Until Penelope attained the age of twenty-one the trustees of the settlement were to have power to apply income for her maintenance whether or not there was any other income available for that purpose and were to accumulate and capitalise surplus income; (ii) If Penelope attained the age of twenty-one the trustees were to be under a duty to pay the income to her until she reached the age of thirty or died under that age; (iii) If Penelope attained the age of thirty the trustees were to hold the capital of the trust fund upon trust for her absolutely; (iv) If Penelope died under the age of thirty, leaving a child or children who attained the age of twenty-one, the trustees were to hold the trust fund and the income thereof in trust for such child or children, and, if more than one, in equal shares.

9–200		Subject to these trusts, the trustees of the settlement were to hold the trust fund in trust equally for all of Richard's children (other than Penelope) who, being male, attained the age of twenty-one, or, being female, attained that age or married under it. In the case of the failure of the trust, the fund was to be held on the trusts of the testator's will which would take effect after Richard's death as if he had died without having been married.

The proposed settlement provided that the power of maintenance contained in section 31 of the Trustee Act 1925, subject to certain modifications, and the power of advancement contained in section 32 of the Act in an unmodified form, should be available to the trustees.

9–201		The trustees of the testator's will took out an originating summons to determine the question whether they could lawfully exercise the powers conferred on them in relation to the expectant interest of the defendant Penelope, in the testator's residuary estate by applying (with the consent of the defendant Richard, her father) some part not exceeding one-half of the capital of such interest in such manner as to make it subject to the trusts, powers and provisions of the settlement proposed to be executed by the plaintiff, the settlor. Danckwerts J.[11] held that the exercise of the power of advancement in this way would not be objectionable; but his decision was reversed by the Court of Appeal.[12] Richard and Penelope appealed.

9–202		VISCOUNT RADCLIFE: "The word 'advancement' itself meant in this context the establishment in life of the beneficiary who was the object of the power or at any rate some step that would contribute to the furtherance of his establishment. Advancement had, however, to some extent a limited range of meaning, since it was thought to convey the idea of some step in life of permanent significance, and accordingly, to prevent uncertainties about the permitted range of objects for which moneys could be raised and made available, such words as 'or otherwise for his or

---

[11] [1959] Ch. 699.
[12] [1961] Ch. 466.

her benefit' were often added to the word 'advancement'. It was always recognised that these added words were 'large words' (see Jessel M.R. in *Re Breeds' Will*[13]) and indeed in another case (*Lowther v Bentinck*[14]) the same judge spoke of preferment and advancement as being 'both large words' but of 'benefit' as being the 'largest of all.' Recent judges have spoken in the same terms—see Farwell J. in *Re Halsted's Will Trusts*[15] and Danckwerts J. in *Re Moxon's Will Trusts*.[16] This wide construction of the range of the power, which evidently did not stand upon niceties of distinction provided that the proposed application could fairly be regarded as for the benefit of the beneficiary who was the object of the power, must have been carried into the statutory power created by section 32, since it adopts without qualification the accustomed wording 'for the advancement or benefit in such manner as they may in their absolute discretion think fit.'

"So much for 'advancement,' which I now use for brevity to cover the combined **9–203** phrase 'advancement or benefit.' It means any use of the money which will improve the material situation of the beneficiary. It is important, however, not to confuse the idea of 'advancement' with the idea of advancing the money out of the beneficiary's expectant interest. The two things have only a casual connection with each other. The one refers to the operation of finding money by way of anticipation of an interest not yet absolutely vested in possession or, if so vested, belonging to an infant: the other refers to the status of the beneficiary and the improvement of his situation. The power to carry out the operation of anticipating an interest is not conferred by the word 'advancement' but by those other words of the section which expressly authorise the payment or application of capital money for the benefit of a person entitled 'whether absolutely or contingently on his attaining any specified age or on the occurrence of any other event, or subject to a gift over on his death under any specified age or on the occurrence of any other event, and whether in possession or in remainder or reversion,' etc.

"I think, with all respect to the Commissioners, a good deal of their argument is **9–204** infected with some of this confusion. To say, for instance, that there cannot be a valid exercise of a power of advancement that results in a deferment of the vesting of the beneficiary's absolute title (Penelope, it will be remembered, is to take at thirty under the proposed settlement instead of at twenty-one under the will) is in my opinion to play upon words. The element of anticipation consists in the raising of money for her now before she has any right to receive anything under the existing trusts: the advancement consists in the application of that money to form a trust fund, the provisions of which are thought to be for her benefit.

"I have not been able to find in the words of section 32, to which I have now referred, anything which in terms or by implication restricts the width of the manner or purpose of advancement. It is true that, if this settlement is made, Penelope's children, who are not objects of the power, are given a possible interest in the event of her dying under thirty leaving surviving issue. But if the disposition itself, by which I mean the whole provision made, is for her benefit, it is no objection to the exercise of the power that other persons benefit incidentally as a result of the exercise. Thus a man's creditors may in certain cases get the most immediate advantage from an advancement made for the purpose of paying them off, as in *Lowther v Bentinck*; and a power to raise money for the advancement of a wife may cover a payment made direct to her husband in order to set him up in business (*Re Kershaw's Trusts*[17]). The exercise will not be bad, therefore, on this ground.

---

[13] [1875] 1 Ch.D. 226 at 228.
[14] [1874] L.R. 19 Eq. 166 at 169.
[15] [1937] 2 All E.R. 570 at 571.
[16] [1958] 1 W.L.R. 165 at 168.
[17] (1868) L.R. 6 Eq. 322.

9–205   "Nor in my opinion will it be bad merely because the moneys are to be tied up in the proposed settlement. If it could be said that the payment or application permitted by section 32 cannot take the form of a settlement in any form but must somehow pass direct into or through the hands of the object of the power, I could appreciate the principle upon which the Commissioners' objection was founded. But can that principle be asserted? Anyone can see, I think, that there can be circumstances in which, while it is very desirable that some money should be raised at once for the benefit of an owner of an expectant or contingent interest, it would be very undesirable that the money should not be secured to him under some arrangement that will prevent him having the absolute disposition of it. I find it very difficult to think that there is something at the back of section 32 which makes such

9–206   an advancement impossible. Certainly neither Danckwerts J. nor the members of the Court of Appeal in this case took the view. . .

9–207   "The truth is, I think, that the propriety of requiring a settlement of moneys found for advancement was recognised as long ago as 1871 in *Roper-Curzon v Roper-Curzon* and, so far as I know, it has not been impugned since. If, then, it is a proper exercise of a power of advancement for trustees to stipulate that the money shall be settled, I cannot see any difference between having it settled that way and having it settled by themselves paying it to trustees of a settlement which is in the desired form.

"The Commissioners' objections seem to be concentrated upon such propositions as that the proposed transaction is 'nothing less than a resettlement' and that a power of advancement cannot be used so as to alter or vary the trusts created by the settlement from which it is derived. Such a transaction, they say, amounts to using the power of advancement as a way of appointing or declaring new trusts different from those of the settlement. The reason why I do not find that these propositions have any compulsive effect upon my mind is that they seem to me merely vivid ways of describing the substantial effect of that which is proposed to be done and they do not in themselves amount to convincing arguments against doing it. Of course, whenever money is raised for advancement on terms that it is to be settled on the beneficiary, the money only passes from one settlement to be caught up in the other. It is therefore the same thing as a resettlement. But, unless one is to say that such moneys can never be applied by way of settlement, an argument which, as I have shown, has few supporters and is contrary to authority, it merely describes the inevitable effect of such an advancement to say that it is nothing less than a resettlement. Similarly, if it is part of the trusts and powers created by one settlement that the trustees of it should have power to raise money and make it available for a beneficiary upon new trusts approved by them, then they are in substance given power to free the money from one trust and to subject it to another. So be it: but, unless they cannot require a settlement of it at all, the transaction they carry out is the same thing in effect as an appointment of new trusts.

"In the same way I am unconvinced by the argument that the trustees would be improperly delegating their trust by allowing the money raised to pass over to new trustees under a new settlement conferring new powers on the latter. In fact, I think that the whole issue of delegation is here beside the mark. The law is not that trustees cannot delegate: it is that trustees cannot delegate unless they have authority to do so. If the power of advancement which they possess is so read as to allow them to raise money for the purpose of having it settled, then they do have the necessary authority to let the money pass out of the old settlement into new trusts. No question of delegation of their powers or trusts arises."

9–208   "I ought to note for the record (1) that the transaction envisaged does not actually involve the raising of money, since the trustees propose to appropriate a block of shares in the family's private limited company as the trust investment, and

(2) there will not be any actual transfer, since the trustees of the proposed settlement and the will trustees are the same persons. As I have already said, I do not attach any importance to these factors, nor, I think, do the Commissioners. To transfer or appropriate outright is only to do by short cut what could be done in a more roundabout way by selling the shares to a consenting party, paying the money over to the new settlement with appropriate instructions and arranging for it to be used in buying back the shares as the trust investment. It cannot make any difference to follow the course taken in *Re Collard's Will Trusts*[18] and deal with the property direct. On the other point, so long as there are separate trusts, the property effectually passes out of the old settlement into the new one, and it is of no relevance that, at any rate for the time being, the persons administering the new trusts are the same individuals.

"I have not yet referred to the ground which was taken by the Court of Appeal as their reason for saying that the proposed settlement was not permissible. To put it shortly, they held that the statutory power of advancement could not be exercised unless the benefit to be conferred was 'personal to the person concerned, in the sense of being related to his or her own real or personal needs.'[19] Or, to use other words of the learned Master of the Rolls,[20] the exercise of the power 'must be an exercise done to meet the circumstances as they present themselves in regard to a person within the scope of the section, whose circumstances call for that to be done which the trustees think fit to do.' Upjohn L.J.[21] expressed himself in virtually the same terms.

9–209

"My Lords, I differ with reluctance from the views of judges so learned and experienced in matters of this sort: but I do not find it possible to import such restrictions into the words of the statutory power which itself does not contain them. First, the suggested qualification, that the considerations or circumstances must be 'personal' to the beneficiary, seems to me uncontrollably vague as a guide to general administration. What distinguishes a personal need from any other need to which the trustees in their discretion think it right to attend in the beneficiary's interest? And, if the advantage of preserving the funds of a beneficiary from the incidence of death duty is not an advantage personal to that beneficiary, I do not see what is. Death duty is a present risk that attaches to the settled property in which Penelope has her expectant interest, and even accepting the validity of the supposed limitation, I would not have supposed that there was anything either impersonal or unduly remote in the advantage to be conferred upon her of some exemption from that risk. I do not think, therefore, that I can support the interpretation of the power of advancement that has commended itself to the Court of Appeal, and, with great respect, I think that the judgments really amount to little more than a decision that in the opinion of the members of that court this was not a case in which there was any occasion to exercise the power. That would be a proper answer from a court to which trustees had referred their discretion with a request for its directions; but it does not really solve any question where, as here, they retain their discretion and merely ask whether it is impossible for them to exercise it.

9–210

"To conclude, therefore, on this issue, I am of opinion that there is no maintainable reason for introducing into the statutory power of advancement a qualification that would exclude the exercise in the case now before us. It would not be candid to omit to say that, though I think that that is what the law requires, I am

9–211

[18] [1961] Ch. 293.
[19] [1961] Ch. 466 at 484.
[20] [1961] Ch. 466 at 481.
[24] *ibid.*

uneasy at some of the possible applications of this liberty, when advancements are made for the purposes of settlement or on terms that there is to be a settlement. It is quite true, as the Commissioners have pointed out, that you might have really extravagant cases of resettlements being forced on beneficiaries in the name of advancement, even a few months before an absolute vesting in possession would have destroyed the power. I have tried to give due weight to such possibilities, but when all is said I do not think that they ought to compel us to introduce a limitation of which no one, with all respect, can produce a satisfactory definition. First, I do not believe that it is wise to try to cut down an admittedly wide and discretionary power, enacted for general use, through fear of its being abused in certain hypothetical instances. And moreover, as regards this fear, I think that it must be remembered that we are speaking of a power intended to be in the hands of trustees chosen by a settlor because of his confidence in their discretion and good sense and subject to the external check that no exercise can take place without the consent of a prior life-tenant; and that there does remain at all times a residual power in the court to restrain or correct any purported exercise that can be shown to be merely wanton or capricious and not to be attributable to a genuine discretion. I think, therefore, that, although extravagant possibilities exist, they may be more menacing in argument than in real life . . ."

9–212   [However, their Lordships also held that the power of advancement under section 32 was to be regarded in the same way as a special power of appointment so far as the application of the rule against perpetuities was concerned so that the proposed advancement would be void.]

C. Payment of Trust Funds to Beneficiaries

Trustees must pay trust moneys to the right beneficiaries, for otherwise it is a breach of trust. In *Eaves v Hickson*,[22] trustees were induced by a forgery to pay trust funds to persons not entitled, and Romilly M.R. held that, as between trustee and beneficiary, the loss fell on the former.[23]

Section 61 of the Trustee Act 1925, is now available as a defence to a trustee who honestly and reasonably makes a wrongful payment through circumstances similar to those in *Eaves v Hickson*, or through an erroneous construction of the trust instrument.[24]

9–213   Before paying trust funds to an alleged *assignee* from a beneficiary a trustee must investigate the assignee's title. If he relies merely on the alleged assignee's statement, he is not acting reasonably. If the assignee happens also to be solicitor to the trust the trustee will still be liable[25] unless excused under s.61 of the Trustee Act.[26] But although the trustee must investigate the assignee's title, he cannot require actual delivery up to him of the assignee's document of title.[27]

---

[22] (1861) 30 Beav. 136. However, only if the forger or the wrong recipients could not compensate the beneficiary.
[23] See also *Ashby v Blackwell* (1765) 2 Eden 299 at 302; *Sutton v Wilders* (1871) L.R. 12 Eq. 373, *Boulton v Beard* (1853) 3 De G.M. & G. 608; *Sporle v Barnaby* (1864) 10 Jur. 1142.
[24] *Re Smith, Smith v Thompson* (1902) 71 L.J.Ch. 411; *National Trustees Company of Australasia v General Finance Co. of Australasia* [1905] A.C. 381; *Re Allsop* [1914] 1 Ch. 1.
[25] *Davis v Hutchings* [1907] 1 Ch. 356.
[26] *Re Allsop* [1914] 1 Ch. 1. It is possible protection may be available under Trustee Act 2000, ss.11 and 23.
[27] *Re Palmer* [1907] 1 Ch. 486; see *Warter v Anderson* (1853) 11 Hare 301.

If a trustee, through inadvertence or a mistake of construction or of fact, has overpaid one beneficiary at the expense of another, and the court is administering the estate, it will adjust accounts out of future payments.[28] If the estate is not being administered by the court, an adjustment can be made with the court's assistance; and might presumably be made without any application to the court. If the underpaid beneficiary can identify the fund erroneously paid, he has, in addition, the remedy of tracing it into the hands of the overpaid beneficiary or an assignee (except a bona fide purchaser or a person with the defence of change of position),[29] and if beneficiary under a will he will also have a personal action against a recipient under *Ministry of Health v Simpson* principles.[30]

But if a *trustee-beneficiary* underpays *himself*, then, according to *Re* **9–214**
Horne,[31] he suffers by his mistake though it may be that, nowadays, he should be allowed to recoup himself out of trust property in his hands.[32]

The Law Reform Committee (Cmnd. 8733, para.5.4) made the following recommendation: "where it appears that the cost of taking out a summons is out of all proportion to the amount at stake, trustees should be empowered to take the advice of counsel (in the case of trusts having adult beneficiaries only) or Chancery Queens Counsel or conveyancing counsel of the court (where there are infant beneficiaries) and to distribute on the basis of that advice if no adult beneficiary starts proceedings within three months of being sent a copy of the relevant opinion." As a half-way measure s.48 of the Administration of Justice Act 1985 gives the court power (without an oral hearing) to authorise action to be taken concerning the construction of a will or trust in reliance on a written opinion of a person with a ten year High Court qualification within s.71 of the Courts and Legal Services Act 1990.

IV. STATUTORY AND JUDICIAL PROTECTION OF TRUSTEES IN RESPECT OF TRUSTEESHIP FUNCTIONS

The Trustee Act 1925

Protection against liability in respect of rents and covenants

Section 26.—(1) Where a personal representative or trustee liable as such[33] for— **9–215**

(a) any rent, covenant, or agreement reserved by or contained in any lease; or

---

[28] *Dibbs v Goren* (1849) 11 Beav. 483; *Re Musgrave* [1916] 2 Ch. 417. Not until *Kleinwort Benson Ltd v Lincoln C.C.* [1999] 2 A.C. 349 did the common law allow recovery for mistakes of law as well as fact.
[29] *Re Diplock* [1948] Ch. 465; *Lipkin Gorman v Karpnale Ltd* [1991] 2 A.C. 548.
[30] [1951] A.C. 251, see para.11–26.
[31] [1905] 1 Ch. 76.
[32] See *Re Reading* [1916] W.N. 262, *Lewin on Trusts* (17th ed.), para.42.08.
[33] The protection of the section avails a personal representative or trustee in respect of his representative liability *as such*. Personal liability, unprotected by the section, is incurred if the personal representative or trustee takes possession of the leaseholds and so becomes personally liable by privity of estate or enters into a lease in course of administration so becoming personally liable by privity of contract. It seems a trustee is liable "as such" only where liability on a contract is limited to the value of the trust fund, the trustee not being personally liable beyond that. *Re Owers (No.2)* [1941] Ch. 389; *Re Bennett* [1943] 1 All E.R. 467; *Youngmin v Health* [1974] 1 W.L.R. 135 at 138.

(b) any rent, covenant or agreement payable under or contained in any grant made in consideration of a rentcharge; or

(c) any indemnity given in respect of any rent, covenant or agreement referred to in either of the foregoing paragraphs:

satisfies all liabilities under the lease or grant which may have accrued, or been claimed, up to the date of the conveyance hereinafter mentioned, and where necessary, sets apart a sufficient fund to answer any future claim that may be made in respect of any fixed and ascertained sum which the lessee or grantee agreed to lay out on the property demised or granted, although the period for laying out the same may not have arrived, then and in any such case the personal representative or trustee may convey the property demised or granted to a purchaser, legatee, devisee or other person entitled to call for a conveyance thereof and thereafter—

9–216   (i) he may distribute the residuary real and personal estate of the deceased testator or intestate, or, as the case may be, the trust estate (other than the fund, if any, set apart as aforesaid) to or amongst the persons entitled thereto, without appropriating any part, or any further part, as the case may be, of the estate of the deceased or of the trust estate to meet any future liability under the said lease or grant;

(ii) notwithstanding such distribution, he shall not be personally liable in respect of any subsequent claim under the said lease or grant.

(1A) Where a personal representative or trustee has as such entered into, or may as such[34] be required to enter into, an authorised guarantee agreement[35] with respect to any lease comprised in the estate of a deceased testator or intestate or a trust estate (and, in a case where he has entered into such an agreement, he has satisfied all liabilities under it which may have accrued and been claimed up to the date of distribution)—

(a) he may distribute the residuary real and personal estate of the deceased testator or intestate, or the trust estate, to or amongst the persons entitled thereto—

(i) without appropriating any part of the estate of the deceased, or the trust estate, to meet any future liability (or, as the case may be, any liability) under any such agreement, and

(ii) notwithstanding any potential liability of his to enter into any such agreement; and

(b) notwithstanding such distribution, he shall not be personally liable in respect of any subsequent claim (or as the case may be, any claim) under any such agreement.

9–217   (2) This section operates without prejudice to the right of the lessor or grantor, or the persons deriving title under the lessor or grantor, to follow the assets of the deceased or the trust property into the hands of the persons amongst whom the same may have been respectively distributed, and applies notwithstanding anything to the contrary in the will or other instrument, if any, creating the trust.

(3) In this section "lease" includes an underlease and an agreement for a lease or underlease and any instrument giving any such indemnity as aforesaid or varying the

---

[34] See preceding footnote.
[35] Defined in the Landlord and Tenant (Covenants) Act 1995.

liabilities under the lease; "grant" applies to a grant whether the rent is created by limitation, grant, reservation, or otherwise, and includes an agreement for a grant and any instrument giving any such indemnity as aforesaid or varying the liabilities under the grant; "lessee" and "grantee" include persons respectively deriving title under them.

Protection by means of advertisements

Section 27.[36]—(1) With a view to the conveyance to or distribution among the persons entitled to any real or personal property, the trustees of a settlement, trustees of land,[37] trustees for sale of personal property or personal representatives, may give notice by advertisement in the Gazette, and in a newspaper circulating in the district in which the land is situated, and such other like notices, including notices elsewhere than in England and Wales, as would, in any special case, have been directed by a court of competent jurisdiction in an action for administration, of their intention to make such conveyance or distribution as aforesaid, and requiring any person interested[38] to send to the trustees or personal representatives within the time, not being less than two months, fixed in the notice or, where more than one notice is given, in the last of the notices, particulars of his claim in respect of the property or any part thereof to which the notice relates.

9–218

(2) At the expiration of the time fixed by the notice the trustees or personal representatives may convey or distribute the property or any part thereof to which the notice relates, to or among the persons entitled thereto, having regard only to the claims, whether formal or not, of which the trustees or personal representatives then had notice[39] and shall not, as respects the property so conveyed or distributed, be liable to any person of whose claim the trustees or personal representatives have not had notice[40] at the time of conveyance or distribution; but nothing in this section—

9–219

(a) prejudices the right of any person to follow the property, or any property representing the same, into the hands of any person, other than a purchaser, who may have received it; or

(b) frees the trustees or personal representatives from any obligation to make searches or obtain official certificates of search similar to those which an intending purchaser would be advised to make or obtain.

(3) This section applies notwithstanding anything to the contrary in the will or other instrument, if any, creating the trust.

---

[36] For the form which the advertisement should take, see *Re Aldhous* [1955] 1 W.L.R. 459.

[37] "Trustees of land" extends to a trust comprising partly land and partly personalty under the Trusts of Land and Appointment of Trustees Act 1996.

[38] Protection is afforded against belated claims of creditors, next of kin or beneficiaries under a will: *Re Aldhous* [1955] 1 W.L.R. 459 at 462.

[39] The Law Reform Committee (Cmnd. 873, para.5.1) recommend that trustees should be empowered to write to any potential creditors, enclosing a copy of counsel's opinion, informing them they should make their claim within three months of receiving the opinion. If no claim is then made the trustees should be free to make the proposed distributions without liability, but without prejudice to the creditor's right to follow the trust assets.

[40] In view of s.27(2)(b) this may well cover constructive notice as well as actual notice. See also Law Com. No.157 (Illegitimacy) 1986, para.3.10, n.22. If they have notice of a claim it cannot be ignored even if the claimant fails to respond to the advertisements: *Guardian Trust & Executor Co. of New Zealand v Public Trustee* [1942] A.C. 115 at 127.

Payment into court by trustees

9–220　　**Section 63.**[41]—(1) Trustees, or the majority of trustees, having in their hands or under their control money or securities belonging to a trust, may pay the same into court; and the same shall, subject to rules of court, be dealt with according to the orders of the court.

(2) The receipt or certificate of the proper officer shall be a sufficient discharge to trustees for the money or securities so paid into court.

(3) Where money or securities are vested in any persons as trustees, and the majority are desirous of paying the same into court, but the concurrence of the other or others cannot be obtained, the court may order the payment into court to be made by the majority without the concurrence of the other or others.

(4) Where any such money or securities are deposited with any banker, broker, or other depositary, the court may order payment or delivery of the money or securities to the majority of the trustees for the purpose of payment into court.

(5) Every transfer payment and delivery made in pursuance of any such order shall be valid and take effect as if the same had been made on the authority by the act of all the persons entitled to the money and securities so transferred, paid, or delivered.

Miscellaneous statutory protection

9–221　Trustees and personal representatives have protection under the Adoption Act 1976, s.45 and the Legitimacy Act 1976, s.7, if they do not have notice of illegitimate or legitimated or adopted persons where the existence of such persons affects entitlement to the trust property. However, protection under s.27 of the Trustee Act may be sufficient.[42]

Judicial Protection and Intervention

Civil Procedure Rules Part 64

General

64.1

9–222　(1) This Part contains rules—

　　(a) in Section I, about claims relating to—

　　　　(i) the administration of estates of deceased persons, and
　　　　(ii) trusts; and

　　(b) in Section II, about charity proceedings.

(2) In this Part and its practice directions, where appropriate, references to trustees include executors and administrators.

---

[41] Unless trustees have reasonable cause, they may be made liable for the costs of paying funds into, and getting them out of, court. In case of doubt as to the claim, share or identity of a beneficiary the practice today is to submit the matter to the court for determination by way of Pt.8 claim under CPR pt.64. See A. J. Hawkins (1968) 84 L.Q.R. 65.

[42] See repeal of Family Law Reform Act 1969, s.17 by F.L.R.A. 1987, s.20 and comments of G. Miller [1988] Conv. 410 at 417–419.

(3) All proceedings in the High Court to which this Part applies must be brought in the Chancery Division.

I CLAIMS RELATING TO THE ADMINISTRATION OF ESTATES AND TRUSTS

Scope of this Section

64.2

This Section of this Part applies to claims—   **9–223**
  (a) for the court to determine any question arising in—
        (i) the administration of the estate of a deceased person; or
        (ii) the execution of a trust;
  (b) for an order for the administration of the estate of a deceased person, or the execution of a trust, to be carried out under the direction of the court ('an administration order');
  (c) under the Variation of Trusts Act 1958; or
  (d) under section 48 of the Administration of Justice Act 1985.

Claim form

64.3

A claim to which this Section applies must be made by issuing a Part 8 claim form. **9–224**

Parties

64.4

(1) In a claim to which this Section applies, other than an application under section **9–225**
48 of the Administration of Justice Act 1985—
  (a) all the trustees must be parties;
  (b) if the claim is made by trustees, any of them who does not consent to being a claimant must be made a defendant; and
  (c) the claimant may make parties to the claim any persons with an interest in or claim against the estate, or an interest under the trust, who it is appropriate to make parties having regard to the nature of the order sought.
  (2) In addition, in a claim under the Variation of Trusts Act 1958, unless the court directs otherwise any person who—
  (a) created the trust; or
  (b) provided property for the purposes of the trust,
must, if still alive, be made a party to the claim.

(The court may, under rule 19.2, order additional persons to be made parties to a claim.)

. . .

This Practice Direction Supplement Part 64

I CLAIMS RELATING TO THE ADMINISTRATION OF ESTATES AND TRUSTS

Examples of claims under rule 64.2(a)

1 The following are examples of the types of claims which may be made under rule **9–226**
64.2(a)—

(1) a claim for the determination of any of the following questions—

(a) any question as to who is included in any class of persons having—

> (i) a claim against the estate of a deceased person;
> (ii) a beneficial interest in the estate of such a person; or
> (iii) a beneficial interest in any property subject to a trust;

(b) any question as to the rights or interests of any person claiming—

> (i) to be a creditor of the estate of a deceased person;
> (ii) to be entitled under a will or on the intestacy of a deceased person; or
> (iii) to be beneficially entitled under a trust;

(2) a claim for any of the following remedies—

(a) an order requiring a trustee—

> (i) to provide and, if necessary, verify accounts;
> (ii) to pay into court money which he holds in that capacity; or
> (iii) to do or not to do any particular act;

(b) an order approving any sale, purchase, compromise or other transaction by a trustee; or
(c) an order directing any act to be done which the court could order to be done if the estate or trust in question were being administered or executed under the direction of the court.

. . .

9–227 It is noteworthy that under Pt. 64 when a court is asked to adjudicate upon a course of action proposed by trustees there are three distinct categories of issues, as explained by Robert Walker J.[43]:

> (i) whether some proposed action is within the trustees' powers as a matter of construction of the trust instrument or statute or both;
> (ii) whether a proposed action, apparently within the trustees' power and representing their decision on a particularly significant matter, will be declared by the court to be a proper exercise of the trustees' power, so that the trustees may safely proceed to implement their decision;
> (iii) whether the court itself will exercise a discretion vested in the trustees but surrendered by them to the court where there is some good reason for the court to accept this surrender; *e.g.* because the trustees are disabled by a conflict of interest or by a fair and honest deadlock so that the issue cannot be resolved by removing one trustee rather than another.

> However, a situation may straddle these categories as where a conflict of interest of a trustee who wishes to join in a joint decision of the other independent trustees leads the trustees to seek a

---

[43] In an unreported Chambers judgment cited by Hart J. in *Public Trustee v Cooper* [2001] W.T.L.R. 901 at 923.

declaration that they may properly implement such decision.[44] Where it is the court itself exercising a discretion surrendered to it, then it must be put into an adequately informed position to make a considered decision[45]: it will not accept a proferred general surrender of discretion as to future income.[46] If the trustees are not up to this, then they should be replaced by new trustees.

Section 8. Judicial Control of Trustees

Wherever trustees have a discretion to exercise, the question arises as to the extent to which the court can control or sanction the exercise of the discretion at the behest of a complaining beneficiary. The discretion may be a distributive discretion (under a discretionary trust or a power of appointment or of maintenance or of advancement) or an administrative or managerial discretion (under a power of investment, for example). A purported appointment may be held void or voidable, compensation may need to be paid on surcharging or falsifying the accounts, trustees may be removed or declarations made as to the scope of trustees' duties. **9–228**

Scope for positive intervention

Under a discretionary trust the trustees, of course, have a duty to exercise their discretion by distributing income (or, ultimately, capital) in some sort of amounts to some of the beneficiaries (unless, under a power to accumulate, they have decided to accumulate income). If the trustees neglect or refuse or are unable (till the outcome of a case), to discharge their duty, then the court will let them remedy this[47] or will positively have the settlor's intentions carried out, as Lord Wilberforce pointed out, "by appointing new trustees or by authorising or directing representative persons of the classes of beneficiaries to prepare a scheme for distribution, or even, should the proper basis for distribution appear, by itself directing the trustees so to distribute."[48] **9–229**

In the case of distributive powers of appointment, advancement or maintenance, the trustees have a duty to consider from time to time whether or not to exercise the power but they need not exercise the power.[49] Thus, if a power to distribute income to X instead of to trust beneficiaries is not exercised within a reasonable period (in default of an expressly specified period) the power lapses in respect of that income so that the income devolves on the trust beneficiaries entitled in default of a valid exercise of the power.[50]

If a trustee's attitude is that she is not going to bother about using any powers to benefit a beneficiary, B, as B does not deserve any consideration, (*e.g.* because B married against her wishes) the court will intervene to **9–230**

[44] *Public Trustee v Cooper* above, *Re Drexel Burnham Lambert Pension Plan* [1995] 1 W.L.R. 32.
[45] *Marley v Mutual Security Merchant Bank* [1991] 3 All E.R. 198.
[46] *Re Allen-Meyrick's W.T.* [1966] 1 W.L.R. 499.
[47] *Re Locker's S.T.* [1978] 1 All E.R. 216, above, para.3–59.
[48] *McPhail v Doulton* [1971] A.C. 424 at 451, A.J. Hawkins (1967) 31 Conv.(N.S.) 117.
[49] *Re Hay's S.T.* [1981] 3 All E.R. 786 at 792–793, above, para.3–137.
[50] *Re Allen-Meyrick's W.T.* [1966] 1 W.L.R. 499.

remove the trustee or direct a payment that no trustee could refuse to make unless being spiteful or malicious: *Klug v Klug*.[51] In that case legacy duty had to be paid by a beneficiary in four equal instalments but the beneficiary's income was insufficient to pay these instalments. Neville J. said,[52] "When the summons was previously before me, I decided that the trustees could in the exercise of their discretion under the powers of advancement, if they thought fit, advance out of capital a sum sufficient to pay this legacy duty. The public trustee thinks that their discretion should be so exercised, but his co-trustee, the mother, declines to join him in so doing, not because she has considered whether or not it would be for her daughter's welfare, that the advance should be made, but because her daughter has married without her consent, and her letters show, in my opinion, that she has not exercised her discretion at all ... In such circumstances, it is the duty of the court to interfere and to direct a sum to be raised out of capital sufficient to pay off ... the legacy duty." It seems that no other course of action could be taken by the trustees (unless they acted in a way that no rational adequately informed body of trustees could act) so the court should direct such course.

9–231   Exceptionally in the pensions fund context the courts[53] have also been prepared positively to exercise fiduciary powers to augment pensions of beneficiaries where there is no one who can exercise the power, the employer-trustee being a company in liquidation and the liquidator being in the irreconcilable position of acting for the creditors interested in a non-exercise of the power to benefit the ordinary beneficiary-members of the pension scheme, while acting as trustee required to look after such members' interests. The court[54] acts in the manner in which a reasonable trustee could be expected to act in the light of all the material circumstances so as to do what is just and equitable.

9–232   One accepts this in the pensions context where the member-beneficiaries have earned their entitlements as deferred pay and as settlors have some justified expectations that powers to augment their entitlement out of surpluses will be seriously considered for exercising in certain circumstances. In the private family trust context however, where the trustees are in a position to exercise their powers in favour of persons who are not beneficiaries at all but only objects of a power of appointment but the trustees choose not to exercise them, having stated that they fairly considered exercising their powers but chose not to, then one would expect that should be the end of the matter, despite dicta of Warner J.[55] (not

---

[51] [1918] 2 Ch. 67. See *Re Lofthouse* (1885) 29 Ch.D. 921 (where trustees had refused to pay maintenance to a beneficiary under a discretionary power and Bacon V.-C. ordered £400 p.a. to be paid; on appeal his order was discharged without more ado since the trustees were agreeable to pay £250 p.a.) There was an interventionist attitude in some 19th century cases concerning powers to benefit a beneficiary, especially if the beneficiary was a ward of court: *Re Hodges* (1878) 7 Ch.D. 754, *Re Roper's Trusts* (1879) 11 Ch.D. 271.
[52] *ibid.* at 71.
[53] *Mettoy Pension Trustees Ltd v Evans* [1991] 2 All E.R. 513.
[54] *Thrells Ltd v Lomas* [1993] 1 W.L.R. 456. Now, under Pensions Act 1995, s.25(2) an independent person as trustee exists to exercise the power.
[55] *Mettoy Pension Trustees Ltd v Evans* [1991] 2 All E.R. 513 at 549 citing Lord Wilberforce on discretionary trusts in *McPhail v Doulton* [1971] A.C. 424 at 457 set out *supra* in para.3–135.

restricted expressly to the pensions context he was concerned with) that discretionary powers can be positively exercised by the court in any of the ways that discretionary trusts can be carried into effect by the court according to Lord Wilberforce.

However, in *Schmidt v Rosewood Trust Ltd*[56] Lord Walker cited the **9–233** remarks of Warner J in asserting the court's inherent jurisdiction to supervise, and if necessary to intervene in, the administration of trusts, whether dealing with the rights of beneficiaries under discretionary trusts or the rights of objects of fiduciary powers of appointment. Thus, in an extreme case where, in the light of the settlor's letters of wishes, the trustees are not exercising their fiduciary powers of appointment in the manner intended by the settlor the trustees can be replaced by more amenable trustees or even a particular exercise of the power could be directed by the court if it would be perverse to any sensible expectation of the settlor to exercise—or no rational trustee could possibly exercise— the power other than in the directed fashion.[57]

Wide-ranging internal duties over distributive discretions

A trustee must **9–234**

(1) consider from time to time the exercise of its distributive discretions[58];
(2) obtain any requisite consent in due form;
(3) implement its decisions in due form[59];
(4) comply with mandatory rules as to perpetuities and accumulations and illegality in creating any new trusts[60];
(5) not (unless authorised) profit from the trust or place itself in a position where there is a conflict between its fiduciary duty and its self-interest or its fiduciary duty to others[61];
(6) personally exercise its powers itself (unless delegation is authorised)[62];
(7) not fetter its future exercise of discretions (unless authorised)[63];
(8) not go beyond the scope of its discretionary powers so as to try to do something that is unauthorised[64];
(9) consciously exercise its own independent discretion, not automatically doing what the settlor or a beneficiary or anyone else tells it to do[65] (though it should take account of the settlor's wishes[66]);
(10) act fairly and disinterestedly in discriminating between those beneficiaries or objects or classes of beneficiaries or objects whom it may benefit in its absolute discretion[67];

---

[56] [2003] 2 A.C. 709, para.51.
[57] Compare *Klug v Klug* [1918] 2 Ch. 67.
[58] *Re Hay's S.T.* [1981] 3 All E.R. 786, *Schmidt v Rosewood Trust Ltd* [2003] 2 A.C. 709.
[59] *Kain v Hutton* [2004] 1 N.Z.L.R. 318.
[60] *Pilkington v I.R.C.* [1964] A.C. 612, *Re Abrahams W.T.* [1969] 1 Ch. 463.
[61] *Bristol & West B.S. v Mothew* [1998] Ch. 1.
[62] *Speight v Gaunt* (1883) 9 App Cas 1.
[63] *Re Vestey's Settlement* [1950] 2 All E.R. 89 at 895, *Re Gibson's S.T.* [1981] Ch. 179 at 182.
[64] *Re Morris' S.T.* [1951] 2 All E.R. 528.
[65] *Turner v Turner* [1984] Ch. 100, *Wilson v Turner* (1883) 22 Ch.D. 21.
[66] *Abacus Trust Co. v Barr* [2003] Ch. 409, *Shalson v Russo* [2003] W.T.L.R. 1165.
[67] *Edge v Pensions Ombudsman* [2002] Ch. 602.

(11) must exercise its powers responsibly with a view to achieving the purposes for which the settlor vicariously[68] conferred the powers upon it and not in a manner that is arbitrary, capricious or perverse to any sensible expectation of the settlor,[69] so

   (a) it must not exercise a power to achieve an ulterior or corrupt purpose of itself, thereby committing "a fraud on the power"[70]; and

   (b) it must adequately ascertain for itself the relevant considerations and then ensure that it does not reach a decision which it would not have reached but for ignoring those ascertained considerations or taking account of an irrelevant consideration.[71]

As explained in *Wong v Burt* para.9–260 the circumstances in which a fraud on a power arises involve a power being exercised to achieve an ulterior or corrupt purpose. However, if a personal power is released so as to benefit the person entitled in default of the exercise of such power so such person can then benefit the releasor of the power, this is outside the fraud on a power doctrine, the releasor not being in a conflict of interest situation and the default beneficiary being the owner of the property (subject to divestment by exercise of the power) and capable of dealing with it as he or she likes.[72] However, if the donee of a personal power positively exercises it, then like the donee of a fiduciary power, he is subject to the fraud on a power doctrine.[73]

9–235   The Court of Appeal decision in *Re Hastings-Bass*[74] has recently obtained the status of a "rule" or "principle". A statutory advancement into a new settlement was made out of an old settlement with intent to avoid estate duty at 75 per cent. It transpired that the advancement of capital out to trustees for B for life, with remainders over to his family was void for perpetuity as to these remainders. The Revenue argued that an advancement of capital only for B's life did not fully dispose of the capital, so that this fell outside the scope of s.32 so as to be void, or was not "for the benefit of B" when the remainders failed so that it was outside s.32 and void.[75] The Court of Appeal held[76] that where the trustee "acts in good faith" the court should not interfere with his action,

   "notwithstanding that it does not have the full effect which he intended, unless

---

[68] *Re Wills Trust Deeds* [1964] Ch. 219 at 228–229.
[69] *Re Manisty's Settlement* [1974] Ch. 17, *Re Hay's S.T.* [1981] 3 All E.R. 786, *Edge v Pensions Ombudsman* [2000] Ch. 602.
[70] *Wong v Burt* [2004] N.Z.C.A. 174, *Vatcher v Paull* [1915] A.C. 372.
[71] *Re Hastings-Bass* [1975] Ch. 25, *Abacus Trust Co. v Barr* [2003] Ch. 409.
[72] *Re Somes* [1896] 1 Ch. 250. Similarly revocation of a revocable appointment made under a personal special power of appointment, even coupled with a release of the power, falls outside the fraud on a power doctrine unless the revocation is solely for the purpose of making a new appointment which is a fraud on the power: *Re Greaves* [1954] Ch. 434.
[73] *Hillsdown Holdings plc v Pensions Ombudsman* [1997] 1 All E.R. 862.
[74] [1975] Ch. 25.
[75] As in *Re Abrahams W.T.* [1969] 1 Ch. 463.
[76] [1975] Ch. 25 at 41.

(1) what he has achieved is unauthorised by the power conferred on him or
(2) it is clear that he would not have acted as he did

    (a) had he not taken into account considerations which he should not have taken into account or
    (b) had he not failed to take into account considerations which he ought to have taken into account".

The trustee's action in advancing capital only to B for life was not void **9–236** because it was authorised under s.32 and the overlooking of the voidness of the remainders after B's lifetime, so that there was a resulting trust of the capital to the old settlement, did not prevent the advancement of capital to B for his life being for his benefit and so valid when this achieved the substantial tax-saving intended by the trustee. B would still have received his life-interest if the trustee had appreciated the need to restrict the remainders to the perpetuity period provided for in the old settlement.

As held in *Abacus Trust Co. v Barr*, para.9–266, assuming that the **9–237** overlooked material consideration does not make the impugned action of the trustee void in equity[77] as unauthorised,[78] the action of the trustee will be voidable if it is clear that it would not have acted as it did had it not failed to take into account a consideration which it ought to have taken into account. Thus three questions arise:

(1) what were the trustees under a duty to consider?
(2) did they fail to consider it?
(3) would they have acted differently if they had considered it?

Normally one will expect a beneficiary to invoke the *Hastings-Bass* principle **9-238** against the trustees, but they may invoke it against themselves to try to protect themselves against liability for a breach of trust. Thus, in two cases[79] the trustees executed a deed of appointment doing exactly what they intended the deed to achieve in benefiting the persons specified therein. However, some time later they appreciated that they had overlooked the disastrous tax consequences of their action, and there was no doubt that they would have acted differently if they had appreciated their mistake when about to execute the deed. The Court held the appointments void under the *Hastings-Bass* principle, so undoing what the trustees had done which looks far too good to be true.

The deeds by their wording meant what they said and had fully achieved **9-239** what they were intended to achieve at the time, so there could be no question of rectification of the deeds or of setting the deeds aside for

---

[77] At law corporate or individual trustees have in their own right full power to transfer legal title to property to another even if the exercise of the equitable power (leading to such transfer) is void: *Cloutte v Storey* [1911] 1 Ch. 18; *De Vigier v I.R.C.* [1964] 2 All E.R. 907, 914; *Rolled Steel Products (Holdings) Ltd v British Steel Corp.* [1986] Ch. 246 at 303.

[78] As in *Re Abrahams W.T.* [1969] 1 Ch. 463 and as alleged by the Revenue in *Re Hastings-Bass* [1975] Ch. 25.

[79] *Green v Cobham* [2000] W.T.L.R. 1101, *Abacus Trust Co. (Isle of Man) Ltd v NSPCC* [2001] W.T.L.R. 953.

mistake.[80] After all, there was no mistake as to the effect of the transaction carried into effect by the deed, only as to the subsequently discovered disadvantageous tax consequences. Should not the *Hastings-Bass* principle be unavailable in such circumstances? Appellate courts may take this view in due course, but until then *Abacus Trust Co. v Barr* deals with the issue by having such principle make the impugned transaction voidable, thereby affording the court a discretion (taking account of the lapse of time and the interests of third parties) as to whether it should be avoided and, if so, on what terms.

9–240   In the context of family trusts the patriarchal settlor will not want the discretionary beneficiaries of his bounty to be able to whine from time to time that the trustees *might* have done this or that or the other, rather than what they actually did, so that their actual action is voidable unless the trustees discharge the onus of positively showing that they *would* not have done anything other than what they did. Thus, the onus is on the volunteer-beneficiaries to establish that the trustees *would* have done something different but for overlooking a significant consideration or taking account of an irrelevant consideration.[81]

9–241   In the pensions context, however, the settlor-beneficiaries having strenuously earned their pension rights and claims, so as to be able to have a decent standard of living, can require negative decisions of trustees against them to be struck down for the issue to be reconsidered if the trustees might have been more positive but for overlooking a significant consideration or taking account of an irrelevant consideration.[82]

The public law test of Wednesbury Corporation irrationality

9–242   Recently, judges[83] have introduced into private trust law the public law doctrine of *Wednesbury*[84] unreasonableness whereby a decision of a public body (that could otherwise not be impugned under private law principles) can be set aside if the court considers the decision to be one that no properly informed reasonable body could have reached, there being a legitimate expectation of persons capable of being affected by the decision that such a public body should not make a decision that no reasonable body could make. Thus, in *Edge v Pensions Ombudsman*,[85] after holding that discretionary trustees of a pension trust were entitled honestly to favour some beneficiaries over others, Scott V-C stated, "The judge may disagree with the manner in which the trustees have exercised their discretion, but unless they can be seen to have taken into account irrelevant, improper or

---

[80] *Gibbon v Mitchell* [1990] 3 All E.R. 338, *Wolff v Wolff*, infra para.14–297.

[81] *Re Green GCG Trust* [2003] W.T.L.R. 377, D. J. Hayton, "Pension Trusts and Traditional Trusts: Drastically Different Species of Trusts" [2005] Conv. 229.

[82] *Hearn v Younger* [2002] W.T.L.R. 1317, *Stannard v Fisons Pension Trust Ltd* [1992] I.R.L.R. 27; and see para.9–000.

[83] *Harris v Lord Shuttleworth* [1995] O.P.L.R 79, 86–87; *Wild v Pensions Ombudsman* [1996] O.P.L.R. 129, 135; *Edge v Pensions Ombudsman* [1998] Ch. 512, 534, 536 affd [2000] Ch. 602, 628–630.

[84] *Associated Provincial Picture House v Wednesbury Corp.* [1948] 1 K.B. 223.

[85] [1998] Ch. 512 at 534. The Court of Appeal rejected the apellant's criticisms of the approach of Scott V.-C. but considered it unnecessary to examine how far to press the analogy with *Wednesbury* public law principles; [2000] Ch. 602 at 628–630.

irrational factors, or unless their decision can be said to be one that no reasonable body of trustees properly directing themselves could have reached, the judge cannot interfere."

In public law, judicial review principles require the public body to afford **9–243** the claimants an opportunity to make their case so that both sides' arguments can be fully considered. In trust law, trustees are only under a duty to ensure they have adequate factual and/or legal background information to enable them to reach an informed decision.[86] They do not, for example, need to inform objects of powers or default beneficiaries that the trustees are contemplating doing something that may affect them and, *a fortiori*, do not need to give a fair hearing to objects of a power of appointment and those beneficiaries entitled in default of exercise of the power.[87] Once in possession of such information they cannot exercise their discretions in a way that is capricious, irrational or perverse to any sensible expectation of the settlor.[88] In the light of such traditional terminology that creates rights under private trust law there is surely no need by analogy with public law to hold that trustees cannot exercise their discretions in a way that no reasonable body of trustees would have done. After all, is it not perverse to any sensible expectation of the settlor to permit trustees to make a decision that no adequately informed reasonable body of trustees could possibly have made?

Robert Walker J. opined in *Scott v National Trust*[89] that "legitimate **9–244** expectation may have some part to play in trust law as well as in judicial review" when indicating that, if trustees had paid £1,000 a quarter to an elderly impoverished beneficiary for the last ten years, the latter has a legitimate expectation that no reasonable body of trustees would discontinue the payment without any warning and without giving her the opportunity of trying to persuade the trustees to continue the payment, at least temporarily. Under the traditional approach it would surely be perverse to any sensible expectation of the settlor for the trustees to dispense or withhold his bounty in such arbitrary fashion. Specialist trust-law judges surely have enough techniques at their disposal for controlling trustees without introducing some public law considerations which could mislead non-specialist judges into wrongfully introducing other public law notions, *e.g.* so that all 70 discretionary beneficiaries or objects of powers of appointment have to be sent a standardised grant application form to fill in or at least be informed when the trustees are about to make significant distributive decisions.

The advantage of the test whether the trustees' decision was perverse to **9–245** any sensible expectation of the settlor or was one that no rational body of trustees could have reached is that it is an objective test. Discretionary

---

[86] *R v Charity Commissioners Ex p. Baldwin* [2001] W.T.L.R. 137, 148–151. In the pensions context, however, of earned rights where the trustees have to form an opinion (*e.g.* as to whether the claimant is disabled or could be "able" but for an unreasonable refusal to submit to treatment) trustees may need to take more steps to be properly informed so that a proper decision can be made, and a breach of duty may be inferred if the decision is one which no reasonable trustee could make on the material before it: *Telstra Super Pty. Ltd v Flegeltaub* [2002] V.R. 276, para.26.
[87] *Re B* [1987] 2 All E.R. 475 at 478; *Scott v National Trust* [1998] 2 All E.R. 705 at 718.
[88] *Re Manisty's Settlement* [1974] Ch. 17.
[89] [1998] 2 All E.R. 705 at 718.

decision-making is a subjective process[90] that affords the trustees plenty of autonomous leeway so they may properly reach a poor decision that many trustees or the court might consider unreasonable, although not irrational in the sense of a decision that no rational trustees could possibly reach.[91] So long as the trustees appear to have given a real and genuine consideration to the relevant matters the courts will not interfere.

9–246   However, a claimant will often not be in a position to challenge how the decision-maker reached the decision and so has to fall back, if possible, on alleging that something must have gone wrong with the decision-making process because the decision objectively is *Wednesbury Corporation* irrational one or one that is perverse to any sensible expectation of the settlor. With increasing numbers of judicial review cases in the public law area many judges and counsel are very conversant with *Wednesbury Corporation* irrationality and happier dealing with it[92] rather than with perversity.

Management discretions concerning external matters

9–247 The *Hastings-Bass* principle cannot be used to invalidate appointments of new trustees[93] or decisions made in the investment sphere. Here it has been seen[94] that trustees are *inter alia* under a duty to act fairly as between beneficiaries interested in income and beneficiaries interested in capital and to exhibit the statutory standard of care that is essentially that of a prudent man of business would take in conducting another's affairs. In determining whether there has been a breach of the duty of care the court focuses on what the trustees did and what they should have done objectively if they had exhibited the due standard of care.[95]

In *Tempest v Lord Camoys,*[96] the trustees on selling real estate had to purchase real estate "in their absolute discretion." One trustee wanted to purchase particular real estate for £60,000 with £30,000 borrowed on mortgage pursuant to the trustees' power to raise money by mortgage "at their absolute discretion." The other trustee refused to concur in the purchase, considering it not to be a prudent exercise of the power. The Court of Appeal held that it could not interfere with the dissenting trustee's discretion. Jessel M.R. pointed out that all the court will do is prevent the trustees from exercising their power "improperly."

9–248   As Slade L.J. subsequently said,[97] "In other words the court was of opinion that even a power expressed in terms that it should be exercisable at the trustees' absolute discretion was subject to the implicit restriction that it should be exercised properly within the limits of the general law."

---

[90] See L. Smith; "The Motive not the Deed" in J. Getzler (ed.) *Rationalising Property Equity and Trusts: Essays in Honour of Edward Burn*, Lexis Nexis, 2003, pp. 67–33.

[91] *Edge v Pensions Ombudsman* [2000] Ch. 602; *Re Beloved Wilkes' Charity* (1851) 3 Mac. & G. 440.

[92] *E.g.* as affecting a mortgagee's power to raise interest rates as it sees fit: *Paragon Finance plc v Staunton* [2002] 2 All E.R. 248 paras 37–42

[93] *Re Dubury's S.T.* [1995] 3 All E.R. 145.

[94] See, above, paras 9–53 *et seq.*

[95] *Nestlé v National Westminster Bank* [1994] 1 All E.R. 118; *Wight v Olswang (No.2)* [2001] W.T.L.R. 291.

[96] (1882) 21 Ch.D. 571.

[97] *Bishop v Bonham* [1988] 1 W.L.R. 742 at 751–752; also see *Elder's Trustee and Executor Co. Ltd v Higgins* (1965) 113 C.L.R. 426 at 448.

For example, they must act within their powers and comply with their duty of undivided loyalty to their beneficiaries.

Because trustees must act unanimously[98] (unless charitable trustees or pension trustees or otherwise provided by the trust instrument) any trustee with some fairly slight basis for doubt about the proposed exercise of a discretion can prevent such an exercise. A beneficiary can obtain an injunction against a proposed exercise of an investment discretion only if such exercise is plainly improper or not in accordance with the trustees' duty of safe investment. If the beneficiary does not find out about an improper or unsafe investment until after the event, then his remedy will be to have the investment sold and to make the trustees liable to account for any losses[99] that arise.

Exceptionally, where the trustees are trustees of land then the court has a vast positive discretion under ss.14 and 15 of the Trusts of Land and Appointment of Trustees Act 1996 to make such order as it thinks fit, taking account of the factors in s.15(1). Normally, it will not enforce a sale if so to do would defeat the purpose of the trust.[1]

Exemption clauses

It should first be noted that the jurisdiction of the court as to pure matters **9–249** of law cannot be ousted by provisions in the trust instrument giving the trustees power to determine all questions arising in the execution of the trusts under the instrument.[2] However, the decision of trustees or of a third party can be binding and conclusive on matters of fact, assuming that the specified factual circumstances are conceptually certain,[3] while the decision of someone with expert knowledge in the relevant factual area can even conclusively determine an incidental question of construction.[4]

If trustees prove that the settlor knew of, and approved, a clause in the trust instrument exempting the trustees from liability for the complained of breach of trust upon a fair non-restrictive construction of the clause,[5] then the trustees escape liability for such breach unless it was a dishonest or reckless breach of trust. This was held by the Court of Appeal in *Armitage v Nurse*[6] in giving effect to a clause protecting the trustee from liability "unless such loss or damage shall be caused by his own actual fraud." "Fraud" was held simply to mean dishonesty which[7] "connotes at the minimum an intention on the part of the trustee to pursue a particular course of action, either knowing that it is contrary to the interests of the

---

[98] *Luke v South Kensington Hotel Ltd* (1879) 11 Ch.D. 121.
[99] For difficulties in establishing that (i) losses flowed from (ii) a breach of duty see *Nestlé v National Westminster Bank* [1993] 1 W.L.R. 1290 and *Wight v Olswang (No.2)* [2001] W.T.L.R. 291.
[1] *Edwards v Lloyds TSB Bank plc* [2005] 1 F.C.R. 139. In bankruptcy cases see the Insolvency Act 1986, s.335A.
[2] *Re Wynn* [1952] Ch. 271.
[3] *Re Coxen* [1948] Ch. 747; *Re Jones* [1953] Ch. 125; *Re Wright's W.T.* [1981] Law.S. Gaz 841.
[4] *The Glazier* (1996) 1 Ll. Rep.370; *Re Tuck's S.T.* [1978] Ch. 49; *Dundee General Hospitals Board v Walker* [1952] 1 All E.R. 896.
[5] *Walket v Stones* [2001] Q.B. 902, 935 at 941.
[6] [1998] Ch. 241.
[7] *ibid*, 251, below at 9–279.

beneficiaries or being recklessly indifferent whether it is contrary to their interests or not."

9–250   Thus, it is permissible for an exemption clause to exempt a trustee from liability for loss arising from gross negligence as well as ordinary negligence. The Court of Appeal, unfortunately, did not have bailment cases[8] cited to it, so it erroneously assumed that in English law no distinction could be made between ordinary and gross negligence. It therefore erroneously assumed that exemption from all varieties of negligence either had to be accepted or outlawed, while in modern conditions one could not possibly hold that exemption from liability for ordinary negligence was contrary to public policy or repugnant to the trust concept. Scope therefore remains to challenge the view of the Court of Appeal and try to establish that exemption clauses (as in Scotland[9]) cannot extend to protect trustees from liability for gross negligence.

9–251   Further uncertainty exists where trustees consciously act beyond their powers (*e.g.* making an investment which they know to be unauthorised, like buying a villa in Lanzarote) so deliberately committing a breach of trust, but do so in good faith and in the honest belief that they are acting in the best interests of the beneficiaries as a whole. Lord Nicholls[10] considered this to be fraudulent because the trustees are taking a risk to the prejudice of another's rights, which risk is known to be one which there is no right to take. Millett L.J.[11] (as he then was) considered this not to be fraudulent, perhaps assuming that if the trustees honestly think there is a risk which they ought to take, then they can justifiably believe they have a right to take it, although he accepted that[12] "a trustee who relied on the presence of an exemption clause to justify what he proposed to do would thereby lose its protection: he would be acting recklessly in the proper sense of the term."

The retired Slade L.J., faced with these two approaches, in *Walker v Stones*[13] held that if the trustee, deliberately committing a breach of trust and taking a risk honestly believing it to be in the interests of the beneficiaries, is a solicitor, then he cannot rely on a clause exempting him from liability unless fraudulent if no reasonable solicitor-trustee could have held such belief.

9–252   Trustees will be well-advised to accept Lord Nicholl's view and not to commit a deliberate breach of trust in the belief it will be profitable or, if not, will be covered by a wide exemption clause. They should not proceed except with extended powers conferred by the court[14] or, perhaps, if they

---

[8] *Gibbon v McMullen* (1865) L.R. 2 P.C. 317; *Beal v Smith Devon Rly. Co.* (1864) 3 H. 8 C. 332: gratuitous bailees are liable for gross negligence only. Note also that victims of horseplay can recover against a co-participant who was reckless or grossly negligent: *Wooldridge v Sumner* [1963] 2 Q.B. 43 at 69; *Blake v Galloway* [2004] 1 W.L.R. 2844.

[9] *Lutea Trustees Ltd v Orbis Trustees* [1997] S.C.L.R. 735, [1998] S.L.T. 471.

[10] *Royal Brunei Airlines v Tan* [1995] 2 A.C. 378 at 390.

[11] *Armitage v Nurse* [1998] Ch. 241 at 252.

[12] *ibid.*, 254.

[13] [2000] W.T.L.R. 975, [2000] 4 All E.R. 412, [2001] Q.B. 902. However, he accepted that there is a single test of dishonest assistance in a breach of trust and in the construction of exemption clauses and so applied an objective test based on the appeal in *Royal Brunei Airlines v Tan* interpreted in *Twinsectra Ltd v Yardley* [2002] 2 A.C. 164 however as requiring a dishonest trustee to know that he was transgressing ordinary standards of honest behavior and Stones did not know this according to the first instance judge.

[14] Under Trustee Act 1925, s.57.

have sufficient beneficiaries of full capacity to provide them with an indemnity backed with some security.

A trustee who is a solicitor who inserts a clause into the settlor's trust instrument to exempt himself from liability for breaches of trust unless fraudulent, will also be well-advised if he tells the settlor to seek independent legal advice. After all, such solicitor-prospective trustee is in a fiduciary relationship with the settlor, so that one would expect that he would be disabled from relying on such a broad clause unless independent legal advice was suggested.[15] Somewhat surprisingly, however, the Court of Appeal[16] has held that the solicitor as prospective executor and trustee, who drafted the testamentary trusts, did not have to prove he had advised the testator to take independent legal advice, so long as it was proved the testator knew and approved the will—which must be the case where probate of the will had been granted.

Millett L.J. stated:

"The fundamental fallacy in the [plaintiffs'] argument is that clause 12 **9–253** does not confer a benefit on the persons responsible for advising the testator on the contents of the will. In the first place, it does not discriminate between the persons who advised the testator in connection with his will and other persons who become executors or trustees and who have had no part in the preparation of his will. In the second place, it does not confer a benefit on the executors and trustees but defines the extent of the potential liabilities. Unlike a trustee charging clause, it does not enable the executors and trustees to profit from their position, but it protects them from loss thereby. The inclusion of the clause does not, therefore, conflict with the rule that, in the absence of clear words, a trustee may not profit form his trust."

With respect, is there not much to be said for the view that the solicitor-executor-trustee did profit from being unjustly enriched at the expense of the beneficiaries?[17] Did he not profit from saving the insurance premiums otherwise needed to protect against liability for losses? Did he not profit from being saved from liability to pay the beneficiaries the £8 million losses flowing from his alleged gross and ordinary negligence? Should he not have been under a fiduciary duty to advise the testator to obtain independent legal advice; and should breach of such duty not have prevented him from relying on the clause?

So far, it has been the basic type of exemption clause that has been **9–254** considered, namely a clause exempting from liability for a breach of duty. However, a clause may oust any duty in the first place so that there can then be no breach of duty.

In *Hayim v Citibank*,[18] for example, Citibank was appointed executor of the testator's American will on terms that the executor "shall have no

---

[15] *Rutanen v Ballard* 1997 424 Mass. 723 at 733; *Baskerville v Thurgood* [1992] Sask. LR. 214.
[16] *Bogg v Raper* (1998)/99) 1 I.T.E.L.R. 267 at 285 for the cited passage in the text.
[17] The saving of expense is a benefit or profit: *Peel v Canada* (1992) 98 D.L.R. (4th) 140, *Peter v Beblow* (1993) 101 D.L.R. 621, 645.
[18] [1987] A.C. 730.

responsibility or duty with respect to" a Hong Kong house until the deaths of the testator's very elderly brother and sister who resided in the house. This house was given by a Hong Kong will to another executor on trust for Citibank as executor of the American will. Citibank declined to take steps to have the house sold for the benefit of the beneficiaries under the American will who wanted the house to be sold and the siblings to be evicted from it. Substantial losses flowed from the delayed sale of the house. The Privy Council held the clause was "understandable and explicable". To avoid death duties (payable if the siblings had interests in possession in the house) and to avoid placing them at the mercy of the beneficiaries, the clause enabled Citibank to permit the siblings to remain living in the house without Citibank owing any duties to the beneficiaries (other than to account to them if Citibank used the house for its own purposes).

9–255   It is also not uncommon to see clauses that oust the trustee's duty to diversify investments, *e.g.* where 90 per cent of the value of the trust fund is in the controlling shareholding of a company transferred by the settlor to the trustees. The statutory duty of care when investing can also be excluded. Thus, a big lottery winner might settle £2 million on trustees to speculate with it for 21 years as if they were the absolute beneficial owners of it and could afford to lose all of it without it affecting their standard of living in any way.

Of course, all the duties of trustees cannot be ousted or the trustees would either be nominee-resulting trustees for the settlor or themselves be absolute beneficial owners. The trustees must be left under a duty to perform the trust honestly and in good faith for the benefit of beneficiaries having a correlative right to make the trustees account for performance of their duty.[19]

While it seems the Unfair Contract Terms Act 1977 does not apply to trustees entitled to their remuneration as a beneficial incident of their burdensome office,[20] some other statutes apply to particular types of trust to outlaw exemption clauses in the public interest.

9–256   Section 192 of the Companies Act 1985 specifically intervenes where there is a trust deed for securing an issue of debentures. In such a deed a borrower, which is a company, charges some of its property by way of fixed or floating charges in favour of the trustees as security for money lent. The trustees hold these secured rights on trust for the debenture holders who hold debenture stock in proportion to the amounts provided by them by way of loan. This device is very useful for raising a large sum of money from a large number of people. The deed states when the security will become enforceable and confers much discretion on the trustees subject to varying degrees of control by the debenture holders. Any provision in the deed is void under s.192 "in so far as it would have the effect of exempting a trustee of the deed from, or indemnifying him against, liability for breach

---

[19] *Armitage v Nurse* [1998] Ch. 241 at 253.
[20] W. Goodhart (1996) 10 Trust L.I. 38, 43 (changing his mind from [1980] Conv. 333) based on *Re Duke of Norfolk's S.T.* [1982] Ch. 61.

of trust where he fails to show the degree of care and diligence required of him as trustee, having regard to the provisions of the trust deed conferring on him any powers, authorities or discretions." Section 192(2) makes it clear that subsection (1) does not invalidate any release given to a trustee for things done or undone under a power for a three-quarters majority of debenture holders to give such a release.[21] For authorised unit trusts s.84 of the Financial Services Act 1986 makes any provision void so far as it would have the effect of exempting the manager or trustee from liability for failing to exercise due care and diligence. For pension trusts s.34 of the Pensions Act 1995 prohibits exclusion or restriction of liability for breach of an obligation under any rule of law to take care or exercise skill in the performance of any investment functions.

9–257

The Law Commission, has issued a Consultation Paper, "Trustee Exemption Clauses.[22] Its provisional conclusion is that there is little reason to allow professional trustees, whether corporate or individual, in selling their skilled services to exempt themselves from liability for grossly negligent breaches of trust or even ordinarily negligent breaches. Its report is due October 2005.

RE BELOVED WILKES'S CHARITY[23]

Lord Chancellor (1851) 3 Mac. & G. 440

Charitable trustees had to select a boy to be educated at Oxford for the Anglican ministry, preference to be given to boys from four named parishes if in the trustees' judgment a fit and proper candidate therefrom could be found. Without giving any reasons, but stating that they had acted impartially, the trustees selected Charles Joyce who did not come from the named parishes but who had a brother who was a minister who had put forward Charles's merits to the trustees. The court was asked to set aside the selection, and to select William Gale, whose father was a respectable farmer residing in one of the specified parishes.

9–258

Held. In the absence of evidence that the trustees had exercised their discretion unfairly or dishonestly, the court would not interfere.

LORD TRURO L.C.: "The question, therefore, is, whether it was the duty of the trustees to enter into particulars, or whether the law is not, that trustees who are appointed to execute a trust according to discretion, that discretion to be influenced by a variety of circumstances (as, in this instance, by those particular circumstances which should be connected with the fitness of a lad to be brought up as a minister of the Church of England), are not bound to go into a detail of the grounds upon which they come to their conclusion, their duty being satisfied by shewing that they have considered the circumstances of the case, and have come to their conclusion accordingly. Without occupying time by going into a lengthened examination of the decisions, the result of them appears to me so clear and reasonable, that it will be sufficient to state my conclusion in point of law to be, that in such cases as I have mentioned it is to the discretion of the trustees that the execution of the trust is

9–259

---

[21] For the relationship between s.192 and Table A article 85 see *Movitex Ltd v Bulfield* [1988] B.C.L.C. 104.
[22] No.171.
[23] Applied in *Wilson v Law Debenture Trust Corp.* [1995] 2 All E.R. 337 at 343.

confided, that discretion being exercised with an entire absence of indirect motive, with honesty of intention, and with a fair consideration of the subject. The duty of supervision on the part of this Court will thus be confined to the question of the honesty, integrity, and fairness with which the deliberation has been conducted, and will not be extended to the accuracy of the conclusion arrived at, except in particular cases. If, however, as stated by Lord Ellenborough in *The King v The Archbishop of Canterbury* ((1812) 15 East 117), trustees think fit to state a reason, and the reason is one which does not justify their conclusion, then the Court may say that they have acted by mistake and in error, and that it will correct their decision; but if, without entering into details, they simply state, as in many cases it would be most prudent and judicious for them to do, that they have met and considered and come to a conclusion, the court has then no means of saying that they have failed in their duty, or to consider the accuracy of their conclusion. It seems, therefore, to me, that having in the present case to look to the motives of the trustees as developed in the affidavits, no ground exists for imputing bad motives. The Petitioners, indeed, candidly state, on the face of their petition, that they do not impute such motives, they merely charge the trustees with a miscarriage as regards the duty which they had to perform. I cannot, therefore, deal with the case as if the petition had contained a statement of a different kind, and if I could, still I should say, having read the affidavits, that I see nothing whatever which can lay the foundation for any judicial conclusion that the trustees intentionally and from bad motives failed in their duty, if they failed at all."

WONG v BURT

New Zealand Court of Appeal [2004] N.Z.C.A. 174 (Anderson P., Hammond and Wiliam Young J.J.)

HAMMOND J "[8] The essential facts relating to this issue can be shortly stated.

9–260   [9] Clause 5 of William Wong's will, in summary, provided as follows:

- The residuary estate was to be held in trust with the net annual income payable to Estelle Wong until her death.
- After the death of Estelle Wong, the net annual income was to be payable in equal shares to those of Phillipa and Wong Liu Sheung who were still alive. It is of singular importance to this case that there was no substitutionary provision in favour of grandchildren, if one of those daughters predeceased Estelle; in that event, all the income was to be paid to the other surviving daughter.
- After the death of the last surviving child, the estate is to be distributed amongst the children, or grandchildren, or great grandchildren of Phillipa. The exclusion of Wong Liu Sheung's children appears to have been quite deliberate, as a result of a family falling out.

[10] Clause 6 of the will conferred upon the trustees a discretion to pay to Estelle, out of the capital of the estate:

. . . such sum or sums as they in their absolute discretion may think fit if they shall consider it necessary, desirable or expedient so to do by reason of the state of my wife's health or her desire to travel or to acquire a home or by reason of a fall in the purchasing power of money or for any other reasons whatsoever whether similar or dissimilar to the foregoing.

[11] When Phillipa Wong died in 1995 Mrs Estelle Wong became concerned as to the position of Mei-Ling and Matthew. She viewed the inability of these two

children to take their mother's share of the estate income, in the event of their mother's death, as inappropriate, and unfair.

[12] To overcome this disability, in 1996 the trustees distributed $250,000 of the capital of the William Wong estate to Estelle. Estelle then lent this sum of $250,000 to the Phillipa Estelle Wong Trust (PEW Trust). The beneficiaries of PEW are Mei-Ling and Matthew.

[13] In effecting this payment of $250,000, the trustees relied on their powers under clause 6 of the will. The debt was then periodically forgiven over a period of years, and by this will.

The claim in the High Court

[14] Wong Liu Sheung bought proceedings in the High Court claiming that, in so **9–261** proceeding, the trustees:

- had acted *ultra vires* the terms of the trust;
- breached their duty to exercise their discretion for a proper purpose; and
- breached their duty to act impartially and even handedly towards all classes of beneficiaries.

The judgment in the High Court

[15] Ronald Young J dismissed this claim, in its entirety, in a judgment delivered on **9–262** 6 May 2003.

. . .

The grounds of appeal

[20] Ms Peters argued that the exercise of the discretion by the trustees in the **9–263** impugned respect was for an improper purpose. This submission rested essentially on two propositions. First, that the sole purpose of the exercise of the discretion was to "remedy" a perceived inequality that had arisen under clause 5 of the will (the appellants really say as a device to circumvent the plain meaning of clause 5). Secondly, that the distribution made was to benefit a person who was not an object of the clause 6 discretion (i.e. not Estelle).

[21] As to remedies, Ms Peters submitted that the $250,000 can be traced to the PEW Trust, and as such, the trustees of that trust hold the funds as constructive trustees for the William Wong estate.

[22] Alternatively, the appellants submit that the trustees are personally liable. The essential issue both under clause 13 of the will (the exoneration provision) and s73 is whether the trustees acted dishonestly. The appellants submit that the trustees' actions, particularly when they were specifically warned that the will prohibited the course of conduct proposed, amounted (at least) to "recklessness".

. . .

The law

[27] The notion of a fraud on a power itself rests on the fundamental juristic **9–264** principle that any form of authority may only be exercised for the purposes conferred, and in accordance with its terms. This principle is one of general application.

[28] The particular expression, a "fraud on a power", applies to both a power and a discretion. The word "fraud" here denotes an improper motive, in the sense that a power given for one purpose is improperly used for another purpose.

[29] Over the years a number of attempts have been made to categorise the circumstances in which a fraud on a power will arise. For instance, Hanbury and Martin *Modern Equity* (16 ed 2001) at 188 divides the cases into three categories. The first arises where the appointment is made as a result of a prior agreement or bargain with the appointee as to what he or she will do with the proceeds. Secondly, there are those cases where the power is exercised improperly so as to benefit the appointor. The third category are those cases in which an appointment is drafted so that the intent appears to benefit objects of the power, but the real intent is to benefit non-objects.

[30] These distinctions are useful for analytic and descriptive purposes, but it is necessary to recall that the *sine qua non* which makes the exercise of a discretion or power "improper" is the improper intention of the person exercising it. The central principle is that if the power is exercised with the intention of benefiting some non-object of the discretionary power, whether that person is the person exercising it, or anybody else for that matter, the exercise is void. If, on the other hand, there is no such improper intention, even although the exercise does in fact benefit a non-object, it is valid. See *Vatcher v Paull* [1915] AC 372 at 378 per Lord Parker (PC Jersey).

[31] In the case of a discretionary power to be exercised in favour of one of its objects, but in the "hope" that the recipient will benefit a non-object, the validity of such an exercise will depend upon whether the recipient had legal and moral freedom of action (*Birley v Birley* (1858) 25 Beav 299; 53 ER 651).

[32] The case law in this area is difficult, not so much for the underlying principles, which seem plain enough, but in their application to often quite complex estates, or inter-related transactions. Assume, for instance, a case in which a discretionary power is exercisable in favour of an adult male (X) who states that, if it is in fact exercised in his favour, he will give part of the relevant fund to his parents, Y and Z, who are not objects of the discretionary power. If the true intention of the appointment is to benefit the parents, the exercise is invalid. If that is not the case, but X is under some distinct pressure to benefit Y and Z, the exercise would also be invalid (*re Dick* [1953] Ch 343). On the other hand, if X has genuine freedom of action and wishes to give Y and Z a benefit, then it appears that the exercise of the power would be good (*Re Marsdens Trusts* (1859) 4 Drew 594; 62 ER 228; and see Parker and Mellows, *The Modern Law of Trusts* (8 ed, Oakley) at 222).

[33] As to the effect of a finding of a fraud on a power, it has long been held that where a power is successfully impugned, its exercise is totally invalid (*Re Cohen* [1911] 1 Ch 37), unless the improper element in the appointment can be severed from the remainder of that appointment (*Topham v Duke of Portland* (1858) 1 De GJ & S. 517; 46 ER 205).

This case

9–265 [34] It is necessary at this point to add some further facts. On the evidence, Mrs Estelle Wong was devastated by the death from cancer of her daughter Phillipa, in August of 1995. Phillipa was then only 43 years old, and Matthew and Mei-Ling were teenagers. Estelle was very close to Phillipa. Although Phillipa's family were in Australia, Estelle spoke regularly to Phillipa, and she would frequently go to Australia to visit her daughter.

[35] On one occasion, after she had returned from Australia, Estelle expressed concern to Mr Burt (who is now a retired chartered accountant and had a long association with the Wong family) "about the effect of Bill Wong's will". Estelle

suddenly came to appreciate that, under the will, Phillipa's share of the income would not pass to her children.

[36] It was in those circumstances that advice was sought from Chapman Tripp on this issue. It seems that it was Mr Burt who calculated various figures, and "concluded that $250,000 would partly redress the situation and should be loaned to the PEW Trust, and successively forgiven". As Mr Burt put it, "the purpose of the loan and forgiveness programme was to restore the expected benefit that Mei-Ling and Matthew would have received on their mother's death had they been entitled under Bill's will to her life interest in the PW Estate Trust.

. . .

[39] In their opinion (which was disclosed to the Court) Chapman Tripp advised that clause 5 must be read in "its plain words". The solicitors said, "In other words there is no statutory remedy to allow Phillipa's two children to receive the income that she would have received". The solicitors then detailed three options which, as they saw it, were "available to remedy this matter". One was to resort to the discretionary power available to the trustees under clause 6 of the will, which "[Estelle] could then invest in [her] own name". Estelle could then amend her will to provide for that sum to be left equally to Mei-Ling and Matthew. Secondly, the capital sum received from the estate could be loaned to the PEW Trust and then, on Estelle's death, the assets of that trust automatically vest in Mei-Ling and Matthew. A third option was identified as being an interest-free loan from the husband's estate, but repayable on Janice's death.

[40] Although some disadvantages in each of these alternatives were identified, it was at no point suggested by the solicitors that the potential difficulties relating to a fraud on a power might have to be addressed in relation to the first option.

[41] The evidence in the case in this respect is well documented and quite clear. In summary, on Phillipa's premature death, Mrs Estelle Wong became concerned that there was no gift-over provision as to income for Phillipa's children. A member of Chapman Tripp recorded in a file note: "this is of great concern to Mrs Wong and although she accepts that her late husband may never have anticipated their daughter predeceasing Mrs Wong she is adamant that it would have been his intention for Phillipa's share of the income to pass to her children". Thus it was that a scheme was settled by Mrs Wong, with the trustees, and after taking legal advice, which had the overt and pre-determined idea that the trustees would utilise clause 6 of the will to avoid the effect of clause 5 of the will, in the circumstances which had arisen. This exercise was not undertaken as a distinct, or separate advance to Mrs Wong or in the "hope" that Estelle Wong would benefit a non-object. The exercise was already constrained by a pre-considered course of action which also avoided Mrs Estelle Wong having to resort to any assets under her control or direction to assist her grandchildren.

[42] In our view, this deliberate, and pre-conceived, device amounted to a fraud on the power. If Mrs Estelle Wong had simply been advanced the money out of the estate and had then exercised genuine freedom of action to benefit the children (as for instance by setting up a trust for them), that would not have been unlawful. But what was knowingly erected was a deliberate scheme to subvert the terms of the will. What was overlooked was that the property was vested in those entitled in default of the exercise of the power, subject to its being divested by a proper exercise of the power in clause 6, and the steps in fact taken gave rise to a fraud on those entitled in default."

Held to the extent the $250,000 could not be recovered by tracing into the PEW Trust, the trustees were personally accountable and not protected by exemption clause "not liable for any loss not attributable to dishonesty".

ABACUS TRUST COMPANY (ISLE OF MAN) v BARR

Chancery Division [2003] Ch 409; [2003] 1 All ER 763

9–266　LIGHTMAN J: "[17] The Rule as stated in Hastings-Bass was expressed in a negative form to the effect that the court should not interfere with the exercise in good faith of a trustee's discretion, notwithstanding that it does not have the full effect which the trustee intended, unless the trustee exceeded the authority given by the trust or:

> "it is clear that he would not have acted as he did (a) had he not taken into account considerations which he should not have taken into account, or (b) had he not failed to take into account considerations which he ought to have taken into account" [1975] Ch at 41G.

9–267　[18] The Rule was restated in a positive form by Warner J in *Mettoy Pension Trustees v Evans* [1990] 1 WLR 1587 at 1621H, namely that:

> "where a trustee acts under a discretion given to him by the terms of the trust the court will interfere with his action if it is clear that he would not have so acted as he did had he not failed to take into account considerations which he ought to have taken into account."

[19] Warner J went on to state (at p.1625B) the exercise to be undertaken by the court in deciding whether the trustee has so acted:

> "In a case such as this, where it is claimed that the rule in Hastings-Bass applies, three questions arise:
>
> (1)　What were the trustees under a duty to consider?
> (2)　Did they fail to consider it?
> (3)　If so, what would they have done if they had considered it?"

9–268　[20] A series of subsequent cases (all save one at first instance) have considered and (with only one substantive modification) applied or sought to apply the Rule as reformulated by Warner J. It is unnecessary to consider the question raised by Lord Walker whether the holding in two such cases that the actual or potential adverse tax consequences of the exercise of the power are relevant facts for the purposes of the Rule is a step too far. (In this regard it may be noted that in *Gibbon v Mitchell* [1990] 1 WLR at 1304 Millett J limited the jurisdiction to set aside for mistake to cases where there is a mistake of law or fact as to the effect of the transaction itself as opposed merely to the consequence or advantages to be gained by entering into it). The one substantive modification was made by the Court of Appeal in the case of Stannard. In that case the trustees of a pension scheme had to make a transfer in respect of transferring employees to a new fund. Sometime ahead of the proposed transfer they decided its quantum in the light of the value of the pension fund as it then stood. Thereafter prior to the date that the transfer was made, there was a recent substantial increase in value of the pension fund, which might have occasioned a change in the trustee's decision. The trustees were not however informed of the increase and accordingly did not have the opportunity to reconsider their previous decision in the light of the new facts. The Court of Appeal held that the failure of the trustees to consider this relevant consideration flawed their decision and that it was sufficient for the court to hold the decision invalid that the trustees only might, and not would, have taken a different decision if they had done so. It is not apparent from the judgments in that case that the Court of Appeal appreciated that it was departing from the Rule in this regard as laid down in Hastings-Bass. The choice between the two criteria remains open: see Scott at 718. Fortunately no such choice is required in this case, for clearly the Trustee would not have appointed 60% of the Trust Fund if it had known of the Settlor's true wishes in that regard. I shall need later to refer to a passage in the judgment of Staughton LJ in Stannard on the issue whether under the Rule the exercise of the power is rendered void or voidable.

. . .

[23] In my view it is not sufficient to bring the Rule into play that the Trustee **9–269** made a mistake or by reason of ignorance or a mistake did not take into account a relevant consideration or took into account an irrelevant consideration. What has to be established is that the Trustee in making his decision has (in the language of Warner J in Mettoy) failed to consider what he was under a duty to consider. If the Trustee has in accordance with his duty identified the relevant considerations and used all proper care and diligence in obtaining the relevant information and advice relating to those considerations, the Trustee can be in no breach of duty and its decision cannot be impugned merely because in fact that information turns out to be partial or incorrect. For example, if the Settlor had wished for an appointment of 40% of the Trust Fund in favour of the Sons, but in a letter to the Trustee informing the Trustee of his wishes by reason of a slip by him or a clerical error by his secretary the settlor had stated that he wanted an appointment of 60% of the Trust Fund, and if the Trustee in accordance with that (erroneous) expression of wishes had made an appointment of 60%, neither could the Trustee be criticised nor could the appointment be challenged under the Rule. The Trustee took into account the relevant consideration (the wishes of the Settlor) and acted reasonably and properly in relying on the letter as the expression of those wishes. The fact that the Trustee misapprehended the Settlor's true intentions is irrelevant. Likewise a decision by the Trustee to appoint quoted shares to a particular value to a beneficiary is not flawed if the shares subsequently turn out at the date of the appointment to have been immensely more valuable or less valuable than their quoted price by reason of a fact not reasonably ascertainable at the time e.g. an imminent take-over bid or a massive fraud perpetrated on the quoted company.

[24] In summary the Rule affords to the beneficiaries the protection of a **9–270** requirement that the Trustee performs its duty in exercising of its discretion, and a remedy in case of a default. In the absence of any such breach of duty the Rule does not afford the right to the Trustee or any beneficiary to have a decision declared invalid because the Trustee's decision was in some way mistaken or has unforeseen and unpalatable consequences.

[25] Accordingly turning to the facts of this case, it is not sufficient to invoke the **9–271** Rule that the Trustee mistakenly understood that the Settlor wished the appointment to extend to 60% of the Trust Fund when his true intention was 40%. The Trustee properly identified the Settlor's intention as a relevant consideration. The Trustee was informed by Mr Ward-Thompson that his wish was that the appointment extend to 60%. The fact that Mr Ward-Thompson misunderstood the Settlor's true wish and communicated that misunderstanding to the Trustee does not of itself establish any breach of duty by the Trustee and accordingly scope for application of the Rule. To establish the breach of duty and application of the Rule, the Settlor

must go further and show that the Trustee was in breach of duty in acting on and relying on what Mr Ward-Thompson told him.

. . .

9–272   [28] The fourth issue raised is whether by reason of application of the Rule the appointment is void or voidable. This issue is of critical significance in this case, for the lapse of 10 years since the Appointment, the signal failure by the Settlor (indeed his deliberate decision not) to take any legal advice or any effective action until 2001, his acquiescence until then in the Appointment having full legal effect and in particular the payment to the Sons as fully entitled thereto of some ú400,000 from the Settlement must have the greatest significance if the Settlement is voidable, but none at all if it is void.

9–273   [29] The similarity between the grounds on which a decision by trustees may be attacked and the grounds on which official decision-making is subject to judicial review has been noted: see *Edge v Pensions Ombudsman* [2000] Ch 602 at 627-30 and Walker at pp.227-8. But there are three critical differences between public (or administrative) law and private law proceedings. The first is the discretion vested in the court in public law proceedings whether or not to grant relief. The second is a difference in approach to the distinction between what is "void" and what is "voidable". In public law where an act or order is ultra vires, it is a nullity without existence or effect in law, but the terms "nullity" and "void" have no absolute sense: their meaning is relative depending upon the court's willingness to grant relief in any situation. If the court is willing to grant the necessary legal remedies, the act or order is recognised as having no legal effect at all. But the court may hold the act or order invalid, but refuse relief e.g. because he does not deserve a discretionary remedy, because of delay or for some other legal reason. In such a case the void order remains effective and must be accepted as if it is valid: see Wade & Forsyth, Administrative Law 8th edition pages 306–8. The third is the strict time limits insisted upon for commencement of proceedings for judicial review.

9–274   [30] By contrast with the position in public law proceedings in trust proceedings the legal classifications of void and voidable must be respected and there is no such strict time limit, and the court only has a discretion and can only have regard to the lapse of time between the act under challenge and the challenge when the challenged act is voidable and not void. The need in justice for some regard to the lapse of time in cases such as the present when the Rule is invoked was underlined by Park J in *Breadner v Granville-Grossman* [2001] Ch 523 at 553. Such need can only be satisfied if the decision successfully challenged under the Rule is voidable and not void.

9–275   [31] The authorities leave open the question whether a decision successfully challenged under the Rule is voidable or void. (The problematic judgment of Farwell LJ in *Cloutte v Storey* [1911] 1 Ch 18 on the effect of a fraud on a power raises difficulties pointed out by Lord Walker and cannot be determinative). There are statements in a number of the cases that the decision is void, but it is not clear how far the issue was fully argued, if argued at all, and so far as they do so decide, their weight and otherwise binding effect on me is diluted by the absence of reasoning and accord with principle by the fact that there appears to have been no reference made to the statement by Staughton LJ in Stannard (at para 66 p.237) that in the case of the challenge to the decision in that case the court had a discretion whether to declare the trustees' decision invalid. It is necessarily implicit in this statement in the private law context in which it is to be found that he was holding that the court had a discretion whether to avoid the trustee's decision *i.e.* it was voidable only.

[32] What may appear to have been a decision of trustees may on examination **9–276** prove to have been no decision at all. An example is furnished by the case of *Turner v Turner* [1984] Ch 100 where the trustees for many years signed every document placed before them by their solicitors (including appointments) without understanding that they had any discretion to exercise. But if the trustees have exercised the discretion conferred upon them, but in doing so have failed to take into account a relevant consideration or have taken into account an irrelevant consideration, it cannot in my view fairly or sensibly be held that they made no decision. It may be held that they made a flawed decision which is open to challenge, but that they made a decision is beyond question. The common law doctrine of "Non est factum" has a very narrow and limited application. The transaction must be essentially different in substance or in kind from the transaction intended: *Saunders v Anglia Building Society* [1971] AC 1004 at 1026 per Lord Wilberforce. As Lord Walker suggests, a like requirement as to the essential nature of a transaction is surely called for before the equivalent rule can render a decision in equity no decision at all. The application of the Rule cannot of itself have this effect.

[33] A successful challenge made to a decision under the Rule should in principle **9–277** result in the decision being held voidable and not void. This accords with the ordinary principles of Equity that (leaving aside the separate and distinct self-dealing rule) a decision challenged on grounds of breach of fiduciary duty is voidable and not void. That applies to the Appointment which, as I have held, falls foul of the Rule.

[34] In my view accordingly the Appointment in this case is voidable and not void. **9–278** Whether in the circumstances of this case the Appointment should or should not be avoided and, if so, on what terms is a matter on which I have not been addressed and on which the parties are at liberty to adduce further evidence and make further submissions. I must accordingly adjourn the hearing of this matter until a date when this issue can be argued and determined. There is however every reason to believe that to save further expensive contentious litigation the parties can and will seek to settle and agree the outstanding issue and seek any necessary approval by the court of the compromise reached.

ARMITAGE v NURSE

Court of Appeal [1998] Ch. 241 [1997] 3 W.L.R. 1048 [1997] 2 All E.R. 705 (Hirst, Millett and Hutchison L. JJ.)

Under clause 15 of the settlement, "No Trustee shall be liable for any loss or **9–279** damage which may happen . . . from any cause whatsoever unless such loss or damage shall be caused by his own actual fraud." As a matter of construction, the court first held "clause 15 exempts the trustee from liability for loss or damage to the trust property no matter how indolent, imprudent, lacking in diligence, negligent or wilful he may have been, so long as he has not acted dishonestly."

MILLETT L.J. (with whom Hirst and Hutchison L.JJ. concurred)

"The permitted scope of trustee exemption clauses

It is submitted on behalf of Paula that a trustee exemption clause which purports to exclude all liability except for actual fraud is void, either for repugnancy or as contrary to public policy. . . . What is pleaded is, at the very lowest, culpable and probably gross negligence. So the question reduces itself to this: can a trustee exemption clause validly exclude liability for gross negligence?

9–280   It is a bold submission that a clause taken from one standard precedent book and to the same effect as a clause found in another, included in a settlement drawn by Chancery counsel acting for an infant settlor and approved by the court on her behalf, should be so repugnant to the trusts or contrary to public policy that it is liable to be set aside at her suit. But the submission has been made and we must consider it. In my judgment it is without foundation.

There can be no question of the clause being repugnant to the trust. In *Wilkins v Hogg* (1861) 31 L.J.Ch. 41 at 42 Lord Westbury LC challenged counsel to cite a case where an indemnity clause protecting the trustee from his ordinary duty had been held so repugnant as to be rejected. Counsel was unable to do so. No such case has occurred in England or Scotland since.

9–281   I accept the submission made on behalf of Paula that there is an irreducible core of obligations owed by the trustees to the beneficiaries and enforceable by them which is fundamental to the concept of a trust. If the beneficiaries have no rights enforceable against the trustees there are no trusts. But I do not accept the further submission that these core obligations include the duties of skill and care, prudence and diligence. The duty of the trustees to perform the trusts honestly and in good faith for the benefit of the beneficiaries is the minimum necessary to give substance to the trusts, but in my opinion it is sufficient. As Mr Hill pertinently pointed out in his able argument, a trustee who relied on the presence of a trustee exemption clause to justify what he proposed to do would thereby lose its protection: he would be acting recklessly in the proper sense of the term.

It is, of course, far too late to suggest that the exclusion in a contract of liability for ordinary negligence or want of care is contrary to public policy. What is true of a contract must be equally true of a settlement. It would be very surprising if our law drew the line between liability for ordinary negligence and liability for gross negligence. In this respect English law differs from civil law systems, for it has always drawn a sharp distinction between negligence, however gross, on the one hand and fraud, bad faith and wilful misconduct on the other. The doctrine of the common law is that: "Gross negligence may be evidence of mala fides, but is not the same thing." (See *Goodman v Harvey* (1836) 4 A & E 870 at 876, 111 ER 1011 at 1013 per Lord Denman C.J.) But while we regard the difference between fraud on the one hand and mere negligence, however gross, on the other as a difference in kind, we regard the difference between negligence and gross negligence as merely one of degree. English lawyers have always had a healthy disrespect for the latter distinction. In *Hinton v Dibbin* (1842) 2 Q.B. 646, 114 ER 253 Lord Denman C.J. doubted whether any intelligible distinction exists; while in *Grill v General Iron Screw Collier Co* (1866) 35 LJCP 321 at 330 Willes J. famously observed that gross negligence is ordinary negligence with a vituperative epithet. But civilian systems draw the line in a different place. The doctrine is *culpa lata dolo aequiparetur*; and although the maxim itself is not Roman the principle is classical. There is no room for the maxim in the common law; it is not mentioned in Broom *Selection of Legal Maxims Classified and Illustrated* (10th edn, 1939).

9–282   The submission that it is contrary to public policy to exclude the liability of a trustee for gross negligence is not supported by any English or Scottish authority. The cases relied on are the English cases of *Wilkins v Hogg* (1861) 31 L.J.Ch. 41 and *Pass v Dundas* (1880) 43 LT 665; and the Scottish cases of *Knox v Mackinnon* (1888) 13 App.Cas. 753 and *Rae v Meek* (1889) 14 App.Cas. 558, *Wyman or Ferguson (Pauper) v. Paterson* [1900] A.C. 271 and *Clarke v Clarke's Trustees* 1925 SC 693. These cases, together with two other Scottish cases, *Seton v Dawson* (1841) 4 D 310 and *Carruthers v Carruthers* [1896] A.C. 659, and cases from the Commonwealth and America, were reviewed by the Jersey Court of Appeal in *Midland Bank Trustee*

(Jersey) Ltd v Federated Pension Services Ltd [1995] Jersey L.R. 352, [1996] PLR 179 in a masterly judgment delivered by Sir Godfray Le Quesne Q.C.

I agree with the conclusion of the Jersey Court of Appeal that all these cases are **9–283** concerned with the true construction of the particular clauses under consideration or of similar clauses in standard form in the nineteenth century. None of them deals with the much wider form of clause which has become common in the present century, and none of them is authority for the proposition that it is contrary to public policy to exclude liability for gross negligence by an appropriate clause clearly worded to have that effect.

At the same time, it must be acknowledged that the view is widely held that these clauses have gone too far, and that trustees who charge for their services and who, as professional men, would not dream of excluding liability for ordinary professional negligence, should not be able to rely on a trustee exemption clause excluding liability for gross negligence. Jersey introduced a law in 1989 which denies effect to a trustee exemption clause which purports to absolve a trustee from liability for his own "fraud, wilful misconduct or gross negligence". . . . If clauses such as cl 15 of the settlement are to be denied effect, then in my opinion this should be done by Parliament."

Section 9. The Control of Occupational Pension Funds

Introduction

Occupational pension schemes are of two types, defined benefit (or final **9–284** salary) schemes and defined contribution (or money-purchase) schemes. Usually, both employer and employee pay contributions to trustees. In the case of defined benefit schemes the contributions are used by the trustees for themselves to build up a large trust fund that is security[24] for payment to scheme members of their pensions and for payment of death-in-service benefits and pensions to surviving spouses, partners, cohabitants or dependants: the company is at risk as liable to make up any shortfall in the scheme. In the case of defined contribution schemes, the contributions are used by the trustees for regular investment on behalf of each contributing employee with an assurance company which invests in a range of shares or unit trusts, so that, on retirement or death-in-service, funds will be available to purchase an annuity and provide a limited lump sum as well; no question of any shortfall arises for the company to meet. However, employees do less well under these schemes than under defined benefit schemes, not least because their contributions are less than under defined benefit schemes.

The employee's contract of employment leads to him becoming a **9–285** member of the pension scheme upon its terms and conditions, so his rights arise under the scheme.[25] Each employee is settlor of a separate settlement within the head trust established originally by the employer.[26] The employee

---

[24] *Wrightson Ltd v Fletcher Challenge Nominees Ltd* [2001] UKPC 23, para.28. This does not mean that any surplus belongs to the employer which is liable to make up any deficit, because scheme members have expectations of enhanced benefits: the terms of the scheme and the exercise of powers of amendment thereof are crucial, coupled with Pensions Act 1995, s.37 as substituted by Pensions Act 2004, s.25. Further see *National Grid plc v Mayes* [1999] Pensions L.R. 37.

[25] *Imperial Group Pension Trust Ltd v Imperial Tobacco Ltd* [1991] 1 W.L.R. 589.

[26] *Air Jamaica Ltd v Charlton* [1999] 1 W.L.R. 1399 at 1408.

is normally contractually obliged to contribute to the pension fund via deduction from his wages or salary while the employer is also contractually obliged to contribute. These bilateral contributions, which arise from the employee's unilateral work, are the source of the benefits to which the employee is entitled as a scheme member. The employee is thus directly and indirectly the settlor of the amount of money needed as security for his entitlements to benefits. It is thus the employee's expectations as settlor that the trustees must focus upon in exercising their discretions.

9–286 Moreover, over many years the employee has strenuously earned his secured rights under the pension scheme as deferred remuneration. He expects his trustees to give very serious and special consideration to any claims he may have to take early retirement or to any partial or total disability benefits and to any claims of his cohabitants or dependants in respect of benefits arising from his death. These matters will often be crucial to living standards. Furthermore, the discretion afforded to the trustees will often be much more limited than in the case of ordinary family discretionary trusts because the trustees' discretionary fiduciary obligation is restricted to deciding whether a person is entitled to a payment on establishment of certain factual requirements.[27]

9–287 In the case of a family discretionary trust the expectation of the patriarchal settlor is for his trustees to have as much autonomous leeway over the trust period to make the sorts of gifts in their discretion as he would have made if still alive and absolute beneficial owner of the property.[28] Any whining, whingeing beneficiaries or objects of discretionary powers are not intended to have much scope at all to complain that they received less bounteous "icing on their cake" than others, except in blatant circumstances where the trustees' integrity can be challenged, *e.g.* in reaching a decision perverse to any sensible expectation of the settlor or a decision that no rational body of trustees could reach.

9–288 Moreover, in such family trusts a holder of a personal, as opposed to a fiduciary, power can exercise it spitefully and capriciously,[29] but if an employer holds a personal power in a pensions trust structure it must not exercise the power in a manner likely seriously to damage the relationship of confidence between employee and employer.[30]

No need for a fair hearing but reasons need be disclosed for pension trusts

9–289 In the context of traditional family trusts there is clearly no need for a fair hearing even if there may be said to be two sides involved with a particular issue; *e.g.* the objects of a power of appointment and the beneficiaries entitled in default of exercise of such power.[31] Where the trustees know

---

[27] *Telstra Super Pty Ltd v Flegeltaub* [2000] 2 V.R. 276, para.25.
[28] *Re Wills Trust Deeds* [1964] Ch. 219 at 228–229, *Sayseng v Kellog Superannuation Pty Ltd* [2003] N.S.W.S.C. 945, para.59
[29] *Re Wright* [1920] 1 Ch. 108 at 118.
[30] *Imperial Group Pension Trust Ltd v Imperial Tobacco Ltd* [1991] 1 W.L.R. 589, *National Grid plc v Laws* [1997] Pens L.R. 157, 177. Further see D. J. Hayton, "Pension Trusts and Traditional Trusts: Drastically Different Species of Trusts" [2005] Conv. 229.
[31] *Scott v National Trust* [1998] 2 All E.R. 705 at 718; *R v Charity Commissioners Ex p. Baldwin* [2001] W.T.L.R. 137 at 148–149; *re B* [1987] 2 All E.R. 475 at 478; *Yates v Air Canada* [2004] B.C.S.C. 3.

what the settlor wanted, then it is permitted for them to do what he wanted without giving much consideration to the interests of other persons capable of benefiting under the trust.[32] Such persons may think this is rough on them, so all they are getting is "rough justice", but if this is what the settlor intended, then so be it. If a settlor could have lived for 130 years and then would likely have done with his own property what his trustees did with the trust property under the terms of his trust created when he was 60 years old, then the trustees' conduct cannot be impugned unless their integrity can be challenged.

However, the pension trust context is very different indeed. This is so **9–290** whether a scheme member has a specific individual interest in an early retirement pension or a permanent disability payment, or a more general class interest in the amount of pension fund to be transferred to the new employer taking over the business in which the class members work or in the amount of augmented benefits for the class if there is a fund surplus available for such augmentation, or whether a third party claims a pension as a cohabitant or a lump sum as designee of a member's indicative power of designation of death-in-service benefits.

The interest at stake of a scheme member or third party is so important **9–291** to him as relating to his expected standard of living that the Pensions Ombudsman has held that it is "injustice in consequence of maladministration" to fail to give reasons to a claimant for rejecting his claim because how can be understand or appeal to the Pensions Ombudsman against a decision for which no reasons are given.[33] Acceptable standards of administration require provision of a reasoned decision together with copies of documents relied upon in the decision[34] (with appropriate deletions of any confidential information concerning others). This reflects the common law approach to decisions of administrative bodies where cases where reasons are not required are becoming exceptions to a general rule.[35]

When someone capable of benefiting under a trust goes to court to seek **9–292** significant information withheld by the trustee, the Privy Council in *Schmidt v Rosewood Trust Ltd*,[36] in a seminal advice provided by Lord Walker extolling the broad flexible power of the "court's inherent jurisdiction to supervise (and where appropriate intervene in) the administration of trusts", has emphasised the need to look at the strength of such person's claim. A claim can hardly be much stronger than that of an employee who claims his health circumstances justify an early retirement with a pension and payment of a hefty lump sum for permanent disablement, even though the trustee in its discretion needs to hold the opinion that such is justified by the employee's health circumstances.

---

[32] *Karger v Paul* [1984] V.R. 161; *Breadner v Granville-Grossman* [2001] Ch. 523; *Re Esteem Settlement* [2004] W.T.L.R. 1.
[33] *Allen v TKM Group Pension Trust Ltd* [2002] Pensions L.R. 333; *Manship v IMI Pensions Trust Ltd* (26 Nov. 2002); Annual Report 2001–2002, p.7.
[34] Very relevant for internal appeals: consider Pensions Act 1995 s.50, now as substituted by Pensions Act 2004, s.273.
[35] *Stefan v General Medical Council* [1999] 1 W.L.R. 1293; *R. v Higher Education Funding Council Ex p. Institute of Dental Surgery* [1994] 1 W.L.R. 241.
[36] [2003] 2 A.C. 709, para.66, applied in *Foreman v Kingston* [2004] 1 N.Z.L.R. 841.

9–293   The claimant will produce as much medical evidence as he can to support his claim and, if the trustees' delegate to deal with these matters then requires it, the delegate will seek further evidence from the claimant's doctors or independent doctors and perhaps from an inquiry agent; he should then afford the claimant the opportunity to deal with matters then arising that are adverse to the claim so that all relevant considerations are present in the adjudicatory framework. No formal oral hearing with rights of reply is needed: all that is needed is that the trustee has in place procedures[37] to ensure that it is adequately informed of relevant considerations [38] so that a real and genuine determination of the claim is made.[39] It is up to the trustees sensibly to decide how it goes about being adequately informed of relevant considerations.

9–294   What then if the trustees determine to reject the claim stating "We have properly taken account of all relevant considerations and ignored all irrelevant considerations but in our opinion your claim fails" or "We have taken account of the original material supplied by you, of further material obtained by us and of your response (with supporting materials) to queries raised by us, but in our opinion your claim fails"? The trustees refuse to do anything more.

9–295   In 1994 Rattee J in *Wilson v Law Debenture Trust Corp plc*[40] upheld the entitlement of pension trustees to refuse to provide any reasoning for their decisions, just as under *Re Londonderry's Settlement*[41] trustees of a family trust are entitled to refuse to provide any reasons, despite the key differences already detailed above, which subsequently led Lord Walker (when Robert Walker J.) in a scholarly paper to be critical[42] of the judge's view. In support of his criticism Lord Walker cited the remarks of Lord Browne-Wilkinson in 1995 in *Target Holdings Ltd v Redferns*,[43] "It is important . . . to distinguish between the basic principles of trust law and those specialist rules developed in relation to traditional trusts and the rationale of which has no application to trusts of quite a different kind." Indeed, in February 1992 in addressing the Annual Conference of Australian Superannuation Funds on the topic "Equity and its relevance to superannuation today",[44] Lord Browne-Wilkinson had opined that *Re Londonderry's Settlement* should not be applied to pension trusts.Lord Walker in *Schmidt v Rosewood Trust Ltd* has now stressed the greater the strength of the claimant's interest the greater the likelihood of the court

---

[37] *Stannard v Fisons Pension Trust Ltd* [1991] P.L.R. 225, para.65; *Hearn v Younger* [2002] W.T.L.R. 1317 para.91, *Tonkin v Western Mining Corporation* [1998] 10 ANZ Ins. Cas. 61–397. Now see Pensions Act 2004, s.273 substituting new Pensions Act 1995, s.50.

[38] *Edge v Pensions Ombudsman* [2002] Ch. 602.

[39] *Maciejewski v Telstra Super Pty Ltd* (1998) 44 N.S.W.L.R. 601, *Knudsen v Kara Kar Holdings Pty Ltd* [2000] N.S.W.S.C. 715 para.55; *Telstra Super Pty Ltd v Flegeltaub* [2000] 2 V.R. 276, paras 29–30; *Dundee General Hospitals Board v Walker* [1952] 1 All E.R. 896 at 905.

[40] [1995] 2 All E.R. 337.

[41] [1965] Ch. 918.

[42] "Some Trust Principles in the Pensions Context" in A. J. Oakley (ed.) *Trends in Contemporary Trust Law*, (Clarendon, Oxford, 1996), p.123 at p.131.

[43] [1996] A.C. 421 at 435.

[44] Privately published by the Leo Cussen Institute, cited in *Crowe v Stevedoring Employees Retirement Fund* [2003] V.S.C. 316, para.34.

exercising its broad inherent jurisdiction to supervise and, if appropriate, intervene in trust affairs. In my firm opinion, the exceptional strength of the interest of a pension scheme member whose claim has been rejected to be able to know the reasons and to see any supporting documents (subject to any deletions of confidential material) is such that he should now be entitled to obtain such reasons and supporting documents from the trustee.[45]

After all, the claimant has the core right to an early retirement pension **9–296** and a lump sum if the relevant factual circumstances are established in the fiduciary opinion of the trustee and he has the vital ancillary right to strike down the trustee's opinion if it would or might have been different but for ignoring a relevant consideration or taking account of an irrelevant consideration.[46] Surely these rights are not meaningful and without substance unless the claimant can ascertain whether or not he has such rights[47] by ascertaining the reasoning of the trustee. We must not forget that the claimant was led to become an employee and to continue in employment as settlor of the contributions giving rise to his rights as deferred remuneration on the basis that he did have meaningful and substantial rights.

Thus, in the field of pension trusts, while there is no need for a fair **9–297** hearing as such, there is a need for an adequately informed reasoned decision after procedures enabling the trustee to be adequately informed to come to a fair conclusion. In the field of traditional family trusts there just needs to be an adequately informed decision, often requiring the trustees to do very little to be adequately informed where the settlor's wishes as to whom he wants benefited are clear.

Decisions that "would" or "might" have been different if trustee adequately informed

Unless and until restricted by the House of Lords,[48] the rule in *Hastings* **9–298** *Bass*,[49] as summarised by Warner J. in *Mettoy Pension Trustees Ltd v Evans*[50] is that "where a trustee acts under a discretion given to him by the terms of the trust, the court will interfere with his action if it is clear that he *would* not have acted as he did had he not failed to take into account considerations which he *ought* to have taken into account". This relates to the duty to ascertain, and so be adequately informed of, the relevant considerations before reaching a decision.[51] As emphasised by Warner J.[52]

---

[45] It would appear that *Schmidt* has even undermined *Re Londonderry's Settlement* so that disclosure of reasons could be ordered in an appropriate family trust case according to Lord Hoffmann in the October 2003 Nottingham Lecture in Miami and Lightman J. in the February 2004 Withers Lecture at King's College London, though Balmford J. in *Crowe v Stevedoring Employees Retirement Fund* [2003] V.S.C. 316 felt she had to follow *Re Londonderry's Settlement* but found the relevant documents not to reveal reasons, and so ordered them to be disclosed.

[46] *Stannard v Fisons Pension Trust Ltd* [1991] Pensions L.R. 225.

[47] See, *e.g. Re Murphy's Settlements* [1999] 1 W.L.R. 282; *Scally v Southern Health and Social Services Board* [1992] 1 A.C. 294 at 306–307. Beneficiaries need a meaningful right to make the trustee account for its actions: *Foreman v Kingston* (2004) 6 I.T.E.L.R. 841, [2004] 1 N.Z.L.R. 841.

[48] See Lord Walker (when L.J.) in "The Limits of the Principle in *Re Hastings-Bass*", (2002) 13 K.C.L.J. 173 and E. G. Nugee Q.C. [2003] P.C.B. 173.

[49] [1975] Ch. 25.

[50] [1990] 1 W.L.R. 1587 at 1621.

[51] *Stannard v Fisons Pension Trust Ltd* [1991] P.L.R. 225 at 233.

[52] [1990] 1 W.L.R. 1587 at 1621.

and by Lightman J in *Re Barr's S.T*[53] three questions therefore arise: (1) what were the relevant considerations to be taken into account by the trustee under such duty to be adequately informed (the settlor's wishes being a key consideration[54])? (2) did the trustee fail to take account of them? (3) if so, what "would" the trustee have done if the trustee had taken into account the relevant considerations? If the trustee would not have acted differently despite failing to take account of a relevant consideration or ignoring an irrelevant consideration, then the court will not interfere.[55] It will interfere if the trustee would have acted differently.

9–299   The Court of Appeal in 1975 used "would" in formulating the so-called Rule in *Re Hastings-Bass*,[56] a family trust case, so naturally in 1990 Warner J.[57] also used "would", though dealing with a pension trust case. "Would" makes perfect sense in the family trust context where the patriarchal settlor[58] would not wish his discretionary beneficiaries to be able to whine from time to time that the trustees "might" have done this, that or the other, and so put the trustees to the trouble and expense of proving that they *would* not have made a different decision.

9–300   However, in the pensions context the wish of the beneficiary-settlors strenuously earning their pension rights and claims so as to be able to have a decent retired standard of living, will surely be not to have the high hurdle of having to prove that the trustees *would* have acted differently rather than *might* have acted differently, especially as a complex evaluation of circumstances may well be involved.

9–301   Thus, in *Kerr v British Leyland (Staff) Trustees Ltd*[59] Fox LJ, without citing any cases, held the duty of pension trustees whose beneficiaries "have purchased their rights" was "to give properly informed consideration to the application" concerning a total disability claim, but, due to the trustees not being informed by their delegate of a particular relevant consideration, "I think that it might materially have affected their decision", so the decision "to reject Mr Kerr's claim was of no effect and the trustees should reconsider the claim."

9–302   Subsequently, Dillon L.J. in *Stannard v Fisons Pension Trust Ltd*[60] followed *Kerr* in holding a trustees' decision of no effect because it "might" materially have affected their decision if they had been properly informed of the then current value of the trust fund and the implications of such for the basis of ascertaining the amount of the fund to be transferred to provide for pensions of employees transferring to another company.

---

[53] [2003] Ch. 409, para.19, applied in *Burrell v Burrell* [2005] W.T.L.R. 313. The need for a breach of duty is crucial despite the contrary view of Brian Green Q.C. (2003) 17 Trust L.I. 114.

[54] *ibid.*, paras 23 and 25, *Re Esteem Settlement* [2004] W.T.L.R. 1 para.122.

[55] *Stannard v Fisons Pension Trust* [1992] I.R.L.R. 27 at 33–34, para.66 (Staughton L.J.), *Nestlé v National Westminster Bank* [1994] 1 All E.R. 118; *Fox v Fox Estate* (1996) 28 O.R. (3d) 493 (Ontario CA).

[56] [1975] Ch. 25 at 41.

[57] *Mettoy Pension Trust Ltd v Evans* [1990] 1 W.L.R. 1587 at 1621, 1625.

[58] *Re Wills Trust Deeds* [1964] Ch. 219 at 228–229, *Sayseng v Kellog Superannuation Pty Ltd* [2003] N.S.W.S.C. 945, para.59.

[59] (1986) [2001] W.T.L.R. 1071 at 1079.

[60] [1991] P.L.R. 225.

Since then, first instance judges[61] have rightly, in my respectful opinion, **9–303** used "might" in the context of pension cases. However, as pointed out earlier, "would" is perfectly appropriate for traditional family trust cases as accepted by the Jersey Royal Court in *Re Green GLG Trust*[62] (though it there made no difference whether "would" or "might" was the better approach), especially when the Court of Appeal in the family trust case of *Re Hastings-Bass* itself had used "would".

Negative and positive judicial interference with trustees' decisions

Recent decisions have been concerned with whether or not application of **9–304** the rule in *Hastings-Bass* makes a decision "void" as if "void" or "null" or "ineffective" had some absolute sense.[63] One also needs to remind oneself that a transfer of the legal title by trustees to beneficiaries or new trustees will be effective where the trustees hold legal title and so can transfer it,[64] though the transfer will be subject to equitable claims,[65] not being a transfer to a bona fide purchaser for value of a legal or equitable interest. Thus, it does not matter whether the claimant has an equitable interest, due to a void or ineffective exercise of an equitable power, or a mere equity to rescind a voidable exercise of an equitable power except in so far as more weight may be given to discretionary bases to equitable relief in the case of a mere equity.

One also needs to note that in English administrative law[66] the courts **9–305** have moved away from terminology like "void" or "null", preferring to intervene as remedially appropriate, whether so that a decision has no effect at all from the outset or only after a person justifiably acted on the assumption the decision was valid or perhaps refusing relief because of delay,[67] waiver or some other reason.

It is submitted that such a flexible remedial approach should be taken in **9–306** the trust context. Where a beneficiary's claim to particular benefits under a pension scheme is wrongly rejected, then since nothing has happened it is easy to declare the rejection ineffective (or void), so that the matter must be reconsidered in proper fashion. However, where the trustees' wrongful decision has achieved positive ends, then the court should investigate matters carefully and, if favouring restricting or undoing such decision, should consider whether there is some discretionary factor against this, *e.g.* delay or change of position. In the pensions context it may be significant that section 67 of the Pensions Act 1995 has been substituted by a provision making amendments of the trust deed affecting subsisting rights voidable

---

[61] *AMP(UK) plc v Barker* [2001] W.T.L.R. 1237; *Hearn v Younger* [2002] W.T.L.R. 1317.

[62] [2003] W.T.L.R. 377, para.29.

[63] See *Re Barr's S.T.* [2003] Ch. 409, paras 28–30.

[64] *Rolled Steel Products (Holdings) Ltd v British Steel Corporation* [1986] Ch. 246 at 303; *De Vigier v IRC* [1964] 2 All E.R. 907 at 914. An exception arises under Trusts of Land and Appointment of Trustees Act 1996, s.8(1) if the trustees' power to dispose of the land is excluded.

[65] *Re Newen* [1894] 2 Ch. 297; *Re Osiris Trustees* [2000] W.T.L.R. 933.

[66] See P. P. Craig, *Administrative Law* (5th ed. 2003) pp. 692 *et seq.*

[67] Under CPR 54.5 judicial review must be sought within three months anyhow, while time limits may be imposed on internal pension appeals by interested persons: Pensions Act 1995, s.50 as substituted by Pensions Act 2004, s.273.

rather than void.[68] In the case of a family trust, if overlooking a relevant consideration prevents the exercise of a power for the "benefit" of a person actually being for that person's benefit, then the exercise of the power will be *ultra vires* and void as alleged in *Re Hastings- Bass* but rejected by the Court of Appeal.

9–307   In one area, however, the court should be prepared to make a positive decision itself, rather than just negate the trustees' decision and leave it to the trustees properly to reconsider the matter and come up with a proper decision within the large leeway afforded to trustees. English[69] and Canadian[70] administrative law on abuse of discretionary powers is beginning to indicate that where all other decisions would be irrational ones that no sensible adequately informed decision-maker could make, then the matter should not be referred back for re-consideration: the court itself should make the only rational decision and implement it.

9–308   Support for this in the trusts context can already be found in *Mettoy Pension Trustees Ltd v Evans*[71] where Warner J. in 1989 concluded that discretionary powers of trustees will be enforced by the court appointing new trustees or, should the proper basis for distribution appear, by itself directing the trustees so to distribute trust property, in the same way that Lord Wilberforce in *McPhail v Doulton*[72] had indicated discretionary trusts could be enforced by the courts "in the manner best calculated to give effect to the settlor's intentions" In 2003 Warner J.'s views were endorsed in Lord Walker's advice in *Schmidt v Rosewood Trust Ltd*[73] where the underlying emphasis is that in the court's broad "inherent jurisdiction to supervise and (where appropriate intervene in) the administration of trusts", the more strength to the beneficiary's claim the more likely it is that the court will intervene.

9–309   Where the beneficiary's claim is an all or nothing one as in most pension claims, but not as in claims to have a discretionary family trust distribution within a broad value range, it is easier for the court to find that the only rational possibility is to accept the claim in the light of the evidence produced by the claimant and the trustees to justify their conflicting attitudes, so that the court can substitute the only rational decision for the flawed decision of the trustees.[74] If further evidence is required, then the court can quash the trustees' rejection of the claim, direct the trustees as to

---

[68] Pensions Act 2004, s.262. On void under old s.67 see *AON Trust Corporation Ltd v KPMG* [2004] Pensions L.R. 337.

[69] *R (on Bibi's application) v Newham LBC* [2002] 1 W.L.R. 237; *R v North and East Devon HA* [2001] Q.B. 213.

[70] *Mount Sinai Hospital v Quebec* [2001] 2 S.C.R. 281, paras 67–68.

[71] [1990] 1 W.L.R. 1587, 1617–1618, noting the advancement ordered by the court in *Klug v Klug* [1918] 2 Ch. 67. In the circumstances the court itself exercised the power so that the employer received one third and the beneficiaries two thirds of the available fund. The case was followed in *Thrells v Lomas* [1993] 2 All E.R. 546 before the Pensions Act 1995, s.25(2) avoids the need for court intervention where the liquidator is conflicted out of exercising the company's power, his power being vested in an independent person as trustee.

[72] [1971] A.C. 424 at 457.

[73] [2003] 2 A.C. 709, para.51 favouring this broad view cited in para.41.

[74] See *Minehan v AGL Employees Superannuation Pty Ltd* (1998) 134 A.C.T.R. 1, paras 66–69, following *Dillon v Burns Philp Finance Ltd* (NSW Sup Ct, Bryson J, July 20, 1988 unreported); *Dunstone v Irving* [2000] Vic S.C. 488, paras 131–134.

the nature of the further evidence needed and direct the trustees to exercise their discretion afresh in the light of such further evidence and of the guidance in the Court's judgment.[75]

Where a claim relates to the claimant having become totally and permanently disabled "in the opinion of the trustee" in circumstances where the trustee has effected a policy of insurance to cover only beneficiaries who become so disabled, it will almost invariably be irrational for the trustee not to pay the proceeds of the policy to the claimant if the insurer in its opinion has considered the claimant to be so disabled. The claimant's difficulties thus lie with persuading the insurer that he has become totally and permanently disabled. **9–310**

The grounds upon which "the opinion of the insurer" can be challenged are generally similar to the grounds on which the opinion of the trustee can be challenged but the consequences of a successful challenge are more radical. As stated by Bryson J in *Sayseng v Kellogg Superannuation Pty Ltd*,[76] "The Court regards the reference to the insurer's opinion as means adopted by the parties for ascertainment of the facts to which the opinion relates: contractual entitlement depends on the facts, not primarily on the opinion which is the means of ascertaining them, and if the insurer has actually failed to form the opinion, or has constructively failed by acting on some wrong basis, the Court proceeds to determine the facts." If the incidental machinery to give effect to a contract breaks down then the court gives effect to the contract.[77] Thus, the decision of the Court can take the place of the insurer's opinion[78] (*e.g.* as to whether the claimant is totally and permanently disabled or whether the deceased's death was self-inflicted) if the Court decides that the insurer's opinion is to be disregarded as in breach of its contractual and fiduciary duties. If the court then decides that the insurable event has occurred, it can direct the insurer to pay the requisite amount to the trustee, whose only rational course is to pay it to the beneficiary, or the court can simply order payment directly to the beneficiary. **9–311**

In the traditional trust context, rights of beneficiaries are to be determined solely by means of the machinery of the trustee exercising its discretion, so that if such an exercise has to be disregarded as in breach of the trustee's fiduciary duties, then the exercise of the discretion has to be referred back to those same trustees or, in an extreme case, to new trustees after removal of the old trustees.[79] **9–312**

---

[75] As in administrative law cases: *R (on Bibi's application) v Newham LBC* [2002] 1 W.L.R. 237.

[76] [2003] N.S.W.S.C. 945, para.77.

[77] E.g. *Beaufort Developments (NI) Ltd v Gilbert-Ash (NI) Ltd* [1999] 1 A.C. 266 at 288–289, 291–292.

[78] *McArthur v Mercantile Mutual Life Insurance Co Ltd* [2002] Qd. R. 197; *Sayseng v Kellogg Superannuation Pty Ltd* [2003] N.S.W.S.C. 945, paras 82–85, 94–97; *Butcher v Port* [1985] 1 N.Z.L.R. 491 at 496–497, N.Z.C.A.; the defendant cannot take advantage of his own wrongdoing: *Edward v Aberayron Mutual Ship Assurance Society* (1876) 1 Q.B.D. 563.

[79] *Edge v Pensions Ombudsman* [1998] Ch. 512 at 534 endorsed [2000] Ch. 602 at 627, 630 (a pensions case involving a discretionary power of amendment to take account of an actuarial surplus, not a power relating to a factual issue), *Kerr v British Leyland (Staff) Trustees Ltd* (1986) [2001] W.T.L.R. 1071 (CA, p.1080, assumed traditional rules applied to pension trustees so the court could not substitute its view for that of the trustees).

9–313   However, in the pensions trust context why should the courts, in the light of the broad discretion to intervene emphasised by the Privy Council in *Schmidt*,[80] not treat the discretion of the trustee in *certain* areas involving complex consideration as the sole machinery for determining the rights of beneficiaries but in *other* areas merely to be the incidental machinery for giving effect to beneficiaries' rights on establishment of particular facts. If the incidental machinery does not duly operate, then the court intervenes to determine whether or not particular facts have been established. In the pensions trust context there is not the rationale that there is in family trusts for the all-pervasive centrality of the trustees' discretion as the sole machinery for determining the rights of beneficiaries.[81]

9–314   Thus, where the opinion of the trustee as to the establishment of certain facts is required before payment out of benefits, *e.g.* as to a permanent disability or whether death was self-inflicted or whether a person was a dependant or cohabitant of the beneficiary at his death, the court should be able to decide the matter itself if the opinion of the trustee is a nullity for breach of its fiduciary obligations.[82] The court should decide the matter itself if it has enough material to reach a decision. If it does not have enough material, then it should afford the claimant and the trustees the opportunity to obtain further evidence for the trustees then to act in accordance with the court's earlier guidance. Failure so to act will then lead to the court resolving the matter.

9–315   However, in other areas where there is plenty of scope for discretion (*e.g.* as to distributing death-in-service benefits where trustees have a discretion after taking account of person(s) designated by the beneficiary in his lifetime, but circumstances may have changed significantly since the making of such indicative designation, or as to augmenting the benefits of different classes of beneficiary) if the discretionary decision is fatally flawed, then the court should refer the exercise of the discretion back to the trustees (or replacement trustees if more appropriate).

Legislative intervention

9–316   The facilitative simple nature of trust law permits the creation of a ring-fenced fund protected against the insolvency of its trustee-owner, but otherwise stacked with provisions favouring the employer at the expense of the employee-beneficiaries. In a *laisser-faire* era the employer, influenced by the trade union, was hopefully left to be trusted to look after the pension fund for employees in benevolent altruistic fashion, whether as itself trustee or having its directors as trustees. The only statutory intervention needed was to exempt these long-running trust funds from the rule against

---

[80] [2003] 2 A.C. 709.

[81] Note Lord Browne-Wilkinson's remarks in *Target Holdings Ltd v Redferns* [1996] A.C. 421 at 435, "It is important . . . to distinguish between the basic principles of trust law and those specialist rules developed in relation to traditional trusts which are applicable only to such trusts and the rationale of which has no application to trusts of quite a different kind" endorsed by Lord Walker (when Walker J.) in A. J. Oakley (ed.) *Trends in Contemporary Trust Law*, p.131.

[82] See *Minehan v AGL Employees Superannuation Pty Ltd* (1998) 134 A.C.T.R. 1 paras 66–69 following *Dillon v Burns Philp Finance Ltd* (NSW Sup Ct, Bryson J, July 20, 1988, unreported).

remoteness,[83] while much on-going fiscal regulation has prevented exploitation of favourable tax provisions in Finance Acts, with caps placed upon the amount of contributions and of the amount ultimately available for a senior employee's pension.

In defined benefit schemes if the contributions of employees and **9–317** employer prove inadequate to provide the promised pension benefits then the onus lies on the employer to make up the deficit. For a substantial period this caused no worries due to a rising stock market for investments and due to a good job market causing many employees to leave their jobs before reaching retirement age. Also dividends from shares were tax- free for pension funds until the Government in 1998 removed this valuable benefit worth £5 billion p.a.

However, it was appreciated that there was a need for a Pensions **9–318** Ombudsman to provide cheap speedy relief for scheme members where there was maladministration.[84] This involves "bias, neglect, inattention, delay, incompetence, ineptitude, perversity, turpitude, arbitariness and so on".[85] For such he can direct apologies be made, order the holding of another meeting, award compensation for financial loss or even for distress,[86] order specific performance as by making someone a scheme member from a particular date. However, where the maladministration amounts to a breach of trust the range of his remedies is limited to those available to the High Court,[87] though this is not too restrictive if that range is fairly wide in the light of *Schmidt v Rosewood Trust Ltd* and other matters discussed above.[88]

A crisis then arose in respect of significant pension funds the property of **9–319** which was misappropriated by the well-known, swash-buckling Robert Maxwell before his mysterious death by drowning. The Government set up a Committee under (now Sir) Roy Goode which reported[89] that trust law was a good basis for pension funds but only if the freedom to minimise the obligations of the trustees was drastically restricted and if actuarially supervised minimum funding requirements were imposed. The Pensions Act 1995 was thus enacted, also setting up an Occupational Pensions Regulatory Authority ("OPRA"). Thereafter, the Government removed the tax free perquisite for dividends received by pension trusts and there was a poor three year performance of the stock markets. Accounting standards also tightened, so that companies found that notional actuarial surpluses had become deficits which the companies needed to provide for out of their

---

[83] Now Pension Schemes Act 1993 s. 163, originally Superannuation and other Funds (Validation) Act 1927.
[84] Post created in Social Security Act 1990, but currently governed by Pensions Scheme Act 1993 as amended by Pensions Act 1995 and 2004.
[85] *Hillsdown Holdings plc v Pensions Ombudsman* [1997] 1 All E.R. 862 at 884.
[86] *Wild v Smith* [1996] O.P.L.R. 129.
[87] *Wakelin v Read* [2000] Pens L.R. 319, CA. but the P.O can order a claimant be made a member of a scheme retrospective to a particular date subject to paying contributions rather than order damages even if in the High Court damages would have to be ordered if the claimant did not seek specific performance: *Henderson v Stephenson* 2005, *The Times* 27 January.
[88] See para.9–233 above.
[89] See "Pension Law Reform", 1993 Cm. 2342, and the case for trust law in D. J. Hayton, "Trust Law and Occupational Pension Schemes" [1993] Conv. 283; also see note of R. Nobles on Pensions Act 1995 in (1996) 59 M.L.R. 241.

own resources—and which affected the price of the shares. Many companies closed their defined benefit schemes and switched to direct contribution schemes. Indeed, some companies went into liquidation and wound up their pension funds in circumstances where there was a large deficit. Employees, who thought they would be well-provided for, found there was very little for them, throwing them back on a very basic State pension.

9–320   These matters led to the Pensions Act 2004. This replaces OPRA with the Pensions Regulator, inheriting OPRA's powers but with extra powers[90] for a more pro-active role, much assisted by obligations[91] upon persons involved with pension schemes to report breaches of the legislation to the Regulator, so he can protect members' benefits, promote good administration of pension schemes, and take steps to reduce the likelihood of claims against the new Pension Protection Fund.

9–321   The Regulator's most significant determinations have to be made on his behalf by a Determinations Tribunal.[92] An appeal lies to the Pension Regulator Tribunal[93] from which appeal on a point of law may be made, with leave, to the Court of Appeal.

9–322   The 2004 Act also establishes a Pension Protection Fund ("PPF") to provide compensation for members of defined benefit schemes if the sponsoring employer is insolvent and the scheme underfunded.[94] A £15 per head flat-rate levy in respect of the members of such pension schemes is made on the trustees thereof, though 80 per cent of the money raised is due to come from a risk-based levy according to different risk ratings of different pension trusts. The Board of the PPF may be required to review its decision and a PPF Ombudsman may then deal with matters.[95]

9–323   The Act provides for at least one third of trustees (or of directors of a corporate trustee) in every scheme to be nominated and selected by the members,[96] while the trustees (or directors of a corporate trustee) are required to be conversant with relevant scheme documentation and have appropriate knowledge and understanding of pensions and trust law and of the principles underpinning investment of assets and funding of liabilities.[97] The Regulator has to issue a Code of Practice to provide practical guidance on these matters.[98]

9–324   The old Minimum Funding Requirement with its "one size fits all" approach is replaced with new scheme funding requirements which are flexible enough to take into account scheme-specific factors when determining the most appropriate funding strategy and to allow for a longer-term view of investments and for correcting funding deficiencies.[99] The trustees and the employer must in the light of actuarial valuations (at least once

---

[90] Pensions Act 2004 ss.13 to 32.
[91] *ibid.* ss.70–71.
[92] *ibid.* ss.9–10.
[93] *ibid.* ss.102–105.
[94] *ibid.* ss.107–119.
[95] *ibid.* ss.209–217.
[96] *ibid.* ss.241–243.
[97] *ibid.* ss.247–248.
[98] *ibid.* s.90.
[99] *ibid.* ss.221–233.

every three years) agree a strategy, with the Pensions Regulator having powers of last resort to help resolve differences.[1] The Regulator also has to issue a Code of Practice for trustees on scheme funding.[2]

There is a morass of cumbersome protective legislation to be found in **9–325** the Pension Schemes Act 1993, the Pensions Act 1995 (181 sections and 7 Schedules), the Welfare Reform and Pensions Act 1999, and the Pensions Act 2004 (325 sections and 13 schedules). It is beyond the scope of this book to deal with pension trusts any further, other than to note that the power to amend the trust deed so as to affect subsisting rights is closely circumscribed.[3]

Pensions Act 1995

32.—(1) Decisions of the trustees of a trust scheme may, unless the scheme **9–326** provides otherwise, be taken by agreement of a majority of the trustees.

(2) Where decisions of the trustees of a trust scheme may be taken by agreement of a majority of the trustees—

(a) the trustees may, unless the scheme provides otherwise, by a determination under this subsection require not less than the number of trustees specified in the determination to be present when any decision is so taken, and

(b) notice of any occasions at which decisions may be so taken must, unless the occasion falls within a prescribed class or description, be given to each trustee to whom it is reasonably practicable to give such notice.

(3) Notice under subsection (2)(b) must be given in a prescribed manner and not later than the beginning of a prescribed period.

33.—(1) Liability for breach of an obligation under any rule of law to take care or **9–327** exercise skill in the performance of any investment functions, where the function is exercisable—

(a) by a trustee of a trust scheme, or

(b) by a person to whom the function has been delegated under section 34,

cannot be excluded or restricted by any instrument or agreement.

(2) In this section, references to excluding or restricting liability include—

(a) making the liability or its enforcement subject to restrictive or onerous conditions,

(b) excluding or restricting any right or remedy in respect of the liability, or subjecting a person to any prejudice in consequence of his pursuing any such right or remedy, or

---

[1] *ibid.* s.231.
[2] *ibid.* s.90.
[3] *ibid.* s.262 substituting an extended Pensions Act 1995, s.67. Generally see further R. Ellison, *Pensions Law & Practice*, and Sweet & Maxwell, *The Law of Pension Schemes* and G. Thomas and A. Hudson, *The Law of Trusts*, (Oxford; 2004), Chap. 43; and The First Report of the Pensions Commission, October 12, 2004 at www.pensionscommission.org.uk.

(c) excluding or restricting rules of evidence or procedure.

(3) This section does not apply—

    (a) to a scheme falling within any prescribed class or description, or
    (b) to any prescribed description of exclusion or restriction.

9–328   **34.**—(1) The trustees of a trust scheme have, subject to section 36(1) and to any restriction imposed by the scheme, the same power to make an investment of any kind as if they were absolutely entitled to the assets of the scheme.

(2) Any discretion of the trustees of a trust scheme to make any decision about investments—

    (a) may be delegated by or on behalf of the trustees to a fund manager to whom subsection (3) applies to be exercised in accordance with section 36, but
    (b) may not otherwise be delegated except under section 25 of the Trustee Act 1925 (delegation of trusts during absence abroad) or subsection (5) below.

9–329   (3) This subsection applies to a fund manager who, in relation to the decisions in question, falls, or is treated as falling, within any of paragraphs (a) to (c) of section 191(2) of the Financial Services Act 1986 (occupational pension schemes: exemptions where decisions taken by authorised and other persons).

(4) The trustees are not responsible for the act or default of any fund manager in the exercise of any discretion delegated to him under subsection (2)(a) if they have taken all such steps as are reasonable to satisfy themselves or the person who made the delegation on their behalf has taken all such steps as are reasonable to satisfy himself—

    (a) that the fund manager has the appropriate knowledge and experience for managing the investments of the scheme, and
    (b) that he is carrying out his work competently and complying with section 36.

(5) Subject to any restriction imposed by a trust scheme—

9–330   (a) the trustees may authorise two or more of their number to exercise on their behalf any discretion to make any decision about investments, and
    (b) any such discretion may, where giving effect to the decision would not constitute carrying on investment business in the United Kingdom (within the meaning of the Financial Services Act 1986), be delegated by or on behalf of the trustees to a fund manager to whom subsection (3) does not apply to be exercised in accordance with section 36;

but in either case the trustees are liable for any acts or defaults in the exercise of the discretion if they would be so liable if they were the acts or defaults of the trustees as a whole.

(6) Section 33 does not prevent the exclusion or restriction of any liability of the trustees of a trust scheme for the acts or defaults of a fund manager in the exercise of a discretion delegated to him under subsection (5)(b) where the trustees have taken all such steps as are reasonable to satisfy themselves, or the person who made the delegation on their behalf has taken all such steps as are reasonable to satisfy himself—

    (a) that the fund manager has the appropriate knowledge and experience for managing the investments of the scheme, and

    (b) that he is carrying out his work competently and complying with section 36;

and subsection (2) of section 33 applies for the purposes of this subsection as it applies for the purposes of that section.

(7) The provisions of this section override any restriction inconsistent with the provisions imposed by any rule of law or by or under any enactment, other than an enactment contained in, or made under, this Part or the Pension Schemes Act 1993. **9–331**

Pensions Act 2004

244 Investment principles

For section 35 of the Pensions Act 1995 (investment principles) substitute— **9–332**

"35 Investment principles

(1) The trustees of a trust scheme must secure—

    (a) that a statement of investment principles is prepared and maintained for the scheme, and

    (b) that the statement is reviewed at such intervals, and on such occasions, as may be prescribed and, if necessary, revised.

(2) In this section "statement of investment principles", in relation to a trust scheme, means a written statement of the investment principles governing decisions about investments for the purposes of the scheme.

(3) Before preparing or revising a statement of investment principles, the trustees of a trust scheme must comply with any prescribed requirements.

(4) A statement of investment principles must be in the prescribed form and cover, amongst other things, the prescribed matters.

(5) Neither a trust scheme nor a statement of investment principles may impose restrictions (however expressed) on any power to make investments by reference to the consent of the employer.

(6) If in the case of a trust scheme—

    (a) a statement of investment principles has not been prepared, is not being maintained or has not been reviewed or revised, as required by this section, or

    (b) the trustees have not complied with the obligation imposed on them by subsection (3),

section 10 applies to any trustee who has failed to take all reasonable steps to secure compliance.

(7) Regulations may provide that this section is not to apply to any scheme which is of a prescribed description."

. . .

247 Requirement for knowledge and understanding: individual trustees

(1) This section applies to every individual who is a trustee of an occupational pension scheme. **9–333**

(2) In this section, "relevant scheme", in relation to an individual, means any occupational pension scheme of which he is a trustee.

(3) An individual to whom this section applies must, in relation to each relevant scheme, be conversant with—

(a) the trust deed and rules of the scheme,
(b) any statement of investment principles for the time being maintained under section 35 of the Pensions Act 1995 (c. 26),
(c) in the case of a relevant scheme to which Part 3 (scheme funding) applies, the statement of funding principles most recently prepared or revised under section 223, and
(d) any other document recording policy for the time being adopted by the trustees relating to the administration of the scheme generally.

(4) An individual to whom this section applies must have knowledge and understanding of—

(a) the law relating to pensions and trusts,
(b) the principles relating to—

(i) the funding of occupational pension schemes, and
(ii) investment of the assets of such schemes, and

(c) such other matters as may be prescribed.

(5) The degree of knowledge and understanding required by subsection (4) is that appropriate for the purposes of enabling the individual properly to exercise his functions as trustee of any relevant scheme.

248 Requirement for knowledge and understanding: corporate trustees

9–334 (1) This section applies to any company which is a trustee of an occupational pension scheme.

(2) In this section, "relevant scheme", in relation to a company, means any occupational pension scheme of which it is a trustee.

(3) A company to which this section applies must, in relation to each relevant scheme, secure that each individual who exercises any function which the company has as trustee of the scheme is conversant with each of the documents mentioned in subsection (4) so far as it is relevant to the exercise of the function.

(4) Those documents are—

(a) the trust deed and rules of the scheme,
(b) any statement of investment principles for the time being maintained under section 35 of the Pensions Act 1995,
(c) in the case of a relevant scheme to which Part 3 (scheme funding) applies, the statement of funding principles most recently prepared or revised under section 223, and
(d) any other document recording policy for the time being adopted by the trustees relating to the administration of the scheme generally.

(5) A company to which this section applies must secure that any individual who exercises any function which the company has as trustee of any relevant scheme has knowledge and understanding of—

(a) the law relating to pensions and trusts,
(b) the principles relating to—

(i) the funding of occupational pension schemes, and
(ii) investment of the assets of such schemes, and

(c) such other matters as may be prescribed.

(6) The degree of knowledge and understanding required by subsection (5) is that appropriate for the purposes of enabling the individual properly to exercise the function in question.

(7) References in this section to the exercise by an individual of any function of a company are to anything done by the individual on behalf of the company which constitutes the exercise of the function by the company.

(8) In this section "company" means a company within the meaning given by section 735(1) of the Companies Act 1985 (c. 6) or a company which may be wound up under Part 5 of the Insolvency Act 1986 (c. 45) (unregistered companies).

249 Requirement for knowledge and understanding: supplementary

(1) For the purposes of sections 247 and 248, a person's functions as trustee of a relevant scheme are any functions which he has by virtue of being such a trustee and include, in particular— **9–335**

(a) any functions which he has as one of the trustees authorised under section 34(5)(a) of the Pensions Act 1995 (c. 26) (delegation of investment discretions) in the case of the scheme, and
(b) any functions which he otherwise has as a member of a committee of the trustees of the scheme.

(2) Regulations may provide for any provision in section 247 or 248—

(a) not to apply, or
(b) to apply with modifications,
to a trustee in prescribed circumstances.

(3) Nothing in either of those sections affects any rule of law requiring a trustee to have knowledge of, or expertise in, any matter.

. . ."

Section 10. Indemnity of Trustees[4]

I. Indemnity and Lien Against the Trust Property[5]

By s.31(1) of the Trustee Act 2000 "A trustee (a) is entitled to be reimbursed from the trust funds, or (b) may pay out of the trust funds, **9–336**

---

[4] See generally A. W. Scott, "Liabilities Incurred in the Administration of Trusts" (1915) 28 H.L.R. 725; Stone. "A Theory of Liability of Trust Estates for the Contracts and Torts of the Trustee" (1922) 22 Col. L.R. 527; A. J. Hawkins, "The Personal Liability of Charity Trustees" (1979) 95 L.Q.R. 99; D. J. Hayton, "Trading Trusts", Chapter in J. Glasson (ed.), *International Trust Laws*.
[5] For indemnity against the beneficiaries personally, see Part II of this section, para.9–341; for indemnity against the beneficiary's beneficial interest under s.62 of the Trustee Act 1925, see para.10–115; for a trustee's indemnity against his co-trustee, see para.10–162.

expenses *properly* incurred by him when acting on behalf of the trust." What then, if he employs an agent or nominee or custodian and such appointee incurs expenses and charges remuneration? By s.32 (3) "The trustees may reimburse the agent, nominee or custodian out of the trust funds for any expenses *properly* incurred by him in exercising functions as an agent, nominee or custodian." However, by s.32 (2) the trustees can only "remunerate the agent, nominee or custodian out of the trust funds for services" if "the amount does not exceed such remuneration as is *reasonable* in the circumstances for the provision of those services by him to or on behalf of that trust."

9–337   These provisions reflect the established position that trustees only have power to pay "proper costs incident to the execution of the trust."[6] As Lord Templeman stated in *Carver v Duncan*,[7] "Trustees are entitled to be indemnified out of the capital and income of their trust fund against all obligations incurred by the trustees in the due performance of their duties and the due exercise of their powers. The trustees must then debit each item of expenditure either against income or against capital. The general rule is that income must bear all ordinary outgoings of a recurrent nature, such as rates and taxes and interest on charges and incumbrances. Capital must bear all costs, charges, and expenses incurred for the benefit of the whole estate."

In *Stott v Milne*[8] the Earl of Selborne L.C. stated, "The right of trustees to indemnity against all costs and expenses properly incurred by them in the execution of the trust is a first charge on all the trust properly, both income and *corpus*. The trustees, therefore, had a right to retain the costs out of the income until provision could be made for raising them out of the *corpus*." Similarly if mortgage interest is paid out of capital because no income is available, capital must be reimbursed out of future income.[9]

9–338   Section 39 (1) of the Trustee Act 2000 defines "the trust funds" to mean "income or capital funds of the trust",[10] which, on the face of it, appears to cover both the initial payment and the ultimate incidence of costs and expenses. This is supported by the fact that the Law Commission specifically intended trustees to have complete discretion to allocate the ultimate incidence of "the costs of employing a nominee or custodian between income and capital"[11] and believed this was achieved by the definition of "trust funds", which applies also to reimbursement of expenses in s.31 (1) and to remuneration of agents (as to which no general or specific recommendations were made by the Commission).

---

[6] *Holding and Management Ltd v Property Holding and Investment Trust plc* [1998] 1 W.L.R. 1313 at 1324 per Nicholls L.J.; *Re Grimthorpe* [1958] Ch. 615 at 623.
[7] [1985] 2 All E.R. 645 at 652.
[8] (1884) 25 Ch.D. 710 at 715.
[9] *Honywood v Honywood* [1902] 1 Ch. 347.
[10] The new s.19(5) of the Trustee Act 1925 substituted by Trustee Act 2000 has the same definition which the Law Commission believed gave trustees discretion as to the ultimate incidence of insurance premiums: "Trustees' Powers and Duties", Law Com No.260, paras 6.6 and 8.39 and p.119 note on clause 34.
[11] "Trustees' Powers and Duties" Law Com No.260 paras 5.13 and 8.33 and p.117 note on clauses 31 and 32 of the draft Bill; but *Lewin on Trusts* (17th ed.), paras 25–26B takes a contrary view.

No indemnity can be claimed by a trustee in respect of a liability improperly[12] incurred to X, *e.g.* because of:

(i) lack of power under the trust instrument;
(ii) lack of due authorisation under internal requirements (*e.g.* for trustee unanimity, or consent of B, or for a meeting to be duly held before any decision is taken);
(iii) breach of equitable duties (*e.g.* to diversify investments, to supervise agents, to invest with the statutory duty of care).

Moreover, (iv), a trustee cannot reimburse itself if indebted to the trust by reason of some unconnected breach of trust.[13] After all, its right to reimbursement depends ultimately on the state of accounts between it and the beneficiaries and is limited to the balance, if any, in its favour.

Finally, (v) no right of indemnity exists to the extent that it has been **9–339** excluded in the trust instrument, as may happen where the trustee has a liberal right to remuneration under a charging clause intended to cover expenses,[14] but a trustee of a family trust would normally refuse to act if the indemnity right was to be excluded.

The trustee can protect itself against the problems in (i) and (ii) above by taking the advice of lawyers or even the guidance of the court but this takes time and money. It can also protect itself against allegations that, in breach of its equitable duties, it involved itself as claimant or defendant in an action involving the trust and a third party, so that it should personally pay its own costs and the costs of the other (winning) side in the action. To do this, it seeks in private a Beddoe's Order[15] from the court which will entitle it to be reimbursed costs out of the trust fund no matter the result of the litigation, so long as full and frank disclosure was made to the court. However, where the claim seeks to undermine the trust wholly or partly (*e.g.* claims by the settlor's creditors or trustee in bankruptcy[16] or an adverse proprietary tracing claim) the trustee may be required to be neutral and only have a right of indemnity for the costs of acting neutrally,[17] unless no other person is appropriate to represent the interests of beneficiaries who are unborn or otherwise unascertained.[18]

---

[12] Exceptionally, if the trustee acted in good faith and the transaction benefited the trust fund he should have a right of indemnity to the extent of the benefit to prevent unjust enrichment of the beneficiaries: *Vyse v Foster* (1872) 8 Ch.App. 309, 336–337, *Conway v Fenton* (1888) 11 Ch.D. 512, 518—or the trust deed might expressly permit indemnity even beyond the extent of the benefit to the whole expense.

[13] *Ex p. Edmonds* (1862) 4 De G.F. & J. 488, 498; *Re Johnson* (1880) 15 Ch.D. 548; *Re British Power Traction & Lighting Co.Ltd* [1910] 2 Ch. 470.

[14] *Ex p. Chippendale, Re German Mining Co* (1854) 4 De G.M. & G 19, 52; *McLean v Burns Philip Trustee Co. Pty. Ltd* [1985] 2 N.S.W.L.R. 623 (the right to indemnity excluded in unit trusts so as not to affect the marketability of units).

[15] *Re Beddoe* [1893] 1 Ch. 547: this is in a separate action and the judge who hears it will not hear the main action. For details see *Lewin on Trusts* (17th ed.) paras 21–106 to 21–119.

[16] See ss.339–342, 423–425 Insolvency Act 1986.

[17] *Alsop Wilkinson v Neary* [1996] 1 W.L.R. 1220.

[18] *Re Hall* [1994–95] Cayman I.L.R. 456, *Lloyds Bank v Bylevan Corp. S.A.* [1994–95] C.I.L.R. 519.

9–340   The right of indemnity of a trustee is bolstered by an equitable proprietary right in the nature of a non-possessory lien,[19] which enables the trustee to retain assets against actual, contingent or possible liabilities[20] or to seek a sale of the assets[21] if in the ownership of a sucessor trustee. The equitable lien will continue to bind successor trustees[22] but will not bind beneficiaries to whom the assets are distributed unless expressly preserved by the distributing trustee(s), the recipient beneficiary normally receiving the assets (whether expressly or by necessary implication) discharged from the interests of other beneficiaries and from the prior equitable interests of trustees.[23]

Trustees should reimburse themselves as soon as possible because they are not entitled to interest on the money they paid out to meet expenses.[24]

II. INDEMNITY AGAINST THE BENEFICIARY PERSONALLY

9–341   A trustee's right of indemnity in respect of expenses properly incurred—*e.g.* in respect of costs, a call on shares, solicitor's, stockbroker's or auctioneer's charges—is a right of indemnity against the trust *estate*, not *against* the beneficiary. Hence, the trustees of an ordinary club are entitled to be indemnified out of the club property, not by the club members,[25] unless, as is often the case, the club rules allow this. But in the following circumstances a trustee's indemnity extends beyond the estate to the *beneficiary* personally:

First, where the trustee accepted the trust at the request of the settlor who is also a beneficiary so as to raise an implied contract of indemnity[26] and secondly, where the beneficiary is a *sole* beneficiary *sui juris* and entitled absolutely[27] or there are *several* beneficiaries who are *sui juris* and between them collectively entitled absolutely.[28] This can prove very useful where a trustee for such beneficiaries properly borrows money to carry out

---

[19] *Jennings v Mather* [1901] 1 K.B. 108 at 113–114, [1902] 1 K.B. 1 at 6, 9; *Stott v Milne* (1884) 25 Ch.D. 710 at 715; *Commissioner of Stamp Duties v ISPT* (1999) 2 I.T.E.L.R. 1, 18; *Octavo Investments Pty Ltd v Knight* (1979) 114 C.L. R 360; *Dimos v Dikeatos Nominees Ltd* (1997) 149 A.L.R. 113, [1996] 68 F.C.R. 39. Further see Trust Law Committee, "The Proper Protection by Liens, Indemnities or Otherwise of those who cease to be Trustees": www.kcl.ac.uk/depsta/law/tlc.

[20] *X v A* [2000] 1 All E.R. 490.

[21] *Re Pumfrey* (1882) 22 Ch.D. 255 at 262.

[22] *Dimos v Dikeatos Nominees Ltd* (1997) 149 Aust L.R. 113, (1996) 68 F.C.R. 39.

[23] Australian cases (like *Dimos, supra,* and *Chief Commissioner of Stamp Duties v Buckle* (1998) 72 A.L.J.R. 242) treat the trustee's right not as an "encumbrance" but as a proprietary right equivalent to (but ranking ahead of) the equitable interests of beneficiaries. Further see *Lewin on Trusts* (17th ed.), paras 14–50 and 26–22 and Trust Law Committee Consultation Paper, December 1999, "The Proper Protection by Liens, Indemnities or otherwise of Those who Cease to be Trustees."

[24] *Foster v Spencer* [1996] 2 All E.R. 672.

[25] *Wise v Perpetual Trustee Co.* [1903] A.C. 139.

[26] *Ex p. Chippendale* (1854) 4 De G.M. & G. 19 at 54; *Jervis v Wolferstan* (1874) L.R. 18 Eq. 18 as explained by Lord Blackburn in *Fraser v Murdoch* (1881) 6 App.Cas. 855 at 872; *Matthews v Ruggles-Brise* [1911] 1 Ch. 194. In that case it was also held that where a beneficiary is personally liable to indemnify his trustee, an assignment by him of his beneficial interest does not affect that liability as it stood at the date of the assignment.

[27] *Hardoon v Belilios* [1901] A.C. 118.

[28] *Buchan v Ayre* [1915] 2 Ch. 474 at 477; *Re Reid* (1971) 17 D.L.R. (3d) 199. *Balkin v Peck* (1997) 43 N.S.W.L.R. 766, (1998) 1 I.T.E.L.R. 717. (English executor recovered from Australian beneficiaries when he overlooked the tax payable on proceeds remitted to Australia).

authorised trading or investing and the borrowings exceed the assets when things go dreadfully wrong as occurred in *J. W. Broomhead (Vic.) Pty. Ltd (in liq.) v J. W. Broomhead Pty. Ltd*[29] where McGarvie J. held "where there are several beneficiaries entitled to separate benefits, a beneficiary who gets a proportion of the benefit should bear that proportion of its burdens unless he can show why the trustee shold bear the proportion of them himself." He further held that where a beneficiary is insolvent the loss in respect of his proportion falls on the trustee and not the other beneficiaries. He also accepted that "a request from a beneficiary to the trustee to assume the office of trustee or to incur liabilities obviously justifies the imposition of a personal liability to indemnify on the beneficiary and this should be so even if the beneficiary has only a limited interest."

Section 11: Third Parties and Trustees

In carrying out the trusts or powers a trustee is personally liable to the extent of his whole fortune or patrimony for debts, contracts, torts or taxes arising in respect of his acts or omissions as trustee. After all, the trust property is not an entity that can be regarded as a person to be made liable. Having transferred his property, usually by way of gift, to the trustees the settlor has disappeared from the picture. The trustees are not agents for the beneficiaries nor are they in a partnership with them so there is no legal connection between the beneficiaries and any creditors. Thus, the trustees are personally liable and remain so even after retiring as trustees: hence the need for an indemnity from the new trustees or reliance upon their equitable lien. **9–342**

As a matter of contract law a trustee and a third party may agree that the trustee may limit or exclude his personal liability and that the trustee shall pay the debt out of the trust property under his statutory right of indemnity.[30] The onus lies on the trustee to displace the strong presumption of personal liability so that contracting descriptively "as trustee" is not sufficient,[31] but contracting "as trustee and not otherwise" will suffice since the phrase would be meaningless if not excluding personal liability.[32]

Where a trustee does not pay a creditor out of her own moneys or out of trust moneys available under her statutory right of indemnity the creditor may have a claim by way of subrogation to the trustee's right of indemnity.[33] **9–343**

---

[29] [1985] V.R. 891 at 936–939.

[30] *Muir v City of Glasgow Bank* (1879) 4 App.Cas. 337 at 355. It is possible for the trustee, if authorised, to go further and charge the trust property with payment of the debt: such an intention to create a charge is not likely to be inferred merely from an agreement that the creditor is to look to the trust property and not to the trustee for payment: *cf.* Swiss Bank Corporation v Lloyds Bank [1980] 2 All E.R. 419 at 426; affd. [1981] 2 All E.R. 449. See also Law Reform Committee's proposals at para.9–455 concerning a floating, as opposed to a fixed, charge.

[31] *Watling v Lewis* [1911] 1 Ch. 414 at 424, *Marston Thompson & Evershed plc. v Benn* [1998] C.L. 6.3. The Trust Law Committee in paras 3.14 and 10.4 of "Creditors' Right against Trustees and Trust Funds" (June 1999) recommends removal of this trap for unwary trustees or executors so that contracting "as trustee" (or "executor") should exclude personal liability for properly incurred contractual liabilities, if the trust fund (or estate) is inadequate.

[32] *Re Robinson's Settlement* [1912] 1 Ch. 717 at 729; *Muir v City of Glasgow Bank* (1879) 4 App.Cas. 337 at 362.

[33] *Re Johnson* (1880) 15 Ch.D. 548 at 552; *Re Blundell* (1889) 44 Ch.D. 1, 11; *Vaccum Oil Pty. Ltd v Wiltshire* (1945) 72 C.L.R. 319 at 325, 336; *Re Raybould* [1900] 1 Ch. 199.

The problem is that the creditor's right is derivative: he stands in the shoes of the trustee and has no better right than the trustee.[34] Thus, for the creditor to be paid out of the trust assets he will need to show that the right of indemnity was not excluded by the trust instrument,[35] that the debt was properly incurred in the authorised carrying-on of the trust, and that the state of accounts between the trustee and the beneficiaries (taking into account any losses caused by any breach of trust on the trustee's part) is such that there is some balance in the trustee's favour to which the right of indemnity may attach.[36] However, where there are two or more trustees and one of them does not have a clear account (*e.g.* because of an outstanding claim against him for a breach of trust) the creditor can rely on the right to indemnity enjoyed by the other trustee.[37]

9–344 In addition to his proprietary right of indemnity, a trustee in some limited circumstances (already discussed above, para.9–341) may have a personal right of indemnity against a beneficiary personally. The right of subrogation in respect of the proprietary right of a trustee to an indemnity from the trust property arose out of the Court of Chancery's practice in administration of trust estates in an administration action. There was no similar practice for allowing a right of subrogation in respect of a trustee's right of indemnity against a beneficiary personally but, in principle, it seems there should be such a right of subrogation.[38]

A person contracting with a trustee is in a particularly invidious position due to her derivative right being worthless if the trustee happens to be or become indebted to the trust fund for some unconnected breach of trust or if the trustee happens to be in breach of some equitable duty of care in negotiating the contract. In the absence of a power to create a fixed charge over specific assets or to create an equitable interest in the fluctuating trust fund in the nature of a floating charge,[39] what can be done to protect the creditor's interests?

9–345 To deal with the unconnected indebtedness problem it seems possible[40] to negotiate as part of the price of the contract a necessarily incidental, but express, term that the trustee is in no way personally liable upon the

---

[34] *Ex p. Edmonds* (1862) 4 De G.F. & J. 488 at 498; *Re Johnson* (1880) 15 Ch.D. 548; *Re British Power Traction & Lighting Co. Ltd* [1910] 2 Ch. 470.

[35] Unlike Trustee Act 1925, s.69(2) which expressly allowed s.30(2) to be subject to contrary intent, no provision in Trustee Act 2000 allows this in respect of s.31 (the successor to s.30(2) of the 1925 Act), but it is considered that no court would permit a trustee to exploit s.31 if its generous remuneration was premised upon no recovery of expenses. A court could hold s.31 inapplicable on the basis the trustee was acting not "on behalf of the trust" but on behalf of itself in order to earn its generous remuneration or could hold the benefit of the remmuneration was only available as burdened by the obligation not to claim expenses.

[36] See section 10, above, para.9–336.

[37] *Re Frith* [1902] 1 Ch. 342 at 346; "The indemnity is not to the trustees as a body but to each of the trustees. Each of them who has acted properly is entitled to be indemnified against the debts properly incurred by him in the performance of the trusts. The Court prevents a trustee from insisting upon that right unless he comes in with clear accounts; but if he comes in with clear accounts he is no the less entitled to be indemnified because he has a co-trustee who has run away with certain moneys. I am, of course, excluding the case where a trustee who has a clear account is responsible for a co-trustee who has not."

[38] Para.2.29 of Trust Law Commitee consultations paper on Rights of Creditors against Trustees and Trust Funds, April 1997.

[39] See para.9–000 for proposal of Law Reform Committee.

[40] Trust Law Committee Consultation Paper "Rights of Creditors against Trustees and Trust Funds" (April 1997) para.2.35; *Scott on Trusts* (4th ed.) Vol. IIIA pp 499–500; Stone (1922)22 Col.L.R.527; J.G. Merralls (1993) 10 Austr. Bar Rev. 248.

contract, but the creditor shall have a personal[41] non-proprietary direct independent right of recourse to the trust fund, so that it is immaterial whether or not the trustee's right of indemnity has been extinguished by indebtedness to the trust fund. It would be better, however, if statute were to provide (as recommended by the Trust Law Committee)[42] that the indebtedness of a trustee to the trust at the time a contractual creditor (or a victim of a tort) seeks an indemnity out of the trust fund should not be a reason for refusing such an indemnity to such creditor (or victim).

Dealing with a trustee who may be in breach of his equitable duty of care **9–346** is fraught with danger. If the creditor believes he is getting too good a bargain perhaps he should disclose this to help ensure that the trustee satisfies the equitable duty—but this would seem to place intending contractors with trustees under a fiduciary obligation which seems inappropriate and impractical in the commercial context. Perhaps, the House of Lords or even the Court of Appeal might restrict "properly incurred" to mean incurred by virtue of authority in the trust instrument and complying with any internal procedures[43] so that it would be immaterial[44] that there had been a breach of equitable duties of care in investing or in supervising agents. It would be better if statute were to provide (as recommended by the Trust Law Committee)[45] that a trustee's breach of equitable duties should not prevent a creditor having a right of indemnity out of the trust fund unless dishonestly implicated in such breach. Furthermore, where a trustee's conduct made him a tortfeasor and such conduct amounted to a breach of his equitable duties (*e.g.* of care) this should not prevent the victim from having a right of indemnity out of the trust fund. In *Re Raybould* it was fortunate for the claimant that the subsidence damage was caused by the proper management of the colliery by the trustee. In *Re Christian Brothers of Ireland in Canada*[46] the Brothers operated schools where some of its teachers unlawfully sexually abused pupils. It was held that all the property of the charity was available to satisfy pupils' claims.

Where a deceased's estate includes a business, special problems arise **9–347** since it is necessary to consider not just the beneficiaries interested in the estate, but also the claims of creditors of the deceased and the claims of creditors of the business carried on by the deceased's executors. The applicable principles appear most clearly from a judgment of the High Court of Australia in *Vacuum Oil Company Pty. Ltd v Wiltshire*.

In dealing with third parties, especially in borrowing money, it is useful if **9–348** the trustees have power to create a charge over the trust *fund* (as distinct from particular assets happening at the time to be comprised in the trust fund) so to provide security for third parties. The Law Reform Committee (Cmnd. 8733) discussed this issue as follows:

"2.20 . . . our conclusion is that where the trust is of such a kind that the trustees are likely to wish to engage in commercial operations such

---

[41] So affording no priority over other creditors.
[42] Report on "Rights of Creditors against Trustees and Trust Funds" (June 1999) paras 3.4 and 10.2.
[43] See para.9–338 above.
[44] Assuming the problem of indebtedness to the trust fund for such breach of trust was overcome.
[45] Paras 3.11 and 10.3 of Report in note 42 above.
[46] (2000) 184 D.L.R. (4th) 445.

as large scale borrowing, the right solution would be for the trust deed to confer upon the trustees a power to create a charge upon the trust fund in favour of a creditor. The effect of such a charge would be to make the third party, in whose favour it was created, a *cestui que trust*. His rights as chargee would be analogous to those conferred by a floating charge, just as the rights of any other *cestui que trust* subsist in the assets from time to time comprised in the trust fund. The trustees would retain all their powers of dealing with the trust fund although they would, of course, have to exercise them with due regard for the interest of the chargee as of any other beneficiary.

9–349   2.21 We see no reason to doubt that a trust instrument could be so worded under the present law as to confer on trustees just the sort of power that we have in mind. Trustees can be, and frequently are, given power to appoint beneficial interests without consideration and we think it would in fact be possible to empower them to create beneficial interests for valuable consideration, the consideration being part of the trust fund in which the beneficial interest will thereafter subsist. However, because there is some doubt whether this would be permissible under the present law, we think that legislation is needed to make it clear that a power to create a charge upon the trust fund as a continuing entity can be conferred upon trustees by the trust deed, thus enabling them to give the maximum possible security tothird parties. However, we do not think that the trustees of an existing trust should be able to make use of this new statutory provision: in our view it would not be right to allow the imposition of such a power on an existing trust where the settlor had not envisaged it would be needed. If the power is needed, it will always be possible for a trustee in this position to apply to the court under the Variation of Trusts Act 1958 . . .

9–350   2.24 Whilst the form of any legislation following our report is, of course, a matter for Parliamentary Counsel to determine, we do not think that it should be necessary to define or in any way to limit the nature of the power that we envisage. The suggested new clause below, which is no doubt capable of a good deal of improvement, is intended simply to draw attention to the fact that trustees can, under existing law, be given the sort of powers we have in mind:

Charges for value on trust funds

(1)   Where under the terms of any trust instrument the trustees have power to charge the trust fund or any part thereof (as distinct from any assets for the time being comprised in the trust fund) to secure obligations created by them for valuable consideration, the persons in whose favour such obligations are created shall take equitable interests in the trust fund or part with such priority and subject to such conditions and provisions as the trustees have power under the trust instrument and are expressed by the instrument creating the charge to create.

(2) Subject to subsection (4) of this section, a person in whose favour such a **9–351**
charge is created may require that
  (a) a memorandum of the charge be endorsed, written on or permanently
  annexed to the instrument creating the trust;
  (b) the instrument be produced to him by the person having the possession or custody thereof to prove that a sufficient memorandum has
  been placed thereon or annexed thereto.
Without prejudice to any other manner in which persons dealing with
trustees may acquire notice of such a charge, such memorandum shall, as
respects priorities, be deemed to constitute actual notice to all persons and
for all purposes of the matters therein stated.
(3) Subsections (5) and (6) of section 137 of the Law of Property Act 1925 shall
apply in relation to any memorandum authorised by this section.
(4) Section 138 of the Law of Property Act 1925 (power to nominate a trust
corporation to receive notices) shall apply for the purposes of this section
with the omission of subsection (7), and the obligation imposed on the trust
corporation by subsection (9) shall extend to any person authorised by the
trustees to inspect and take copies of the register and notices held by the
trust corporation."

RE RAYBOULD

Chancery Division [1900] 1 Ch. 199, 69 L.J. Ch. 249.

The surviving trustee and executor of a deceased's estate properly worked one of **9–352**
the testator's collieries. Earthworks caused a subsidence damaging the buildings and
machinery of the adjoining owners, Roberts & Cooper. They obtained a judgment
against the trustee for damage and costs. In the present proceedings they sought an
order that this amount and cost be paid out of the testator's estate.

BYRNE J.: "The first question I have to consider is whether the same principle **9–353**
ought to be applied to the case of a trustee claiming a right to indemnity for liability
for damages for a tort, as is applied to the simpler case of claims made against a
trustee by ordinary business creditors, where they have been allowed the benefit of
his right to indemnity, by proving directly against the assets: the kind of case of
which *Dowse v Gorton* [1891] A.C. 190 is a recent illustration. It has been argued
that there is no authority to justify me in holding that, where damages have been
recovered against a trustee in respect of a tort, the person so recovering can avail
himself of the trustee's right to indemnity, and so go direct against the trust estate;
but the authority of *Bennett v Wyndham* (1862) D.F. & J. 259 goes to show that if a
trustee in the course of the ordinary management of his testator's estate, either by
himself or his agent, does some act whereby some third person is injured, and that
third person recovers damages against the trustee in an action for tort, the trustee, if
he has acted with due diligence and reasonably, is entitled to be indemnified out of
his testator's estate. When once a trustee is entitled to be this indemnified out of his
trust estate, I cannot myself see why the person who has recovered judgment against
the trustee should not have the benefit of this right to indemnify and go direct
against the trust estate or the assets, as the case may be, just as an ordinary creditor
of a business carried on by a trustee or executor has been allowed to do, instead of
having to go through the double process of suing the trustee, recovering the
damages from him and leaving the trustee to recoup himself out of the trust estate. I
have the parties interested in defending the trust estate before me, and I have also

the trustee, and he claims indemnity, and, assuming that a proper case for indemnifying him is made out by the evidence, I think his claim should be allowed.

"The next question I have to decide is whether this trustee has worked the colliery in such a way as to be entitled to be indemnified. Having considered all the evidence, I am not prepared to say that the injury done to the applicants' land was occasioned by reckless or improper working, or otherwise than by the ordinary and reasonable management of the colliery; and I therefore come to the conclusion that the trustee is entitled to be indemnified out of the assets against the damages and costs which he has been ordered to pay to Messrs. Roberts & Cooper. It follows, therefore, for the reasons already given, that Messrs. Roberts & Cooper are entitled to stand in the trustee's place for the purpose of obtaining this indemnity direct from this testator's estate. The result, therefore, is that this summons succeeds . . ."

VACUUM OIL COMPANY PTY LTD v WILTSHIRE

High Court of Australia (1945) 72 C.L.R. 319

9–354 Questions arose as to the priority of the claims of creditors of a testator (such as Vacuum Oil) and creditors of the business carried on by the testator's executor, in the course of administration of the testator's bankrupt estate.

LATHAM C.J.: "In the first place I refer to the general principles of law which have been developed in relation to the rights and liabilities of the parties concerned when an executor carries on the business of his testator. These parties are the executor, the beneficiaries who claim under the will, the creditors of the testator (who may be called estate creditors) and the creditors to whom debts have been incurred in the course of trading by the executor (who may be called trading creditors).

"1. an executor is entitled (apart from any express authority given by the will) as against both beneficiaries and estate creditors to carry on the business of his testator for the purpose of realisation, but only for that purpose (*Collinson v Lister* (1855) 20 Beav. 356). In respect of debts incurred by him in so carrying on the business he is personally liable to the trading creditors—the debts are his debts, and not the debts of his testator (*Labouchere v Tupper* (1857) 11 Moo.P.C. 198; *Ex p. Garland* (1804) 10 Yes. Jun. 110). But as against beneficiaries and both classes of creditors he is entitled to indemnity in respect of those debts out of the assets of the estate (*Dowse v Gorton* [1891] A.C. 190 at 199).

9–355 "2. If an executor is authorised by the will to carry on the business not merely for the purpose of realisation, then it is still the case that debts incurred by him are his debts for which he is liable to the new creditors. The authority given by the testator is part of his disposition of his estate and binds beneficiaries under his will. Thus, as against the beneficiaries in such a case the executor is entitled to an indemnity against the new debts out of the assets of the estate which the testator authorised to be used for the purpose of carrying on the business and out of any assets acquired in the course of carrying on (*Ex p. Garland*).

"But the testator cannot by his will prejudice the rights of his own creditors (*Re Oxley* [1914] 1 Ch. 604 at 613). They may insist upon payment of the debts and upon realisation of the assets of the estate in due course in order to obtain payment, notwithstanding any provisions in the will with respect to the carrying on of the business. They can make the executor account upon the basis of the assets which came to his hands or which he has subsequently acquired as executor, leaving the new creditors to get such remedy as they can against the executor himself, but with the added right of subrogation to his indemnity against the estate—an indemnity which will be worth nothing if the old creditors exhaust the estate (*Dowse v Gorton*).

"3. If an executor carries on a business otherwise than for the purpose of **9–356** realisation and without authority given by the will of his testator, he acts at his own risk, the debts which he incurs are his debts, and he has no authority as against either beneficiaries or creditors to come upon the assets of the estate for the purpose of meeting them (*Labouchere v Tupper*).

"4. But if a beneficiary actually authorises him to carry on the business, he is entitled as against that beneficiary to indemnity out of the estate in respect of the debts which, in the course of such carrying on, he incurs to the trading creditors. Similarly, if a creditor of the testator actually authorises him to carry on the business he is entitled as against that creditor to a similar indemnity, which in each case enures by subrogation for the benefit of the new creditors (*Dowse v Gorton*).

"5. The position is the same if a creditor of the testator *actively* and positively **9–357** *assents* to the executor carrying on the business, but it is not easy to determine, on the authorities, what kind of conduct should be held to amount to the necessary active and positive assent. The principle upon which the right of the executor in such a case to indemnity out of assets of the estate as against an estate creditor has been variously stated. In *Dowse v Gorton* (at 208), Lord Macnaghten said: 'If the business is carried on by the executors at the instance of the creditors without regard to the terms of the will, the executors, I suppose, have the ordinary rights of agents against their principals.; In *Re Millard; Ex p. Yates* (1895) 72 L.T. 823, Smith L.J. referred to the words of Lord Macnaghten and applied the principle suggested by him. In the same case, however, Lord Esher M.R. pointed out that it could hardly be said that the executor in such a case was the agent of the creditors, because, if he were, the creditors would be undisclosed principals in the business and would be liable to new creditors for goods supplied to the business. The law, however, had held otherwise. Lord Esher took the view that the executor carrying on was in the position of a trustee for the creditors and that Lord Herschell in *Dowse v Gorton* had based his judgment in that case upon the view that the executor was such a trustee. Upon either view the result followed that the executor was entitled to an indemnity as against the estate creditors—in one case the indemnity to which an agent is entitled against his principal and in the other case the indemnity which a *cestui que trust* is bound to give to his trustee against liabilities reasonably incurred in performing the trust—to use the words of Lord Esher M.R. in *Millard's* case.

"There are difficulties in adopting the theory of agency (as pointed out by Lord **9–358** Esher) and there is no clear binding decision of any court (as distinct from *obiter dicta*) that the executor is a trustee in respect of creditors who have assented to the carrying on, but is not a trustee in the same sense with respect to creditors who have not assented to the carrying on.

"6. The principle which has been developed in the cases appears to be *sui generis*. It was decided in *Dowse v Gorton* that knowledge by estate creditors that the business is being carried on otherwise than for purposes of realisation does not amount to such an assent as to entitle the executors to an indemnity out of assets of the estate as against those creditors. There must be something more than mere knowledge and inaction—more than 'standing by' with knowledge.

"7. But the principle which has been applied is not an example of the application **9–359** of the equitable doctrine of acquiescence. A person may lose his rights by acquiescence, that is, by quiescence in such circumstances that assent to an infringement of his rights which is taking place may reasonably be inferred. Acquiescence is an instance of estoppel by words or conduct. (*De Bussche v Alt* (1878) 8 Ch.D. 286 at 314.) A person who so acquiesces is not allowed in equity to complain of the violation of his right because he has really induced the person infringing his right to pursue a course of action from which the latter person might otherwise have abstained. It is a condition, however, of the application of the doctrine of acquiescence that the person who acts in infringement of the right should be acting under a mistake as to his own rights. If he knows that he is infringing the right of another person he takes the risk of those rights being asserted against him (*Ramsden v Dyson* (1866) L.R. 1 H.L. 129 at 141). Further, the person whose rights are infringed must know that other person is acting under a mistaken belief (*Ramsden v Dyson; Russell v Watts* (1883) 25 Ch.D. 559 at 576). A case of acquiescence by an estate creditor in this sense in the executor trading might be made out in some cases. But there is no evidence of such acquiescence in the present case—no evidence of any such mistake or inducement—and I therefore set the equitable doctrine of acquiescence on one side.

9–360   "8. There is one other matter to which reference may be made before endeavouring to apply the law to the present case. In *Dowse v Gorton*, Lord Macnaghten expressed the opinion that estate creditors could not claim the assets of the business which had been acquired after the death of the testator and then refuse the executors indemnity in respect of liabilities incurred in carrying on the business. If they so acted, it was said, they would be reprobating after approbating. The same view is expressed in *Re Oxley*, by Cozens-Hardy M.R. at 610 and by Buckley L.J. at 614. These observations were not necessary for the decision of either case, because Lord Macnaghten in *Dowse v Gorton* and the majority in *Re Oxley* held that the creditors were not making any claim in respect of assets acquired subsequently to the death of the testator. I find much difficulty in reconciling these observations with the clearly established rule of law that assets acquired by an executor in carrying on the business of his testator are assets of the testator's estate in every respect in the same way as the testator's assets which came to the hands of the executor at the time of his testator's death. See the statement of the law by Herschell L.C. in *Dowse v Gorton* (at 198) and the many cases cited in *Williams on Executors & Administrators* (11th ed., 1921), Vol. 2, 1271 *et seq.*, where the law is stated as it existed before the Administration of Estates Act 1925 (Imp.). When an estate creditor sues an executor for his debt or takes an administration order the assets upon which execution can be levied under a judgment *de bonis testatoris* or which can be administered in the suit are all the assets which the executor has obtained in his capacity as executor. A creditor so suing does not "claim against" any particular part of the assets. He is entitled as of course to the application to estate liabilities of all the estate assets, including assets acquired after the death. He may not have known that the business had been carried on. It would be a remarkable thing if the result of such a creditor taking the only possible steps to compel payments of his debt should be that he must be taken to have assented to the carrying on so as to be postponed to the trading creditors.

9–361   "9. In the present case the testator's estate is being administered in bankruptcy under the provisions of section 155 of the Bankruptcy Act. It is clear that all the assets in the hands of the executor as executor will be administered and that no distinction will be drawn between assets which belonged to the testator and assets which have been subsequently acquired by the executor in the course of carrying on the business. Thus all the estate creditors in the present case are, simply because they have lodged proofs of debt, claiming against all the assets. If the *obiter dicta* in *Dowse v Gorton* and *Oxley's* case to which I have referred were to be taken as accurately stating the relevant law the result would be that all the estate creditors, independently of any assent by them in fact to the business being carried on, would be treated as having assented on the ground that they could not "approbate' the business being carried on by claiming the after-acquired assets, and 'reprobate' by refusing to allow the executor an indemnity out of those assets. If this were the law, then the result would be that all the estate creditors would be deemed to have assented because they have made claims to the satisfaction of which any assets in the executor's hands can be applied, even though some of them may have been completely unaware that the business had been carried on. The statements to which I have referred were not necessary for the decision of the cases mentioned and should not, I think be regarded as an authoritative statement of the law.

"10. Strictly it would appear, the trading creditors, whose debts are owed only by **9–362** the executor personally, should not be admitted as creditors in the administration under the Bankruptcy Act section 155 of the estate of the testator. They are not creditors of the testator's estate. But, as the executor may have a right of indemnity out of the estate assets in respect of the trading debts against some beneficiaries or some estate creditors, the trading creditors will be entitled to the benefit of his indemnity, and so will be entitled, through him, though not directly, to the application of estate assets to the satisfaction of their debts in priority to the claims of such beneficiaries or creditors. It is only in this way that the claims of trading creditors can come into consideration in these proceedings."

QUESTIONS

1. David, Eric and Ferdinand are trustees of a fund whose portfolio of **9–363** investments includes some 10,000 shares out of an issued 30,000 shares in a private company. The Fund is held upon protective trusts for Ferdinand during his life and after his death for George and Harry equally. Ian, who is the trustees' solicitor, discussed with them the possibility of them acquiring a sufficient number of shares in the company to give them a majority holding. The trustees refused for though they had power to retain their existing shares they had no power to invest in further shares in any private companies. Ian told them that they had a chance of applying successfully to the court for such a power but the trustees considered that it would not be worth it. In consideration of Ian agreeing not to charge legal fees for his unbilled work for the preceding year they told Ian that if he wished he could personally go ahead and try to obtain control for himself for as far as they could see this could only enhance the value of the trust's shareholding.

Ian then acquired all the remaining shares in the company, disposed of **9–364** some of its assets, reorganised the business and increased the value of the shares from £1 each to £4 each. In the meantime, Ferdinand had become bankrupt and David and Eric removed him from his trusteeship on the ground of his unfitness to act (without replacing him) and refused to apply any income for his benefit.

How far is Ian entitled to keep the profit on these transactions?

How far is the conduct of David and Eric legally justified?

Can Ferdinand call for the correspondence which passed between David and Eric, on the one hand, and Ian, on the other, relating to his removal from office and to the decision not to pay him any money?

2. David Rockechild is beneficially interested under a will trust of his **9–365** grandfather who died on April 1, 1990. Sir Malcolm Place and Sir Frank Haddock are the trustees of the settlement (with the broadest possible powers of investment) currently holding investments worth about £4 million

upon trust for Alan Rockechild for life, with overriding power for the trustees to appoint that upon or before Alan Rockechild's death the capital be distributed to any one or more of Alan's children in such shares as the trustees in their absolute discretion may think fit, but with remainder in default of appointment to Alan's three children, Brian, Charles and David equally if they attain 30 years of age.

The trustees have recently refused to pay an already agreed advancement of money to David in the following circumstances. David is a qualified pharmacist and he was offered the opportunity to become co-owner of a good chemist's shop for £150,000. His father and the trustees recognised that this was a very worthwhile opportunity so arrangements were made for David to call upon the trustees to receive the moneys under an exercise of the statutory power of advancement and David gave three months' notice of leaving his present job.

9–366   When David arrived he was told that he would have to sign a particular document before he could have the moneys. Upon examining the document he discovered it to be a deed already signed by his father and his brothers consenting to certain share transactions carried out in 2000 and authorising the trustees to retain any profits made by them in respect of those transactions.

Apparently, at tea at the 2000 Annual General Meeting of Quickgains Ltd attended by the trustees as representatives of the settlement, which had a not insubstantial shareholding, the trustees had obtained information about some prospective profitable contracts, that might lead to a take-over bid in a year or so, from one of the directors who was an old friend of theirs. The trustees discussed this information with Alan, Brian and Charles (for David, then aged 15 years and the youngest son by 5 years, was away at boarding school) and they all agreed that it would be worth risking investing a further £100,000 (but no more) of trust moneys in the company and that the trustees could spend as much of their moneys as they wished once the £100,000 trust moneys had been invested.

The trustees invested the £100,000 and then their own moneys and the shares had quadrupled in value between 2000 and 2005 when the trust shareholding was sold upon the written advice of the trust's stockbrokers.

9–367   When pressed by David the trustees refused to disclose how much of their own moneys had been invested in Quickgains Ltd, how much profit they had made or when or if they had sold their shares. The trustees merely pointed out that David should be very grateful for the profits which they had enabled the trust to make. However, David refused to sign the deed whereupon the trustees refused to advance any moneys to him. They also pointed out that if he did not be sensible like his father and his brothers and sign the deed, then it might well be that the power of appointment might be exercised in a way that might not be favourable to him. Two days later David received a letter from his father saying that as the father's personal circumstances had changed he was no longer prepared to consent to any advancement being made to David. Instructing solicitors imagine that the trustees put the father up to this.

Consider what courses of action may be available to David.

3. In September 2002 Tim died, bequeathing his coin collection and **9–368** £800,000 to his executor and trustee, Eric, on trust for his widow for life, remainder to his children Alan, Brian and Charles equally. Their children were then aged 30, 25 and 15 years respectively. The will contained various administrative provisions including wide powers of investment, and also a clause exempting the trustee from liability for any breach of trust that is not dishonest.

Although Eric was himself an experienced investor, upon winding up Tim's estate in March 2003 he gave the £800,000 for investment to Whizz Kid & Co. which specialises in discretionary portfolio management for clients and for itself. Eric signed the Company's current customer agreement in 2003. Its terms enable the Company *inter alia* to sell its own shares to the trust at a price no higher than that generally available at the time and to purchase for itself the trust's shares at a price no lower than that generally available at the time and provide that the Company shall not be liable for any loss arising from its negligence. The Company reports back to Eric every six months and follows his written policy statement concerning income and capital growth.

The investments are now only worth £400,000. At the end of 2003 the **9–369** Company sold £30,000 of its own AB.C. plc shares to the trust and these shares are now only worth £5,000. In 2003 the Company bought from the trust for £20,000 XYZ plc shares now worth £80,000. About £200,000 of the loss is due to the negligence of Jason, an employee of the Company, who is addicted to cocaine. Eric's son knew about Jason's addiction and had told Eric about it.

A year ago Eric gave the coin collection to Donald, an apparently reputable dealer in coins, to sell as soon as someone was found prepared to pay about £25,000 for the collection. At first Eric phoned Donald every new month to see if a purchaser had materialised. After four months Donald told Eric not to bother phoning because he would phone Eric if a sale occurred. Last week Eric tried to phone Donald and discovered that Donald had sold the collection for £22,500 six months ago, had used the proceeds in his business and then been made bankrupt a month ago.

Advise Tim's widow, who has heard that Whizz Kid & Co.is having financial problems and would also like to have the trust property sold up and its proceeds divided between her and her children.

4. A domineering, secretive, prospective settlor seeks your advice on how much he can keep in the dark persons interested under a very flexible discretionary trust and whether he can sensibly insert a provision, "No breach of trust action may be brought where the trustees have received written permission from the settlor in the relevant matter unless the action is brought within one month of the grant of such permission."

Chapter 10

PERSONAL LIABILITY OF TRUSTEES FOR BREACH OF TRUST

Section 1. Remedies for Breach of Trust

10–01 Any act or neglect on the part of a trustee which is contrary to the duties imposed upon him, and which is not excused by law,[1] or by the terms of the trust instrument,[2] is a breach of trust. Thus, as Millett L.J. observed in *Armitage v Nurse*[3]:

> "A breach of trust may be deliberate or inadvertent; it may consist of an actual misappropriation or misapplication of the trust property or merely of an investment or other dealing which is outside the trustees' powers; it may consist of a failure to carry out a positive obligation of the trustees or merely of a want of skill and care on their part in the management of the trust property; it may be injurious to the interests of the beneficiaries or be actually to their benefit."

10–02 Trustees are liable only for their *own* breaches of duty. Note, though, that it constitutes a breach of duty for a trustee to leave the trust affairs in the hands of a co-trustee to be dealt with as he sees fit,[4] or to leave trust property in his sole control,[5] or to stand by with knowledge that he is committing a breach of duty,[6] or to take no steps to obtain redress on becoming aware that he has committed a breach of trust,[7] or to retire from being a trustee with the object of facilitating a breach of trust which the remaining, or new, trustees then commit.[8]

---

[1] Note the Trustee Act 1925, s.61, discussed at para.10–110.

[2] Where a trust instrument contains a clause qualifying the extent of the trustee's duties, or otherwise exempting him from liability unless guilty of dishonesty, the court should construe the clause restrictively, against the trustee, but should bear in mind that the clause was inserted by the settlor, rather than the trustee himself, so that a strict *contra proferentem* approach would be unjustified: *Midland Bank Trustee (Jersey) Ltd v Federated Pension Services Ltd* [1996] P.L.R. 179 at 192; *Bogg v Raper* (1999) 1 I.T.E.L.R. 267 at 281. See too *Wight v Olswang (No.1)* (1999) 1 I.T.E.L.R. 783; *Wight v Olswang (No.2)* (2000) 2 I.T.E.L.R. 689.

[3] [1998] Ch. 241 at 250, adding that breaches of trust can be committed fraudulently or in good faith. Various rules turn upon this distinction, *e.g.* the rules governing exemption clauses (paras 9–249 *et seq*, above), limitation periods (paras 10–141 *et seq.*), and the release of a trustee's bankruptcy debts by discharge (Insolvency Act 1986, s.281(3), considered in *Woodland-Ferrari v UCL Group Retirement Benefits Scheme* [2002] 3 W.L.R. 1154).

[4] *Wynne v Tempest* (1897) 13 T.L.R. 360; *Re Lucking's W.T.* [1968] 1 W.L.R. 866. This assumes that there has been no proper delegation, *e.g.* under the Trustee Act 2000 ss.11, 12. Exceptionally a settlor may provide that a trustee must act as his co-trustee directs, in which case he will not be liable unless he dishonestly assists his co-trustee to commit a breach: *Re Arnott* [1899] I.R. 201.

[5] *Lewis v Nobbs* (1878) 8 Ch.D. 591. This assumes that the co-trustee is not an authorised nominee or custodian under the Trustee Act 2000, s.19.

[6] *Booth v Booth* (1838) 1 Beav. 125; *Gough v Smith* [1872] W.N. 18.

[7] *Wilkins v Hogg* (1861) 8 Jur. 25 at 26.

[8] *Head v Gould* [1898] 2 Ch. 250; *Kingdom v Castleman* (1877) 36 L.T. 141.

Trustees who cause the same damage to their beneficiaries by their **10–03** respective breaches of duty are jointly and severally liable: *i.e.* the beneficiaries can require two or more of them jointly, or one of them individually, to discharge their common liability.[9] If a trustee is obliged to pay more than his fair share, then he can recover a contribution from the others, or even require them to reimburse him in full.[10]

Remedies for breach of trust

Various remedies are available for breach of trust, but the focus of this **10–04** chapter is on compensatory awards. Two types of compensatory award can be made against trustees: an order that they should pay a money substitute for performance of their primary obligation to hold the trust assets for the beneficiaries and deliver them *in specie* when required to do so; and an order that they should pay money to redress harm which the beneficiaries have sustained through the trustees' breach of duty. Both types of award have traditionally been mediated through proceedings to make the trustees account for their stewardship of the trust property, but they are different in nature, essentially because the second type of claim depends on the assertion that the trustees have committed a breach of trust, while the first type of claim does not.

Where trustees misapply trust property, the beneficiaries may be able to **10–05** follow and/or trace the assets or their identifiable proceeds into the hands of the recipients, and they may then be entitled to assert a proprietary claim to the assets or their traceable proceeds.[11] If they prefer to assert such a proprietary claim, rather than pursuing the trustees with a view to fixing them with a personal compensatory liability, then the beneficiaries may do so at their election.[12]

Other remedies may also be available. As previously discussed in Chapter **10–06** 6, trustees must account for gains made contrary to their fiduciary duty to subordinate their personal interests to those of the beneficiaries.[13] Transactions between trustees and third parties entered in breach of trust can be set aside at the beneficiaries' suit, although not if the third party is a *bona fide* purchaser for value without notice of the trust.[14] Declarations can be made, setting out the nature and extent of a beneficiary's interest,[15] or a trustee's duty.[16] Prohibitory injunctions can be issued, restraining trustees

---

[9] *Charitable Corp. v Sutton* (1742) 2 Atk 400 at 406; *Walker v Symonds* (1818) 3 Swan 1 at 75; *Ashurst v Mason* (1875) L.R. 20 Eq. 225 at 233; *Re Duckwari plc* [1999] Ch. 253 at 262.
[10] See paras 10–161 to 10–163.
[11] See Chap. 12.
[12] Denning J., "The Recovery of Money" (1949) 65 L.Q.R. 37, 44; *Hagan v Waterhouse* (1994) 34 N.S.W.L.R. 308 at 369–370; *Wong v Burt* (2004) 7 I.T.E.L.R. 263 at [59].
[13] See paras 6–10 *et seq.*, above.
[14] *Peffer v Rigg* [1977] 1 W.L.R. 285.
[15] The courts have an unfettered discretion to make binding declarations under CPR rule 40.20, but they will not normally entertain theoretical questions with no practical application: *Padden v Arbuthnot Pensions and Investments Ltd*. [2004] EWCA Civ 582 at [24] and [31]. The proper form of a declaration of equitable interest under rule 40.20 is discussed in *Powell v Wilshire* [2005] 1 Q.B. 117 at [39]–[45], *per* Arden L.J. The Trusts of Land and Appointment of Trustees Act 1996 s.14(2)(b) enables a person with an interest in property that is subject to a trust of land to obtain an order declaring the nature or extent of his interest, as in, *e.g. Oxley v Hiscock* [2004] 2 F.L.R. 669.
[16] *Cowan v Scargill* [1985] Ch. 270.

from committing a breach of trust.[17] Trustees can be removed and new trustees appointed.[18] Judicial trustees and, exceptionally, receivers of trust property[19] can also be appointed, where this is necessary to preserve the trust assets and no other remedy, *e.g.* the appointment of new trustees, is feasible.

10–07   Can an award of exemplary damages be made in a case of outrageous misconduct by a trustee? In *Re Brogden*,[20] North J. said that "the court will not punish a trustee pecuniarily for his breach of trust except so far as loss has resulted therefrom to the trust estate", and historically no English court has ever awarded exemplary damages against a defaulting trustee.[21] Until recently, it was thought that the English courts had no power to award exemplary damages in respect of equitable wrongdoing because there was no case pre-dating 1964 where this had been done.[22] However, they may wish to reconsider their position, now that the cause of action test for the award of exemplary damages has been discredited in *Kuddus v Chief Constable of Leicestershire*.[23] Elsewhere, the appellate courts of Canada and New Zealand have held that an award of exemplary damages can be made in relation to a breach of fiduciary duty.[24] In Australia, the leading case is now *Harris v Digital Pulse Pty. Ltd*,[25] where Heydon J.A. vehemently opposed the award of exemplary damages for equitable wrongdoing, but Mason P. strongly favoured their award in suitable cases. The third judge, Spigelman C.J., considered it unnecessary and undesirable to decide the case on the basis that a punitive monetary award can never be awarded in equity because remedial flexibility is a characteristic of equity jurisprudence. In our view, the courts should be able to award exemplary damages in cases of outrageous misconduct by trustees and other fiduciaries.

Standing to sue

10–08   Proceedings to have a breach of trust redressed "may be taken by a beneficiary against a trustee or a former trustee or the estate of a former trustee".[26] This includes the beneficiary of a discretionary trust, who can

---

[17] *Fox v Fox* (1870) L.R. 11 Eq. 142 (improper distribution of assets); *Dance v Goldingham* (1873) L.R. 8 Ch. App. 902; *Buttle v Saunders* [1950] 2 All E.R. 193 (sale of assets at an undervalue).

[18] See Chap. 8.

[19] *Att.-Gen. v Schonfield* [1980] 1 W.L.R. 1182; *Clarke v Heathfield* [1985] I.C.R. 203; *Derby & Co. Ltd v Weldon (Nos.3 and 4)* [1990] Ch. 65 (freezing injunction); *Younghams v Candoora No.19 Pty. Ltd.* (2000) 3 I.T.E.L.R. 154; *ASIC v Takaran Pty Ltd (No.2)* (2002) 43 A.C.S.R. 334.

[20] (1886) 38 Ch.D. 546 at 557. See too *Att.-Gen. v Alford* (1855) 4 De G.M. & G. 843; *Vyse v Foster* (1872) L.R. 3 Ch. App. 309 at 333, affirmed (1874) L.R. 7 H.L. 318.

[21] The Pensions Act 1995, s.10 permits penalty fines for maladministration of occupational pension schemes, but to date no such fine has been imposed in a reported case.

[22] *AB v South West Water Services Ltd* [1993] Q.B. 507. See too Law Commission, *Aggravated, Exemplary, and Restitutionary Damages* (Law Com. No.247, 1997) paras.[5.54]–[5.56], recommending legislation to give the courts a power to award exemplary damages in relation to breaches of equitable duty. This recommendation has not been acted upon by Parliament.

[23] [2002] 2 A.C. 122.

[24] Canada: *Norberg v Wynrib* [1992] 2 S.C.R. 226; *KM v HM* [1992] 3 S.C.R. 6; *Whiten v Pilot Insurance Co.* [2002] 1 S.C.R. 595. New Zealand: *Aquaculture Corp v New Zealand Green Mussel Co. Ltd* [1990] 3 N.Z.L.R 299; *Cook v Evatt (No.2)* [1992] 1 N.Z.L.R. 676.

[25] (2003) 56 N.S.W.L.R. 298.

[26] *Young v Murphy* [1996] 1 V.R. 279 at 281. See too *Re Cross* (1881) 20 Ch.D. 109; *Space Investments Ltd v Canadian Imperial Bank of Commerce Trust Co. (Bahamas) Ltd* [1986] 1 W.L.R. 1072 at 1074.

obtain an injunction to compel the proper administration of the trust even though his interest is nothing more than a mere expectancy.[27] Proceedings to redress a breach of trust can also be taken by a trustee against a co-trustee or former trustee,[28] without joining the beneficiaries,[29] and it is no answer to the claim that the trustee himself participated in the breach.[30]

Section 2. Compensation Claims against Trustees

In his valuable study of the law in this area,[31] Dr Steven Elliott has **10–09** explained that Equity recognises two different types of compensation claim against trustees, which he terms substitutive performance claims and reparation claims. Substitutive performance claims are claims for a money payment as a substitute for performance of the trustees' obligation to deliver trust assets *in specie*. Claims of this sort are apposite when trust property has been misapplied, and the amount claimed is the objective value of the property which the trustees should have delivered. Reparation claims are claims for a money payment to make good the damage caused by a breach of trust, and the amount claimed is measured by reference to the loss sustained by the beneficiaries. Claims of this sort are often brought where trustees have carelessly mismanaged trust property, but they lie more generally wherever a fiduciary has harmed his principal by committing a breach of duty. Both types of claim have traditionally been mediated through proceedings for an account, as we shall discuss.[32]

I. SUBSTITUTIVE PERFORMANCE CLAIMS

"The duty of a trustee is properly to preserve the trust fund, to pay the **10–10** income and the corpus to those who are entitled to them respectively, and to give all his *cestuis que trust* on demand information with respect to the

---

[27] *Gartside v I.R.C.* [1968] A.C. 553 at 617. See too *Spellson v George* (1987) 11 N.S.W.L.R. 300 at 316, considered in *Schmidt v Rosewood Trust Ltd* [2003] 2 A.C. 709 at [59]–[60]; *Johns v Johns* [2004] 3 N.Z.L.R. 202 at [34]; *Armitage v Nurse* [1998] Ch. 241 at 261. The objects of a fiduciary power of appointment are similarly entitled.

[28] *Young v Murphy* [1996] 1 V.R. 279, at 281.

[29] *ibid.* at 283. See too *Greenwood v Wakeford* (1839) 1 Beav 576; *Re Cross* (1881) 20 Ch.D. 109; *Williams v Barton* [1927] 2 Ch. 9; *Montrose Investment Ltd v Orion Nominees Ltd* [2004] W.T.L.R. 133 at [24]. If a trustee pursues proceedings against a co-trustee to judgment, the beneficiaries are generally bound by the outcome of the proceedings and forbidden to bring subsequent proceedings in their own right against the same defendant in respect of the same breach of trust: *Norton v Levy* (1883) 48 L.T. 703 at 704; *Re De Leeuw* [1922] 2 Ch. 540 at 550–551.

[30] *ibid.* at 283. See too *Baynard v Woolley* (1855) 20 Beav. 583 at 585, *Butler v Butler* (1877) 7 Ch.D. 116 at 120–121 and 121.

[31] Dr. Elliott's work is most fully elaborated in his Oxford D.Phil. thesis: *Compensation Claims against Trustees* (2002), parts of which have been published as: S. B. Elliott, "Restitutionary Compensatory Damages for Breach of Fiduciary Duty?" [1998] R.L.R. 135; S. B. Elliott, "Fiduciary Liability for Client Mortgage Frauds" (1999) 13 Tru. L.I. 74; S. B. Elliott, "Remoteness Criteria in Equity" (2002) 65 M.L.R. 588; S. B. Elliott and C. Mitchell, "Remedies for Dishonest Assistance" (2004) 67 M.L.R. 16, esp. 23–34; S. B. Elliott and J. Edelman, "Money Remedies against Trustees" (2004) 18 Tru. L.I. 116. See also: *Lewin on Trusts* (17th ed., 2000), chap. 39; R. Chambers, "Liability" in P. Birks and A. Pretto (eds.) Breach of Trust (2002) 1; C. E. F. Rickett, "Equitable Compensation: Towards a Blueprint?" (2003) 25 Sydney L.R. 31.

[32] See paras 10–66 *et seq.*.

mode in which the trust fund has been dealt with, and where it is."[33] The beneficiaries have corresponding rights to obtain trust accounts and to insist that the trust assets are maintained or disbursed solely in accordance with the trust instrument.[34] The beneficiaries can obtain a court order commanding the trustees to perform their duties,[35] and to obtain such an order they need not assert that the trustees have done anything wrong. Their claim resembles[36] a claim for specific performance of the primary obligations owed under a contract,[37] rather than a claim for damages for breach of contract or tort.[38]

10–11	If a trustee cannot perform his core obligation to account for and deliver a trust asset *in specie*, for example because he has lost or misapplied it, then the court can order him instead to pay money as a substitute for performance of his duty. In this situation, the trustee has obviously committed a breach of trust, but there is no need for the beneficiaries to plead or prove the breach in order to obtain their remedy.[39] The reason is that their claim is still a claim for performance of the trustee's primary obligation to deliver the asset, but with the difference that it is a claim for *substitute* performance of this obligation by the payment of a money sum. It is not a claim for money to compensate the beneficiaries for any harm which they may have suffered as a consequence of the trustee's failure to perform his obligation *in specie*. The amount payable is accordingly measured by the objective value of the property which the trustee should have delivered: it "looks not so much to the loss suffered as to what is required to restore the trust fund".[40]

---

[33] *Low v Bouverie* [1891] 3 Ch. 82 at 99, *per* Lindley L.J.

[34] *Target Holdings Ltd v Redferns* [1996] A.C. 421 at 434. These rights and duties arise immediately that the trustee receives trust assets in a fiduciary capacity: *Att.-Gen v Cocke* [1988] Ch. 414 at 420.

[35] *Re Locker's S.T.* [1977] 1 W.L.R. 1323 (trustees ordered to exercise obligatory discretionary power of appointment). The courts can also make a vesting order directing trustees to transfer trust assets to an absolutely entitled beneficiary: Trustee Act 1925, ss.44(vi) and 51(1)(d); *Re Knox's Trusts* [1895] 2 Ch. 483; *cf. Quinton v Proctor* [1998] 4 V.R. 469; *Mok Chi Keung v Mok Chi Hoi* (2003) 215 HKCU 1; *Davis v Williams* [2003] NSWCA 371 at [41]. Where one or more beneficiaries are absolutely beneficially entitled to land held on a trust of land, so that they have rights to replace the trustees under the Trusts of Land and Appointment of Trustees Act 1996, s.19, the English courts should also be willing to vest the land directly in the beneficiaries, preferring the approach in *Re Godfrey's Trusts* (1883) 23 Ch.D. 205 to that in *Re Holland* (1881) 16 Ch.D. 672 and *Re Carrie* (1878) 10 Ch.D. 93.

[36] Note, however, that a court can order trustees to perform their obligations without regard to the adequacy of other remedies, whereas an order for specific performance of a contract will be made only where common law damages are an inadequate remedy: see para.14–134.

[37] A claim for specific performance may succeed even though it is issued before the date when contractual performance is required, so that by definition no breach of contract can yet have occurred: *Hasham v Zenab* [1960] A.C. 316, noted R. E. Megarry (1960) 76 L.Q.R. 200.

[38] Compare the statement in *Ex p. Adamson* (1878) 8 Ch. App. 807 at 819, that Chancery suits for breach of trust were always for "an equitable debt or liability in the nature of a debt", with the comment in *Jervis v Harris* [1996] Ch. 195 at 202–203, that "The plaintiff who claims payment of a debt need not prove anything beyond the occurrence of the event or condition on the occurrence of which the debt becomes due. He need prove no loss; the rules as to remoteness of damage and mitigation of loss are irrelevant."

[39] *Bacon v Clarke* (1837) 2 My. & Cr. 294; *Re Stevens* [1898] 1 Ch. 162; *Ahmed Angullia bin Hadjee Mohamed Salleh Angullia v Estate and Trust Agencies (1927) Ltd* [1938] A.C. 624 at 637.

[40] *New Cap Reinsurance Corp. Ltd v General Cologne Re Australia Ltd* (2004) 7 I.T.E.L.R. 295 at [55], *per* Young C.J. in Eq. See too *Re Anglo-French Co-operative Soc.* (1882) 21 Ch.D. 492 at 506; *Re Windsor Steam Coal Co. (1901) Ltd* [1929] 1 Ch. 151 at 166–167; *Knight v Haynes Duffell, Kentish & Co. (a firm)* [2003] EWCA Civ 223 at [36]–[39]. It is often said that the trustee must effect "restitution" or "restoration" of the trust assets which he has improperly withheld, or their money equivalent: *e.g. Re Dawson* [1966] 2 N.S.W.R. 211 at 216, at para.10–18; *Bartlett v Barclays Bank Trust Co. Ltd (No.2)* [1980] Ch. 515 at 543; *Target Holdings Ltd v Redferns* [1996] A.C. 421 at 433, *infra* at para.10–26; *Re French Caledonia Travel Service Pty Ltd (in liq.)* (2003) 59 N.S.W.L.R. 361 at [64]; *Alexander v Perpetual Trustees (W.A.) Ltd* (2004) 204 A.L.R. 417 at [104] and [116]. See too Pensions Act 1995, s.14.

Because their claim is not founded on an assertion that the trustee has **10–12** committed a breach of duty, the beneficiaries need not prove that the trustee's actions or omissions have caused them a loss,[41] nor do the concepts of remoteness[42] and contributory negligence[43] have any bearing on their claim. Moreover, no deduction will be made for tax which would have been payable by the trustees on the relevant property but for their default,[44] and the beneficiaries' tax liabilities do not enter the picture because they arise when capital or income is distributed out of the fund, and not when the trustee pays the value of the relevant asset back into the trust fund.

To give some examples of substitutive performance claims, let it be **10–13** supposed that a trustee T makes an unauthorised distribution of £x to A, who is now bankrupt; that T makes an unauthorised investment of £y in a villa in South Africa, which has now halved in value; and that T makes an unauthorised transfer of assets worth £z to an agent, B, who has now absconded with the money. Because T had no power under the trust to distribute the £x to A or to spend the £y on the villa, he will be treated as though he carried out these transactions with his own money, and he will be required to pay £x and £y back into the trust fund,[45] with compound interest at 1% above the clearing banks' base rate.[46] So far as the assets worth £z are concerned, T will now have to pay their replacement value back into the trust fund, even if this has risen to £2z in the interim,[47] and it makes no difference whether the assets were lost through an innocent accident or through B's negligence or dishonesty: see *Clough v Bond*[48] and *Caffrey v Derby*,[49] which are discussed in the extract from *Re Dawson*.

In *Target Holdings Ltd v Redferns*, the claimant agreed to lend money to a **10–14** borrower to purchase property. Repayment of the loan was to be secured by a charge on the property. The money was placed with the defendant solicitors on trust for payment to the borrower's order, once a duly executed charge over the property and supporting documents of title were delivered. The solicitors paid the money over to the borrower's order without first obtaining the charge or other documents, although these were later delivered. The borrower defaulted on the loan and it then transpired

---

[41] *Cocker v Quayle* (1830) 1 Russ. & M. 353; *Salway v Salway* (1831) 2 Russ. & M. 215; *Youyang Pty. Ltd v Minter Ellison Morris Fletcher* (2003) 212 C.L.R. 484 at [63] and [69].
[42] *Clough v Bond* (1838) 3 My. & Cr. 490; *Magnus v Queensland National Bank* (1888) 37 Ch.D. 466; *Re Dawson* [1966] 2 N.S.W.R. 211 at 214, at para.10–11; *Re Duckwari plc (No.2)* [1999] Ch. 268 at 272; *McCann v Switzerland Insurance Australia Ltd* (2000) 203 C.L.R. 579 at 621–622.
[43] *Nationwide B.S. v Bulmer Radmore (a firm)* [1999] P.N.L.R. 606, *per* Blackburne J.: "contributory negligence has never been a defence open to a trustee sued by his beneficiary for breach of trust in wrongfully paying away the trust fund" (N.B. this passage of Blackburne J.'s judgment is not reproduced in the report). See too *Alexander v Perpetual Trustees (W.A.) Ltd* (2004) 204 A.L.R. 417 at [44], citing *Pilmer v Duke Group Ltd (in liq.)* (2001) 207 C.L.R. 165 at [86] and [170]–[173], but the *dicta* in *Pilmer* were concerned with reparation claims.
[44] *Bartlett v Barclays Bank Trust Co. Ltd (No.2)* [1980] Ch. 515 at 543; *Re Bell's Indenture* [1980] 1 W.L.R. 1217; *John v James* [1986] S.T.C. 352 at 361.
[45] *Knott v Cottee* (1852) 19 Beav. 77; *Re Duckwari plc (No.2)* [1999] Ch. 268 at 272; *Royal Trust Corp. of Canada v Barter* [2000] BCSC 1842 at [46]–[50]; *Wong v Burt* (2004) 7 I.T.E.L.R. 263 at [59].
[46] *Wallersteiner v Moir (No.2)* [1975] Q.B. 373 at 397.
[47] *Shepherd v Mouls* (1845) 24 Hare 500 at 504; *Re Massingberd* (1890) 63 L.T. 296.
[48] (1838) 3 My. & Cr. 490 at 496-497, *per* Lord Cottenham L.C., endorsed in *Target Holdings Ltd v Redferns* [1996] 1 A.C. 421 at 434, *per* Lord Browne-Wilkinson.
[49] (1801) 6 Ves 488.

that the property had been fraudulently over-valued, so that the claimant was left substantially out of pocket after it had exercised its power of sale. The Court of Appeal held that the solicitors had committed a breach of trust by releasing the money before receiving the documents, and that at this moment there had been "an immediate loss placing the trustee under an immediate duty to restore the moneys to the trust fund".[50] They concluded that the solicitors were liable for the full amount of the money, but to prevent double recovery they required the claimant to give credit for the amount realised by the sale of the property.

10–15   The House of Lords agreed that there had been a breach of trust, but disagreed that the clock should be stopped at the date of breach for the purpose of quantifying the solicitors' liability. Their Lordships held that the relevant date was the date of judgment, *i.e.* after the transaction had been completed, and that the solicitors would therefore be liable only if the claimant could prove that its loss would not have occurred but for the early payment of the money without taking any security. Hence the case was sent back to the High Court for determination of this point.

10–16   Unfortunately, Lord Browne-Wilkinson's leading speech is hard to follow.[51] He clearly thought that the claimant should have to prove a causal link between its loss and the solicitor's breach of duty. Yet, as Lord Millett has since observed,[52] the claim was for substitutive performance of the solicitor's duty to hold and disburse the trust money in accordance with the terms of the trust, and so the question whether the claimant had suffered a loss as a result of the solicitor's breach of duty was beside the point. In Lord Millett's view, the case should have been decided on the different basis that the solicitor's payment without taking the documents was a breach of trust, but that where a trustee has misapplied trust assets, his "obligation to restore the trust property is not an obligation to restore it in the very same form in which he disbursed it, but an obligation to restore it in any form authorized by the trust."[53] Hence, when the solicitor acquired the title deeds and delivered them to the claimant, it performed its obligation to restore the trust property, not *in specie*, but in the form of an authorised substitute. Hence the solicitor should not have been liable for anything.

10–17   This rationalisation of the case leaves intact Lord Browne-Wilkinson's finding that the quantum of the liability owed by a trustee who misapplies trust property is not determined at the date of breach, even though he comes under an immediate liability to restore the property.[54] However, this does not mean that the court can look at events occurring after the breach to see whether the beneficiaries would ultimately have suffered the same

---

[50] [1994] 1 W.L.R. 1089 at 1103, *per* Peter Gibson L.J.
[51] Essentially he failed to distinguish substitutive performance claims and reparation claims. The source of this confusion was the Supreme Court of Canada's decision in *Canson Enterprises Ltd v Boughton & Co.* [1991] 3 S.C.R. 534, as explained in J. Edelman and S. B. Elliott, "Money Remedies against Trustees" (2004) 18 Tru L.I. 116, 122–125.
[52] Sir P. Millett, "Equity's Place in the Law of Commerce" (1998) 114 L.Q.R. 214, 225–227. See too Lord Millett, "Proprietary Restitution" in S. Degeling and J. Edelman (eds.), *Equity in Commercial Law* (2005).
[53] *ibid*, 227.
[54] See too *Youyang Pty. Ltd v Minter Ellison Morris Fletcher* (2003) 212 C.L.R. 484 at [35].

loss anyway.[55] Instead, its significance lies in the fact that the court can look to see whether the trustee has rectified matters in an authorised fashion since the date of breach. Also, if the trustee has not done this, the value of his obligation to hand over the property will vary according to its current market value, or, where the property is money, according to the amount of (compound) interest accrued on the money between the date of breach and the date of judgment.

RE DAWSON

[1966] 2 N.S.W.R. 211 at 214–216, endorsed by Brightman L.J. in *Bartlett v Barclays Bank Trust Co. Ltd (No.2)* [1980] Ch. 515 at 543

STREET J.: "The obligation of a defaulting trustee is essentially one of effecting a **10–18** restitution to the estate. The obligation is of a personal character and its extent is not to be limited by common law principles governing remoteness of damage. In *Caffrey v Darby*,[56] trustees were charged with neglect in failing to recover possession of part of the trust assets. The assets were lost and it was argued by the trustees that the loss was not attributable to their neglect. The Master of the Rolls, in stating his reasons, asked 'will they be relieved from that by the circumstance that the loss has ultimately happened by something that is not a direct and immediate consequence of their negligence?' His answer to this question was that, even supposing that 'they could not look to the possibility' of the actual event which occasioned the loss, 'yet, if they have already been guilty of negligence they must be responsible for any loss in any way to that property; for whatever may be the immediate cause the property would not have been in a situation to sustain that loss if it had not been for their negligence. If they had taken possession of the property it would not have been in his possession. If the loss had happened by fire, lightning, or any other accident, that would not be an excuse for them, if guilty of previous negligence. That was their fault.' *Caffrey v Darby* is consistent with the proposition that if a breach has been committed then the trustee is liable to place the trust estate in the same position as it would have been in if no breach had been committed. Considerations of causation, foreseeability and remoteness do not readily enter into the matter. To the same effect is the case of *Clough v Bond*.[57] It was argued before Lord Cottenham L.C. that 'the principle of the court is to charge persons in the situation of trustees as parties to the breach of trust, wherever they have acted irregularly, and the irregularity, however well intended, has in the result enabled their co-trustees to commit a breach of trust, or has been, however remotely, the origin of the loss.' . . . The principles embodied in this approach do not appear to involve any inquiry as to whether the loss was caused by or flowed from the breach. Rather the inquiry in each instance would appear to be whether the loss would have happened if there had been no breach.

". . . The cases to which I have referred demonstrate that the obligation to make **10–19** restitution, which courts of equity have from very early times imposed on defaulting trustees and other fiduciaries, is of a more absolute nature than the common-law obligation to pay damages for tort or breach of contract. . . . Moreover the

---

[55] *Cocker v Quayle* (1830) 1 Russ. & M. 535.
[56] (1801) 6 Ves. 488.
[57] (1838) 3 My. & Cr. 490.

distinction between common law damages and relief against a defaulting trustee is strikingly demonstrated by reference to the actual form of relief granted in equity in respect of breaches of trust. The form of relief is couched in terms appropriate to require the defaulting trustee to restore to the estate the assets of which he deprived it. Increases in market values between the date of breach and the date of recoupment are for the trustee's account: the effect of such increases would, at common law, be excluded from the computation of damages but in equity a defaulting trustee must make good the loss by restoring to the estate the assets of which he deprived it notwithstanding that market values may have increased in the meantime. The obligation to restore to the estate the assets of which he deprived it necessarily connotes that, where a monetary compensation is to be paid in lieu of restoring assets, that compensation is to be assessed by reference to the value of the assets at the date of restoration and not at the date of deprivation. In this sense the obligation is a continuing one and ordinarily, if the assets are for some reason not restored *in specie*, it will fall for quantification at the date when recoupment is to be effected, and not before."

TARGET HOLDINGS LTD. v REDFERNS (A FIRM)

House of Lords (Lords Keith, Ackner, Jauncey, Browne-Wilkinson and Lloyd)
[1996] 1 A.C. 421; [1995] 3 W.L.R. 352; [1995] 3 All E.R. 785

10–20 The claimant mortgagee alleged that it had been the victim of a mortgage fraud as part of which the insolvent second defendant had over-valued the mortgaged property at £2 million. The first defendant, a firm of solicitors, had acted not just for the claimant but also for the mortgagor, Crowngate Ltd., and also for Kohli Ltd. and Panther Ltd. The owner of the property, Mirage Ltd., had agreed to sell to Crowngate for £775,000 but Crowngate had arranged matters so that Mirage would sell to Panther for £775,000, which would then sell the property on to Kohli for £1,250,000, which would then sell to Crowngate for £2 million. The claimant knew nothing of these arrangements. It paid £1,525,000 to the defendant solicitors to be held on a bare trust to pay the money to Crowngate's order only when the property was transferred to Crowngate and charges over it were executed in the claimant's favour.

10–21 In breach of trust the money was paid over a month before the charges were executed. Crowngate became insolvent and the claimant sold the property for only £500,000. The claimant sued the defendant solicitors for breach of their duty of care as the claimant's solicitor in failing to alert the claimant to the suspicious circumstances, and also for breach of trust in paying the money away without authority. The claimant sought summary judgment for breach of trust; Warner J. granted leave to defend conditional upon payment into court of £1 million. The Court of Appeal granted summary judgment.

10–22 LORD BROWNE-WILKINSON (with whom all the other Law Lords simply agreed): "Peter Gibson L.J., with whom Hirst L.J. agreed, held that the basic liability of a trustee in breach of trust is not to pay damages but to restore to the trust fund that which has been lost to it or to pay compensation to the beneficiary for what he has lost. He held that, in assessing the compensation payable to the beneficiary, causation is not irrelevant but common law rules of causation, as such, do not apply: the beneficiary is to be put back in the position he would have been in but for the breach of trust. He held that in cases where the breach of trust does not involve paying away trust money to a stranger (*e.g.* making an unauthorised investment), the answer to the question whether any loss has been thereby caused and the quantification of such loss will depend upon events subsequent to the commission of the breach of trust. But he held that in cases such as the present where the trustee has paid away trust moneys to a stranger, there is an immediate loss to the trust fund and the causal connection between the breach and the loss is obvious: the trustee comes under an immediate duty to restore the moneys to the trust fund. He held that the remedies of equity are sufficiently flexible to require Target (as it has always accepted) to give credit for the moneys received on the subsequent realisation of its security. But otherwise Redferns' liability was to pay to Target the whole of the moneys wrongly paid away . . .

"Before considering the technical issues of law which arise, it is appropriate to look at the case more generally. Target alleges, and it is probably the case, that it was defrauded by third parties (Mr. Kohli and Mr. Musafir and possibly their associates) to advance money on the security of the property. If there had been no breach by Redferns of their instructions and the transaction had gone through, Target would have suffered a loss . . . [which] would have been wholly caused by the fraud of the third parties. The breach of trust committed by Redferns left Target in exactly the same position as it would have been if there had been no such breach: Target advanced the same amount of money, obtained the same security and received the same amount on the realisation of that security. In any ordinary use of words, the breach of trust by Redferns cannot be said to have caused the actual loss ultimately suffered by Target unless it can be shown that, but for the breach of trust, the transaction would not have gone through, *e.g.* if Panther could not have obtained a conveyance from Mirage otherwise than by paying the purchase money to Mirage out of the moneys paid out, in breach of trust, by Redferns to Panther on 29 June. If that fact can be demonstrated, it can be said that Redferns' breach of trust was a cause of Target's loss: if the transaction had not gone through, Target would not have advanced the money at all and therefore Target would not have suffered any loss. But the Court of Appeal decided,[58] and it is common ground before your Lordships, that there is a triable issue as to whether, had it not been for the breach of trust, the transaction would have gone through. Therefore the decision of the Court of Appeal in this case can only be maintained on the basis that, even if there is no causal link between the breach of trust and the actual loss eventually suffered by Target (*i.e.* the sum advanced less the sum recovered) the trustee in breach is liable to bear (at least in part) the loss suffered by Target . . .

10–23

"At common law there are two principles fundamental to the award of damages. First, that the defendant's wrongful act must cause the damage complained of. Second, that the plaintiff is to be put 'in the same position as he would have been in if he had not sustained the wrong for which he is now getting his compensation or reparation'.[59] Although, as will appear, in many ways equity approaches liability for making good a breach of trust from a different starting point, in my judgment those two principles are applicable as much in equity as at common law. Under both systems liability is fault based: the defendant is only liable for the consequences of the legal wrong he has done to the plaintiff and to make good the damage caused by such wrong. He is not responsible for damage not caused by his wrong or to pay by way of compensation more than the loss suffered from such wrong. The detailed rules of equity as to causation and the quantification of loss differ, at least ostensibly, from those applicable at common law. But the principles underlying both

10–24

---

[58] See [1994] 1 W.L.R. 1089 at 1100 and 1104, *per* Ralph Gibson and Peter Gibson L.JJ.
[59] See *Livingstone v Rawyards Coal Co.* (1880) 5 App. Cas. 25 at 39, *per* Lord Blackburn.

systems are the same. On the assumptions that had to be made in the present case until the factual issues are resolved (*i.e.* that the transaction would have gone through even if there had been no breach of trust), the result reached by the Court of Appeal does not accord with those principles. Redferns as trustees have been held liable to compensate Target for a loss caused otherwise than by the breach of trust. I approach the consideration of the relevant rules of equity with a strong predisposition against such a conclusion.

10–25   "The considerations urged before your Lordships, although presented as a single argument leading to the conclusion that the views of the majority in the Court of Appeal are correct, on analysis comprise two separate lines of reasoning, *viz.*:

> (A) an argument developed by Mr Patten Q.C. (but not reflected in the reasons of the Court of Appeal) that Target is now (*i.e.* at the date of judgment) entitled to have the 'trust fund' restored by an order that Redferns reconstitute the trust fund by paying back into client account the moneys paid away in breach of trust. Once the trust fund is so reconstituted, Redferns as bare trustee for Target will have no answer to a claim by Target for the payment over of the moneys in the reconstituted 'trust fund'. Therefore, Mr. Patten says, it is proper now to order payment direct to Target of the whole sum improperly paid away, less the sum which Target has received on the sale of property; and
> (B) the argument accepted by the majority of the Court of Appeal that, because immediately after the moneys were paid away by Redferns in breach of trust there was an immediate right to have the 'trust fund' reconstituted, there was then an immediate loss to the trust fund for which loss Redferns are now liable to compensate Target direct.

10–26   "The critical distinction between the two arguments is that argument (A) depends upon Target being entitled now to an order for restitution to the trust fund whereas argument (B) quantifies the compensation payable to Target as beneficiary by reference to a right to restitution to the trust fund at an earlier date and is not dependent upon Target having any right to have the client account reconstituted now.

10–27   "Before dealing with these two lines of argument, it is desirable to say something about the approach to the principles under discussion. The argument both before the Court of Appeal and your Lordships concentrated on the equitable rules establishing the extent and quantification of the compensation payable by a trustee who is in breach of trust. In my judgment this approach is liable to lead to the wrong conclusions in the present case because it ignores an earlier and crucial question, viz is the trustee who has committed a breach under any liability at all to the beneficiary complaining of the breach? There can be cases where, although there is an undoubted breach of trust, the trustee is under no liability at all to a beneficiary. For example, if a trustee commits a breach of trust with the acquiescence of one beneficiary, that beneficiary has no right to complain and an action for breach of trust brought by him would fail completely. Again there may be cases where the breach gives rise to no right to compensation. Say, as often occurs, a trustee commits a judicious breach of trust by investing in an unauthorised investment which proves to be very profitable to the trust. A carping beneficiary could insist that the unauthorised investment be sold and the proceeds invested in authorised investments: but the trustee would be under no liability to pay compensation either to the trust fund or to the beneficiary because the breach has caused no loss to the trust fund. Therefore, in each case the first question is to ask what are the rights of the beneficiary: only if some relevant right has been infringed so as to give rise to a loss is it necessary to consider the extent of the trustee's liability to compensate for such loss.

"The basic right of a beneficiary is to have the trust duly administered in **10–28** accordance with the provisions of the trust instrument, if any, and the general law. Thus, in relation to a traditional trust where the fund is held in trust for a number of beneficiaries having different, usually successive, equitable interests (*e.g.* A for life with remainder to B), the right of each beneficiary is to have the whole fund vested in the trustees so as to be available to satisfy his equitable interest when, and if, it falls into possession. Accordingly, in the case of a breach of such a trust involving the wrongful paying away of trust assets, the liability of the trustee is to restore to the trust fund, often called 'the trust estate', what ought to have been there.

"The equitable rules of compensation for breach of trust have been largely **10–29** developed in relation to such traditional trusts, where the only way in which all the beneficiaries' rights can be protected is to restore to the trust fund what ought to be there. In such a case the basic rule is that a trustee in breach of trust must restore or pay to the trust estate either the assets which have been lost to the estate by reason of the breach or compensation for such loss. Courts of Equity did not award damages but, acting *in personam*, ordered the defaulting trustee to restore the trust estate.[60] If specific restitution of the trust property is not possible, then the liability of the trustee is to pay sufficient compensation to the trust estate to put it back to what it would have been had the breach not been committed.[61] Even if the immediate cause of the loss is the dishonesty or failure of a third party, the trustee is liable to make good that loss to the trust estate if, but for the breach, such loss would not have occurred.[62] Thus the common law rules of remoteness of damage and causation do not apply. However, there does have to be some causal connection between the breach of trust and the loss to the trust estate for which compensation is recoverable, viz the fact that the loss would not have occurred but for the breach.[63]

"Hitherto I have been considering the rights of beneficiaries under traditional **10–30** trusts where the trusts are still subsisting and therefore the right of each beneficiary, and his only right, is to have the trust fund reconstituted as it should be. But what if at the time of the action claiming compensation for breach of trust those trusts have come to an end? Take as an example again the trust for A for life with remainder to B. During A's lifetime B's only right is to have the trust duly administered and, in the event of a breach, to have the trust fund restored. After A's death, B becomes absolutely entitled. He of course has the right to have the trust assets retained by the trustees until they have fully accounted for them to him. But if the trustees commit a breach of trust, there is no reason for compensating the breach of trust by way of an order for restitution and compensation to the trust fund as opposed to the beneficiary himself. The beneficiary's right is no longer simply to have the trust duly administered: he is, in equity, the sole owner of the trust estate. Nor, for the same reason, is restitution to the trust fund necessary to protect other beneficiaries. Therefore, although I do not wholly rule out the possibility that even in those circumstances an order to reconstitute the fund may be appropriate, in the ordinary case where a beneficiary becomes absolutely entitled to the trust fund the court

---

[60] See *Nocton v Lord Ashburton* [1914] A.C .932 at 952, *per* Viscount Haldane L.C.
[61] See *Caffrey v Darby* (1801) 6 Ves. 488 and *Clough v Bond* (1838) 3 My. & Cr. 490.
[62] See *Underhill and Hayton Law of Trusts and Trustees* 14th edn. (1987) pp.734–736, *Re Dawson (decd.)* [1966] 2 N.S.W.R. 211 and *Bartlett v Barclays Bank Trust Co. Ltd (No.2)* [1980] 2 Ch. 515.
[63] See also *Re Miller's Deed Trusts* (1978) 75 L.S. Gaz. 454 and *Nestlé v National Westminster Bank plc* [1993] 1 W.L.R. 1260.

orders, not restitution to the trust estate, but the payment of compensation directly to the beneficiary. The measure of such compensation is the same, *i.e.* the difference between what the beneficiary has in fact received and the amount he would have received but for the breach of trust . . .

Argument (A)

10–31   "As I have said, the critical step in this argument is that Target is now entitled to an order for reconstitution of the trust fund by the repayment into client account of the moneys wrongly paid away, so that Target can now demand immediate repayment of the whole of such moneys without regard to the real loss it has suffered by reason of the breach.

10–32   "Even if the equitable rules developed in relation to traditional trusts were directly applicable to such a case as this, as I have sought to show, a beneficiary becoming absolutely entitled to a trust fund has no automatic right to have the fund reconstituted in all circumstances. Thus, even applying the strict rules so developed in relation to traditional trusts, it seems to me very doubtful whether Target is now entitled to have the trust fund reconstituted. But in my judgment it is in any event wrong to lift wholesale the detailed rules developed in the context of traditional trusts and then seek to apply them to trusts of quite a different kind. In the modern world the trust has become a valuable device in commercial and financial dealings. The fundamental principles of equity apply as much to such trusts as they do to the traditional trusts in relation to which those principles were originally formulated. But in my judgment it is important, if the trust is not to be rendered commercially useless, to distinguish between the basic principles of trust law and those specialist rules developed in relation to traditional trusts which are applicable only to such trusts and the rationale of which has no application to trusts of quite a different kind.

10–33   "This case is concerned with a trust which has at all times been a bare trust. Bare trusts arise in a number of different contexts: *e.g.* by the ultimate vesting of the property under a traditional trust, nominee shareholdings, and, as in the present case, as but one incident of a wider commercial transaction involving agency. In the case of moneys paid to a solicitor by a client as part of a conveyancing transaction, the purpose of that transaction is to achieve the commercial objective of the client, be it the acquisition of property or the lending of money on security. The depositing of money with the solicitor is but one aspect of the arrangements between the parties, such arrangements being for the most part contractual. Thus, the circumstances under which the solicitor can part with money from client account are regulated by the instructions given by the client: they are not part of the trusts on which the property is held. I do not intend to cast any doubt on the fact that moneys held by solicitors on client account are trust moneys or that the basic equitable principles apply to any breach of such trust by solicitors. But the basic equitable principle applicable to breach of trust is that the beneficiary is entitled to be compensated for any loss he would not have suffered but for the breach. I have no doubt that, until the underlying commercial transaction has been completed, the solicitor can be required to restore to client account moneys wrongly paid away. But to import into such trust an obligation to restore the trust fund once the transaction has been completed would be entirely artificial. The obligation to reconstitute the trust fund applicable in the case of traditional trusts reflects the fact that no one beneficiary is entitled to the trust property and the need to compensate all beneficiaries for the breach. That rationale has no application to a case such as the present. To impose such an obligation in order to enable the beneficiary solely entitled (*i.e.* the client) to recover from the solicitor more than the client has in fact lost flies in the face of common sense and is in direct conflict with the basic principles of equitable compensation. In my judgment, once a conveyancing transaction has been completed the client has no right to have the solicitor's client account reconstituted as a 'trust fund'.

Argument (B)

" . . . The key point in the reasoning of the Court of Appeal is that where moneys **10–34** are paid away to a stranger in breach of trust, an immediate loss is suffered by the trust estate: as a result, subsequent events reducing that loss are irrelevant. They drew a distinction between the case in which the breach of trust consisted of some failure in the administration of the trust and the case where a trustee has actually paid away trust moneys to a stranger. There is no doubt that in the former case, one waits to see what loss is in fact suffered by reason of the breach, *i.e.* the restitution or compensation payable is assessed at the date of trial, not of breach. However, the Court of Appeal considered that where the breach consisted of paying away the trust moneys to a stranger it made no sense to wait: it seemed to Peter Gibson L.J. obvious that in such a case 'there is an immediate loss, placing the trustee under an immediate duty to restore the moneys to the trust fund'.[64] The majority of the Court of Appeal therefore considered that subsequent events which diminished the loss in fact suffered were irrelevant, save for imposing on the compensated beneficiary an obligation to give credit for any benefit he subsequently received. In effect, in the view of the Court of Appeal one 'stops the clock' at the date the moneys are paid away: events which occur between the date of breach and the date of trial are irrelevant in assessing the loss suffered by reason of the breach.

"A trustee who wrongly pays away trust money, like a trustee who makes an **10–35** unauthorised investment, commits a breach of trust and comes under an immediate duty to remedy such breach. If immediate proceedings are brought, the court will make an immediate order requiring restoration to the trust fund of the assets wrongly distributed or, in the case of an unauthorised investment, will order the sale of the unauthorised investment and the payment of compensation for any loss suffered. But the fact that there is an accrued cause of action as soon as the breach is committed does not in my judgment mean that the quantum of the compensation payable is ultimately fixed as at the date when the breach occurred. The quantum is fixed at the date of judgment, at which date, according to the circumstances then pertaining, the compensation is assessed at the figure then necessary to put the trust estate or the beneficiary back into the position it would have been in had there been no breach. I can see no justification for 'stopping the clock' immediately in some cases but not in others: to do so may, as in this case, lead to compensating the trust estate or the beneficiary for a loss which, on the facts known at trial, it has never suffered.

"Moreover, in my judgment the distinction is not consistent with the decision in **10–36** *Re Dawson (decd.).*[65] In that case a testator had established separate executors for his New Zealand and his Australian estates. In 1939 the New Zealand estate was under the administration of attorneys for, amongst others, PSD. PSD arranged that New Zealand £4,700 should be withdrawn from the New Zealand estate and paid away to a stranger, X, who in turn was supposed to lend the moneys to an Australian company in which PSD was interested. X absconded with the money. In

---

[64] [1994] 1 W.L.R. 1089 at 1103.
[65] [1966] 2 N.S.W.R. 211.

that case, therefore, the trust money had been paid away to a stranger. Street J. had to decide whether the liability of PSD to compensate the estate was to be satisfied by paying sufficient Australian pounds to buy New Zealand £4,700 at the rate of exchange at the date of breach (when there was parity between the two currencies) or at the date of judgment (when the Australian pound had depreciated against the New Zealand pound). He held that the rate of exchange was to be taken as at the date of judgment. Although, contrary to the present case, this decision favoured the beneficiaries at the expense of the defaulting trustee, the principle is of general application whether operating to the benefit or the detriment of the beneficiaries. The equitable compensation for breach of trust has to be assessed as at the date of judgment and not at an earlier date.

10–37   "In *Canson Enterprises Ltd. v Boughton & Co.*[66] the plaintiffs had bought some property in a transaction in which they were advised by the defendant, a solicitor. To the knowledge of the solicitor, but not of the plaintiffs, there was an improper profit being made by the vendors. If the plaintiffs had known that fact, they would not have completed the purchase. The defendant solicitor was in breach of his fiduciary duties to the plaintiffs. After completion the plaintiffs built a warehouse on the property, which due to the negligence of engineers and builders, was defective. The question was whether the defendant solicitor was liable to compensate the plaintiffs for the defective building, the plaintiffs contending that 'but for' the defendant's breach of fiduciary duty they would not have bought the property and therefore would not have built the warehouse. Although the Supreme Court of Canada were unanimous in dismissing the claim, they reached their conclusions by two differing routes. The majority considered that damages for breach of fiduciary duty fell to be measured by analogy with common law rules of remoteness, whereas the minority considered that the equitable principles of compensation applied. Your Lordships are not required to choose between those two views. But the judgment of McLachlin J. (expressing the minority view) contains an illuminating exposition of the rules applicable to equitable compensation for breach of trust. Although the whole judgment deserves study, I extract the following statements:

10–38   'While foreseeability of loss does not enter into the calculation of compensation for breach of fiduciary duty, liability is not unlimited. Just as restitution *in specie* is limited to the property under the trustee's control, so equitable compensation must be limited to loss flowing from the trustee's acts in relation to the interest he undertook to protect. Thus, Davidson states "It is imperative to ascertain the loss *resulting from breach of the relevant equitable duty.*"[67] . . .

          'A related question which must be addressed is the time of assessment of the loss. In this area tort and contract law are of little help . . .The basis of compensation at equity, by contrast, is the restoration of the actual value of the thing lost through the breach. The foreseeable value of the items is not in issue. As a result, the losses are to be assessed as at the time of trial, *using the full benefit of hindsight* . . .[68]

          'In summary, compensation is an equitable monetary remedy which is available when the equitable remedies of restitution and account are not appropriate. By analogy with restitution, it attempts to restore to the plaintiff what has been lost as a result of the breach, *i.e.* the plaintiff 's lost opportunity.

---

[66] [1991] 3 S.C.R. 534.
[67] I. Davidson, "The Equitable Remedy of Compensation" (1982) 3 Melb. U.L.R. 349, 354 (McLachlin J.'s emphasis).
[68] McLachlin J.'s emphasis.

The plaintiff's actual loss as a consequence of the breach is to be assessed with the full benefit of hindsight. Foreseeability is not a concern in assessing compensation, but it is essential that the losses made good are only those which, on a common sense view of causation, were caused by the breach.'[69]

"In my view this is good law. Equitable compensation for breach of trust is designed **10–39** to achieve exactly what the word compensation suggests: to make good a loss in fact suffered by the beneficiaries and which, using hindsight and common sense, can be seen to have been caused by the breach . . .

"Mr. Patten for Target relied on *Nant-y-glo and Blaina Ironworks Co. v Grave*[70] as **10–40** showing that a trustee can be held liable to recoup to the trust fund the value of shares at the highest value between the date of breach and the date of judgment. In my view that case has no relevance. The claim there was not for breach of trust but for account of profits made by a fiduciary (a company director) from shares which he had improperly received in breach of his duty. The amount recoverable in an action claiming an account of profits is dependent upon the profit made by the fiduciary, not the loss suffered by the beneficiary.

"Mr. Patten also relied on *Jaffray v Marshall*,[71] where the principles applicable in **10–41** an action for an account of profits were, to my mind wrongly, applied to a claim for compensation for breach of trust. In my judgment that case was wrongly decided not only because the wrong principle was applied but also because the judge awarded compensation by assessing the quantum on an assumption (*viz.* that the house in question would have been sold at a particular date) when he found as a fact that such sale would not have taken place even if there had been no breach of trust.

"For these reasons I reach the conclusion that, on the facts which must currently **10–42** be assumed, Target has not demonstrated that it is entitled to any compensation for breach of trust. Assuming that moneys would have been forthcoming from some other source to complete the purchase from Mirage if the moneys had not been wrongly provided by Redferns in breach of trust, Target obtained exactly what it would have obtained had no breach occurred, *i.e.* a valid security for the sum advanced. Therefore, on the assumption made, Target has suffered no compensatable loss. Redferns are entitled to leave to defend the breach of trust claim.

"However, I find it very difficult to make that assumption of fact. There must be a **10–43** high probability that, at trial, it will emerge that the use of Target's money to pay for the purchase from Mirage and the other intermediate transactions was a vital feature of the transaction. The circumstances of the present case are clouded by suspicion, which suspicion is not dissipated by Mr. Bundy's untruthful letter dated 30 June informing Target that the purchase of the property and the charges to Target had been completed. If the moneys made available by Redferns' breach of trust were essential to enable the transaction to go through, but for Redferns' breach of trust Target would not have advanced any money. In that case the loss suffered by Target by reason of the breach of trust will be the total sum advanced to Crowngate less the proceeds of the security. It is not surprising that Mr Sumption Q.C. was rather muted in his submission that Redferns should have had unconditional leave to defend and that the order for payment into court of £1m. should be set aside. In my judgment such an order was fully justified.

"I would therefore allow the appeal, set aside the order of the Court of Appeal **10–44** and restore the order of Warner J."

---

[69] Lord Browne-Wilkinson's emphasis.
[70] (1878) 12 Ch.D. 738.
[71] [1993] 1 W.L.R. 1285.

II. REPARATION CLAIMS

10–45   Reparation claims are claims that trustees should make good the harm which the beneficiaries have suffered as a consequence of the trustees' breach of duty. They depend on the assertion that the trustees have committed a wrong,[72] and the award made is calculated by reference to the loss suffered by the beneficiaries,[73] including the loss of a chance to avoid a detriment or make a gain.[74] The beneficiaries must prove that their loss has been factually caused by the trustees' breach of duty, using a "but-for" causation test in all cases, regardless of whether the breach was innocent, negligent, or fraudulent.[75] Canadian authorities also indicate that their claims are subject to the principle of *novus actus interveniens*,[76] and that where the beneficiaries have become aware that their trustees are not to be trusted, losses flowing from clearly unreasonable behaviour by the beneficiaries thereafter will be judged to have been caused by this behaviour and not by the breach.[77]

10–46   A reparation claim might be brought, for example, where a trustee T fails to exhibit the requisite duty of care in negligently making an authorised investment which subsequently declines in value, or again, where T has failed to do something, *e.g.* to diversify investments,[78] or to sell particular assets,[79] or to monitor the activities of a 99 per cent owned company, as in *Bartlett v Barclays Bank Trust Co. Ltd.* In cases of the latter sort, it must be shown that the loss could not have occurred, but for T's failure to do what no reasonable trustee (*viz.* a properly informed trustee exhibiting the due standard of care) could have failed to do. Proving this can be difficult,[80] but it seems that a claim would lie where trustees take a positive decision to take specific action, *e.g.* to sell particular shares as soon as practicable, and then fail to implement their decision without any conscious reason. Another way of analysing this situation, however, would be to draw an

---

[72] *Partington v Reynolds* (1858) 4 Drew 253, 255–256; *Dowse v Gorton* [1891] A.C. 190 at 202; *Re Stevens* [1898] 1 Ch. 162 at 170.

[73] *Elder's Trustee and Executor Co. Ltd v Higgins* (1963) 113 C.L.R. 426 at 453; *Fales v Canada Permanent Trust Co.* [1977] 2 S.C.R. 302 at 320. Confusingly, claims of this kind are also often described as claims for "restitutionary", as in, *e.g. Hodgkinson v Simms* [1994] 3 S.C.R. 377 at 440; *Re Mulligan* [1998] 1 N.Z.L.R. 481 at 507; *Swindle v Harrison* [1997] 4 All E.R. 705 at 733. But this usage is best avoided, as in this context the word "restitution" simply means "compensation": *Bartlett v Barclays Bank Trust Co. Ltd (No.2)* [1980] Ch. 515 at 545, *per* Brightman L.J.

[74] *Sanders v Parry* [1967] 1 W.L.R. 753 at 767; *Nestlé v National Westminster Bank plc* [1993] 1 W.L.R. 1260 at 1269; *Colour Control Centre Pty. Ltd v Ty* N.S.W. Sup. Ct. (Eq. Div.) July 24, 1995; *Bank of New Zealand v New Zealand Guardian Trust Co. Ltd* [1999] 1 N.Z.L.R. 664 at 685–686.

[75] *Target Holdings Ltd v Redferns* [1996] A.C. 421 at 436; *Collins v Brebner* [2000] Lloyds Rep. P.N. 587; *Hulbert v Avens* [2003] EWHC 76 (Ch) at [56]; *Gwembe Valley Development Co. Ltd v Koshy (No.3)* [2004] 1 B.C.L.C. 131 at [147]. But *cf. Bairstow v Queen's Moat Houses plc* [2001] 2 B.C.L.C. 531 at [53]–[54]. On the question whether reparation claims are subject to a remoteness cap, see S. B. Elliott, "Remoteness Criteria in Equity" (2002) 65 M.L.R. 588; and also *Olszanecki v Hillocks* [2002] EWHC 1997 (Ch).

[76] *Hodgkinson v Simms* [1994] 3 S.C.R. 377 at 443, *per* La Forest J.; *Waxman v Waxman* (2004) 7 I.T.E.L.R. 162 at [663], *per curiam* (Ont. CA).

[77] *Canson Enterprises Ltd v Boughton & Co.* [1991] 3 S.C.R. 534 at 554, *per* McLachlin J., endorsed in *Corporaçion del Cobre de Chile v Sogemin Metals Ltd* [1997] 1 W.L.R. 1396 at 1403-1404. See too *Lipkin Gorman v Karpnale Ltd* [1992] 4 All E.R. 331 at 361.

[78] *Nestlé v National Westminster Bank* [1993] 1 W.L.R. 1265 at 1281; *Re Mulligan* [1998] 1 N.Z.L.R. 181.

[79] *Wight v Olswang (No.2)* [2000] W.T.L.R. 783, reversed [2001] W.T.L.R. 291; *Re Ambrazevicius Estate* (2002) 164 Man. R. (2d) 5.

[80] Consider *Nestlé v National Westminster Bank* [1993] 1 W.L.R. 1265.

analogy with the case where a trust instrument requires a particular original investment to be sold as soon as practicable. If the trustees fail to perform this duty, then a substitutive performance claim will lie against them for the amount that would have been realised if they had sold investment within a reasonable time.[81]

In *Bartlett v Barclays Bank Trust Co. Ltd (No.2)*, Brightman L.J. thought **10–47** that in cases where trustees are ordered to pay money to make good the harm caused to the beneficiaries by the trustees' negligence, the award made is "not readily distinguishable from damages except with the aid of a powerful legal microscope."[82] This comment was later echoed by Millett L.J. in *Bristol & West B.S. v Mothew*, where he held that:[83]

> "Equitable compensation for breach of the duty of skill and care [owed by a fiduciary] resembles common law damages in that it is awarded by way of compensation to the plaintiff for his loss. There is no reason in principle why the common law rules of causation, remoteness of damage and measure of damages should not be applied by analogy in such a case. It should not be confused with equitable compensation for breach of fiduciary duty, which may be awarded in lieu of rescission or specific restitution."

It is a controversial question whether trustees and other fiduciaries who **10–48** harm their principals by their negligent acts or omissions should be treated in the same way as tortfeasors at common law, or whether the fact that they are fiduciaries justifies treating them more stringently. When considering this question it is important to distinguish clearly between substitutive performance claims and reparation claims, and to bear in mind that either type of claim might lie on some sets of facts, *e.g.* where trustees make an unauthorised negligent investment. As Millet L.J. stresses in the passage quoted above, analogies with tort claims are simply inapt if a *substitutive performance* claim is brought, but we may legitimately ask whether a *reparation* claim should be governed by rules of causation, remoteness, and contributory negligence which are identical with, or more claimant-friendly than, the rules which apply to tort claims for compensatory damages.

The authorities are divided on this point. Proponents of the stringent **10–49** view emphasise that a fiduciary and his principal are not "independent and equal actors, concerned primarily with their own self-interest" but parties in a special relationship under which one "pledges itself to act in the best

---

[81] *Fry v Fry* (1859) 27 Beav. 144; *Fales v Canada Permanent Trust Co.* (1976) 70 D.L.R. (3d) 257 at 274. What if the trustees decide to appoint capital to O by executing the requisite deed before the date when the power expires, and then fail to execute the deed in time, so that the deed is void and the beneficiaries get the capital, as in *Breadner v Granville-Grossman* [2001] 1 Ch. 523? Should the trustees compensate O for his loss? Falsification of accounts would be impossible but equitable compensation should be payable as happened out of court in *Breadner*. Further, see D.J. Hayton "Unique Rules for the Unique Institution, the Trust" in S. Degeling and J. Edelman (eds) *Equity in Commercial Law* (2005).
[82] [1980] Ch. 515 at 545.
[83] [1998] Ch. 1 at 18, adopting *Permanent B.S. v Wheeler* (1994) 11 W.A.R. 187 at 237, *per* Ipp J. See too *Bank of New Zealand v New Zealand Guardian Trust Co. Ltd* [1999] 1 N.Z.L.R. 664 at 687; *Hilton v Barker Booth & Eastwood (a firm)* [2005] UKHL 8 at [29], *per* Lord Walker.

interest of the other", so that "when breach occurs, the balance favours the person wronged."[84] Proponents of the opposite view deny that there is a valid reason to treat a trustee or other fiduciary differently from anyone else who injures another person by his negligence, and that "regardless of the doctrinal underpinning, plaintiffs should not be able to recover higher damage awards merely because their claim is characterized as a breach of fiduciary duty, as opposed to breach of contract or tort."[85]

10–50　　This debate is often conducted in all-or-nothing terms, but in our view the best way forward is for the courts to acknowledge that it can be appropriate to treat different kinds of fiduciary in different ways.[86] For example, there is an important difference between traditional family trusts and modern commercial trusts for absolutely entitled beneficiaries where the parties are on a more equal footing and the management role of the trustee is extensive and complex. In the latter case at least, there is no justification for imposing the same stringent liability for negligent conduct as for unauthorised conduct.

BARTLETT v BARCLAYS BANK TRUST CO. LTD

Chancery Division [1980] Ch. 515; [1980] 1 All E.R. 139

10–51　The claimant sued the trustees for failing to exercise proper supervision over the management of the family company, "BTL", which they controlled through possession of a 99.8 per cent shareholding. Subsequently BTL became a wholly-owned subsidiary of another company, "BTH", which the trustees also controlled through a 99.8 per cent shareholding. The trustees' failure to supervise BTL and then BTH led to the company losing over £1/2 million in a disastrous property speculation.

10–52　　BRIGHTMAN J.: "The situation may be summed up as follows. BTH made a large loss as a result of the involvement of itself and BTL in the Old Bailey project. This loss reduced the value of the BTH shares and thereby caused a loss to the trust fund of the 1920 settlement. The bank, had it acted in time, could be reason of its shareholding have stopped the board of BTL embarking on the Old Bailey project;

---

[84] *Canson Enterprises Ltd v Boughton & Co.* [1991] 3 S.C.R. 534 at 543, *per* McLachlin J., quoted with approval in *Youyang Pty. Ltd v Minter Ellison Morris Fletcher* (2003) 212 C.L.R. 484 at [40]. See too *Norberg v Wynrib* [1992] 2 S.C.R. 226 at 272, *per* McLachlin J., quoted with approval in *Pilmer v Duke Group Ltd (in liq.)* (2001) 207 C.L.R. 165 at [71]; *Maguire v Makaronis* (1997) 188 C.L.R. 449 at 473. The argument that equity should exert prophylactic pressure on fiduciaries by stringent treatment of their breaches of skill and care as well as their breaches of fiduciary duty has been made by Joshua Getzler in three articles: "Equitable Compensation and the Regulation of Fiduciary Relationships" in P. Birks and F. D. Rose (eds.) *Restitution and Equity: Resulting Trusts and Equitable Compensation* (2000) 235; "Duty of Care" in P. Birks and A. Pretto (eds.), *Breach of Trust* (2002) 41; "Am I My Beneficiary's Keeper? Fusion and Loss-Based Fiduciary Remedies" in S. Degeling and J. Edelman (eds.), *Equity in Commercial Law* (2005).

[85] *Martin v Goldfarb* (1998) 41 O.R. (3d) 161 at 173, *per* Finlayson J.A. See too *Day v Mead* [1987] 2 N.Z.L.R. 443 at 451, *per* Cooke P; *Canson Enterprises Ltd v Boughton & Co.* [1991] 3 S.C.R. 534 at 585–589, *per* La Forest J.; *Waxman v Waxman* (2004) 7 I.T.E.L.R. 162 at [660]-[662]; J. Edelman and S. B. Elliott, "Money Remedies against Trustees" (2004) 18 Tru L.I. 116, 119–122; A.S. Burrows, *Remedies for Torts and Breach of Contract* 3rd ed. (2004), 600–606.

[86] See further C. E. F. Rickett, "Compensating for Loss in Equity: Choosing the Right Horse for Each Course" in P. Birks and F. D. Rose (eds), *Restitution and Equity, vol. 1* (2000) 178; D. J. Hayton "Unique Rules for the Unique Institution, the Trust" in S. Degeling and J. Edelman (eds.), *Equity in Commercial Law* (2005).

and, had it acted in time, could have stopped the board of BTL and later the board of BTH (it is unnecessary to differentiate) from continuing with the project; and could, had it acted in time, have required BTH to sell its interest in Far to Stock Conversion on the no-loss or small-loss terms which (as I find) were available for the asking. This would not have necessitated the draconian course of threatening to remove, or actually removing, the board in favour of compliant directors. The members of the board were reasonable persons, and would (as I find) have followed any reasonable policy desired by the bank had the bank's wishes been indicated to the board. The loss to the trust fund could have been avoided (as I find) without difficulty or disruption had the bank been prepared to lead, in a broad sense, rather than to follow.

"What, then, was the duty of the bank and did the bank fail in its duty? It does **10–53** not follow that because a trustee could have prevented a loss it is therefore liable for the loss. The questions which I must ask myself are: (i) what was the duty of the bank as the holder of 99.8% of the shares in BTL and BTH? (2) was the bank in breach of duty in any and if so what respect? (3) if so, did that breach of duty cause the loss which was suffered by the trust estate? (4) if so, to what extent is the bank liable to make good that loss? In approaching these questions, I bear in mind that the attack on the bank is based, not on wrongful acts, but on wrongful omissions, that is to say, non-feasance not misfeasance.

"The cases establish that it is the duty of a trustee to conduct the business of the **10–54** trust with the same care as an ordinary prudent man of business would extend towards his own affairs: see *Re Speight*[87] *per* Jesse M.R. and Bowen L.J. (affirmed on appeal[88] and see Lord Blackburn[89]). In applying this principle, Lindley L.J. added in *Re Whitely*[90]:

'. . . care must be taken not to lose sight of the fact that the business of the trustee, and the business which the ordinary prudent man is supposed to be conducting for himself, is the business of investing money for the benefit of persons who are to enjoy it at some future time, and not for the sole benefit of the person entitled to the present income. The duty of a trustee is not to take such care only as a prudent man would take if he had only himself to consider; the duty rather is to take such care as an ordinary prudent man would take if he were minded to make an investment for the benefit of other people for whom he felt morally bound to provide. The is the kind of business the ordinary prudent man is supposed to be engaged in; and unless this is borne in mind the standard of a trustee's duty will be fixed too low; lower than it has ever yet been fixed, and lower certainly than the House of Lords or this Court endeavoured to fix it in [*Re Speight*].'

". . . If the trust had existed without the incorporation of BTL, so that the **10–55** bank held the freehold and leasehold properties and other assets of BTL directly on the trusts of the settlement, it would in my opinion have been a clear breach of trust for the bank to have hazarded trust money in the Old Bailey development project in partnership with Stock Conversion. The Old Bailey project was a gamble, because it involved buying into the site at prices in excess of the investment values of the properties, with no certainty or

---

[87] (1883) 22 Ch.D. 727 at 739, 762.
[88] (1883) 9 App. Cas. 1.
[89] *ibid.* at 19.
[90] (1886) 33 Ch.D. 347 at 355.

probability, with no more than a chance, that planning permission could be obtained for a financially viable redevelopment, that the numerous proprietors would agree to sell out or join in the scheme, that finance would be available on acceptable terms, and that the development would be completed, or at least become a marketable asset, before the time came to start winding up the trust. However one looks at it, the project was a hazardous speculation on which no trustee could properly have ventured without explicit authority in the trust instrument. I therefore hold that the entire expenditure in the Old Bailey project would have been incurred in breach of trust, had the money been spent by the bank itself. The fact that it was a risk acceptable to the board of a wealthy company like Stock Conversion has little relevance.

10–56   "I turn to the question, what was the duty of the bank as the holder of shares in BTL and BTH? I will first answer this question without regard to the position of the bank as a specialist trustee, to which I will advert later. The bank, as trustee, was bound to act in relation to the shares and to the controlling position which they conferred, in the same manner as a prudent man of business. The prudent man of business will act in such manner as is necessary to safeguard his investment. He will do this in two ways. If facts come to his knowledge which tell him that the company's affairs are not being conducted as they should be, or which put him on enquiry, he will take appropriate action. Appropriate action will no doubt consist in the first instance of enquiry of and consultation with the directors, and in the last but most unlikely resort, the convening of a general meeting to replace one or more directors. What the prudent man of business will not do is to content himself with the receipt of such information on the affairs of the company as a shareholder ordinarily receives at annual general meetings. Since he has the power to do so, he will go further and see that he has sufficient information to enable him to make a responsible decision from time to time either to let matters proceed as they are proceeding, or to intervene if he is dissatisfied. This topic was considered by Cross J. in *Re Lucking's Will Trusts*.[91] In that case nearly 70 per cent of the shares in the company were held by two trustees, L and B, as part of the estate of the deceased; about 29 per cent belonged to L in his own right, and 1 per cent belonged to L's wife. The directors in 1954 were Mr. and Mrs. L and D, who was the manager of the business. In 1956 B was appointed trustee to act jointly with L. The company was engaged in the manufacture and sale of shoe accessories. It had a small factory employing about 20 people, and one or two travellers. It also had an agency in France. D wrongfully drew some £15,000 from the company's bank account in excess of his remuneration, and later became bankrupt. The money was lost. Cross J. said this[92]:

10–57   'The conduct of the defendant trustees is, I think, to be judged by the standard applied in *Re Speight*, namely, that a trustee is only bound to conduct the business of the trust in such a way as an ordinary prudent man would conduct a business of his own. Now, what steps, if any, does a reasonably prudent man who finds himself a majority shareholder in a private company take with regard to the management of the company's affairs? He does not, I think, content himself with such information as to the management of the company's affairs as he is entitled to as shareholder, but ensures that he is represented on the board.

[91] [1968] 1 W.L.R. 866.
[92] *ibid.* at 874–875.

He may be prepared to run the business himself as managing director or, at least, to become a non-executive director while having the business managed by someone else. Alternatively, he may find someone who will act as his nominee on the board and report to him from time to time as to the company's affairs. In the same way, as it seems to me, trustees holding a controlling interest ought to ensure so far as they can that they have such information as to the progress of the company's affairs as directors would have. If they sit back and allow the company to be run by the minority shareholder and receive no more information than shareholders are entitled to, they do so at their risk if things go wrong.'

"I do not understand Cross J. to have been saying that in every case where **10–58** trustees have a controlling interest in a company it is their duty to ensure that one of their number is a director or that they have a nominee on the board who will report from time to time on the affairs of the company. He was merely outlining convenient methods by which a prudent man of business (as also a trustee) with a controlling interest in a private company, can place himself in a position to make an informed decision whether any action is appropriate to be taken for the protection of his asset. Other methods may be equally satisfactory and convenient, depending on the circumstances of the individual case. Alternatives which spring to mind are the receipt of the copies of the agenda and minutes of board meetings if regularly held, the receipt of monthly management accounts in the case of a trading concern, or quarterly reports. Every case will depend on its own facts. The possibilities are endless. It would be useless, indeed misleading, to seek to lay down a general rule. The purpose to be achieved is not that of monitoring every move of the directors, but of making it reasonably probable, so far as circumstances permit, that the trustee or (as in *Re Lucking's Will Trusts*) one of them will receive an adequate flow of information in time to enable the trustees to make use of their controlling interest should this be necessary for the protection of their trust asset, namely the shareholding. The obtaining of information is not an end in itself, but merely a means of enabling the trustees to safeguard the interest of their beneficiaries.

"... So far, I have applied the test of the ordinary prudent man of business. **10–59** Although I am not aware that the point has previously been considered, except briefly in *Re Waterman's Will Trusts*,[93] I am of opinion that a higher duty of care is plainly due from someone like a trust corporation which carries on a specialised business of trust management. A trust corporation holds itself out in its advertising literature as being above ordinary mortals. With a specialist staff of trained trust officers and managers, with ready access to financial information and professional advice, dealing with and solving trust problems day after day, the trust corporation holds itself out, and rightly, as capable of providing an expertise which it would be unrealistic to expect and unjust to demand from the ordinary prudent man or woman who accepts, probably unpaid and sometimes reluctantly from a sense of family duty, the burdens of a trusteeship. Just as, under the law of contract, a professional person possessed of a particular skill is liable for breach of contract if he neglects to use the skill and experience which he professes, so I think that a professional corporate trustee is liable for breach of trust if loss is caused to the trust fund because it neglects to exercise the special care and skill which it professes to have. The advertising literature of the bank was not in evidence (other than the scale of fees) but counsel for the bank did not dispute that trust corporations,

---

[93] [1968] 1 W.L.R. 866.

including the bank, hold themselves out as possessing a superior ability for the conduct of trust business, and in any event I would take judicial notice of that fact. Having expressed my view of the higher duty required from a trust corporation, I should add that the bank's counsel did not dispute the proposition.

10–60   "In my judgment the bank wrongfully and in breach of trust neglected to ensure that it received an adequate flow of information concerning the intentions and activities of the boards of BTL and BTH. It was not proper for the bank to confine itself to the receipt of the annual balance sheet and profit and loss account, detailed annual financial statements and the chairman's report and statement, and to attendance at the annual general meetings and the luncheons that followed, which were the limits of the bank's regular sources of information. Had the bank been in receipt of more frequent information it would have been able to step in and stop, and ought to have stopped, Mr Roberts and the board embarking on the Old Bailey project. That project was imprudent and hazardous and wholly unsuitable for a trust whether undertaken by the bank direct or through the medium of its wholly owned company. Even without the regular flow of information which the bank ought to have had, it knew enough to put it on enquiry. There were enough obvious points at which the bank should have intervened and asked questions. Assuming, as I do, that the questions would have been answered truthfully, the bank would have discovered the gamble on which Mr Roberts and his board were about to embark in relation to the Old Bailey site, and it could have, and should have, stopped the initial move towards disaster, and later on arrested further progress towards disaster . . .

10–61   "I hold that the bank failed in its duty whether it is judged by the standard of the prudent man of business or of the skilled trust corporation. The bank's breach of duty caused the loss which was suffered by the trust estate. If the bank had intervened as it could and should have, that loss would not have been incurred. By 'loss', I mean the depreciation which took place in the market value of the BTL and BTH shares, by comparison with the value which the shares would have commanded if the loss on the Old Bailey project had not been incurred, and reduction of dividends through loss of income. The bank is liable for the loss so suffered by the trust estate, except to the extent that I shall hereafter indicate . . .

10–62   "The bank also relies on clause 18 of the settlement. Clause 18 entitled the bank to:

> 'act in relation to [BTL] or any other company and the shares securities and properties thereof in such way as it shall think best calculated to benefit the trust premises and as if it was the absolute owner of such shares securities and property.'

In my judgment this a clause which confers on the bank power to engage in a transaction which might otherwise be outside the scope of its authority; it is not an indemnity protecting the bank against liability for a transaction which is a breach of trust because it is one that a prudent man of business would have eschewed . . .

10–63   "Section 61 of the Trustee Act 1925 is pleaded. There is no doubt that the bank acted honestly. I do not think it acted reasonably. Nor do I think it would be fair to excuse the bank at the expense of the beneficiaries.

10–64   "There remains this defence, which I take from paragraph 26 of the amended pleading:

> 'In about 1963 the Old Company purchased a site at Woodbridge Road, Guildford, pursuant to the policy pleaded in paragraph 19 hereof, for the sum of £79,000, and re-sold the same for £350,000 to MEPC Ltd. in 1973. The net

profit resulting from such sale was £271,000. If, which is denied, the Defendant is liable for breach of trust, whether as alleged in the amended Statement of Claim or otherwise, the Defendant claims credit for such sum of £271,000 or other sum found to be gained in taking any accounts or inquiries.'

"The general rule as stated in all the textbooks, with some reservations, is that **10–65** where a trustee is liable in respect of distinct breaches of trust, one of which has resulted in a loss and the other in a gain, he is not entitled to set off the gain against the loss, unless they arise in the same transaction . . . The relevant cases are, however, not altogether easy to reconcile. All are centenarians and none is quite like the present. The Guildford development stemmed from exactly the same policy and (to a lesser degree because it proceeded less for) exemplified the same folly as the Old Bailey project. Part of the profit was in fact used to finance the Old Bailey disaster. By sheer luck the gamble paid off handsomely, on capital account. I think it would be unjust to deprive the bank of this element of salvage in the course of assessing the cost of the shipwreck. My order will therefore reflect the bank's right to an appropriate set-off . . ."

III. Accountability

Before the Judicature Acts, beneficiaries could only make hostile claims **10–66** against their trustees by bringing an administration suit. This was a suit for the judicial execution of the trust, asking the court to assume responsibility for the trust's performance. Beneficiaries can still bring full execution proceedings, but they can now also bring narrower proceedings for discrete relief by asking the court for an order that the trustees should present an account of their dealings for judicial scrutiny, adding the common form plea for administration of the trust estate "if and so far as necessary".[94]

As explained in *Glazier v Australian Men's Health (No.2)*,[95] there are **10–67** three types of accounting order which a court might make. An order for an *account in common form* is the most common, as the name suggests. The trustees are directed to submit a set of accounts which identify the original trust property, what the trustees have received, what they have disbursed for costs and expenses,[96] what they have distributed to the beneficiaries, and what they have left in hand. These accounts can then be challenged by the beneficiaries, but the fact that a court has ordered trustees to present accounts in this form need not imply that they have done anything wrong, as orders for common accounts can be made simply in order to clarify matters.[97] In contrast, an order for an *account on the basis of wilful default* is entirely grounded on the trustees' misconduct,[98] and requires them to

---

[94] *Iliffe v Trafford* [2001] EWHC 469 (Ch) at [8].
[95] [2001] NSWSC 6. Austin J.'s decision was overturned on appeal, but nothing was said by the N.S.W.C.A. that contradicted his structural analysis of accounting in equity: *Meehan v Glazier Holdings Pty. Ltd* (2002) 54 N.S.W.L.R. 146.
[96] Note the Trustee Act 2000, s.31, discussed at paras 9–336 *et seq.*, above, which empowers trustees to take properly incurred expenses out of the trust funds. For discussion of the question whether trustees can recover an indemnity for expenses incurred in the course of unauthorised conduct, see *Fitzwood Pty. Ltd v Unique Goal Pty. Ltd (in liq.)* (2001) 188 A.L.R. 566.
[97] *Partington v Reynolds* (1858) 4 Drew 253 at 256.
[98] *ibid.*

account not only for what they have received but also for what they would have received if they had not committed a breach of duty.[99] The term "wilful default" is a misleading one in this context since it encompasses all breaches of duty, running from inadvertent non-compliance with the terms of the trust through to deliberate fraud.[1] Finally, an order for an *account of profits* requires the trustees to account for specific gains.

10–68   An account of profits will be ordered in connection with a claim that the trustees should be required to hand over improper gains, and an account on the basis of wilful default will be ordered in connection with a reparation claim. An account in common form can be ordered where the beneficiaries make a claim for substitutive performance; however, it can also be used where they seek to recover compensation for loss. In all cases, the onus lies on the trustees to prove and justify their records, and evidential presumptions are made against them if they fail to do so.[2] In the event that a court decides, following its scrutiny of the trustees' accounts, that they owe the beneficiaries a personal liability of some kind, then different forms of order can be made against them, according to the nature of the trust. Where the trust is absolute and there is no need to reconstitute the fund, the court can simply order them to transfer trust assets or pay money directly to the beneficiaries.[3] Where the trust is still on foot, the trustees will be ordered to reconstitute the fund in a proper state, or where they have been replaced by new trustees, to transfer assets or pay money to the new trustees, to be held by them under the terms of the trust.[4]

10–69   The various types of claim which can be brought against trustees are mediated through proceedings for an account in different ways. In the case of a substitutive performance claim where the trustees have made an unauthorised distribution, the court will not permit the trustees to enter the distribution into the accounts as an outgoing as it will not allow them to say that they acted in breach of duty.[5] Instead, they will be treated as though they have spent their own money and kept the trust assets in hand. The accounts will be "falsified" to delete the unauthorised outgoing, and the trustees will be required to produce the relevant trust property *in specie* or pay a money substitute out of their own pockets.[6]

10–70   Reparation claims are brought into the conceptual scheme of the accounts in a different way. The loss claimed by the beneficiaries is translated into an accounting item by "surcharging" the trustees with the

---

[99] *Re Tebbs* [1976] 1 W.L.R. 924; *Bartlett v Barclays Bank Co. Ltd* [1980] Ch. 15; *Coulthard v Disco Mix Club Ltd* [1999] 2 All E.R. 457 at 481; *Armitage v Nurse* [1998] Ch. 241 at 252; *Iliffe v Trafford* [2001] EWHC 469 (Ch) at [9]; *Garcia v Delfino* [2003] NSWSC 1001 at [31]–[33].

[1] *Walker v Symonds* (1818) 3 Swans 1 at 69; *Re Chapman* [1896] 2 Ch. 763 at 776 and 779–780. See too J.H. Stannard "Wilful Default" [1979] Conv. 345, esp. 348.

[2] *Maintemp Heating & Air Conditioning Inc. v Monat Developments Inc.* (2002) 59 O.R. (3d) 270, esp. at [40]–[44]; *Wong v Wong* [2002] BCSC 779 at [25].

[3] *Target Holdings Ltd v Redferns* [1996] A.C. 421 at 435; *Roxborough v Rothmans of Pall Mall Australia Ltd* (2002) 185 A.L.R. 335 at 353.

[4] *Partridge v Equity Trustees Executors and Agency Co. Ltd* (1947) 75 C.L.R. 149; *Hillsdown plc v Pensions Ombudsman* [1997] 1 All E.R. 862 at 897; *Chellaram v Chellaram (No.2)* [2002] 3 All E.R. 17 at [159]; *Patel v London Borough of Brent* [2003] EWHC 3081 (Ch) esp. at [32].

[5] *Re Smith* [1896] 1 Ch. 71 at 77; *Re Biss (deceased)* [1903] 2 Ch. 40.

[6] *Knott v Cottee* (1852) 16 Beav. 77 at 79–80; *Re Bennion* (1889) 60 L.T. 859; *Re Salmon* (1889) 42 Ch.D. 351 at 357.

amount of the loss as if the trustees had already received this amount for the beneficiaries. They must then pay an equivalent amount into the trust funds out of their pockets in order to balance the accounts.[7] Essentially the same procedure is followed in the case of a claim for unauthorised profits: the trustees are treated as though they had received this sum for the benefit of the beneficiaries, and the accounts are surcharged accordingly. As a sanction to underpin and emphasise the trustee's duty of loyalty in cases where trustees have improperly received particular assets, *e.g.* shares, in breach of duty, they will be liable to account to the beneficiaries for the highest market value of the assets between the date of breach and the date of judgment. The justification for this rule is that the trustees owe a continuing duty throughout this period to realise the assets for the beneficiaries at the most opportune moment.[8] Where trustees divert business contracts to themselves in breach of fiduciary duty, they must account for all the profits which are properly attributable to the breach, but need not account for profits which they make through their legitimate business activities.[9]

GLAZIER v AUSTRALIAN MEN'S HEALTH (NO.2)

[2000] NSWSC 6, New South Wales Supreme Court; decision reversed in *Meehan v Glazier Holdings Pty. Ltd* (2002) 54 N.S.W.L.R. 146, without casting doubt on the following summary of legal principles.

Austin J.:

Accounting for administration in common form or for wilful default, and accounting for profit or replenishing loss

"In equity an order for the taking of accounts may be made in a wide variety of **10–71** circumstances. In the present context it is important to distinguish between two kinds of orders. One kind (which I shall call an order for an account of administration) is made where the overall administration of a business enterprise or fund or other property is to be established or accounted for. Another kind (which I shall call an order for an account of profits) is made to provide a remedy for specific equitable wrongdoing.

Order for account of administration

"An order for an account of administration is made for the taking of accounts of **10–72** money received and disbursed by the person who is responsible for the administration of a business enterprise or fund or other property, and for payment of any amount found to be due by that person upon the taking of the accounts. For

---

[7] *Meehan v Glazier Holdings Pty. Ltd* (2002) 54 N.S.W.L.R. 146 at 149–150; *Re Ambrazevicius Estate* (2002) 164 Man. R. (2d) 5; *Man Fong Hang v Man Ping Nam* [2003] 1383 HKCU 1.

[8] *Nant-y-glo and Blaina Ironworks Co. v Grave* (1878) 12 Ch.D. 738, accepted in *Target Holdings Ltd v Redferns* [1996] A.C. 421 at 440; *Re Caerphilly Colliery Co.* (1877) L.R. 5 Ch.D. 336 at 341, endorsed in *Att.-Gen. for Hong Kong v Reid* [1994] 1 A.C. 324 at 335.

[9] *C.M.S. Dolphin Ltd v Simonet* [2001] 2 B.C.L.C. 704 at [97]. The timing of the account is helpfully discussed in *Crown Dilmun v Sutton* [2004] 1 B.C.L.C. 468 at [205]–[214].

example, the court routinely orders the taking of accounts of the administration of an estate by an executor, or upon the dissolution of a partnership, or of the administration of property by a mortgagee in possession, or of a trust fund such as a solicitor's trust account. In such a case the making of the order need not imply any wrongdoing by the defendant.

Order for an account of administration in common form

10–73 "The usual form of order, referred to as an order in common form or for common accounts, requires the defendant to account only for what he or she has actually received, and his or her disbursement and distribution of it. The defendant prepares accounts and it is open to the other parties to surcharge or falsify items in those accounts. A surcharge is the showing of an omission for which credit ought to have been given, while a falsification is the showing of a charge which has been wrongly inserted, the falsifying party alleging that money shown in the account as paid was either not paid or improperly paid[10] . . .

Order for an account of administration on basis of wilful default

10–74 "Sometimes the court orders that accounts be taken on the basis of wilful default (or in the earlier cases, wilful neglect or default). The order is 'entirely grounded on misconduct', the defendant being required to account not only for what he or she has received, but also for what he or she might have received had it not been for the default.[11] To obtain an order for the taking of accounts in common form against an executor, for example, the plaintiff need only show that the defendant is the executor, and need not show anything about the defendant's dealings with the estate; whereas to obtain an order on the basis of wilful default the plaintiff must allege and prove 'that there is some part of the deceased's personal estate which ought to have been and might have been received by the defendant, and which he has omitted to receive by his own wilful neglect or default'.[12]

10–75 "It appears that in the present context, the concept of 'wilful default' is confined to cases where there has been 'a loss of assets received, or assets which might have been received'.[13] In that case the failure of executors to cause the proceeds of an insurance policy to be paid to the policy's mortgagee for nearly seven years, during which time interest accrued to the mortgagee, was held not to amount to wilful default for the purposes of an application for an accounting on that basis. However, the concept is evidently not confined to cases of conscious wrongdoing.[14] Obviously the concept here is not necessarily the same as the concept of 'wilful default' used in other parts of the law.[15]

10–76 "As will be seen the court may make an order that general accounts be taken on the footing of wilful default if at least one instance of wilful default has been proved. However the court has a discretion whether to make such an order. The test is this: 'is the past conduct of the trustees such as to give rise to a reasonable *prima facie* inference that other breaches of trust not yet known to the plaintiff or the court have occurred?'[16]

---

[10] G. P. Stuckey and C. D. Parker (eds.) *Parker's Practice in Equity (New South Wales)* 2nd ed. (1949), p.269.
[11] *Partington v Reynolds* (1858) 4 Drew 253 at 255–6.
[12] *ibid.* at 256.
[13] *Re Stevens* [1898] 1 Ch. 162 at 171.
[14] *Bartlett v Barclays Trust Co. Ltd* [1980] 1 Ch. 515 at 546.
[15] See, *e.g. Wilkinson v Feldworth Financial Services Pty. Ltd* (1998) 29 A.C.S.R. 642 at 696–700.
[16] *Re Tebbs* [1976] 1 All E.R. 858 at 863; see also *Russell v Russell* (1891) 17 V.L.R. 729.

"An order for accounts based on wilful default has the effect of casting a much **10–77** more substantial burden of proof on the accounting party than applies in the case of common accounts. On a falsification, the onus is on the accounting party to justify the account, unless the account is a settled account . . .[17] An accounting on the footing of wilful default leads to an order requiring the defendant to replenish funds wrongfully depleted by him or her and in that sense to make restitution for the benefit of the plaintiff.

Order for account of profits for specific equitable wrongdoing

"An order for an account of profits is made where specific wrongdoing such as **10–78** breach of trust or fiduciary duty has been found or is suspected. It is usually ancillary to the grant of an injunction.[18] An order for an account of profits typically requires the wrongdoer to account to the plaintiff for profits made in consequence of the wrongdoing, although the court has a discretion to fashion the order to suit the circumstances of the case, and (for example) will not order the defendant to account for the entire profits of a business established in breach of fiduciary duty, where it would be inequitable to do so.[19] The accounting relates to specified gains rather than the general administration of a fund. Since the order is premised upon a finding of specific wrongdoing, the distinction between an order in common form and an order on the basis of wilful default is irrelevant.

Comparison of order for account of profits with orders for account of administration in common form and on basis of wilful default

"The contrast between an order for an account of profits and an order for an **10–79** account of administration in common form is obvious. The former provides a remedy for specific wrongdoing, while the latter 'supposes no misconduct'.[20] The difference between an order for an account of profits and an order for an account of administration on the basis of wilful default is much less sharp. This is especially so when one bears in mind that an order on the footing of wilful default can be limited to an account of part only of the administration, and even to that part of the administration in respect of which wilful default has been proved (as in *Re Tebbs*). Confusion has arisen because in both cases, it is necessary to establish at least one instance of wrongdoing, and yet in one case the order is directed only to the specific wrongdoing that has been proved, while in the other case proof of an instance of wrongdoing leads to a process which 'assumes the probability that other improper transactions may have occurred'[21] throughout the administration or some specified part of it.

"There is another source of confusion between cases where it is appropriate to **10–80** order the taking of accounts on the basis of wilful default, and cases where relief is sought because of a specific breach of trust or duty. In action for breach of trust or duty, an order for an account of profits is one of the many equitable remedies available if the plaintiff makes out an appropriate case. Another remedy is an order that the defendant replenish the fund that he or she has wrongfully depleted (in an

---

[17] *Parker*, p 269; *Daniell's Practice of the High Court of Chancery* (5th edn., 1871), 1120ff. and 575ff.; *Seton's Forms of Judgment and Orders* (6th edn., 1901), Vol II, 1356ff. and 1382ff.; and note the forms of falsification and surcharge in *Miller and Horsell's Equity Forms and Precedents* (1934), 195–196; and as to settled accounts, see *Pit v Cholmondeley* (1754) 2 Ves. 565.
[18] *Colbeam Palmer Ltd v Stock Affiliates Pty. Ltd* (1968) 122 C.L.R. 25 at 34.
[19] *Warman International Ltd v Dwyer* (1995) 182 C.L.R. 544.
[20] *Partington v Reynolds* at 256.
[21] *Re Tebbs* at 864.

administration action, this may take the form of an order charging the executor with the asset). Confusion can arise because an order of that kind is similar in effect to, though more specific than, an order for the taking of accounts on the basis of wilful default, since the latter order includes a provision requiring that the defendant replenish the fund by the amount certified to be due when accounts have been taken.

Active and passive misconduct

10–81 "In a case where an account of administration on the basis of wilful default is appropriate, emphasis is placed on whether the defendant has failed to discharge his or her duty, rather than whether the plaintiff has established active conduct in breach of duty. This could lead one to infer that the difference between accounting on the basis of wilful default and accounting for profit is that in the first case the wrongdoing is passive whereas in the second case there is active wrongdoing. In my view that would be an oversimplification.

10–82 [His Lordship then considered *Re Wrightson*,[22] *Bartlett v Barclays Bank Trust Co. (No.2)*,[23] and *Gava v Grljusich*,[24] and continued:] "In my view the distinction drawn in these cases is not the mere distinction between active and passive conduct. The circumstances that give rise to a breach of trust will commonly involve active and passive elements. For example, in *Re Tebbs* the wrongdoing was active conduct, involving the sale of land at an undervalue, but it was regarded as wilful default by Slade J. and his characterisation of it was accepted by Kennedy J. in *Gava v Grljusich*.[25] In *Bartlett v Barclays Trust Co. Ltd.* the wrongdoing was found to be wilful default, although it involved the 'active' conduct of allowing directors to occupy residential premises at an undervalue as well as the 'passive' default of not intervening to prevent the unauthorised investment. In *Re Symons*,[26] the plaintiffs' complaints related to conduct with active and passive elements but the case was treated as one of wilful default. Similarly, in the present case there is evidence that the trustee failed to keep proper accounting records. That involved omission to make accurate and complete entries recording the receipt and disbursement of trust money (passive breaches), and preparation and maintenance of accounting records that were not in proper form for a trust (active conduct). More importantly, it is hard to see why in principle there should be such a dramatic difference in consequences between cases where the breach is active and cases where it is passive. The true distinction identified by the quoted passages is the distinction between an order for administration, made in cases where the defendant is required to administer a fund for the benefit of others over time, and fails to do so properly (and is therefore guilty of 'passive' breaches by not doing what he or she ought to have done), and an order for an account of profits or replenishment of a fund, made in cases where the complaint is about specific instances of wrongdoing ('active' breaches, although they may be as much non-feasance as misfeasance) . . ."

IV. EXAMPLES

Making unauthorised investments and negligently investing

10–83 Where trustees make an unauthorised investment they are liable for the amount of the money improperly invested, but they are entitled to claim a credit for the sale proceeds of the property when it is sold, as held in *Knott*

---

[22] [1908] 1 Ch. 789.
[23] [1980] Ch. 539.
[24] [1999] W.A.S.C. 13.
[25] *ibid.* at [31].
[26] (1882) 21 Ch.D. 757.

v Cottee, para.10–85. However, "what the prudent man should do at any time depends on the economic and financial conditions of that time—not on what judges of the past, however eminent, have held to be the prudent course in the conditions if 50 or 100 years before" as Dillon L.J. has indicated.[27] Thus, he and his brethren further indicated[28] that if a negligent investment policy (one that no prudent trustee could have pursued) causes loss, the trustee can be required to make good to the trust fair compensation for the capital growth there would have been if a proper investment policy had been followed *i.e.* compensation for loss of profit taking account, it seems, of the average performance of authorised investments during the period. It would seem to follow that if trustees invest in unauthorised investments (as contrasted with negligent investment in authorised investments) they could be similarly accountable for the profit that would have been made if they had properly invested in authorised investments.

In *Re Mulligan*[29] in order to favour the life tenant the trustees did not **10–84** diversify by investing in equities. It was held that they should have diversified in 1972 to the extent of 40 per cent of the capital and such 40 per cent holdings in equities would have appreciated at 75 per cent of an appropriate index of equities. The 25 per cent discount took account of dealing costs and the fact that the fund was not large enough for the trustees to be expected to rival the index. Nowadays investment can be in "tracker funds" which track and reflect the index, so obviating the need for such a discount.

KNOTT V COTTEE

Master of the Rolls (1852) 16 Beav. 77; 16 Jur.(o.s.) 752

A testator who died in January 1844 directed his executor-trustees to invest in **10–85** "the public or Government stocks or funds of Great Britain, or upon real security in England and Wales." In 1845 and 1846, the defendant executor-trustee invested part of the estate in Exchequer bills, which in 1846 were ordered into court, and in the same year sold at a loss. By a decree made in 1848, the court declared that the investment in Exchequer bills was improper. If, however, the investment had been retained, its realisation at the time of the decree of 1848 would have resulted in a profit.

Held, "that the executor ought to be charged with the *amount improperly invested*, and credited with the produce of the Exchequer bills in 1846."

Romilly M.R.: "Here is an executor who had a direct and positive trust to **10–86** perform, which was, to invest the money upon government stocks or funds, or upon real securities, and accumulate at compound interest all the balances after maintaining the children. He has made certain investments, which the court has declared to be improper. The case must either be treated as if these investments had not been made, or had been made for his own benefit out of his own moneys, and that he had

---

[27] *Nestlé v National Westminster Bank plc* [1994] 1 All E.R. 118 at 126.
[28] *ibid.* at 126–127 (criticising *Robinson v Robinson* (1851) 1 De. G.M. & G. 247).
[29] [1998] 1 N.Z.L.R. 481.

at the same time retained moneys of the testator in his hands. I think, therefore, that there must be a reference back, to ascertain what balances the executor retained from time to time, it being clear that he has retained some balances . . .

10–87   "As to the mode of charging the executor in respect of the Exchequer bills, I treat the laying out in Exchequer bills in this way: The persons interested were entitled to earmark them, as being bought with the testator's assets, in the same manner as if the executor had bought a house with the trust funds; and though they do not recognise the investment, they had a right to make it available for what was due; and though part of the property of the executor, it was specifically applicable to the payment. When the Exchequer bills were sold and produced £3,955, the court must consider the produce as a sum of money refunded by the executor to the testator's estate on that day; and on taking the account, the master must give credit for this amount as on the day on which the Exchequer bills were sold . . ."

10–88   If a trustee makes an unauthorised investment, the beneficiaries may, if they choose, and if they are all *sui juris*, adopt the investment as part of the trust.[30] The difficulty is as to the *extent* of their remedy. If they decide to adopt the investment, but it has caused a loss to the estate, can they also require the trustee to replace that loss? According to *Re Lake*,[31] they apparently can. But Wood V.-C. in *Thornton v Stokill*[32] seems to have held that if they adopt the investment, it settles the matter. To play safe the beneficiaries should refuse to authorise or adopt the investment but accept the investment *in specie* as part satisfaction of the trustees' personal liability to perform the trust substitutively by making a money payment.

10–89   Where the unauthorised investment has not been or cannot be adopted (*e.g.* where the beneficiaries are not each *sui juris*) the beneficiaries have a lien over it until the trust fund loss is made up, whether by the trustees using their own resources to replace the loss so that they can take over the investment themselves, or by the sale of the investment with the balance to make up the loss coming from the trustees' own resources. Of course, if the investment is of an *authorised* nature, the beneficiaries have no option of adopting or rejecting it, for it is necessarily part of the trust.[33]

Improper Retention of Unauthorised Investments[34]

10–90   Where trustees retain an unauthorised investment they are liable for the difference between the price obtainable on sale at the proper time and the proceeds of sale of the unauthorised investment when eventually sold.

FRY V FRY

Master of the Rolls (1859) 27 Beav. 144; 28 L.J.Ch. 591; 34 L.T.(o.s.) 51; 5 Jur. 1047

10–91   A testator who died in March 1834, after devising his residuary real estate to two trustees on trust to pay the rents (except those of the Langford Inn) to his wife during her widowhood, with remainder over, and bequeathing his residuary personal

---

[30] *Re Patten* (1883) 52 L.J. Ch. 787; *Re Jenkins* [1903] 2 Ch. 362; *Wright v Morgan* [1926] A.C. 788 at 799.
[31] [1903] 1 K.B. 439; and see *Ex p. Biddulph* (1849) 3 De. G. & Sm. 587.
[32] (1855) 1 Jur. 751. See also *Re Cape Breton* (1885) 29 Ch.D. 795.
[33] *Re Salmon* (1889) 42 Ch.D. 351.
[34] The assumption being that the investment has depreciated; otherwise any gain belongs of course to the trust. See Arden M.R. in *Piety v Stace* (1799) 4 Ves. 620 at 622, 623.

estate upon trust for conversion for his wife during her widowhood, with remainder over, directed the trustees: "And as for and concerning all that messuage or dwelling-house called Langford Inn . . . upon trust, as soon as convenient after my decease, to sell and dispose of the same, either by auction or private sale, and for the most money that could be reasonably obtained for the same." In April 1836 the trustees advertised the Langford Inn for sale for £1,000. They refused an offer of £900, made in 1837. One of the trustees died in 1842. A railway opened in 1843 caused the property to depreciate in value through the diversion of traffic. The property was again advertised for sale in 1845, but no offer was received. The other trustee died in 1856. Langford Inn was still unsold and could not be sold except at a low price.

Held, by Romilly M.R., the trustees had committed a breach of trust by reason of **10–92** their negligence in not selling the property for so many years, that the property must be sold, and that the estates of the trustees were "liable to make good the deficiency between the amount which should be produced by the sale of the inn and the sum of £900, in case the purchase-money thereof should not amount to that sum."[35]

It was held by the Court of Appeal in *Re Chapman*[36] and in *Rawsthorne v* **10–93** *Rowley*,[37] that a trustee is not liable for a loss arising through the retention of an *authorised* investment unless he was guilty of *wilful default*,[38] which requires proof of want of ordinary prudence on the part of the trustee.[39] The position is now governed by sections 1, 4 and 5 of the Trustee Act 2000. The trustees must from time to time obtain and consider proper advice on whether retention of the investment is satisfactory having regard to the need for diversification and the suitability of the investments. In deciding what to do the statutory duty of care needs to be observed (except to the extent excluded).

Improper realisation of proper investments

It is clearly a breach of trust if trustees sell an authorised investment for the **10–94** purpose of investing in an unauthorised investment or for the purpose of paying the proceeds to the life-tenant in breach of trust. In such cases the trustees are liable to replace the authorised investment or the proceeds of sale of the authorised investment, whichever is the greater burden.[40] Replacement of the authorised investment will be at its value at the date it

---

[35] See also *Grayburn v Clarkson* (1868) 3 Ch.App. 605; *Dunning v Gainsborough* (1885) 54 L.J.Ch. 891. Where the proper time during which the unauthorised investments, *e.g.* shares, should have been sold is a period during which fluctuations occur in the value of the shares one may take half the sum of the lowest and highest prices at which the shares might have been sold in the period commencing when the shares could first have been sold to advantage and ending at the date by which they should reasonably have been sold: *Fales v Canada Permanent Trust Co.* (1976) 70 D.L.R. (3d) 257 at 274.

[36] [1896] 2 Ch. 763.

[37] [1909] 1 Ch. 409n.

[38] See also *Baud v Fardell* (1855) 4 W.R. 40; *Henderson v Hunter* (1843) 1 L.T.(o.s.) 359 at 385; *Robinson v Murdoch* (1881) 45 L.T. 417; Joyce J. in *Re Oddy* (1910) 104 L.T. 128 at 131; *Re Godwin* (1918) 87 L.J.Ch. 645.

[39] *per* Lindley L.J. in *Re Chapman* [1896] 2 Ch. 763 at 776.

[40] Thus, if an authorised investment is sold for £10,000, then invested in an unauthorised investment sold for £8,000 and when matters are discovered the authorised investment can be repurchased for £7,000, the trustees must top up the £8,000 to £10,000, the true figure that should be in the accounts (after falsifying them) as retained for the beneficiaries: *Shepherd v Mouls* (1845) 4 Hare 500, 504; *Watts v Girdlestone* (1843) 6 Beav. 188.

is actually replaced or at the date of the court judgment if not earlier replaced or, exceptionally, at the date the authorised investment would, in any event, have been sold.[41]

PHILLIPSON v GATTY

Vice-Chancellor (1848) 6 Hare 26; affirmed (1850) 7 Hare 516; 2 H. & Tw. 459; 12 L.T.(o.s.) 445; 13 Jur.(o.s.) 318

10–95 The trustees of a sum of consols, who had power to convert and reinvest in the public funds or upon real security, realised part of the stock and invested it in an unauthorised investment.

10–96 WIGRAM V.-C.: ". . . Then comes another material question—are the trustees to replace the stock, or the money produced by the sale? Mr. Wood argued that they were liable to make good the money only, distinguishing the sale, which he said was lawful, from the investment, which I have decided to have been a breach of trust. My opinion is, that the trustees must replace the stock. There was no authority to sell, except with a view to the reinvestment; and here the sale was made with a view to the investment I have condemned. It was all one transaction, and the sale and investment must stand or fall together . . ."

10–97 *Held*, therefore, the trustees must replace the stock improperly realised. *Affirmed on appeal.*[42]

Non-Investment of trust funds

10–98 A trustee ought not to leave trust moneys uninvested for an unreasonable length of time. If he unnecessarily retains trust moneys which he ought to have invested, he is chargeable with interest.[43]

10–99 While an investment is being sought, however, a trustee has statutory powers to pay trust moneys into an interest-bearing account.[44] If a trustee, having been *directed* to invest in a *specific* investment, *makes no investment at all*, and the price of the specified investment rises, he may be required to purchase so much of that investment as would have been obtained by a purchase at the proper time.[45] This applies equally where he is directed to invest in a specific investment and he makes some investment other than the one specified.[46] But if he is directed to invest in a specified *range* of investments, and he makes no investment at all, it has been held that he is chargeable only with the trust fund itself, and not with the amount of one or other of the investments which might have been purchased.[47] The reason was stated by Wigram V.-C in *Shepherd v Mouls*[48] as follows: "The

---

[41] *Re Bell's Indenture* [1980] 3 All E.R. 425 at 437–439, pointing out that in *Re Massingberd* (1890) 63 L.T. 296 the reference to the date of the writ for ascertaining the value of the property sold in breach of trust was *per incuriam* and should be the date of the judgment.
[42] Followed in *Re Massingberd* (1890) 63 L.T. 296.
[43] *Re Jones*, (1883) 49 L.T. 91. For lost capital appreciation see *Midland Bank Trustee Ltd v Federated Pension Services* [1995] Jersey L.R. 352.
[44] Trustee Act 2000 ss. 3, 16–24.
[45] *Byrchall v Bradford* (1822) 6 Madd. 235.
[46] *Pride v Fooks* (1840) 2 Beav. 430 at 432.
[47] *Shepherd v Mouls* (1845) 4 Hare 500; *Robinson v Robinson* (1851) 1 De G.M. & G. 247.
[48] *ibid.* at 504.

discretion given to the trustees to select an investment among several securities makes it impossible to ascertain the amount of the loss (if any) which has arisen to the trust from the omission to invest, except, perhaps, in the possible case (which has not occurred here) of a particular security having been offered to the trustees, in conformity with the terms of the trust." Nowadays, however, in view of *Nestlé v National Westminster Bank*[49] as discussed above, para.9–82 the trustees would be charged with the loss of profit that would have been made taking account of the average performance of the investments within the specified range.

Trust funds in trade

If a trustee in breach of trust lends funds to a third party who knows they **10–100** are trust funds but not that the loan is a breach of trust and employs the trust funds in trade, the beneficiaries cannot claim from the third party a share of the profits. For example, a trustee in breach of trust lends £1,000 of trust moneys to X, who employs the fund in his trade. The agreement between the trustee and X provides that X is to pay interest at the rate of 15 per cent. By employing this fund of £1,000 in his trade, X makes a profit during the first year of £300. The beneficiaries cannot claim from X a share of that profit; all that they can require is that he replace, with interest, the fund which he borrowed. What is the position if X knew, not merely that the funds were trust funds, but also *that the loan was itself a breach of trust*? In this latter case, it would seem that X is a constructive trustee, that he may not "traffic in his trust," and must therefore account for his profit.[50] Of course, if the instrument of trust authorises a loan of trust funds to a third party, and such a loan is made, the beneficiaries have no right to claim profits.[51]

On the other hand, if it is the trustee himself who in breach of trust **10–101** employs trust funds in *his own* trade, the beneficiaries may, instead of taking interest, require him to account for the profit. Thus, if in breach of trust he employs £1,000 of trust moneys in his own trade and thereby makes a profit during the first year of £200, the beneficiaries (on calling upon him to replace the fund of £1,000), may, instead of taking interest on that sum, claim the profit of £200.[52]

Even if the trust funds so employed by the trustee in his own trade were **10–102** mixed up with his private moneys, so that the fund used by him was a mixed one, the beneficiaries may still claim a proportionate share of the profits.[53]

---

[49] [1994] 1 All E.R. 118.
[50] See *Stroud v Gwyer* (1860) 25 Beav. 130; *Vyse v Foster* (1872) 8 Ch.App. 309 at 334; *Belmont Finance Co. Ltd v Williams Furniture Ltd* [1979] Ch. 250; *Beach Petroleum N.L. v Johnson* (1993) 43 F.C.R. 1; *Farrow Finance Co. Ltd (in liq.) v Farrow Properties Pty. Ltd (in liq.)* [1999] 1 V.R. 584; *Robins v Incentive Dynamics Pty Ltd (in liq.)* (2003) 45 A.C.S.R. 244.
[51] *Parker v Bloxam* (1855) 20 Beav. 295 at 302–304; *Evans v London Co-operative Society Ltd, The Times*, July 6, 1976.
[52] *Jones v Foxall* (1852) 15 Beav. 388; *Williams v Powell* (1852) 15 Beav. 461; *Townsend v Townsend* (1859) 1 Giff. 201; *Re Davis* [1902] 2 Ch. 314.
[53] *Docker v Somes* (1834) 2 My. & K. 655; *Edinburgh T.C. v Lord Advocate* (1879) 4 App.Cas. 823. Indeed, if the trust funds were the *sine qua non* of the purchase of a valuable asset later sold at a profit it is arguable that the trust should take the whole profit for to allow the trustee a proportion for himself would be to allow him to profit from his position.

But it is either the one or the other, *either* interest *or* profit. They cannot, even if they find it advantageous to do so, claim interest for part of the time and profit for the other part.[54]

Summary of income position

(a) **Rate of interest**

10–103 If the life-tenant has lost income owing to the trustee's default he is entitled to interest on the capital moneys at what one may term the "trustees' rate" or, exceptionally, at a higher rate. In the nineteenth century the trustees' rate was 4 per cent, with 5 per cent in cases of fraud or active misconduct in using money for trading purposes of the trustee. The rate depends on the court's discretion but the trustees' rate in the 1980s and 1990s became the rate of the court's special account[55] replacing the short-term investment account, reflecting the rate a trust fund would have earned if invested in authorised securities. *Lewin*[56] states "These rates ceased to be generally available and now the judgment rate is a possible substitute but, at eight per cent, is at present more than could be obtained on deposit." Clearly, in its discretion the court must award less than the higher rate and so award in the region of five or, perhaps, six per cent.

10–104 However, a higher rate will be charged:

(i) where the trustee actually received a higher rate—when the life tenant takes the actual interest[57];

(ii) where the trustee ought to have received a higher rate (*e.g.* if he realised an authorised investment bearing 10 per cent and bought an unauthorised investment bearing five per cent[58]) when the life-tenant is entitled to interest at that higher rate;

(iii) where the trustee is presumed to have received a commercial rate as where he has made unauthorised use of trust moneys for his own purposes and the profits actually made by the trustee are unascertainable[59] or are less than the amount produced by applying the commercial rate—when the life-tenant is entitled to interest at the commercial rate instead of the actual interest or profit.[60] The commercial rate that is now presumed is one per cent above the

---

[54] *Heathcote v Hume* (1819) 1 Jac. & W. 122; *Vyse v Foster* (1872) 8 Ch. App. 309 at 334; *Tang Man Sit v Capacious Investments Ltd* [1996] 1 All E.R. 193.

[55] *Bartlett v Barclays Bank Trust Co. Ltd* [1980] Ch. 515 at 547; *Jaffray v Marshall* [1994] 1 All E.R. 143; *West v West* Ch.D. June 3, 2003. The Court Fund Rules 1987, rules 26, 27 deal with special account rates for funds invested with the court. The rates change much less frequently than commercial bank rates: usually. they keep in line with National savings rates.

[56] 17th ed. (2000) paras 39–32.

[57] *Re Emmet's Estate* (1881) 17 Ch.D. 142; *Matthew v T. M. Sutton Ltd* [1994] 1 W.L.R. 1455. This should include the case where the trustee has used the money to reduce his overdraft and to save paying an actual interest rate: *Farnell v Cox* (1898) 19 L.R.(N.S.W.)Eq. 142.

[58] *Jones v Foxall* (1852) 15 Bcav. 388; *Att.-Gen. v Alford* (1855) 4 De G.M. & G. 843 explained in *Mayor of Berwick v Murray* (1857) 7 De G.M. & G. 497.

[59] *Wallersteiner v Moir (No.2)* [1975] Q.B. 373.

[60] *Burdick v Garrick* (1870) 5 Ch.App. 233; *Vyse v Foster* (1872) 8 Ch.App. 309 at 329 (affd. L.R. 7 H.L. 318); *Gordon v Gonda* [1955] 1 W.L.R. 885; *O'Sullivan v Management Agency Ltd* [1985] Q.B. 428.

London and Scottish clearing banks' base lending rate now that Bank of England minimum lending rate no longer exists.[61]

(b) Simple or compound interest

Nowadays there seems to be a presumption that in its discretion the court **10–105** will award compound interest with yearly rests not just where there was a duty to accumulate income,[62] not just where the trustee or fiduciary was fraudulent or actually used the money in his own trade,[63] but where it is presumed against the wrongdoing fiduciary that he retained the misapplied money and used it for his own purposes most beneficially.[64] Compound interest is not to be awarded only as a punishment but as representing what the fiduciary should reasonably have obtained.

(c) Apportioning only real rate to life tenant

Where the trustee rate or the higher rate of the clearing banks reflects the **10–106** continued erosion in the value of money by reason of significant inflation then a proportion of the income should be added to capital leaving the beneficiaries only with a real rate of interest. Thus in *Jaffray v Marshall*[65] the interest at the special investment account rate was divided equally between capital and income, though the equitable life interest of the instigating life tenant benefiting from the breach was impounded under s.62 of the Trustee Act 1925.

Section 3. Impounding the Trustee's Beneficial Interest; Rule in *Re Dacre*[66]

If a beneficiary is also trustee, but is in default to the estate in his character **10–107** of trustee, he is not entitled to receive any further part of his beneficial interest until his default is made good. His beneficial interest may also be applied in satisfaction of his liability. Take X who is a trustee, for himself for life, remainder to Y. X commits a breach of trust, and has not yet satisfied his liability. Until he does so, he cannot receive any further part of his beneficial interest, and that interest may be applied in satisfaction of his liability. The rule holds good where X's beneficial interest is *derivative* as well as where it is original. For example, X holds on trust for several

---

[61] *Belmont Finance Ltd v Williams Furniture Ltd (No.2)* [1980] 1 All E.R. 393; *O'Sullivan v Management Agency Ltd* [1985] Q.B. 428; *John v James* [1986] S.T.C. 352 at 363; *Shearson Lehman Inc. v Maclaine Watson & Co. Ltd* [1990] 3 All E.R. 723 at 732–734; *Guardian Ocean Cargoes Ltd v Banco da Brazil (No.3)* [1992] 2 Lloyd's Rep. 193; *Westdeutsche Landesbank Girozentrale v Islington B.C.* [1994] 4 All E.R. 890.

[62] *Re Barclay* [1899] 1 Ch. 674; *Wallersteiner v Moir (No.2)* [1975] Q.B. 373.

[63] *Jones v Foxall* (1852) 15 Beav. 388; *Re Barclay* [1899] 1 Ch. 674; *Burdick v Garrick* (1870) 5 Ch.App. 233; *O'Sullivan v Management Agency Ltd* [1985] Q.B. 428; *John v James* [1986] S.T.C. 352 at 363–364.

[64] See *Wallersteiner v Moir (No.2)* [1975] Q.B. 373 at 388 where Lord Denning MR stated, "It should be presumed that the wrongdoer made the most beneficial use of it" while Buckley L.J. pointed out (p. 397) that a trustee who misapplied trust funds was forthwith liable to replace them with interest "on the notional ground that the money so applied was, in fact, the trustee's own money and that he has retained the misapplied trust money in his own hands and used it for his own purposes."

[65] [1993] 1 W.L.R. 128.

[66] [1916] 1 Ch. 344; *Jacubs v Rylance* (1874) L.R. 17 Eq. 341; *Re Brown* (1886) 32 Ch.D. 597.

beneficiaries, of which he is not himself one. He is in default to the estate in his character of trustee. One of the beneficiaries dies, and then X becomes entitled to that beneficiary's share as intestate successor or as legatee or devisee. X is now derivatively a beneficiary, and the rule applies as stated above.

10–108   What is the position of an *assignee* from the trustee-beneficiary X? The assignee is in the same position as his assignor, *i.e.* he takes subject to the equity available against the trustee-beneficiary.[67] He takes subject to that equity even if the trustee-beneficiary's default to the estate was *subsequent* to the assignment.[68]

10–109   It can, in fact, be most unsafe to take an assignment of the beneficial interest of a trustee-beneficiary, especially if that interest is reversionary. But it was held in *Re Towndrow*[69] that the rule does not apply to a case in which the trustee-beneficiary's liability relates to one trust (of a specific legacy) and his beneficial interest is derived from another trust (of the residuary estate), even though he is trustee of both trusts and both trusts are created by the same will. The rule in *Re Dacre* therefore applies only where the default relates to, and the beneficial interest is derived from, the same trust.

Section 4. Defences

I. POWER OF THE COURT TO RELIEVE TRUSTEES FROM PERSONAL LIABILITY

10–110   Section 61[70] of the Trustee Act 1925 states, "If it appears to the court that a trustee, whether appointed by the court or otherwise, is or may be[71] personally liable for any breach of trust, whether the transaction alleged to be a breach of trust occurred before or after the commencement of this Act, but has acted honestly and reasonably, and ought fairly to be excused for the breach of trust and for omitting to obtain the directions of the court in the matter in which he committed such a breach, then the court *may* relieve him either wholly or partly from personal liability for the same." This enables the court to excuse not just breaches of trust in the management of trust property but also payments to the wrong persons.[72] The question of fairness should be considered separately from whether the trustee acted honestly and reasonably: is it fair for the trustee to be excused

---

[67] *Irby v Irby (No.3)* (1858) 25 Beav. 632.
[68] *Doering v Doering* (1889) 42 Ch.D. 203; *Re Knapman* (1881) 18 Ch.D. 300 at 307.
[69] [1911] 1 Ch. 662.
[70] Re-enacting s.3 of the Judicial Trustees Act 1896. See Sheridan, "Excusable Breaches of Trust" (1955) 19 Conv.(N.S.) 420; Lord Maugham, "Excusable Breaches of Trust" (1898) 14 L.Q.R. 159; C Stebbings, *The Private Trustee in Victorian England* (2002), Chap.6; J. Lowry and R. Edwards, "Excuses" in P. Birks and A. Pretto (eds.) *Breach of Trust* (2002) 269. For similar protection of officers of a company, see s.727 of the Companies Act 1985.
[71] This does not authorise relief in respect of future anticipated breaches of trust: it relates to an existing situation where the trustee may or may not be liable for breach of trust: *Re Rosenthal* [1972] 1 W.L.R. 1273.
[72] *Re Alsop* [1914] 1 Ch. 1; *Ward-Smith v Jebb* (1964) 108 So. Jo. 919; *Re Wightwick* [1950] 1 Ch. 260; *Re Evans* [1999] 2 All E.R. 777.

when the inevitable result is to deny compensation to the beneficiaries? The burden is on the trustee[73] to satisfy the threefold obligation[74] of proving he acted honestly, reasonably and ought fairly to be excused. An appellate court will be reluctant to interfere with the lower court's exercise of discretion.[75]

The court is rather reluctant to grant relief to a paid trustee but may do **10–111** so in special circumstances.[76] The taking of legal advice will be a significant consideration if such advice is followed but a breach of trust occurs because the advice was erroneous: the standing of the legal adviser and the value of the property affected by the advice will be relevant considerations.[77] If the adviser were a negligent solicitor then the trustee should sue the solicitor to recover the loss for the trust and it seems hardly likely that the court would excuse the trustee if he failed to sue.[78] One must distinguish between trustees obtaining advice on behalf of the trust beneficiaries and trustees obtaining advice for their own personal protection and benefit. In the former case any cause of action arising from negligent advice will be a trust asset so that, if not barred by the limitation period, the beneficiaries could sue for themselves on joining the trustees as co-defendants with the adviser if the trustees refused to sue; in the latter case the beneficiaries generally have no rights against the adviser, being able only to sue the trustees for any breach of trust.[79]

II. An Instigating or Consenting Beneficiary Cannot Sue the Trustee and the Court has Power to Make Such Beneficiary Indemnify Trustee for Breach of Trust

A beneficiary[80] who is of full capacity[81] and knowingly[82] concurs in a breach **10–112** of trust cannot afterwards complain of it against the trustees[83] unless they knew or ought to have known that the beneficiary's concurrence was the

---

[73] *Re Stuart* [1897] 2 Ch. 583; *Re Turner* [1897] 1 Ch. 536.

[74] *Marsden v Regan* [1954] 1 W.L.R. 423 at 434–435, *per* Evershed M.R. See too *Mitchell v Halliwell* [2005] EWHC 937 (Ch) at [49] (no relief for honest trustee who unreasonably failed to ensure that beneficiaries took independent advice).

[75] *Marsden v Regan* [1954] 1 W.L.R. 423, CA.

[76] *National Trustees Co. of Australasia v General Finance Co.* [1905] A.C. 373; *Re Windsor Steam Coal Co.* [1929] 1 Ch. 151; *Hawkesley v May* [1956] 1 Q.B. 304; *Re Pauling's S.T.* [1964] Ch. 303 (partial relief); *Re Rosenthal* [1972] 1 W.L.R. 1273.

[77] *National Trustees Co. of Australasia*, above; *Re Allsop* [1914] 1 Ch. 1 at 13; *Marsden v Regan* [1954] 1 All E.R. 475 at 482. See too *Wong v Burt* (2004) 7 I.T.E.L.R. 263 at [49]–[58].

[78] *National Trustees Co. of Australasia*, above.

[79] *Wills v Cooke* (1979) 76 L.S.G. 706 *per* Slade J.; *Parker-Tweedale v Dunbar Bank plc* [1990] 2 All E.R. 577 at 583. But for exceptions to this rule, see discussion in *Hayim v Citibank N.A.* [1987] A.C 730 at 747–748; *Bradstock Trustee Services Ltd v Nabarro Nathanson* [1995] 1 W.L.R. 1405; *H.R. v J.A.P.T.* [1997] P.L.R. 99.

[80] In charitable trusts only the Attorney-General can consent or acquiesce in a breach of trust: *Re Freeston's Charity* [1978] 1 All E.R. 481 at 490, though the Court of Appeal found it unnecessary to say anything on this point: [1979] 1 All E.R. 51 at 63.

[81] *Wilkinson v Parry* (1828) 4 Russ. 272 at 276; *Montford v Cadogan* (1816) 19 Ves. 635. He may not fraudulently misrepresent his age to obtain money and then claim the money again on majority: *Overton v Banister* (1844) Hare 503.

[82] *Phipps v Boardman* [1964] 2 All E.R. 187 at 204–205, 207; the point was not appealed.

[83] *Fletcher v Collis* [1905] 2 Ch. 24, *infra*, para.10–117. If he instigates or requests the breach then *a fortiori* he cannot sue.

result of undue influence.[84] The position is summarised by Wilberforce J.[85] (as he then was) in a passage approved by the Court of Appeal[86]: "The court has to consider all the circumstances in which the concurrence of the *cestui que trust* was given with a view to seeing whether it is fair and equitable that, having given his concurrence, he should afterwards turn round and sue the trustees: that, subject to this, it is not necessary that he should know that what he is concurring in is a breach of trust, provided that he fully understands what he is concurring in, and that it is not necessary that he should himself have directly benefited by the breach of trust." It would thus seem that if B consents to an act which the trustees know to be unauthorised but refrain from so telling B then B may still sue the trustees. The trustees must put the beneficiaries fully in the picture and must not withhold crucial information.[87] If, however, they themselves do not appreciate that what they propose is a breach of trust and B fully understands and agrees with the proposal then B should not be able to sue them if things turn out badly.

10–113   The above equitable principles apply whether the beneficiary's consent or acquiescence[88] is before or after the breach of trust. They operate to prevent that particular beneficiary from suing for breach of trust, whether or not he benefited from consenting to such breach: *Fletcher v Collis*.

10–114   Where the beneficiary instigated, requested or consented to a breach of trust which the trustees then committed and another beneficiary called upon the trustee to make good the breach of trust, the court has always had jurisdiction to order the trustee to be indemnified out of the interest of the beneficiary who, being of full capacity, either instigated, requested or concurred in the breach. A motive of personal benefit on the part of the beneficiary was sufficient to invoke the jurisdiction in cases of instigation[89] or request[90]; but personal benefit actually derived by the beneficiary was necessary in cases of concurrence.[91] In order to succeed in claiming an indemnity, the trustee had to show that the beneficiary knew the facts which constituted the breach of trust although it was not necessary to show that the beneficiary knew that these facts amounted in law to a breach of trust: *Re Somerset*.[92]

---

[84] *Re Pauling's S.T.* [1964] Ch. 303 at 338. Trustees must take special care in the case of young adults living with their parents.

[85] *Re Pauling's S.T.* [1962] 1 W.L.R. 86 at 108.

[86] *Holder v Holder* [1968] Ch. 353; *Re Freeston's Charity* [1978] 1 W.L.R. 741.

[87] *Phipps v Boardman* [1964] 2 All E.R. 187 at 204–205; *Mitchell v Halliwell* [2005] EWHC 937 (Ch) esp. at [41]–[52].

[88] Mere delay (subject to Limitation Act 1980) is not enough; there must be conduct and circumstances making it inequitable to assert a claim *e.g.* having knowledge of entitlement to sue but doing nothing, so trustee does things that would otherwise not have been done: *De Busche v Alt* (1877) 8 Ch.D. 286, 314; *Nelson v Rye* [1996] 1 W.L.R. 1378.

[89] *Trafford v Boehm* (1746) 3 Atk. 440 at 442; *Raby v Ridehalgh* (1855) 7 De G.M. & G. 104.

[90] *M'Gachen v Dew* (1851) 15 Beav. 84; *Hanchett v Briscoe* (1856) 22 Beav. 496.

[91] *Cocker v Quayle* (1830) 1 Russ. & M. 535 at 538; *Booth v Booth* (1838) 1 Beav. 125 at 130; *Blyth v Fladgate* [1891] 1 Ch. 337 at 363. It makes no difference that the concurring beneficiary became a beneficiary after the date of his concurrence; *Evans v Benyon* (1887) 37 Ch.D. 329 at 344. These factors of motive and actual benefit may still influence the exercise of discretion of the court determining whether all or any part of the beneficial interest should be impounded: *Bolton v Curre* [1895] 1 Ch. 544 at 549; *Re Somerset* [1894] Ch. 231 at 275.

[92] See also *Rehden v Wesley* (1861) 29 Beav. 213 at 215.

Section 62 of the Trustee Act 1925[93] enlarges the jurisdiction as follows: **10–115**
"Where a trustee commits a breach of trust at the instigation or request or
with the consent in writing[94] of a beneficiary, the court may if it thinks fit
make such order as to the court seems just for impounding all or any part
of the interest of the beneficiary in the trust estate by way of indemnity to
the trustee[95] or persons claiming through him."[96] However, the factors of
motive and actual benefit are likely to continue to influence the court in
exercising its discretion.

The section provides for impounding the interest of the "beneficiary in **10–116**
the trust estate." In *Ricketts v Ricketts*[97] there was a marriage settlement for
a mother for her life, remainder to her son. The son, on his marriage,
assigned his reversionary interest under that settlement to the trustees of
his own marriage settlement, under which latter settlement he was a
beneficiary for life. Notice of the assignment was given to the trustees of
the first settlement. By that assignment the son divested himself of his
character of beneficiary under the first settlement, and substituted in his
place the trustees of the second settlement. Afterwards the son instigated
the trustees of the first settlement to commit a breach of trust in his favour
by applying trust capital in discharging his debts, and when those trustees
proceeded against him under the section for an indemnity, they discovered
that he was not a beneficiary against whom they could proceed. Their
beneficiary was now to be found in the trustees of the second settlement,
who were trustees for the son who instigated the breach of trust to pay off
his debts. He was not a "beneficiary in the trust estate."

FLETCHER v COLLIS

Court of Appeal [1905] 2 Ch. 24 (Vaughan Williams, Romer and Stirling L.JJ)

Securities were settled on trust for the husband for life, remainder to the wife for **10–117**
life, remainder to children. At the request of the wife and with the (written) consent
of the husband, the trustee in 1885 sold off the whole of the trust fund and handed
the proceeds to the wife, who spent them. In June 1891 the husband was
adjudicated bankrupt. In August 1891 the present action was commenced by the
remaindermen against the trustee to make him replace the loss, but proceedings
were stayed on an undertaking by the trustee, on the security of (*inter alia*) certain
policies on his life, to make good the trust fund. By means of payments by the
trustee and of the policies which fell in on his death in 1902, the whole of the trust
fund was replaced, together with interest from August 1891.

The personal representative of the deceased trustee then took out a summons for **10–118**
a declaration that she was entitled, during the life of the husband, to the income of
the trust fund replaced by the deceased trustee. It was argued for her that a

---

[93] Replacing Trustee Act 1893, s.45 replacing Trustee Act 1888, s.6.
[94] The requirement of writing only refers to consent and not instigation or request: *Re Somerset* [1894] 1 Ch.
231.
[95] An order for indemnity can be made in favour of a former trustee: *Re Pauling's S.T. (No.2)* [1963] Ch.
576. It would be absurd if the trustee who, ex hypothesi, is in breach of trust had to remain trustee in
order to have an impounding order for an indemnity.
[96] Would the section be available if the sole trustee had fled the country leaving only trust assets behind and
the remaindermen claimed to be subrogated to the trustee's right to impound the instigating life-tenant's
income?
[97] (1891) 64 L.T. 263.

beneficiary who concurs in a breach of trust cannot afterwards complain of it against his trustee. The capital had in fact been replaced by the trustee at the instance of the remaindermen, but since the husband himself had by virtue of his concurrence no claim against the trustee, the income of the capital so replaced should (during the life of the husband) go to her as personal representative of the trustee who replaced it.

10–119   For the husband's trustee in bankruptcy, who resisted the claim of the personal representative, it was contended that the authorities showed that mere concurrence by a beneficiary does not preclude him from complaining against his trustee: it must be shown that the beneficiary also derived a personal benefit from the breach of trust, which was not the case here.

10–120   ROMER L.J.: "There was one proposition of law urged by the counsel on behalf of the respondents before us to which I accede. It is this: If a beneficiary claiming under a trust does not *instigate* or *request* a breach of trust, is not the active moving party towards it, but merely *consents* to it, *and* he obtains no personal benefit from it, then his interest in the trust estate would not be impoundable in order to indemnify the trustee liable to make good loss occasioned by the breach. I think this is what was meant and referred to by Chitty J. in his judgment in *Sawyer v Sawyer*,[98] where he says: 'It strikes me as a novelty in law, and a proposition not founded on principle, to say that the person who merely consents is bound to do more than what he says he consents to do. It does not mean that he makes himself personally liable, nor does he render any property liable to make it good.' But that proposition of law must be taken to be subject to the following right of the trustee as between himself and the beneficiaries. In the case I have before referred to in respect to the general proposition, the beneficiary who knowingly consented to the breach could not, if of full contracting age and capacity, and in the absence of special circumstances, afterwards be heard to say that the conduct of the trustee in committing the breach of trust was, as against him the particular beneficiary, improper, so as to make the trustee liable to the beneficiary for any damage suffered in respect of that beneficiary's interest in the trust estate by reason of the loss occasioned by the breach, and of course if satisfactorily proved the consent of the beneficiary to the breach need not be in writing.

10–121   "I will illustrate what I have said by a concrete case, not only to make my meaning perfectly plain, but also because the illustration will have a bearing upon the case now before us. Take a simple case of a trust under a settlement, say, of £3,000, for a tenant for life, and after the death of the tenant for life for certain remaindermen. Suppose the trustee commits a breach of trust and sells out £1,000, and pays it over to some third person, so that the *cestui que trust* does not benefit by it himself, and suppose that the tenant for life, being of full age and *sui juris*, knows of that act of the trustee and consents to it. What would be the position of the trustee in reference to that breach of trust if he were made liable at the instance of the remaindermen for the loss accruing to the trust estate by the breach of trust, assuming the £1,000 to have been lost? The remaindermen would have the right of saying, so far as their interest in remainder is concerned, the capital must be made good by the trustee; but the tenant for life who consented could not himself have brought an action against the trustee to make him liable for the loss of income suffered by the tenant for life by reason of the breach of trust as to the £1,000. On the other hand, the trustee would not have had a right, as against the *cestui que*

---

[98] (1885) 28 Ch.D. 595 at 598.

trust, the tenant for life, to have impounded the tenant for life's interest on the remaining £2,000 of the trust fund in order to indemnify himself. Now suppose the remaindermen having brought an action to make good the breach of trust against the trustee, and the tenant for life is a co-plaintiff, a defence is put in by the trustee raising his right as against the tenant for life seeking relief in respect of the loss of income, but admitting the right of the remaindermen: what would the court in such a case do if the question between the tenant for life and the trustee had to be tried out, and the tenant for life was found to have consented knowingly to the breach of trust? To my mind the right thing for the court to do would have been clear. It might order the £1,000 to be paid into court by the trustee; but, pending the life of the tenant for life, it might also order the income to be paid to the trustee, because the income of the £1,000 would have been out of the pocket of the trustee just as much as the corpus from which it proceeded, and not to have given that relief to the trustee would have been to ignore his right, and to have acceded to the claim of the tenant for life in the action by him that I have indicated. Now suppose that the tenant for life is not a plaintiff, but co-defendant with the trustee, so that the question cannot be tried out at the trial as between the tenant for life and the trustee: what might the court do, if so advised, in that case? It might order the £1,000 to be paid into court by the trustee, and it might reserve the question of the right as between the tenant for life and the trustee to the income to be determined at some later period. It will be found that that illustration is pertinent to the case that is now before us. In such a case when the question as to income arose the trustee would be able to say: "The remaindermen are clearly not entitled to the income on the trust fund I have replaced, if the tenant for life is not entitled to it as against me. I replaced it; it is my money, and I am entitled to it"; and, therefore, when the question came to be tried out ultimately as between the tenant for life and the trustee, if that income was still under the control of the court, the court would again have the right to say to the trustee who replaced the corpus: "The income is yours in the absence of the right of the beneficiary, the tenant for life, to claim as against you to make you liable for that income."

"Now that right of a trustee which I have been dealing with, the right to resist the **10–122** claim by the beneficiary to make good as against him the income, has clearly not been affected either by section 6 of the Trustee Act of 1888, or by section 45 of the Trustee Act of 1893. As I pointed out in *Bolton v Curre*,[99] those sections were intended to and did *extend* the powers of the court for the benefit of the trustee. They clearly extended the powers of court so far as concerns the case of a married woman restrained from anticipation; but they also extended them in another respect by giving power to the court to impound any part of the interest in the trust property of any beneficiary who consented to a breach of trust, provided that consent was in writing. But clearly there was nothing in those sections which was intended to, and nothing in my opinion which operated so as to, deprive the trustee of the right I previously indicated, namely, the right of saying as against a beneficiary who has consented to a breach of trust that the beneficiary cannot make him, the trustee, personally liable to recoup, to the beneficiary who consented, the loss accruing to that beneficiary by the breach of trust committed with his consent. The beneficiary, if he consented to the breach of trust, could not be heard to make that a ground of complaint or a ground of action as against the trustee . . .

Is not this matter that we have to deal with on this appeal in substance one where **10–123** a beneficiary who has consented to a breach of trust is now for his own benefit calling upon the trustee to make good the loss accruing to the beneficiary by reason of the breach? I think it is . . ."

---

[99] [1895] 1 Ch. 544 at 549.

10–124   *Held*, therefore, by the Court of Appeal that the personal representative of the deceased trustee was entitled, during the life of the husband tenant for life, to the income of the fund replaced by the trustee.

HOLDER v HOLDER

Court of Appeal [1968] Ch. 353; [1968] 2 W.L.R. 237; [1968] 1 All E.R. 665

10–125   The plaintiff was seeking to set aside a sale made to the third defendant by the first two defendant trustees when the third defendant was technically a trustee. The facts have already been set out at para.9–08 and Harman L.J. with whom Danckwerts and Sachs L.JJ. expressly agreed on this point dealt as follows with the defence of the plaintiff's consent or acquiescence.

10–126   HARMAN L.J.: ". . . There arises a further defence, namely, that of acquiescence, and this requires some further recital of the facts.

10–127   "Completion of the sale was due for Michaelmas, 1961, but by that time the third defendant was not in a position to find the purchase money. The proving executors served a notice to complete in October, 1961, and, the validity of this notice being questioned, served a further notice in December. In February 1962 the plaintiff's solicitor pressed the defendants to forfeit the third defendant's deposit and this was a right given by the contract of sale and is an affirmation of it. Further, in May, 1962, the plaintiff issued a writ for a common decree of administration against the proving executors, seeking thus to press them to complete the contract and wind up the estate. The contract was in fact completed in June, 1962, and in the same month £2,000 on account was paid to and accepted by the plaintiff as his share and he thereupon took no further steps with his action. In order to complete, the third defendant borrowed £21,000 from the Agricultural Mortgage Corporation with interest at $7^1/_2$ per cent. He also borrowed £3,000 from his mother with interest at 6 $^1/_2$ per cent, and a like sum from his sister at a similar rate of interest. In November 1962 the third defendant demanded possession of Glebe Farm house from the plaintiff, who at that time changed his solicitors, and it was suggested by the new solicitors in February 1963 that the third defendant was disqualified from bidding at the auction. This was the first time any such suggestion had been made by anyone. The writ was not issued till a year later.

10–128   "I have found this question a difficult one. The plaintiff knew all the relevant facts but he did not realise nor was he advised till 1963 that the legal result might be that he could object to his brother's purchase because he continued to be a personal representative. There is no doubt strong authority for the proposition that a man is not bound by acquiescences until he knows his legal rights. In *Cockerell v Cholmeley*[1] Sir John Leach M.R. said this:

> 'It has been argued that the defendant, being aware of the facts of the case in the lifetime of Sir Henry Englefield has, by his silence, and by being a party to the application to Parliament, confirmed the title of the plaintiffs. In equity it is considered, as good sense requires it should be, that no man can be held by any act of his to confirm a title, unless he was fully aware at the time, not only of the fact upon which the effect of title depends, but of the consequence in point of law; and there is no proof that the defendant, at the time of the acts referred to, was aware of the law on the subject . . .'

---

[1] (1830) 1 Russ. & M. 418 at 425.

There, however, the judge was asked to set aside a legal right. In *Wilmott v Barber*[2] **10–129**
Fry J. said this:

> 'A man is not to be deprived of his legal rights unless he has acted in such a
> way as would make it fraudulent for him to set up those rights. What, then, are
> the elements or requisites necessary to constitute fraud of that description? In
> the first place the plaintiff must have made a mistake as to his legal rights.
> Secondly, the plaintiff must have expended some money or must have done
> some act (not necessarily upon the defendant's land) on the faith of his
> mistaken belief. Thirdly, the defendant, the possessor of the legal right, must
> know of the existence of his own right which is inconsistent with the right
> claimed by the plaintiff. If he does not know of it he is in the same position as
> the plaintiff, and the doctrine of acquiescence is founded upon conduct with a
> knowledge of your legal rights.'

On the other hand, in *Stafford v Stafford*[3] Knight Bruce L.J. said this:

> 'Generally, when the facts are known from which a right arises, the right is
> presumed to be known . . .'

"Like the judge, I should desire to follow the conclusion of Wilberforce J. who **10–130**
reviewed the authorities in *Re Pauling's Settlement Trusts*[4]; and this passage was
mentioned without dissent in the same case in the Court of Appeal[5]:

> 'The result of these authorities appears to me to be that the court has to
> consider all the circumstances in which the concurrence of the *cestui que trust*
> was given with a view to seeing whether it is fair and equitable that, having
> given his concurrence, he should afterwards turn round and sue the trustees:
> that, subject to this, it is not necessary that he should know that what he is
> concurring in is a breach of trust, provided that he fully understands what he is
> concurring in, and that it is not necessary that he should himself have directly
> benefited by the breach of trust.'

There is, therefore, no hard and fast rule that ignorance of a legal right is a bar, but
the whole of the circumstances must be looked at to see whether it is just that the
complaining beneficiary should succeed against the trustee.[6]
     "On the whole I am of the opinion that in the circumstances of this case it would **10–131**
not be right to allow the plaintiff to assert his right (assuming he had one) because
with full knowledge of the facts he affirmed the sale. He has had £2,000 as a result.
He has caused the third defendant to embark on liabilities which he cannot recoup.
There can in fact be no *restitutio in integrum* which is a necessary element in
rescission.
     "The plaintiff is asserting an equitable and not a legal remedy. He has by his **10–132**
conduct disentitled himself to it. It is extremely doubtful whether the order if
worked out would benefit anyone, I think we should not assent to it, on general
equitable principles."

---

[2] (1880) 15 Ch.D. 96 at 105.
[3] (1857) 1 De G. & J. 193 at 202.
[4] [1961] 3 All E.R. 713 at 730.
[5] [1964] Ch. 303.
[6] Endorsed in *Re Freeston's Charity* [1979] 1 All E.R. 51 at 62. The third proposition of Fry J. in *Wilmott v
Barber* (1880) 15 Ch.D. 96 at 105 has also been rejected in *Taylor Fashions Ltd v Liverpool Victoria
Trustees Co. Ltd* [1981] 1 All E.R. 897 at 915–918 and *Habib Bank Ltd v Habib Bank A.G. Zurich* [1981] 2
All E.R. 650 at 666, 668. See above, paras 2–33 to 2–34.

RE SOMERSET, SOMERSET v EARL POULETT

Court of Appeal [1894] 1 Ch. 231 (Lindley, A. L. Smith and Davey L.JJ.)

10–133   Kekewich J. held that a £34,612 mortgage was a proper investment except in so far as the trustees had advanced too much, so that they were liable for a breach of trust in respect only of the amount excessively advanced: Trustee Act 1888, s.5. He considered that the largest sum which in the circumstances the trustees could properly have advanced was £26,000. He further held that the trustees were entitled to have the plaintiff's life interest impounded by way of indemnity under the Trustee Act 1888, s.6; as to which the plaintiff appealed.

10–134   LINDLEY L.J.: ". . . The second question is whether, in order to indemnify the trustees, the court ought to impound the income of the trust funds during the life of the appellant. This question turns on the construction of section 6, and on the conduct of the parties. [Section 6 is now Trustee Act 1925, s.62.]

10–135   "Did the trustees commit the breach of trust for which they have been made liable at the instigation or request, or with the consent in writing, of the appellant? The section is intended to protect trustees, and ought to be construed so as to carry out that intention. But the section ought not, in my opinion, to be construed as if the word 'investment' had been inserted instead of 'breach of trust.' An enactment to that effect would produce great injustice in many cases. In order to bring a case within this section the *cestui que trust* must instigate, or request or consent in writing to some act or omission which is itself a breach of trust and not to some act or omission which only becomes a breach of trust by reason of want of care on the part of the trustees. If a *cestui que trust* instigates, requests or consents in writing to an investment not in terms authorised by the power of investment, he clearly falls within the section; and in such a case his ignorance or forgetfulness of the terms of power would not, I think, protect him—at all events, not unless he could give some good reason why it should, *e.g.*, that it was caused by the trustee. But if all that a *cestui que trust* does is to instigate, request or consent in writing to an investment which is authorised by the terms of the power, the case is, I think, very different. He has a right to expect that the trustees will act with proper care in making the investment, and if they do not they cannot throw the consquences on him unless they can show that he instigated, requested or consented in writing to their non-performance of their duty in this respect. This is, in my opinion, the true construction of this section.

10–136   "As regards the necessity for a writing, I agree with the decision of Mr. Justice Kekewich in *Griffith v Hughes*,[7] that an instigation or request need not be in writing, and that the words 'in writing' apply only to the consent.

10–137   "I pass now to the facts. It is, in my opinion, perfectly clear that the appellant instigated, requested and consented in writing to the investment by the trustees of the trust money on a mortgage of Lord Hill's estate. This, indeed, was not disputed. But the evidence does not, that I can see, go further than this. He certainly never instigated, requested or consented in writing to an investment on the property without inquiry; still less, if upon inquiry the rents payable in respect of the lands mortgaged were found to be less than the interest payable on the mortgage.

10–138   "Whether the appellant knew the rental is a very important question. Mr. Justice Kekewich has found that he did. But the evidence does not, in my opinion, warrant this inference . . .

---

[7] [1892] 3 Ch. 105.

"The solicitors obtained the valuation for and on behalf of the trustees; they **10–139** obtained the second opinion of the valuers for the benefit of the borrower, and for the protection of the trustees. In obtaining the valuation and opinion the solicitors were not acting for or on behalf of the appellant; and considering that they never disclosed the valuation or opinion to the appellant, and never informed him of their effect, he cannot, in my opinion, be held to have known them. It is important to observe that the statute does not make a *cestui que trust* responsible for a breach of trust simply because he had actual or constructive notice of it; he must have instigated or requested it, or have consented to it in writing. Even if the knowledge of his solicitors could be imputed to him for some purposes, it is not true in fact that the appellant did by himself or his agent instigate, request or consent in writing to a breach of trust.[8] Even if the appellant had constructive notice through his solicitors of the valuation, the court, in exercising the power conferred on it by the statute, would, in my opinion, be acting unjustly, and not justly, if, under the circumstances of this case, it held the appellant liable to indemnify the trustees. The court would be treating the appellant as having done more than he did, and I can see no justification for such a course. It must be borne in mind that the plaintiff was not seeking to benefit himself at the expense of the remaindermen as in *Raby v Ridehalgh*.[9] He was seeking a better security for the trust money for the benefit of everyone interested in it . . ."

Held, therefore, by the Court of Appeal that the defendants were not entitled to **10–140** have the plaintiff's life interest impounded by way of indemnity.[10]

III. STATUTES OF LIMITATION[11]

Equitable rules

The doctrine of "laches" is expressly preserved by the Limitation Act 1980, **10–141** section 36 of which provides that "nothing in the Act shall affect any equitable jurisdiction to refuse relief on the ground of acquiescence or otherwise." The doctrine is available "where it would be practically unjust to give a remedy, either because the party has, by his conduct, done that which might fairly be regarded as equivalent to a waiver of it, or where by his conduct and neglect he has, though perhaps not waiving that remedy, yet put the other party in a situation in which it would not be reasonable to place him if the remedy were afterwards asserted."[12] The doctrine really

---

[8] On this point, A. L. Smith L.J. observed (at 270): "In my opinion, upon the true reading of this section, a trustee, in order to obtain the benefit conferred thereby, must establish that the beneficiary knew the facts which rendered what he was instigating, requesting or consenting to in writing a breach of trust." Davey L.J. observed (at 274): ". . . in order to bring the case within the section the beneficiary must have requested the trustee to depart from and go outside the terms of his trust. It is not, of course, necessary that the beneficiary should know the investment to be in law a breach of trust."

[9] (1855) 7 De G.M. & G. 104.

[10] In accordance with this case is *Mara v Browne* [1892] 2 Ch. 69 at 92–93, where North J. held that the trustee was not entitled to impound the interest of the beneficiary because the beneficiary, though she had consented in writing, had not consented to those acts which constituted the breach of trust. On appeal [1896] 1 Ch. 199 the point did not arise. The life tenant's interest was impounded in *Jaffray v Marshall* [1993] 1 W.L.R. 1285.

[11] For discussion of the history of equity's limitation rules, see W. Swadling, "Limitation" in P. Birks and A. Pretto (eds.). *Breach of Trust* (2002), 319.

[12] *per* Lord Selborne L.C. in *Lindsay Petroleum Co. v Hurd* (1874) L.R. 5 P.C. 221 at 239–240. See also *Weld v Petre* [1929] 1 Ch. 33 at 51–52; *Holder v Holder* [1968] Ch. 353; *Nelson v Rye* [1986] 2 All E.R. 186, 200–205, although incorrect on other points: *Paragon Finance plc v Thakerar & Co.* [1999] 1 All E.R. 400, 415–416; *Companhia de Seguros Imperio v Heath Ltd* [2001] 1 W.L.R. 112; *J.J. Harrison (Properties) Ltd v Harrison* [2002] 1 B.C.L.C. 162.

consists of a substantial lapse of time coupled with the existence of circumstances which make it inequitable to enforce the plaintiff's claim.

10–142 The field of operation of the doctrine has been narrowed by statute.[13] Nowadays, it is the statutory six-year period which operates against a beneficiary in respect of a claim against the trustee for a breach of trust[14] and not the equitable doctrine of "laches." But there are cases outside the Act (*e.g.* claims against trustees who have fraudulently concealed their breaches of trust from the beneficiaries[15]) and cases under the Act[16] in which the liability of the trustee is subject to no *statutory* period of limitation at all (*e.g.* a claim against trustees for property or proceeds thereof retained by them). In such a case the right of the beneficiary will only be barred by an unreasonably long period of delay amounting to laches.[17]

10–143 The ability of equity to act by analogy to the statute is expressly recognised and preserved, for s.36(1) of the 1980 Act provides that the six-year period which it lays down is not to apply to "any claim for specific performance of a contract or for an injunction or for *other equitable relief*" save in so far as a court of equity may apply it by analogy.[18] But the analogous application of s.36(1) is limited to claims for which no express provision is to be found elsewhere in the statute.[19]

10–144 Thus it was held in *Re Diplock*[20] that even if the claims in equity were analogous to the common law action for money had and received (which they were not), they were also "actions in respect of a claim to the personal estate of a deceased person" for which under s.20 of the 1939 Act (now s.22 of the 1980 Act) the relevant period of limitation was one of 12 years from the date when the right to receive the share or interest accrued; accordingly, there was no scope for applying any other period by way of analogy or otherwise.

---

[13] Trustee Act 1888, s.8; Limitation Act 1939 replaced by Limitation Act 1980.

[14] See Limitation Act 1939, s.19(2) replaced by Limitation Act 1980, s.21(3), para.10–150; *Re Pauling's S.T.* [1964] Ch. 303. For reform see Law Com No.270, *Limitation of Actions.*

[15] Limitation Act 1980, s.32(1)(b), para.10-146. In *Tito v Waddell (No.2)* [1977] Ch. 106 at 248–251, Megarry J. held that breaches of the self-dealing rule would also be outside the Act, but the CA declined to follow him on this point in *Gwembe Valley Development Co. Ltd v Koshy (No.3)* [2004] 1 B.C.L.C. 131, holding at [108] that it would be anomalous and unnecessarily complicated to apply different limitation periods to claims for breach of fiduciary duty and claims against trustees who purchase trust property.

[16] Limitation Act 1980, s.21(1), para.10–148.

[17] See *McDonnell v White* (1865) 11 H.L.C. 271; *Sleeman v Wilson* (1871) L.R. 13 Eq. 36; *Tito v Waddell (No.2)* [1977] Ch. 106 at 248–250.

[18] On this and actions for accounts, see *Tito v Waddell (No.2)* [1977] Ch. 106 at 250–252 discussing Limitation Act 1939, s.2(7) replaced by Limitation Act 1980, s.36(1).

[19] A case like *Re Robinson* [1911] 1 Ch. 502 would be decided today in accordance with the provisions of s.21(3) of the Limitation Act 1980 and not by the use of any analogy to the statute. But note that in *Gwembe Valley Development Co. Ltd v Koshy (No.3)* [2004] 1 B.C.L.C. 131 the CA resolved a limitation point in relation to a claim against a company director *both* on the basis that he was a constructive trustee and so a trustee within s.21 *and* on the basis that the rules governing claims by beneficiaries for recovery of trust property should apply by way of analogy under s.36.

[20] [1948] Ch. 465 at 502–516; when the case reached the House of Lords, *sub nom. Ministry of Health v Simpson* [1951] A.C. 251, their Lordships approved the views of the Court of Appeal on the applicability of s.20 of the Limitation Act 1939 (now s.22 of the 1980 Act) and it therefore became unnecessary to express an opinion on the applicability of s.26 thereof (now s.32 of the 1980 Act). It seems s.22 of the 1980 Act applies even after the personal representatives have become trustees.

However, the six-year period applicable to an action for damages for **10–145** fraud at common law has been held[21] to apply by analogy to equitable claims to make a person who is not a trustee personally liable for dishonest assistance in a breach of fiduciary duty or for knowingly dealing inconsistently with fiduciary obligations affecting property received even if not initially aware that it was trust property.

The equitable rule that time would not run against the plaintiff in cases **10–146** of fraud and mistake is adopted by section 32(1) of the 1980 Act (replacing and amending s.26 of the 1939 Act) which provides[22]:

> "Where in the case of any action for which a period of limitation is prescribed by this Act, either:
>
> (a) the action is based upon the fraud of the defendant or his agent or of any person through whom he claims or his agent, or
> (b) any fact relevant to the plaintiff's right of action has been deliberately concealed from him by any such person as aforesaid, or
> (c) the action is for relief from the consequences of mistake,
>
> the period of limitation shall not begin to run until the plaintiff has discovered the fraud concealment or mistake, as the case may be, or could with reasonable diligence have discovered it."

Subsection (3) goes on to protect purchasers taking under transactions without notice of the fraud having been committed or the concealment or mistake having been made, as the case may be. "Deliberate commission of a breach of duty in circumstances in which it is unlikely to be discovered for some time amounts to deliberate concealment of the facts involved in that breach of duty."[23] The House of Lords[24] has held that where after a cause of action has arisen there was a deliberate concealment of facts relevant to the plaintiff's cause of action time does not begin to run until the concealment was or should have been discovered. In a separate case, the House of Lords has also held that a defendant does not deliberately commit a breach of duty unless he intends to commit the act which constitutes the breach of duty and realizes that the act involves a breach of duty.[25]

It was decided in *Phillips-Higgins v Harper*[26] that paragraph (c) does not **10–147** apply to the case of a right of action concealed from the plaintiff by a mistake. Its scope is limited to actions where a mistake has been made and

---

[21] *Coulthard v Disco Mix Club Ltd* [1999] 2 All E.R. 457; *Companhia de Seguros Imperio v Heath Ltd* [2001] 1 W.L.R. 112.

[22] See *Nocton v Lord Ashburton* [1914] A.C. 932 at 936, 958; *Kitchen v R.A.F. Association* [1958] 1 W.L.R. 563 at C.A. (solicitor's negligence); *Baker v Medway Supplies* [1958] 1 W.L.R. 1216 (fraudulent conversion of money); *Bartlett v Barclays Bank Trust Co.* [1980] 1 All E.R. 139 at 154; *Peco Arts Inc. v Hazlitt Gallery Ltd* [1983] 3 All E.R. 193 (reasonable diligence in discovering drawing not an original).

[23] Limitation Act 1980 s.32(2); *King v Victor Parsons & Co.* [1973] 1 W.L.R. 29 at 33, *per* Lord Denning M.R. This reflects the old case law on (b) when it was known as fraudulent concealment in Limitation Act 1939, s.26.

[24] *Sheldon v R. H. Outhwaite (Underwriting Agencies) Ltd* [1996] A.C. 102. The meaning of deliberate concealment in sub-s.32(1)(b) and 32(2) is also reviewed in *Williams v Fanshaw Porter Hazelhurst* [2004] P.N.L.R. 544 and *Newgate Stud Co. v Penfold* [2004] EWHC 2993 (Ch).

[25] *Cave v Robinson Jarvis and Rolf* [2003] 1 A.C. 384.

[26] [1954] 1 Q.B. 411.

has had certain consequences and the plaintiff is seeking to be relieved from those consequences, *e.g.* actions to recover money paid under a mistake; to rescind or rectify contracts on the ground of mistake; to reopen accounts settled in consequence of mistakes. It applies, in fact, only where mistake is an essential ingredient of the cause of action, and it does not help a plaintiff to ascertain the amount still due to him after the ordinary period of limitation has expired. The anomalous result is that a person who has by mistake paid too much can take advantage of the section, but the person who has by mistake received too little cannot avail himself of it.

Statutory rules affording little protection to trustees

10–148 Section 21 of the Act reads as follows:

"(1) No period of limitation prescribed by this Act shall apply to an action by a beneficiary under a trust, being an action:

(a) in respect of any fraud or fraudulent breach of trust to which the trustee was a party or privy; or

(b) to recover from the trustee trust property or the proceeds thereof in the possession of the trustee, or previously received by the trustee and converted to his use.

10–149 (2) Where a trustee who is also a beneficiary under the trust receives or retains trust property or its proceeds as his share on a distribution of trust property under the trust, his liability in any action brought by virtue of subsection (1)(b) above to recover that property or its proceeds after the expiration of the period of limitation prescribed by this Act for bringing an action to recover trust property shall be limited to the excess over his proper share.

This subsection only applies if the trustee acted honestly and reasonably in making the distribution.

10–150 (3) Subject to the preceding provisions of this section an action by a beneficiary to recover trust property or in respect of any breach of trust, not being an action for which a period of limitation is prescribed by any other provision of this Act,[27] shall not be brought after the expiration of six years from the date on which the right of action accrued. For the purposes of this subsection the right of action shall not be treated as having accrued to any beneficiary entitled to a future interest in the trust property until the interest fell into possession.

10–151 (4) No beneficiary as against whom there would be a good defence under this Act shall derive any greater or other benefit from a judgment or order obtained by any other beneficiary than he could have obtained if he had brought the action and this Act had been pleaded in defence."

10–152 The word "trustee" is defined for the purposes of s.21 by reference to section 68(17) of the Trustee Act 1925. This definition excludes persons owing the duties incident to an estate conveyed by way of mortgage,[28] but

---

[27] Where personal representatives have become trustees upon completing administration of an estate the relationship between s.21(3) and s.22 is unclear. It would seem that the breadth of s.22 (formerly s.20 of the 1939 Act) makes the 12-year period applicable: *Re Diplock* [1948] Ch. 465 at 511–513; *Ministry of Health v Simpson* [1951] A.C. 251 at 276–277.

[28] But a prior mortgagee of land exercising his power of sale is a trustee of the surplus for subsequent mortgagees after meeting his own claims. See *Thorne v Heard* [1894] 1 Ch. 599; the Law of Property Act 1925, s.105.

includes constructive trustees and personal representatives. It has been held to include the directors of a company,[29] but not trustees in bankruptcy[30] nor apparently the liquidators of companies in voluntary liquidation.[31]

The Court of Appeal[32] has distinguished two classes of "constructive **10–153** trustees": (1) where the defendant acquired the property, agreeable to it being held by him as a trustee or as a fiduciary before the conduct complained of by the claimant; (2) where the wrongful conduct of the defendant in asserting his selfish interest led to him being a constructive trustee of property or personally liable to account as a constructive trustee for dishonest assistance in a breach of trust or fiduciary duty or for receiving trust or fiduciary property for his own benefit when unaware it was such property but later dealing inconsistently with it after becoming aware it was such property. Instances within (1) include trustees *de son tort* (assuming trusteeship functions in the beneficiaries' interests) but not the type of executor *de son tort* who acts in her own interest,[33] and include agents, like solicitors receiving trust property knowing it to be such and agreeing to treat it as such but who subsequently treat it as if not trust property but their own. Perpetual liability under section 21(1) only applies to the first class of constructive trustee.

The section is limited to actions by *beneficiaries* in respect of trust **10–154** property. It is thought, however, that a newly-appointed trustee would have the same rights as the beneficiaries themselves against the surviving trustees.[34] A claim by the Attorney-General against trustees of a charitable trust (which has no beneficiary) is outside the section.[35]

Perpetual liability is confined under this section as under the 1888 Act **10–155** for express trustees to cases of (a) fraudulent[36] breaches of trust and (b) of retention or conversion of the trust property. It appears from *Thorne v Heard*[37] that the negligence of a trustee, resulting in his solicitor embezzling the trust funds, was insufficient to render the trustee "party or privy" to the fraud. On the face of it it appears that there could be perpetual liability for an innocent recipient of trust property from a fraudulent trustee,[38] although it would be fairer for there only to be such liability if the recipient were privy to the fraud.

[29] *Re Lands Allotments Co.* [1894] 1 Ch. 616 at 631, 638, 643 and *Whitwam v Watkin* (1898) 78 L.T. 188.
[30] *Re Cornish* [1896] 1 Q.B. 99.
[31] *Re Windsor Steam Coal Co. (1901) Ltd* [1928] Ch. 609; affd. on a different ground [1929] 1 Ch. 151.
[32] *Paragon Finance plc v Thakerar & Co* [1999] 1 All E.R. 400 at 408–409; *Companhia de Seguros Imperio v Heath Ltd* [2001] 1 W.L.R. 112. It seems that a company director who obtains the company's property for himself by the misuse of his power is a constructive trustee within (1): *J.J. Harrison (Properties) Ltd v Harrison* [2002] 1 B.C.L.C. 162 at [29]. See too *Gwembe Valley Development Co. Ltd v Koshy (No.3)* [2004] 1 B.C.L.C. 131 at [77]–[102].
[33] *Jones v Williams* [2000] Ch. 1 was decided in ignorance of the above two-fold classification, with the second class seemingly being the appropriate one.
[34] See *Re Bowden* (1890) 45 Ch.D. 444, a case decided under the 1888 Act which was not limited to actions by beneficiaries. Also see *Lewin on Trusts* (17th ed.) para.44–21; and the comments in para.10–08, above.
[35] *Att.-Gen. v Cocke* [1988] Ch. 414.
[36] See *North American Land Co. v Watkins* [1904] 1 Ch. 242; [1904] 2 Ch. 233; *Vane v Vane* (1872) L.R. 8 Ch. 383; *Armitage v Nurse* [1998] Ch. 241 at 260.
[37] [1895] A.C. 495.
[38] *G. L. Baker Ltd v Medway Building and Supplies Ltd* [1958] 1 W.L.R. 1216 at 1221–1222.

10–156   The section speaks of property "previously received by the trustee and converted to his use." In *Re Howlett*[39] it was contended that this referred to an *actual* receipt of property, but Danckwerts J. held that it included a *notional* receipt, and so he was able to charge a trustee who had occupied trust property for some 20 years with an occupation rent. To fall foul of s.21(1)(b) a trustee's retention or conversion must be some wrongful application in his own favour.[40]

10–157   Exceptionally, he has some protection under s.21(2) so that if he had distributed one-third of the trust property to himself, honestly and reasonably believing that only three beneficiaries existed, he will be liable to a fourth beneficiary turning up after six years not for a quarter share but only for the one-twelfth difference between the one-third share he took and the one-quarter share which was truly his.

10–158   Section 21(3) of the Act prescribes a six-year period of limitation for breach of trust cases not falling within s.21(1) or (2) or within any other provision of the Act. Thus, if a trustee can show that an innocent or negligent breach of trust led him to part with the trust property the six-year period is the appropriate one to limit his liability. The six-year period will also be appropriate if the trust funds were dissipated by a co-trustee.[41] It is also applicable for personal and proprietary claims against third parties who received trust property[42] for their own benefit unless, perhaps, from a fraudulent trustee.[43]

10–159   The last sentence of s.21(3) protects reversionary interests by enacting that time shall not run against a beneficiary until his interest has fallen into possession.[44] Even before that date a remainderman can sue for breach of trust. In such a case if the prior beneficiary is himself barred the trustees must nevertheless replace the fund at the suit of the remainderman, but during the continuance of the prior beneficiary's interest they will be entitled to the income of the property: for a judgment recovered by one beneficiary is not to improve the position of one who is already barred.[45]

10–160   Where a beneficiary is merely interested under a discretionary trust until obtaining a life interest in possession on attaining 25 years, the Court of Appeal has held[46] that time does not run until the beneficiary obtains the interest in possession on his 25th birthday. It matters not that at 18 a beneficiary, whether her interest is in possession or not, is entitled to see trust accounts, etc., so as to be able to discover a breach of trust. The rationale for s.23(1) "is not that a beneficiary with a future interest has not the means of discovery, but that the beneficiary should not be compelled to

---

[39] [1949] Ch. 767.
[40] *Re Gurney* [1893] 1 Ch. 590; *Re Page* [1893] 1 Ch. 304; *Re Fountaine* [1909] 2 Ch. 382.
[41] *Re Tufnell* (1902) 18 T.L.R. 705; *Re Fountaine* [1909] 2 Ch. 382.
[42] But not the personal estate of a deceased where the 12-year limit under s.22 Limitation Act 1980 applies: *Ministry of Health v Simpson* [1951] A.C. 251.
[43] See note 38 above.
[44] Consent by a life-tenant to an advance in favour of a remainderman does not amount to a release of the life interest so as to convert the remainderman's interest into an interest in possession: *Re Pauling's S.T.* [1964] Ch. 303.
[45] *Re Somerset* [1894] 1 Ch. 231; s.19(3) of the Limitation Act 1939 and s.21(4) of the 1980 Act; *Mara v Browne* [1895] 2 Ch. 69 reversed on another point [1896] 1 Ch. 199.
[46] *Armitage v Nurse* [1998] Ch. 241.

litigate (at considerable personal expense) in respect of an injury to an interest which he may never live to enjoy. Similar reasoning would apply to exclude a person who is merely the object of a discretionary trust or power which may never be exercised in his favour."[47] This might seem to suggest that the liability of trustees of a discretionary trust is open-ended, except for those objects who received a distribution (thereby acquiring an absolute interest in possession before the relevant breach of trust and so have six years in which to act). However, in *Johns v Johns*[48] the New Zealand Court of Appeal reviewed Millett L.J.'s words, and concluded that a discretionary beneficiary would fit the rationale identified by his Lordship only if he had a further interest in the trust fund capable of falling into possession at a future date. Otherwise he "would not fit the clear requirement of a future interest in the trust property".[49]

Section 5. Liability of Trustees *inter se*

Contribution claims between trustees formerly lay in equity: they now lie under the Civil Liability (Contribution) Act 1978 between trustees who are liable "in respect of the same damage."[50] Because trustees in this position are jointly and severally liable to the beneficiaries',[51] one trustee may find himself obliged to pay more than his fair share of their common liability to restore the trust fund or compensate the beneficiaries for loss. In this case, he can recover a contribution of between 1 and 100 per cent of his payment from one or more of the others,[52] depending on the court's assessment of the proportions in which their common liability should be borne.

10–161

It seems likely that when apportioning liability between trustees the courts will continue to draw on the principles which were developed in the Chancery jurisdiction prior to the enactment of the 1978 Act. Thus, they will start with the presumption that co-trustees should share equal responsibility towards the beneficiaries,[53] and they will then look to see whether there are any reasons for departing from this rule. A trustee who has wrongfully misapplied trust funds to his own exclusive use,[54] or who has exclusively benefited as a beneficiary from the breach of trust,[55] must reimburse the others in full in the event that they are ordered to restore the trust fund. So too must a trustee who has acted fraudulently if the others have acted in good faith.[56]

10–162

---

[47] *ibid*, 261, *per* Millett L.J.
[48] [2004] 3 N.Z.L.R. 202.
[49] *ibid.* at [40].
[50] Civil Liability (Contribution) Act 1978, ss.1, 6. Hence a trustee cannot recover a contribution from a co-trustee who is liable only respect of some other damage, or who is not liable to the beneficiaries at all: *cf. Alexander v Perpetual Trustee (W.A.) Ltd* (2004) 204 A.L.R. 417.
[51] See para.10–03, above.
[52] Complete reimbursement is expressly allowed for by s.2(2) of the 1978 Act.
[53] *Lingard v Bromley* (1812) 1 V. & B. 114: *Jesse v Bennett* (1856) 6 De G. M. & G. 609; *Robinson Lingard v Bromley* (1812) 1 V. & B. 114: *Jesse v Bennett* (1856) 6 De G.M. & G. 609; *Robinson v Harkin* [1896] 2 Ch. 415 at 426; *Gilchrist v Dean* [1960] V.R. 266 at 270–271.
[54] *Lincoln v Wright* (1841) 4 Beav. 427; *Thompson v Finch* (1856) 22 Beav. 316 at 327; *Bahin v Hughes* (1886) 31 Ch.D. 390 at 395; *Wynne v Tempest* [1897] 1 Ch. 110; *Goodwin v Duggan* (1996) 41 N.S.W.L.R. 158 at 166.
[55] *Chillingworth v Chambers* [1896] 1 Ch. 685.
[56] *Baynard v Woolley* (1855) 20 Beav. 583 at 585–586; *Elwes v Barnard* (1865) 13 L.T. 426; *Bellemore v Watson* (1885) 1 T.L.R. 241 at 242; *Re Smith* [1896] 1 Ch. 71; *Deloitte Haskins & Sells v Coopers & Lybrand Ltd* Alberta Q.B. 29 November 1996, at [92].

10–163 The courts' general tendency in the cases pre-dating the 1978 Act was to reject the argument that a trustee who played an active part in the management of trust affairs should be liable for a greater share of trust losses than a passive trustee who did nothing and so failed to prevent the losses from occurring.[57] However, this tough line was moderated to the extent that lay trustees were permitted to shift the burden of paying for trust losses onto professional trustees, upon whose expertise the lay trustees had reasonably relied.[58] It may be that the modern proliferation of trust companies will invest this line of authority with increasing significance.[59]

BAHIN v HUGHES

Court of Appeal (1886) 31 Ch.D. 390; 55 L.J.Ch. 472; 54 L.T. 188; 34 W.R. 311; 2 T.L.R. 276 (Cotton, Bowen and Fry L.JJ.)

10–164 A testator, Robert Hughes, bequeathed a legacy of £2,000 to his three daughters—Eliza Hughes, Mrs. Burden and Mrs. Edwards—on trust to invest in specified securities and in real securities in England and Wales. Eliza Hughes, who was the active trustee, and Mr. Burden invested the fund on the (unauthorised) security of leasehold properties, an investment discovered by Mr. Burden. Mrs Edwards had been informed of the proposal, but her concurrence was not obtained. The security proving insufficient, the tenant for life and remaindermen brought this action against Eliza Hughes, Mr. Edwards (whose wife had died) and Mr. and Mrs. Burden, claiming that the defendants were liable to make good the trust fund.[60] Edwards served a third-party notice on Eliza Hughes claiming to be indemnified by her, on the ground that she had assumed the role of sole trustee, that the investment had been made at her instigation, and that she had represented to Mrs. Edwards that the mortgage was a proper and sufficient security.

10–165 *Held*, by Kay J., that the defendants were jointly and severally liable to replace the £2,000, and that the defendant Edwards had no right of indemnity against Eliza Hughes. Edwards appealed.

10–166 COTTON L.J.: ". . . On going into the authorities, there are very few cases in which one trustee, who has been guilty with a co-trustee of breach of trust and held answerable, has successfully sought indemnity as against his co-trustee. In *Lockhart v Reilly*[61] it appears from the report of the case in the *Law Journal* that the trustee by whom the loss was sustained had been not only trustee, but had been and was a solicitor, and acting as solicitor for his self and his co-trustee, and it was on his advice that Lockhart had relied in making the investment which gave rise to the action of the *cestui que trust*. The Lord Chancellor (Lord Cranworth) refers to the

---

[57] *Lingard v Bromley* (1812) 1 V. & B.114 at 117; *Wilson v Moore* (1833) 1 My. & K. 126 at 147; *Bahin v Hughes* (1886) 31 Ch.D. 390 at 396. per Cotton L.J., at para.10–167; *Bacon v Camphausen* (1888) 55 L.T. 851 at 852.

[58] *Lockhart v Reilly* (1856) 25 L.J. Ch. 697, affirmed (1857) 27 L.J. Ch. 54: *Thompson v Finch* (1856) 22 Beav. 316; *Wilson v Thomson* (1875) L.R. 20 Eq. 459: *Re Partington* (1887) 57 L.T. 654; *Re Turner* [1897] 1 Ch. 536; *Re Linsley* [1904] 2 Ch. 785; and *cf. Linsley v Kirstiuk* (1986) 28 D.L.R. (4th) 495.

[59] *Cf. Fales v Canada Permanent Trust Co.* [1977] 2 S.C.R. 302; *Blair v Canada Trust Co.* (1986) 32 D.L.R. (4th) 515.

[60] Prior to s.18 of the Married Women's Property Act of 1882 (which did not apply to the present case) a married woman could not act as trustee without the participation of her husband (Mr. Edwards); he was necessarily a trustee through her trusteeship, and was responsible for her breaches of trust.

[61] (1856) 25 L.J.Ch. 697 at 702.

fact that he was a solicitor, and makes the remark: 'The whole thing was trusted to him. He was the solicitor, and, independently of the consideration that one cannot help seeing it was done with a view of favouring his own family, yet if that had not been so, the co-trustee leaves it with the solicitor-trustee, by whose negligence (I use no harsher word) all this evil, in a great degree, has arisen.' Therefore the Lord Chancellor, in giving his decision, relies upon the fact of the trustee being a solicitor. In *Thompson v Finch*[62] was conceded to prove against the estate of the deceased trustee for the full loss sustained; but it appears that in this case also he was a solicitor, and that he really took this money to himself, for he mixed it with his own money, and invested it on a mortgage; and therefore it was held that the trustee was entitled to indemnity from the estate of the co-trustee, who was a solicitor. This was affirmed in the Court of Appeal; and the Court of Appeal took so strong a view of the conduct of the solicitor that both of the judges concurred in thinking that he ought to be called on to show cause why he should not be struck off the rolls. Of course, where one trustee has got the money into his own hands, and made use of it, he will be liable to his co-trustee to give him an indemnity. Now I think it wrong to lay down any limitation of the circumstances under which one trustee would be held liable to the other for indemnity, both having been held liable to the *cestui que trust*; but so far as cases have gone at present, relief has only been granted against a trustee who has himself got the benefit of the breach of trust, or between whom and his co-trustees there has existed a relation which will justify the court in treating him solely liable for the breach of trust . . .

"Miss Hughes was the active trustee and Mr. Edwards did nothing, and in my opinion it would be laying down a wrong rule that where one trustee acts honestly, though erroneously, the other trustee is to be held entitled to indemnity who by doing nothing neglects his duty more than the acting trustee. That Miss Hughes made an improper investment is true, but she acted honestly, and intended to do the best she could, and believed that the property was sufficient security for the money, although she made no inquiries about their being leasehold houses. In my opinion the money was lost just as much by the default of Mr. Edwards as by the innocent though erroneous action of his co-trustee, Miss Hughes. All the trustees were in the wrong, and every one is equally liable to indemnify the beneficiaries." *Appeal dismissed.*

10–167

HEAD v GOULD

Chancery Division [1898] 2 Ch. 250; 67 L.J.Ch. 480; 78 L.T. 739

Miss Head and Mr. Gould were appointed new trustees of certain marriage settlements (the beneficial interests being the same under both settlements), and thenceforth Gould acted as solicitor to the trusts. Miss Head was one of the remaindermen under these settlements, the tenant for life being her mother. The new trustees sold a house forming part of the trust, and in breach of trust handed the proceeds of sale to the tenant for life. Part of the trust property consisted also of certain policies on the life of Mrs. Head, policies which Mrs. Head had mortgaged to the trust by way of security for advances of trust capital which the former trustees had made to her at her urgent request for the purpose of assisting the family. These policies were (in breach of trust) surrendered by the new trustees with the concurrence of Mrs. Head.

10–168

---

[62] (1856) 25 L.J.Ch. 681.

10–169   Miss Head claimed to be indemnified by her co-trustee, Gould, under circumstances which appear from the judgment:

10–170   KEKEWICH J.: ". . . It will be convenient here at once to deal with the claim made by Miss Head against her co-trustee, Gould. By her third party notice she seeks to be indemnified by him against loss by reason of the breaches of trust, on the ground that the loss and misapplication (if any) of the trust funds, or any part thereof, were occasioned entirely by his acts or defaults, and that he assumed to act as solicitor to the trust estate and as the sole trustee thereof, and exercised control of the administration of the trust funds, and that whatever was done by herself in connection with the trust was at his instigation and in reliance upon his advice.

10–171   "This is a serious charge, and if it had been proved would have entitled her to the relief claimed according to well-known and well-recognised principles. . . There is before me no evidence bringing the case within those principles, or showing that the charge which is correctly formulated on them is consistent with the facts. My conclusion from such evidence as there is before the court is distinctly adverse to the claim. I know that, before the appointment of herself and Gould as trustees, Miss Head was an active party to the importunities of her mother which induced the former trustees to commit a breach of trust for their benefit, and that she looked to the change of trustees as a means of, in some way or other, obtaining further advances. I know, further, that she was well acquainted with the position of the trust, and that it was all-important to maintain the policies and to appropriate the rents of the house to that purpose. She now affects to ignore all that has been done since her appointment, and professes not to remember having executed the several instruments which must have been executed by her for the sale of the house and the surrender of the policies, or the receipt of moneys arising therefrom. With regret, and under a painful sense of duty, I am bound to say that I do not credit her testimony. True it is that the defendant, Gould, is a solicitor, and that he was appointed a trustee for that very reason. True no doubt, also, that the legal business was managed by him, and I do not propose to absolve him from any responsibility attaching to him on that ground; but I do not myself think that Byrne J. or any other judge ever intended to hold that a man is bound to indemnify his co-trustee against loss *merely* because he was a solicitor, when that co-trustee was an active participator in the breach of trust complained of, and is not proved to have participated merely in consequence of the *advice and control* of the solicitor. . . ."

10–172   *Held* therefore, the trustee, Miss Head, had no claim of indemnity against her co-trustee.[63]

QUESTIONS

10–173   1. What should the measure of liability be in the following alternative circumstances where, in breach of trust, Samantha Smith and Roger Robinson, trustees of a family trust:

  (a) transfer the £2 million portfolio of investments and cash to a discretionary portfolio manager and either (i) two months later before any of the investments have been replaced there is a stock-

---

[63] *Cf. Re Mulligan* [1998] 1 N.Z.L.R. 181, where a lay trustee (and life tenant) insisted on her solicitor co-trustees pursuing an investment policy to the disadvantage of the remaindermen.

market collapse, so that the portfolio is worth only £1$\frac{1}{2}$ million or (ii) four years later, after the original investments have all been replaced, there is a stock-market collapse, so that the portfolio is worth only £1$\frac{1}{2}$ million, having been work £2$\frac{1}{4}$ million earlier;

(b) transfer investments worth £200,000 to their children Amanda Smith and Jack Robinson in consideration of their marriage and either (i) two months later before any of the investments have been sold there is a stock-market collapse, so that the investments are worth only £150,000 or (ii) four years later, after the investments have been sold and used to purchase a £200,000 house (now worth £280,000) there is a stock-market collapse, so that if the investments had been retained they would suddenly have depreciated from £250,000 to £175,000.

2. Ted and Tom are trustees of a £500,000 fund held on trust for Ted **10–174** himself, Arthur, Brian, Charles and David in equal shares contingent upon each attaining 30 years of age. To allay any suspicions of the other beneficiaries Ted takes little part in running the trust affairs, relying to a large extent on Tom, a 50-year old solicitor.

Tom and Arthur consider in 1998 that it would be desirable to buy shares in Exploration Syndicate Co. Ltd but realise that the trustees have no power to do so under the Trustees Investments Act 1961, the will creating the trust conferring no express powers of investment. Nevertheless, Tom writes to Ted telling him that his City connections lead him to consider it a very good idea to buy shares in Exploration Syndicate Co. Ltd For this purpose they can call in £30,000 deposited with the Countrywide Building Society bringing in a gross 8 per cent interest. Ted replies by letter, "If you wish us to invest that £30,000 in the Exploration Syndicate Co. Ltd that is all right by me."

Tom then wrote to Brian, Charles and David, "Ted and I as trustees are considering investing £30,000 of the trust funds in buying shares in the Exploration Syndicate Co. Ltd That is quite a lot of money but we would consider it well spent on such shares. However, before we go ahead we would like to have your consent. Arthur has already consented and we look forward to receiving replies from you and the other beneficiaries quite soon."

Brian and David replied briefly consenting. Charles replied, "I am quite happy for the £30,000 to be invested in the shares proposed. Of course, I assume they are authorised investments." The beneficiaries, Ted, Arthur, Brian, Charles and David were then respectively aged 29, 27, 25, 23 and 17 years. After the replies had been received the £30,000 was invested in buying the proposed shares.

Three years later the company collapsed and the whole £30,000 was lost, the shares only having produced a gross 3 per cent yield in the first year and nothing thereafter.

Advise the trustees of their position *vis-à-vis* (1) the beneficiaries and (2) themselves.

Chapter 11

PERSONAL LIABILITY OF THIRD PARTIES INVOLVED IN A BREACH OF TRUST

Section 1. Introduction

11–01 Third parties involved in a breach of trust can become personally liable to the beneficiaries in various ways. First, a person who is neither a trustee, nor authorised by the trustees, but who takes it upon himself to intermeddle with trust affairs, or to perform acts characteristic of the trustee's office, is personally liable to account to the beneficiaries for trust assets which come into his hands, as a trustee *de son tort*.

11–02 Secondly, a person who dishonestly assists in a breach of trust can become personally liable to restore the trust fund, to compensate the beneficiaries for loss, to pay them the amount of profits made by the wrongdoing trustee, or to pay them the amount of his own profits.

11–03 Thirdly, a person who dishonestly receives misdirected trust property for his own benefit with knowledge that it has been paid to him in breach of trust, or who receives such property innocently but then acquires knowledge of its improper provenance before dishonestly dealing with it for his own benefit, is personally liable to repay the value of the property and any profits deriving from it. It also seems likely that a recipient of misdirected trust funds who does not know of their improper provenance at the time of receipt, and who does not acquire such knowledge by the time that he innocently deals with them for his own benefit, is nonetheless personally liable to repay the value of the property, on the ground that he has been unjustly enriched at the beneficiaries' expense, unless he can establish a change of position defence.

11–04 We have already discussed the position of a trustee *de son tort* in Chapter 6.[1] In this chapter, we shall discuss dishonest assistants and knowing recipients.

Personal liability to account as a constructive trustee

11–05 The defendants in these situations are all commonly said to owe a personal liability to account as constructive trustees. Confusingly, however, the courts do not always mean the same thing when they use this expression. In the case of a trustee *de son tort*, they mean that when the defendant acquires trust property through his intermeddling he holds this property on constructive trust, so that he is personally liable to account for it in his

---

[1] See paras 6–220 to 6–222, above.

capacity as trustee of the constructive trust. It seems likely that the courts also use the phrase in this way when describing the liability of knowing recipients, given that constructive trusts are imposed on misdirected trust funds received by third parties who are not *bona fide* purchasers for value without notice of the beneficiaries' equitable proprietary interest.[2]

In the case of dishonest assistants, however, the expression means **11–06** something different. A dishonest assistant can be liable whether or not he has received trust property which might be impressed with a constructive trust for the beneficiaries.[3] Hence when the courts say that he is personally liable to account as a constructive trustee, they do not mean that he is himself a trustee of property for which he must account: "there is no real trust and usually no chance of a proprietary remedy" against him,[4] and "he is in fact not a trustee at all."[5] Instead, they mean that he should be treated, by a legal fiction, as though he were one of the trustees in whose breach of trust he has participated, so as to fix him with the same personal liabilities as the trustees owe to the beneficiaries: his liability derives from and duplicates theirs.[6] Another way of putting this is to say that liability for dishonest assistance is a civil secondary liability, analogous to the criminal secondary liability of those who procure, aid, or abet a crime.[7] This has important consequences for the rules on causation and quantification of remedies which govern dishonest assistance claims, which we shall discuss below.[8]

Section 2. Dishonest Assistants

The primary breach

Claims for dishonest assistance clearly lie against defendants who assist in **11–07** misapplications of property by trustees, whether express, constructive, or resulting,[9] and other fiduciaries, *e.g.* company directors.[10] It is unclear

---

[2] See para.12–101. If this trust is imposed in order to reverse the recipients' unjust enrichment at the beneficiaries' expense, then it might be preferable to describe it as a resulting trust: see para.6–228, above.

[3] *Royal Brunei Airlines Sdn. Bhd. v Tan* [1995] 2 A.C. 378 at 382, *per* Lord Nicholls; at para.11–59; *Houghton v Fayers* [2000] Lloyd's Rep. Bank. 145 at 149.

[4] *Coulthard v Disco Mix Club Ltd* [2000] 1 W.L.R. 707 at 731.

[5] *Dubai Aluminium Co. Ltd v Salaam* [2003] 2 A.C. 366 at [141], *per* Lord Millett. See too *Belmont Finance Corp. Ltd v Williams Furniture Ltd* [1979] Ch. 250 at 272. But *cf. Westdeutsche Landesbank Girozentrale v Islington L.B.C.* [1996] A.C. 669 at 705, *per* Lord Browne-Wilkinson, above at para.5–188; *Giumelli v Giumelli* (1999) 196 C.L.R. 101 at 112.

[6] *Rolfe v Gregory* (1865) 4 De G. J. & S. 576 at 579, *per* Lord Westbury L.C.; *U.S. Surgical Corp. v Hospital Products International Pty. Ltd* (1982) 2 N.S.W.L.R. 766 at 817 (not considered on appeal); *Arab Monetary Fund v Hashim* Q.B.D. 29 July 1994, *per* Chadwick J.; *Royal Brunei Airlines Sdn. Bhd. v Tan* [1995] 2 A.C. 378 at 385; *Australian Securities Commission v A.S. Nominees Ltd* (1995) 62 F.C.R. 504 at 523; *Equiticorp Industries Ltd v R. (No.47)* [1998] 2 N.Z.L.R. 481 at 658; *Bankgesellschaft Berlin A.G. v Makris* Q.B.D. (Comm. Ct.) 22 January 1999, *per* Cresswell J.; *Grupo Torras v Al-Sabah (No.5)* [2001] Lloyd's Rep. Bank. 36 at 61–62.

[7] P. Sales, "The Tort of Conspiracy and Civil Liability" [1990] C.L.J. 491; D J. Cooper, *Secondary Liability for Civil Wrongs* (PhD thesis, University of Cambridge, 1996).

[8] See paras 11–15 to 11–18.

[9] For the latter, see: *Bank Tejerat v Hong Kong and Shanghai Banking Corp. (C.I.) Ltd* [1995] 1 Lloyd's Rep. 239; *Heinl v Jyske Bank (Gibraltar) Ltd* [1999] Lloyd's Rep. Bank. 511.

[10] *Selangor United Rubber Estates Ltd v Cradock (No.3)* [1968] 1 W.L.R. 1555; *Belmont Finance Corp. Ltd v Williams Furniture Ltd (No.2)* [1980] 1 All E.R. 393; *Heinl v Jyske Bank (Gibraltar) Ltd* [1999] Lloyd's Rep. Bank. 511.

whether claims also lie against defendants who assist in breaches of fiduciary duty that do not entail the misapplication of property,[11] but in our view they should, to reinforce the integrity of fiduciary relationships.

11–08   There was originally no requirement that a defendant should have assisted in a dishonest breach of duty.[12] Then, in an unreserved judgment not discussing the earlier cases, Lord Selborne L.C. held that assistants in a breach of trust could not be liable unless "they assist with knowledge in a dishonest and fraudulent design on the part of the trustees".[13] In his speech for the Privy Council in *Royal Brunei Airlines Sdn Bhd v Tan*, Lord Nicholls declined to apply this rule, holding that the claimant did not need to show that the breach of trust assisted by the defendant had been a dishonest breach.[14] This finding has now been affirmed by the House of Lords, in *Twinsectra Ltd v Yardley*.[15]

The defendant's state of mind

11–09   Turning to the defendant's own state of mind, the cases on this point had got into a sorry state prior to *Royal Brunei*. In *Baden, Delvaux v Société Générale pour Favoriser le Développement du Commerce et de l'Industrie en France S.A.*,[16] Peter Gibson J. had held that a defendant might be liable for assisting in a breach of trust even if his behaviour fell short of dishonesty,[17] and he had accepted that any of five types of knowledge would serve to render a defendant liable as an assistant in a breach of trust: (i) actual knowledge; (ii) wilfully shutting one's eyes to the obvious; (iii) wilfully and recklessly failing to make such inquiries as an honest and reasonable man would make; (iv) knowledge of circumstances which would indicate the facts to an honest and reasonable man; (v) knowledge of circumstances which would put an honest and reasonable man on inquiry.[18] He also held that types (ii)-(v) could all be distinguished from type (i), as examples of "imputed" or "constructive knowledge".[19]

11–10   The *Baden, Delvaux* classification of knowledge subsequently formed the starting point for discussion in a series of English cases on liability for assisting in a breach of trust. The points were made in these cases, that categories (ii) and (iii) should more properly be understood as types of actual, rather than constructive knowledge;[20] that constructive knowledge is

---

[11] No: *Cowan de Groot Properties Ltd v Eagle Trust plc* [1991] B.C.L.C. 1045 at 1103; *Satnam Investments Ltd v Dunlop Heywood & Co. Ltd* [1999] 1 B.C.L.C. 385 at 404; *Petrotrade Inc. v Smith* [2000] 1 Lloyd's Rep. 486 at 491–492. Maybe: *Brown v Bennett* [1999] 1 B.C.L.C. 649 at 657–659; *Fyffes Group Ltd v Templeman* [2000] 2 Lloyd's Rep. 643; *Gencor A.C.P. Ltd v Dalby* [2000] 2 B.C.L.C. 734 at 757. Yes: *Waxman v Waxman* (2004) 7 I.T.E.L.R. 162 at [546].
[12] *Fyler v Fyler* (1841) 3 Beav. 550; *Att.-Gen v Corporation of Leicester* (1844) 7 Beav. 176.
[13] *Barnes v Addy* (1874) L.R. 9 Ch. App. 244 at 252, confirmed in *Belmont Finance Corp. v Williams* [1979] Ch. 250 at 257.
[14] [1995] 2 A.C. 378 at 385, at para.11–85.
[15] [2002] 2 A.C. 164 at 171 and 195; *infra* at paras 11–89 and 11–113.
[16] [1993] 1 W.L.R. 509 (the case was decided in 1983).
[17] *ibid.* at 577.
[18] *ibid.* at 575–587.
[19] *ibid.* at 576.
[20] *Agip (Africa) Ltd v Jackson* [1990] Ch. 265 at 293; *Cowan de Groot Properties Ltd v Eagle Trust plc* [1991] B.C.L.C. 1045 at 1103.

not the same thing as constructive notice;[21] that businessmen do not normally make inquiries unless the facts are such as to raise suspicion, suggesting that constructive notice, as that term is generally understood in relation to dealings with land, has only a limited role to play in the context of commercial transactions;[22] that categories (i), (ii), and (iii) certainly suffice for liability as an assistant;[23] and that categories (iv) and (v) could take in dishonest as well as negligent states of mind.[24] A consensus also emerged that, contrary to Peter Gibson J's view, a defendant must have been dishonest to incur liability.[25]

The view that dishonesty is a pre-requisite for liability was not beyond **11–11** doubt, however, as a line of cases pre-dating *Baden, Delvaux* and holding that a defendant can be liable if he has honestly but negligently failed to investigate the circumstances of an impugned transaction, was never overruled.[26] The body of law founded on the *Baden, Delvaux* classification also suffered from the more general problem that it was over-theorized: as Lord Nicholls put it in *Royal Brunei*, the courts were led into "tortuous convolutions" in their efforts to investigate the "sort" of knowledge possessed by defendants, "when the truth is that 'knowingly' is inapt as a criterion when applied to the gradually darkening spectrum where the differences are of degree and not kind."[27]

In *Royal Brunei*, Lord Nicholls therefore determined to start afresh. He **11–12** held that knowledge is best avoided as a defining ingredient of liability, and that the *Baden, Delvaux* scale is best forgotten in this context.[28] He rejected the idea that unconscionability should be the touchstone for liability, unless it is made clear "what, in this context, unconscionable *means*",[29] and he held that to fix a defendant with liability, it must be shown that he has acted dishonestly. He emphasised that the test for dishonesty in this context is not purely subjective, in the sense that individuals are not "free to set their own standards of honesty in particular circumstances",[30] and must be judged by reference to the standards of right-thinking members of society. So, as the courts have put it in subsequent cases, there is no "Robin Hood" defence to an action for dishonest assistance.[31]

---

[21] *Re Montagu's S.T.* [1987] Ch. 264 at 277–9; at paras 11–36 *et seq.*

[22] *Cowan de Groot Properties Ltd v Eagle Trust plc* [1991] B.C.L.C. 1045 at 1112; *Eagle Trust plc v S.B.C. Securities Ltd* [1993] 1 W.L.R. 484 at 492–493; *El Ajou v Dollar Land Holdings plc* [1993] B.C.L.C. 735 at 758.

[23] *Lipkin Gorman v Karpnale Ltd* [1989] 1 W.L.R. 1340 at 1355, not considered on appeal [1991] 2 A.C. 548.

[24] *Agip (Africa) Ltd v Jackson* [1990] Ch. 265 at 293; *Cowan de Groot Properties Ltd v Eagle Trust plc* [1991] B.C.L.C. 1045 at 1112.

[25] e.g. *Agip (Africa) Ltd v Jackson* [1990] 1 Ch. 265 at 292–293, on appeal: [1991] Ch. 547 at 569; *Lipkin Gorman v Karpnale Ltd* [1989] 1 W.L.R. 1340 at 1354–5.

[26] *Selangor United Rubber Estates Ltd v Cradock (No.3)* [1968] 1 W.L.R. 1555; *Karak Rubber Co. Ltd v Burden (No.2)* [1972] 1 W.L.R. 602; *Rowlandson v National Westminister Bank Ltd* [1978] 1 W.L.R. 798.

[27] [1995] 2 A.C. 378 at 391; at para.11–79.

[28] *ibid.* at 392; at para.11–85.

[29] *ibid* at 392 (his emphasis).

[30] *ibid.* at 389; at para.11–71.

[31] *Grupo Torras S.A. v Al-Sabah (No.5)* [2001] Lloyd's Rep. Bank. 36 at 60; *Walker v Stones* [2001] Q.B. 902 at 939; *Twinsectra Ltd v Yardley* [2002] 2 A.C. 164 at 172. *Cf Consul Developments Pty. Ltd v D.P.C. Estates Pty. Ltd* (1975) 132 C.L.R. 373 at 398.

11–13   Did Lord Nicholls mean to lay down a test of self-conscious dishonesty analogous to the test laid down in criminal law by Lord Lane C.J. in *R. v Ghosh*[32]; *i.e.* must a defendant have done something that right-thinking people would regard as dishonest, and also have been aware that they would view his actions in this light? There are strong pointers in Lord Nicholls' speech that he did not mean to say this, particularly his statement that:[33]

> "Whatever may be the position in some criminal or other contexts (see, for instance, *R. v Ghosh*), in the context of the accessory liability principle acting dishonestly, or with a lack of probity, which is synonymous, means simply not acting as an honest person would in the circumstances. This is an objective standard."

11–14   Notwithstanding this, however, and notwithstanding the fact that in his dissenting speech in the House of Lords in *Twinsectra Ltd v Yardley*, Lord Millett concluded that Lord Nicholls did not mean to introduce a test of self-conscious dishonesty, the majority of their Lordships held in *Twinsectra* that this was what he meant to do. With respect to Lord Hutton, who gave the leading speech, his reading of Lord Nicholls' words was strained, and considered as a matter of textual interpretation, Lord Millett's reading is more convincing.[34] However, Lord Hutton offered one policy justification for his conclusion, namely that "a finding by a judge that a defendant has been dishonest is a grave finding, and it is particularly grave against a professional man, such as a solicitor."[35] To this it can be added that because liability for dishonest assistance is a civil secondary liability, the causation rules that govern the claim are much more claimant-friendly than those which govern most claims for wrongdoing, suggesting that such liability should be incurred only by those whose state of mind renders them particularly blameworthy.[36]

Causation

11–15   Generally speaking, the law of civil wrongs, like the criminal law, is "moulded on the philosophy of autonomy",[37] with the result that it does not generally regard loss flowing from the actions of a primary wrongdoer as having been caused by the actions of a participant who has induced or assisted in the commission of the wrong.[38] However, civil secondary liability is an exception to this general rule: a defendant fixed with liability of this

---

[32] [1982] Q.B. 1053.
[33] [1995] 2 A.C. 378 at 389; at para.11–71.
[34] The NZCA displayed little enthusiasm for the majority view in *U.S. International Marketing Ltd v National Bank of New Zealand Ltd* [2004] 1 N.Z.L.R. 589, but did not have to decide whether self-conscious dishonesty is required in New Zealand.
[35] [2002] 2 A.C. 164 at 174.
[36] For precisely this reason, the English courts have refused to hold that civil secondary liability can be incurred by those who assist the commission of a tort: *Credit Lyonnais Bank Nederland N.V. v Export Credits Guarantee Dept* [2000] 1 A.C. 164.
[37] G. Williams, "Complicity, Purpose and the Draft Code" [1990] Crim. L.R. 4, 6.
[38] H.L.A. Hart and A.M. Honoré, *Causation in the Law* 2nd edn (1985), p.385.

sort is liable for loss flowing from the primary wrong even where there is no direct causal link between his actions and the loss. Thus, as Mance L.J. held in the specific context of a dishonest assistance claim, in *Grupo Torras S.A. v Al-Sabah (No.5)*[39]:

"The starting point . . . is that the requirement of dishonest assistance relates not to any loss or damage which may be suffered, but to the breach of trust or fiduciary duty. The relevant enquiry is . . . what loss or damage resulted from the breach of trust or fiduciary duty which has been dishonestly assisted."

This was affirmed on appeal,[40] and then reaffirmed by another Court of Appeal, in *Casio Computer Ltd v Sayo*, where Tuckey L.J. stated that[41]:

"*Grupo Torras* . . . establishes that in a claim for dishonest assistance it is not necessary to show a precise causal link between the assistance and the loss . . . [and that loss] caused by the breach of fiduciary duty is recoverable from the accessory."

Of course, where a defendant's actions have made no difference at all to **11–16** the implementation of a breach of trust or fiduciary duty, "there is no causative effect and therefore no assistance . . . [so that] the requirements of conscience [do not] require any remedy."[42] Hence a claimant must at least show that the defendant's actions have made the fiduciary's breach of duty easier than it would otherwise have been. But the causation require-ment for dishonest assistance is no stronger than this, and it is no answer to a claim, for example, that the claimant's loss would have occurred anyway, because the wrongdoing fiduciary would have committed the breach even if the defendant had not assisted him. Thus a defendant can be liable for actions or omissions which precede the commission of the breach,[43] although he cannot be liable if his actions or omissions only occurred after the breach was fully implemented.[44] However, where the breach has entailed the misapplication of funds, the courts are likely to hold that it was not fully implemented until the funds were hidden away where the beneficiaries could not find them, with the consequence that those who assist in money-laundering activities after trust funds have been removed from a trust account can be fixed with liability for dishonest assistance.[45]

Remedies

Because liability for dishonest assistance is a civil secondary liability which **11–17** derives from and duplicates the liability of the trustee or fiduciary whose breach has been assisted, the remedies available against the dishonest

---

[39] QBD (Comm. Ct.) 24 June 1999.
[40] [2001] Lloyd's Rep. Bank. 36 at 61.
[41] [2001] EWCA Civ 661 at [15].
[42] *Brown v Bennett* [1999] 1 B.C.L.C. 649 at 659, *per* Morritt L.J.
[43] R. P. Austin, "Constructive Trusts" in P. D. Finn (ed.), *Essays in Equity* (1985), pp.196, 236–237, discussing *Adama v Bank of New South Wales* [1984] 1 N.S.W.L.R. 285. See too *Aequitas Ltd v Sparad No. 100 Ltd* [2001] N.S.W.S.C. 14.
[44] *Brown v Bennett* [1998] 2 B.C.L.C. 97 at 105.
[45] *Heinl v Jyske Bank (Gibraltar) Ltd* [1999] Lloyd's Rep. Bank. 511 at 523, approving *Agip (Africa) Ltd v Jackson* [1990] Ch. 265 at 293. See too *Casio Computer Co. Ltd v Sayo* [2001] EWCA Civ 661 at [22].

assistant are identical with the remedies available against the trustee or fiduciary.' Thus, dishonest assistants can be ordered to account for the value of misapplied trust property as a form of secondary substitutive performance of the trustees' obligation to apply the property in accordance with the trust.[46] They can be ordered to pay the same measure of compensation as the trustee or fiduciary would have to pay if the principal sued him for reparation.[47] They can also be ordered to pay the amount of unauthorised profits made by the wrongdoing trustee or fiduciary,[48] and it is "nothing to the point" that they have not enjoyed these profits for themselves.[49] ?

11–18   It sometimes happens that a dishonest assistant makes a profit for himself by assisting in a breach of trust or fiduciary duty which does not correspond to a loss suffered by the claimant. In these circumstances, the trustee or fiduciary owes no primary liability for the assistant's gain, and so the dishonest assistant cannot be made liable to pay over the amount of his profit on the basis that he is secondarily liable to do so. To avoid the conclusion that he is therefore not liable to disgorge his profit, the courts have dealt with cases of this sort by abandoning the theory that liability for dishonest assistance is a civil secondary liability, and ordering an account of profits against the dishonest assistant.[50]

Section 3. Knowing Recipients

11–19   To make a defendant personally liable where he has received misapplied trust assets (or their traceable proceeds) and dealt with them for his own benefit, the beneficiaries must currently show that at the time when the defendant dealt with the property his conscience was affected with knowledge of the breach of trust. This requirement is reflected in the language that is commonly used to describe recipient liability: defendants are said to be liable for "knowing receipt and dealing". The degree of knowledge required for liability under this head has been exhaustively discussed by the courts, but it still cannot be said that they have reached a clear consensus. Moreover, some recent judicial observations on the nature of liability under this head suggest that the time is now ripe for the courts to take a more radical approach altogether, by recognizing not only that it

---

[46] See paras 10–10 *et seq.*, above. Awards of this sort were made against dishonest assistants in, *e.g. Macdonald v Hauer* (1976) 72 D.L.R. (3d) 110 at 129; *Re Bell's Indenture* [1980] 1 W.L.R. 1217 at 1231–1233; *Commercial Union Life Assurance Co. of Canada v John Ingle Insurance Group Inc.* (2002) 22 C.C.L.I. 221, affirmed (2002) 217 D.L.R. (4th) 178; *NCR Australia v Credit Connection Pty. Ltd (in liq.)* [2004] NSWSC 1 at [150]; *Barlow Clowes International Ltd v Eurotrust International Ltd* [2004] W.T.L.R. 45.

[47] See paras 10–45 *et seq.* above. Awards of this sort were made against dishonest assistants in, *e.g. Colour Control Centre Pty. Ltd v Ty* N.S.W. Sup. Ct. (Eq. Div.) 24 July 1995; *Equiticorp Industries Group Ltd v R. (No.47)* [1998] 2 N.Z.L.R. 481 at 658; *Fyffes Group Ltd v Templeman* [2000] 2 Lloyd's Rep. 643.

[48] See paras 6–10 *et seq.*

[49] *Comax Secure Business Services Ltd v Wilson* Q.B.D. June 21, 2001, *per* Richard Seymour Q.C. (sitting as a deputy High Court judge). See too *Canada Safeway Ltd v Thompson* [1951] 3 D.L.R. 295; *Glenko Enterprises Ltd v Keller* [2001] 1 W.W.R. 229 at 257–258.

[50] *Consul Development Pty. Ltd v D.P.C. Estates Pty. Ltd* (1972) 132 C.L.R. 373 at 397, followed in *U.S. Surgical Corp. v Hospital Products International Pty. Ltd* (1982) 2 N.S.W.L.R. 766 at 817, and quoted with approval in *Fyffes Group Ltd v Templeman* [2000] 2 Lloyd's Rep. 643 at 672. See too *Crown Dilmun v Sutton* [2004] 1 B.C.L.C. 468 at [204].

is a fault-based equitable wrong to receive and deal with misapplied trust property for one's own benefit with a dishonest state of mind, but also that a strict liability claim in unjust enrichment concurrently lies against a recipient of misapplied trust property, subject to his ability to raise the defence of change of position.

Ingredients of liability

Before discussing these issues, some points must be made about other **11–20** aspects of liability for knowing receipt. First, liability is not confined to cases concerning misapplied trust property: it may also be incurred where a defendant receives misdirected assets which were controlled by a person, such as a company director, who owed fiduciary duties to a principal in respect of his handling of the property.[51] Secondly, there is no need to show that the trustee or fiduciary misapplied the relevant property with a dishonest state of mind.[52] Thirdly, receipt of trust property includes receipt of the traceable proceeds of trust property, as identified in accordance with the relevant tracing rules.[53] Fourthly, the defendant must have received legal title to the property; for if he has not, then he is strictly liable to repay the amount of the property and no question arises of his holding the property on constructive trust for the claimant, whose remedy will lie at common law.[54] Fifthly, the defendant must have received the property beneficially for himself: he will not be liable if he receives property ministerially, *i.e.* in his capacity as agent for a third party to whom he owes an immediate duty to account for the property, and who is himself immediately liable to the beneficiaries on the defendant's receipt.[55] Sixthly, the defendant must not be in a position to raise the defence of *bona fide* purchase for value of the legal estate without notice of the beneficiaries' interest.[56]

---

[51] *Russell v Wakefield Waterworks Co.* (1875) L.R. 20 Eq. 474 at 479; *Belmont Finance Corp. Ltd v Williams Furniture Ltd (No.2)* [1980] 1 All E.R. 393; *Agip (Africa) Ltd v Jackson* [1991] Ch. 547; *C.M.S. Dolphin Ltd v Simonet* [2001] 2 B.C.L.C. 704.

[52] *Polly Peck International plc v Nadir (No.2)* [1992] 4 All E.R. 769 at 777; *El Ajou v Dollar Land Holdings plc* [1994] 2 All E.R. 685 at 700.

[53] *Agip (Africa) Ltd v Jackson* [1990] Ch. 265 at 289–292; *El Ajou v Dollar Land Holdings plc* [1994] 2 All E.R. 685 at 700; *Boscawen v Bajwa* [1996] 1 W.L.R. 328 at 334; *Foskett v McKeown* [2001] 1 A.C. 102 at 128; *Trustor A.B. v Smallbone (No.2)* [2001] 3 All E.R. 987 at 994. For the rules of tracing, see Chap. 12.

[54] *Criterion Properties plc v Stratford* [2004] 1 W.L.R. 1846; *cf. Trustee of the Property of F.C. Jones & Sons (a firm) v Jones* [1997] Ch. 159. Trustees generally have the power to transfer legal title to trust property even where they act in breach of trust: *Rolled Steel Products (Holdings) Ltd v British Steel Corp.* [1986] Ch. 246 at 304.

[55] *Barnes v Addy* (1874) 9 Ch. App. 244 at 254-5; *Agip (Africa) Ltd v Jackson* [1990] Ch. 265 at 291–2; *Twinsectra Ltd v Yardley* [2002] 2 A.C. 164 at 194; *Evans v European Bank Ltd* (2004) 7 I.T.E.L.R. 19 at [164]–[176]. In these circumstances, the defendant may still be liable for dishonest assistance, depending on his state of mind, as in, *e.g. British North American Elevator Co. v Bank British North American* [1919] A.C. 658; *Papamichael v National Westminster Bank plc* [2003] 1 Lloyd's Rep. 341. The implications of the beneficial receipt requirement for banks are helpfully explored in J P. Moore. *Restitution from Banks* (DPhil thesis, University of Oxford, 2000), discussed in C. Mitchell, "Assistance" in P. Birks and A. Pretto (eds.), *Breach of Trust* (2002) 139, pp.184–187.

[56] *Re Diplock* [1948] Ch. 465 at 535 and 544; *Carl Zeiss Stiftung v Herbert Smith & Co. (a firm) (No.2)* [1969] 2 Ch. 276 at 289; *Cowan de Groot Properties Ltd v Eagle Trust plc* [1992] 4 All E.R. 700 at 767.

Requirement of knowledge

11–21   Like the cases on assistance that pre-date *Royal Airlines Sdn. Bhd. v Tan*,[57] the cases on receipt have often adopted the five-fold classification of knowledge which was approved by Peter Gibson J. in *Baden Delvaux*.[58] There is no clear alignment between actual knowledge, *Baden, Delvaux* categories (i)-(iii), and dishonesty on the one hand, and between constructive knowledge, *Baden, Delvaux* categories (iv)-(v), and negligence on the other. Hence it is difficult to translate decisions which are expressed in the language of *Baden, Delvaux* into the language of dishonesty and negligence. Some cases suggest that carelessness of the kind which is typically exhibited by defendants falling into categories (iv)-(v) will not suffice for liability.[59] But the weight of authority indicates that something less than dishonesty of the sort typically displayed by defendants falling into categories (i)-(iii) will be enough.[60]

11–22   Clearly, though, a person who receives trust or fiduciary property for his own benefit in circumstances where he has actual, "Nelsonian" or "naughty" knowledge of a misapplication will be liable. "Nelsonian" knowledge (after Admiral Nelson putting his telescope to his blind eye to avoid knowledge of flag signals ordering him to withdraw at the Battle of Copenhagen) covers the deliberate shutting of eyes to what would otherwise be obvious.[61] A defendant has "naughty" knowledge where he deliberately or recklessly fails to make the inquiries that an honest, reasonable man would make in circumstances where the defendant's suspicions were aroused.[62] Moreover, if the circumstances were such that the suspicions of an honest, reasonable man would have been aroused then the court will be slow to accept the defendant's protestations that his suspicions were not aroused, and so will be ready to infer that his suspicions were aroused.[63] Essentially it is a matter of fact—a jury question[64]—whether the defendant exhibited a sufficient degree of fault by virtue of having actual, Nelsonian, or naughty knowledge of the misapplication, bearing in mind that where he "knows of circumstances which may on the one hand

---

[57] [1995] 2 A.C. 378.
[58] [1993] 1 W.L.R. 509 at 577; at para.11–09, above.
[59] *Re Montagu's S.T.* [1987] Ch. 264; at para.11–33; *Lipkin Gorman v Karpnale Ltd* [1987] 1 W.L.R. 987 at 1005; *Barclays Bank plc v Quincecare Ltd* [1992] 4 All E.R. 363 at 375; *Eagle Trust plc v S.B.C. Securities Ltd* [1992] 4 All E.R. 488 at 509; *Cowan de Groot Properties Ltd v Eagle Trust plc* [1992] 4 All E.R. 700 at 759; *Polly Peck International plc v Nadir (No.2)* [1992] 4 All E.R. 769 at 777; *Jonathan v Tilley* (1988) 12 Tru. L.I. 36.
[60] *Selangor United Rubber Estates Ltd v Cradock (No.3)* [1968] 1 W.L.R. 1555; *Belmont Finance Corp. v Williams Furniture Ltd (No.2)* [1980] 1 All E.R. 399 at 405; *International Sales and Agencies Ltd v Marcus* [1982] 3 All E.R. 551 at 558; *Baden, Delvaux v Société Générale pour Favoriser le Dıveloppement du Commerce et de l'Industrie en France S.A.* [1993] 1 W.L.R. 509 at 582; *Houghton v Fayers* [2000] 1 B.C.L.C. 511.
[61] *Baden, Delvaux* [1993] 1 W.L.R. 509 at 576. See too *The Star Sea* [2003] 1 A.C. 469 at [112], *per* Lord Scott: "an imputation of blind-eye knowledge requires an amalgam of suspicion that certain facts may exist and a decision to refrain from taking any step to confirm their existence".
[62] As pointed out in *Assets Co. Ltd v Mere Roihi* [1905] A.C. 176 at 201: "If it can be shown that his suspicions were aroused and that he abstained from making inquiries for fear of learning the truth . . . fraud may be ascribed to him."
[63] *Eagle Trust plc v S.B.C. Securities Ltd* [1992] 4 All E.R. 488 at 509; *El Ajou v Dollar Land Holdings plc* [1993] 3 All E.R. 717 at 739.
[64] *Agip (Africa) Ltd v Jackson* [1990] Ch. 265 at 293.

make the payment a misapplication but which may on the other hand be consistent with perfect propriety . . . such a case might be determined on its particular facts by the principle that a party to a commercial agreement should not be fixed with notice simply because in a loose sense he has been put on inquiry".[65]

A defendant will not be liable if he knows that it would constitute a **11–23** breach of trust if he were to receive trust property from the trustees, but he genuinely forgets this before he receives and deals with the property for his own benefit.[66] If a defendant knows at the time of receiving the property that it is misapplied trust property, then his conscience will be affected and he will hold the property on constructive trust for the beneficiaries from that time onwards, with the result that he will be liable by way of surcharging and falsifying his accounts to restore the trust fund, to compensate the beneficiaries, or to disgorge his gains to them, in the event that he deals with the property for his own benefit.[67] Moreover, if he spends money improving the property he is not entitled to be reimbursed for this expenditure, save for the extent that he can set if off against rents and profits for which he is also accountable.[67a] If a defendant receives misapplied trust property innocently, however, and only subsequently acquires knowledge of its improper provenance, then he will only be personally liable to the beneficiaries in respect of those dealings with the property that have taken place after he acquired knowledge.[68] On the basis that the defendant holds the property on constructive trust for the beneficiaries from the time that his conscience is affected with knowledge that the property is theirs, he will be strictly liable to restore the trust fund by way of falsification of his accounts even in the exceptional case where the property is stolen or destroyed by an act of God after he knows that it should be returned to the beneficiaries.

Developing the law

In *B.C.C.I. (Overseas) Ltd v Akindele*,[69] Nourse L.J. recently sought to cut **11–24** through the problems engendered by the *Baden, Delvaux* classification. His Lordship held that dishonesty will suffice, but is not required, to make a defendant liable where he has received and dealt with misapplied trust property for his own benefit,[70] and that as a general rule a defendant will be liable whenever his "state of knowledge [is] . . . such as to make it unconscionable for him to retain the benefit of the receipt."[71] With respect to his Lordship, however, unconscionability is an uncertain concept,

---

[65] *Criterion Properties plc v Stratford U.K. Properties L.L.C.* [2002] 2 B.C.L.C. 151 at 173; not doubted on appeal.
[66] *Re Montagu's S.T.* [1987] Ch. 264; at para.11–33.
[67] *Rolled Steel Products (Holdings) Ltd v British Steel Corp.* [1986] 1 Ch. 246 at 303–4; *Westdeutsche Landesbank Girozentrale v Islington L.B.C.* [1996] A.C. 669 at 707.
[67a] *Re Loftus (deceased)* [2005] EWHC 406 (Ch) at [201].
[68] *Re Diplock* [1948] Ch. 465 at 477; *Allen v Rea Brothers Trustees Ltd* (2002) 4 I.T.E.L.R. 627 at 642–643 and 645–646.
[69] [2001] Ch. 437.
[70] *ibid.* at 448.
[71] *ibid.* at 455.

reference to which seems unlikely to bring clarity to this area of the law.[72] Indeed, unconscionability was expressly rejected by Lord Nicholls in *Royal Brunei* as the test for assistance liability for precisely this reason.[73]

11–25   It is submitted that the courts would do better to develop the law in this area by holding that dishonestly receiving and dealing with misapplied trust property for one's own benefit is a fault-based equitable wrong analogous to the wrong of dishonest assistance. This could be achieved by interpreting the cases requiring fault for liability in this area as having been concerned with equitable wrongdoing. At the same time, the courts should also hold that a strict liability claim in unjust enrichment lies concurrently against the recipients of misapplied trust property. These twin developments have been advocated extra-judicially by Lord Nicholls[74] and Lord Walker.[75] They have also been urged by Lord Millett in *Dubai Aluminium Co. Ltd v Salaam*, where he held *obiter* that[76]:

> "Dishonest receipt gives rise to concurrent liability, since the claim can be based on the defendant's dishonesty, treating the receipt itself as incidental, being merely the particular form taken by the defendant's participation in the breach of fiduciary duty; but it can also be based simply on the receipt, treating it as a restitutionary claim independent of any wrongdoing."

11–26   Three further strands of authority could also be drawn upon by a claimant arguing for the introduction of a strict liability claim in unjust enrichment against the recipients of misapplied trust property. First, it was held by the House of Lords in *Ministry of Health v Simpson*[77] that the recipients of funds improperly distributed in the administration of a deceased person's estate are strictly liable to repay the persons properly entitled to the estate, and there is no compelling reason of principle why this situation should be treated differently from the situation where trust assets are misdirected. Secondly, it was held by the House of Lords in *Lipkin Gorman v Karpnale Ltd*[78] that a common law action for money had and received would lie where a claimant's property was wrongfully taken from him by a third party and transferred without his knowledge to the defendant, and again there is no compelling reason of principle why this

---

[72] Consider the different readings of *Akindele* in *Papamichael v National Westminster Bank plc* [2003] 1 Lloyd's Rep. 341 at [246]–[247] and *Criterion Properties plc v Stratford U.K. Properties LLC* [2003] 2 B.C.L.C. 129 at [20]–[39], not reviewed on appeal [2004] 1 W.L.R. 1846.

[73] [1995] 2 A.C. 378 at 392.

[74] In his article "Knowing Receipt: The Need for a New Landmark", in W. R. Cornish *et al.* (eds.) *Restitution: Past, Present and Future* (1998) 231. See too P. Birks, 'Receipt', in P. Birks and A. Pretto (eds.), *Breach of Trust* (2002) p.213; but for a different view, see L. D. Smith, 'Unjust Enrichment, Property, and the Structure of Trusts' (2000) 116 L.Q.R. 412, reviewed in M. Bryan, "The Liability of the Recipient: Restitution at Common Law or Wrongdoing in Equity?" in S. Degelman and J. Edelman (eds.), *Equity in Commercial Law* (2005).

[75] In his John Lehane Memorial Lecture 2004, "Dishonesty and Unconscionable Conduct in Commercial Life: Some Reflections on Accessory Liability and Knowing Receipt"; available on-line at: www.ucc.ie/law/restitution/arti_property.htm.

[76] [2003] 2 A.C. 366 at [87], citing *John v Dodwell & Co. Ltd* [1918] A.C. 563.

[77] [1951] A.C. 251.

[78] [1991] 2 A.C. 548.

situation should be treated differently from the situation where trust assets are misdirected. Thirdly, it has been held that where trust assets are misappropriated by a trustee and used to pay off a security charged on property belonging to an innocent third party, the beneficiaries are entitled to be subrogated to the extinguished rights which were formerly possessed by the charge-holder, and to be treated, by a legal fiction, as though these rights were not extinguished, but were instead assigned to the beneficiaries in order that they might enforce them against the innocent third party for their own benefit.[79] The English courts have now explicitly acknowledged that subrogation is a remedy awarded to reverse unjust enrichment,[80] and if beneficiaries are entitled to acquire proprietary rights against innocent third parties via subrogation on the ground of unjust enrichment, then *a fortiori* they should also be entitled to a direct personal claim in unjust enrichment against innocent third parties who are enriched at the beneficiaries' expense.

In the event that the recipients of misapplied trust property were made **11–27** strictly liable to make restitution to the beneficiaries on the ground of unjust enrichment, the question arises whether any room would then be left in practice for a wrong-based knowing receipt action, where proof of fault was required: *i.e.* would circumstances ever arise in which a claimant might wish to bring a wrong-based claim? One answer is that a defendant who received trust property ministerially would have a good defence to the unjust enrichment claim, but would not have a defence against the wrong-based claim.[81] Another is that a claimant might suffer a loss that is greater than the benefit received by the defendant, with the result that the claimant would be better off seeking a compensatory rather than a restitutionary remedy, particularly if the view were taken that the wrong-based liability is a civil secondary liability with the result that the defendant would be liable to the same extent as the trustees.[82]

Change of position defence

If the courts do hold that a claim in unjust enrichment lies against the **11–28** recipients of misapplied trust property, it seems likely that recipients who are sued on this basis will often attempt to raise a change of position defence. It therefore seems apposite to give a brief account here of the circumstances in which this defence is available.

---

[79] *McCullough v Marsden* (1919) 45 D.L.R. 645 at 646–647; subsequent proceedings: *McCullough v Elliott* (1922) 62 D.L.R. 257. *Boscawen v Bajwa* [1996] 1 W.L.R. 328 might also be viewed as a relevant authority, assuming that the claimant's entitlement to subrogation in this case derived from the fact that the money used to pay off the charge to which it was subrogated had been impressed with a *Quistclose* trust in its favour. See paras 12–106 and 12–118 *et seq.*, below.

[80] *Banque Financière de la Cité v Parc (Battersea) Ltd* [1999] A.C. 221 at 228 and 234, *per* Lord Steyn and Lord Hoffmann, followed in *Cheltenham & Gloucester plc v Appleyard* [2004] EWCA Civ 291 at [33]; *Niru Battery Manufacturing Co. v Milestone Trading Ltd (No.2)* [2004] 2 All E.R. (Comm.) 289, at [27]–[28]; *Filby v Mortgage Express (No.2) Ltd* [2004] EWCA Civ 759 at [62].

[81] See para.11–20 n.55 and text.

[82] See para.11–17, above. As pointed out by Lord Walker in his John Lehane Memorial Lecture, above n.75, the defendant would be liable to pay compound interest if he were ordered to pay a money substitute for the trustees' obligation to restore the trust fund. Failure to understand this point led to the wrong outcome in *Alers-Hankey v Solomon* [2004] BCSC 1368, attempting to quantify the remedies awarded in *Alers-Hankey v Teixeira* (2002) 5 I.T.E.L.R. 171.

11–29   In practice, the defence of change of position is most often relied upon by defendants who have incurred extraordinary expenditure in reliance on their receipt of the benefit which forms the subject-matter of the claim: *i.e.* because they have received the benefit, they have been led to spend their money on something which they would not otherwise have bought. However, the defence is available to a wider class of defendants than this, and there is no need to show that the change in a defendant's position came about because he consciously incurred expenditure in reliance on his receipt of the benefit, although there must be a causal link 'at least on a "but-for" test' between the receipt of the benefit and the change in the defendant's position.[83] Thus, a defendant who is paid £5,000 and then immediately loses it when his wallet is stolen can raise the defence even though it cannot be said that he changed his position in reliance on his receipt. A defendant who changes his position in anticipation of a benefit which is subsequently paid to him can also raise the defence.[84] In the event that a defendant changes his position by purchasing an asset which remains in his possession at the time when the claim is made, he cannot rely on the defence to the extent that he remains enriched by his possession of the asset.[85]

11–30   In *Lipkin Gorman v Karpnale Ltd*,[86] Lord Goff held that the defence is not available to those who act in bad faith nor to wrongdoers. This good faith requirement clearly excludes defendants who have been self-consciously dishonest, but it can also exclude those who have failed "to act in a commercially acceptable way" and those who have engaged in "sharp practice of a kind that falls short of outright dishonesty".[87] On the other hand, "mere negligence on the part of the recipient is not sufficient to deprive him of the defence of change of position".[88]

11–31   In *Barros Mattos Junior v MacDaniels Ltd*,[89] the question arose whether a defendant is relevantly a "wrongdoer" debarred from relying on the defence if he does something illegal. Relying on the House of Lords' decision in *Tinsley v Milligan*,[90] Laddie J. held that the answer to this question is always affirmative, and he denied that the courts have any discretion in the matter:[91] subject to a *de minimis* threshold, they must always disallow the change of position defence in line with the maxim *ex*

---

[83] For *obiter dicta* to this effect, see *Scottish Equitable plc v Derby* [2001] 3 All E.R. 818 at 827; *Rose v A.I.B. Group (U.K.) plc* [2003] 2 B.C.L.C. 374 at [49]; *Cressman v Coys of Kensington (Sales) Ltd* [2004] 1 W.L.R. 2775 at [49]. In principle these *dicta* are preferable to the contrary findings in *Streiner v Bank Leumi (U.K.) plc* Q.B.D. 31 October 1985; *Credit Suisse (Monaco) S.A. v Attar* [2004] EWHC 374 (Comm).

[84] *Dextra Bank & Trust Co. Ltd v Bank of Jamaica* [2002] 1 All E.R. (Comm.) 193.

[85] *Lipkin Gorman v Karpnale Ltd* [1991] 2 A.C. 548 at 560; *Campden Hill Ltd v Chakrani* [2005] EWHC 911 (Ch) at [86]–[87].

[86] *ibid.* at 580.

[87] *Niru Battery Manufacturing Co. v Milestone Trading Ltd (No.1)* [2002] 2 All E.R. (Comm.) 705 at [125], *per* Moore-Bick J., affirmed [2004] 1 Lloyd's Rep. 344.

[88] *ibid.* at [125], *per* Moore-Bick J., relying on *Dextra Bank & Trust Co. Ltd v Bank of Jamaica* [2002] 1 All E.R. (Comm.) 193, where at [42]–[45] the Privy Council declined to hold that the relative fault of the claimant and the defendant can affect the availability of the defence, and also held that "if fault is to be taken into account at all, it would surely be unjust to take into account the fault of one party (the defendant) but to ignore fault on the part of the other (the [claimant])."

[89] [2005] 1 W.L.R. 247.

[90] [1994] 1 A.C. 340; at para.5–130, above.

[91] [2005] 1 W.L.R. 247 at [22]–[30] and [42]–[43].

dolo malo non oritur actio, even if this effectively means imposing an arbitrarily heavy penalty on a defendant. This led him to conclude that the defendants could not raise the defence, even though they had acted in good faith when they had received stolen money and paid it on to third parties, because they had converted the money from U.S. dollars into Nigerian naira before paying it away, contrary to a law requiring foreign exchange dealings in Nigeria to be conducted through authorised intermediaries. In the result, the defendants were liable to repay U.S. $8 million.

On Laddie J.'s reasoning, the defendants would have escaped liability if **11–32** they had paid the money away without converting it into naira first. Why should so much have turned on a breach of the Nigerian foreign exchange laws that was unconnected with the circumstances in which the claimant's money had been stolen and placed in the defendants' hands? The courts would do better to take a more nuanced approach to assessing the gravity of the illegal acts committed by defendants, along with all the other circumstances of a case, before jumping to the conclusion that the change of position defence should be disallowed. It is by no means obvious that the rule in *Tinsley* debarring *Tinsley* founded on evidence of illegality should necessarily be extended to knock out *defences*, even assuming that the rule for claims works well, something which may be doubted.[92]

RE MONTAGU'S SETTLEMENT

Chancery Division [1987] 1 Ch. 264; [1992] 4 All E.R. 308 [1987] 2 W.L.R. 1192.

Sir Robert Megarry V.-C.: ". . . What is in issue is the result of the receipt by **11–33** the tenth Duke of a large number of settled chattels, and his disposal of them during his lifetime. On many matters the evidence is slender or obscure, since the tenth Duke (whom I shall call simply 'the Duke') received the chattels in the late 1940s and disposed of many of them then; he died in 1977 and others concerned have also died. What has to be resolved was whether the Duke held the chattels as a constructive trustee so that his estate is accountable for them or their proceeds.

"The issue centred on clause 14(B) of the 1923 settlement. That settlement **11–34** assigned a large number of chattels to the trustees of the settlement upon certain trusts. In the events which happened, the trustees had a fiduciary duty on the death of the ninth Duke to select and make an inventory of such of the chattels as they considered suitable for inclusion in the settlement, and to hold the residue of the chattels in trust for the Duke absolutely. In the event, the trustees made no selection or inventory but instead treated all the chattels as being the absolute property of the Duke. The Duke's solicitor, Mr. Lickfold, undoubtedly knew the terms of clause 14(B) and understood its effect, and the Duke had a copy of the settlement: but the time came when Mr. Lickfold, Col. Nicholl (a solicitor advising the trustees), the trustees themselves and Mr. Gilchrist, an American lawyer advising the Duke, all seemed to have treated clause 14(B) as allowing the trustees to assent to the Duke taking any of the chattels that he wished and either keeping them or else selling them and keeping the proceeds of sale. In 1949 there were two large sales of the chattels; and many chattels were shipped out to Kenya, where the Duke was living.

---

[92] See paras 5–126 to 5–128, above.

11–35   "There is no suggestion that anyone concerned in the matter was dishonest. There was a muddle, but however careless it was, it was an honest muddle. Further, I do not think that the Duke was at any relevant time conscious of the fact that he was not entitled to receive the chattels and deal with them as beneficial owner. Of course, if clause 14(B) is singled out for attention and read carefully it could be seen by a reasonably intelligent layman not to empower the trustees simply to release chattels to the Duke, but to require them first to select chattels for inclusion in the settlement and to provide that only when they had done that would the chattels not selected become the Duke's property. But clause 14(B) was deeply embedded in a long and complex document, and in view of the advice and information that the Duke received from his solicitor I can see no reason why the Duke should be expected to attempt to construe the settlement himself. If expressed in terms of the doctrine of notice, I have held, ante, p.268F-G, that the Duke had notice, both actual and imputed, of the terms of clause 14(B)." But I have also said, ante, pp.271H–272 A:

> 'I do not think that the tenth Duke had any knowledge at any material time that the chattels that he was receiving or dealing with were chattels that were still subject to any trust. I think that he believed that they had been lawfully and properly released to him by the trustees.'

11–36   "That brings me to the essential question for decision. The core of the question is what suffices to constitute a recipient of trust property a constructive trustee of it. I can leave on one side the equitable doctrine of tracing: if the recipient of trust property still has the property or its traceable proceeds in his possession, he is liable to restore it unless he is a purchaser without notice. But liability as a constructive trustee is wider, and does not depend upon the recipient still having the property or its traceable proceeds. Does it suffice if the recipient had 'notice' that the property he was receiving was trust property, or must he have not merely notice of this, but knowledge, or 'cognizance,' as it has been put?

11–37   "In the books and the authorities the word 'notice' is often used in place of the word 'knowledge,' usually without any real explanation of its meaning. This seems to me to be a fertile source of confusion; for whatever meaning the layman may attach to those words, centuries of equity jurisprudence have attached a detailed and technical meaning to the term 'notice,' without doing the same for 'knowledge.' The classification of 'notice' into actual notice, constructive notice and imputed notice has been developed in relation to the doctrine that a bona fide purchaser for value of a legal estate takes free from any equitable interests of which he has no notice. I need not discuss this classification beyond saying that I use the term 'imputed notice' as meaning any actual or constructive notice that a solicitor or other agent for the purchaser acquires in the course of the transaction in question, such notice being imputed to the purchaser. Some of the cases describe any constructive notice that a purchaser himself obtains as being 'imputed' to him; but I confine 'imputed' to notice obtained by another which equity imputes to the purchaser.

11–38   "Now until recently I do not think there had been any classification of 'knowledge' which corresponded with the classification of 'notice.' However, in the *Baden* case [1992] 4 All E.R. at p.235, the judgment sets out five categories of knowledge, or of the circumstances in which the court may treat a person as having knowledge. Counsel in that case were substantially in agreement in treating all five types as being relevant for the purpose of a constructive trust; and the judge agreed with them: at 415. These categories are (i) actual knowledge; (ii) wilfully shutting one's eyes to the obvious; (iii) wilfully and recklessly failing to make such inquiries as an honest and reasonable man would make; (iv) knowledge of circumstances which would indicate the facts to an honest and reasonable man; and (v) knowledge of circumstances which would put an honest and reasonable man on inquiry. If I pause there, it can be said that these categories of knowledge correspond to two categories of notice: Type (i) corresponds to actual notice, and types (ii), (iii), (iv) and (v) correspond to constructive notice. Nothing, however, is said (at least in terms) about imputed knowledge. This is important, because in the case before me Mr. Taylor strongly contended that Mr. Lickfold's knowledge must be imputed to the Duke, and that this was of the essence of his case.

"It seems to me that one must be very careful about applying to constructive **11–39** trusts either the accepted concepts of notice or any analogy to them. In determining whether a constructive trust has been created, the fundamental question is whether the conscience of the recipient is bound in such a way as to justify equity in imposing a trust on him. The rules concerning a purchaser without notice seem to me to provide little guidance on this and to be liable to be misleading. First, they are irrelevant unless there is a purchase. A volunteer is bound by an equitable interest even if he has no notice of it; but in many cases of alleged constructive trusts the disposition has been voluntary and not for value, and yet notice or knowledge is plainly relevant. Second, although a purchaser normally employs solicitors, and so questions of imputed notice may arise, it is unusual for a volunteer to employ solicitors when about to receive bounty. Even if he does, he is unlikely to employ them in order to investigate the right of the donor to make the gift or of the trustees or personal representatives to make the distribution; and until this case came before me I had never heard it suggested that a volunteer would be fixed with imputed notice of all that his solicitors would have discovered had he employed solicitors and had instructed them to investigate his right to receive the property.

"Third, there seems to me to be a fundamental difference between the questions **11–40** that arise in respect of the doctrine of purchaser without notice and constructive trusts. As I said in my previous judgment, ante, pp.272ʜ–273ʙ:

'The former is concerned with the question whether a person takes property subject to or free from some equity. The latter is concerned with whether or not a person is to have imposed upon him the personal burdens and obligations of trusteeship. I do not see why one of the touchstones for determining the burdens on property should be the same as that for deciding whether to impose a personal obligation on a man. The cold calculus of constructive and imputed notice does not seem to me to be an appropriate instrument for deciding whether a man's conscience is sufficiently affected for it to be right to bind him by the obligations of a constructive trustee.'

I can see no reason to resile from that statement, save that to meet possible susceptibilities I would alter 'man' to 'person.' I would only add that there is more to being made a trustee then merely taking property subject to an equity.

"There is a further consideration. There is today something of a tendency in **11–41** equity to put less emphasis on detailed rules that have emerged from the cases and more weight on the underlying principles that engendered those rules, treating the rules less as rules requiring complete compliance, and more as guidelines to assist the court in applying the principles. A good illustration of this approach is to be found in the judgment of Oliver J. in *Taylors Fashions Ltd v Liverpool Victoria Trustees Co. Ltd (Note)* [1981] Q.B. 133 at 145–155. This view was adopted by Robert Goff J. in *Amalgamated Investment & Property Co. Ltd v Texas Commerce International Bank Ltd* [1982] Q.B. 84 at 104, 105, and it was, I think, accepted, though not cited, by the Court of Appeal in the latter case: see at pp.116–132. Certainly it was approved in terms by the Court of Appeal in *Habib Bank Ltd v Habib Bank A.G. Zurich* [1981] 1 W.L.R. 1265 at 1285, 1287. The *Taylors Fashions case* [1981] Q.B. 133 concerned equitable estoppel and the five probanda to be found in the judgment of Fry J. in *Willmott v Barber* (1880) 15 Ch.D. 96, 105; and on the facts of the case before him Oliver J. in the *Taylors Fashions* case concluded that the question was not whether each of those probanda had been satisfied but whether it would be unconscionable for the defendants to take advantage of the mistake there in question. Accordingly, although I readily approach the five categories of knowledge set out in the *Baden* case [1983] B.C.L.C. 325 as useful guides, I regard them primarily as aids in determining whether or not the Duke's conscience was affected in such a way as to require him to hold any or all of the chattels that he received on a constructive trust.

11–42   "There is one further general consideration that I should mention, and that is that 'the court should not be astute to impute knowledge where no actual knowledge exists': see the *Baden* case at 415, *per* Peter Gibson J. This approach goes back at least as far as *Barnes v Addy* (1874) 9 Ch. App.244, 251, 252. The view of James L.J., at 256, was that the court had in some cases

'gone to the very verge of justice in making good to cestuis que trust the consequences of the breaches of trust of their trustees at the expense of persons perfectly honest, but who have been, in some more or less degree, injudicious.'

11–43   "Of the five categories of knowledge set out in the *Baden* case [1983] B.C.L.C. 325, Mr. Chadwick, as well as Mr. Taylor, accepted the first three. What was in issue was nos. (iv) and (v), namely, knowledge of circumstances which 'would indicate the facts to an honest and reasonable man' or 'would put an honest and reasonable man on inquiry.' On the view that I take of the present case I do not think that it really matters whether or not categories (iv) and (v) are included, but as the matter has been argued at length, and further questions on it may arise, I think I should say something about it.

11–44   "First, as I have already indicated, I think that one has to be careful to distinguish the notice that is relevant in the doctrine of purchaser without notice from the knowledge that suffices for the imposition of a constructive trust. This is shown by a short passage in the long judgment of the Court of Appeal in *In Re Diplock* [1948] Ch. 465 at 478, 479. There, it was pointed out that on the facts of that case persons unversed in the law were entitled to assume that the executors were properly administering the estate, and that if those persons received money bona fide believing themselves to be entitled to it, 'they should not have imposed upon them the heavy obligations of trusteeship.' The judgment then pointed out:

'the principles applicable to such cases are not the same as the principles in regard to notice of defects in title applicable to transfers of land where regular machinery has long since been established for inquiry and investigation.'

11–45   "With that, I turn to the cases on constructive knowledge. Mr. Taylor relied strongly on *Selangor United Rubber Estates Ltd v Cradock (No. 3)* [1968] 1 W.L.R. 1555 and *Karak Rubber Co. Ltd v Burden (No. 2)* [1972] 1 W.L.R. 602. Each was a knowing assistance case. In the *Selangor* case at 1582, Ungoed-Thomas J., immediately after speaking of tracing property into the hands of a volunteer, said that equity

'will hold a purchaser for value liable as constructive trustee if he had actual or constructive notice that the transfer to him was of trust property in breach of trust . . .';

and at 1583 he went on to refer to equitable rights and to say that in general 'it is equitable that a person with actual notice or constructive notice of those rights should be fixed with knowledge of them.' I find this view hard to reconcile with the passage in *Re Diplock* [1948] Ch. 465 (a case not cited to the judge) which I have just mentioned; and with all respect, it also seems to me to tend to confuse the absence of notice which shields a purchaser from liability under the doctrine of tracing, with the absence of knowledge of the trust which will prevent the imposition of a constructive trust. The judge went on to consider the meaning of 'knowledge' in various judgments, and reached a conclusion that knowledge was not confined to actual knowledge; and with this, as such, Mr. Chadwick had no quarrel. But he strongly contended that the cases cited on the extended meaning of 'knowledge' were cases within the 'wilful and reckless' head in the classification in the *Baden* case [1983] B.C.L.C. 325 (*i.e.* type (iii)), and that there was nothing to justify the inclusion of types (iv) an (v). The essential difference, of course, is that types (ii) and (iii) are governed by the words 'wilfully' or 'wilfully and recklessly,' whereas types (iv) and (v) have no such adverbs. Instead, they are cases of carelessness or negligence being tested by what an honest and reasonable man would have realised or would have inquired about, even if the person concerned was, for instance, not at all reasonable. Yet Ungoed-Thomas J. in his conclusion, at p.1590, applied the standard of what would have been indicated to an honest and reasonable man, or would have put him on inquiry, and so, I think, included all five of the *Baden* types of knowledge, and not only the first three.

In the *Karak* case [1972] 1 W.L.R. 602, Brightman J. considered this conclusion. **11–46** Again *Re Diplock* [1948] Ch. 465 was not cited, but *Williams v Williams* (1881) 17 Ch.D. 437, another case not cited to Ungoed-Thomas J. in the *Selangor* case [1968] 1 W.L.R. 1555, was duly examined. Brightman J. distinguished that case by pointing out that it was a knowing receipt case, whereas the case before him was a knowing assistance case; and he said, at 638, that *Williams v Williams* had 'no relevance at all to the case before me.' In *Williams v Williams* Kay J. had held that the recipient of the trust property, a solicitor, was not liable as a constructive trustee, and, at 445, the judge said that the case would be 'very different' if the recipient had 'wilfully shut his eyes.' He then referred to the 'very great negligence' of the solicitor, qua solicitor, in ignoring the trust, though holding that he was not liable as a constructive trustee. I do not see how Kay J. could have reached that conclusion if he had thought that knowledge of *Baden* types (iv) and (v) had sufficed; and, of course, what is before me is a case of knowing receipt, like *Williams v Williams* and unlike the *Karak* case.

"There is also *In Re Blundell* (1888) 40 Ch.D. 370, a case not cited in the *Selangor* **11–47** case [1968] 1 W.L.R. 1555. It was cited but not mentioned in the judgment in the *Karak* case [1972] 1 W.L.R. 602, but like *Williams v Williams*, 17 Ch.D. 437 and *In Re Diplock* [1948] Ch. 465 it does not appear in the *Baden* case [1983] B.C.L.C. 325: all three, I may say, were duly cited in the *Carl Zeiss* case [1969] 2 Ch. 276. In *Re Blundell*, Stirling J. refused to hold that a solicitor was a constructive trustee of costs that a trustee of property had allowed him to take out of the estate, even though he knew that the trustee was guilty of a breach of trust, 'unless there are facts brought home to him which show that to his knowledge the money is being applied in a manner which is inconsistent with the trust': see p.381. Both *Williams v Williams* and *In Re Blundell* figure prominently in the judgments of Sachs and Edmund Davies L.JJ. in the *Carl Zeiss* case, in support of their conclusion that negligence is not enough and that there must be dishonesty, a conscious impropriety or a lack of probity before liability as a constructive trustee is imposed . . .

"I shall attempt to summarise my conclusions.

11–48   (1) The equitable doctrine of tracing and the imposition of a constructive trust by reason of the knowing receipt of trust property are governed by different rules and must be kept distinct. Tracing is primarily a means of determining the rights of property, whereas the imposition of a constructive trust creates personal obligations that go beyond mere property rights.

11–49   (2) In considering whether a constructive trust has arisen in a case of the knowing receipt of trust property, the basic question is whether the conscience of the recipient is sufficiently affected to justify the imposition of such a trust.

11–50   (3) Whether a constructive trust arises in such a case primarily depends on the knowledge of the recipient, and not on notice to him; and for clarity it is desirable to use the word 'knowledge' and avoid the word 'notice' in such cases.

11–51   (4) For this purpose, knowledge is not confined to actual knowledge, but includes at least knowledge of types (ii) and (iii) in the *Baden* case [1983] B.C.L.C. 325, 407, *i.e.* actual knowledge that would have been acquired but for shutting one's eyes to the obvious, or wilfully and recklessly failing to make such inquiries as a reasonable and honest man would make; for in such cases there is a want of probity which justifies imposing a constructive trust.

11–52   (5) Whether knowledge of the *Baden* types (iv) and (v) suffices for this purpose is at best doubtful; in my view, it does not, for I cannot see that the carelessness involved will normally amount to a want of probity.

11–53   (6) For these purposes, a person is not to be taken to have knowledge of a fact that he once knew but has genuinely forgotten: the test (or a test) is whether the knowledge continues to operate on that person's mind at the time in question.

11–54   (7)(a) It is at least doubtful whether there is a general doctrine of 'imputed knowledge' that corresponds to 'imputed notice.' (b) Even if there is such a doctrine, for the purposes of creating a constructive trust of the 'knowing receipt' type the doctrine will not apply so as to fix a donee or beneficiary with all the knowledge that his solicitor has, at all events if the donee or beneficiary has not employed the solicitor to investigate his right to the bounty, and has done nothing else that can be treated as accepting that the solicitor's knowledge should be treated as his own. (c) Any such doctrine should be distinguished from the process whereby, under the name 'imputed knowledge,' a company is treated as having the knowledge that its directors and secretary have.

11–55   (8) Where an alleged constructive trust is based not on 'knowing receipt' but on 'knowing assistance,' some at least of these considerations probably apply; but I need not decide anything on that; and I do not do so.

11–56   "From what I have said, it must be plain that in my judgment the Duke did not become a constructive trustee of any of the chattels. I can see nothing that affected his conscience sufficiently to impose a constructive trust on him."

Order accordingly.

ROYAL BRUNEI AIRLINES v TAN

Privy Council [1995] 2 A.C. 378 [1995] 3 W.L.R. 64 [1995] 3 All E.R. 97.

11–57   The judgment of their Lordships was delivered by LORD NICHOLLS OF BIRKENHEAD: "The proper role of equity in commercial transactions is a topical question. Increasingly plaintiffs have recourse to equity for an effective remedy when the person in default, typically a company, is insolvent. Plaintiffs seek to obtain relief from others who were involved in the transaction, such as directors of the company, or its bankers, or its legal or other advisers. They seek to fasten fiduciary obligations directly onto the company's officers or agents or advisers, or to have them held personally liable for assisting the company in breaches of trust or fiduciary obligations.

"This is such a case. An insolvent travel agent company owed money to an airline. **11–58** The airline seeks a remedy against the travel agent's principal director and shareholder. Its claim is based on the much-quoted dictum of Lord Selborne L.C., sitting in the Court of Appeal in Chancery, in *Barnes v Addy* (1874) L.R. 9 Ch.App.244 at 251–252:

> '[The responsibility of a trustee] may no doubt be extended in equity to others who are not properly trustees, if they are found . . . actually participating in any fraudulent conduct of the trustee to the injury of the cestui que trust. But . . . strangers are not to be made constructive trustees merely because they act as the agents of trustees in transactions within their legal powers, transactions, perhaps of which a court of equity may disapprove, unless those agents receive and become chargeable with some part of the trust property, or unless they assist with knowledge in a dishonest and fraudulent design on the part of the trustees.'

"In the conventional shorthand, the first of these two circumstances in which third **11–59** parties (non-trustees) may become liable to account in equity is 'knowing receipt,' as distinct from the second, where liability arises from 'knowing assistance.' Stated even more shortly, the first limb of Lord Selborne L.C.'s formulation is concerned with the liability of a person as a *recipient* of trust property or its traceable proceeds. The second limb is concerned with what, for want of a better compendious description, can be called the liability of an *accessory* to a trustee's breach of trust. Liability as an accessory is not dependent upon receipt of trust property. It arises even though no trust property has reached the hands of the accessory. It is a form of secondary liability in the sense that it only arises where there has been a breach of trust. In the present case the plaintiff airline relies on the accessory limb. The particular point in issue arises from the expression 'a dishonest and fraudulent design on the part of the trustees . . .'

"In short, the issue on this appeal is whether the breach of trust which is a **11–60** prerequisite to accessory liability must itself be a dishonest and fraudulent breach of trust by the trustee.

The honest trustee and the dishonest third party

"It must be noted at once that there is a difficulty with the approach adopted on this **11–61** point in the *Belmont* case [1979] Ch. 250. Take the simple example of an honest trustee and a dishonest third party. Take a case where a dishonest solicitor persuades a trustee to apply trust property in a way the trustee honestly believes is permissible but which the solicitor knows full well is a clear breach of trust. The solicitor deliberately conceals this from the trustee. In consequence, the beneficiaries suffer a substantial loss. It cannot be right that in such a case the accessory liability principle would be inapplicable because of the innocence of the trustee. In ordinary parlance, the beneficiaries have been defrauded by the solicitor. If there is to be an accessory liability principle at all, whereby in appropriate circumstances beneficiaries may have direct recourse against a third party, the principle must surely be applicable in such a case, just as much as in a case where both the trustee and the third party have been dishonest. Indeed, if anything, the case for liability of the dishonest third party seems stronger where the trustee is innocent, because in such a case the third party alone was dishonest and that was the cause of the subsequent misapplication of the trust property.

11–62   "The position would be the same if, instead of *procuring* the breach, the third party dishonestly *assisted* in the breach. Change the facts slightly. A trustee is proposing to make a payment out of the trust fund to a particular person. He honestly believes he is authorised to do so by the terms of the trust deed. He asks a solicitor to carry through the transaction. The solicitor well knows that the proposed payment would be a plain breach of trust. He also well knows that the trustee mistakenly believes otherwise. Dishonestly he leaves the trustee under his misapprehension and prepares the necessary documentation. Again, if the accessory principle is not to be artificially constricted, it ought to be applicable in such a case.

11–63   "These examples suggest that what matters is the state of mind of the third party sought to be made liable, not the state of mind of the trustee. The trustee will be liable in any event for the breach of trust, even if he acted innocently, unless excused by an exemption clause in the trust instrument or relieved by the court. But *his* state of mind is essentially irrelevant to the question whether the *third party* should be made liable to the beneficiaries for the breach of trust. If the liability of the third party is fault-based, what matters is the nature of his fault, not that of the trustee. In this regard dishonesty on the part of the third party would seem to be a sufficient basis for his liability, irrespective of the state of mind of the trustee who is in breach of trust. It is difficult to see why, if the third party dishonestly assisted in a breach, there should be a further prerequisite to his liability, namely that the trustee also must have been acting dishonestly. The alternative view would mean that a dishonest third party is liable if the trustee is dishonest, but if the trustee did not act dishonestly that of itself would excuse a dishonest third party from liability. That would make no sense.

Earlier authority

11–64   "The view that the accessory liability principle cannot be restricted to fraudulent breaches of trust is not to be approached with suspicion as a latter-day novelty. Before the accessory principle donned its *Barnes v Addy*, L.R. 9 Ch. App.244 straitjacket, judges seem not to have regarded the principle as confined in this way. In *Fyler v Fyler* (1841) 3 Beav. 550, 568, Lord Langdale M.R. expressed the view that, if trustees invested in an unauthorised investment, solicitors who knowingly procured that to be done for their own benefit 'ought to be considered as partakers in the breach of trust' even though the trustees intended in good faith that the investment would be beneficial to the life tenant and not prejudicial to the beneficiaries with interests in capital. The same judge. Lord Langdale M.R., in *Attorney-General v Corporation of Leicester* (1844) 7 Beav. 176 at 179, stated:

> 'it cannot be disputed that, if the agent of a trustee, whether a corporate body or not, knowing that a breach of trust is being committed, interferes and assists in that breach of trust, he is personally answerable, although he may be employed as the agent of the person who directs him to commit that breach of trust.'

In *Eaves v Hickson* (1861) 30 Beav. 136 trustees, acting in good faith, paid over the fund to William Knibb's adult children on the strength of a forged marriage certificate produced to them by William Knibb. Sir John Romilly M.R. held that William Knibb was liable to replace the fund, to the extent that it was not recovered from his children, and to do so in priority to the liability of the trustees. Far from this being a case of fraud by the trustees, Sir John Romilly M.R., at p.141, described it as a very hard case on the trustees, who were deceived by a forgery which would have deceived anyone who was not looking out for forgery or fraud.

"This point did not arise in *Barnes v Addy*, L.R. 9 Ch. App.244. There the new **11–65** sole trustee was engaged in a dishonest and fraudulent design. He intended to misapply the trust fund as soon as it reached his hands. The two solicitors were held not liable because there was no evidence that either of them had any knowledge or suspicion of this.

"What has gone wrong? Their Lordships venture to think that the reason is that, **11–66** ever since the *Selangor* case [1968] 1 W.L.R. 1555 highlighted the potential uses of equitable remedies in connection with misapplied company funds, there has been a tendency to cite and interpret and apply Lord Selborne L.C.'s formulation in *Barnes v Addy*, L.R. 9 Ch. App.244 at 251–252, as though it were a statute. This has particularly been so with the accessory limb of Lord Selborne L.C.'s apothegm. This approach has been inimical to analysis of the underlying concept. Working within this constraint, the courts have found themselves wrestling with the interpretation of the individual ingredients, especially 'knowingly' but also 'dishonest and fraudulent design on the part of the trustees,' without examining the underlying reason why a third party who has received no trust property is being made liable at all . . .

"To resolve this issue it is necessary to take an overall look at the accessory **11–67** liability principle. A conclusion cannot be reached on the nature of the breach of trust which may trigger accessory liability without at the same time considering the other ingredients including, in particular, the state of mind of the third party. It is not necessary, however, to look even more widely and consider the essential ingredients of recipient liability. The issue on this appeal concerns only the accessory liability principle. Different considerations apply to the two heads of liability. Recipient liability is restitution-based; accessory liability is not . . .

Fault-based liability

"Given, then, that in some circumstances a third party may be liable directly to a **11–68** beneficiary, but given also that the liability is not so strict that there would be liability even when the third party was wholly unaware of the existence of the trust, the next step is to seek to identify the touchstone of liability. By common accord dishonesty fulfils this role. Whether, in addition, negligence will suffice is an issue on which there has been a well-known difference of judicial opinion. The *Selangor* decision [1968] 1 W.L.R. 1555 in 1968 was the first modern decision on this point. Ungoed-Thomas J., at p.1590, held that the touchstone was whether the third party had knowledge of circumstances which would indicate to 'an honest, reasonable man' that the breach in question was being committed or would put him on inquiry. Brightman J. reached the same conclusion in *Karak Rubber Co. Ltd v Burden (No. 2)* [1972] 1 W.L.R. 602. So did Peter Gibson J. in 1983 in *Baden v Société Générale pour Favoriser le Développement du Commerce et de l'Industrie en France S.A. (Note)* [1993] 1 W.L.R. 509. In that case the judge accepted a five-point scale of knowledge which had been formulated by counsel.

"Meanwhile doubts had been expressed about this test by Buckley and Goff L.JJ. **11–69** in the *Belmont* case [1979] Ch. 250 at 267, 275. Similar doubts were expressed in Australia by Jacobs P. in *D. P. C. Estates Pty, Ltd v Grey and Consul Development Pty. Ltd* [1974] 1 N.S.W.L.R. 443 at 459. When that decision reached the High Court of Australia, the doubts were echoed by Barwick C.J., Gibbs and Stephen JJ.: see *Consul Development Pty. Ltd v D.P. Estates Pty. Ltd* (1975) 132 C.L.R. 373 at 376, 398, 412.

11–70   "Since then the tide in England has flowed strongly in favour of the test being one of dishonesty: see, for instance, Sir Robert Megarry V.-C. in In *Re Montagu's Settlement Trusts* [1987] Ch. 264, 285, and Millett J. in *Agip (Africa) Ltd v Jackson* [1990] Ch. 265 at 293. In *Eagle Trust Plc. v S.B.C. Securities Ltd* [1993] 1 W.L.R. 484 at 495, Vinelott J. stated that it could be taken as settled law that want of probity was a prerequisite to liability. This received the imprimatur of the Court of Appeal in *Polly Peck International Plc. v Nadir (No. 2)* [1992] 4 All E.R. 769 at 777, *per* Scott L.J. . . .

Dishonesty

11–71   "Before considering this issue further it will be helpful to define the terms being used by looking more closely at what dishonesty means in this context. Whatever may be the position in some criminal or other contexts (see, for instance, *Reg. v Ghosh* [1982] Q.B. 1053), in the context of the accessory liability principle acting dishonestly, or with a lack of probity, which is synonymous, means simply not acting as an honest person would in the circumstances. This is an objective standard. At first sight this may seem surprising. Honesty has a connotation of subjectivity as distinct from the objectivity of negligence. Honesty, indeed, does have a strong subjective element in that it is a description of a type of conduct assessed in the light of what a person actually knew at the time, as distinct a from what a reasonable person would have known or appreciated. Further, honesty and its counterpart dishonesty are mostly concerned with advertent conduct, not inadvertent conduct. Carelessness is not dishonesty. Thus for the most part dishonesty is to be equated with conscious impropriety. However, these subjective characteristics of honesty do not mean that individuals are free to set their own standards of honesty in particular circumstances. The standard of what constitutes honest conduct is not subjective. Honesty is not an optional scale, with higher or lower values according to the moral standards of each individual. If a person knowingly appropriates another's property, he will not escape a finding of dishonesty simply because he sees nothing wrong in such behaviour.

11–72   "In most situations there is little difficulty in identifying how an honest person would behave. Honest people do not intentionally deceive others to their detriment. Honest people do not knowingly take others' property. Unless there is a very good and compelling reason, an honest person does not participate in a transaction if he knows it involves a misapplication of trust assets to the detriment of the beneficiaries. Nor does an honest person in such a case deliberately close his eyes and ears, or deliberately not ask questions, lest he learn something he would rather not know, and then proceed regardless. However, in the situations now under consideration the position is not always so straightforward. This can best be illustrated by considering one particular area: the taking of risks.

Taking risks

11–73   "All investment involves risk. Imprudence is not dishonesty, although imprudence may be carried recklessly to lengths which call into question the honesty of the person making the decision. This is especially so if the transaction serves another purpose in which that person has an interest of his own.

11–74   "This type of risk is to be sharply distinguished from the case where a trustee, with or without the benefit of advice, is aware that a particular investment or application of trust property is outside his powers, but nevertheless he decides to proceed in the belief or hope that this will be beneficial to the beneficiaries or, at least, not prejudicial to them. He takes a risk that a clearly unauthorised transaction will not cause loss. A risk of this nature is for the account of those who take it. If the risk materialises and causes loss, those who knowingly took the risk will be accountable accordingly. This is the type of risk being addressed by Peter Gibson J. in the *Baden* case [1993] 1 W.L.R. 509 at 574, when he accepted that fraud includes taking 'a risk to the prejudice of another's rights, which risk is known to be one which there is no right to take.'

"This situation, in turn, is to be distinguished from the case where there is **11–75** genuine doubt about whether a transaction is authorised or not. This may be because the trust instrument is worded obscurely, or because there are competing claims, as in *Carl Zeiss Stiftung v Herbert Smith & Co. (No. 2)* [1969] 2 Ch. 276, or for other reasons. The difficulty here is that frequently the situation is neither clearly white nor clearly black. The dividing edge between what is within the trustee's powers and what is not is often not clear-cut. Instead there is a gradually darkening spectrum which can be described with labels such as clearly authorised, probably authorised, possibly authorised, wholly unclear, probably unauthorised and, finally, clearly unauthorised.

"The difficulty here is that the differences are of degree rather than of kind. So **11–76** far as the trustee himself is concerned the legal analysis is straightforward. Honesty or lack of honesty is not the test for his liability. He is obliged to comply with the terms of the trust. His liability is strict. If he departs from the trust terms he is liable unless excused by a provision in the trust instrument or relieved by the court. The analysis of the position of the accessory, such as the solicitor who carries through the transaction for him, does not lead to such a simple, clear-cut answer in every case. He is required to act honestly; but what is required of an honest person in these circumstances? An honest person knows there is doubt. What does honesty require him to do?

"The only answer to these questions lies in keeping in mind that honesty is an **11–77** objective standard. The individual is expected to attain the standard which would be observed by an honest person placed in those circumstances. It is impossible to be more specific. Knox J. captured the flavour of this, in a case with a commercial setting, when he referred to a person who is 'guilty of commercially unacceptable conduct in the particular context involved:' see *Cowan de Groot Properties Ltd v Eagle Trust Plc* [1992] 4 All E.R. 700 at 761. Acting in reckless disregard of others' rights or possible rights can be a tell-tale sign of dishonesty. An honest person would have regard to the circumstances known to him, including the nature and importance of the proposed transaction, the nature and importance of his role, the ordinary course of business, the degree of doubt, the practicability of the trustee or the third party proceeding otherwise and the seriousness of the adverse consequences to the beneficiaries. The circumstances will dictate which one or more of the possible courses should be taken by an honest person. He might, for instance, flatly decline to become involved. He might ask further questions. He might seek advice, or insist on further advice being obtained. He might advise the trustee of the risks but then proceed with his role in the transaction. He might do many things. Ultimately, in most cases, an honest person should have little difficulty in knowing whether a proposed transaction, or his participation in it, would offend the normally accepted standards of honest conduct.

"Likewise, when called upon to decide whether a person was acting honestly, a **11–78** court will look at all the circumstances known to the third party at the time. The court will also have regard to personal attributes of the third party, such as his experience and intelligence, and the reason why he acted as he did.

"Before leaving cases where there is real doubt, one further point should be **11–79** noted. To inquire, in such cases, whether a person dishonestly assisted in what is later held to be a breach of trust is to ask a meaningful question, which is capable of being given a meaningful answer. This is not always so if the question is posed in terms of 'knowingly' assisted. Framing the question in the latter form all too often leads one into tortuous convolutions about the 'sort' of knowledge required, when the truth is that 'knowingly' is inapt as a criterion when applied to the gradually darkening spectrum where the differences are of degree and not kind.

Negligence

11–80   "It is against this background that the question of negligence is to be addressed. This question, it should be remembered, is directed at whether an honest third party who receives no trust property should be liable if he procures or assists in a breach of trust of which he would have become aware had he exercised reasonable diligence. Should he be liable to the beneficiaries for the loss they suffer from the breach of trust?

11–81   "The majority of persons falling into this category will be the hosts of people who act for trustees in various ways: as advisers, consultants, bankers and agents of many kinds. This category also includes officers and employees of companies in respect of the application of company funds. All these people will be accountable to the trustees for their conduct. For the most part they will owe to the trustees a duty to exercise reasonable skill and care. When that is so, the rights flowing from that duty form part of the trust property. As such they can be enforced by the beneficiaries in a suitable case if the trustees are unable or unwilling to do so. That being so, it is difficult to identify a compelling reason why, in addition to the duty of skill and care vis-à-vis the trustees which the third parties have accepted, or which the law has imposed upon them, third parties should also owe a duty of care directly to the beneficiaries. They have undertaken work for the trustees. They must carry out that work properly. If they fail to do so, they will be liable to make good the loss suffered by the trustees in consequence. This will include, where appropriate, the loss suffered by the trustees, being exposed to claims for breach of trust.

11–82   "Outside this category of persons who owe duties of skill and care to the trustees, there are others who will deal with trustees. If they have not accepted, and the law has not imposed upon them, any such duties in favour of the trustees, it is difficult to discern a good reason why they should nevertheless owe such duties to the beneficiaries.

11–83   "There remains to be considered the position where third parties are acting for, or dealing with, dishonest trustees. In such cases the trustees would have no claims against the third party. The trustees would suffer no loss by reason of the third party's failure to discover what was going on. The question is whether in this type of situation the third party owes a duty of care to the beneficiaries to, in effect, check that a trustee is not misbehaving. The third party must act honestly. The question is whether that is enough.

11–84   "In agreement with the preponderant view, their Lordships consider that dishonesty is an essential ingredient here. There may be cases where, in the light of the particular facts, a third party will owe a duty of care to the beneficiaries. As a general proposition, however, beneficiaries cannot reasonably expect that all the world dealing with their trustees should owe them a duty to take care lest the trustees are behaving dishonestly . . .

The accessory liability principle

11–85   "Drawing the threads together, their Lordships' overall conclusion is that dishonesty is a necessary ingredient of accessory liability. It is also a sufficient ingredient. A liability in equity to make good resulting loss attaches to a person who dishonestly procures or assists in a breach of trust or fiduciary obligation. It is not necessary that, in addition, the trustee or fiduciary was acting dishonestly, although this will usually be so where the third party who is assisting him is acting dishonestly. 'Knowingly' is better avoided as a defining ingredient of the principle and in the context of this principle the *Baden* [1993] 1 W.L.R. 509 scale of knowledge is best forgotten.

Conclusion

"From this statement of the principle it follows that this appeal succeeds. The **11–86** money paid to B.L.T. on the sale of tickets for the airline was held by B.L.T. upon trust for the airline. This trust, on its face, conferred no power on B.L.T. to use the money in the conduct of its business. The trust gave no authority to B.L.T. to relieve its cash flow problems by utilising for this purpose the rolling 30-day credit afforded by the airline. Thus B.L.T. committed a breach of trust by using the money instead of simply deducting its commission and holding the money intact until it paid the airline. The defendant accepted that he knowingly assisted in that breach of trust. In other words, he caused or permitted his company to apply the money in a way he knew was not authorised by the trust of which the company was trustee. Set out in these bald terms, the defendant's conduct was dishonest. By the same token, and for good measure, B.L.T. also acted dishonestly. The defendant was the company, and his state of mind is to be imputed to the company.

"The Court of Appeal held that it was not established that B.L.T. was guilty of fraud or dishonesty in relation to the amounts it held for the airline. Their Lordships understand that by this the Court of Appeal meant that it was not established that the defendant intended to defraud the airline. The defendant hoped, maybe expected, to be able to pay the airline, but the money was lost in the ordinary course of a poorly-run business with heavy overhead expenses. These facts are beside the point. The defendant had no right to employ the money in the business at all. That was the breach of trust. The company's inability to pay the airline was the consequence of that breach of trust."

TWINSECTRA LTD v YARDLEY

House of Lords [2002] 2 A.C. 164 (Lords Slynn, Steyn, Hoffmann, Hutton, and Millett)

The claimant lent £1 million to Yardley for the sole purpose of buying property. It **11–87** paid the money to Sims, a solicitor who was associated with Yardley, but who was not acting for him in this matter. Sims undertook not to release the money to Yardley except in accordance with the loan conditions. In breach of this undertaking Sims released the money to Yardley's solicitor, Leach, who released it to Yardley, who used £3570,000 of the money to pay off a debt. When Yardley failed to repay the loan the claimant sued Leach (*inter alia*) for dishonest assistance in Sims' breach of the *Quistclose* trust with which the money had been impressed (see para.5–40, above). The House of Lords held unanimously that the loan money had indeed been impressed with a *Quistclose* trust, but they also held by a majority that Leach had not acted with the requisite degree of dishonesty for accessory liability. The extracts from Lord Hutton's speech reproduced below are representative of the majority view; Lord Millett's dissenting analysis of the issue is also reproduced here.

LORD HUTTON: "My Lords, I have had the advantage of reading in draft the **11–88** speeches of my noble and learned friends Lord Hoffmann and Lord Millett. For the reasons which they give I agree that the undertaking given by Mr. Sims to

Twinsectra Ltd. (Twinsectra) created a trust, and I turn to consider whether the Court of Appeal was right to hold that Mr. Leach is liable for assisting in Mr. Sims' breach of trust. Carnwath J. held that the undertaking did not create a trust, but he also held that Mr. Leach had not been dishonest. The Court of Appeal reversed his findings and held that the undertaking gave rise to a trust and that Mr. Leach had acted dishonestly and was liable as an accessory to Mr. Sims' breach of trust.

11–89   "My Lords, in my opinion, the issue whether the Court of Appeal was right to hold that Mr. Leach had acted dishonestly depends on the meaning to be given to that term in the judgment of Lord Nicholls of Birkenhead in *Royal Brunei Airlines Sdn. Bhd. v Tan*.[93] In approaching this question it will be helpful to consider the place of dishonesty in the pattern of that judgment. Lord Nicholls considered the position of the honest trustee and the dishonest third party and stated that dishonesty on the part of the third party was a sufficient basis for his liability notwithstanding that the trustee, although mistaken and in breach of trust, was honest.[94] He then turned to consider the basis on which the third party, who does not receive trust property but who assists the trustee to commit a breach, should be held liable. He rejected the possibility that such a third party should never be liable and he also rejected the possibility that the liability of a third party should be strict so that he would be liable even if he did not know or had no reason to suspect that he was dealing with a trustee. Therefore Lord Nicholls concluded that the liability of the accessory must be fault-based and in identifying the touchstone of liability he stated: 'By common accord dishonesty fulfils this role.'[95] Then, he cited a number of authorities and the views of commentators and observed that the tide of authority in England had flowed strongly in favour of the test of dishonesty and that most, but not all, commentators also preferred that test.[96]

11–90   "Whilst in discussing the term 'dishonesty' the courts often draw a distinction between subjective dishonesty and objective dishonesty, there are three possible standards which can be applied to determine whether a person has acted dishonestly. There is a purely subjective standard, whereby a person is only regarded as dishonest if he transgresses his own standard of honesty, even if that standard is contrary to that of reasonable and honest people. This has been termed the 'Robin Hood test' and has been rejected by the courts. As Sir Christopher Slade stated in *Walker v Stones*:[97]

> 'A person may in some cases act dishonestly, according to the ordinary use of language, even though he genuinely believes that his action is morally justified. The penniless thief, for example, who picks the pocket of the multi-millionaire is dishonest even though he genuinely considers the theft is morally justified as a fair redistribution of wealth and that he is not therefore being dishonest.'

Secondly, there is a purely objective standard whereby a person acts dishonestly if his conduct is dishonest by the ordinary standards of reasonable and honest people, even if he does not realise this. Thirdly, there is a standard which combines an objective test and a subjective test, and which requires that before there can be a finding of dishonesty it must be established that the defendant's conduct was dishonest by the ordinary standards of reasonable and honest people and that he

---

[93] [1995] 2 A.C. 378.
[94] *ibid.* at 384–385.
[95] *ibid.* at 387.
[96] *ibid.* at 388–389.
[97] [2001] Q.B. 902 at 939.

himself realised that by those standards his conduct was dishonest. I will term this 'the combined test'.

"There is a passage in the earlier part of the judgment in the *Royal Brunei* case **11–91** which suggests that Lord Nicholls considered that dishonesty has a subjective element. Thus in discussing the honest trustee and the dishonest third party he stated:[98]

> 'These examples suggest that what matters is the state of mind of the third party . . . But [the trustee's] state of mind is essentially irrelevant to the question whether the third party should be made liable to the beneficiaries for the breach of trust.'

"However, after stating that the touchstone of liability is dishonesty,[99] Lord **11–92** Nicholls went on to discuss the meaning of dishonesty:[1]

> 'Before considering this issue further it will be helpful to define the terms being used by looking more closely at what dishonesty means in this context. Whatever may be the position in some criminal or other contexts (see, for instance, *R. v Ghosh*[2]), in the context of the accessory liability principle acting dishonestly, or with a lack of probity, which is synonymous, means simply not acting as an honest person would in the circumstances. This is an objective standard.'

"My noble and learned friend Lord Millett has subjected this passage and **11–93** subsequent passages in the judgment to detailed analysis and is of the opinion that Lord Nicholls used the term 'dishonesty' in a purely objective sense so that in this area of the law a person can be held to be dishonest even though he does not realise that what he is doing is dishonest by the ordinary standards of honest people. This leads Lord Millett on to the conclusion that in determining the liability of an accessory dishonesty is not necessary and that liability depends on knowledge.

"In *R. v Ghosh* Lord Lane C.J. held that in the law of theft dishonesty required **11–94** that the defendant himself must have realised that what he was doing was dishonest by the ordinary standards of reasonable and honest people. The three sentences in Lord Nicholls' judgment which appear to draw a distinction between the position in criminal law and the position in equity, do give support to Lord Millett's view. But considering those sentences in the context of the remainder of the paragraph and taking account of other passages in the judgment, I think that in referring to an objective standard Lord Nicholls was contrasting it with the purely subjective standard whereby a man sets his own standard of honesty and does not regard as dishonest what upright and responsible people would regard as dishonest. [He quoted the passage of Lord Nicholls' speech that is reproduced at para.11–71, above] . . . Further Lord Nicholls said:[3]

> 'Ultimately, in most cases, an honest person should have little difficulty in knowing whether a proposed transaction, or his participation in it, would offend the normally accepted standards of honest conduct. Likewise, when

---

[98] [1995] 2 A.C. 378 at 385.
[99] *ibid.* at 387.
[1] *ibid.* at 389.
[2] [1982] Q.B. 1053.
[3] [1995] 2 A.C. 378 at 391.

called upon to decide whether a person was acting honestly, a court will look at all the circumstances known to the third party at the time. The court will also have regard to personal attributes of the third party such as his experience and intelligence, and the reason why he acted as he did.'

11–95   "The use of the word 'knowing' in the first sentence would be superfluous if the defendant did not have to be aware that what he was doing would offend the normally accepted standards of honest conduct, and the need to look at the experience and intelligence of the defendant would also appear superfluous if all that was required was a purely objective standard of dishonesty. Therefore I do not think that Lord Nicholls was stating that in this sphere of equity a man can be dishonest even if he does not know that what he is doing would be regarded as dishonest by honest people.

11–96   " . . . There is, in my opinion, a further consideration which supports the view that for liability as an accessory to arise the defendant must himself appreciate that what he was doing was dishonest by the standards of honest and reasonable men. A finding by a judge that a defendant has been dishonest is a grave finding, and it is particularly grave against a professional man, such as a solicitor. Notwithstanding that the issue arises in equity law and not in a criminal context, I think that it would be less than just for the law to permit a finding that a defendant had been 'dishonest' in assisting in a breach of trust where he knew of the facts which created the trust and its breach but had not been aware that what he was doing would be regarded by honest men as being dishonest.

11–97   "It would be open to your Lordships to depart from the principle stated by Lord Nicholls that dishonesty is a necessary ingredient of accessory liability and to hold that knowledge is a sufficient ingredient. But the statement of that principle by Lord Nicholls has been widely regarded as clarifying this area of the law and, as he observed, the tide of authority in England has flowed strongly in favour of the test of dishonesty. Therefore I consider that the courts should continue to apply that test and that your Lordships should state that dishonesty requires knowledge by the defendant that what he was doing would be regarded as dishonest by honest people, although he should not escape a finding of dishonesty because he sets his own standards of honesty and does not regard as dishonest what he knows would offend the normally accepted standards of honest conduct.

11–98   " . . . Therefore I turn to consider the judgment of Carnwath J. and the Court of Appeal on the basis that a finding of accessory liability can only be made against Mr. Leach if, applying the combined test, it were established on the evidence that he was dishonest.

11–99   "At the trial Mr. Leach was cross-examined very closely and at length about his state of mind when he paid to Mr. Yardley the moneys transferred to him by Mr. Sims. The tenor of his replies was that he paid the moneys to his client because his client instructed him to do so. . . .

11–100   "[After] holding that the undertaking given by Mr. Sims did not create a trust the judge stated:

'Were any of the defendants knowing recipients or accessories?

'The above conclusion makes it unnecessary to resolve the more difficult question whether any of the defendants (that is, the Yardley companies, or Mr. Leach) had the necessary state of mind to make them liable under these headings. For these purposes the companies must realistically be taken to have had the same knowledge and state of mind as Mr. Yardley. I have already given my views as to the extent to which I regard him as having acted dishonestly. In Mr. Leach's case, I have found that he was not dishonest, but that he did deliberately shut his eyes to the implications of the undertaking. Whether in either case this would be sufficient to establish accessory liability depends on the application of the *Royal Brunei* principles to those facts. Although that case was concerned with "knowing assistance" rather than "knowing receipt", I would find it very difficult, in the light of the current state of the authorities to which I have referred, to define the difference in the mental states required; and I doubt if there is one.'

"It would have been open to the judge to hold that Mr. Leach was dishonest, in **11–101** that he knew that he was transferring to Mr. Yardley or to one of his companies moneys which were subject to an undertaking that they would be applied solely for the acquisition of property and that the moneys would not be so applied. But the experienced judge who was observing Mr. Leach being cross-examined at length found that Mr. Leach, although misguided, was not dishonest in carrying out his client's instructions.

"The judge did not give reasons for this finding or state what test he applied to **11–102** determine dishonesty, but I think it probable that he applied the combined test and I infer that he considered that Mr. Leach did not realise that in acting on his client's instructions in relation to the moneys he was acting in a way which a responsible and honest solicitor would regard as dishonest. The judge may also have been influenced by the consideration that as he did not find that Mr. Sims' undertaking created a trust Mr. Leach would not have realised that he was dealing with trust property.

"It is only in exceptional circumstances that an appellate court should reverse a **11–103** finding by a trial judge on a question of fact (and particularly on the state of mind of a party) when the judge has had the advantage of seeing the party giving evidence in the witness box. Therefore I do not think that it would have been right for the Court of Appeal in this case to have come to a different conclusion from the judge and to have held that Mr. Leach was dishonest in that when he transferred the moneys to Mr. Yardley he knew that his conduct was dishonest by the standards of responsible and honest solicitors. . . .

"However, in the present case, the Court of Appeal considered that it was **11–104** entitled to differ from the judge and to find that Mr. Leach had been dishonest on the ground that the judge had deliberately refrained from considering a particular aspect of the case, namely 'Nelsonian' dishonesty. . . .

"Delivering the judgment of the Court of Appeal and after referring to the **11–105** passage in the judgment of Carnwath J., citing Lord Nicholls, Potter L.J. stated[4]:

'Bearing in mind the inclusion within Lord Nicholl's definition of dishonesty of the position where a party deliberately closes his eyes and ears, it can only be assumed that at that point, when the judge referred to Mr. Leach as "not dishonest", he was referring to the state of conscious, as opposed to "Nelsonian", dishonesty, and it is plain that he deliberately refrained from resolving the latter question on the basis that it was unnecessary to do so.

'Had the judge undertaken that task, Mr. Tager submits that he could only have been driven to one conclusion, namely that Nelsonian dishonesty was established.'

---

[4] [1999] Lloyd's Rep. Bank. 438 at 462.

11–106   " . . . I agree with Lord Hoffmann that it is unfortunate that Carnwath J. referred to Mr. Leach deliberately shutting his eyes to the problems and to the implications of the undertaking, but like Lord Hoffmann I do not think it probable that having cited the passage from the judgment of Lord Nicholls the judge then overlooked the issue of Nelsonian dishonesty in finding that Mr. Leach was not dishonest. I also consider, as Lord Millett has observed, that this was not a case where Mr. Leach deliberately closed his eyes and ears, or deliberately did not ask questions, lest he learned something he would rather not know—he already knew all the facts, but the judge concluded that nevertheless he had not been dishonest. I also think that Potter L.J. applied too strict a test when he stated[5]:

> 'It seems to me that, save perhaps in the most exceptional circumstances, it is not the action of an honest solicitor knowingly to assist or encourage another solicitor in a deliberate breach of his undertaking.'

This test does not address the vital point whether Mr. Leach realised that his action was dishonest by the standards of responsible and honest solicitors. In the light of the judge's finding, based as it clearly was, on an assessment of Mr. Leach's evidence in cross-examination in the witness box before him, I consider the Court of Appeal should not have substituted its own finding of dishonesty."

11–107   LORD MILLETT (dissenting on the dishonest assistance point): "My Lords, there are two issues in this appeal. The first is concerned with the nature of the so-called '*Quistclose* trust' and the requirements for its creation.[6] The second arises only if the first is answered adversely to the appellant. It is whether his conduct rendered him liable for having assisted in a breach of trust. This raises two questions of some importance. One concerns the extent of the knowledge of the existence of a trust which is required before a person can be found civilly liable for having assisted in its breach. In particular, is it sufficient that he was aware of the arrangements which created the trust or must he also have appreciated that they did so? The other, which has led to a division of opinion among your Lordships, is whether, in addition to knowledge, dishonesty is required and, if so, the meaning of dishonesty in this context. . . .

Knowing (or dishonest) assistance

11–108   "Before turning to the critical questions concerning the extent of the knowledge required and whether a finding of dishonesty is a necessary condition of liability, I ought to say a word about the distinction between the 'knowing receipt' of trust money and 'knowing (or dishonest) assistance' in a breach of trust; and about the meaning of 'assistance' in this context.

11–109   "Liability for 'knowing receipt' is receipt-based. It does not depend on fault. The cause of action is restitutionary and is available only where the defendant received or applied the money in breach of trust for his own use and benefit.[7] There is no basis for requiring actual knowledge of the breach of trust, let alone dishonesty, as a condition of liability. Constructive notice is sufficient, and may not even be necessary. There is powerful academic support for the proposition that the liability

---

[5] *ibid.* at 465.
[6] See *Barclays Bank Ltd v Quistclose Investments Ltd* [1970] A.C. 567.
[7] See *Agip (Africa) Ltd v Jackson* [1990] Ch. 265 at 291–292; *Royal Brunei Airlines Sdn. Bhd. v Tan* [1995] 2 A.C. 378 at 386.

of the recipient is the same as in other cases of restitution, that is to say strict but subject to a change of position defence.

"Mr. Leach received sums totalling £22,000 in payment of his costs for his own **11–110** use and benefit, and Twinsectra seek their repayment on the ground of knowing receipt. But he did not receive the rest of the money for his own benefit at all. He never regarded himself as beneficially entitled to the money. He held it to Mr. Yardley's order and paid it out to Mr. Yardley or his companies. Twinsectra cannot and does not base its claim in respect of these moneys in knowing receipt, not for want of knowledge, but for want of the necessary receipt. It sues in respect of knowing (or dishonest) assistance.

"The accessory's liability for having assisted in a breach of trust is quite different. **11–111** It is fault-based, not receipt-based. The defendant is not charged with having received trust moneys for his own benefit, but with having acted as an accessory to a breach of trust. The action is not restitutionary; the claimant seeks compensation for wrongdoing. The cause of action is concerned with attributing liability for mis-directed funds. Liability is not restricted to the person whose breach of trust or fiduciary duty caused their original diversion. His liability is strict. Nor is it limited to those who assist him in the original breach. It extends to everyone who consciously assists in the continuing diversion of the money. Most of the cases have been concerned, not with assisting in the original breach, but in covering it up afterwards by helping to launder the money. Mr. Leach's wrongdoing is not confined to the assistance he gave Mr. Sims to commit a breach of trust by receiving the money from him knowing that Mr. Sims should not have paid it to him (though this is sufficient to render him liable for any resulting loss); it extends to the assistance he gave in the subsequent misdirection of the money by paying it out to Mr. Yardley's order without seeing to its proper application.

The ingredients of accessory liability

"The classic formulation of this head of liability is that of Lord Selborne L.C. in **11–112** *Barnes v Addy*.[8] Third parties who were not themselves trustees were liable if they were found 'either making themselves trustees de son tort, or actually participating in any fraudulent conduct of the trustee to the injury of the *cestui que trust*'. In the next passage of his judgment he amplified this by referring to those who 'assist with knowledge in a dishonest and fraudulent design on the part of the trustees'.[9]

"There were thus two conditions of liability: the defendant must have assisted (i) **11–113** with knowledge (ii) in a fraudulent breach of trust. The second condition was discarded in the Royal Brunei case. Henceforth, it was sufficient that the defendant was accessory to any breach of trust whether fraudulent or not. The question for present decision is concerned with the first condition. Since that case it has been clear that actual knowledge is necessary; the question is whether it is sufficient, or whether there is an additional requirement of dishonesty in the subjective sense in which that term is used in criminal cases.

"Prior to the decision in the *Royal Brunei* case the equitable claim was described **11–114** as 'knowing assistance'. It gave a remedy against third parties who knowingly assisted in the misdirection of funds. The accessory was liable if he knew all the relevant facts, in particular the fact that the principal was not entitled to deal with the funds entrusted to him as he had done or was proposing to do. Unfortunately,

---

[8] (1874) L.R. 9 Ch. App. 244 at 251.
[9] *ibid.* at 252.

the distinction between this form of fault-based liability and the liability to make restitution for trust money received in breach of trust was not always observed, and it was even suggested from time to time that the requirements of liability should be the same in the two cases. Authorities on one head of liability were applied in cases which concerned the other, and judges embarked on sophisticated analyses of the kind of knowledge required to found liability.

11–115   "Behind the confusion there lay a critical issue: whether negligence alone was sufficient to impose liability on the accessory. If so, then it was unnecessary to show that he possessed actual knowledge of the relevant facts. Despite a divergence of judicial opinion, by 1995 the tide was flowing strongly in favour of rejecting negligence. It was widely thought that the accessory should be liable only if he actually knew the relevant facts. It should not be sufficient that he ought to have known them or had the means of knowledge if he did not in fact know them.

11–116   "There was a gloss on this. It is dishonest for a man deliberately to shut his eyes to facts which he would prefer not to know. If he does so, he is taken to have actual knowledge of the facts to which he shut his eyes. Such knowledge has been described as 'Nelsonian knowledge', meaning knowledge which is attributed to a person as a consequence of his 'wilful blindness' or (as American lawyers describe it) 'contrived ignorance'. But a person's failure through negligence to make inquiry is insufficient to enable knowledge to be attributed to him.[10]

11–117   "In his magisterial opinion in the *Royal Brunei* case, every word of which merits close attention, Lord Nicholls firmly rejected negligence as a sufficient condition of accessory liability. The accessory must be guilty of intentional wrongdoing. But Lord Nicholls did not, in express terms at least, substitute intentional wrongdoing as the condition of liability. He substituted dishonesty. Dishonesty, he said, was a necessary and sufficient ingredient of accessory liability. 'Knowingly' was better avoided as a defining ingredient of the principle, and the scale of knowledge accepted in *Baden v Société Générale pour Favoriser le Developpement du Commerce et de l'Industrie en France S.A.*[11] was best forgotten. His purpose, as he made clear, was to get away from the refinements which had been introduced into the concept of knowledge in the context of accessory liability.

The meaning of dishonesty in this context

11–118   "In taking dishonesty to be the condition of liability, however, Lord Nicholls used the word in an objective sense. He did not employ the concept of dishonesty as it is understood in criminal cases. He explained the sense in which he was using the word as follows. [Here, his Lordship quoted the passage of Lord Nicholls' speech that is reproduced at paras 11–71 and 11–72, above.]

Dishonesty as a state of mind or as a course of conduct?

11–119   "In *R. v Ghosh*,[12] Lord Lane C.J. drew a distinction between dishonesty as a state of mind and dishonesty as a course of conduct, and held that dishonesty in s.1 of the Theft Act 1968 referred to dishonesty as a state of mind. The question was not whether the accused had in fact acted dishonestly but whether he was aware that he was acting dishonestly. The jury must first of all decide whether the conduct of the accused was dishonest according to the ordinary standards of reasonable and honest

---

[10] See *Agip (Africa) Ltd v Jackson* [1990] Ch. 265 at 293.
[11] [1993] 1 W.L.R. 509.
[12] [1982] Q.B. 1053.

people. That was an objective test. If he was not dishonest by those standards, that was an end of the matter and the prosecution failed. If it was dishonest by those standards, the jury had secondly to consider whether the accused was aware that what he was doing was dishonest by those standards. That was a subjective test. Given his actual (subjective) knowledge the accused must have fallen below ordinary (objective) standards of honesty and (subjectively) have been aware that he was doing so.

"The same test of dishonesty is applicable in civil cases where, for example, **11–120** liability depends upon intent to defraud, for this connotes a dishonest state of mind. *Aktieselskabet Dansk Skibsfinansiering v Brothers*[13] was a case of this kind (trading with intent to defraud creditors). But it is not generally an appropriate condition of civil liability, which does not ordinarily require a guilty mind. Civil liability is usually predicated on the defendant's conduct rather than his state of mind; it results from his negligent or unreasonable behaviour or, where this is not sufficient, from intentional wrongdoing.

"A dishonest state of mind might logically have been required when it was **11–121** thought that the accessory was liable only if the principal was guilty of a fraudulent breach of trust, for then the claim could have been regarded as the equitable counterpart of the common law conspiracy to defraud. But this requirement was discarded in the *Royal Brunei* case.

"It is, therefore, not surprising that Lord Nicholls rejected a dishonest state of **11–122** mind as an appropriate condition of liability. This is evident from the opening sentence of the passage cited above, from his repeated references both in that passage and later in his judgment to the defendant's conduct in 'acting dishonestly' and 'advertent conduct', and from his statement that 'for the most part' (ie not always) it involves 'conscious impropriety'. 'Honesty', he said, 'is a description of a type of conduct assessed in the light of what a person actually knew at the time'. Usually ('for the most part'), no doubt, the defendant will have been guilty of 'conscious impropriety'; but this is not a condition of liability. The defendant, Lord Nicholls said was 'required to act honestly';[14] and he indicated that Knox J. had captured the flavour of dishonesty in *Cowan de Groot Properties Ltd v Eagle Trust plc* when he referred to a person who is 'guilty of commercially unacceptable conduct in the particular context involved'.[15] There is no trace in Lord Nicholls' opinion that the defendant should have been aware that he was acting contrary to objective standards of dishonesty. In my opinion, in rejecting the test of dishonesty adopted in *R. v Ghosh*, Lord Nicholls was using the word to characterise the defendant's conduct, not his state of mind.

"Lord Nicholls had earlier drawn an analogy with the tort of procuring a breach **11–123** of contract. He observed that a person who knowingly procures a breach of contract, or who knowingly interferes with the due performance of a contract, is liable in damages to the innocent party.[16] The rationale underlying the accessory's liability for a breach of trust, he said, was the same. It is scarcely necessary to observe that dishonesty is not a condition of liability for the common law cause of action. This is a point to which I must revert later; for the moment, it is sufficient to say that procuring a breach of contract is an intentional tort, but it does not depend on dishonesty. Lord Nicholls was not of course confusing knowledge with dishonesty.

---

[13] [2001] 2 B.C.L.C. 324.
[14] [1995] 2 A.C. 378 at 390.
[15] [1992] 4 All E.R. 700 at 761.
[16] [1995] 2 A.C. 378 at 387.

But his approach to dishonesty is premised on the belief that it is dishonest for a man consciously to participate in the misapplication of money.

11–124   "This is evident by the way in which Lord Nicholls dealt with the difficult case where the propriety of the transaction is doubtful. An honest man, he considered, would make appropriate enquiries before going ahead. This assumes that an honest man is one who would not knowingly participate in a transaction which caused the misapplication of funds. But it is most clearly evident in the way in which Lord Nicholls described the conduct of the defendant in the case under appeal. The question was whether he was personally liable for procuring or assisting in a breach of trust committed by his company. The trust was created by the terms of a contract entered into between the company, which carried on the business of a travel agency, and an airline. The contract required money obtained from the sale of the airline's tickets to be placed in a special trust account. The company failed to pay the money into a special account but used it to fund its own cash flow. Lord Nicholls described the defendant's conduct: 'In other words, he caused or permitted his company to apply the money in a way he knew was not authorised by the trust of which the company was trustee. Set out in these bald terms, [the defendant's] conduct was dishonest.'[17] There was no evidence and Lord Nicholls did not suggest that the defendant realised that honest people would regard his conduct as dishonest. Nor did the plaintiff put its case so high. It contended that the company was liable because it made unauthorised use of trust money, and that the defendant was liable because he caused or permitted his company to do so despite his knowledge that its use of the money was unauthorised. This was enough to make the defendant liable, and for Lord Nicholls to describe his conduct as dishonest.

11–125   "In my opinion Lord Nicholls was adopting an objective standard of dishonesty by which the defendant is expected to attain the standard which would be observed by an honest person placed in similar circumstances. Account must be taken of subjective considerations such as the defendant's experience and intelligence and his actual state of knowledge at the relevant time. But it is not necessary that he should actually have appreciated that he was acting dishonestly; it is sufficient that he was. . . .

Should subjective dishonesty be required?

11–126   "The question for your Lordships is not whether Lord Nicholls was using the word dishonesty in a subjective or objective sense in the *Royal Brunei* case. The question is whether a plaintiff should be required to establish that an accessory to a breach of trust had a dishonest state of mind (so that he was subjectively dishonest in the *R. v Ghosh* sense); or whether it should be sufficient to establish that he acted with the requisite knowledge (so that his conduct was objectively dishonest). This question is at large for us, and we are free to resolve it either way.

11–127   "I would resolve it by adopting the objective approach. I would do so because: (1) consciousness of wrongdoing is an aspect of *mens rea* and an appropriate condition of criminal liability: it is not an appropriate condition of civil liability. This generally results from negligent or intentional conduct. For the purpose of civil liability, it should not be necessary that the defendant realised that his conduct was dishonest; it should be sufficient that it constituted intentional wrongdoing. (2) The objective test is in accordance with Lord Selborne LC's statement in *Barnes v Addy* and traditional doctrine. This taught that a person who knowingly participates in the

---

[17] [1995] 2 A.C. 378 at 393.

misdirection of money is liable to compensate the injured party. While negligence is not a sufficient condition of liability, intentional wrongdoing is. Such conduct is culpable and falls below the objective standards of honesty adopted by ordinary people. (3) The claim for 'knowing assistance' is the equitable counterpart of the economic torts. These are intentional torts; negligence is not sufficient and dishonesty is not necessary. Liability depends on knowledge. A requirement of subjective dishonesty introduces an unnecessary and unjustified distinction between the elements of the equitable claim and those of the tort of wrongful interference with the performance of a contract.

"If Mr. Sims' undertaking was contractual, as Mr. Leach thought it was, then Mr. **11–128** Leach's conduct would have been actionable as a wrongful interference with the performance of the contract. Where a third party with knowledge of a contract has dealings with the contract breaker which the third party knows will amount to a breach of contract and damage results, he commits an actionable interference with the contract.[18]

"In *British Motor Trade Association v Salvadori*,[19] the defendant bought and took **11–129** delivery of a car in the knowledge that it was offered to him by the vendor in breach of its contract with its supplier. There is a close analogy with the present case. Mr. Leach accepted payment from Mr. Sims in the knowledge that the payment was made in breach of his undertaking to Twinsectra to retain the money in his own client account until required for the acquisition of property.

"In the *Earl of Sefton's case* the defendant bought land in the knowledge that the **11–130** use to which it intended to put the land would put the vendor in breach of his contractual obligations to the plaintiff. Again the analogy with the present case is compelling. Mr. Leach knew that by accepting the money and placing it at Mr. Yardley's free disposal he would put Mr. Sims in breach of his contractual undertaking that it would be used only for the purpose of acquiring property.

"In both cases the defendant was liable for any resulting loss. Such liability is **11–131** based on the actual interference with contractual relations, not on any inducement to break them, so that it is no defence that the contract-breaker was a willing party to the breach and needed no inducement to do so. Dishonesty is not an ingredient of the tort.

"It would be most undesirable if we were to introduce a distinction between the **11–132** equitable claim and the tort, thereby inducing the claimant to attempt to spell a contractual obligation out of a fiduciary relationship in order to avoid the need to establish that the defendant had a dishonest state of mind. It would, moreover, be strange if equity made liability depend on subjective dishonesty when in a comparable situation the common law did not. This would be a reversal of the general rule that equity demands higher standards of behaviour than the common law.

"If we were to reject subjective dishonesty as a requirement of civil liability in this **11–133** branch of the law, the remaining question is merely a semantic one. Should we return to the traditional description of the claim as 'knowing assistance', reminding ourselves that nothing less than actual knowledge is sufficient; or should we adopt Lord Nicholls' description of the claim as 'dishonest assistance', reminding ourselves that the test is an objective one?

"For my own part, I have no difficulty in equating the knowing mishandling of **11–134** money with dishonest conduct. But the introduction of dishonesty is an unnecessary distraction, and conducive to error. Many judges would be reluctant to brand a

---

[18] See *D. C. Thomson & Co. Ltd v Deakin* [1952] Ch. 646 at 694, *Earl of Sefton v Tophams Ltd* [1965] Ch. 1140, where the action failed only because the plaintiff was unable to prove damage.
[19] [1949] Ch. 556.

professional man as dishonest where he was unaware that honest people would consider his conduct to be so. If the condition of liability is intentional wrongdoing and not conscious dishonesty as understood in the criminal courts, I think that we should return to the traditional description of this head of equitable liability as arising from 'knowing assistance'.

Knowledge

11–135   "The question here is whether it is sufficient that the accessory should have actual knowledge of the facts which created the trust, or must he also have appreciated that they did so? It is obviously not necessary that he should know the details of the trust or the identity of the beneficiary. It is sufficient that he knows that the money is not at the free disposal of the principal. In some circumstances it may not even be necessary that his knowledge should extend this far. It may be sufficient that he knows that he is assisting in a dishonest scheme.

11–136   "That is not this case, for in the absence of knowledge that his client is not entitled to receive it there is nothing intrinsically dishonest in a solicitor paying money to him. But I am satisfied that knowledge of the arrangements which constitute the trust is sufficient; it is not necessary that the defendant should appreciate that they do so. Of course, if they do not create a trust, then he will not be liable for having assisted in a breach of trust. But he takes the risk that they do.

11–137   "The gravamen of the charge against the principal is not that he has broken his word, but that having been entrusted with the control of a fund with limited powers of disposal he has betrayed the confidence placed in him by disposing of the money in an unauthorised manner. The gravamen of the charge against the accessory is not that he is handling stolen property, but that he is assisting a person who has been entrusted with the control of a fund to dispose of the fund in an unauthorised manner. He should be liable if he knows of the arrangements by which that person obtained control of the money and that his authority to deal with the money was limited, and participates in a dealing with the money in a manner which he knows is unauthorised. I do not believe that the man in the street would have any doubt that such conduct was culpable.

The findings below

11–138   "Mr. Leach's pleaded case was that he parted with the money in the belief, no doubt engendered by Mr. Yardley's assurances, that it would be applied in the acquisition of property. But he made no attempt to support this in his evidence. It was probably impossible to do so, since he was acting for Mr. Yardley in the acquisition of the three properties which had been identified to him on 23 December 1992, and must have known that some of the payments he was making were not required for their acquisition. In his evidence he made it clear that he regarded the money as held by him to Mr. Yardley's order, and that there was no obligation on his part to see that the terms of the arrangements between Twinsectra and Mr. Sims were observed. That was Mr. Sims' responsibility, not his.

11–139   "The judge found that Mr. Leach was not dishonest. But he also found as follows:

'He was clearly aware of [the terms of the undertaking]. Indeed, his pleaded defence asserts . . . that he believed their "substance . . . to be that the advance would be applied in the acquisition of property" and that he had received them on the footing that they would be so applied. Yet, in evidence, he frankly admitted that he had regarded the money as held simply to the order of Mr. Yardley, without restriction. Again, I have to conclude that he simply shut his eyes to the problems. As far as he was concerned, it was a matter solely for Mr. Sims to satisfy himself whether he could release the money to Mr. Yardley's account.'

"The Court of Appeal thought that the judge's two conclusions (i) that Mr. Leach **11–140** was not dishonest and (ii) that he 'simply shut his eyes to the problems' (or, as he put it later in his judgment 'deliberately shut his eyes to the implications') were inconsistent. They attempted to reconcile the two findings by saying that the judge had overlooked the possibility of wilful blindness. . . .

Conclusion

"I do not think that this was a case of wilful blindness, or that the judge overlooked **11–141** the possibility of imputed knowledge. There was no need to impute knowledge to Mr. Leach, for there was no relevant fact of which he was unaware. He did not shut his eyes to any fact in case he might learn the truth. He knew of the terms of the undertaking, that the money was not to be at Mr. Yardley's free disposal. He knew (i) that Mr. Sims was not entitled to pay the money over to him (Mr. Leach), and was only prepared to do so against confirmation that it was proposed to apply the money for the acquisition of property; and (ii) that it could not be paid to Mr. Yardley except for the acquisition of property. There were no inquiries which Mr. Leach needed to make to satisfy himself that the money could properly be put at Mr. Yardley's free disposal. He knew it could not. The only thing that he did not know was that the terms of the undertaking created a trust, still less a trust in favour of Twinsectra. He believed that Mr. Sims' obligations to Twinsectra sounded in contract only. That was not an unreasonable belief; certainly not a dishonest one; though if true it would not have absolved him from liability.

"Yet from the very first moment that he received the money he treated it as held **11–142** to Mr. Yardley's order and at Mr. Yardley's free disposition. He did not shut his eyes to the facts, but to 'the implications', that is to say the impropriety of putting the money at Mr. Yardley's disposal. His explanation was that this was Mr. Sims' problem, not his.

"Mr. Leach knew that Twinsectra had entrusted the money to Mr. Sims with only **11–143** limited authority to dispose of it; that Twinsectra trusted Mr. Sims to ensure that the money was not used except for the acquisition of property; that Mr. Sims had betrayed the confidence placed in him by paying the money to him (Mr. Leach) without seeing to its further application; and that by putting it at Mr. Yardley's free disposal he took the risk that the money would be applied for an unauthorised purpose and place Mr. Sims in breach of his undertaking. But all that was Mr. Sims' responsibility.

"In my opinion this is enough to make Mr. Leach civilly liable as an accessory (i) **11–144** for the tort of wrongful interference with the performance of Mr. Sims' contractual obligations if this had been pleaded and the undertaking was contractual as well as fiduciary; and (ii) for assisting in a breach of trust. It is unnecessary to consider whether Mr. Leach realised that honest people would regard his conduct as dishonest. His knowledge that he was assisting Mr. Sims to default in his undertaking to Twinsectra is sufficient."

QUESTIONS

1. In *Barnes v Addy* (1874) 9 Ch. App. 244 at 252, Lord Selborne L.C. **11–145** thought that "if persons dealing honestly as agents are at liberty to rely on the legal power of the trustees, [and] are not to have the character of

trustees constructively thrust upon them, then the transactions of mankind can safely be carried through; and I apprehend those who create trusts do expressly intend, in the absence of fraud and dishonesty, to exonerate such agents of all classes from the responsibilities which are expressly incumbent by reason of the fiduciary relation upon the trustees." In light of these comments do you think that fault should be a pre-requisite for third party liability for breach of trust; and if so, what degree of fault?

11–146   2. A stockbroker is directed by trustees to sell an authorised investment and to apply the proceeds to the purchase of an unauthorised investment. He knowingly does so because he *bona fide* believes this to be in the beneficiaries' best financial interests. Most surprisingly the unauthorised investment halves in value within a year. Can the beneficiaries sue the stockbroker if the trustees are now insolvent; and if so, what might be the measure of his liability?

11–147   3. Four years ago under the terms of the Hazzard Settlement Trust, the 13th Duke of Hazzard forfeited his life interest by marrying a Roman Catholic after the death of his first wife. The terms of the Settlement then required the trustees to retain in the Settlement such settled chattels as they saw fit and to allow the new life tenant, the 13th Duke's son, Timon, to choose for himself absolutely any of the remaining chattels. The trustees were a solicitor, Sharp, and Colonel Bluster, an old friend of the family who was accustomed to relying on Sharp in matters of trust administration.

The 13th Duke secretly paid Sharp £5,000 to let Timon have first choice of the settled chattels, and so Timon then innocently took for himself chattels to the value of £200,000, and left in the Settlement chattels worth only £50,000.

Timon forthwith sold the chattels for £200,000 and spent half the proceeds on the wedding reception of his only daughter Ophelia, and the other half on shares in Grockle plc which are now worth £10,000. Meanwhile, Sharp invests his £5,000 in shares in Whizzo plc which are now worth £50,000.

Timon has now died and Yorick has become life tenant under the Settlement. Assuming that all the above facts have come to light, advise Yorick what remedies may be available to him.

Chapter 12

PROPRIETARY CLAIMS FOLLOWING A BREACH OF TRUST

Section 1. Introduction

Various proprietary claims can lie where trustees make an unauthorised **12–01** investment or misappropriate trust property for themselves or misdirect trust property to third parties. The beneficiaries[1] may be entitled to assert a continuing equitable proprietary interest in misdirected trust assets; to assert a new equitable proprietary interest in the traceable proceeds of trust assets, arising under a constructive trust; to acquire an equitable lien over property in a defendant's hands; or to acquire a charge over a defendant's property via subrogation.

The key features of proprietary claims

These claims differ in that the first and second are claims to *ownership* of **12–02** property, while the third and fourth are claims to *security* over property belonging to a defendant. However, all four claims bring the advantage of priority in a defendant's insolvency. If a defendant has never owned an asset free from a claimant's ownership interest, then this interest will be unaffected by his insolvency because the asset can never have formed part of his estate. If the claimant has a charge over a defendant's property, then this will give him priority over the defendant's unsecured creditors, and possibly over his other secured creditors as well, depending on the relevant priority rules.

If a claimant has an ownership right in an asset which appreciates in **12–03** value, then the increase will accrue to the claimant. If a claimant has a charge over a defendant's property to secure the repayment of a particular sum, and the property depreciates in value, then the claimant can still enforce the whole amount of his charge against the property, and if necessary recover any outstanding difference via a personal action.

Pending the hearing of a proprietary claim a claimant is entitled almost **12–04** as of right to an interim injunction preserving the claimed assets until the outcome of the trial.[2]

Following, tracing, and claiming

If a trustee takes trust property for himself and retains the property in its **12–05** original form, then it will often be a simple matter for the beneficiaries to identify the property which forms the subject-matter of their proprietary

---

[1] In the case of misdirected funds, claims can also be made by the trustees: *Montrose Investment Ltd v Orion Nominees Ltd* (2004) 7 I.T.E.L.R. 255 at [24]–[25].
[2] If part of his proprietary claim is weak the court has discretion to grant the requested injunction only over part of the claimed assets: *Polly Peck International plc v Nadir (No.2)* [1992] 4 All E.R. 769.

claim. However, matters are often less straightforward than this. If a trustee transfers a trust asset to a third party, then the beneficiaries must *follow* the asset from the trustee's hands into the third party's hands as a necessary evidential preliminary to asserting a proprietary claim against the asset: *i.e.* they must first prove that the asset held by the third party was formerly held for them by the trustee. Again, if a trustee or a third party recipient exchanges trust property for a new asset, then the beneficiaries must *trace* the value inherent in the trust property into the value inherent in the new asset before they can assert a proprietary claim to the new asset.[3]

12–06   In *Foskett v McKeown* Lord Millett explained the relationship between the rules of following, tracing, and claiming in these terms:[4]

> '[Following and tracing] are both exercises in locating assets which are or may be taken to represent an asset belonging to the plaintiffs and to which they assert ownership. The processes of following and tracing are, however, distinct. Following is the process of following the same asset as it moves from hand to hand. Tracing is the process of identifying a new asset as the substitute for the old. Where one asset is exchanged for another, a claimant can elect whether to follow the original asset into the hands of the new owner or to trace its value into the new asset in the hands of the same owner . . . Tracing is also distinct from claiming. It identifies the traceable proceeds of the claimant's property. It enables the claimant to substitute the traceable proceeds for the original asset as the subject matter of his claim. But it does not affect or establish his claim. That will depend on a number of factors including the nature of his interest in the original asset . . . [and] his claim may also be exposed to potential defences as a result of intervening transactions.'

12–07   Thus, "the rules of following and tracing . . . [are] evidential in nature", and they are distinct from "rules which determine substantive rights": "the former are concerned with identifying property in other hands or in another form; the latter with the rights that a claimant can assert against the property in its present form".[5] Consistently with this, the discussion in this chapter is divided into two sections, the first dealing with the rules of following and tracing, and the second with the rules that govern proprietary claims following a breach of trust.

Common law and equitable tracing rules

12–08   For many years it has traditionally been thought that there are different tracing rules in equity and at common law, and that the equitable rules are more favourable to claimants than the common law rules, most significantly

---

[3] Different rules apply to "clean substitutions" and "mixed substitutions", the former occurring where the new asset is acquired solely with trust property, the latter occurring where the new asset is acquired with a mixture of trust property and the defendant's own property: *Foskett v McKeown* [2001] 1 A.C. 102 at 130; at para.12–78.

[4] *Foskett v McKeown* [2001] 1 A.C. 102 at 127–128; at paras 12–65 and 12–69.

[5] *Glencore International A.G. v Metro Trading International Ltd* [2001] 1 Lloyd's Rep. 284 at [180], *per* Moore-Bick J. See too *Boscawen v Bajwa* [1996] 1 W.L.R. 328 at 334, *per* Millett L.J.; at para.12–120; *Waxman v Waxman* (2004) 7 I.T.E.L.R. 162 at [582].

because claimants at common law cannot trace through mixtures of money in bank accounts, something which equity allows.[6] Traditionally it has also been thought that a claimant must show that his property was held on trust or subject to some other fiduciary relationship before he can take advantage of the equitable tracing rules with a view to tracing through mixtures in bank accounts.[7]

As Professor Lionel Smith has explained, these findings were always suspect as a matter of authority.[8] They were inconsistent with a long line of subrogation cases in which claimants were not required to establish a fiduciary relationship before invoking the equitable tracing rules to show that their money was used to discharge securities to which they sought to be subrogated.[9] They were also inconsistent with *Marsh v Keating*,[10] where the House of Lords advised by twelve common law judges was willing to accept that the common law could trace through a mixed bank account. Finally, Viscount Haldane L.C.'s finding in *Sinclair v Brougham*[11] that there can be no tracing at common law where money has been lent and placed in a bank account was founded on a misunderstanding of Thesiger L.J.'s statement in *Re Hallett's Estate*[12] that a claimant who makes an unsecured loan cannot generally make a proprietary claim against the borrower's assets to secure repayment of the loan.

12–09

These objections to the traditional view are now of subsidiary importance, however, following *Foskett v McKeown*, where Lord Steyn[13] and Lord Millett[14] both considered that there is now only one set of tracing rules in English law, applicable to common law and equitable claimants alike. Their comments on this point were *obiter*, but it seems likely that they will be followed in future cases.[15] Developing the law in this way would certainly be desirable in principle. In the past, the courts have been apt to discover fiduciary relationships between the parties to litigation, not because their relationship has been of the sort that would normally attract the imposition of fiduciary duties, but because the courts have wished to let the claimant take advantage of the "equitable" tracing rules. So, for example, it has been held that a thief owes a fiduciary duty to his victim, with the result that the victim can invoke the "equitable" rules in order to trace through the thief's

12–10

---

[6] *Sinclair v Brougham* [1914] A.C. 398 at 419–420; *Banque Belge pour l'ÉEtranger v Hambrouck* [1921] 1 K.B. 321 at 328 and 330; *Re Diplock* [1948] Ch. 465 at 518; *Agip (Africa) Ltd v Jackson* [1991] Ch. 547 at 566. The point was conceded in *Lipkin Gorman v Karpnale Ltd* [1991] 2 A.C. 548. See too *Taylor v Plumer* (1815) 3 M. & S. 562, which has often been said to stand for the proposition that tracing through mixtures in bank accounts is not possible at common law, but which in fact lays down a rule about claiming; moreover, the case was ultimately decided on equitable principles, as confirmed in *Trustee of F.C. Jones & Son (a firm) v Jones* [1997] Ch. 159 at 169.
[7] *Sinclair v Brougham* [1914] A.C. 398 at 421; *Re Diplock* [1948] Ch. 465 at 536–537; *Agip (Africa) Ltd v Jackson* [1991] Ch. 547 at 566.
[8] L. D. Smith, *The Law of Tracing* (1997), 123–130 and 168–174.
[9] e.g. *Marlow v Pitfeild* (1719) 1 P. Wms. 558; *Baroness Wenlock v River Dee Co.* (1887) 19 Q.B.D. 15; *Orakpo v Manson Investments Ltd* [1978] A.C. 95.
[10] (1834) 2 Cl. & Fin. 250.
[11] [1914] A.C. 398 at 419–421.
[12] (1880) 13 Ch.D. 696 at 723–724.
[13] [2001] 1 A.C. 102. at 113.
[14] *ibid.* at 128–9; at paras 12–70 and 12–71.
[15] But compare *Bracken Partners Ltd v Gutteridge* [2003] 2 B.C.L.C. 83 at [131] (not considered on appeal [2004] 1 B.C.L.C. 377) with *Shalson v Russo* [2003] W.T.L.R. 1165 at [103]–[104].

sale of the stolen property and mixing of the proceeds in a bank account.[16] Instrumental findings of this sort debase the currency of the fiduciary concept.

Section 2. Following and Tracing

I. FOLLOWING

12–11   In many cases, following a misdirected trust asset into the hands of a third party recipient presents no great evidential difficulty. However, problems can arise when the recipient mixes the asset with other assets in such a way that they lose their discrete identity.[17] Different rules are used to resolve these problems, depending on whether the asset has been incorporated into a fungible mixture, *i.e.* a mixture composed of mutually interchangeable units, each of which can readily be separated from the others without causing any damage.[18]

Fungible mixtures

12–12   Suppose that trust assets are mixed with other assets in such a way that no one can tell who has contributed what to the mixture, but it remains possible to divide the mixture into identical parts: suppose, for example, that trust crude oil is mixed with other crude oil,[19] or trust shares with other shares.[20] Where the whole mixture is still intact, the beneficiaries' contribution must still be somewhere in the mixture even though it has lost its discrete identity, and so the rule in this case is that the beneficiaries can identify any proportionate part of the mixture as their property.[21]

12–13   However, if part of the mixture is consumed or transferred to a third party, then the evidential problem becomes more acute. In this case no one can know whether the beneficiaries' contribution subsists in the remainder. Two rules are used to resolve this problem. In the absence of wrongdoing, the remainder is apportioned rateably between contributors to the mixture: *e.g.* if 20,000 barrels of trust oil are mixed with 100,000 barrels of oil belonging to others, and 30,000 barrels are consumed, then one-sixth of the

---

[16] *Black v Freedman* (1910) 12 C.L.R. 105 at 110, endorsed by Lord Templeman in *Lipkin Gorman v Karpnale Ltd* [1991] 2 A.C. 548 at 565–6; *Bishopsgate Investment Management Ltd v Maxwell* [1993] 1 Ch. at 70; *Westdeutsche Landesbank Girozentrale v Islington L.B.C.* [1996] A.C. 669 at 716.

[17] See generally P. Birks, "Mixtures of Goods" in N. Palmer and E. McKendrick (eds.), *Interests in Goods* 2nd ed. (1993); P. Matthews, "The Limits of Common Law Tracing" in P. Birks (ed.), *Laundering and Tracing* (1995), pp.42–46; L. D. Smith, *The Law of Tracing* (1997), chap. 2; R. J. W. Hickey, "Dazed and Confused: Accidental Mixtures of Goods and the Theory of Acquisition of Title" (2003) 66 M.L.R. 368.

[18] *Rysaffe Trustee Co. (C.I.) Ltd v I.R.C.*. [2002] S.T.C. 872 at [32]; *Glencore International A.G. v Alpina Insurance Co. Ltd (No.2)* [2004] 1 All E.R. (Comm.) 858 at [16]. See too J. Austin, *Lectures on Jurisprudence* 4th edn. (1879) p.807; R. Goode, "Are Intangible Assets Fungible?" in P. Birks and A. Pretto (eds) *Themes in Comparative Law* (2002) 97.

[19] *Indian Oil Corp. v Greenstone Shipping S.A.* [1988] Q.B. 345; *Glencore International A.G. v Metro Trading International Ltd* [2001] 1 Lloyd's Rep. 284.

[20] *Brady v Stapleton* (1952) 88 C.L.R. 322.

[21] *Lupton v White* (1808) 15 Ves. Jun. 432 at 441; *Indian Oil Corp. v Greenstone Shipping S.A.* [1988] Q.B. 345 at 369–371; *Foskett v McKeown* [2001] 1 A.C. 102 at 143; *Glencore International A.G. v Metro Trading International Ltd* [2001] 1 Lloyd's Rep. 284 at [185].

90,000 barrels remaining (*i.e.* 15,000 barrels) are deemed to be trust oil.[22] However, where the mixing is done wrongfully, as in the case where a trustee fails to segregate trust assets from his own assets, a different rule applies, namely that evidential uncertainty created by wrongdoing is resolved against the wrongdoer.[23] This does not mean that the wrongdoer is debarred from following his own contribution into the mixture, but simply that losses from the mixture are deemed to have come out of his portion first.[24] So, for example, if a trustee mixes 100 tons of trust gravel with 100 tons of his own gravel, and 80 tons of gravel are then stolen out of the mixture, the trustee can identify 20 tons of the remaining gravel as his own, but he must allow the beneficiaries to identify the remainder as theirs.

Non-fungible mixtures

The process of following an asset inevitably comes to an end if the asset is **12–14** destroyed. The law provides that it also comes to an end because the asset is deemed to have been destroyed, in three situations:

(1) where the asset is physically attached to another, "dominant", asset so that it would cause serious damage, or be disproportionately expensive, to separate the two: here the asset is said to "accede" to the dominant asset;[25]

(2) where the asset is physically attached to land in such a way that it would cause serious damage, or be disproportionately expensive, to separate the two: here the asset is said to become a "fixture" on the land;[26] and

(3) where the asset is combined with other items to create a wholly new product, under the doctrine of "specification".[27]

At least in the case of specification, however, these rules are modified **12–15** where the mixing is performed by a wrongdoer. Here, despite the creation of the new thing, the owner of the assets which are wrongfully used to create the new asset can follow his property into the new asset. So, in *Jones v De Marchant*,[28] a husband wrongfully took eighteen beaver skins belonging to his wife and used them, together with four skins of his own, to have a

---

[22] *Spence v Union Marine Insurance Co.* (1868) L.R. 3 C.P. 427.

[23] This is a rule of general application in the law of evidence: *Armory v Delamirie* (1722) 1 Str. 505; *Infabrics Ltd v Jaytex Ltd* [1985] F.S.R. 75.

[24] *Harris v Truman* (1881) 7 Q.B.D. 340 at 358, affirmed (1882) 9 Q.B.D. 264; *Indian Oil Corp. v Greenstone Shipping S.A.* [1988] Q.B. 345 at 370–371, *Foskett v McKeown* [2001] 1 A.C. 102 at 132; at para.12–86; *Glencore International A.G. v Metro Trading International Ltd* [2001] 1 Lloyd's Rep. 284 at [159] and [182].

[25] *Hendy Lennox (Industrial Engines) Ltd v Grahame Puttick Ltd* [1984] 1 W.L.R. 485; *McKeown v Cavalier Yachts Pty. Ltd* (1988) 13 N.S.W.L.R. 303 at 311. Which of two assets accedes to the other depends on which is the "dominant" entity, a point which is decided rather impressionistically by reference to overall significance rather than monetary value. The doctrine of "accession" derives from the Roman doctrine of *accessio*.

[26] *Elitestone Ltd v Morris* [1997] 1 W.L.R. 687. See too H. N. Bennett, "Attachment of Chattels to Land" in N. Palmer and E. McKendrick (eds.), *Interests in Goods* 2nd edn (1993).

[27] *International Banking Corp. v Ferguson, Shaw & Sons* 1910 S.C. 182; *Borden (U.K.) Ltd v Scottish Timber Products Ltd* [1981] Ch. 25. The doctrine derives from the Roman doctrine of *specificatio*.

[28] (1916) 28 D.L.R. 561, endorsed in *Foskett v McKeown* [2001] 1 A.C. 102 at 132–133; at para.12–86. See too *Spence v Union Marine Insurance Co. Ltd* (1868) L.R. 3 C.P. 427 at 437–438; *Sandeman & Sons v Tyzack and Branfoot Steamship Co. Ltd* [1923] A.C. 680 at 694–695.

fur coat made up which he gave to his mistress. The wife was allowed to recover the coat, a result which can only be explained on the basis that she was permitted to follow her property into the new asset.

II. Tracing

12–16   The rules on tracing resemble the rules on following, insofar as they provide that gains and losses to a mixture must be shared rateably between innocent contributors to the mixture. They also provide that evidential uncertainty created by wrongdoing must be resolved against the wrongdoer.

Where a trustee mixes trust money with his own money

12–17   Suppose that a trustee mixes £25,000 of his own money with £25,000 of trust money in such a way that the funds lose their separate identities. Suppose that he takes £20,000 out of the mixture and loses it, and then takes a further £20,000 out of the mixture and uses it to buy a painting which triples in value. It is impossible to say whose money was lost, whose money bought the painting, and whose money is left. Because the trustee is a wrongdoer, Equity resolves the evidential problem against him,[29] by allowing the beneficiaries to "cherry-pick" from two rules in order to reach the best result for themselves.[30] The rule in *Re Hallett's Estate*[31] provides that the trustee may not say that the beneficiaries' money was lost, and that the beneficiaries may say that the trustee lost his own money. The rule in *Re Oatway*[32] provides that the trustee may not say that he used his own money to buy the painting, and that the beneficiaries may say that their money was used for this purpose. This produces the result that the beneficiaries can trace their money into the painting and £5,000 of the remaining cash, the balance being attributable to the trustee. Note that the rule in *Clayton's* case, considered below, does not apply in this situation.[33]

12–18   The rules in *Re Hallett's Estate* and *Re Oatway* are designed to resolve evidential uncertainty. Hence they have no bite in a situation that is not evidentially uncertain. Suppose that a trustee mixes £50,000 of his own money and £50,000 of trust money and places the mixture in an empty bank account. Suppose that he withdraws £80,000, loses it, and then adds another £30,000 of his own money, so that there is now £50,000 in the account. Here, the beneficiaries cannot invoke the rule in *Re Hallett's Estate* to identify more than £20,000 in the account as their property because it is not evidentially uncertain that at least £30,000 of the remaining funds came from the trustee's own resources.[34] This rule, established in *James Roscoe*

---

[29] *Gray v Haig* (1855) 20 Beav. 214 at 226.
[30] *Shalson v Russo* [2003] W.T.L.R. 1165 at [144], *per* Rimer J.
[31] (1880) 13 Ch.D. 696, esp. at 727, *per* Jessel M.R.: "where a man does an act which may be rightfully performed . . . he is not allowed to say against the person entitled to the property or the right that he has done it wrongfully." See too *Halley v Law Society* [2002] EWHC 139; (Ch) at [160].
[32] [1903] 2 Ch. 356, esp. at 360, *per* Joyce J.: the trustee "cannot maintain that the investment which remains represents his money alone and what has been spent and can no longer be traced or recovered was money belonging to the trust." See too *Grey v Haig* (1855) 20 Beav. 214 at 226.
[33] *Re Hallett's Estate* (1880) 13 Ch.D. 696 at 728.
[34] Cf. *Law Society of Upper Canada v Toronto-Dominion Bank* (1999) 169 D.L.R. (4th) 353, where the Ontario CA failed to grasp this point, as noted by L. D. Smith (2000) 33 Can. Bus. L.J. 75.

(Bolton) Ltd v Winder,[35] is known as "the lowest intermediate balance rule": "absent any payment in of money with the intention of making good earlier depredations, tracing cannot occur through a mixed account for any larger sum than is the lowest balance in the account between the time the beneficiary's money goes in, and the time the remedy is sought."[36]

Where a trustee mixes trust funds together

If trust funds are mixed together and the beneficiaries are equally innocent **12–19** victims of the trustee's wrongdoing, then the beneficiaries will generally have equally strong claims to a rateable share of gains, and equally weak claims to avoid taking a rateable share of losses, to the mixed fund.[37] Hence, gains and losses are generally shared between the beneficiaries *pro rata*.[38]

Until recently, there was thought to be an exception to this principle, **12–20** deriving from *Clayton's* case.[39] This concerned a dispute centring on the appropriation of payments as between a bank and its customer, but it came to be seen as authority for the rule that if a trustee places money belonging to two different sets of beneficiaries into the same unbroken running account,[40] any withdrawals that he makes from the account are deemed to be made in the same order as the payments in, on a "first in, first out" basis.[41] Thus, for example, if he puts £10,000 from Trust A into a current bank account, and then puts in £10,000 from Trust B, and then withdraws £10,000 and loses it (or uses it to buy an asset which triples in value), then the loss (or gain) will be attributed solely to the beneficiaries of Trust A.

As between the beneficiaries of Trust A and Trust B this is an arbitrary **12–21** and unfair result, and for this reason the "first in, first out" rule has been discarded in many Commonwealth jurisdictions, in favour of a *pro rata* approach.[42] In *Barlow Clowes International Ltd v Vaughan*,[43] the Court of

---

[35] [1915] 1 Ch. 62, endorsed in *Re Goldcorp Exchange Ltd* [1995] 1 A.C. 74 at 107–108, also in *Bishopsgate Investment Management Ltd v Homan* [1995] Ch. 211 at 219 and 220, at paras 12–48 and 12–52.

[36] *Re French Caledonia Travel Service Pty. Ltd* (2003) 59 N.S.W.L.R. 361 at [175], *per* Campbell J. For application of the principle where goods are successively withdrawn and deposited in a mixed bulk, see *Glencore International A.G. v Metro Trading International Ltd* [2001] 1 Lloyd's Rep. 284 at [201]–[202], revisited in *Glencore International A.G. v Alpina Insurance Co. Ltd (No.2)* [2004] 1 All E.R. (Comm.) 858 at [14]–[20]. For a case falling within the scope of Campbell J.'s proviso, see *Westdeutsche Landesbank Girozentrale v Islington L.B.C.* [1994] 4 All E.R. 890 at 939 (not considered on appeal).

[37] But it seems that if a trustee mixes two trust funds in one account and then purports to withdraw a sum for the beneficiary of one trust but actually uses it for his own purposes then that sum should be allocated to that particular trust: *Re Stillman and Wilson* (1950) 15 A.B.C. 68; *Re Registered Securities Ltd* [1991] 1 N.Z.L.R. 545.

[38] *Edinburgh Corp. v Lord Advocate* (1879) 4 App. Cas. 823; *Re Diplock* [1948] Ch 465 at 533, 534, and 539.

[39] (1816) 1 Mer. 529. For the history of the case see L. D. Smith, *The Law of Tracing* (1997), pp.183–194; *Re French Caledonia Travel Service Pty. Ltd* (2003) 59 N.S.W.L.R. 361 at [20]–[172].

[40] *e.g.* a current bank account, a solicitor's trust account, or a moneylender's account. The rule does not apply where there are distinct and separate debts: *The Mecca* [1897] A.C. 286; *Re Sherry* (1884) 25 Ch.D. 692 at 702. Nor does the rule apply to entries on the same day: it is the end-of-day balance which counts: *The Mecca* at 291.

[41] *Pennell v Deffell* (1853) 4 De G.M. & G. 372; *Hancock v Smith* (1889) 41 Ch.D. 456 at 461; *Re Stenning* [1895] 2 Ch. 433; *Re Diplock* [1948] Ch. 465 at 553–554.

[42] *Re Ontario Securities Commission* (1985) 30 D.L.R. (4th) 1, affirmed (1998) 52 D.L.R. (4th) 767; *Re Registered Securities Commission* [1991] 1 N.Z.L.R. 545; *Keefe v Law Society of New South Wales* (1998) 44 N.S.W.L.R. 451; *A.S.I.C. v Enterprise Solutions 2000 Pty. Ltd* [2001] QSC 82; *Re Esteem Settlement* 2002 J.L.R. 53; *Re French Caledonia Travel Service Pty. Ltd* (2003) 59 N.S.W.L.R. 361; *Re International Investment Unit Trust* [2005] 1 N.Z.L.R. 270.

[43] [1992] 4 All E.R. 22.

Appeal reaffirmed the general application of *Clayton's* case in English law, except where its application would be impracticable or would result in injustice between the parties. However, more recent English cases suggest that the rule will not often be applied, for the courts are now swift to find that the rule is an impracticable or unjust method of resolving disputes between the victims of shared misfortune, particularly in cases of large-scale fraud.[44]

12–22   *Barlow Clowes* concerned the liquidation of an investment company whose fraudulent managers had stolen most of the company's assets, leaving thousands of investors out of pocket. The question arose as to how the surviving assets should be distributed between the investors. The court held that the rule in *Clayton's* case should not be used to resolve this question because the investors had all intended that their money should be pooled in a single fund for investment purposes, so that it would conform with their original intentions if they all shared rateably in what remained in the pool. However, Woolf and Leggatt L.JJ.[45] also indicated that a "rolling charge" solution might be fairer than rateable sharing so that claimants should share losses and gains to the fund in proportion to their interest in the fund immediately prior to each withdrawal.

12–23   This would work as follows. Suppose that a trustee pays £2,000 from Trust A and then £4,000 from Trust B into an empty current bank account. He then withdraws £3,000 and loses it. He then pays in £3,000 from Trust C before withdrawing another £3,000 to buy shares whose value increases tenfold. He then withdraws the remaining £3,000 and loses it. Applying the "rolling charge" rule, the first loss must be borne by A and B in the ratio 1:2, and C need not bear this loss at all. Immediately after the first withdrawal the remaining £3,000 would be attributed to A and B in the ratio 1:2, and after the next deposit, the £6,000 in the account would be attributable to A, B, and C in the ratio 1:2:3. Hence, the shares should be attributed to them in the same proportion, leaving A with shares worth £5,000, B with shares worth £10,000 and C with shares worth £15,000. In contrast, the *pro rata* rule would attribute all gains and losses in proportion to the total contributions made by each Trust, giving a ratio of 2:4:3, and leaving A with shares worth £6,667, B with shares worth £13,333, and C with shares worth £10,000. The "first in, first out" rule, meanwhile, would produce the result that all of A's money is lost, that £1000 of B's money is lost, that all the shares belong to B, and that all of C's money is lost.

12–24   In *Shalson v Russo*,[46] Rimer J. suggested that the rolling charge rule should always be used to resolve cases of this kind, because the *pro rata* rule ignores evidence of what has actually happened to the claimants' money:

---

[44] *El Ajou v Dollar Land Holdings plc (No.2)* [1995] 2 All E.R. 213 at 222; *Russell-Cooke Trust Co. v Prentis* [2003] 2 All E.R. 478 at 495; *Commerzbank Aktiengesellschaft v I.M.B. Morgan plc* [2005] Lloyd's Rep. 298 at [43]–[49]. Note too that in *El Ajou (No. 2)*, at 223—4, Robert Walker J. held that where A and B's money is mixed in an account and *Clayton's* case deems A's money (and not B's) to have been paid to D, B can still trace into the money received by D and claim against him if A makes no claim and is unlikely to do so. This finding was followed in *Campden Hill Ltd v Chakrani* [2005] EWHC 911 (Ch) at [76]—[77].
[45] *ibid.* at 35 and 44.
[46] [2003] W.T.L.R. 1165 at [150].

thus, in the example, we know that no part of Trust C's £3,000 can have gone into the trustee's first withdrawal, suggesting that Trust C should not have to share this loss with Trust A and Trust B. Rimer J.'s position can certainly be supported by reference to *Roscoe v Winder*,[47] but in a case involving thousands of investors and hundreds of thousands of deposits and withdrawals, the expense and practical difficulties of calculation using the rolling charge rule may be prohibitive, leaving the claimants with a choice between the rough justice of the *pro rata* rule, and the even rougher justice of "first in, first out".

Where recipients of trust money mix it with their own money

Where a trustee misdirects trust funds to a *bona fide* purchaser for value **12–25** without notice of the trust interest the beneficiaries may be able to follow the property into his hands and trace its inherent value through his subsequent mixtures and substitutions, but it will be pointless for them to do this as he will have a defence to any proprietary claim that they might bring.[48] However, where a trustee misdirects trust property to a recipient who is not a *bona fide* purchaser, the beneficiaries may well wish to follow the property into the recipient's hands and then trace its inherent value through subsequent mixtures and substitutions into some new asset.

The tracing rules that apply in this case will vary according to whether **12–26** the recipient has acted in good faith. If he is a *bona fide* volunteer, then the rules governing the situation will be the same as those which govern the case where money belonging to the innocent beneficiaries of separate trust funds is mixed together by the trustee[49]: gains and losses will be shared rateably, possibly subject to the rule in *Clayton's* case[50] if the court sees fit to apply it.[51] If the recipient takes the property with knowledge of the breach of trust, however, then he cannot innocently mix the property with his own property. He will owe the beneficiaries a duty as constructive trustee to account to them for the trust property. Hence if he mixes it with his own property he will be counted as a wrongdoer,[52] and the case will be governed by the same rules as those which govern the case where an express trustee wrongfully mixes trust funds with his own money: evidential uncertainties will be resolved against the trustee.[53]

---

[47] [1915] 1 Ch. 62, discussed in para.12–18, above.
[48] *Miller v Race* (1758) 1 Burr. 542; *Pilcher v Rawlins* (1872) L.R. 7 Ch. App. 259; *Taylor v Blakelock* (1886) 32 Ch.D. 560; *Re Diplock* [1948] Ch. 465 at 539; *Foskett v McKeown* [2001] 1 A.C. 102 at 130; at para.12–77. See too D. Fox, "*Bona Fide* Purchase and the Currency of Money" (1996) 55 C.L.J. 547.
[49] *Re Diplock* [1948] Ch. 465 at 524 and 539.
[50] *Re Diplock* [1948] Ch. 465 at 554.
[51] See paras 12–20 to 12–24, above. If the recipient pays the trust money into an interest-bearing account designated as a trust account as soon as he learns of the trust claim, this will be regarded as effectively unmixing the fund so that the trust claim will then relate only to the money in the designated account: *Re Diplock* [1948] Ch. 465 at 551–2, dealing with the claim against the National Institute for the Deaf, reversed on an amended statement of the facts: *ibid.* at 559.
[52] *Boscawen v Bajwa* [1996] 1 W.L.R. 328 at 336–8; at paras 12–129 to 12–134; *Banton v C.I.B.C. Trust Corp.* (2001) 197 D.L.R. (4th) 212.
[53] See paras 12–17 and 12–18, above.

Payment of debts

12–27   Like the process of following property from hand to hand, the process of tracing the value inherent in property through mixtures and substitutions must come to an end if the asset in which the value resides is dissipated or destroyed. So, if a trustee (or third party recipient) uses trust funds to buy a meal, or a house which burns down, then his purchases leave no traceable residue (assuming that the house is uninsured): nothing is left in his hands to which the beneficiaries might assert a proprietary claim. As the Court of Appeal stated in *Re Diplock*[54]:

> "The equitable remedies [available to beneficiaries making proprietary claims] presuppose the continued existence of the [trust] money either as a separate fund or as part of a mixed fund or as latent in property acquired by means of such a fund. If such continued existence is not established equity is . . . helpless."

12–28   The rule that the tracing process comes to an end when the value being traced is dissipated generally applies in the case where a defendant uses trust money to pay off a debt: if the creditor is a *bona fide* purchaser then there is no point following the money into his hands, and nothing is usually left in the hands of the defendant.[55] However, there are two exceptions to this principle. First, if the debt was secured by a charge over the defendant's property then Equity can treat the debt and the charge, by a legal fiction, as though they were not extinguished by the payment, thereby enabling the beneficiaries to trace the value inherent in their money into the value inherent in the creditor's fictionally subsisting *chose* in action against the defendant.[56] Secondly, if a defendant borrows money and uses it to buy an asset, and subsequently uses trust money to repay his creditor, then the beneficiaries can trace "backwards" through the loan transaction into the asset and identify the value inherent in the asset as the proceeds of the value inherent in the trust money.[57]

The role of intention

12–29   Backwards tracing was an issue in *Foskett v McKeown* in the Court of Appeal, where Scott V.-C. expressed the view that beneficiaries should be allowed to trace "backwards" through the payment of a debt with trust

---

[54] [1948] Ch. 465 at 521.
[55] *Northern Counties of England Fire Insurance Co. v Whipp* (1884) 26 Ch.D. 482 at 495–496; *Thomson v Clydesdale Bank Ltd* [1893] A.C. 282.
[56] *Boscawen v Bajwa* [1996] 1 W.L.R. 328 at 340, rejecting *Re Diplock* [1948] Ch. 465 at 549–550. See paras 12–140 and 12–141. As discussed at para.12–105, the point of this is that the beneficiaries can acquire the fictionally subsisting security via subrogation and enforce it for their own benefit.
[57] L.D. Smith, "Tracing into the Payment of a Debt" [1995] C.L.J. 290, esp. 292–295, expanded in L. D. Smith, *The Law of Tracing* (1997), pp.146–152. This analysis has the support of Dillon L.J. in *Bishopsgate Investment Management Ltd v Homan* [1995] Ch. 211 at 216–217, at paras 12–40 to 12–41 (but was disapproved by Leggatt L.J. at 221 and 222, at paras 12–56 and 12–61). It was also adopted by Hobhouse J. in *Westdeutsche Landesbank Girozentrale v Islington L.B.C.* [1994] 4 All E.R. 890 at 939–940 (approved by CA without comment); by Scott V.-C. in *Foskett v McKeown* [1998] Ch. 265 at 283–4 (not considered on appeal to HL); by Rimer J. in *Shalson v Russo* [2003] W.T.L.R. 1165 at [144] (*obiter*); and (in effect) by David Richards Q.C., sitting as a deputy High Court judge in *Law Society v Haider* [2003] EWHC 2486 (Ch) at [40]–[41].

money into an asset purchased with the borrowed money only if they could prove that it was the trustee's intention at the time of borrowing the money to repay the lender with trust money.[58] However, the tracing rules are not concerned with a defendant's intentions, but with establishing transactional links between assets in order to identify the current whereabouts of the value which was formerly in the claimant's property.[59] As Ungoed-Thomas J. stated in *Re Tilley's Will Trusts*[60]:

> "if, having regard to all the circumstances of the case objectively considered, it appears that the trustee has in fact, whatever his intention, laid out trust moneys in or towards a purchase, then the beneficiaries are entitled to the property purchased and any profits which it produces to the extent to which it has been paid for out of the trust money."

The law's focus on transactional links may seem to produce some **12–30** unpalatable results. Suppose that a trustee misdirects £5 of trust money to an innocent donee X who uses it to buy a winning lottery ticket that pays out £1 million. X can prove that he could have used his own resources to buy the ticket, and that he would have done so if he had known the improper provenance of the trust money. Nonetheless, the beneficiaries can say that the £1 million are the traceable proceeds of the trust money. Again, suppose that a trustee steals £5,000 of trust money and uses it to pay his rent, and then uses another £5,000 of his own to buy a diamond. The beneficiaries cannot trace into the ring even if they can prove that the trustee could not have afforded to pay the rent and buy the jewel out of his own resources. In our view, however, the answer to problems of the former sort does not lie in reformulating the *tracing* rules by requiring beneficiaries to prove causal rather than transactional links between misapplied trust property and substitute assets,[61] but in revisiting the rules of *claiming* the fruits of misdirected trust property.[62] So far as the problems of the latter sort are concerned, we are not convinced that the beneficiaries should have anything more than a personal claim against the trustee, a view which is borne out by the courts' treatment of Lord Templeman's "swollen assets theory" in *Space Investments Ltd v Canadian Imperial Bank of Commerce Trust Co.*[63]

The swollen assets theory

Space Investments concerned a bank trustee that was empowered by the **12–31** trust instrument to lend trust money to itself. The bank lawfully exercised this power, and then went into liquidation. The beneficiaries were unable to

---

[58] [1998] Ch. 265 at 283–284.
[59] Similarly, the rules of following are concerned with identifying the current whereabouts of particular assets, and with deeming them to be in particular locations when no-one can say where they have actually gone. See further L. D. Smith, *The Law of Tracing* (1997) pp.69–70, 82–85, and 136–139.
[60] [1967] Ch. 1179 at 1193.
[61] As urged in D. A. Oesterle, "Deficiencies of the Restitutionary Right to Trace" (1983) 68 Cornell L.R. 172; C. Rotherham, "The Metaphysics of Tracing: Substituted Title and Property Rhetoric" [1996] Osgoode Hall L.J. 321; S. Evans, "Rethinking Tracing and the Law of Restitution" (1999) 115 L.Q.R. 469.
[62] See further para.12–102.
[63] [1986] 3 All E.R. 75.

trace their money into any particular surviving asset and so the Privy Council held that their claims ranked as unsecured debts. In *obiter dicta*, however, Lord Templeman contrasted the situation with the case where a trustee unlawfully dissipates trust money and the beneficiaries cannot trace their money into a particular surviving asset. Here, in his Lordship's view, "equity allows the beneficiaries to trace the trust money to all the assets of the bank and to recover the trust money by the exercise of an equitable charge over all the assets of the bank."[64]

12–32   In support of this conclusion he cited Jessel M.R.'s comment in *Re Hallett's Estate*,[65] that "if a man mixes trust funds with his own, the whole will be treated as trust property". However, this was to misread Jessel M.R.'s judgment, which was concerned with the case where a trustee mixes £X of trust money with £Y of his own money in a particular account and then dissipates part of the mixture. Jessel M.R. said nothing to support Lord Templeman's assertion that in such a case the *whole* of the trustee's assets constitutes one colossal fund which should be regarded as having been mixed with the trust money, so that if the money in the account is dissipated the beneficiaries can switch their attention to some other asset in the trustee's hands.

12–33   Moreover, Lord Templeman's analysis is inconsistent with the *Roscoe v Winder* principle discussed earlier,[66] that presumptions are made against wrongdoing trustees only where there is evidential uncertainty. In a case where it is certain that a trustee has dissipated trust money out of a particular bank account, this principle prevents the beneficiaries from arguing that some other asset in the trustee's hands should be deemed to represent the traceable proceeds of their property. For this reason, Lord Templeman's *dicta* were restrictively distinguished by the Privy Council in *Re Goldcorp Exchange Ltd*,[67] and again by the Court of Appeal in *Bishopsgate Investment Management Ltd v Homan*.

BISHOPSGATE INVESTMENT MANAGEMENT LTD v HOMAN

Court of Appeal [1995] Ch. 211; [1994] 3 W.L.R. 1270; [1995] 1 All E.R. 347

12–34   DILLON L.J.: "This is an appeal, by leave of the judge, by Bishopsgate Investment Management Ltd. ("B.I.M.") against an order of Vinelott J. made on 21 December 1993. B.I.M., which is now in liquidation, is the trustee of certain of the assets of various pension schemes for employees of companies with which the late Robert Maxwell was associated.

12–35   "The respondents to the appeal, Mr. Homan and three colleagues who are partners in Price Waterhouse & Co., are the court-appointed administrators of Maxwell Communication Corporation Plc. ("M.C.C."). The judge's order was made on an application by the administrators under the Insolvency Act 1986 for directions. M.C.C., which was known at an earlier stage as the British Printing

---

[64] *ibid.* at 76–77, overlooking *Re Hallett & Co.* [1894] 2 Q.B. 237 at 245, *per* Davey L.J.
[65] (1880) 13 Ch.D. 696 at 719.
[66] See para.12–18, above.
[67] [1995] 1 A.C. 74. See too *Jones v Southall & Bourke Pty. Ltd* [2004] FCA 539 at [79].

Corporation Ltd., was a publicly quoted company and the most prominent of a large number of companies, for which it was the holding company. There is a second group of companies, which have been referred to as the Maxwell private sector companies; essentially they were companies the share capitals of which were beneficially owned, directly or indirectly, by Robert Maxwell and members of his family or trusts established by him.

"On the unexpected death of Robert Maxwell on 5 November 1991 it was **12–36** discovered that very large amounts of pension fund moneys of B.I.M. had been improperly paid, during his lifetime, directly or indirectly into various bank accounts of the private sector companies and of M.C.C. with National Westminster Bank. At the time of each wrongful payment of B.I.M.'s pension fund moneys into M.C.C.'s accounts those accounts were overdrawn, or later became overdrawn. It was also found that M.C.C. was hopelessly insolvent. . . .

"The administrators, who have realised a substantial amount of M.C.C.'s assets **12–37** although the administration is far from complete, wanted to make an interim distribution among the creditors of M.C.C. But the liquidators claimed that B.I.M. was entitled to an equitable charge, in priority to all other unsecured creditors of M.C.C., on all the assets of M.C.C. for the full amount of the pension moneys of B.I.M. wrongly paid to M.C.C. Accordingly the administrators applied to the Companies Court for directions.

"Vinelott J. approached the application on the basis that if the claims of B.I.M. **12–38** were plainly not maintainable in law the court ought to make a declaration to that effect, in order that an interim distribution could be made without regard to unfounded claims. But, if it was possible that on a further investigation of the facts there might be a claim, valid in law, by B.I.M. to an equitable charge on a particular asset, the proceeds of that asset ought not to be distributed until the particular facts had been investigated.

"The judge declared by his order that the administrators were entitled to deal **12–39** with specified notices of claim as if they do not give rise to any proprietary claims, and he declared also that B.I.M. was not entitled to any equitable charge over the assets of M.C.C. in respect of proprietary claims notified to the administrators to the extent that such assets were acquired before any moneys or assets misappropriated from B.I.M. were paid or transferred to or so as to be under the control of M.C.C. and were not acquired in anticipation of or otherwise in connection with the misappropriation of such assets or moneys. In essence the judge held that B.I.M. could only claim an equitable charge on any assets of M.C.C. in accordance with the recognised principles of equitable tracing and these principles do not permit tracing through an overdrawn bank account—whether an account which was already overdrawn at the time the relevant moneys were paid into it or an account which was then in credit, but subsequently became overdrawn by subsequent drawings.

"The judge reserved, however, the position if it were shown that there was a **12–40** connection between a particular misappropriation of B.I.M.'s moneys and the acquisition by M.C.C. of a particular asset. The judge gave as an instance of such a case what he called 'backward tracing'—where an asset was acquired by M.C.C. with moneys borrowed from an overdrawn or loan account and there was an inference that when the borrowing was incurred it was the intention that it should be repaid by misappropriations of B.I.M.'s moneys. Another possibility was that moneys misappropriated from B.I.M. were paid into an overdrawn account of M.C.C. in order to reduce the overdraft and so make finance available within the overdraft limits for M.C.C. to purchase some particular asset.

"By a respondent's notice by way of cross-appeal, the administrators ask us to **12–41** overrule these reservations of the judge, and hold that even if the possible facts which the judge envisages were clearly proved that could not in law give B.I.M. any equitable charge on the particular asset acquired. For my part I would not interfere at all with this aspect of the judge's exercise of his discretion. In my judgment, if the connection he postulates between the particular misappropriation of B.I.M.'s money and the acquisition by M.C.C. of a particular asset is sufficiently clearly proved, it is at least arguable, depending on the facts, that there ought to be an equitable charge in favour of B.I.M. on the asset in question of M.C.C.

12–42   "But the main claims of B.I.M. are put much more widely as claims to an equitable charge on all the assets of M.C.C. These claims are not founded on proving any particular intention of Robert Maxwell or others in charge of M.C.C. but on general principles which it is said that the court ought to apply. They are founded primarily on certain observations of Lord Templeman in giving the judgment of the Privy Council in *Space Investments Ltd. v Canadian Imperial Bank of Commerce Trust Co. (Bahamas) Ltd.*[68] In particular, in that case Lord Templeman said[69]:

> 'In these circumstances it is impossible for the beneficiaries interested in trust money misappropriated from their trust to trace their money to any particular asset belonging to the trustee bank. But equity allows the beneficiaries, or a new trustee appointed in place of an insolvent bank trustee . . . to trace the trust money to all the assets of the bank and to recover the trust money by the exercise of an equitable charge over all the assets of the bank.. . . [That] equitable charge secures for the beneficiaries and the trust priority over the claims of the customers . . . and . . . all other unsecured creditors.'

12–43   "What Lord Templeman there said was strictly *obiter*, in that on the facts the Privy Council held that the bank trustee was authorised by the trust instruments to deposit trust money with itself as banker and so there had been no misappropriation. The beneficiaries or their new trustee therefore could merely prove with the other general creditors of the insolvent bank trustee for a dividend in respect of the moneys so deposited.

12–44   "Vinelott J. rejected the submissions of B.I.M. founded on the *Space Investments* case. He considered that Lord Templeman could not have intended to effect such a fundamental change to the well-understood limitations to equitable tracing; Lord Templeman was only considering the position of an insolvent bank which had been taking deposits and lending money.

12–45   "In the notice of appeal to this court, B.I.M.'s first ground of appeal relies on the *Space Investments* case and it is said that the judge erred in his interpretation of what Lord Templeman had said. There is a second, and alternative, ground of appeal to which I will refer later. . . .

12–46   "As I read the judgment of the Privy Council in *Re Goldcorp Exchange Ltd.*[70] delivered by Lord Mustill, it makes it clear that Lord Templeman's observations in the *Space Investments* case were not concerned at all with the situation we have in the present case where trust moneys have been paid into an overdrawn bank account, or an account which has become overdrawn. Lord Mustill said in the clearest terms[71]:

> 'Their Lordships should, however, say that they find it difficult to understand how the judgment of the Board in *Space Investments Ltd v Canadian Imperial*

---

[68] [1968] 1 W.L.R. 1072.
[69] *ibid.* at 1074.
[70] [1995] 1 A.C. 74.
[71] *ibid.* at 104.

Bank of Commerce Trust Co. (Bahamas) Ltd. on which the claimants leaned heavily in argument, would enable them to overcome the difficulty that the moneys said to be impressed with the trust were paid into an overdrawn account and thereupon ceased to exist.[72] The observations of the Board in the *Space Investments* case were concerned with a mixed, not a non-existent, fund.'

"Thus the wide interpretation of those observations put forward by Cooke P. [in the New Zealand Court of Appeal in *Re Goldcorp*[73]], which is the basis of the first ground of appeal in the present case, is rejected. Instead the decision of the Court of Appeal in *Re Diplock* is endorsed. There it was said[74]: **12–47**

'The equitable remedies presuppose the continued existence of the money either as a separate fund or as part of a mixed fund or as latent in property acquired by means of such a fund. If, on the facts of any individual case, such continued existence is not established, equity is as helpless as the common law itself.'

"Also endorsed, in my judgment, in the decision of the Board delivered by Lord Mustill is the long-standing first instance decision in *James Roscoe (Bolton) Ltd v Winder*,[75] which Mr. Heslop for B.I.M., in his submissions in March, invited us to overrule. That was a decision that, in tracing trust moneys into the bank account of a trustee in accordance with *Re Hallett's Estate*,[76] tracing was only possible to such an amount of the balance ultimately standing to the credit of the trustee as did not exceed the lowest balance of the account during the intervening period. Thus as is said in the headnote to the report: **12–48**

'Payments into a general account cannot, without proof of express intention, be appropriated to the replacement of trust money which has been improperly mixed with that account and drawn out.'

That reflects the statement by Sargant J. in the *James Roscoe* case[77];

'it is impossible to attribute to him"—*i.e.* the account holder—"that by the mere payment into the account of further moneys, which to a large extent he subsequently used for purposes of his own, he intended to clothe those moneys with a trust in favour of the plaintiffs.'

"Mr. Heslop, for B.I.M., referred, however, to later passages in the opinion of Lord Mustill. First Lord Mustill stated that the law relating to the creation and tracing of equitable proprietary interests is still in a state of development.[78] He referred to two recent decisions[79] on facts not particularly relevant to the present case as instances where equitable proprietary interests have been recognised in circumstances which might previously have been regarded merely as circumstances for common law relief . . . **12–49**

---

[72] See, *e.g. Re Diplock* [1948] Ch. 465.
[73] *Liggett v Kensington* [1993] 1 N.Z.L.R. 257 at 274.
[74] [1948] Ch. 465 at 521.
[75] [1915] 1 Ch. 62.
[76] (1880) 13 Ch.D. 696.
[77] [1915] 1 Ch. 62 at 69.
[78] [1995] 1 A.C. 74 at 109.
[79] *Att.-Gen. for Hong Kong v Reid* [1994] A.C. 324 and *Lord Napier and Ettrick v Hunter* [1993] A.C. 713.

12–50   "Mr. Heslop submitted that the beneficiaries under the pension schemes of which B.I.M. is trustee are in a different position from the other creditors, who are mainly banks, of B.I.M. He did not, of course, adopt the simple populist approach that pensioners, like widows and orphans, are 'goodies' while banks, like usurers, are 'baddies' and so the court should use its powers to ensure that the goodies are paid in full ahead of the baddies. But he did say that the beneficiaries under the pension schemes never undertook the risk that their pension funds would be misappropriated and paid into the overdrawn bank account of an insolvent company, whereas all the banks which lent money to M.C.C. took their chance, as a commercial risk, on M.C.C.'s solvency.

12–51   "Mr. Heslop therefore relied on the second ground in the notice of appeal, whereby B.I.M. claims (as it has been explained to us) to be entitled to an equitable charge as security for its claims against M.C.C. (i) over any moneys standing to the credit at the time of the appointment of the administrators of M.C.C. of any banking account maintained by M.C.C. into which any moneys of B.I.M. or the proceeds of any assets of B.I.M. misappropriated from it were paid and (ii) over any assets acquired out of any such bank account, whether or not in credit as at the date such assets were acquired.

12–52   "So far as (i) is concerned, the point is that the National Westminster Bank account into which the misappropriated B.I.M. trust moneys were paid happened to be in credit when the administrators were appointed. B.I.M. therefore claims a lien on that credit balance in the National Westminster Bank account for the amount of the misappropriated trust moneys. It is difficult to suppose, however, in the circumstances of Robert Maxwell's last days—and I know no evidence—that Robert Maxwell intended to make good the misappropriation of the B.I.M. pension moneys by the cryptic expedient of arranging to put M.C.C.'s account with National Westminster Bank into credit—but without repaying the credit balance this created to B.I.M. But in the absence of clear evidence of intention to make good the depredations on B.I.M. it is not possible to assume that the credit balance has been clothed with a trust in favour of B.I.M. and its beneficiaries.[80]

12–53   "As to (ii), this seems to be going back to the original wide interpretation of what Lord Templeman said in the *Space Investments* case and applying it to an overdrawn account because the misappropriated moneys that went into the account were trust moneys and thus different from other moneys that may have gone into that account. But the moneys in the *Space Investments* case were also trust moneys, and so, if argument (ii) is valid in the present case, it would also have been valid, as a matter of law, in the *Space Investments* case. But that was rejected in *Re Goldcorp Exchange Ltd.* because equitable tracing, though devised for the protection of trust moneys misapplied, cannot be pursued through an overdrawn and therefore non-existent fund. Acceptance of argument (ii) would, in my judgment, require the rejection of *Re Diplock*, which is binding on us, and of Lord Mustill's explanation of Lord Templeman's statement in the *Space Investments* case in *Re Goldcorp Exchange Ltd.*

12–54   "It is not open to us to say that because the moneys were trust moneys the fact that they were paid into an overdrawn account or have otherwise been dissipated presents no difficulty to raising an equitable charge on assets of M.C.C. for their amount in favour of B.I.M. The difficulty Lord Mustill referred to is not displaced. Accordingly I would reject both grounds of appeal, and dismiss both the appeal and the cross-appeal.

12–55   "On consideration, I do not regard it as appropriate to give any further directions to the judge."

---

[80] See *James Roscoe (Bolton) Ltd v Winder* [1915] 1 Ch. 62.

LEGGATT L.J.: ". . . There can be no equitable remedy against an asset acquired **12–56** *before* misappropriation of money takes place, since ex hypothesi it cannot be followed into something which existed and so had been acquired before the money was received and therefore without its aid.

"The concept of a 'composite transaction' is in my judgment fallacious. What is **12–57** envisaged is (a) the purchase of an asset by means of an overdraft, that is, a loan from a bank, and (b) the discharge of the loan by means of misappropriated trust money. The judge thought that the money could be regarded as having been used to acquire the asset. His conclusion was that 'It is sufficient to say that proof that trust moneys were paid into an overdrawn account of the defaulting trustee may not always be sufficient to bar a claim to an equitable charge.'

"I see the force of Mr. Kosmin's submission that, if an asset were used as security **12–58** for an overdraft which was then discharged by means of misappropriated money, the beneficiary might obtain priority by subrogation. But there can ordinarily be no tracing into an asset which is already in the hands of the defaulting trustee when the misappropriation occurs.

"In *Liggett v Kensington*[81] Cooke P. applied the principle which he derived from **12–59** the *Space Investments* case that those who do not take a risk of insolvency are entitled to an equitable charge over all the assets of the trustee, giving them priority over those who are to be regarded as having taken such a risk. That decision is authority for no wider proposition than that, where a bank trustee wrongly deposits money with itself, the trustee can trace into all the bank's credit balances.

"Consistently with Mr. Kosmin's submissions on this appeal, Lord Mustill, **12–60** delivering the judgment of the Board in *Re Goldcorp Exchange Ltd.*,[82] stated that their Lordships found it difficult to understand how it would enable the claimants in that case to 'overcome the difficulty that the moneys said to be impressed with the trust were paid into an overdrawn account and thereupon ceased to exist.' Lord Mustill emphasised that the observations of the Board were concerned with a mixed, not a non-existent, fund. He also cited with approval *James Roscoe (Bolton) Ltd. v Winder* as conventionally exemplifying the principles of tracing.

"I therefore consider that the judge came to the right conclusion, though I do not **12–61** accept that it is possible to trace through an overdrawn bank account or to trace misappropriated money into an asset bought before the money was received by the purchaser. I agree that the appeal should be dismissed."

HENRY L.J.: "I agree with both judgments." *Appeal dismissed with costs.* **12–62**

FOSKETT v MCKEOWN

House of Lords [2001] 1 A.C. 102, [2000] 2 W.L.R. 1299, [2000] 3 All E.R. 97. Lords Browne-Wilkinson, Hoffmann and Millett (with Lords Steyn and Hope dissenting).

The claimant purchasers paid money to Murphy on trust for themselves, **12–63** intending that the money should be used to buy land for investment purposes in Portugal. Murphy had previously bought a life insurance policy on his own life, on trust for his children (who would receive 90 per cent of the policy proceeds in the event of his death) and his mother (who would receive 10 per cent). Murphy paid the first two annual premiums with his own money; the source of the money which

---

[81] [1993] 1 N.Z.L.R. 257.
[82] [1995] 1 A.C. 74 at 104.

he used to pay the third premium was disputed; and in breach of trust he used the claimants' money to pay the fourth and fifth premiums. Murphy then committed suicide and the insurer paid £1 million to the surviving trustees of the policy settlement. The claimants sued the trustees, arguing that at least 40 per cent of the insurance proceeds was held on constructive trust for them because at least 40 per cent of the insurance premiums had been paid with trust money misappropriated by Murphy. A majority of the House of Lords allowed the claim, and refused to restrict the claimants to a lien over the proceeds for the amount of money paid towards the premiums.

12–64   LORD MILLETT: "My Lords, this is a textbook example of tracing through mixed substitutions. At the beginning of the story the purchasers were beneficially entitled under an express trust to a sum standing in the name of Mr. Murphy in a bank account. From there the money moved into and out of various bank accounts where in breach of trust it was inextricably mixed by Mr. Murphy with his own money. After each transaction was completed the purchasers' money formed an indistinguishable part of the balance standing to Mr. Murphy's credit in his bank account. The amount of that balance represented a debt due from the bank to Mr. Murphy, that is to say a chose in action. At the penultimate stage the purchasers' money was represented by an indistinguishable part of a different chose in action, *viz.* the debt prospectively and contingently due from an insurance company to its policyholders, being the trustees of a settlement made by Mr. Murphy for the benefit of his children. At the present and final stage it forms an indistinguishable part of the balance standing to the credit of the respondent trustees in their bank account.

Tracing and following

12–65   "The process of ascertaining what happened to the purchasers' money involves both tracing and following. These are both exercises in locating assets which are or may be taken to represent an asset belonging to the purchasers and to which they assert ownership. The processes of following and tracing are, however, distinct. Following is the process of following the same asset as it moves from hand to hand. Tracing is the process of identifying a new asset as the substitute for the old. Where one asset is exchanged for another, a claimant can elect whether to follow the original asset into the hands of the new owner or to trace its value into the new asset in the hands of the same owner. In practice his choice is often dictated by the circumstances. In the present case the purchasers do not seek to follow the money any further once it reached the bank or insurance company, since its identity was lost in the hands of the recipient (which in any case obtained an unassailable title as a *bona fide* purchaser for value without notice of the purchasers' beneficial interest). Instead the purchasers have chosen at each stage to trace the money into its proceeds, *viz..* the debt presently due from the bank to the account holder or the debt prospectively and contingently due from the insurance company to the policy holders.

12–66   "Having completed this exercise, the purchasers claim a continuing beneficial interest in the insurance money. Since this represents the product of Mr. Murphy's own money as well as theirs, which Mr. Murphy mingled indistinguishably in a single chose in action, they claim a beneficial interest in a proportionate part of the money only. The transmission of a claimant's property rights from one asset to its traceable proceeds is part of our law of property, not of the law of unjust enrichment. There is no 'unjust factor' to justify restitution (unless 'want of title' be one, which makes the point). The claimant succeeds if at all by virtue of his own title, not to reverse unjust enrichment. Property rights are determined by fixed rules and settled principles.

They are not discretionary. They do not depend upon ideas of what is 'fair, just and reasonable'. Such concepts, which in reality mask decisions of legal policy, have no place in the law of property.

"A beneficiary of a trust is entitled to a continuing beneficial interest not merely in the trust property but in its traceable proceeds also, and his interest binds every one who takes the property or its traceable proceeds except a *bona fide* purchaser for value without notice. In the present case the purchasers' beneficial interest plainly bound Mr. Murphy, a trustee who wrongfully mixed the trust money with his own and whose every dealing with the money (including the payment of the premiums) was in breach of trust. It similarly binds his successors, the trustees of the children's settlement, who claim no beneficial interest of their own, and Mr. Murphy's children, who are volunteers. They gave no value for what they received and derive their interest from Mr. Murphy by way of gift. **12–67**

Tracing

"We speak of money at the bank, and of money passing into and out of a bank account. But of course the account holder has no money at the bank. Money paid into a bank account belongs legally and beneficially to the bank and not to the account holder. The bank gives value for it, and it is accordingly not usually possible to make the money itself the subject of an adverse claim. Instead a claimant normally sues the account holder rather than the bank and lays claim to the proceeds of the money in his hands. These consist of the debt or part of the debt due to him from the bank. We speak of tracing money into and out of the account, but there is no money in the account. There is merely a single debt of an amount equal to the final balance standing to the credit of the account holder. No money passes from paying bank to receiving bank or through the clearing system (where the money flows may be in the opposite direction). There is simply a series of debits and credits which are causally and transactionally linked. We also speak of tracing one asset into another, but this too is inaccurate. The original asset still exists in the hands of the new owner, or it may have become untraceable. The claimant claims the new asset because it was acquired in whole or in part with the original asset. What he traces, therefore, is not the physical asset itself but the value inherent in it. **12–68**

"Tracing is thus neither a claim nor a remedy. It is merely the process by which a claimant demonstrates what has happened to his property, identifies its proceeds and the persons who have handled or received them, and justifies his claim that the proceeds can properly be regarded as representing his property. Tracing is also distinct from claiming. It identifies the traceable proceeds of the claimant's property. It enables the claimant to substitute the traceable proceeds for the original asset as the subject matter of his claim. But it does not affect or establish his claim. That will depend on a number of factors including the nature of his interest in the original asset. He will normally be able to maintain the same claim to the substituted asset as he could have maintained to the original asset. If he held only a security interest in the original asset, he cannot claim more than a security interest in its proceeds. But his claim may also be exposed to potential defences as a result of intervening transactions. Even if the purchasers could demonstrate what the bank had done with their money, for example, and could thus identify its traceable proceeds in the hands of the bank, any claim by them to assert ownership of those proceeds would be defeated by the *bona fide* purchaser defence. The successful completion of a tracing exercise may be preliminary to a personal claim[83] or a proprietary one, to the enforcement of a legal right,[84] or an equitable one. **12–69**

---

[83] As in *El Ajou v Dollar Land Holdings plc* [1993] 3 All E.R. 717.
[84] As in *Trustees of the Property of F.C. Jones & Sons (a firm) v Jones* [1997] Ch. 159.

12–70   "Given its nature, there is nothing inherently legal or equitable about the tracing exercise. There is thus no sense in maintaining different rules for tracing at law and in equity. One set of tracing rules is enough. The existence of two has never formed part of the law in the United States.[85] There is certainly no logical justification for allowing any distinction between them to produce capricious results in cases of mixed substitutions by insisting on the existence of a fiduciary relationship as a precondition for applying equity's tracing rules. The existence of such a relationship may be relevant to the nature of the claim which the plaintiff can maintain, whether personal or proprietary, but that is a different matter. I agree with the passages which my noble and learned friend Lord Steyn has cited from Professor Birks' essay 'The Necessity of a Unitary Law of Tracing',[86] and with Dr Lionel Smith's exposition in his comprehensive monograph *The Law of Tracing*.[87]

12–71   "This is not, however, the occasion to explore these matters further, for the present is a straightforward case of a trustee who wrongfully misappropriated trust money, mixed it with his own, and used it to pay for an asset for the benefit of his children. Even on the traditional approach, the equitable tracing rules are available to the purchasers. There are only two complicating factors. The first is that the wrongdoer used their money to pay premiums on an equity linked policy of life assurance on his own life. The nature of the policy should make no difference in principle, though it may complicate the accounting. The second is that he had previously settled the policy for the benefit of his children. This should also make no difference. The claimant's rights cannot depend on whether the wrongdoer gave the policy to his children during his lifetime or left the proceeds to them by his will; or if during his lifetime whether he did so before or after he had recourse to the claimant's money to pay the premiums. The order of events does not affect the fact that the children are not contributors but volunteers who have received the gift of an asset paid for in part with misappropriated trust moneys.

The cause of action

12–72   "As I have already pointed out, the purchasers seek to vindicate their property rights, not to reverse unjust enrichment. The correct classification of the purchasers' cause of action may appear to be academic, but it has important consequences. The two causes of action have different requirements and may attract different defences.

12–73   "A plaintiff who brings an action in unjust enrichment must show that the defendant has been enriched at the plaintiff's expense, for he cannot have been unjustly enriched if he has not been enriched at all. But the plaintiff is not concerned to show that the defendant is in receipt of property belonging beneficially to the plaintiff or its traceable proceeds. The fact that the beneficial ownership of the property has passed to the defendant provides no defence; indeed, it is usually the very fact which founds the claim. Conversely, a plaintiff who brings an action like the present must show that the defendant is in receipt of property which belongs beneficially to him or its traceable proceeds, but he need not show that the defendant has been enriched by its receipt. He may, for example, have paid full value for the property, but he is still required to disgorge it if he received it with notice of the plaintiff's interest.

12–74   "Furthermore, a claim in unjust enrichment is subject to a change of position defence, which usually operates by reducing or extinguishing the element of enrichment. An action like the present is subject to the *bona fide* purchaser for value defence, which operates to clear the defendant's title.

---

[85] See Scott, *The Law of Trusts* (4th ed., 1989), 605–609.
[86] In R. Cranston (ed.), *Making Commercial Law: Essays in Honour of Roy Goode* (1997).
[87] L. D. Smith *The Law of Tracing* (1997). See particularly pp.120–130, 277–279, and 342–347.

The tracing rules

"The insurance policy in the present case is a very sophisticated financial instru- **12–75** ment. Tracing into the rights conferred by such an instrument raises a number of important issues. It is therefore desirable to set out the basic principles before turning to deal with the particular problems to which policies of life assurance give rise.

"The simplest case is where a trustee wrongfully misappropriates trust property **12–76** and uses it exclusively to acquire other property for his own benefit. In such a case the beneficiary is entitled at his option either to assert his beneficial ownership of the proceeds or to bring a personal claim against the trustee for breach of trust and enforce an equitable lien or charge on the proceeds to secure restoration of the trust fund. He will normally exercise the option in the way most advantageous to himself. If the traceable proceeds have increased in value and are worth more than the original asset, he will assert his beneficial ownership and obtain the profit for himself. There is nothing unfair in this. The trustee cannot be permitted to keep any profit resulting from his misappropriation for himself, and his donees cannot obtain a better title than their donor. If the traceable proceeds are worth less than the original asset, it does not usually matter how the beneficiary exercises his option. He will take the whole of the proceeds on either basis. This is why it is not possible to identify the basis on which the claim succeeded in some of the cases.

"Both remedies are proprietary and depend on successfully tracing the trust **12–77** property into its proceeds. A beneficiary's claim against a trustee for breach of trust is a personal claim. It does not entitle him to priority over the trustee's general creditors unless he can trace the trust property into its product and establish a proprietary interest in the proceeds. If the beneficiary is unable to trace the trust property into its proceeds, he still has a personal claim against the trustee, but his claim will be unsecured. The beneficiary's proprietary claims to the trust property or its traceable proceeds can be maintained against the wrongdoer and anyone who derives title from him except a *bona fide* purchaser for value without notice of the breach of trust. The same rules apply even where there have been numerous successive transactions, so long as the tracing exercise is successful and no *bona fide* purchaser for value without notice has intervened.

"A more complicated case is where there is a mixed substitution. This occurs **12–78** where the trust money represents only part of the cost of acquiring the new asset. As James Barr Ames pointed out in 'Following Misappropriated Property into its Product',[88] consistency requires that, if a trustee buys property partly with his own money and partly with trust money, the beneficiary should have the option of taking a proportionate part of the new property or a lien upon it, as may be most for his advantage. In principle it should not matter (and it has never previously been suggested that it does) whether the trustee mixes the trust money with his own and buys the new asset with the mixed fund or makes separate payments of the purchase price (whether simultaneously or sequentially) out of the different funds. In every case the value formerly inherent in the trust property has become located within the value inherent in the new asset.

"The rule, and its rationale, were stated by Samuel Williston in 'The Right to **12–79** Follow Trust Property when Confused with Other Property'[89]:

'If the trust fund is traceable as having furnished in part the money with which a certain investment was made, and the proportion it formed of the whole

---

[88] (1906) 19 Harvard L.R. 511.
[89] (1888) 2 Harvard L.R. 28, 29.

money so invested is known or ascertainable, the *cestui que trust* should be allowed to regard the acts of the trustee as done for his benefit, in the same way that he would be allowed to if all the money so invested had been his; that is, he should be entitled in equity to an undivided share of the property which the trust money contributed to purchase-such a proportion of the whole as the trust money bore to the whole money invested. The reason in one case as in the other is that the trustee cannot be allowed to make a profit from the use of the trust money, and if the property which he wrongfully purchased were held subject only to a lien for the amount invested, any appreciation in value would go to the trustee.'

If this correctly states the underlying basis of the rule (as I believe it does), then it is impossible to distinguish between the case where mixing precedes the investment and the case where it arises on and in consequence of the investment. It is also impossible to distinguish between the case where the investment is retained by the trustee and the case where it is given away to a gratuitous donee. The donee cannot obtain a better title than his donor, and a donor who is a trustee cannot be allowed to profit from his trust.

12–80   "In *Re Hallett's Estate*,[90] Jessel M.R. acknowledged that where an asset was acquired exclusively with trust money, the beneficiary could either assert equitable ownership of the asset or enforce a lien or charge over it to recover the trust money. But he appeared to suggest that in the case of a mixed substitution the beneficiary is confined to a lien. Any authority that this dictum might otherwise have is weakened by the fact that Jessel M.R. gave no reason for the existence of any such rule, and none is readily apparent. The dictum was plainly *obiter*, for the fund was deficient and the plaintiff was only claiming a lien. It has usually been cited only to be explained away.[91] It was rejected by the High Court of Australia in *Scott v Scott*.[92] It has not been adopted in the United States.[93] In *Primeau v Granfield* Learned Hand J. expressed himself in forthright terms: 'On principle there can be no excuse for such a rule.'[94]

12–81   "In my view the time has come to state unequivocally that English law has no such rule. It conflicts with the rule that a trustee must not benefit from his trust. I agree with Burrows that the beneficiary's right to elect to have a proportionate share of a mixed substitution necessarily follows once one accepts, as English law does, (i) that a claimant can trace in equity into a mixed fund and (ii) that he can trace unmixed money into its proceeds and assert ownership of the proceeds.

12–82   "Accordingly, I would state the basic rule as follows. Where a trustee wrongfully uses trust money to provide part of the cost of acquiring an asset, the beneficiary is entitled at his option either to claim a proportionate share of the asset or to enforce a lien upon it to secure his personal claim against the trustee for the amount of the misapplied money. It does not matter whether the trustee mixed the trust money with his own in a single fund before using it to acquire the asset, or made separate payments (whether simultaneously or sequentially) out of the differently owned funds to acquire a single asset.

12–83   "Two observations are necessary at this point. First, there is a mixed substitution (with the results already described) whenever the claimant's property has contributed in part only towards the acquisition of the new asset. It is not necessary for the

---

[90] (1880) 13 Ch.D. 696 at 709.
[91] See *e.g. Re Tilley's Will Trusts* [1967] Ch. 1179 at 1186, *per* Ungoed-Thomas J.; A. Burrows, *The Law of Restitution* (1993), p.368.
[92] (1963) 109 C.L.R. 649 at 661–662, cited by Morritt L.J. below: [1998] Ch. 265 at 300–301.
[93] See the American Law Institute, *Restatement of the Law, Trusts 2d* (1959) at §202(h).
[94] (1911) 184 F. 480 at 482.

claimant to show in addition that his property has contributed to any increase in the value of the new asset. This is because, as I have already pointed out, this branch of the law is concerned with vindicating rights of property and not with reversing unjust enrichment. Secondly, the beneficiary's right to claim a lien is available only against a wrongdoer and those deriving title under him otherwise than for value. It is not available against competing contributors who are innocent of any wrongdoing. The tracing rules are not the result of any presumption or principle peculiar to equity. They correspond to the common law rules for following into physical mixtures (though the consequences may not be identical). Common to both is the principle that the interests of the wrongdoer who was responsible for the mixing and those who derive title under him otherwise than for value are subordinated to those of innocent contributors. As against the wrongdoer and his successors, the beneficiary is entitled to locate his contribution in any part of the mixture and to subordinate their claims to share in the mixture until his own contribution has been satisfied. This has the effect of giving the beneficiary a lien for his contribution if the mixture is deficient.

"Innocent contributors, however, must be treated equally inter se. Where the **12–84** beneficiary's claim is in competition with the claims of other innocent contributors, there is no basis upon which any of the claims can be subordinated to any of the others. Where the fund is deficient, the beneficiary is not entitled to enforce a lien for his contributions; all must share rateably in the fund.

"The primary rule in regard to a mixed fund, therefore, is that gains and losses **12–85** are borne by the contributors rateably. The beneficiary's right to elect instead to enforce a lien to obtain repayment is an exception to the primary rule, exercisable where the fund is deficient and the claim is made against the wrongdoer and those claiming through him. It is not necessary to consider whether there are any circumstances in which the beneficiary is confined to a lien in cases where the fund is more than sufficient to repay the contributions of all parties. It is sufficient to say that he is not so confined in a case like the present. It is not enough that those defending the claim are innocent of any wrongdoing if they are not themselves contributors but, like the trustees and Mr. Murphy's children in the present case, are volunteers who derive title under the wrongdoer otherwise than for value. On ordinary principles such persons are in no better position than the wrongdoer, and are liable to suffer the same subordination of their interests to those of the claimant as the wrongdoer would have been. They certainly cannot do better than the claimant by confining him to a lien and keeping any profit for themselves.

"Similar principles apply to following into physical mixtures.[95] There are relatively **12–86** few cases which deal with the position of the innocent recipient from the wrongdoer, but *Jones v De Marchant*[96] may be cited as an example. A husband wrongfully took 18 beaver skins belonging to his wife and used them, together with four skins of his own, to have a fur coat made up which he then gave to his mistress. Unsurprisingly the wife was held entitled to recover the coat. The mistress knew nothing of the true ownership of the skins, but her innocence was held to be immaterial. She was a gratuitous donee and could stand in no better position than the husband. The coat was a new asset manufactured from the skins and not merely the product of intermingling them. The problem could not be solved by a sale of the coat in order to reduce the disputed property to a divisible fund, since (as we shall see) the

---

[95] See *Lupton v White* (1808) 15 Ves. Jun. 432; and *Sandeman & Sons v Tyzack and Branfoot Steamship Co. Ltd* [1913] A.C. 680 at 695, where Lord Moulton said: "If the mixing has arisen from the fault of 'B', 'A' can claim the goods."
[96] (1916) 28 D.L.R. 561.

realisation of an asset does not affect its ownership. It would hardly have been appropriate to require the two ladies to share the coat between them. Accordingly it was an all or nothing case in which the ownership of the coat must be assigned to one or other of the parties. The determinative factor was that the mixing was the act of the wrongdoer through whom the mistress acquired the coat otherwise than for value.

12–87   "The rule in equity is to the same effect, as Page Wood V.-C. observed in *Frith v Cartland*:[97]

> '. . . if a man mixes trust funds with his own, the whole will be treated as the trust property, except so far as he may be able to distinguish what is his own.'

This does not, in my opinion, exclude a pro rata division where this is appropriate, as in the case of money and other fungibles like grain, oil or wine. But it is to be observed that a pro rata division is the best that the wrongdoer and his donees can hope for. If a pro rata division is excluded, the beneficiary takes the whole; there is no question of confining him to a lien. *Jones v De Marchant* is a useful illustration of the principles shared by the common law and equity alike that an innocent recipient who receives misappropriated property by way of gift obtains no better title than his donor, and that if a proportionate sharing is inappropriate the wrongdoer and those who derive title under him take nothing.

Insurance policies

12–88   "In the case of an ordinary whole-life policy the insurance company undertakes to pay a stated sum on the death of the assured in return for fixed annual premiums payable throughout his life. Such a policy is an entire contract, not a contract for a year with a right of renewal. It is not a series of single premium policies for one year term assurance. It is not like an indemnity policy where each premium buys cover for a year after which the policyholder must renew or the cover expires. The fact that the policy will lapse if the premiums are not paid makes no difference. The amounts of the annual premiums and of the sum assured are fixed in advance at the outset and assume the payment of annual premiums throughout the term of the policy. The relationship between them is based on the life expectancy of the assured and the rates of interest available on long term government securities at the inception of the policy.

12–89   "In the present case the benefits specified in the policy are expressed to be payable 'in consideration of the payment of the first Premium already made and of the further Premiums payable'. The premiums are stated to be '£10220.00 payable at annual intervals from 06 Nov 1986 throughout the lifetime of the life assured'. It is beyond argument that the death benefit of £1m paid on Mr. Murphy's death was paid in consideration for all the premiums which had been paid before that date, including those paid with the purchasers' money, and not just some of them. Part of that sum, therefore, represented the traceable proceeds of the purchasers' money.

12–90   "It is, however, of critical importance in the present case to appreciate that the purchasers do not trace the premiums directly into the insurance money. They trace them first into the policy and thence into the proceeds of the policy. It is essential not to elide the two steps. In this context, of course, the word 'policy' does not mean the contract of insurance. You do not trace the payment of a premium into the

---

[97] (1865) 2 H. & M. 417 at 420.

insurance contract any more than you trace a payment into a bank account into the banking contract. The word 'policy' is here used to describe the bundle of rights to which the policyholder is entitled in return for the premiums. These rights, which may be very complex, together constitute a chose in action, *viz.* the right to payment of a debt payable on a future event and contingent upon the continued payment of further premiums until the happening of the event. That chose in action represents the traceable proceeds of the premiums; its current value fluctuates from time to time. When the policy matures, the insurance money represents the traceable proceeds of the policy and hence indirectly of the premiums.

"It follows that, if a claimant can show that premiums were paid with his money, **12–91** he can claim a proportionate share of the policy. His interest arises by reason of and immediately upon the payment of the premiums, and the extent of his share is ascertainable at once. He does not have to wait until the policy matures in order to claim his property. His share in the policy and its proceeds may increase or decrease as further premiums are paid; but it is not affected by the realisation of the policy. His share remains the same whether the policy is sold or surrendered or held until maturity; these are merely different methods of realising the policy. They may affect the amount of the proceeds received on realisation but they cannot affect the extent of his share in the proceeds. In principle the purchasers are entitled to the insurance money which was paid on Mr. Murphy's death in the same shares and proportions as they were entitled in the policy immediately before his death.

"Since the manner in which an asset is realised does not affect its ownership, and **12–92** since it cannot matter whether the claimant discovers what has happened before or after it is realised, the question of ownership can be answered by ascertaining the shares in which it is owned immediately before it is realised. Where A misappropriates B's money and uses it to buy a winning ticket in the lottery, B is entitled to the winnings. Since A is a wrongdoer, it is irrelevant that he could have used his own money if in fact he used B's. This may seem to give B an undeserved windfall, but the result is not unjust. Had B discovered the fraud before the draw, he could have decided whether to keep the ticket or demand his money back. He alone has the right to decide whether to gamble with his own money. If A keeps him in ignorance until after the draw, he suffers the consequence. He cannot deprive B of his right to choose what to do with his own money; but he can give him an informed choice.

"The application of these principles ought not to depend on the nature of the **12–93** chose in action. They should apply to a policy of life assurance as they apply to a bank account or a lottery ticket . . ."

Section 3. Claiming

In this section we describe the different proprietary claims that can be **12–94** made against trust property or its traceable proceeds, assuming that all necessary following and tracing processes have been successfully completed. We then consider possible sources of the beneficiaries' proprietary rights.

I. PROPRIETARY CLAIMS

Where a trustee misappropriates trust property for himself

If a trustee misappropriates trust assets for himself and retains them in **12–95** their original form, then the beneficiaries can demand that he reconstitute the trust estate, where necessary by conveying legal title to the assets to new trustees who have been appointed in the meantime.[98] If a trustee misappropriates trust property and uses it exclusively to acquire other property for his own benefit (a "clean substitution"), then the beneficiaries can elect either to claim the new property *in specie*, or to enforce an equitable lien over the new property to secure their personal claim against the trustee to restore the trust fund.[99] If a trustee misappropriates trust property and mixes it with his own property before buying a new asset out of the mixture (a "mixed substitution"), then again the beneficiaries can elect either to claim a proportionate ownership interest in the new asset, or to enforce an equitable lien over the property to secure their personal claim against the trustee.[1]

12–96   If a trustee misappropriates money from two different trust sources and uses it to buy a new asset, then[2]:

> "neither set of beneficiaries can claim a first charge over the asset to recover its money. The equities as between the two sets of beneficiaries will be equal. Neither will be entitled to priority as against the other. It follows that they must share proportionately in the asset, bearing *pro rata* any shortfall and enjoying *pro rata* any increase in value."

12–97   If beneficiaries assert an ownership interest in property which generates income, then they can claim the income as well: so, for example, if they trace into a house which has been let for rent, then they can claim the rental income as well as the house.[3] If a trustee uses trust funds to buy a house in the trustee's name, with the help of a mortgage loan that the trustee personally covenants to repay, the courts do not treat the trustee as having personally contributed the mortgage money when calculating the quantum of the beneficiaries' claim. So, for example, if the trustee uses £25,000 of trust money to buy a house with the help of a £75,000 purchase loan secured by a mortgage on the property, and the house increases in value, then the beneficiaries can claim the whole house, subject to a counter-claim for any mortgage payments actually made by the trustee: but for the £25,000 of trust funds the trustee would not have been able to provide the necessary security for the mortgage loan and so the fruits of the transaction should go to the beneficiaries.[4]

12–98   An equitable lien is "essentially a positive right to obtain . . . an order for sale of the subject property or for actual payment from the subject fund"

---

[98] See para.10–10, above. Before the Judicature Acts it would have been necessary for the beneficiaries to bring full execution proceedings, although these would usually have been aborted once relief had been granted in respect of the particular misapplication: see *e.g. Re Medland* (1889) 41 Ch.D. 476 at 482. Today there is almost never a call for full judicial execution of a trust, but the same principles are applied, the overriding object being to enforce the performance of the trust according to its terms.

[99] *Re Hallett's Estate* (1880) 13 Ch.D. 696 at 709; *Foskett v McKeown* [1998] Ch. 265 at 277; [2001] 1 A.C. 102 at 130, above at para.12–76.

[1] *Scott v Scott* (1962) 109 C.L.R. 649; *Re Tilley's W.T.* [1967] Ch. 1178 (where the point was conceded); *British Columbia Teachers' Credit Union v Betterley* (1975) 61 D.L.R. (3d) 755; *Foskett v McKeown* [1998] Ch. 265 at 277; [2001] 1 A.C. 102 at 130–131; at paras 12–78 to 12–82.

[2] *Foskett v McKeown* [1998] Ch. 265 at 278, *per* Scott V.-C. See too Lord Millett's comments on appeal: [2001] 1 A.C. 102 at 132; above at para.12–84.

[3] *Banton v C.I.B.C. Corp.* (1999) 182 D.L.R. (4th) 486 at 504–505; *Greenwood v Lee* Ch.D. May 21, 2001.

[4] *Paul Davies Pty. Ltd v Davies* [1983] N.S.W.L.R. 440; *Re Marriage of Wagstaff* (1990) 99 F.L.R. 390.

and it "may, in general, be enforced in the same way as any other equitable charge, namely, by sale in pursuance of court order or, where the lien is over a fund, by an order for payment thereout."[5] Since an ownership interest in property will "rise or fall in value with the property"[6] it will be to the beneficiaries' advantage to elect for an equitable lien in cases where the property has decreased in value, and pursue a personal claim against the defendant for the difference. An equitable lien can also be a potent remedy in a case where the beneficiaries can trace into a number of different assets and funds. Suppose that a trustee has several bank accounts and mixes £100,000 of trust money with his own money in his No.1 account, then transfers money from the No.1 account to his No.2 and No.3 accounts, and then buys a painting with money from the No.1 account, a car with money from the No.2 account, and a flat with money from the No.3 account. In this case, "as against the wrongdoer and his successors in title, the beneficiary is entitled to locate his contribution in any part of the mixture [*i.e.* in any part of the value remaining in the three accounts, the painting, the car, and the flat] and to subordinate their claims to share in the mixture till his own contribution has been satisfied."[7]

If the trustee reinstates the trust by returning the trust property then the beneficiaries will have no claim against him. However, if a trustee uses trust money to buy assets which increase in value it is not enough for him to repay the value of the trust money originally taken: he must account to the beneficiaries for the increase in value as well.[8]   **12–99**

If a trustee has honestly done work or spent money improving an asset claimed by the beneficiaries then he may be entitled to an allowance at the court's discretion.[9]   **12–100**

Where trust property is misdirected to a third party

Where trust property is misdirected to a third party recipient, then again, the beneficiaries can assert an ownership right in the property or its traceable proceeds unless the recipient is a *bona fide* purchaser for value without notice of the beneficiaries' equitable interest.[10] Even if he has acted in good faith, the recipient must "yield up any [trust property that remains], or the traceable proceeds of any that [has been exchanged for a new asset]".[11] This proprietary liability is not dependent on proof of fault and it must be distinguished from the *personal* liability which the recipient may additionally incur for knowing receipt if he has acted with the requisite   **12–101**

[5] *Hewett v Court* (1983) 149 C.L.R. 638 at 664, *per* Deane J.
[6] *Australian Postal Corp. v Lutak* (1991) 21 N.S.W.L.R. 584 at 590, *per* Bryson J.
[7] *Foskett v McKeown* [2001] 1 A.C. 102 at 132, *per* Lord Millett; at para.12–83. See too *El Ajou v Dollar Land Holdings plc* [1993] 3 All E.R. 713 at 735–736; on appeal: [1994] 2 All E.R. 685 at 701; *Re Goldcorp Exchange Ltd* [1994] 2 All E.R. 806 at 831.
[8] *Scott v Scott* (1962) 109 C.L.R. 649; *Re Hughes* [1970] I.R. 237.
[9] *Re Berkeley Applegate (Investment Consultants) Ltd* [1988] 3 All E.R. 71 at 83; *Badfinger Music Ltd v Evans* [2001] W.T.L.R. 1.
[10] *Foskett v McKeown* [2001] 1 A.C. 102 at 127 and 130; above at paras 12–67 and 12–77.
[11] *Re Montagu's S.T.* [1987] Ch. 264 at 272, *per* Megarry V.-C.

degree of fault.[12] If the recipient has mixed trust property with his own, then the beneficiaries can claim the traceable residue of their property,[13] the identity of the residue being determined by rules which vary according to whether the recipient has acted in good faith, as discussed above.[14]

12–102   As previously noted,[15] the rules of tracing permit beneficiaries to trace into assets bought by an innocent recipient even though he can prove that he could have bought the asset with his own money, and that he would have done so, had he known that the money which he actually used to buy the asset belonged to the beneficiaries. In the event that the asset increases in value, then it follows from the foregoing discussion that the beneficiaries can capture the whole of the increase by asserting an ownership claim to the asset. In a case where the defendant is a wrongdoing trustee, or a donee from a wrongdoing trustee, as in *Foskett v McKeown*, above, this outcome may not offend us, but where he has acted in good faith, it is "an affront to our notions of justice" that he should be liable in this way, as Lord Millett has observed.[16] Suppose that an innocent recipient uses £5 of misapplied trust funds to buy a lottery ticket which pays out £5 million where he could and would have used his own £5 for the purpose, had he known of the trust money's tainted source. In our view, the most to which the beneficiaries should be entitled in this situation is an equitable lien over the winnings to secure repayment of the £5.[17]

Where a trustee makes an unauthorised investment

12–103   When an express trust is declared, "the trust fund" is generally defined in the trust deed in terms such as "property transferred to the trustees to hold on the terms of this settlement and all the property from time to time representing the same", but the latter clause can simply be regarded as spelling out what is inevitably involved in the settlor creating a trust. The reason is that the trustees will be given powers of disposition, sale, and investment, and for these to be effective, the trustees must be able to transfer their legal title to trust assets clear of the beneficiaries' equitable interest. Hence the doctrine of overreaching provides that whenever the trustees exercise a power to sell or dispose of trust assets in an authorised fashion, the recipient takes clear legal title, and in the case of sale, the trust will instantly attach instead to the proceeds of sale.[18] Again, if the trustees

---

[12] *Allan v Rea Brothers Trustees Ltd* [2002] P.L.R. 169 at [55], *per* Robert Walker L.J.; *Waxman v Waxman* (2004) 7 I.T.E.L.R. 162 at [583], *per curiam* (Ont. CA); *Clark v Cutland* [2004] 1 W.L.R. 783 (D can hold property on constructive trust for C even though C concedes that D not personally liable to account); *Nabb Brothers Ltd v Lloyds Bank International (Guernsey) Ltd* [2005] EWHC 405 (Ch) at [72]: "the concept of constructive trust is used in relation to proprietary claims where the liability of the defendant to restore the property is not dependant on any 'knowing receipt'." Personal liability for knowing receipt is discussed at paras 11–19 *et seq.*

[13] *Re Diplock* [1948] Ch. 465 at 524 and 539.

[14] See para.12–26, above.

[15] See para.12–30, above.

[16] "Proprietary Restitution" in S. Degeling and J. Edelman (eds.), *Equity in Commercial Law* (2005). See too S. Worthington, "Justifying Claims to Secondary Profits" in E.J.H. Schrage *Unjust Enrichment and the Law of Contract* (2001) p.451; S. Worthington, *Equity* (2003), 1, pp.10–12.

[17] An outcome which is supported by *Re Tilley's W.T.* [1967] Ch. 1179, as discussed in D. J. Hayton, "Equity's Identification Rules" in P. Birks (ed.) *Laundering and Tracing* (1995) pp.1, 10–12.

[18] *State Bank of India v Sood* [1997] Ch. 276. See too C. Harpum, "Overreaching, Trustees' Powers, and the Reform of the 1925 Property Legislation" [1990] C.L.J. 277; D. Fox, "Overreaching" in P. Birks and A. Pretto (eds.) *Breach of Trust* (2002) 95; R.C. Nolan "Property in a fund" (2004) 120 L.Q.R. 108, pp.111–117.

use trust money to buy a new asset in a valid exercise of their powers of investment, then the same thing happens: the beneficiaries' equitable interest in the money is overreached, the vendor gets clear legal title to the money, and the trust attaches to the new asset.

Now consider the case where trustees act in an unauthorised way when **12–104** they sell trust assets or use trust money to buy new assets. In *Wright v Morgan*, Viscount Dunedin held that where[19]:

> "a trustee has made an improper investment, the law is well settled. The *cestuis que trustent* as a whole have a right, if they choose, to adopt the investment and to hold it as trust property. But if there is not unanimity then it is not trust property, but the trustee who has made it must keep the investment himself. He is debtor to the trust for the money which has been applied in its purchase."

These rules would be worked out in proceedings for an account either by affirming the purchase in a case where the beneficiaries all consent to that outcome, or else, in a case where they do not, by falsifying the account to delete the unauthorised expenditure from the record and requiring the trustees to reconstitute the trust fund by paying over the amount of the outgoing from their own pockets.[20] In a case where the trustee uses trust money to make an unauthorised investment which triples in value, and the beneficiaries cannot all consent to take the investment because some are minors or unborn, can the trustee keep it for himself and repay the amount of the purchase money plus interest? Presumably he cannot. In this case, the adult beneficiaries could apply (at the trustee's expense) to the court under the Trustee Act 1925, s.57, for an order authorising the purchase; alternatively, they could move to replace the trustee, and the new trustee could then demand the investment on the beneficiaries' behalf.[21]

Where trust funds are used to pay off a mortgage

Suppose that a trustee misappropriates trust money and uses it to pay off a **12–105** debt secured by a mortgage on his house, or suppose that a trustee misdirects trust money to a third party who does the same thing. Here, the courts can allow the beneficiaries, by means of a legal fiction, to trace their money into the discharged mortgage,[22] and acquire it as a security for the repayment of their money as though it had never been discharged.[23] This remedy is termed "subrogation", which literally means "substitution": the beneficiaries are treated, by a legal fiction, as though they were substitutes for the original mortgagee.[24]

---

[19] [1926] A.C. 788 at 798, citing *Parker v McKenna* (1874) L.R. 10 Ch. 96. See too *Re Patten* (1883) 52 L.J. (Ch.) 787; *Power v Banks* [1901] 2 Ch. 487 at 496; *Re Jenkins and H.E. Randall and Co.'s Contract* [1903] 2 Ch. 362.

[20] *Re Biss (deceased)* [1903] 2 Ch. 40. See further paras 10–11 to 10–13 and 10–69, above.

[21] *Young v Murphy* [1996] 1 V.R. 279.

[22] See para.12–28, above.

[23] *M'Mahon v Fetherstonhaugh* [1895] 1 I.R. 83; *McCullough v Marsden* (1919) 45 D.L.R. 645; *McCullough v Elliott* (1922) 62 D.L.R. 257.

[24] Because subrogation entails a fictional process of revival and transfer of the mortgagee's extinguished rights, the courts have a discretion to decide how many of the mortgagee's advantages should accrue to a claimant: *Halifax Mortgage Services Ltd v Muirhead* (1998) 76 P. & C.R. 418, noted C. Mitchell (1998) 12 Tru. L.I. 175; *Banque Financière de la Cité v Parc (Battersea) Ltd* [1999] 1 A.C. 221, noted C. Mitchell [1998] R.L.R. 144; *Cheltenham & Gloucester plc v Appleyard* [2004] EWCA Civ 291 at [32]–[44].

12–106   *Boscawen v Bajwa*, was arguably a case of this kind. The claimant building society lent money to a borrower for the sole purpose of buying a house, and the borrower's solicitors paid the money over to the vendor prematurely, before the sale documents were properly completed. The vendor used the money to discharge a mortgage over the property, and then the sale fell through. The Court of Appeal allowed the claimant to acquire the mortgage via subrogation, and although it was not pleaded in this way, the case can be explained on the basis that the claimant's money was subject to a *Quistclose* trust[25] that was breached when the money was transferred to the vendor before the sale documents were completed.[26]

II. SOURCES OF PROPRIETARY RIGHTS

12–107   It is easier to describe the different types of proprietary claim which the beneficiaries can bring following a breach of trust than it is to explain why the beneficiaries are entitled to bring such claims. In *Foskett v McKeown*, above, the majority of the House of Lords held that the beneficiaries are given a proprietary claim to the whole or part of a traced asset in order to vindicate their proprietary rights in the trust fund. The following discussion considers what this means.

Rights in traceable substitutes

12–108   We must first distinguish proprietary claims to trust assets in their original form from proprietary claims to the traceable proceeds of trust assets. Suppose that a trustee misappropriates a trust painting for himself, or misdirects it to a recipient who is not a *bona fide* purchaser for value without notice. In this case, nothing happens to interrupt the beneficiaries' continuing equitable ownership of the painting, and they can enforce their continuing rights by obtaining a declaration of ownership and an order for reconveyance if necessary.

12–109   Now contrast the case where a trustee uses trust assets to buy an unauthorised investment for the beneficiaries, or a new asset for himself, or where a trustee misdirects trust property to a third party who uses it to buy a new asset. Here, assuming that the beneficiaries can trace and follow as necessary into the new asset, they can assert a proprietary claim to the new asset. But, strictly speaking, their proprietary right to the new asset cannot be the same right as their proprietary right to the original trust property. The reason is that a property right is a right to a specific thing which cannot be detached from the thing to which it relates and reattached to some new thing.[27] For example, an ownership right in land relates to the land, and so

---

[25] See para.5–40, above.
[26] *Cf. Hillel v Christoforides* (1991) 63 P. & C.R. 301 at 307; *Chohan v Saggar* [1992] B.C.C. 750 at 756; *Filby v Mortgage Express (No.2) Ltd* [2004] EWCA Civ 759 at [19].
[27] P. Birks, "Tracing, Property, and Unjust Enrichment" (2002) 54 C.L.P. 231, 244–245; R. Chambers, "Tracing and Unjust Enrichment" in J. W. Neyers *et al.* (eds.) *Understanding Unjust Enrichment* (2004) 263, 273–274. See too A. Burrows, "Proprietary Restitution: Unmasking Unjust Enrichment" (2001) 117 L.Q.R. 412.

it cannot be the same right as the right to the sale proceeds of the land, even if one right is exchanged for the other.

In *Foskett v McKeown*, above, their Lordships averted their eyes from **12–110** this, focussing their attention on the beneficiaries' interests as interests in the trust fund established by the settlor. Lord Browne-Wilkinson held that[28]:

> "The only trusts at issue are the express trusts of the purchasers' trust deed. Under those express trusts the purchasers were entitled to equitable proprietary interests in the original moneys [which they paid over to the trustee]. Like any other equitable proprietary interest, those equitable proprietary interests under the purchasers' trust deed which originally existed in the moneys paid to [the trustee] now exist in any other property which, in law, now represents the original trust assets. . . . If, as a result of tracing, it can be said that certain of the policy moneys are what now represent part of the assets subject to the trusts of the purchasers trust deed, then as a matter of English property law the purchasers have an absolute interest in such moneys."

Similarly, Lord Millett held that the beneficiaries have "a continuing beneficial interest not merely in the trust property but in its traceable proceeds also",[29] and he has since written extra-judicially that "'the fiction of persistence' is not a fiction [because the] beneficiaries' interests in the new investment are exactly the same as their interest in the old."[30] However, this cannot be true: the new asset is not the old asset, and prior to the acquisition of the new asset with trust funds, no one owed any obligation to the beneficiaries in respect of the new asset. It follows that the beneficiaries' right in the new asset after it has been acquired must be a new right whose existence calls for explanation.

Sources of rights in traceable substitutes

To the extent that they recognised this, the majority of the House of Lords **12–111** in *Foskett* explained the beneficiaries' new right as a right which arose in order to "vindicate their property rights" in the trust fund.[31] However, it should be stressed that the mere fact of the beneficiaries' ownership of the original trust property is not enough in itself to explain their acquisition of a new proprietary right in a traceable substitute.[32] In Professor Birks' terms,

---

[28] [2001] 1 A.C. 102 at 110. *Cf. Taylor v Plumer* (1815) 3 M. & S. 562 at 575.
[29] *ibid.* at 127; at para.12–67.
[30] Lord Millett, "Proprietary Restitution" in S. Degeling and J. Edelman (eds.) *Equity in Commercial Law* (2005), adding that "wrongfully substituted assets are [not] held on a constructive trust . . . [but] continue to be held on the same trusts throughout. If the claimant was the beneficiary under an express trust, the substituted assets are held on the same express trusts."
[31] [2001] 1 A.C. 102 at 129, *per* Lord Millett; above at para. 12–72. See too Lord Browne-Wilkinson's comments at 110 and Lord Hoffmann's comments at 115.
[32] As suggested in R. Grantham and C. Rickett, "Property and Unjust Enrichment" [1997] N.Z.L.Rev. 668, 675–684; G. Virgo, *The Principles of the Law of Restitution* (1999), pp.15–17 and 592–601; R. Grantham and C. Rickett, *Enrichment and Restitution in New* Zealand (2000), chap. 3; G. Virgo, "Vindicating Vindication" in A. Hudson (ed.), *New Perspectives on Property Law: Obligations and Restitution* (2003); R. Grantham and C. Rickett, "Property Rights: A Legally Significant Event" [2003] C.L.J. 417.

it is not an "event" to which the new right can respond.[33] For this event, one must look instead to the substitution by means of which the new asset was acquired with the trust property.

12–112   Take the case where a trustee uses trust funds to purchase an authorised investment.[34] Here, by virtue of an agreement between the settlor and the trustee, the trustee holds the original trust property, subsequently added property, and property substituted for such property as a trust fund for the beneficiaries. When the trustee buys an authorised investment with trust funds, the beneficiaries' interest in the funds is overreached, and they acquire a new interest in the new investment, by a process which the beneficiaries cannot subsequently dispute. In our view, the source of the beneficiaries' new rights in this case is the settlor's intention, agreed to by the trustee, to give the beneficiaries' proprietary rights in the original trust assets and the proceeds thereof, mediated through the trustee's authorised exercise of his powers of sale and investment to acquire new assets for the beneficiaries, to be held by him on the same terms as those on which he held the original trust assets.[35]

12–113   The same analysis can also be used to explain the case where the trustees purport to acquire new assets for the beneficiaries, but act beyond the scope of their powers. As noted above,[36] the beneficiaries can retrospectively adopt the unauthorised investment, which looks like an *ad hoc* variation of the trust, retrospectively giving the beneficiaries rights whose source, again, is the settlor's intention, agreed to by the trustee, to create such rights in their favour.

12–114   The case where a trustee misappropriates trust funds and uses them to acquire new assets for himself resembles the case where a trustee makes an unauthorised profit from his position. As argued in Chapter 6, the constructive trust imposed on the trustee's gain in the latter situation responds to the fact that a trustee binds himself by agreement at the moment when he assumes office to hold all the profits of his office for the beneficiaries as and when he receives them.[37] *A fortiori*, one can also say that a trustee binds himself to hold whatever traceable proceeds of trust funds come into his hands for the beneficiaries, and that the beneficiaries' proprietary right to these therefore responds to the trustee's intention that the beneficiaries should have them. Obviously it is tempting to say of this situation that the trustee does not intend the beneficiaries to acquire the new assets, but intends to take them for himself. As explained in Chapter 6, however, it is not the trustee's *current* intention, but his *original* intention at the time of taking office, to which the beneficiaries' proprietary right responds.[38]

---

[33] See, *e.g.* P. Birks, "Tracing, Property, and Unjust Enrichment" (2002) 54 C.L.P. 231, 245. And for an explanation of event-based analyses of rights, see para.5–05, above.

[34] See para.12–103, above.

[35] See too R. Chambers, "Tracing and Unjust Enrichment" in J. W. Neyers *et al.* (eds.) *Understanding Unjust Enrichment* (2004) 263, p.267.

[36] See para.12–104, above.

[37] See paras 6–10 and 6–11, above.

[38] *ibid.*

Finally, we come to the case where the traceable proceeds of misdirected **12–115** trust assets are in the hands of third party recipients. Here, the recipients have not previously agreed to hold the new assets for the beneficiaries, and the beneficiaries' right to them should therefore be explained either on the basis that the recipient commits a wrong (analogous to conversion at common law) when he interferes with the beneficiaries' rights in the original trust property, or else that he is unjustly enriched at the beneficiaries' expense when trust assets are used to acquire new assets for the benefit of the recipient.[39]

In *Foskett*, Lord Millett denied that beneficiaries can claim the traceable **12–116** proceeds of trust property in the hands of third parties on the ground of unjust enrichment.[40] However, his Lordship's reasons for saying this do not stand up to scrutiny. They depend on the premise that the law of property and the law of unjust enrichment cannot both be in issue in a single claim. Yet this premise entails a categorical error, since property and unjust enrichment are not categories that can be opposed: the first is a type of right, and the second a source of rights.[41] Moreover, his Lordship purports to analyse claims to traceable proceeds in the hands of third parties in the same way that he analyses claims to traceable proceeds in the hands of trustees. Yet the two types of claim are different, since the trustees have previously agreed to hold the proceeds for the beneficiaries while the third parties have not.

Does it matter?

There are practical reasons why all this matters, as noted by Lord Millett in **12–117** *Foskett*.[42] Most significantly, it seems from his Lordship's comments there that the defence of change of position is not available to a third party recipient of trust funds unless the beneficiaries' claim is founded on unjust enrichment.[43] Extra-judicially, however, he has suggested that even where this is not the basis of the claim, such a third party should have an equitable allowance for work done improving any trust asset that he has received.[44]

BOSCAWEN v BAJWA

Court of Appeal [1995] 4 All E.R. 769; [1996] 1 W.L.R. 328 (Stuart-Smith, Waite, and Millett L.J.)

Dave & Co., solicitors for the prospective purchaser of Bajwa's house acted also **12–118** for the Abbey National, which transferred £140,000 to Dave & Co. to be used only to complete the purchase and until then to be held for the Abbey National. In

---

[39] P. Birks, "Property and Unjust Enrichment: Categorical Truths" [1997] N.Z.L.Rev. 623, 661; A. Burrows, *The Law of Restitution* 2nd ed. (2002), pp.64–66 and 208–209.

[40] [2001] 1 A.C. 102 at 127; above, at para 12–66.

[41] P. Birks, *Unjust Enrichment* 2nd ed. (2005), pp.32–38.

[42] [2001] 1 A.C. 102 at 129; above, at paras 12–72 to 12–74.

[43] For general discussion of the change of position defence, see paras 11–28 *et seq.*, above; and for discussion of the question whether the defence should be available in response to proprietary claims, see P. Birks, "Change of Position and Surviving Enrichment" in W. Swadling (ed.), *The Limits of Restitutionary Claims: A Comparative Analysis* (1997), 36, pp.42 *et seq.*

[44] "Proprietary Restitution" in S. Degeling and J. Edelman (eds.), *Equity in Commercial Law* (2005).

breach of trust Dave paid £137,405 to Bajwa's solicitors to hold to Dave's order till completion and then sent them Dave's cheque for £2,595 which "bounced" just after Bajwa's solicitors had precipitately paid £140,000 to Bajwa's mortgagee, the Halifax B.S. to discharge its mortgage on Bajwa's house.

12–119   The sale fell through. The plaintiff, a judgment creditor of Bajwa, obtained a charging order absolute over the house, which was sold and the £105,311 net proceeds of sale were paid into court. It was held that the Abbey National was entitled to all these proceeds. It had priority over the plaintiff because its moneys could be traced into the payment to the Halifax B.S. and it was entitled to be subrogated to Halifax's legal charge. Bajwa's freehold was subject to a charge in equity by way of subrogation in favour of the Abbey National when the plaintiff obtained his interest under the charging order.

12–120   MILLETT L.J. *"Tracing and subrogation.*: The submission that the deputy judge illegitimately conflated two different causes of action, the equitable tracing claim and the claim to a right of subrogation, betrays a confusion of thought which arises from the admittedly misleading terminology which is traditionally used in the context of equitable claims for restitution. Equity lawyers habitually use the expressions "the tracing claim" and "the tracing remedy" to describe the proprietary claim and the proprietary remedy which equity makes available to the beneficial owner who seeks to recover his property in specie from those into whose hands it has come. Tracing properly so-called, however, is neither a claim nor a remedy but a process. Moreover, it is not confined to the case where the plaintiff seeks a proprietary remedy; it is equally necessary where he seeks a personal remedy against the knowing recipient or knowing assistant. It is the process by which the plaintiff traces what has happened to his property, identifies the persons who have handled or received it, and justifies his claim that the money which they handled or received. Unless he can prove this, he cannot (in the traditional language of equity) raise an equity against the defendant or (in the modern language of restitution) show that the defendant's unjust enrichment was at his expense.

12–121   "In such a case, the defendant will either challenge the plaintiff's claim that the property in question represents his property (*i.e.* he will challenge the validity of the tracing exercise), or he will raise a priority dispute (*e.g.* by claiming to be a bona fide purchaser without notice). If all else fails, he will raise the defence of innocent change of position. This was not a defence which was recognised in England before 1991, but it was widely accepted throughout the common law world. In *Lipkin Gorman (a firm) v Karpnale Ltd* [1991] 2 A.C. 548 the House of Lords acknowledged it to be part of English law also. The introduction of this defence not only provides the court with a means of doing justice in future, but allows a re-examination of many decisions of the past in which the absence of the defence may have led judges to distort basic principles in order to avoid injustice to the defendant.

12–122   "If the plaintiff succeeds in tracing his property, whether in its original or in some changed form, into the hands of the defendant and overcomes any defences which are put forward on the defendant's behalf, he is entitled to a remedy. The remedy will be fashioned to the circumstances. The plaintiff will generally be entitled to a personal remedy; if he seeks a proprietary remedy he must usually prove that the property to which he lays claim is still in the ownership of the defendant. If he succeeds in doing this, the court will treat the defendant as holding the property on a constructive trust for the plaintiff and will order the defendant to transfer it in specie to the plaintiff. But this is only one of the proprietary remedies which is available to a court of equity. If the plaintiff's money has been applied by the defendant, for example, not in the acquisition of a landed property but in its improvement, then the court may treat the land as charged with the payment to the plaintiff of a sum representing the amount by which the value of the defendant's land has been enhanced by the use of the plaintiff's money. And if the plaintiff's money has been used to discharge a mortgage on the defendant's land, then the court may achieve a similar result by treating the land as subject to a charge by way of subrogation in favour of the plaintiff.

"Subrogation, therefore, is a remedy, not a cause of action (see Goff and Jones **12–123** *Law of Restitution* (4th ed., 1993) at 589 ff, *Orakpo v Manson Investments Ltd* [1978] A.C. 95 at 104 *per* Lord Diplock and *Re TH Knitwear (Wholesale) Ltd* [1988] Ch. 275 at 284 *per* Slade L.J.). It is available in a wide variety of different factual situations in which it is required in order to reverse the defendant's unjust enrichment. Equity lawyers speak of a right of subrogation, or of an equity of subrogation, but this merely reflects the fact that it is not a remedy which the court has a general discretion to impose whenever it thinks it just to do so. The equity arises from the conduct of the parties on well-settled principles and in defined circumstances which make it unconscionable for the defendant to deny the proprietary interest claimed by the plaintiff. A constructive trust arises in the same way. Once the equity is established the court satisfies it by declaring that the property in question is subject to a charge by way of subrogation in the one case or a constructive trust in the other.

"Accordingly, there was nothing illegitimate in the deputy judge's invocation of **12–124** the two doctrines of tracing and subrogation in the same case. They arose at different stages of the proceedings. Tracing was the process by which the Abbey National sought to establish that its money was applied in the discharge of the Halifax's charge; subrogation was the remedy which it sought in order to deprive Mr Bajwa (through whom the appellants claim) of the unjust enrichment which he would thereby otherwise obtain at the Abbey National's expense.

Tracing

"It is still a prerequisite of the right to trace in equity that there must be a fiduciary **12–125** relationship which calls the equitable jurisdiction into being (see *Agip (Africa) Ltd v Jackson* [1991] Ch. 547 at 566 *per* Fox L.J.). That requirement is satisfied in the present case by the fact that from the first moment of its receipt by Dave in its general client account the £140,000 was trust money held in trust for the Abbey National. The appellants do not dispute that the Abbey National can successfully trace £137,405 of its money into Hill Lawson's client account. But they do dispute the judge's finding that it can trace the sum further into the payment to the Halifax.

"The £137,405 was paid into Hill Lawson's general client account at the bank **12–126** because it was only intended to be kept for a short time. Funds which were held for clients for any length of time were held in separate designated accounts. Hill Lawson's ledger cards showed Mr Bajwa as the relevant client. According to Mr Duckney, Hill Lawson also held other funds for Mr Bajwa which were the result of an inheritance which he had received. These were the source from which Hill Lawson made good the shortfall of £2,595 which arose when Dave's cheque was dishonoured. The amount of these other funds is unknown, though it was certainly nothing like £140,000. The evidence does not show whether they were held in Hill Lawson's general client account or whether they were held in a separate designated account. If they were held in the general client account, the £137,405 received from Dave was (quite properly) mixed not only with moneys belonging to other clients but also with money belonging to Mr Bajwa. Hill Lawson can be presumed not to have committed a breach of trust by resorting to moneys belonging to other clients, but they were perfectly entitled to use Mr Bajwa's own money to discharge the Halifax's charge on his property. Whether they did so or not cannot be determined in the absence of any evidence of the amount involved. Accordingly, it is submitted, the Abbey National has failed to establish how much of its money was applied in the discharge of the Halifax's charge and how much of the money which was applied for this purpose was Mr Bajwa's own money.

12–127 "The Abbey National answers this submission in two ways. First, it submits that Hill Lawson's ledger cards show that Hill Lawson appropriated the £137,405 which it had received from Dave towards the payment of the sum of £140,000 to the Halifax, and resorted to Mr Bajwa's other funds only when Dave's cheque for the balance was dishonoured. The ledger cards were, of course, made up after the event, though long before any litigation ensued, so they are not primary evidence of actual appropriation; but they are reliable evidence of the appropriation which Hill Lawson believed that they had made.

12–128 "I accept this submission. It is not necessary to apply artificial tracing rules where there has been an actual appropriation. A trustee will not be allowed to defeat the claim of his beneficiary by saying that he has resorted to trust money when he could have made use of own; but if the beneficiary asserts that the trustee has made use of the trust money there is no reason why he should not be allowed to prove it.

12–129 "The second way in which the Abbey National answers the appellants' submission is by reliance on equity's ability to follow money through a bank account where it has been mixed with other moneys by treating the money in the account as charged with the repayment of his money. As against a wrongdoer the claimant is not obliged to appropriate debits to credits in order to ascertain where his money has gone. Equity's power to charge a mixed fund with the repayment of trust moneys enables the claimant to follow the money, not because it is his, but because it is derived from a fund which is treated as if it were subject to a charge in his favour (see *Re Hallett's Estate; Knatchbull v Hallett* (1880) 13 Ch.D. 696; *Re Oatway, Hertslet v Oatway* [1903] 2 Ch. 356 and *El Ajou v Dollar Land Holdings plc* [1993] 3 All E.R. 717).

12–130 "The appellants accept this, but submit that for this purpose Mr Bajwa was not a wrongdoer. He was, as I have said, not guilty of any impropriety or want of probity. He relied on his solicitors, and they acted unwisely, perhaps negligently, and certainly precipitately, but not dishonestly. Mr Bajwa, it is submitted, was an innocent volunteer who mixed trust money with his own. As such, he was not bound to give priority to the Abbey National, but could claim parity with it. Accordingly, Mr Bajwa and the Abbey National must be treated as having contributed pari passu to the discharge of the Halifax's charge; and in the absence of the necessary evidence the amounts which were provided by Mr Bajwa and the Abbey National respectively cannot be ascertained. (In fact, on this footing the Abbey National would be entitled to succeed to the extent of one-half of its claim, but that is by the way.)

12–131 "For this proposition the appellants rely on a passage in *Re Diplock's Estate, Diplock v Wintle* [1948] Ch. 465 at 524 as follows:

'Where an innocent volunteer (as distinct from a purchaser for value without notice) mixes "money" of his own with "money" which in equity belongs to another person, or is found in possession of such a mixture, although that other person cannot claim a charge on the mass superior to the claim of the volunteer, he is entitled, nevertheless, to a charge ranking *pari passu* with the claim of the volunteer . . . But this burden on the conscience of the volunteer is not such as to compel him to treat the claim of the equitable owner as paramount. That would be to treat the volunteer as strictly as if he himself stood in a fiduciary relationship to the equitable owner which *ex hypothesi* he does not. The volunteer is under no greater duty of conscience to recognise the interest of the equitable owner than that which, lies on a person having an equitable interest in one of two trust funds of "money" which have become mixed towards the equitable owner of the other. Such a person is not in conscience bound to give precedence to the equitable owner of the other of the two funds.'

"This would be highly relevant if the distinction which the court was there making **12–132** was between the honest and the dishonest recipient. But it was not. The distinction was between the innocent recipient who had no reason to suspect that the money was not his own to dispose of as he pleased, and the recipient who knew or ought to have known that the money belonged to another. In *Re Diplock's Estate* the defendants were the recipients of grants made to them by the personal representatives of a deceased testator in accordance with the terms of the residuary gift in his will. The gift was afterwards held by the House of Lords to be ineffective, with the result that the testator's residue passed on intestacy. The next of kin then brought proceedings to recover the moneys paid away. The defendants found themselves in an unenviable position. Not only had they received the money honestly and in good faith, but they had had no reason to think that it was not theirs. There was no question of their having consciously mixed money which belonged to another with their own.

"But the present case is very different. Neither Mr Bajwa nor his solicitors acted **12–133** dishonestly, but nor were they innocent volunteers. Hill Lawson knew that the money was trust money held to Dave's order pending completion and that it would become available for use on behalf of their client only on completion. They were manifestly fiduciaries. Mr Bajwa, who was plainly intending to redeem the Halifax's mortgage out of the proceeds of sale of the property, must be taken to have known that any money which his solicitors might receive from the purchasers or their mortgagees would represent the balance of the proceeds of sale due on completion and that, since he had made no arrangement with the purchasers to be advanced any part of that amount before completion, it would be available to him only on completion. He cannot possibly have thought that he could keep both the property and the proceeds of sale. Had he thought about the matter at all, he would have realised that the money was not his to mix with his own and dispose of as he saw fit. The only reason that he and his solicitors can be acquitted of dishonesty is that he relied on his solicitors and they acted in the mistaken belief that, save for the tidying up of some loose ends, they were on the point of completing.

"It follows that Mr Bajwa cannot avail himself of the more favourable tracing **12–134** rules which are available to the innocent volunteer who unconsciously mixes trust money with his own.

Subrogation

"The appellants submit that the mere fact that the claimant's money is used to **12–135** discharge someone else's debt does not entitle him to be subrogated to the creditor whose debt is paid. There must be 'something more': *Paul v Speirway Ltd (in liq)* [1976] Ch. 220 at 230 *per* Oliver J; and see *Orakpo v Manson Investments Ltd* [1978] A.C. 95 at 105. From this the appellants derive the proposition that in order to be subrogated to the creditor's security the claimant must prove (i) that the claimant intended that his money should be used to discharge the security in question (that being the 'something more' required by Oliver J) and (ii) that he intended to obtain the benefit of the security by subrogation.

12–136   "I cannot accept that formulation as a rule of general application regardless of the circumstances in which the remedy of subrogation is sought. The cases relied on were all cases where the claimant intended to make an unsecured loan to a borrower who used the money to discharge a secured debt. In such a case the claimant is not entitled to be subrogated to the creditor's security since this would put him in a better position than he had bargained for.

12–137   "The mere fact that the payer of the money intended to make an unsecured loan will not preclude his claim to be subrogated to the personal rights of the creditor whose debt is discharged if the contractual liability of the original borrower proves to be unenforceable: see *e.g. Re Wrexham, Mold & Connah's Quay Rly Co* [1899] 1 Ch. 440 (where the borrowing was *ultra vires*) and *B Liggett (Liverpool) Ltd v Barclays Bank Ltd* [1928] 1 K.B. 48 (where the borrowing was unauthorised) . . .

12–138   "In cases such as *Butler v Rice* [1910] 2 Ch. 277 and *Ghana Commercial Bank v Chandiram* [1960] A.C. 732, where the claimant paid the creditor direct and intended to discharge his security, the court took the claimant's intention to have been to keep the original security alive for his own benefit save in so far as it was replaced by an effective security in favour of himself. In the present case the Abbey National did not intend to discharge the Halifax's charge in the events which happened, that is to say in the event that completion did not proceed. But it did not intend its money to be used at all in that event. If *Butler v Rice* and similar cases are relied upon to support the proposition that there can be no subrogation unless the claimant intended to keep the original security alive for its own benefit save in so far as it was replaced by a new and effective security, with the result that the remedy is not available where the claimant had no direct dealings with the creditor and did not intend his money to be used at all, then I respectfully dissent from that proposition. I prefer the view of Slade L.J. in *Re TH Knitwear (Wholesale) Ltd* [1988] Ch. 275 at 286 that in some situations the doctrine of subrogation is capable of applying even though it is impossible to infer a mutual intention to this effect on the part of the creditor and the person claiming to be subrogated to the creditor's security. In the present case the payment was made by Hill Lawson, and it is their intention which matters. As fiduciaries, they could not be heard to say that they had paid out their principal's money otherwise than for the benefit of their principal. Accordingly, their intention must be taken to have been to keep the Halifax's charge alive for the benefit of the Abbey National pending completion. In my judgment this is sufficient to bring the doctrine of subrogation into play.

12–139   "The application of the doctrine in the present case does not create the problem which confronted Oliver J in *Paul v Speirway*. The Abbey National did not intend to be an unsecured creditor of anyone. It intended to retain the beneficial interest in its money unless and until that interest was replaced by a first legal mortgage on the property. The factual context in which the claim to subrogation arises is a novel one which does not appear to have arisen before, but the justice of its claim cannot be denied. The Abbey National's beneficial interest in the money can no longer be restored to it. If it is subrogated to the Halifax's charge its position will not be improved nor will Mr Bajwa's position be adversely affected. Both parties will be restored as nearly as may be to the positions which they were respectively intended to occupy."

12–140   "The appellants place much reliance on a passage in *Re Diplock* [1948] Ch. 465, 549-550, where the court was dealing with the claim against the Leaf Homeopathic Hospital. The hospital received a grant for the specific purpose of enabling it to pay off a secured bank loan. The passage in question reads:

'Here, too, we think that the effect of the payment to the bank was to extinguish the debt and the charge held by the bank ceased to exist. The case cannot, we think, be regarded as one of subrogation, and if the appellants were entitled to a charge it would have to be a new charge created by the court. The position in this respect does not appear to us to be affected by the fact that the payment off of this debt was one of the objects for which the grant was made. The effect of the payment off was that the charity, which had previously held the equity of redemption, became owners of unincumbered property. That unencumbered property derived from a combination of two things, the equity of redemption contributed by the charity and the effect of the Diplock money in getting rid of the incumbrance. If equity is now to create a charge (we say "create" because there is no survival of the original charge) in favour of the judicial trustee, it will be placing him in a position to insist upon a sale of what was contributed by the charity. The case, as it appears to us, is in effect analogous to the cases where Diplock money is expended on improvements to charity land. The money was in this case used to remove a blot on the title; to give the judicial trustee a charge in respect of the money so used would, we think, be equally unjust to the charity who, as a result of such a charge, would have to submit to a sale of the interest in the property which it brought in. We may point out that if the relief claimed were to be accepted as a correct application of the equitable principle, insoluble problems might arise in a case where in the meanwhile fresh charges on the property had been created or money been expended upon it.'

"The passage is not without its difficulties and is in need of reappraisal in the **12–141** light of the significant developments in the law of restitution which have taken place in the last 50 years. The second sentence is puzzling. The discharge of the creditor's security at law is certainly not a bar to subrogation in equity; it is rather a precondition. But the court was probably doing no more than equating the remedy to the creation of a new charge for the purpose of considering whether this was justified.

"It is also unclear what conclusion was thought to follow from the observation **12–142** that the unencumbered property derived from two sources, the equity of redemption contributed by the charity and the money belonging to the next of kin which was used to redeem the mortgage. If the money had been used to buy the property without any contribution from the charity, the next of kin would have sought a declaration that they were solely and beneficially entitled to the property under a constructive trust. Their claim to be subrogated to the security which had been discharged with their money reflected the respective contributions which they and the charity had made, and did not encroach upon the charity's equity of redemption at all.

"Nor is it clear to me why insoluble problems would arise in a case where there **12–143** had been fresh charges created on the property in the meantime. The next of kin would obtain a charge by subrogation with the same priority as the charge which had been redeemed except that it would not enjoy the paramountcy of the legal estate. A subsequent incumbrancer who obtained a legal estate for value without notice of the interest of the next of kin would take free from it . . .

"Taken as a whole, however, the passage cited is an explanation of the reasons **12–144** why, in the particular circumstances of that case, it was considered unjust to grant the remedy of subrogation. The hospital had changed its position to its detriment. It had in all innocence used the money to redeem a mortgage held by the bank, which, no doubt, was willing to allow its advance to remain outstanding indefinitely so long as it was well secured and the interest was paid punctually. The next of kin were seeking to be subrogated to the bank's security in order to enforce it and enable a proper distribution of the estate to be made. This would have been unjust to the hospital. It may be doubted whether in its anxiety to avoid injustice to the hospital the court may not have done an even greater injustice to the next of kin, who were denied even the interest on their money. Justice did not require the withholding of any remedy, but only that the charge by subrogation should not be enforceable until the hospital had had a reasonable opportunity to obtain a fresh advance on suitable terms from a willing lender, perhaps from the bank which had held the original security.

12–145   "Today, considerations of this kind would be regarded as relevant to a change of position defence rather than as going to liability . . ."

QUESTIONS

12–146   **1.** "Debtor-creditor relationships where the recipient is intended to be able to use the moneys as its own and so mix them with its own moneys subject to an obligation to repay a corresponding amount with interest with interest cannot create equitable interests in favour of the payer." Discuss.

12–147   **2.** When is it appropriate to claim an equitable charge rather then whole or part ownership?

12–148   **3.** "The flexibility of the charge where money is traced from a bank account, *e.g.* into other mixed bank accounts and assets purchased with mixed moneys provides in the light of *El Ajou* strong remedies against the wrongdoer and third parties with notice." Discuss.

12–149   **4.** "A beneficiary can pick and choose his tracing rules under *Re Hallett's Estate* and *Re Oatway* when the trustee has mixed trust moneys in his private currect account at his bank though this is unnecessary if only a charge is sought." Discuss.

12–150   **5.** "The rule in *Clayton's* case is too arbitrary for a court of equity to apply it." Discuss.

12–151   **6.** "The tracing rules are too harsh on innocent volunteers, though wicked volunteers deserve their strict treatment. An innocent volunteer, in the sense of one without actual Nelsonian or naughty knowledge, should not be liable to share his profits if he would have been able to make them without the assistance of the claimants' moneys." Discuss.

12–152   **7.** "Lord Templeman in *Space Investments* has odd ideas on tracing." Discuss in light of the views in *Re Goldcorp* and *Bishopsgate v Homan*.

12–153   **8.** "It is not obvious why if T wrongfully mixes £50,000 of trust funds with £50,000 of his own money to buy a house now worth £200,000 the beneficiaries should have a lesser claim than if T had used the beneficiaries' £50,000 to buy a £100,000 house with the assistance of a £50,000 endowment mortgage thereon (under which interest alone is paid until maturity of the endowment policy)." Discuss.

12–154   **9.** Trevor, who is trustee, deposits £6,000 of trust moneys in his personal current account which is £100 in credit though he has overdraft facilities limited to £1,400. On the following day he attends an auction of paintings and buys a painting which he has always wanted for £6,500. He pays for it by a cheque drawn on his personal account. A month later he opens a trustee account into which he pays £6,000. The painting is now worth £13,000. Advise the beneficiaries. Would your advice be different if a fire had destroyed the painting?

10. Darby and Joan were trustee of a family trust for Joan for life, remainder to **12–155** Darby for life, remainder to their two children equally. On Joan's death, Darby became trustee of her testamentary trust for Darby for life, remainder as to one half for their grandchildren and the other half for the R.S.P.C.A.

In May 2000, Darby had £5,000 in his current bank account. On June 1 Darby paid into it £30,000, the proceeds of sale of some family trust investments. On 8 June he withdrew £5,000 to purchase shares in Whizzo Ltd; on June 15 he withdrew £20,000 to purchase shares in Zomko Ltd; on June 22 he withdrew £10,000 to pay the last instalment due on a painting he had purchased on an instalment basis for himself a year earlier.

In July, Darby decided to advance out of the testamentary trust £50,000 each to his grandson, Simon, and to the R.S.P.C.A. However, by mistake he paid them out of family trust moneys. As it happened, the R.S.P.C.A. had an option conferred by a benefactor to purchase for £50,000 some land worth £500,000, so it simply endorsed the £50,000 cheque over to the benefactor.

Simon paid his £50,000 into his building society deposit account containing £10,000. He then paid £600 thereout into his current bank account already containing £600, before withdrawing £100 cash and giving £50 thereof to his wife, Tara, who used £6 thereof to buy lottery tickets. One ticket won £6 million.

Later Simon withdrew £29,400 to buy a racehorse, which shortly afterwards broke a leg, so it had to be destroyed, while the remaining £30,000 was used to discharge Simon's mortgage on his home. This is now up for sale because Simon and Tara are going to emigrate to The Bahamas.

Advise Simon's childless uncle Jasper, who has discovered the above facts on Darby's recent death and seeks to maximise his entitlement under the family trust, taking account of the fact that the Whizzo shares have quadrupled in value, the Zonko shares are worthless, and the painting has doubled in value.

11. Bill died in 1975, having left his residuary estate to Charles and David upon **12–156** trust for his sister, Samantha, for life, remainder to such of her legitimate children as attained 21 years if more than one in equal shares, but in default thereof for University College, Durham, which now seeks your advice.

Having spent a year in Italy, Samantha had returned to England in October 1954 with Romeo Mondello, pretending they had married each other in Rome on September 3, 1969. In 1970 Samantha gave birth to Luigi. In 1975 Romeo died. In 1976 Samantha had an illness which left her incapable of having further children.

In 1993 at Samantha's request the trustees were happy to advance £28,000 so that Luigi could purchase a house.

In 1997 Samantha married a wealthy Greek. She then released her life interest in the trust fund. Before transferring the trust fund to Luigi the trustees asked Samantha as a mere formality to produce her marriage certificate. Through the services of Mario an Italian hairdresser to whom she had confided her problem, Samantha managed to obtain a forged Italian marriage certificate. After seeing it the trustees transferred the trust fund, consisting of £110,000 cash and £10,000 gilt-edged securities, to Luigi.

Luigi opened a deposit account for the cash and spent £101,000 on buying an Italian restaurant. He transferred the £9,000 balance into his current account then containing £1,000. He withdrew £5,000 therefrom to buy shares in Go-go Hi-Sci Ltd Within a year payment of bills for his restaurant put his account into overdraft.

In March 2001 Samantha told Luigi to his astonishment that he was illegitimate but that he need not worry about his inheritance since his uncle had really intended him to benefit believing he was legitimate.

Luigi then sold the gilt-edged securities and, to comfort Samantha, spent £6,000 of the proceeds on a holiday for them both, whilst spending the balance on bills for his restaurant.

At present Luigi's current account contains £2,500, though he has heavy outstanding debts in respect of his restaurant. However, the Go-go shares and Luigi's house have quadrupled in value. Mario has just won £50,000 on the football pools.

12–157   **12.** Is the following approach sensible for a claimant beneficiary?

(a) Go for a *proprietary* claim to trust assets or their traceable proceeds, if possible.

(b) Go for *personal* liability:
  (i) of trustee or other fiduciary for breach of trust or other fiduciary obligation;
  (ii) of third party who dishonestly assists in a breach of trust or other fiduciary obligation and so becomes personally liable to the same extent as the trustee or beneficiary whose breach he has assisted;
  (iii) of third party who received for his own benefit trust or fiduciary property but parts with it after having actual, Nelsonian, or naughty knowledge that he had improperly received the property;
  (iv) of third party who received for his own benefit trusts or fiduciary property and who has parted with it, on basis that he is strictly liable to repay in unjust enrichment unless he can establish a change of position defence.

Chapter 13

TRUST AND THE CONFLICT OF LAWS

Section 1. Preliminary Matters

The conflict of laws is that part of the private law of the English and Welsh **13-01** system of law which deals with issues which concern elements connected with other legal systems, *e.g.* of Scotland, Northern Ireland, the Republic of Ireland, Jersey, the Isle of Man, each of the American and Australian states, each of the Canadian or Spanish provinces. A settlor of British nationality domiciled[1] in California may create a trust of assets, half of which are in Bermuda and half in Ontario, and appoint four trustees, one habitually resident in Bermuda, one habitually resident in Ontario and two habitually resident in England. One-third of the beneficiaries may be habitually resident in California, one-third in England and one-third in Jersey. The trust instrument may specify Californian law as governing the validity of the trust, and Bermudian law as governing administration of trust assets there and Ontario law as governing administration of the assets there. It may also confer express powers on the trustees to change the law governing the validity of the trust and to change the place of administration and the law governing administration. An alleged breach of trust may lead the beneficiaries to bring an action against the trustees before the Chancery Division of the English High Court.

The two questions that arise are (1) does the English court have **13-02** jurisdiction to hear the case, and, if so, (2) what system of law shall apply to each point in issue? Sometimes, the case may be an exceptional one where, though the English court technically has jurisdiction, it will stay or strike out the proceedings on the ground of *forum non conveniens*, because the defendant shows there is another forum to whose jurisdiction he is amenable, in which justice can be done at substantially less inconvenience and expense, and where the claimant will not be deprived of a legitimate personal or juridical advantage which would be available to him under the English jurisdiction.[2] Sometimes, the question arises whether the English

---

[1] Domicile is a technical concept: it does not mean habitual residence. No one can be without a domicile since it is this that connects him with some legal system for many conflict of laws purposes. A person has a domicile of origin at birth (being his father's domicile or if illegitimate, his mother's domicile) a domicile of dependency when the infant's parents change domicile and may acquire a domicile of choice by the *factum* of permanent residence with the *animus* of residing there permanently or indefinitely. Upon giving up a domicile of choice the domicile of origin applies until acquisition of a new domicile of choice. However, for the purposes of the Civil Jurisdiction and Judgments Act 1982 by s.41 an individual's domicile simply requires residence in and a substantial connection with a territorial unit having its own system of law.

[2] *Spiliada Maritime Corp. v Cansulex Ltd* [1987] A.C. 460 and *Chelleram v Chellaram (No.2)* [2002] 3 All E.R. 17, but in E.U. and EFTA countries jurisdiction under the EC Council Regulation 44/2001 and the Lugano Convention, Arts 23 and 27 is on a first come (or "first seised") basis.

court will recognise or enforce a foreign judgment purporting to determine an issue that relates to the action before the court.

13–03   Detailed matters relating to questions of jurisdiction, of *forum non conveniens*, and of recognition or enforcement of foreign judgments are best left to the major works on conflict of laws,[3] though the EC Council Regulation 44/2001 and the Lugano EFTA Convention on Civil Jurisdiction and Enforcement of Judgments in force in the United Kingdom will be considered in outline at the end of the chapter. For the moment it is the choice of law issue—determining the law applicable to the matter in question—that will be examined. However, as will be seen, there are some situations where if the English court has jurisdiction it will apply English domestic law. One is used to this in family matters relating to divorce, separation and maintenance, and guardianship, custody and adoption of children, but in *Chellaram v Chellaram*, below at 13–38, Scott J. held that the machinery for the enforcement of beneficiaries' rights determined under the proper law, particularly the removal of trustees and the appointment of new ones, is a matter to be governed by English law where the English court has jurisdiction to hear the case,[4] even though the proper law governing the validity of the trust may not be English but Indian and regardless of whether the law governing administration may be English or Indian.[5] He was strongly influenced by the maxim "Equity acts *in personam*" enabling the court to make orders effective against trustees within the jurisdiction of the court.

Antecedent Matters and "Characterisation"

13–04   A distinction needs to be made between the testator's will or the settlor's trust document, which may be considered as the "rocket-launcher" on the one hand, and the trust itself—the "rocket"—on the other hand.[6] The law that governs whether or not the property of the testator or settlor has been effectively vested under a valid will or other instrument in personal representatives or trustees, free or not from third-party rights (*e.g.* under forced heirship regimes,[7] matrimonial property regimes[8] or bankruptcy or

---

[3] Dicey and Morris on *Conflict of Laws*, Cheshire & North on *Private International Law*. On trusts and conflict of laws there is a very useful chapter in Glassen (ed.), *International Trust Laws* and in Underhill & Hayton, *Law of Trusts and Trustees*, 16th ed. (2003).

[4] The English Court (ignoring the E.U. and EFTA Brussels and Lugano Conventions and Council Regulation 44/2001) has jurisdiction against persons served with proceedings in England, those voluntarily submitting to the jurisdiction, and those served abroad with the court's leave if a necessary or proper party to a claim against a duly served person or if a trustee of a trust governed by English law or if the subject-matter is located within England: Civil Procedure Rule 6.20.

[5] Essentially, Scott J. seems to be regarding the enforcement of beneficiaries' rights as a matter of procedure and so governed by the *lex fori*: *Chellaram v Chellaram (No.2)* [2002] 3 All E.R. 17, para.142. Also see *Stirling-Maxwell v Cartwright* (1879) 11 Ch.D. 5 at 22; *Re Lord Cable* [1976] 3 All E.R. 417 at 431–432.

[6] *Re Lord Cable* [1976] 3 All E.R. 417 at 431. *Att.-Gen. v Campbell* (1872) L.R. 5 H.L. 524, Art.4 of Hague Convention, see para.13–29.

[7] *e.g.* under French law a deceased's children have rights to part of his estate so that if he has three children he may only freely dispose of, say, one-quarter of his estate; *Re Annesley* [1926] Ch. 692; *Re Adams* [1967] I.R. 424. In ascertaining the size of his estate, gifts of capital in his lifetime are notionally added back to the value of his estate and if the actual estate at death is insufficient to satisfy the heirs' claims they have personal claims to make up the amount of their fixed or forced shares from donees, starting with the most recent donee. In some states gifts are safe if made 10 years before the donor's death.

[8] *e.g.* a husband cannot dispose of property within the matrimonial regime without his wife's participation: cp *Pullan v Koe* position, para.4–55 above.

defranding creditor[9] laws) may well be different from the law that governs the trust provisions once the intended trust property has wholly or partly survived the application of the law, or laws, relating to the preliminary issues.

Clearly, the formal requirements of the *lex situs* (the law of the jurisdiction of the location of the assets) need to be satisfied for transferring assets or declaring trusts thereof. If H wrongfully transfers to trustees property subject to a matrimonial property regime without W's written consent it may be that she will have a personal claim in tort or unjust enrichment against the trustees or a proprietary half share in the transferred assets and their traceable product. It is up to the *lex fori* (the law of the jurisdiction whose court is hearing the case) to characterise the issue which arises[10] and then give effect to a personal or a proprietary claim as the case may be.

This raises difficult problems where a forced heirship claim arises[11] **13–05** because the deceased died domiciled in Civilopia which requires three quarters of his estate to pass to his three children absolutely, such estate being notionally increased for this purpose by earlier lifetime gifts of capital made by the deceased. Let us assume, the deceased, D, a widower, left an actual estate worth £6 million, but nine years before death transferred English assets worth £18 million to English trustees of a trust governed by English law. Thus, the three children sue the trustees for £12 million to make up their £18 million forced heirship claim.[12] Civilopia[13] characterises their claims as succession claims governed by the Civilopian *lex successionis* as the jurisdiction of D's last habitual residence, which as D's last domicile is also regarded by the English court as the *lex successionis*.

The heirs' claims would not, of course, have arisen but for D's death, but the central issue is how to treat the lifetime gift when, of course, no-one could know what would ultimately be D's *lex successionis* and whether he would die with sufficient actual estate to satisfy his heirs' claims or whether he would even be survived by any descendants. It would appear that the English *lex fori* would characterise the £18 million gift as a lifetime transfer valid by the English *lex situs*,[14] although potentially impeachable by the Insolvency Act 1986 or if he died domiciled in England within six years, having intended to defeat claims of his children to reasonable maintainance, by the Inheritance (Provision for Family and Dependants) Act 1975 when s.13 thereof protects trustees against being liable beyond the value of the property in their hands. No such potential having materialised, the

---

[9] Insolvency Act 1986 ss.339–342, 423–425.
[10] *Macmillan Inc. v Bishopsgate Investment Trust (No.3)* [1996] 1 All E.R. 585; *RZB v Five Star LLC* [2001] 3 All E.R. 257.
[11] See D. J. Hayton (ed.), *European Succession Laws*, 2nd ed. (2002), for the mainland European forced heirship rules. The issue is not one of capacity (like infancy or lunacy). It is because the lifetime gift was effective that the forced heirship claim arises.
[12] This could even occur if the trustees had transferred the assets on to trustees of a Cayman or Bermudan trust where legislation ousts forced heirship claims so no such claims could be brought there.
[13] Thus, assets found to be located in civil law jurisdictions can be frozen by the forced heirs in pursuing their claims.
[14] D. J. Hayton (ed.), *European Succession Laws*, 2nd ed. (2002), paras 1–67 to 1–69: *Lewin on Trusts* (17th ed.) paras 11–59 to 11–60; P. Matthews (2001) 5 Chase Journal 15.

lifetime transfer is unimpeachable and so falls outside D's estate[15] to which the Civilopian *lex successionis* applies. Such conclusion is reinforced when considering Art.15(1)(d) and (f) of The Hague Trust Convention (made English law by the Recognition of Trusts Act 1987) which require the application of the mandatory provisions of the *lex situs* designated by the English forum's choice of law rules concerning "the transfer of title to property" and "the protection, in other respects, of third parties acting in good faith", whether the trustees or the beneficiaries are regarded as "third parties".

13–06   Characterisation of a transaction as testamentary and so governed by the *lex successionis*, or as a lifetime disposition (governed by the *lex situs*) is crucial from the perspective of formalities and forced heirship claims where the deceased opened a joint account with X some years before death. The North American,[16] English[17] and Irish[18] approach is to treat property passing on death by virtue of being surviving joint tenant as being by virtue of an earlier lifetime disposition and not a testamentary disposition.

Once the court of the forum has held that, under the applicable *lex situs*, the owner of assets has effectively vested them in a person as trustee (including settlor-trustee), it seems it should be the applicable (or proper) law governing the trust that determines what interests have then arisen in favour of intended beneficiaries.[19] Capacity to alienate property and capacity to create a trust must thus be considered separately.

In the case of immovables the *lex situs* has particular significance, especially for succession on the death of the owner thereof, while succession to movables is governed by the law of the deceased's last domicile in England and other common law countries—some civil law countries applying the law of the deceased's last habitual residence, some the law of the last nationality, and some applying such *lex successionis* to immovables as well as movables.[20]

This distinction is not the same as that between real property and personal property. Leasehold interests in land, though personal property, are immovables.[21] Where Settled Land Act 1925 capital moneys have been invested in stocks and shares but by s.75(5) such capital moneys and

---

[15] If the settlement were revocable or subject to the settlor's general power of appointment, there is a plausible case for permitting the trustees thereof to be subject (by analogy) to the forced heirship claims of heirs under the Civilopian mandatory family protection rules since the trust fund would automatically be regarded as part of the deceased's net estate subject to children's family provision claims under English family protection rules if the settlor had died domiciled in England: see Inheritance (Provision for Family and Dependants) Act 1975, s.25(1) "net estate" definition. The section 10 position is very different: it only applies if D died within 6 years, had the requisite intent to defeat his children's claims and had not by virtue of lifetime and testamentary provisions (including trusts) made reasonable provision for them, in which circumstances the court may invade the trust to the extent necessary to make reasonable provision, but the trustees under s.13 cannot be liable beyond the trust assets then in their hands. Any analogy between this specific narrow provision and general forced heirship rules would be false.

[16] *Hutchinson v Ross* 211 NE 2d 637 (1965); *Sanchez v Sanchez* 547 So 2d 945 (1989); *Re Reid* (1921) 64 D.L.R. 598; *Edwards v Bradley* [1956] O.R. 225.

[17] *Young v Sealey* [1949] Ch. 278; *Re Figgis* [1969] 1 Ch 123, 149.

[18] *Lynch v Burke* [1995] 1 IR 159.

[19] Further see J. Harris, *The Hague Trusts Convention* (Hart Publishing, 2003), pp.7–20.

[20] Generally see D. J. Hayton (ed.), *European Succession Laws*, 2nd ed. (2002).

[21] *Freke v Carberry* (1873) L.R. 16 Eq. 461.

investments therewith are regarded as "land" then the stocks and shares are immovables.[22]

General equitable principles of the Court of Chancery have a significant role, especially the maxim "Equity acts *in personam*."[23] Other maxims that may be applicable are, for example, "equity will do nothing in vain" and "equity will not require persons to do acts illegal by the law of the place where the acts are to be performed," *e.g.* where foreign exchange laws prevent trustees from getting money out of the country for the beneficiaries.[24]

Section 2. Choice of Applicable Law

As provided by Arts 6 and 7 of The Hague Convention, implemented by the Recognition of Trusts Act 1987, a trust is governed by the law expressly or impliedly chosen by the settlor, or in the absence of such choice, by the law with which the trust is most closely connected. It is easy to assume that there can be only one applicable law governing the trust except where the trust assets are physically situate in two or more countries where different applicable laws may be chosen to cover the assets situate in different countries. Upon a little reflection it can be seen that there may well be one law governing the validity of the trust provisions, often referred to as the "proper" law, and one law governing the administration of the trust. Upon further reflection, quite apart from preliminary issues concerning form or capacity with respect to the instrument creating the trust, there may be questions relating to formal validity of the trust itself[25] or capacity to act as trustee,[26] as well as questions relating to the substantive (or essential) validity of the trust provisions or questions affecting the interpretation (or construction) of such provisions. A settlor might thus state that his trust is to be governed by English law except that Scots law is to govern matters of interpretation[27] and Cayman Isles law is to govern matters of administration.

13–07

Where there is an express choice[28] the position is clear enough, except for the finer points of the distinction between matters of validity and matters of administration and except for any rule of public policy that

13–08

---

[22] *Re Cutcliffe's W.T.* [1940] Ch. 565.

[23] *e.g.* See also *Cook Industries Ltd v Galliher* [1979] Ch. 439; *Derby & Co. Ltd v Weldon (No.2)* [1989] 1 All E.R. 1002, *Webb v Webb* [1994] 3 All E.R. 911; [1992] 1 All E.R. 17.

[24] *Re Lord Cable* [1976] 3 All E.R. 417, for analogous contracts, see *Kahler v Midland Bank Ltd* [1950] A.C. 24. See Arts 15 and 16, Hague Convention, paras 13–34, 13–35.

[25] *e.g.* if the proper law applicable to the transfer of property allowed it to be done by conduct or by writing, whilst the proper law applicable to the creation of a trust of such property required use of a deed.

[26] *e.g.* if the proper law applicable to the transfer of property allowed transfer to any person of full capacity but the proper law applicable to the creation of a trust requires a trustee to be an official trust corporation or a male over 35 years of age.

[27] At first sight a Chancery lawyer might wonder how substantive validity and interpretation can be governed by different laws: validity almost inevitably depends on interpretation or construction. However, a trust provision may be valid whatever the interpretation, *e.g.* if "children" is legitimate children or children whether legitimate or illegitimate. Even if a trust provision would have been void under the old rule against remoteness if "issue" meant "descendants" and not just "children" the meaning of "issue" may be determined by the law expressly chosen by the testator even if different from the law governing validity. A testator may create his own dictionary of meanings whether by using specific foreign legal phrases or, generally incorporating a foreign law to govern interpretation: *Studd v Cook* (1883) 8 App.Cas. 577.

[28] For split laws in a contractual context see *Forsikrings Vesta v Butcher* [1986] 2 All E.R. 488 at 504–505; *Libyan Arab Bank v Bankers Trust Co.* [1989] 3 All E.R. 252 at 267, and the Contracts (Applicable Law) Act 1990 implementing the 1980 Rome Convention, especially Arts 3 and 4.

might invalidate such choice. Leaving these aside for the moment, a settlor may expressly[29] go further and empower his trustees to change the law governing the validity of the trust (with the proviso that it does not invalidate the rights of the beneficiaries under the original law governing validity) and to change the law governing the administration of the trust, with or without changing the principal place of administration of the trust. It would seem that the law governing validity at the time of the disputed issue should determine whether that issue was a matter for the law governing validity or for the law governing administration and should, indeed, determine whether or not and by what formal methods the law governing administration may be replaced by another law.[30] This last point is particularly significant where there is no express power to change the law governing administration.

13–09   This leads one to implied choice of law for matters of validity or matters of administration and to implied powers to change the law governing administration. If the addresses of the settlor and the trustees are English and the trust instrument refers to the English Trustee Act 1925 (*e.g.* in extending the powers in ss. 31 and 32 thereof) then there will be an implied choice of English law as the applicable law governing the trust in all its aspects. At some stage implied subjective intent shades off into an imputed objective intent that the trust shall be governed by the law with which it is most closely connected at the time of its creation.[31] In ascertaining such objective law various factors are taken into account, with the weight to be attached to each factor varying according to the particular circumstances. In a testamentary trust the domicile of the testator at his death traditionally had much significance.[32] It still should have significance[33] under Art.7 (which enumerates four indicators "in particular" for ascertaining the law with which a trust is most closely connected) as will obviously be the case where the home trust jurisdiction considers the matter as will normally be the position for matters concerning the internal trustee—beneficiary relationship. In the case of an *inter vivos* trust the domicile or habitual residence of the settlor at the time he created the trust has some significance as well as the place of execution of the trust instrument. Regard will also be had to the trustee's place of residence or business[34], though it must not be overlooked that trustees (other than professional corporate trustees) are often chosen for their personal qualities irrespective

---

[29] *Chellaram v Chellaram (No.2)* [2002] 3 All E.R. 17, paras 160–161.

[30] In England we consider the law governing validity as the "mother" law to which the law governing administration is attached by an umbilical cord: *cf. Marlborough v Att.-Gen.* [1945] Ch. 78 at 85, *Iveagh v I.R.C.* [1954] Ch. 364 at 370, *Fattorini v Johannesburg Trust* (1948) 4 S.A.L.R. 806 at 812. The original settlement's perpetuity period applies to property transferred thereout to a separate settlement: *Trennery v West* [2005] U.K.T.H.L. 5, para.41. See Art.10, Hague Convention, para.13–31.

[31] *Iveagh v I.R.C.* [1954] Ch. 364.

[32] *Re Lord Cable* [1976] 3 All E.R. 417 at 431. Older cases tended to assume that the law of the testator's domicile because it governed the validity of the will must govern trust dispositions in that will: this may happen to be the case but such does not necessarily follow: *Chelleram v Chelleram (No.2)*, above.

[33] But will not necessarily be determinative (see *Tod v Barton* (2002) 4 I.T.E.L.R. 715).

[34] As in *Chellaram v Chellaram (No.2)* [2002] 3 All E.R. 17 where the judge considered that there was not any significant difference between Art.7 and the common law, but held the trust to have an Indian proper law despite the majority of trustees being resident in England.

of where they live or work. Thus, if the testator or settlor expressly designates where the trust is to be administered this will be a more significant factor. Account will also be taken of the *situs* of the trust assets and the objects of the trust and the places where they are to be fulfilled.[35]

It seems there will be a presumption in favour of one implied or imputed applicable law governing all aspects of the trust,[36] the onus being upon he who alleges that one law governs validity and another law governs administration. If the original trustees appointed to administer the trust are foreign there will usually be other foreign elements and rarely will there be no express choice of the applicable law—in such rare case if there is a preponderant connection with one foreign system of law it is very likely that such law will govern both validity and administration and not just administration. If the trust instrument authorises the trustees to retire in favour of foreign trustees and to transfer the assets to such foreign trustees it seems likely that this power to change the place of administration impliedly carries with it the power to change the law governing administration to the law with which those foreign trustees are familiar, so far as this will be the law of a state that has its own internal law of trusts. For the law governing validity to be changed as well, the authority to transfer assets to foreign trustees will need to state that this is so,[37] so that such assets shall thereafter be exclusively governed by such foreign law so far as not contravening mandatory rules of the original "mother" law. As Lord Walker remarked in *Trennery v West*[38] the second settlement serves "as a vehicle to receive and continue the act of bounty effected by the first settlement, with the rule against perpetuities acting as a sort of umbilical cord between the two settlements". Declaring the trust to be governed henceforth by the law of Suntrustopia so far as not invalidating any beneficial interests under the original English trust will have Suntrustopian law operating under the continuing umbrella of English law even if the Suntrustopian trust is a new separate settlement for capital gain tax purposes.

13–10

Matters of Validity Contrasted with Matters of Administration

Where there is an express power to replace the law governing administration a wise settlor will specify what are matters of administration since there is precious little case law guidance on what amounts to matters of administration as opposed to matters of validity.

13–11

Some guidance may be found in *Pearson v I.R.C.*,[39] which was concerned with "dispositive" powers of trustees that prevent a beneficiary having an interest in possession and "administrative" powers that do not. After all, dispositive powers affect the nature or *quantum* of a beneficiary's beneficial

---

[35] *Fordyce v Bridges* (1848) 2 Ph. 497; *Re Mitchner* [1922] St.R.Qd. 252. See Art.7, Hague Convention, para.12–00.
[36] *Chelleram v Chelleram* [1985] Ch. 409.
[37] *Chellaram v Chellaram (No.2)* [2002] 3 All E.R. 17.
[38] [2005] U.K.H.L. 5.
[39] [1981] A.C. 753. A dispositive power prevents any beneficiary having an interest in possession because it enables net income to be diverted away from him after its has arisen: see above, para.1–111.

interest and so would appear not to be matters of administration. From *obiter dicta* in *Chellaram v Chellaram*, para.13–38, it appears that the rights of the beneficiaries are matters of validity so that the corresponding duties of the trustees must also be matters of validity. This is obviously true where the beneficial interests are concerned but not as concerns the beneficiaries' rights and the trustees' duties relating to investments authorised only under the Trustee Act 2000. Matters of investment are clearly matters of administration. If the law governing administration changes from one jurisdiction to another which permits investment in "x" then beneficiaries have no right to object to investment in "x" if the trustees exhibit the requisite standard of care—even if this be of a lower standard than that required by the previous jurisdiction's law.[40]

13–12 Matters of administration, it seems, must include the powers of trustees to administer and dispose and acquire trust assets, their powers of investment, their powers of delegation, their powers to pay debts and expenses and compromise claims, their rights to remuneration, their rights to contribution and indemnity between themselves, the appointment, retirement and removal of trustees and the devolution of trusteeship, the powers of the court to give advice and to confer powers upon trustees.

Powers of maintenance and advancement can affect the nature and extent of beneficiaries' interests, *e.g.* if the law of administration is changed to a foreign law which allows up to three-quarters of a beneficiary's contingent share to be advanced to him or gives no right to income at the age of 18 years to a beneficiary whose interest in capital is contingent on acquiring a greater age such as 30 years.[41] Thus ss 31 and 32 of the English Trustee Act should continue to apply even if the place and law of administration are changed to a different system of law, unless the clause that empowers such change can be broadly construed as authorising the foreign state's Trustee Act to apply to the exclusion of the English Act.

13–13 Matters pertaining to the original validity of the trust provisions (*e.g.* the rules against remoteness, accumulations and inalienability and prohibiting purpose trusts unless charitable trusts) are for the law governing validity. However, if an English testator in his will directs his executors to transfer some Scottish property, whether movable or immovable, that he himself had earlier inherited to two Scottish trustees on public but non-charitable trusts (valid according to Scots law but not English law) then although the law governing the testator's will and other trust dispositions in it may be English it should be Scots law that governs and upholds the validity of the public trusts.[42] The position should be similar if the English domiciled testator had directed his executors to transfer his shares in a Jersey

---

[40] It would be a fraud on the power if trustees exercised their power to change the law governing administration—or validity—for the purpose of benefiting themselves by reducing their duties of care.

[41] He will only be entitled to income on attaining the specified age in some jurisdictions. Some jurisdictions, indeed, exclude a beneficiary's rights under *Saunders v Vautier* either altogether or only with the court's leave. The distinction between capital and income is probably a matter of validity because it affects beneficiaries' entitlements.

[42] *cf. Jewish National Fund v Royal Trust Co.* (1965) 53 D.L.R. (2d) 577. The courts tend, where possible, to choose as the applicable law one which will sustain the validity of the trust: *Augustus v Permanent Trustee Co. (Canberra) Ltd* (1971) 124 C.L.R. 245.

company to a Jersey trustee for furthering the purposes of the Jersey Conservative Party to be enforceable by its leader from time to time.

The Variation of Trusts Act 1958 and the Matrimonial Causes Act 1973

The Variation of Trusts Act position is special. Most jurisdictions have such **13–14** Acts. Since the legislation can drastically alter the nature and extent of beneficiaries' interests one might have expected that the court's jurisdiction should be restricted to those trusts whose validity is governed by the *lex fori*. Nevertheless, the English courts have arrogated to themselves unlimited jurisdiction in the absence of restricting words in the Variation of Trusts Act 1958.[43] "However, where there are substantial foreign elements in the case, the court must consider carefully whether it is proper to exercise the jurisdiction. If, for example, the court were asked to vary a settlement which was plainly a Scottish settlement, it might well hesitate to exercise its jurisdiction to vary the trusts simply because some of, or even all, the trustees and beneficiaries were in this country. It may well be that the judge would say that the Court of Session was the appropriate tribunal to deal with the case."[44] In the light of Art.8(2)(h) of the Hague Convention it is very likely that an English court will decline jurisdiction for trusts governed by a foreign law (unless legislation thereof specifically authorised the English court). One must remember that all the parties before the court will be anxious for the jurisdiction to be exercised for family or for taxation reasons and that the interests of infant or unborn beneficiaries will hardly ever[45] be prejudiced by any variation. However, the taxation authorities in a particular country may take the point that the variation is ineffective except to the extent that adult beneficiaries are estopped from reverting to the pre-variation position.

Court orders varying nuptial settlements[46] under Matrimonial Causes Act 1973, s.24(1)(c) and (d) can be made even in respect of foreign trusts of foreign property held by foreign trustees[47] but will not be made if they would be likely to be ineffective in the relevant foreign country.[48] One can invoke Art.15 generally or 15(1)(b) specifically to justify such English jurisdiction so that there can be a proper determination of all matters arising out of the divorce, application of the Act being an effect of the marriage. The Variation of Trusts Act jurisdiction is different in requiring the consent of all adult beneficiaries coupled with the court's consent, while the trustees have a non-partisan co-operative function.

---

[43] *Re Ker's Settlement* [1963] Ch. 553; *Re Paget's Settlement* [1965] 1 W.L.R. 1046. The same has happened in Alberta and in Western Australia: *Commercial Trust Co. v Laing* unreported (Waters *Law of Trusts in Canada*, at 1134); *Faye v Faye* [1973] W.A.R. 66.

[44] *Re Paget's Settlement* [1965] 1 W.L.R. 1046 at 1050, *per* Cross J.

[45] See *Re Remnant's W.T.* [1970] 1 Ch. 560.

[46] *Brooks v Brooks* [1995] 3 All E.R. 257, 263.

[47] *E v E* [1990] F.L.R. 233, 242; *T v T* [1996] 2 F.L.R. 357, 363: *Charalambous v Charalambous* [2004] EWCA Civ 1030, [2004] 2 F.L.R. 1093, though local foreign proceedings to recognise the English court order will also be necessary to protect the trustees giving effect to such order, *e.g. Compas Trustees v McBarnett* [2002] Jersey L.R. 321 where the order was required as a matter of comity.

[48] *Goff v Goff* [1934] p.107, 113.

Limitations upon Free Choice of Law

13–15 Obvious problems exist where immovables are concerned but under the Trusts Convention the *lex situs* does not need to govern the validity of trusts of immovables. Take land in Spain (which does not have the trust concept within its code of law) or in Jersey (which allows trusts so long as they are not of land in Jersey). There are practical problems if recourse has to be had to Spanish or Jersey courts and so far as title to the land is concerned the trustees would appear as ordinary private beneficial owners. However, if the land comprised say one-twentieth of the aggregate of property subjected to trusts with an English proper law why should the English trustees not be under valid *in personam* trusteeship obligations to the English beneficiaries in respect of the land, *e.g.* to pay rents over to the beneficiaries and to keep the premises in reasonable repair?[49]

13–16 A settlor has total freedom of choice of law unless such choice is manifestly incompatible with public policy.[50] Art.13 of the Hague Convention affords a discretion to refuse to recognise a trust or a category of trust if its significant elements, except for the choice of law, the place of administration and the habitual residence of the trustee, are more closely connected with a non-trust-State. The United Kingdom considered it unhelpful for its courts to have such a discretion and so the Recognition of Trusts Act 1987 deliberately omits the uncertainties of Art.13.

If, in what would otherwise be a trust governed by English law, an Englishman purports to create a trust of English land but expressly chooses a foreign law with the intent of enabling the land to be held for ever on valid public but non-charitable purpose trusts it is clear that the land will not be so held. The English court will have to give effect to the English policy rules as to the administration of land within the jurisdiction. Indeed, the policy rules recognising the unenforceability of purpose trusts, where no one has *locus standi* to apply to the court to have the purposes positively carried out, would prevent the trust being effective even if the property was not land.

13–17 If, however, it was movable or immovable property in Scotland subjected to public non-charitable purpose trusts expressed to be subject to Scots law (and valid by Scots law) then there seems no policy reason for the English court to invalidate such trusts of an English testator in his English will. Indeed, if the trusts were private non-charitable purpose trusts of movables

---

[49] *cf. Re Fitzgerald* [1904] 1 Ch. 573; *Webb v Webb* [1994] 3 All E.R. 911. Sufficient scope is afforded to the *lex situs* to govern preliminary or policy issues, *e.g. Re Ross* [1930] 1 Ch. 377 (*legitima portio*); *Re Hoyles* [1911] 1 Ch. 179, *Duncan v Lawson* (1889) 41 Ch.D. 394 (Mortmain Acts); *Freke v Carberry* (1873) L.R. 16 Eq. 461 (perpetuities and accumulations); *Re Pearse's Settlement* [1909] 1 Ch. 304 (Jersey land could not be conveyed by a married woman to someone except for adequate pecuniary compensation so that her after-acquired property covenant in an English settlement was construed as not intended to include after-acquired Jersey land within the scope of the covenant).
[50] See Arts 6 and 18 but note the safeguards in Arts 15 and 16 of The Hague Convention. English courts are likely to invoke public policy where a settlor uses Belize or Cook Islands law to settle his own property on protective trusts for himself for life (see *Re Lawrence* (2003) 5 I.T.E.L.R. 1) or creates a Cook Islands asset protection trust which can only be upset if the creditor intended to be defrauded brings an action within one year of the property being transferred to the trustees and proves his case beyond reasonable doubt.

in the Isle of Man, Jersey, Bermuda or Cayman valid under special legislation with there being an expressly designated enforcer with standing to enforce the trust, the English court should not invalidate them, nor should it if such trusts purchase English assets as investments or even if such assets are directly transferred to the trustees to become original settled assets.[51] However, the purposes must not amount to a mere investment clause[52] or to a device purporting to put beneficial ownership in suspense protected from claims of creditors and tax inspectors.[53]

One should note that a choice of law (*e.g.* English law) to govern a trust makes that law govern the relationship between the trustees and the beneficiaries: that law governs the "internal" aspects of the trust. As far as the trustees' "external" relations with third parties are concerned, *e.g.* in contracting with them or transferring property to them one has to apply the conflict of laws rules applicable to contracts or to the transfer of property. Thus, a trustee of a trust governed by the law of Jersey may rely when contracting in Jersey on Art.32(1) of the Trusts Jersey Law 1983, "Where in any transaction or matter affecting a trust a trustee informs a third party that he is acting as trustee a claim by such third party in relation thereto shall extend only to the trust property." If the trustee contracts in England under English law (not expressly choosing Jersey law to govern the contract) he will be personally liable since any person contracting under English law is personally liable except to the extent he expressly restricts liability, for example to trust property to which he has a right of recourse for paying trust expenses.[54]

Section 3. The Recognition of Trusts Act 1987 and Limited Scope of Trusts Convention

Since August 1, 1987, Articles 1 to 18 (except 13 and 16 para.2) and 22 of **13–18** The Hague Trusts Convention, have been in force in the United Kingdom in respect of trusts whenever created, but this does not affect the law to be applied to anything done or omitted before August 1, 1987.[55] Section 1(2)

---

[51] See D. J. Hayton, "Developing the Obligation Characteristic of the Trust" (2001) 117 L.Q.R. 96. Further on offshore developments see D. J. Hayton (ed.) *Modern International Developments in Trust Law* (Kluwer 1999) Chapters 1 and 15; A. G. D. Duckworth, "The Role of Offshore Jurisdictions in the Development of the International Trust" (1999) 32 Vanderbilt Jo. Transnational Law 879; A. G. D. Duckworth "Trust Law in the New Millennium: Fundamentals" *Trusts & Trustees*, Feb 2001, at 9–15 and D. J. Hayton (ed.), *Extending the Boundaries of Trusts and Similar Ring-Fenced Funds* (Kluwer, 2002), chapter by D. Waters, "Reaching for the Skies".

[52] *e.g.* a trust for the purpose of developing the income yield and capital growth of the trust fund, so in default of any disposal of the beneficial interest there will be a resulting trust for the settlor.

[53] *e.g.* a trust to develop the business of X Co.Ltd where X Co.or its owner should be regarded as beneficiary or a trust to maintain a collection of paintings together as a private collection when the settlor should be regarded as beneficiary under a resulting trust. Under the Cayman Special Trusts Alternative Regime Law 1997 s.7 "beneficiaries" have no interests whatsoever in the trust property and have no rights to sue the trustees or the expressly appointed "enforcer", so unless a "beneficiary" has been appointed an enforcer the English court seems likely to treat "beneficiaries" as objects of a power, leaving a resulting trust for the settlor: *cf Armitage v Nurse* [1998] Ch. 241, 253.

[54] See above, para.9–342.

[55] SI 1987/1177. The Convention is regarded as clarifying the common law position (on which see Wallace (1987) 36 I.C.L.Q. 454) but the non-retrospective provision was inserted in s.1(5) of the 1987 Act *ex abundante cautela*.

extends the Convention's provisions to any other trusts of property arising (*e.g.* orally or by statute) under the law of any part of the United Kingdom or by virtue of a judicial decision in the United Kingdom or elsewhere. This is because Art.3 restricts the Convention to trusts created voluntarily and evidenced in writing.[56] Despite the superficial width of Art.2 the Convention does not extend beyond trusts to agency or mandate as earlier explained.[57]

Limited Scope of Trusts Convention

13–19   1. This (private international law) Convention does not introduce the trust into the internal private law of States that do not have the concept of the trust; it simply makes foreign States recognise trusts of property as a matter of private international law, although, for recognition to mean something, the internal private law needs to recognise that the trust fund is separate from the owner's private patrimony, so as to be immune from claims of the owner's creditors heirs and spouse.[58]

2. This (private international law) Convention does not affect the internal private law of States that have the trust concept: the extent to which the applicable law can be expressly or impliedly changed and the distinction between matters of validity and matters of administration may vary according to the appropriate applicable law because State A's internal trust rules may differ from such rules of State B.

3. Non-trust states expect the home jurisdiction to resolve matters concerning the internal trustee—beneficiary relationship, so the Trusts Convention will help them where the external relationship of the trustees with third parties is concerned.

4. The Convention applies only to a trust ("the rocket") and not to the instrument launching the trust ("the rocket-launcher"). Antecedent preliminary issues that may affect the validity of wills, deeds or other acts by which property is allegedly subjected to a trust fall outside the Convention: Art.4. The Convention only applies if whatever is the applicable law governing capacity or formal or substantive validity of wills or *inter vivos* declarations of trust by the settlor or transfers of property to trustees has not operated to prevent the relevant property being available to be subjected to trusts.

13–20   5. While the Convention recognises the equitable proprietary right of beneficiaries in trust property and its traceable product in States that have such equitable concept, it does not introduce such proprietary right into States that have no concept of equitable proprietary interest in their fixed

---

[56] The French text is "et dont la preuve est *apportée par écrit*" which appears to need dilution to reflect "evidenced" in writing and so to cover most trusts which are first established in respect of a nominal sum, with substantial assets being added subsequently and with written evidence subsequently arising, whether produced by the settlor or the trustees, *e.g.* in their accounts.

[57] See paras 1–5, 1–6. A settlor's declaration of himself as trustee of assets now controlled by him as trustee should be within Art.2, but, in any event, if valid by its own governing law should be recognised under Arts 11 *et seq*.

[58] The Dutch implementing legislation provides for this: D.J. Hayton (1996) 5 J. Int. P. 127.

scheme of property interests. If trust property is transferred in such a State to X the *lex situs* will govern the effect of such transfer and deny the existence of any equitable proprietary interest except to the extent that any actual knowledge by X of a breach of trust may make it possible to take advantage of any *lex situs* rules on fraud: see the last sentence of Art.11 para.3(d) and also Art.15(d)(f) and para.113 of the Von Overbeck Official Report on the Trusts Convention.[59] However, in *El Ajou v Dollar Landholdings plc*[60] the equitable tracing process was held not to be defeated if traceable assets passed through various civil law jurisdictions so as to end up in a common law jurisdiction.

6. Art.15 detracts hugely from Art.11. It ensures the application of the **13–21** internal mandatory rules of a State whose law is applicable according to the conflicts rules of the forum, irrespective of the law applicable to the trust. A forum will have choice of law rules in areas such as succession, property, bankruptcy, divorce, matrimonial property regimes. Many Civil law states[61] know little of a distinction between a private patrimony and a fiduciary patrimony so that a separate fiduciary fund as a type of quasi-security for the personal claims of beneficiaries may only arise if the implementing legislation expressly ousts Art.15 para.(d) and (e) as in the Netherlands, unless one can boldly regard Art.11 as requiring recognition of a fiduciary patrimony separate from a private patrimony which alone is subject to Art.15. After all para.108 of the Von Overbeck Report states that Art.11 para.2 "determines that the assets of the trust are separate from those of the trustee. This is an essential element of the trust, without which its recognition would have no meaning." Mandatory succession rules (*réserve héréditaire, legitima portio, pflichtteil*) have special significance, especially if a settlor's trust assets are found in the civil law forum of a forced heir who seeks such assets: *Holzberg v Sasson* 1986 Rev. crit. de dr. int. pr. 685. Choice of law rules may lead to the *lex successionis, lex situs* or *lex fori* being invoked so as wholly or partly to undo the effects of a trust. While an English court should characterise a Frenchman's transfer of assets in England to English trustees as a straightforward *inter vivos* transfer of property governed by the English *lex situs,* protected by Art.15(d) of the Convention, and then by the English applicable law of the trust, a French court will characterise such transfer as pertaining to the French *lex successionis* so far as it affects property subject to *réserve héréditaire*. So long as the trust property remains in England (or another common law country) it should remain intact but if the property is found in France (or a sympathetic civil law country) then the heirs may claim it in satisfaction of their *réserves héréditaires*.

---

[59] The Report is reproduced in Glasson (ed.) *International Trust Laws* and will be taken account of by the court in construing the Convention as implemented by the 1987 Recognition of Trusts Act: *e.g. Three Rivers D. C. v Bank of England (No.2)* [1996] 2 All E.R. 363.

[60] [1993] 3 All E.R. 717, 736–737, [1995] 2 All E.R. 213, 221 in respect of a personal claim but the position should be the same for a proprietary remedy despite the continuing interest in property vindication approach in *Foskett v McKeown* [2001] 1 A.C. 102: the life of the law has not always been logical.

[61] See Hayton, Kortmann & Verhagen (eds.), *Principles of European Trust Law* (Kluwer, 1999). Some States accept that property of an undisclosed principal in the apparent ownership of his agent must, on the insolvency of the agent, be preserved exclusively for the principal.

13–22   7. Under the first paragraph of Art.16 the *lex fori* court must of course apply its own international mandatory rules, *e.g.* if a beneficiary is suing the trustee for failure to export to the beneficiary some thing or animal whose export is prohibited by the *lex fori*.

Under the second paragraph the *lex fori* court has a discretion, to be exercised only in the most exceptional case, to apply the international mandatory rules of some other State with a sufficiently close connection with the case, where the State's law is neither the *lex fori* nor the law applicable to the trust as such.

Trust States find it difficult to appreciate the need for such a provision since a Court of Equity will do nothing in vain (*i.e.* will not make orders which cannot be carried out as where foreign immovables are concerned) and will not require a person to do an act that is illegal in the place where it is to be done.[62] Thus, if the law of the trust is that of State A, the law of the forum that of State B, and the law of State C makes it illegal to take certain sorts of assets out of State C, any action by a beneficiary against the trustees for not getting such assets out to the beneficiary will fail, regardless of the second paragraph. The uncertain ambit of the paragraph is also unsatisfactory for lawyers and for courts. The United Kingdom government therefore made the reservation allowed by the third paragraph.

13–23   8.   By Art.13 a court in a trust or non-trust State has a discretionary power to refuse to recognise a trust or a category if the significant elements of the trust (*e.g.* situs of assets, settlor's and beneficiaries' habitual residence) are more closely connected with non-trust, than with trust, States, except for the choice of the applicable law, the place of administration and the habitual residence of the trustee. It seems that it is up to the court to decide in a particular case what are the significant elements which connect the trust closely to a non-trust State. The relevant time for these significant elements to be so connected seems to be the time of the events occasioning the claim for recognition and not the time of creation of the trust. The United Kingdom Recognition of Trusts Act 1987 deliberately omitted Art.13 because it was considered unnecessary for such a discretion to be available.

9. The Convention is only concerned with trusts of property created voluntarily and evidenced in writing[63] and not with the imposition of constructive trusteeship upon a defendant so that he is personally liable to account as a constructive trustee if he dishonestly assisted in a breach of trust, whether or not any trust property was ever in his hands. Where a defendant cannot be made personally liable in tort or contract but has acted with want of probity equity constructively treats him as if he had been a trustee as a formula for an equitable personal (as opposed to proprietary) remedy, which will be of no assistance if the defendant is deeply insolvent. A defendant in a State not having the trust and any equitable jurisdiction can never be liable as a constructive trustee in that State.

---

[62] *Re Lord Cable* [1976] 3 All E.R. 417 at 435.
[63] Seemingly of the settlor or the trustees in signing trust accounts, *e.g.* in relation to property subsequently added to trusts of nominal sums.

**Section 4. Civil Jurisdiction & Judgments Acts 1982 & 1991 and
Regulation 44/2001**

These Acts make special provision for E.U. countries and for EFTA   **13–24**
countries as required by the Brussels 1968 Convention on Civil Jurisdiction
and Enforcement of Judgments and the parallel Lugano Convention of
1988 for EFTA countries. For EU countries (other then Denmark) the
Brussels Convention has been replaced by Council Regulation 44/2001. The
basic principle is that jurisdiction is conferred on the courts of the
"domicile" of the defendant,[64] but a person may be sued as settlor trustee
or beneficiary in the courts of the contracting State in which the trust is
"domiciled".[65] A trust is domiciled in the state having the system of law
with which the trust has its closest and most real connection,[66] which seems
to be the system that provides the applicable (or governing) law of the trust,
so giving birth to the trust. The court first "seised" of the action hears it,[67]
even if a trust instrument confers jurisdiction on a another system of law to   **13–25**
have exclusive jurisdiction in any proceedings brought against a settlor,
trustee or beneficiary if relations betwen these persons or their rights or
obligations under the trust are involved.[68] However, such first court in its
discretion may refer the matter to the courts in the designated exclusive
jurisdiction. Where the proceedings have as their object rights *in rem* in
immovable property or tenancies of immovable property, then the courts of
the state in which such property is situated have exclusive jurisdiction.[69] If a
father claims that French immovable property vested in his son is held on a
resulting trust for the father this is regarded as a personal matter between
them so that the French court does not have exclusive jursidiction: English
Equity acts *in personam* and the English court has jurisdiction if the son is
resident in England or the trust is an English trust.[70]

The Conventions and Regulation No.44 of 2001 do not apply to rights in
property arising out of a matrimonial relationship, wills or succession or
bankruptcy or insolvency,[71] thus excluding ante-nuptial marriage settlements. However, once under the relevant law governing wills and succession a testamentary trust has been permitted to arise, it seems that any
subsequent breach of trust dispute (*e.g.* arising 20 or 30 years later) should
fall within the Conventions and the Regulation, just as in the case of a
dispute arising under a trust set up in the settlor's lifetime. Once the right
in property has been established as vested in a trustee, T, or an absolute

---

[64] Requisting only residence in and a substantial connection with the relevant jurisdiction.
[65] Art.5(6).
[66] s.45 of the 1982 Act.
[67] Articles 21 and 23 respectively of the Brussels and Lugano Conventions, Article 27 of Regulation 44/2001.
[68] Art.17 as restricted by *Grasser v Mirat* [2004], Lloyds Reg 222 (Case C–116/82 of European Court of Justice).
[69] Art.16(1) of Convention and Art.22 of Regulation 64/2001.
[70] *Webb v Webb* [1994] Q.B. 696; [1994] 3 All E.R. 911 applied by CA in *Pollard v Ashurst* [2001] 2 All E.R. 75 upholding judge's order on behalf of husband's trustee in bankruptcy that husband and wife should sell their jointly owned Portugese villa to enable the trustee to obtain the husband's share of the proceeds.
[71] Art.1 of the Convention and Regulation.

owner, O, then matters arising years later concerning breaches of trust or contract or delicts surely cannot be matters of succession.[72]

13–26   Judgments on trusts and other matters given in a contracting State are to be recognised and enforced in the other contracting States.[73] However, a judgment will not be recognised[74]:

(1) if such recognition is manifestly contrary to public policy in the State in which recognition is sought;

(2) where it was given in default of appearance if the defendant was not duly served with the relevant proceedings in sufficient time to enable him to arrange for his defence, unless the defendant failed to commence proceedings to challenge the judgment when it was possible to do so;

(3) if the judgment is irreconcilable with a judgment in a dispute between the same parties in the State in which recognition is sought;

(4) if the judgment is irreconcilable with an earlier judgment given in another Member State or in a third State involving the same cause of action and between the same parties, provided that the earlier judgment fulfils the conditions necessary for its recognition in the Member State addressed.

CONVENTION ON THE LAW APPLICABLE TO TRUSTS AND ON THEIR RECOGNITION[75]

13–27 The States signatory to the present Convention,

Considering that the trust, as developed in courts of equity in common law jurisdictions and adopted with some modifications in other jurisdictions, is a unique legal institution,

Desiring to establish common provisions on the law applicable to trusts and to deal with the most important issues concerning the recognition of trusts,

Have resolved to conclude a Convention to this effect, and have agreed upon the following provisions—

---

[72] Further on this and what are "trusts" within the Conventions and the Regulation see D. J. Hayton, "The Trust in European Commercial Life" in J. Lowry (ed.), *Commercial Law Essays in Honour of Sir Roy Goode* (2005).

[73] Arts 33 and 38 of Regulation 44/2001.

[74] Art.34 of the Regulation.

[75] Generally see J. Harris, *The Hague Trusts Convention* (Hart Publishing, 2002); Explanatory Report by A.E. von Overbeck published by Permanent Bureau of The Hague Conference in Acts and Documents of the 15th Session of the Hague Conference pp.370 *et seq.*, D. J. Hayton (1987) 36 I.C.L.Q. 260; Underhill & Hayton (16th ed.) Chapter 23; *Lewin on Trusts* (17th ed) Chapter 11; O'Sullivan [1993] 2 J.Int. P. 85; Albisini & Gambino [1993] 2 J.Int. P. 73; Schoenblum [1994] 1 J.Int. P. 5; Hayton [1994] J.Int. P. 23; Dicey & Morris, Chap.29; Hayton in Borras (ed.) *Liber Amicorum Georges Droz* (1996). The Convention has been ratified (*i.e.* implemented) by Italy, Malta, Australia, Netherlands, Luxembourg, Canada (for Alberta, New Brunswick, British Columbia, Newfoundland, Prince Edward Island, Manitoba, Saskatchewan) and the United Kingdom (including Isle of Man, Jersey, Guernsey, Gibraltar, Bermuda, Hong Kong, British Virgin Islands, Turks & Caicos, Montserrat, but not Cayman Islands). The Swiss have announced their intention to ratify in 2005, while the French are seriously considering ratifying in 2006 after establishing a French fiduciary concept filed in the Senate by Senator Philippe Marini on February 8, 2005.

CHAPTER I—SCOPE

Article 1

This Convention specifies the law applicable to trusts and governs their recognition. **13–28**

Article 2

For the purposes of this Convention, the term "trust" refers to the legal relation-ships created—*inter vivos* or on death—by a person, the settlor, when assets have been placed under the control of a trustee for the benefit of a beneficiary or for a specified purpose.

A trust has the following characteristics—

(*a*) the assets constitute a separate fund and are not a part of the trustee's own estate;
(*b*) title to the trust assets stands in the name of the trustee or in the name of another person on behalf of the trustee;
(*c*) the trustee has the power and the duty, in respect of which he is accountable, to manage, employ or dispose of the assets in accordance with the terms of the trust and the special duties imposed upon him by law.

The reservation by the settlor of certain rights and powers and the fact that the trustee may himself have rights as a beneficiary, are not necessarily inconsistent with the existence of a trust.

Article 3

The Convention applies only to trusts created voluntarily and evidenced in writing. **13–29**

Article 4

The Convention does not apply to preliminary issues relating to the validity of wills or of other acts by virtue of which assets are transferred to the trustee.

Article 5

The Convention does not apply to the extent that the law specified by Chapter II does not provide for trusts or the category of trusts involved.

CHAPTER II—APPLICABLE LAW

Article 6

A trust shall be governed by the law chosen by the settlor. The choice must be **13–30** express or be implied in the terms of the instrument creating or the writing evidencing the trust, interpreted, if necessary, in the light of circumstances of the case.

Where the law chosen under the previous paragraph does not provide for trusts or the category of trust involved, the choice shall not be effective and the law specified in Art.7 shall apply.

Article 7

Where no applicable law has been chosen, a trust shall be governed by the law with which it is most closely connected.

In ascertaining the law with which a trust is most closely connected reference shall be made in particular to—

(*a*) the place of administration of the trust designated by the settlor;
(*b*) the situs of the assets of the trust;
(*c*) the place of residence or business of the trustee;
(*d*) the objects of the trust and the places where they are to be fulfilled.

Article 8

13–31   The law specified by Art.6 or 7 shall govern the validity of the trust, its construction, its effects, and the administration of the trust. In particular that law shall govern—

(*a*) the appointment, resignation and removal of trustees, the capacity to act as a trustee, and the devolution of the office or trustee;
(*b*) the rights and duties of trustees among themselves;
(*c*) the right of trustees to delegate in whole or in part the discharge of their duties or the exercise of their powers;
(*d*) the power of trustees to administer or to dispose of trust assets, to create security interests in the trust assets, or to acquire new assets;
(*e*) the powers of investment of trustees;
(*f*) restrictions upon the duration of the trust, and upon the power to accumulate the income of the trust;
(*g*) the relationships between the trustees and the beneficiaries including the personal liability of the trustees to the beneficiaries;
(*h*) the variation or termination of the trust;
(*i*) the distribution of the trust assets;
(*j*) the duty of trustees to account for their administration.

Article 9

In applying this Chapter a severable aspect of the trust, particularly matters of administration, may be governed by a different law.

Article 10

The law applicable to the validity of the trust shall determine whether that law or the law governing the severable aspect of the trust may be replaced by another law.

CHAPTER III—RECOGNITION

Article 11

13–32   A trust created in accordance with the law specified by the preceding Chapter shall be recognized as a trust. Such recognition shall imply, as a minimum, that the trust property constitutes a separate fund, that the trustee may sue and be sued in his capacity as trustee, and that he may appear or act in this capacity before a notary or any person acting in an official capacity.

In so far as the law applicable to a trust requires or provides, such recognition shall imply, in particular—

(*a*) that personal creditors of the trustee shall have no recourse against the trust assets;

(*b*) that the trust assets shall not form part of the trustee's estate upon his insolvency or bankruptcy;
(*c*) that the trust assets shall not form part of the matrimonial property of the trustee or his spouse nor part of the trustee's estate upon his death;
(*d*) that the trust assets may be recovered when the trustee, in breach of trust, has mingled trust assets with his own property or has alienated trust assets. However, the rights and obligations of any third party holder of the assets shall remain subject to the law determined by the choice of law rules of the forum.

Article 12

Where the trustee desires to register assets, movable or immovable, or documents **13–33** of title to them, he shall be entitled, in so far as this is not prohibited by or inconsistent with the law of the State where registration is sought, to do so in his capacity as trustee or in such other way that the existence of the trust is disclosed.

Article 13

No State shall be bound to recognize a trust the significant elements of which, except for the choice of the applicable law, the place of administration and the habitual residence of the trustee, are more closely connected with States which do not have the institution of the trust or the category of trust involved.

Article 14

The Convention shall not prevent the application of rules of law more favourable to the recognition of trusts.

CHAPTER IV-GENERAL CLAUSES

Article 15

The Convention does not prevent the application of provisions of the law **13–34** designated by the conflicts rules of the forum, in so far as those provisions cannot be derogated from by voluntary act, relating in particular to the following matters—

(*a*) the protection of minors and incapable parties;
(*b*) the personal and proprietary effects of marriage;
(*c*) succession rights, testate and intestate, especially the indefeasible shares of spouses and relatives;
(*d*) the transfer of title to property and security interests in property;
(*e*) the protection of creditors in matters of insolvency;
(*f*) the protection, in other respects, of third parties acting in good faith.

If recognition of a trust is prevented by application of the preceding paragraph, the court shall try to give effect to the objects of the trust by other means.

Article 16

The Convention does not prevent the application of those provisions of the law of **13–35** the forum which must be applied even to international situations, irrespective of rules of conflict of laws.
    If another State has a sufficiently close connection with a case then, in exceptional circumstances, effect may also be given to rules of that State which have the same character as mentioned in the preceding paragraph.

Any Contracting State may, by way of reservation, declare that it will not apply the second paragraph of this article.

Article 17

In the Convention the word "law" means the rules of law in force in a State other than its rules of conflict of laws.

Article 18

The provisions of the Convention may be disregarded when their application would be manifestly incompatible with public policy (*ordre public*).

Article 19

Nothing in the Convention shall prejudice the powers of States in fiscal matters.

Article 20

13–36 Any Contracting State may, at any time, declare that the provisions of the Convention will be extended to trusts declared by judicial decisions.

This declaration shall be notified to the Ministry of Foreign Affairs of the Kingdom of the Netherlands and will come into effect on the day when this notification is received.

Article 31 is applicable to the withdrawal of this declaration in the same way as it applies to a denunciation of the Convention.

Article 21

Any Contracting State may reserve the right to apply the provisions of Chapter III only to trusts the validity of which is governed by the law of a Contracting State.

Article 22

13–37 The Convention applies to trusts regardless of the date on which they were created.

However, a Contracting State may reserve the right not to apply the Convention to trusts created before the date on which, in relation to that State, the Convention enters into force.

Article 23

For the purpose of identifying the law applicable under the Convention, where a State comprises several territorial units each of which has its own rules of law in respect of trusts, any reference to the law of that State is to be construed as referring to the law in force in the territorial unit in question.

CHELLARAM v CHELLARAM

Chancery Division [1985] 1 All E.R. 1043; [1985] Ch. 409

13–38 SCOTT J.: "The bedrock of counsel for the defendants' case is that these two settlements are foreign settlements, the proper law of which is the law of India. Counsel for the plaintiffs contends, on the contrary, that the proper law is the law of England.

"It is important to be clear at the outset as to the relevance of this issue on the present application. The application seeks to prevent the plaintiffs from prosecuting in England a claim for the removal of the trustees and for the appointment of new trustees. Counsel for the defendants argues that the law by which the proposition that the trustees should be removed must be tested, and by which the question of who should be appointed in their places must be answered, is the proper law of the settlement. Counsel for the plaintiffs submits, however, that it is not the proper law of the settlement but the law of the place of administration that should govern such issues as removal of trustees and appointment of new ones. The place of administration, he submits, is London.

"The proper law of the settlement is, *per* Lord Greene M.R. in *Duke of Marlborough v A.-G. (No. 1)* [1945] Ch. 78 at 83, the law which governs the settlement. He went on:

"This law can only be the law by reference to which the settlement was made and which was intended by the parties to govern their rights and liabilities."

In Dicey and Morris on the *Conflict of Laws* (10th ed., 1980), p.678, r. 120 states:

"The validity, the interpretation and the effect of an *inter vivos* trust of movables are governed by its proper law, that is, in the absence of any express or implied selection of the proper law by the settlor, the system of law with which the trust has its closest and most real connection."

"When counsel for the defendants first opened the case to me, I was strongly **13–39** inclined to regard the law of India as the obvious proper law of these two settlements, but as argument progressed I found myself progressively less certain. The beneficiaries are an Indian family. The trustees were all Indian in origin although one or other may have held a British passport. The settlements were drawn up in Bombay by Mr. Advani, an Indian practitioner, acting apparently in the course of his profession. The settlors were Indian in origin and Indian-domiciled at the date of the settlement. All these factors point, and I think point strongly, to the law of India being the proper law.[76]

"Mr. Advani has sworn an affirmation in which he has stated in terms that he intended Indian law to apply to these settlements which he drafted. This evidence is inadmissible as evidence of the intentions of the parties to the settlements, but I may, I think, take it as indicating that the settlements are appropriate in form for the purposes of Indian law. Nevertheless, I am left with doubts. The trust property was Bermudian. The underlying assets, in the form of the operating companies, were all situated outside India. The purpose of the settlements was, it seems, in part to escape Indian taxation and, in part, to escape Indian exchange control regulations. But most important of all, it seems to me, is the identity of the three original trustees. Two, Mr. Rupchand and Mr. Bharwani, were permanently resident in England. The third, Ram Chellaram, was the member of the family who, in 1975, appeared to have the closest connection with England. The inference is inescapable that the parties to the settlements contemplated that administration thereof would take place in London. Indeed, counsel for the defendants accepted that this was an inference which was open to be drawn.

"The question why, if the parties intended the settlements to be governed by **13–40** Indian law they should have arranged for an English administration, is a difficult one to answer. The parties' contemplation of an English administration seems to me

---

[76] As was later the view of Lawrence Collins J. in *Chellaram v Chellaram (No.2)* [2002] 3 All E.R. 17, paras 165–167.

to point strongly in favour of an English proper law. For the moment, however, I propose to leave the question open and to assume that counsel for the defendants is right that the law of India is the proper law of the settlement and to see where that leads. It leads, counsel for the defendants submitted, to the conclusion that the English courts should have nothing to do with the plaintiffs' claim for the removal of the trustees. You cannot have, he said, English courts removing foreign trustees of foreign settlements any more than you can have foreign courts removing English trustees of English settlements. Tied up in this *cri de coeur* are, in my view, three separate points. First, there is the question of jurisdiction. Does an English court have jurisdiction to entertain such a claim? Second, there is the question of power. If an English court does have jurisdiction, can it make an effective order removing foreign trustees of foreign settlements? Third, there is the *forum conveniens* point. Is this an action which an English court ought to be trying?

13–41   "I start with jurisdiction. In a sense, there is no doubt at all but that the court has jurisdiction. Each of the defendants was either served personally or service was effected on Norton Rose Botterell & Roche who had authority to accept service. By reason of due service of the writ, the court has jurisdiction over each of the defendants in respect of each of the issues raised by the writ.

"As to subject matter, also there is in my judgment no doubt that the court has jurisdiction. In *Ewing v Orr Ewing* (1883) 9 App.Cas. 34 it was held by the House of Lords that the English courts had jurisdiction to administer the trusts of the will of a testator who died domiciled in Scotland. The will was proved in Scotland by executors, some of whom resided in Scotland and some in England. The assets, the subject of the trusts, consisted mainly of hereditable and personal property in Scotland. An infant beneficiary resident in England brought an action in England for the administration of the trusts of the will by the English courts. It was clear that the proper law of the trusts was the law of Scotland. None the less, the House of Lords, affirming the Court of Appeal, upheld the jurisdiction of the English courts. The Earl of Selborne L.C. said (at 40–41):

13–42   "... the jurisdiction of the English Court is established upon elementary principles. The Courts of Equity in England are, and always have been, Courts of conscience, operating *in personam* and not *in rem*; and in exercise of this personal jurisdiction that have always been accustomed to compel the performance of contracts and trusts as to subjects which were not either locally or *ratione domicilii* within their jurisdiction. They have done so as to land, in Scotland, in Ireland, in the Colonies, in foreign countries. ... A jurisdiction against trustees, which is not excluded *ratione legis rei sitae* as to land, cannot be excluded as to movables, because the author of the trust may have had a foreign domicil; and for this purpose it makes no difference whether the trust is constituted *inter vivos*, or by a will, or *mortis causâ* deed."

Lord Blackburn agreed (at 46):

"The jurisdiction of the Court of Chancery is *in personam*. It acts upon the person whom it finds within its jurisdiction and compels him to perform the duty which he owes to the plaintiff."

          . . .

13–43   Current authority establishes that the court does have a discretion to decline jurisdiction on *forum non conveniens* grounds. But the principle that the English court has jurisdiction to administer the trusts of foreign settlements remains unshaken. The jurisdiction is *in personam*, is exercised against the trustees on whom the foreign trust obligations lie, and is exercised so as to enforce against the trustees the obligations which bind their conscience.

"The jurisdiction which I hold the court enjoys embraces, in my view, jurisdiction to remove trustees and appoint new ones. In *Letterstedt v Broers* (1884) 9 App.Cas. 371 at 385–386, Lord Blackburn referred to a passage in Story's *Equity Jurisprudence* (12th ed., 1877), section 1289, which reads:

'. . . Courts of equity have no difficulty in interposing to remove trustees who have abused their trust . . .'

Lord Blackburn then continued:

'It seems to their Lordships that the jurisdiction which a Court of Equity has no difficulty in exercising under the circumstances indicated by Story is merely ancillary to its principal duty, to see that the trusts are properly executed.'

Accordingly, in my judgment, the courts of this country, having jurisdiction to administer the trusts of the two settlements, have jurisdiction ancillary thereto to remove the trustees.

"The argument of counsel for the defendants that the court did not have **13–44** jurisdiction to remove the trustees of a foreign settlement was based in part on the proposition that an order of removal would be ineffective to divest the present trustees of the fiduciary duties they owed under the proper law of the settlements. To some extent, this submission was based on the form of the relief sought in paragraph 4 of the writ. It seeks:

'An order removing the defendants as trustees of Mohan's Settlement and Harish's Settlement and appointing some fit and proper persons to be trustees in their place.'

An order in that form would not of itself, however, divest existing trustees and vest trust property in new trustees. Consequently, such an order would usually be accompanied by a vesting order under section 44 (in the case of land) section 51 (in the case of stocks and shares) of the Trustee Act 1925. It could not, in my opinion, sensibly be suggested (and counsel for the plaintiffs has not suggested) that a vesting order under section 51 could divest the defendants of the trust shares in the Bermudan holding companies or could vest those shares in new trustees. A vesting effect could be achieved by a vesting order only in respect of stocks and shares situated within the territorial jurisdiction of the court. Further, so long as the trust shares remain vested in the defendant trustees, their fiduciary obligations in respect thereof must remain. So, counsel for the defendants submitted, the court lacks the power to grant relief sought by paragraph 4 of the writ.

"This argument is, in my judgment, based on a point of form and not of **13–45** substance. The jurisdiction of the court to administer trusts, to which the jurisdiction to remove trustees and appoint new ones is ancillary, is an *in personam* jurisdiction. In the exercise of it, the court will inquire what personal obligations are binding on the trustees and will enforce those obligations. If the obligations are owed in respect of trust assets abroad, the enforcement will be, and can only be, by *in personam* orders made against the trustees. The trustees can be ordered to pay, to sell, to buy, to invest, whatever may be necessary to give effect to the rights of the beneficiaries, which are binding on them. If the court is satisfied that, in order to give effect to or to protect the rights of the beneficiaries, the trustees ought to be replaced by others, I can see no reason in principle why the court should not make *in personam* orders against the trustees requiring them to resign and to vest the trust assets in the new trustees. The power of the court to remove trustees and to appoint new ones, owes its origin to an inherent jurisdiction and not to statute, and it must follow that the court has power to make such *in personam* orders as may be necessary to achieve the vesting of the trust assets in the new trustees. This is so, in my judgment, whether or not the trust assets are situated in England, and whether or not the proper law of the trusts in question is English law. It requires only that the individual trustee should be subject to the jurisdiction of the English courts. It does not matter, in my view, whether they have become subject to the jurisdiction by reason of service of process in England or because they have submitted to the jurisdiction, or because under R.S.C., Ord. 11 the court has assumed jurisdiction.[77] In every case, orders *in personam* are made by the courts on the footing that those against whom they are made will obey them.

13–46   "Accordingly, and for these reasons, I do not accept counsel for the defendants' submission that the English courts have no power to remove the defendants as trustees of these two settlements. Since, however, such removal would have to be effected by *in personam* orders, the plaintiffs have put before me an amended statement of claim which seeks such orders. In my judgment, the court would have power, if it thought it right to do so, to make those orders.

"There are two other associated points which I should now deal with. As an adjunct to his submission that the English courts lack the power to remove trustees of foreign settlements, counsel for the defendants submitted that if such an order in the *in personam* form were made the defendants could not safely obey the order without first obtaining confirmation from the Indian courts that it would be proper for them to do so. Further, he submitted, his clients ought not to be subjected to such an order unless it were clear that Indian law would regard them, if they did obey, as discharged from their fiduciary obligations under the settlement.

13–47   "It would be a matter entirely for the defendants and their advisers what steps they take in the Indian courts, but for my part I am not impressed by the proposition that such confirmation would be necessary. The English courts have jurisdiction over these defendants. An objection to the exercise of jurisdiction on *forum conveniens* grounds has been taken and I must deal with it, but, if in the end the case continues in England, I would expect that the Indian courts, for reasons of comity would afford the same respect to orders of this court as in like circumstances and for the same reasons English courts would afford to theirs.

"Counsel for the defendants suggested to me that I would give short shrift to an order of a foreign court removing a trustee of an English trust; but if the English trustee had been subject to the jurisdiction of the foreign court exercised in like circumstances to those in which English courts claim and exercise jurisdiction, I can see no reason why I should recoil from an order *in personam* made by the foreign court against an English trustee. And if the order had been given effect to by, for example, the trustee transferring trust assets in England into the names of new trustees, I see no reason why an English court should question the efficacy of the transfer. All of this assumes, of course, that there were no vitiating features in the manner in which the foreign order was obtained.

13–48   "As to the point that the defendants might, notwithstanding that they had transferred the Bermudan shares to new trustees, still owe fiduciary duties under the settlements, there is, in my view, no substance to that point. Firstly, no party to the

---

[77] Now see Civil Procedure Rule 6.20(11) to (15).

English action could so contend. Mohan and Lachmibai Chellaram are not parties to the action but could easily be joined, as also could any of the sisters who wished to be joined. This does not therefore seem to me to be a practical problem. Secondly, the point could be raised as a defence to the plaintiffs' claim for the removal of trustees, and, if the court were satisfied that the point was a sound one, I cannot imagine that the defendants would be ordered to transfer the shares. Thirdly, the status of trustee and the burden of the fiduciary obligations arising therefrom have, as it seems to me, no reality except in relation to assets which are vested in or under the control of the trustee. If a trustee is divested of the trust assets, I do not understand how it can be supposed that he can retain any fiduciary obligation thereafter in respect of those assets or in respect of the income derived from them.

"I do not, therefore, think, there is anything in counsel for the defendants' **13–49** objections to the efficacy of the *in personam* orders, if such orders were made.

"I have dealt with counsel for the defendants' submission on jurisdiction and on the power of an English court to make the orders sought on the footing that Indian law is the proper law of the settlements. As an adjunct to his arguments on those matters, counsel for the defendants submitted that, if Indian law was the proper law of the settlements, then Indian law was the system of law which ought to be applied to the matter of removal of trustees of the settlements and to the appointment of new ones. He drew my attention to the relevant provisions of the Indian Trusts Act 1882, as amended up to 1969, and commented, rightly in my opinion, that the various provisions in that Act relevant to the removal and appointment of trustees by the Indian court could not be applied by an English court in the present case.

"Counsel for the defendants wielded this point as part of his argument on **13–50** jurisdiction and also as relevant to his *forum conveniens* point. Counsel for the plaintiffs has contended that the proper law of the settlement is English law but he has submitted that, even if that is wrong, England is the place where the trusts were intended to be administered and the place where, in fact, the trusts have been administered, that the administration of a trust is governed not by the proper law of the trust but by the law of the place where administration takes place, and that the removal of trustees and the appointment of new ones is a matter of administration. It is a feature of the history of these settlements that there has been remarkably little administration. The reason for this is that the trust property has been represented simply by shares in Bermudan holding companies, and no trust income has been derived therefrom. Until recently, when in response to the plaintiffs' demand trust accounts were prepared, there were no such accounts. However, counsel for the plaintiffs is, in my view, right in pointing out that such administration as there has been has taken place in London. It was in London that the deeds of retirement and appointment of new trustees were prepared and executed; such legal advice as has been taken by the trustees seems to have been taken by Mr. Advani from Norton Rose Botterell & Roche in London, and there seems to me to be no room for any real doubt that the parties to the settlement contemplated that the administration would take place in London.

"Accordingly, in my judgment, the factual basis on which counsel for the plaintiffs **13–51** makes his submission is sound. As to law, counsel for the plaintiffs relies on the proposition stated in *Dicey and Morris*, p.683, r. 121 that:

> 'The administration of a trust is governed (*semble*) by the law of its place of administration.'

Among the matters classified in the notes to rule 121 as matters of administration is "the question who can appoint a trustee and what persons may be so appointed." If this rule correctly states the law, it would seem to follow that the issue regarding removal of the trustees of these settlements should be governed by the law of the place of administration of the settlements. However, the tentative manner in which the rule is expressed is justified, in my view, by the lack of clear authority provided by the cases cited in the footnotes.

"There are two categories of case which must be distinguished from cases as the present case. Firstly, there are cases which establish that the administrative powers conferred on personal representatives by the Administration of Estates Act 1925 can be exercised by English personal representatives in relation to assets in England, whether or not the deceased died domiciled in England (see *Re Wilks*, [1935] Ch. 645). These cases exemplify the well-settled proposition that the administration of a deceased's assets is governed by the law of the country from which the administrator derives his authority.

13–52   "Secondly, there are cases which support the view that the provisions of English trust legislation apply to trust property situated in England whether or not the trusts on which the trust property is held are the trusts of foreign settlements: see *Re Kehr (decd.), Martin v Foges* [1952] Ch. 26, although Danckwerts J. doubted 'whether trustees constituted by the law of a foreign country would have the powers conferred on trustees regulated by English law' (see [1952] Ch. 26 at 30); see also *Re Ker's Settlement Trusts* [1963] Ch. 553. But neither of these lines of cases supports the proposition in *Dicey and Morris*, r. 121 when applied to a foreign settlement which is being administered in England but where the trust property is not in England.

"More cogent support is provided by *Re Pollak's Estate* [1937] T.P.D. 91. In that case the testator was domiciled in the Transvaal. He left movables in England and in South Africa as well as in other countries. By his will he appointed as his executor and trustee an English bank which had no branch in South Africa and left his residuary estate on trust for beneficiaries, the majority of whom were domiciled in England. A number of questions were raised for the decision of the Transvaal court, including a question as to the law which should determine the rights and duties of the bank as trustee in the execution of the testamentary trust. Since the testator was domiciled in the Transvaal, South African law governed the construction of the will, but the court concluded that the testator had intended the trust to be administered in England, and Davis J., with whose judgment Greenberg J. concurred, said (at 101):

'I have no doubt that in appointing an English bank . . . to administer a trust fund wherein the great majority of the persons interested were at the time domiciled in England, the testator . . . intended English law to govern.'

13–53   He cited with approval this passage in the American Law Institute's Restatement of the Law of Conflict of Laws (see [1937] T.P.D. 91 at 101–102):

'If the testator appoints as trustee a trust company of another state, presumptively his intention is that the trust should be administered in the latter state; the trust will therefore be administered according to the law of the latter state.'

Accordingly, the court held that the rights and duties of the bank as trustee were to be governed by English law, notwithstanding that the essential validity of the trust and the construction of the will were governed by the law of South Africa, the domicile of the testator. The reasoning which led the Transvaal court to this decision I respectfully accept. The court concluded that the testator in establishing a settlement to be administered in England must have intended English law to govern its administration. The court gave effect to that intention. But it does not follow from *Re Pollak's Estate* that the law of the place of the administration of a trust would govern the rights and duties of the trustee in a case where the circumstances did not enable the inference to be drawn that such was the testator's or settlor's intention. *Re Pollak's Estate* was a case of testamentary trust. It is well-established English law that the essential validity of a testamentary trust of movables is governed by the law of the testator's domicile. But there is no reason why a testator should not by will establish a trust to be governed by some law other than the law of his domicile. His ability to create the trust may be subject to the law of his domicile but subject thereto he is, in my view, as able by will to make a foreign settlement as he is able to do so *inter vivos*. *Re Pollak's Estate* supports the proposition that a testator can do so. It does not, in my view, support anything further and does not really support rule 121.

"As a matter of principle, I find myself unable to accept the distinction drawn by **13–54** rules 120 and 121 in *Dicey and Morris* between 'validity, interpretation and effect' on the one hand and 'administration' on the other hand.[78] The rights and duties of trustees, for example, may be regarded as matters of administration but they also concern the effect of the settlement. The rights of the trustees are enjoyed as against the beneficiaries; the duties of the trustees are owed to the beneficiaries. If the rights of the beneficiaries are to be ascertained by applying the proper law of the settlement, I do not understand how the duties of the trustees can be ascertained by applying a different law, and vice versa. In my judgment, a conclusion that the law of the place of administration of a settlement governs such matters as the rights and duties of the trustees can only be right if that law is the proper law governing the settlement.

"But the right of beneficiaries to have trustees removed and new ones appointed is a right of a rather special nature. It is not, at least in the usual case, a right conferred by the settlement. If it were the case that a settlement conferred on particular beneficiaries or on a particular person such as the settlor the right to remove trustees and appoint new ones, that right (like any other rights conferred by the settlement on beneficiaries or trustees) would, in my view, require to be given effect in accordance with the proper law of the settlement. That would, in my view, be so, regardless of where the settlement was being administered. But no such right is conferred by the two settlements with which I am concerned.

"The plaintiffs' claim for the removal of trustees and the appointment of new **13–55** ones is, in this case, as in most cases, not an attempt to enforce a corresponding right conferred by the settlements, but is an appeal to the inherent jurisdiction of the court to which Lord Blackburn referred in *Letterstedt v Broers* (1884) 9 App.Cas. 371 at 385–386. The function of English courts in trust litigation is to enforce or protect the rights of the beneficiaries which bind the conscience of the trustee defendants. The identification and extent of those rights is a matter for the proper law of the settlement, but the manner of enforcement is, in my view, a matter of machinery which depends on the powers enjoyed by the English courts. Among the powers available to English courts is the power to order the removal of trustees and the appointment of new ones. This power is, in my view, machinery which, under English domestic law, can be exercised by English courts where necessary in order

---

[78] Dicey & Morris, *Conflict of Laws* now reads, "The validity, construction, effects and administration of a trust are governed by the law chosen by the settlor, or, in the absence of any such choice, by the law with which the trust is most closely connected."

to enable the rights of beneficiaries to be enforced or protected. The exercise of the domestic power does not, in my view, depend on whether the rights of the beneficiaries are enjoyed under domestic settlements or foreign settlements, or on whether the trust property is situated in England or abroad. The locality of the trust property will, however, determine whether the removal can be achieved by an *in rem* order or whether an *in personam* order is appropriate. Accordingly, except where rights conferred by the settlement are under consideration, the removal of trustees and the appointment of new ones are not, in my judgment, a matter to be governed by the proper law of the settlement. Nor, in my opinion, is it a matter governed by the law of the place where the administration of the settlement has taken place. It is, in my judgment, a matter to be governed by the law of the country whose courts have assumed jurisdiction to administer the trusts of the settlement in question.

13–56   "In the view of the matter I take, therefore, I do not think that the identification of the proper law of the settlement is a critical issue on this application. Any court before which the plaintiffs' case is litigated will have to consider the rights of the beneficiaries under these discretionary settlements in order to form an opinion whether the enforcement or protection of those rights requires the removal of the present trustees but no one has suggested that the nature of those rights is going to be different if tested under Indian law than if tested under English law. Any such difference is likely to be marginal only and to be immaterial for the purposes of the plaintiffs' claim for the removal of the trustees.

"It is, therefore, not necessary for me to decide on this application whether Indian law or English law is the proper law of the settlements. I am dealing with an interlocutory application. The relevant evidence has not been tested by cross-examination. In these circumstances, I would, I think, be unwise to express a conclusion on the proper law question and I do not do so.

13–57   "I have held, contrary to counsel for the defendants' submission, that the English courts have both jurisdiction and power to deal with the plaintiffs' claim for the removal of trustees and for the appointment of new ones. In that event, counsel for the defendants submits that the court ought nevertheless to decline to exercise that jurisdiction on the ground, shortly stated, that there is another competent jurisdiction, India, in which justice can be done between the parties, and that by comparison with India, England is a *forum non conveniens* . . .

"In my judgment, the defendants have failed to cast England as a *forum non conveniens*. It is settled on authority that the onus lies on the defendants to satisfy me that I ought, in my discretion, to grant a stay. They have not done so, and I therefore refuse a stay and dismiss their application." *Application dismissed*.

QUESTIONS

13–58   1. S, an Italian national domiciled in Italy but resident in England, visits Dublin in 1975 and pays 100 Irish punts to A and B as Dublin resident trustees on specified trusts which confer on the trustees a power to accumulate income for 100 years or, if later, until the expiry of 20 years from the death of the last survivor of all the descendants of Queen Elizabeth II living at the date of his trust instrument which expressly makes Irish law govern the trust (so the accumulation power is valid).

On his return to his London residence S has £1 million transferred to A and B in Dublin who then use it to purchase shares in English companies for £500,000 and an English house for £500,000. A month later S transfers English company shares worth £1 million to A and B as well as two Italian restaurants in London worth £1 million.

A beneficiary claims that the trustees can no longer exercise their power of accumulation in respect of income from the above assets. Advise the trustees.

Would your advice differ if S had stayed in London and paid £100 to London resident trustees, though still creating such an extensive power of accumulation and expressly choosing Irish law to govern the trust and subsequently transferring the above assets to such English trustees? Is it significant that the United Kingdom Government has let Turks & Caicos Islands (and Cayman for STAR trusts) abolish the rule against perpetuities and accumulations and did not extend *The Thellusson Act* 1800 to Ireland when part of the United Kingdom, while also accepting (though not yet implementing) a Law Commission Report recommending abolition of the rule against accommodations?

S died recently, and his widow and two children who are Italian nationals claim to have the trust set aside *pro tanto* to satisfy their reserved shares for three quarters of his estate, which under Italian law includes capital given away in the deceased's lifetime. Advise the trustees.

2. "In the light of *Pullan v Koe* [1913] 1 Ch. 9 and *RZB v Five Star LLC* [2001] 3 All E.R. 257, trustees need to check whether property about to be transferred to them is not subject to a foreign matrimonial community of property regime because the settlor's spouse (if not a party to such transfer) may well have a proprietary interest in such property." Discuss.

Chapter 14

EQUITABLE REMEDIES

Section 1. Equitable and Common Law Remedies

14–01 In this chapter we shall consider the following equitable remedies: injunctions; specific performance; damages awarded in addition to, or in lieu of, injunctions and specific performance; rescission; and rectification.[1] Equitable remedies are those which, historically, were granted by the courts exercising an exclusive equitable jurisdiction prior to the fusion of the courts by the Judicature Acts 1873–5. It is a controversial issue whether it desirable to fence equitable remedies off and treat them separately from common law remedies as though the two had no connection with one another, retaining and emphasising the differences which existed between them prior to fusion of the court system.

14–02 On one view,[2] this is desirable because equitable remedies possess unique characteristics, most notably that they are discretionary, and are subject to discretionary defences. In this, they are said to differ from common law remedies which may be claimed as of right on proof of a wrong known to the law (with or without proof of consequent loss, depending on the cause of action). Equitable remedies are also said to possess the distinctive feature that their effect is to force a defendant, through the threat of punishment or otherwise, to comply with his legal obligations *in kind*.[3] So, for example, a defendant who is made the subject of injunctive relief or a decree of specific performance may not leave his primary contractual or tortious obligations unfulfilled, and may not choose to fulfil the "secondary" obligation to pay damages which arises on breach of a primary duty of performance, as he is able to do at common law. In equity he must, on pain of punishment, act or refrain from acting in the manner specified in the court order. Indeed, even if he chooses to take the punishment rather than act as he should, the court may simply by-pass him and in an appropriate case empower someone else to do the act instead.[4] On this view of the law, it makes sense to consider equitable remedies alongside one another, because this enables us to gain a better understanding of their common features.

---

[1] Others include declarations; cancellation and delivery up of documents; and discovery, now called disclosure, being the process whereby a party to a suit is obliged to divulge the existence of documentation relevant to the issues in the claim.

[2] *Meagher, Gummow, and Lehane's Equity: Doctrines and Remedies*, 4th ed. (2002) paras [2-270]–[2-320].

[3] *In specie* in Latin, from which root the term "specific performance" derived.

[4] For example, it is possible for the court to order that a conveyance or transfer of the defendant's land which he has promised to convey to the claimant be executed by someone other than the defendant if he will not execute it himself.

On another view,[5] it is misleading to distinguish equitable and common   **14–03**
law remedies on the ground that the former are discretionary and the latter
are not, given that both are granted and withheld in line with clearly
established rules and principles. Granted that some of these principles
allow the courts a wide discretion when exercising their equitable jurisdiction, the same can also be said of certain common law principles (*e.g.* the
rules limiting the award of compensatory damages, and the rules authorising the award of punitive damages). Moreover, it is untrue that the
common law lacks the means to compel the performance of primary
obligations, for this is the function of the award of an agreed sum in
contract cases.

More profoundly, it is said to diminish our understanding of the law to   **14–04**
consider equitable and common law remedies separately, because this
obscures the full range of the courts' remedial armoury in the law of
obligations, and it disguises the similarities which exist between some
equitable and common law remedies, *e.g.* an account of profits in equity
and an order that the defendant account for and pay over a sum of money
made pursuant to an action for unjust enrichment at common law. Granted
that there are some differences between equitable and common law
remedies (*e.g.* common law damages, in contrast to equitable damages
awarded in lieu of an injunction, cannot be awarded in response to an
anticipated wrong), "nothing would be lost, and some simplicity and
rationality would be gained, if one took the small steps necessary to move
to a fully-fused system of remedies where it would be unnecessary to use
the labels common law and equitable."[6] On this, second, view of the law,
the discussion which follows in this chapter would serve a better purpose if
it appeared alongside a discussion of common law remedies in books on
contract, tort, unjust enrichment, and remedies.

Section 2. Injunctions

(1) Definition and classification

An injunction is an order of the court forbidding the initiation or the   **14–05**
continuance of some act or state of affairs or commanding that an act be
done.[7] An injunction may therefore be *prohibitory* or *mandatory* and the
distinction, as in the case of positive and negative covenants in regard to
land, is one of substance not form[8]: while an order of the court requiring
the demolition of a house wrongfully erected could be framed as an order
not to leave it standing, the order would nonetheless be mandatory. A tell-
tale sign is that mandatory injunctions normally require some expenditure

---

[5] A. Burrows, *Fusing Common Law and Equity: Remedies, Restitution and Reform* (Hochelaga Lecture,
2002) pp.1–26; A. Burrows, "We Do This at Common Law But That in Equity" (2002) 22 O.J.L.S. 1. *Cf.*
S. Worthington *Equity* (2003), chap. 2; J. Edelman, "A 'Fusion Fallacy' Fallacy?" (2003) 119 L.Q.R. 375.

[6] A. Burrows, *Remedies for Torts and Breach of Contract* 3rd ed. (2004) pp.11–12.

[7] An exception to this definition appears to be the order of prohibition in judicial review proceedings.

[8] *Truckell v Stock* [1957] 1 W.L.R. 161.

on the part of the defendant. In addition, whereas the execution of prohibitory injunctions generally needs no supervision (the defendant simply has to refrain from committing the prohibited act), the execution of a mandatory order may do so *e.g.* in the case of an order to demolish a house in a particular manner.

(2) Distinguished from specific performance

14–06 *Positive* contractual obligations of certain kinds are normally enforced, in equity, by orders for specific performance[9] rather than mandatory injunctions.[10] What is the point of insisting on this difference? Does it really matter to a claimant or defendant whether the claimant obtains a mandatory injunction or a decree of specific performance? In terms of enforcement, it could not seriously matter for both remedies are enforced in the same way: in the case of an individual defendant, by imprisonment,[11] fine, or sequestration of assets (or any combination of these) and in the case of a corporation (whose officers may, additionally, be punished in their individual capacities), by fine or sequestration of assets or both.[12] Yet, it *does* matter which a claimant is required to apply for because, as will be seen, the number of grounds on which a decree for specific performance may be refused is considerably greater than the number of grounds on which a final injunction may be refused. And this appears to be for a justifiable reason: by contract an individual may either, by negative stipulation, put himself under disabilities that he does not have under the general law (apart from the contract) or, by positive stipulation, impose on himself obligations which he does not have under the general law (apart from the contract). In the former case, he is merely restricting his freedom to act, which restriction can, within limits, be enforced by a prohibitory injunction without imposing burdens on him over and above those which the general law imposes. But in the latter case, when the defendant has (albeit freely and for valuable consideration) taken upon himself the burden of doing something which the general law does not require him to do, a court of equity will be astute to enquire into the justice of making him do *in kind* that which he has promised. In particular, it will want to be certain that, for example, the claimant is ready, willing and able to perform the obligations which *he* has undertaken pursuant to the contract; it will want to ensure, moreover, that there is "mutuality" between the parties[13] and so on. When a defendant is required, at the behest of a claimant, to do more than the

---

[9] See section 3 below.
[10] *Evans v B.B.C. and I.B.A., The Times*, February 26, 1974 provides an exception to this rule. Additionally, the injunction granted was interloculory.
[11] Contempt of Court Act 1981, s.14(1) considered by Laddie J. in *Re Swaptronics Ltd, The Times*, August 17, 1998, and by Thorpe L.J. in *Harris v Harris (No.2)* [2002] 1 F.L.R. 248.
[12] Rules of the Supreme Court, Orders 45 and 52, as incorporated into the Civil Procedure Rules 1998. On the court's inherent power, see *Webster v Southwark L.B.C.* [1983] Q.B. 698.
[13] See below, para.14–143.

law generally requires of him, a court of conscience will test the justice of the claimant's claim more keenly than otherwise.[14]

Moreover, it is often said that, unlike the case with mandatory injunctions, no decree of specific performance will lie on an interim (formerly referred to as "interlocutory") basis (*i.e.* pending trial). If true, it would matter very much whether a claimant's claim were for a mandatory injunction or a decree of specific performance for, in the first case he might obtain interim relief but in the second could not. The case of *Sky Petroleum Ltd v VIP Petroleum Ltd*,[15] however, tends to blur the distinction and, moreover, suggests that it is not true that specific performance will not lie on an interim basis. There, the claimant applied for an interlocutory prohibitory injunction restraining the defendant from failing to supply it with petrol, which failure was allegedly in breach of contract. Goulding J. treated the motion as one for an interlocutory decree of specific performance, looking at the substance rather than the form, and granted it.

14–07

(3) Perpetual or interim

All injunctions may be classified, in addition, as either *interim*[16] or *perpetual*.[17] Interim injunctions are those granted pending the final resolution of an issue between the parties or some earlier specified event[18] and the courts have developed a special approach to the granting of them, quite different from those applicable to perpetual injunctions.[19] It will be convenient to consider the principles on which perpetual injunctions are granted first. Before doing so, however, three other general points may usefully be made about the jurisdiction to grant injunctions.

14–08

(4) The statutory basis of the modern jurisdiction

The equitable and therefore discretionary nature of the jurisdiction to grant injunctions does not absolve a claimant from the requirement to show some legal or equitable cause of action, despite the wording of s.37(1) of the Supreme Court Act 1981 which provides:

14–09

---

[14] It might be objected that some negative contractual obligations (*e.g.* not to build on land) can only be enforced by mandatory injunctions (*e.g.* where the building has gone up and the only way of satisfactorily remedying the wrong is to require it to be pulled down) and, yet, here, the plaintiff will not be required to satisfy the requirements which he would have had to satisfy on an application for specific performance of a positive contractual stipulation. Is the distinction morally defensible? It is suggested that it is: in this case, the defendant has not taken upon himself any burden over and above that imposed by the law. The burden which will be imposed on him by requiring him to demolish the building is both self-inflicted *and* the consequence of his own wrong-doing. It would be odd to allow him to plead that wrong in his own defence. In contrary fashion, the burden which is imposed on a defendant who has promised to do something *positive* is, of course, self-inflicted but not the result of wrong-doing and if a claimant promisee claims a remedy which will achieve more perfect justice than an award of damages (*i.e.* a decree of specific performance), then his moral entitlement to more justice than the law normally affords can legitimately be tested.

[15] [1974] 1 W.L.R. 576.

[16] Formerly *interlocutory*.

[17] Also termed "permanent" and "final". Although "perpetual" is the preferred terminology under the Civil Procedure Rules, it is potentially misleading in that the injunction might not, on its terms, be intended to have perpetual effect at all. Indeed, all that is meant is that the injunction granted is finally decisive of the issue between the parties. The actual order granted, for example, in the case of a one year restrictive covenant being enforced against a former employee, will endure only for one year.

[18] Such as the disposal of an appeal against the dismissal of a motion seeking interim relief pending trial. The grant of an injunction in such case is purely so that, should the appeal against the substantive refusal succeed, an order made on appeal will not be in vain.

[19] See below, para.14–26.

"The High Court[20] may by order (whether interlocutory or final) grant an injunction . . . in all cases in which it appears to the court to be just and convenient to do so."

The case of *Normid Housing Association Ltd v Ralphs*[21] illustrates this point. There, an injunction was refused to the claimants who were suing their architects, the defendants, for negligence. The defendants, as would be expected, had professional insurance. The insurers, however, were desirous of settling whatever claim the defendants might have against them. The sum which the insurers offered the defendants was less than the sum claimed by the claimants from the defendants. When the claimants discovered this, they sought an injunction preventing the defendants from accepting the insurers' offer. They failed because the defendants owed no legal duty to the claimants to insure at all, let alone for any particular sum.

(5) The quia timet jurisdiction

14–10 Second, the foregoing principle has not prevented the issuing of injunctions *quia timet*.[22] Equity, achieving more perfect justice than the common law (which was limited to the award of damages to make good injury which had already occurred), acted to restrain *future* wrongs. Indeed, all (perpetual) prohibitory injunctions achieve as much, in that, although normally sought only where there has been an actual wrong done, they ensure, so far as any court order can, that the wrong will not be repeated, thus rendering unnecessary a multiplicity of suits. It was only one step from that to hold that a threatened future wrong should be restrained before it had occurred.[23] However, "mere vague apprehension is not sufficient to support an action for a *quia timet* injunction. There must be an immediate threat to do something".[24] Nor is it sufficient, in order to obtain an injunction *quia timet* against a defendant, to show that he would *technically* be a joint tortfeasor with another defendant if the latter were not restrained: one

---

[20] By the County Courts Act 1984, section 38 (as substituted by the Courts and Legal Services Act 1990, section 3), the County Court may make any order within its jurisdiction that could be made by the High Court except those of a "prescribed kind", *i.e.* specified under regulations made by the Lord Chancellor. To date, such regulations have been made in the County Court Remedies Regulations 1991 where, by regulation 2, *Anton Piller* (now called "search") orders and *Mareva* (now called "freezing") injunctions are prescribed *except* in (i) family proceedings, (ii) for the purpose of preserving property forming the subject matter of proceedings or (iii) in aid of execution of county court orders or judgments for the purpose of preserving assets until execution.

[21] [1989] 1 Lloyd's Rep. 265. See also *Day v Brownrigg* (1878) 10 Ch.D. 294. The principle appears to be subject to two exceptions: the jurisdiction of the High Court (1) to restrain the prosecution or defence of proceedings in a lower court or in another country and (2), when proceedings are on foot to resolve a dispute, to grant an order to protect or further the functioning of the tribunal. One academic has argued, against the judicial trend, for the concept of the entirely autonomous injunction: A.M. Tettenborn, "Injunctions without Damages" (1987) 38 N.I. Legal Q. 118.

[22] Literally, "because (the claimant) fears".

[23] *Quia timet* injunctions can also be awarded to prevent a defendant's imminent unjust enrichment at a claimant's expense: C. Mitchell, *The Law of Contribution and Reimbursement* (2003), paras 14–38 to 14–45; *Padden v Arbuthnot Pensions & Investments Ltd* [2004] EWCA Civ 582.

[24] *Per* Lord Buckmaster in *Graigola Merthyr Co. Ltd v Swansea Corporation* [1929] A.C. 344 at 353. See too *Morris v Redland Bricks Ltd* [1970] A.C. 652; *Hooper v Rogers* [1975] Ch. 43; *British Telecommunications plc v One In A Million Ltd* [1999] 1 W.L.R. 903 (where D was said to have equipped himself with "the instruments of fraud" by registering internet domain names).

must go further in such cases and show an inclination to join in the threatened act. Thus an injunction was issued in anticipation of a threatened wrong (the erection of a car wash) against a lessee but not against his freeholder who, despite being a technical joint tortfeasor, showed no inclination to join in the act.[25]

(6) In personam or in rem

The fact that the jurisdiction is equitable means that, in theory, the order of **14–11** the court operates *in personam* rather than *in rem*. These Latin tags refer to a traditional distinction between rights against *particular* persons (such as arise under contracts) and rights against persons *generally* (such as arise in ownership). Historically, the Chancellor acted to perfect the injustices of the operation of the common law, administered in the King's courts, not by changing any substantive rule of law but, rather, by requiring a legal rightholder not to enforce his right. The Chancellor's method of securing compliance was to threaten imprisonment. The jurisdiction, therefore, was said to be solely *in personam*: directed against particular persons. However the modern trust, which is descended from the practice of the Chancellors who would regularly require a legal owner to hold property for the benefit and enjoyment of another, is a good example of how blurred the distinction between personal and property rights can become: no-one nowadays would seriously defend the thesis that a beneficiary's rights under a trust are merely personal rights.[26] Far from it, the reason that a beneficiary's rights prevail over the rights of a trustee's creditors where the trustee becomes insolvent is precisely that the beneficiary's rights in the trust property are rights of ownership. It is necessary to treat with caution, therefore, statements that the equitable jurisdiction is purely personal.

In relation to the equitable jurisdiction to issue injunctions a similar **14–12** blurring of the traditional distinction may also be seen. In practice, injunctions may operate against people to whom they are not immediately directed, for example, as in *Att.-Gen. v Newspaper Publishing Plc*[27] where it was said that "if C's conduct, in knowingly doing acts which would, if done by B, be a breach of the injunction against [B], results in impedance to or intereference with the administration of justice by the court in the action between A and B, then, so far as the question of C's conduct being a contempt of court is concerned, it cannot make any difference whether such

---

[25] *Celsteel Ltd v Alton House Holdings Ltd* [1986] 1 W.L.R. 512. Given that breach of an injunction could expose a defendant to severe penalties this sort of limitation on the availability of the remedy is not a merely technical requirement.

[26] Although personal accountability of the trustee to the beneficiary is the hallmark of the trust and part of the "irreducible core content" of *trusteeship: Armitage v Nurse* [1998] Ch. 241 *per* Millett L.J. This does not preclude, however, the idea that as against the rest of the world, the beneficiary's rights are *in rem*. For further discussion, see P. Matthews, "From Obligation to Property, and Back Again?" in D.J. Hayton (ed.) *Extending the Boundaries of Trusts and Similar Ring-Fenced Funds* (2002), 203, L.D. Smith, *Unravelling Proprietary Restitution* (2004) C.B.L.J. 317.

[27] [1988] Ch. 333 and *sub nom. Att.-Gen. v Times Newspaper Ltd* [1992] 1 A.C. 191. See also *Jockey Club v Buffham* [2003] 2 W.L.R. 178; *Att.-Gen. v Punch Ltd* [2003] 1 A.C. 1046. And for general discussion, see P. Devonshire, "Freezing Orders, Disappearing Assets and the Problem of Enjoining Non-Parties" (2002) 118 L.Q.R. 124.

conduct takes the form of aiding and abetting B on the one hand or acting solely of his own volition on the other"[28] Thus anyone *with notice*[29] of an injunction directed at another may independently contemn the court and will do so, for example, where "the subject matter of the action[30] is such that, if it is destroyed in whole or in part before the trial of the action, the purpose of the action will be wholly or partly nullified".[31]

(7) General equitable principles governing the grant of final injunctions

(i) Adequacy of common law remedies

14–13   Equity had no cause to supplement an existing legal remedy which was adequate and it came to be a requirement of the first order that before any equitable remedy would lie, the legal remedy be shown to be inadequate—a matter to be determined having regard to the nature of the injury (whether it is assessable in monetary terms), the prospect of its being repeated (when, otherwise, a multiplicity of suits would be necessary) and, to a lesser extent, the ability of a defendant to satisfy an award of damages. In *Beswick v Beswick*,[32] a case on specific performance, D had promised P to pay a weekly sum of £5 to P's widow for the rest of her life. When D indicated that he would not do so, P's estate succeeded in an application for specific performance of the agreement. One of the reasons why it succeeded was the fact that damages for D's breach would be nominal (on the principle that neither P nor his estate suffered any loss: that fell on his impoverished widow). That, it was felt, would be an inadequate remedy in a situation which, morally, cried out for something more to be done. Another reason given in that case to justify the award of a decree was that as the obligation to pay the weekly sum was a continuing one of indefinite duration, P's estate would have to institute a multiplicity of suits—on a weekly basis!—in order to obtain justice. A decree would obviously constitute a more adequate remedy.

14–14   There is, moreover, something to be said for the view that the nominal nature of damages is taken into account quite routinely outside contractual cases: in tort, the fact that even a relatively trivial threatened trespass, may be restrained by injunction[33] suggests that this is so. Were it otherwise the law would be seen to tolerate serious inroads into the notion of ownership (*i.e.* with quiet enjoyment) of real property. But, still, it might plausibly be said that the court's willingness to grant injunctive relief in such situations is dependent not so much on the cause of action (distinguishing between

---

[28] [1992] 1 A.C. 103 *per* Lord Brandon.
[29] Knowledge is, of course, the touchstone of (personal) equitable liability: see Lord Browne-Wilkinson in *Westeutsche Landesbank Girozentrale v Islington B.C.* [1996] A.C. 669 at 709.
[30] In that case, the confidential nature of certain information.
[31] [1992] 1 A.C. at 104.
[32] [1968] A.C. 58. See, further, the discussion of this case in section 4 at para.14–252. It is clear that the same principle governs the grant of injunctions, as in *e.g. The Sea Hawk* [1968] 1 Lloyd's Rep. 317: *The Angelic Grace* [1995] 1 Lloyd's Rep. 87 at 96, *per* Millett L.J.
[33] *Woollerton and Wilson Ltd v Richard Costain Ltd* [1970] 1 W.L.R. 411. But note *Jaggard v Sawyer* [1995] 1 W.L.R. 269, below at para.14–254.

contract and tort, for example) as on the fact that in these cases the wrong is *threatened* (*i.e.* future rather than present or past) and this allows the *quia timet* jurisdiction to be invoked. It is a curious feature of this jurisdiction that the "inadequacy of damages" requirement seems to diminish to vanishing point: if a promisor is either honest or silly enough to announce, in advance of the time for performance of his obligations, that he does not intend to fulfil them then, on the promisee's application, a court of equity will have no hesitation in giving him an added reason (threat of contempt proceedings) to do as he promised. And this appears to be the case even if the promise is one which, if breached, would cause loss which could be easily assessed in damages.

(ii) Equity will not act in vain

This principle (or "maxim" of equity), like the last, is common to specific **14–15** performance.[34] The idea is that if issuing an injunction would be futile, no injunction will be issued. In *Wookey v Wookey*,[35] a family case, it was said that where there was evidence that an order would not be complied with and that nothing would be done about the non-compliance in judicial terms (because the subject of the order would, on account of youth, not be imprisoned and, on account of impecuniosity, not be fined) then the order should not be made. This is perhaps an extreme application of the principle but can be defended. More regular applications of the principle are to be found in cases where it would be *impossible* for the defendant to comply with the order (because, for example, in a case where a mandatory injunction was sought requiring him to tear down a building, he no longer owned the land and had no right to tear down any building upon it) or, as in the *Spycatcher* litigation,[36] where a final injunction was refused against a newspaper preventing it from publishing certain information. Although that information was initially confidential it had already been published in a book that had become widely available in the United Kingdom.

(iii) Delay and acquiescence

The requirement that one who seeks equitable relief must do so without **14–16** delay, even within the statutory limitation period (the doctrine of laches[37]) is often factually indistinguishable from the doctrine of acquiescence whereby knowing failure to object to a wrong may give rise to an inability to resurrect an objection to it at a later date. The cases on delay diverge on the question whether *mere* delay (*i.e.* unaccompanied by acquiescence) will bar the grant of relief.[38] As to acquiescence, the test is whether the plaintiff represented that he would no longer enforce his rights.[39]

---

[34] See section 3, at para.14–141.
[35] [1991] Fam. 121.
[36] See *Att.-Gen. v Observer Ltd* [1990] 1 A.C. 109.
[37] Pronounced "lay-cheese".
[38] *Fullwood v Fullwood* (1878) 9 Ch.D. 176, *per* Fry J., no.; *H.P. Bulmer Ltd & Showerings Ltd v J. Bollinger S.A.* [1977] 2 C.M.L.R. 625: only if "inordinate", *per* Goff L.J.
[39] *Allen v Veranne Builders Ltd* [1988] E.G.C.S. 2.

14–17   An example of how acquiescence may operate to bar not just equitable but *any* relief is to be found in *Gafford v Graham*.[40] There, the defendant was in breach of a restrictive covenant which prevented him from converting his bungalow or extending his barn without the claimant's consent. He breached the covenant in 1986 but, as the Court of Appeal said, "the [claimant] made no complaint until his solicitor wrote to the defendant about three years after the acts complained of", despite full knowledge of the breaches. At first instance, the judge had awarded the claimant damages in respect of the conversion and extension. The Court of Appeal, however, held that his acquiescence was a bar not just to equitable relief but *all* relief and discharged the order for damages. It held that, in all the circumstances, it would be unconscionable for the claimant to enforce the (legal) rights which he undoubtedly had in 1986. This, notwithstanding that the claimant's action was begun well within the limitation period. The case is an example (closely related to proprietary estoppel) of how equity can operate to *extinguish* accrued legal rights. Not all cases in which equitable relief is refused, however, are so draconian: normally, a claimant's delay will, if it has any effect, merely serve to deprive him of his (presumably more adequate) *equitable* remedy. His legal rights (and the remedies he has in respect of infringements thereof) remain, in the absence of something like an estoppel, intact.

14–18   But even a claimant who, knowing of a threatened or incipient wrong, begins proceedings for an injunction timeously must weigh carefully the decision whether or not at an early stage of the action to seek interim injunctive relief: *Jaggard v Sawyer*[41] shows how the very possibility of obtaining perpetual injunctive relief may turn on that decision (the court awarded damages in lieu), though it may be contrasted with *Mortimer v Bailey*[42] where the claimants' delay in seeking an interim injunction did not prevent them from obtaining a perpetual injunction, given the speed with which they had begun their proceedings.

(iv) Clean hands

14–19 A claimant who has behaved improperly may be denied equitable relief, although the "clean hands" principle will not be triggered where the claimant's conduct is morally shabby but legally unimpeachable.[43] There must also exist a close connection between the impropriety of the claimant's behaviour and the relief which he seeks: "Equity does not demand that its suitors shall have led blameless lives",[44] and mere general depravity is not enough in itself to deny a claimant relief.[45] Thus, in *Grobelaar v News Group Newspapers Ltd*.[46] the House of Lords granted the claimant footballer an injunction restraining the defendant newspaper from repeating its

---

[40] [1995] 3 E.G.L.R. 75.
[41] [1995] 1 W.L.R. 269 and below, at para.14–254.
[42] [2005] 2 E.G. 102.
[43] *Dering v Earl of Winchelsea* (1787) 1 Cox Eq. Cas. 318; *Loosley v N.U.T.* [1988] I.R.L.R. 157; *Lonhro plc v Fayed (No.5)* [1993] 1 W.L.R. 1489.
[44] *Loughran v Loughran* (1934) 292 U.S. 216 at 292. *per* Brandeis J.
[45] *Meyers v Casey* (1913) 17 C.L.R. 90: *A.-G. v Equiticorp Industries Group Ltd* [1996] 1 N.Z.L.R. 528.
[46] [2002] 1 W.L.R. 3024.

unproven allegation that he had thrown football matches, even though he had been proven to have taken bribes, to have told his co-conspirator that he had thrown matches in exchange for the bribe money, and to have lied about this in court.

Further discussion of this requirement, also common to specific perfor- **14–20** mance, is to be found in section 3.[47] It is accepted that a claimant who has himself defaulted on a contract cannot obtain injunctive relief to enforce any of its terms.[48] That is an application, in the field of contract, of the clean hands maxim. It is, however, a different requirement from the similar doctrine that he who comes to equity must do equity, which looks not to whether the claimant's hands are already soiled by wrong-doing, but rather to the future question whether the claimant is prepared to fulfil his outstanding obligations.[49] In applications for specific performance, this translates into a requirement that the claimant demonstrate that he is "ready, willing and able" to perform his side of the bargain. Both requirements are morally defensible in that, by seeking an equitable remedy over and above the legal one to which he is entitled, a claimant must appeal to a court of conscience. He cannot do so if his is not clear.

(v) No undue hardship

Interim and mandatory injunctions in particular provide scope for an **14–21** argument that an injunction ought to be refused as a matter of discretion on the ground of hardship to the defendant. In the former case, this is so because, by definition, the claimant has not yet established his right to any relief (because there has not yet been a trial) and in the latter because often, as was suggested above, what is distinctive of a mandatory injunction is that compliance will involve the defendant in expenditure which may be out of all proportion to the benefit which the claimant will derive from the grant of an injunction.

Some cases which sought to circumvent hardship to the defendant by **14–22** granting an injunction but suspending its operation for a period[50] are now suspect in light of the decision in *Jaggard v Sawyer*[51] where that practice was specifically disapproved. The jurisdiction to award damages in lieu of an injunction, now contained in s.50 of the Supreme Court Act 1981 (which jurisdiction was analysed closely in that case), is a statutory recognition of the fact that sometimes the award of an injunction (particularly a manda-tory one requiring, for example, the demolition of a building) can be oppressive to a defendant. By giving courts of equity the power to award damages in lieu, Parliament made it easier to justify declining to grant injunctions in such cases. But the practice of doing so existed prior to the

---

[47] at para.14–150.
[48] *Measures Bros. Ltd v Measures* [1910] 2 Ch. 248.
[49] Although Lord Denning M.R. appears to have confused the doctrines in *Shell (U.K.) Ltd v Lostock Garage Ltd* [1976] 1 W.L.R. 1187.
[50] e.g. *Woollerton and Wilson Ltd v Richard Costain Ltd* [1970] 1 W.L.R. 411. See also Lane L.J.'s proposed solution to the problem raised in *Miller v Jackson* [1977] Q.B. 966.
[51] [1995] 1 W.L.R. 269, and below, at para.14–254.

statutory provision where undue hardship would have resulted. A claimant would, in those circumstances, be confined to his legal remedy of damages. The innovation of the provision (first introduced by Lord Cairns in 1858) was that where the injunction had been sought to restrain *future* wrongs, for which common law damages could not be awarded, a plaintiff would not be put out of court without *any* remedy: he might be given damages instead.

(vi) The public interest

14–23 Although in specific performance cases the notion has long been accepted that public considerations might affect the availability of equitable remedies in contract[52] (in which branch of the law, more generally, it is well accepted that private individuals cannot create rights and duties for each other which contravene public policy), the matter is more controversial as regards those torts which create a perimeter of inviolability around the notion of private ownership of land. In *Miller v Jackson*[53] Lord Denning M.R. opined *obiter* that if the defendants in that case had committed the tort of nuisance (he held to the contrary), then an injunction should have been refused on the ground that the public interest in (i) protecting the environment achieved by the preservation of playing fields and (ii) enabling youth to enjoy the benefits of outdoor games prevailed over the private interest in securing the privacy of home and garden without the intrusion or interference caused by cricket balls hit out of the defendants' neighbouring cricket ground. That aspect of the decision was disavowed by a later Court of Appeal in *Kennaway v Thompson*,[54] which held that the public interest in motor-boat racing could not prevail over the private right of quiet enjoyment of the home.

14–24 More recently, in *Dennis v Ministry of Defence*,[55] Buckley J. declined to hold that the public importance of the defendant's activities in training fighter jet pilots prevented the claimant from suing in private nuisance in respect of the noise made by the jets flying over his house. However, the judge also held that the public interest did affect the question of remedy, and concluded that it would not be in the public interest to grant the claimant an injunction, although he would be entitled to damages. This was consistent with the result, if not with the reasoning in *Kennaway*, where the Court of Appeal did not order the claimant to desist from his activities altogether, but instead struck a balance between the parties by specifying the number of events that would henceforth be allowed, the number of boats which would be allowed to race, and the timing of the events.

14–25 It is suggested that the distinction which is drawn between tort and contract (or, indeed, between tort and trust) is defensible: both contract and trust are, at the most general level, facilitative institutions which allow individuals to write "local law", creating for themselves powers, disabilities,

---

[52] See, below, at para.14–142.
[53] [1977] Q.B. 966.
[54] [1981] Q.B. 88.
[55] [2003] 2 E.G.L.R. 121.

rights and obligations that do not otherwise exist. The danger that individuals might achieve or attempt to achieve undesirable purposes through these institutions has always been guarded against judicially in the doctrines which invalidate contracts and trusts on grounds of illegality and public policy. The law of tort (which comprises all the non-voluntary, non-statutory private law rules regulating behaviour) is itself a statement of public policy: the availability of an effective remedy for the unwelcome intrusion of cricket balls or over-flying jets upon the quiet enjoyment of one's home is merely an acknowledgement of the importance that is attached, as a matter of public policy, to such enjoyment. If there is some doubt about how much importance should be given to quiet enjoyment of home and garden it seems misleading to dress that up as a clash between public and private right: it is either a clash between two desirable public goals or between two desirable private goals. Either way, in the face of long-established authority, a judicial re-setting of the balance seems constitutionally inappropriate. With contract and trust, on the other hand, there is truly a potential clash between private right or obligation and public policy.

(8) Interim injunctions

(i) General principles

Unlike perpetual injunctions, where the lawyer finds himself considering **14–26** principles of equity, interim injunctions are granted or refused on grounds which have nothing to do, either historically or logically, with the maxims of equity. The principles on which the court acts, or has acted up to the introduction of the Civil Procedure Rules at least, are designed to achieve justice between the parties under circumstances of ignorance or uncertainty (*i.e.* when it is not known whether the claimant's claim is well founded). It must be cautioned at this stage, however, that both the Civil Procedure Rules and the Human Rights Act 1998 have an effect on the substance of these principles and it will be necessary to qualify what follows.[56]

In order to circumvent the necessity, at an early stage of an action, of **14–27** deciding disputed questions of fact or determining points of law with insufficient argument, the House of Lords laid down guidelines in *American Cyanamid Co. v Ethicon Ltd*[57] for the exercise of judicial discretion whether to grant an interim injunction. The House had previously held in *J.T. Stratford & Son Ltd v Lindley*[58] that a claimant had to show a prima facie case that he would succeed at trial in obtaining injunctive relief. The decision in *Cyanamid* is to the effect that a claimant need only show that he has a case that is not frivolous or vexatious and that there is a serious question to be tried. Once that is established, the question whether an

---

[56] See para.14–37 to 14–39.
[57] [1975] A.C. 396 and below at para.14–51.
[58] [1965] A.C. 269. *Cyanamid* has been said to be irreconcilable with this decision but as *Cyanamid* was the later case, that is the one the Court of Appeal should follow: *Hubbard v Pitt* [1976] Q.B. 142.

injunction should be granted turns on the balance of convenience, a much used shorthand phrase to describe the balancing exercise in which the court engages in order to minimize the risk of doing injustice.

14–28   That balancing exercise is undertaken as follows: once a serious question for trial is raised, unless there is no arguable defence to the claimant's claim (in which case an injunction should be granted until trial[59]), the court considers whether damages would be an adequate remedy for loss caused to the claimant by *not* granting an injunction pending trial. If so, *and* the defendant can afford to pay, then the balance favours no injunction. If the loss likely to be caused is not remediable in damages (either as a matter of legal principle or practice, *i.e.* the defendant could not pay them) then the court considers to what extent the claimant would be able to compensate the defendant for any loss caused to him by *granting* an injunction pending trial. (Thus making the claimant's relief conditional on the provision of what is called a cross-undertaking in damages.[60]) This has the result that if damages would not be an adequate remedy for the claimant (either as a matter of principle or practice) then *if* the defendant's potential loss is compensable, the balance favours an injunction. Where damages would be inadequate for both parties, however, (either as a matter of principle or practice) then injustice is best avoided by maintaining the *status quo*.[61] "Special factors" might properly be taken into account, but only as a last resort can the merits be examined and, even then, only if the strength of one case is disproportionate to the other.

14–29   Much judicial ink has been spilled over the relationship of these guidelines to instant cases and, in particular, on the question whether apparent exceptions to the *Cyanamid* approach are truly exceptions or merely different ways of striking the balance of convenience in instant cases. An instance of judicial divergence on that (rather semantic) issue is to be found in *Cambridge Nutrition Ltd v B.B.C.*[62] There certainly appear to

---

[59] Unless, with the defendant's consent, the hearing of the motion is treated as the trial of the action in which case a perpetual injunction will lie.

[60] This undertaking is extracted, if the injunction is granted, as a matter of course. Not, however, from the Crown when it is seeking to enforce the law (as opposed to its own proprietary or contractual rights): *Hoffman-La Roche (F.) & Co. v Secretary of State for Trade and Industry* [1975] A.C. 295. The same is true of (i) relator actions where an undertaking will be required of the relator but not of the Attorney-General and (ii) local authorities enforcing the law: *Kirkless B.C. v Wickes Building Supplies Ltd* [1992] 3 W.L.R 170. Where the Attorney-General is seeking to enforce a charitable trust as *parens patriae* the position is otherwise and public funds ought not to be risked (as proprietary rights are being asserted). Rather, if there were someone (such as a receiver of charitable property) to give an undertaking, it would be right to require an undertaking from that person (rather than the Attorney-General) limited to the funds available to the charity: *Att.-Gen. v Wright* [1988] 1 W.L.R. 164, Hoffmann J. The same judge, in *Oxy Electric Ltd v Zainuddin* [1991] 1 W.L.R. 115, doubted the decision of Sir Nicolas Browne-Wilkinson V.-C. in *Blue Town Investments Ltd v Higgs & Hill Plc.* [1990] 1 W.L.R. 696 to strike out a claim for final injunctive relief as vexatious unless the claimant was prepared to apply for interlocutory relief and offer the usual cross-undertaking. Requiring a claimat to put his money where his mouth is in this way underestimates what a claimant is risking in not applying for interlocutory relief (see *Jaggard v Sawyer* [1995] 1 W.L.R. 269) and, of course, as Hoffmann J. pointed out (at 120) with a rhetorical question, "Is a poor claimant's claim struck out when a rich claimant's claim would survive?"

[61] Which, in effect, means letting any alleged wrong already initiated continue and, in the case of *quia timet* relief, prohibiting the occurrence of any alleged wrong. See Lord Diplock in *Garden Cottage Foods Ltd v Milk Marketing Board* [1984] A.C. 130, 140.

[62] [1990] 3 All E.R. 523.

be categories of cases (whether *Cyanamid* "exceptions" or not) where the claimant has to show more than that his case is not frivolous or vexatious, raising merely a serious question to be tried. They are as follows.

(i) *trade disputes*: The Trade Union and Labour Relations (Consolida- **14–30** tion) Act 1992, s.221(2) provides that, on an application for an interlocutory injunction, where the defendant claims that he acted in contemplation or furtherance of a trade dispute, the court is to have regard to the likelihood of the defendant's establishing at the trial any of the matters which, under the Act, confer immunity from tortious liability.

(ii) *trial of action unlikely or delayed*: In *Cambridge Nutrition Ltd v* **14–31** *B.B.C.*[63] the claimants sought an injunction preventing the defendant from broadcasting a programme (in the making of which they had participated) until after the imminent publication of a government report on the claimant low calorie diet, the subject matter also of the programme. The programme, however, would have had no impact if broadcast after the publication of the report and, if an injunction were granted to trial, it would effectively prevent the broadcast for good. Clearly, if the *Cyanamid* principles are designed to achieve a fair resolution pending trial, others must be used to achieve such resolution where there is likely to be no trial. The court therefore looked at the merits of the claim and, finding the basis of it to be implausible (an oral agreement not to broadcast until after publication of the report—for which there was remarkably little evidence) declined to grant an injunction.

(iii) *no arguable defence*: This has already been mentioned in the **14–32** discussion above of *Cyanamid*.

(iv) *injunctions to restrain the presentation of winding-up petitions*: It has **14–33** been held since *Cyanamid* that the guidelines do not apply to an interlocutory injunction to restrain the bringing of other proceedings on the ground that these latter would be an abuse of the court's process: the grant of such injunction finally determines the matter.[64] So a claimant would fail unless he demonstrated not merely a serious issue whether the defendant's proceedings would be an abuse but, over and above that, that the defendant was bound to fail in those proceedings. In *Ward v Coulson Sanderson and Ward Ltd.*[65] the Court of Appeal followed that reasoning to hold that *Cyanamid* did not apply to injunctions to restrain the presentation of a winding-up petition by a creditor.

---

[63] [1990] 3 All E.R. 523. See also *Cayne v Global Natural Resources Plc.* [1984] 1 All E.R. 225.
[64] *Bryanston Finance v De Vries (No.2)* [1976] Ch. 63, per Stephenson L.J. and Sir John Pennycuick. Buckley L.J. concurred in refusing the injunction but purported to follow *Cyanamid*.
[65] [1986] P.C.C. 57.

14–34   (v) *mandatory interlocutory injunctions*: For the grant of a mandatory injunction on an interlocutory basis there must be a "high degree of assurance" that it will appear at trial that the injunction was rightly granted.[66]

14–35   In cases where the nature of the interlocutory relief sought requires that the defendant be taken by surprise, or where the relief sought is urgent, in that it must be granted right away, if it is to be granted at all, interim injunctions may be applied for without notice (formerly termed *ex parte*): *i.e.* in the absence of the party against whom the order is sought. An order can then be made, normally effective only over a short period, which will be reviewed at a hearing with notice to the other side at the end of that period (or at an earlier time if the defendant applies before the end of the period to have the order discharged). On applications without notice, applicants must fully and frankly disclose all the facts in their knowledge which are relevant to the exercise of the court's discretion, and this extends to disclosing possible defences which the defendant may have. Breach of this duty is a serious matter that will entitle (though not oblige) the court to discharge the injunction without more, and leave the applicant to apply again.[67]

14–36   The court's power to grant interim injunctions is not limited to forbidding actions which are inherently unlawful. Freezing orders[68] often restrain defendants from actions which are lawful in themselves (*e.g.* withdrawing money from a bank account); and in harassment cases, the courts have granted interim injunctions forbidding defendants to enter specified "exclusion zones", even though they have the same basic right as any other member of the public to use the public highway running through these zones.[69]

(ii)The effect of the Civil Procedure Rules ("CPR")

14–37   By virtue of section 2 of the Civil Procedure Act 1997 and the Civil Procedure Rules 1998,[70] all civil claims brought after April 25, 1999 fall to be dealt with according to the CPR. Based on a review of Civil Justice by Lord Woolf, the then Master of the Rolls, they were intended to effect a fundamental change in the administration of civil justice in this country. For present purposes, it is pertinent to note that the principles according to which the courts have, since *Cyanamid*, awarded interim relief, must now be

---

[66] *Shepherd Homes Ltd v Sandham* [1971] Ch. 340, Megarry J.; *Locabail International Finance Ltd v Agroexport* [1986] 1 W.L.R. 657, holding that Megarry J.'s approach was not affected by *Cyanamid* which it had preceded. Note, however, Hoffmann J. in *Films Rover International Ltd v Cannon Film Sales Ltd* [1987] 1 W.L.R. 670 observing that in exceptional cases where the risk of injustice was greater in not granting an injunction, the *Shepherd Homes* test need not be met.

[67] *Lloyd's Bowmaker Ltd v Britannia Arrow Holdings plc* [1988] 1 W.L.R. 1337 at 1343–1344. *per* Glidewell L.J.: *Memory Corporation Plc v Sidhu (No.2)* [2000] 1 W.L.R. 1443 at 1459, *per* Mummery L.J.: *Network Telecom (Europe) Ltd v Telephone Systems International Inc.* [2004] 1 All E.R. (Comm.) 418.

[68] See para.14–41.

[69] *e.g. Burris v Azadani* [1995] 1 W.L.R. 1372: *Dailchi Pharmaceuticals U.K. Ltd v S.H.A.C.* [2004] 1 W.L.R. 1503.

[70] SI 3132/1998.

read subject to the "overriding objective" of allowing the court (through, amongst other things, active "case management") to deal with cases justly. This may include taking steps to ensure that the parties are on an equal footing, saving expense, and dealing with a case in ways which are appropriate to the amount involved, the importance of the case, the complexity of the case and the financial situation of the parties. Some or all of these might well militate in favour of the approach boldly (and, it is suggested, sensibly) advocated by Laddie J in *Series 5 Software v Clark*[71] which cannot be interpreted as anything other than a first instance rejection of the *Cyanamid* approach.

(iii) The effect of the Human Rights Act 1998

The Human Rights Act 1998 most obviously affects the award of interim **14–38** injunctions through s.12(3), which imposes a special threshold test which must be satisfied before a court may grant an interim injunction which might affect the exercise of a defendant's right to freedom of expression under Art.10 of the European Convention. The section sets a higher threshold for the grant of interim injunctions against the news media than the *American Cyanamid* guideline of a "serious question to be tried" or a "real prospect of success" at the trial, as it provides that interim injunctions should not be granted "so as to restrain publication before trial unless the court is satisfied that the applicant is likely to establish that publication should not be allowed." In *Cream Holdings Ltd v Banerjee*[72] the House of Lords held that the word "likely" in s.12(3) will generally mean "more likely than not", although there are some cases where a lesser degree of likelihood may suffice: for example, "where the potential adverse consequences of the disclosure are particularly grave".[73] Applying this test, their Lordships concluded that the applicants were not entitled to an interim injunction preventing the disclosure of confidential information because the matters which the defendant newspaper wished to publish were of serious public interest, suggesting that the applicants' prospects of success at trial were insufficiently strong to justify an interim injunction.

In *Greene v Associated Newspapers Ltd*[74] the question arose whether the **14–39** *Cream Holdings* test also applies where an applicant seeks an interim injunction restraining the publication of material which is alleged to be defamatory. The Court of Appeal held that it does not, reasoning that defamation cases raise different issues from cases concerned with breach of confidence and breach of privacy,[75] given that confidentiality and privacy, once lost, are lost forever, unlike reputations which can be rebuilt. Defamation cases therefore continue to be governed by the rule in *Bonnard*

---

[71] [1996] All E.R. 853, below, at para.14–82.
[72] [2005] 1 A.C. 253. for a case where the s.12(13) threshold test was satisfied, see *Douglas V Hello! Ltd.*[2005] EWCA Civ 595 at [250]-[259], disapproving the earlier decision by a differently constituted C.A to lift the interim injunction granted by the judge at first instance: [2001] Q.B. 967.
[73] *ibid.* at [22], *per* Lord Nicholls.
[74] [2005] 1 All E.R. 30.
[75] *cf. Campbell v MGN Ltd* [2004] A.C. 457: *Re S (a child)* [2005] 1 F.L.R. 591.

v Perryman:[76] if a defendant in a libel action makes a statement verified as true in which he maintains that he can and will justify his alleged libel, then the claimant cannot have an interim injunction to restrain the publication of an allegedly defamatory statement unless it is plain that the plea of justification is bound to fail.

(9) Two special cases of interim injunction[77]

14–40   Both *Mareva* (now "freezing") injunctions and *Anton Piller* (now "search") orders are interim orders. As Lord Donaldson M.R. made plain in *Polly Peck International v Nadir (No. 2)*,[78] there is no question of *Cyanamid* applying to *Mareva* injunctions ". . . which proceed on principles quite different from those applicable to other interlocutory injunctions." The same is true of *Anton Piller* or search orders. Together they have been described by the same judge as the law's "nuclear weapons".[79]

(i) Freezing injunctions

14–41   Section 37 of the Supreme Court Act 1981 provides:

> "(1) The High Court may by order (whether interlocutory or final) grant an injunction or appoint a receiver in all cases in which it appears to the court to be just and convenient to do so . . .
>
> (3) The power of the High Court under subsection (1) to grant an interlocutory injunction restraining a party to any proceedings from removing from the jurisdiction of the High Court, or otherwise dealing with, assets located within that jurisdiction shall be exercisable in cases where that party is, as well as in cases where he is not, domiciled, resident or present within that jurisdiction."

14–42   This provision is now the statutory basis for the injunction that was first granted in *Nippon Yusen Kaisha v Karageorgis*[80] but which took its name from the second case of its grant, *Mareva Compania Naveira S.A. v International Bulkcarriers S.A.*[81] The criteria for obtaining a freezing injunction are: (1) a good arguable case[82]; (2) that there is a real risk that any judgment will go unsatisfied by reason of the disposal by the defendant of his assets, unless he is restrained by court order from disposing of them; and (3) it would be just and convenient in all the circumstances of the case to grant the relief sought.

14–43   On (1), it has been said that this amounts to a case "which is more than barely capable of serious argument, but not necessarily one which the judge considers would have a better than 50 per cent chance of success".[83] The

---

[76] [1891] 2 Ch. 269.
[77] See generally *Gee on Commercial Injunctions*, 5th edn. (2004).
[78] [1992] 4 All E.R. 769.
[79] *Bank Mellat v Nikpour* [1985] F.S.R. 87 at 91–92.
[80] [1975] 1 W.L.R. 1093.
[81] [1975] 2 Lloyd's Rep. 509.
[82] The court is bound therefore to consider the merits of the case.
[83] Per Mustill J. in *Ninemia Corporation v Trave Schiffahrtsgesellschaft GmbH (The "Niedersachsen")* [1983] 2 Lloyd's Rep. 600 at 605.

requirement in (2) is not that of "nefarious intent" (*i.e.* that the defendant will dissipate assets *so that* a judgment will be unsatisfied) but, rather an objective risk that there will be dissipation making it likely that the result of his dissipation will be that the judgment goes unsatisfied.[84] The requirement in (3) is no mere formula: it may be regarded as justifying the approach taken in *Polly Peck International v Nadir (No.2)* with regard to banks whose business, depending on the confidence of their investors, might be destroyed at a stroke: the claimant's cross-undertaking in damages would be of little consolation or utility.

It is important for third parties who, it has been seen, can contemn the **14–44** court if they have notice of the terms of an injunction with which they act inconsistently,[85] to know just what acts are prohibited by the order.[86]

The injunction is available both before and after judgment and may **14–45** restrict dealings with *all* assets of the defendant or merely assets up to a certain value (*i.e.* the value of the claimant's claim plus costs). However, it gives the claimant no right *in rem* or security or priority over the defendant's creditors (of which the claimant has not yet shown himself to be one).

Prior to the enactment of the Civil Jurisdiction and Judgments Act 1982, **14–46** there was no power in the High Court to grant a freezing injunction against a defendant who had assets in the jurisdiction but against whom there was no substantive claim subject to the jurisdiction, the claimant asserting no proprietary interest in the assets.[87] The Act, which gives effect to the Convention on Jurisdiction and the Enforcement of Judgments in Civil and Commercial Matters,[88] has been interpreted by the Court of Appeal[89] to provide that such injunction can be obtained in England before trial or

---

[84] In *Derby & Co. Ltd v Weldon* [1990] Ch. 48, the Court of Appeal rejected the subjective interpretation of the requirement even in the case of the wide ("draconian", per May L.J.) relief granted in that case. *A fortiori*, then, in a standard case.

[85] In the particular case of freezing injunctions, note Eveleigh L.J.'s comments in *Z Ltd v A-Z and AA-LL* [1982] Q.B. 558 at 583, but *cf. Z Bank v D* [1994] 1 Lloyd's Rep. 656.

[86] Third parties such as banks may also be liable for the tort of negligence if they break the terms of a freezing, *e.g.* by allowing withdrawals from a frozen bank account: *C & E Commissioners v Barclays Bank plc* [2005] 1 Lloyd's Rep. 165. Such an order is not appropriate in matrimonial cases: *Ghoth v Ghoth* [1992] 2 All E.R. 920. On the question whether a freezing injunction is available against property which appears to be jointly owned by the defendant and another, the standard form recognises that, in the case of bank accounts, moneys held to the account of the defendant are subject to the order whether held in the defendant's own name or jointly with some other party. In practice, in order to obtain such order, a claimant must be prepared to satisfy the court that the asset constituted by the chose in action would be available in execution of the claimant's judgment or for distribution in the defendant's bankruptcy. The claimant might show this by establishing a tracing claim to the "contents" of the account or by showing that the defendant is the sole beneficial owner of them. If he cannot, then the third party's share will be released to him. Where the joint property is land, the defendant's interest (under the statutory trust) may be the subject of an injunction and, after judgment, a charging order. If the court is satisfied that the property is owned in equity solely by the defendant it may grant relief against both the defendant and the co-owning third party: *S.S.F. v Masri* [1985] 1 W.L.R. 876.

[87] *Siskina (Owners of Cargo Lately Laden on Board) v Distos Compania Naveira S.A.* [1979] A.C. 210 although in *Mercedes-Benz A.G. v Leiduck* [1995] 3 All E.R. 929 at 946–950, Lord Nicholls considered the law should move on to allow "free-standing" freezing injunctions auxiliary to foreign proceedings and in 1999 the Privy Council gave leave for an appeal from the Bahamas to raise the point, but the appeal ultimately was not proceeded with.

[88] Set out in Sch. 1 to the Act. See para.14–112

[89] *Babanaft International Co. S.A. v Bassatne* [1990] Ch. 13. See also *Republic of Haiti v Duvalier* [1990] Q.B. 202; *Baltic Shipping Co. v Translink Shipping Ltd* [1995] 1 Lloyd's Rep. 673; *Bank of China v NBM LLC* [2002] 1 WLR 864.

after judgment even though the claimant has no cause of action, in England, against the defendant: so long as a court in another contracting state has jurisdiction, it suffices.

(ii) Search orders[90]

14–47 In *Anton Piller K.G. v Manufacturing Process*[91] the Court of Appeal approved the making of an order, in substance an interim mandatory injunction, requiring the defendants to allow the claimant's solicitors to enter the defendants' premises to inspect documents and remove them to the claimant's solicitors' custody. Failure to comply with the order is a contempt by the defendant and so, even though the order does not *entitle* the claimant to enter as if he had a search warrant, the defendant has good reason to allow him so to do. The order is made so as to safeguard vital evidence which is needed to prove the claim although it may be granted simply to obtain information necessary to safeguard the claimant's rights, to locate assets against which a judgment might be enforced and to preserve property which might otherwise be dissipated or destroyed.

14–48 Because of the truly draconian effect of an order of this sort which, to a greater extent than the freezing injunction, involves serious inroads into basic civil liberties,[92] it is now accepted that they are to be granted sparingly.[93] The three essential requirements (*per* Ormrod L.J in *Anton Piller*[94]) are (1) an extremely strong *prima facie* case; (2) the potential or actual damage to the claimant (if an order is not made) must be very serious; and (3) there must be clear evidence that the defendant has in his possession incriminating documents or things and that there is a real possibility that he may destroy such material before any application with notice can be made.[95] Even if all the conditions are met, the court still has to be satisfied that the need for the order outweighs the injustice of making an order against a defendant without his having been heard.[96] This has the

---

[90] The standard order now made, as with freezing injunctions, is provided for by CPR. Close scrutiny of its provisions (it was designed to be comprehensible to the lay reader) reveals much of what is judicially thought desirable in future practice and, by implication, undesirable in past practice. The jurisdiction has now been placed on a statutory footing by section 7 of the Civil Procedure Act 1997.

[91] [1976] Ch. 55. The first reported case of such order was in *E.M.I. v Pandit* [1975] 1 W.L.R. 302 (Templeman J.).

[92] *i.e.* the right to be heard before the making of an order against one (a feature which, in virtue of its essential *ex parte* nature, it shares with the freezing injunction), the right to be free from arbitrary search and seizure, and the right to privacy in one's own home (orders were commonly made against defendants to be executed at their places of residence).

[93] The frequency with which orders came to be granted (see Oliver L.J.'s reference to them as "very, very commonly employed" and "almost commonplace" in *Dunlop Holdings Ltd v Staravia Ltd* [1982] Com. L.R. 3) led to the expression of judicial concern in a number of cases about claimants' failures to demonstrate, and judicial failure to insist on demonstration, of the necessity of making an order (see Hoffmann J. in *Lock International plc. v Beswick* [1989] 1 W.L.R. 1268) and led to the establishment of a committee under Staughton L.J. which made recommendations (largely followed in the model orders which preceded the current model orders contained in CPR) on future practice.

[94] [1976] Ch. 55 at 62.

[95] The Staughton Committee added a fourth requirement (*cf.* Hoffmann J.'s view in *Lock International plc. v Beswick* [1989] 1 W.L.R. 1268) that the harm likely to be caused by the execution of the order to the defendant and his business affairs must not be excessive or out of proportion to the legitimate object of the order.

[96] This is no mere formula and is a more important element in the judicial balancing exercise in search order cases than in freezing injunction or other cases of applications without notice. This is for the reason that although interlocutory, once executed the order cannot be "unexecuted". There is often no sense in a defendant's bothering to discharge a search order at a hearing with notice to the other side once it has been executed (but see Hoffmann J. in *Lock International Plc v Beswick*, below, at para.14–117).

effect that an order will not be made against persons of good standing who are likely to obey an order of the court to deliver up.[97] *Emmanuel v Emmanuel*[98] makes it plain that in matrimonial proceedings an order will only be granted on strong evidence.

There is a common law principle enshrined in s.14(1) of the Civil **14-49** Evidence Act 1968 that no person may be obliged in civil proceedings to produce any document or thing which may incriminate him (or his spouse). There are two important exceptions to this, for present purposes, namely s.72 of the Supreme Court Act 1981[99] and s.31 of the Theft Act 1968.[1] *Emmanuel v Emmanuel*[2] clarifies, however, that an order may be made if the risk of incrimination extends only to a charge of perjury in the proceedings in the context of which the order is sought.

On the question of the court's jurisdiction to make orders in support of **14-50** actions other than those proceeding in an English court, the principle in *Siskina*[3] has been reversed to the extent that s.25 of the Civil Jurisdiction and Judgments Act 1982 applies to search orders. The limitation arises from the restriction of "interim relief" in subsection (7) (to which the section applies) to interim orders *other than* those making provision for "obtaining evidence". Clearly most search orders are intended to do just that. Those which seek merely to preserve assets in jeopardy, on the other hand, clearly are not and the *Siskina* principle will not apply to them.

AMERICAN CYANAMID v ETHICON LTD

House of Lords [1975] A.C. 396, [1975] 1 All E.R. 504.

LORD DIPLOCK: "In my view the grant of interlocutory injunctions in actions for **14-51** infringement of patents is governed by the same principles as in other actions. I turn to consider what those principles are.

"My Lords, when an application for an interlocutory injunction to restrain a **14-52** defendant from doing acts alleged to be in violation of the plaintiff's legal right is made upon contested facts, the decision whether or not to grant an interlocutory injunction has to be taken at a time when ex hypothesi the existence of the right or the violation of it, or both, is uncertain and will remain uncertain until final judgment is given in the action. It was to mitigate the risk of injustice to the plaintiff during the period before that uncertainty could be resolved that the practice arose of granting him relief by way of interlocutory injunction; but since the middle of the 19th century this has been made subject to his undertaking to pay damages to the defendant for any loss sustained by reason of the injunction if it should be held at the trial that the plaintiff had not been entitled to restrain the defendant from doing

---

[97] *e.g.* barristers and their clerks: *Randolph M Fields v Watts* (1985) 129 S.J. 67.
[98] [1982] 1 W.L.R. 669.
[99] Intellectual property cases. See para.14–107.
[1] Para. 14–106. Although, having regard to the decision in *Sociedade Nacionale de Combustiveis de Angola U.E.E. v Lundqvist* [1991] 2 Q.B. 310, which held that the section did not apply to charges of conspiracy under s.1 of the Criminal Law Act 1977, nor at common law, the practical effect of s.31 in commercial (non-intellectual property) cases will therefore be reduced: no search order may be granted where there is a real possibility of a conspiracy charge.
[2] [1982] 1 W.L.R. 669.
[3] *Siskina v Distos S.A.* [1979] A.C. 210. For section 25 see para.14–112.

what he was threatening to do. The object of the interlocutory injunction is to protect the plaintiff against injury by violation of his right for which he could not be adequately compensated in damages recoverable in the action if the uncertainty were resolved in his favour at the trial; but the plaintiff's need for such protection must be weighed against the corresponding need of the defendant to be protected against injury resulting from his having been prevented from exercising his own legal rights for which he could not be adequately compensated under the plaintiff's undertaking in damages if the uncertainty were resolved in the defendant's favour at the trial. The court must weigh one need against another and determine where 'the balance of convenience' lies.

14–53   "In those cases where the legal rights of the parties depend upon facts that are in dispute between them, the evidence available to the court at the hearing of the application for an interlocutory injunction is incomplete. It is given on affidavit and has not been tested by oral cross-examination. The purpose sought to be achieved by giving to the court discretion to grant such injunctions would be stultified if the discretion were clogged by a technical rule forbidding its exercise if upon that incomplete untested evidence the court evaluated the chances of the plaintiff's ultimate success in the action at 50 per cent or less, but permitting its exercise if the court evaluated his chances at more than 50 per cent.

14–54   "The notion that it is incumbent upon the court to undertake what is in effect a preliminary trial of the action upon evidential material different from that upon which the actual trial will be conducted, is, I think, of comparatively recent origin, though it can be supported by references in earlier cases to the need to show 'a probability that the plaintiffs are entitled to relief' (*Preston v Luck* (1884) 27 Ch.D. 497 at 506, *per* Cotton L.J.) or 'a strong prima facie case that the right which he seeks to protect in fact exists' (*Smith v Grigg Ltd* [1924] 1 K.B. 655 at 659, *per* Atkin L.J.). These are to be contrasted with expressions in other cases indicating a much less onerous criterion, such as the need to show that there is 'certainly a case to be tried' (*Jones v Pacaya Rubber and Produce Co. Ltd* [1911] 1 K.B. 455 at 457, *per* Buckley L.J.) which corresponds more closely with what judges generally treated as sufficient to justify their considering the balance of convenience upon applications for interlocutory injunctions, at any rate up to the time when I became a member of your Lordships' House . . .

14–55   "*Hubbard v Vosper* [1972] 2 Q.B. 84 was treated by Graham J. and the Court of Appeal in the instant appeal as leaving intact the supposed rule that the court is not entitled to take any account of the balance of convenience unless it has first been satisfied that if the case went to trial upon no other evidence than is before the court at the hearing of the application the plaintiff would be entitled to judgment for a permanent injunction in the same terms as the interlocutory injunction sought.

14–56   "Your Lordships should in my view take this opportunity of declaring that there is no such rule. The use of such expressions as 'a probability,' 'a prima facie case,' or 'a strong prima facie case' in the context of the exercise of a discretionary power to grant an interlocutory injunction leads to confusion as to the object sought to be achieved by this form of temporary relief. The court no doubt must be satisfied that the claim is not frivolous or vexatious; in other words, that there is a serious question to be tried.

14–57   "It is no part of the court's function at this stage of the litigation to try to resolve conflicts of evidence on affidavit as to facts on which the claims of either party may ultimately depend nor to decide difficult questions of law which call for detailed argument and mature considerations. These are matters to be dealt with at the trial. One of the reasons for the introduction of the practice of requiring an undertaking as to damages upon the grant of an interlocutory injunction was that 'it aided the court in doing that which was its great object, viz. abstaining from expressing any opinion upon the merits of the case until the hearing': *Walkefield v Duke of Buccleugh* (1865) 12 L.T. 628 629. So unless the material available to the court at the hearing of the application for an interlocutory injunction fails to disclose that the plaintiff has any real prospect of succeeding in his claim for a permanent injunction at the trial, the court should go on to consider whether the balance of convenience lies in favour of granting or refusing the interlocutory relief that is sought.

"As to that, the governing principle is that the court should first consider whether, **14–58** if the plaintiff were to succeed at the trial in establishing his right to a permanent injunction, he would be adequately compensated by an award of damages for the the loss he would have sustained as a result of the defendant's continuing to do what was sought to be enjoined between the time of the application and the time of the trial. If damages in the measure recoverable at common law would be adequate remedy and the defendant would be in a financial position to pay them, no interlocutory injunction should normally be granted, however strong the plaintiff's claim appeared to be at that stage. If, on the other hand, damages would not provide an adequate remedy for the plaintiff in the event of his succeeding at the trial, the court should then consider whether, on the contrary hypothesis that the defendant were to succeed at the trial in establishing his right to do that which was sought to be enjoined, he would be adequately compensated under the plaintiff's undertaking as to damages for the loss he would have sustained by being prevented from doing so between the time of the application and the time of the trial. If damages in the measure recoverable under such an undertaking would be an adequate remedy and the plaintiff would be in a financial position to pay them, there would be no reason upon this ground to refuse an interlocutory injunction.

"It is where there is doubt as to the adequacy of the respective remedies in **14–59** damages available to either party or to both, that the question of balance of convenience arises. It would be unwise to attempt even to list all the various matters which may need to be taken into consideration in deciding where the balance lies, let alone to suggest the relative weight to be attached to them. These will vary from case to case.

"Where other factors appear to be evenly balanced it is a counsel of prudence to **14–60** take such measures as are calculated to preserve the status quo. If the defendant is enjoined temporarily from doing something that he has not done before, the only effect of the interlocutory injunction in the event of his succeeding at the trial is to postpone the date at which he is able to embark upon a course of action which he has not previously found it necessary to undertake; whereas to interrupt him in the conduct of an established enterprise would cause much greater inconvenience to him since he would have to start again to establish it in the event of his succeeding at the trial.

"Save in the simplest cases, the decision to grant or to refuse an interlocutory **14–61** injunction will cause to whichever party is unsuccessful on the application some disadvantages which his ultimate success at the trial may show he ought to have been spared and the disadvantages may be such that the recovery of damages to which he would then be entitled either in the action or under the plaintiff's undertaking would not be sufficient to compensate him fully for all of them. The extent to which the disadvantages to each party would be incapable of being compensated in damages in the event of his succeeding at the trial is always a significant factor in assessing where the balance of convenience lies; and if the extent of the uncompensatable disadvantage to each party would not differ widely, it may not be improper to take into account in tipping the balance the relative strength of each party's case as revealed by the affidavit evidence adduced on the hearing of the application. This, however, should be done only where it is apparent upon the facts disclosed by evidence as to which there is no credible dispute that the strength of one party's case is disproportionate to that of the other party. The court is not justified in embarking upon anything resembling a trial of the action upon conflicting affidavits in order to evaluate the strength of either party's case.

14–62   "I would reiterate that, in addition to those to which I have referred, there may be many other special factors to be taken into consideration in the particular circumstances of individual cases. The instant appeal affords one example of this."

14–63   Viscount Dilhorne, Lord Cross of Chelsea Lord Salmon and Lord Edmund-Davies all simply agreed with Lord Diplock.

CAMBRIDGE NUTRITION LTD V. BRITISH BROADCASTING CORPORATION

14–64   Court of Appeal [1990] 3 All E.R 523. Kerr and Ralph Gibson L.JJ. and Eastham J.)

14–65   The claimants were manufacturers of a widely used low-calorie diet and agreed to participate in the making of a programme thereon by the defendants. The claimants contended and the defendants denied that it was a contractual term of their agreement that the programme would not be broadcast until after the publication of a government report on the medical aspects of diets such as the claimants'. Having become increasingly concerned about the tone of the proposed programme, the claimants applied for injunctive relief preventing broadcast until after publication of the government report and sought an interlocutory injunction pending trial. The nature of the programme as proposed was such that it was only appropriate for transmission before publication of the government report. The judge granted an injunction and the defendants appealed.

14–66   Kerr L.J.: "I would unhesitatingly refuse such an injunction in this case, and I summarise my reasons as briefly as I can.

14–67   "First, I do not consider that the question whether or not an injunction should be granted should in this case be tested simply by reference to the guidelines laid down in the *American Cyanamid* case. I accept that the judge was entitled to conclude that he should be guided by that case, but in my view it is not suitable for that purpose. Although *Cayne v Global Natural Resources plc* [1984] 1 All E.R. 225 was clearly an exceptional case, I would reiterate without repeating what I then said (at 234–235) and I refer equally to the tenor of the judgments of Eveleigh and May L.J.J. in that case, which are much to the same effect. It is important to bear in mind that the *American Cyanamid* case contains no principle of universal application. The only such principle is the statutory power of the court to grant injunctions when it is just and convenient to do so. The *American Cyanamid* case is no more than a set of useful guidelines which apply in many cases. It must never be used as a rule of thumb, let alone as a strait-jacket. Admittedly, the present case is miles away on its facts from the *Global Natural Resources* case, and it is also much weaker than *NWL Ltd v Woods* [1979] 3 All E.R. 614, [1979] 1 W.L.R. 1294, where Lord Diplock himself recognised the limitations of the *Cyanamid* guidelines. But nevertheless, I do not consider that it is an appropriate case for the *Cyanamid* guidelines because the crucial issues between the parties do not depend on a trial, but solely or mainly on the grant or refusal of the interlocutory relief. The *American Cyanamid* case provides an authoritative and most helpful approach to cases where the function of the court in relation to the grant or refusal of interlocutory injunctions is to hold the balance as justly as possible in situations where the substantial issues between the parties can only be resolved by a trial. In my view, for reasons which require no further elaboration, the present case is not in that category. Neither side is interested in monetary compensation, and once the interlocutory decision has been given, little, if anything, will remain in practice.

"But for present purposes the point can be put more narrowly. It seems to me **14–68** that cases in which the subject matter concerns the right to publish an article, or to transmit a broadcast, whose importance may be transitory but whose impact depends on timing, news value and topicality, do not lend themselves easily to the application of the *Cyanamid* guidelines. Longer term publications, such as films or books, may not be in the same category. I think that it would be an inappropriate test for the grant or refusal of interlocutory injunctions in such cases if the transmission of a broadcast, or the publication of an article, whose value and impact depended on their timing, could be prevented merely by the plausible, or not implausible, allegation of a term alleged to have been agreed orally in an informal conversation. In such cases it *should* matter whether the chances of success in establishing some binding agreement are 90 per cent or 20 per cent. I use that phraseology because counsel for the plaintiffs referred us to the decision of this court in *Alfred Dunhill Ltd v Sunoptic SA* [1979] FSR 337 at 373, where Megaw L.J. said that in the application of the *Cyanamid* test it did not matter whether the chances of success in establishing liability were 90 per cent or 20 per cent. The *Dunhill* case, like *Cyanamid* itself, was a typical case in which the *Cyanamid* guidelines are of great value, because everything depended on the trial and the long-term rights of the parties. The present type of case is not in the same category.

"Accordingly, since I would not follow the structured approach of the *American* **14–69** *Cyanamid* case in the present case, in carrying out the necessary balancing exercise I would have some regard to the relative weakness of the plaintiffs' case in establishing the contract on which they rely. Counsel for the plaintiffs conceded that clearly no contract of any kind had been made in the telephone conversations themselves. It is obvious that neither party was bound to anything at that stage. The conversations were no more than preliminary discussions. At most, as suggested by counsel for the plaintiffs, they resulted in a statement of terms which would apply if the BBC went ahead with the programme and the plaintiffs co-operated in making it. Even then, either side could no doubt have resiled from the project; for some time at least. The whole situation was by its nature undefined, and not easily definable in legal terms. Moreover, the alleged conditions were to be confirmed in writing, but never were. The second alleged condition, concerning the featuring of users of the diet 'before and after' was never pursued. And no reference to the existence of any condition was made for five months or so, despite all that intervened.

"In my view it would be highly undesirable if, on evidence of that nature, which **14–70** the judge rightly characterised as being no more than 'plausible' in support of the alleged condition, the court were driven to grant an injunction because of the application of the *Cyanamid* guidelines. In situations of this kind, quite apart from the alleged express reference to a written confirmation in the original telephone calls, it is essential that there should indeed be written confirmation of any fetter on transmission or other publication. In the absence of clear evidence of a contract having been made, I consider that the court should be extremely slow to grant an interlocutory injunction in such situations. And if the application of the *Cyanamid* test were to lead to a different conclusion, then that would demonstrate that it is not appropriate in these situations.

14–71   "However, in the same way as the judge, I do not think that it makes any difference whether this case is decided in accordance with the *Cyanamid* test or not. On either basis the answer is the same. The judge and I agree about that, even though our answers are different. That in itself serves to demonstrate that one must be careful not to lose sight of the real demands of justice in any given case by attaching too much importance to the *Cyanamid* guidelines. The only real difference of substance in the court's approach concerns the extent to which it is permissible or otherwise to have some regard to the relative strength of the parties' contentions on the merits. But in that connection it should also be remembered that the speech of Lord Diplock in the *American Cyanamid* case [1975] 1 All E.R. 504 at 511, [1975] A.C. 396 at 409 itself contains a later passage where he appears himself to qualify to some extent the earlier passage on this aspect. I can summarise the position by saying that in a context such as the present a doubtful contract should never prevail over the right of free speech, all other things being even.

14–72   "In these circumstances it seems to me to be obviously contrary to the public interest that the plaintiffs should be entitled to an order which has the effect of suppressing similar discussion of this topic by the BBC in a programme made with the plaintiffs' full co-operation, merely on the basis of a shadowy claim of an oral agreement concerning the timing of this programme alleged to have been made on the telephone some eight months ago.

14–73   "I would allow this appeal and lift the injunction."

14–74   RALPH GIBSON L.J.: "It is necessary to go back to the *Cyanamid* principles as set out by Lord Diplock. The judge had reached the point that the plaintiffs had a good arguable case for the injunction sought, and that the plaintiffs would not be adequately compensated by an award of damages at trial. The finding that the BBC would be adequately compensated by an award of damages, which the plaintiffs could pay, could have been regarded by the judge as sufficient to establish that, in the absence of any other relevant factor, there could be no reason to refuse an interlocutory injunction: see the *American Cyanamid* case [1975] 1 All E.R. 504 at 510, [1975] A.C. 396 at 408 *per* Lord Diplock. The judge in fact went on to consider the balance of justice or convenience, as I have said, and it is important to note that in my view it was essential that that balance be considered, because on the evidence, contrary to the judge's view, the remedy in damages was not adequate to compensate for the loss which would be suffered by either party if the injunction was wrongly granted or wrongly withheld.

14–75   "Since neither party would be adequately compensated by an award of damages, the guidance offered in the following paragraph in Lord Diplock's speech was of crucial importance [1975] 1 All E.R. 504 at 511, [1975] A.C. 396 at 408–409):

> 'Save in the simplest cases, the decision to grant or to refuse an interlocutory injunction will cause to whichever party is unsuccessful on the application some disadvantages which his ultimate success at the trial may show he ought to have been spared and the disadvantages may be such that the recovery of damages to which he would then be entitled either in the action or under the plaintiff's undertaking would not be sufficient to compensate him fully for all of them. The extent to which the disadvantages to each party would be incapable of being compensated in damages in the event of his succeeding at the trial is always a significant factor in assessing where the balance of convenience lies; and if the extent of the uncompensatable disadvantage to each party would not differ widely, it may not be improper to take into account in tipping the balance the relative strength of each party's case as revealed by the affidavit evidence

adduced on the hearing of the application. This, however, should be done only where it is apparent on the facts disclosed by evidence as to which there is no credible dispute that the strength of one party's case is disproportionate to that of the other party. The court is not justified in embarking on anything resembling a trial of the action on conflicting affidavits in order to evaluate the strength of either party's case.'

"It is clear that what is there said is the setting out of guidelines for the assistance **14–76** of the judges. I quote this passage again:

'. . . if the extent of the uncompensatable disadvantage to each party would not differ widely, it may not be improper to take into account in tipping the balance the relative strength of each party's case . . .'

"For my part, I would hold that on the evidence before the judge this case was at **14–77** best for the plaintiffs clearly within that principle. The uncompensatable disadvantage of each party in this case is difficult to assess separately for this purpose, and therefore even more difficult to compare with any confidence that one is more grave than the other.

"This is a case, therefore, in which I think that the relative strength of the parties' **14–78** cases should be taken into account, and this can be done by reference to the undisputed evidence on the affidavits and documents . . .

"There is one further matter to be taken into account on the balance of justice. **14–79** Since I am following the judge through the principles stated in the *American Cyanamid* case, I should point out that it comes under the heading: '. . . many other special factors to be taken into consideration in the particular circumstances of individual cases' (see [1975] 1 All E.R. 504 at 511, [1975] A.C. 396 at 409). I refer to the public interest in the exercise by the BBC of their rights and duties in communication to the people of this country . . .

"I would allow this appeal." **14–80**

EASTHAM J: "I agree that this appeal should be allowed . . . [following the **14–81** approach of Ralph Gibson L.J.].

SERIES 5 SOFTWARE v CLARKE

Chancery Division [1996] 1 All E.R. 853

LADDIE J.: "It is, of course, comparatively rare for applications for interlocutory **14–82** relief to reach the House of Lords. However, 1975 was an exception. In that year two cases, both of which involved an analysis of the courts' power to grant interlocutory injunctions, were heard more or less one after the other. The first was *F. Hoffmann-La Roche & Co. Att.-Gen. v Secretary of State for Trade and Industry* [1973] A.C. 295. . . . In the course of that case their Lordships considered the circumstances in which interlocutory injunctions were granted and the conditions to which their grant could be subject. In particular Lord Diplock said ([1975] A.C. 295 at 360–361):

'An interim injunction is a temporary and exceptional remedy which is available before the rights of the parties have been finally determined and, in the case of an ex parte injunction, even before the court had been apprised of the nature of the defendant's case. *To justify the grant of such a remedy the plaintiff must*

*satisfy the court first that there is a strong prima facie case that he will be entitled
to a final order restraining the defendant from doing what he is threatening to do*,
and secondly that he will suffer irreparable injury which cannot be compensated
by a subsequent award of damages in the action if the defendant is not
prevented from doing it between the date of the application for the interim
injunction and the date of the final order made on trial of the action.
Nevertheless, at the time of the application it is not possible for the court to be
absolutely certain that the plaintiff will succeed at the trial in establishing his
legal right to restrain the defendant from doing what he is threatening to do. If
he should fail to do so the defendant may have suffered loss as a result of
having been prevented from doing it while the interim injunction was in force;
and any loss is likely to be damnum absque injuria for which he could not
recover damages from the plaintiff at common law. So unless some other
means is provided in this event for compensating the defendant for his loss
there is a risk that injustice may be done.' (My emphasis.)

14–83   Then, having explained that the imposition of the cross-undertaking is designed to
mitigate the risk to the defendant, Lord Diplock proceeded:

'Beside mitigating the risk of injustice to the defendant the practice of exacting
an undertaking as to damages facilitates the conduct of the business of the
courts. It relieves the court of the necessity to embark at an interlocutory stage
upon an enquiry as to the likelihood of the defendant's being able to establish
facts to destroy *the strong prima facie case which ex hypothesi will have been
made out by the plaintiff*. The procedure on motion is unsuited to inquiries into
disputed facts. This is best left to the trial of the action . . .' (My emphasis.)

14–84   "This was consistent with the approach which was followed in many, but not all,
cases before *American Cyanamid*. The court had to pay regard to the strength or
otherwise of the plaintiff's case as revealed by a consideration of all the affidavit
evidence.

14–85   "Judgment in *Hoffmann-La Roche* was given just before the long vacation on July
3, 1974.

14–86   "That brings me to *American Cyanamid*, the hearing for which commenced after
the long vacation on November 12, 1974. It can be assumed that the panel read the
parties' briefs before that date. The panel consisted of Lord Diplock, Viscount
Dilhorne, Lord Cross, Lord Salmon and Lord Edmund-Davies—that is, it included
two members of the panel which decided *Hoffmann-La Roche*. If the House of
Lords intended to say that it was inappropriate on an application for interlocutory
relief, save in rare cases, to take into account the apparent strength of the plaintiff's
case, it would mean that Lord Diplock performed a volte face on this issue in a
matter of four months. In my view it is inconceivable that Lord Diplock and Lord
Cross could have forgotten what was said in the *Hoffmann-La Roche* judgment a
few months earlier. Therefore, if they were saying the opposite of what was said in
Hoffmann-La Roche, they must have been aware that they were doing so but chose
not to mention that fact or explain it in *American Cyanamid*. That is a proposition I
find difficult to accept. It seems to me that it is therefore appropriate to consider
whether what Lord Diplock said in *Hoffmann-La Roche* is incompatible with what
he said in *American Cyanamid* only a few months later. For this it is necessary to
consider the *American Cyanamid* decision with some care.

14–87   "The *American Cyanamid* case was concerned with the alleged infringement of
the main claim in the plaintiff's patent for absorbable surgical sutures. In response
to the allegation of infringement, Ethicon presented a classic squeeze argument

beloved of patent lawyers. It said that its sutures did not fall within the monopoly defined by the claim—that is it did not infringe, or, in the alternative, if the claim was construed widely enough to include its product, the patent was invalid on a number of grounds under the Patents Act 1949.

"In the House of Lords, as in the High Court and the Court of Appeal, both **14–88** parties had addressed the question of whether the plaintiff had demonstrated a strong prima facie case. In the course of his judgment, Lord Diplock said [1975] 1 All E.R. 504 at 510, [1975] A.C. 396 at 407:

> 'Your Lordships should in my view take this opportunity of declaring that there is no such rule. The use of such expressions as "a probability", "a prima facie case", or "a strong prima facie case" in the context of the exercise of a discretionary power to grant an interlocutory injunction leads to confusion as to the object sought to be achieved by this form of temporary relief. The court no dubt must be satisfied that the claim is not frivolous or vexatious; in other words, that there is a serious question to be tried.'

"The first question to be answered is precisely what was 'such rule' the existence **14–89** of which the House of Lords disapproved. This can be found in the early part of Lord Diplock's judgment. In the High Court, Graham J. had held that the plaintiff had made out a strong prima facie case and went on to say that the balance of convenience favoured the grant of interlocutory relief. The way in which the Court of Appeal dealt with the application was set out in the following passage in Lord Diplock's judgment [1975] A.C. 396 at 404–405):

> 'As Russell L.J. put it in the concluding paragraph of his reasons for judgment **14–90** with which the other members of the court agreed—". . . if there be no prima facie case on the point essential to entitle the plaintiff to complain of the defendant's proposed activities, that is the end of the claim to interlocutory relief." "Prima facie case" may in some contexts be an elusive concept, but the sense in which it was being used by Russell L.J. is apparent from an earlier passage in his judgment. After a detailed analysis of the more conflicting expert testimony he said: "I am not satisfied on the present evidence that on the proper construction of this specification, addressed as it is to persons skilled in the relevant art or science, the claim extends to sterile surgical sutures produced not only from a homopolymer of glycolide but also from a copolymer of glycolide and up to 15 per cent of lactide. That is to say that I do not consider that a prima facie case of infringement is established." In effect what the Court of Appeal was doing was trying the issue of infringement on the conflicting affidavit evidence as it stood, without the benefit of oral testimony or cross-examination. They were saying: "If we had to give judgment in the action now without any further evidence we should hold that Cyanamid had not satisfied the onus of proving that their patent would be infringed by Ethicon's selling sutures made of XLG." The Court of Appeal accordingly did not find it necessary to go into the questions raised by Ethicon as to the validity of the patent or to consider where the balance of convenience lay.'

As Lord Diplock put it ([1975] A.C. 396 at 405):

> '[The Court of Appeal] considered that there was a *rule of practice so well established as to constitute a rule of law* that precluded them from granting any interim injunction unless on the evidence adduced by both the parties on the

hearing of the application the applicant had satisfied the court that on the balance of probabilities the acts of the other party sought to be enjoined would, if committed, violate the applicant's legal rights.' (My emphasis.)

Lord Diplock then made it clear that it was in order to enable the existence of that rule of law to be considered that leave to appeal had been granted.

14–91   "The result of applying that rule of law was that in the Court of Appeal the motion lasted for two working weeks while the parties argued questions of polymer chemistry, infringement and validity. In the House of Lords the defendant tried to do the same thing. The note of argument there shows that sophisticated arguments of patent ambiguity, construction, inutility, false suggestion, insufficiency and unfair basis were advanced. In effect, the Court of Appeal had abandoned any attempt to evaluate the pros and cons of granting an interlocutory injunction and had said that there was a mandatory initial hurdle at which the plaintiff had fallen. The flexibility and absence of strict rules which had been advocated by the Court of Appeal in *Hubbard v Vosper* was ignored. If such a rule of law as envisaged by the Court of Appeal in *American Cyanamid* did exist, it would inevitably force the parties to engage in trying to prove at the interlocutory stage all those issues which were for determination at the trial. In a case as complicated as *American Cyanamid* it was likely to be impossible to show a strong prima facie case of infringement and validity and any attempt to do so would force the parties to expound at length on complicated technical and legal issues. But those were issues which at an interlocutory stage the court could not hope to resolve. It would have followed that if such a rule of law existed, interlocutory injunctions in patent cases, or in any other complicated case, would become a thing of the past no matter how severe was the damage to be suffered by the plaintiff in the interim.

14–92   "When Lord Diplock said that there was no such rule, he was referring to the so-called rule of law which the Court of Appeal had followed. In dismissing this approach, the House of Lords approved of the decision in *Hubbard v Vosper* and in particular that part of the decision in which the Court of Appeal deprecated any attempt to fetter the discretion of the court by laying down any rules which would have the effect of limiting the flexibiity of the remedy (see [1975] A.C. 396 at 407).

14–93   "Once it had disposed of the inflexible rule as applied by the Court of Appeal in the instant case, the House of Lords went on to consider what principles a court should bear in mind when deciding whether to grant interlocutory relief. First, it said ([1975] A.C. 396 at 408):

> '. . . [the court should] consider whether if the plaintiff were to succeed at the trial in establishing his right to a permanent injunction he would be adequately compensated by an award of damages for the loss he would have sustained as a result of the defendant's continuing to do what was sought to be enjoined between the time of the application and the time of the trial. If damages in the measure recoverable at common law would be adequate remedy and the defendant would be in a financial position to pay them, no interlocutory injunction should *normally* be granted, *however strong the plaintiff's claim appeared to be at that stage*.' (My emphasis.)

It should be noticed from the emphasised words in that passage that this approach was not said to be invariably the correct one and furthermore the words used suggest that where damages for the plaintiff was *not* an adequate remedy the apparent strength of the plaintiff's claim might well be a relevant consideration.

14–94   "Having considered the issue of adequacy of damages, Lord Diplock proceeded as follows ([1975] A.C. 396 at 408):

'It is where there is doubt as to the adequacy of the respective remedies in damages available to either party or to both, that the question of balance of convenience arises. It would be unwise to attempt even to list all the various matters which may need to be taken into consideration in deciding where the balance lies, let alone to suggest the relative weight to be attached to them. These will vary from case to case.'

"The reality is that the balance of convenience issue will need to be considered in **14–95** most cases because evidence relating to the adequacy of damages normally will be contradictory and there will be no possibility of resolving the differences by cross-examination. In the result, normally there will be doubt as to the adequacy of damages. It follows that in most cases it will be the exercise of taking into account all the issues relevant to the balance of convenience which will be the major task of the court faced with an application for interlocutory relief. As Lord Diplock went on to point out ([1975] A.C. 396 at 408–409):

'Save in the simplest cases, the decision to grant or to refuse an interlocutory injunction will cause to whichever party is unsuccessful on the application some disadvantages which his ultimate success at the trial may show he ought to have been spared and the disadvantages may be such that the recovery of damages to which he would then be entitled either in the action or under the plaintiff's undertaking would not be sufficient to compensate him fully for all of them. The extent to which the disadvantages to each party would be incapable of being compensated in damages in the event of his succeeding at the trial is always a significant factor in assessing where the balance of convenience lies . . .'

"In many cases before *American Cyanamid* the prospect of success was one of the **14–96** important factors taken into account in assessing the balance of convenience. The courts would be less willing to subject the plaintiff to the risk of irrecoverable loss which would befall him if an interlocutory injunction was refused in those cases where it thought he was likely to win at the trial than in those cases where it thought he was likely to lose. The assessment of the prospects of success therefore was an important factor in deciding whether the court should exercise its discretion to grant interlocutory relief. It is this consideration which *American Cyanamid* is said to have prohibited in all but the most exceptional case. so it is necessary to consider with some care what was said in the House of Lords on this issue.

"Lord Diplock said ([1975] A.C. 396 at 409): **14–97**

'. . . if the extent of the uncompensatable disadvantage to each party would not differ widely, it may not be improper to take into account in tipping the balance the relative strength of each party's case as revealed by the affidavit evidence adduced on the hearing of the application. . . . The court is not justified in embarking on anything resembling a trial of the aciton on conflicting affidavits in order to evaluate the strength of either party's case.'

It appears to me that there is nothing in this which is inconsistent with the old **14–98** practice. Although couched in terms 'it may not be improper', this means that it is legitimate for the court to look at the relative strength of the parties' case as disclosed by the affidavits. The warning contained in the second of the quoted sentences is to avoid courts at the interlocutory stage engaging in mini-trials, which is what happened, at least in the Court of Appeal, in *American Cyanamid* itself.

Interlocutory applications are meant to come on quickly and to be disposed of quickly.

14–99   "The supposed problem with *American Cyanamid* centres on the following statement by Lord Diplock ([1975] A.C. 396 at 409):

> '[Assessing the relative strength of the parties' case], however, should be done only where it is apparent upon the facts disclosed by evidence as to which there is no credible dispute that the strength of one party's case is disproportionate to that of the other party.'

If this means that the court *cannot* take into account its view of the strength of each party's case if there is any dispute on the evidence, as suggested by the use of the words 'only' and 'no credible dispute', then a new inflexible rule has been introduced to replace that applied by the Court of Appeal. For example, all a defendant would have to do is raise a non-demurrable dispute as to relevant facts in his affidavit evidence and then he could invite the court to ignore the apparent strength of the plaintiff's case. This would be inconsistent with the flexible approach suggested in *Hubbard v Vosper* [1972] 2 Q.B. 84 which was cited with approval earlier in *American Cyanamid* [1975] A.C. 396 at 407. Furthermore, it would be somewhat strange, since *American Cyanamid* directs courts to assess the adequacy of damages and the balance of convenience, yet these too are topics which will almost always be the subject of unresolved conflicts in the affidavit evidence.

14–100   "In my view Lord Diplock did not intend by the last-quoted passage to exclude consideration of the strength of the cases in most applications for interlocutory relief. It appears to me that what is intended is that the court should not attempt to resolve difficult issues of fact or law on an application for interlocutory relief. If, on the other hand, the court is able to come to a view as to the strength of the parties' case on the credible evidence, then it can do so. In fact, as any lawyer who has experience of interlocutory proceedings will know, it is frequently the case that it is easy to determine who is most likely to win the trial on the basis of the affidavit evidence and any exhibited contemporaneous documents. If it is apparent from that material that one party's case is much stronger than the other's then that is a matter the court should not ignore. To suggest otherwise would be to exclude from consideration an important factor and such exclusion would fly in the face of the flexibility advocated earlier in *American Cyanamid*. As Lord Diplock pointed out in *Hoffmann-La Roche*, one of the purposes of the cross-undertaking in damages is to safeguard the defendant if this preliminary view of the strength of the plaintiff's case proves to be wrong.

14–101   "Accordingly, it appears to me that in deciding whether to grant interlocutory relief, the court should bear the following matters in mind. (1) The grant of an interlocutory injunction is a matter of discretion and depends on all the facts of the case. (2) There are no fixed rules as to when an injunction should or should not be granted. The relief must be kept flexible. (3) Because of the practice adopted on the hearing of applications for interlocutory relief, the court should rarely attempt to resolve complex issues of disputed fact or law. (4) Major factors the court can bear in mind are (a) the extent to which damages are likely to be an adequate remedy for each party and the ability of the other party to pay, (b) the balance of convenience, (c) the maintenance of the status quo, and (d) any clear view the court may reach as to the relative strength of the parties' cases.

14–102   "In coming to this conclusion I am encouraged by the following considerations.

> (1) The House of Lords in *American Cyanamid* did not suggest that it was changing the basis upon which most courts had approached the exercise of discretion in this important area.

(2) The only issue which it was expressly addressing was the existence of the inflexible rule of law which had been applied as a mandatory condition by the Court of Appeal.

(3) It would mean that there was no significant inconsistency between the *Hoffmann-La Roche* and *American Cyanamid* decisions.

(4) It would be consistent with the approval given by the House of Lords to the decision in *Hubbard v Vosper* and, implicitly, the decision to the same effect in *Evans Marshall & Co. Ltd v Bertola SA* [1973] 1 W.L.R. 349 (a decision of Lord Edmund-Davies when in the Court of Appeal).

(5) It would preserve what is one of the great values of interlocutory proceedings, namely an early, though non-binding, view of the merits from a judge. Before *American Cyanamid* a decision at the interlocutory stage would be a major ingredient leading to the parties resolving their differences without the need for a trial. There is nothing inherently unsatisfactory in this. Most clients ask for and receive advice on prospects from their lawyers well before there has been cross-examination. In most cases the lawyers have little difficulty giving such advice. It should also be remembered that in many jurisdictions on the continent trials are conducted without discovery or cross-examination. There is nothing inherently unfair in a court here expressing at least a preliminary view based on written evidence. After all, it is what the courts managed to do for a century and a half.

(6) Allowing parties to come to an earlier view on prospects would assist in reducing the costs of litigation. This is an issue to which much attention is being given at the moment.

(7) It would mean that the approach of the courts in England and Wales to the grant of interlocutory relief would be the same as that followed in Scotland . . ."

CIVIL EVIDENCE ACT 1968

14 Privilege against incrimination of self or spouse

(1) The right of a person in any legal proceedings other than criminal proceedings **14–103** to refuse to answer any question or produce any document or thing if to do so would tend to expose that person to proceedings for an offence or for the recovery of a penalty—

(a) shall apply only as regards criminal offences under the law of any part of the United Kingdom and penalties provided for by such law; and

(b) shall include a like right to refuse to answer any question or produce any document or thing if to do so would tend to expose the husband or wife of that person to proceedings for any such criminal offence or for the recovery of any such penalty.

(2) In so far as any existing enactment conferring (in whatever words) powers of **14–104** inspection or investigation confers on a person (in whatever words) any right otherwise than in criminal proceedings to refuse to answer any question or give any evidence tending to incriminate that person, subsection (1) above shall apply to that right as it applies to the right described in that subsection; and every such existing enactment shall be construed accordingly.

14–105   (3) In so far as any existing enactment provides (in whatever words) that in any proceedings other than criminal proceedings a person shall not be excused from answering any question or giving any evidence on the ground that to do so may incriminate that person, that enactment shall be construed as providing also that in such proceedings a person shall not be excused from answering any question or giving any evidence on the ground that to do so may incriminate the husband or wife of that person.

THEFT ACT 1968

31 Effect on civil proceedings and rights

14–106   (1) A person shall not be excused, by reason that to do so may incriminate that person or the wife or husband of that person of an offence under this Act—

  (a) from answering any question put to that person in proceedings for the recovery or administration of any property, for the execution of any trust or for an account of any property or dealings with property; or

  (b) from complying with any order made in any such proceedings;

but no statement or admission made by a person in answering a question put or complying with an order made as aforesaid shall, in proceedings for an offence under this Act, be admissible in evidence against that person or (unless they married after the making of the statement or admission) against the wife or husband of that person.

SUPREME COURT ACT 1981

72 Withdrawal of privilege against incrimination of self or spouse in certain proceedings

14–107   (1) In any proceedings to which this subsection applies a person shall not be excused, by reason that to do so would tend to expose that person, or his or her spouse, to proceedings for a related offence or for the recovery of a related penalty—

  (a) from answering any question put to that person in the first-mentioned proceedings; or

  (b) from complying with any order made in those proceedings.

14–108   (2) Subsection (1) applies to the following civil proceedings in the High Court, namely—

  (a) proceedings for infringement of rights pertaining to any intellectual property or for passing off;

  (b) proceedings brought to obtain disclosure of information relating to any infringement of such rights or to any passing off; and

  (c) proceedings brought to prevent any apprehended infringement of such rights or any apprehended passing off.

14–109   (3) Subject to subsection (4), no statement or admission made by a person—

(a) in answering a question put to him in any proceedings to which subsection (1) applies; or

(b) in complying with any order made in any such proceedings,

shall, in proceedings for any related offence or for the recovery of any related penalty, be admissible in evidence against that person or (unless they married after the making of the statement or admission) against the spouse of that person.

(4) Nothing in subsection (3) shall render any statement or admission made by a person as there mentioned inadmissible in evidence against that person in proceedings for perjury or contempt of court. **14–110**

(5) In this section— **14–111**

"intellectual property" means any patent, trade mark, copyright, design right, registered design, technical or commercial information or other intellectual property;

"related offence", in relation to any proceedings to which subsection (1) applies, means—

(a) in the case of proceedings within subsection (2)(*a*) or (*b*)—

   (i) any offence committed by or in the course of the infringement or passing off to which those proceedings relate; or

  (ii) any offence not within sub-paragraph (i) committed in connection with that infringement or passing off, being an offence involving fraud or dishonesty;

(b) in the case of proceedings within subsection (2)(*c*), any offence revealed by the facts on which the plaintiff relies in those proceedings;

"related penalty", in relation to any proceedings to which subsection (1) applies means—

(a) in the case of proceedings within subsection (2)(a) or (b), any penalty incurred in respect of anything done or omitted in connection with the infringement or passing off to which those proceedings relate;

(b) in the case of proceedings within subsection (2)(c), any penalty incurred in respect of any act or omission revealed by the facts on which the plaintiff relies in those proceedings.

CIVIL JURISDICTION & JUDGMENTS ACT 1982

25 Interim relief in England and Wales and Northern Ireland in the absence of substantive proceedings

(1) The High Court in England and Wales or Northern Ireland shall have power to grant interim relief where— **14–112**

(a) proceedings have been or are to be commenced in a *Contracting State* other than the United Kingdom or in a part of the United Kingdom other than that in which the High Court in question exercises jurisdiction; and

(b) they are or will be proceedings whose subject-matter is within the scope of the 1968 Convention as determined by Art.1 (whether or not *the Convention* has effect in relation to the proceedings).

14–113   (2) On an application for any interim relief under subsection (1) the court may refuse to grant that relief if, in the opinion of the court, the fact that the court has no jurisdiction apart from this section in relation to the subject-matter of the proceedings in question makes it inexpedient for the court to grant it.

14–114   (3) Her Majesty may by Order in Council extend the power to grant interim relief conferred by subsection (1) so as to make it exercisable in relation to proceedings of any of the following descriptions, namely—

    (a) proceedings commenced or to be commenced otherwise than in a *Contracting State*;

    (b) proceedings whose subject-matter is not within the scope of the 1968 Convention as determined by Art.1;

    (c) arbitration proceedings.

14–115   (4) An Order in Council under subsection (3)—

    (a) may confer power to grant only specified descriptions of interim relief;

    (b) may make different provision for different classes of proceedings, for proceedings pending in different countries or courts outside the United Kingdom or in different parts of the United Kingdom, and for other different circumstances; and

    (c) may impose conditions or restrictions on the exercise of any power conferred by the Order . . .

14–116   (7) In this section "interim relief", in relation to the High Court in England and Wales or Northern Ireland, means interim relief of any kind which that court has power to grant in proceedings relating to matters within its jurisdiction, other than—

    (a) a warrant for the arrest of property; or

    (b) provision for obtaining evidence.

LOCK PLC v BESWICK

Chancery Division [1989] 1 W.L.R. 1268

14–117   HOFFMANN J.: "*The Anton Piller jurisdiction*

The growth in the *Anton Piller* jurisdiction, from the original invention of such orders in 1974 as the ultimate weapon against fraudulent copyright pirates, to their widespread use today has been described by Scott J. in *Columbia Picture Industries Inc. v Robinson* [1987] Ch. 38. As Scott J. pointed out, they potentially involve serious inroads on principles which bulk large in rhetoric of English liberty, such as the presumption of innocence, the right not to be condemned unheard, protection against arbitrary searches and seizures, the sanctity of the home. My common experience of the evident surprise of counsel when I have refused applications leads me to indorse Scott J.'s observation, at 76:

    'the practice of the court has allowed the balance to swing much too far in favour of plaintiffs and that *Anton Piller* orders have been too readily granted and with insufficient safeguards for respondents.'

14–118   "In the original *Anton Piller* case, *Anton Piller KG v Manufacturing Processes Ltd* [1976] Ch. 55, 61, Lord Denning M.R. said:

'It seems to me that such an order can be made by a judge ex parte, but it should only be made where it is essential that the plaintiff should have inspection so that justice can be done between the parties: and when, if the defendant were forewarned, there is a grave danger that vital evidence will be destroyed, that papers will be burnt or lost or hidden, or taken beyond the jurisdiction, and so the ends of justice be defeated: and when the inspection would be no real harm to the defendant or his case. . . . We are prepared, therefore, to sanction its continuance, but only in an extreme case where there is grave danger of property being smuggled away or of vital evidence being destroyed.'

Ormrod L.J. said, at 62:   **14–119**

'There are three essential pre-conditions for the making of such an order, in my judgment. First, there must be an extremely strong prima facie case. Secondly, the damage, potential or actual, must be very serious for the applicant. Thirdly, there must be clear evidence that the defendants have in their possession incriminating documents or things, and that there is a real possibility that they may destroy such material before any application inter partes can be made.'

"These strict requirements were indorsed by the Court of Appeal in *Booker*   **14–120**
McConnell Plc. v Plascow [1985] R.P.C. 425, where Dillon L.J. referred to the passages from Lord Denning M.R. and Ormrod L.J., which I have cited, and commented, at p.441:

'The phrase "a real possibility" [used by Ormrod L.J.] is to be contrasted with the extravagant fears which seem to afflict all plaintiffs who have complaints of breach of confidence, breach of copyright or passing off. Where the production and delivery up of documents is in question, the courts have always proceeded, justifiably, on the basis that the overwhelming majority of people in this country will comply with the court's order, and that defendants will therefore comply with orders to, for example, produce and deliver up documents without it being necessary to empower the plaintiff's solicitors to search the defendant's premises.'

"*Anton Piller* orders are frequently sought in actions against former employees   **14–121**
who have joined competitors or started competing businesses of their own. I have learned to approach such applications with a certain initial scepticism. There is a strong incentive for employers to launch a pre-emptive strike to crush the unhatched competition in the egg by causing severe strains on the financial and management resources of the defendants or even a withdrawal of their financial support. Whether the plaintiff has a good case or not, the execution of the *Anton Piller* order may leave the defendants without the will or the money to pursue the action to trial in order to enforce the cross-undertaking in damages.

"Some employers seem to regard competition from former employees as pre-   **14–122**
sumptive evidence of dishonesty. Many have great difficulty in understanding the distinction between genuine trade secrets and skill and knowledge which the employee may take away with him. In cases in which the plaintiff alleges misuse of trade secrets or confidential information concerning a manufacturing process, a lack of particularity about the precise nature of the trade secrets is usually a symptom of an attempt to prevent the employee from making legitimate use of the knowledge and skills gained in the plaintiff's service. That symptom is particularly evident in

this case. Judges dealing with ex parte applications are usually also at a disadvantage in dealing with alleged confidential knowledge of technical processes described in technical language, such as the electric circuitry in this case. It may look like magic but turn out merely to embody a principle discovered by Faraday or Ampère.

14–123   "Even in cases in which the plaintiff has strong evidence that an employee has taken what is undoubtedly specific confidential information, such as a list of customers, the court must employ a graduated response. To borrow a useful concept from the jurisprudence of the European Community, there must be *proportionality* between the perceived threat to the plaintiff's rights and the remedy granted. The fact that there is overwhelming evidence that the defendant has behaved wrongfully in his commercial relationships does not necessarily justify an *Anton Piller* order. People whose commercial morality allows them to take a list of the customers with whom they were in contact while employed will not necessarily disobey an order of the court requiring them to deliver it up. Not everyone who is misusing confidential information will destroy documents in the face of a court order requiring him to preserve them.

14–124   "In many cases it will therefore be sufficient to make an order for delivery up of the plaintiff's documents to his solicitor or, in cases in which the documents belong to the defendant but may provide evidence against him, an order that he preserve the documents pending further order, or allow the plaintiff's solicitor to make copies. The more intrusive orders allowing searches of premises or vehicles require a careful balancing of, on the one hand, the plaintiff's right to recover his property or to preserve important evidence against, on the other hand, violation of the privacy of a defendant who has had no opportunity to put his side of the case. It is not merely that the defendant may be innocent. The making of an intrusive order ex parte even against a guilty defendant is contrary to normal principles of justice and can only be done when there is a paramount need to prevent a denial of justice to the plaintiff. The absolute extremity of the court's powers is to permit a search of a defendant's dwelling house, with the humiliation and family distress which that frequently involves . . .

Should the order have been made?

14–125   "I am conscious of the fact that I have had the benefit of adversarial argument and a much longer time to read the evidence than the judge in chambers had when he made the order. But I am bound to say that it did not in my view justify any form of ex parte relief, let alone an *Anton Piller* order. The evidence came nowhere near disclosing an 'extremely strong prima facie case' or 'clear evidence that the defendants [had] in their possession incriminating documents or things' or that there was a 'grave danger' or 'real possibility' that the defendants might destroy evidence. The lack of specificity in the plaintiff's affidavit was such that I have some doubt whether it could be said to have raised a triable issue. Furthermore, these defendants were no fly-by-night video pirates. They were former long service employees with families and mortgages, who had openly said that they were entering into competition and whom the plaintiff knew to be financed by highly respectable institutions.

14–126   "As for the searches of the private homes of Messrs. Dearman, Ives and Lock, including the seizure of Mr. Dearman's private diary and other papers relating to his industrial tribunal proceedings against the plaintiff, none of which have been subsequently relied on, I can only sympathise with the sense of outrage which they must have felt.

"Nor do I understand why it was necessary to make an order ex parte which had **14–127** the effect of allowing the plaintiff's employees to have immediate access to all of Safeline's confidential documents and prototypes. In the *Anton Piller* case, one of the conditions mentioned by Lord Denning M.R. for the grant of an order was that 'inspection would do no real harm to the defendant or his case.' [1976] Ch. 55, 61. Even if it was thought that the defendants were the kind of dishonest people who would conceal or destroy incriminating documents, it would surely have been sufficient at the ex parte stage to allow the plaintiff's solicitors to remove the documents and make copies for their own retention pending an application by the plaintiff inter partes for leave to inspect them. The defendants would then have had the opportunity to object or to ask for a restricted form of inspection, such as by independent expert only. I do not regard the right to apply to discharge the order as a sufficient protection for the defendants. The trauma of the execution of the *Anton Piller* order means that in practice it is often difficult to exercise until after substantial damage has been done."

Evidence obtained under the order

"The plaintiff says that whether or not its case was strong enough on the original **14–128** application, the material recovered when the order was executed amply justifies the order he made. I agree that in deciding whether the defendants have suffered injustice as a result of the order, I should not ignore evidence which the order itself has brought to light: *WEA Records Ltd v Visions Channel 4 Ltd* [1983] 1 W.L.R. 721. In my judgment, however, the material seized by the plaintiff improves its case very little and comes nowhere near demonstrating that the defendants were indeed the kind of dishonest people who would, but for the order, have destroyed incriminating documents . . .

The discharge order

"I shall order that the *Anton Piller* order be discharged, that the defendants have **14–129** leave to proceed to an inquiry before the master on the cross-undertaking in damages and that all copies retained by the plaintiff or its advisers of the documents, computer records and prototypes seized under the order be returned to the defendants."

Section 3. Specific Performance

A decree of specific[4] performance is an order[5] of the court[6] compelling the **14–130** defendant[7] personally to do what he has promised to do.[8] While the

---

[4] Referring to the performance in kind (in Latin, *in specie*) of a contractual (or primary) obligation rather than the performance of the secondary obligation to pay damages for loss caused by breach of a primary obligation. Meagher, Gummow and Lehane's *Equity, Doctrines and Remedies* (4th ed.) observes the technical distinction between specific performance *proper* (which applies only to executory contracts requiring something to be done such as the execution of a deed or conveyance) and specific performance of executed agreements (whereby the performance of *any* contractual obligation may be decreed): the principles applying to both are the same, but the distinction makes it easier to understand decisions such as *C.H. Giles & Co. Ltd v Morris* [1972] 1 W.L.R. 307 and *Posner v Scott-Lewis* [1987] Ch. 25.

[5] *i.e.* a final order. An interim decree is not possible but see *Sky Petroleum Ltd v VIP Petroleum Ltd* [1974] 1 W.L.R. 576 and *Hill v C.A. Parsons & Co. Ltd* [1972] Ch. 305, cases where injunctions amounting in substance to the specific performance of obligations were granted on an interlocutory (now "interim") basis.

[6] Both the High Court and the County Court have jurisdiction to grant specific performance and, whereas

common law allows a defendant to choose to be a "bad man" and break his contractual obligations and pay damages for the privilege, where equity intervenes it will compel a defendant to be a "good man" and fulfil his obligations.[9] Compulsion may take various forms, *e.g.* empowering a person other than the defendant to execute a conveyance which the latter has promised but refused to execute,[10] or, more generally, committing the defendant to prison on account of his contempt[11] (*i.e.* disobedience to the order of the court) until he complies with the court order and purges his contempt.

14–131   If a decree is granted, the contract is not merged in the judgment of the court but still exists so that, if the decree is not or cannot be complied with, the claimant may return to court,[12] seek dissolution of the decree, and obtain an award of common law damages.[13]

14–132   Not all positive contractual stipulations or promises will be specifically enforced[14] and the purpose of this section is to examine the principles upon which the court's discretion will be exercised. It is nowadays refused only according to reasonably settled principles, the most important of which are[15]: (i) lack of consideration; (ii) adequacy of common law remedies, (iii) equity will not act in vain, (iv) illegality or public policy, (v) lack of mutuality of a sort irremediable by imposition of terms, (vi) that the contract is incapable of being enforced in its entirety, (vii) that the order could not be enforced without the constant supervision of the court, (viii) delay, (ix) lack of clean hands, (x) undue hardship, (xi) performance would involve the defendant in a breach of contract (or trust), (xii) set-off, (xiii) mistake and misrepresentation and (xiv) misdescription of subject-matter. These will be looked at in turn.

---

the County Court jurisdiction is limited in the case of contracts to sell or lease land to cases where the purchase price (or, in the case of leases, the value of the property) does not exceed the County Court limit, the County Court must give effect to every defence or counterclaim to which effect would be given in the High Court: County Courts Act 1984, s.38. Even where a case falls outside the County Court's jurisdiction to *decree* specific performance, that court might still *declare* that a party would be entitled to such decree: *Rushton v Smith* [1976] Q.B. 480.

[7] Specific performance does not lie against the Crown (Crown Proceedings Act 1947, s.21(1)(a)) but a declaration may be made as to the Crown's position.

[8] It is only available to enforce positive obligations. Negative ones must be enforced by injunction.

[9] See Sir Peter Millett in 1993 Restitution L.R. 7 at 19–20, developing the celebrated view of O.W. Holmes in *The Common Law* (1881) and in "The Path of the Law" (1897) 10 Harv. L.R. 457. The availability of specific performance enables "Equity to treat as done that which ought to be done" *e.g. Attorney-General for Hong Kong v Reid* [1994] 1 A.C. 324.

[10] Supreme Court Act 1981, s. 39.

[11] Sequestration of assets until compliance is also available against both individuals and corporations and is the only way of proceeding against corporations for contempt, although their directors may, of course, be imprisoned. Fines may also be imposed. See, generally, R.S.C. Ord. 45 and Miller's *Contempt of Court* (2nd ed.), Chap.14.

[12] In fact, he *must* return to court if he does not want to follow through with the decree: *GKN Distributors Ltd v Tyne Tees Fabrication Ltd* (1985) 50 P. & C.R. 403 (sale to another purchaser): *Singh v Nazeer* [1979] Ch. 474.

[13] *Johnson v Agnew* [1980] A.C. 367.

[14] It is important to keep distinct the notion of a contract's enforceability in general terms, whether at law (where it might be unenforceable, *e.g.* for mistake, uncertainty, illegality *etc.*) or in equity (likewise, *e.g.*, for undue influence, misrepresentation *etc.*) from its ability to be enforced specifically. The latter notion implies that there is no legal or equitable ground for avoiding the contract and that the claimant will not be confined to a remedy in damages. A non-specifically enforceable contract may nonetheless, therefore, be said to be enforceable.

[15] See generally Jones and Goodhart *Specific Performance* (1996).; *Fry on Specific Performance* (6th ed.); Spry's *Equitable Remedies* (6th ed.) Ch. 3; Sharpe's *Injunctions and Specific Performance* (1983), Part II and Meagher, Gummow and Lehane's *Equity, Doctrines and Remedies* (4th ed.), Chaps 20 and 36.

(i) Lack of consideration

Lack of consideration in fact prevents there being a contract at law at all **14–133** and, if so, there is nothing to perform,[16] *in specie* or otherwise. But the consideration provided by a deed, although sufficient at law, is insufficient in equity.[17] Yet there is no equitable test of adequacy of consideration (it follows the law in that respect) and the provision of money or money's worth, however small the sum, suffices.[18] Likewise, past consideration will not support a suit in equity.[19]

(ii) Inadequacy of damages

The best way of illustrating how this principle operates in relation to the **14–134** enforcement of positive contractual stipulations is to examine different categories of contracts. First, some that have been held to be specifically enforceable and then some that have been held not to be.

(a) Contracts for the disposition of an interest in land

Each piece of real estate is regarded as unique and, therefore, damages will **14–135** be an inadequate remedy for a purchaser in the sense that damages will not enable him to buy a replacement in the market.[20] Although damages will, clearly, be an adequate remedy for a vendor (who wants only money), a decree will lie against a purchaser on grounds of mutuality.[21] "A contract to mortgage property, real or personal, will, normally at least, be specifically enforceable, for a mere claim to damages or repayment is obviously less valuable than a security in the event of the debtor's insolvency".[22]

(b) Chattels of especial value

The Court of Chancery had always claimed jurisdiction to order the return **14–136** of a specific chattel wrongly retained by another[23] not properly a contractual claim) but, as rationalised by Lord Eldon,[24] its justification for so doing was that such chattels possessed a *pretium affectionis*[25] which could not be

---

[16] A similar consideration requires that, for example, contracts for the sale or disposition of interests in land must comply with s.2 of the Law of Property (Miscellaneous Provisions) Act 1989 before specific performance may be ordered. Likewise contracts void at law for other reasons, *e.g.* mistake, illegality, and uncertainty.

[17] *Re Pryce* [1917] 1 Ch. 234 at 241 *per* Eve J. Mere covenantees are therefore volunteers in equity and can only enforce the covenant at law: *Cannon v Hartley* [1949] Ch. 213. Children of a marriage are, in marriage settlement cases, treated in equity, however, as having provided consideration: *Re Pryce, above; Re Kay's Settlement* [1939] Ch. 329 and may obtain specific performance.

[18] *Mountford v Scott* [1975] Ch. 258. But cp. *Milroy v Lord* (1862) 4 De G.F. & J. 264 and *Peffer v Rigg* [1977] 1 W.L.R. 285.

[19] *Robertson v St John* (1786) 2 Bro. C.C. 140

[20] *Hall v Warren* (1804) 9 Ves. 605; *Adderley v Dixon* (1824) 1 Sim. & St. 607. In *Verrall v Great Yarmouth Borough Council* [1981] 1 Q.B. 202, the Court of Appeal affirmed the grant of specific performance to enforce a contractual licence to occupy premises. As no other premises could be found damages would have been an inadequate remedy (the promisee being unable to hire any premises with any damages awarded).

[21] So the vendor can "thrust the property down the purchaser's throat", *per* Lindley L.J. in *Hope v Walter* [1900] 1 Ch. 257 at 258. But, on mutuality, see below, para.14–143.

[22] *Swiss Bank Corp v Lloyd's Bank Ltd* [1980] 2 All E.R. 419 at 425, *per* Buckley L.J.

[23] *Pusey v Pusey* (1684) 1 Vern. 273 (an ancient horn, reputedly a gift of Canute).

[24] *Nutbrown v Thornton* (1804) 10 Ves. 160 at 163.

[25] Roughly, a "sentimental value".

estimated in damages.[26] Extending that reasoning by one step in *Sky Petroleum Ltd v VIP Petroleum Ltd*,[27] Goulding J. held that the court had jurisdiction to order specific performance of a contract to sell non-specific chattels in a case where the remedy of damages would be inadequate.

(c) Shares in a private limited company

14–137 There being no readily available market in such shares, in light of the restriction on the transferability of shares in private companies and of the criminal prohibition in s.81 of the Companies Act 1985,[28] damages will normally be an inadequate remedy.

(d) Contracts for sale of personal property not within (b) or (c) above

14–138 Such contracts are not specifically enforceable so that, for example, contracts for the sale of shares in which there is a ready market, *i.e.* those of a quoted public company,[29] and, indeed, any other contract[30] for the disposition of personal property, tangible or intangible, will not be specifically enforced unless it can be shown in the instant case that damages would not be an adequate remedy.[31] A contract to leave personal or real property by will is not enforceable directly (which would interfere with freedom of testamentary power) but a legatee who receives it in breach will be ordered to yield it up[32] and, before death of the testator, the promisee can obtain a declaration of right and an injunction restraining any inconsistent disposition.[33]

---

[26] *Falcke v Gray* (1859) 4 Dr. 651; *Thorn v Commissioners of Public Works* (1863) 32 Beav. 490 (stones from Old Westminster Bridge); *Phillips v Lamdin* [1949] 2 K.B. 33 (ornate Adam door). Damages would clearly be an inadequate remedy if an award would not enable the promisee to go into the market place and purchase a similar chattel. By definition it could not do so in cases of this sort. Note also that s.52 of the Sale of Goods Act 1979 enables the court, additionally, to decree specific performance of contracts for the sale of "specific or ascertained goods", *i.e.* identified and agreed upon when the contract is made. Neither under the statutory nor equitable jurisdictions (both being discretionary) will specific performance be decreed of contracts for the sale of "ordinary articles of commerce", even though specific or ascertained goods within the Act, as damages would be an adequate remedy: *Cohen v Roche* [1927] 1 K.B. 169 (set of Hepplewhite chairs); *Whiteley Ltd v Hilt* [1918] 2 K.B. 808, at 819. Inadequacy of damages seems, therefore, to be the touchstone.

[27] [1974] 1 W.L.R. 576 (enforcement of obligation to supply petrol during petrol shortage, no alternative source available), para.14–162.

[28] Prohibiting a private company (other than a company limited by guarantee and not having a share capital) from offering its securities to the public directly or indirectly.

[29] It seems doubtful whether a life interest under a settlement of such shares would be sufficiently unique to merit specific performance of a contract for its disposition.

[30] Note, however, that in the case of contracts to assign choses in action there is no need (save for the purpose of perfecting legal title) to obtain specific performance at all as an assignment for value operates without more as an assignment in equity on the principle that equity considers that done which ought to be done: *per* Lord Macnaghten in *Tailby v Official Receiver* (1888) App. Cas. 523 at 547–548. The operation of that principle does not depend on the specific enforceability of the contract to assign.

[31] Additionally, a contract for the transfer of the goodwill of a business is too uncertain to enforce *in specie*: *Darbey v Whitaker* (1857) 4 Drew. 134 (unless premises or other business assets are contracted to be transferred with it). This appears to be an example of a contract sufficiently certain at law but not specifically enforceable for lack of certainty, an odd conclusion save that, for specific performance to lie, the court must be able to supervise the exact performance of the contract (*per* Lord Hardwicke L.C. in *Buxton v Lister* (1746) 3 Atk. 383 at 386. As imprisonment may result from non-compliance, this requirement is understandable.

[32] *Synge v Synge* [1894] 1 Q.B. 466 (on the ground that he is a volunteer and takes subject to the equity).

[33] *Schaefer v Schumann* [1972] A.C. 572 (Privy Council).

(e) Contracts for personal services

Contracts of employment, by statute,[34] are non-specifically enforceable. The **14–139** equitable approach is illustrated in *De Francesco v Barnum*[35]; "The courts are bound to be jealous lest they should turn contracts of service into contracts of slavery", *per* Fry L.J. This approach applies to contracts *of* service not covered by the statute and any contract *for* personal services but there seems to be no hard and fast *rule*.[36]

(f) Contracts to pay money

In *South African Territories Ltd v Wallington*,[37] a contract to make a loan **14–140** was not specifically enforced because damages would be an adequate remedy. In *Beswick v Beswick*[38] the contract was to pay an annuity to a third party. It was enforced because damages would have been an inadequate remedy in the sense that either (i) damages awarded to the promisee would have been nominal or (ii) a multiplicity of suits might need to be brought if there were future breaches or (iii) the worth of an annuity, depending on the longevity of the annuitant, might be too conjectural to quantify.[39] It remains doubtful whether a promisee could obtain specific performance of a promise to pay a lump sum to a third party: if he could, it would require an English court to uphold (i) as a sufficient reason for enforcing a promise *in specie* and, moreover, one which the promisee could not have enforced for his own benefit.[40]

(iii) Equity never acts in vain

Equity never acts in vain and, therefore, it will not decree performance of **14–141** the impossible or the futile. Therefore, a vendor of land who has wrongfully conveyed away the property will not be ordered to convey to a purchaser what he no longer has unless the transferee is, for example, a company controlled by the vendor and used as a crude device or sham to avoid specific performance.[41] Likewise, an agreement for a lease which has

---

[34] Trade Union and Labour Relations (Consolidation) Act 1992, section 236; "no court shall . . . by way of an order of specific performance . . . compel an employee to do any work or to attend at any place for the doing of any work."

[35] (1890) 45 Ch.D. 430. The authorities cited in *Fry on Specific Performance*, at pp.50–51 suggest that other (earlier) justifications were that equity would not act in vain and even the absence of a property right in the plaintiff.

[36] In *Giles (C.H.) & Co.Ltd v Morris* [1972] 1 W.L.R. 307, Megarry J. denied that there was a rule preventing enforcement: it was, rather, a question of looking at the particular obligations in question. In *Hill v C.A. Parsons & Co.Ltd* [1972] Ch. 305 the Court of Appeal by a majority enforced a contract for personal services in what were described as exceptional circumstances. See also *Lumley v Wagner* (1852) 1 De G.M. & G. 604, where a singer was prevented by injunction from breaching her promise to sing only at the plaintiff's theatre, effectively thereby being forced to sing for the plaintiff. This and other cases were reviewed by Mance L.J in *Lady Navigation Inc. V Laurintzencod A.B.* [2005] EWCA Civ 579, concluding that there is no general rule that injunctive relief will be withheld if the practical effect would be to compel performance of a contract for personal services.

[37] [1898] A.C. 309.

[38] [1968] A.C. 58.

[39] But query: actuaries and judges in personal injury cases do it routinely.

[40] Because in *that* case, damages clearly would be adequate. Note that it is not to be thought that the question whether such promise be specifically enforceable is an academic one. A defendant is at risk of imprisonment for failure to comply with a decree of specific performance but cannot nowadays (since abolition of debtors' prison) be gaoled for inability to pay a civil debt.

[41] *Jones v Lipman* [1962] 1 W.L.R. 832.

already expired will not be enforced,[42] nor an agreement for a partnership not being of fixed duration,[43] nor an agreement to purchase property when the claimant has no funds to pay the purchase price.[44] But *Verrall v Great Yarmouth Borough Council*[45] makes clear that authorities from the last century on transient interests[46] are now suspect: an agreement to occupy premises for two days is, other things being equal, specifically enforceable.

(iv) Illegality and public policy

14–142   A contract which is illegal is void and there is nothing to enforce, specifically or otherwise. A contract which is valid but which, if executed, might achieve some goal contrary to public policy might not be enforced specifically. *Wroth v Tyler*[47] provides a good example of this. In that case, a husband contracted to sell his property. After conclusion of the contract, his wife registered a charge against the property under the Matrimonial Homes Act 1967 which gave her the right (but no more than the right) not to be evicted. The vendor sought either specific performance or damages in lieu. Specific performance was refused on, amongst others, the ground that if it were ordered, the vendor would have to take the property subject to the wife's occupation. But he would be able to evict the husband and other members of the family. The splitting up of a family in that way would be an end contrary to public policy and the vendor would be awarded damages in lieu.

(v) Mutuality

14–143   It used to be said that specific performance will not be granted to a promisee who could not himself be the subject of a decree,[48] *i.e.* all the obligations imposed by the contract upon the plaintiff promisee must themselves be specifically enforceable. This is the traditional statement of the requirement of mutuality. Fry's statement of it, which required mutuality at the time of entering into the contract (rather than it sufficing at the date of the hearing) was rejected in *Price v Strange*.[49] Goff L.J.[50] stated

---

[42] *Turner v Clowes* (1869) 20 L.T. 214 It might be otherwise if the lessee would derive some benefit by being granted legal rights under the lease: *Walters v Northern Coal Mining Board Co* (1855) 5 De G.M. & G. 629.

[43] *Henry v Birch* (1804) 9 Ves. 357: either partner might dissolve it at will.

[44] *Wilkie v Redsell* [2002] EWCA Civ 926.

[45] [1981] Q.B. 202 at 220. Contrast, *e.g. Glasse v Woolgar and Roberts (No.2)* (1897) 41 Sol. Jo. 573: "It was almost ludicrous to ask for specific performance of a lease for a single day", per Lindley L.J.

[46] *e.g. Lavery v Pursell* (1888) 39 Ch.D. 508 where, at 519, one reason for refusing specific performance of a contract for a one year lease was that it was not often possible to get a decree made within a year and therefore a decree would be in vain.

[47] [1974] Ch. 30.

[48] *Flight v Bolland* (1828) 4 Russ. 298 (minor failing to obtain decree because, *qua* minor, suit could not be maintained against him).

[49] [1978] 1 Ch. 337.

[50] *ibid.* at 354. At 368–369 Buckley L.J. stated: "The court will not compel a defendant to perform his obligations specifically if it cannot at the same time ensure that any unperformed obligations of the plaintiff will be specifically performed unless, perhaps, damages would be an adequate remedy to the defendant for any default on the plaintiff's part." There is some tension between this finding and the HL's decision in *White & Carter (Councils) Ltd v McGregor* [1962] A.C. 413, that the court has no general equitable discretion to prevent the innocent party to a contract from forcing performance onto the other party and claiming payment. For discussion, see *Ministry of Sound (Ireland) Ltd v World Online Ltd* [2003] 2 All E.R. (Comm.) 823 at [67]–[72].

"want of mutuality raises a question of the court's discretion to be exercised according to everything that has happened up to the decree" so that "the court will grant specific performance if it can be done without injustice or unfairness to the defendant" which may involve some payment to the defendant as in *Price v Strange*.[51] Where injustice can be avoided by the imposition of terms on the plaintiff or an award of damages to the defendant, a decree may be made subject thereto. Indeed, since the decision in that case, there has been a steady academic and judicial retreat from the doctrine of mutuality as a coherent explanation for the outcome of older, decided cases or, indeed, as a sound objection as a matter of moral principle.[52] This is to be welcomed for it appears at times to have been used as a principle to justify the specific enforcement of certain types of contract (such as those for the disposition of land, when, quite plainly, damages would be an adequate remedy for a vendor[53]) and, capriciously, to deny the specific enforceability of others. In other words, it was serving a dual role in the case law. The judicial retreat from it must now be almost complete in light of the decision of the High Court in *Rainbow Estates v Tokenhold Ltd*.[54]

A word of background explanation about this decision is necessary. A **14–144** landlord's repairing covenant is enforceable by statute notwithstanding any equitable rule restricting the tenant's remedy "whether based on mutuality or otherwise".[55] This provision was enacted precisely because it was thought that repairing covenants were not specifically enforceable either because, the tenant's covenants not being so enforceable, the landlord's covenants could not be so for want of mutuality or, alternatively, because of the need for constant supervision. The court in this case, however, decided that neither of these reasons had been the *ratio* of any decided case and, there being no reason in principle why a tenant's repairing covenant should not be specifically enforced (so long as oppression was avoided and the work required to be done was sufficiently defined[56]), the court in an appropriate case would order specific performance of a tenant's repairing covenant. The qualifications in parentheses would mean, however, that appropriate cases were rare.

In any event, it appears that, so far as mutuality is a decisive doctrine in **14–145** English law today, a defendant may disentitle himself by waiver to rely on lack of mutuality as a reason for refusing specific performance.[57]

---

[51] *ibid.* p.357.
[52] For a summary of the academic attack, see Jones & Goodhart, *op. cit.*, at 38 *et seq.*
[53] But, as may be seen from para.14–135, he is said to be entitled to specific performance on the ground of mutuality.
[54] [1999] Ch. 64 (Mr Lawrence Collins Q.C, sitting as a deputy judge of the Chancery Division), noted P. Luxton [1998] J.B.L. 564.
[55] Landlord and Tenant Act 1985, section 17.
[56] On this last requirement para.14–148.
[57] *Price v Strange, above; Halkett v Dudley* [1907] 1 Ch. 590.

(vi) Entire contracts only

14–146   That the contract sought to be enforced *in specie* should be capable of being enforced in its entirety[58] is an old rule[59] but one which may now be more flexible. In *CH Giles & Co.Ltd v Morris*,[60] a case where specific performance was sought of a contract for the sale of shares, one of the terms of which required the vendors to procure the appointment of a particular individual as managing director of the company, Megarry J. said "the court may refuse to let the disadvantages and difficulties of specifically enforcing the obligation to perform personal services outweigh the suitability of the rest of the contract for specific performance . . .".[61] Where the contract can properly be construed as two distinct contracts, specific performance may be obtained to enforce one of them.[62]

(vii) The need for constant supervision

14–147   There is authority to the effect that breach of a contract which would need constant supervision by the court if it were to be performed *in specie* will only sound in damages.[63] In *Posner v Scott-Lewis*,[64] however, Mervyn Davies J. at a tenant's request and on facts difficult to distinguish from *Ryan v Mutual Tontine Westminster Chambers Association*,[65] made an order against the landlord for the appointment of a resident porter whom the landlord had covenanted to employ for the purpose of carrying out certain duties at a block of flats: he found that there was a sufficient definition of what had to be done in order to comply with the order of the court. The more recent and important case of *Co-operative Insurance Society Ltd v Argyll Stores (Holdings) Ltd*[66] provided the House of Lords with the opportunity to review and reconcile the authorities clustered around this principle. In that case the tenant (owners of Safeway supermarkets) had given a covenant to keep the demised premises open for retail trade during normal business hours. The tenant was the anchor-tenant in a new shopping mall in Hillsborough but had made a decision, based on national performance, to close all of its loss-making stores of which the demised premises were one. The tenant was content to pay damages for breach but resisted an order for

---

[58] Distinguish this requirement, which stresses the need for all of the *defendant's* obligations to be enforceable from the requirement of mutuality which focuses on the (alleged) need for all the *claimant's* obligations to be enforceable against him.

[59] *Ogden v Fossick* (1862) 4 De G.F. & J. 426.

[60] [1972] 1 W.L.R. 307. See too *Rainbow Estates Ltd v Tokenhold Ltd* [1997] Ch. 64 at 73; *Internet Trading Clubs Ltd v Freeserve (Investments) Ltd* Ch. June 19, 2001 at [30] *per* Tomkinson J., considering *Odessa Tramways Co. v Mendel* (1878) 8 Ch.D. 235.

[61] *ibid.* at p.317–318.

[62] *e.g. Lewin v Guest* (1826) 1 Russ. 325 (Separate contracts to purchase two plots; purchaser obliged to take one plot even though vendor could not show title to other). It would be otherwise where, *e.g.*, a vendor knew that from purchaser's point of view the purchases were interdependent: *Poole v Shergold* (1786) 1 Cox Eq. Cas. 273.

[63] *Ryan v Mutual Tontine Westminster Chambers Association* [1893] 1 Ch. 116 (lessor's covenant to provide resident porter who would always be in attendance at block of flats). See also *Dowty Boulton Paul Ltd v Wolverhampton Corporation* [1971] 2 All E.R. 277 (mandatory injunction refused to enforce covenant to maintain acrodrome for period of over 60 years: same principle applied)

[64] [1987] Ch. 25.

[65] *supra*. n.63.

[66] [1998] A.C. 1, below, at para.14–219.

specific performance. The Court of Appeal, by a majority, granted a decree[67] which the House of Lords discharged.

Lord Hoffmann, speaking for the whole court, approved a long line of **14–148** authority to the effect that the court will not order anyone to run a business. He examined the normal reason for this: the need for constant supervision. In *C.H. Giles & Co. v Morris* Megarry J.[68] had suggested that difficulties of supervision were "a narrow consideration": performance would normally be secured by the defendant's realisation that he is liable to contempt for failure to obey the order and, therefore, there would in practice be little need for the court to "supervise". This kind of consideration had been relied on by the Court of Appeal to justify its order. The House, however, distinguished between orders to carry on an activity, such as running a business over time, and orders requiring a defendant merely to achieve a result. In the former case, the risk of repeated, expensive and cumbersome applications to the court for guidance is much higher than in the latter: even if the result which the court has ordained that the defendant shall bring about is a complex thing (such as erecting a building in accordance with complex plans) the court will still only have to rule once, after the fact, to say whether or not there has been compliance. If a defendant, on the other hand, were ordered to run a retail grocery business during ordinary business hours, there might be innumerable applications. It was with this distinction in mind, said Lord Hoffmann, that courts had in the past ordered the specific performance of repairing covenants and building contracts. What the courts had been prepared to do in those cases (of orders to achieve a result) was not to be confused with the approach to orders to carry on an activity. That was where the majority in the Court of Appeal had fallen into error.[69]

(viii) Delay or laches

There being no statutory limit on the time after which a claim for specific **14–149** performance may be brought[70] equitable considerations govern and may deprive a claimant of the right to performance *in specie* where there is delay either sufficient to be evidence of the plaintiff's abandonment of the contract[71] or coupled with circumstances which make it unjust to order specific performance.[72]

---

[67] [1996] 3 W.L.R. 27 (Millett L.J. forcefully dissenting).

[68] [1972] 1 W.L.R. 307.

[69] In a Scottish case with essentially identical facts, *Highland & Universal Properties Ltd v Safeway Properties Ltd* [2000] 3 E.G.L.R. 110, the Inner House granted specific implement of the defender's obligation to keep its premises open, noting that Scots law differs from English law in this area, but suggesting that in *Argyll Stores* Lord Hoffmann overstated the difficulties of superintending orders to carry on an activity in cases of this kind.

[70] Limitation Act 1980, s.36. Nor do the Limitation Acts apply by analogy: *Talmash v Mugleston* (1826) 4 LJOS Ch. 200.

[71] *Parkin v Thorold* (1852) 16 Beav. 59 at 73. The claimant will still have his legal remedy.

[72] *Lindsay Petroleum Co.v. Hurd* (1874) L.R. 5 P.C. 221. Where the plaintiff took possession and waited 10 years before seeking a decree to have the legal title vested in him, mere delay with no injustice to the defendant was no bar: *Williams v Greatrex* [1957] 1 W.L.R. 31. See too *Ridgeway Motors (Isleworth) Ltd v Michael* Ch.D. June 13, 1996 (claim for S.P. after 17 years struck out for laches).

(ix) Lack of clean hands

14–150   If the claimant is guilty of some impropriety connected to the contract[73] ("reprehensible", "unfair" or "tricky" conduct being required) he may be disentitled to an equitable remedy. The jurisdiction of the court to consider this matter cannot be ousted by agreement.[74] However, this last point was decided in a case where a clause in a sale agreement, which provided that the consideration was to be paid in cash "free from any equity cross-claim set-off or other deduction whatsoever", was held not to prevent the purchaser from raising an unclean hands defence. This was for the reason that the wording was not apt to exclude such a claim but alternatively for the reason that, even if it had been apt, "it could not have the effect of fettering the discretion of the court. Once the court is asked for the equitable remedy of specific performance, its discretion cannot be fettered".[75] Although defensible on its own, this decision does not sit easily with the long-established practice[76] of parties contracting that a particular obligation, if breached, shall "sound only in damages". This is just as much an attempt to oust the discretionary jurisdiction of the court to award a specific remedy. Perhaps all that can be said about it is that it is not, all other things being equal, an objectionable one.

(x) Undue hardship

14–151   Specific performance may be refused if hardship will be caused to either of the parties or a third party.[77] The decisions in individual cases tend to turn on the facts (see, for an example, *Wroth v Tyler*).[78] Although there is Commonwealth authority requiring the hardship to have existed at the date of contract,[79] in England it has been held that specific performance could be refused on the ground of hardship arising after contract.[80]

(xi) Breach of contract

14–152   It is a well-established principle that the court will not grant a decree if compliance with it would involve the defendant in breach of a prior contract (or, indeed, trust).[81]

---

[73] *van Gestel v Cann, The Times*, August 7, 1987 (claim that plaintiff guilty of fraud unconnected with contract of no assistance to defendant).

[74] *Quadrant Visual Communications Ltd v Hutchison Telephone (U.K.) Ltd* [1993] B.C.L.C. 442. See, generally, Snell's *Equity* (29th ed.) at 30 *et seq.*; 611 *et seq.*

[75] [1993] B.C.L.C. 442 at 451.

[76] Endorsed by the Court of Appeal in *Co-operative Insurance Society Ltd v Argyll Stores (Holdings) Ltd*, above and not criticised on this point by the House of Lords.

[77] *Thomas v Dering* (1837) 1 Keen 729 at 747–748.

[78] [1974] Ch. 30, para.14–178. Other situations, *e.g.* include: trustee vendors, contractually obliged to discharge personally incumbrances on property, relieved from so doing as purchase price insufficient to cover secured amounts (*Wedgwood v Adams* (1843) 6 Beav. 600); purchaser not obliged to take property which had no right of access, so no possibility of enjoyment (*Denne v Light* (1857) 8 De G.M. & G. 774.

[79] *e.g. Nicholas v Ingram* [1958] N.Z.L.R. 972.

[80] *Patel v Ali* [1984] Ch. 283 at 288 (husband and wife vendors; husband bankrupted, causing delay; wife seriously ill; young children; wife dependent on proximity of relatives so moving difficult).

[81] *Harvela Investments Ltd v Royal Trust Co. of Canada Ltd* [1985] Ch. 103 at 122, *per* Peter Gibson J.

(xii) Set-off

In *BICC Plc. v Burndy Corpn.*[82] the Court of Appeal accepted by a majority **14–153** that a right of equitable set-off (where a defendant seeks to defend a claim on the basis that the plaintiff is liable, under a related cross-claim, to him in a sum equal to or greater than the claim made by the plaintiff) could stand as a complete defence to a claim by a plaintiff not merely for a debt but also for specific performance.

(xiii) Mistake and misrepresentation

A contract which is not avoidable in equity for mistake or misrepresenta- **14–154** tion might sound only in damages if, owing to misrepresentation or (even unilateral) mistake, performance *in specie* would involve real hardship for the defendant amounting to injustice.[83]

(xiv) Misdescription of subject-matter[84]

Although the authorities on this relate to sales of land the principles ought **14–155** to apply to contracts for the disposition of personalty which are otherwise specifically enforceable. A misdescription *in the contract* will amount to a breach because the vendor cannot then convey what he has contracted to convey. Quite apart from the common law rules determining the rights of an innocent party equity developed the following rules[85] to deal specifically with this kind of breach when a question arose, assuming the contract was not discharged at law, whether it should be performed *in specie*.

If the misdesription is substantial (so that the purchaser does not get **14–156** what he wanted (*i.e.* but for the misdescription it is reasonable to suppose he would never have contracted at all[86]), the vendor cannot enforce either at law or in equity even with abatement of price. If insubstantial, the vendor can enforce though with abatement of price by way of compensation.[87] Whether substantial or not, the *purchaser* can enforce and take whatever the vendor has *and* secure an abatement.[88]

---

[82] [1985] Ch. 232.
[83] *Tamplin v James* (1880) 15 Ch.D. 215 (land correctly described in plans, not consulted by purchaser; purchaser obliged to buy despite unilateral error in thinking adjacent land included. No injustice.) Contrast *Denny v Hancock* (1870) 6 Ch. App. 1 (similar error was caused by vendor's unsatisfactory plans: no decree). See also *Riverlate Properties v Paul* [1975] Ch. 133; *Geest plc v Fyffes plc* Q.B.D. (Comm. Ct.) March 23, 1998.
[84] See, for a summary, Farrand's *Contract & Conveyance* (4th ed.) at pp.52–55.
[85] Applicable to open contracts. In practice, parties to contracts for the sale of land use Standard Conditions which moderate the position. These, however, are subject to the Unfair Contract Terms Act 1977 and to a judicial reluctance to allow parties to escape their equitable duties, *qv Rignall Developments Ltd v Halil* [1988] Ch. 190. See also, for a discussion of the applicability to contracts relating to dealings in land of European Community Directive 93/13, [1993] C.J. L 95/29. Bright & Bright, "Unfair Terms in Land Contracts: Copy Out or Cop Out?" (1995) 11 L.Q.R. 655.
[86] *Flight v Booth* (1834) 1 Bing. N.C. 370.
[87] *Jacobs v Revell* [1900] 2 Ch. 858.
[88] *Rutherford v Acton-Adams* [1915] A.C. 866 at 870.

ADDERLEY v DIXON

High Court of Chancery (1824) 1 Sim. & St. 607

14–157 The claimants took assignments of certain debts which had been proven in the estates of two bankrupts. This entitled them to whatever dividend might be declared on the debts in the bankruptcy. The claimants then contracted to sell their rights under the assignments for 2 shillings and sixpence in the pound to the defendant. The claimants sought specific performance of the purchaser's obligation to pay the price.

14–158   SIR JOHN LEACH V.-C.: "Courts of Equity decree the specific performance of contracts not upon any distinction between realty and personalty, but because damages at law may not in the particular case, afford a complete remedy. Thus a Court of Equity decrees performance of a contract for land, not because of the real nature of the land, but because damages at law, which must be calculated upon the general money value of land, may not be a complete remedy to the purchaser, to whom the land may have a peculiar and special value. So a Court of Equity will not, generally, decree performance of a contract for the sale of stock or goods, not because of their personal nature, but because damages at law, calculated upon the market price of the stock or goods, are as complete a remedy to the purchaser as the delivery of the stock or goods contracted for; inasmuch as, with the damages, he may purchase the same quantity of the like stock or goods.

14–159   "In *Taylor v Neville*, cited in *Buxton v Lister* (1746) 3 Atk 383 at 384), specific performance was decreed of a contract for sale of 800 tons of iron, to be delivered and paid for in a certain number of years and by instalments; and the reason given by Lord Hardwicke is that such sort of contracts differ from those that are immediately to be executed and they do differ in this respect, that the profit upon the contract, being to depend upon future events, cannot be correctly estimated in damages where the calculation must proceed upon conjecture. In such a case, to compel a party to accept damages for the non-performance of his contract, is to compel him to sell the actual profit which may arise from it, at a conjectural price. In *Ball v Coggs* (1710) 1 Bro. P.C. 140, specific performance was decreed in the House of Lords of a contract to pay the plaintiff a certain annual sum for his life, and also a certain other sum for every hundred weight of brass wire manufactured by the defendant during the life of the plaintiff. The same principle is to be applied to this case. Damages might be no complete remedy, being to be calculated merely by conjecture; and to compel the plaintiff in such a case to take damages would be to compel him to sell the annual provision during his life for which he had contracted at a conjectural price. In *Buxton v Lister* Lord Hardwicke puts the case of a ship carpenter purchasing timber which was peculiarly convenient to him by reason of its vicinity; and also the case of an owner of land covered with timber contracting to sell his timber in order to clear his land; and assumes that as, in both those cases, damages would not, by reason of the special circumstances, be a complete remedy, equity would decree specific performance.

14–160   "The present case being a contract for the sale of the uncertain dividends which may become payable from the estates of the two bankrupts, it appears to me that, upon the principle established by the cases of *Ball v Coggs* and *Taylor v Neville*, a Court of Equity will decree specific performance, because damages at law cannot accurately represent the value of the future dividends; and to compel this purchaser to take such damages would be to compel him to sell these dividends at a conjectural price.

"It is true that the present bill is not filed by the purchaser, but by the vendor, **14–161** who seeks, not the uncertain dividends, but the certain sum to be paid for them. It has, however, been settled, by repeated decision, that the remedy in equity must be mutual; and that, where a bill will lie for the purchaser, it will also lie for the vendor."

SKY PETROLEUM LTD v VIP PETROLEUM LTD

Chancery Division [1974] 1 W.L.R. 576 **14–162**

The claimants had contracted to purchase all their petrol, at fixed prices, from the defendants. During a petrol shortage the defendants purported to terminate the contract on the ground of breach of certain credit provisions therein by the claimants. Pending trial of that issue, the claimants sought an injunction to restrain the defendants from witholding supplies.

"GOULDING J.: "What I have to decide is whether any injunction should be **14–163** granted to protect the plaintiffs in the meantime. There is trade evidence that the plaintiffs have no great prospect of finding any alternative source of supply for the filling stations which constitute their business. The defendants have indicated their willingness to continue to supply the plaintiffs, but only at prices which, according to the plaintiffs' evidence, would not be serious prices from a commercial point of view. There is, in my judgment, so far as I can make out on the evidence before me, a serious danger that unless the court interferes at this stage the plaintiffs will be forced out of business. In those circumstances, unless there is some specific reason which debars me from doing so, I should be disposed to grant an injunction to restore the former position under the contract until the rights and wrongs of the parties can be fully tried out. The most serious hurdle in the way of the plaintiffs is the well known doctrine that the court refuses specific performance of a contract to sell and purchase chattels not specific or ascertained. That is a well-established and salutary rule, and I am entirely unconvinced by Mr. Christie, for the plaintiffs, when he tells me that an injunction in the form sought by him would not be specific enforcement at all. The matter is one of substance and not of form, and it is, in my judgment quite plain that I am, for the time being, specifically enforcing the contract if I grant an injunction. However, the ratio behind the rule is, as I believe, that under the ordinary contract for the sale of non-specific goods, damages are a sufficient remedy. That, to my mind, is lacking in the circumstances of the present case. The evidence suggests, and indeed it is common knowledge that the petroleum market is in an unusual state in which a would-be buyer cannot go out into the market and contract with another seller, possibly at some sacrifice as to price. Here, the defendants appear for practical purposes to be the plaintiffs' sole means of keeping their business going, and I am prepared so far to depart from the general rule as to try to preserve the position under the contract until a later date. I therefore propose to grant an injunction."

BESWICK v BESWICK

House of Lords [1968] A.C. 58 [1967] 2 All E.R. 1197 (Lords Pearce, Upjohn, Reid, Hodson and Guest).

Peter Beswick agreed with his nephew to transfer to him his business in **14–164** consideration of the nephew's (a) employing Peter as a consultant for life and (b) paying thereafter to Peter's widow an annuity at the rate of £5 per week for life.

Peter died and the nephew refused to make any payments to the widow but the first. She sued for specific performance in her capacity as administratix of Peter's estate and in her personal capacity. The House unanimously rejected her personal claim as a *ius quaesitum tertio* but allowed her representative claim.

14–165 LORD UPJOHN: "As it is necessary to keep clear and distinct the right of the widow as administratix of her husband and personally, I think it will be convenient to use letters: letter A represents the deceased and A1 the widow, as personal representative. B the widow in her personal capacity and C the appellant. And in other examples I shall give, these letters will serve the same purpose.

14–166 "Much is common ground between the parties: (1) B was not a party to the agreement: (2) A did not enter into the agreement as trustee for B in relation to the annuity to be paid to her; (3) A1 stands for all relevant purposes in the shoes of A and is entitled to sue C for breach of his admitted repudiation of the agreement (see paragraph 5 of the defence), but the parties differ fundamentally as to the remedy to which A1 is entitled in such an action . . .

14–167 "Leaving section 56 out of account, there was no real dispute between the parties as to their respective rights (as distinct from remedies) under the agreement. (a) B has no rights thereunder. But it was clear from the whole tenor of the agreement that the annuity was to be paid to her for her own beneficial enjoyment, so if C paid it to her she could keep it and did not hold it as a constructive trustee for A1; (b) C would completely perform his obligation under the contract by continuing to pay the annuity to B during her life. Neither A nor A1 could compel C to pay it to A or A1, but (c) A or A1 and C could, if they pleased, agree to modify, compromise or even discharge further performance of the contract by C, and B would have no right to complain. If authority be wanted for these fundamental propositions, it is to be found in *Re Schebsman* and *Re Stapleton-Bretherton*.

14–168 "But when A dies and his rights pass to A1, it is said that the remedy of specific performance is no longer appropriate against C. The argument was first that the estate of A suffered no damage by reason of C's failure to pay B, so A1 is entitled to nominal damages but as she is not otherwise interested in the agreement as such it would be wrong to grant specific performance; for that remedy is available only where damages will be an inadequate remedy. Here nominal damages are adequate. Further, it was argued, to do so would really be to confer upon B a right which she does not have in law or equity to receive the annuity. Then, secondly, it was said that if the remedy of specific performance is granted it might prejudice creditors of A so that the parties ought to be left to their strict rights at law. Thirdly, it is said that there are procedural difficulties in the way of enforcing an order for specific performance in favour of a third party. I will deal with these points, though in reverse order.

14–169 "As to procedural difficulties, I fear I do not understand the argument. The point if valid applies to an action for specific performance by A just as much as by A1 yet in the authorities I have quoted no such point was ever taken; in *Drimmie v Davies* indeed the action was by executors. Further, it seems to me that if C fails to obey a four-day order obtained by A1, B could enforce it under the clear and express provisions of R.S.C. Ord. 45. r.9 (formerly Ord. 42. r.26). Alternatively A1 could move for and obtain the appointment of a receiver of the business upon which the annuity is charged and the receiver would then be directed by the Court to pay the annuity to B out of the profits of the business. Finally, A1 could issue a writ of fi. fa. under Ord. 45, r.1, but as A1 would then be enforcing the contract and not modifying or compromising it the court would obviously in executing its order compel her to carry out the contract in toto and hand the proceeds of execution to B. This point is entirely without substance.

"Then as to the second point. Let me assume (contrary to the fact) that A died **14-170** with substantial assets but also many creditors. The legal position is that prima facie the duty of A1 is to carry out her intestate's contracts and compel C to pay B; but the creditors may be pressing and the agreement may be considered onerous; so it may be her duty to try and compromise the agreement with C and save something for the estate even at the expense of B. See *Ahmed Angullia v Estate & Trust Agencies* (1927) *Ltd per* Lord Romer. So be it, but how can C conceivably rely upon this circumstance as a defence by him to an action for specific performance by A1? Of course not; he, C, has no interest in the estate; he cannot plead a possible jus tertii which is no concern of his. It is his duty to fulfil his contract by paying C. A1 alone is concerned with the creditors, beneficiaries or next of kin of A and this point therefore can never be a defence by C if A1 in fact chooses to sue for specific performance rather than to attempt a compromise in the interest of the estate. This point seems to me misconceived. In any event, on the facts of this case there is no suggestion that there are any unpaid creditors and B is sole next of kin, so the point is academic.

"Then, as to the first point. On this question we were referred to the well-known **14-171** dictum of Lush L.J. in *Lloyd's v Harper*:

> 'I consider it to be an established rule of law that where a contract is made with A for the benefit of B, A can sue on the contract for the benefit of B and recover all that B could have recovered if the contract had been made with B himself.'

While in the circumstances it is not necessary to express any concluded opinion thereon, if the learned Lord Justice was expressing a view on the purely common law remedy of damages, I have some difficulty in going all the way with him. If A sues for damages for breach of contract by reason of the failure to pay B he must prove his loss; that may be great or nominal according to circumstances.

"I do not see how A can, in conformity with clearly settled principle in assessing **14-172** damages for breach of contract, rely at common law on B's loss. I agree with the observations of Windeyer J, in the as yet unreported case of *Coulls v Bagot's Executor and Trustee Co. Ltd* in the High Court of Australia. But I note, however, that in *Lloyd's v Harper* James and Cotton L.JJ. treated A as trustee for B and I doubt whether Lush L.J. thought otherwise.

"However, I incline to the view that on the facts of this case damages are nominal **14-173** for it appears that A died without any assets save and except the agreement which he hoped would keep him and then his widow for their lives. At all events let me assume that damages are nominal. So it is said nominal damages are adequate and the remedy of specific performance ought not to be granted. That is, with all respect, wholly to misunderstand that principle. Equity will grant specific performance when damages are inadequate to meet the justice of the case.

"But in any event quantum of damages seldom affects the right to specific **14-174** performance. If X contracts with Y to buy Blackacre or a rare chattel for a fancy price because the property or chattel has caught his fancy he is entitled to enforce his bargain and it matters not that he could not prove any damage.

"In this case the court ought to grant a specific performance order all the more **14-175** because damages *are* nominal. C has received all the property: justice demands that he pay the price and this can only be done in the circumstances by equitable relief. It is a fallacy to suppose that B is thereby obtaining additional rights: A1 is entitled to compel C to carry out the terms of the agreement. The observations of Holmes L.J. already quoted are very much in point.

14–176   "My Lords, in my opinion the Court of Appeal were clearly right to grant a decree of specific performance."

14–177   Lords Pearce, Reid, Hodson and Guest delivered speeches concurring in the grant of such decree.

WROTH v TYLER

Chancery Division [1974] Ch. 30

14–178   The defendant contracted to sell his property to the claimants for £6,000. The next day, the defendant's wife registered a charge against the property under the Matrimonial Homes Act 1967 which gave her the right not to be evicted or excluded from the property. She refused to remove the charge and the defendant told the claimants he could not complete. The claimants sought specific performance or damages in lieu. The property was worth £7,500 at the date fixed for completion and £11,500 at the date of the hearing.

14–179   MEGARRY J.: "The issues before me may be summarised as follows. (1) Delay apart, are the plaintiffs entitled to specific performance of the contract with [missing page 1012 in .pdf file] vacant possession? If they are, a form of order is sought that will require the defendant to make an application to the court for an order against his wife terminating her rights of occupation under the Matrimonial Homes Act 1967 in accordance with section 1(2). (2) Delay apart, are the plaintiffs, as an alternative, entitled to specific performance of the contract subject to the rights of occupation of the defendant's wife, with damages or an abatement of the purchase price in respect thereof? If they are, they will be able to make the application to the court under the Act of 1967, by virtue of section 1(2) and section 2(3). (3) If, apart from delay, the plaintiffs would be entitled to an order for specific performance under either of these two heads, is their right to it barred by delay? (4) If the plaintiffs have no right to specific performance, then it is common ground that they are entitled to damages. There is, however, an acute conflict as to the measure of damages . . .

14–180   "The defendant says that the damages must be assessed as at the date of the breach, in accordance with the normal rule: the plaintiffs says that this is a case where damages must be assessed as at the date of assessment, that is, today, if I assess the damages. . . . Damages assessed as at the date of breach would be £1,500, but as at the date of the hearing would be £5,500. At which figure should damages for the loss of the bargain be assessed? The defendant says that the former figure applies, in accordance with the general rule, but the plaintiffs say that the latter figure applies, for unless it does, they will be unable to acquire an equivalent house at today's prices . . .

14–181   "I may summarise my conclusions as to the essentials of the right given by the Act to an occupying spouse as follows. The right is in essence a personal and non-assignable statutory right not to be evicted from the matrimonial home in question during marriage or until the court otherwise orders; and this right constitutes a charge on the estate or interest of the owning spouse which requires protection against third parties by registration. For various reasons, the right may be said to be one which readily fits into no category known to conveyancers before 1967; the phrase sui generis seems apt, but of little help.

14–182   "With that in mind, I turn to the first question before me. Delay apart, are the plaintiffs entitled to specific performance of the contract with vacant possession? If they are, the form of order sought will require the defendant to make an application to the court under section 1(2) to terminate his wife's rights of occupation which arose and became a charge on the defendant's estate on January 1, 1968, and were protected by registration on May 28, 1971 . . .

"It seems to me that where a third party has some rights over the property to be **14–183** sold, there are at least three categories of cases. First, there are those cases where the vendor is entitled as of right to put an end to the rights of the third party, or compel his concurrence or co-operation in the sale. Second, and at the other extreme, there are cases where the vendor has no right to put an end to the third party's rights, or compel his concurrence or co-operation in the sale, and can do no more than to try to persuade him to release his rights or to concur in the sale.

"A vendor must do his best to obtain any necessary consent to the sale; if he has **14–184** sold with vacant possession he must, if necessary, take proceedings to obtain possession from any person in possession who has no right to be there or whose right is determinable by the vendor, at all events if the vendor's right to possession is reasonably clear; but I do not think that the vendor will usually be required to embark upon difficult or uncertain litigation in order to secure any requisite consent or obtain vacant possession. Where the outcome of any litigation depends upon disputed facts, difficult questions of law, or the exercise of a discretionary jurisdiction, then I think the court would be slow to make a decree of specific performance against the vendor which would require him to undertake such litigation. In such a case, the vendor cannot know where the litigation will end. If he succeeds at first instance, the defendant may carry him to appeal; if he fails at first instance, the purchaser may say that there ought to be an appeal. No doubt the line between simple and difficult cases will sometimes be hard to draw; and it may be that specific performance will be readily decreed only where it is plain that the requisite consent is obtainable without difficulty. The form of decree appropriate to such cases might specifically require the defendant to undertake such litigation; the court moulds the decree as need be. But it may be that the court will do no more than direct the defendant to procure the requisite consent: see *Long v Bowring* (1864) 33 Beav. 585; *Seton's Judgments and Orders*, 7th ed. (1912), p.2204.

"In the present case the defendant has endeavoured to persuade his wife to **14–185** concur in the sale, but has failed. It is true that after the failure of his initial attempt on the Friday night he then instructed his solicitors to withdraw from both the sale and his Norfolk purchase; but he again tried to persuade his wife on the Sunday, and there is some evidence of later attempts. As the evidence stands, I think that the defendant has sufficiently attempted to obtain her consent, short of litigation. The mere fact that he sought to withdraw from the contract before he had made all his attempts does not seem to me to make much difference; if a later attempt had succeeded, he could still have completed at the date fixed for completion.

"Persuasion having failed, I think that the court should be slow to grant a decree **14–186** of specific performance that would require an unwilling husband to make an application to the court under section 1(2) of the Act of 1967, particularly as the decision of the court depends upon the application of phrases such as 'just and reasonable' under section 1(3). In any case, the court would be reluctant to make an order which requires a husband to take legal proceedings against his wife, especially while they are still living together. Accordingly, although this is a contract of a type which the court is normally ready to enforce by a decree of specific performance, in my judgment it would, in Lord Redesdale L.C.'s phrase, be 'highly unreasonable' to make such a decree if there is any other form of order that could do justice; and that I must consider in due course. Let me add that I would certainly not regard proceedings under the Act by the defendant against his wife as being without prospect of success. As the evidence stands (and of course I have not heard the defendant's wife) there is at least a real prospect of success for the defendant. He does not in any way seek to deprive his wife of a home; the difference between them is a difference as to where the matrimonial home is to be. In that, the conduct of the wife towards the plaintiffs and the defendant must play a substantial part.

14–187   "In turn to the second main question, that of Mr. Blackburne's alternative claim to specific performance for which he contended if he failed in his main claim to specific performance, and if he also was limited to damages assessed as at the date of the breach. This alternative claim was for specific performance of the contract, but with the plaintiffs taking subject to the charge in favour of the defendant's wife, and receiving damages or an abatement of the purchase money. By virtue of section 2(3) of the Act of 1967, section 1(2) to (5) would apply to the plaintiffs as they apply to the defendant, in that the plaintiffs would be persons deriving title under the defendant, and affected by the charge. If the plaintiffs took subject to the charge in favour of the defendant's wife, the result would be remarkable, for reasons which I have already indicated. The defendant has no rights of occupation under the Act, for his right of occupation stems from his estate in the land, and so section 1(1) of the Act gives him no statutory rights of occupation. The defendant's daughter has no rights of occupation under the Act, for the Act does not purport to confer such rights on anyone except a spouse. The defendant's wife alone has statutory rights of occupation, and on the facts of this case, these are expressed as being no more than 'a right not to be evicted or excluded from the dwelling house or any part thereof.' It has not been contended that this language is wide enough to empower the wife to authorise others to occupy the house with her, so that on that footing the plaintiffs, after completion, would be unable to evict the wife without an order of the court made under the Act, whereas the defendant and the daughter would have no defence to proceedings to evict them.

14–188   "There seems to be considerable force in the contention that this would be the result. Neither the defendant nor the daughter would have any rights of their own to remain in the house, and what the statute gives the wife is not a positive right of occupation, whether a licence or otherwise, but a mere negative right not to be evicted or excluded. A person who is given a positive right of occupation might be envisaged as having been given the right to permit others to occupy with him or her: but a mere negative right not to be evicted or excluded cannot so readily be construed in this sense . . .

14–189   "If one leaves the position of the children on one side as being debatable, there remains the position of the defendant vis-à-vis the plaintiffs. Even if the wife not only is protected against eviction or exclusion, but also has the right to permit others to occupy the dwelling with her, the defendant has contracted to give vacant possession to the plaintiffs. Could he, then, in breach of his contract, remain in occupation under cover of his wife's statutory right not to be evicted or excluded? Would a decree of specific performance of the contract subject only to his wife's statutory rights in effect be nugatory as to his contractual obligation not himself to remain in occupation but to give vacant possession? The Act seems to me to have created much doubt and uncertainty in this sphere, but there is at least a real possibility that a decree of specific performance subject to the wife's right not to be evicted or excluded would enable the plaintiffs, by taking suitable proceedings, to evict the defendant and perhaps the daughter, and thus split up the family. These circumstances seem to me to make the case one in which the court should be slow to decree specific performance if any reasonable alternative exists. I shall accordingly turn to the question of damages to see whether they would provide the plaintiffs with an adequate remedy . . ."

[He then held that the measure of damages perhaps at common law but certainly **14–190** in lieu of specific performance was to be assessed at the date of judgments and so awarded £5,500 damages; *Johnson v Agnew, infra*, now makes it clear that common law and equitable damages have the same measure.]

JOHNSON v AGNEW

House of Lords [1980] A.C. 367 (Lords Wilberforce, Salmon, Fraser, Keith and Scarman).

The claimants, in arrears of mortgage, contracted to sell their properties to the **14–191** defendant at a price in excess of the amount owing on mortgage and sufficient to allow them to purchase another property. The defendant failed to complete and an order for specific performance was made. Before it was carried out the claimants' mortgagees enforced their securities so that (a) the claimants could no longer convey the properties and (b) there was insufficient even to pay off the mortgages, let alone purchase another property with the proceeds. The claimants therefore sought an order that the defendant should pay the purchase price, less the moneys received on the mortgagees' sales, and an inquiry as to damages.

LORD WILBERFORCE: "My Lords, this appeal arises in a vendors' action for specific **14–192** performance of a contract for the sale of land, the appellant being the purchaser and the vendors respondents. The factual situation is commonplace, indeed routine. An owner of land contracts to sell it to a purchaser; the purchaser fails to complete the contract; the vendor goes to the court and obtains an order that the contract be specifically performed; the purchaser still does not complete; the vendor goes back to the court and asks for the order for specific performance to be dissolved, for the contract to be terminated or 'rescinded,' and for an order for damages. One would think that the law as to so typical a set of facts would be both simple and clear. It is no credit to our law that it is neither, . . .

"By April 3, 1975, specific performance of the contract for sale had become **14–193** impossible. The vendors took no action upon the order for specific performance [entered on November 26 1974] until November 5, 1976, when they issued a notice of motion seeking (*a*) an order that the purchaser should pay the balance of the purchase price and an inquiry as to damages or (*b*) alternatively a declaration that they were entitled to treat the contract as repudiated by the purchaser and to forfeit the deposit and an inquiry as to damages.

"On February 25, 1977, Megarry V.-C. dismissed the motion. He rejected the first **14–194** claim on the ground that, as specific performance was no longer possible, it would be unjust to order payment of the full purchase price. The second claim was not pressed, on the ground that it was precluded by authority: *Capital and Suburban Properties Ltd, v Swycher* [1976] Ch. 319.

"The vendors appealed to the Court of Appeal who again rejected each **14–195** alternative: they followed the previous decision in *Swycher's* case. However they held that the vendors could recover damages under the Chancery Amendment Act 1858 (Lord Cairns' Act), which enables the court to award damages in addition to or in substitution for specific performance. They accordingly made an order discharging the order for specific performance and an order for an inquiry as to damages. They fixed the date on which damages should be assessed as November 26, 1974, being the date of entry of the order for specific performance. The purchaser is now appealing against this order.

"In this situation it is possible to state at least some uncontroversial propositions **14–196** of law.

14–197 "First, in a contract for the sale of land, after time has been made, or has become, of the essence of the contract, if the purchaser fails to complete, the vendor can *either* treat the purchaser as having repudiated the contract, accept the repudiation, and proceed to claim damages for breach of the contract, both parties being discharged from further performance of the contract; *or* he may seek from the court an order for specific performance with damages for any loss arising from delay in performance. (Similar remedies are of course available of purchasers against vendors.) This is simply the ordinary law of contract applied to contracts capable of specific performance.

14–198 "Secondly, the vendor may proceed by action for the above remedies (*viz*, specific performance or damages) in the alternative. At the trial he will however have to elect which remedy to pursue.

14–199 "Thirdly, if the vendor treats the purchaser as having repudiated the contract and accepts the repudiation, he cannot thereafter seek specific performance. This follows from the fact that, the purchaser having repudiated the contract and his repudiation having been accepted, both parties are discharged from further performance.

14–200 "At this point it is important to dissipate a fertile source of confusion and to make clear that although the vendor is sometimes referred to in the above situation as 'rescinding' the contract, this so-called 'rescission' is quite different from rescission ab initio, such as may arise for example in cases of mistake, fraud or lack of consent. In those cases, the contract is treated in law as never having come into existence. (Cases of a contractual right to rescind may fall under this principle but are not relevant to the present discussion.) In the case of an accepted repudiatory breach the contract has come into existence but has been put an end to or discharged. Whatever contrary indications may be disintered from old authorities, it is now quite clear, under the general law of contract, that acceptance of a repudiatory breach does not bring about 'rescission ab initio.'

14–201 "Fourthly, if an order for specific performance is sought and is made, the contract remains in effect and is not merged in the judgment for specific performance. This is clear law, best illustrated by the judgment of Sir Wilfrid Greene M.R. in *Austins of East Ham Ltd v Macey* [1941] Ch. 338, 341 in a passage which deals both with this point and with that next following. It repays quotation in full.

14–202 'The contract is still there. Until it is got rid of, it remains as a blot on the title, and the position of the vendor, where the purchaser has made default, is that he is entitled, not to annul the contract by the aid of the court, but to obtain the normal remedy of a party to a contract which the other party has repudiated. He cannot, in the circumstances, treat it as repudiated except by order of the court and the effect of obtaining such an order is that the contract, which until then existed, is brought to an end. The real position, in my judgment, is that, so far from proceeding to the enforcement of an order for specific performance, the vendor, in such circumstances is choosing a remedy which is alternative to the remedy of proceeding under the order for specific performance. He could attempt to enforce that order and could levy an execution which might prove completely fruitless. Instead of doing that, he elects to ask the court to put an end to the contract, and that is an alternative to an order for enforcing specific performance.'

14–203 "Fifthly, if the order for specific performance is not complied with by the purchaser, the vendor may *either* apply to the court for enforcement of the order, *or* may apply to the court to dissolve the order and ask the court to put an end to the contract. This proposition is as stated in *Austins of East Ham Ltd v Macey* [1941] Ch. 338 (and see *Singh (Sudagar) v Nazeer* [1979] Ch. 474 at 480, *per* Megarry V.-C.) and is in my opinion undoubted law, both on principle and authority. It follows, indeed, automatically from the facts that the contract remains in force after the order for specific performance and that the purchaser has committed a breach of it of a repudiatory character which he has not remedied, or as Megarry V.-C. puts it [1979] Ch. 474 at 480, 790, that he is refusing to complete.

"These propositions being, as I think they are, uncontrovertible, there only **14–204** remains the question whether, if the vendor takes the latter course, *i.e.*, of applying to the court to put an end to the contract, he is entitled to recover damages for breach of the contract. On principle one may ask 'Why ever not?' If, as is clear, the vendor is entitled, after, and notwithstanding that an order for specific performance has been made, if the purchaser still does not complete the contract, to ask the court to permit him to accept the purchaser's repudiation and to declare the contract to be terminated, why, if the court accedes to this, should there not follow the ordinary consequences, undoubted under the general law of contract, that on such acceptance and termination the vendor may recover damages for breach of contract?

"I now consider the arguments which are said to support the negative answer. **14–205**

"The principal authority lies in the case of *Henty v Schröder*, 12 Ch.D. 666, 667 in which Sir George Jessel M.R. is briefly reported as having laid down that a vendor 'could not at the same time obtain an order to have the agreement rescinded and claim damages against the defendant for breach of the agreement.'

At first instance, if has been followed usually uncritically . . . Finally, *Henty v Schröder* was endorsed by the Court of Appeal in *Capital and Suburban Properties Ltd v Swycher* ("*Swycher's* case") [1976] Ch. 319, but on a new basis which I shall shortly consider, and in the present case.

This is however the first time that this House has had to consider the right of an **14–206** innocent party to a contract for the sale of land to damages on the contract being put an end to by accepted repudiation, and I think that we have the duty to take a fresh look. I should certainly be reluctant to invite your Lordships to endorse a line of authority so weak and unconvincing in principle. Fortunately there is support for a more attractive and logical approach from another bastion of the common law whose courts have adopted a more robust attitude . . .

[He then considered *McDonald v Dennys Lascelles Ltd*. (1933) 43 C.L.R. 457; **14–207** *Holland v Wiltshire* (1954) 90 C.L.R. 409 and *Mckenna v Richey* [1950] V.L.R. 360.]

"My Lords, I am happy to follow the latter case. In my opinion *Henty v Schröder*, **14–208** 12 Ch.D. 666, cannot stand against the powerful tide of logical objection and judicial reasoning. It should no longer be regarded as of authority: the cases following it should be overruled . . .

"The second basis for denying damages in such cases as the present is that which **14–209** underlines the judgment of the Court of Appeal in *Swycher's* case. This is really a rationalisation of *Henty v Schröder*, 12 Ch.D. 666, the weakness of which case the court well perceived. The main argument there accepted was that by deciding to seek the remedy of specific performance the vendor (or purchaser) has made an election which either is irrevocable or which becomes so when the order for specific performance is made. A second limb of this argument (but in reality a different argument) is that the vendor (or purchaser) has adequate remedies under the order for specific performance so that there is no need, or equitable ground, for allowing him to change his ground and ask for damages.

14–210   "In my opinion, the argument based on irrevocable election, strongly pressed by the appellant's counsel in the present appeal, is unsound. Election, though the subject of much learning and refinement, is in the end a doctrine based on simple considerations of common sense and equity. It is easy to see that a party who has chosen to put an end a contract by accepting the other party's repudiation cannot afterwards seek specific performance. This is simply because the contract has gone—what is dead is dead. But it is no more difficult to agree that a party, who has chosen to seek specific performance, may quite well thereafter, if specific performance fails to be realised, say, 'Very well, then, the contract should be regarded as terminated.' It is quite consistent with a decision provisionally to keep alive, to say, 'Well, this is no use—let us now end the contract's life.' A vendor who seeks (and gets) specific performance is merely electing for a course which may or may not lead to implementation of the contract—what he elects for is not eternal and unconditional affirmation, but a continuance of the contract under control of the court which control involves the power, in certain events, to terminate it. If he makes an election at all, he does so when he decides not to proceed under the order for specific performance, but to ask the court to terminate the contract: see the judgment of Sir Wilfrid Greene M.R. in *Austins of East Ham Ltd v Macey* [1941] Ch. 338 quoted above. The fact is that the election argument proves too much. If it were correct it would deny the vendor not just the right to damages, but the right to 'rescind' the contract, but there is no doubt that this right exists: what is in question is only the right on 'rescission,' to claim damages.

14–211   "In my respectful opinion therefore *Swycher's* case [1976] Ch. 319, whether it should be regarded as resting upon *Henty v Schröder*, 12 Ch.D. 666, or upon an independent argument based on election was wrongly decided in so far as it denied a right to contractual damages and should so far be overruled. The vendors should have been entitled, upon discharge of the contract, on grounds of normal and accepted principle, to damages appropriate for a breach of contract.

14–212   "There is one final point, on this part of the case, on which I should make a brief observation. Once the matter has been placed in the hands of a court of equity, or one exercising equity jurisdiction, the subsequent control of the matter will be exercised according to equitable principles. The court would not make an order dissolving the decree of specific performance and terminating the contract (with recovery of damages) if to do so would be unjust, in the circumstances then existing, to the other party, in this case to the purchaser. This is why there was, in the Court of Appeal, rightly, a relevant and substantial argument, repeated in this House, that the non-completion of the contract was due to the default of the vendors: if this had been made good, the court could properly have refused them the relief sought. But the Court of Appeal came to the conclusion that this non-completion, and the ultimate impossibility of completion, was the fault of the purchaser. I agree with their conclusion and their reasons on this point and shall not repeat or add to them.

14–213   "It is now necessary to deal with questions relating to the measure of damages. The Court of Appeal, while denying the vendors' right to damages at common law, granted damages under Lord Cairns' Act. Since, on the view which I take, damages can be recovered at common law, two relevant questions now arise. (1) Whether Lord Cairns' Act provides a different measure of damages from the common law; if so, the respondents would be in a position to claim the more favourable basis to them. (2) If the measure of damages is the same, on what basis they should be calculated.

14–214   "Since the decision of this House, by majority, in *Leeds Industrial Co-operative Society Ltd v Slack* [1924] A.C. 851 it is clear that the jurisdiction to award damages in accordance with section 2 of Lord Cairns' Act (accepted by the House as surviving the repeal of the Act) may arise in some cases in which damages could not be recovered at common law; examples of this would be damages in lieu of a quia timet injunction and damages for breach of a restrictive covenant to which the plaintiff was not a party. To this extent the Act created a power to award damages which did not exist before at common law. But apart from these, and similar cases where damages could not be claimed at all at common law there is sound authority for the proposition that the Act does not provide for the assessment of damages on any new basis. The wording of section 2 'may be assessed in such manner as the court shall direct' does not so suggest, but clearly refers only to procedure . . .

[He examined various cases and continued:] "On the balance of these authorities **14–215** and also on principle, I find in the Act no warrant for the court awarding damages differently from common law damages, but the question is left open on what date such damages, however awarded, ought to be assessed.

"The general principle for the assessment of damages is compensatory, *i.e.*, that **14–216** the innocent party is to be placed, so far as money can do so, in the same position as if the contract had been performed. Where the contract is one of sale, this principle normally leads to assessment of damages as at the date of the breach—a principle recognised and embodied in section 51 of the Sale of Goods Act 1893. But this is not an absolute rule: if to follow it would give rise to injustice, the court has power to fix such other date as may be appropriate in the circumstances.

"In cases where a breach of a contract for sale has occurred, and the innocent **14–217** party reasonably continues to try to have the contract completed, it would to me appear more logical and just rather than tie him to the date of the original breach, to assess damages as at the date when (otherwise than by his default) the contract is lost. Support for this approach is to be found in the cases. In *Ogle v Earl Vane* (1867) L.R. 2 Q.B. 275; L.R. 3 Q.B. 272 the date was fixed by reference to the time when the innocent party, acting reasonably, went into the market; in *Hickman v Haynes* (1875) L.R. 10 C.P. 598 at a reasonable time after the last request of the defendants (buyers) to withhold delivery. In *Radford v De Froberville* [1977] 1 W.L.R. 1262, where the defendant had convenanted to build a wall, damages were held measurable as at the date of the bearing rather than at the date of the defendant's breach, unless the plaintiff ought reasonably to have mitigated the breach at an earlier date.

"In the present case if it is accepted, as I would accept, that the vendors acted **14–218** reasonably in pursuing the remedy of specific performance, the date on which that remedy became aborted (not by the vendor's fault) should logically be fixed as the date on which damages should be assessed. Choice of this date would be in accordance both with common law principle, as indicated in the authorities I have mentioned, and with the wording of the Act 'in substitution for . . . specific performance.' The date which emerges from this is April 3, 1975—the first date on which mortgages contracted to sell a portion of the property. I would vary the order of the Court of Appeal by substituting this date for that fixed by them—viz. November 26, 1974. The same date (April 3, 1975) should be used for the purpose of limiting the respondents' right to interest on damages. Subject to these modifications I would dismiss the appeal." [Lords Salmon, Fraser, Keith of Kinkel and Scarman agreed.]

CO-OPERATIVE INSURANCE SOCIETY LTD & ARGYLL STORES (HOLDINGS) LTD

House of Lords [1998] A.C. 1 (Lords Hoffman, Browne–Wilkinson Slynn of Hadley, **14–219** Hope of Craighead & Clyde)

LORD HOFFMANN

"1. The issue

In 1955 Lord Goddard C.J. said:

> 'No authority has been quoted to show that an injunction will be granted
> enjoining a person to carry on a business, nor can I think that one ever would
> be, certainly not where the business is a losing concern:' *Attorney-General v
> Colchester Corporation* [1955] 2 Q.B. 207, 217.

In this case his prediction has been falsified. The appellant defendants. Argyll Stores
(Holdings) Ltd ('Argyll'), decided in May 1995 to close their Safeway supermarket
in the Hillsborough Shopping Centre in Sheffield because it was losing money. This
was a breach of a covenant in their lease, which contained in clause 4(19) a positive
obligation to keep the premises open for retail trade during the usual hours of
business. Argyll admitted the breach and, in an action by the landlord. Co-operative
Insurance Society Ltd ('C.I.S.') consented to an order for damages to be assessed.
But the Court of Appeal [1996] Ch. 286, reversing the trial judge. ordered that the
covenant be specifically performed. It made a final injunction ordering Argyll to
trade on the premises during the remainder of the term (which will expire on 3
August 2014) or until an earlier subletting or assignment. The Court of Appeal
suspended its order for three months to allow time for Argyll to complete an
assignment which by that time had been agreed. After a short agreed extension, the
lease was assigned with the landlord's consent. In fact, therefore, the injunction
never took effect. The appeal to your Lordships is substantially about costs. But the
issue remains of great importance to landlords and tenants under other commercial
leases . . .

14–220   "The judge refused to order specific performance. He said that there was on the
authorities a settled practice that orders which would require a defendant to run a
business would not be made. He was not content, however, merely to follow
authority. He gave reasons why he thought that specific performance would be
inappropriate. Two such reasons were by way of justification for the general
practice. An order to carry on a business, as opposed to an order to perform a
'single and well-defined act,' was difficult to enforce by the sanction of committal.
And where a business was being run at a loss, specific relief would be "too far-
reaching and beyond the scope of control which the court should seek to impose."
The other two related to the particular case. A resumption of business would be
expensive (refitting the shop was estimated to cost over £1m.) and although Argyll
had knowingly acted in breach of covenant, it had done so 'in the light of the settled
practice of the court to award damages.' Finally, while the assessment of damages
might be difficult, it was the kind of exercise which the courts had done in the past.

4. The settled practice

14–221   "There is no dispute about the existence of the settled practice to which the judge
referred. It sufficient for this purpose to refer to *Braddon Towers Ltd v International
Stores Ltd*. [1987] 1 E.G.L.R. 209, 213, where Slade J. said:

> 'Whether or not this may be properly described as a rule of law. I do not doubt
> that for many years practitioners have advised their clients that it is the settled
> and invariable practice of this court never to grant mandatory injunctions
> requiring persons to carry on business.'

But the practice has never, so far as I know, been examined by this House and it is open to C.I.S. to say that it rests upon inadequate grounds or that it has been too inflexibly applied.

"Specific performance is traditionally regarded in English law as an exceptional **14–222** remedy, as opposed to the common law damages to which a successful plaintiff is entitled as of right. There may have been some element of later rationalisation of an untidier history, but by the 19th century it was orthodox doctrine that the power to decree specific performance was part of the discretionary jurisdiction of the Court of Chancery to do justice in cases in which the remedies available at common law were inadequate. This is the basis of the general principle that specific performance will not be ordered when damages are an adequate remedy. By contrast, in countries with legal systems based on civil law, such as France, Germany and Scotland, the plaintiff is prima facie entitled to specific performance. The cases in which he is confined to a claim for damages are regarded as the exceptions. In practice, however, there is less difference between common law and civilian systems than these general statements might lead one to suppose. The principles upon which English judges exercise the discretion to grant specific performance are reasonably well settled and depend upon a number of considerations, mostly of a practical nature, which are of very general application. I have made no investigation of civilian systems, but a priori I would expect that judges take much the same matters into account in deciding whether specific performance would be inappropriate in a particular case.

"The practice of not ordering a defendant to carry on a business is not entirely **14–223** dependent upon damages being an adequate remedy. In *Dowty Boulton Paul Ltd v Wolverhampton Corporation* [1971] 1 W.L.R. 204. Sir John Pennycuick V.-C. refused to order the corporation to maintain an airfield as a going concern because: 'It is very well established that the court will not order specific performance of an obligation to carry on a business:' see p.211. He added: 'It is unnecessary in the circumstances to discuss whether damages would be an adequate remedy to the company:' see p.212. Thus the reasons which underlie the established practice may justify a refusal of specific performance even when damages are not an adequate remedy.

"The most frequent reason given in the cases for declining to order someone to **14–224** carry on a business is that it would require constant supervision by the court. In *J.C. Williamson Ltd v Lukey and Mulholland* (1931) 45 C.L.R. 282, 297–298, Dixon J. said flatly: 'Specific performance is inapplicable when the continued supervision of the court is necessary in order to ensure the fulfillment of the contract.'

"There has, I think, been some misunderstanding about what is meant by **14–225** continued superintendence. It may at first sight suggest that the judge (or some other officer of the court) would literally have to supervise the execution of the order. In *C.H. Giles & Co. Ltd v Morris* [1972] 1 W.L.R. 307, 318 Megarry J. said that 'difficulties of constant superintendence' were a 'narrow consideration' because:

> 'there is normally no question of the court having to send its officers to supervise the performance of the order ... Performance ... is normally secured by the realisation of the person enjoined that he is liable to be punished for contempt if evidence of his disobedience to the order is put before the court; ...'

This is, of course, true but does not really meet the point. The judges who have said that the need for constant supervision was an objection to such orders were no doubt well aware that supervision would in practice take the form of rulings by the court, on applications made by the parties, as to whether there had been a breach of the order. It is the possibility of the court having to give an indefinite series of such rulings in order to ensure the execution of the order which has been regarded as undesirable.

14–226   "Why should this be so? A principal reason is that, as Megarry J. pointed out in the passage to which I have referred, the only means available to the court to enforce its order is the quasi-criminal procedure of punishment for contempt. This is powerful weapon: so powerful, in fact, as often to be unsuitable as an instrument for adjudicating upon the disputes which may arise over whether a business is being run in accordance with the terms of the court's order. The heavy-handed nature of the enforcement mechanism is a consideration which may go to the exercise of the court's discretion in other cases as well, but its use to compel the running of a business is perhaps the paradigm case of its disadvantages and it is in this context that I shall discuss them.

14–227   "The prospect of committal or even a fine, with the damage to commercial reputation which will be caused by a finding of contempt of court, is likely to have at least two undesirable consequences. First, the defendant, who ex hypothesi did not think that it was in his economic interest to run the business at all, now has to make decisions under a sword of Damocles which may descend if the way the business is run does not conform to the terms of the order. This is, as one might say, no way to run a business. In this case the Court of Appeal made light of the point because it assumed that, once the defendant had been ordered to run the business, self-interest and compliance with the order would thereafter go hand in hand. But, as I shall explain, this is not necessarily true.

Secondly, the seriousness of a finding of contempt for the defendant means that any application to enforce the order is likely to be a heavy and expensive piece of litigation. The possibility of repeated applications over a period of time means that, in comparison with a once-and-for-all inquiry as to damages, the enforcement of the remedy is likely to be expensive in terms of cost to the parties and the resources of the judicial system.

14–228   "This is a convenient point at which to distinguish between orders which require a defendant to carry on an activity, such as running a business over or more or less extended period of time, and orders which require him to achieve a result. The possibility of repeated applications for rulings on compliance with the order which arises in the former case does not exist to anything like the same extent in the latter. Even if the achievement of the result is a complicated matter which will take some time, the court, if called upon to rule, only has to examine the finished work and say whether it complies with the order. This point was made in the context of relief against forfeiture in *Shiloh Spinners Ltd v Harding* [1973] A.C. 691. If it is a condition of relief that the tenant should have complied with a repairing covenant, difficulty of supervision need not be an objection. As Lord Wilberforce said, at p.724:

> 'what the court has to do is to satisfy itself, ex post facto, that the covenanted work has been done, and it has ample machinery, through certificates, or by inquiry, to do precisely this.'

This distinction between orders to carry on activities and orders to achieve results explains why the courts have in appropriate circumstances ordered specific performance of building contracts and repairing covenants: see *Wolverhampton Corporation v Emmons* [1901] 1 K.B. 515 (building contract) and *Jeune v Queens Cross Properties Ltd.* [1974] Ch. 97 (repairing covenant). It by no means follows, however, that even obligations to achieve a result will always be enforced by specific performance. There may be other objections, to some of which I now turn.

"One such objection, which applies to orders to achieve a result and a fortiori to **14–229** orders to carry on an activity, is imprecision in the terms of the order. If the terms of the court's order, reflecting the terms of the obligation, cannot be precisely drawn, the possibility of wasteful litigation over compliance is increased. So is the oppression caused by the defendant having to do things under threat of proceedings for contempt. The less precise the order, the fewer the signposts to the forensic minefield which he has to traverse. The fact that the terms of a contractual obligation are sufficiently definite to escape being void for uncertainty, or to found a claim for damages, or to permit compliance to be made a condition of relief against forfeiture, does not necessarily mean that they will be sufficiently precise to be capable of being specifically enforced. So in *Wolverhampton Corporation v Emmons*. Romer L.J. said, at p.525, that the first condition for specific enforcement of a building contract was that

'the particulars of the work are so far definitely ascertained that the court can sufficiently see what is the exact nature of the work of which it is asked to order the performance.'

"Similarly in *Morris v Redland Bricks Ltd*. [1970] A.C. 652, 666, Lord Upjohn **14–230** stated the following general principle for the grant of mandatory injunctions to carry out building works:

'the court must be careful to see that the defendant knows exactly in fact what he has to do and this means not as a matter of law but as a matter of fact, so that in carrying out an order he can give his contractors the proper instructions.'

Precision is of course a question of degree and the courts have shown themselves willing to cope with a certain degree of imprecision in cases of orders requiring the achievement of a result in which the plaintiffs' merits appeared strong; like all the reasons which I have been discussing, it is, taken alone, merely a discretionary matter to be taken into account: see *Spry. Equitable Remedies*, 4th ed. (1990). p.112. It is, however, a very important one.

"I should at this point draw attention to what seems to me to have been a **14–231** misreading of certain remarks of Lord Wilberforce in *Shiloh Spinners Ltd v Harding*. at p.724. He pointed out, as I have said, that to grant relief against forfeiture subject to compliance with a repairing covenant involves the court in no more than the possibility of a retrospective assessment of whether the covenanted work has been done. For this reason, he said:

'Where it is necessary, and, in my opinion, right, to move away from some 19th century authorities, is to reject as a reason against granting relief, the impossibility for the courts to supervise the doing of work.'

This is plainly a remark about cases involving the achievement of a result such as doing repairs, and, within that class, about making compliance a condition of relief against forfeiture. But in *Tito v Waddell (No. 2)* [1977] Ch. 106, 322 Sir Robert Megarry V.-C. took it to be a generalisation about specific performance and, in particular, a rejection of difficulty of supervision as an objection, even in cases of orders to carry on an activity. Sir Robert Megarry V.-C. regarded it as an adoption of his own views (based, as I have said, on incomplete analysis of what was meant by difficulty of supervision) in *C.H. Giles & Co. Ltd v Morris* [1972] 1 W.L.R. 307, 318. In the present case [1996] Ch. 286, 292–293. Leggatt L.J. took this claim at face value. In fact, Lord Wilberforce went on to say that impossibility of supervision 'is a reality, no doubt, and explains why specific performance cannot be granted of agreements to this effect . . .' Lord Wilberforce was in my view drawing attention to the fact that the collection of reasons which the courts have in mind when they speak of difficulty of supervision apply with much greater force to orders for specific performance, giving rise to the possibility of committal for contempt, than they do to conditions for relief against forfeiture. While the paradigm case to which such objections apply is the order to carry on an activity, they can also apply to an order requiring the achievement of a result.

14–232   "There is a further objection to an order requiring the defendant to carry on a business, which was emphasised by Millett L.J. in the Court of Appeal. This is that it may cause injustice by allowing the plaintiff to enrich himself at the defendant's expense. The loss which the defendant may suffer through having to comply with the order (for example, by running a business at a loss for an indefinite period) may be far greater than the plaintiff would suffer from the contract being broken. As Professor R. J. Sharpe explains in 'Specific Relief for Contract Breach,' ch. 5 of *Studies in Contract Law* (1980), edited by Reiter and Swan. p.129:

> 'In such circumstances, a specific decree in favour of the plaintiff will put him in a bargaining position vis-à-vis the defendant whereby the measure of what he will receive will be the value to the defendant of being released from performance. If the plaintiff bargains effectively, the amount he will set will exceed the value to him of performance and will approach the cost to the defendant to complete.'

14–233   This was the reason given by Lord Westbury L.C. in *Isenberg v East India House Estate Co. Ltd*. (1863) 3 De G.J. & S. 263, 273 for refusing a mandatory injunction to compel the defendant to pull down part of a new building which interfered with the plaintiff's light and exercising instead the Court of Chancery's recently-acquired jurisdiction under Lord Cairns's Act 1858 (21 & 22 Vict. c. 27) to order payment of damages:

> '. . . I hold it . . . to be the duty of the court in such a case as the present not, by granting a mandatory injunction, to deliver over the defendants to the plaintiff bound hand and foot, in order to be made subject to any extortionate demand that he may by possibility make, but to substitute for such mandatory injunction an inquiry before itself, in order to ascertain the measure of damage that has been actually sustained.'

14–234   It is true that the defendant has, by his own breach of contract, put himself in such an unfortunate position. But the purpose of the law of contract is not to punish wrongdoing but to satisfy the expectations of the party entitled to performance. A remedy which enables him to secure, in money terms, more than the performance due to him is unjust. From a wider perspective, it cannot be in the public interest for the courts to require someone to carry on business at a loss if there is any plausible alternative by which the other party can be given compensation. It is not only a waste of resources but yokes the parties together in a continuing hostile relationship. The order for specific performance prolongs the battle. If the defendant is ordered to run a business, its conduct becomes the subject of a flow of complaints, solicitors' letters and affidavits. This is wasteful for both parties and the legal system. An award of damages, on the other hand, brings the litigation to an end. The defendant pays damages, the forensic link between them is severed, they go their separate ways and the wounds of conflict can heal.

"The cumulative effect of these various reasons, none of which would necessarily **14–235** be sufficient on its own, seems to me to show that the settled practice is based upon sound sense. Of course the grant or refusal of specific performance remains a matter for the judge's discretion. There are no binding rules, but this does not mean that there cannot be settled principles, founded upon practical considerations of the kind which I have discussed, which do not have to be re-examined in every case, but which the courts will apply in all but exceptional circumstances. As Slade J. said, in the passage which I have quoted from *Braddon Towers Ltd v International Stores Ltd* [1987] 1 E.G.L.R. 209, 213, lawyers have no doubt for many years advised their clients on this basis. In the present case. Leggatt L.J. [1996] Ch. 286, 294 remarked that there was no evidence that such advice had been given. In my view, if the law or practice on a point is settled, it should be assumed that persons entering into legal transactions will have been advised accordingly. I am sure that Leggatt L.J. would not wish to encourage litigants to adduce evidence of the particular advice which they received. Indeed, I doubt whether such evidence would be admissible.

The decision of the Court of Appeal

"I must now examine the grounds upon which the majority of the Court of Appeal **14–236** [1996] Ch. 286 thought it right to reverse the judge. In the first place, they regarded the practice which he followed as outmoded and treated Lord Wilberforce's remarks about relief against forfeiture in *Shiloh Spinners Ltd v Harding* [1973] A.C. 691, 724 as justifying a rejection of the arguments based on the need for constant super-vision. Even Millett L.J., who dissented on other grounds, said, at p.303, that such objections had little force today. I do not agree. As I have already said, I think that Lord Wilberforce's remarks do not support this proposition in relation to specific performance of an obligation to carry on an activity and that the arguments based on difficulty of supervision remain powerful.

"The Court of Appeal said that it was enough if the contract defined the tenant's **14–237** obligation with sufficient precision to enable him to know what was necessary to comply with the order. Even assuming that this to be right. I do not think that the obligation in clause 4(19) can possibly be regarded as sufficiently precise to be capable of specific performance. It is to 'keep the demised premises open for retail trade.' It says nothing about the level of trade, the area of the premises within which trade is to be conducted, or even the kind of trade, although no doubt the tenant's choice would be restricted by the need to comply with the negative covenant in clause 4(12)(a) not to use the premises 'other than as a retail store for the sale of food groceries provisions and goods normally sold from time to time by a retail grocer food supermarkets and food superstores . . .' This language seems to me to provide ample room for argument over whether the tenant is doing enough to comply with the covenant.

"The Court of Appeal thought that once Argyll had been ordered to comply with **14–238** the covenant, it was, as Roch L.J. said, at p.298, 'inconceivable that they would not operate the business efficiently.' Leggatt L.J. said, at p.292, that the requirement

'was quite intelligible to the defendants, while they were carrying on business there . . . If the premises are to be run as a business, it cannot be in the defendants' interest to run it half-heartedly or inefficiently . . .'

This treats the way the tenant previously conducted business as measuring the extent of his obligation to do so. In my view this is a non sequitur: the obligation depends upon the language of the covenant and not upon what the tenant has previously chosen to do. No doubt it is true that it would not be in the interests of the tenant to run the business inefficiently. But running the business efficiently does not necessarily mean running it in the way it was run before. Argyll had decided that, from its point of view, the most efficient thing to do was to close the business altogether and concentrate its resources on achieving better returns elsewhere. If ordered to keep the business open, it might well decide that the next best strategy was to reduce its costs as far as was consistent with compliance with its obligations, in the expectation that a lower level of return would be more than compensated by higher returns from additional expenditure on more profitable shops. It is in my view wrong for the courts to speculate about whether Argyll might voluntarily carry on business in a way which would relieve the court from having to construe its order. The question of certainty must be decided on the assumption that the court might have to enforce the order according to its terms.

14–239 "C.I.S. argued that the court should not be concerned about future difficulties which might arise in connection with the enforcement of the order. It should simply make the order and see what happened. In practice Argyll would be likely to find a suitable assignee (as it in fact did) or conduct the business so as to keep well clear of any possible enforcement proceedings or otherwise come to terms with C.I.S. This may well be true, but the likelihood of Argyll having to perform beyond the requirements of its covenant or buy its way out of its obligation to incur losses seems to me to be in principle an objection to such an order rather than to recommend it. I think that it is normally undesirable for judges to make orders in terrorem, carrying a threat of imprisonment, which work only if no one inquires too closely into what they mean.

14–240 "The likelihood that the order would be effective only for a short time until an assignment is an equivocal argument. It would be burdensome to make Argyll resume business only to stop again after a short while if a short stoppage would not cause any substantial damage to the business of the shopping centre. On the other hand, what would happen if a suitable assignee could not be found? Would Argyll then have to carry on business until 2014? Mr. Smith, who appeared for C.I.S., said that if the order became oppressive (for example, because Argyll were being driven into bankruptcy) or difficult to enforce, they could apply for it to be varied or discharged. But the order would be a final order and there is no case in this jurisdiction in which such an order has been varied or discharged, except when the injuncted activity has been legalised by statute. Even assuming that there was such a jurisdiction if circumstances were radically changed. I find it difficult to see how this could be made to apply. Difficulties of enforcement would not be a change of circumstances. They would have been entirely predictable when the order was made. And so would the fact that Argyll would suffer unquantifiable loss if it was obliged to continue trading. I do not think that such expedients are an answer to the difficulties on which the objections to such orders are based.

14–241 "Finally, all three judges in the Court of Appeal took a very poor view of Argyll's conduct. Leggatt L.J. said [1996] Ch. 286, 295, that they had acted 'with gross commercial cynicism;' Roch L.J. began his judgment by saying that they had 'behaved very badly' and Millett L.J. said, at p.301, that they had no merits. The principles of equity have always had a strong ethical content and nothing which I say is intended to diminish the influence of moral values in their application. I can envisage cases of gross breach of personal faith, or attempts to use the threat of non-performance as blackmail, in which the needs of justice will override all the considerations which support the settled practice. But although any breach of covenant is regrettable, the exercise of the discretion as to whether or not to grant specific performance starts from the fact that the covenant has been broken. Both landlord and tenant in this case are large sophisticated commercial organisations and I have no doubt that both were perfectly aware that the remedy for breach of the covenant was likely to be limited to an award of damages. The interests of both were purely financial: there was no element of personal breach of faith, as in the Victorian cases of railway companies which refused to honour obligations to build stations for landowners whose property they had taken: compare *Greene v West Cheshire Railway Co.* (1871) L.R. 13 Eq. 44. No doubt there was an effect on the businesses of other traders in the Centre, but Argyll had made no promises to them and it is not suggested that C.I.S. warranted to other tenants that Argyll would remain. Their departure, with or without the consent of C.I.S., was a commercial risk which the tenants were able to deploy in negotiations for the next rent review. On the scale of broken promises, I can think of worse cases, but the language of the Court of Appeal left them with few adjectives to spare.

"It was no doubt discourteous not to have answered Mr. Wightman's letter. But to say, as Roch L.J. did, at p.299, that they had acted 'wantonly and quite unreasonably' by removing their fixtures seems to me an exaggeration. There was no question of stealing a march, or attempting to present C.I.S. with a fait accompli, because Argyll had no reason to believe that C.I.S. would have been able to obtain a mandatory injunction whether the fixtures had been removed or not. They had made it perfectly clear that they were closing the shop and given C.I.S. ample time to apply for such an injunction if so advised. **14–242**

Conclusion

"I think that no criticism can be made of the way in which Judge Maddocks **14–243** exercised his discretion. All the reasons which he gave were proper matters for him to take into account. In my view the Court of Appeal should not have interfered and I would allow the appeal and restore the order which he made."

All of their Lordships agreed with Lord Hoffmann. **14–244**

Section 4. Damages in Addition to or in Lieu of Injunction and Specific Performance

Section 50 of the Supreme Court Act 1981[89] provides: **14–245**

> "Where the Court of Appeal or the High Court has jurisdiction to entertain an application for an injunction or specific performance, it may award damages in addition to, or in substitution for, an injunction or specific performance."

This provision embodies and confers upon the named courts the jurisdiction that was conferred upon the Court of Chancery by s.2 of the Chancery Amendment Act 1858 (Lord Cairns' Act) which was later repealed.[90]

---

[89] See generally Jolowicz, *Damages in Equity—A Study of Lord Cairns' Act*, [1975] C.L.J. 224.
[90] The wording of the section is set out in the judgment of Sir Thomas Bingham M.R in *Jaggard v Sawyer*, [1995] 1 W.L.R. 269.

Jaggard v Sawyer[91] is now the leading case on the jurisdiction so far as it relates to damages in lieu of injunctions, and the Court's findings also affect the question of how the section might apply to awards of damages in substitution for specific performance. It is convenient, however, to take injunctions first.

14–246   Lord Cairns' Act enabled the Court of Chancery (i) to award damages (previously only awardable in common law courts) for *past* unlawful conduct "in addition to" awarding injunctions to restrain *future* unlawful conduct and (ii) to award damages "in substitution for" the grant of an injunction to restrain future unlawful conduct. Authoritative guidance on the exercise of the discretion in (ii) was given by A. L. Smith L.J. in *Shelfer v City of London Electric Lighting Co*[92] in the form of four conditions that required, as a working rule, to be met: the injury to the claimant's rights had to be small, capable of being estimated in money, and adequately compensable by a small sum; it must also be oppressive to the defendant to grant the injunction.[92a] Despite judicial zeal not to allow a wrong-doer merely to purchase the right to engage in wrongful activity, the net effect of an award of damages under (ii) is to allow a wrong-doer to engage lawfully in conduct that infringed a plaintiff's legal or other right. This is because, *per* Sir Thomas Bingham M.R., "a succession of future actions based on that conduct would, if brought, be dismissed or struck out, since a plaintiff could not complain of that for which he had already been compensated"[93] or, per Millett L.J., "the doctrine of res judicata operates to prevent the plaintiff and his successors from bringing proceedings thereafter to recover even nominal damages in respect of further wrongs for which the plaintiff has already been fully compensated." In addition, damages are awardable under (ii) if injunctive relief is refused on the grounds of delay, acquiescence etc. A.L. Smith L.J.'s "working rule" was, after all, no more than a crystallisation of the perceived practice of the courts of equity which, in the last analysis, awarded remedies according to the justice of the case.

14–247   On the measure of damages to be awarded in lieu, despite the *dicta* of Lord Wilberforce in *Johnson v Agnew*[94] to the effect that there could be no difference between the bases of assessment at common law and in equity, *Jaggard v Sawyer* makes clear that as regards injunctions, Lord Wilberforce cannot be taken to have intended to deny that some awards of damages under Lord Cairns' Act compensate for *future* wrongs—wrongs, therefore, not compensable at law. It is submitted, with respect, that the view of Millett L.J. to the effect that "Lord Wilberforce's statement . . . must be taken to be limited to the case where [the damages] are recoverable in respect of the same cause of action"[95] is clearly correct in principle. This

---

[91] [1995] 1 W. L. R. 269. at para.14–254. See too *Deakins v Hoskings* [1994] 1 E.G.L.R. 190; *Gafford v Graham* [1995] 3 E.G.L.R. 75; *Daniells v Mendonca* [1999] 78 P. & C.R. 401: *Marcic v Thames Water Utilities Ltd (No.2)* [2002] Q.B. 1003, overtaken by the HL's findings on liability in *Marcic (No.1)* [2004] 2 A.C. 42; *Midtown Ltd v City of London Real Property Co. Ltd* [2005] EWHC 33 (Ch) at [66]–[77].
[92] [1895] 1 Ch. 287 at 322–323.
[92a] [1995] 1 W.L.R. 269 at 280–281.
[93] *ibid.* at 286.
[94] [1980] A.C. 367 at 400.
[95] [1995] 1 W.L.R. 269 at 291.

view, moreover, may have consequences even for contractual cases where the duty breached, as in *Beswick v Beswick*,[96] is an on-going one so that, should specific performance be refused on some discretionary ground, an award of damages in lieu could properly be assessed, indeed, would *require* to be assessed, on a basis other than that adopted by courts of common law. This is a convenient moment at which to turn to damages in lieu of specific performance.

The extent of the jurisdiction, preserved by s.50 of the Supreme Court **14–248** Act 1981 is a matter of some doubt. It is clear that, in order for there to arise a power to award damages in lieu of specific performance, there must have been *jurisdiction* to order specific performance (even if, as a matter of discretion it was likely to be refused) as at the date of the writ.[97] But which of the grounds for refusing a decree go to jurisdiction and which to discretion? Ultimately the matter is one of statutory construction. It is here suggested that the first seven grounds covered in the preciding section ought to be seen as going to jurisdiction but the remainder only to discretion. This suggestion is put forward without any appeal to authority but principle enough can be advanced to defend it: it is impossible to enforce a promise made without consideration, unnecessary to grant a remedy where the common law remedy is adequate, pointless or impossible to act in vain, obnoxious to act contrary to public policy (and so on). Matters such as delay, hardship, mistake (and so on) can fairly be characterised as grounds on which, if appropriate, to exercise some grace but nothing more.

There is authority for the view that no damages can be awarded unless **14–249** specific performance is claimed[98] but that must be read subject to the *dicta* of Millett L.J. in *Jaggard v Sawyer*[99] which, in relation to injunctions, dissent from that view: if a claimant omitted to claim an injunction because, realistically, it would not be granted, the jurisdiction to award damages in lieu still existed. As a matter of principle, that ought to apply to specific performance.

Note that the jurisdiction also allows damages *in addition* to specific **14–250** performance. The purpose of this provision in relation to injunctions has already been explained[1] but in the present context, they might be awarded where, exceptionally, only part of a contract is specifically enforced the claimant being awarded damages for the defendant's failure to perform the rest.[2]

As to the measure of damages, Lord Wilberforce in *Johnson v Agnew*[3] **14–251** rejected the view that damages could be assessed on different bases under the Act and at common law. Megarry J., in *Wroth v Tyler*[4] had said that the

---

[96] [1968] A.C. 58.
[97] *Jaggard v Sawyer* [1995] 1 W.L.R. 269 at 284–285.
[98] *Horsler v Zorro* [1975] Ch. 302.
[99] above, at 289–290.
[1] See paras 14–21 and 14–22 and *Jaggard v Sawyer*, above, at 284–286.
[2] *e.g. Soames v Edge* (1860) John 669 (agreement to build house and lease to plaintiff: damages for failure to build, decree that lease of land be executed).
[3] [1980] A.C. 367.
[4] [1974] Ch. 30.

purpose of an award was to offer a true substitute for specific performance—which could only be refused at trial. That date, rather than the date of breach, might be the relevant one, therefore, in assessing compensation. This view is, with respect, clearly right, and is reconcilable with Lord Wilberforce's view. The common law rule did not invariably select the date of breach as the relevant one in determining loss: that was merely the *normal* rule in commercial contracts. But as it is always reasonable to seek specific performance of a contract for the sale of land[5] any increase in loss caused by denial of the relief at trial (so late in the day) ought, as a matter of justice, to be taken into account because "if to follow [the normal rule] would give rise to injustice, the court has power to fix such other date as may be appropriate in the circumstances."[6]

14–252   Millett L.J.'s view in *Jaggard v Sawyer*[7] arguing against, so far as injunctions are concerned, the abstraction of Lord Wilberforce's view from its context must, by its nature, apply across the board: it is impossible to see why, if Mrs Beswick had been refused a decree of specific performance merely on the ground of hardship to the defendant, she should not have been awarded substantial damages in lieu. It clearly would not be a true substitute for specific performance (an adequate remedy) to award her nominal damages which according to the reasoning in the case would be an inadequate remedy. It should be no objection that Peter Beswick's estate would thus get substantial damages for loss in reality suffered by another if the estate was in principle held entitled to specific performance. On the question whether the estate would be obliged to hand the damages over to Mrs Beswick personally, one would have to resolve the conflict between the principles (a) that, as a matter of law, it would have no duty so to do and, in equity,[8] Mrs Beswick is a volunteer, and (b) the view of Lord Pearce[9] who saw "no objection in principle to the estate enforcing the judgment, receiving the fruits on behalf of the widow and paying them over to the widow, *just as a bailee does when he recovers damages which should properly belong to the true owner of the goods*", which is tantamount to recognising (through, presumably, a constructive trust) a proprietary interest in a volunteer in rather special circumstances.

14–253   It should be noted, of course, that by reason of the Contract (Rights of Third Parties) Act 1999, applying to all contracts entered into after May 11, 2000, a claim like Mrs Beswick's personal claim might well now succeed. However, section 5 makes an oblique reference to the situation contemplated here: it provides that where a promisee has recovered in respect of a third party's loss, then, in any proceedings by the third party, the court shall reduce the award to the third party accordingly. The draftsman (and thus Parliament) seems to have assumed in this case that the promisee, contrary

---

[5] Except, perhaps, if one knows or ought to know that one's own hands are unclean.
[6] per Lord Wilberforce at 401. Note also Millett L.J.'s explanation, in *Jaggard v Sawyer*, above, at 290–291, of Lord Wilberforce's view as it affects injunction cases concerned with the prevention of future wrongs.
[7] above.
[8] See paras 4–30 *et seq.*
[9] *Beswick v Beswick* [1968] A.C. 58 at 92 (emphasis supplied); further see Lord Upjohn on enforcement rights *ibid.* at 100.

to the argument advanced here, might be able to resist either a personal or proprietary claim by the third party to receive any damages awarded to the promisee in respect of the third party's loss. Still, what Parliament *assumes* to be law is not itself law: only the *enactments* of the Queen in Parliament are recognised as law and the argument advanced in this paragraph must stand or fall independently of any assumption thought to underlie the Act.[10]

JAGGARD v SAWYER

Court of Appeal [1995] 1 W.L.R. 269; [1995] 2 All E.R. 189 (BINGHAM M.R., KENNEDY and MILLETT L.JJ.)

In a cul-de-sac residential development consisting of ten plots, the claimant and **14–254** defendants each owned one, together with part of the private road immediately fronting each. Each plot was bound by a restrictive covenant preventing the user of any part of any plot not built upon from being used other than as a private garden. The defendants purchased land adjacent to their plot but inaccessible from the private road other than through their plot. They obtained, in 1988, planning permission to build on the adjacent land and (wrongly believing the road to be a public one) to construct a driveway leading to it, over their garden, from the road. The claimant threatened injunctive proceedings on the ground of (i) breach of covenant and (ii) trespass over her portion of the road but did not act on the threat. On 14 June 1989 the defendants began building and on 10 August 1989, the building at an advanced stage, the claimant began proceedings for an injunction. No interlocutory relief was sought and the building was completed thereafter. At trial it was common ground that the road was private but was the only means of access to the plot. The judge held that although the defendants were in breach of covenant, had committed trespass and would by using the road in future, continue to commit trespass, it would, in the circumstances, have been oppressive to grant an injunction and that damages should be awarded in lieu under section 50 of the Supreme Court Act 1981. The award would be £694.44, one ninth share of £6,250, the sum which the nine plot-owners might reasonably have demanded from the defendants as the price of release from the covenant and for the grant of a right of way. The claimant appealed.

SIR THOMAS BINGHAM M.R.: "The judge recognised that a plaintiff who can show **14–255** that his legal right will be violated by the defendant's conduct is prima facie entitled to the grant of an injunction. He accepted that the court will only rarely and reluctantly permit such violation to occur or continue. But he held that this case fulfilled the four tests laid down by A. L. Smith L.J. in *Shelfer's* case to bring this case within the exception. The real question in this appeal is whether that judgment is sustainable.

"(1) He regarded the injury to the plaintiff's right as small. This is in my view so. **14–256** It is not suggested that the increase in traffic attributable to the existence of No. 5A will be other than minimal, or that the cost of keeping up the road will be significantly increased. The defendants have in any event offered throughout to contribute to the cost of upkeep and are willing, if a draft is tendered to them, to execute a deed binding themselves by the same covenants as other residents of the

---

[10] There is further support for the argument that the damages would be held on constructive trust from *Hunt v Severs* [1994] 2 A.C. 350 (tort claimant holding damages on trust for carer).

Avenue. It is not suggested that the driveway to No. 5A impairs the visual amenity of the plaintiff's house or affects its value. There is of course a violation of the plaintiff's strict legal right, but that will be so in any case of this kind.

14–257   "(2) The judge considered the value of the injury to the plaintiff's right as capable of being estimated in money. He based himself on the *Wrotham Park* approach. In my view he was justified. He valued the right at what a reasonable seller would sell it for. In situations of this kind a plaintiff should not be treated as eager to sell, which he very probably is not. But the court will not value the right at the ransom price which a very reluctant plaintiff might put on it. I see no error in the judge's approach to this aspect.

14–258   "(3) The judge held that the injury to the plaintiff's legal right was one which could be adequately compensated by a small money payment. I agree, and I do not think this conclusion can be faulted.

14–259   "(4) The judge concluded that in all the circumstances it would be oppressive to the defendants to grant the injunctions sought. Most of the argument turned on this condition, and in particular on the significance which the judge attached to the plaintiff's failure to seek interlocutory relief.

14–260   "It is important to bear in mind that the test is one of oppression, and the court should not slide into application of a general balance of convenience test. But oppression must be judged as at the date the court is asked to grant an injunction, and (as Brightman J. recognised in the *Wrotham Park* case) the court cannot ignore the reality with which it is then confronted. It is relevant that the plaintiff could at an early stage have sought interlocutory relief, which she would seem very likely to have obtained; but it is also relevant that the defendants could have sought a declaration of right. These considerations are not decisive. It would weigh against a finding of oppression if the defendants had acted in blatant and calculated disregard of the plaintiff's rights, of which they were aware, but the judge held that this was not so, and the plaintiff's solicitors may be thought to have indicated that damages would be an acceptable remedy. . . . The judge was in my view entitled to hold on all the facts before the court at trial that the grant of an injunction would be oppressive to the defendants, and I share that view.

14–261   "I am of the clear opinion that the appeal must be dismissed."

KENNEDY L.J.: "I agree."

14–262   MILLETT L.J.: "This appeal raises yet again the question: what approach should the court adopt when invited to exercise its statutory jurisdiction to award damages instead of granting an injunction to restrain a threatened or continuing trespass or breach of a restrictive covenant? And if the court accedes to the invitation on what basis should damages be assessed?

14–263   "Before considering these questions, it is desirable to state some general propositions which are established by the authorities and which are, or at least ought to be, uncontroversial.

14–264   "(1) The jurisdiction was originally conferred by section 2 of the Chancery Amendment Act 1858, commonly known as Lord Cairns's Act. It is now to be found in section 50 of the Supreme Court Act 1981. It is a jurisdiction to award damages 'in addition to or in substitution for such injunction or specific performance.'

14–265   "(2) The principal object of Lord Cairns's Act is well known. It was described by Turner L.J. in *Ferguson v Wilson* (1866) L.R. 2 Ch. App.77, 88. It was to enable the Court of Chancery, when declining to grant equitable relief and leaving the plaintiff to his remedy at law, to award the plaintiff damages itself instead of sending him to the common law courts to obtain them. From the very first, however, it was recognised that the Act did more than this. The jurisdiction of the Court of Chancery was wider than that of the common law courts, for it could give relief where there was no cause of action at law. As early as 1863, Turner L.J. himself had recognised the potential effect of Lord Cairns's Act. In *Eastwood v Lever* (1863) 4 De G.J. & S. 114, 128, he pointed out that the Act had empowered the courts of equity to award damages in cases where the common law courts could not. The Act, he said, was not "confined to cases in which the plaintiffs could recover damages at law." Damages at common law are recoverable only in respect of causes of action which are complete at the date of the writ; damages for future or repeated wrongs must be made the subject of fresh proceedings. Damages in substitution for an injunction, however, relate to the future, not the past. They inevitably extend beyond the damages to which the plaintiff may be entitled at law. In *Leeds Industrial Co-operative Society Ltd v Slack* [1924] A.C. 851 the House of Lords confirmed the jurisdiction of the courts to award damages under the Act in respect of an injury which was threatened but had not yet occurred. No such damages could have been awarded at common law.

"(3) The nature of the cause of action is immaterial; it may be in contract or tort. **14–266** Lord Cairns's Act referred in terms to 'a breach of any covenant, contract, or agreement, or against the commission or continuance of any wrongful act.' The jurisdiction to award damages in substitution for an injunction has most commonly been exercised in cases where the defendant's building has infringed the plaintiff's right to light or where it has been erected in breach of a restrictive covenant. Despite dicta to the contrary in *Woollerton and Wilson Ltd v Richard Costain Ltd* [1970] 1 W.L.R. 411 there is in my opinion no justification for excluding cases of threatened or continuing trespass on the ground that trespass is actionable at law without proof of actual damage. Equitable relief, whether by way of injunction or damages under Lord Cairns's Act, is available because the common law remedy is inadequate; but the common law remedy of damages in cases of continuing trespass is inadequate not because the damages are likely to be small or nominal but because they cover the past only and not the future.

"(4) The power to award damages under Lord Cairns's Act arises whenever the **14–267** court 'has jurisdiction to entertain an application' for an injunction or specific performance. This question must be determined as at the date of the writ. If the court would then have had jurisdiction to grant an injunction, it has jurisdiction to award damages instead. When the court comes to consider whether to grant an injunction or award damages instead, of course, it must do so by reference to the circumstances as they exist at the date of the hearing.

"(5) The former question is effectively one of jurisdiction. The question is **14–268** whether, at the date of the writ, the court *could* have granted an injunction, not whether it *would* have done: *City of London Brewery Co. v Tennant* (1873) L.R. 9 Ch.App.212. Russell L.J. put it neatly in *Hooper v Rogers* [1975] Ch. 43 at 48 when he said that the question was 'whether . . . the judge could have (however unwisely . . .) made a mandatory order.' There have been numerous cases where damages under Lord Cairns's Act were refused because at the date of the writ it was impossible to grant an injunction or specific performance: for one well known example, see *Lavery v Pursell* (1888) 39 Ch.D. 508. The recent case of *Surrey County Council v Bredero Homes Ltd* [1993] 1 W.L.R. 1361 appears to have been a case of this character.

"(6) It is not necessary for the plaintiff to include a claim for damages in his writ. **14–269** As long ago as 1868 Lord Chelmsford L.C. held that damages may be awarded under Lord Cairns's Act 'though not specifically prayed for by the bill, the statute having vested a discretion in the judge, which he may exercise when he thinks the case fitting without the prayer of the party:' see *Betts v Neilson* (1868) L.R. 3 Ch.App. 429 at 411.'

It would be absurd as well as misleading to insist on the plaintiff including a claim for damages in his writ when he is insisting on his right to an injunction and opposing the defendant's claim that he should be content to receive damages instead. By a parity of reasoning it is not in my opinion necessary for a plaintiff to include a claim for an injunction in order to found a claim for damages under the Act. It would be absurd to require him to include a claim for an injunction if he is sufficiently realistic to recognise that in the circumstances he is unlikely to obtain one and intends from the first to ask the court for damages instead. But he ought to make it clear whether he is claiming damages for past injury at common law or under the Act in substitution for an injunction.

14–270   "(7) In *Anchor Brewhouse Developments Ltd v Berkley House (Docklands Developments) Ltd* (1987) 38 B.L.R. 87 Scott J. granted an injunction to restrain a continuing trespass. In the course of his judgment, however, he cast doubt on the power of the court to award damages for future trespasses by means of what he described as a 'once and for all payment.' This was because, as he put it, the court could not by an award of damages put the defendant in the position of a person entitled to an easement; whether or not an injunction were granted, the defendant's conduct would still constitute a trespass; and a succession of further actions for damages could accordingly still be brought. This reasoning strikes at the very heart of the statutory jurisdiction; it is in marked contrast to the attitude of the many judges who from the very first have recognised that, while the Act does not enable the court to license future wrongs, this may be the practical result of withholding injunctive relief; and it is inconsistent with the existence of the jurisdiction, confirmed in *Leeds Industrial Co-operative Society Ltd v Slack* [1924] A.C. 851, to award damages under the Act in a quia timet action. It is in my view fallacious because it is not the award of damages which has the practical effect of licensing the defendant to commit the wrong, but the refusal of injunctive relief. Thereafter the defendant may have no right to act in the manner complained of, but he cannot be prevented from doing so. The court can in my judgment properly award damages 'once and for all' in respect of future wrongs because it awards them in substitution for an injunction and to compensate for those future wrongs which an injunction would have prevented. The doctrine of res judicata operates to prevent the plaintiff and his successors in title from bringing proceedings thereafter to recover even nominal damages in respect of further wrongs for which the plaintiff has been fully compensated . . .

14–271   "When the plaintiff claims an injunction and the defendant asks the court to award damages instead, the proper approach for the court to adopt cannot be in doubt. Clearly the plaintiff must first establish a case for equitable relief, not only by proving his legal right and an actual or threatened infringement by the defendant, but also by overcoming all equitable defences such as laches, acquiescence or estoppel. If he succeeds in doing this, he is prima facie entitled to an injunction. The court may nevertheless in its discretion withhold injunctive relief and award damages instead. How is this discretion to be exercised? In a well known passage in *Shelfer v City of London Electric Lighting Co.* [1895] 1 Ch. 287 at 322–323, A. L. Smith L.J. set out what he described as 'a good working rule' that

'(1) If the injury to the plaintiff's legal right is small, (2) And is one which is capable of being estimated in money, (3) And is one which can be adequately compensated by a small money payment, (4) And the case is one in which it would be oppressive to the defendant to grant an injunction:—then damages in substitution for an injunction may be given.'

Laid down just 100 years ago, A. L. Smith L.J.'s check-list has stood the test of time; but it needs to be remembered that it is only a working rule and does not purport to be an exhaustive statement of the circumstances in which damages may be awarded instead of an injunction.

"Reported cases are merely illustrations of circumstances in which particular **14–272** judges have exercised their discretion, in some cases by granting an injunction, and in others by awarding damages instead. Since they are all cases on the exercise of a discretion, none of them is a binding authority on how the discretion should be exercised. The most that any of them can demonstrate is that in similar circumstances it would not be wrong to exercise the discretion in the same way. But it does not follow that it would be wrong to exercise it differently.

"The outcome of any particular case usually turns on the question: would it in all **14–273** the circumstances be oppressive to the defendant to grant the injunction to which the plaintiff is prima facie entitled? Most of the cases in which the injunction has been refused are cases where the plaintiff has sought a mandatory injunction to pull down a building which infringes his right to light or which has been built in breach of a restrictive covenant. In such cases the court is faced with a fait accompli. The jurisdiction to grant a mandatory injunction in those circumstances cannot be doubted, but to grant it would subject the defendant to a loss out of all proportion to that which would be suffered by the plaintiff if it were refused, and would indeed deliver him to the plaintiff bound hand and foot to be subjected to any extortionate demands the plaintiff might make. In the present case, as in the closely similar case of *Bracewell v Appleby* [1975] Ch. 408, the plaintiff sought a prohibitory injunction to restrain the use of a road giving access to the defendants' house. The result of granting the injunction would be much the same; the house would not have to be pulled down, but it would be rendered landlocked and incapable of beneficial enjoyment . . .

"In considering whether the grant of an injunction would be oppressive to the **14–274** defendant, all the circumstances of the case have to be considered. At one extreme, the defendant may have acted openly and in good faith and in ignorance of the plaintiff's rights, and thereby inadvertently placed himself in a position where the grant of an injunction would either force him to yield to the plaintiff's extortionate demands or expose him to substantial loss. At the other extreme, the defendant may have acted with his eyes open and in full knowledge that he was invading the plaintiff's rights, and hurried on his work in the hope that by presenting the court with a fait accompli he could compel the plaintiff to accept monetary compensation. Most cases, like the present, fall somewhere in between.

"In the present case, the defendants acted openly and in good faith and in the not **14–275** unreasonable belief that they were entitled to make use of Ashleigh Avenue for access to the house that they were building. At the same time, they had been warned by the plaintiff and her solicitors that Ashleigh Avenue was a private road, that they were not entitled to use it for access to the new house, and that it would be a breach of covenant for them to use the garden of No. 5 to gain access to No. 5A. They went ahead, not with their eyes open, but at their own risk. On the other hand, the plaintiff did not seek interlocutory relief at a time when she would almost certainly have obtained it. She should not be criticised for that, but it follows that she also took a risk, namely, that by the time her case came on for trial the court would be presented with a fait accompli. The case was a difficult one, but in an exemplary judgment the judge took into account all the relevant considerations, both those which told in favour of granting an injunction and those which told against, and in the exercise of his discretion he decided to refuse it. In my judgment his conclusion cannot be faulted.

14–276   "Having decided to refuse an injunction and to award the plaintiff damages instead, the judge had to consider the measure of damages. He based them on her share of the amount which, in his opinion, the plaintiff and the other residents of Ashleigh Avenue could reasonably have demanded as the price of waiving their rights. In this he applied the measure of damages which had been adopted by Brightman J. in *Wrotham Park Estate Co. Ltd v Parkside Homes Ltd* [1974] 1 W.L.R. 798, a case which has frequently been followed. It would not be necessary to consider this matter further but for the fact that in the recent case in this court of *Surrey County Council v Bredero Homes Ltd* [1993] 1 W.L.R. 1361 doubts were expressed as to the basis on which this measure of damages could be justified and whether it was consistent with the reasoning of Lord Wilberforce in *Johnson v Agnew* [1980] A.C. 367. It is, therefore, necessary to examine those cases further.

14–277   "In *Surrey County Council v Bredero Homes Ltd* [1993] 1 W.L.R. 1361 the plaintiffs claimed damages from the original covenantor, a developer, for breach of a restrictive covenant against building more than 72 houses, and sought to measure the damages by reference to the additional profit which the defendant had made by building the extra houses. Their claim to substantial damages failed. The case is not authority on the proper measure of damages under Lords Cairns's Act, since (as Dillon L.J. made clear, at p.1367c) the plaintiffs' claim was for damages at common law and not under the Act . . .

14–278   "Examination of the facts stated in the headnote reveals that the defendant had disposed of all the houses on the estate before the plaintiffs commenced proceedings, and that the purchasers were not joined as parties. Any claim to damages under Lord Cairns's Act must have failed; at the date of the writ the court *could* not have ordered the defendant to pull down the houses, since this was no longer something which was within its power to do.

14–279   "Unfortunately, however, Dillon L.J. cast doubt on the correctness of the measure of damages which had been adopted by Brightman J. in *Wrotham Park Estate Co. Ltd v Parkside Homes Ltd* [1974] 1 W.L.R. 798 a case which was decided under Lord Cairns's Act. He said [1993] 1 W.L.R. 1361 at 1366:

> 'The difficulty about the decision in the *Wrotham Park* case is that in *Johnson v Agnew* [1980] A.C. 367 at 400G, Lord Wilberforce, after citing certain decisions on the scope and basis of Lord Cairns's Act which were not cited to Brightman J., stated in the clearest terms that on the balance of those authorities and on principle he found in the Act no warrant for the court awarding damages differently from common law damages.'

14–280   "This statement must not be taken out of context. Earlier in his speech Lord Wilberforce had clearly recognised that damages could be awarded under Lord Cairns's Act where there was no cause of action at law, and he cannot have been insensible to the fact that, when the court awards damages in substitution for an injunction, it seeks to compensate the plaintiff for loss arising from future wrongs, that is to say, loss for which the common law does not provide a remedy. Neither *Wroth v Tyler* nor *Johnson v Agnew* [1980] A.C. 367 was a case of this kind. In each of those cases the plaintiff claimed damages for loss occasioned by a single, once and for all, past breach of contract on the part of the defendant. In neither case was the breach a continuing one capable of generating further losses. In my view Lord

Wilberforce's statement that the measure of damages is the same whether damages are recoverable at common law or under the Act must be taken to be limited to the case where they are recoverable in respect of the same cause of action. It cannot sensibly have any application where the claim at common law is in respect of a past trespass or breach of covenant and that under the Act is in respect of future trespasses or continuing breaches of covenant.

"Accordingly I am of opinion that the judge was not precluded by the decision of **14–281** the House of Lords in *Johnson v Agnew* from adopting the measure of damages which he did. It is, however, necessary to notice the observations of Steyn L.J. in *Surrey County Council v Bredero Homes Ltd* [1993] 1 W.L.R. 1361 at 1369.

> 'In my view *Wrotham Park Estate Co. Ltd v Parkside Homes Ltd* [1974] 1 W.L.R. 798 is only defensible on the basis of the third or restitutionary principle . . . The plaintiffs' argument that the *Wrotham Park* case can be justified on the basis of a loss of bargaining opportunity is a fiction.'

I find these remarks puzzling. It is plain from his judgment in the *Wrotham Park* case that Brightman J.'s approach was compensatory, not restitutionary. He sought to measure the damages by reference to what the plaintiff had lost, not by reference to what the defendant had gained. He did not award the plaintiff the profit which the defendant had made by the breach, but the amount which he judged the plaintiff might have obtained as the price of giving its consent. The amount of the profit which the defendant expected to make was a relevant factor in that assessment, but that was all.

"Both the *Wrotham Park* and *Bredero Homes* cases (unlike the present) were **14–282** concerned with a single past breach of covenant, so that the measure of damages at common law and under the Act was the same. Prima facie the measure of damages in either case for breach of a covenant not to build a house on neighbouring land is the diminution in the value of the plaintiff's land occasioned by the breach. One element in the value of the plaintiff's land immediately before the breach is attributable to his ability to obtain an injunction to prevent the building. Clearly a defendant who wished to build would pay for the release of the covenant, but only so long as the court could still protect it by the grant of an injunction. The proviso is important. It is the ability to claim an injunction which gives the benefit of the covenant much of its value. If the plaintiff delays proceedings until it is no longer possible for him to obtain an injunction, he destroys his own bargaining position and devalues his right. The unavailability of the remedy of injunction at one and the same time deprives the court of jurisdiction to award damages under the Act and removes the basis for awarding substantial damages at common law. For this reason, I take the view that damages can be awarded at common law in accordance with the approach adopted in the *Wrotham Park* case, but in practice only in the circumstances in which they could also be awarded under the Act.

"This may be what Steyn L.J. had in mind when he said that the loss of bargaining **14–283** opportunity was a fiction. If he mean it generally or in relation to the facts which obtained in the *Wrotham Park* case, then I respectfully disagree. But it was true in the circumstances of the case before him, and not merely for the reason given by Rose L.J. (that the plaintiffs did not object to the extra houses and would have waived the breach for a nominal sum). The plaintiffs did not bring the proceedings until after the defendant had sold the houses and was no longer susceptible to an injunction. The plaintiffs had thereby deprived themselves of any bargaining position. Unable to obtain an injunction, they were equally unable to invoke the jurisdiction to award damages under Lord Cairns's Act. No longer exposed to the risk of an injunction, and having successfully disposed of the houses, the defendant had no reason to pay anything for the release of the covenant. Unless they were able to recover damages in accordance with restitutionary principles, neither at common law nor in equity could the plaintiffs recover more than nominal damages.

14–284   "In the present case the plaintiff brought proceedings at a time when her rights were still capable of being protected by injunction. She has accordingly been able to invoke the court's jurisdiction to award in substitution for an injunction damages which take account of the future as well as the past. In my view there is no reason why compensatory damages for future trespasses and continuing breaches of covenant should not reflect the value of the rights which she has lost, or why such damages should not be measured by the amount which she could reasonably have expected to receive for their release.

14–285   "In my judgment the judge's approach to the assessment of damages was correct on the facts and in accordance with principle. I would dismiss the appeal."

Section 5. Rescission

14–286   The equitable right to rescind[11] is the right of a party to a transaction to set it aside and so to be restored to his former position. It must be distinguished as a voidable transaction from a transaction that is void *ab initio* (*e.g.* a contract void for illegality or a very fundamental mistake). It must also be distinguished from the case where a contract with no inherent invalidity is said to be rescinded for the future when the innocent party accepts the wrongdoer's repudiatory breach of contract as terminating the contract, but leaving the innocent party free to sue the wrongdoer for his past breaches of a valid contract.[12]

14–287   Equity can set aside a transaction in circumstances where the common law would not and is more flexible in its view of the requirement that the claimant make counter restitution *e.g.* taking accounts and making an allowance for services rendered or for deterioration of property.[13] Moreover, equity by applying the maxim "he who comes to equity must do equity" can grant relief on terms, *e.g.* so that a contract is set aside so long as the vendor offers the property in question to the purchaser at a proper price.[14]

14–288   The grounds for rescission include cases:[15]

    (i) where a party was induced to enter into a contract by a fraudulent misrepresentation—or even an innocent misrepresentation, but the court now has a discretion to award damages in lieu of rescission if it would be equitable to do so[16];

---

[11] See *Alati v Kruger* (1955) 94 C.L.R. 216 at 223–224 endorsed by Dunn L.J. in *O'Sullivan v Management Agency & Music Ltd* [1985] 3 All E.R. 352 at 364–365.

[12] *Johnson v Agnew* [1980] A.C. 367 at 396–398, para.14–200; *Photo Production Ltd v Securicor Transport Ltd* [1980] A.C. 827 at 844.

[13] See cases in n.11 above.

[14] *Grist v Bailey* [1967] Ch. 532, *Magee v Pennine Insurance Co. Ltd* [1969] 2 Q.B. 507. Further see Goff & Jones, Law of Restitution Chap. 9.

[15] There is no equitable jurisdiction to grant rescission of a contract on the ground of common mistake where the contract is valid at common law: *Great Peace Shipping Ltd v Tsavlisis Salvage (International) Ltd* [2003] Q.B. 679, disapproving *Solle v Butcher* [1950] 1 K.B. 671.

[16] Misrepresentation Act 1967, s. 2(2). Indeed s.2(1) allows damages of a tortious measure to be awarded for a negligent misrepresentation: *Royscot Trust Ltd v Rogerson* [1991] 2 Q.B. 297. See also *Witter Ltd v TBP Industries* [1996] 2 All E.R. 573.

(ii) where a party entered into a transaction as a result of another's undue influence[17];

(iii) where a poor ignorant person entered into a disadvantageous transaction (*e.g.* at an undervalue) without any independent legal advice[18];

(iv) where the other party to a contract uberrimae fidei (*e.g.* a contract of insurance) is in breach of his duty of full disclosure[19];

(v) where the other party to a transaction is in breach of his fiduciary duty of full disclosure[20];

(vi) where a donor made a gift under a unilateral mistake as to the effect of the gift (*e.g.* causing a forfeiture of a protected life interest[21] or causing a[22] beneficiary to be benefited twice forgetful of an earlier gift to that beneficiary); and

(vii) where a donor made a gift by reason of another's misrepresentation or undue influence.[23]

The English Court of Appeal in *TSB Bank v Camfield*[24] has taken the **14–289** strict view that if a claimant can set aside a transaction, like a mortgage, for misrepresentation (or undue influence) then it must be set aside entirely rather than partially, even where a wife would have agreed to a maximum liability of £15,000 (rather than of £30,000) irrespective of the misrepresentation (or unde influence). The Australian High Court[25] has subsequently rejected that view and applied the maxim, "He who seeks equity must do equity" so as to do what is practically just. Thus, in the above type of case the mortgage should be entirely set aside but on the terms that the wife affords the mortgagee security for £15,000 because she was prepared to undertake that liability independently of any misrepresentation (or undue influence). In England a first instance judge has held[26] that where (unlike *Camfield*) the wife had actually benefited from the loan sought to be set aside she had to make restitution of such benefit to be granted rescission. It seems likely that the House of Lords in due course will overrule *Camfield* and follow the Australian approach.

The right to rescind is lost if: **14–290**

(i) the party entitled to rescind affirms the transaction[27];

---

[17] *Barclays Bank plc v O'Brien* [1994] 1 A.C. 180; *CIB.C. Mortgages plc v Pitt* [1994] 1 A.C. 200.
[18] *Cresswell v Potter* [1978] 1 W.L.R. 255 *Crédit Lyonnais Nederland NV v Burch* [1997] 1 All E.R. 144; *Portman B.S. v Dusangh* [2001] W.T.L.R 117.
[19] *Pan Atlantic Insurance Co. Ltd v Pine Top Insurance Co. Ltd* [1994] 3 All E.R. 581.
[20] *Daly v Sidney Stock Exchange* (1986) 160 C.L.R. 371.
[21] *Gibbon v Mitchell* [1990] 1 W.L.R. 1304.
[22] *Hood (Lady) of Avalon v Mackinnon* [1909] 1 Ch. 476.
[23] *Re Glubb* [1900] 1 Ch. 354.
[24] [1995] 1 All E.R. 951.
[25] *Vadasz v Pioneer Concrete SA* (1995) 69 A.L.J.R. 678. Similarly in *Maguire v Makaronis* (1998) 188 C.L.R. 449 it allowed mortgagors to rescind a mortgage (for non-disclosure that their solicitors were the mortgagees) on condition they repaid the capital with interest at a commercial rate, but not the higher rate in the mortgage deed.
[26] *Dunbar Bank plc v Nadeem* [1997] 2 All E.R. 253 (£210,000 of the loan to H and W was used to buy a lease in the names of H and W, so to obtain rescission W had to pay the bank £105,000 plus interest).
[27] *Peyman v Lanjani* [1985] Ch. 457; *Leaf v International Galleries* [1950] 2 K.B. 86; *Mitchell v Homfray* (1881) 8 Q.B.D. 587.

(ii) *restitutio in integrum* is not substantially possible, taking account of services rendered or for property deterioration[28];

(iii) an innocent third party acquires rights for value before the claimant sets the transaction aside or does everything he can to set it aside by communicating his intention to the other party[29]; or

(iv) the right is not exercised within a reasonable time.[30]

Section 6. Rectification

14–291   Rectification is a discretionary remedy to rectify a document so that it accords correctly with what the parties agreed[31] or in the case of a settlement with what the settlor intended.[32] For this purpose there is an exception to the "parole evidence rule" so that oral evidence may be given to establish the error with the "convincing proof"[33] that is required. When rectification occurs it is retrospective.[34]

14–292   In bilateral transactions the mistake must normally be common to both parties so that the document fails to record what they agreed.[35] Exceptionally, rectification will be available where there was a unilateral mistake in circumstances where the party who was not mistaken is fraudulent or estopped from resisting rectification by virtue of his unconscionable conduct.[36]

14–293   Rectification of a voluntary deed, like a settlement, can be obtained if the donor's real intention was not accurately reflected in the deed.[37] Strong evidence of her precise real intention will be required so that the judge can be convinced that the document which was executed differed by reason of some mistake from that which the settlor intended *e.g.* an accidental departure from his instructions to the draftsman.[38] It is not enough that it would have been better if the settlor had executed a deed which was from

---

[28] *Erlanger v New Sombrero Phosphate Co* (1873) 3 App. Cas. 1218; *O'Sullivan v Management Agency & Music Ltd* [1985] Q.B. 428.

[29] *Oakes v Turquand* (1869) L.R. 2 H.L 325; *Car & Universal Finance Co. Ltd v Caldwell* [1965] 1 Q.B. 525.

[30] *Car and Universal Finance Co. Ltd v Caldwell* [1965] 1 Q.B. 525 at 554; *Leaf v International Galleries* [1950] 2 K.B. 86 at 92.

[31] *Joscelyne v Nissen* [1970] 2 Q.B. 86; *Racal Group Services Ltd v Ashmore* [1994] S.T.C. 416.

[32] *Re Butlin's S.T.* [1976] Ch. 251; *Lake v Lake* [1989] S.T.C. 865.

[33] *Joscelyne v Nissen* [1970] 2 Q.B. 86; *Thor Navigation Inc. v Ingosstrakh Insurance Co. Ltd* [2005] EWHC 19 (Comm) at [51], *per* Gloster J. Note that "subsequent conduct [by the parties to an instrument[is both relevant and highly persuasive as to what a party's intention was at and leading up to the execution of the instrument in question": *Westland Savings Bank v Hancock* [1987] 2 N.Z.L.R. 21 at 31 *per* Tipping J.

[34] *Lake v Lake* [1989] S.T.C. 865.

[35] *The Nai Genova* [1984] 1 Lloyd's Rep. 353 at 359, *per* Slade L.J. It is not enough that the parties can be shown to have made a common mistake as to the effect of their transaction: it must be shown that they commonly intended to include or exclude something in their document which was not included or excluded: *Frederick Rose (London) Ltd v William Pimm Jr Co. Ltd* [1953] 2 Q.B. 450; *Lloyd v Stanbury* [1971] 1 W.L.R. 535 at 543; *Jones v Kaiser* [1999] EWCA Civ 1135. *James Hay Pension Trustees Ltd v Hird* [2005] EWHC 1093 (Ch), para.113.

[36] *Thomas Bates & Son Ltd v Wyndham's (Lingerie) Ltd* [1981] 1 All E.R. 1077 at 1086; *Commission for New Towns v Cooper (GB) Ltd* [1995] Ch. 259; *Thor Navigation Inc. v Ingosstrakh Insurance Co. Ltd* [2005] EWHC 19 (Comm) at [57]–[62] *per* Gloster J. A person is not necessarily dishonest for the purposes of this rule simply because he has Nelsonian or naughty knowledge of the other party's mistake: *George Wimpey U.K. Ltd v V.I. Construction Ltd* [2005] EWCA Civ 77.

[37] *Re Butlin's S.T.* [1976] Ch. 251.

[38] *Tankel v Tankel* [1999] 1 F.L.R. 676; *Re Smouha Family Trust* [2000] W.T.L.R. 133.

the outset in the form to which she seeks it to be changed, nor is it enough that if the settlor's attention had been drawn to the actual terms of the deed and she had been asked if she would rather have them changed, she would have said that she would. Thus, where the deed excluded the trustees from benefiting under the trust and the original trustees were replaced as trustees by the settlor's daughters who were primary beneficiaries and who subsequently received significant benefits, the court[39] refused to rectify the deed so that beneficiaries who were trustees could benefit. It is immaterial that the purpose of rectification is to obtain an intended fiscal advantage, but the court must be convinced that the clause to be rectified was intended to be in some precisely different form from that ultimately appearing in the deed.[40]

14–294 As alternatives to rectification, it is worth noting that if the donor did not intend the transaction to have the effect which it did (*e.g.* a surrender to have the effect of forfeiting his life interest under a protective trust) it may be totally set aside,[41] while the exercise of a power may be declared void if it would not have been so exercised but for ignoring a key factor.[42]

14–295 Rectification will not be granted where a bona fide purchaser for value without notice has acquired a proprietary interest under the document.[43] Laches or acquiescence will also bar the claim.[44] In the case of a voluntary settlement the court may refuse to rectify if a trustee, who took office in ignorance of the mistake, has a reasonable objection to rectification.[45]

14–296 Section 20 of the Administration of Justice Act 1982 allows a will to be rectified if the court is satisfied that it fails to carry out the testator's intentions in consequence of a clerical error or a failure to understand his instructions.[46]

WOLFF v WOLFF

Chancery Division [2004] EWHC 2110 (Ch); [2004] W.T.L.R. 1349

14–297 The claimants intended to enter into an inheritance tax saving scheme with the assistance of a solicitor who was not clear as to what he was doing. On June 4, 1997 he had them execute a reversionary lease of their home in favour of their two daughters for 125 years commencing June 4, 2017 at a peppercorn rent. The same day the claimants as settlors by deed purported to assign to trustees the lease (held by their daughters) and £1,000, and declared trusts giving a life interest to their

---

[39] *Tankel v Tankel* [1999] 1 F.L.R. 676.
[40] *Racal Group Services v Ashmore* [1995] S.T.C. 1151: a covenant in favour of charitable trustees for a period exceeding 3 years was clearly intended, so as to attract tax relief, but mistakenly the period in the covenant could not exceed 3 years; Court of Appeal refused rectification because not clear on what particular dates over what particular period payments would be made, the company's controller only having a general idea. Some offshore jurisdictions have a more benevolent approach: *Briggs v Integritas Trust Management (Cayman) Ltd* [1988] C.I.L.R. 456.
[41] *Gibbon v Mitchell* [1990] 1 W.L.R. 1304; *Wolgg v Wolgg* [2004] W.T.L.R. 1349.
[42] *Re Hastings–Bass* [1975] Ch. 25; *Abacus Trust Co. v Barr* [2003] Ch. 409.
[43] *Smith v Jones* [1954] 1 W.L.R. 1089, or nowadays, presumably if an innocent volunteer has changed his position.
[44] *Beale v Kyte* [1907] 1 Ch. 564.
[45] *Re Butlin's S.T.* [1976] Ch. 251.
[46] *e.g. Wordingham v Royal Exchange Trust Co* [1992] Ch. 412.

daughters, and the capital to such of the daughters' *children* as attained 18 in such proportions as the trustee might appoint, but otherwise in equal shares, while then declaring that after 80 years the trust property should be held for the *daughters* in equal shares (with substitutionary gifts in favour of the daughters' issue then living); there was no power to advance or appoint capital to the daughters.

The claimants intended to make a gift of their home to their daughters but only on the basis it did not deprive them of their right to live there free of charge, while the lease did so deprive them from June 2017; and they intended their daughters to have capital or access to it, which was not the case under the trust in any meaningful way (as they were unlikely to survive for 80 years with their children all having died before 18).

14–298 MANN J. "So far as the lease and trust deed are concerned Mr Brownbill, on behalf of the Wolffs, relies on each of what he says is two lines of cases. The first line is said to show that a voluntary settlor can claim to have a settlement set aside if he made it under a mistake as to its effect. That, says Mr Brownbill, applies in this case because the Wolffs made such a mistake in believing, wrongly, that the lease did not affect their right to live in the property for as long as they wished. They also made a relevant mistake in relation to the trust deed, believing that it gave the daughters an interest in capital. The second line of cases is said to entitle a voluntary settlor to have a settlement set aside where there has been an inadequate explanation of the transaction and a lack of understanding of it—it will be set aside unless there is a sufficient level of understanding which brings home its effect, particularly where it is so improvident as to expose the settler to the risk of destitution or something close to it. The Wolffs did not have that understanding or explanation in relation to the effects of the lease on their rights of occupation (and indeed their lack of understanding went further), and in relation to the effect of the trust deed. Although these lines of cases might sound as though they were so close as to be aspects of the same thing, Mr Brownbill submitted they were different and distinct.

14–299 "The law on the first line of cases was considered by Millett J. in *Gibbon v Mitchell* [1990] 1 W.L.R. 1304. In that case a protected life interest was surrendered by the life tenant, who thereby intended to accelerate the absolute interest of the remainderman. He had not appreciated that the effect of the surrender was in fact to forfeit his life interest and bring into operation the discretionary trusts which followed it. Millett J. set aside the deed under the 'much wider equitable jurisdiction to relieve from the consequences of a mistake' (p1307F). Having considered a number of cases (all of which have been shown to me by Mr Brownbill) he concluded (p1309E–F):

> 'In my judgment, these cases show that, wherever there is a voluntary transaction by which one party intends to confer a bounty on another, the deed will be set aside if the court is satisfied that the disponor did not intend the transaction to have the effect which it did. It will be set aside for mistake whether the mistake is a mistake of law or of fact, so long as the mistake is as to the effect of the transaction itself and not merely as to its consequences or the advantages to be gained by entering into it.'

14–300 "Mr Brownbill seeks to deploy that principle. He says that the Wolffs made a mistake, and it was not merely as to the consequences of the transaction—it was a mistake as to its nature and what it had achieved and therefore as to its effect. They intended a transaction with a lease which left them with a right of occupation, and they got a transaction which was a lease which deprived them of a right of occupation.

"I confess that originally I had thought that the mistake of the Wolffs (which I **14–301** have found they made as a matter of fact) was more as to the consequences of their transaction than as to its effect (though that distinction is not always easy to grasp). They intended a lease to their daughters, and they knew that that would give their daughters an interest. The fact that the lease deprived them of their right of possession seemed to me to be more of a 'conseq uence', the words of Millett J. On the facts, depriving them of their actual occupation was not even clearly a necessary consequence, because there is no suggestion that the daughters would evict them or even charge them rent. Were that to happen there would be tax consequences, but that is clearly a 'consequence' in Millett J.'s terminology.

"However, I have been persuaded that my initial reaction was wrong. The Wolffs **14–302** intended to give away an interest to their daughters, but there were limits to that gift. It was to take effect in the future, but even then it was not to deprive them of the rights of occupation free of charge that they had enjoyed hitherto. In fact and in law the lease deprives them of that right from June 2017. That seems to me to be an effect of the transaction—they have given away more than they intended. The matter can be tested in this way. Suppose that the lease took effect one day after its execution rather than 20 years, but the Wolffs still had the belief that they could continue to live in the property. Those stark facts show more clearly that their mistake was as to the effect of the transaction. In *AMP (UK) Plc v Barker* [2001] P.L.R. 77 at paragraph 70 Lawrence Collins J. observed, in relation to Millett J's distinction between effects and consequences:

> 'If anything, it is simply a formula designed to ensure that the policy involved in equitable relief is effectuated to keep it within reasonable bounds and to ensure that it is not used simply when parties are mistaken about the commercial effects of their transactions or have second thoughts about them. The cases certainly establish that relief may be available if there is a mistake as to law or the legal consequences of an agreement or settlement. . .'

If that is indeed the significance of the distinction, then the mistake of the Wolffs in this case falls on the right side of the line (so far as they are concerned). They made a mistake as to the legal effects of the transaction, and it was a significant one. It is certainly serious enough to give rise to the equity of setting it aside.

"In those circumstances the lease falls to be set aside. **14–303**

"That conclusion renders a decision on the other points academic. However, I **14–304** make the following observations on them.

"So far as Mr Brownbill's alternative line of cases is concerned, I rather doubt if it **14–305** can now be taken to exist. The jurisdiction seems to me to be based on mistake. One of the high water marks of this alternative line, so far as Mr Brownbill was concerned, was *Philippson v Kerry* (1863) 32 Beav. 628, where an elderly lady gave away a material part of her wealth believing that the donee would give her the dividends for the rest of her life. She received no explanation of the consequences of the transaction. On analysis I think that this can be treated as a mistake case, and Millett J. certainly treated it as one—see his rationale of it at 1309D. Mr Brownbill did cite other cases on the point, but I do not need to deal with them.

"Had it been necessary for me to do so, I would have held that the trust deed fell **14–306** to be set aside for the same reason as the lease. The Wolffs clearly intended their daughters to have capital or access to it, and the trust deed, whatever else it might did not do that (or at least not in any meaningful way—they might have had capital if they survived for 80 years). However, I do not need to consider this further since the setting aside of the lease will mean that there is no asset in the trust."

AMP (UK) PLC v BARKER

Chancery Division [2001] 1 W.T.L.R. 1256, (2001) Pensions L.R. 77

14–307 The trustees of the non-contributory Pension Scheme ("the Scheme") of the National Provident Institution ("NPI") in 1998 amended the Scheme rules with the required approval of the board of NPI. The amendment was designed to increase the benefits of those forced to retire as a result of incapacity and was regarded as a minor one, costing NPI only a comparatively small amount. After AMP (UK) plc took over NPI in 2000, it discovered that it had been overlooked that the deferred pension payable to those leaving after two or more years was to be calculated as if the leaver was leaving because of incapacity, and so t he cost to the employer was potentially enormous. Thus, AMP sought and obtained rectification of the rule changes so as to remove the link between incapacity leavers and early leavers (though the Court would also have been prepared to set aside the changes whether for mistake or because under the rule in *Re Hastings-Bass* the trustees and the employer would not have done what they did if they had known that the wording used gave extra rights also to early leavers).

14–308 LAWRENCE COLLINS J.: The starting point is free from difficulty. In the case of a bilateral transaction, there must be convincing proof that the concluded instrument does not represent the common intention of the parties. The policy reason for the need for convincing proof is that certainty and ready enforceability of transactions would otherwise be hindered by constant attempts to cloud the issue: *The Olympic Pride* [1980] 2 Lloyd's Rep 67, 72. The claimant does not have to meet more than the civil standard of balance of probabilities, but convincing proof is required to counteract the cogent evidence of the parties' intention displayed by the instrument: *Thomas Bates and Sons Ltd v Wyndham's Ltd* [1981] 1 W.L.R. 505, 521 (CA); *Grand Metropolitan Plc v William Hill Group Ltd* [1997] 1 B.C.L.C. 390; *Lansing Linde Ltd v Alber* [2000] P.L.R. 15, 44.

14–309 The claimant must show some outward expression of accord or evidence of a continuing common intention, outwardly manifested. But it is not necessary to have a concluded and binding contract antecedent to the agreement which it is sought to rectify. In a well-known passage in *Frederick E Rose Ltd v William H Pim & Co Ltd* [1953] 2 Q.B. 450, 461–462 (CA) Denning L.J. said:

> 'Rectification is concerned with contracts and documents, not with intentions. In order to get rectification it is necessary to show that the parties were in complete agreement on the terms of their contract, but by an error wrote them down wrongly; and in this regard, in order to ascertain the terms of their contract, you do not look into the inner minds of the parties—into their intentions—any more than you do in the formation of any other contract. You look at their outward acts, that is, at what they said or wrote to one another in the coming to their agreement, and then compare it with the document that they have signed. If you can predicate with certainty what their contract was, and that it is, by a common mistake, wrongly expressed in the document, then you rectify the document; but nothing less will suffice. It is not necessary that all the formalities of the contract should have been executed so as to make it enforceable at law but, formalities apart, there must have been a concluded contract. There is a passage in *Crane v Hegenzan—Harris Co Inc* [1939] 1 All E.R. 662, 664 which suggests that a continuing common intention alone will suffice; but I am clearly of the opinion that a continuing common intention is not sufficient unless it has found expression in outward agreement. There could

be no certainty at all in business transactions if a party who had entered into a—firm contract could afterwards turn round and claim to have it rectified on the ground that the parties intended something different. He is allowed to prove, if he can, that they *agreed something different*. . . but not that they *intended* something different.'

"In *Joscelyne v Nissen* [1970] 2 Q.B. 86, 97, however, the Court of Appeal said **14–310** that *Rose v Pim* did not assert or re-instate the view that an antecedent complete concluded contract was required for rectification. It only showed that prior accord on a term or meaning of a phrase to be sued must have been outwardly expressed or communicated between the parties. The Court of Appeal expressly approved the reference by Simonds J. in *Crane v Hegeman-Harris Co Inc, supra,* to common continuing intention', with the qualification that some outward expression of accord is required. I accept the submissions of Mr Brian Green Q.C. that these are not two separate conditions, but rather different sides of the same coin, since an uncommunicated inward intention is wholly irrelevant."

In the case of unilateral transactions, i.e transactions which create rights for **14–311** persons other than the maker of the instrument, but which are not the result of a bargain, *e.g.* voluntary settlements, the court has a discretion to rectify in the case of mistake. In this type of case there is, of course, no question of having to show common mistake. The jurisdiction to rectify in such cases has a long history: see *Walker v Armstrong* (1856) 8 De G.M. & G. 531. The leading modem authority is *Re Butlin's Settlement* [1976] Ch. 251. In that case the settlor, Sir Billy Butlin, had executed a voluntary settlement which was intended to give a majority of five trustees power to exercise the power given them by the settlement over capital and income. As a result of a drafting error by counsel, the settlement did not give effect to this intention. It was held that the court had power to rectify the settlement notwithstanding that only one of the original trustees knew of the intention. Brightman J. said (at 260–261):

'There is, in my judgement, no doubt that the court has power to rectify a settlement notwithstanding that it is a voluntary settlement and not the result of a bargain, such as an ante—nuptial marriage settlement. *Lackersteen v Lackersteen* (1860) 30 L.J. Ch. 5, a decision of Page-Wood V.-C. and *Behrens v Heilbut* (1956) 222 L.J. Jo. 290, a decision of Harman J., are cases in which voluntary settlements were actually rectified. There are also *obiter dicta* to the like effect in cases where rectification was in fact refused; see *Bonhote v Henderson* [1895] 1 Ch. 742; [1895] 1 Ch. 202.'

"I have had the benefit of a more elaborate argument on the requirement of **14–312** common accord in a case like the present one . . .

"Consequently, the intentions of the trustees and the principal employer must **14–313** converge. But they do not have to agree *inter se*. The resolution, however, cannot be rectified to reflect the intentions of the trustees when that is not also the intention of the principal employer, for otherwise the resolution could take a form to which the principal employer had not consented, and the consent of the principal employer is an essential part of the machinery of amendment.

"There must, therefore, be cogent evidence of the intentions both of the trustees **14–314** and of NPI, but not necessarily of their agreement or accord.[47] In some of the earlier cases on voluntary settlements, rectification was ordered on the uncontradicted affidavit: see, eg *Hanley v Pearson* (1879) 13 Ch.D. 545. Mr Nigel Inglis-

---

[47] Followed in *Gallaher Ltd v Gallaher Pensions Ltd* [2005] EWHC 42 (Ch) at [117].

Jones Q.C. for the trustees suggested that a similar approach would be appropriate in a case such as this. It may be that the need for objective manifestation in the case of a unilateral transaction is simply one element of the need for convincing proof of the mistake. It was present in the two leading modern cases on mistake in unilateral transactions, *Re Butlin's Settlement* and *Gibbon v Mitchell* [1990] 1 W.L.R. 1304, p.1263E–H. The certainty of transactions would be undermined if the court could act, otherwise than in exceptional circumstances, simply on the assertion of a party to the transaction. But when one is considering the intentions of a collective body such as a group of trustees or a committee of a board it is their collective intention which is relevant, and it would be a very odd case (and certainly not this one) if that collective intention were not objectively manifested.

14–315   "Consequently what AMP has to show convincingly is a continuing common intention by the trustees and the NPI to affect only incapacity benefits. It is clear from the factual findings that there is overwhelming evidence that their intentions were limited to improving the benefits for those leaving on account of incapacity, and they had not the slightest intention to benefit early leavers in general. If objective manifestation of their intentions is a separate requirement, then there can be no doubt that it is fulfilled in abundance.

. . .

14–316   "The next question is whether the right to rectification is affected by the fact that the trustees and the board sub-committee intended to pass, or consent to, the very wording in the resolution It is plain that it is not so affected. *Re Butlin's Settlement* illustrates another general proposition in the law of rectification, which is that rectification may be available even if the parties have quite deliberately used the wording in the instrument. Brightman J. said (at 261–2):

'. . . rectification is available not only in a case where particular words have been added, omitted or wrongly written as a result of careless copying or the like. It is also available where the words of the document are purposely used but it was mistakenly considered that they bore a different meaning as a matter of true construction. In such a case. . . the court will rectify the wording so that it expresses the true intention. . .'

14–317   "Consequently rectification may be available if the document contains the very wording that it was intended to contain, but it has in law or as a matter of true construction an effect or meaning different from that which was intended: *Whiteside v Whiteside* [1950] Ch. 65, 74; *Grand Metropolitan Plc v William Hill Group Ltd*, above. It is sometimes said that equitable relief against mistake is not available if the mistake relates only to the consequences of the transaction or the advantages to be gained by entering into it: cf *Whiteside v Whiteside*, above; Gibbon v Mitchell [1990] 1 W.L.R. 1304, 1309. This distinction seems to have been derived in the former case from the 1929 edition of *Kerr on Fraud and Mistake*. If anything, it is simply a formula designed to ensure that the policy involved in equitable relief is effectuated to keep it within reasonable bounds and to ensure that it is not used simply when parties are mistaken about the commercial effects of their transactions or have second thoughts about them. The cases certainly establish that relief may be available if there is a mistake as to law or the legal consequences of an agreement or settlement, and in the present case Mr Simmonds Q.C. ultimately accepted that, if there was a mistake, it was a mistake as to legal effect and not merely as to consequences.

"It is therefore quite unreal to contend that the intention of the trustees and NPI **14–318** was simply to pass a resolution containing the words which it did in fact contain, or that they did not intend or agree to abolish the link between the calculation of benefits under rules 4.1 and 8.4(1). Nor can it be said that they intended (as was held in *Lansing Linde*) simply to sign anything which was put before them. The resolution was the subject of preparation, advice and discussion. It was not the result of a rubber—stamping exercise, and the fact that, as result of an oversight or of negligence (see *Walker v Armstrong, ante)* it had an effect going far beyoind the intentions of the trustees and NPI not only does not prevent rectification, but is a ground for it."

INDEX